D1806878

MESSIANIC MYSTICISM

MOSES HAYIM LUZZATTO AND THE PADUA SCHOOL

THE LITTMAN LIBRARY OF
JEWISH CIVILIZATION

Dedicated to the memory of
LOUIS THOMAS SIDNEY LITTMAN
who founded the Littman Library for the love of God
and as an act of charity in memory of his father
JOSEPH AARON LITTMAN
יהא זכרם ברוך

'Get wisdom, get understanding:
Forsake her not and she shall preserve thee'
PROV. 4: 5

The Littman Library of Jewish Civilization is a registered UK charity
Registered charity no. 1000784

MESSIANIC MYSTICISM

Moses Hayim Luzzatto and the Padua School

ISAIAH TISHBY

Translated by
MORRIS HOFFMAN

Oxford · Portland, Oregon
The Littman Library of Jewish Civilization
2008

The Littman Library of Jewish Civilization

Chief Executive Officer: Ludo Craddock
Managing Editor: Connie Webber

PO Box 645, Oxford OX2 OUJ, UK
www.littman.co.uk

Published in the United States and Canada by
The Littman Library of Jewish Civilization
c/o ISBS, 920 N.E. 58th Avenue, Suite 300
Portland, Oregon 97213-3786

© *The Littman Library of Jewish Civilization* 2008

All rights reserved.
No part of this publication may be reproduced,
stored in a retrieval system, or transmitted, in any form or by
any means, without the prior permission in writing of
The Littman Library of Jewish Civilization

A catalogue record for this book is available from the British Library

Library of Congress Cataloging-in-Publication Data
Tishby, Isaiah.
[Hikre kabalah u-sheluhoteha. English. Selections]
Messianic mysticism : Moses Hayim Luzzatto and the Padua school / Isaiah Tishby;
translated by Morris Hoffman Oxford.
p. cm.
Includes bibliographical references and index.
1. Cabala—History. 2. Luzzatto, Moshe Hayyim, 1707–1747. 3. Sabbathaians.
4. Messianic era (Judaism) I. Title.
BM526 .T57213
296.8'33—dc22 2007034192
ISBN 978–1–874774–09–9

Publishing co-ordinator: Janet Moth
Production: John Saunders
Design: Pete Russell, Faringdon, Oxon.
Copy-editing: George Tulloch
Proof-reading: Philippa Claiden
Index: Meg Davies (Fellow of the Society of Indexers)
Typeset by Hope Services (Abingdon) Ltd
Printed in Great Britain on acid-free paper by
MPG Books, Bodmin, Cornwall

Contents

Note on Transliteration

THE transliteration of Hebrew in this book reflects consideration of the type of book it is, in terms of its content, purpose, and readership. The system adopted therefore reflects a broad approach to transcription, rather than the narrower approaches found in the *Encyclopaedia Judaica* or other systems developed for text-based or linguistic studies. The aim has been to reflect the pronunciation prescribed for modern Hebrew, rather than the spelling or Hebrew word structure, and to do so using conventions that are generally familiar to the English-speaking reader.

In accordance with this approach, no attempt is made to indicate the distinctions between *alef* and *ayin*, *tet* and *taf*, *kaf* and *kuf*, *sin* and *samekh*, since these are not relevant to pronunciation; likewise, the *dagesh* is not indicated except where it affects pronunciation. Following the principle of using conventions familiar to the majority of readers, however, transcriptions that are well established have been retained even when they are not fully consistent with the transliteration system adopted. On similar grounds, the *tsadi* is rendered by 'tz' in such familiar words as bar mitzvah. Likewise, the distinction between *ḥet* and *khaf* has been retained, using *ḥ* for the former and *kh* for the latter; the associated forms are generally familiar to readers, even if the distinction is not actually borne out in pronunciation, and for the same reason the final *he* is indicated too. As in Hebrew, no capital letters are used, except that an initial capital has been retained in transliterating titles of published works (for example, *Shulḥan arukh*).

Since no distinction is made between *alef* and *ayin*, they are indicated by an apostrophe only in intervocalic positions where a failure to do so could lead an English-speaking reader to pronounce the vowel-cluster as a diphthong—as, for example, in *ha'ir*—or otherwise mispronounce the word.

The *sheva na* is indicated by an *e*—*perikat ol*, *reshut*—except, again, when established convention dictates otherwise.

The *yod* is represented by *i* when it occurs as a vowel (*bereshit*), by *y* when it occurs as a consonant (*yesodot*), and by *yi* when it occurs as both (*yisra'el*).

Names have generally been left in their familiar forms, even when this is inconsistent with the overall system.

Thanks are due to Jonathan Webber of Birmingham University for his help in elucidating the principles to be adopted.

Translator's Note

THE present work translates a set of Isaiah Tishby's essays that appeared in volume iii of his *Ḥikrei kabalah usheluḥoteiha: meḥkarim umekorot/Studies in Kabbalah and its Branches: Researches and Sources* (Magnes Press, Hebrew University; Jerusalem, 1993).

In the essays, Tishby referred several times to essays on related themes which he proposed to publish and the titles of some of which he had already chosen. Where it has been possible to trace the publications I have added the details. Where no such details are given it may be taken that, so far as I know, Tishby did not live to fulfil his intention.

Additions to the text in square brackets: where these are Tishby's own, his initials are added only where he himself inserted them. I have added a number of biblical and talmudic references without comment; similarly with some minor or translational additions which are self-evidently mine. My other additions are indicated as by 'Trans.', except in the case of the Bibliography, which is entirely an addition. In the Bibliography, I have offered translations of titles except where they appear to be little more than a play on the author's name.

In translating scriptural verses I have often had to depart from the various recognized versions (which sometimes differ substantially from each other) so as to convey the meaning which, in the particular context, seems most likely to have been intended by the users.

In the Psalms, the consistent difference in the verse numbering between Jewish and non-Jewish versions results from the fact that the non-Jewish versions do not count the superscriptions (e.g. 'A Psalm of David') as verses, whereas in the Jewish versions the superscription counts as verse 1, or, if lengthy, may even count as more than one verse.

My thanks are due to Dr Ada Rapoport-Albert, of University College London (who suggested that I undertake this translation), for much help with many difficulties and obscurities.

M.H.

Introduction

JOSEPH DAN

TISHBY, LUZZATTO, AND MODERN HEBREW LITERATURE

IN THE 1950s, when Isaiah Tishby began to work on the series of studies many of which are included in this volume in an English translation, Rabbi Moses Hayim Luzzatto was regarded as one of the founding fathers of modern Jewish culture. He was acclaimed as the cornerstone of modern Hebrew literature, which was regarded as a major component of the emergence of contemporary Jewish culture, which served as a foundation for the integration of Jews into modern European life, and which opened the door to the development of Jewish nationalism and Zionism, and eventually to the establishment of the Jewish state, Israel. It might be said that he was regarded as the major writer who opened the canon of modern Hebrew literature. When I was in elementary school, in the 1940s, and we started to learn Hebrew poetry, Luzzatto was the first poet we read. When the State of Israel established its curriculum in Hebrew literature, Luzzatto was presented in a prominent position. His plays were studied by every student who prepared himself for the matriculation examination. This is no longer the case. Later in these pages I shall try to review the process which caused a drastic decline in Luzzatto's position in contemporary Israeli culture.

Isaiah Tishby, who presented his Ph.D. thesis in kabbalah to Gershom Scholem in 1945, and started teaching at the Department of Hebrew Literature in the Hebrew University of Jerusalem in 1949, was close to two scholars who were responsible, probably more than anyone else, for the elevated position of Luzzatto at that time. One was Fischel Lachower, who was regarded as the most important historian of Hebrew literature. His volumes on the history and development of modern Hebrew literature, which were written against the background of intense Zionist faith, dictated the canon of texts, writers, and poets. This history started with Luzzatto and reached its peak with the poetry of Hayim Nahman Bialik, who was regarded as the national poet of the young state. Lachower was an erudite scholar in many aspects of traditional Jewish culture, and was interested especially in kabbalah.

He found in the works of Luzzatto a combination of mysticism and modernity, and dedicated several articles to the study of Luzzatto's plays, which were written in the eighteenth-century conventions of Italian plays, in magnificent biblical Hebrew, and contained—so Lachower believed—a layer of meaning based on the secrets of kabbalah. A volume of articles by Lachower, which included the studies of Luzzatto, was entitled *On the Border between Old and New*: he viewed Luzzatto as partly belonging to traditional Jewish culture, and at the same time as one who opened the gates of that culture to enlightenment and modernity.

It was Lachower who initiated the great project which became Isaiah Tishby's most influential and best-known work, the volumes on the *Wisdom of the Zohar*, which include a vast anthology of sections from the Zohar, translated from the original Aramaic into Hebrew, with detailed introductions to the main subjects and a commentary explaining the texts. Lachower started to translate some paragraphs from the Zohar, and presented his plan to the major publisher in Jerusalem at that time, the Bialik Institute, the publishing house of the Jewish Agency. He soon realized that he could not undertake the vast project himself, and asked Tishby to join him. Lachower died soon after that, and it was Tishby who actually did almost everything, though Lachower's name was included as a co-author of the first volume. Thus, the interest in the Zohar brought Lachower and Tishby together, and it served as a background for Tishby's interest in Luzzatto.

It is impossible to understand this connection between Luzzatto, Lachower, and Tishby without taking into account the influence of H. N. Bialik. Bialik, though he died long before these events (in 1935), was still a dominant figure in Hebrew culture. It was Bialik who initiated, in the 1920s, the great project of the *kinus*—the assembling, editing, and republishing of the great cultural and spiritual treasures of Jewish traditional creativity and presenting them in a modern, secular format to the emerging Hebrew civilization in Palestine, and later in Israel. It was his vision of integrating Jewish tradition and modern culture by scholarly and popular presentation of the achievements of the past. Bialik himself contributed to this endeavour by publishing, together with Rabnitzki, the great anthology of talmudic–midrashic heritage in their *Sefer ha'agadah*. Bialik wrote a very influential article on the subject, and the Jewish Agency (which was at that time actually the government of the Jewish community in Palestine) established its publishing house, the Bialik Institute, for this purpose. Bialik himself was not particularly interested in kabbalah, but he did ask Gershom Scholem in 1926 to put forward a programme for the publication of kabbalistic texts within the framework of the *kinus*. It seems that Bialik played a meaningful part in the establishment of the study of kabbalah at the Hebrew University (founded in 1925), and the appointment of Scholem as one of its teachers. What is important to us in this context is that Bialik wrote a profound, sensitive article on Luzzatto, 'The Young Man from Padua', which contributed to the establishment of Luzzatto at the centre of the emerging canon of modern Hebrew literature.

The other person, besides Lachower, who may have influenced Tishby's interest in the works of Luzzatto was Professor Simon Halkin, who was the head of the Department of Hebrew Literature at the Hebrew University when Tishby became a teacher in that department. Halkin was invited by the university to hold the chair of Modern Hebrew Literature after the retirement of the previous teacher, Joseph Klausner, who had held this position since the founding of the university. Klausner wrote a six-volume history of Hebrew literature during the period of the Enlightenment, which completely contradicted the views held by Lachower. According to Klausner, the beginning of modern Hebrew literature should be found in the establishment of the first Hebrew Enlightenment journal, *Hame'asef*, in Germany in the end of the eighteenth century, two generations after Luzzatto. Halkin, however, was closer to Lachower, and in his lectures and publications presented a picture of gradual transition in Hebrew creativity from the traditional forms to more modern ones, a process in which Luzzatto held a central position.

There was no direct clash concerning Luzzatto between Halkin and Klausner, but the subject provoked fierce controversy between Halkin and another scholar and literary critic, Baruch Kurzweil (who was rejected for the position of Halkin's chair, and who blamed for this Gershom Scholem, against whom he wrote extensively later). When the notes of Halkin's lectures were published, Kurzweil wrote a series of critical articles which were later assembled into a book, *Our Modern Literature: Continuation or Revolution?* His main thesis was that the essential characteristic of modern Hebrew literature was its secular attitude and the rejection of Jewish rabbinic values, and that therefore it represented a rebellion against Jewish traditional culture. There was no place for Luzzatto or similar writers in the history of the modern phenomenon. Halkin was deeply hurt by Kurzweil's harsh criticism, but did not respond. Tishby, however, published an article in the daily newspaper *Ha'arets* which defended his colleague and supported him.

Halkin shaped the Department of Hebrew Literature according to his conceptions of the history of the subject. He included many new subjects which were not a part of the curriculum before, including Jewish prayers, the literature of the aggadah, Jewish folklore, Jewish Hellenistic literature, and especially Hebrew ethical literature, which was Tishby's domain, in which Luzzatto was a central figure, being the author of the most successful Hebrew work of ethics of all times—*Mesilat yesharim* [The Highway of the Upright]. Tishby taught several seminars on the ethical and kabbalistic works of Luzzatto; I had the pleasure to participate in two of them.

Thus, the connections between Tishby and Luzzatto are to be found on several levels: personal, academic, ideological, and thematic. Bialik, Lachower, and Halkin were among the figures who brought them together, beyond scholarly and historical interest. Tishby's scholarly work in general contains an element of passion and devotion—concerning the Zohar, the Shabatean messianic movement, and other subjects—yet Luzzatto had a special place, and Tishby most probably felt a particular closeness to the tragic figure of the 'young man from Padua'.

It should be pointed out that these discussions and controversies were characteristic of the cultural discourse in Israel in the 1950s and 1960s, but have been marginalized or even completely ignored in the last few decades. The historical conceptions of the development of modern Hebrew literature presented by Lachower and Halkin were not accepted by the next generation of scholars in this field (most of whom were direct disciples of Halkin's), while those of Klausner and Kurzweil dominate today the image of Hebrew Enlightenment and modern literature. Within the context of this radical change in attitude, the writings of Luzzatto have been completely marginalized in current Israeli culture. The plays of Luzzatto are no longer part of the curriculum of Israeli schools, and most Israeli intellectuals are completely unaware of their existence. The curriculum of the Department of Hebrew Literature at the Hebrew University no longer includes many of the traditional subjects that Halkin introduced. Israeli culture as a whole adopted the European definition of 'literature', and finds no place in it for traditional Jewish genres, subjects, and authors. The secular nature of the contemporary conception of literature relegates complex, multi-layered figures like Luzzatto to a position of ancient, irrelevant religious thinkers who may be the concern of historians but do not convey any message to the Israeli public today.

TISHBY AND THE NEW MANUSCRIPTS: THE LUZZATTO CIRCLE

Isaiah Tishby started his scholarly study of the writings of Rabbi Moses Hayim Luzzatto in the 1950s. In his visits to libraries of Hebrew manuscripts in England and other European countries he became aware that there was a wealth of material concerning Luzzatto and his circle of disciples to be found in manuscripts that had not been studied by previous scholars, and that these works—some of them found in Luzzatto's own handwriting—contain important information which can lead to a meaningful revision of the image of Luzzatto's world view. He acquired photocopies of several important manuscripts, and started to study them. At that time (1958) he appointed me his teaching and research assistant, and he entrusted to me the reading and copying of several sections of these manuscripts. From then, I became his associate and a party to his work in this field, and was privileged to follow closely the development of his conclusions concerning this unique chapter in the history of Jewish mysticism.

One of the first assignments which Tishby gave me was to decipher and copy the personal, mystical diary which Luzzatto's disciple, Rabbi Moses David Valle, wrote in the margins of his own commentary on the Bible. Tishby proved that Valle was Luzzatto's closest follower, and that he was designated to be Messiah ben David in the messianic programme that Luzzatto's circle devised (Luzzatto himself was designated as the reincarnation of Moses, a messianic figure above all others). His commentary transforms the text of the Scriptures into a detailed biography of the Messiah, which Valle believed to be the story of his own soul. This commentary is present in several manuscript volumes, and it is very probable that Tishby was the first (and, as yet, the only) modern reader of all of them. While the commentary is written in the formal script of a copyist of manuscripts, the notes in the margins are written in cursive, personal handwriting, probably often written in the morning, after waking from a particularly significant dream, or connected to a daily event. Whereas the commentary is presented in non-personal, abstract language, the notes convey the impression of personal, intimate remarks. Many of these notes include a full date—year, month, and day—thus making it possible to connect each of them to actual events in the lives of Luzzatto and Valle. Here was a record of personal mystical visions and experiences, written in short, often enigmatic notes, a rare example of an immediate recording of such experiences in the history of Jewish mysticism. Tishby studied this diary in detail, and the essay he published is translated in the present volume. The Valle diary and commentary are undoubtedly a most meaningful discovery of Tishby's, which changed the image of Luzzatto and his circle in a dramatic way.

Another subject which fascinated Tishby was Luzzatto's great endeavour of writing a 'new Zohar', imitating the language and style of the great medieval masterpiece. Tishby devoted a study to the controversy surrounding the printing of the Zohar in Italy in the sixteenth century, and was familiar with the messianic role given to the publication of the Zohar in many circles of kabbalists. Luzzatto shared the view that the real Zohar, or the inner meaning of the Zohar, would be revealed in messianic times. However, he believed that it would be a new Zohar, dedicated completely to the elaboration of the process of the Redemption, and would be written by the Messiah himself, namely Moses Hayim Luzzatto. The text which Luzzatto wrote was scattered through some printed works and some manuscripts, and Tishby set out to collect all the sections and reconstruct the entire work. This endeavour served him in elucidating many aspects of the messianic message of

Luzzatto and his circle, which he presented in several of the studies translated in this volume. Tishby, who dedicated so much effort to the presentation of the original, classical Zohar in his *Wisdom of the Zohar*, was deeply touched by this 'second edition' of the work written by the young, passionate messianic pretender in eighteenth-century Padua.

This work was one of the main reasons for the criticism, and ultimately the expulsion, of Luzzatto by the Jewish Italian communities. Even his closest supporters, such as his teacher Rabbi Isaiah Bassano, were taken aback by the daring and radical ideas in this 'new Zohar', and demanded that Luzzatto stop writing it and hide whatever he had written so far. Luzzatto claimed that the work was dictated to him by a heavenly emissary, a *magid*, who was first revealed to him in his youth. His critics demanded that he refrain from writing the messages of the *magid*, and Luzzatto had to accept this injunction. It was later discovered, however, that he did continue to write the 'new Zohar', and this was one of the reasons why he was forced to emigrate from Italy and settle in Amsterdam.

Tishby was most interested in Luzzatto's poetry, his hymns and religious poems (*piyutim*). Luzzatto had already earned a place among the most important Hebrew poets of all times, so Tishby was gratified to find a treasure of hitherto unknown and unpublished poems by Luzzatto in the manuscripts he studied. Ephraim Broido, the editor of the influential intellectual journal *Molad*, and a good friend of Halkin and Tishby, dedicated a complete issue to the publication of Luzzatto's newly discovered poems, edited by Tishby.

MESSIANISM AND THE MYSTICAL MARRIAGE

This volume, which offers the best modern study of Luzzatto to English-speaking readers, is the proper place to present and emphasize the importance of one text, which Tishby discovered and published, which I consider to be one of the most meaningful mystical texts ever written, in any language, period, and culture. It is the *ketubah* of Rabbi Moses Hayim Luzzatto, to which the young bridegroom added a detailed commentary, ascribing radical mystical and messianic significance to the wedding ceremony. The *ketubah* is an ancient Jewish legal document, written in Aramaic, in which the bridegroom undertakes to support his wife throughout their marriage, and to compensate her in case of divorce. It is a rather dry document, signed by the bridegroom and witnesses, and read in the marriage ceremony. It is technical and legal, its language is fixed, and the only indication of the specific event is the compulsory insertion of the date, the place, the names of the bride and bridegroom, the names of the witnesses, and the exact sum of money promised by the bridegroom in case of divorce. The reading of the *ketubah* by the rabbi officiating in the marriage ceremony is the boring part of the event;

most of the gathered people do not understand the Aramaic, and pay little attention; besides, no one likes to think about divorce when a marriage is celebrated.

Luzzatto, however, perceived his marriage and the signing of the *ketubah* as the culmination of a cosmic and divine mystical and messianic process, and expressed it in a detailed commentary which he wrote on the text of his own *ketubah*. It is an exegesis of that text as a whole, both the traditional, technical, legal portions and the individual ones—the date, place, and names inserted on that particular occasion. The following remarks do not add any details to Tishby's analysis of this text. They are an attempt to place the document in a wider spiritual context.

Early critics of Luzzatto in Padua pointed out that he remained single after the age at which young Jews usually got married. He was called by the pejorative Aramaic phrase *plag gufa*, 'half a body'. Marriage was a most important point in the process of growing up and becoming a member of the community. A mature unmarried person could hardly be found in Jewish society, and certainly not among scholars and rabbis. When Luzzatto claimed to have had contact with a celestial power, the *magid*, and to be the recipient of supreme secrets, his case was weakened by his being single: it is unimaginable that God will choose an incomplete, unmarried person to whom to reveal profound secrets. When Luzzatto did marry, in 1731, when he was in his early twenties, the reason for the delay became obvious. He married (under pressure from his teacher and benefactor, Rabbi Isaiah Bassano) the daughter of the rabbi of Mantua, Rabbi David Finzi, whose name was Zipporah. The marriage, therefore, was one between Moses and Zipporah, the daughter of Jethro—the re-emergence of the biblical couple (see Exod. 2: 21, and cf. 4: 25, 18: 2). It is inconceivable, after knowing Luzzatto's spiritual world, that he could marry anyone with any other name.

Tishby discovered this document in a photocopy of manuscript Guenzburg 376 which was housed in the Ben Tsevi Institute in Jerusalem. The manuscript includes several kabbalistic treatises, published and unpublished, by Luzzatto. Tishby identified it as the Coronel MS 28, which has been described in the catalogue of that collection. The text and Tishby's study were published in 1960 in the Y. F. Baer jubilee volume in Jerusalem, and then included in Tishby's first volume of collected studies, *Netivei emunah uminut* [Paths of Faith and Heresy] (Ramat Gan, 1964). Despite the fact that the text was published more than forty years ago, I have seen very few references to it in any context, and its religious significance seems to have escaped most of the scholars in the field. I have dedicated to it a chapter in my *On Sanctity* (Jerusalem, 1997; pp. 435–55).

The connection between mysticism and erotic metaphors is as ancient as the discipline itself. The erotic encounters vividly described in Solomon's

Song of Songs have been a major source of images and expressions since the great commentary on that work by Origen. In kabbalah, which introduced the conception of a female figure as part of the Godhead, the erotic encounters between masculine and feminine divine powers became a major theme, and it included also references to an erotic relationship between the mystic and the female power in the divine realm, the Shekhinah. The imperfection of the present world was often expressed in terms of the distance between the bride and bridegroom in the divine world, and redemption was described as the reinstitution of sexual harmony.

All these materials, which abound in kabbalistic literature, in the Zohar, and in Lurianic kabbalah, were used extensively by Luzzatto. What is new in his presentation, however, is the intense personal character that the abstract metaphors acquired in his world view. Tishby collected, in his introduction to the text, several unambiguous statements in Luzzatto's poetry and kabbalistic works in which the marriage of the biblical Moses with Zipporah is defined as the union between the Shekhinah and the masculine part of the Godhead. In the commentary on the *ketubah* the biblical text and the kabbalistic interpretation are transferred to the personal realm. The ceremony in Padua, the marriage of Moses Luzzatto and Zipporah Finzi, is identified completely with the sexual union in the divine world. According to the statements collected by Tishby from all Luzzatto's works as well as those of his disciples, it is clear that the occasion was understood by them not only as a union in the divine world, but as the ultimate union, the eradication of all the obstacles on the way to redemption, and it represented, in the most actual and literal manner, the arrival of the messianic age.

Tishby followed the documents concerning the messianic expectation of the Luzzatto circle in great detail, and succeeded in presenting a coherent and comprehensive picture of their messianic vision. There is no doubt that Moses David Valle was designated, by Luzzatto and by himself, as the key messianic figure, that of Messiah ben David. Concerning the equation of Moses with Luzzatto, he was identified as the supreme messianic figure, above that of the messiahs of the tribes of Judah and of Joseph. Luzzatto made use of numerous references to the redeeming aspect of Moses in the kabbalistic tradition, but developed it further in a systematic way. The conclusion Tishby reached, which is supported by unambiguous textual evidence, is that Luzzatto, as the contemporary presence of Moses, is the main power and the supreme coordinator of the messianic process.

Two problems remained. First, what was the role of Rabbi Jekutiel Gordon of Vilna, a medical student who came from Poland to Padua to study medicine, and became Luzzatto's closest associate and his partner in leading the messianic circle? And second, what about the figure of Messiah ben Joseph? Who was he, and what was his role in this messianic group?

Concerning Rabbi Jekutiel, the documents supplied Tishby with a clear picture: he was identified with the figure of Seraiah of the tribe of Dan, who was portrayed in the Zohar and other sources as the military leader of the armies of the Messiah, a central figure in the messianic process. Tishby discovered references to Seraiah in Luzzatto's writings that insist that Seraiah was born in Poland and joined the Messiah by leaving his homeland. Luzzatto also defended his friend against the accusation that he dedicated himself to the study of 'the wisdom of the Gentiles', and explained it as being needed to fulfil a divine design. It is probable that the image of Jekutiel–Seraiah is described in some of Luzzatto's poems. Luzzatto, Valle, and Jekutiel were the three figures in the messianic hierarchy of Luzzatto's circle.

The problem of Messiah ben Joseph was a more complex one. In the first publication by Tishby of this material in 1960 he presented this question as one which he was not yet ready to resolve, and which needed more study—though at that time he had expressed his conclusion clearly in conversations with me. One of the reasons for his hesitation was the direct impact of his conclusions on the controversy which raged around Luzzatto in his own lifetime and had continued to simmer ever since: was Luzzatto an adherent of the Shabatean messianic movement and doctrine? The core of the criticism which made Luzzatto's life bitter and frustrating and caused him exile from his homeland was the accusation that he was a secret worshipper of Shabetai Tsevi, the messiah who converted to Islam in 1666. To defend himself, Luzzatto wrote a special treatise, *Milḥamot hashem* [The Wars of the Lord], to express his rejection of Shabatean messianism. His critics found many flaws in his arguments and were not convinced. Tishby hesitated, because his presentation may be interpreted as supporting the enemies of Luzzatto. However, he finally did publish the material and analysed it in great detail. He had no doubt that Shabetai Tsevi was identified by Luzzatto and his circle as the failed Messiah, the victim of the messianic process, Messiah ben Joseph. Talmudic tradition and early medieval apocalyptic literature described Messiah ben Joseph as a hero, a victim, a saint, who was killed by the demonic opponent of the Messiah, Armilus, in a series of victories which led him almost to rule the whole earth; then Messiah ben David appears, and he is the one who ultimately overcomes Armilus and establishes the victory of the holy hosts. In some sources we find a statement that Messiah ben Joseph will be resurrected by Messiah ben David in the culmination of the redemption process. In the many decades which have passed since Tishby first published his conclusion I have not seen any argument presented which may cast doubt on this identification of Shabetai Tsevi with Messiah ben Joseph in Luzzatto's messianic teachings.

If so, was Luzzatto a secret Shabatean? On the one hand, he certainly was. He did not designate Shabetai Tsevi as a false messianic pretender, as a sinner, heretic, and apostate, but rather assigned him an important traditional role in the messianic process. We do not know whether he intended to revive him during this process. On the other hand, was Shabetai Tsevi, according to Luzzatto, the Messiah? Obviously, the true Messiah was Luzzatto himself, assisted by Valle—Messiah ben David—and Jekutiel of Vilna, the chief commander of the messianic armies. Shabetai Tsevi represented a preliminary, unsuccessful stage in the messianic apocalypse. His teachings were not the ones that messianic believers had to follow: they had to receive the teachings of Luzzatto himself.

An even more complex question is whether Luzzatto followed the messianic doctrines of the Shabatean movement, which were formulated mainly by the 'prophet' of Shabetai Tsevi, Nathan of Gaza. In this respect, Tishby's conclusions were more definite: the concept of the messianic process in Luzzatto's circle was very close to the doctrines presented in the previous century by Nathan and other Shabatean thinkers. The most important document concerning this process was the detailed, multi-volume commentary on the Bible by Rabbi Moses David Valle. Valle, as Tishby showed, interpreted almost every verse in the Bible as relating to the endeavours of a messianic figure, which he called *hatsadik hamevarer*, 'the righteous one who separates good from evil'. The Bible, in this work, is actually the mythical biography of the Messiah, indicating the past, present, and future events in the great apocalyptic drama of the struggle against evil and the bringing about of the Redemption. This tsadik is obviously Valle himself, and the biography of the Messiah as related in the biblical texts is the spiritual autobiography of the tsadik-Messiah, Valle himself.

The conceptions of the role of the Messiah in Valle's work differ in a most meaningful way from the kabbalistic tradition on the process of the Redemption as formulated by Rabbi Isaac Luria Ashkenazi, the Ari, and his disciples in sixteenth-century Safed. These kabbalists presented a profound, powerful myth, according to which it is the duty of every Jew to take part in a cosmic struggle to bring about the purification of the lower and higher realms from the domination of the powers of evil. A central metaphor employed by Lurianic myth is that of the assembling and redeeming of the scattered sparks—sparks of divine light which were captured by the forces of Satan, and which in their captivity are sustaining the powers of evil. These sparks can be set free by the performance of the commandments and by ethical deeds, and every person has to take part in this. An evil deed committed by a person causes another spark to fall into the dark realm, whereas every blessing, every prayer, every righteous act makes a spark return to the divine realm and be united with its source, thus weakening the domination of evil. Ultimate messianic redemption will arrive, according to Luria, when all the sparks have been liberated and elevated, depriving evil of its sources of sustenance and thus destroying it. In the seventeenth century Lurianic kabbalah spread throughout the Jewish world and became the dominant Jewish world view.

Lurianic kabbalah did not specify the role of the Messiah. Despite the fact that Luria's main disciple, Rabbi Hayim Vital, believed himself to be the Messiah, and some messianic role was also attributed to Luria himself, the Messiah in the Lurianic doctrine is the result of the process of redemption rather than its cause. The Messiah, as an individual, has no specific function in bringing about the liberation and elevation of the captive sparks; he participates in it like every other person. This attitude was dramatically transformed in the theology presented by Nathan of Gaza, which dominated the messianic movement of the adherents of Shabetai Tsevi. According to Nathan, there is a core of utter evil at the heart of the realm ruled by the satanic forces, which is so dark and difficult that the efforts of ordinary Jews are incapable of overcoming it. There must come a divine emissary, an incarnated divine power, who could focus the spiritual power of the Jewish people as a whole and who would face this core of evil and vanquish it. This is the mission of the Messiah, who thus assumes the role of the leader of the people, the representative of God on earth, and it is he who leads the final struggle against the powers of evil. This was the first time in the history of Jewish messianism that the role of the Messiah was theologically defined, and he was presented as the intermediary between God and the people of Israel. Every person has to express his faith in the Messiah, and the divine incarnation uses this spiritual power to enhance and achieve the ultimate goal of redemption.

The commentary on the Bible by Moses David Valle, the biography of the Messiah and the autobiography of the author, follows the principles of Nathan of Gaza's messianic theology. The fate of the messianic process resides in the efforts and struggles of the Messiah as an individual. He is portrayed as the leader of the redemptive process, and he is personally responsible for every achievement and every failure. It is he who has to vanquish the powers of evil, and all his efforts are dedicated to that purpose, while he suffers all the wounds inflicted on him by his cruel enemies. This detailed, comprehensive picture of the Messiah is dependent to a very large extent on the teachings of Nathan of Gaza and the other theologians of Shabatean messianism. If Shabateanism is defined as a belief in the messianic mission of the person Shabetai Tsevi, Valle was not a Shabatean, because he believed that it was he himself who bore the messianic burden, rather than the messianic pretender of the previous century. However, if Shabateanism is defined as a messianic theology formulated by Nathan of Gaza, then Valle, and Luzzatto with him, should be regarded as belonging to that spiritual camp.

Another element common to the Luzzatto circle and the Shabateans is not only the sincere, unshakeable belief in the imminence of messianic redemption but the complete faith that it has actually arrived and is culminating now, in the present. The great message which the 'prophet' Nathan brought to the Jewish world was that the process described in detail in Lurianic kabbalah, that of the liberation and elevation of the captive sparks, had been completed, and in the divine realms the messianic era had actually begun. It takes time—argued Nathan and other Shabatean thinkers—for the perfection achieved in the divine realms to be manifested on earth, but the battle has been decided and the messianic victory is no longer in doubt. According to the evidence assembled by Tishby, Luzzatto and Valle were absolutely confident that the Lurianic process had reached its goal with complete success, and that the messianic era was here and now. Every event in their earthly lives was interpreted as another indication of this fact. The mystical diary which Valle wrote in the margins of his biblical commentary can be understood in many cases as stressing this fact, and it is evident also in statements in the letters written by Jekutiel of Vilna. The circle which assembled around Luzzatto was dedicated not only to the enhancement of the Redemption, but to celebrating the achievement of that process. They were not future-oriented; they viewed themselves as the expression of the present, the few who recognized the beginning of the new era before everybody became aware of it. The most potent expression of this conception was the celebration of Luzzatto's marriage, and the document which Tishby discovered and published concerning that event, Luzzatto's commentary on his own *ketubah*.

This document is written in short sentences, in the style of exegetical works, quoting the original text and commenting on it in dry, technical phrases. It is expressed in technical kabbalistic terminology, often using midrashic techniques. The Hebrew text cannot be understood without detailed knowledge of kabbalistic literature; Tishby did his best to explain it in the notes he added to the publication of the text, yet these notes were intended more for scholars in the field than for the general reader. Luzzatto presents here a human experience—marriage and sexual union—as the culmination of a divine process, the achievement of complete erotic union in the divine world, which is the ultimate achievement of the purpose of cosmic and divine existence, the emergence of the redeemed universe and divine world. This is not a vision, nor is it a metaphor: this is what actually happened on that day when Moses and Zipporah were united. Behind the succinct, technical words of Luzzatto—and of Tishby—is hidden one of the most potent mystical and messianic experiences ever recorded, an experience of self-deification within the framework of an actual erotic event which transforms the universe and state of the divine powers; it is the end of history and the beginning of a new world, that of messianic redemption.

LUZZATTO AND HASIDISM

During the nineteenth century it seemed that Moses Hayim Luzzatto 'belonged' to the camp of the mitnagedim, the 'opponents' of the hasidic movement, after the great schism which began in 1772 and continues to this very day. One of the characteristics of the activity of the mitnagedim was the renewed emphasis on the study of Hebrew ethical literature, which was a central demand of the Musar movement that began in the middle of the nineteenth century and reached its peak at the end of that century and the beginning of the twentieth. The activity of the mitnagedim in general, and of the Musar movement teachers in particular, was centred in the Torah academies, the yeshivas, and in many of them the study of ethical texts was introduced as a central subject. Among these, the ethical works of Luzzatto were highly regarded. In Jerusalem of the 1940s and 1950s and even later one could see on every bus a person or two deeply immersed in reading *Mesilat yesharim* or some other of Luzzatto's popular treatises on ethics, such as *Da'at tevunot* [Knowledge with Understanding] or *Derekh hashem* [The Way of the Lord]. Some people knew these works by heart, in the same way that they knew talmudic tractates. It seems that these ultra-Orthodox opponents of any change in Jewish tradition embraced Luzzatto despite the accusations that he was a secret adherent of Shabetai Tsevi. The ethical treatises, which Luzzatto wrote mainly in Amsterdam after he was forced to leave Italy, appealed to these readers because of the inner stratum of kabbalistic world view which was hidden in them, despite their dominant style of Hebrew philosophical discourse. Luzzatto was forbidden to write any more kabbalistic works, and he found in this literary genre an avenue for expressing his ideas without using kabbalistic terminology or citing kabbalistic sources. Many of these treatises were published again and again, some of them reprinted almost every year in popular editions. Luzzatto was thus regarded as a saint and as a pietist, highly revered by intellectuals and common people in this segment of Orthodox Jewish society.

At the same time, some hasidic groups began to take an interest in Luzzatto's kabbalistic works. These were circles of spiritualists within some of the leading hasidic courts. Tishby was once very offended when a text of Luzzatto's Zohar which he copied and lent to one of his students in a seminar was acquired by such a group and printed as a book, without his knowledge and permission. The 'forbidden' messianic texts began to reappear in the Orthodox bookshops in Jerusalem, and Luzzatto acquired semi-secret adherents in twentieth-century Jerusalem.

Tishby was engaged in the 1960s and 1970s by several aspects of the history and thought of the hasidic movement. He published, in collaboration with me, the extensive article 'Hasidic Thought and Literature' in the seventeenth volume of the *Hebrew Encyclopedia*, which is still the only comprehensive survey of all aspects of hasidic spiritual creativity. He studied in great detail the messianic element in hasidism, a subject which led him to confront and criticize some of Gershom Scholem's conclusions concerning this subject. When he immersed himself in the study of the writings of Luzzatto and his circle, he discovered, rather unexpectedly, that early hasidic teachers made use of key terms and central concepts of the Luzzatto circle, and the role of Luzzatto as a source of hasidic thought became one of Tishby's main subjects of research. He proved that the hasidic slogan 'God, the Torah, and Israel are one and the same', which is often quoted as a Zoharic dictum, was actually formulated by Luzzatto and his circle. More important, the central hasidic concept of the leader of a hasidic community, the tsadik, as the one who fights evil and redeems the divine sparks which are captive in that realm, follows the biographical-messianic figure of the tsadik who separates good from evil, *hatsadik hamevarer*, which is at the centre of Valle's biblical commentary. The theory of the tsadik as a divine emissary who represents his community in the struggle against evil and brings about the individual redemption of his followers as well as contributing to the salvation of the whole people is central to hasidic ideology and practice, and Tishby demonstrated that meaningful components of this theory were derived from the writings of Luzzatto and Valle. He suggested that the avenue by which this influence extended from Italy to eastern Europe was the work of Rabbi Jekutiel of Vilna, who returned from Padua to his country and preached his teacher's ideas to the intellectuals from among whom the early hasidic teachers emerged. According to Tishby's thesis, therefore, the modern hasidic adherents of Luzzatto's kabbalistic and messianic teaching are actually returning to the sources which were used by their spiritual ancestors two and a half centuries ago.

*

The image of Luzzatto emerging from all these seemingly separate and independent realms of activity and creativity is rather unusual. Luzzatto stands as a central figure at the origins of all segments of modern Jewish movements. He is revered—for radically different reasons—by the modern adherents of integration of Jewish and European culture, the inheritors of the Enlightenment movement. He is regarded as an ethical teacher, a saint, by the mitnagedim, and as a great kabbalistic teacher by circles of hasidim. His teachings represented an original version of Shabatean messianism, while continuing and developing the Lurianic kabbalistic tradition. Dozens of his works in different editions are to be found on the shelves of every traditional bookshop. Tishby brought to the attention of the public an unknown body of meaningful treatises and poems. These writings, and especially Luzzatto's *ketubah* with his commentary, place him as one of the most profound mystics in the history of Jewish culture, one who should be included in the annals of mysticism in general.

ONE

A Collection of Kabbalistic Works from the Unpublished Manuscripts of Rabbi Moses Hayim Luzzatto: MS Oxford 2593

In memory of my friend and colleague, the late
HAYIM WIRSZUBSKY

PART 1

WHEN I began my search, during my stay in England in 1956, for unpublished manuscripts by R. M. H. Luzzatto (Ramhal), my most important find was the collection in MS Oxford 2593.[1] In Neubauer's catalogue this was described as a collection of unidentified kabbalistic writings by anonymous authors. The only work attributed was Luzzatto's *Ḥoker umekubal*, and even in that case the description did not identify the important foreword which appears, out of order, after the main body of the text. From my examination of the collection it was clear to me that all the works in it were by Luzzatto, and this collection, which was my starting point, has served me ever since as a basis for the discovery of further manuscripts which had been put away unpublished. In my lecture at the Institute of Jewish Studies in Jerusalem in 1961 I discussed one item in the collection, a homily and prayer for a formal meal [*se'udah*] on the night of 17 Shevat. More recently I have specifically

[1] Opp. Add. 8° 79. I am most grateful to the curators of the Bodleian Library at Oxford, who, on the occasion of my first visit in 1956 and again when I returned there in 1976, allowed me access to the manuscript treasures in the library, met all my requests for photocopies, and granted me permission to publish this manuscript and others in whole or in part. My thanks are due also to the staff of the Institute for the Photography of Hebrew Manuscripts at the National and University Library in Jerusalem for their help and dedicated service. I availed myself of the photographs in the Institute to read many of the manuscripts which I required for the purposes of my research.

categorized the collection as follows:[2] 'My researches have shown this collection be a rich store of unpublished kabbalistic writings by Luzzatto, and I am about to provide them with a commentary and publish them separately and collectively.'

In the survey and explanatory comments presented here I discuss in detail every item in the collection and draw attention, as necessary, to links with other writings in the corpus of Luzzatto's works. In a continuation of the present essay I shall publish a selection of short compositions and fragments from the collection, adding introductions and notes, under the title 'Pirkei kabalah meḥiburim genuzim shel ramḥa"l mitokh ketav-yad oksford 2593' ['Kabbalistic Writings from Unpublished Works by Luzzatto in MS Oxford 2593']. [This appears to be the supplementary part—not separately titled—of the present essay, from Section IX onward, as noted in the Appendix to this volume.—Trans.] At the same time I am preparing for print, in a similar form, a selection of compositions which came to my notice in a variety of sources in the course of my investigations. The latter selection will be entitled 'Pirkei kabalah meḥiburim genuzim shel ramḥa"l mitokh kitvei-yad shonim' ['Kabbalistic Writings from Unpublished Works by Luzzatto in Various Manuscripts'].

In an appendix [not traced—Trans.] I have added some letters which shed fresh light on the methods employed by the members of Luzzatto's school in Padua in copying and disseminating their master's writings. These letters, which also contain some surprising revelations about the practice of magic among the members of the school, are connected with the explanation of *yiḥud hayirah*, which I shall discuss in presenting *Yiḥud gan-eden* in the present collection.[3]

The number of pages in the codex is 170, including blank folios or pages amounting to some thirty pages in all,[4] as well as some pages left partly blank. The last folio with any writing on it is 168^{r}; its contents, however, are not part of the collection of compositions, but are a list of payments to the writer, together with the names of the payers. The names are written in Latin characters, with the name Bonfil at their head, and only in the last line does there appear in Hebrew 'talmidim 2' ['pupils, 2']. There is no doubt that the word *talmidim* was written by R. Jekutiel of Vilna, one of Luzzatto's chief disciples, and that he drew up the whole list while engaged in teaching at the Torah Or yeshiva in Venice after his return to Italy from Lithuania.[5] On fo. 105^{r-v} of MS Oxford 2237, which consists mostly of writings by R. Jekutiel and

[2] In 'Shirim ufiyutim miginzei rabi mosheh ḥayim lutsato', now Essay 2 below.

[3] See Section IX below.

[4] The following are the completely blank pages: 10^{v}, 39^{r}–42^{v}, 47^{v}–50^{v}, 73^{v}–74^{v}, 115^{v}, 127^{v}, 134^{v}, 148^{r-v}, 166^{v}–167^{v}, 168^{v}–170^{v}. Only in two places is it evident that pages are missing: before 128^{r} and between 162^{v} and 163^{r}.

[5] See Essay 8, pp. 438–43.

Luzzatto in R. Jekutiel's hand, there is a prayer for Jacob Bonfil, who is mentioned as a supporter of R. Jekutiel's work in the school. Apparently the collection came into the possession of R. Jekutiel while he was living in Venice.

The works are written in various hands, and sometimes the handwriting is not uniform even within one composition. The codex is in small format, corresponding to the pattern of the notebooks in which Luzzatto, or copyists working under his supervision in his school, entered his writings.[6] It is clear to me that several works and fragments are in Luzzatto's own hand, whereas I can say with certainty that no composition in the collection is in the handwriting of R. Jekutiel. However, with regard to some of the compositions which appear to me to be autographs, it is hard to establish with certainty that the handwriting is that of Luzzatto, even though many manuscripts have been preserved which he undoubtedly wrote himself. His manuscripts display many pronounced differences in the form of the letters and the penstrokes, and sometimes the writing changes constantly in appearance even from line to line on the same page.[7] Only in the case of one copyist,[8] who prepared many of the copies in the collection, is the handwriting uniform throughout and identifiable without hesitation. In the description of each item I shall express my opinion on the handwriting.

Evidence of various kinds confirms that these documents are by Luzzatto: their identity with compositions known from other sources to have been his handiwork, their presence in other collections containing writings by him, elements of form, structure, or style characteristic of his works, or motifs or ideas which occur frequently in his writings or bear the stamp of his personal philosophy. In this essay I shall adduce only part of the material internal evidence; I shall draw attention to the rest in the notes which will accompany the published texts.

I. 'LINKED DISCOURSES'
(FOS. 1^r–10^r, 163^r–165^r)

The collection begins with three series of homilies (fos. 1^r–10^r)[9] constructed on the same pattern, which by its character would justify the description

[6] See M. Benayahu, 'Ha"magid" shel ramḥa"l', in I. Ben-Zvi and M. Benayahu (eds.), *Sefer zikaron liyeshayahu zoneh/Isaiah Sonne Memorial Volume* (= *Sefunot*, 5) (Jerusalem, 1961), 326.

[7] Ibid. 306–7. Attention is drawn there to signs tending to identify the handwriting of Luzzatto in the journal of the *magid*; these are also found in other autographs, as I shall point out in several places below.

[8] Referred to below as 'the unmistakable copyist'.

[9] The last two series are distinguished by the letters *beit* and *gimel*.

'linked discourses'. Each series is composed of seven short homilies in a linked succession which together form a single unit, the first six relating to the same set of scriptural verses[10] while the seventh provides an exposition of a particular group of masoretic accents.[11] Other scriptural verses and sayings of the sages and the Zohar which are quoted vary from one homily to another, but two verses recur regularly in each series, one in the first homily[12] and one in the second.[13] A further series of this sort, the beginning of which is missing, is to be found at the end of the collection (fos. 163^{r}–165^{r}).[14]

MS Oxford 2237, which contains compositions by Luzzatto copied by Jekutiel, has an extract from these homilies on fos. 158^{r}–159^{v}, from the middle of 'Vayotse ha'eved' ['The servant brought out'—Gen. 24: 53] in the first series to the penultimate line in 'Venatata hakesef' ['You shall spend the money'—Deut. 14: 26] in the second series. Apparently Jekutiel copied the homilies at Padua, perhaps in a more extensive form than that found in MS 2593, and took them with him when he returned home in 1733.[15] At any rate his possession of them is evidence in favour of Luzzatto's authorship.

The identity of the author is also evident from motifs and ideas which are clearly typical of Luzzatto. I will point out and exemplify several important themes: the *tikun* ['restoration'] of the Shekhinah and her elevation to her mystical union and perfect *yiḥud* up to the level of Ein Sof, which run like a continuous thread through all the homilies; it appears that in the prayer 'to ensure that the *tikunim* which have already been performed will never be

10 I note here, word for word, the verses used in the homilies: 'And you shall spend the money on whatever your soul desires, on oxen, or sheep, or wine or strong drink, or whatever your soul asks of you, and you shall eat there before the Lord your God, and you shall rejoice, both you and your household' (Deut. 14: 26); 'And the servant brought forth jewels of silver and jewels of gold and raiment and gave them to Rebecca, and he gave costly gifts to her brother and her mother' (Gen. 24: 53); 'You are wholly fair, my love; there is no flaw in you' (S. of S. 4: 7); 'And Jacob kissed Rachel and lifted up his voice and wept' (Gen. 29: 11); 'When a man takes a new wife, he shall not go out [to serve] with the army or be charged with any public duty; he shall be free for his house for one year, and make the wife he has taken happy' (Deut. 24: 5); 'And God said "Let there be light", and there was light' (Gen. 1: 3). This last verse is expounded three times in succession in each series.

11 *Zarka*, *makef*, *shofar holekh*, *segolta*. In the second series, the interpretation of the accents is followed by a short homily on 'O Lord, open my lips' [the verse from Ps. 51: 17 which opens the Amidah prayer—Trans.] (fo. 7^{r-v}), but it is out of place here; it belongs to the series of homilies described in Section IV below.

12 'And Boaz said to her at mealtime: "Come here, and eat some bread, and dip your morsel into the sour wine." So she sat beside the reapers, and he passed some parched grain to her and she ate and was satisfied, and had some left over' (Ruth 2: 14).

13 'And you became exceedingly beautiful, and grew to regal estate' (Ezek. 16: 13).

14 The truncated beginning contains the last six lines of the homily on Deut. 14: 26 [n. 10 above]. The preceding composition, *Ta'amei mitsvot*, has the end missing, and it is therefore impossible to determine how many pages are missing between it and the homilies.

15 See Essay 8, nn. 92 and 96.

annulled' (fo. 9ᵛ) there is an allusion to *tikunim* performed in Luzzatto's group;[16] a messianic eschatological bent, in particular the trinity of redeemers in the shape of Moses and the two Messiahs:[17] 'Cause three lights to shine upon us in the three *vavs* of *tsadik ḥay olamim* [the sefirah Tsadik (Yesod), 'the eternally living'], and let them all be bound together as one in the letter *shin* of *mashiaḥ*,[18] which is to say the two Messiahs together with Moses' (fo. 7ʳ); '"and you became exceedingly beautiful"[19] with two Messiahs the perfection of man, "and you grew to regal estate", which alludes to Moses, of whom it was said "and he was king in Jeshurun"'[20] (fo. 163ᵛ); the cleaving [*devekut*] of the soul to the Godhead as the highway to the service of

[16] As we know, 'the *tikun* of the holy Shekhinah', together with 'the *tikun* of all Israel', was itself presented in the rules of the group as the exclusive aim to be pursued in the service of the Lord. See *R' mosheh ḥayim lutsato uvenei doro: osef igerot ute'udot*, ed. S. Ginzburg [hereafter *Igerot*] (Tel Aviv, 1937), i. 8–11. There, and in Luzzatto's writings, the *tikun* of the Shekhinah is a concept with a distinctly messianic meaning. Rivkah Schatz, commenting on the teaching of the Maggid of Mezhirech and his disciples that prayer must be directed solely towards the needs of the Shekhinah (and it should be added that the same is also found in the writings of R. Jacob Joseph of Polonnoye, expressed in his own way), states that this teaching implies the necessity of personal resignation, quietistic in character, in the service of the Lord: R. Schatz [Schatz-Uffenheimer], *Haḥasidut kemistikah* (Jerusalem, 1968), 81, 91–5. This statement is based on the idea common in hasidic literature that the Shekhinah inhabits the soul and that Israel and, in particular, the tsadikim are organs of the Shekhinah, and on similar ideas. Schatz sees this as an outstanding innovation by the Maggid of Mezhirech, transforming the Shekhinah 'from a transcendental concept . . . into a psychological concept of immanence' (ibid. 92); moreover, she adduces that idea in support of G. Scholem's view on the neutralization of messianism in hasidism (ibid. 176–7; and see ibid. 100–1, 110–21). The instruction 'that one should pray for the Shekhinah and for the whole of Israel' (quoted ibid. 92, as a common hasidic formula) sounds like a paraphrase of the instruction in the rules of Luzzatto's group; and the basic elements of the presence of the Shekhinah in the soul, with which it is so closely associated as to merge with it, are also found expressed in Luzzatto's writings in terms closely resembling the language of the teachers of hasidism, as I shall point out below in connection with passages of prayer and interpretations of the accent *zarka*. And see n. 41 below. In my opinion, solely in the light of the kabbalah of the Zohar and that of Luria, and taking no cognizance of the powerful links between the doctrine of hasidism and the activist messianic kabbalah of Luzzatto, any diversion of the *tikun* of the Shekhinah and its offshoots into channels of quietism and neutralization of messianism would amount to detaching a clear and unambiguous idea from its root, and I see no basis for the opinion that such a diversion took place in the literature of hasidism.

[17] See Essay 4, p. 237, and Essay 3, pp. 198–206; and n. 31 below.

[18] [In *gematriyah*, the consonants *ḥet* and *yod* of *ḥay* = 8+10 = 18; three *vavs* have the same value, 6×3 = 18. The 'three *vavs*' of the letter *shin* (ש) are its three upright strokes. The letter *ḥet* (ח) could similarly be regarded as made up of three *vavs*. On *vav*, see also Essay 2, text referring to nn. 30 and 31.—Trans.]

[19] Ezek. 16: 13. This verse, which is quoted unfailingly in every series, is interpreted as relating to the Shekhinah. See n. 13 above. Here the word *me'od* [*bime'od me'od*, 'exceedingly'], consisting of the letters *aleph*, *dalet*, *mem*, is turned into 'Adam', the first man, alluding to the well-known notarikon: **A**dam—**D**avid—**M**essiah.

[20] Deut. 33: 5.

the Lord.[21] Among matters connected with *devekut* special attention should be drawn to two particular kinds of approach which are characteristic of Luzzatto's general philosophy:

1. *Tikunim* and *devekut* in physical actions, especially eating, so as to draw down divine lights into material things.[22] In the homily 'You shall spend the money' in the first series, after a description of the thirsting of the soul for

[21] Contrary to the opinion of G. Scholem (on the basis of 'the exalted level of the holy man' in *Mesilat yesharim*, ch. 26) that, for Luzzatto, *devekut* was still 'the last stop on the highway of ascent' reached only by the chosen few 'through the special lovingkindness that is bestowed on the hasid', and that therefore it ought not to be assumed that Luzzatto influenced the view of *devekut* in hasidism. See his essay '"Devekut" o "hitkasherut intimit im elohim" bereshit haḥasidut' in his book *Devarim bego* (Tel Aviv, 1976), 328–9, and, in parallel with this, his essay 'Hatsadik' in his *Pirkei-yesod behavanat hakabalah usemaleiha* (Jerusalem, 1976), 239–41. This opinion concerning Luzzatto's outlook is not correct even with regard to *Mesilat yesharim*, which was published during his lifetime (Amsterdam, 1740), a few years after the storm of persecution and excommunications which embittered his life, when he was of course formulating his ideas with great caution. In the preface to this book he presented *devekut* as a general aim while pointing the way to achieving it, and in ch. 19 ('Beve'ur ḥelkei haḥasidut' ['In Explanation of the Elements which Go to Make Up Piety']) he enlarged on this. Moreover, in ch. 1 ('Beve'ur kelal ḥovat ha'adam be'olamo' ['In Explanation of the Whole Duty of Man in his Lifetime']), in which he stated that 'true perfection resides only in *devekut* to Him, blessed be He', he taught—expressing himself with restraint—that the elevation and sanctification of corporeality (which in ch. 26 are reserved to the possessor of the quality of holiness) are included in the general duties and rights of man. This is what he says: 'And if he has control over himself and cleaves to his Creator and makes use of [the things of] this world only to help him serve his Creator, he is raised up and the world itself is raised up with him, for all mankind are greatly exalted by serving the perfect man who is sanctified by His holiness, blessed be He.' In certain compositions written in Padua and published after his death, he opened still wider the gates of self-purification and sanctification; and in compositions removed from public view in this collection he emphasized that every Jew must strive to attain, and can attain, the exalted level of *devekut* described at the end of *Mesilat yesharim* as a gracious gift to the holy man. This will be shown clearly in the course of our discussion.

[22] [Tishby refers here to an intended section, to have been numbered XI, on the homily on the mystical significance of the formal meal on the night of 17 Shevat. The intended section was not written for reasons explained in his headnote to Section XI below.—Trans.] In Tevet 5490 [end of 1729/beginning of 1730] Luzzatto declared: 'And in particular [Luria] left one large area for me, namely the matter of the link between the worlds and the manner in which God's conduct of them *is revealed, through emanation, to corporeal levels of existence*. And these are all matters sweeter than honey, and there are many of them in the *tikunim* [*Tikunim ḥadashim*] and more in *Kohelet*' (*Igerot*, i. 52). The commentary on Ecclesiastes [*Kohelet*], which was the first extensive treatise inspired by the *magid*, was written in Aramaic. Luzzatto regarded it and his *Ḥibur al hatorah* as two sections of his 'book of the Zohar'. See *Igerot*, i. 19, 31, 39, 52, 53, 61, 62, 70, 76, 89, 93–4, 114, 143; ii. 223, 285, 290, 408. It emerges from the letters that this treatise and other Zoharic works were in the possession of R. Isaiah Bassano, who discussed their subject matter with Luzzatto after the signature of the undertaking to withdraw them from circulation. And see n. 61 below. As regards Luzzatto's *Tikunim ḥadashim*, which appeared in print not long ago (Jerusalem, 1958), see my *Netivei emunah uminut* (Ramat Gan, 1964), 187, 188–9, 323 n. 13.

closeness to God in mutual love, as in 'his right hand embraces me' [S. of S. 2: 6], we find the following: 'And just as this desire is awakened in us, so may You draw down to us Your lovingkindness . . . in oxen and sheep and wine and strong drink [Deut. 14: 26], *tikunim* which are attached to the four letters of Your holy name, for some supernal lights descend and clothe themselves in the food of Israel in order to feed their souls with heavenly sustenance . . . and to the Tetragrammaton, with the names of its letters spelt out in full, are attached many other foods . . . and it is all contained in the heavenly bread [divine bounty which flows down from the sefirah Binah]' (fo. 1^{r}).

2. The operation of *devekut* as a means of restoring the honour of the people of Israel and renewing their holiness as of old: '[With regard to] so many tears which we shed before You in loving *devekut*, it is forthwith said of us "When a man takes" etc.,[23] and this taking is *kidushin* [the sacred marriage of the sefirot Tiferet and Malkhut—Trans.], [through the sefirah] Hokhmah, in which effect is given to the verse "and you shall be to Me a kingdom of priests and a holy nation"' (fos. 163^{v}–164^{r}).[24] The context in this sentence and in the immediately succeeding text shows that this is a petition and expression of hope for early messianic redemption.[25]

The stamp of Luzzatto's personality can also be recognized in formal and linguistic elements drawn from *Tikunei hazohar*, in the spirit of which he was steeped and which he strove to imitate in his writings.[26] As had been done in *Tikunei hazohar*, he wove passages of prayer into these homilies. This is not common in homiletic literature. In fact it is a more essential element here than in the 'Zohar' original. Whereas in *Tikunei hazohar* the passages of prayer are generally superimposed literary adornments, here they are in the nature of actual liturgical compositions, so that the great majority of these homilies may be numbered together with the wealth of liturgical works by Luzzatto, most of which have recently been discovered in manuscript.[27]

[23] Deut. 24: 5: 'When a man takes a new wife . . .'.

[24] Exod. 19: 6.

[25] On the problem of the relationship between *devekut* and messianic eschatological *tikun*, see n. 128 below, and Sections IX and XI [but as to XI, see n. 22 above—Trans.].

[26] Luzzatto wrote that all his Zoharic works were written 'exactly according to the laws and ordinances of the *Tikunim* [*ḥadashim*]' (*Igerot*, i. 52), that is to say, on the pattern of *Tikunei hazohar*. And see ibid. 94 for his reliance on *Tikunei hazohar* and *Raya meheimna* to justify the multiplicity of messianic references in his writings.

[27] I have sent for printing a prayer for the night of Shavuot, two prayers for the night of 17 Shevat, and a series of confessional prayers. These will be published in *Molad* [they appeared in *Molad*, NS 8 (31) (1980), and are republished in Essay 2 below—Trans.]. In Essay 2, p. 117 ff. I have also considered other prayers preserved in manuscript. M. Benayahu, in his essay 'Tefilot shenityaḥasu leramḥa"l ve'einan lo utefilot shelo nizkar bahen shemo vehen lo', *Sinai*, 78 (1976), 217–54, published three prayers and listed other prayers which had been put away

The following are the opening words of the various passages of prayer:[28] 'Master of all the worlds, behold, Your Shekhinah rises up before You out of the desire for You which fills our heart in exile' (fo. 1r); 'Master of the worlds, You are the strength of Israel, as it is written: "The name of the Lord is a strong tower",[29] and this is their strength, that they can endure exile and do not change in spite of all their misfortunes' (fo. 1v); 'Behold, the Shekhinah [ascends] towards You in the prayers of Israel, which are prayers woven as with a thread of the lips' (fo. 2r); 'Master of the worlds, behold, the Shekhinah ascends towards You from within the walls of our heart' (fo. 4r); 'Master of all the worlds, behold, the holy Shekhinah is a covering for the tsadik, of which it is said "for that is his only covering".[30] May it be Your will to enwrap [*sheta'atif*] him in it so that there may be said of him "A prayer of the afflicted *ki ya'atof*" [in Ps. 102: 1, 'when he fainteth', but here interpreted as 'when he enwraps'—Trans.], followed immediately by "and pours out his complaint [*siḥo*] before the Lord",[31] this *siaḥ* being [the second syllable] of *mashiaḥ* [Messiah]' (fo. 5r); 'Master of all worlds, all the world is yours, and this is the Shekhinah, the lower world in which "may the glory of the Lord endure for ever"[32] [*le'olam*, but quite probably taken here as *la'olam*, 'for the world'—

unpublished. With regard to Benayahu's 'discovery'—which is given prominence in the title of the essay and which he reports at some length (ibid. 221–3)—that the prayers printed in *Sefer hashirim*, ed. S. Ginzburg and B. Klar (Jerusalem, 1945), under the heading 'Prayer to be recited over the graves of tsadikim' were attributed in error to Luzzatto and actually came from *Ma'avar yabok*, I must point out that I reported this in full detail in my essay 'Ha'imut bein kabalat ha'ar"i lekabalat harema"k bikhetavav uveḥayav shel r' aharon berekhyah mimodena', *Zion*, 39 (1974), 22 n. 38. My essay was published in the middle of 5736 [1976] and his in 5737.

28 I have included in the quotations two paragraphs which do not contain the formula 'Master of the worlds' because they address God in the second person. Appeals to Heaven in the second person are also woven into paragraphs which I have not quoted. The result is to impart a liturgical character to the homilies as a whole.

29 Prov. 18: 10.

30 Exod. 22: 26.

31 Ps. 102: 1. The homily continues as follows: 'And that is the *siaḥ* referred to in "no shrub [*siaḥ*] of the field was yet [*terem*] in the earth" (Gen. 2: 5). Why not? Because He had not caused it to rain [*lo himtir*, which contains the consonants of *terem*] [ibid.]. And as for the *mem* of Messiah, it is the forty days [letter *mem* = 40] of the formation of the embryo to perfect the likeness [of the Messiah] in the mystical form of Adam' (fo. 5r–v). The origin of the messianic interpretation of 'the shrub of the field' is the Zohar I, 25*a* (which belongs to *Tikunei hazohar*), but it owes its development to the homily *Kodesh yisra'el lashem* by A. M. Cardozo. See G. Scholem, 'Shenei mekorot ḥadashim lidiat torato shel avraham mikha'el kardozo', in I. Ben-Zvi and M. Benayahu (eds.), *Sefer hayovel lishene'ur zalman shazar/Shneur Zalman Shazar Jubilee Volume* (= *Sefunot*, 3–4) (Jerusalem, 1959–60), 259–60. Similarly in the development of the concept of the messianic trinity, which also had its origin in *Raya meheimna* and *Tikunei hazohar* (see Zohar I 25*b*, II 120*a*, III 153*b*, 246*b*; *Zohar ḥadash*, ed. R. Margaliot (Jerusalem, 1953), *tikunim*, 110*b*), Luzzatto was influenced by Cardozo. See G. Scholem, 'Shenei mekorot ḥadashim', 253, 259, 264–8. And see Essay 4, p. 237, and Essay 3, pp. 198–206.

32 Ps. 104: 31.

Trans.]' (fo. 7ᵛ); 'Behold, she is Your handmaid,[33] of whom it was said "And spread your skirt over your handmaid, for you are her redeemer [*go'el*]",[34] and this is *tsadik ḥay olamim*, the redeeming angel [*hamalakh hago'el*], and Mtt [Metatron], the servant whose name is like that of his Master [BT *San.* 38*b*]' (fo. 163ʳ).[35]

Another factor which has its origin in *Tikunei hazohar* is the use of the group of masoretic accents *zarka*, *makef*, *shofar holekh*, *segolta* as material for kabbalistic interpretations. This group is expounded many times in *Tikunei hazohar*, especially in the *tikunim* in *Zohar ḥadash*,[36] and in nearly all of the passages *zarka* is made to refer to the Shekhinah in two senses: her elevation

[33] 'Your handmaid' is meant to include the congregation of Israel in the world below, for the text continues: 'And by this [Your] skirt you will save us from Esau and Ishmael and the mixed multitude'.

[34] Ruth 3: 9.

[35] The frequency of prayers in Luzzatto's Zoharic works is irregular. In *Tikunim ḥadashim* there are only two prayers, one in the name of Elijah (p. 10) and one in the name of Metatron (p. 131). By contrast, the remnants of *Zohar tinyana* (apparently all from *Ḥibur al hatorah*) show that that work was full of passages of prayer. Two fragments were known and had been published: the text which was sent by R. Jekutiel in his letter to Vilna and published by R. Jacob Emden in *Zot torat hakenaot* (Altona, 1752), 45*b* (reprinted in *Igerot*, ii. 408–9); two prayers in Aramaic, one in the name of Moses (*Raya meheimna*) and one in the name of Metatron, which were sent by Luzzatto to his teacher in a letter (*Igerot*, i. 96, 97). Luzzatto regarded the prayers in his writings as proof that the revelations of the *magid* were not from the Sitra Ahra, and said so at the end of the second prayer (ibid. 97–8) and in a general declaration preceding the prayers (ibid. 94). The discourse on the beginning of the weekly portion 'Mikets', a copy of which Luzzatto sent to Hamburg, to Livorno, and to his teacher, and which played an important part in the polemic against him, has remained unknown up to now because S. Ginzburg published only the text of the preface (ibid. 98), but it has been preserved in two copies in a collection of the letters in the Jewish Theological Seminary, New York, MS Mic. 4022, nos. 22, 25. And see *Igerot*, i. 73, 75–6, 91, 95, 98–9, 104, 108–9, 113–14, 126, 134, 159, 161, 164; A. Ben-Ish, 'Te'udot letoledot ramḥa"l', *Metsudah*, 3–4 (1945), 225, 228; my *Netivei emunah uminut*, 169–70, 185. The content of the discourse provides no basis whatever for the charge by R. Moses Hagiz that it contains an apologia for the apostasy of Shabetai Tsevi. For our purpose it is important to note that it contains a prayer in the name of *avraham sava ḥasida* ['Abraham the pious old man']. In MS Jewish Theological Seminary Mic. 1585 I found another fragment which takes up two folios (187ʳ–188ᵛ), apparently in Luzzatto's handwriting. From the beginning up to fo. 188ʳ, end of line 2, there are three previously unknown prayers in Aramaic in the names of R. Hamnuna Sava, Elijah, and Abraham. These are followed by the two prayers printed in *Igerot*. These folios had undoubtedly fallen out of a complete or partial copy of *Ḥibur al hatorah*; they have no connection with the letter. Thus, of all the fragments which remain, only the discourse which was sent to Vilna contains no prayer, but its text was deliberately abbreviated and cut, and it may be that it, too, contained liturgical passages.

[36] *Tikunei hazohar*, ed. R. Margaliot (Tel Aviv, 1948), *tikun* 21, 61*a*–62*b*; *Zohar ḥadash*, *tikunim*, 97*c*–98*b*, 99*c*–100*d*, 103*c*, 109*a*–110*a*. The last pages contain the passage to be found in the Zohar I, 24*a*–*b*, which belongs to *Tikunei hazohar*. In the Zohar II, 158*a* (*Raya meheimna*), the group of accents is mentioned but not explained. A. Shiloah's *Nose'ei musikah bazohar* (Jerusalem, 1977) entirely omits the discourses in the *tikunim* of *Zohar ḥadash*, which are crammed with references to cantillation and the accents.

from her place in the system of sefirot to the level of Keter or even Ein Sof, and her use, when she is brought down, as ammunition in the war against the forces of evil, the Sitra Ahra ['Other Side'],[37] while in a few places the movements of the Shekhinah are linked to redeemers and to messianic redemption.[38] The four expositions of the accents in the 'linked discourses' refer only to the ascent and descent of the Shekhinah, but in two well-known works we find the other aspects also—the war against the Sitra Ahra, and messianic redemption.[39] I will quote two passages from the discourses. The first exposition is a paraphrase of its source in the Zohar, whereas in the second one Luzzatto showed the ascent of the Shekhinah in a different light: '*Zarka* etc.—the Shekhinah will ascend to Ein Sof, *makef* ['a binder', hyphen]—just as she ascended to Ein Sof and bound together in unity those on high, so she will descend endlessly by the same paths and bind them together so that all are joined together in unity' (fo. 3^{v});[40] '*Zarka*—the Shekhinah will be thrown [*tizdarek*, from verbal root *z-r-k*] from our mouths towards You, *compounded of all our organs and all our inward parts*, and the *makef* has the purpose of binding together as one those above and those below' (fo. 165^{r}).[41]

The last point which marks the connection with the literature of the Zohar, and in the present context not necessarily with *Tikunei hazohar*, is the use of Hebrew words to convey the same meaning as do the equivalent forms in the Aramaic of the Zohar: *lehazmin lemata*, 'to prepare below' [the Hebrew

[37] See the commentary on the group of accents in R. Moses Cordovero's *Pardes rimonim*, Gate 29, ch. 1. The explanation of *zarka* says that the Shekhinah 'is thrown [*nizreket*] towards its hidden source and ascends and is united through the mystery of Hokhmah, reaching [the sefirah] Keter'. The ascent to Ein Sof is omitted.

[38] See *Zohar ḥadash*, *tikunim*, 97*d*–98*a*, 109*c*–*d*; and Section IX below.

[39] *Tikunim ḥadashim*, 141–2; *Adir bamarom* (Warsaw, 1886), 31–5, commentary on the *tikunim* of *Zohar ḥadash*, 97*c*–98*a*. In *Tikunim ḥadashim*, *makef shofar holekh* is related to the redeeming activity of the Messiah ben Joseph in his descent to the husks [the forces of evil—Trans.] and his ascent through the power of Luzzatto's holy Zohar.

[40] Cf. *Zohar ḥadash*, *tikunim*, 109*a*. And see *Adir bamarom*, 33–4.

[41] In *Tikunei hazohar*, too, it is stated that the Shekhinah rises into the mouths of the righteous when they pray (see e.g. p. 100*c* of that work), but I have not found any indication there that it is part of the bodily and spiritual being of the worshippers. This description and several others in the passages of prayer I have quoted are consistent with the psychological concept of immanence which is put forward by R. Schatz, in *Haḥasidut kemistikah*, as an innovation of hasidism. To supplement what has been said on this important point, I will quote, by way of example, one sentence from the commentary on *Idra raba*: 'But indeed it is a great hidden truth that a part of Mal[khut] clothes itself in the souls of Israel, and it is a holy mystery that dwells within his [Israel's] bowels, which is what is meant by "*elohai bekirbi*" [understanding this as 'my God is within me', instead of 'in my midst', as in Deut. 31: 17—Trans.], and this is like marrow and inward parts to the soul . . . and that is the hidden meaning of the matter mentioned many times in the Zohar and the *tikunim*, which describe how the Shekhinah is a soul to souls and dwells in the heart' (*Adir bamarom*, 50). And see ibid. 136.

verb normally means 'to invite'], *lesalek yekarekha*, 'to raise up Your glory' [Hebrew normally 'to remove'] (fo. 3^{r}), and in similar senses *shemistaleket* (fo. 3^{v}), *lehizdamen*, *mizdamen* (fo. 6^{r}), *mizdamen*[*ot*] *neged hizdamenutah shel hashekhinah*, from the roots *s-l-k* and *z-m-n* (fo. 165^{r}); *lehatkif*, 'to strengthen' [Hebrew normally 'to attack'] (fo. 6^{r}); *mitpareshet mimekha*, 'departs from you' [normal Hebrew 'is separated' or 'is explained'] (fo. 164^{r}). This odd linguistic phenomenon shows that the author was accustomed to using the Aramaic of the Zohar in both speech and writing.[42]

With regard to the handwriting of the discourses, I am of the opinion that it is entirely that of Luzzatto. It is true that the impression gained from a superficial inspection is that the four series are written in four different hands, none of which is that of Luzzatto or 'the unmistakable copyist' (see n. 8 above). But close scrutiny reveals that the shape and slope of the letters as well as the general appearance of the handwriting vary in the same series and even on a single page, and some sheets have been written with such haste and lack of clarity and in such an unsteady hand that they cannot possibly be attributed to a copyist.[43] It follows that if the writer was not Luzzatto we must reach the absurd conclusion that different authors were responsible for each series and even for parts of the same series. The only reasonable possibility, therefore, is that we have before us Luzzatto's handwriting in various shapes and forms.

The characteristic references I have given here, and many similar ones which could be added, show that these homilies are infused with an overwhelming love for the Shekhinah and were composed in a state of enthusiasm and spiritual exaltation under the inspiration of the author's *magid*—his messenger from Heaven. However, in speaking of the part played by the *magid* in Luzzatto's compositions we must draw a distinction between the different kinds of composition. From his letters we learn that most of his kabbalistic writings from the time that the *magid* revealed himself to him in Sivan 5487 [early summer 1727] until Luzzatto's capitulation in Padua in Av 5490 [late summer 1730] were connected with his consciousness of revelations from on high,[44] and it appears from hints which he drops that this applies also to the forty or more compositions that he wrote between 5491 and 5494 [1731–4], when he was obliged by the undertaking he had given to suppress all reference to the *magid*.[45] It is clear, however, that only some of the revelations

[42] The small number of these words and their sporadic use obscure their peculiarity and they merge into Luzzatto's Hebrew style without jarring unduly. The situation is different in the interpretations of the commandments, which are considered in Section XII below.

[43] In these pages, and especially in the fourth series, the unevenness of the handwriting is even more conspicuous than in the journal of the *magid*. See M. Benayahu, 'Ha"magid" shel ramḥa"l', 306–7.

[44] See Tishby, *Netivei emunah uminut*, 185.

[45] See *Igerot*, ii. 254, 267–8; Benayahu, 'Ha"magid" shel ramḥa"l', 313–14; Tishby, *Netivei emunah uminut*, 187–8.

were recorded in the terms in which they were communicated and at the time they were heard or shortly afterwards, whereas the rest were embodied in the compositions in a version adapted and expanded by logical and discursive thought-processes and worked into a planned literary form.[46] These homilies and other writings very similar to them in character and tone belong to the category of direct revelations.[47] Apparently writings of this kind were read in gatherings of the group at fixed times or on special occasions,[48] which means that by getting to know them we gain entry into the mysteries of the life of the group.

[46] This distinction is based on Luzzatto's own words. In his statements on his works he ascribed them all to the revelations of the *magid*, including even his *Kelalim leḥokhmat ha'emet*, which are concise summaries of the intricacies of the Lurianic myth in a systematic speculative form. See *Igerot*, i. 31, 53, 70. However, when R. Joseph Ergas asserted that the subject matter of *Ma'amar haḥokhmah* and the *Kelalim*, which had been handed over to him as revelations of the *magid*, was gathered from well-known kabbalistic books and that 'the *magid* would not communicate what was found in books' (ibid. 102), Luzzatto's reply with regard to *Ma'amar haḥokhmah* was equivocal: 'I, too, already knew *that it was not necessary to say of it that it was done in accordance with the word of the magid* . . . but it contains new interpretations of the Scriptures—these were spoken by the mouth of the *magid*.' He characterized the *Kelalim ketsarim* ['Brief Principles'] similarly (ibid. 114). In the comments which accompanied the new insights transmitted in his letters he stated clearly that he had recorded the revelations together with additions of his own: ibid. 32, 44. Elsewhere, however (ibid. 53), it is stated that he abbreviated revelations in committing them to writing. And see Benayahu, 'Ha"magid" shel ramḥa"l', 308–9.

[47] Of the writings in the collection, I regard the following, in addition to these homilies, as being in the category of direct revelations: the homilies on 'You are wholly fair, my love' [S. of S. 4: 7] (Section III); 'O Lord, open my lips' [Ps. 51: 17] (Section IV); 'El shadai' etc. (Section VII); and *Yiḥud gan-eden* (Section IX). The homily on 'Se'udat leil tu"v bishevat 5493' [a ceremonial meal on the night of 17 Shevat, 5493/1733] ['Section XI', but see n. 22 above] and 'Expositions of the Commandments' (Section XII) may also belong to this category. With regard to *Mishkenei elyon*, see below, end of Section II.

[48] Such as the poem, prayer, and the homily for the night of 17 Shevat. It appears to me that at least some of the kabbalistic poems published in Essay 2 below, as well as the kabbalistic prayers, in particular those included in MS Guenzburg 745, were direct revelations and were recited in the group. In my lecture on the Guenzburg collection in 1961 I dealt in detail with the recitation of the poems and prayers in the group, and with regard to the poems I quoted two clear items of evidence: (*a*) the rules of the group state: 'During the midday period of study [the] four who are successful in the ballot will stand at the four corners of the table *to recite the poems which are prepared for them for that period*' (*Igerot*, i. 13); (*b*) in a letter in Italian to R. Isaiah Bassano dated the New Moon of Adar 5496 [early spring 1736] (published in Hebrew translation), R. Jacob Hazak [Forti] wrote: 'The page on which *were written all the arrangements and the* [prescriptions for] *studies* [*hasedarim vehalimudim*] *instituted by R. Moses Hayim* has been torn out of the book, and the poems, too, are no longer recited' (ibid. ii. 416; the words *hasedarim vehalimudim* were written in Hebrew in the original letter, as is pointed out ibid. 450 n. 432). These *sedarim velimudim*, too, were certainly, at least in part, written at the instruction of the *magid*.

II. SECRETS OF THE TEMPLE: *MISHKENEI ELYON* ['DWELLINGS OF THE MOST HIGH'] (FOS. 11^r–38^v)

This work, the only one of any size among the unpublished writings in the collection[49] to have been preserved in its entirety, begins with a statement of its intention: 'In this discourse my purpose is to explain matters connected with the Temple on High mentioned by our sages of blessed memory, its form, its character, and all its laws and statutes, and to show how the one of this world below corresponds to it in its design and dimensions, explaining all very plainly' (fo. 11^r). The intention outlined in this sentence underlies this composition from beginning to end, but its execution differs in form and content from what the opening words lead us to expect. The Temple on High and the relationship between it and the Temple of the world below are depicted here on a broad canvas rich in intricate and colourful descriptions. So far as I know there is no real parallel for these descriptions in the literature of aggadah or that of kabbalah.[50] I will present this composition in its main outlines, in the order in which the various subjects are dealt with.

The introduction (fos. 11^r–13^r) states that the foundation and place of origin of the Temple on High are in the foundation stone [*even shetiyah*] which stands in the middle of the last light in the system of lights or sefirot, i.e. in the centre of the Shekhinah, which is 'Mother of the children', and in which 'all beings have their roots'. The site of the foundation stone is 'the house of the holy congregation', 'the place of great delight and the place of love and peace' which is 'hidden away and concealed for the king alone to enter', that is to say the womb of the Shekhinah, and 'all the rest of the House' begins from the foundation stone. From it radiate roads and highways and paths both great and small for the transmission of heavenly bounty and food to enable the worlds to carry on their existence, and it serves as a watchtower from which the divine oversight is exercised, 'for this stone stands at the heart of the world'.

The section of the text which follows this (fos. 13^r–16^r), which is similarly in the nature of an introduction, explains the relationship between the

49 With the exception of the dialogue 'Philosopher and Kabbalist' (Section VIII), which in spite of the particular version in the collection, as will become apparent, is not to be classed as a text withdrawn from circulation.

50 See A. Aptowitzer, 'Beit hamikdash shel malah al pi ha'agadah', *Tarbiz*, 2 (1931), 137–53, 257–87; I. Tishby, *The Wisdom of the Zohar*, trans. D. Goldstein (Oxford, 1989), vol. iii, pt. v, sect. 1.

Temples on their different planes and at their different times. The Temple on High came into existence before the creation of the world as a product of 'the force of tranquillity' engendered in the first coupling of Malkhut [Sovereignty, feminine] and Melekh [King]. But in its primordial existence it was not in a state of complete perfection, for only Hokhmah [Wisdom], the second beginning in order of divinity, was active in establishing it, whereas Keter [the Crown], the supernal beginning, 'was hidden within Hokhmah and could not be seen from without' (fo. 13ᵛ); and the world, too, which is carried on through the power of the Temple on High, was not created perfect. Had Adam not stumbled into sin, he would have brought about the perfection of the Temple and the world by causing the 'hidden beginning' to operate openly, but when he sinned the world was spoilt and fell below even its original imperfect level. Solomon was privileged to rectify the defects and build the Temple of this world, 'but nevertheless the whole was within the mystical category of Hokhmah alone, and because they did not attain the ultimate perfection, that tranquillity was interrupted and the House was destroyed' (fo. 14ʳ). The First Temple, then, corresponded to the Temple on High at the time, and as soon as it was destroyed the Temple on High was transformed and established 'in a new form, which is the form and pattern of the future', i.e. at the perfect level of Keter, 'and therefore Ezekiel saw it standing already built'. If Israel had shown themselves worthy by their deeds when they returned from Babylon, the redemption under Ezra would have been a perfect redemption and they would have built the earthly Temple to the highest degree of perfection as it was revealed in the vision of Ezekiel, but because they were not properly rehabilitated in spirit, 'they constructed it according to [the advice of] the prophets among them, partly like the former one and partly like the latter one which had already been renewed in the world above'. The Third Temple would be erected 'according to the lights of Keter', and 'not only will they be alike but the Temple above will stretch out and come down . . . and then there will be built round it a building of earthly substance . . . and building will be joined to building so that they become one . . . and the divine glory will dwell in it, completely revealed'[51] (fos. 14ᵛ–15ᵛ).

The main body of this work (fos. 16ʳ–33ᵛ) contains detailed descriptions of the external and internal structure according to the vision of Ezekiel, in which Luzzatto saw the pattern of the perfect Temple above and below. I doubt if architects could construct a building according to these plans, but Luzzatto regarded them as a realistic design, as is evident from the appendix described below. I will confine myself here to pointing out and exemplifying one aspect. The relationship between mystical entities, holy names and their combinations, and lights etc. on the one hand, and, on the other, parts of the

[51] See *Tikunim ḥadashim*, 91.

Temple which are presented in Ezekiel as concrete objects, is not described as a relationship between abstract models and physical likenesses. The same tangible components appear to exist in the world above too, but the description of their existence is ambivalent, and without warning they shed material forms and take on spiritual ones. Below are a few passages which reflect these extraordinary metamorphoses: 'And these gates are formed when the light has grown strong at a particular place in this wall. Through the strength of the light, that place is filled with great compassion, and that place becomes a gateway through which the light can pass out. And you must understand that when this name is spelt out in full as I have said, its numerical value rises [to] *tav resh ayin alef* [671], which [in Aramaic] is a gate' (fo. 18^r); 'The right-hand light has spread out in the greatness of its might and glory and appears like a candelabrum entirely of gold, with seven great lights extending on each side of it . . . and on the left there is also another light which spreads out along its length and breadth into the form of a table on which they arrange all sorts of pleasant and delightful foods, and there the shewbread is always displayed' (fos. 19^v–20^r); 'and you must know that the wall is Adonai, and the doors which form the gate are also the lights of Adonai which are spread out and close the gate, *alef yod* on the right and *dalet nun* on the left [a rearrangement of the four consonants of 'Adonai'—Trans.], and the light which shines within the wall is entirely contained in the Tetragrammaton, blessed be He' (fo. 30^v). These passages are characteristic of the whole of the main body of the composition. Only on a few pages (fos. 23^r–25^v) is there an appreciable difference in the nature of the discussion, where the subject considered is 'the order of service', and especially the mystical significance of the sacrifices. I deal with that below from a different point of view.

The composition is followed by an appendix (fos. 34^r–38^v) headed by this statement: 'I give you here a brief account of all the dimensions of the house with all the rules relating to them in five chapters, in concise language and in their proper order.' The appendix is arranged in mishnaic form, on the pattern and in the style of the Mishnah tractate *Midot* ['Dimensions']. In its substance, too, there are many points of correspondence and parallels, and occasionally the text is word for word the same. Here and there a few verses of Ezekiel[52] are quoted, but only one of them (44: 2) is the same [as in *Midot*]. The subject order and the contents under each head differ for the most part from the model, and of course the whole is here formulated as a straightforward *mishnah* free of any differences of opinion among the sages. Luzzatto regarded these mishnaic chapters as a crystallization into exact architectonic form of the colourful visionary descriptions in his mystical composition. I do not see a congruence between the one and the other, but a decision on

[52] And see *Shishah sidrei mishnah*, 'Kodashim', ed. H. Albeck (Jerusalem and Tel Aviv, 1956), 313, 431–2, 434.

this point is not within the competence of a layman in matters of architecture.[53]

Most of the motifs and ideas in this unique composition have no exact counterpart in Luzzatto's other writings, but comparable references are not entirely lacking. I will offer and comment on two examples. On the mystical interpretation of the sacrifices there is quite a close parallel in the *Kitsur sefer hakavanot*, which was likewise withdrawn from circulation but preserved in manuscript.[54] I quote here a continuous passage from one document and short extracts from the other:

Those below must draw near every day to those above, the significance of this being the binding of the branch together with the root, so that the angels are joined with their root and so are the souls. Indeed, the significance of the sacrificial offering [*korban*] is to bring the angels near [*lehakriv*, which in other contexts means 'to sacrifice', and has the same verbal root *k-r-b* as *korban*—Trans.] and that of the incense is to bring the souls near, and you should clearly understand that this is mystically interpreted as 'man' and 'beast': those within [i.e. the souls] are called 'man' and those of them who are on the outside [the angels] are called 'beast'. (MS Oxford 2593, fo. 24[v])

'And this is the mystical significance of the *korban*; its inner meaning is "nearness" [*kerevut*], that is, to draw all the branches near to their root' (MS BL Or. 10860, fo. 1[r]); 'Know that the significance of the *korbanot* in general is the *tikun* ['restoration'] of the root of living creatures . . . and what it means is

[53] This work and the appendix are both in the handwriting of 'the unmistakable copyist'. Mistakes, and lacunae indicated by dots, show that the copyist had difficulty in reading the text from which he was working.

[54] In my book *Netivei emunah uminut*, 325 n. 53, I drew attention to the copy in MS Oxford Heb. f. 120 and described its title-page and colophon. I later observed that in MS BL Or. 10860 (Gaster Collection) there is another copy, minus the title-page and the title *Sefer hakavanot shel kol hashanah*, but the text of the colophon, including the date 13 Shevat 5493 [1733] and the statement by R. Israel Hezekiah Treves that he wrote out the book for R. Jekutiel of Vilna, is word for word the same. In the Oxford copy the handwriting varies, whereas the London copy is all in one hand that is unlike any found in the other manuscript. On most of the pages of the London copy there are erasures, corrections, and additions both long and short between the lines and in the margins. On a partial comparison it was apparent to me that most of the corrections and additions were embodied in the Oxford copy. It follows that the latter was prepared from the London copy, which was apparently written out by R. Israel Hezekiah Treves. I have found indications which afford grounds for a reasonable hypothesis as to the relationship between the two copies: Luzzatto produced various editions of the *Kitsur sefer hakavanot*. Treves first copied it from an early edition; he afterwards corrected and supplemented it from an expanded later edition and asked his colleagues to prepare an orderly copy for R. Jekutiel. Luzzatto's *Sefer hakavanot* was widely circulated, as is shown by the existence of partial copies in manuscript, most of them in Italian handwriting but some written by Ashkenazis. Rabbi Hayim Friedlaender of Benei Berak, to whom I supplied information on the discovery of the two copies, will shortly be publishing the book in full. [See Bibliography.]

that in essence, all living creatures are either souls or angels, and both kinds enter into the *korban*, for "the beast" mystically alludes to the angels and the souls are man' (ibid., fo. 40^{v}); 'For it is entirely this that was the restorative power of the sacrifice, to draw the lower worlds near to their root' (ibid., fo. 54^{v}).[55] In spite of differences of detail the sentiments are essentially the same and can be recognized as the product of a single author's mind.

Secondly, eschatological elements occupy a central position here in the actual vision of the Third Temple, on which the whole composition is founded. True, there is no explicit mention of a redeemer or of messianism until the last page, and even there the reference is simply to a Messiah without any indication of the triad of Moses and the two Messiahs.[56] However, there is no doubt that at the time this composition was written—between 1728 and 1730, as will be shown below—Luzzatto was already an advocate of the concept of the messianic trinity,[57] although not all his writings give expression to it.

But there is no need to look for textual support to establish that Luzzatto was the author of this composition, for I have discovered evidence which

[55] The name Shoresh ['root'] is commonly used for Ein Sof or Keter in *Kitsur sefer hakavanot*, especially in connection with the processes of elevation to the supreme Divine Source, and there is even reference to copulation with the 'root' on the part of the lower entities [the *taḥtonim*], the *heikhalot*, and the sefirot. These matters occupy a central position in the last section (from 254 on), beginning 'And now I will explain to you a general *kavanah* with regard to prayer'. They are not found in the original Lurianic *kavanot*, but matters to do with the 'root', among them ascent to the 'root' and copulation with the 'root', are a principal topic in the Shabatean work *Va'avo hayom el ha'ayin*, the attribution of which to R. Jonathan Eybeschuetz has been confirmed on investigation. See M. A. Perlmutter, *R' yehonatan aibeshits veyaḥaso el hashabeta'ut* (Jerusalem and Tel Aviv, 1947), item *shoresh* in the index. In Essay 8, n. 93, I stated that Luzzatto, even before his departure from Padua—that is, a short time after the accusation linking R. Jonathan Eybeschuetz with *Va'avo hayom el ha'ayin*—had been giving thought to the character of Eybeschuetz, and certainly knew that he had been charged with Shabatean heresy. It is therefore possible that *Va'avo hayom el ha'ayin* had come into his hands and that he had absorbed some ideas from it. Another possibility is that they both drew the topics connected with the 'root' from a Shabatean source common to them both. The points to which I have drawn attention do not prove a connection between Luzzatto and Shabatean literature in this regard, for the term *shoresh* as an indication of an exalted level of divinity is found in early sources too, but the manner of its use in Luzzatto's writings raises a question which requires clarification.

[56] The closing sentence expresses an acute messianic longing: 'It follows that the powers of compassion [*raḥamim*] will spread greatly in the world in the time of the Messiah, and all things will be restored to a state of very great perfection, and all the luminaries will shine with a great light such as there has never been before, and holiness will spread without limit, and then tranquillity and joy will multiply in all the worlds . . . May it be the will of our Father in Heaven, in his compassion, to hasten our redemption so that the city may be rebuilt on its mound and the palace stand in its proper place [Jer. 30: 18], speedily in our days, Amen' (fo. 33^{v}). On the previous page (fo. 33^{r}) he says of the prince [*nasi*] in Ezekiel: 'He is the king-Messiah.'

[57] The messianic trinity is a main topic in *Tikunim ḥadashim*, which was written in 1729. And see Essay 4, p. 237, and Essay 3, pp. 198–206.

proves clearly that it is identical with a work entitled *Mishkenei elyon* ['Dwellings of the Most High'] which is mentioned in correspondence between Luzzatto and his mentor in 1730 and 1731. Among the writings of R. Isaac Pacifico (a Venetian rabbi who was a strong opponent of Luzzatto) in MS Montefiore 111, which consists for the most part of letters and responsa of eighteenth-century Italian scholars, I found the draft of a sharply polemical letter attacking Luzzatto (fos. 13^{r}–14^{r}). The names of the writer and the addressee are not recorded in the draft and Luzzatto is referred to in it only by derogatory epithets ('babe and suckling', 'the empty-headed boy'), but there is no doubt that this is a letter from Pacifico to R. Moses Hagiz written in the second half of 1730.[58] The following is an extract relating to the work we are considering:

And the trouble is that it is again being said that the empty-headed boy *has produced a commentary on Ezekiel's Temple* [and] *on the Temple on High and has called it Mishkenei elyon*. And this is in line with the opinion of the Christians who chirp and mutter [Isa. 8: 19]; when their foot strikes against the wall, they know not, neither do they discern, for their eyes are bedaubed so that they cannot see, their hearts so that they cannot understand [Isa. 44: 18]. And they say that the words of the prophet related only to the Temple on High, and by means of this ['this' = *Mishkenei elyon*] a sword has been placed into their hand with which to kill us, while they say 'By your own hand has this befallen you; you shall lie down in sorrow' [cf. Isa. 50: 11].[59] (fo. 13^{v})

58 It was apparently a reply to the letter which Hagiz wrote on the eve of the New Moon of Iyar 5490 [1730], of which only a summary of the contents has been preserved (*Igerot*, i. 132–3).

59 The letter is full of venomous accusations against Luzzatto and his supporters. Most of the charges have no foundation in fact, for example the allegation that *Mishkenei elyon* embodied strains of Christianity and that the Christians were likely to be helped by it, but these accusations are important for the history of the dispute and they contain new factual information. A few examples will be given here; I shall publish the whole letter elsewhere, together with other letters bearing on the Luzzatto affair. The following are some of the derogatory expressions used: of R. Isaiah Bassano, 'To the fore in every matter of holiness [or harlotry! The word is spelt so that it can be read as *kedushah* or *kedeshah*—Trans.], not one of the palm trees or one of the cedars but one of the oak trees of Basha"n [a play on 'Bassan'; and see e.g. Isa. 2: 13—Trans.]'; of R. Nehemiah Cohen: 'And the voice of man follows him [a play on Job 21: 33, changing the spelling so as to substitute 'the voice of' for 'every'—Trans.] to bite and strike [verbs chosen for assonance with Job's verb—*yimshokh*, *lishokh*, *linshokh*] like the venom of a snake; the most ostentatious man in Ferrara, who bestowed on him the crown of the rabbinate'; of R. Simeon Morpurgo, 'The physician from Ancona, [his] external appearance uncleanness and, beneath it, cunning'; of R. Judah Mendola, 'the humble hypocrite of Mantua, who fabricates untruths . . . and exalts the immature lad above the elders in the gate'; of R. Raphael Israel Kimhi, 'The serpent of Eden . . . the emissary of Safed, may it be built and established in our days, who dwelt in his house and within his walls for some days . . . and he copied out his book of *tikunim* to show the nations and rulers his beauty in every place where the sole of his foot treads' (fo. 13^{r-v}). In no other source so far known are we informed that R. Nehemiah Cohen ordained Luzzatto as rabbi before he signed the undertaking in Av 5490 [1730]. (On the

In a letter of Kislev 5490 [end of 1729], Luzzatto, enumerating those of his works which had been inspired by the *magid*, wrote: 'And there is also another work of mine, *Mishkenei elyon*, which you, honoured and learned sir, have seen.'[60] R. Isaiah Bassano had this composition in his possession after the signature of the undertaking in Padua [see above, text referring to n. 45—Trans.]. In Heshvan 5491 [autumn 1730], Luzzatto, declaring that he was seeking to recover all the copies of his works which had been circulated outside his group, wrote to his teacher: 'The reason why I have tried hard to have my *Mishkenei elyon* returned to me is that it is a treatise . . . for I am not concerned at all about my commentaries, but as to my treatises—including

personalities mentioned, see the index to *Igerot*.) New and surprising information is given in the charge brought against one of Luzzatto's works: 'Moreover, a grievous vision concerning him is revealed to us [cf. Isa. 21: 2], namely that he has begun to expound the philosophy of Aristo [but as spelt, the word reads *arisato*, 'his cradle']—a twisting serpent, a writhing serpent [Isa. 27: 1]—giving it a mystical interpretation. [Woe] to us on the day of judgement, woe to us on the day of rebuke! for this, too, will be said *in the book of wars against the Lord*, that he has seen or known [i.e. as a witness, cf. Lev. 5: 1—Trans.] "the secret of the Lord with those that fear Him" [Ps. 25: 14] in the great monster skulking in the rivers of heresy and misbelief. And what will the messengers of the [Gentile] nation answer, other than that the children of Israel have renounced their Torah and alleged against the Lord [their] God things which were not right' (fos. 13^v–14^r). This is apparently a reference to the book mentioned in Luzzatto's letter of 20 Nisan 5490 [1730] to his teacher: 'And I am at present writing a book entitled *Milḥamot hashem* [The Wars of the Lord], and the passage which I have copied here is from that book' (*Igerot*, i. 123). However, from the tenor of the passage quoted in the letter (ibid. 121–2) it appears that Pacifico gives a distorted picture of the work. The passage is a revelation in Aramaic of *avraham sava ḥasida* ['Abraham the pious old man'] on the fall [*nefilah*] of a tsadik—Messiah ben Joseph—to the husks, the forces of evil, in the mystical understanding of *bar niflei*, an untimely birth. The conclusion to be drawn from it is that *Milḥamot hashem* was a work of the same type as *Tikunim ḥadashim*. (This important passage, like most of the kabbalistic passages in the letters, is difficult to understand because of the copying errors in S. Ginzburg's edition.) On the other hand, it should not be supposed that the whole affair was a pure figment of the Venetian rabbi's imagination. I would conjecture that in *Milḥamot hashem* Luzzatto revealed in the name of the *magid* that even in the heretical Aristotelian philosophy sparks of holiness existed beneath the surface, and for anyone who was capable of using it in order to raise up sparks and battle against the Sitra Ahra, the camp of Satan, it was permissible and even desirable to study it. Similar ideas are contained in the remarks on the study of secular subjects which I quoted in *Netivei emunah uminut*, 196. On Pacifico's letter, see also below in the discussion of the commentary on *Ma'amar parashat mishpatim* (Section XI).

60 *Igerot*, i. 31. Hence this work was written at latest at the beginning of 1730. Luzzatto mentions it together with other writings (*Ma'amar hage'ulah*, *Ma'amar haḥokhmah*, etc.) after three books which he received 'from the *magid* alone until Elijah, of blessed memory, makes his appearance', and having enumerated them, he adds: 'All these in addition to new insights *which are spoken to me* on Sabbaths and festivals or days when I am not occupied with my long treatise'. But this indication will not serve to fix the exact or approximate time when they were written, for Elijah began to appear to him before the end of 5487 [1727]. See Benayahu, 'Ha"magid" shel ramḥa"l', 302–9.

those that are in your hands—I beg that they may be hidden away.'[61] The emphasis he laid on *Mishkenei elyon* shows that he rated its importance

[61] *Igerot*, ii. 219. At the present time (early in 1978) there has been published an essay by M. Benayahu, 'Shevuat ramḥa"l laḥdol mileḥaber sefarim al-pi ha"magid", mahutah vetotse-'oteiha', *Zion*, 42 (1977), 24–48, which sets out to prove that Luzzatto and his associates faithfully observed the undertakings he had been made to sign and the prohibitions imposed on him in Padua and Frankfurt, and that Luzzatto did not set at naught or contravene the bans issued in 1735–6. This essay is very much in the nature of an apologia, in which the assumptions and conclusions are adapted and subordinated to the purpose determined in advance. One of the outstanding examples of unacceptable tendentiousness relates to the information that after the Padua decree requiring the withdrawal of Luzzatto's kabbalistic writings, and after the decree of burning pronounced in Frankfurt and in consequential bans on the offending works, he, his disciples, and his teacher continued to keep them in their possession and to study them. Here and in n. 22 above I have dealt incidentally with this information, and in Essay 8, pp. 415–24, I discussed it directly and drew what appeared to me to be the conclusions which sprang from it. The information I have given here with regard to *Mishkenei elyon* is not mentioned in Benayahu's essay, but he remarks: 'It appears that writings which were in the hands of R. Isaiah Bassano remained in his possession' and 'without doubt' the treatise on Ecclesiastes and *Tikunim ḥadashim* remained with him, and Luzzatto's disciples, too, did not refrain from using their master's writings, 'and therefore Luzzatto's writings were still available in Padua' (pp. 41–2). In order to reconcile this information with the assumption of faithfulness to the undertakings and the bans, Benayahu states that in all the writings which they retained, 'the *magid* and the souls of holy men are not mentioned' (p. 42); and, expressed in other words: 'No such writings as were forbidden on account of the oath have been found and none has been preserved' (p. 43). According to Benayahu's own arguments (see pp. 27–30, 37), the Paduan decrees and, it would hardly be necessary to add, those of Frankfurt had applied even to writings not composed at the dictation of a *magid*. But the amazing thing is that his statement inverts the facts. *Tikunim ḥadashim* and the treatise on Ecclesiastes are the principal two 'maggidic' books which were pilloried by Luzzatto's opponents at every stage of the dispute, and they received prominent and dishonourable mention in the documents on the prohibitions and bans; and in *Tikunim ḥadashim*, which has been preserved and is in our possession, we find that on nearly every page Metatron, Elijah, the Faithful Shepherd [Moses], Abraham, and the souls of other tsadikim reveal themselves and speak. That is to say, facts which contradict the assumptions on which the essay is based are removed without ceremony, so that the situation is arbitrarily stood on its head by the author. I shall endeavour to show other matters of this kind in their proper light in my further discussion in the next issue of this journal [*Kiryat sefer*] and elsewhere. However, in simple justice, I must immediately draw attention to two matters presented in a mistaken and misleading manner:

(*a*) Benayahu goes to great trouble (pp. 33–9) to show that no special importance should be attached to what happened at Frankfurt; that there was nothing essentially new in the admissions and prohibitions contained in the document which Luzzatto had to sign there, the interrogation which preceded the signature being merely a sort of quiet conversation among scholars; that 'Ramhal sincerely wanted to still the controversy and, for the sake of peace, behaved with a good measure of concessiveness' (p. 37); that Luzzatto saw the results of the pleasant conversation as imposing a valid obligation, and only with regard to the admission of fabricating the revelation of the *magid*, which was extracted from him in a manner hardly pleasant, did he complain of having been wronged. The interpretation of the signed admission and of what Luzzatto said in his letter of the New Moon of Elul 5495 [late summer 1735] (*Igerot*, ii. 303–4), an interpretation intended to gloss over the gravity of the inquisitorial

extremely highly. To date, no other copy of the main body of the text is known, but sections of the mishnaic appendix are copied in MS Harvard 54,[62] fos. 132^{r}–133^{r}, and it seems probable that the copyist had the whole work before him.

As I have said, Luzzatto himself represented *Mishkenei elyon* as a work inspired by the *magid*. The question is whether the whole work was written down as it was received in a series of revelations or whether only basic matters, revealed through the inspiration of the *magid*, were crystallized after a time in an adapted and extended form.[63] From the special character of both its form and its content, it appears to me that, apart from the appendix, what we have here is a maggidic work throughout, on the pattern of the books in the style of the Zohar.[64]

III. HOMILIES ON 'YOU ARE WHOLLY FAIR, MY LOVE' (FOS. 43^{r}–45^{v}, 128^{r-v}, 165^{v}–166^{r})

The first section, which is also the most important (fos. 43^{r}–45^{v}), contains eight short homilies, each of about fifteen to twenty lines.[65] Each one is

scene enacted within the walls of the Beit Din in Frankfurt, is nothing but a chain of distortions of texts. This is not the place to detail them, but the crowning example is the suppression of Luzzatto's declaration at the end of his letter, which completely negates the hair-splitting arguments and apologetic contortions. As regards the fact that he refrained from teaching kabbalah in Amsterdam, he wrote: 'And it is not because of the Frankfurt prohibition that I do this, *for the whole of that affair is nothing to me but a broken shard*' (ibid. 305; and see ibid. 358).

(*b*) Contrary to my demonstration (in Essay 8, n. 19) that the commentary on *Idra raba* was written in 1731, Benayahu discovers (p. 44 n. 82): 'This book was written before the oath, and as early as 26 Tevet 5490 [Jan. 1730] Luzzatto sent his teacher commentaries from it (see *Igerot*, 52, 54).' Any schoolchild who reads that letter attentively will realize that it refers to Luzzatto's *Idra*. The passage expounded there (*Igerot*, i. 54) will be found in *Tikunim ḥadashim*, 117, in the *Idra kadisha* which Luzzatto included in *tikun* 69 of his book. It is disturbing that a person whose knowledge does not suffice to distinguish between the *Idra* of the Zohar and the *Idra* in *Tikunim ḥadashim* offers instruction in the study of Luzzatto's kabbalistic writings.

[62] I have considered the Harvard collection in Essay 2 below. And see below, text referring to n. 117.

[63] See end of Section I above.

[64] In the texture of its characteristic style, and to some extent also in its motifs and speculative elements, *Mishkenei elyon* bears the imprint of *Berit menuḥah* (Amsterdam, 1648), one of the enigmatic books of medieval kabbalistic literature. The influence of *Berit menuḥah*, which also has a bearing on the affair of the *magid*, is acknowledged or implicit both in well-known and in less familiar works by Luzzatto. In *Sod hamerkavah* (Section X below) this source is quoted several times, and in considering it there I will explain the extent of its influence and its significance.

[65] From the fourth one onwards the homilies are numbered in square script with the letters *gimel* (3) to *zayin* (7); that is to say, one homily has been omitted from the reckoning in

headed by three scriptural verses, two of which are the same in every case: Song of Songs 4: 7 ('You are wholly fair, my love, and there is no flaw in you'), and Proverbs 5: 19 ('A lovely hind, a graceful doe; her breasts will satisfy you at all times, and you will always be intoxicated with her love'), while the third verse is always from Ecclesiastes, but different for each homily. At the end of the collection (fos. 165^{v}–166^{r}) there is a ninth homily corresponding to these eight in size and structure.[66] On one folio (128^{r-v}) another homily which has been preserved minus its beginning expounds the same verses from the Song of Songs and Proverbs, but has no verse from Ecclesiastes, and it appears that there was no such verse in the missing portion either. This fragment is more than equivalent in length to three homilies in the group of nine.[67] In MS Oxford 2307, a small collection of writings by Luzzatto, there is a work entitled *Kaf-dalet kishutei kalah* ['Twenty-Four Ornaments of the Bride'] (fos. 40^{v}–42^{v}) containing twenty-four very short homilies, each of three to six lines, on 'You are wholly fair, my love' and on another verse which is different in each one. In the second word of the second verse the first and last letters are consistently pointed with *shuruk* ['u'] and *kamats* [long 'a'] without regard to the rules of vocalization, the odd pointing being adapted to the use of holy names for the purpose of kabbalistic *kavanot* ['mystical meditations'], as will be explained below. The facts given above show that Luzzatto wrote various small works of leaflet length on the same verse from the Song of Songs.[68]

error. However, in this series there are no spaces between the homilies, and the letters used to number them differ in appearance from those used in the next series, the homilies on 'O Lord, open my lips'. Hence it is evident that they were inserted later by another hand and that the mistake was not that of the writer.

66 The verses from Ecclesiastes, in the order in which they are used in the homilies, are 10: 10, 7, 11, 1, 14, 12, 9; 9: 15; 12: 14. In my opinion the whole of this section is in Luzzatto's hand. In the eight homilies the writing resembles that of the first series in the 'linked discourses'; in the ninth one it is identical with the hasty and uneven writing in the fourth series of that section—the series which appears immediately before this homily at the end of the collection. See n. 43 above and the remarks to which that note relates.

67 It appears to me that the missing beginning did not take up a whole folio. If my assumption is correct this may mean that there was another homily of this kind, and perhaps several, and that more than one folio is missing before the fragmentary homily. To judge from the verses expounded on the folio which we have, it may be that alongside the ones from the Song of Songs and Proverbs there was a third verse, 'Hear, O Israel' (Deut. 6: 4) or 'But as for me, my prayer' (Ps. 69: 14); however, it is possible that this homily and others of the same kind were based on only two verses. This folio was written out by a copyist, but not by 'the unmistakable copyist'.

68 It should be added that in the 'linked discourses', too, the third link is 'You are wholly fair, my love'. In *Razin genizin*, which is appended to *Megilat setarim* (Warsaw, 1889), 105–6, there is a homily in Aramaic under the heading 'You are wholly fair etc.', but in the text itself this verse is mentioned only in the concluding sentence, and the entire homily is introduced as a supplement to a series of discourses in Aramaic on the verses 'Behold, you are fair, my love' (S. of S. 1: 15; 4: 1). Next to the heading the name 'R. Jekutiel' is noted, but the names of Luzzatto's

The common denominator of all the homilies on 'You are wholly fair, my love' is their central theme: the virtues of the Shekhinah and her situation.

On the face of it the structure of these homilies, unlike that of the 'linked discourses', follows a simple routine: the placing of two or three different scriptural verses at the head of each homily. But three specific elements which I note here not only distinguish the homilies in terms of substance but also confer on them a special structural character. The incomplete homily might pass for a section of *Tikunei hazohar* in Hebrew. Its Zoharic character finds expression in linguistic elements such as the Aramaizing use of the verb *z-m-n*, or starting sentences with *Bo ure'eh* ['Come and see'] and ending them with *vaday* ['certain'], and in the lines of the discussion and commentary. In 'Twenty-Four Ornaments of the Bride' a prominent and novel feature is the irregular vocalization, a practice followed in *yiḥudim* ['unifications'] in which the scriptural texts are not the subject of speculative or homiletic comment but provide material for bringing divine names together for the purpose of mystical and magical practices.[69] We have here an uncommon combination the object of which is to take scriptural verses and turn them abruptly to different purposes. The most important section, which we must discuss in some detail, is that constituted by the nine homilies on the group of three texts. The meaning assigned to each of the three verses which stand at the head of these homilies alters its complexion from one homily to another and even within the same one, but the function of each is the same, or at any rate similar, in all the homilies: the verse from the Song of Songs displays the beauty of the Shekhinah and her restoration to perfection [*tikun*] by removing the 'husks' [*kelipot*] from her, and particularly by severing the contact between

disciples which appear alongside homilies in that collection are not intended to indicate authorship. See my remarks in Essay 3, p. 199.

69 See my discussion of *Yiḥud gan-eden*, Section IX below. The architectonic basis of the strange vocalizations becomes very clear when we discover their nature. The twenty-four pairs of vowelled letters correspond exactly, with slight variations of order, to the set of twenty-four biliteral names contained in R. Hayim Vital's *Sha'ar hakavanot*, introduction to the section headed 'Inyan yom hakipurim'. It is evident that the twenty-four verses linked with 'You are wholly fair, my love' and expounded together with that verse were chosen for the fact that the first and last letters of their second words matched the set of names. A set of names of the same kind is given in *Kitsur sefer hakavanot* in the section headed 'Inyan avodat yom hakipurim', but most of the names are different from those to which I have just referred. Following them there appears this statement: 'These are 24 [in number], and *they are aspects of the 24 ornaments of the bride*' (MS BL Or. 10860, fo. 41^{v}). The fact that in the pamphlet *Kaf-dalet kishutei kalah* ['Twenty-Four Ornaments of the Bride'] Luzzatto did not make use of the set of names which appears in his *kavanot* shows that *Kitsur sefer hakavanot* was a later work. In *Yiḥud hayirah*, too, which I consider below (Section IX), there is a *kavanah* concerning one of the twenty-four names: 'Then you will meditate on the divine name *uta* so as to combine the whole of the Torah in *at-bash* [i.e. replacing *alef* by *tav*, *beit* by *shin*, etc.], and you will draw down upon yourself fear and humility so that these are always upon your countenance' (MS Guenzburg 745, fo. 169^{v}).

her and her rival, the handmaid Lilith; the verse from Proverbs portrays the function of the Shekhinah in bestowing heavenly bounty and directing the course of the world and all the creatures in it; the object of the verses from Ecclesiastes is to describe the disturbance and harm caused by the Sitra Ahra and ways of removing or rectifying these ill effects, and to set the vices of Lilith against the virtues of the Shekhinah. This fixed apportionment of functions to the scriptural verses imparts to the whole set of homilies the character of a work of literary craftsmanship in the form of variations on a single theme.

I summarize here, taking the homilies in order, the contrasts drawn between the Shekhinah and the Sitra Ahra. These contain features, important in themselves, which are also of importance in helping us to recognize the intellectual and emotional background to Luzzatto's veneration and love of the Shekhinah.

1. The Shekhinah is restored (achieves *tikun*) through the power of the four matriarchs (configurations of the Godhead) and disseminates their light to Israel through the power of her intercourse with her supernal husband, but sometimes, when the Sitra Ahra gains the upper hand, their intercourse is impaired and the light is obscured. Through the merit of the study of the Torah illumination is restored to Israel, and 'forthwith the Sitra Ahra flees from them' and 'the Shekhinah is restored with a restoration [*tikun*] which is perfect in every way' (fo. 43^{r}).

2. Supernal lights gather together in the Shekhinah and pour forth from her in love, and through their power she rules the world. Even when, on the surface, power is in the hands of the servants—the forces of the Sitra Ahra—and the princes of the Shekhinah are under their sway, 'all this is only as it appears to the eye, but in truth everything is in a state of perfect *tikun* and His kingdom rules over all' [Ps. 103: 19] (fo. 43^{r-v}).

3. The Shekhinah is crowned by Binah on the Sabbath with seventy names, which serve in her possession as fountains of blessing and sparks of fire; and then the serpent, which strikes 'when the Shekhinah is in an imperfect state', is deprived of its power and 'cannot suck nourishment' even from the dust, for 'everything is sanctified with supreme holiness' (fos. 43^{v}–44^{r}).

4. The Shekhinah is not content with bestowing the divine flow on the souls of mankind but also restores them to their proper state of perfection. Whereas 'the wicked handmaid does not desire *tikun*' and 'they corrupt even what, at first, was mostly good', the Shekhinah, 'even in a matter which, to begin with, was a little bad', lovingly 'sets [people] right and returns them to [the path of] goodness' (fo. 44^{r}).

5. 'Just as [the Shekhinah] is drawn [to all things] in love, so does she draw all things towards beauty' by her *tikunim*, and she spurs 'the soul to cleave to her

as she cleaves to the souls'. The opposite is the case with the 'wicked handmaid', whose way is to corrupt 'that which is beautiful to look upon, that which is a vessel perfected', and she behaves like a fool who 'despairs, and causes others to despair, of attaining *devekut* and truth' (fo. 44^{v}).

6. The Shekhinah may be described as 'the word of the Lord', and 'in her is the whole of the Torah, all of it consisting of the names of the Holy One, blessed be He'. Therefore when the letters are combined through 'the ardour of the soul' in love, supernal lights and a flow of divine bounty are drawn down from the Shekhinah, whereas the activity of the Sitra Ahra in combining letters is 'witchcraft' which darkens the soul and causes a spirit of defilement to rest upon it (fos. 44^{v}–45^{r}).

7. In the *tikunim* of the Shekhinah the souls of those engaged in the *tikun* are illumined and enjoy the lights of her divine flow, but the occupation of the Sitra Ahra with transgressions weakens the body and saddens the soul. Anyone who makes use of the names of that which is unclean 'exposes himself to danger; [that is] certain', but with the holy names of the Shekhinah, 'in the case of a person who is holy and uses them appropriately, each with its own kind, he does not separate[70] [them], so that no confusion results'[71] (fo. 45$^{r–v}$).

8. The Shekhinah bestows the divine flow on the two Messiahs out of her love for them and frees them from their imprisonment by the husks. Since 'the Messiah is an expression of the mystical essence of the Shekhinah', he is called, while among the husks, 'poor [*misken*] in respect of Malkhut', and then 'the Holy One, blessed be He, blocks all the roads to him and he is not revealed . . . so that the Sitra Ahra should not take hold of him' and he is tormented and 'has no form or comeliness',[72] but when he emerges from the husks he inherits the beauty of the Shekhinah and it is said of him 'Your eyes shall see the King in his beauty'[73] (fo. 45^{v}).

9. The Shekhinah as *ayelet* ['a hind'] is mystically equated with *emet* ['truth'],[74] and *emet* is her seal [cf. BT *Shab.* 55*a* and Tishby, *Wisdom of the*

[70] The Hebrew word is *ḥotsets*; it should perhaps be read as *kotsets* [which could mean 'cut (them) apart'—Trans.].

[71] This matter, which is connected with the activities of Luzzatto and his group, is explained *in extenso* in his *Derekh hashem*, pt. iii, ch. 2: 'Be'inyan hape'ulah beshemot uvekhishuf' ['Concerning Activity with Names and Witchcraft'].

[72] Isa. 53: 2. Similarly, in his *Kinat hashem tsevaot* Luzzatto wrote that the Messiah was 'alluded to in the mystical reference to the Shekhinah'. See the passage I quoted in *Netivei emunah uminut*, 182, and the references to the Shabatean sources ibid. 321 n. 120.

[73] Isa. 33: 17.

[74] In *gematriyah*, *ayelet* has the same numerical value as *emet*. *Emet* is the sefirah Tiferet, and hence *ayelet emet* signifies perfect pairing. The connection between *ayelet* and *emet* is indicated by a similar oblique reference in the first homily also.

Zohar, ii. 562—Trans.]; and although until the Redemption the world is governed by the judgement of actions [as good or bad], 'at the end everything will stand solely by the *devekut* of Israel with the Holy One, blessed be He'. 'This rule of justice is intended to lead ultimately to a state of perfect *devekut* . . . to strengthen the good, and to restore the bad to good ways . . . to achieve a *tikun* which is the manifestation of supreme perfection, lacking nothing'[75] (fo. 165^v).

In these homilies the Godhead is not directly addressed in passages of prayer, but in view of the tone and content and the opening of each homily with the passionate cry 'The Shekhinah is the hind of love', they may be regarded as hymns of praise to the Shekhinah in poetic prose couched in the form of homilies.

'Twenty-Four Ornaments of the Bride', too, is a group of homilies extolling the Shekhinah, but at greater length and with more emphasis on matters connected with exile and redemption and on the figures of the Messiahs. The three 'ornaments' which I quote here verbatim and in full typify the nature of the twenty-four:

(6) 'You are wholly fair, my love' etc., 'Make haste, my beloved' etc.[76] [The word 'my beloved', which should properly be read *dodi*, is pointed with *kubuts* ['u'] under the first letter and *kamats* [long 'a'] under the last, and carries the accent *gershayim* over the first letter.—Trans.] The Shekhinah spreads over the two Messiahs, and they include the whole of Israel,[77] and the bad odour must be removed from Israel to the end that they may be perfumed, and the Holy One, blessed be He, must Himself take up the cause of the two Messiahs, and that is [expressed in] 'And the Lord will be King',[78] and He will ascend 'the mountains of spices', and all of them will become perfumed. Then 'you will be wholly fair, my love', perfuming herself wholly in a single action through the perfecting of the bond of the Messiahs. (MS Oxford 2307, fos. 40^v–41^r)

75 There is an allusion here, which is left unclarified, to one of the central ideas of Luzzatto's doctrine: at the Creation the Sitra Ahra, too, was formed, and because of its existence the world has been governed since the beginning—and all the more so during the Exile—by the rule of *din* and *mishpat* [judgement and law], on the basis of the dualism of good and evil. But evil, which is the antithesis of good, was created only so that it might be nullified, and in time to come it will pass away and there will be perfect unity above and below under the rule of *ahavah* and *ḥesed* [love and mercy]. See *Da'at tevunot*, ed. H. Friedlaender (Benei Berak, 1973), 17–20, in the introduction.

76 S. of S. 8: 14: 'Make haste, my love, and be like a roe or a young hart upon the mountains of spices.' The vowelled letters are also marked with the accent *gershayim*, but here and in a few other homilies the *gershayim* has been omitted from the second vowelled letter through the carelessness of the copyist.

77 In the form of the two kingdoms, Judah and Ephraim.

78 Zech. 14: 9.

(10) 'You are wholly fair, my love' etc., 'for Mordecai the Jew was second' etc.[79] [The consonants *mrdkhy* are pointed with *kubuts* under the first letter and *kamats* under the last, and *gershayim* appears over both of those letters.—Trans.] While the Shekhinah is in exile without a partner above, the Holy One, blessed be He, unites her below with some tsadik, who has the mystical identity of Mordecai, and then whatever fault the prince[80] wishes to perpetrate, Mordecai corrects it, as is to be understood by the expression 'she would immerse herself and sit',[81] and therefore 'you are wholly fair' etc. (Ibid., fo. 41ʳ)

(19) 'You are wholly fair, my love' etc., 'Let every soul [*neshamah*, again with *kubuts/gershayim* and *kamats/gershayim* on first and last letters respectively—Trans.] praise the Lord' etc.[82] The perfection of the Shekhinah [is] in the soul of the King-Messiah, which is an only daughter, but in order for her to attain perfection all the other souls must be joined together in her and become one in her. Then the Shekhinah shines with a great *tikun*, for she is a bride, and then 'you are wholly fair, my love' and no flaw remains, for by virtue of their mutual responsibility they perform *tikun* for each other, so that all is restored to a state of perfection [*hakol metukan*]. (Ibid., fo. 42ʳ)

Luzzatto stresses the erotic character of the relations of the tsadikim to the Shekhinah in other works of his too, especially in his description of the relations between Ramhal = Moses and 'the bride of Moses'.[83] Particularly noteworthy is the idea that in order to achieve perfect *tikun* all the souls of Israel must join together in mutual responsibility and be merged into the Shekhinah together with the soul of the Messiah.[84]

[79] Esther 10: 3: 'second to King Ahasuerus'.

[80] Hebrew *hasar*. The letter *r* should perhaps be read as *d*, and the word would then be *hashed* ['the evil spirit']. In either event the reference is to Sama'el, the leader of the Sitra Ahra. Through his domination over the Shekhinah in exile, he is characterized as King Ahasuerus, who forcibly subdued Esther, while the tsadik—Mordecai, whose communion [*hityaḥadut*] with the Shekhinah is a *tikun* removing the slur which Sama'el seeks to cast upon her by his filth—is called 'second to King Ahasuerus'. For the relations between the Sitra Ahra and the Shekhinah while she is in exile, see Tishby, *Wisdom of the Zohar*, i. 382–5.

[81] A reference to *Meg.* 13*b*: 'She would arise from the bosom of Ahasuerus and immerse herself and sit in the bosom of Mordecai.'

[82] Ps. 150: 6.

[83] See *Sod haketubah* ['The Mystical Interpretation of the Marriage Contract'] in Essay 3, p. 211 ff. In my commentary at pp. 190–5, 202–6, I showed that Luzzatto, elevated by his marriage to the status of husband of the Shekhinah, associated the members of his school with himself in the mystical experience of the holy union. On the position of the Shekhinah in Luzzatto's philosophy, see also S. A. Horodezky, 'R' mosheh ḥayim lutsato kimekubal', *Keneset*, 5 (1940), 314–15.

[84] The influence of Nathan of Gaza can be recognized in this idea. In a section of *Sefer haberiah* ['The Book of the Creation'] published in H. Wirszubsky's essay *Al ha'ahavah haruḥanit: midivrei natan ha'azati* (Tel Aviv, 1941), 180–92, Nathan taught that the *tikun* of the world of

From what has been said here and from my discussion of the 'linked discourses' (Section I above), it is clear that all these homilies belong to the category of the direct revelations which were noted down as they were received under the inspiration of the *magid*. In my opinion it may be said without hesitation that these writings were intended, from the first, to be used for the purposes of study and worship in Luzzatto's group and were read at their meetings in the course of their devotions for 'the *tikun* of the holy Shekhinah' and 'the *tikun* of the whole community of Israel'. There is also reason to suppose that the 'Twenty-Four Ornaments of the Bride' were regularly read in the Friday evening service [*kabalat shabat*, 'Welcoming the Sabbath'] together with the recital of the Song of Songs customary among the kabbalists.[85]

atsilut ['emanation'] would not be complete 'until the complete correction of all that needs to be corrected [*litaken*] in the souls of Israel so that they attain perfect unity, all of them comprised in a single body, which is the Messiah' (ibid. 183). He went on to say that the unification [*yiḥud*] of the souls of Israel depended on their loving each other while cleaving in love to the Holy One, blessed be He, and to the Shekhinah. And see Wirszubsky's remarks ibid. 180–1, and in his essay 'Hate'ologyah hashabeta'it shel natan ha'azati', *Keneset*, 8 (1944), 240–1; G. Scholem, *Shabetai tsevi vehatenuah hashabeta'it bimei ḥayav* (Tel Aviv, 1957), ii. 700.

[85] The rite of adorning the Shekhinah with twenty-four bridal ornaments on the Sabbath was practised in kabbalistic circles in Safed, where it took the form of reciting the twenty-four chapters of the Mishnah in tractate *Shabat* at the times of the statutory services or at the formal meals. The twenty-four chapters were divided into three equal parts. R. Abraham Galante, in his *Hanhagot* ['Ethical Guidelines', rules of conduct], testified to the existence of this practice in Safed, and also mentioned the recitation of the Song of Songs at the Friday evening service. See S. Schechter, *Studies in Judaism*, ser. 2 (Philadelphia, 1908), appendix, 297. See also M. Benayahu, *Sefer toledot ha'ar"i* (Jerusalem, 1967), 330–1, 350; D. Tamar, *Meḥkarim betoledot hayehudim be'erets yisra'el uve'italyah* (Jerusalem, 1970), 153. These two customs are not mentioned in Nathan of Gaza's 'guidelines' so far as we know them at present. See M. Benayahu, 'Hatenuah hashabeta'it beyavan', *Sefunot*, 14 (1971–8), 278–9 and n. 13. However, *Ḥemdat yamim*, pt. i, expatiates with enthusiasm on the reading of the Song of Songs (29[38]*d*–40*c*) and the reading of the twenty-four chapters of Mishnah *Shabat* to represent the twenty-four ornaments of the bride (42*c*, 44*b*–*c*). In the description of the two customs references are introduced to kabbalistic *kavanot*. The directions for the readings similarly include important innovations. The following are two examples which have a bearing on the compilation by Luzzatto: (*a*) the recitation of the Song of Songs takes place 'before the reading of the secrets of the Torah' as a preparation for proper understanding 'in the study of kabbalah' (38[39]*c*); (*b*) the twenty-four chapters of the Mishnah should be read at the Friday evening service in order to adorn the Shekhinah 'at the time of her ascent to lean upon her beloved' [cf. S. of S. 8: 5] (42*c*). (The page references and the Hebrew quotations here translated follow the Venice edition of 1758; see M. Benayahu, *Haskamah ureshut bidefusei venetsiyah* (Jerusalem, 1971), 140–3.) *Ḥemdat yamim* is a treasury of Shabatean practices as followed by Nathan of Gaza, his disciples, and their disciples up to the time the book was printed in 1731–2. As I stated at the end of my second essay enquiring into its sources: 'Several facts which I have been successful in bringing to light but have not yet published give me cause to believe that in the course of my investigation I shall be able to advance some way further through the period which concerns us and get near the years in which *Ḥemdat yamim* was printed' (*Netivei emunah uminut*, 168; and see my allusions to the

IV. HOMILIES ON 'O LORD, OPEN MY LIPS'
(FOS. 46^{r}–47^{r}, 7^{r-v}, 166^{r})

This section consists of nine homilies, each six to nine lines long, seven of them grouped together and numbered in order in the original by square Hebrew letters (fos. 46^{r}–47^{r}), and two others separated from them (fos. 7^{r-v}, 166^{r}).[86] In all of them the same two texts are expounded: 'O Lord, open my lips and my mouth will declare Your praise',[87] and 'You will show faithfulness to Jacob';[88] the differences between the homilies are in the details of the expositions. They also share the same general subject, the *tikun* of the Shekhinah, but the manner of the *tikun* varies according to the level on which it takes place: above, by the relations between the Shekhinah and a particular sefirah or group of sefirot; below, through the agency of Israel or the patriarchs. The name Adonai always relates to the Shekhinah, but *emet* and *ya'akov* are used in various senses, and the subject matter of the homily varies with them. It is clear that these writings, too, were intended for Luzzatto's group and were read at their gatherings.

From the point of view of originality in structure and ideas these homilies are of no great interest, and there is no reason why we need concern ourselves to explain them in the present setting, but they are extremely important as aids to our understanding of the nature of early manifestations

participation of the editor, R. Jacob Algazi, and his colleagues in the compilation of the book, ibid. 129, 146, 161. So, too, in many of the notes to *Netivei emunah uminut*, above all nn. 53 and 64 on pp. 307 and 308). My further researches have completely confirmed this hypothesis. It is therefore probable that the innovations introduced by *Ḥemdat yamim* with regard to the reading of the Song of Songs and the 'Twenty-Four Ornaments of the Bride' had their origin in late Shabatean 'rules of conduct'. Since Luzzatto based 'Twenty-Four Ornaments of the Bride' on a verse from the Song of Songs it is reasonable to suppose that he, too, introduced the use of the *kavanot* and the study of the secrets of the Torah by his group, as in his book, after the recitation of the Song of Songs and the reading of the Mishnah chapters at the Friday evening service. It should be pointed out that the 'Twenty-Four Ornaments of the Bride' are followed by rules of conduct and *kavanot* for the preparations [for the Sabbath] and for the afternoon service [*minḥah*] on the eve of the Sabbath (MS Oxford 2307, fos. 43^{r}–44^{v}).

[86] The first of the separate homilies is sandwiched between the second and third series of the 'linked discourses', on two lines under the second series and four lines above the third series. The second one is the last text in the collection, immediately following the ninth homily in the series on 'You are wholly fair, my love'. The handwriting in the three sections consisting of these homilies is similar to that of the homilies which precede them, which in my opinion, as I have already said, were all penned by Luzzatto himself.

[87] Ps. 51: 17.

[88] Mic. 7: 20.

of the *magid*. Most of them are couched in obscure language, in unfinished sentences, and in veiled allusions. This characteristic is even more conspicuous in them than in the nine homilies on 'You are wholly fair, my love'.

As an example I will quote one homily, adding brief notes:

(4) 'O Lord, open my lips', 'You will show faithfulness [*emet*] to Jacob'. Certainly *emet* contains two females,[89] *alef tav* being Rachel, in whom is 'O Lord, [open] my lip[s] [*sefatai*] etc.' 'Open', it is not the letter *mem* which opens it [Luzzatto may have read *sefati*, 'my lip'—Trans.] but *s(h)in*, the three patriarchs together[90] [represented by the three strokes of the letter *shin*, ש—Trans.]. This means that the *shin* whistles [*shoreket*] with opened mouth, and immediately the *mem*, which had been silent [i.e. a closed final letter, ם], opens also [מ], 'and my mouth will declare Your praise', completing *emet*. An indication of this is 'And You made a name [*shem*] for Yourself, as it is this day',[91] the *shin* whistles, the *mem* is silent,[92] the two of them are combined to be restored in perfect *tikun*. Jacob takes both of them so that all may achieve *tikun* through the mystery of the letter *vav*, the letter of *emet*,[93] and that is certainly 'You will show faithfulness to Jacob'. (fo. 46^v^)

A number of admirably clear and systematic works were undoubtedly produced from raw material of this kind.

V. A DISCUSSION BETWEEN THE SOUL AND THE INTELLECT (FOS. 51^r^–73^r^)

The work I bring to the attention of the reader in this section is unknown from any other source. Like the documents I dealt with in the previous sections, it is not greatly different from Luzzatto's known works in structure, literary character, or the ideas it expresses. Indeed, it belongs to a literary category which is common in Luzzatto's other writings, namely speculative dialogue. Four

[89] Binah–Leah—the letter *mem*; Malkhut–Rachel—*at*, i.e. the letters *alef tav*; together forming the letters of *emet*.

[90] Hesed, Gevurah, and Tiferet.

[91] Neh. 9: 10.

[92] As in *Sefer yetsirah*, 86*a*. The letters *shin* and *mem* are joined together in the word *shem* ['name'] in the verse from Nehemiah.

[93] *Ya'akov-ve'-emet* [*ve-* being the mystically significant letter *vav*—Trans.]: Jacob and Emet ['Truth']. These are names for Tiferet, and perfect *tikun* is achieved by the intercourse of Tiferet with the Shekhinah when she is restored to perfection, the Shekhinah herself having the character of Emet when she is joined with Binah, the supernal female.

books of the same kind are extant in print.[94] However, the very fact of its close relationship to another work of this kind raises bibliographical and literary problems. In the well-known work *Da'at tevunot* ['Knowledge with Understanding']—which, at first, was untitled in nearly all the manuscripts,[95] and certainly had no title in the original—and in the work under consideration here—which likewise has no title in the manuscript—the speakers in the dialogue are the same: the soul and the intellect, which carry on a disputation like a disciple raising questions and a master giving answers.[96] The two dialogues differ from each other with regard to the course of the discussion and its subject matter, but in both of them the intended purpose is the solution of religious and ethical problems by the author's method of applying the principles of kabbalah, and there are also substantial points of contact between them. The question is therefore: why did Luzzatto write two different books in the form of a discussion between the soul and the intellect, and how are the two discussions related? Moreover, *Da'at tevunot* is itself complicated by a problematical relationship with two other works. One of these, which was published a long time ago and was reprinted under the title *Kelalim rishonim* ['First Principles'], has already been considered and compared with *Da'at tevunot*,[97]

[94] *Da'at tevunot* (Warsaw, 1889), *Derekh ḥokhmah* (Amsterdam, 1783), *Ḥoker umekubal* (Shklov, 1785), *Milḥemet mosheh* (Warsaw, 1889). I consider the last-mentioned work in Section VIII below, text referring to n. 167. S. Ginzburg, in the list at the end of his book *The Life and Works of Moses Hayyim Luzzatto* (Philadelphia, 1931), mentioned two dialogues as existing in manuscript: *Vikuaḥ bein hanefesh vehaguf* ['A Discussion between the Soul and the Body'] (142, no. 58) and *Vikuaḥ bein heḥakham veheḥasid* ['A Discussion between the Scholar and the Hasid'] (143, no. 60), but offered no documentary evidence to prove their existence. J. Almanzi's biography of Luzzatto, *Kerem ḥemed*, 3 (1838), 131, describes two works which were apparently arranged for the most part in the form of dialogues between Luzzatto and R. Moses David Valle. See Section IX below, where *Yiḥud gan-eden* is considered.

[95] The work is preserved in many manuscripts. It appears that the title *Da'at tevunot* was coined by R. M. S. Ghirondi. The book was printed from a copy prepared for him in 1818; at its head appears the introduction which he wrote in the same year. It was he who wrote the second title-page in the printed edition, which carries two names: *Sefer da'at tevunot hanikra ma'amar havikuaḥ* ['The Book *Da'at tevunot*, which is Called "The Discussion"']. The same copy with the title-page and the introduction has been preserved in MS Warsaw 174, where the indications of the dates are clear. In MS BL 860 the book is called *Vikuaḥ shebein hasekhel vehaneshamah* ['A Discussion between the Intellect and the Soul'], but the title is in a different handwriting from that of the body of the text. In MS Oxford-Hirsch 1, again, the title *S[efer] havikuaḥ leramḥa"l* ['"The Discussion", by Luzzatto'] is a later addition. Hence it is evident that the titles *Ma'amar havikuaḥ* and *Sefer havikuaḥ* were likewise not in the original.

[96] The earliest example in our literature of a work laid out in the form of a dialogue like this is the discussion between the intellect and the soul in *Ḥovot halevavot* ['Duties of the heart'] by R. Bahya ibn Pakuda, in the 'gate' entitled *Avodat ha'elohim* ['Worship of God'], chs. 5–10.

[97] H. Friedlaender, in the introduction to *Da'at tevunot*, p. 14, and in the introduction to *Kelalim rishonim* in *Sefer hakelalim* ['The Book of Principles'] (which is appended to *Da'at tevunot*), p. 246, stated that there is a close and constant parallelism in content between the 'Principles', which are formulated in kabbalistic terminology, and *Da'at tevunot*, which is

whereas the second, a discussion between 'Mar Yanuka' and 'Mar Kashisha' ['Mr Child' and 'Mr Old'], was hidden away in manuscript. Known only by its title, and falsely attributed to R. Jekutiel of Vilna,[98] it has not, up to now, been the subject of any scholarly research and no connection has been drawn between it and *Da'at tevunot*.[99] After describing and commenting on the text of the dialogue in the present collection I shall offer some preliminary comparisons of the works mentioned.

The dialogue in the collection breaks off in the middle of a sentence on fo. 73^{r}, and the last word is so placed as to mark the end of the page; in other words the reason for the break is that the writer stopped here. Fos. 73^{v} and 74 are blank, and it is probable that the writer intended to continue with the remainder of the dialogue. To judge from the features outlined at the beginning of the discussion and the pointers to matters which will be considered below,[100] it appears that we have before us what was intended to be a book of considerable size, but it may be that the plan conceived by the author was not fully realized. From the point of view of the handwriting, language, and style this work has jarring and anomalous features the like of which can also be found in other writings in the collection, but here they are more numerous

written in a speculative style. In the notes to *Da'at tevunot* he specified the parallels. His statement was undoubtedly correct both as a whole and in detail, but it is not correct to call the work in question *Kelalim rishonim*. It is true that in several manuscripts it is so entitled, but this was clearly a mistake by a copyist, for Luzzatto applied the name *Hakelalim harishonim* to the work which he sent his teacher in Elul 5489 [1729] and which has now been reprinted in *Sefer hakelalim* under the title *Kelalei pitḥei ḥokhmah vada'at* ['Principles of the "Gateways to Wisdom and Understanding"']. See *Igerot*, i. 14–15, 53, 115. In MS Jerusalem 2517 8° (previously MS Warsaw), which contains this work [the essay with the disputed title—Trans.] in Luzzatto's handwriting and on which Friedlaender mainly relied, the title *Kelalim rishonim* was added by a later hand.

98 This dialogue, in the handwriting of R. Jekutiel, is contained in MS Oxford 2237. Neubauer recorded it in his catalogue as a philosophical work by that writer, and Ginzburg (*Life and Works of Moses Hayyim Luzzatto*, 153, no. 72) copied Neubauer's remark. When I read this work in Oxford in 1956 I recognized at once that it was a different and more extensive version of *Da'at tevunot* and that this version, too, was by Luzzatto. My assumption has meanwhile been confirmed beyond doubt by the discovery of two further copies, as I explain below.

99 The only person to have grasped the true nature of this dialogue was M. Glatzer in his recent description of MS Harvard 54, which contains one of the copies. See Essay 2, p. 116.

100 Folio references, together with an indication of the matters alluded to, are as follows: 54^{v} (the link between the soul and the body and between spiritual and corporeal things); 56^{v} (the existence of the righteous and the wicked in the world); 63^{v} (the condition of the souls before their entry into the world and after leaving it); ibid. (the function of the *tselem* ['image'] in joining together the soul and the body); 64^{r} (the relevance of Adam's sin for an understanding of the changes in the condition of souls); 64^{v} (the clothing of the souls in the perfected [*metukanim*] garments of a *tselem* after death); 67^{r} (the question of the righteous man who suffers misfortune); 69^{v} ('guidelines' relating to the tree of knowledge and the tree of life); 72^{v}, 73^{r} (turning evil back to good).

and conspicuous. The shape of the letters frequently changes and at times they are so indistinct that they can only be deciphered by guesswork; many words are split, while, on the other hand, parts of different words are run together and meaningless combinations of letters are formed. Clerical errors and missing or transposed letters and words are plentiful, some of them with corrections and insertions and some left as they were, and in some places one mistake follows closely on another.[101] There are also pretty frequent linguistic errors, involving serious breaches of the rules of grammar and syntax, as well as incoherence and infelicities of style which obscure the substance of the argument.[102] These aberrations in handwriting and language seem at first to point to the conclusion that the writer is not the author, and may even create the impression that the work is not by Luzzatto. The fact is, however, that grave errors are common even in the autographs of great scholars, and there are defects here more appropriate to the handwriting of an author than to that of a copyist, such as letters so malformed as to make them difficult to read. I therefore think that this work, like others in the collection in which the handwriting is similar, was penned by Luzzatto, hurriedly and with his mind not entirely on the matter in hand. His authorship is proved beyond doubt by the speculative elements which form the basis of the work and by its general stylistic texture.

This dialogue, which covers a wide and varied range of topics, takes the form of a genuine discussion.[103] The soul is not limited in its function to putting questions such as a layman would ask and assenting to the answers of the intellect: on the contrary, it raises difficulties and argues vigorously, and in the course of argument and counter-argument the debate branches out and many matters arise which have only a slender connection with the subjects under discussion.

[101] In some words the letter *he* is written instead instead of *pe*—thus *pesiah* ['a step'] is written *hesiah*, which would be read *hasiah* ['the faction'] (fo. 51^{r}); *mishpat* ['justice'] is written *mish'hat* (fo. 53^{r}), and similarly with a derived form of this word (fo. 55^{r}). Examples of other mistakes: the obscure *b-n-z-not* (fo. 53^{v}), which perhaps should read *benizmanot*[?] or *behazmanot*; *hatuv* (fo. 55^{r}) for *hakatuv*; *kena'uha* (fo. 62^{v}), with *alef* after the *nun*, for *kanuha*; *hatakhlilit* (fo. 66^{r}) for *hatakhlit*. For the substitution of *he* for *pe* in Italian handwriting, see Essay 2, p. 170, where I pointed out that in the solution to Luzzatto's riddle in verse 'Haran' had been written instead of 'Paran'. It is possible that most of the other pieces in the collection are also in Luzzatto's own handwriting.

[102] [Two examples (on fos. 58^{r} and 69^{v}) of incoherence and solecisms are given in this footnote. Neither sentence is completely intelligible. To add to the difficulties, some words seem to have been omitted in the first example, and in the second, there is an adjective without a noun.—Trans.] Comparable defects of language and style are unknown to me in other authentic works of Luzzatto; at any rate they do not occur in such abundance as here.

[103] An extremely interesting example of the manner of the discussion and its literary character is provided by the argument and counter-argument on dialectical complications in explaining ideas. The intellect compares these complications to the doubts which beset an artist in his work (fo. 72^{v}).

I outline here the arrangement of the main topics in the order in which they are discussed. The literary framework is set, at the beginning, by the appeal of the soul [a feminine in Hebrew] to the intellect: since the intellect is appointed by the Creator to guide her, will it show her how to extricate herself from the confusion in which she finds herself for lack of knowledge? The intellect declares that the principal reason why souls are confused is that mankind are ignorant of the way in which *hahanhagah vehahashgaḥah* [the providence which governs the world and its inhabitants] operates in accordance with the secret inner thought of God; they are only able to grasp its outward appearance as this is revealed in action, but this is not God's ultimate governance. This inner governance has its origin in the sefirot, in the union of Binah with Tiferet and Malkhut, and in that union the Torah and the souls of Israel also have their source. Hence the inner governance is embodied in the Torah, which was given to Israel alone. The first goal which the soul must strive to reach under the guidance of the intellect is self-knowledge. But before getting to know her own nature, she must properly understand her duty with regard to the worship of the Lord. That duty is founded on the power of choice with which she is endowed (fos. 51^r–53^r). From that point onward the whole of the incomplete dialogue in our possession consists of a discussion aimed at clarifying various aspects of the question of free choice.

I will try to summarize the subjects covered under eight headings:

1. The commandments [*mitsvot*] are the principal medium for the exercise of the power of choice. Through observing them the soul is illumined and fulfils her mission by cleaving to her divine source, whereas through their neglect she is darkened and cut off from her source. Elevation through *devekut* confers eternal life, and the delight experienced in *devekut* is the true reward which awaits the soul, 'for only if a man cleaves to his Cause is he described as living' (fos. 53^r–54^v).

2. The desire for *devekut* exists as a natural urge in every being [*kol mesubav*—literally, everyone who has been caused, i.e. brought into being—Trans.] to establish a bond with its Cause [*sibah*]. However, while, in the angels, this natural desire is fulfilled as a corollary of their existence, and they are in a state of constant *devekut*, man has to arouse the desire [in himself] and give effect to it by making a positive choice (fos. 54^v–56^v).

3. The advantage of free choice is that, by it, man attains his intended level through his own effort, and thereby he is raised above other creatures and even above the angels, whose perfection is bestowed upon them as a gift. Hence the other creatures receive the bounty of the sefirot only so far as it is necessary for their existence; man alone is privileged to receive the 'abundant flow' of divine energy which confers on him the ability to 'restore the Cause to its perfection', and through him is born the *tikun* of the world (fos. 56^v–58^r).

4. Man's exercise of choice necessarily implies the existence of the evil inclination which will draw him towards sin and corruption, and for this purpose the Holy One, blessed be He, devised the Sitra Ahra [the power of evil] and laid upon man the duty of subduing it by overcoming his evil impulse. But God's desire is that man should enjoy eternal and undisturbed delight; He therefore determined in advance that all the souls that were destined to be created 'should be brought to perfection in this world', and that after the seventh millennium the world would be renewed without the Sitra Ahra and without the evil inclination. As an obvious consequence the power of free choice would be abolished (fos. 58^{r}–60^{r}).[104]

5. Even the angels—who are without sin because, having no power to choose, they are obliged to fulfil the commandments laid upon them—may err through 'lack of enlightenment and knowledge', or even fall into error through a deliberate action. That is the secret of the rebellion and fall of Sama'el, a holy angel who was to have acted as the messenger of God but became defiled because he fulfilled his task 'with alien and unholy intent', exalting himself and presuming to act independently as if two powers controlled the world and he were one of them (fos. 60^{r}–62^{r}).[105]

6. In its early existence the soul, like the angels, has no freedom of choice, and only when it wraps itself in the garment called the *tselem* ['image'], on descending to this world, is it enabled to join itself to the physical body and come into contact with the Sitra Ahra (fos. 62^{v}–64^{v}).[106]

7. If Adam had not sinned, complete *tikun* would have taken place at once, the soul and body would have remained united, and they would have enjoyed eternal delight together; but because of his sin it was decreed that they should be parted by death. The light afforded by the sefirot to man, in his blemished existence in this world, is extremely weak, but even the light which reaches

[104] Instability in this world and constant *devekut* in the world when it is renewed are founded on two different divine forces, Hokhmah and Keter, 'and it is all alluded to in the word *bereshit*—"in the beginning"—which is to be interpreted [allegorically] as the letter *beit* plus *reshit*—"two beginnings"' (fos. 59^{v}–60^{r}). The corresponding remarks in *Mishkenei elyon* to which I referred in the third paragraph of Section II above are similarly linked explicitly to the interpretation of *bereshit* as *beit reshit*. The meaning of *beit reshit* is explained *in extenso* in the unpublished part of Luzzatto's *Kinat hashem tsevaot* (MS Oxford 2237, fos. 232^{v}–233^{r}, 238^{r-v}), which I shall shortly be considering elsewhere. And see my *Netivei emunah uminut*, 316 n. 12. The source of the interpretation as *beit reshit* is the Zohar I, 31*b*, but there the intention is plainly to show that the term *reshit* is not applied to Keter.

[105] See R. Margaliot, *Malakhei elyon* (Jerusalem, 1945), 248–51; Tishby, *Wisdom of the Zohar*, ii. 455–8; I. Tishby, *Torat hara vehakelipah bekabalat ha'ar"i* (Jerusalem and Tel Aviv, 1942), 69–70.

[106] See Scholem, *Pirkei-yesod behavanat hakabalah usemaleiha*, 367–80; Tishby, *Wisdom of the Zohar*, ii. 770–3; Tishby, *Torat hara vehakelipah bekabalat ha'ar"i*, 110–13. And cf. *Adir bamarom*, 156–9.

the soul during its separate existence in Paradise is not as strong as that which will illuminate it when it is joined with the body at the resurrection of the dead, for man's perfection consists in the partnership of the soul and the body (fos. 64^{v}–68^{v}).

8. The last section of the subject matter, which breaks off in mid-sentence (fos. 69^{r}–73^{r}), is part of an explanation of the mystical significance of Adam's sin. In the portion which has been preserved the principal idea is that although, as a result of sin, the world and man are in a state of balance between good and evil, *tikun* and corruption, and the scale is tipped according to the way in which man exercises his power to choose, complete *tikun* is nevertheless assured in advance. Even the souls of the most corrupt sinners in Israel will be repaired [*yetukenu*] and purified. The inevitability of complete *tikun* is explained as due to two causes. First, just as the divine vessels destroyed in 'the breaking of the vessels' were repaired through the light of the sparks which adhered to their fragments, so, too, repair is assured to the destroyed souls of the wicked on account of the light shed by whatever few *mitsvot* they have had the merit to perform, or in default of such *mitsvot*, on account of the merit of their forebears or some other merit. Secondly, the very existence of the Emanator, who is the perfection of goodness, 'will oblige all evil to return to good', and even 'the greatest and most absolute evil will also be repaired so that it becomes good'.

Of all the ideas in this dialogue, including those which I have not specifically mentioned, only a few are entirely absent from the rest of Luzzatto's works, but the great majority of them embody essentially new propositions, or at least fresh nuances. For our present purpose I will deal with a few points of comparison between the work in this collection and *Da'at tevunot* together with the other two works connected with the last-mentioned [namely *Kelalim rishonim* and the dialogue between Mar Yanuka and Mar Kashisha—Trans.].

In making the comparison with *Da'at tevunot* we must examine the nature of the relationship between the two dialogues beyond the simple fact that the participants have the same names. In the opening conversation of *Da'at tevunot* we find it stated that the purpose of the debate is to clarify four of the thirteen principles of the faith. This opening statement is scarcely supported by what follows it: the true purpose, as H. Friedlaender showed in his introduction and notes to the book,[107] is to expound the principles of Lurianic kabbalah under the guise of quasi-philosophic speculative explanations. In any event the two debates follow altogether different patterns, and there is no relationship, either open or concealed, between these two works. So far as concerns the subject matter, many of the topics dealt with in the 'Discussion'

[107] See n. 97 above.

are also considered in *Da'at tevunot*, but in general the differences between them are greater than the similarities. The following are some examples.

1. *Hanhagot ha'olam*. The existence of two governing powers [*hanhagot*], one concealed and the other revealed, is briefly described at the beginning of the 'Discussion', but is a central theme treated extensively in *Da'at tevunot*. The latter work speaks of 'the governance of justice', which operates in this world on the basis of a duality consisting of good and evil. A contrast is drawn with 'the governance of unity', free of any conflicting elements, which will manifest itself at the end of days, and which meanwhile lies hidden within the governance of justice, guiding it towards the eschatological turning point of history.[108] In the 'Discussion' the two forms of governance are presented as the ways in which the Godhead operates in this world, and in this connection no reference is made to questions of duality and unity or to eschatological aspects of the subject.[109]

2. Freedom of choice. Essentially everything on this subject in *Da'at tevunot* is in line with what is said in the 'Discussion', but in the former, free choice is an incidental matter, whereas in the latter it is the pivotal question. Moreover, most of the ideas linked with the idea of choice in the 'Discussion' are not mentioned in *Da'at tevunot*.

3. *Devekut*. In both works *devekut* is presented as a vital necessity, of supreme importance in the relations of man with the Godhead. In the 'Discussion' we find the following statements among others: 'And the truth is that a being [*mesubav*] which has not this desire and this bond can only be called half a creature' (fo. 55^r); 'for truly the pinnacle of worship is *devekut*, and it is truly a supreme need on the part of God for what is pleasing to Him in the existence of the world' (fo. 55^v). These statements accord with the evaluation of *devekut* in *Da'at tevunot*.[110] However, the two works are distinguished from each other by specific differences in their perception of the nature of *devekut*. Each has things to say which do not appear in the other. Two matters should be mentioned which are emphasized in the 'Discussion' but are absent from *Da'at tevunot*.

(*a*) *Devekut* and the performance of the *mitsvot* [the commandments in the Torah] are described as two sides of the same coin. The following unequivocal sentence will serve as an example: 'And by the presence of this bond

108 See Friedlaender, introduction to *Da'at tevunot*, 17–20.

109 There is only a brief allusion to show that in his remarks in this work on the ways of divine providence Luzzatto had in mind the same ideas as were expressed in detail in *Da'at tevunot*: 'All the ills of the Exile, even though they make it appear to Israel as if [He were] hiding His face from them, are only preparations to bring *tikunim* into being for the Redemption' (fo. 51^v).

110 *Da'at tevunot*, ed. Friedlaender, 6–7, 165–9, 179–83.

[*devekut*] throughout his [man's] parts is meant the 613 *mitsvot* which correspond to the 613 parts of man, and truly man [insert 'without' to complete the sense] the *mitsvot* is not a complete creature, for he lacks a part which he ought to have for the full realization of his existence, namely the bond which I have mentioned' (fo. 55^{v}).

(*b*) *Devekut* is presented as the ascent of the soul step by step in the system of the sefirot until it reaches Ein Sof: 'And when man acquires his *devekut* [taken as a power of adhesion—Trans.] and the Emanator desires to act through him, then Malkhut, which is the lowest sefirah, will acquire her *devekut* and adhere to Yesod, and Yesod will acquire his *devekut* and adhere to what is above him, and so on up to Ein Sof, as already said, and then every recipient will be ready and every Bestower will bestow the divine flow because of the readiness of the recipient' (fo. 55^{v}). The differences referred to show clearly that the two dialogues between the soul and the intellect are independent of each other and can on no account be considered as two versions of the same work.

The basis for a comparison between the 'Discussion' and the 'First Principles'—which is a wide-ranging kabbalistic work using unmistakably Lurianic terminology and concepts—is provided by the nature and function of the kabbalistic elements in the 'Discussion'. The latter work contains three indirect references to kabbalistic sources.[111] The subjects of Ein Sof, the sefirot, and the Sitra Ahra are mentioned repeatedly and explicitly.[112] However, in only one place (fos. 71^{r}–72^{r}) are unquestionably Lurianic ideas mentioned (the breaking of the vessels, the fallen sparks, and the processes of *tikun*),[113] and even those few cases are only cited incidentally and by way of analogy, to explain the *tikun* which is assured to the souls of the wicked by the

[111] 'The first knowledge which you must acquire is self-knowledge, as we were taught by [Solomon] the Wise in his holy song [S. of S. 1: 8]: "If you do not know for yourself" etc.' (fo. 52^{v}). [The ethical dative *lakh*, rendered here as 'for yourself', is left untranslated in the Authorized Version and others.—Trans.] The allusion in this case is to a passage in *Zohar ḥadash* which I consider below in connection with *Mar yanuka umar kashisha*. 'And it [self-perfection by the performance of the commandments] means the perfect image, which R. Simeon bar Yohai mentions many times' (fo. 55^{v}). 'This matter [the mystical meaning of the tree of knowledge] is explained by the Ari, may his memory be for a blessing, and also by R. Simeon bar Yohai, in many ways, in many places, and on many levels, and all of them are true' (fo. 69^{r}).

[112] *Da'at tevunot* cites many passages from the Zohar, but expresses concepts which are clearly kabbalistic without recourse to kabbalistic terms.

[113] Additionally, two allusions should be mentioned. One relates to the concept of *tsimtsum* in Luzzatto's kabbalah, but its true meaning is wholly obscured: '. . . the Emanator desired not to act of His own accord and according to His will but that His will should be in accordance with the will of those below' (fo. 56^{r}). See *Da'at tevunot*, ed. Friedlaender, 8–9, 43. The second is an incidental remark on terminology: 'And Keter is not numbered among the sefirot of the *partsufim*' (fo. 60^{r}).

presence of sparks of holiness in them.[114] In the 'Principles' and *Da'at tevunot*, on the other hand—explicitly in the former and by coded references in the latter—questions of Lurianic kabbalah are considered directly, methodically, and at length. It follows that there is no particular affinity between the 'Discussion' and the 'Principles' beyond the subject matter which links the 'Discussion' with *Da'at tevunot*.

With regard to the discussion entitled *Mar yanuka umar kashisha*, a virtually unknown work, I propose to offer some introductory information and comments before comparing it with the 'Discussion' in the collection. In the copy in the handwriting of R. Jekutiel of Vilna which has been preserved in MS Oxford 2237, the work consists of two parts (I, fos. 42^v–83^v; II, fos. 84^r–94^r)[115] and an appendix (fos. 95^r–99^r). The appendix is a further copy of two passages from Part I.[116] Another copy of the work, in Sephardi

[114] The transference of the breaking of the vessels and *tikun* to the field of human existence is important for the links between hasidism and Luzzatto's doctrine. The idea of the parallel to be drawn between 'breaking' and *tikun* on the one hand and man's states of descent and ascent on the other is also to be found in *Adir bamarom*, 59. In this connection it should be pointed out that there is clear evidence of Luzzatto's influence on the Maggid of Mezhirech in the Maggid's explanation of the breaking of the vessels: 'For there is a parable presented by R. M[oses] of a tailor who takes a whole piece of stuff and cuts it into tiny pieces . . . in the same way He alone, blessed be He, existed at first, and afterwards He created the worlds . . . and there had to be a breaking so that the light could be perceived' (Dov Baer of Mezhirech, *Magid devarav leya'akov*, ed. Rivkah Schatz (Jerusalem, 1976), 36). The simile is taken unaltered from *Raya meheimna* (Zohar III, 27*b*), but there, of course, the parable relates not to the breaking of the vessels but to questions and answers in the study of halakhah. However, there is a similar parable which sets out to explain the breaking of the vessels in Luzzatto's *Kela"ḥ pitḥei ḥokhmah* ['138 Gateways to Wisdom'], exposition of Gateway 36: '[Ein Sof] acted like a craftsman who can only work gradually, setting the piece before him and shaping it a little, and its form is altered several times before it is perfected.' In Essay 8, pp. 420–4, 444–8, 450–1, I indicated that the '138 Gateways' may have come into the hands of the Maggid of Mezhirech in manuscript.

[115] The following (converted to arabic numerals from the original foliation in Hebrew lettering) are missing in this copy: 1^v, 7^r–11^v (which would have been between 49^v and 50^r according to the new numbering), 14^r–15^v (between 51^v and 52^r). R. Jekutiel, when making his copy, undoubtedly skipped the pages which should have appeared as 1^v and 2^r. Later on, the folio on which 1^r was written became detached and 1^v was left without it. The foliation in Hebrew lettering is continuous as far as fo. *nun-beit* (52, corresponding to fo. 88^r) in the middle of Part II, and breaks off there, but a second series of Hebrew folio numbers starts at the beginning of Part II (84^r) with the letter *beit* (2) and continues to *yod-zayin* (17^r) at the end of the appendix.

[116] The two passages are: (*a*) fos. 95^r–96^v, corresponding to *Da'at tevunot*, 31–40 (section 41 to the middle of section 48); in this manuscript the passage in question was written on some of the folios missing between fos. 49^v and 50^r; (*b*) fos. 97^r–99^r; in *Da'at tevunot*, ed. Friedlaender, 19–27 (section 38 to the middle of section 40), and here in Part I, fos. 47^r–49^v. The two passages, here copied in reverse order, belong in the section divided into chapters in this copy, but in the appendix they are presented as a dialogue, as they are in the other two copies. Apparently the division into chapters was the editorial work of R. Jekutiel, and after a time, when he recopied these passages, he reverted to the form of the original which lay before him. Jekutiel's collection also contains other writings which were copied several times.

handwriting, is contained in the collection of Luzzatto's writings in MS Harvard 54.[117] It, too, consists of two parts (I, fos. 6^v, 31^r–54^r; II, fos. 54^v–59^r).[118] A third copy, in Rashi script written in an Italian hand,[119] exists in MS Jerusalem 2365 8°; it contains only Part I (fos. 1^r–45^r). The first part corresponds closely to the whole of *Da'at tevunot*, of which, indeed, it is mostly an equivalent, though with textual variants and differences of form and substance. In *Da'at tevunot* there is no reference, direct or indirect, to the existence of a second part. On the contrary, the last sentence spoken by the soul is clearly formulated as a final statement. Not so the words of Mar Yanuka ['Mr Child'] at the end of Part I, which pave the way for the continuation in Part II: 'And I shall return again to learn from you [things] which [are] after my own heart at a time that I shall choose[120] for myself, God willing.' The three copies are not altogether identical. I will point out differences in Part I which go beyond such textual variations as can be expected to occur between one manuscript copy and another. In the Oxford copy there is a section consisting of nine chapters drafted as a continuous speech by Mar Kashisha ['Mr Old'],[121] whereas in the other two copies, as well as in *Da'at tevunot*, the same remarks are presented in the form of a dialogue without division into chapters.[122] In the Harvard manuscript the beginning corresponds to the beginning of *Da'at tevunot*, and the page is headed with the inscription: 'A discussion between the intellect and the soul, the disciple asks and the master replies', which tells us that this copyist had seen the text of *Da'at tevunot* and preferred the version which contained two parts. The Jerusalem copy, on the other hand, opens with two preliminary paragraphs in which Mar Kashisha is approached by Mar Yanuka, a distinguished student who has learnt Torah from his celebrated teacher, 'applying the methods of *pilpul* and *sevara* in the sea of the Talmud and the earlier and later *posekim*', and who now desires to be rescued from perplexity in his study of the secrets of the Torah. Mar Kashisha willingly agrees 'to teach a pupil so worthy, whom I have known to be of good repute since your youth'.[123] These differences prove that the three

[117] See n. 62 above.

[118] The folios of this manuscript were bound out of order.

[119] I was so advised by a palaeographer whom I consulted.

[120] In the Jerusalem manuscript: 'that you choose (for me)'.

[121] Only a part of this section (fos. 3^v–12^v in the original Hebrew foliation) has been preserved: from the beginning of ch. 1 to near the end of ch. 3, and ch. 9 (in the new numbering, fos. 45^v–50^v). See n. 115 above.

[122] In *Da'at tevunot*, ed. Friedlaender, the text corresponding to the chapters is on pp. 19–55 (sections 35–70).

[123] This copy has a title-page which bears the inscription: 'Part I, behold before you, dear reader, a ladder set up on the earth, and the top of it reaches to Heaven [Gen. 28: 12]'. It is clear that this copyist, too, had the second part and intended to copy it. It may be that he did so and that Part II has been lost.

copies are independent of each other, and it may be stated without a shadow of doubt that R. Jekutiel was no more than one of the copyists.[124]

The second part concentrates on one subject, that of setting Mar Yanuka's mind at rest over a passage in the Zohar[125] which he found surprising: 'All those who occupy themselves with the Torah, the Gemara, and the *posekim* and are full of *mitsvot* and good deeds will be turned away from all the gates of the Garden of Eden in the world to come, and all their deeds will count as nothing, Heaven forbid' (fo. 84ᵛ),[126] if they have not occupied themselves with the study of kabbalah during their life in this world. Mar Kashisha confirms the truth of this teaching, and in explaining it repeats with great vigour that the gates of the supernal Garden of Eden are indeed closed to anyone who has not studied kabbalah—'the science of truth'—and has not, by its light, accomplished acts of *tikun* and attained *devekut*. The performance of *mitsvot* and the study of the revealed Torah are secondary to the main matter, and 'mankind have erred in this and reversed their importance; this has caused the inner Torah and true knowledge to be forgotten by Israel, and they have been left in utter darkness in this world' (fo. 91ʳ). Luzzatto expressed a similar view in several places in his letters and writings,[127] but here he crystallized it into a sharp polemic against the learning and way of life of those who interpreted Scripture literally and debated minutiae. The following is an extract from his incisive criticism:

124 However, it is difficult to establish whether the copy was made in Padua before he left there in 1733 or in Venice after his return to Italy in 1755. See Essay 8, pp. 435–43.

While I was engaged in the preparation of this essay for the press, the second part was published in duplicated form (Jerusalem, 1978). Here again the publisher-copyist, Y. Spiner, has been drawn into repeating Neubauer's mistake (n. 98 above), and has written on the title-page: 'A discussion between Mar Yanuka and Mar Kashisha by the Gaon and holy kabbalist R. *Jekutiel of Vilna* [the emphasis is that of the publisher] (may the memory of that tsadik be for a blessing), one of the great disciples of our master Moses Hayim Luzzatto (may the memory of that tsadik be for a blessing), in which is explained the virtue of the study of kabbalah.' The text is corrupt and marred by omissions. In all the cases which I have examined the omissions are of whole lines present in the Oxford copy, but if the comparison is made with the Harvard copy, parts of lines are seen to be missing. Hence the note on the reverse of the title-page, 'Copied from the manuscript in the library of Hyotin [*sic*], Cambridge, USA', i.e. from the Harvard manuscript, is incorrect.

125 *Zohar ḥadash* on S. of S., 70*d*. There is an allusion to this passage in the 'Discussion' in the collection (see n. 110 above). The passage is translated into Hebrew in I. Tishby, *Mishnat hazohar* (Jerusalem, 1971), ii. 407–9, and into English in *Wisdom of the Zohar*, iii. 1131–3. And see my remarks [as translated] in *Wisdom of the Zohar*, iii. 1086–7.

126 The quotations follow the text of the Oxford copy.

127 See *Igerot*, ii. 236–7, 239–40. In these two letters, written in the middle of 5492 [1732], there are even verbal parallels with the text of *Mar yanuka umar kashisha*, and on p. 237 we find adduced as evidence the passage from the *Zohar ḥadash* which is explained here. See also ibid. 304, 358–9; *Milḥemet mosheh*, 19–20; Horodezky, 'R' mosheh ḥayim lutsato kimekubal', 305–8; Section VI below, text referring to n. 141.

But let us acknowledge the truth: [what results] from all the great *pilpulim* on all the problems and laws? Do we gain from them any knowledge of the Creator Himself or of His creation and governance? No, that is certain . . . and therefore it is impossible for such knowledge to reveal the light of the Creator, blessed be He, for we know nothing whatsoever of that by means of this knowledge . . . and therefore when the soul goes to render an account of its deeds and to be rewarded according to its actions . . . and it has occupied itself with nothing save this *pilpul* and the laws [and] the performance of *mitsvot*, what will it be able to grasp of this light from the Creator Himself and His governance and the bestowal of His divine flow, since during its lifetime it attained no understanding of this at all, for it did not concern itself with any inner truths. (fo. 88^{r-v})

In contrasting the blameworthy literalists and scholars with the praiseworthy mystics, he depicted the latter in the form of the members of his group:

But the Lord did not choose this but true knowledge and perfect restoration, *and it is they who cleave to the Lord* and of them it is said 'And you who cleave to the Lord' etc. ['. . . are alive every one of you this day': Deut. 4: 4], for they concern themselves with the ordering of the universe in the manner ordained by the Emanator, blessed be He . . . and it is they who serve the Lord with no thought but to serve Him, *for the tikun of the Shekhinah and the tikun of all Israel*[128] . . . And the Lord, blessed be He, in his governance and deep design, acts so that it [the science of kabbalah] should not cease entirely; and He does certain deeds not visible to the eye of all, wonders without number, and in the end will reveal to the eye of all some of the great wonders He has performed: even when Israel were at their lowest pitch there were not wanting among them men chosen of the Lord and those who served Him with no thought but to serve, and who performed *tikunim* for the restoration of the Shekhinah, some of the youngest of the flock [Jer. 49: 20] whom I shall not mention by name.[129] (fo. 91^{r-v})

The last pages contain explanations of the four kinds of knowledge which, according to the *Zohar ḥadash*, are the keys which open the gates of Paradise for the soul: (*a*) Knowledge of 'the emanation of the Godhead, blessed be He, through the mystery of the sefirot' (fo. 92^{r}); as spelt out in detail, this includes the theosophy and cosmology of Luria's kabbalah. (*b*) 'Knowledge of the mystery of this body [of ours] in all its form and its organs and in all that con-

[128] This is the form of words which appears in the rules of the group. See n. 16 above. We have here one of the clear expressions of the unity between *devekut* and *tikun*. It need hardly be said that in the writings of Luzzatto the *tikun* of the Shekhinah is intended to hasten messianic redemption. And see Sections IX and XI [but as to XI, see headnote to Section XI] below.

[129] This statement reflects the tribulations and hopes of Luzzatto and his group during the period of their persecution from 1731 onwards, when they were forced to go underground. An anguished description of the circumstances is given in the confessional prayers shortly to be published [and duly published—Trans.] in *Molad*. [Now Essay 2 below.] And see the poem 'Kaveh kaveh libi' ['Hope, hope, my heart'] and my explanation of the words *yiru kovim* ['those who hope will see'] in Essay 2, pp. 144–5.

cerns its conduct, how it is rooted in the supernal sefirot' (fo. 92^{v}), and the recognition of the ways in which corporeality and spirituality are linked. (*c*) 'Knowledge of the mystery of the soul . . . with regard to the mystery of the transmigrations and impregnations [*iburim*] and levirate marriage . . . and to know the roots of the soul, and why it enters the body' (fo. 93^{r-v}). (*d*) 'The true knowledge of all creatures and their behaviour and the[ir] judgements [passed upon them] in truth' (fo. 93^{v}), the recognition of the operation of the sefirot in the laws of nature and in the divine governance which is above natural law. This set of four kinds of knowledge appeared in print in two versions, a short one[130] and a long one[131] which is basically the same as in the work we are considering here. The most reasonable assumption is that it originated in this work, which is essentially an explanation of the statement in the Zohar on knowledge, and was taken from here and inserted into other works.

Among the points of contact between the 'Discussion' in the collection and Part II of *Mar yanuka umar kashisha* there is one central matter I will deal with here since it can serve to throw further light on the nature of the 'Discussion'. That part, unlike Part I and *Da'at tevunot*,[132] speaks of a hidden governance and a revealed governance in this world, as does the work in the collection. Briefly, what is stated is that Ein Sof emanated one of His lesser powers in order to create and govern the world. This power works in two ways: (*a*) 'superficial governance as it appears in this corporeal world', in which the Emanator 'has clothed his light in garments upon garments wherein He conceals Himself and is not seen at all'. For this reason 'the early naturalists and philosophers' fell into error and heresy and 'went so far as to believe that there is no God in the world (Heaven forbid) but that the world goes its own way' (fo. 87^{v}); (*b*) the 'inner governance' through the operation of the sefirot. This works in two ways: one, 'through the inner quality which permeates them', that is to say, through the operation of the divine lights which reside within living creatures; the other, through 'its mystery and root [the mystery and root of every creature] above, in the sefirot' (fo. 93^{v}), i.e.

130 At the end of *Milḥemet mosheh*; also reprinted in *Sefer hakelalim* ['The Book of Principles'], 360–2. The same version is also found in the dialogue *Ḥoker umekubal* ['Philosopher and Kabbalist'] in the collection, as explained in Section VIII below, text referring to n. 168.

131 At the beginning of *Adir bamarom*, under the heading 'Introduction relating to the study of the science and kinds of knowledge which are required'. The editor, R. S. Luria, did not indicate the source, but of course this is not Luzzatto's introduction to the commentary on *Idra raba*. Variants from the version in *Mar yanuka umar kashisha* at the beginning and end and in the body of the text, including omissions and additions and even personal references ('as I have explained', 'as I have already said'), show that the 'introduction' in the hands of the editor was a separate document, and it seems probable that Luzzatto himself detached the set of 'kinds of knowledge' from the dialogue and arranged it as a short work in its own right.

132 See above, text referring to nn. 108, 109.

through the paradigmatical relationship between the divine sources and their cosmic and human issue.[133] The two forms of governance are contained in the Torah, for 'all the lights which issue from this power are collectively given the name "Torah"' (fo. 87^{r}). The 'superficial governance' was conveyed to Israel in the content of the Torah 'according to its literal interpretation' by the revelation of 'the attributes of the Lord, blessed be He' (fo. 89^{v}) in the operation of natural law, whereas the 'inner governance' through divine lights is hidden in 'the letters of the Torah and their combinations, their vowels, their accents, their juxtapositions, and their interconnection . . . this is because the Holy One, blessed be He, and the Torah are one'[134] (fo. 87^{r}), and [this inner governance] is understood by kabbalists through the esoteric interpretation of the Torah.[135] In other words: in the description of the two forms of governance, the inferior, transcendental aspect of the relationship between the Divinity and the world is contrasted with the superior, immanent aspect of the relationship. In my opinion it is clear that this was also Luzzatto's intention in his obscure distinction between governance in deed and governance in thought in the 'Discussion between the Soul and the Intellect'. Thus, in the tract included in the collection, Luzzatto was giving veiled expression to his kabbalistic viewpoint on the two kinds of governance of the world.[136]

The indications to which I have drawn attention in these four works ought to help to establish their chronological order and contribute to an understanding of the processes by which they took shape, but the evidence points in different directions, and the question needs further study. *Da'at tevunot* and the 'Principles' carry dates, which might be thought enough to establish the order and times of their composition. *Da'at tevunot* ends with this inscription: 'Completed on the fifth day of the week, on the eve of the New Moon of Adar II, in the year 5494 [1734]'; and the end of the 'Principles' is inscribed: 'Completed on the fourth day of the week, on 9 Iyar, 5494'. However, it is surprising to find a camouflaged version of mystical ideas, couched in the style of a speculative document, apparently antedating their presentation in their true colours as kabbalistic concepts and in kabbalistic terminology. It may well be asked, therefore, whether either or both of the dates do not rather indicate the completion of the copy in question. But so long as there is

[133] The source of this concept of the two aspects of the relationship between the Godhead and the world is the Zohar, as explained in Tishby, *Wisdom of the Zohar*, i. 273; see also ii. 654. The Zohar, however, does not assess the relative values of the two ways in which the sefirot operate.

[134] See Essay 9, pp. 454–65, 471.

[135] The perception of the secrets of the Torah as an instrument of the inner governance exercised by the Godhead and as a repository of the knowledge relating to that governance is the principal theme of this work and forms the basis for the exaltation of the science of kabbalah, as expressly stated in its opening remarks (fo. 85^{r}).

[136] And see n. 113 above and the text to which it refers.

no proof of this we must accept that the two works, at any rate in the form in which we have them, were first written in 1734 on the dates given in the colophons. With regard to the order in which *Mar yanuka umar kashisha* and *Da'at tevunot* were written, there are two apparent possibilities: either the second part was dropped or it was added later. I do not consider that the latter possibility can reasonably be entertained, for it is hard to imagine that Luzzatto would write a work of a decidedly spiritualistic bent—presenting the study of halakhah and the fulfilment of practical commandments as of inferior standing on the ladder of religious virtues—late in 1734, just when his opponents were rearing their heads again and reports were increasingly circulating about his clandestine activity within his group and his preparations to have the dialogue *Ḥoker umekubal* printed and published in Amsterdam.[137] I am therefore of the opinion that both parts of *Mar yanuka umar kashisha* were composed in 1731 or 1732, shortly after Luzzatto had overcome his humiliation in the latter part of 1730, and that in 1734 he decided to produce a re-edited version of the dialogue, omitting the second part, which his accusers could have used as ammunition against him. At the same time he decided to expose the kabbalistic foundations of the speculative dialogue and entrust them to the care of the members of his group in the form of 'Principles'. Perhaps this indicates the direction in which we may find a suitable explanation for the dual form of the discussion between the soul and the intellect: Luzzatto embarked on the discussion contained in this collection, expressing its kabbalistic ideas in cautious and restrained language, as a supplement to the truncated version of *Mar yanuka umar kashisha* and on the same literary pattern, but did not manage to complete it. On this hypothesis the collection in question would have been written and assembled in the set of papers which we now have a few months before Luzzatto left Padua.[138]

[137] See *Igerot*, ii. 248 ff.

[138] To my explanation of the forms of governance in the previous paragraph it should be added that *Mar yanuka umar kashisha* and the 'Discussion' in the collection differ markedly from each other in an essential respect: their evaluation of the commandments. In the 'Discussion' these are presented as a most important bridge between man and God (fos. 53^{v}–54^{v}). True, *Mar yanuka umar kashisha* does, likewise, stress the duty to fulfil the commandments, and in one place (fo. 90^{r-v}) it praises them in similar tones and using similar arguments to those in the 'Discussion': the 613 commandments correspond to the ordering of the lights of the world above and to the 613 parts of man and of this world, and they help man 'by his deeds, to move all the worlds and the supernal lights' and to reveal the lights and draw them down. But it makes these statements by way of answer to the question posed by Mar Yanuka: 'From what you have said, the mere study of the Torah is sufficient: then why the 613 commandments?'; and no sooner has the intellect praised the commandments than it again says that the study of 'the literal meaning and the laws' must be a secondary matter. In the 'Discussion', on the other hand, nothing is said to depreciate the commandments.

VI. 'LET NOT THE WISE MAN GLORY IN HIS WISDOM'
(FOS. 75^r–76^v)

This short work, which takes as its text Jeremiah 9: 22–3, is not a homily or an exposition but a sort of essay on a speculative theme which is remarkable for its clarity and concentration.[139] The whole work is devoted to an explanation of the nature of the knowledge which must be acquired and the actions which are demanded in order to realize the aim indicated in the verse 'But let him that glories glory in this: that he understands and knows Me'.

Luzzatto begins by defining the prophet's instruction as meaning 'that mankind should occupy themselves in [acquiring] the knowledge of His glorious greatness', and he declares that it is impossible to achieve this end through learning to understand the nature of the commandments and getting to know 'the order of their performance in all their details'. Philosophers hold that since the supreme values of religion reside not in the study of the commandments but in knowing God, 'it is necessary to pursue investigative and secular studies', but this is a false view, 'because of which they have followed the vain things [cf. 2 Kgs. 17: 15] of the studies of the nations'. The command 'You shall meditate on it day and night'[140] leaves no time for 'other studies', and so it is necessary to discover in the Torah itself, which is specific to Israel, the knowledge of 'His greatness, blessed be He, and the secret of His wonderful deeds' (fo. 75^r)—knowledge which lies beyond the practical commandments contained in the Torah.

Given this introduction, the content of which is on all fours with the principal line of argument of *Mar yanuka umar kashisha*, Part II,[141] we would have expected guidance on learning the secrets of the Torah concerning the mysteries of the Godhead and Creation according to the *kabalot* of the Zohar and Luria; but what then follows is entirely different and surprises us by its novelty. 'The secret of true faith' lies in understanding the holiness of God and the holiness of Israel. God chose Israel in order 'to make them holy exactly as He is holy', and He 'desires them [to serve] below as [do] the ministering angels above'. It was to this end that He created the world and imbued it with His love and holiness. Israel cannot attain the exalted level for which they are intended 'unless they observe every detail of the Torah and the commandments', but the fulfilment of the commandments is only a preparatory step. In order for Israel to realize their unique status as God's own possession,

139 The tract is in the handwriting of 'the unmistakable copyist'.

140 Josh. 1: 8.

141 See above, text referring to nn. 126 and 127.

holiness must permeate all their material affairs, in accordance with the precept 'In all your ways know Him'.[142] That precept is not completely fulfilled by concentrating one's mind on acting for the sake of Heaven when performing corporeal actions, 'in order that one may live and serve the Lord':[143] its meaning is rather 'that all one's actions must be veritably things of holiness' (fo. 75^{v}). To this end the children of Israel must love the Lord as He loves them and must 'adhere to Him, in the true sense of that word, with perfect adherence [*devekut*]'. This close bond will be established in its full strength 'in time to come to all eternity', but even in exile, 'while His face is hidden from them', it is possible 'for them to achieve holiness' (fo. 76^{v}).

The subjects of *devekut* and the sanctification of corporeality occupy a central position in others of Luzzatto's works too,[144] but here, additionally, we find an unusual idea of great importance: the two subjects mentioned are seen as the essence of kabbalah. Thus the final sentence of the treatise sums up in these words:

> It follows that the whole science of truth [kabbalah] rests solely on this question, the question of the holiness of Israel: how the Holy One, blessed be He, adheres to them in His holiness and how Israel must adhere, through their desire and their worship, to His holiness, blessed be He; and how all the affairs of the world and of all creation have rested upon this basis ever since they came into existence and [will do so] to all eternity.

Luzzatto is concerned in many of his writings to define 'the science of truth'. He does so in various ways, but in general he gives primacy to the nature of the Godhead and Creation, subordinating to them the ways of serving God. There is a similar definition to the one in the present treatise, with even greater emphasis on the restoration to perfection [*tikun*] of corporeality and its sanctification, in the introduction to the dialogue *Ḥoker umekubal* ['Philosopher and Kabbalist'], which is another of the works laid up in this collection.[145] The passage of most importance for our present purpose reads as follows:

142 Prov. 3: 6.

143 That is how Maimonides explained the verse. See *Mishneh torah*, 'Hilkhot de'ot', 3: 3. The verse, in the meaning assigned to it by Luzzatto, regularly serves in hasidic literature as a catchword in support of worship through corporeality.

144 See nn. 21 and 22 above. Special importance is attached to this subject in the homily *Se'udat leil tu"v bishevat hatatsa"g* ['The Formal Meal on the Eve of 17 Shevat 5493 [1733]']: see [the intended] Section XI below [as to which, however, see n. 22 above—Trans.]. The prayer at the end of it is included in my essay 'Tefilot miginzei r' mosheh ḥayim lutsato' [subsequently published in *Molad*, and now as Part B of Essay 2 below]. In the prefaces to the poems and prayers in Essay 2, see also pp. 118–19 below.

145 A pirated and very inaccurate version of the introduction was published some years ago. I am about to publish a critical edition of it. See n. 174 below.

Kabbalah is greater [than literal interpretation], for by its very nature, actions themselves revert to goodness and become *tikunim* in the upper world; that is to say, it is because the Supernal Will so ordained matters that the things of this world should become sanctified by man's use of them for his needs and his pleasure . . . so that by this means they, too, are brought to perfection, and the power of holiness that he [man] has drawn down [into his soul] is extended to them too . . . Thus it is evident that the science of truth explains the meaning of holiness and how God, blessed be He, resides in His creatures, and how He cleaves to them . . . For what the Holy One, blessed be He, most desires in His world is that all the affairs of the world should be veritable *tikunim* [acts of restoration in the upper world] and things of holiness . . . for the Supernal Will desired to draw man near, to rest upon him and cleave to him . . . and all these ways and statutes taken together are this science of truth. (fos. 111ʳ–112ʳ)

Luzzatto's utterances on these and similar matters sound as if they could have fallen from the lips of the teachers of hasidism, though the explanations are clearer and the style has a greater precision and consistency than is usual in their homilies. Further strong support for the existence of powerful links between the doctrine of hasidism and Luzzatto's teachings is provided by his transfer of the centre of gravity of kabbalistic doctrine from the heights of theological speculation and theosophical myths to the human condition and the relationship between the soul and its divine source.[146]

VII. HOMILY ON 'GOD ALMIGHTY APPEARED TO ME AT LUZ'
(FOS. 103ᵛ–104ʳ)

This paragraph, which, according to its declared subject, is intended as an exposition of the episode of Jacob's blessing of Joseph's sons (Gen. 48) in the form of a kabbalistic homily, is an assemblage of obscure and fragmentary allusions and hints of allusions to kabbalistic mysteries and to processes of *tikun* in the sefirot and in the 'countenances' or 'configurations' of God [*partsufim*] as well as in Hebrew letters and holy names. There is no sustained

[146] The change which occurred in Luzzatto's kabbalistic thinking—a change in the philosophy of an undoubted kabbalist—is not identical with the alteration in character which kabbalistic terms and concepts underwent in hasidism, but there is a close similarity between the two processes. See Scholem, *Devarim bego*, 364–71. In Essay 9, n. 72, I drew attention to a series of subjects the treatment of which, in my opinion, affords evidence of substantial links between hasidism and Luzzatto and the members of his circle; and in several places in the present essay I point out certain connections. I will explain the matter at greater length in Essay 10 below.

exposition of the scriptural text of any significance. Nor can I see, on the kabbalistic level itself, any well-defined subject matter.

The handwriting is most difficult to decipher because of the number and frequency of the changes in the form of the letters, some of which are broken or distorted. The paragraph is written at the foot of the last page of the dialogue *Ḥoker umekubal* [considered in the following section] and on the page which follows it. The impression is gained that this material was committed to writing in haste following the sudden awakening of the *magid* in the depths of Luzzatto's consciousness. [But now see n. 176 below.—Trans.]

VIII. 'THE DISCUSSION'/ 'PHILOSOPHER AND KABBALIST' (FOS. 77^{r}–103^{v}) AND ITS INTRODUCTION (FOS. 108^{r}–115^{r})

Ḥoker umekubal ['Philosopher and Kabbalist', originally entitled *Ma'amar havikuaḥ*, 'The Discussion'] is the best-known and most widely circulated of Luzzatto's kabbalistic writings, and was an important element in the attack upon him by his critics.[147] The version in the present collection is more extensive than the other known versions and differs from them. It is accompanied by a very interesting introduction, which was mentioned by Luzzatto in a letter to R. Isaiah Bassano[148] but is not in the printed edition. It belongs, of course, in front of the dialogue, but it was moved or bound out of order, and is separated from it by two short compositions. In my review the introduction and the work itself are presented together in their proper order.[149]

The following are the principal subjects covered in the introduction. At Mount Sinai the Holy One, blessed be He, presented Israel with a key, contained in the secrets of the Torah, to the knowledge of the Godhead and recognition of God's manner of governing the world, in order to save them from error and heresy (fos. 108^{r}–109^{v}). Since the destruction of the Temple and the beginning of the Exile, the secrets of the Torah have been ever more dimly understood (fos. 109^{v}–110^{v}); even those who occupy themselves in the study of the Torah and understand it on the literal level are incapable of

[147] See *Igerot*, ii. 248 ff. [148] Ibid. 243.

[149] This is the only work in the collection which has up to now been the subject of a scholarly study, having been considered by Y. Avivi in his essay 'Ma'amar havikuaḥ leramḥa"l', *Hamayan* (Tishrei 5735 [1974]), 49–58. I deal with that essay here and examine its hypotheses and conclusions as necessary.

seeing and giving effect to its principal purpose, which is concealed in 'the science of truth' alone—that purpose being to recognize the need, and [Israel's] ability, to endow all the affairs of this world with divine sanctity (fos. 110ᵛ–112ʳ).[150] In recent times darkness has descended on 'the science of truth' to such an extent that even 'great scholars' in Israel have come to show contempt for it, and on occasion they have denied 'that the holy Zohar was composed by R. Simeon bar Yohai (may he be remembered for life in the world to come) and his companions' (fos. 112ʳ–113ʳ). Because of this dreadful spiritual decline the author has been stirred to clarify 'the science of truth' and reveal its beauty in this long treatise 'by way of a discussion between a philosopher [*ḥoker*] and a kabbalist'. He has divided it 'into five discussions' aimed at teaching, in proper order, the principal ideas of the doctrine of kabbalah; whoever understands them properly will have reached a point at which he loves the Shekhinah with ardour and serves the Lord with distinction (fos. 113ʳ–115ʳ).

In the documents in our possession it is several times stated that the intention of *Ma'amar havikuaḥ* was to refute the arguments in R. Judah Aryeh of Modena's book *Ari nohem* ['A Roaring Lion'].[151] Most of the arguments in that book are aimed at disproving the attribution of the Zohar to R. Simeon bar Yohai and his contemporaries and demonstrating that it is a late work. On the other hand, there is no reference to the question of the date of composition of the Zohar in the well-known work *Ḥoker umekubal*, and doubts therefore arose whether that work is identical with 'The Discussion' mentioned in the documents.[152] The introduction clarifies the matter. In it, Luzzatto commented disparagingly on those who challenged the attribution of the Zohar to R. Simeon bar Yohai, but contented himself with a brief reference because he thought that it was only necessary to prove the truth and importance of the doctrine of kabbalah in order for the arguments against the antiquity of the Zohar to collapse.

This version of 'The Discussion' contains three sections which are also found elsewhere as independent units: (*a*) Ten 'Chapters' which exist in many manuscripts as a separate treatise. (*b*) *Kof-lamed-ḥet* [*kela"ḥ*] *pitḥei ḥokhmah* ['138 Gateways to Wisdom']. The 'Gateways' and their commentary were printed together as a complete book,[153] and the 'Gateways' without the com-

[150] See above, text referring to n. 145, where I quote a relevant passage from the introduction.

[151] See *Igerot*, ii. 256–7, 268, 344, 352–3. In *Igerot*, Modena's book is generally called *Sha'agat aryeh* ['A Lion's Roar': the title is in either event a play on the author's name—Trans.].

[152] See my remarks in *Wisdom of the Zohar*, i. 36. Avivi, in his 'Ma'amar havikuaḥ leramḥa"l', 52 n. 1, misrepresented my position by quoting me in part, omitting the crucial sentence 'But his teacher, R. Isaiah Bassano, testifies explicitly that the dialogue was written to counter Modena.'

[153] See Essay 8, pp. 420–4.

mentary appear in manuscripts as a separate work. (*c*) The four kinds of knowledge required in 'the science of truth'. This section appears in print at the head of the commentary on *Idra raba* which was published under the title *Adir bamarom* ['Mighty [is the Lord] on High'].[154] The 'Chapters' in their entirety were inserted into an edition of 'Philosopher and Kabbalist' printed under the heading *Kelalut kol ha'ilan* ['The Whole Tree'],[155] which, however, contains no mention of the 'Gateways' or the 'four kinds of knowledge'. In the work in the present collection the 'Chapters' (fo. 88^v^) and the 'Gateways' (fo. 101^v^) and their commentary (fo. 102^r^) are represented only by their opening words, and only the 'Kinds of Knowledge' are given in full.

Y. Avivi posed the question whether the 'Chapters' and the 'Gateways' were written from the start as parts of the dialogue [in 'The Discussion'—Trans.]. His answer was that 'the material for "The Discussion" as first written down consisted of fresh insights and principles which came to mind in the course of Luzzatto's studies and which he sent to his teacher'. Then, having decided to compose 'The Discussion' as a defence of kabbalah, 'he condensed the second series of principles into ten chapters in mishnaic style. These he presented as a summary of the Lurianic kabbalah by the kabbalist'; and he 'arranged the responsa in his letters into 138 "gateways", marked off from each other in plain language, and explained them at greater length in a commentary, and presented these two [the 'principles' and the 'gateways'—Trans.] as the response of the kabbalist'. Avivi's answer, then, is that the 'Chapters' and the 'Gateways' and their commentary as we now have them were written up for the purposes of 'The Discussion' on the basis of explanations in a different form which had preceded them.[156] This solution to the

[154] See n. 131 above.

[155] The first edition (Shklov, 5545 [1785]) contained only two of the chapters. The 'Chapters' were printed as a whole for the first time in the edition of M. Frestadt (Leipzig and Königsberg, 1840) from a more complete manuscript. See the introduction to that edition, pp. xiv, xxxi, and the note on p. 45 in the body of the text.

[156] Avivi deals with this in his 'Ma'amar havikuaḥ leramḥa"l', 53–8. The earliest information on the 'second series of principles' dates from Tevet 5490 [end of 1729–beginning of 1730]. In Nisan of that year [Mar. 1730] they had not yet been sent to R. Isaiah Bassano. It is to be supposed that they were delivered to him, but we have no confirmation of this. See *Igerot*, i. 53, 118, 121. This work [the 'second series of principles'—Trans.] was printed in the book entitled *Pitḥei ḥokhmah vada'at* (Warsaw, 1884), 4*b*–19*a*. So too, at 19*a*–30*b*, were the writings sent as letters on which Avivi relies. Although their origin as letters is not specified, their content proves that they were collected from at least three. It seems probable that these were all sent to one person, who, as is indicated by allusions they contain, received writings and kabbalistic teachings from Luzzatto in other letters too, but the addressee is certainly not R. Isaiah Bassano as assumed by Avivi. Many scholars outside Padua sought to learn kabbalah from Luzzatto both orally and by correspondence with him, and the expression 'they [have] asked me' which occurs repeatedly in these letters tells us that the addressee had approached Luzzatto on behalf of a group. Apparently the scholar in question lived in the neighbourhood of Mantua and came to

problem is founded on dubious considerations. In the 'Chapters' and the 'Gateways' the principles of Luria's complex and ramified kabbalah are presented in terse and concentrated form, using difficult technical terms which even kabbalists are unable to understand without a detailed explanation. Even less are those writings suited to the level of understanding of 'philosophers' at the start of their enquiries, for whom 'The Discussion' was intended. In the dialogue itself there is no such explanation. At first sight the position appears to be different with regard to the 'Gateways', a commentary on which is included in the version of 'The Discussion' in our collection; but the commentary, too, is written in a distinctly kabbalistic style which requires a thorough knowledge and profound understanding of kabbalah such as would have been beyond the kabbalist's interlocutor even after the progress he made in the course of the discussion.[157] Moreover, Luzzatto, writing to his teacher, described 'The Discussion' as 'a little book' [*sefer me'at hakamut*],[158] whereas the 'Gateways' and their commentary amount to a book of considerable size compared with the whole of the dialogue even in its longer version, and it is inconceivable that they were intended as an addendum to a 'little book'.

I offer the following conjecture as an answer to this complicated problem: 'The Discussion' was composed in various versions at different stages. The first version, which was the shortest, was written and sent to R. Isaiah

Luzzatto for oral tuition while the latter was staying there, as is shown by one of the letters: 'And this matter I recall explaining to you, learned sir, when we were in Mantua' (ibid. 29*a*). This remark does not, however, exclude the possibility that the reference is to a resident of Mantua, in which case it is to be supposed that the questioner was R. Judah Mendola. See *Igerot*, index, under his name. In *Igerot*, ii. 230, Luzzatto conveys information about a responsum he had given orally to R. Aviad Sar-Shalom Basilea, but the content of that responsum is quoted in a letter in *Pitḥei ḥokhmah vada'at* (21*b*) as an original insight previously unknown to the questioner. And see *Igerot*, ii. 353. The information we have on Luzzatto's residence in Mantua dates it to Iyar 5491 [late spring 1731]. See ibid. 231–3; and Essay 8, n. 84.

[157] The 'Chapters' are undoubtedly a précis of the 'second principles', as was pointed out by R. Samuel Luria in his reissue of *Ḥoker umekubal*, in which he added remarks on every chapter. It is therefore reasonable to conclude that the 'Chapters' were written in the first place for study by the members of the group and their close associates who had the 'principles' in their possession. The relationship between the responsa in *Pitḥei ḥokhmah vada'at* and the '138 Gateways' is different. Avivi demonstrated that there are close parallels between the responsa and the commentary on the 'Gateways', but what we have here are points of contact in certain passages which can be explained in two ways: (*a*) Luzzatto put into the commentary on the 'Gateways' matter which he had previously committed to writing in replies to enquirers; (*b*) the commentary on the 'Gateways' was composed earlier and matter contained in it was inserted in the responsa. The former possibility is the more reasonable, but in any event it is idle to assume that the 'Gateways' with its comprehensive and profound commentary was composed on the basis of the responsa as a part of the popular work 'The Discussion'.

[158] *Igerot*, ii. 243.

Bassano in the summer of 1732.[159] The 'Chapters', and perhaps also the 'Gateways' without the commentary, had already been written at that time. Luzzatto decided to insert the 'Chapters' into his apologia, the dialogue, in order to lay before the philosopher—now freed from his hostility to kabbalah—an example of a profound treatise on 'the science of truth', even though it was as yet beyond the philosopher's comprehension. As early as that summer, Luzzatto asked his teacher to approve the publication of 'The Discussion', but the latter, at that time, withheld his approval. At the end of 5493 or the beginning of 5494 [i.e. in the second half of 1733] Luzzatto again sent the work to his teacher, having meanwhile made some changes to it, and again asked him to authorize its publication.[160] We do not know the nature and extent of the alterations, which Luzzatto characterized as 'new wording', but it is clear that he had produced a different and apparently expanded version, for he states: 'I have no other copy like it.'[161] This version may perhaps have included the 'Gateways' without the commentary,[162] but he certainly

159 On this point Avivi's statement ('Ma'amar havikuaḥ leramḥa"l', 49–50), based on the remarks of R. Isaiah Bassano (*Igerot*, ii. 353), is correct. A reference should be added to what was said by Bassano in his letter of 22 Heshvan 5495 [autumn 1734] to the rabbis of Venice (ibid. 253).

160 I base this assumption on four letters written between 5 Tevet and 17 Sivan 5494 [Dec. 1733–June 1734] (*Igerot*, ii. 242–5). The last letter before Tevet 5494 which has come into our hands, dating from the intermediate days of Passover 5492 [1732], contains as yet no reference to 'The Discussion'. I quote here the passages which are important for our purpose: 'It is, after all, only a little book, and moreover, *you saw* [Luzzatto uses the respectful third person—Trans.] *the substance of it some time ago, and it contains only verbal alterations*; and in any event you could see all of it that you need to in an hour or two . . . As I have already said, *I have not altered the introduction from the form in which you, learned Sir, have already seen it* and approved it, for which reason I have not sent it to you; but in any event, if you wish me to, I will send it' (243); 'I entreat you, learned Sir, if you can read the "Discussion" which is in your hands, to do so quickly and send it to me; *and if you cannot—please send it to me unread.* And I beg you most earnestly to do so, *for I have no other copy like it*' (245). There is no foundation for Avivi's explanations that, from what Luzzatto says, 'it is possible that the introduction, too, was first written as an independent work' ('Ma'amar havikuaḥ leramḥa"l', 57), and that the words 'moreover, you saw the substance of it some time ago' etc. relate to 'letters and principles that had been sent to him' (ibid. 58). It is clear that the reference is to the first edition of 5492 [1732]. And see n. 156 above.

161 *Igerot*, ii. 245. See the quotations in the preceding note.

162 MS Mosad Harav Kook 252, Jerusalem—the greater part of which consists of an important collection of Luzzatto's writings which were copied in Lvov in 5541 [1781] and reproduced with their authorship disguised (see Section IX below)—contains the 'Gateways' without a commentary (fos. 43^{r}–47^{v}) under the heading *Sefer pitḥei haḥokhmah mimaran mhrr me'ir paprsh* [*sic*] *zllh"h* ['The Book of the Gateways to Wisdom, by our master, our teacher and rabbi, R. Meir Poppers, may his memory be for a blessing in the life of the world to come']. In the first place only 137 'gateways' are reproduced, followed by the inscription 'tam venishlam' etc. ['finished and completed, praised be God the Creator']. Then comes the missing 'gateway', with the note: 'Belongs to Section 28.' This addition was certainly inserted from another copy, as

did not intend 'The Discussion' to be coupled in print with the '138 Gateways to Wisdom' plus its commentary. In the same letter Luzzatto said that he wanted to make further changes in the text of 'The Discussion' after receiving his teacher's endorsement.[163] I would suppose that he did indeed prepare a different edition, which is the expanded version in the collection, and that, in his introductory remarks, he made allusions to the 'Chapters', the 'Gateways', and their commentary for the benefit of kabbalists in his group and in the circle of his adherents outside the group who possessed copies of those works. He also introduced into this edition of 'The Discussion' an abbreviated version[164] of the section on the 'four kinds of knowledge' from the discussion known as *Mar yanuka umar kashisha*. This leads us to a new hypothesis with regard to the printed version also: although it is marred by the mistakes and omissions of copyists, its brevity is attributable not to copying errors but to the fact that it is based on the original short version of 1732. The foregoing, as I have said, is only conjectural, and it involves difficulties that are not easily resolved, but on the information available I can see no readier solution of this complex problem.[165]

Of the five discussions described in the introduction, corresponding to five parts, only the middle three are headed so as to show where they begin: 'Second Part'—fo. 88^{v}, 'Third Part'—fo. 99^{r}, 'Fourth Part'—fo. 101^{v}. Interpolated in the middle of Part II (fos. 90^{r}–98^{v}) is a section at the head of which is written 'This belongs at the end', and at the conclusion of that section is another inscription: 'Thus far [the piece which] belongs at the end, from here onward belongs above after the statement of the kabbalist beginning "Both of them are certainly true".' Because of this interpolation and the fact that the beginning of Part V is not marked, only three of the parts can be delimited with certainty: Part I, fos. 77^{r}–88^{v}; Part II, fos. 88^{v}–90^{r}, 98^{v}–99^{r}; Part III, fos. 99^{r}–101^{v}. It is uncertain where Part IV ends and where Part V begins. Avivi states ['Ma'amar havikuaḥ leramḥa"l'], p. 51, that Part V begins

is proved by the different form of the concluding sentence: 'nishlemu kela"ḥ kelalim pitḥei haḥokhmah . . .' ['[the] 138 principles, the gateways to wisdom, have been completed . . . and may the Lord, blessed be He, grant me the privilege of explaining them at length, amen and amen']. It may be that this wish was written in Luzzatto's own hand: if that is the case, it would prove that the 'Gateways' first existed as an independent work and that the commentary was added later. But even if the words were added by a reader, they still prove that the 'Gateways' were circulated as a work which had no commentary.

163 'Please favour me with a reply without delay, for it is possible that the language of that book will not all be understood without me. And I wish to rewrite [literally 'to renew'] all those matters in a different way which will be readily understood. Now that I have safely returned home [from Venice], it will not take me long to do all this, God willing' (*Igerot*, ii. 245).

164 See above, text referring to n. 130.

165 On the basis of this suggestion it must be assumed that the works in the collection in question were assembled after Sivan 5494 [mid 1734]. See end of Section V above.

with the section on the 'kinds of knowledge' (fos. 102^r–103^v) and continues with the section copied in error into the middle of Part II. This conclusion does not square with the description of Part V in the introduction: 'The fifth is a programme of study to teach anyone who is beginning [to learn] the science' (fo. 114^v). The 'kinds of knowledge' are not a suitable way into the subject for a beginner: it seems clear to me that they are the end of Part IV, and that Part V begins at the beginning of the interpolated passage (fo. 90^r), where the philosopher argues that 'not all intellects are equal, and the minds of men are very different from one another, and the way must be broadened not for one intellect alone but for all, if possible'. This means that the section which was dislodged from its proper place is the entire fifth part.[166]

Milḥemet mosheh ['The War of Moses'], which is extant in print (Warsaw, 1889) and manuscripts,[167] is similar in structure, length, and principal contents to 'The Discussion' in the present collection. But there are conspicuous differences between them, both formal and literary: a different title; disciple and master instead of the philosopher and the kabbalist in dialogue; and an introduction by a disciple of Luzzatto who claims to have written the book himself on the basis of oral instruction received from his master.[168] On the title-page of the printed edition the book is presented as a work by Luzzatto, 'arranged by one of his disciples, may his [the disciple's] memory be for a blessing', 'now published for the first time from the actual manuscript of his disciples [*sic*] the aforesaid arranger'. Having regard to the version in the collection, I think that the attribution of authorship to a disciple and the changes in the title, the speakers, and the introduction are so much camouflage applied by Luzzatto's disciples after his death in order to avoid circulating his works exactly as written and under his name.[169]

166 The correctness of my allocation is also shown by the version in MS Harvard 54, which I consider below. The fourth part, including the 'four kinds of knowledge', is missing from that version.

167 The manuscripts are written in Italian and Ashkenazi hands. I must correct the statement I made in Essay 8, n. 129, that the text of *Milḥemet mosheh* was 'of doubtful authenticity'.

168 From the words of the disciple in the introduction: 'As I received from my teacher R. M[oses] H[ayim], may his memory be for a blessing, and as I learned by studying the books [cf. Dan. 9: 2—Trans.] to acquire a complete and enlightened understanding of those matters'.

169 On the title-page of MS Warsaw 99, which was in the possession of R. M. S. Ghirondi (as is evident from that page, the text of which bears the hallmark of his personal style), and on the title-page of MS BL 1075, which is a copy made by J. Almanzi in 1830, the work is attributed to Luzzatto without any mention of the disciple, although the introduction as printed appears in both of these manuscripts. J. Ghirondi, too, in his essay on the life of Luzzatto, numbers *Milḥemet mosheh* among Luzzatto's works: 'Al devar toledot hagaon r' mosheh ḥayim lutsato . . .', *Kerem ḥemed*, 2 (1836), 66.

There is another copy of the longer version in MS Harvard 54 (fos. 7ʳ–30ᵛ, 1ʳ–6ʳ).[170] It differs in three important respects from the version in the collection: the 'Chapters' and the 'Gateways' without the commentary are given in full; Part IV, including both the commentary on the 'Gateways' and the 'Kinds of Knowledge', is altogether missing; after the 'Gateways' at the end of Part III (fo. 27ᵛ according to the alphabetical notation = fo. 2ᵛ) comes the section which is out of order in the collection and which, on the evidence of the introduction, is Part V.[171] There is reason to assume that in the version which was in the hands of this copyist the 'Chapters' and the 'Gateways' were similarly represented only by their opening words and that he supplemented the allusions with material from the collection in MS Guenzburg 745.[172] The question is, however, why is Part IV missing? At first sight it might seem necessary to suppose that this copy was prepared from an interim version consisting of four parts which did not include either a commentary to the 'Gateways' or the 'Kinds of Knowledge'. But this is an untenable hypothesis, for here too the introduction mentions five discussions, and at the beginning of the section which is identical with Part V there is also a reference to the commentary on the 'Gateways': 'A very suitable order of study is first to learn the chapters which you have arranged, then the gateways to wisdom *and then their explanation*.' It is therefore more reasonable to assume that the copyist saw no point in including an allusion to the commentary on the 'Gateways' seeing that it formed the main constituent of Part IV, and while he was about it he also omitted the 'Kinds of Knowledge', which he rightly regarded as a supplement to the matters dealt with in the commentary to the 'Gateways' in this work. It remains to add a point which proves beyond doubt that this copy was not taken from MS Oxford 2593. The dialogue concludes here with words spoken by the kabbalist which are not in that manuscript. The paragraph in question, which is important for its content, is also absent from *Milḥemet mosheh*. It reads as follows:

My son, I desire with all my heart to teach you the first principles, after which [abbreviation unclear in the manuscript] will come all the homilies [two more words unclear], although you will not immediately get to the bottom of these things which I will teach you, they will nevertheless be enough to acquaint you with all the roots necessary for the study of kabbalah as a whole, and after that you may enquire into them. You have already disengaged yourself from the opinion of those who scoff at this science because they have heard that it ascribes material form to

[170] With regard to my assessment of this manuscript, see n. 62 above. The folios are bound out of order. They are numbered at the top, on the Hebrew alphabetical system, in their correct order from *alef-alef* (1ʳ) to *lamed-alef* (30ʳ). (Fo. *kaf-he* (25), between 30ᵛ and 1ʳ, is missing.) Luzzatto's introduction appears here in its proper place at the head of the dialogue (*alef-alef* to *gimel-beit*, corresponding to fos. 7ʳ–9ᵛ).

[171] See n. 166 above.

[172] See Essay 2, pp. 116–17.

the Creator, blessed be He, whereas you have understood that this is not so and that what all concerned speak of is the attributes of His will [apparently the sefirot—Trans.] and [their] actions. Therefore I will set in order for you a systematic general account of the primary roots, and afterwards you may enquire concerning them and I will answer you. Then you will engrave [them?] upon the tablet of your heart and will understand for yourself, with perfect understanding, all the books of the holy rabbi, the Ari [Luria], may he be remembered for eternal life; and afterwards I will enlighten you as to the service [of Heaven], which is the mystical intention [*kavanah*] of all the prayers and commandments, explaining very clearly. [Here I] end.

This paragraph emphasizes that 'The Discussion', even in its longer version, is no more than a preliminary to the full knowledge of kabbalah, the chief concern of kabbalah being instructions for the service of the Lord through mystical *kavanot*.[173]

'The Discussion' and the introduction are written in a hand resembling that of other works in the collection which I have been inclined to regard as Luzzatto's. But in this work the fact that a part has been inserted in the wrong place makes it particularly difficult to feel confident in identifying Luzzatto as the writer. Nevertheless the indications that this and similar handwriting is that of Luzzatto seem to me stronger than the signs which would support an attribution to a copyist. At least the question should be regarded as requiring further study. Many autographs are copies made by authors of their own earlier drafts, and defects often occur in their writing similar to those in the work of copyists. This phenomenon is common in the autographs of Luzzatto.[174]

173 It is possible that this ending is not by Luzzatto but was added later in his school.

174 To my regret, I must conclude this section by making public a sorry story connected with the introduction. In the seminar which I conducted in the Hebrew University in 1957, I lent a student the photograph of the introduction which I had brought back from Oxford, to assist him in preparing a thesis. A short time later there came into my hands a stencilled pamphlet of which the title-page read as follows: 'Introduction to *Ma'amar havikuah* by Rabenu Moses Hayim Luzzatto, may the memory of that tsadik and holy man be for a blessing, now published for the first time (copied from the holy manuscript of the rabbi, its author), Jerusalem 5718 [1958].' In the course of the investigation which followed—and which was pursued by the university's student disciplinary court—the student admitted that he had been persuaded to betray his trust and had handed the photograph to two young yeshiva students for publication. The instigators declared that they had influenced the student 'for the sake of Heaven'. The introduction was printed a second time from that copy in *Yalkut yediot ha'emet*, ii (Tel Aviv, 1966), 298–310. In that case, too, the publication was carried out by fraud; the source and the name of the publisher were suppressed and the list of contents omitted any reference to the introduction. Through their inability to decipher the handwriting and failure to understand the subject matter of the introduction, the text issued by the 'sinners for the sake of Heaven' was confused and corrupt. To make matters worse, they invented nonsensical readings. As a result, it is hard to find any lines in which there are no mistakes. It would be pointless to detail all the blunders,

PART 2

IX. YIḤUD GAN-EDEN
(FOS. 104v–107v)
AND ITS COMMENTARY

A

THIS short work, untitled in the collection, opens with the verse 'See, the smell of my son is as the smell of a field'.[175] One would have expected it, therefore, to be a homily on this verse,[176] but there is no doubt whatever as to

and I shall confine myself to quoting a few by way of awful example: *mosheh tsivah* for *misham zakhu* ['Moses commanded' instead of 'thence they were privileged'] (p. 301); *lehitanot ba'aniyut yediat kevodo* for *lehitaneg beta'anug* . . . ['to afflict oneself with the humility of the knowledge of His glory' instead of 'to delight in the pleasure of . . .'] (302); *nikhbad veshorshi* for *nikhbad venora* ['glorious and radical' instead of 'glorious and awe-inspiring'] (306); *atsato* for *atsmo* ['His counsel' instead of 'Himself'] (306); *mitgaderim* for *menagedim* ['they boast' instead of 'they oppose'] (309). The [intended] republication of the introduction in my essay 'Pirkei kabalah' will serve incidentally to redress the violence done by these people to Luzzatto's text.

175 Gen. 27: 27.

176 This verse serves as an introduction to the action of the soul in ascending to Paradise through the power of the *yiḥud*. This is based on its explanation in the midrashim: 'When Jacob entered into his father's presence, *gan eden* [the Garden of Eden] entered with him' (*Bereshit rabah*, ed. Theodor–Albeck, 68: 22). *Yiḥud gan-eden*, in the handwriting of 'the unmistakable copyist', was interpolated between 'The Discussion/Philosopher and Kabbalist' and its introduction (Section VIII above), together with the homily on 'God Almighty appeared to me at Luz', which I described in Section VII above. M. Benayahu, in his *Kitvei hakabalah sheleramḥa"l* (Jerusalem, 1979), 88, made the unfounded assertion that the homily on 'God Almighty' was the beginning of *Yiḥud gan-eden*. Shortly after the first part [i.e. Sections I–VIII] of the present essay was published, I noticed that Luzzatto had copied the homily on 'God Almighty' in a letter to his teacher, R. Isaiah Bassano, written on the eve of the New Moon, Shevat 5491 [1731], and had presented it as 'a new insight into the Pentateuch portion "Vayeḥi"' [Gen. 47: 28 to end of book]. At the end of it he wrote: 'Here ends the tract, and you, honoured and learned Sir, will see that it is a very beautiful thing: an exposition of the verse letter by letter in accordance with the order of the celestial chariot, to bring blessings to the world' (*Igerot*, ii. 221). It appears that his teacher asked for an explanation of the homily. Concerning this, Luzzatto wrote on 14 Shevat 5491 [1731]: 'And as for an explanation of the tract, I cannot send it at present, for I have neither paper nor time, and I will complete it on another occasion, God willing' (ibid. 225). Benayahu (*Kitvei hakabalah*, 235) mentioned the 'new insight into the portion "Vayeḥi"' contained in the letter of the New Moon of Shevat, and gave a page reference for it, but did not realize that the 'insight' in question was the homily on 'God Almighty'. The 'insight' was

its identity, for alumni of Luzzatto's school stated in writing what it was. There is also the evidence of the shortened version of it printed at the end of Luzzatto's commentary *Perush idra raba*, which was published under the title *Adir bamarom* (Warsaw, 1886). On p. 211 of that publication we read: 'Belongs to the commentary on the passage "Izdarezu betikuneikhon ['be zealous in your *tikunim*'] etc.", and is the mystical meaning of *yiḥud g-e-*.' That is to say, the work reproduced there is called *Yiḥud gan-eden*, and its mystical meaning is explained in *Perush idra raba*, in the commentary on the named passage in the Zohar.[177] The fuller commentary, which clarifies the obscure text of the *yiḥud*, constitutes the main element in our elucidation of its subject matter here.

In the literature of kabbalah, especially Lurianic kabbalah, *yiḥudim* are an instrument of major importance for the elevation of the soul to the heights and for mystical and magical activity in the upper and lower worlds.[178] The term *yiḥud* means various things: the unification of the worlds, the unification of the sefirot, and the entry of the soul into unity with the divine forces in perfect *devekut*. After the performance of the *yiḥud* the soul returns to the body and to this world permeated with a divine flow which confers on it a knowledge of the secrets of the Torah and the mysteries of existence as well as the ability to use them for the *tikun* of the world—that is, its restoration to perfection—and for the personal benefit of the performer of the *yiḥud*. Examples of the principal actions which may be carried out by means of the *yiḥudim* are, on the one hand, war against the forces of evil called the husks [*kelipot*], the raising up of sparks, and the strengthening of holiness; on the other, the expulsion of *shedim* and other evil spirits, the correction of sins, and the cure of disease. The structural pattern common to all the *yiḥudim* is a system of holy names, letters, accents, and vowel-points, combinations of these,

reprinted from Luzzatto's letter in *Otserot ramḥa"l*, ed. H. Friedlaender (Benei Berak, 1986), 340–1. In describing the homily on 'God Almighty' in Section VII above, I recorded my impression that it had been committed to writing in haste because of the sudden awakening of the *magid* in the depths of Luzzatto's consciousness. This impression was certainly incorrect, but I am still inclined to think that this homily is a 'maggidic' revelation, like many 'new insights' which Luzzatto transmitted to his teacher in his letters before the Padua edicts at the end of 5490 [1730]. Thereafter, of course, he avoided mentioning the source of his inspiration.

[177] The location given for the explanation of the *Yiḥud* is imprecise. The *Yiḥud* is divided into two paths, 'The Path of Fear' and 'The Path of Love', and the explanation of 'Izdarezu betikuneikhon' is the beginning of the explanation of 'The Path of Love', which is missing from the shorter version of the *Yiḥud* reproduced at the end of *Adir bamarom*. See below, text referring to n. 190 and the note itself. *Perush idra raba* ['Commentary on *Idra raba*'] was written in 1731. And see Essay 8, pp. 412–14 and n. 19; and n. 61 above.

[178] See G. Scholem, *Kabbalah* (Jerusalem, 1974), 76, 179–80, 372, 425, 446; R. J. Zvi Werblowsky, *Joseph Karo: Lawyer and Mystic* (Oxford, 1962), 46–8, 71–6; L. Fine, 'The Practice of Yihudim in Lurianic Kabbalah', *Jewish Spirituality*, 2 (1987), 64–98.

gematriyot and the like, founded on scriptural verses and fragments of verses and accompanied by indications of *kavanot* and instructions for action. *Yiḥudim* are performed in private, in a state of concentrated meditation, and their results are described as the gaining of access to the mysteries of prophecy and of the Holy Spirit, one of its levels being the reception of 'maggidic' revelations from angels and the souls of the righteous.[179]

The performance of *yiḥudim* was a central factor in Luzzatto's mystical experiences and in the campaign against him. Before the *magid* first appeared to him on the New Moon of Sivan 5487 [summer 1727], Luzzatto, then in his twentieth year, had spent years preparing himself to receive revelations, making frequent use of *yiḥudim* to achieve intense concentration. Once he had succeeded in his aim and the *magid* had revealed himself, Luzzatto received 'personal *yiḥudim*' and 'personal *tikunim*' so that he should be able to strengthen his grasp of mystical matters by the revelations of Elijah, Metatron, and the souls of righteous and holy men.[180] From statements by Luzzatto's supporters we learn that he handed over to them, for study, *yiḥudim* which he used.[181] The gravest and most substantial charge laid against Luzzatto by his accusers was that there were grounds to fear that, in the *yiḥudim*, he brought into operation the forces of the Sitra Ahra [the forces of evil], from whom he received the revelations, or that, at least, the revelations contained an admixture of the Sitra Ahra.[182] The most specific and concrete form taken by this allegation was that Luzzatto's revelations were Shabatean interpretations of secrets of the Torah.[183] His teacher, R. Isaiah

[179] The doctrine of *yiḥudim* in Lurianic kabbalah is crystallized in two books: *Sha'ar ruaḥ hakodesh* (Jerusalem, 1863) and *Sha'ar hayiḥudim* (Korets, 1783), which are parallel collections of the teachings of R. Hayim Vital, differing from each other at many points. Several chapters explain the nature of *yiḥudim*, the ways in which they operate, and how they are performed, and these serve as an introduction to a set of *yiḥudim* which are given as examples.

[180] See *Igerot*, i. 39. M. Benayahu's essay 'Ha"magid" shel ramḥa"l', 300–14, gives the principal available information on Luzzatto's use of *yiḥudim* and on the reception of revelations by their aid. And see Essay 6, pp. 300–3.

[181] The emissary from Safed, R. Raphael Israel Kimhi, testifying before the rabbis of Venice on 3 Kislev 5490 [end of 1729], praised Luzzatto: 'And with my own eyes I saw the *yiḥudim* which he performed, when he fell upon his face, supported on his hands on the table for about half an hour' (*Igerot*, i. 21). It may reasonably be assumed that he also saw the texts of the *yiḥudim*. R. David Finzi, rabbi of Mantua, who became Luzzatto's father-in-law in 1731, wrote about him as follows in a letter dated the 25th day of the Omer 5490 [halfway between Passover and Pentecost, 1730]: 'For verily he acquired wings by means of a certain *yiḥud*, he had a voice—a voice came to him from a *magid*, *and the yiḥudim are laid up in store with us, "concealed in our tent"*' (ibid. 131).

[182] This charge was brought by Luzzatto's principal accusers, R. Ezekiel Katzenellenbogen and R. Moses Hagiz. See *Igerot*, i. 74, 80–1, 82. In a letter to R. Isaiah Bassano dated 14 Shevat 5491 [1731], Luzzatto mentioned that in 1730 R. Jacob Belilios, chief of his accusers among the rabbis of Venice, had likewise voiced the suspicion that he brought the forces of the Sitra Ahra into operation in his *yiḥudim*. See *Igerot*, ii. 223.

[183] See Essay 4, pp. 223–8.

Bassano, sought to defend his pupil's use of *yiḥudim*, but felt doubtful and raised the possibility that the charges of Luzzatto's opponents might be justified.[184] At the conclusion of the inquiry held in Padua into these accusations, Luzzatto undertook upon oath, on 3 Av 5490 [late summer 1730], that until such time as he lived in the Land of Israel he would refrain unreservedly from the use of *yiḥudim*.[185] His responses, both before and after the Padua edicts,

184 See *Igerot*, i. 84–6, 103–5, and Luzzatto's agitated replies, ibid. 93–5, 112–14, 115–17. The correspondence between R. Isaiah Bassano and Luzzatto turned upon the accession by the anti-Shabatean kabbalist R. Joseph Ergas of Livorno to the ranks of those who feared that there was an admixture of the Sitra Ahra in the practice of the *yiḥudim*. The following extracts from what was said by Ergas and Bassano are worth quoting verbatim. Ergas: 'There is good reason to fear that it is the spirit of impurity, as is stated there [in *Sha'ar hanevuah*, see below] in chapter 4, namely that while a person is performing the *yiḥud* and has isolated himself from others, it is possible that the spirits of impurity may attach themselves to him and lead him astray; he may think that it is the spirit of holiness whereas it is none other than the spirit of impurity, Heaven forbid; see what is said there. And I was informed by R. J. Wilna that, for this reason, he does not practise *yiḥudim*; and he was surprised to see me shutting myself away to perform them' (ibid. 101–2); Bassano: 'And because you are most dear to me, I am fearful on your account lest some element of the profane may be mingled with the holy; which is not impossible, seeing that the Ari—may he be remembered for life in the world to come—taught us in *Sha'ar hanevuah*, ch. 2, that a man's degree of merit and his deeds determine the nature of the *magid*; he may have been composed of good and evil, the good declaring the truth and the evil falsehood' (ibid. 103); '. . . although in my opinion his [R. J. Ergas's] statement concerning *yiḥudim* is mistaken, and even if our teacher and master, R. J. Wilna, were to say this to me himself, I would not accept it; for in my humble opinion, the words of the Rabbi [the Ari—(as recorded by) R. Hayim Vital, on the danger that the spirit of uncleanness might be involved] were spoken only with regard to *yiḥudim* performed while prostrating oneself on the graves of the righteous. Moreover: if it were so, you would not allow anyone at all to carry out *yiḥudim* or *kavanot*. And also, as we know: a man who comes to purify himself should be helped [*Shab.* 104]. In any event, my son, know what I learned in my youth from the mouth of a saintly man . . . who was passing through Verona on his way to the Land of Israel, where he died and was buried; he was a disciple of the great rabbi, the author of *Megaleh amukot* [Nathan Nata ben Solomon Spira, d. 1633—Trans.], in whose name he told me that *kavanot* did not become established outside the Land of Israel because of the polluted air of the land[s] of the nations, etc.' (ibid. 105). From the content of the quotations where the Ari is cited, and from the chapter references given, it may be stated with certainty that the work in question was *Sha'ar hayiḥudim*, which was entitled *Sha'ar hanevuah* in the manuscript version in the hands of Ergas and Bassano. To compound the irony, the two scholars, who were fearful of any whiff of Shabatean heresy, regarded R. Jacob Wilna—one of the leading propagandists of Shabateanism in Turkey and Europe—as a guide in these matters. R. J. Wilna was in Italy for a time in 1725: see M. Benayahu, *R' ya'akov vilna uveno veyaḥaseihem lashabeta'ut* (Jerusalem, 1954), 206–7. That Shabatean scholar argued strongly for the abandonment of Lurianic *kavanot*. It is to be supposed that his warning against the practice of Lurianic *yiḥudim* was based on Shabatean considerations, but he succeeded in concealing his true motives in his contacts with the opponents of Shabateanism. And see Benayahu, 'Hatenuah hashabeta'it beyavan', 405–8. R. Raphael Israel Kimhi, a pupil of R. J. Wilna in Safed, spoke with great enthusiasm about Luzzatto's use of *yiḥudim*. See n. 181 above.

185 'Further, my teacher aforesaid has taught me, with regard to the *yiḥudim* that I have been accustomed to perform, and by means of which it appeared to me that I gained insight and

to the campaign of persecution are remarkable for the strength of his expressions of outrage at the attempts to ban the *yiḥudim* and so block the channels of the divine flow to his soul.[186]

None of the letters and other documents on the subject of Luzzatto's *magid* and the controversy associated with it quotes the text of any *yiḥud*, and none conveys any information on the nature of *yiḥudim*. Nor have any studies of Luzzatto dealt with the character of *yiḥudim*. Moreover, the text of *Yiḥud gan-eden* printed, with no title, at the end of *Adir bamarom*[187] was not identified and escaped the attention of scholars, until my own investigations revealed the existence of the same *yiḥud* in MS Oxford 2593. As indicated in Part 1 of this essay,[188] I propose here to offer a clarification of that *yiḥud*. I begin with a short account of the nature of *Yiḥud gan-eden* and the other two *yiḥudim* which have so far come into our hands, go on to discuss the date of their composition, and then consider in detail the subject matter of *Yiḥud gan-eden*, with due regard to the explanations given in the commentary in *Perush idra raba*.

On the basis of its contents, the text of *Yiḥud gan-eden* in MS Oxford 2593—which is also found, with variant readings, in MS Mosad Harav Kook 252[189]

girded myself with strength to compose the works aforesaid, that this matter *is not* [clearly] *distanced from the hindrances of the paths of darkness*, especially in the atmosphere of the land of the Gentiles, and that there is serious doubt concerning it. For this reason my teacher aforesaid has commanded me to withdraw my hand from compositions and *yiḥudim* such as these'; and 'I hereby commit myself by a binding covenant and a solemn oath and a strict ban on [my] utterances . . . *to give up absolutely and withdraw my hand entirely from the performance of yiḥudim* and the composition of kabbalistic works in any language whatsoever in the name of a *magid* or of holy souls so long as I am outside the land [of Israel]' (*Igerot*, ii. 410–11). Two different versions of Luzzatto's undertaking have been preserved, both dated 3 Av 5490 [late summer 1730], and in one of them (*Igerot*, i. 176–7) there is no reference to *yiḥudim*. It is probable that this more lenient version was put forward in the first place by R. Isaiah Bassano and Luzzatto, with the approval of the investigating rabbis, but that in the course of the investigation the rabbis withdrew their approval and sought to impose more stringent terms; at their request the version containing the ban on *yiḥudim* was drafted, and this was the one accepted as having binding force. And see Benayahu, 'Shevuat ramḥa"l laḥdol mileḥaber sefarim al-pi ha"magid"', 27–9.

186 See n. 184 above; *Igerot*, ii. 223, 232.

187 See above, text referring to n. 177, and the note itself.

188 See above, text referring to n. 3, and nn. 47, 69, 94, 128, 162. In my references to *Yiḥud gan-eden* I also mentioned *Yiḥud hayirah* and its commentary, which I will consider here. M. Benayahu, in his essay 'Tefilot veyiḥudim lahasagah shel ramḥa"l', in *Temirin: Texts and Studies in Kabbala and Hasidism*, ii (Jerusalem, 1981), 214–18, published *Yiḥud hayirah* and extracts from its commentary, and another *yiḥud* based on the vowel-points of the verse 'Zokhreni h' biretson amekha' [Ps. 106: 4: 'Remember me, O Lord, when You show favour to Your people'], together with a prayer.

189 Note 162 above. And in my essay on Luzzatto's influence on hasidic doctrine [Essay 10, pp. 488–9] I dealt with other writings by Luzzatto contained in MS Mosad Harav Kook 252. See also nn. 191, 192, 205 below.

(fos. 60^{v}–61^{v})—falls into three parts. The three sections are explicitly indicated in the commentary on the *Yiḥud*:[190] (*a*) *Derekh ha'ahavah* ['The Path of Love']: 'How so? They glean in the field—"and floods cannot overwhelm it" etc. [S. of S. 8: 7]' (fos. 104^{v}–105^{v}); (*b*) *Derekh hayirah* ['The Path of Fear' (i.e. fear of Heaven)]: 'Whoever is in fear [i.e. anyone whose conduct is governed by the fear of Heaven—Trans.]—to him the verse applies: "you are, all of you, alive today" [Deut. 4: 4]' (fo. 106^{r-v}); (*c*) an abbreviated and variant version of 'The Path of Fear': '*saday sadeh*—in the mystery of *vahadikot hamon* ['you shall beat a multitude in pieces': a paraphrase of Mic. 4 :13, *vahadikot amim rabim*, perhaps in order to give a virtual equivalent in the numerical value of the letters to *s(h)aday sadeh*—Trans.]' (fos. 106^{v}–107^{v}).[191] The section consisting of 'The Path of Love' is missing at the end of *Adir bamarom* in the printed version, and similarly it does not appear at the end of *Sefer yiḥud hagan*, a manuscript in the possession of a private collector containing the exposition of the *Yiḥud* as in Luzzatto's *Perush idra raba*, and the text of the *Yiḥud*.[192] In 'The Path of Fear' the person performing the *yiḥud* is raised up to

[190] The following appears in the passage connecting the first section to the second, at the end of the *yiḥud*: 'Whoever is *in* [the state of] *fear* acts thus; whoever is *in* [the state of] *love* makes his way to the tree of life, tends it and waits until its fruits are ripe, takes [them] and eats.' In the commentary on the *yiḥud* (*Adir bamarom*, 35) we find this: 'You have, of course, heard of the procedures of war which are called *the path of fear*; there is another path called *the path of love* which begins after the armour and spears.' On the words 'the path of fear' the foot of the page bears the note: 'See, at the end of the book, *Kitsur yiḥudei hagan* ['Summary of the *yiḥudim* of the Garden (of Eden)'].' After the transitional sentence comes an explanation of the passage in the Zohar entitled 'Izdarezu betikuneikhon' ['be zealous in your *tikunim*']; this explanation is part of the commentary on 'the path of love'. This juxtaposition was responsible for the insertion of an erroneous reference at the head of the *yiḥud* at the end of the book. See n. 177 above.

[191] A note above the third section in MS Mosad Harav Kook 252 (fo. 61^{r}) reads: 'The aforesaid *kavanat* [*sic*] in brief', and at the beginning of the third section in the text of the *yiḥud* at the end of *Adir bamarom* there has been inserted against the word *shaday*: 'This is the well-known *yiḥud*.' Both of these remarks are intended to convey that this text is an abridgement of *Derekh hayirah*. The abridgement was certainly prepared in Luzzatto's school, apparently by Luzzatto himself.

[192] I am indebted to Rabbi Yosef Spiner for his kindness in informing me of the existence of this work and in providing me with a photographic copy of it. It is of great interest from several points of view. Including the *Yiḥud*, it comprises thirty folios, preceded by two additional folios, one a title-page and the other bearing part of an introduction headed 'Introduction by the copyist'. Apparently the end of the introduction was on another folio not included in the photograph. The title-page reads as follows: '*Sefer yiḥud hagan*. Composed by the learned kabbalistic scholar, the rabbi, our teacher, Moses Hayim Luzzatto, and is part of the commentary he wrote on the *Idra*; his purpose in this work being to reveal the secret of study for the *tikun* of the Shekhinah. Copied here in Vitebsk by Samuel ben Benjamin Wolf Segal in the year 5580 [1820].' The text is interspersed with variant readings marked *s"a* (*sefarim aḥerim* ['other books']), and brief explanations. It is not clear whether the additions are the work of the copyist of Vitebsk or had been inserted earlier. Corrections of mistakes and other comments are entered in the margins in a different hand. The text of the *Yiḥud* (fos. 26^{v}–30^{r}) is reproduced

Paradise ('the Garden of Eden') by force of the fear of the Lord; in 'The Path of Love' the ascent takes place by virtue of the love of the Lord, and in both 'Paths' it is hinted that the purpose of the ascent of the soul is to gain a grasp of exalted secrets. The actions required in order to attain this grasp are presented in concrete narrative descriptions accompanied by allusions to their kabbalistic meaning—holy names and letters of the alphabet, lights, and sefirot. 'The Path of Fear' contains descriptions of war against the serpent and an attack on the Tower of Babel—that is, of course, against the forces of

without a heading. It appears that the commentary on the *Yiḥud*, accompanied by the text of the *Yiḥud*, was in circulation as a work in its own right, separately from the *Sefer yiḥud hagan*. And indeed, the collection of Luzzatto's writings in MS Mosad Harav Kook 252, which includes *Yiḥud gan-eden*, also includes the commentary (fos. 37ʳ–42ᵛ), though that is put first and is separated from the text. The commentary there bears the following note at its head: 'Copied from the commentary on the *Idra* of the great and godly scholar and kabbalist which he learned from the servants of the Most High'; and it concludes with the note: 'End of the commentary on *Idra raba*'. The identity of the author was obscured, and undoubtedly the separation of the *Yiḥud* from its commentary by other writings was intended to conceal the true nature of these two and the fact that they belonged together. See Essay 10, pp. 488–9; and n. 162 above. It is reasonable to suppose that the editing of the *Yiḥud* together with its commentary as a combined work was carried out by R. Jekutiel of Vilna in Shklov or Brisk [Brest-Litovsk], and that the members of his group distributed them in Lithuania and Poland. According to evidence given in Altona in 1753 on the activities of R. Jekutiel in Shklov (R. Jacob Emden's *Beit yehonatan hasofer* (n.p., n.d.), 6*a*), '*he* [Jekutiel] *wished to hand over to him* [the witness] *yiḥudim which he should perform with intense devotion* [*kavanah*], *closing his eyes*, whereupon mice and cats [meaning angels and holy spirits coming to reveal secrets of the Torah and visions of the occult] would forthwith come and fill the room in order to obliterate thought, and by this means he would see great wonders.' See Essay 8, pp. 431–4. Luzzatto's *Perush idra raba* as a whole, and the commentary on the *Yiḥud* in particular, were greatly admired in the school of the Vilna Gaon. See Essay 8, nn. 7 and 8 and pp. 437–8; and Essay 9, pp. 471–3. In the present context it is worth reproducing more fully than I did in Essay 8 (p. 450 and n. 132) R. Abraham Simhah of Mestislav's report of the question he put to his uncle, R. Hayim of Volozhin (*Derekh tevunot* (Jerusalem, 1880), 38*b*): 'Seeking his guidance, I once said to him that it seemed that the manuscripts of the aforesaid rabbi [Luzzatto] on the beginning of the *Idra raba* . . . all relate to awe-inspiring revelations from the upper world, *especially so in the explanation of Yiḥud hagan, there being no end to the awful and wonderful matters it contains. He answered me in these words: "It is quite clear and certain."*' The explanation[s] of *Sod milḥemet hashem* and *Sod hakeravah* ['The Secret of the War of the Lord' and 'The Secret of the Battle'], quoted from Luzzatto in the writings of R. Menahem Mendel of Shklov and R. I. E. Haver [Wildmann] to which I referred in my essay 'Kudsha berikh hu' [Essay 9, p. 473], are meant to explain the *Yiḥud*. Similarly with R. Zadok Bloch (a pupil of R. Hayim of Volozhin) to whose quotations from Luzzatto in his commentary to *Sefer habahir* I referred in the same essay (pp. 471–2 below); he relies on the explanation of the *Yiḥud* to clarify the meaning of the war against the Sitra Ahra waged with arms and [with] the study of the Torah for its own sake. See MS Jerusalem 3177 8°, fo. 30ʳ. It should be added that in *Beit olamim, perush idra raba lery*[*od*]"*a*[*lef*] *ḥaver* (Warsaw, 1889), 4*a*–9*a*, the explanation of the passage in the Zohar 'Itkaneshu levei' idra melubashin shiryan veromeḥin' ['Gather together at the house of assembly clad in armour and with spears']—concerning war against the Sitra Ahra with weapons consisting of holy names and *yiḥudim*—was written under the influence of Luzzatto's commentary on the *Yiḥud*, which, however, receives no mention.

evil, the Sitra Ahra—with various weapons, 'the spear and the sword, the bow and the sling', and the result of the armed struggle is that the person performing the *yiḥud* fans 'the embers into a flame . . . and throws off sparks in all directions'. In 'The Path of Love' the performer of the *yiḥud* grasps the tree of life, cultivates it, 'and takes of its fruit and eats'.[193] The allusions in these descriptions are interpreted, in plain words and in esoteric language, in the commentary on the *Yiḥud*.

Another *yiḥud* which has been preserved, *Yiḥud hayirah*, appears in four manuscripts, two containing only the text of the *yiḥud*[194] and two which also have its commentary.[195] I will not enter here into the complexities of the commentary, since even a cursory consideration of them would require ramified explanations of text and subject matter, but will content myself with pointing out the circumstances in which the text as we have it was written and how it came down to us, and with indicating the lines on which the body of that *yiḥud* is to be understood. The manuscript of the commentary was written at Padua before Rosh Hashanah 5493 [i.e. in 1732] by R. Jekutiel of

[193] The descriptions of the actions show that the *kavanot* ['mystical meditations'] of the *Yiḥud* were accompanied by cultic ceremonies not unlike magical rites. From this point of view, *Yiḥud gan-eden*, especially in 'The Path of Fear', is similar to two texts relating to *tikunim*, called *Vikuaḥ* and *Pe'ulah* ['Discussion' and 'Action'], which were in the hands of Joseph Almanzi and whose subject matter he summarized. A close parallel can be observed between the description employed in 'The Path of Fear' and that in the *Pe'ulah*. The purpose of the latter according to Almanzi was 'to hurl stones from a ballista to strike the enemies [who are] the fifth army and Armilus the wicked, and these stones will later serve as great stones for the foundation of the House'. See Essay 6, pp. 308–9. In n. 38 to that essay I put forward the hypothesis that the 'fifth army and Armilus the wicked' represented Edom–Rome–Christianity. There is also some evidence of an anti-Christian tendency in the *Yiḥud*, in 'The Path of Fear': 'He has seen the coiled serpent and pursues it, strikes it with his sword and cuts it to pieces; *the sword does not cut until he takes it from the hand of Esau*, for it is said [Gen. 27: 40] "By your sword you shall live". *He takes it from his hand* and acts for the Name, "the sword of the Lord"' (fo. 105^r). Similarly in the third section, the abridgement of 'The Path of Fear': 'If he finds difficulty with regard to this particular matter *he will take the sword from the hand of Esau* and act for the Lord, the sword of the Lord' (fo. 107^r). This form of words also appears in the other two manuscripts, but in the printed version at the end of *Adir bamarom* the words 'the sword does not cut . . . takes it from his hand' are missing, as are also the words 'from the hand of Esau' further on. It is clear that these are censorial deletions by the editor.

[194] MS Guenzburg 745, fos. 167^r–169^v; MS Harvard 54, fo. 132^v.

[195] MS Columbia 17 *alef* 893, fos. 98^v–100^r, 100^v–118^r; MS Mantua 112, fos. 30^r–31^r, 31^v–41^v. And see Essay 2, pp. 116–17; Benayahu, *Kitvei hakabalah*, 66–71, 71–2. In these manuscripts the *yiḥud* appears in a considerably expanded version. Benayahu, 'Tefilot veyiḥudim', 214–16, published the fuller version, enclosing the additions in square brackets to distinguish them from the original text. In 1988, in Jerusalem, Rabbi Yosef Spiner published parts of Luzzatto's *Perush idra raba*, taken from MS Cincinnati 501, that were not included in *Adir bamarom* (Warsaw, 1886); he entitled them *Sefer adir bamarom, ḥelek sheni* ['*Adir bamarom*, Part II']. Together with these he published the text of *Yiḥud hayirah* and its commentary under the title *Ma'amar yiḥud hayirah* (ibid. 133–64).

Vilna, who undoubtedly copied it from Luzzatto's original. It was sent in two parts or more—the first part accompanying the *yiḥud*—to a member of the group living outside Padua, in letters containing instructions on how to use the *yiḥud* and achieve its aims, as well as instructions to pass it on to 'great, righteous, and pious men'.[196] In spite of the similarity of the title *Yiḥud hayirah* to *Derekh hayirah* in *Yiḥud gan-eden*, the two are different and even contrary to each other in form and content. Whereas in 'The Path of Fear' the central subject is the struggle against the Sitra Ahra, the body of *Yiḥud hayirah* contains no mention of the forces of evil and the war against them; its dominant theme is the strong desire to achieve a peaceful and harmonious unity in the soul of the performer of the *yiḥud* in the process of adherence to the Godhead and to extend this unity to all realms of existence. To put it in another way, 'The Path of Fear' is essentially a description of a set of physical actions designed to elevate the soul by making ritual practices serve mystical and magical ends, whereas *Yiḥud hayirah* gives spiritual instruction for the elevation of the soul through the shedding of corporeality.[197] The structure of this *yiḥud* is homogeneous and balanced. The verse with which it opens is

[196] See Benayahu, 'Tefilot veyiḥudim', 214; and his *Kitvei hakabalah*, 67, 70, 75–9.

[197] A different spirit infuses the commentary, and especially the letters which accompanied it; and the last letter of the batch sent from Padua contains explicit instructions for the outright performance of magic: 'Know now a great secret, *that from this name there issues the making of all forms* [here] *below which can receive the divine flow from above, for the declaration* [*lehagadat*: the same root gives *magid*—Trans.] *of the future or the declaration of other matters which may be conveyed in messages* [from a supernatural source], *whether it be through the medium of the constellations or by means of some other power*. And now I will acquaint you with a *great act* which can be performed through the mystical power of this name: write in four rows twelve combinations of the letters of the Tetragrammaton, twelve combinations of the letters *alef he yod he* [*ehyeh*], and twenty-four combinations of the letters *alef dalet nun yod* [*adonai*] in groups of two combinations to each column. Above them all write the name *m h"sh* [the letters of *m sh"h*—I.T. [= *Metatron sar hapanim*, Metatron the Prince of the Countenance—Trans.]] and, at the foot, *hehahi*. *And when there is something you wish to know, adjure the angel Safriel in the name of m h"sh that he make known to you the thing which you seek in the name of hehahi*. And the writing must be on kosher parchment. Then draw a circle on something else, and if that, too, is on kosher parchment, so much the better, and inside the circle write three [Hebrew] alphabets in circles one inside the other. Look hard at them and you will see some of the letters appear to move. Then write those letters separately and look at them and see the order in which they move. In this way you will compose words and the answer to your question will emerge' (MS Mantua 112, fo. 45^r). (This letter was published along with three earlier letters, all of them from the Columbia manuscript, in the essay by Israel Weinstock, 'Perush [meḥug?] haramḥa"l lamishnah harishonah besefer yetsirah', in *Temirin: Texts and Studies in Kabbala and Hasidism*, ii (Jerusalem, 1981), 221–9; the passage I have quoted appears at the end of the essay. See my opening remarks to Part 1 of the present essay.) Benayahu had these instructions before him but ignored them and turned the matter on its head; he even accused Almanzi of falsely introducing, with anti-kabbalistic intent, the title *Pe'ulah* ['Action'] and the reference to the hurling of 'ballistic' stones into his description of the document in his possession (see n. 193 above). See Benayahu, 'Tefilot veyiḥudim', 204–6.

'. . . to fear this glorious and awful name, the Lord your God',[198] and the series of *kavanot*—names and their combinations—turns upon the concept of the fear of God's majesty and on the word *yirah* ['fear'], with its letters and vowel-points. The purpose of the *yiḥud*, too, is conveyed in clear and unambiguous language: the attachment of the soul, step by step, to the Godhead and the drawing down of supernal light and profound secrets.[199]

The third extant *yiḥud* which is important for our present purpose is headed 'For Sabbath nights'. It appears in MS Oxford 1901, where it is written in Luzzatto's own hand on the last folio (125^r^) of his *Tikunim ḥadashim*,[200] and it is dated at the end: 'Night of the conclusion of the holy Sabbath, 23 Heshvan 5495 [late 1734]'. It is arranged in three paragraphs, the first letters of which together form the name Yeho (*yod he vav*). Each paragraph opens with its own scriptural verse. The verses and the content of the *yiḥud* show that its principal aim is the unification of the sefirot Hesed and Gevurah and Tiferet, without any express practical purpose in this world and in the life of the performer of the *yiḥud*.

The times at which the three *yiḥudim* were composed, and several matters connected with them, put it beyond all doubt that Luzzatto regarded the sworn undertakings obtained from him in Padua and Frankfurt as given under compulsion and having no binding force: he broke them in his personal conduct and in his instructions to the members of his group. At the beginning of 5495 [late 1734] renewed controversy raged around him over his plan to move to Amsterdam; the rabbis of Venice were in uproar and demanded that an edict of *ḥerem* be issued against him and 'that his books be burned like the books of infidels and heretics'.[201] At that time, on the very eve of his departure from Padua,[202] he wrote the *yiḥud* 'for Sabbath nights'. Leaving it in his school as a parting gift, he set out for Frankfurt, where he fell into the trap set for him by his opponents. *Yiḥud hayirah* and its commentary were sent from Padua, with Luzzatto's approval, at the end of 5492 [1732], as stated above, and in my opinion there is no doubt that they were composed just

[198] Deut. 28: 58.

[199] Attention should be drawn to a phenomenon which is unusual in kabbalistic practices of this kind: at the outset and at the moment of greatest exaltation the instructions to the performer of the *yiḥud* direct him towards the establishment of firm contact with Ein Sof: 'Then begin to apply your mind to thinking of the majesty of Ein Sof, blessed be He . . . and consider that He is standing looking at you from there, and let it be in your thought as if you could see his splendour and glory [standing next to you] . . . then meditate, [for] just as you meditate on His majesty, so does He draw you near, to give you light' (Benayahu, 'Tefilot veyiḥudim', 214); 'And integrate your *nara"n* [the three parts of your soul: *nefesh*, *ruaḥ*, *neshamah*] in great humility, and Ein Sof, blessed be He, will cause the light to shine within you [or 'the light of Ein Sof, blessed be He, will shine within you']' (ibid. 216).

[200] See Tishby, *Netivei emunah uminut*, 323 n. 13.

[201] *Igerot*, ii. 276.

[202] See ibid. 256, in the addition to Luzzatto's letter of 21 Heshvan 5495 [late 1734].

before being sent. At any rate the very fact that they were sent, together with instructions as to how the *yiḥud* was to be performed and disseminated, proves conclusively that the ban on the use of *yiḥudim* was treated as null and void in Luzzatto's school. This conclusion applies also to *Yiḥud gan-eden*, the commentary on which appears in *Perush idra raba*, which was composed in 1731.[203] There, too, instructions are given, accompanied by warnings, as to the methods of using the *yiḥud*.[204]

B

The commentary on *Yiḥud gan-eden*, which was intended to throw light on the secrets of the *yiḥud*, is likewise written on two levels, the revealed and the occult.[205] While emphasizing the depth of the secrets of the *yiḥud*, Luzzatto utters stern warnings of the dangers they involve, and declares that he has deliberately confused matters so as to prevent them from being understood by anyone whose soul is not purified and whose mind is not properly pre-

[203] See Essay 8, n. 19.

[204] In discussing this matter previously I stated, without any reliance on the *yiḥudim* under consideration here, that Luzzatto refused to regard the undertakings which had been forced upon him as valid, and I refuted the apologetic arguments by which M. Benayahu sought to contradict my conclusion. See n. 61 above. In the introduction to his book *Kitvei hakabalah*, 8–9, 13–14, and in several places in the body of the text, Benayahu continued to argue at wordy length in support of his contrary hypothesis that Luzzatto kept meticulously to his undertakings, but in describing the *yiḥudim* which have been preserved (ibid. 63, 67, 88, 99, 101, 103, 105) he evaded the question how these fitted his hypothesis. Only in his essay 'Tefilot veyiḥudim', 214, did he pose this question with regard to the *Yiḥud hayirah* and its commentary, and the conjectures he put forward in answer to it are odd: 'it appears' that *Yiḥud hayirah* was composed 'in the first period' before the *magid* revealed himself to Luzzatto in Sivan 5487 [summer 1727]; and with regard to the manuscript in which *Yiḥud hayirah* and its commentary have come down to us he offered the following lame and self-defeating explanation: 'This manuscript was undoubtedly copied after the oath', but 'it may be that this manuscript was overlooked by Luzzatto, and it may be that this *yiḥud*, which is concerned with fear, was not reckoned among the things to which the oath applied'.

[205] In the version in MS Mosad Harav Kook 252 the commentary begins: 'The reapers of the field are young' (*Adir bamarom*, 24), and concludes: 'in the mystical significance of the intercourse which turns study into action, and understand this well' (ibid. 39). In the manuscript *Sefer yiḥud hagan* (see n. 192 above) the commentary extends from 'Colleagues, gather together in the house of assembly clad in armour and [bearing] spears' (*Adir bamarom*, 25) to 'and therefore he desired that they should deliver themselves up to death etc. and he said etc. to decree words of truth' (ibid. 38). In Luzzatto's *Perush idra raba* in MS Warsaw 149, fo. 17^r, above the commentary on the words of the Zohar 'Colleagues, gather together in the house of assembly', appears a note: 'Yiḥud hagan'. This note, in a different hand from that of the copyist, accords with the beginning of the commentary on the *yiḥud* in *Sefer yiḥud hagan*. From examination of the subject matter it is clear that the full extent of the commentary is as contained in MS Mosad Harav Kook 252.

pared for them.[206] I think I have succeeded in interpreting his coded symbols, and their clarification has made all the clearer the importance of *Yiḥud gan-eden* for our knowledge of Luzzatto's spiritual world in its mystical and messianic aspects.

The commentary, read literally, summarizes the ideas and actions described in 'The Path of Fear' as follows. The study of the Torah and the fulfilment of the commandments are duties which must be carried out solely for the *tikun* of the Shekhinah [her restoration to perfection], 'so that there should be no trace in one's thoughts of any other intent, not even that of perfecting oneself and one's soul so as to find favour in the eyes of the King, but only to do His will'.[207] The service of God by the performance of *mitsvot* ['commandments'] is, in mystical terms, 'the cultivation of the field . . . for the *mitsvot* act through sowing, the lights being sown in the female, which is the field'.[208] In the existing sorry situation it is not in man's power to reap the harvest of the seeds of the *mitsvot* that have been sown in the Shekhinah in 'the cultivation of the field', and to draw down the lights—that is, sublime secrets—that have sprung from them, because the Sitra Ahra which dominates the air of this world lies in wait to snatch the lights away as they descend. For this reason the Holy One, blessed be He, has opened a path by which a chosen few, who apply themselves single-mindedly to mystical meditations [*kavanot*] for the *tikun* of the Shekhinah, may raise their souls up to the Garden of Eden and there, permeated and enveloped by its air, take the lights of the *mitsvot* from the realm of the Shekhinah and bring them down without being attacked by the Sitra Ahra; for 'when it [the light] is taken by man it is protected, because all the danger occurs in the transmission from

[206] The following quotations will serve as examples: 'And furthermore, I will explain this to you clearly, although I cannot clarify it all in writing, for it requires to be conveyed by word of mouth. *Therefore what I say* [about it] *to you* [here] *is disconnected*, for taking this path is greatly to be dreaded, even though it is truly the path of the Lord . . . and therefore *I do not explain the matter to you in its proper order*, so that not everyone who wishes to acquire the name [i.e. gain access to the secret: an adaptation of Mishnah *Ber.* 2: 8—Trans.] can come and acquire it . . . *and I have already confused the order of things* for the reason I gave above so that you should not be able to rely on my words to justify any action' (*Adir bamarom*, 27); 'And do not be hasty, and let not your heart too readily come to terms with the beginning of an understanding of these matters, nor should you think that your mind has encompassed them, that you have them in your grasp and that you are their master, for I know that it is not in my power to explain them to you as clearly as would be necessary and to give you a thorough understanding of them' (ibid. 30–1); 'And herein are exceedingly great and hidden secrets . . . but I cannot specify them here, for they may not be imparted to any but a most worthy and proper recipient, in a whisper and in fear, awe, trembling, and sweat' (ibid. 35).

[207] Ibid. 27. Cf. *Igerot*, i. 8 (*Takanot rishonot* ['First Rules'], sect. 3), 10 (*Takanot nosafot* ['Supplementary Rules'], sects. 1–2). The rules were fixed at the time that the group was reorganized in 1731. See Essay 6, pp. 292–3.

[208] *Adir bamarom*, 24–5.

Malkhut [the Shekhinah—Trans.] to man'.[209] The action of those who are thus raised up, carried out in the air of Paradise, involves war against the Sitra Ahra with weapons supplied to them by the Shekhinah 'in the mystical form of a bow or sword or spear or sling'.[210] In their assault on the Sitra Ahra, especially with sling-stones—the sling being their most powerful armament, since the Shekhinah herself is the holy sling—the warriors topple the tower of impurity, which is, as it were, a Tower of Babel, and 'the deepest secrets are revealed through the power of this sling'.[211] In short, the purpose of using the *yiḥud gan-eden* by 'the path of fear' is to uncover mysteries, otherwise beyond reach during the Exile, which exist in the realm of the Shekhinah in the Garden of Eden, and to save them from the clutches of the Sitra Ahra while they are being brought down to this world.

However, it is evident that these complicated descriptions are not to be taken simply at their face value. We need to strip away the literal meaning of the commentary in order to reveal the main purpose of the *yiḥud*. Citing a passage in *Tikunei hazohar*,[212] Luzzatto wrote that what was meant by Pharaoh's decree that all newborn males were to be cast into the river, and by the concealment of Moses in 'the ark of bulrushes',[213] was the retention of 'the light of the Torah' and 'the spirit of the Messiah' in the Garden of Eden.[214] This surprising exposition ('into the river' = to the Garden of Eden, 'cast him' = conceal the secrets of the Torah and the Messiah in the Garden of Eden) has no support in the passage in the Zohar on which it is alleged to be based[215] or in Luzzatto's lame explanation of the subject matter of the exposition. But it contains the key to the understanding of his true intention, which he declared he had purposely obscured. What he really meant by 'the river' was the abyss of the *kelipot*—the evil spirits known as the husks—and since the secrets of the Torah and the soul of the Messiah were being held captive in the prison of the Sitra Ahra for so long as the Temple lay in ruins and Israel was in exile, it was said of them that they were cast 'into the river'. As for the kabbalistic

209 *Adir bamarom*, 25.

210 Ibid. 26.

211 Ibid. 34. Luzzatto's instruction to those performing *yiḥudim* is in the following terms: 'Make use of the sling to draw forth the deep significance of the secrets, and by hurling stone after stone, *tikun* after *tikun*, you [will] always discover great lights and secrets.'

212 *Zohar ḥadash*, *tikunim*, 112*d*–113*a*.

213 As in Exod. 1: 22 ('Every son that is born you shall cast into the river') and 2: 3 ('And she laid it in the reeds on the brink of the river').

214 See *Adir bamarom*, 27–9, for this and all the other references to 'casting into the river' of which I have made use here.

215 In the passage quoted here, and in parallel passages (*Zohar ḥadash*, *tikunim*, 98*b*; *Tikunei zohar*, *tikun* 21, 53*b*) the casting into the river is made to apply to the degradation of esoteric doctrine; that is to say, Pharaoh's order 'Cast him into the river' is understood as alluding to the decree that the secrets of the Torah should be cast out and besmirched in exile. None of the three passages contains any reference to 'the Garden of Eden'.

scholars who sought to attain a knowledge of the mysteries hidden in the river of the husks, they, too, must cast themselves into it in order to extract those mysteries. 'The son that is born' is the Moses-Messiah, by which designation is meant that 'when the Temple was destroyed, truly the Messiah was born, as is well known'. Contained within the spirit of the Messiah were secrets of the Torah and holy powers which had to be known and understood in order to bring about the Redemption, but the Holy One, blessed be He, decreed that during the Exile 'the transmission of the divine spirit to the Messiah will be blocked, and he will be unable to draw the emanation down into Israel as he should, but will be cast into the river'. Thus, so long as the Messiah and the secrets of the Torah he carried within him remained plunged in the river of the husks of evil, the Exile would continue, and therefore 'the reapers of the field' [kabbalists] were given the ability to attach themselves to them and

> all to be contained within this spirit of the Messiah . . . and to hold strongly to him, so that they should all be cast into the river; and *that is the tikun which I am expounding to you* . . . and so they will receive there what is proper for them to receive and afterwards bring it down, and will be called *maskilim* ['enlightened' or 'enlighteners'] . . . and the reason that the scriptural expression *tashlikhuhu* ['cast him'] has become *taskiluhu* ['enlighten him'] is that they are perfected through the mystical action of [the sefirah] Yesod, so as subsequently to bestow this bounty on others.

In freeing the captive secrets from the dominion of the husks they would also liberate the soul of the Messiah and help him to complete the Redemption, 'for the Messiah is called *tsadik* ['righteous'], as in the allusion in Scripture: "he is righteous and saved",[216] and those who hold fast to his strength are called *tsadikim*'.

A careful reading of the commentary to *Yiḥud gan-eden* proves, in my opinion, that in quoting Luzzatto selectively and with deliberate omissions, I have not misrepresented him but have followed his instructions,[217] and that I am correct in ascribing a messianic-eschatological purpose to the *Yiḥud* on the basis of the homiletic interpretation of Pharaoh's decree. I have found convincing evidence elsewhere in writings from Luzzato's school to confirm my understanding of the underlying meaning of the homily. The text of the verse describing the hiding of Moses in the rush basket ('and she laid it in the reeds by the river's brink'), which is ostensibly interpreted here as relating to the hiding of the Moses-Messiah in Paradise, is applied to the descent of the Messiah, son of Joseph, to the husks; we find the following explicit statement:

[216] Zech. 9: 9.

[217] 'Put together all my words, the first and the last, and [meditate] deeply on each and every word so as to form a good picture in your mind, and then these things will be as clear to you as if you saw them with your own eyes; and know that until you have pictured them with this clarity you have not grasped them' (*Adir bamarom*, 31).

'"By the river's brink"—on the brink of the sea of *sa'ad* [this should undoubtedly read *sa'ir* ['satyr'][218]] which is the *s*[*itra*] *a*[*ḥra*], "in the river"—the place of the *s*[*itra*] *a*[*ḥra*]'.[219] I must point out, however, that in the body of the *Yiḥud* and in the commentary, 'the Garden of Eden' is generally to be understood literally, that is, as an exalted region close to the realm of the sefirot, a region whose air is holy and confers holiness. Only in some of his references to the river did Luzzatto use the term 'the Garden of Eden' as a veiled allusion to the Sitra Ahra; that is to say, the regular location of the soul of the Messiah and the secrets of the Torah is actually Paradise, and it is only because of the rise in power of the Sitra Ahra that they descend into the depths of that evil realm. So, too, the soul of the person performing the *yiḥud* literally ascends to Paradise, is armed there with holy weapons, hurls itself down into the midst of the husks, and battles against them to rescue captives and hasten the Redemption. In this respect the intention of *yiḥud gan-eden* in 'the path of fear' is similar to the intention of *nefilat apayim* ['falling on one's face', prostrating oneself] in Lurianic kabbalah: ascent for the purpose of descending and raising up.[220]

The idea that the secrets of the Torah are in the possession of the Sitra Ahra for the duration of the Exile is Lurianic. R. Hayim Vital wrote: 'From the day that the Temple was destroyed and the Torah was burnt, its secrets and mysteries were handed over to the spirits of evil [*ḥitsonim*, 'the external ones'], and this is called *the exile of the Torah* in the world to come.'[221]

218 As is suggested in the margin of the printed homily [*sa'ir* but spelt with a *samekh* as first letter—Trans.].

219 *Megilat setarim verazin genizin* (Warsaw, 1889), 86–7. This homily, which is 'the first commentary' in a series of homiletic commentaries in Aramaic on Exod. 29: 6 ('You shall place the mitre on his head, and put the holy crown on the mitre') and Prov. 12: 4 ('A good wife is the crown of her husband'), is of great importance for an understanding of the attitude towards Shabateanism in Luzzatto's school. The allusions it contains are intended to explain and justify Shabetai Tsevi's descent to the husks in his apostasy, which in Shabateanism is called *sod hamitsnefet* ['the secret of the mitre']. In my addendum to Essay 6, n. 37, I dealt briefly with the meaning of the allusions relating to the mitre in the above-mentioned homily, and I explained them more fully in Essay 5, pp. 277–80.

220 See Tishby, *Torat hara vehakelipah*, 128–30.

221 H. Vital, *Sha'ar hakavanot* (Jerusalem, 1902), 58*d*. In the middle of the year 5490 [about the spring of 1730] R. Isaiah Bassano quoted this passage on the exile of the Torah among the husks (ascribing it to *S*[*eder*?] *hakavanot betik*[*un*] *ḥatsot* ['The Order [or 'Book'] of *kavanot* at the Midnight Study Session']) (*Igerot*, i. 103–4) in response to Luzzatto's argument that it was out of the question that the Sitra Ahra should reveal 'holy things'. Luzzatto, in his reply, explained the meaning of the Exile of the Torah as he understood it. He said he had not meant 'that it is impossible for the Sitra Ahra to communicate secrets of the Torah', but that the revelations of his *magid* 'through the power of the *yiḥud*' should not be attributed to the Sitra Ahra, 'for matters are already clear to me with regard to a subject which is beyond the reach of the Sitra Ahra' (ibid. 115–16). The explanation is weak, and certainly did not convince his opponents. And see n. 225 below.

Luzzatto, however, had important reasons for caution in expressing the ideas he advanced in the commentary to the *Yiḥud*. The descent of the Messiah to the husks and the need for the redemption of those who have descended are a fundamental element of Shabatean ideology, and Luzzatto's outlook on this subject was so close to the views of the Shabateans that even in dissociating himself from such views in his anti-Shabatean apologia he failed to obliterate the traces of their influence.[222] On the question of secrets of the Torah in the hands of the husks, it was charged against Luzzatto that when he was being investigated in Padua in 1730 a manuscript book of incantations was found in his possession, containing the following: '. . . because, when the Temple was destroyed, the mysteries of the Torah were delivered to "the external ones", and whoever wishes to know its secrets must invoke *s"m* [Sama'el] . . . until finally he reveals himself to you in human form and becomes a slave subservient to you, to disclose whatever you want to know'.[223] This accusation was voiced in public in 1735, and Luzzatto and his teacher denied it utterly.[224] Compelling the husks by force of arms to disclose the secrets of the Torah is akin to the coercion of Sama'el by conjuration, and therefore it is understandable that Luzzatto would use coded language in an endeavour to disguise the reference to the raising of mysteries out of the river of the husks.[225]

222 See Essay 4, pp. 229–47.

223 *Igerot*, ii. 262, and see ibid. 265, 268–9, 273–4, 278, 338, 347, 388, 391.

224 See ibid. 303, 339, 356, 358, 415.

225 A record of the court of the rabbis of Modena stated (ibid. 339) that R. Isaiah Bassano laid before them all the writings found in Luzzatto's house when Luzzatto was being investigated in Padua and that these did not include 'any complete book' of incantations but only 'scattered pages and small pamphlets . . . on matters to do with efficacious formulae etc.'; and that in a rigorous search through these documents they had not found them to contain 'this evil and bitter thing', namely 'conjuring up the Sitra Ahra to reveal secrets of the Torah'. The argument that the whole story was a fabrication by Luzzatto's persecutors is undermined first by the fact that the beginning of the extract produced to the rabbinical court of Venice (ibid. 262) as a passage from the book of incantations corresponds to the language of *Sha'ar hakavanot*, and secondly by the close parallel between the instruction in the commentary on *Yiḥud gan-eden* and the act of conjuration. A passage in *Sha'ar ruaḥ hakodesh* (Jerusalem, 1912), 5*b*–6*a*, shows that the extraction of secrets of the Torah from the forces of impurity was regarded as a legitimate activity in practical Lurianic kabbalah. In that work R. Hayim Vital writes that ever since the powers and secrets of the Torah were delivered into the hands of the husks, the ministers [*sarim*] appointed to have charge of 'unclean creatures such as domestic and wild animals, birds, and creeping things', i.e. the emissaries of the Sitra Ahra, 'know the mysteries and secrets of the Torah', and they will make ready in their mouths [those of unclean creatures] deep secrets of the Torah, expressed in their chirping and their voice; and anyone who understands their voice and their chirping will be able to learn many secrets of the Torah. Some generations have righteous men in their midst who know them ['them' probably refers to the languages of animals and birds—Trans.], *as I saw with my own eyes in the case of my teacher, of blessed memory*, and therefore the ministers make ready the secrets in them and make them known and understood to those who are

Similarly in 'the path of love', which leads to the tree of life, daring and dangerous ideas lie hidden. In place of the assault by means of magic in 'the path of fear', here the main action is the upward struggle of the soul in mystical *devekut*, but this too is described as surrendering oneself to death, which only an elite are able and entitled to experience. Here are two relevant passages:

And the root of all is the strength of [one's] love and the might of [one's] *devekut*; therefore do not let your heart beguile you into approaching its paths; if you do not find your heart perfect in this love as it should be, you will not succeed . . . for whoever does not take it upon himself to remain attached to God in this love will not enter by this path, for he will achieve nothing other than to be grievously punished.[226]

And it shall not be called love unless he goes so far as to value life and death equally . . . for they will leave everything to Him to do as He wishes, either to return the soul to the body and to life or to leave it attached to its root.[227]

The purpose of 'the path of love', too, is 'to draw down to oneself the lights of wisdom', that is, to gain access in 'the Garden of Eden' to hidden secrets which are beyond reach in this world. For this purpose the performer of the *yiḥud* must 'turn himself into the veritable likeness of a being in the upper world . . . and therefore he must make his whole body a chariot for the sefirot, his head for Keter . . . and his brain for Habad [Hokhmah, Binah, Da'at]'. In this state of ecstatic *devekut*, in which the soul combines with divine forces, the person performing the *yiḥud* reaches the tree of life 'to take hold of it and eat of its fruit'.[228]

The tree of life is a symbol of the sefirah Tiferet, which is the equivalent of the Written Law in the world of the Godhead, and eating the fruit of the tree of life means attaining an understanding of the secrets of the Torah which it contains. It may be, however, that this description has an eschatological undertone, for in *Raya meheimna* and in Shabatean literature 'the Torah of the tree of life' is the spiritual Torah which is destined, in the messianic era, to be revealed in the fullness of its mystical essence.[229] The eschatological aspect emerges, in a different way, from between the lines of another descriptive passage. An account of the preparations for *devekut* in 'The Path of Love' says that anyone who seeks to attain that state must fix his mind upon the tree

fit to understand them, as already mentioned'. Which means that some secrets in Lurianic kabbalah were received from the realm of the Sitra Ahra, and it may be deduced that a person who is qualified and fit to do so is entitled to compel the ministers responsible for unclean creatures, or their leader Sama'el, to surrender captive secrets of the Torah to him. And see n. 221 above.

226 *Adir bamarom*, 36.

227 Ibid. 38.

228 Ibid. 35–6. And see Luzzatto's *Da'at tevunot*, ed. Friedlaender, 113–14.

229 See Tishby, *Wisdom of the Zohar*, iii. 1103–8; Scholem, *Shabetai tsevi*, i. 10, 257–60; ii. 694–8, 704.

that appeared to Nebuchadnezzar in his dream, and that from it he will get to know the appearance and nature of the tree of life and understand the lines of conduct to be followed in its domain. To set at rest doubts likely to be evoked by this instruction, Luzzatto writes:

And do not object that 'surely that tree was the sign given to Nebuchadnezzar, and it is certainly unclean; how can we profess to explain it in a way which links it to the tree of life?' . . . for *in Nebuchadnezzar there was a great reshimu* [a residue of divine light] *of holiness*, for which reason he was described in Scripture as 'Nebuchadnezzar My servant';[230] and this was because he came from the strength of Solomon, being the issue of Solomon's union with the Queen of Sheba. And this *reshimu* spread through him with great glory, *so that he actually had the appearance of a celestial being*; and therefore, from what has been said with regard to him you will be able to understand what there is of holiness [in this].[231]

In the surprising statement that 'a great residue of holiness' resides in something unclean and that Nebuchadnezzar's unclean tree mirrors the tree of life, we can detect echoes of the dialectical distortions to be found in Shabatean philosophy.[232] These echoes are yet stronger in the immediately succeeding instructions that 'all these things a man must order and arrange in his mind *and turn himself into a chariot for all these things*', and that *tikunim*—corrections or actions to restore perfection—must be made in all the parts of the tree of life and in the system of sefirot, even to 'the *tikun* of the King's head'—to accord with the features of Nebuchadnezzar's tree. The text is obscure, but its meaning is clear: those who are engaged in elevating the soul in *devekut* thereby raise the fallen lights of holiness in Nebuchadnezzar's tree and return them to their source in the tree of life; and by these actions the unclean tree, too, undergoes *tikun* and is raised up. In other words, the processes of redemption which, in 'the path of fear', result from subduing evil in battle take place in 'the path of love' through turning evil back to good by acts of *tikun*. Luzzatto himself stated this distinction clearly:

230 See Jer. 25: 9; 27: 6; 43: 10.

231 *Adir bamarom*, 36–7. On Nebuchadnezzar as having sprung from the union between Solomon and the Queen of Sheba, see *Alfa beita deven sira*, ed. M. Steinschneider (Berlin, 1858), 21*b*.

232 It is true that aggadic literature has much to say in praise of Nebuchadnezzar in addition to what is said about him in Daniel: see S. Bernstein, *König Nebucadnezar von Babel* (Berlin, 1908), 27 n. 1, 35–6, 37–41, 58–63. But those expressions of praise should not be regarded as affording any basis for Luzzatto's statement that his main purpose was to prove the existence of grains of holiness in impurity. Nor need these remarks by Luzzatto be linked with R. Hayim Vital's statement (*Likutei torah* (Vilna, 1880), 139*a*) that the dimensions of Nebuchadnezzar's image (60 cubits high by 6 cubits wide: Dan. 3: 1) 'corresponded to the six edges [constituent sefirot—Trans.] of Ze'ir Anpin' and 'the six edges of Nukba [the female aspect of Ze'ir Anpin—Trans.]': Vital's intention was solely to compare opposites, in accordance with the common idea that the forces of evil—the Sitra Ahra—were arrayed on the pattern of the sefirot, 'each facing the other'.

When man has raised himself up to the Garden and been clothed in *mitsvah* [the performance of the divine commandments] there are two paths by which he may draw down to himself the lights of wisdom: either the path of fear, in which he subdues the Sitra Ahra by mighty deeds of war, or the path of love, which means adhering [*lehitdabek*] to the lights in great *devekut* and drawing the lights to him through lovingkindness. The choice must be made according to the times and the *tikunim*.[233]

The Messiah is not mentioned in this part of the commentary on the *Yiḥud*, but there seems no doubt to me that the redemption of the imprisoned Redeemer is likewise intended in 'the path of love', which is essentially a road running parallel to 'the path of fear' on a higher plane.

The material of a speculative nature which I have noted in analysing the commentary on *Yiḥud gan-eden* shows that there are points in this *yiḥud* which support the principal allegations made by Luzzatto's opponents with regard to his use of earlier *yiḥudim*.[234] The secrets of the Torah revealed to him through his operation of the *yiḥud* contained 'an admixture of the Sitra Ahra', for they were sunk in the abyss of the husks, the forces of evil, and were raised up from it. The descriptions of the actions involved in raising them show an essential affinity with the processes of redemption in Shabatean messianism, and even embody the proposition which is a principal tenet of Shabateanism that mystical meditations [*kavanot*] must comprise efforts to liberate the Messiah from his captivity among the husks.

I conclude this section by supplementing the information which I have given in previous studies with regard to the links between Luzzatto's *yiḥudim* and *yiḥudim* in Shabatean works.

Nathan of Gaza and A. M. Cardozo, the two spiritual leaders of Shabateanism from its inception, constantly carried out *tikunim* and received revelations through the performance of *yiḥudim*. Their mystical activities were very well known, and written descriptions of them were widely distributed in the circles of believers. In correspondence with his teacher, R. Isaiah Bassano, Luzzatto stated explicitly that *yiḥudim* by Nathan were in his possession and, in cautious language, he expressed appreciation of their importance. Even when he had already been sharply accused of Shabatean heresy, he wrote, 'concerning the writings of R. Nathan': '*A wise man can certainly eat their substance* and discard their husk.'[235] This statement undoubtedly applied to *yiḥudim* too, but we do not know the nature of the *yiḥudim* whose substance the 'wise man' Luzzatto ate.

Cardozo spent about four months in Livorno in 1675, during which time Shabatean scholars received oral instruction from him in matters theological

233 *Adir bamarom*, 35. 234 See above, text referring to nn. 182–3.

235 *Igerot*, i. 155. And see Essay 4, pp. 224–8.

and messianic.[236] R. Samuel of Fez, who had been one of his pupils in Livorno, received a letter from him concerned with ideology in 1690 or thereabouts, in which Cardozo said that some years previously R. Samuel had received the *Derush raza derazin* ['Discourse on the Most Secret of Secrets'].[237] Cardozo's writings contain detailed descriptions of mystical-magical *tikunim* and revelations by *magidim*; these *tikunim* were executed by means of ritual acts, using holy names and combinations of letters of a kind clearly characteristic of *yiḥudim*. Two texts abounding in such descriptions are the discourse *Kodesh yisra'el lashem*[238] and a letter to R. Abraham Rovigo[239] dating from the end of 5461 or the beginning of 5462 [i.e. the second half of 1701] which mentions several works by Cardozo, chief among them being the discourse *Boker de'avraham*. I advanced the hypothesis that Luzzatto was influenced by Cardozo in his use of *yiḥudim* and in the matter of revelations from a *magid*,[240] and I pointed particularly to the traces of the influence of the

[236] See I. Tishby, 'Igerot rabi me'ir rofe lerabi avraham rovigo mishenot tala"h–ta"m [5435–40/1675–80]', in I. Ben-Zvi and M. Benayahu (eds.), *Sefer hayovel lishene'ur zalman shazar/Shneur Zalman Shazar Jubilee Volume* (= *Sefunot*, 3–4) (Jerusalem, 1959–60), 93–5; Tishby, *Netivei emunah uminut*, 231, 346 n. 43. As those references show, R. Abraham Rovigo was preparing to visit Livorno in order to study with Cardozo, but was prevented by Cardozo's departure from that city.

[237] See *Beit hamidrash*, ed. I. H. Weiss (Vienna, 1865), 63–71, 100–3. *Derush raza derazin* is mentioned ibid. 101. And see Tishby, 'Igerot rofe', 110 n. 89; Benayahu, 'Hatenuah hashabeta'it beyavan', 112–17.

[238] Published in G. Scholem's essay 'Shenei mekorot ḥadashim', 253–70. And see Scholem's remarks, ibid. 245–50.

[239] Published in the essay by I. Molkho and A. Amarillo, 'Igerot otobiografiyot shel kardozo', in I. Ben-Zvi and M. Benayahu (eds.), *Sefer hayovel lishene'ur zalman shazar/Shneur Zalman Shazar Jubilee Volume* (= *Sefunot*, 3–4) (Jerusalem, 1959–60), 202–35. This long and very interesting letter was written by Cardozo on receiving [Rovigo's publication] *Eshel avraham ler' mordekhai ashkenazi* (Fürth, 1701), which was sent to him by Rovigo shortly after publication. It is probable that the letter did not reach Rovigo before he left for the Land of Israel at the end of Tevet 5462 [Dec. 1701] and it was left in his house in Modena. Cardozo's comments on *Eshel avraham* at the beginning of the letter make it clear that Rovigo had disclosed to him that [Ashkenazi's] book had been composed under the inspiration of a *magid*. Cardozo expressed a critical view of that work, writing, *inter alia*: 'It is true that the *magid* is of holy provenance but he pitches his remarks at a low level, so that the book is very suitable for those beginning this study; the book of the Zohar [itself] is written on many levels, and this *magid* restricts the knowledge he imparts so as to suit the recipient, or else he is a disciple of the Remak [Cordovero].' The letter shows clearly that there were strong personal bonds between the two scholars, and there is no doubt that Rovigo possessed writings by Cardozo. From a letter sent by Rovigo to R. Benjamin Hakohen in 1705 it is known that in that year Rovigo visited Cardozo's pupils in Constantinople. See G. Scholem, 'R' eliyahu hakohen ha'itamari vehashabeta'ut', in S. Lieberman (ed.), *Alexander Marx: Jubilee Volume on the Occasion of his Seventieth Birthday*, Hebrew vol. *Sefer hayovel likhevod aleksander marks* (New York, 1950), 466–7 n. 46.

[240] See Essay 6, p. 301 and n. 27; and Benayahu, 'Ha"magid" shel ramḥa"l', 302–3. Benayahu pointed out that there is an affinity between Luzzatto and Cardozo in [their references to] the

discourse *Kodesh yisra'el lashem* in several important respects,[241] but I was unable to offer any clear proof that Luzzatto had studied Cardozo's writings. I can now add new evidence which puts the point beyond doubt. I had noticed and drawn attention to the fact that in Luzzatto's poetry and prayers, and in R. Moses David Valle's homiletic writings, the scriptural adjectives *dal* and *evyon* [both meaning 'poor'] were applied respectively to the Messiah ben David and the Messiah ben Joseph.[242] I have since become aware that this messianic terminology also occurs in the discourse *Kodesh yisra'el lashem*, and in this context there is complete accord between Luzzatto's prayer and Cardozo's discourse: both use the words in the interpretation of the same verse.[243] Accord of this kind proves the influence of the one on the other. Hence, with regard to other points of contact also, it may be taken that Luzzatto's direct source was the discourse *Kodesh yisra'el lashem*. For our present purpose this influence is extremely important, for Cardozo supports the messianic interpretation of the terms *dal* and *evyon* by reference to two *yiḥudim*: '. . . and you have already seen in the *Yiḥud keriat shema* . . . and so, too, *Yiḥud b' meshiḥim* ['The *yiḥud* of the Two Messiahs']'.[244]

Finally: certain allusions to the preparation of kabbalistic messianic discourses, preserved and published together with other remnants of Luzzatto's writings,[245] include one which is noted: 'In the work *Boker de'avraham*'. The meaning of this allusion is clear: it is a reference for Luzzatto's own benefit to

system of *yiḥudim*, but he doubted whether Luzzatto had been influenced by Cardozo because the latter's works 'were not widely circulated in Italy'. The reason offered for his doubts is surprising in the light of the information presented here.

241 See Essay 9, n. 58; and n. 31 above. 242 See Essay 2, pp. 124–5; Essay 6, pp. 327–8 and n. 95.

243 Ps. 113: 3. *Takta"v tefilot leramḥa"l*, ed. S. Ulman (Benei Berak, 1979), prayer 'Va'etḥanan' (no. 515 [= *takta"v*]), 348: 'The two Messiahs of whom it is said "He lifts the poor out of the dust, and raises the needy from the dunghill" '. *Kodesh yisra'el lashem* (Scholem, 'Shenei mekorot ḥadashim', 260): 'And then [following the Hebrew word order in Ps. 113: 7] He lifts out of the dust the poor—*mb"d* [*mashiaḥ ben david*], from the dunghill He raises the needy—*mb"e* [*mashiaḥ ben efrayim*].' Scholem, ibid. n. 66, observed that 'the two Messiahs' here meant Shabetai Tsevi and Cardozo. And see what is said by Scholem in the introduction, ibid. 246–7.

244 Apparently the reference is to textual *yiḥudim* which were intended for use in mystical acts designed to unite the divine forces and unite the Messiahs. Luzzatto's prayers, too, display traces of the influence of Cardozo's prayers. It is worth noting, in particular, a series of prayers by Cardozo headed 'Yiḥud leharema"k yetsa"v' ['*Yiḥud* by the Remak [R. Miguel Abraham Cardozo], may his Rock protect and preserve him'] (published in Molkho and Amarillo, 'Igerot otobiografiyot shel kardozo', 238–46). These should be compared with the group of prayers now included in Essay 2 under the heading 'Confessional Prayers of Luzzatto and his Group' (p. 176 ff.), which parallel them in their general tone and particular turns of phrase. The characteristics which I outlined in my introduction to the 'Confessional Prayers' are, for the most part, equally applicable to the series of prayers by Cardozo.

245 *Otserot ramḥa"l*, 295–7, under the heading 'Rashei perakim shel divrei torah' ['Précis of Words of Torah']. The allusion to *Boker de'avraham* is at 295.

Cardozo's *Boker de'avraham* as a source for a discourse he is planning.[246] *Boker de'avraham*, Cardozo's first and most important theological work, was widely circulated in Shabatean circles, and an attempt was even made to publish it in Amsterdam;[247] it is now clear that it also came into the hands of Luzzatto and provided him with some ideas. It is reasonable to assume that, in addition to *Kodesh yisra'el lashem* and *Boker de'avraham*, he read other works by Cardozo and drew guidance from him on the performance of *yiḥudim* and messianic *tikunim*.

X. *SODOT*: 'MYSTERIES', MYSTICAL INTERPRETATIONS

(FOS. 116^{r}–127^{r})

[This section of the manuscript was published in *Ginzei ramḥa"l*, ed. H. Friedlaender (Benei Berak, 1980), 259–71. In general, the quotations and page references below follow that edition. The manuscript copy is in the handwriting of 'the unmistakable copyist' (see n. 8 above).]

'THE MYSTERY OF THE CHARIOT', 'THE MYSTERY OF THE IMAGE OF UNIVERSAL MAN', 'THE MYSTERY OF THE *YIḤUD*'

This series of three short works, each of which has its own subject heading, forms a single section in the nature of a treatise on 'mysteries', a genre which is widely encountered in the literature of kabbalah. The three vary greatly in length (in the manuscript: fos. 116^{r}–119^{r}, 119^{v}, 119^{v}–127^{r}), and at first sight there appears to be no particular link between their subjects. However, as will be shown below, they do have a fundamental theme in common: the nature of

246 There are several allusions to Luzzatto's book *Tikunim ḥadashim* in such forms as *ayin tikunim* [letter *ayin* = 70], *shivim tikunim* [seventy *tikunim*], *tikunim de'vekhol hayadot'* [*tikunim* of 'and all the hands'], this last being a reference to the quotation 'ulekhol hayad haḥazakah' ['and in all the strong hand'—Deut. 34: 12] which opens every *tikun* in *Tikunim ḥadashim*. Apparently the note 'Beḥibur hayad' ['in the "hand" treatise'] is another reference to that work. In the obscure sentence 'h' hamenorah aletah orah, *va'avo hayom* av avot vedavid[?] mitḥaberim betikunim' ['Letter *he* of the menorah [lampstand] light went up, "and I came today"—forebear of ancestors and David(?) joining together in *tikunim*'] (*Otserot ramḥa"l*, 296), it may be that the words *va'avo hayom* allude to the Shabatean work *Va'avo hayom el ha'ayin* ['I Came Today to the Spring'—Gen. 24: 42], which is known to have been written by R. Jonathan Eybeschuetz and was the main cause of the campaign against him in 1725. On the relations between Luzzatto and Eybeschuetz, see Essay 8, n. 93. And see n. 55 above.

247 See Scholem, *Kabbalah*, 273, 277, 397, 399.

the relation between the celestial order and non-divine beings. The third and last of the series, *Sod hayiḥud*, was not completed in the copy which has come down to us, as is evident from a note near the end: 'But in view of a serious oversight, we shall give an important correction [or *tikun*] here, and [this is] as written at the end.' The matter alluded to is not in the copy, and possibly it is not only the end of *Sod hayiḥud* that is missing; there may also have been other 'mysteries' in the complete work. In several places the copyist had difficulty in reading the text, and used dots to indicate the omission of words. Characteristics of style, terminology, and ideas show with certainty that the treatise is by Luzzatto, but there is no need for a meticulous examination of such signs; conclusive proof is afforded by linguistic parallels, some of them verbatim, between *Sod hayiḥud* and the commentary on the passage from the Zohar 'Arimat yaday bitselotin' ['I lifted up my hands in prayer'] which is contained in Luzzatto's *Perush idra raba*.[248]

Sod hamerkavah ['The Mystery of the Chariot'] (fos. 116^r–119^r)

Topics connected with the celestial chariot are dealt with in many of Luzzatto's writings. A list of his works which he delivered to his teacher in Kislev 5490 [end of 1729] included one entitled *Perush hamerkavah*.[249] That 'commentary on the chariot' is not extant but it seems probable that it centred upon the chariot as described in Ezekiel's vision, consisting of living creatures and wheels and a throne, and the likeness of a man (the glory of the Lord) on the throne.

The early Jewish mystics of the Heikhalot literature showed no knowledge of any chariot other than the one so constituted, which, for them, was the domain of the secrets of *ma'aseh merkavah* ['the structure of the chariot'], the secrets of *merkavah* mysticism which were the exalted goal aspired to by *yoredei hamerkavah* (those who 'descended to the chariot'). However, in the doctrine of kabbalah, Ezekiel's chariot was taken to be the lower chariot or a secondary chariot which existed in the world of creation, below the system of the divine sefirot which was the upper chariot.[250] In two of Luzzatto's works matters to do with the chariot form a central theme:

1. *Kelalim sheniyim* ['Second Principles'], printed in a book to which its editor, R. David Luria, gave the title *Pitḥei ḥokhmah vada'at* ['Gateways to Wisdom and Understanding'] (Warsaw, 1884).[251] This work states expressly

[248] See below, text referring to nn. 281–2, and the notes themselves.

[249] See *Igerot*, i. 31. This work, we are told (ibid. 53), was written in Hebrew.

[250] In both systems the chariot is perceived as a sort of vehicle ridden by supernal powers which operate it and act by means of it. See Tishby, *Wisdom of the Zohar*, ii. 587–95. And see G. Scholem, *Jewish Gnosticism, Merkabah Mysticism and Talmudic Tradition* (New York, 1960).

[251] Repr. in *Sha'arei ramḥa"l*, ed. H. Friedlaender (Benei Berak, 1986), 137–256; text corrected by reference to manuscripts, and preceded by an introduction (105–35). And see n. 156 above.

that its subject is 'the upper chariot', but the celestial order is presented here in the figure of 'a chariot' in many different patterns and in a series of procedures and actions which follow the intricacies of Lurianic kabbalah. The sequence of events from the contraction [*tsimtsum*] of the light of Ein Sof to the establishment of the system of the *partsufim* [the 'countenances' of God], by way of the shock of the breaking of the vessels, is described under four headings; this is not the place to go into their exact meaning but they are as follows: *ḥibur hamerkavah*, *tsurat hamerkavah*, *binyan hamerkavah*, and *hanhagat hamerkavah* [which may be rendered approximately as 'the construction of the chariot', 'the form of the chariot', 'the structure of the chariot', and 'the driving of the chariot'—Trans.].

2. *Pinot hamerkavah*.[252] In this work, which is divided into four 'corners' [*pinot*] and has four prayers appended to it, the chariot is that of Ezekiel. This is an eschatological work which sets out to describe the actions of the forces of the chariot in four stages of redemption: the liberation of Israel from the rule of the husks, which is portrayed as the opening of the graves, and turning evil back to good; the renewal of prophecy; peace and tranquillity, an end to wars, the removal of jealousy [or 'fanaticism'], the destruction by fire of 'the two unclean houses which now exist in Jerusalem the holy city', and the descent to this world of the celestial Temple, ready-built, in the midst of the fire; quietude and rest, the annulment of pride and the strengthening of humility, the cleansing of mankind from filth, the elevation of souls. The four stages of redemption are presented as the conditions of love, fear, peace, and strength.

The way in which the chariot is perceived in *Sod hamerkavah* is unique. It is founded on the understanding of the word for a chariot, *merkavah*, as equivalent to *harkavah* ['combination', 'assembly' in the sense of putting parts together to form a whole: the two Hebrew words are derived from the same verb—Trans.]. The actions involved in assembly take place in two steps, the central factor in each being the sefirah Malkhut, the Shekhinah:

1. *Ḥesed*, *din*, and *raḥamim*, the three divine attributes of lovingkindness, judgement, and mercy which are the three sefirot Hesed, Gevurah, and Tiferet, all higher than the Shekhinah, combine within her and impart to her the authority and ability to govern the inhabitants of this world (the non-divine creatures whose root is the Shekhinah) by those attributes, through reward and punishment, reflecting the duality of good and evil, and through *yiḥud* ['unification'], the purpose of which is the annulment of evil and its restoration to good.[253]

252 MS Guenzburg 745, fos. 2r–19v (the main body of the text), 22r–41v (*Merkavah* prayers). Printed in *Ginzei ramḥa"l*, ed. H. Friedlaender (Benei Berak, 1980), 313–32, 333–46.

253 'And this is the mystical significance of the fact that Malkhut is called the lower thought, and Hokhmah the upper thought. That is to say, [the sefirah] Hokhmah arranges her affairs,

2. The Shekhinah exercises governance over earthly creatures by penetrating into them in her compound form, whereupon the forces of lovingkindness, judgement, and mercy which are united within her separate from each other and combine with the beings of this world in accordance with the nature of those beings and the governance they need. The Shekhinah dwells within the creatures of this world [*taḥtonim*, 'those below'] as a soul in the body, and together they form 'the likeness of a man'. In the light of these processes the Shekhinah is *ma'aseh merkavah* ['the making of the chariot'] in two senses: the combination [*harkavah*] within her of the divine forces, and her combination [*hitrakevut*—from the same verbal root] with the non-divine beings of this world.[254]

the affairs of governance and transmission of the divine flow, which is [*sic*] wholly dependent on the sefirot Hesed, Din, and Rahamim [lovingkindness, judgement, and mercy] in all their details and combinations and the ways in which they exercise control, this being the secret meaning of the *partsufim*, as [I have] said elsewhere. And that is what is necessary for the path of reward and punishment. And there everything is explained in accordance with the mystical concept of reward and punishment, and unification [*yiḥud*] which exercises control and turns all evil back to good, as explained in its proper place' (*Ginzei ramḥa"l*, 259). Divine governance is thus seen as exercised in two different ways, 'reward and punishment'—which is presented briefly here to define the functions of the Shekhinah in regard to governance—as opposed to the control exercised by 'unification', about which no more is said here than that it 'turns all evil back to good'. This view of divine governance is one of the important themes in Luzzatto's writings, and it occupies a central position in *Da'at tevunot*. See *Da'at tevunot* and *Sefer hakelalim*, ed. H. Friedlaender (Benei Berak, 1973), 129–98. 'The governance of reward and punishment' is also called 'the governance of good and evil' and 'the governance of justice', while other names for 'the governance of unification' are 'the governance of restoration to perfect good' [*hahatavah hashelemah*] and 'the governance of love'. See n. 277 below. On this question, as on many others, Luzzatto's kabbalistic writings express different and even contradictory ideas. Y. Avivi considered these contradictions and offered suggestions for their resolution in his essay 'Kavanat haberiah beḥiburei ramḥa"l', *Hamayan* (Tamuz 5745 [1985]), 1–18; and see esp. 3–5.

254 The following three quotations exemplify the ideas of 'combination' [*harkavah*] as formulated by Luzzatto: 'And indeed the disclosure of this matter is the mystery of *merkavah* [not here solely in its literal sense of 'chariot'—Trans.], which completes the sefirah Malkhut, and therefore *ma'aseh merkavah* is explained by reference to Malkhut, for Malkhut is truly *ma'aseh merkavah* ['the work of assembly']; that is to say, the individual elements of Malkhut consist in the lights of the chariot, and together their significance is as the soul of man with all its strengths and concerns' (*Ginzei ramḥa"l*, 259); 'But the individual elements of the restoration of Malkhut to perfection [*tikun malkhut*] lie in the mystery of these lights of the chariot; through these lights the divine flow is transmitted to the servants, to each one separately, and, as you have previously heard, all these are none other than parts of Malkhut . . . which, being assembled in various combinations [*harkavot*] [and] bound together by many ties, form a root for all beings' (ibid. 260); 'And when we take Malkhut as a whole—it is the whole existence of the inhabitants of the lower world, and it is the tenth sefirah [along with] the nine sefirot, which assembles and binds together whatever is necessary at any time, in accordance with the coupling which needs to be performed. In particular it is the totality of all these combinations [*harkavot*] by way of the mystery of *ma'aseh hamerkavah*' (ibid.). The ways in which Hesed, Din,

The relations between the Shekhinah and the inhabitants of this world are illustrated in extensive detail in a description of the particular make-up of man's soul which is called *seder maḥashevet haneshamah* [the order of thought of the soul], that is, the ways in which the soul recognizes and comes to understand the affairs of this world. The light of the Shekhinah dwells within the soul, whose root the Shekhinah is; and a superior soul which functions as it should will strive to contemplate and hold fast [*lehitdabek*] to the root to which it is attached. The light of the Shekhinah which resides in the depths of the soul is the Holy Spirit, which is also called 'spirit of understanding' [*ruaḥ sekhel*]; and the soul, through the strength of its attachment to its divine root, is enabled by the Holy Spirit within it to gain true and complete cognizance of everything in the world 'without any weakness or error'.[255]

The idea which reads the act of *harkavah* ['combination'], both as a matter of linguistics and in substance, into the terms *merkavah* and *ma'aseh merkavah* [which mean literally the chariot and the manner of its construction—Trans.] is found in early kabbalistic writings. One of the passages in the Zohar on the seven halls in the world of creation declares that in the seventh and uppermost hall, which is called 'the holy of holies', spirit combines with spirit, the reference being to the coupling of Yesod and Malkhut. The passage goes on to state that Adam, who was created by that divine intercourse, was called *ma'aseh merkavah* [the work, i.e. the product, of combination], and that generally speaking, Adam, that is, Adam's soul, 'is the work of this *merkavah* in which one combined with the other'.[256] On the strength of this passage, but

and Rahamim operate in their governance of the world are likewise described as the combination of the divine forces in Luzzatto's '138 Gateways to Wisdom' [*Kela"ḥ pitḥei ḥokhmah*], commentary to Gateway 7, in the following terms: 'All this combination [*harkavah*] and weaving together is visible to the prophets or to the souls, and it is this which is called *merkavah*.' Malkhut is called *ma'aseh merkavah*, without any connection with *harkavah*, in the Zohar III, 223*b* (*Raya meheimna*): 'They are three in all [Netsah, Hod, and Yesod], they are a chariot for *Tiferet adam* ['the Glory of Man'], forming together *merkavah*, which is Malkhut.'

255 'And indeed the order of thought of the soul, which is the order of these lights, is as follows: within the soul there is an outspreading of light from the Shekhinah, as [I have] said in another place; the soul surrounds it, and all her desire is towards it, and she thinks and considers what to do in order to cleave to it, so that the whole concern of the soul, if there is no one to disturb her, is only to cleave to her root' (*Ginzei ramḥa"l*, 261); 'But there is another divine flow coming from the root: this is the light of the Shekhinah which is within the soul, and this flow of light gathers together the parts of the soul so completely that they will not need to wander about but will absorb this flow; and all of them at once will blaze up and come to understand all that they need to understand in truth, without any weakness or error. And this is the mystery of the Holy Spirit, and in proportion as the spirit increases, the soul attains greater understanding, and so, too, in proportion as the spirit settles within the soul. This was called by the early sages *ruaḥ sekhel*' (ibid.). On the idea of the existence of the light of the Shekhinah in the soul, and a parallel idea in hasidism, see nn. 16 and 41 above. On the ways in which this idea appears in early kabbalistic sources, see Werblowski, *Joseph Karo*, 58–9.

256 Zohar II, 260*a*. And see Tishby, *Wisdom of the Zohar*, ii. 593–4.

by an elaboration going far beyond its literal meaning, R. Meir ibn Gabbai stated that the inclusion of the halls in the sefirot, which were the upper chariot, constituted an act of *harkavah*, and it was this which was *ma'aseh merkavah*.[257] It is likely that in the composition of *Sod hamerkavah* Luzzatto was influenced by these passages, but there is no doubt that he came under the direct and extremely powerful influence of *Berit menuḥah* ['Covenant of Rest'] (Amsterdam, 1648), for that work is quoted four times in *Sod hamerkavah*.[258]

257 See R. Meir ibn Gabbai's *Avodat hakodesh* (Venice, 1567–8), pt. iv, chs. 15–16. Succeeding chapters, nos. 18–19, contain explanations of matters relating to the 'second chariot' in an extensive exegesis of verses from Ezekiel 1, ending as follows: 'Thus far the mystery of the secrets of the chariot and the explanation of the chariot in accordance with the Scriptures, and as it [the chariot] was explained by the rabbi and kabbalist R. Moses de León (may the memory of that tsadik be for a blessing) in the book *Mishkan ha'edut*, according to what he received and drew from the springs of wisdom, and according to what he saw in the words of the true sages who stand in the council of the Lord, namely the sages of the Mishnah, peace be upon them.'

258 The following are the actual quotations: 'The ten sefirot in *beit yod ayin* [*beriah*, *yetsirah*, *asiyah*: creation, forming, making—the three worlds or stages of creation which follow *atsilut*, emanation—Trans.] allude to the inward quality in the soul which, *in the book Berit menuḥah*, *is called hametsi'ut* ['existence' or 'reality']' (*Ginzei ramḥa"l*, 262); 'And these lights at first are together one light on three levels, as mentioned there in the book *Berit menuḥah* . . . and [the sefirah] Hokhmah strips apart the powers of these levels, and it is these individual lights which are called the lower chariot, *as explained there*' (ibid.); '*And therefore he said in the book Berit menuḥah* that all the lights are full of intelligence and wisdom' (ibid. 263); 'And the intellect, too, occurs wherever necessary, and *as is written in the book Berit menuḥah*, *in the Seventh Path* [*sic*: the Sixth Path is meant, see 33*a*], the intellect extends everywhere' (ibid.). I add a paragraph which is not quoted here but the substance of which bears a close relationship to the principles of *Sod hamerkavah*: 'Happy is the man who knows the principle of the tenth level [Malkhut—the Shekhinah], for that level receives into its light and radiance all things and all the supernal lights [the sefirot], *and in this tenth light all the lights appeared combined* . . . and the radiance that issues and spreads from the place of *hametsi'ut* [the supernal source], the hidden place, covers these pillars; *these are the lights which became combined in the tenth light*, and the radiance which issues from the First Cause covers these pillars like a throne, and *"merkavah" means "harkavah"* ['assembly, combination'], *in which all the lights which nourish living creatures were combined* . . . and from that splendid radiance which spreads out from this place, this place was depicted in [physical] forms and came down, and that is the chariot supported by four creatures' (*Berit menuḥah*, 22*b*–*c*). Preceding the references to *Berit menuḥah* in *Sod hamerkavah* there is a mention of 'the book *Mayan haḥokhmah*' (Amsterdam, 1651), which was one of the main works in the literature of the 'circle of contemplation' [*ḥug ha'iyun*]: 'And this is the secret of the radiance which issues from the Splendour [*hazohar*], *which is mentioned in the book Mayan haḥokhmah*. As said in another place, the Splendour is the ten sefirot with everything that is required in them, and they are still hidden from the recipients, but the radiance is this *merkavah* which spreads out and is revealed to the recipients, and [so] they receive some of its lights' (*Ginzei ramḥa"l*, 260). At the end of *Mayan haḥokhmah* we find the statement 'And from the Splendour a radiance goes forth', but in this case there is no allusion to the sefirot. In my opinion Luzzatto attributed the source of the radiance to the sefirot on the basis of the description of the radiance in *Berit menuḥah*, and mentioned the two works alongside each other because he saw an essential affinity between *Berit menuḥah* and the writings of the 'circle of contemplation'. And see n. 268 below.

I conclude this section by examining the traces of *Berit menuḥah* in Luzzatto's kabbalistic works as a whole. In general he refrains from indicating sources, except for the Zohar and the writings of Luria, but he refers to *Berit menuḥah* by name in five of his treatises, quoting it as his authority and adding extravagant words of praise.[259] In other works, especially *Pinot*

[259] The following are the actual references in four works in addition to *Sod hamerkavah*.

(*a*) 'But when He desired to act through the mystery of the sefirot, He arranged His powers in order within Himself, *as stated by the author of Berit menuḥah*' ('138 Gateways', commentary on Gateway 10); 'That is the mystery of all matters concerning *heikhalot* ['palaces'] and all matters concerning the Chariot which are explained in the book *Berit menuḥah*' (ibid., commentary on Gateway 138).

(*b*) 'And by that is meant the upper chariot and the lower chariot, *which are explained in the book Berit menuḥah*, and in which is imprinted the form of all the inhabitants of the lower world . . . and, in truth, from there the souls are cut out, *as explained* [in that book] *Berit menuḥah*' (Commentary on *Idra raba*, MS Cincinnati 501, fo. 278ʳ); 'And the Divine Glory itself arranges itself in the order necessary for it to undertake its actions, *and these are the mystery of the ten points referred to in the book Berit menuḥah, as explained in its proper place*' (ibid., fo. 288ʳ). These two passages occur in the part of the Commentary on *Idra raba* which was not included in *Adir bamarom* and was published by Y. Spiner as *Sefer adir bamarom, ḥelek sheni* ['*Adir bamarom*, Part II'; hereafter *Adir bamarom* II] (Jerusalem, 1988), where they are on pp. 52 and 69. The second passage is taken from a text incorporated as a separate section in manuscripts and printed in *Ginzei ramḥa"l* under the title *Perush ma'amar arimat yaday bitselotin* ['Commentary on the Passage "I lifted up my hands in prayer" '], where the reference to *Berit menuḥah* is on p. 224. In a different version of the same composition printed in *Ginzei ramḥa"l* under the title *Ma'amar hare'utin* the mention of *Berit menuḥah* is on p. 254. And see the editor's introduction, ibid. 216–18.

(*c*) 'And they [the holy names in the three confessional prayers (*viduyim*) in the Yom Kippur order of service] have special vowel-points, and they are mentioned in the book *Berit menuḥah*' (*Sefer kitsur hakavanot*, ed. H. Friedlaender and Y. Spiner (Benei Berak, 1978), 125); 'After that, in the mystery of the *yiḥud*, it is necessary to arouse the Glory [*hakavod*] to illuminate all the lights in Creation; *these are those that are mentioned in the book Berit menuḥah*' (ibid. 166).

(*d*) 'And that is the ascent until the tenth millennium *to which the author of Berit menuḥah referred, and with which he concluded*. And hence it can be seen, incidentally, that R. H. V[ital] (may his memory be for a blessing in the world to come) rightly regarded as mistaken the opinion that the world would be renewed at the end of seven sabbatical periods [7×7,000 years], *for the above-mentioned book* [*Berit menuḥah*], *a book greatly to be respected, most valuable, and reliable in all that it says*, assigns the end of the world [to] the tenth millennium, as explained in its foreword' (*Pitḥei ḥokhmah vada'at* (Warsaw, 1884), 24*a*); 'The configuration of Ze'ir Anpin originated in [stern] judgement, that is to say, it is that which comes forth straight out of the mighty judgements of [the configuration of] Ima ['Mother'—which lies above it and is associated with stern judgements—Trans.]. This is the esoteric meaning of the reference to the letter *vav* as the letter of [stern] judgement in the book *Berit menuḥah*' (ibid. 27*b*). [*Vav* is one of the standard designations of the sefirah Tiferet, corresponding to the configuration of the sefirah Ze'ir Anpin.—Trans.] The section containing these two references to *Berit menuḥah* was printed as a separate work entitled *Igerot pitḥei ḥokhmah vada'at* ['Letters Relating to "Gateways to Wisdom and Understanding" '] in *Sha'arei ramḥa"l*, ed. Friedlaender, where the references in question appear on pp. 380, 392. And see ibid., editor's introduction, 359.

hamerkavah[260] and *Mishkenei elyon*,[261] the influence of *Berit menuḥah* is recognizable though not acknowledged.[262] In addition, the appearance of the *magid* to Luzzatto in the form of the angel Shemui'el bears the hallmark of *Berit menuḥah*.

Shemui'el (or Shamu'el) appears in *heikhalot* literature and in the Zohar, especially in *Tikunei hazohar*, but it was only in *Berit menuḥah* that he earned a central position in the world of the angels[263] and was credited with the revelation of secrets of the Godhead.[264] R. Moses Cordovero wrote in two of his works that *Berit menuḥah* was composed under the inspiration of an angel or a *magid* conveying revelations from on high.[265] Most important in the present

[260] *Ginzei ramḥa"l*, 313–32, 333–40. See above, text referring to n. 252, and the note itself. In describing the 'corners' [*pinot*] as states of love, fear, peace, and strength, Luzzatto was following in the footsteps of *Berit menuḥah*, 3*a–b*. See *Ginzei ramḥa"l*, editor's introduction, 310–12. *Berit menuḥah*, 3*a–b*, speaks of four paths or places linked with four holy names, without any connection with the subject of the chariot. The four corners of the chariot appear at pp. 22*b*–(27)[26]*a* of *Berit menuḥah*, and the form given to them by Luzzatto accords with what was said on the paths of the divine names at the beginning of the book. Echoes of a prayer in *Berit menuḥah*, 30*a*–31*a*, found their way into the prayers Luzzatto appended to *Pinot hamerkavah*.

[261] See n. 64 above.

[262] It is also probable that Luzzatto was influenced by *Berit menuḥah* in his choice of the title *Mesilah ha'olah b*[*eit*]*"a*[*lef*] ['A Highway Going Up to Bethel'] for a treatise, since lost, which was in the possession of R. Zadok Bloch, a pupil of R. Hayim of Volozhin (see Essay 9, n. 62). Similar expressions are, indeed, used in Scripture (Judg. 20: 31, 21: 19) but the language is not identical and is unsuited for application to a kabbalistic-mystical work. The following are two passages from *Berit menuḥah* which, in my opinion, moved Luzzatto to fix on this title for his treatise: 'And this light, when it issues and spreads out from that fine and choice root, without any admixture and exceedingly pure and to be feared, *ascends by the highway that goes up to Bethel*' (15*b*); 'For when the great light issues from the root of roots, from the *metsi'ut* [the supernal source], it darkens some lights and makes others blaze up, makes some seraphim burn and weakens some mighty ones, and, *in going out, it ascends by the highway that goes up to Bethel*; and on this highway it is a journey of six hundred parasangs from the way of the *ḥashmalim*, possessors of the power and the dominion' (25*b*).

[263] See R. Margaliot, *Malakhei elyon* (Jerusalem, 1945), 194–6; Benayahu, 'Ha"magid" shel ramḥa"l', 304–5.

[264] 'These three angels [Shemui'el, Metatron, Yeho'el] *reveal the secrets of this name* [the Tetragrammaton] *to* [all] *creatures* in order to make known His glory and His majestic power, which is the root of our Torah and the basis of our faith' (*Berit menuḥah*, 2*b*). This passage is quoted by R. Judah Kuriyat in his *Ma'or vashemesh* (Livorno, 1839), 124*a*, where he names *Berit menuḥah* as his source. His text reads: 'And they reveal the secrets of God [*ha'el*] to [all] creatures.'

[265] 'And we will present a further proof from the book *Berit menuḥah* . . . And from his words it can be seen with certainty that they are a tradition transmitted from mouth to mouth or from the mouth of an angel, things which cannot be grasped by much study or intellectual subtlety but [show] a wonderful understanding, approaching close to the holy spirit' (*Pardes rimonim*, *Sha'ar hanekudot* (Gate 28)); 'I regard all the words of that book [*Berit menuḥah*] as the words of the holy spirit, transmitted from mouth to mouth or by the mouth of a faithful *magid* to a saintly and holy man' (*Derishot be'inyenei hamalakhim* (published by R. Margaliot at the end of his book *Malakhei elyon*), 9–10).

context is the praise accorded to *Berit menuḥah* in R. Hayim Vital's foreword to *Sha'ar hahakdamot* and in Vital's note in the name of the Ari which was placed at the head of Vital's *Otserot ḥayim*.[266] This note also heads *Otserot ḥayim* in MS Jewish Theological Seminary, New York, Mic. 1615, which was in Luzzatto's possession when he was beginning to concern himself with the study of kabbalah.[267] The note in the manuscript reads as follows:

The book called *Berit menuḥah* is true and was composed by a scholar greatly learned in the science [of kabbalah] and trustworthy, hiding the words of the science very deep. *It was written at the dictation of the soul of a certain tsadik of long ago.* (M[oses] Z[acuto] said: 'In my collection of pamphlets it is written that it was R. Hamai Gaon—may his memory be for a blessing—who revealed himself to him and taught him.')[268]

[266] The foreword and the note were also printed at the head of *Ets ḥayim* (Korets, 1782). The statement by Vital in the foreword to *Sha'ar hahakdamot* [one of the eight 'gates' which make up *Ets ḥayim*—Trans.] reads as follows: 'The book entitled *Berit hamenuḥah* was also composed in the above-mentioned manner, as in the case of my late teacher and master, for the soul of a certain tsadik appeared to him and taught him, and all his words are closed up and sealed, for he was of a faithful spirit, concealing a matter [cf. Prov. 11: 13], and deep, very deep, who can find it out? [Eccles. 7: 24]'

[267] See Essay 6, Plates 1 and 2.

[268] According to R. M. Zacuto's note, the tsadik who taught the anonymous author of *Berit menuḥah* was R. Hamai Gaon. Other scholars attributed the authorship of *Berit menuḥah* to R. Hamai. See H. J. D. Azulai, *Shem hagedolim*, ed. I. A. Benjacob (Vilna, 1856), 'ma'arekhet sefarim' ['books listed by titles'] 10*b* (*Berit menuḥah*), 63*b* (heading 'last part, "kabalah"'). Both versions show that kabbalists saw a close relationship between *Berit menuḥah* and *Sefer ha'iyun*, which was attributed to R. Hamai Gaon. In n. 258 above I offered evidence, based on the juxtaposition of the references to *Berit menuḥah* and *Mayan haḥokhmah* in *Sod hamerkavah*, indicating that Luzzatto associated the subject matter of *Berit menuḥah* with the writings of the 'circle of contemplation' [*ḥug ha'iyun*]. I draw attention here to one particular literary matter which links *Berit menuḥah* indirectly with *Mayan haḥokhmah*. At the head of *Mayan haḥokhmah* this note appears: 'This is the book *Mayan haḥokhmah* which was given by Mikhael to Pali [see below] and by Pali to our master Moses, peace be upon him, and our master Moses revealed [it] so that wisdom might be gained through it for all time to come.' According to this note *Mayan haḥokhmah* was regarded as a pseudepigraphic work attributed to Moses, but doubt is cast on that assumption by the fact that Moses is referred to in the third person in this work where it describes his struggles to grasp 'the primordial darkness' (2*a*–*b*), in language which would be quite inappropriate if the writer were attributing authorship to Moses. Since there is no reference to the angel Pali in any known source other than *Berit menuḥah* (see R. Margaliot, *Malakhei elyon*, 144), I am of the opinion that his name found its way late into the note at the head of *Mayan haḥokhmah* on the strength of the information about his greatness in *Berit menuḥah* or in the source on which the author of *Berit menuḥah* relied. The following is the principal mention of Pali: '*I found it written* that the teacher of Shem the son of Noah was named Pal"i, and therefore it is to be understood that Shemui'el the great servant [*shamash*] may have been so called. In the account of Manoah it is written [Judg. 13: 18]: "Why do you ask my name, seeing that it is *peli* ['hidden' or 'wonderful']?", whence you may draw your own conclusion' (*Berit menuḥah*, 5*b*). [The name rendered 'Pali' above is spelt *pe alef lamed yod*; the word *peli* in Judges is spelt *pe lamed alef yod*, but the Masoretes mark the *alef* as superfluous.—Trans.] Another item of information on Shemui'el is relevant here: '*It was also said* that it was

It seems probable that it was this note which so aroused Luzzatto's enthusiasm that he was impelled to study *Berit menuḥah* in depth.

Sod demut ha'adam hakelali ['The Mystery of the Image of Universal Man'] (fo. 119v)

The image of man, one of the principal patterns in kabbalistic symbolism, is variously depicted. It generally appears in two fundamental forms: (*a*) the image of man is constituted by the sum of the parts of the sefirotic system in the world of the Godhead, and similarly by those of a secondary system of sefirot in the non-divine domain; (*b*) through the intercourse of male and female powers in the sefirotic system, the image of man is brought into existence in the dual form of the bestower of the divine flow and its recipient.[269]

This short 'mystery' describes a different way in which the image of man arises through the processes of divine intercourse: Malkhut, which is the last sefirah in the celestial system and is the female recipient, includes within itself the non-divine levels of existence when it copulates with the male powers of the Divinity, and the image of man which comes into existence through such intercourse is in the nature of an 'image of universal man', in that 'the Godhead and the *nifradim* ['the separated ones': the non-divine beings]' unite

from the angel Shemui'el that Abraham and Moses received [sc. divine wisdom] when they penetrated to the furthest limits of wisdom, as it is written [Exod. 20: 21] "And Moses drew near to the thick darkness where God was", that is the angel Shemui'el' (*Berit menuḥah*, 17*d*). (Incidentally, the perception of Shemui'el as the revealer of the secrets of divine wisdom to Moses may also have served as background to the fact that the *magid* revealed himself to Luzzatto in the form of that angel.) *Berit menuḥah* was written in the first decades of the fourteenth century, as I showed in my book *Meshiḥiyut bedor gerushei sefarad uportugal* (Jerusalem, 1985), 137 n. 14. The writings of the 'circle of contemplation', and especially *Sefer ha'iyun* and *Mayan haḥokhmah*, are considered in detail by Scholem, *Kabbalah*, 273–92.

[269] See Tishby, *Wisdom of the Zohar*, i. 295–302, and many similar references. Particular attention should be drawn to the perception of the angels as patterned on the image of man. In addition to descriptions of individual angels as being in the image of man, kabbalistic literature also applies anthropomorphism to angelological systems in the realm of the Chariot and below the Chariot. See *Wisdom of the Zohar*, i. 297; ii. 624–5. Basing myself on the Zohar III, 143*a*–*b* (*Idra raba*), I indicated that, unlike the angels, the Sitra Ahra is not constructed in the image of man (*Wisdom of the Zohar*, ii. 623). And see ibid. 464–5. On the basis of the Zohar I, 245*a*–*b*, I wrote: 'The forces of the chariot are like the body of the Shekhinah, which works in them and through them just as the soul works in and through the body' (*Wisdom of the Zohar*, ii. 590). I presented the same idea in different terms, ibid. 624 (and see ibid. 635), on the basis of the Zohar II, 142*a*–*b*, and I, 136*b* (*Midrash hanelam*). Most of the passages on which I have relied are translated into Hebrew in my anthology [and thence into English in *Wisdom of the Zohar*] and in accordance with the practice followed in all my introductions I have quoted their headings in the anthology without giving specific references to their position in the Zohar itself. [In the body of the anthology, however, references are given at the head of each text.—Trans.]

in it and adhere to each other.[270] The combination of the non-divine aspects of existence in Malkhut with the divine entity which bestows the divine flow is 'the essence of the union'.

With regard to the nature of the connection between Malkhut and 'the separated ones' in the formation of the 'image of universal man', Luzzatto writes: 'In this mystery there are three female [elements]': that is to say, by the inclusion of 'the separated ones' in Malkhut, Malkhut appears with three aspects, called Shekhinah, *Keneset yisra'el* ['the assembly of Israel'], and *Kalat mosheh* ['the bride of Moses']. In Shekhinah, union exists because Malkhut dwells within 'the separated ones';[271] in *Keneset yisra'el* 'she [Malkhut] is the sum of the "separated ones" who are joined together in her'; in *Kalat mosheh* 'an outspreading from the Shekhinah itself' develops strongly. The description of the image of man which results from the union with 'the bride of Moses' is also entirely novel in its view of the masculine influence, for 'intercourse can take place between it [Malkhut] and the souls, which become male in relation to her'.[272]

[270] In *Igerot pitḥei ḥokhmah vada'at* matters relating to the image of man are explained at length. Distinctions are drawn between the image of man without further definition, or 'the image of individual man', and 'the image of universal man'; and Luzzatto says, *inter alia*, 'This one is in the universal image, and also in the image of man in the combination of "emanation, creation, formation, and making", which, too, is universal' (*Sha'arei ramḥa"l*, ed. Friedlaender, 369).

[271] My assumption that the appellation 'Shekhinah' denotes the unity of Malkhut with 'the separated ones' [i.e. those who are not divine], inasmuch as Malkhut dwells in them, is not confirmed here in explicit terms. But the context requires that the vague remark 'i.e. the Shekhinah, which is Malkhut among the lights' should be spelt out in this way. In the Zohar emphasis is laid on the essential difference between the position of the Shekhinah in relation to the upper worlds, as a sefirah belonging to the divine system, and its position with regard to the lower worlds of 'creation, formation, and making', with which it is joined as their head. The difference is presented as a contradiction which is hard to resolve. See Tishby, *Wisdom of the Zohar*, i. 372–5; ii. 550–1. Luzzatto's distinction between Malkhut, on the one hand, and 'Shekhinah', 'the Assembly of Israel', and 'the bride of Moses', on the other—Malkhut being entirely in the world of emanation while the other three include 'the separated ones'—comes close in principle to the distinction drawn in Joseph Caro's *Magid meisharim* between Malkhut, which is divine, and Shekhinah and Matronita, 'the matron'. See Werblowsky, *Joseph Karo*, 216–33.

[272] The intercourse with 'the bride of Moses' is more clearly described in the commentary on 'arimat yaday bitselotin': 'And the secret of *hbl* [apparently for *hkl* = *hakol*, 'everything'] is *the bride* [*kalat*, absolute form *kalah*, consonants *klh*] *of Moses* . . . for the Shekhinah becomes the [sexual] partner of every Jew . . . and that is the essence of the activity of the righteous, [namely] that the Emanator, blessed be His name, has given them an existence in which they may draw out light from holiness itself; that is to say, when the soul of the righteous man adheres to the Shekhinah there will be renewed from above the light which ought to be renewed, and it will extend to that level of the Shekhinah to which I have referred, at which she becomes their partner' (*Ginzei ramḥa"l*, 244). The 'light of holiness' which the souls of the righteous draw down upon the Shekhinah is the light of the male sefirot which bestow the divine flow; and therefore, also, the union of the souls with 'the bride of Moses' is the union of 'the Godhead and the

At the end of this 'mystery' it becomes clear that the union of 'the separated ones' with the sefirah Malkhut, apart from its universal element, has a particular Jewish national significance, as is stated in this sentence: 'In the assembly of Israel all Israel are included in David; and for the purpose of "the bride of Moses" all Israel are included in Moses, and he has intercourse with her.' David and Moses are the symbols of Malkhut and Tiferet, but this statement contains an unmistakably messianic allusion: David is Messiah ben David, and our master Moses is destined to head the two Messiahs, unify them, and lead them. Luzzatto ascribed to himself, as others did to him, the eschatological rank of Moses, and R. Moses David Valle regarded himself, and was regarded in Luzzatto's circle, as Messiah ben David.[273]

Sod hayiḥud ['The Mystery of the *yiḥud*'] (fos. 119v–127r)

'The mystery of the *yiḥud*' as commonly understood in the teachings of kabbalah means principally the reinforcement of unity in the system of the ten divine sefirot; this is achieved by strengthening the bond between them through processes of intercourse, and by elevating them to their source in the realm of the Emanator (Keter or Ein Sof). The establishment of unity occurs in the particular rhythm of divine life and in man's theurgic activities—mystical meditation in prayer, and the fulfilment of the commandments.[274]

At the beginning of his treatise *Sod hayiḥud*, Luzzatto draws a distinction between the state of 'beginning and end' and that of 'the middle' in the existence of the Godhead and in the nature of the relations between divine and non-divine existence. On the basis of this distinction two different levels are portrayed in the processes of the *yiḥud*: 'couplings of the middle' and, on the other hand, 'couplings of the beginning and end'. For the better understanding of this novel distinction and the processes it involves, I quote Luzzatto's statements verbatim, adding an explanation based on ideas to be found in other writings:[275]

> Ein Sof was perfect long ago as it is now and as it will be, quite unchanged, in time to come, but at the beginning perfection was not revealed in actuality; later on it was revealed in actuality. And because [Ein Sof—Trans.] desired to bring about this revelation, three situations were distinguished: beginning [*rosh*], end [*sof*], and middle [*emtsa*], 'beginning' meaning the perfection which was potentially existent from the start, 'end' the perfection which will be revealed in actual existence here-

separated ones'. In *Wisdom of the Zohar*, iii. 990–2, I showed that the righteous man's love of God created an erotic relationship between him and the Shekhinah like that between her and Moses, who had the rank of 'husband of the Shekhinah'. Luzzatto's view corresponds to that of the Zohar.

273 See Essay 3, pp. 198–206; and Essay 6, pp. 306–14, 324–36.

274 See Tishby, *Wisdom of the Zohar*, i. 238–42.

275 The quotations and references are in accordance with the text printed in *Ginzei ramḥa"l*.

after, and 'middle' applying to it while it has not yet been revealed. And neither in beginning nor in end does evil exist, for everything is for the good; but the middle contains what previously appeared to be evil but is in truth good, and that is called *shem vekhinuy* ['name and appellation'].[276] (*Ginzei ramḥa"l*, 264)

The existence of perfection, the longed-for ideal state, is conditional on the universality of absolute good, with no evil in existence in any shape or form. In the character of Ein Sof, the supreme divine being, perfection is present at all the levels of existence, but at the very beginning [*rosh*], before there were any beings other than Ein Sof, its perfection was only potential, because it was not in contention with imperfection. From this point of view the purpose of Creation was to invent imperfection, by the removal of which the perfection of Ein Sof would be revealed and firmly established in actuality (*sof* ['end']). For the fulfilment of this purpose it was necessary to create evil, the opposite and total negation of the uniform perfection of the Godhead. Evil strives to gain mastery over existence by its destructive power, but is destined to be annulled with the help of action by holy souls (*emtsa* ['middle']). Evil, whose own existence is an imagined reality, will be annulled by its restoration to good, from which it developed through the desire of the Godhead to bring its own perfection from the potential to the actual state.[277]

[276] The terms *rosh* ['beginning'], *emtsa* or *tavekh* ['middle'], and *sof* ['end'] to describe the past, present, and future existence of the Godhead on the pattern of 'was, is, and shall be' are found in the writings of German hasidism and those of R. Abraham Abulafia. See M. Idel, 'Hasefirot sheme'al hasefirot', *Tarbiz*, 51 (1982), 261 n. 110. See also Y. Liebes, 'Sefer "Tsadik yesod olam": mitos shabeta'i', *Da'at*, 1 (1978), 98 n. 131, 101 n. 152, on the subject of *str*—the initial letters of *sof*, *tavekh*, *rosh* (see above), which together spell *seter* ['secrecy']. In Luzzatto's writings these terms are used with different and more complex meanings.

[277] Here, for example, is a paragraph on the subject of the invention of evil as the opposite of the Godhead so that the Godhead may realize its own unity by annulling evil and restoring it to good: 'The esoteric meaning of the matter is that the Emanator, blessed be He, wished to demonstrate His unity, which is actually seen in the restoration of evil to good, in this way, that what seems to be His opposite is not other than He, but that He is everything, and the opposite is only apparently so, since in the end it is good; so that certainly His existence alone is what exists, and none other than He has existence . . . and as against all these He created evil, which is His opposite . . . and when it was finally seen how this opposite is not other than He, His unity was made absolutely clear' (*Adir bamarom* II, 38–9). The idea of the amelioration [*tikun*] of evil—in the sense of original cosmic evil, i.e. the Sitra Ahra—and its restoration to good is contrary to authentic Lurianic kabbalah, which pinned its belief to the destruction of evil in time to come (see n. 285 below). The view that evil was destined to undergo *tikun* was introduced into the system of Lurianic thought by Nathan of Gaza's kabbalah, in which that idea occupied a central position. See Wirszubsky, 'Hate'ologyah hashabeta'it shel natan ha'azati', 234–41. Nathan's teaching was succinctly stated by Wirszubsky: 'The purpose of Ein Sof in bringing into existence the structures of the husks . . . was principally to create the possibility of purifying and annulling evil . . . the structure of the husks has to arise so as to make it possible to refine and cleanse it until it is entirely restored to purity.' It appears that Luzzatto borrowed the idea from Nathan of Gaza and developed and altered it to accord with his pattern of thought. I point

out here two fundamental alterations: on the one hand Luzzatto omitted the allocation of the *tikun* of evil to the Messiah Shabetai Tsevi; on the other, he added the statement that evil was invented to provide a practical manifestation of the perfect unity of the divine Emanator through the annulment of the imagined existence of His opposite. In this regard as in other speculative topics which I have discussed in previous essays, Luzzatto furnishes a bridge between Shabateanism and hasidism. His influence is most conspicuous in the formulations of 'the restoration of evil to good' in Habad hasidism, and especially in the writings of R. Aaron Halevi of Starosielce. See Tishby and Dan, under 'Ḥasidut', in *Ha'entsiklopedyah ha'ivrit*, xvii. 790–5. I stated (ibid. 777–8): 'R. Aaron Halevi takes evil as the work of the Holy One, blessed be He, who invented His opposite in order that His unity should be revealed by the annulment of the opposite in time to come.' And in Essay 9, n. 72, I wrote: 'There are also clear signs of Luzzatto's influence in some characteristic ideas of the Habad movement: among others, one of the central ideas in the writings of R. Aaron Halevi of Starosielce—that when bringing evil into existence God created its opposite so that it could be annulled in time to come—is rooted in the view of evil and the purpose of its existence in Luzzatto's doctrine.' R. Aaron Halevi's views on this subject were explained in detail by Rachel Elior in her book *Torat ha'elohut bador hasheni shel ḥasidut ḥaba"d* (Jerusalem, 1982), chapter headed 'Torat hahipukh', 244–88. However, she did not there report my statement that the doctrine of opposites—*torat hahipukh*—had its origin in the writings of Luzzatto. It should be pointed out that the view that the Sitra Ahra would one day turn back to good and holiness is present as an esoteric idea in Luzzatto's doctrine. In most of his writings in which 'the restoration of evil to good' is presented and explained without reference to 'unification of the middle' and 'unification of the beginning and end', his theme in general is that of turning the results of evil actions by the Sitra Ahra into good; that is, correcting the misdeeds and corruption in the ways of man and the world and firmly establishing the unity of perfect goodness in the realm of the Godhead, free of any clash between Hesed, lovingkindness, and Din, judgement. He does sometimes say explicitly that the Sitra Ahra will be destroyed, which accords with the authentic Lurianic view. To demonstrate the esoteric character of his use of the 'restoration of evil to good' to apply to the Sitra Ahra itself, I will quote the summary of the principles of kabbalah which appears at the end of *Igerot pitḥei ḥokhmah vada'at* (see n. 270 above): 'There are three kinds of knowledge, *one within the other*, in the science of truth [kabbalah]. They are drawn successively from knowledge of the purpose [*kavanah*] of the Creation. The superficial purpose is that the Emanator, blessed be His name, created His world in order to provide a place for the attributes . . . that He might be called merciful and gracious, slow to anger, and so on . . . The second [degree of] knowledge relating to the purpose is that the Emanator, blessed be His name, created the world in order to bestow perfect good on living creatures—which they would receive through merit and not out of charity . . . *finally, after the evil comes the good, and the Sitra Ahra perishes, and holiness becomes complete*; and then all souls will receive, through their merit . . . the third [degree of] knowledge of the purpose, which is wonderful knowledge indeed, namely that the Emanator, blessed be His name, wished to reveal His unity, to show that "I am the first and I am the last" [Isa. 44: 6], and in any event *every curse would be turned into a blessing and all evil would revert to good* . . . and after that there follows the acquisition of knowledge of all the sefirot—that they all return to the supernal unity of Ein Sof, blessed be He. This has not been so well grasped in our times; it is indeed the essence of the faith of Israel—to know the unity of the Emanator, blessed be His name' (*Sha'arei ramḥa"l*, ed. Friedlaender, 404). The first degree of knowledge, 'the superficial purpose', is limited to an understanding of the activity of the sefirot in the governance of the world before the Redemption, with Hesed and Din, the opposing principles of lovingkindness and judgement, existing side by side. Luzzatto calls this 'the governance of justice [*mishpat*]', or 'the governance of reward and punishment'. The second degree of knowledge extends to awareness of the perfect and enduring good to be bestowed on humanity at the end of days, when the world will be

The two ways by which 'the mystery of the *yiḥud*' proceeds are two routes to the establishment of perfect unity, as is explained in *Ginzei ramḥa"l*:

Thus there are two kinds of coupling: the couplings of the middle and those of the beginning and end. That is to say, [divine] unity must become manifest, and it is revealed to a small extent through the couplings in which the left submits to the right, goodness rules, and evil changes back to good. And when it has finished revealing itself in the middle, as a matter of course the beginning and the end remain joined together, for then we find that all are one—beginning and end and middle, all is good, without any evil whatsoever . . . Indeed, all the couplings of the middle are those which are mentioned [as occurring] in *atsilut*, the world of emanation. But the coupling of beginning and end is another matter, being the coupling of Emanation with the glory in *beriah* [the world of Creation]; for the essence of the *tikun* is that the beings below should be[278] firmly attached [*nidbakim*] to those above, until all are attached to Ein Sof, blessed be He. [This] is then called [the state in which] all are one; it is the completion of the middle and the joining of the beginning and end; it is the whole essence of the service of Heaven in truth. (*Ginzei ramḥa"l*, 264)

Unity is brought about by means of sexual couplings. In situations occurring in the 'middle', in the modes of existence before the Redemption, couplings take place between the divine sefirot in the realms of *atsilut* ['Emanation'], and the divine flow so created weakens the power of evil and gradually helps to establish and stabilize the unification of 'beginning' and 'end', in which 'all is good, without any evil whatsoever'. The 'couplings of the middle', then, are equivalent in principle to the well-known couplings in the doctrine of kabbalah. Quite different from them are the 'couplings of beginning and end', which are described as 'the coupling of Emanation with the glory in Creation'. The text goes on to explain that 'the glory in Creation' is the Shekhinah which resides in the palaces of the world of Creation.[279] 'The separated ones' are engendered through the alliance of the Shekhinah with the palaces, and the Shekhinah functions in them as a soul in the body. Hence 'the glory in Creation' is, in fact, a divine force and 'the separated ones' constitute a single female entity: 'This soul [the Shekhinah in the palaces] counts as female in relation to Emanation, and then intercourse takes place between Emanation and Creation.'[280]

ruled under 'the governance of unity', the Sitra Ahra will be destroyed, and the sole authority will be the holiness of God. And see n. 253 above. The third degree of knowledge, which remains hidden 'in our times', achieves the discovery of the absolute unity which comes about through the return of all existence to the depths of the Emanator, Ein Sof, but even in the description of this kind of knowledge the restoration of the Sitra Ahra to good is expressed only in indirect terms: 'and all evil returns to good'. And see n. 289 below.

278 As in the manuscript. There is an error in the printed version: 'were' instead of 'will be'.

279 See Tishby, *Wisdom of the Zohar*, i. 589–94.

280 *Ginzei ramḥa"l*, 265.

The theosophical and cosmogonic ideas which picture divine unity manifesting itself in actuality, along with the annulment of the imagined existence of evil and its restoration to good, often figure prominently in Luzzatto's writings as a major factor in the processes which take place in Emanation and Creation. But in only a few of his works do we find these processes described as conditions of 'beginning and end' as opposed to conditions of the 'middle'. Chief of these few is *Perush idra raba*, in particular one section of it which was circulated as a separate work in two versions—in the commentary on the passage of the Zohar headed 'Arimat yaday bitselotin' ['I lifted up my hands in prayer'] and under the title *Ma'amar hare'utin*.[281] The connection between *Sod hayiḥud* and the particular section of *Perush idra raba* is very close, and in many cases identical expressions are used. On the other hand several important matters which in *Sod hayiḥud* are passed over with no more than obscure allusions or are not mentioned at all are emphasized and clarified in *Perush idra raba*.[282] By way of example I cite below three central subjects in relation to which the explanation in *Sod hayiḥud* is amplified.

1. The 'unification' of 'name and appellation' as opposed to the 'unification' of 'My name and My memorial'.[283] The Tetragrammaton YHVH, all the sefirot above the Shekhinah, particularly Tiferet, and the name Elohim which denotes the sefirah Malkhut, constitute 'name and appellation'. Malkhut, too, referred to as *kinuy* ['appellation'], is an integral part of the sefirotic system, but represents the attribute of strict judgement that came into existence in the processes of differentiating the divine powers into the two opposites, mercy and judgement (Hesed and Din), from which those other opposites, good and evil, sprang and took shape outside the Godhead. Thus the presence of 'name and appellation' in the world of emanation reflects the state called the 'middle' in the existence of the Godhead, i.e. the absence of perfect unity because of the existence of the principle of mutual opposition; and through the joining together of 'name and appellation' in the 'couplings of the middle' between Tiferet and Malkhut, the 'separated ones', too, are exalted, and evil changes back to good. However, the processes of unification of the opposites—symbolized by *yod alef he lamed vav he he yod mem*, a combination of the letters of the Tetragrammaton with those of Elohim—take place solely in the realm of the Godhead. In contrast, 'My name and My memorial', the Tetragrammaton together with the name Adonai, stands for the male sefirot in the divine system in relation to

[281] The section in *Perush idra raba* is printed in *Adir bamarom* II, 61–95. The different versions contained in the two works mentioned are printed in *Ginzei ramḥa"l*, 219–45, 246–58.

[282] The matters dealt with in this section, among them the 'unification' [*yiḥud*] of 'name and appellation', are considered from another point of view by Avivi in his essay 'Kavanat haberiah beḥiburei ramḥa"l'.

[283] As in Exod. 3: 15.

Malkhut–Shekhinah when she dwells within 'the separated ones' and is merged with them as 'the glory in Creation'. Therefore the joining together of 'My name and My memorial' takes place in the 'couplings of beginning and end', in which 'the separated ones' are contained actually in the divine female participant in the coupling, and the existence of mutual opposition is entirely nullified through the 'unification of the separated ones with their root'. This process is symbolized by *alef he dalet vav nun he yod*, a combination of the letters of the Tetragrammaton with those of Adonai.[284]

2. The relationship between *atsilut* ['emanation'] and *beit yod ayin* (*beriah*, *yetsirah*, and *asiyah* ['creation, formation, and making', the three worlds of creation below *atsilut*]) in the acts of intercourse. The ways in which the various couplings proceed, and the relationship between them, are more precisely explained by the statement that there are two, or—subdividing one of them—three, arrangements or patterns [*sedarim*] according to which bonds are established between Emanation and *beit yod ayin*—the Godhead and 'the separated ones'. In the first pattern, Emanation is the root and *beit yod ayin* the many branches which spread outwards from the root, 'and in this way all the *tikunim* [the processes of restoration to perfection] take place in *atsilut*, the world of emanation, as do all the couplings; and the worlds of *beit yod ayin* become wings for the female'. In the second pattern '*atsilut* is reckoned entirely as the soul and *beit yod ayin* as its body, the one corresponding to the other'. The bond between soul and body, sharing as they do a joint image, is closer than that between root and branches or body and wings; nevertheless in the second arrangement, too, the *tikunim* and the couplings take place solely in the realms of *atsilut*, and only the influence which flows from the couplings reaches the worlds of *beit yod ayin*. In the third pattern '*atsilut* is entirely male, and the Glory [the Shekhinah] with all its branches [*beit yod ayin*] is entirely female'; that is to say, *beit yod ayin*, all of the 'separated ones', participate in the couplings as an organic part of the copulating female. In the first two patterns the action is the joining together of 'name and appellation', producing the composite name *yod alef he lamed vav he he yod mem* [see above], in 'the couplings of the middle', but the second pattern constitutes a kind of transition to the joining together of 'My name and My memorial' by the composite *yod alef he dalet vav nun he yod*, in 'the couplings of beginning and end'. It is in the last-mentioned couplings, says Luzzatto, that 'the essence of the *yiḥud*' occurs, 'for this is a truly universal unification in which even the separated ones unite in adherence to their root, since they are entitled to be so unified. Not so the couplings of *atsilut* alone; in that case the *yiḥud* takes place only within *atsilut*'.[285]

[284] See *Ginzei ramḥa"l*, 264–5; *Adir bamarom* II, 65–9.

[285] *Adir bamarom* II, 69–70. A work by Luzzatto published under the title *Sefer kitsur haka-*

3. Final *tikun* and preliminary *tikunim*. 'The turning back of evil to good', 'the manifestation of unity' [*giluy hayiḥud*], and 'the unification of "the separated ones" with their root' are eschatological goals, which when realized will bring about a *tikun*, a return to perfection, completely overturning the existing order of the worlds and the celestial system. On the other hand the actions carried out by those who perform *yiḥudim* in their worship of God are partial and preliminary *tikunim* which lead gradually to the completion of the 'manifestation of unity'. Here is a description of the significance of the preliminary *tikunim*:

And only according to the [degree of] preparation which the end receives from the worship [the performance of *yiḥudim*], only by so much will the beginning draw near to it, little by little, and unity reveal itself; and we shall gain one degree each time, until when all the couplings which take place in six thousand years are gath-

vanot, ed. H. Friedlaender and Y. Finer (Benei Berak, 1978), sets out in detail a comprehensive series of *kavanot* ['mystical meditations'] for use in prayer (pp. 1–161), which are described as *kavanot* for the 'couplings' of *atsilut* ['emanation'] in accordance with the instructions in Luria's kabbalah. At the end of this work there is a small section (pp. 162–71) headed 'General *kavanah* of prayer' which, in point of size, is no more than a short appendix, but which is important for its content. Turning time and again for support to the commentaries *Perush 'arimat yaday bitselotin'* and *Perush idra raba*, this section presents a complete set of higher *kavanot* of prayer alluding to the mystery of the coupling of *beit yod ayin* [the three lower worlds of creation, formation, and making] with *atsilut* (p. 162), that is to say, the 'couplings of beginning and end'. This set is called 'the order of the *kavanah* for the manifestation of union' (p. 170). At the end of the section we find the following: 'Know that this *kavanah* should not be undertaken if one does not first undertake the *kavanah* of *the couplings of atsilut*, for it is not possible to stimulate *the joining together of beginning and end* without first having brought about *the joining of the middle*, but you can undertake that *kavanah* without this [one]' (p. 171). At first sight it appears that the *kavanot* for 'the couplings of the middle' are identical to the Lurianic *kavanot* for 'the couplings of *atsilut*' which were previously presented in the body of *Kitsur hakavanot*, but in fact these are two essentially different groups. The purpose of the *kavanot* for 'the couplings of the middle' is to further the eschatological mission of 'turning evil back to good'; this is contrary to authentic Lurianic kabbalah, which teaches, as a matter of both theory and practice, the destruction of evil in time to come, except in the case of the husk Nogah and the inner substance of the husks which is of holy origin. See Tishby, *Torat hara vehakelipah*, 137–42. And indeed, even in Luria's *kavanot* as embodied by Luzzatto in *Kitsur hakavanot*, there is no mention of 'turning evil back to good'; the actions of the *tikun* are described, in conformity with Luria's original teachings, as processes of raising up sparks from the husks, which means in essence depriving the husks of their vitality in order to destroy them. It follows, then, that 'the couplings of *atsilut*' in the sense of 'the couplings of the middle' are not the same as 'the couplings of *atsilut*' in Lurianic *kavanot*. The two levels in 'the couplings of *atsilut*' are identical with the first two patterns of such couplings which I have explained in this essay by reference to their description in *Perush idra raba*; and *Kitsur hakavanot*, in its presentation of the patterns of these couplings (pp. 164–5), states plainly that the Lurianic *kavanot* are arranged on the basis of the first of them, namely the 'open' level of 'the couplings of *atsilut*' in which the three lower worlds of creation—*beriah*, *yetsirah*, *asiyah*—serve as branches and wings for the Shekhinah. The inferior status of Lurianic *kavanot* in the patterns of these couplings is also alluded to in *Kitsur kavanot*, 7.

ered together, unity [*hayiḥud*] is revealed in its full perfection. And understand this well, that every coupling is a manifestation of unity in the measure which is proper to be revealed in that period, until it is revealed in its entirety.[286]

However, even in the final *tikun* there will be stages in the establishment of complete oneness [*aḥdut*]. In the messianic redemption which will take place in the sixth millennium, oneness will come about through the restoration of evil to good, like the twilight of a Sabbath eve 'which causes all the secular affairs of the week to enter into the holiness of the Sabbath'.[287] In the seventh millennium, which is a mystical Sabbath, 'there will occur the revelation of [i.e. belonging to—Trans.] the end', but 'the equalization of beginning and end by which it is known that all is one' will be realized only in the renewal of the world in the eighth millennium: 'And this is the difference between the seventh millennium and the eighth, for in the seventh the beginning will reach the end and be joined to it, and in the eighth they will all become equal as [they were] at first. That is the mystery of perfect unity [*hayiḥud hashalem*], to which Scripture alludes in "the Lord shall be One and His name One" [Zech. 14: 9].'[288] In other words, the era of 'the manifestation of unity' in all its perfection will come after the period of 'the end of days' and after the destruction of the world.[289]

286 *Adir bamarom* II, 41. 287 Ibid. 61. 288 Ibid. 40.

289 And see '138 Gateways to Wisdom', Gateway 49, end of commentary, which describes the ways in which the 'manifestation of union' will occur in the days of the Messiah in the sixth millennium, in the period of rest during the destruction of the world in the seventh millennium, and when the pinnacle of perfection is reached in the renewal of the world in the eighth millennium. In two important works by Luzzatto which have recently been discovered and published—*Yiḥud hayirah*, with its commentary (see Section IX above, text referring to nn. 194–9, and the notes themselves), and *Takta"v tefilot* ['515 Prayers'], ed. Ulman—matters described as 'beginning', 'middle', and 'end' are referred to but in meanings different from those that I identified for them in my consideration of *Sod hayiḥud*. I have prepared a detailed explanation of these passages, particularly with regard to the many wide-ranging aspects of '515 Prayers', but I must content myself here with some brief remarks. In *Yiḥud hayirah* the *kavanot* for 'the couplings of the middle' and 'the couplings of the beginning and end' have a personal purpose, the entry of the performer of the *yiḥud* into union [*hitḥaberut*] with the divine order through the ascent of an ecstatic soul, by way of the sefirot and the forces above the sefirot, culminating in contact with Ein Sof. These *kavanot* were intended first and foremost to earn for Luzzatto himself the privilege of experiencing these spiritual ascents and close contact [*hitdabekut*] with the Godhead, and to enable his soul to receive supernal lights and exalted secrets. However, *Yiḥud hayirah* was secretly circulated in his school for the use of the members of the group also. I quote here some passages from this *yiḥud* and its commentary, in the version printed under the title *Ma'amar yiḥud hayirah* as an appendix to *Adir bamarom* II, 133–64. In the body of the *yiḥud*, 'beginning, end, and middle' are referred to in the final instructions: 'And then you must meditate on including all the Name in the mystery of *alef' yod-vav-yod*, in the mystery of the supernal *yiḥud* [the letter *alef* (א), representing the unity of the sefirot, is described as made up of a *vav*—the diagonal stroke—and two *yods*—Trans.] and *join beginning and end and middle together* . . . and you will draw upon yourself fear and humility so that they are always present on your face

. . . and then apply yourself with devotion to *drawing out of this the manifestation of union* [*yiḥud*] so far as it is appropriate to that period, *in the mystery of yod-alef-he-lamed-vav-he-he-yod"mem*, which is the Lord your God' (p. 139, sects. 14–15). The explanation of these instructions in the commentary, *Perush hayiḥud*, presents more clearly the ecstatic personal experiences which are their aim: 'And meditate on combining [all the letters of] the whole Torah in this way, in which beginning and end are joined together, and *it will shine upon your soul and give you great light*' (p. 163). The instructions preceding this in the body of the *yiḥud* lay clear emphasis on mystical exaltation as a principal aim without specifically mentioning 'beginning, end, and middle'. The following are examples: 'Then begin to apply yourself to thinking of the majesty of Ein Sof, blessed be He . . . and let your thoughts be as if, so to speak, you could *see His glorious majesty standing by you*' (p. 137, sect. 1); 'Then meditate on this, that in the same measure that you concentrate your thoughts on His majesty, *so does He bring you near to give you light*' (ibid., sect. 2); 'And through this mystery *you will have an entrance to the world above*' (p. 138, sect. 8); 'Then you will unify your tripartite soul [*nefesh*, *ruaḥ*, and *neshamah*] in great humility, and *the light of Ein Sof, blessed be He, will shine upon you*' (p. 139, sect. 12). In '515 Prayers' most of the prayers—and this is their central motif—look forward to the speedy strengthening of divine unity [*yiḥud*], and its assumption of control, in the upper and lower realms. The hoped-for 'unification' is described in terms of the coming together of 'beginning, end, and middle', to which the words *emet* ['truth'] and *seter* ['secrecy'] are applied, because *emet* is composed of the first, middle, and last of the letters of the Hebrew alphabet, and the meaning of *seter* is embodied in the initial letters of *sof*, *tavekh*, *rosh* ['end, middle, beginning'] (see n. 276 above). The following is an extract from the first prayer, in which these combinations of letters are already given prominence: 'For thus You created Your world with these twenty-two [letters], with three [the letters of *emet*] which bear crowns, to show, through them, Your unity—that You are One, alone, and unique in *rosh*, *sof*, and *emtsa* ['beginning, end, and middle'], which is *seter*, *sof tavekh rosh*, in which You have hidden Your face from Israel until the time when Your unity will be manifested among them' (*Takta"v tefilot*, 37). For other examples see prayers 117, 148, 324. However, in the series of prayers the meaning and results of 'the manifestation of unity' were perceived differently. In *Sod hayiḥud* and *Perush idra raba* the principal meaning of the expected revolution was a universal overturning of the existing order in the realms of cosmic and divine existence; in '515 Prayers', on the other hand, its principal eschatological purpose was *the messianic and nationalistic redemption of the Jewish people*, whose very being was informed with the unity of God, whereas the urgent aim towards which 'the manifestation of unity' should be directed was the salvation of the group, and of Jewish society as a whole, in the immediate present. The performer of the *yiḥud*, Luzzatto, who composed the prayers, acts as 'emissary of the congregation', striving to put the achievements of his mystical ascent to work for the benefit of the humiliated assembly of Israel in the Diaspora and of the persecuted messianic group in Padua. By way of example I will mention three prayers, clearly designed for the group, which also display strong messianic and nationalistic tendencies: nos. 177 (pp. 151–2), 205 (pp. 180–5), and 212 (p. 192). Nor is the series of prayers at one with *Sod hayiḥud* in its perception of 'bringing back evil to good', for it does not treat the Sitra Ahra as destined to be restored to perfection and to be included in the realm of God's holiness. Even in the prayers which foretell the restoration of the nations to perfection at the end of days there is no mention of any such destiny awaiting the Sitra Ahra itself. All that is said is that the results of the actions of the forces of evil will be turned back to good through the transformation of the attribute of Judgement [*din*] into the attribute of Mercy [*raḥamim*]. See e.g. prayers nos. 190, 333, 389, 396, 399, 411, 445. And see nn. 277 and 285 above.

XI. COMMENTARY ON *MA'AMAR PARASHAT MISHPATIM* IN THE ZOHAR (FOS. 135ʳ–147ᵛ)

[This section of the manuscript was published in *Ginzei ramḥa"l*, ed. H. Friedlaender (Benei Berak, 1980), 272–84. The quotations and folio references here are as in the manuscript, with the addition of the corresponding references in *Ginzei ramḥa"l*. In the collection in MS Oxford 2593, between the 'mysteries' dealt with in Section X above (fos. 116ʳ–127ʳ in the manuscript) and the present section, there is a kabbalistic homily ending in a prayer. It is headed 'Formal meal for the night of 17 Shevat [*tu"v bishevat*] 5493 [1733]'. In my essay 'Shirim ufiyutim' [Essay 2, pp. 118–19] I introduced the homily and gave a brief explanation of its subject matter, and in a continuation, 'Tefilot miginzei r' mosheh ḥayim lutsato', which first appeared in *Molad*, NS 8 (31) (1980) [and is now printed here in Essay 2], I published the concluding prayer [see pp. 174–6 below]. I gave a detailed explanation of the subject matter of the homily in my essay 'Ikevot rabi mosheh ḥayim lutsato bemishnat haḥasidut' [Essay 10], in the section on rituals for the sanctification of corporeality by *devekut* in Luzzatto's group [see p. 519 ff. below]. I have therefore thought it unnecessary to elaborate [as he had earlier intended: see n. 22 above—Trans.] on the section containing the homily in the present context. The whole homily has been published in *Sefer otserot ramḥa"l*, ed. H. Friedlaender (Benei Berak, 1986), 239–45.]

The passage headed *Ma'amar p'* [*parashat*] *mishpatim*, which is expounded in this treatise, comprises a single folio at the beginning of the section of the Zohar (II, 94*a*–*b*) on the weekly Torah reading 'Mishpatim' (Exod. 21–4). The passage is a kind of foreword to *Sava demishpatim* [in the Zohar], but was written by the author of *Tikunei hazohar*.[290] The expositor assumed that it was an integral part of the Zohar, but he recognized its affinity in style and ideas to *Tikunei hazohar*, and in his commentary he drew support mainly from statements in that part of the literature of the Zohar. The greater part of the treatise is not an explanation of the Zoharic text but a speculative consideration of some kabbalistic problems tenuously associated with remarks in the passage in question.[291] The copy of the exposition breaks off at the top of fo. 147ᵛ, and it seems probable that that side and fo. 148 were left blank to provide space for the copy to be completed. The exposition, as preserved,

290 Part of it, beginning with the words 'Come and see, there is a soul called Ima [Mother]' (94*b*), occurs in *Zohar ḥadash, tikunim*, 117*a*. The concluding paragraph is quoted in Cordovero's *Pardes rimonim*, Gate 31 ('On the Soul'), ch. 3, where it is noted 'Further explained in *Tikunim*'.

291 Luzzatto adopted a similar expository method in his commentary on *Idra raba*.

goes as far as the [grant of the] soul [*nefesh*] from the holy *ofanim*, and the spirit [*ruaḥ*] from the holy *ḥayot*, in the middle of the last paragraph of the Zoharic passage with which it deals.[292]

In considering this text here I select certain topics, explain their main lines, and quote extracts from the treatise to illustrate the subject matter.

1. Principles of the doctrine of transmigration (fos. 135^{r}–137^{r}).[293]

The central idea is that the transmigration of souls is not intended as a punishment:[294] its chief purpose is rather to give man a chance to rectify the faults and shortcomings of which he was guilty in his previous existence in this world; less, however, with the aim of self-perfection than in order to help complete the *tikun* of the whole world and of the Shekhinah. The following are examples of statements which point clearly in this direction: 'Know that there are two kinds of transmigration. There is the transmigration undergone by souls according to their deeds, for their own *tikun*, and there are the transmigrations which souls undergo for the purification of Malkhut' (fo. 135^{r}); 'Every soul has its own *tikun* according to [its] service and its individual transmigrations' (fo. 136^{r});

For this is the supernal judgement which the Holy One, blessed be He, passes upon the souls to bring them to the world in order, through them, to purify Malkhut . . . and on this depends the *tikun* of the entire world . . . and he says that they are sentenced each one to receive his punishment[295] [but] you will see that transmigration was instituted not so that they should receive their punishment but so that they might perfect their deeds. Even though they sometimes bear the sins of their earlier incarnations in their later ones, the purpose of transmigration is nevertheless not that but the completion of the *tikunim* they failed to perform. (fos. 136^{v}–137^{r})[296]

The sin of Adam, the first man, is placed at the head of the defects of the world at large which require *tikun* through transmigrations.

Another major idea more closely connected to the text which is expounded—an idea considered also in the other parts of the commentary—is the distinction between superior souls on the side of the Shekhinah and inferior souls on Metatron's side, by reference to their nature and the changes they undergo in transmigration. The distinction is summarized as follows:

Indeed there are souls mystically associated with the Shekhinah, and souls associated with Mt-t [Metatron]. And these are the chief two forms of governance which

[292] On the matters dealt with in this paragraph see Tishby, *Wisdom of the Zohar*, ii. 713–14.

[293] *Ginzei ramḥa"l*, 272–4.

[294] Contrary to the explicit statement at the beginning of the passage in the Zohar which is the subject of this exposition: 'These are the provisions arranged for transmigration, the judgements of souls which have been sentenced each one to bear its punishment.' This statement is quoted in the exposition but is immediately rejected. See below, text referring to n. 295.

[295] See preceding note.

[296] *Ginzei ramḥa"l*, 272, 273, 274.

exist on high, namely governance by the Shekhinah acting on her own account and governance through the mystery clothed in the form of Mt-t; and the roots exist on both sides, and from their transformations the other souls are made . . . and the soul and all its sparks are all judged according to the highest level on which the soul depends. (fo. 136^{r-v})[297]

2. Links between the Godhead and the creatures of the lower worlds [*hanivra'im*] (fos. 137^{r}–140^{r}).[298]

The Godhead rules by the transmission of its flow from the upper to the lower worlds, from the world of Emanation to the realms of the worlds inhabited by created beings. These processes of divine governance are generally presented in the literature of kabbalah as the products of intercourse between Ze'ir Anpin and his female partner (Tiferet and Malkhut). This document emphasizes at the outset that the bonds between the Godhead and His creatures are essentially those of 'couplings between male and female':

for the Holy One, blessed be He, wishes to cleave to His creatures—He sends forth His flow and they receive it, and [He] has rooted this thing in male and female—everything to do with [those] who send forth the flow in Z[e'ir] A[npin] and everything to do with those who receive it in Nuk' [Nukba, 'the female']; for truly this is the essence of divine governance, that the supernal Will desires to spread His holiness among His creatures and cleave to them; and so this process is perfected in the couplings of male and female . . . That is the mystical significance of the bond which the supernal Will desired to exist between Him and His creatures. (fo. 137^{r-v})[299]

By this we are given to understand that Nukba, which is the Shekhinah, the root and origin of all creatures, carries them within herself in the processes of intercourse.[300]

In virtually the same breath the author explains, taking as his authority the name *Keneset yisra'el* used for the Shekhinah, that the creatures carried within the divine female to receive the flow from the Godhead in intercourse are meant to be understood as the Jews, who are the central pivot of divine governance.[301] The text reads as follows:

And indeed when the divine rule is perfected and Israel are worthy, this mystery of the covenant [the sefirah Yesod, the masculine force] is very much in control, that is

[297] Ibid. 273. [298] Ibid. 274–7. [299] Ibid. 274.

[300] This idea is spelt out more clearly in 'The mystery of the image of universal man' (see above, text referring to nn. 270–2, and the notes themselves). In *Sod hayiḥud* an extensive section is devoted to the inclusion of all creatures [*hanivra'im*] in the acts of divine intercourse (see p. 90 ff. above).

[301] In 'The mystery of the image of universal man' the generality of created beings, called there 'the separated ones', are identified with the community of Israel by obscure allusions. See above, text referring to n. 273.

to say, this bond is strongly aroused, and correspondingly the Holy One, blessed be He, and His Shekhinah join together in a great and close union . . . This is meant to refer to the greatness of the love and desire between Israel and the Holy One, blessed be He, the whole desire of the Holy One, blessed be He, being for Israel and the whole desire of Israel being for the Holy One, blessed be He. That is the basis on which all Creation takes place, for perfect happiness resides in the cleaving of the Lord, blessed be He, to His children so that they cannot be separated from Him, whereas Israel give themselves entirely to Him, and He reveals the greatness of His lights and the power of His glorious holiness to them . . . and that is complete perfection. (fo. 138^{r})[302]

When 'matters are not in a state of perfection, since there is no worthiness in Israel', which is the general situation while Israel are in Exile, the coupling cannot take place properly. However, to safeguard the existence of the Jewish people, the coupling is not completely broken off but is continued in concealment by clothing Metatron—the servant of the Godhead and, as it were, 'the minister for the world'—in the divine powers. 'And in the unions of his chariot male and female indeed join together. He has in him what is needed for the unions of his chariot to be performed for the purposes of the world—for the world must continue to exist—not, however, to show Israel's love and their bond with the Lord, but simply [to do] what is necessary for the governance of the world.'

During the period of the Exile the coupling takes place 'in concealment' on weekdays in order to avoid jealousy and denunciation on the part of the Sitra Ahra, 'for the jealousy of the Sitra Ahra is directed solely at Israel'. Only on the Sabbath, which partakes of the character of the world to come, does the act of coition take place 'in tranquillity without donning other garments and without difficulty . . . for it will be thus in time to come [in the days of the Messiah], which is the true Sabbath'.[303] The eschatological note struck here imparts a messianic character to the hastening of the 'couplings of male and female'.

3. The level of the righteous and the level of the angels (fos. 140^{r}–142^{r}).[304]

Even during the period of the Exile, while the divine powers Yesod [Tsadik] and Malkhut [Shekhinah] are, on the whole, governing the world through the agency of Metatron, the superior souls of the righteous are directly bound up with the Shekhinah, and these souls act and institute action in the world in the same ways as the Shekhinah exercises its rule. The lesser souls in Israel, on the other hand, 'being in the mystery of Metatron', are bound up

302 *Ginzei ramḥa"l*, 275.

303 The shorter extracts quoted here are from fos. 138^{r}–139^{v} of the manuscript; *Ginzei ramḥa"l*, 275–6.

304 *Ginzei ramḥa"l*, 277–8.

with Metatron and subordinated to his rule. In other words the righteous operate independently, as children of the Holy One, blessed be He, whereas the possessors of the other Jewish souls, 'which exist on M-t-t's side', are servants, as it were, whose rank is that of the angels, and therefore they 'must be in servitude'. The fundamental difference between the two kinds of soul, corresponding to the difference between the rank of the righteous and that of the angels, consists in the ways of serving God:

The essential point is that there is a great difference between the angels' service and that of the righteous: it is the mystery of [the difference between] children and servants. The righteous in their service cleave to the Shekhinah in mystical intercourse, so that everything they do is done out of attachment [*hitdabekut*] and love. But Metatron and all the other angels have none of this attachment and intercourse but are described as standing below the Shekhinah and bearing her burden in fear and awe, which is the awe of the servant for his master.[305]

The writer goes on to place great emphasis on the erotic element in the experience of *devekut*: 'And they [the righteous] are veritably in the mystical situation of Yesod, who unites with the Shekhinah and performs all the acts out of love as a husband does for his wife and not as a servant for his master.'[306]

On the face of it the classification of Jewish souls as either children or servants seems highly discriminatory, for they are all born of the Shekhinah and rooted in her.[307] The answer is:

It is not so, for certainly all the acts of the Holy One, blessed be He, are performed in righteousness, but within the mystery of His supernal abode he has given a root to all kinds of being, each for itself, and has granted to each thing as much contentment and tranquillity as is appropriate to its root . . . and for the souls which descend into this level of Metatron, that is actually [the means to] their *tikun* [restoration to perfection], [namely] that they should be thus and serve in this way . . . for truly, being at this level, they do not desire more; on the contrary, this is their *tikun*. And in the end, when the *tikun* of every branch is gathered together to complete the universal *tikun*, all souls, depending on their service, will remain ranked as an only daughter. (fo. 141^{r-v})[308]

4. **The Holy Spirit** (fos. 142^{r}–144^{v}).[309]

Whereas the *neshamah* is the highest of the three powers constituting the soul (*nefesh*, *ruaḥ*, *neshamah*), a higher power still, the Holy Spirit, is present in the

[305] Ibid. 277.

[306] In perceiving the devoted attachment [*devekut*] of the righteous man to the Shekhinah as an erotic relationship, Luzzatto follows in the footsteps of the Zohar. See Tishby, *Wisdom of the Zohar*, iii. 990–2, and n. 272 above.

[307] This difficult question is also considered, and the same forced explanation offered, in other works by Luzzatto. See *Ginzei ramḥa"l*, 217–18, foreword by the editor, H. Friedlaender.

[308] *Ginzei ramḥa"l*, 278.

[309] Ibid. 279–81.

Jew; it is clothed in the *neshamah*. The special eminence of the Holy Spirit lies in its very nature: its source and its activity are rooted in the sefirah Yesod, Tsadik, at a level higher than that of the Shekhinah, which animates the *neshamah*. For this reason the Holy Spirit is called *nishmata detsadik* ['the soul of Tsadik']. The following is a description of the essential nature and status of the Holy Spirit: 'Truly this is [the explanation of] the mystery of the Holy Spirit, namely that it is the realization of the spirit of God which comes from Yesod and unites with the soul itself . . . This Holy Spirit, too, is actually a kind of *neshamah* which unites with the soul of man himself, but this kind of soul is called the soul of Tsadik, unlike the actual souls which are the souls of Malkhut' (fo. 142^{r-v}).[310]

While the 'souls of Malkhut' receive and actuate a divine flow from on high, the Holy Spirit, 'the soul of Tsadik', is 'a soul which gives out influence, not one which receives it'. It is present and active both in the exalted souls of Jewish sages and in 'lowly souls', but the extent of its influence differs according to the rank of the souls: 'for in some cases it reveals itself in large measure, and in others less, and sometimes it may be completely hidden'. Through the Holy Spirit 'the Godhead, blessed be He, is revealed to [superior] souls', whereas in inferior souls the Holy Spirit acts to strengthen them and improve their status.[311]

5. Body and soul [*neshamah*] (fos. 144^{v}–147^{v}).[312]

Bodies, the garments of the souls, may appear to be equal to each other in status, but they, too, are divided into different categories, the ranks of the right and those of the left, on the side of holiness and on the side of uncleanness: 'that is to say, there are bodies the structure of which is actually entered by the Sitra Ahra, i.e. by the husk Nogah ['Brightness'] in the mystical form of a serpent's skin, and there are other bodies built of the holy essence coming from a supernal source'. Both kinds of body need to be restored to perfection, since their corporeal condition is wretched and the evil inclination is bound up with them. Therefore '[their] *tikun* [restoration] may take place in two ways: either the Holy Spirit, when it comes down to unite in intercourse with the only daughter [the soul—*neshamah*], will also unite with the body and illuminate it, or else [the Holy Spirit] will make the body submit to the *neshamah*' (fo. 144^{v}).[313]

[310] *Ginzei ramḥa"l*, 279.

[311] In the manuscript the extracts quoted are at fos. 142^{v}–143^{v}; in *Ginzei ramḥa"l*, at pp. 279–80. In *Sod hamerkavah*, too, the Holy Spirit appears as a force permanently present in the soul, but contrary to what is said here, it is there said to be the light of the Shekhinah dwelling in the soul, and its modes of action are described in an entirely different way. See above, text referring to n. 255, and the note itself.

[312] *Ginzei ramḥa"l*, 281–4.

[313] Ibid. 281.

The action of the Holy Spirit within the body is the highest stage in the process of the body's *tikun*. Even possessors of bodies on the right attain that level only gradually and by virtue of good deeds, the body deserving such elevation having previously been illuminated by the soul [*neshamah*] which dwells within it. The body worthy to receive the light of the soul is called *ḥolo shel shabat* ['the secular Sabbath day'], whereas the body whose *tikun* is accomplished by submission to the soul is simply *ḥol* ['secular'], the husk Nogah, as it were. Correspondingly, there is also a difference in the way the evil inclination is treated in the processes of *tikun*: 'The *tikun* [of bodies on the right] consists in cleaving to holiness, and therefore there must be no connection with the evil inclination. But this is not so for the bodies on the left, whose *tikun* consists in having to suffer obstacles; in their case there is no harm if there is a connection with the evil inclination, for, on the contrary, they must be made to submit.'[314]

The ideas described above, and others associated with them, bear the hallmark of Luzzatto's philosophy, and by their very nature they put it beyond doubt that this is another work by him.[315]

The doctrine of transmigration, which is the central subject of this treatise, is dealt with at various points scattered through a number of Luzzatto's works, and two of his treatises[316] contain systematic but brief and concise discussions of it. R. Isaac Pacifico, in the draft of the letter directed against Luzzatto which I considered earlier,[317] attacks him, *inter alia*, for his views on this subject:

It is also said that among all his other lies and stupidities, he has stated in one of his writings that the soul [*neshamah*] is divided into 613 parts and that it cannot ascend to its resting-place unless it has perfected itself by [performing the] 613 commandments, for which reason it must transmigrate even as many as a hundred times until it has set everything right. In any case, [according to him,] the parts which have been corrected will rise by degrees into the highest heavens, and the impregnated parts will transmigrate on the earth [two words doubtful in the manuscript; the second appears to be a clerical error for *neshamah*] in man who is like a breath [Ps. 144: 4] or in wild and domestic animals. The Merciful One save us from this opinion, which is in line with the opinion of the Christians who say that their god is in Heaven and is on earth [one doubtful word] the year. May those words be sunk in oblivion [which are spoken] in the name of other gods [cf. Deut. 18: 20—Trans.] and never be heard again.[318]

314 Ibid. 282.

315 On the position of exegesis of the Zohar—the category to which this work belongs—in Luzzatto's writings, see Essay 10, pp. 489–92.

316 *Ma'amar haḥokhmah* (Amsterdam, 1783), chapter headed 'Be'inyan hagilgul' ['On Transmigration']; *Derekh hashem*, pt. ii, ch. 3, sect. 10.

317 See above, p. 18 and n. 59.

318 MS Montefiore 111, fo. 14^r.

In what is here alleged to have been said by Luzzatto some of the details are undoubtedly garbled, as also occurs in the other accusations in this letter, but in principle they correspond to the view he expressed in *Ma'amar haḥokhmah*.[319]

With regard to the treatise under consideration here, special attention must be drawn to the styles of handwriting. From the beginning of the work to fo. 142r the style is hurried and varies frequently, especially with respect to the form of the letters, similarly to the hasty writing in other works in the collection which in my opinion may be regarded as being in Luzzatto's own hand.[320] At fo. 142r, in the middle of a sentence, after the first word in the line, the style changes,[321] and from there to the end the writing is that of 'the unmistakable copyist'.[322] This exceptional phenomenon shows clearly that the preceding part was also copied from a prepared text. In my opinion we must conclude from the complicated details of the case that we have here a hasty copy made by the author, Luzzatto, from a previous version in his own handwriting.

XII. EXPOSITIONS OF THE COMMANDMENTS

(FOS. 149r–162v)

[This work was published in *Sefer otserot ramḥa"l*, ed. H. Friedlaender (Benei Berak, 1986), 222–38. The quotations and folio references, which follow the manuscript, are accompanied by the corresponding references in *Otserot ramḥa"l*.]

The commandments [*mitsvot*] expounded in this tract are lettered in sequence from *ḥet* to *yod dalet*, i.e. 8 to 14, as follows: *mitsvah* no. 8—redemption of the first-born of an ass (fos. 149r–150v); no. 9—breaking the neck of the first-born of an ass if it is not redeemed (fos. 150v–152v); no. 10 (not lettered in the manuscript)—the unity of the Lord (fos. 153r–155r); no. 11—loving the Lord (fos. 155v–158r); no. 12—the study of the Torah (fos. 158r–159r); no. 13—the recital of the Shema (fos. 159v–161v); no. 14—phylacteries (fos. 161v–162v). In *mitsvah* no. 12 (study of the Torah) the copy breaks off at the

319 This work was written under the inspiration of the *magid* before 1730. See *Igerot*, i. 31, 102, 114.

320 See above, text referring to nn. 7 and 43; nn. 66 and 86; and text referring to nn. 101–2 and 174.

321 The last words in the handwriting of the first writer are 'amar sheya'an hatsadik oseh menuḥah' (*Ginzei ramḥa"l*, 279).

322 See n. 8 above.

second line on the page (fo. 159[r]). It is probable that the copy from which the writer—'the unmistakable copyist'—was working was incomplete, and that he expected to receive another copy containing the end of the exposition. The end of the last of these *mitsvot* (phylacteries) is also missing, and at the foot of the page (fo. 162[v]) a word has been written in order to keep the folio open. Undoubtedly some folios are missing here, for the work which follows (fo. 163[r]) is without its beginning,[323] but it is impossible to say how many have been lost.

The *mitsvot* relating to the first-born of an ass (nos. 8 and 9 [from Exod. 13: 13]), together with the missing ones nos. 1–7, on the one hand; and, on the other, nos. 10–14 and three more, missing from the end of this document (they would be nos. 15–17), which are presented jointly as being eight commandments in the *parashah* 'Va'etḥanan' [Deut. 5 and 6],[324] constitute a single work formed of two parts which have been joined together. On a literal reading of the *mitsvot* this structure seems very odd: how did fundamental principles of faith and the service of God, His unity, and the other commandments in 'Va'etḥanan' come to be bundled up with those relating to the first-born of an ass, and even be placed *after* them? There is an answer to the riddle. In line with the well-known principle that the 248 positive commandments correspond to the 248 organs of the body, the *mitsvot* in the work we are considering are arranged, unusually enough, in exact accordance with the anatomical system adopted in the enumeration of 'the two hundred and forty-eight organs in man' in Mishnah *Ohol.* 1: 8. However, the order of the groups of organs is head, neck, and body, which is not the same as their order in the Mishnah. Thus the two sets of organs given precedence here are those of the head and neck, with regard to which the Mishnah says 'nine in the head, eight in the neck'. The two commandments relating to the first-born of an ass reflect the mysteries of the two cheeks, including 'the mystery of the teeth, which are thirty-two paths of wisdom' (fo. 149[r]).[325] Hence the first seven *mitsvot*, which are missing in the surviving copy and which I cannot identify, reflect the mystical significance of the organs of the head which come first. The eight *mitsvot* of 'Va'etḥanan' reflect the mysteries of the organs of the neck, consisting of eight vertebrae. It can be stated with certainty that the three *mitsvot* missing at the end of this section, corresponding to the last three vertebrae in the neck, are *mezuzah* ['. . . write them upon the doorposts of your house'], the fear of the Lord, and swearing in the name of the Lord. This is shown by the fact that the five *mitsvot* from 'Va'etḥanan' we actually have here (nos. 10–14) appear in the *parashah* (Deut. 6: 4–8) in the same order as in the tract, and are followed in verses 9 and 12 by the three *mitsvot* I have named.

323 See n. 14 above. 324 *Otserot ramḥa"l*, 227. 325 Ibid. 222.

The pattern of the mystical anatomy underlying the interpretations of the *mitsvot* in this tract is summarized in *mitsvah* no. 10, the unity of the Lord, in the following paragraph detailing the organs of the head:

Come and see a supernal mystery: the body is certainly constructed in two parts—body and head. The neck stands in the middle to join the one to the other. The head—in which there stand arrayed supernal mysteries to send out lights in every direction, the light of wisdom, so that darkness should not rule in the world. They are arranged in the following order: the head [the skull and brain] above all else—the *tikun* of the moon to restore everything to perfection; two temples [together with the ears]—for a foreskin which covers the body; the forehead—the will, so that [strict] judgements should not prevail in the world; the nose—the light of the soul to take up residence in the body; two eyes—to send out light to the world, as it is written:[326] *adonai yireh* [in the biblical context, 'the Lord will provide', but can be read as '. . . will see', or 'will be seen', or 'will cause to see'—Trans.]; two cheeks—to strengthen wisdom in the world, although it is hidden from the children of men. So greatly have the various ranks been perfected [*nitkenu*] on high, [and] the *tikun* of the world [follows, that is] certain. (fo. 153^{r})[327]

Earlier in this text it is stated that the neck is the mystical equivalent of the Temple, and further on there is a description and explanation of various links between the neck and its vertebrae and the Temple.

The whole work is written on the same lines as interpretations of *mitsvot* in the Zohar; in other words, it is of the same type as Luzzatto's *Zohar tinyana* and his *Tikunim ḥadashim*. In addition to its imitation of the style of the Zohar, it has another characteristic in which it resembles *Tikunim ḥadashim*. Here, as there, separate sections of the text conclude with the formula 'Happy are Israel in this world and in the world to come'. On the other hand there is a marked and surprising difference between the two: all the parts of the work we are considering are in Hebrew, but a Hebrew which conveys the clear impression of being a Hebraization of an artificial Aramaic—the sort of Aramaic in which the literature of the Zohar is written. Here are some typical examples of formations of this kind which occur frequently in this work:

(*a*) Word patterns: *mitakef*, *nitkaf*, *hitkif*, to mean 'strengthening' or 'strengthened' [a typical meaning of the Hebrew root *takaf* is 'to attack'—Trans.]; *he'emiduha* ['they made it stand', a literal translation of the Aramaic of the Zohar *okmuha*] instead of *pershuha*, 'they explained it'; *mitaber* [normal Hebrew 'to become pregnant', but here used as a form of *avar*, 'to pass'] to mean 'passing by or away' or 'removed', instead of *ḥolef* or *mesulak*; *meforash* [normally 'explained' or 'explicit'] to mean *nifrad*

326 'And Abraham called the name of that place Adonai Yireh ['the Lord sees', or 'the Lord will provide'], as it is said to this day: "in the mountain of the Lord it will be seen"' (Gen. 22: 13).

327 *Otserot ramḥa"l*, 227.

['separated']; *mistalek* [normal Hebrew 'departs' or 'dies'] for *oleh* or *mitaleh* ['ascends' or 'is raised'].

(*b*) Phrases and idioms: *mishtadel besodot hatorah* [literally 'strives in (i.e. strives to grasp) the mysteries of the Torah']; *dinim mitorerim* ['judgements are aroused']; *kan madregah noda'at besodot hashem hakadosh* ['here there is a known level in the mysteries of the Holy Name']; *sod hasodot leḥakhmei halev* ['the mystery of mysteries for the wise of heart'].

How and to what end was this linguistic farrago created? The most reasonable answer is that Luzzatto wrote this work in the Aramaic of the Zohar, but that because, in 1730, he had to swear not to write or circulate writings in that language, the work was translated into Hebrew, apparently by a member of Luzzatto's group, who stuck meticulously to the Zoharic character of the original. The copy is full of clerical errors, and many sentences have gaps in them, sometimes indicated by dots and sometimes not indicated at all—evidence that the copyist found it difficult to decipher the handwriting of the copy he was using.

With regard to the text as a whole it must be borne in mind that the Zohar follows two distinct patterns in expounding the commandments. The traditional view, in general, has been that all the passages devoted to this topic were concentrated in *Raya meheimna*, the sections of which are scattered through the Zohar on the Torah. But this is an unsound opinion which gained currency as a result of erroneous references which first appeared in the Mantua edition of the Zohar (1558–60). In fact the author of the main body of the Zohar, who lived earlier than the fourteenth-century author of *Raya meheimna* and *Tikunei hazohar*, himself wrote a treatise on the commandments; it is called *Pikuda* or *Pikudin* in manuscripts of the Zohar and in the Cremona edition (1559–60). Only parts of that treatise have been preserved, and apparently it was never completed. In the Mantua edition its expositions of the commandments were interspersed in *Raya meheimna*.[328] The two sets of expositions differ greatly in form and content.

Kabbalists distinguished between the two works, though they ascribed them to a single author. Luzzatto thought that all the expositions of the commandments in the Zohar were part of *Raya meheimna*, as is evident from what he says in his commentary on *Idra raba*: 'In the days of R. Simeon bar Yohai great *tikunim* were created and treatises composed according to the revelation(s) which had been vouchsafed, *for Raya meheimna, the faithful shepherd, took it upon himself to explain the pikudin, and the book R"m was written.* Additionally a book of *tikunim* was written. Both of these are great works

328 The matter was made quite clear in E. Gottlieb's meticulous study 'Ma'amrei ha"pikudin" shebazohar', *Kiryat sefer*, 48 (1973), 490–508 [included in his book *Meḥkarim besifrut hakabalah*, ed. Y. Hacker (Tel Aviv, 1976), 215–30].

containing great revelations from on high in which heavenly beings manifested themselves.'[329] But it is clear from the text by Luzzatto we are considering here that he realized there were two different strata, and in his desire to follow in the footsteps of *Raya meheimna*, as he saw it, he made use of both. In his expositions of the commandments relating to the first-born of the ass he performed feats of homiletical legerdemain based on association of ideas, after the manner of *Raya meheimna*; skipping from one subject to another, he bundled together scraps of various ideas which had no relevance to the commandments he was expounding, and brought into them expressions and descriptions characteristic of *Raya meheimna*. Yet in the expositions of the other commandments his style is pseudo-midrashic in the manner of the *Pikudin*, and in general the explanations are linked to the subject matter of the commandments, with which they form coherent units; only to a minor extent can distinct elements of *Raya meheimna* be detected in them. Every commandment is expounded differently from its exposition in the Zohar,[330] but for the most part Luzzatto's remarks are simply particular formulations of ideas and inclinations which were crystallized in the literature of the Zohar; only here and there do traces of his personal style and original thought break through.

The examples I give here will illustrate the variety of topics woven into the various chapters of this work. *Mitsvah* no. 8 opens with the verse 'Every first-born of an ass you shall redeem with a lamb'.[331] This is followed by a sentence which reads 'This has great mystical significance for masters of the science [of kabbalah]. It is the mystery of the upper jawbone, as it is written: "With the jawbone of an ass, heaps upon heaps" [*beleḥi ḥamor ḥamor ḥamorotayim*].'[332] On the strength of these words, spoken by Samson with regard to his own exploit, we are given a medley of matters unconnected with the commandment which is the subject of the exposition—on 'the mystery of the teeth' [between the jawbones] which are 'the thirty-two paths of wisdom'; on the blocking of the lights and the darkening of the Torah because of things that went wrong through the sin of Adam and the destruction of the Temple, which injured the operation of the upper teeth; and on ways to put right what had gone wrong. The transition to the redemption of the first-born of an ass is made by way of reference to the *tikun* of the ignorant [their redemption

[329] *Adir bamarom leramḥa"l* (Warsaw, 1886), 18.

[330] The commandments relating to the first-born of an ass are expounded only in *Raya meheimna* (Zohar II, 43*a*). The other *mitsvot* are expounded both in *Pikudin* and in *Raya meheimna*. For a list of the *mitsvot* in *Pikudin* see Gottlieb, *Meḥkarim besifrut hakabalah*, 224–9. All the *mitsvot* in the two Zoharic works in question are listed together by R. Margaliot in *Haraya meheimna sefer hamitsvot* (printed at the head of *Zohar*, ed. Margaliot, i. 1–8), together with references for expositions of *mitsvot* in the other parts of the Zohar.

[331] Exod.13: 13.

[332] Judg. 15: 16.

from the state of ignorance—Trans.], in relation to Manoah, the father of Samson, who according to the Talmud 'was an ignoramus'.[333] When an ignoramus achieves personal *tikun*, he 'is called *ḥamor de'orayta*, a *ḥamor* of the Torah—[the word for an ass being an acronym for] e.g. *ḥakham mufla verav rabanan*, a wonderful scholar and teacher of our rabbis'[334] (fo. 150r);[335] this is the mystical significance of redeeming the first-born of the ass.

Mitsvah no. 9 opens with the second limb of the same verse: 'if you do not redeem it, you shall break its neck [*va'arafto*]',[336] and its exposition begins as follows: 'This is the lower jawbone—that is certain; it is these of which it was said: "My teaching shall drop [*ya'arof*] like the rain"'[337] (fo. 150v).[338] On the basis of inferences drawn from the different meanings of *araf*, we are presented with a long and varied series of topics which are threaded together in the flimsiest fashion by association of ideas. The central motif is light and darkness, good and evil, in the creation and governance of the world, in the life of the Jewish people and Jews as individuals, and in the restoration of the world to perfection [*tikun ha'olam*] in time to come. In this mishmash the commandment relating to the breaking of the first-born ass's neck is applied to the ignorant who fail to attain the rank of '*ḥamor* of the Torah'. An ignoramus who does not achieve his own *tikun* 'goes down below and He [the Holy One, blessed be He] breaks his neck in Gehinnom until darkness spreads out from him . . . and he is expelled from the holy community so that he should not cause the light to be confused' (fo. 152r).[339]

In the exposition of *mitsvah* no 10, the unity of the Lord, which is the first of the eight commandments in the Torah portion 'Va'etḥanan' mentioned above, the central theme is the high importance of that commandment and its role as the first of the eight cervical vertebrae according to the mystical anatomical pattern corresponding to the 248 positive precepts.[340] The neck vertebrae are assigned the mission of bringing down a flow of lights and blessings from the organs of the head. The mission of Moses was to prepare or perfect the vertebrae for the conveyance of the flow, but he did not succeed in this and was obliged to content himself with the *tikun* of the upper lights in the organs of the head; as a result defects occurred in the world: 'Certainly Moses was the head of Israel, and he had not (yet?) completed [the task of] bringing them down to the earth . . . and because Moses did not complete them, the Temple was destroyed and all those defects dominated the world. He desired indeed to make this crossing, as it is written: "Let me cross over and see",[341] but the Holy One, blessed be He, wished him to remain above with the *tikun* of the head, and from there he gave the light which he

333 *Ber.* 61*a*.
334 Both expressions are part of the normal vocabulary of *Raya meheimna*.
335 *Otserot ramḥa"l*, 223–4.
336 Exod. 13: 13.
337 Deut. 32: 2.
338 *Otserot ramḥa"l*, 224.
339 Ibid. 226.
340 See above, text referring to nn. 325–7.
341 Deut. 3: 25.

did' (fo. 153^v^).[342] In fulfilling the commandment relating to the unity of the Lord, Jews bring the celestial flow down to the world in limited measure and for a limited time: 'Happy are Israel, who bring about this unity every day, [so that] the supernal light can descend to the world, for this is the very beginning—the whole head—which spreads out below in order to descend into the whole [of humanity]' (fo. 155^r^).[343] Moses, who was not allowed to perfect the operation of all eight vertebrae of the neck, and was able to perfect only the topmost one, will complete their *tikun* at the end of days: 'And in time to come he [Moses] will come and complete the seven others, and then he will perfect [them] with a perfect *tikun*' (fo. 154^r^).[344]

In *mitsvah* no. 11, the love of the Lord, Luzzatto explains that *devekut* is attained by breaking off the yoke of the Sitra Ahra—which bows man down, subjecting him to the rule of the evil inclination and the commission of sins—and by accepting the yoke of the kingdom of Heaven through the study of Torah, prayer, and good deeds. There is nothing particularly novel here: these ideas can readily be found in the Zohar.

The same remark applies to most of the points made in the fragmentary exposition of *mitsvah* no. 12, the study of the Torah. Only in one of its ideas does Luzzatto's highly personal approach stand out, namely in his explanation of the existence of the Sitra Ahra, which, he says, was brought into being by God so that, by subduing evil, He could reveal His absolute unity. This opinion, which figures prominently in Luzzatto's philosophical works,[345] is here expressed in these words: 'Come and see: the Cause of all causes ordered matters so as to reveal His unity. What did He do? He gave power to this unclean one and shut in His light to make room for this unclean one' (fo. 158^r^).[346] This action had as its aim 'the mystery of unity [*hayiḥud*], which hides its power in order to reveal it stage by stage, until all is brought to perfection in perfect unity' (fo. 158^v^).[347]

In *mitsvah* no. 13 the recitation of the Shema is explained as the service of the Lord by the song of the Jew, which is superior to the song of the angels:

> When it [the soul] goes out into the world in the morning, descends into the body, and sets about its work of bringing the world to its proper state of perfection [*tikun*], one must sing a song before the King. What song is this? It is the recitation of the Shema, for there is no one appointed to a task in the world who has not his own song, according to the power that is invested in him; the song of man is superior to all the songs in the world, it takes precedence over the ascent of all the other songs. And it must be said twice a day: when he leaves the presence of the King and when he returns towards Him at night. He must then render service to his Lord, and this he can only do through song. (fo. 159^v^)[348]

[342] *Otserot ramḥa"l*, 227. [343] Ibid. 229. [344] Ibid. 228.
[345] See above, text referring to nn. 275–7, and n. 277 itself. [346] *Otserot ramḥa"l*, 233.
[347] Ibid. 234. [348] Ibid. 234–5.

Through the power of this song the beings of the lower and the upper worlds are exalted in *devekut*, and perfect *yiḥud* ['unification'] is created. The *yiḥud* draws down lights and divine flow by which the whole community of Israel and every part of every Jew are blessed and sanctified.

Mitsvah no. 14, the end of which is missing, is devoted entirely to an explanation of the holiness and high worth of the phylacteries. It emphasizes the strong bond between them and Israel and describes how, in reward for laying the phylacteries, the children of Israel are inspired with God's holiness. Once again, all this is an expression of ideas from the Zohar in a different form.

To sum up: from the point of view of their ideas and style, the expositions of the commandments are of no particular importance, and they are certainly not among the best of Luzzatto's kabbalistic writings. But their special character confers a respectable literary status on them. They are important, too, in another noteworthy respect: the wealth of veils and disguises which Luzzatto drew over his true self, both willingly and under compulsion, constitute a unique kind of camouflage. Utterances in the Zoharic mould, couched in Aramaic, which apparently Luzzatto imagined had been revealed to him from on high, and in which he may have heard the voice of 'the faithful shepherd' [*raya meheimna*] himself, are here dressed up in artificial Hebrew. Under this cloak we can detect the many twists and turns he adopted out of fear of his persecutors, who strove to silence him and obliged him at times to resort to substantial modifications of thought and language.[349]

349 It is not beyond the bounds of possibility that the author of this work was one of Luzzatto's disciples, but I have not found enough evidence to put this to the test.

TWO

Poems, *Piyutim*, and Prayers from Unpublished Manuscripts by Rabbi Moses Hayim Luzzatto: MS Guenzburg 745

A. POEMS AND *PIYUTIM*

FOREWORD BY THE EDITOR OF *MOLAD*

LUZZATTO'S previously known poetic productions, both poems and prayers, are collected in *Sefer hashirim* (Jerusalem, 1945), which was prepared and edited by Simon Ginzburg and published by Benjamin Klar with supplements and a general introduction. At the end of the book (pp. 219–21) Ginzburg gave a 'list of missing poems by Ramhal', based on references by Joseph Almanzi. He appended to the list an emotional appeal to 'all lovers of Ramhal and admirers of his poetry' who could lay hands on any poem by Luzzatto which was not included in the book 'to be so kind as to put themselves out for the sake of the honour of Ramhal and the honour of our literature, and provide the Bialik Foundation with a copy of the text in their possession, and their name will be remembered for a blessing. At any rate would they be so kind as to inform us of the existence of such poems so that no word of Ramhal's may be lost for ever from the treasury of Jewish poetry.'

Isaiah Tishby, in the course of his search for unpublished writings by Luzzatto, found a rich store of poems, *piyutim*, prayers, and other liturgical writings in MS Guenzburg 745 (photograph, Ben Tsevi Institute). This manuscript collection does not bear the name of the author and contains no mention whatsoever of Luzzatto, but on studying the writings Tishby became convinced that most of them were the work of Luzzatto and that a few of those which were not by him had been copied by him or included in the collection on his instructions.

The poems and prayers in the collection do not simply add to the quantity of Luzzatto's poetic work: the great majority of them are of unique quality. There is nothing like them in the other poetic and liturgical works of his which were previously known to us, for they are imbued with the unmistakable spirit of kabbalah and messianism and replete with elements which strongly reflect his personality and the characteristics of his group. The publication and elucidation of these poetic works can therefore shed fresh light on the character of Luzzatto as poet and composer of *piyutim*. They are also of great assistance in the solution of complicated problems relating to the course of his life and his activity as leader of a kabbalistic-messianic group in Padua.

In 1961, at the Institute of Jewish Studies, Jerusalem, Tishby delivered his lecture (at which I was present) entitled 'Ginzei tefilot veshirei kodesh leramḥa"l' ['Unpublished Prayers and Religious Poems by Luzzatto']. He gave a description of the Guenzburg collection as a whole and the principal poems and prayers in it, and read some poems which served to demonstrate the significance of this addition to Luzzatto's poetry and assist in reassessing this poetry and its author. In the same year Tishby published two messianic sonnets from the collection, together with comments on them, in an appendix to his essay 'Hatesisah hameshiḥit beḥugo shel ramḥa"l' in the Festschrift for Isaac Baer (Jerusalem, 1960), 396–7 (reprinted in I. Tishby, *Netivei emunah uminut* (Ramat Gan, 1964), 202–3 [and again as Essay 3 below; but the sonnets are now included and annotated in the present essay: see below—Trans.]). In the essay itself, section C, there was a short description of the whole of the Guenzburg collection, and the two messianic sonnets were explained against the background of their relationship to two central figures who stood at Luzzatto's side in the leadership of the group in Padua, R. Moses David Valle and R. Jekutiel of Vilna. The author declared at the same time (Essay 3, n. 85): 'I hope to be able soon to publish all the important compositions in this collection, making clear their authorship by Luzzatto, their meaning, and their importance.'

After hearing Tishby's lecture I urged him repeatedly to complete his research and publish its results, and above all, of course, to publish the poems themselves. However, the publication of the writings in the Guenzburg collection was delayed by the broadening and ramification of Tishby's research into the writings of Luzzatto and his circle, as well as by illness and other obstacles. In 1976 Tishby spent about six months in Oxford as a visiting fellow at the Centre for Postgraduate Hebrew Studies [now the Oxford Centre for Hebrew and Jewish Studies], which was headed by Dr David Patterson. There he pursued his study of the compositions of Luzzatto in the Guenzburg manuscript and prepared the original poems and *piyutim* in the collection, and some prayers connected with them, for publication in *Molad*.

He planned to head the article in question with a comprehensive introduction containing a description of the writings in the collection, together with a comparison with other works by Luzzatto in various fields of his literary and speculative production, and a detailed explanation of the compositions which are here published. But after his return to Jerusalem he fell ill and has so far been unable to complete the introduction which he has in draft.

For this reason the study of the texts in this first publication by Tishby based on MS Guenzberg 745 is limited in extent, but the poems, *piyutim*, and prayers, and the explanations of them, are given here in full as was always intended: ten poems and *piyutim*, among them the two messianic sonnets published previously, and four prayers. The first three prayers (one for the night of Shavuot and two for the night of 17 Shevat) are directly connected with two of the *piyutim*. The fourth prayer, actually a cycle of prayers ('Confessional Prayers of Luzzatto and his Group'), appears in the collection as a separate section; but in the personal note which it strikes and its reflection of the outlook of the group, as well as in its literary qualities, it is close to the best of the poems and *piyutim*, especially the poem 'Hope, hope, my heart', and it belongs together with them. In addition to the texts some major points emerging from Tishby's research, which were to have been included in the introduction, are presented here in six short prefaces.

The article is divided into two parts [published in two successive issues of *Molad*]: the first consisting of the poems and *piyutim*, with their five prefaces, and the second containing the prayers and the preface relating to them, which is printed at the head of the 'confessional prayers'.

E.B. [Ephraim Broido]

*

PREFACES TO THE POEMS

The Three Poems 'Open to me', 'Hope, hope, my heart', and *Piyut* for the Night of Shavuot

The poems 'Open to me' and 'Hope, hope, my heart' are copied in full in MS Harvard 54, which also has a copy of the first six stanzas of the *piyut* (for the night of Shavuot) which follows them. In the study, which I hope to publish shortly, of the poems and prayers I have discovered in unpublished manuscripts of Luzzatto, I shall describe in detail the collection of his writings contained in MS Guenzburg 745 and the collection in MS Harvard 54. I am grateful to Mr Mordecai Glatzer, who brought the important Harvard collection to my notice and supplied me with a copy of the list of works in it which he had prepared for the Houghton Library of Harvard University. I am also deeply indebted to the directorate of the library, who kindly provided me with a microfilm of this manuscript for the purpose of my research into the writings of Luzzatto. In the Harvard manuscript the division of the verses does not correspond to the metre, and in many places the text is corrupt. The mistakes and other indications show clearly that the copyist was working from the text in the Guenzburg collection. Textual variants in the Harvard collection are pointed out in the notes. [The translation of the notes omits references to variant spellings which do not affect the meaning.—Trans.] Where readings in the Guenzburg collection are doubtful for technical reasons (blurred letters, defects at the margins of the photocopy, etc.) and there is no doubt as to the correctness of the Harvard version, I have included the Harvard readings in my text without comment. In the separate notes on each text, the Harvard manuscript is indicated by the letter H, the Guenzburg manuscript by the letter G.

As well as the two poems and the *piyut*, the Harvard collection contains the following which also appear in the Guenzburg collection: (*a*) four prayers for the festivals, as detailed below in the preface to the *piyut* and prayer for the night of Shavuot; (*b*) mystical prayers, the beginning of which is missing. In the course of my research I realized that these formed about half of the first of the two cycles of mystical prayers in the Guenzburg collection; (*c*) *Yiḥud hayirah*. I also found this in another collection of Luzzatto's writings which I discovered (MS Columbia—New York, 17 *alef* 893). At its head is written: 'This is the order of the *Yiḥud* in brief', and it is followed by a long and important work entitled *Pe*[*rush*] *hayiḥud* ['Commentary on the *Yiḥud*']; (*d*) 137 of the 138 'gateways' in *Kela"ḥ pitḥei ḥokhmah*, minus the commentary. These are headed 'From the Gateways to Wisdom'; (*e*) ten chapters of kabbalistic *mishnayot* which are contained in the printed edition of the book *Ḥoker umekubal* ['Philosopher and Kabbalist'] under the title 'Kelalut kol ha'ilan' ['The Whole Tree']. It became evident to me that the copyist of the Harvard manuscript copied all these works from the Guenzburg collection, as I have already indicated in relation to the two poems and the *piyut* for the night of Shavuot.

Piyut and Prayer for the Night of Shavuot

This *piyut* and the prayer which belongs with it were available to J. Almanzi in a different manuscript. In his biography of Luzzatto, *Kerem ḥemed*, 3 (1838), 155 n. 86, he had this to say about them: 'Prayer and poem on the giving of the Torah for the festival of Shavuot, manuscript in the possession of his [for which read 'my'] friend Mr Abraham Shalom. The prayer is written in clear and pure style, although some element of mysticism enters into it, and the poem consists of ten octaves in the metre of the poem on the redemption from Egypt which I quoted in the previous note.' In the Guenzburg collection, before the *piyut* for Shavuot, there is a 'song for the completion of the [session of] study at Passover' (fos. 107^{r}–110^{r}), and the *piyut* for Shavuot is followed by a 'song to be recited after the study session at Hoshana Rabah' (fos. 113^{r}–114^{r}). Before and after the prayer for Shavuot there are six further prayers for the festivals: 'Prayer to be said on the eve of Passover when burning the leaven' (fo. 60^{r}), 'Prayer to be said before the Passover *seder*' (fos. 60^{v}–61^{r}), 'Prayer for the [first] night of Passover before the study session' (fos. 61^{r}–64^{r}), 'Prayer for the eve of Rosh Hashanah in the cemetery' (fos. 65^{r}–68^{v}), 'Prayer for the eve of Yom Kippur in the cemetery' (fos. 69^{r}–71^{v}), 'Prayer for the night of Hoshana Rabah' (fo. 72^{r-v}). The prayers and *piyutim* for the study sessions on the night of Passover and the night of Hoshana Rabah are printed in *Sefer hashirim*, ed. S. Ginzburg and B. Klar (Jerusalem, 1945), 173–82, 194–7. The 'Esoteric interpretation of the song for the night of Passover' (ibid. 183–92) is not in the Guenzburg collection. MS Harvard 54 contains copies of four of the Guenzburg manuscript prayers for the festivals, in the following order: 'Prayer for the eve of Rosh Hashanah in the cemetery', 'Prayer for the eve of Yom Kippur in the cemetery', 'Prayer to be said on the eve of Passover when burning' [the words 'the leaven' have been omitted in error], 'Prayer for the night of Shavuot before the study session'. I have previously pointed out (in 1961, in my lecture at the Institute of Jewish Studies, Jerusalem, on 'Unpublished Prayers and Religious Poems by Luzzatto') that the 'Prayer for the eve of Rosh Hashanah in the cemetery' is to be found, 'together with a kabbalistic introduction and an esoteric interpretation', in MS Jerusalem 5217 8° (formerly MS Warsaw), fos. 413^{r}–415^{r}. When I publish this prayer I will add a critical edition of the kabbalistic interpretation.

Piyut and Two Prayers for the Night of 17 Shevat

This *piyut* for an occasion which does not figure in the calendar of Jewish festivals, and the prayer associated with it, appear in the Guenzburg collection after the *piyutim* and prayers for the known religious festivals. They show that Luzzatto's group arranged a festivity to mark 17 Shevat, and that at the formal meal on the night of their festival they recited a prayer and sang a song both of which had been composed by Luzzatto for ritual use by the group on that occasion. In two other Oxford manuscripts, nos. 2237 and 2593, there is a kabbalistic homily for the night of 17 Shevat, ending with a prayer. In MS 2237—consisting for the most part of a collection of compositions by R. Jekutiel of Vilna, Luzzatto's well-known disciple, and by Luzzatto himself—the homily appears in R. Jekutiel's handwriting, without any superscription and with no mention of 17 Shevat. However, in MS 2593, which is a collection of unattributed writings—except for one work identified in Neubauer's catalogue as Luzzatto's famous kabbalistic dialogue *Ḥoker umekubal* ['Philosopher and Kabbalist']—the homily is headed 'Formal meal for the night of 17 Shevat 5493 [1733]'. ['17' is written *tet vav" beit* (15+2) =

tov = 'good'.—Trans.] (My researches have shown this collection to be a rich store of unpublished kabbalistic writings by Luzzatto, and I am about to provide them with a commentary and publish them separately and collectively.) From the content of the homily it is apparent that the communal meal was organized as a mystical-messianic rite and that its principal direct purpose was the sanctification of corporeality by the sublimation of the food and drink of the meal and the *tikun* ['bringing to perfection'] of the bodies and organs of the participants. It is hard to say why Luzzatto and the members of his group fixed 17 Shevat as the date of their special festival. On the basis of the date 5493 in MS Oxford 2593 I took it at first, and said as much in my 1961 lecture at the Jerusalem Institute of Jewish Studies, that this group celebration took place only once and was in the nature of a farewell gathering in honour of R. Jekutiel of Vilna on his departure from Padua to return to the lands of Poland and Lithuania. (I have shown elsewhere that R. Jekutiel left Padua not long after 17 Shevat 5493: see my book *Netivei emunah uminut*, 325 n. 53, and Essay 8, text referring to n. 96, and the note itself.) However, that hypothesis proved to be incorrect. I found that one of the homilies by R. Moses David Valle in MS BL 387 (fos. 184v–185r) bears at its head the note 'On the night of 17 Shevat [5492/1732], "and wine gladdens the heart of man" [cf. Ps. 104: 15]'. At the beginning of this homily we find the following:

It has long been well known that there is nothing better for man, nor is there any greater joy for him, than rejoicing in the Torah when he is privileged to be among companions who listen attentively to him as he develops new insights into the Torah and expounds them to his hearers; all the more so when it is a word in season that he speaks, so as to perform for every thing the *tikun* appropriate to it, as these holy companions do on this night at the ceremonial meal [*se'udah shel mitsvah*] which is before us, carrying out *tikunim* for the sake of Heaven . . . and *I, too, unworthy as I am, have been privileged* to perform the *tikun* of the wine that gladdens.

This splendid autobiographical testimony to the character of the meal for which Luzzatto's group assembled on the night of 17 Shevat shows clearly that the ceremony was instituted a few years before 1732 and was observed annually. In the discussion on my lecture the late Professor Cecil Roth remarked that 17 Shevat was the date of the 'Saragossa Purim', which was celebrated by some eastern communities to commemorate the miraculous salvation of the Jews of Saragossa from a false charge. I have not found any connection between the ceremony in Luzzatto's group and the 'Saragossa Purim', but it is nevertheless possible that the group sought to attach their ceremony to the date of a known festival. Perhaps, however, the date of the ceremony was determined by an important event in Luzzatto's life or in the history of the group on which we have no information.

I publish here the prayer which appears at the end of the above-mentioned homily. I will publish the two homilies in their entirety in an essay on 'The homilies of Ramhal and R. Moses David Valle for the meal of their group on the night of 17 Shevat, and related homilies by [members of] their school'.

Two Messianic Sonnets

I have published these two sonnets from MS Guenzburg 745 previously, first in my essay 'Hatesisah hameshiḥit beḥugo shel ramḥa"l le'oram shel ketubah veshirim meshiḥiyim', in S. W. Baron *et al.* (eds.), *Sefer-yovel leyitsḥak ber bimelot lo shivim shanah/Yitzhak F. Baer Jubilee Volume on the Occasion of his Seventieth Birthday* (Jerusalem, 1960), 396–7 [this is reproduced as Essay 3 below—Trans.] and again in my book *Netivei emunah uminut*, 202–3, with some additions to the commmentary. Here I publish the commentary in its extended version. To enable the subject matter of the sonnets to be better understood I quote below some remarks from Section C of the commentary (Essay 3, pp. 207–11):

The first sonnet is a blessing and message of encouragement for the Messiah ben Joseph. The term 'Messiah' is not used, but unmistakable expressions such as 'Son of Joseph, the fruitful one, dear Ephraim' and 'his majestic ox will be exalted', as well as the content of the poem as a whole, show clearly that the warring and avenging Messiah is meant. The poet expresses joy at the coming of the time of vengeance and redemption and declares his confidence that the Messiah ben Joseph will successfully complete his mission by subduing his opponents and will dwell 'in a peaceful place, secure for ever'. The poem is replete with kabbalistic and messianic symbols, such as the epithet 'tsadik' for the Messiah ben Joseph on the basis of his mystical status in relation to the sefirah Yesod, the names *beit akeret* [the barren woman's house] and 'serpent' for the forces of evil, and the description of the divine flow which descends upon the head of the Messiah. The poem is founded on an apocalyptic sense that the end is at hand and that the wars leading to it will terminate in the victory of the Messiah.

The second sonnet concerns Dan, that is, Seraiah, the commander of the army of the Messiah [ben Joseph]. The identity of Dan with Seraiah is proved by a description of his deeds, by the allusions to the scriptural words [Gen. 49: 17] 'its rider falls backward', and especially by the last verse 'a mighty warrior, leap out upon the army's head'. Here some of the events are described in the present tense and even in the past, and the verses of the third stanza put it beyond doubt that Seraiah is very much alive and has already begun to operate successfully.

I went on to offer evidence supporting my statement (Section B: Essay 3, p. 205) that 'Seraiah of the tribe of Dan . . . commander of the messianic army in Luzzatto's group was R. Jekutiel of Vilna'. I relied principally on two poems signed 'Jekutiel of Vilna', copies of which appear after the messianic sonnets in the Guenzburg collection (fo. 203^{r-v}). With regard to those two poems by Jekutiel I said: 'The second poem was doubtless written for Luzzatto's wedding. The subject of the first poem is not clear, but from the names mentioned in it, it appears to me that it was composed as a song of praise for R. Moses David Valle [Messiah ben David in Luzzatto's group, as I stated ibid., Section B]. Both poems have a messianic ring to them and bring in the name "Dan".' After quoting extracts from the poem in honour of R. M. D. Valle and reproducing the last stanza of the epithalamium for Luzzatto, I continued: 'In both poems the content is obscure . . . but there is no doubt that Dan, Judah, and Joseph [who are mentioned in the poems] are Seraiah and the two Messiahs, and that "Dan who leaps" is Seraiah. In both places the mention of Dan comes as a surprise, and the context, especially in the second poem, shows that Dan is another name for the author, that is to say that Seraiah is Jekutiel.' I added:

Luzzatto's poetry as hitherto known to us does not give expression to his love of the Shekhinah and the messianic visions by which he was possessed and which inspired him with such fervent devotion. Did Luzzatto the poet really stifle or silence his mystical and messianic aspirations and experiences, which without doubt were what he valued most highly and held most sacred for many years? This would be surprising, but a 'hidden treasure' which I chanced upon and have been able to identify has shown that any such assumption is unwarranted. The discovery is a collection of religious poems and prayers by Luzzatto which may entirely alter our assessment of the character of his poetic œuvre. In these compositions the poet-artist and the kabbalist-seer, between whom many scholars had sought to draw a distinction, are united.

Riddle in Verse

This riddle in verse is set out in accordance with the rules laid down by Luzzatto in the first version of *Leshon limudim*. That version of his treatise on the theory of literary writing was written in 1724, when the author was 17 years old, but it was put away in manuscript and has only recently appeared in print (see *Sefer leshon limudim*, ed. A. M. Habermann (Jerusalem and Tel Aviv, 1951), pt. 2, *limud* 10, 'The riddle and its rules', 146–7). Two riddles in verse on this pattern have appeared in print, and B. Klar succeeded in solving them by following Luzzatto's instructions (see *Sefer hashirim*, ed. Ginzburg and Klar, 44–6, 49–51, 60, 65–7). The poem under consideration here is likewise headed with 'The form of the riddle', and near its end the Italian name of the subject of the riddle is inserted, with the note *lo'ez* ['foreign']. These are the two principal keys to the solution of a riddle in verse according to the instructions in *Leshon limudim*. All my efforts over a period of more than fifteen years failed to find the hidden answer, nor were colleagues whom I consulted any more successful in breaking the code, but from some of the lines and motifs it was clear to me that this was a religious poem, or even one of a kabbalistic and mystical character. By good fortune last summer, in the relaxed atmosphere of Oxford, an idea occurred to me which led me to my goal. My starting point was a proper understanding of the two lines of 'the form of the riddle':

Mi atem likedoshim tevakeshun
kiftsu pikhem bal taḥarishun

[Who are you who seek holy things
Shut your mouths, do not hold your peace.]

I had long recognized that an important clue was concealed in the second line, which, taken literally, is self-contradictory. I suddenly realized that the two letters of the word *bal* ['not'] should be reversed so that they read *lev* ['heart']. This transforms the text into a poetic version of a famous *mishnah* in *Sefer yetsirah*, 1: 8: 'Eser sefirot belimah, belom pikha miledaber velibekha mileharher' ['Ten sefirot of [or 'founded on'] nothingness [*belimah*],[1] restrain [*belom*] your mouth from speaking and your heart from thinking']. (The whole chapter is reproduced in the Guenzburg collection at fos. 213^r–214^r; I presume it was copied there for the purpose of its use in the riddle.) Thus 'the form of the riddle' is intended as an instruction that when you come to investigate the wonder of the system of the sefirot, the exalted forces of the Godhead, you must approach the holy of holies with trembling: 'Shut your mouth(s), silence your heart[s]'. From this, with the aid of hints in the lines of the poem, I was able to reach the conclusion that the subject of the riddle was *reshit* ['beginning'], in the sense of 'the beginning of wisdom', i.e. the sefirah Hokhmah and the virtues of wisdom [*ḥokhmah*] in general. In *Sefer yetsirah*, Hokhmah–Reshit heads the system of the sefirot, and there is no mention of Keter, which kabbalistic works regularly place above Hokhmah in drawings of the sefirotic tree. The book begins in *mishnah* 1: 'By thirty-two paths the wonders of *ḥokhmah* . . .' and in representing the 'ten sefirot *belimah*' as ten depths (1: 5), it describes the first depth [*omek*] as *omek reshit*.

The other two verse riddles of this kind by Luzzatto which were printed in *Sefer hashirim* appear alongside poems in celebration of weddings, and this indeed was the general purpose of such riddles (see *Sefer hashirim*, ed. Ginzburg and Klar, 46). Apparently the present riddle, too, was read and offered for solution at an earthly wedding, but it was principally intended for the rejoicing of bridegroom and bride at the holy wedding of the divine couple, the Holy One, blessed be He, and the Shekhinah, in the days of the Messiah: see the last two verses: 'We shall look upon the city of our solemn festivals—Zion the release of prisoners / The bridegroom with his bride—the upright will rejoice.'

[1] [The proper rendering of *sefirot belimah* is doubtful: see G. Scholem, *Major Trends in Jewish Mysticism* (New York, 1961), 77.—Trans.]

THE POEMS

[As the poems are of literary interest, it has been thought worth while to give the Hebrew text here in parallel with the translation.—Trans.]

[God who works wonders]

[99[r]] God who works wonders
I will fill my tongue with the glory of Your name; answer me,
Requite me with the joy of Your deliverance
And grant me a willing spirit to uphold me.

Lo, Your faithfulness is from afar
O wondrous in counsel and mighty in power
Let Your holy strength breathe its spirit [upon me]
Which alone gives rest to the weary
Or what else but Your spirit endows with wisdom
The poor man crushed, the lowly poor bowed down
Let the flame of Your light lighten my darkness
I will bend my head low to You
My soul will be filled with Your praise
My God, guide me with Your strength
God who works wonders etc.

Lights of dew, purer than crystal
Shine in Your holy heights

Requite me . . . Ps. 51: 14 (51: 12). [In view of the context this translation is offered as an alternative to the standard renderings of the Psalm: 'Restore to me . . .'.—Trans.]

Lo . . . from afar From Isa. 25: 1: 'I will praise Your name, for You have done wonderful things, designs from afar, faithful and sure.' The reference could be understood in accordance with the literal meaning of the scriptural verse: Your faithfulness in fulfilling Your promises has been demonstrated since the distant past ['from afar' = 'from long ago']; but it appears that the meaning is, above all, kabbalistic and symbolic: Your Shekhinah, the sefirah Malkhut which is also called Emunah—faithfulness—acts 'from afar', from the world of Emanation [*atsilut*]. The Shekhinah is the source of human wisdom, considered as the 'lower wisdom' in the celestial system, and is also the source of inspiration from the Holy Spirit.

breathe its spirit [*yashev ruḥo*, apparently borrowed from Ps. 147: 18, but there it means 'He makes His wind blow'.—Trans.] Only the Holy Spirit which rests upon the poet [as if the verb is from the root *yashav*, 'to sit' or 'to dwell'—Trans.] can relieve his weariness.

Or what . . . bowed down The Holy Spirit confers wisdom on the poor man [*evyon*] who is oppressed and the needy man [*dal*] who has been humbled. At first sight it would seem clear that *evyon* and *dal* are synonymous here and that both refer to Luzzatto himself. But from a statement by R. Moses David Valle, Luzzatto's colleague and his partner in the leadership of the messianic group in Padua, it appears that the reference is to the two Messiahs. The statement in question appears in Valle's commentary on the Psalms, MS BL 387, fo. 72[v]: 'As to the significance of his [the Psalmist's] juxtaposing the words "***p**aletu **d**al **v**e'**e**vyon* [dots over the letters *p, d, v, e* (*alef*)] *miyad resha'i*[*m*] *hatsilu*" [Ps. 82: 4: 'Rescue the poor and the needy, deliver them from the hand of the wicked'], *dal* and *evyon* are mystical references to the two Messiahs, Messiah ben

[האל מפליא]

הָאֵל מַפְלִיא כְּבוֹד שְׁמֶךָ
אֲמַלֵּא לְשׁוֹנִי תַּעֲנֵנִי
הָשִׁיבָה לִי שְׂשׂוֹן יִשְׁעֶךָ
וְרוּחַ נְדִיבָה תִסְמְכֵנִי.

הֵן מֵרָחוֹק אֱמוּנָתֶךָ
עֵצוֹת מַפְלִיא וְאַמִּיץ כֹּחַ
יַשֵּׁב רוּחוֹ עֱזוּז קָדְשֶׁךָ
זֶה לֶעָיֵף לְבַד מָנוֹחַ
אוֹ מַה יַּחְכֵּם וְלֹא רוּחֶךָ
אֶבְיוֹן נִדְכֶּה וְדַל יָשׁוֹחַ
יָאֵר חָשְׁכִּי שְׁבִיב אוֹרֶךָ
יִכַּף רֹאשִׁי לְךָ שָׁחוֹחַ
תִּשְׂבַּע נַפְשִׁי תְהִלּוֹתֶיךָ
אֱלֹקַי בְּעָזְּךָ נַהֲלֵנִי
הָאֵל וכו׳

אוֹרוֹת טַל מִבְּדוֹלַח צַחוּ
בִּמְרוֹם קָדְשָׁךְ הֲלֹא יַזְהִירוּ

David and Messiah ben Joseph, who, after the *tikun* has taken place on high, will finally be disgorged by the husk [*hi poletetan*] which had swallowed them. That explains the use of the term *paletu*, which signifies the spewing out of what had been swallowed. The place is alluded to by the initial letters—look well and you will find it—and [they will] finally be delivered from the *ḥitsonim* ['external ones'], who are the wicked referred to here.' The allusion to the place is in the initial letters of *paletu dal ve'evyon*—Padua. We have here an explicit statement that the two Messiahs, called *dal* and *evyon*, were present in Luzzatto's group in Padua. I have pointed out elsewhere that Valle, in his own writings, presents himself in the role of Messiah ben David, whereas Luzzatto saw himself as the biblical Moses, who was superior to both Messiahs. See I. Tishby, *Netivei emunah uminut* (Ramat Gan, 1964), 186–201. It seems probable, therefore, that by the words 'the *evyon* crushed, the *dal* bowed down' Luzzatto meant to join with himself the two Messiahs who were his associates. Further on, in stanza 7, there is a clear reference to the two Messiahs under the names of *evyon* and *hadar*, as explained in my notes below.

I will bend my head low to You Luzzatto himself, as well as an eyewitness, testified that in his preparations for the revelations of the *magid* and while receiving those revelations his posture was that of *nefilat apayim* ['falling on one's face'], that is, with head and back bent. See *R' mosheh ḥayim lutsato uvenei doro: osef igerot ute'udot*, ed. S. Ginzburg [hereafter *Igerot*] (Tel Aviv, 1937), i. 21, 39, 86, 95, 104. It is to be supposed that the description in this verse which is coupled with a request for divine enlightenment refers to Luzzatto's physical attitude during the mystical experience in which the *magid* revealed himself within the poet's soul.

Lights of dew . . . This expression comes from Isa. 26: 19: 'For Your dew is a dew of light(s)'. Here it refers to the divine lights which pour down from above in the world of Emanation.

Shine . . . On those who . . . trust [*el ḥosei*

On those who, joyful, trust in You
Turning to You alone their shining face.
There they have gathered, and there emerges into light
[99v] The secret place of every mystery that had been hidden
In all the profundities of Your mighty thoughts
O turn towards me also, grant me joy
God who etc.

The chosen shepherd whom You drew near to You
For whom [Your] hand fought there, and triumphed there—
A nation which he made Yours, the son You loved,
Great in faithfulness and great in trust,
[That nation] You have again removed, as long ago You did.
How long must he weep [as one who] gasps for breath,
When will You favour the footstool in which You took delight
The throne set firmly as the moon
There set apart, let us look our fill upon You
Put forth Your right hand, draw me near to You
God who etc.

No counsel avails against You
And every plan You turn back towards Yourself
Your actions prosper as You rule in majesty;
You extend Your strong dominion over all
[100r] I will come and declare Your mighty deeds
[With] all my heart I will obey You alone
Your sceptre rules from sea to sea

bakh] The verse 'On those who, joyful, trust in You' is based on Ps. 5: 12: 'All those who take refuge [or 'who trust'] in You shall rejoice.' But what is meant here is not just people who are confident in their faith but a mystical group of *ḥosim* ['those who trust'] who are privileged to receive divine illumination and come to understand the secrets of the Godhead, as explained in the succeeding verses. These *ḥosim* are the members of Luzzatto's group. The second prayer for the night of 17 Shevat, published in the second part of this essay, contains the following request in the name of the members of the group: 'Endow us with the Holy Spirit, so that we may be illumined by Your light and our souls be bound together with Your holiness . . . and Your holy lights will encompass us and surround us on every side.'

There they have gathered The rays of light are gathered together within 'those who trust', and there they illumine the secrets hidden in the depths of God's thoughts.

The chosen shepherd Moses, *raya meheimna*, the faithful shepherd.

אֶל חוֹסֵי בָךְ אֲשֶׁר יִשְׂמָחוּ
אַךְ בָּךְ פָּנִים לְבַד יָאִירוּ
נֶאֶסְפוּ שָׁם וְשָׁם יִזְרָחוּ
כָּל מִסְתַּר סוֹד אֲשֶׁר הִסְתִּירוּ
כָּל עִמְקֵי מַחְשְׁבוֹת עוּזֶּךָ
וְגַם לִי פְּנֵה נָא, שַׂמְּחֵנִי
הָאֵל וכו׳

רוֹעֶה נִבְחָר אֲשֶׁר קֵרַבְתָּ
שָׁם יָד רָב לוֹ וְשָׁם נוֹצֵחַ
עַם לָךְ הִקְנָה וּבֵן אָהַבְתָּ
רַב אֵמוּן בּוֹ וְרַב בּוֹטֵחַ
לַשְׁבִיתוֹ שׁוּב כְּמֵאָז שַׁבְתָּ
עַד אָן יִבְכֶּה [כְּמִ]תְיַפֵּחַ
מָתַי תִּרְצֶה הֲדוֹם תָּאַבְתָּ
כִּסֵּא נָכוֹן כְּמוֹ יָרֵחַ
שָׁם בָּדָד נִשְׁבְּעָה פָּנֶיךָ
שְׁלַח נָא יְמִינְךָ, קָרְבֵנִי
הָאֵל וכו׳

הֵן אֵין עֵצָה לְעוּמָּתֶךָ
וּמְזִימָּה כָּל לְךָ תָּשִׁיבָה
תִּצְלַח תִּמְשׁוֹל בְּהַדְרָתֶךָ
עַל כָּל עוֹז מָשְׁלְךָ תַּרְחִיבָה
אָבוֹא בִּדְבַר גְּבוּרוֹתֶיךָ
כָּל לָךְ לִבִּי לְבַד אַקְשִׁיבָה
הֵן יֵרְדְּ מִיָּם לְיָם שִׁבְטֶךָ

A nation Israel.

the son You loved . . . An allusion by contraries to the language of Scripture (Deut. 32: 20): 'Children in whom there is no faithfulness'.

You have again removed, as long ago You did You have again driven Israel into exile, just as he was in exile in Egypt 'long ago', before Moses redeemed the people and made them over to You.

the footstool A description applied to the Temple. See Ps. 132: 7; Lam. 2: 1; 1 Chr. 28: 2.

The throne set firmly as the moon See Ps. 89: 37–8.

set apart Trusting in God and alone with Him, free from subjection to foreign rulers.

No counsel avails against You See Prov. 21: 30.

And every plan . . . towards Yourself All understanding returns to You, is under Your control.

Your sceptre rules from sea to sea See Ps. 72: 8.

Then rule my heart, I pray; comfort me
God who etc.

If I was made in secret in time past
[And] on my unformed substance You turned Your eye
I give thanks to You, for I am fearfully and wonderfully made
You have opened a path towards Your spirit
The ignorant You enlighten, the simple You make wise
There You gladden the longing soul
And so I am filled with joy [as I ascend] to Your crown
You have inscribed them all in Your book
[Their] seed will come and serve You
Look now on my affliction, rescue me
God who etc.

You are One, and beside You there is none
O High One, glory is Yours in the splendour of holiness
What man dare raise his eyes to look
[100v] O God in concealment, You whose way is holiness
Better than wine is Your love
I will lower my head and look upon holiness
I will look again on the majesty of Your holiness
Send Your holiness, I pray You, hallow me
God who etc.

Pour out [Your] spirit on all flesh
Heal wounds, bind up our broken limbs
Let majesty increase and there let rest

If I was made . . . eye Based on Ps. 139: 15–16: 'When I was made in secret . . . Your eyes saw my unformed substance.' You watched over me when I was an embryo in my mother's womb.

fearfully and wonderfully made Ps. 139: 14.

You have opened . . . spirit After I emerged from my mother's womb You opened a way for me towards Your spirit and drew me near to You.

the longing soul Longing to cleave [*lehitdabek*] to God.

as I ascend . . . Ascending in *devekut*.

Your crown [*nizrekha*] Perhaps 'Your crown' in the most direct sense, i.e. the sefirah Keter Elyon; or perhaps what is meant is the whole world of the sefirot, each one of which is called Keter.

You have inscribed . . . book From Ps. 139: 16: 'And in Your book they were all written.' Here the meaning is apparently: You inscribed all the children of Israel in Your book with the intent that they should be a holy seed worthy of serving You.

my affliction . . . See Ps. 119: 153.

O High One . . . All the attributes ascribed to

רְדָה נָא לְבָבִי, נַחֲמֵנִי
הָאֵל וכו׳.

בַּסֵּתֶר אִם כְּבָר עוּשֵּׂיתִי
עַל גָּלְמִי עֵינְךָ פָּקַחְתָּ
נוֹרָאוֹת אוֹדְךָ נִפְלֵאתִי
אוֹרַח אֶל רוּחֲךָ פָּתַחְתָּ
בּוֹעֵר תַּשְׂכִּיל וְתַעְרִים פֶּתִי
שָׁם שׁוֹקֵקָה הֲלֹא שִׂמַּחְתָּ
כֵּן גִּיל עַד נִזְרְךָ מָלֵאתִי
כֻּלָּם עַל סִפְרְךָ פִּתַּחְתָּ
זֶרַע יָבֹא וְיַעַבְדֶךָּ
לְעָנְיִי רְאֵה נָא, חַלְּצֵנִי
הָאֵל וכו׳

אֶחָד אַתָּה וּבִלְתָּךְ אָיִן
רָם כָּבוֹד לָךְ בְּהַדְרַת קֹדֶשׁ
מִי אִישׁ יָרִים לְהַבִּיט עָיִן
אֵל מִסְתַּתֵּר וְדַרְכָּךְ קֹדֶשׁ
טוֹבִים דוֹדִים לְךָ מִיָּיִן
אַשְׁפִּיל רֹאשִׁי וְאַבִּיט קֹדֶשׁ
אוֹסִיף הַבִּיט הֲדַר קָדְשֶׁךָ
שְׁלַח קָדְשְׁךָ נָא, קַדְּשֵׁנִי
הָאֵל וכו׳

עַל כָּל בָּשָׂר שְׁפוֹךְ נָא רוּחַ
מַכָּה תִרְפָּא חֲבוֹשׁ שִׁבְרֵנוּ
יִגְדַּל הָדָר וְשָׁם יָנוּחַ

God in this stanza are pregnant with kabbalistic-mystical meaning. They are directed towards God's concealment as Ein Sof and His manifestation in the world of the sefirot ('in the splendour of holiness', 'You whose way is holiness'). From there a flow of delight pours down on the soul of the poet who sings of the love of God ('Better than wine is Your love'), and a window is opened for him to contemplate the sefirot in his mind's eye ('I will . . . look upon holiness').

Better than wine is Your love From S. of S. 1: 2.

I will lower my head It is impossible to look upon the holiness of God with raised eyes, but the poet looks at it with head bowed. See my comment above on 'I will bend my head low to You'.

Pour out [Your] spirit on all flesh A messianic petition, based on Joel 3: 1 [2: 28 in English versions]: 'And it shall come to pass afterwards that I shall pour out My spirit upon all flesh.' Every line of this stanza is messianic.

majesty Messiah ben Joseph: Deut. 33: 17 ('His firstling ox, majesty is his') is expounded as applying to him. See also, below, the

The poor man wounded for our transgressions
The shadows flee, the day draws breath
All our joyous music is for You
Rescue the only one, weak, though anointed king
Bless and show favour to our slender forces
Lift up, I pray, the cup of Your salvation
Accept my reverence, draw me near
God who etc.

Head greatly exalted above all heads,
High is Your wisdom and not to be grasped
[101r] From the lowly man You did indeed accept
Many an offering, and there
Your sovereignty was clothed in strength when You revealed Yourself
Diademed, on splendid seraphim
Your treasured people long ago You taught
The pleasantness of Splendour [*zohar*] and they were betrothed to You
A way of bright light was Your path
I, too, am as a son to You, give me Your blessing
God who etc.

reference to Messiah ben Joseph in the sonnet 'Son of Joseph, the fruitful one': 'His majestic ox will be exalted'.

The poor man wounded for our transgressions Messiah ben David, in accordance with the interpretation of Isa. 53: 5: 'But he was wounded because of our transgressions'. And see above, in the stanza beginning 'Lo, Your faithfulness is from afar', the phrase 'the poor man crushed' and my comment thereon.

The shadows . . . breath Based on S. of S. 2: 17: 'Until the day breathes and the shadows flee'. The verse is interpreted as referring to the messianic redemption. See the midrash *Shir hashirim* [Song of Songs] *rabah*, end of *parashah* 2.

Rescue the only . . . king This verse, too, refers to Messiah ben David, quoting the words of David in 2 Sam. 3: 39: 'I am this day weak, though anointed king.' The phrase 'Rescue the only one [*yaḥid*]' is an allusion to Ps. 22: 21: 'Deliver my soul from the sword, my only one from the power of the dog.' Interpreted mystically, this is a prayer for the deliverance of the soul from the clutches of the husks; and according to Lurianic kabbalah 'the only one' [*yeḥidah*], which is the highest part of the fivefold soul consisting of *nefesh*, *ruaḥ*, *neshamah*, *ḥayah*, *yeḥidah*, is the inheritance of the Messiah. The *yeḥidah* as the soul of the Messiah, and its deliverance from the husks, are central to Luzzatto's doctrine of redemption. See Essay 4, p. 229 ff.

Lift up . . . salvation Cf. Ps. 116: 13.

Head . . . above all heads The highest of the degrees of divinity is in the sefirah Keter, which in the Zohar is called *resha dekhol resha* ['head of every head'] and the like.

High is Your wisdom . . . The sefirah Hokhmah, too, is high above the reach of

אֶבְיוֹן חוֹלַל אֱנוֹשׁ פִּשְׁעֵנוּ
יָנוּס הַצֵּל וְיוֹם יָפוּחַ
חֶדְוַת לָךְ כָּל נְגִינוֹתֵינוּ
יָחִיד הַצֵּל וְרַךְ מָשׁוּחַ
בָּרֵךְ וּרְצֵה מְעַט חֵילֵינוּ
אָנָּא שָׂא כוֹס יְשׁוּעוֹתֶיךָ
וְכָבוֹד קְחָה לִי, תִּמְשְׁכֵנִי
הָאֵל וכו׳

רֹאשׁ עַל כָּל רֹאשׁ מְאֹד נִשֵּׂאתָ
רָמָה חָכְמָה וְלֹא נִתְפָּשָׂה
מִנִּי שָׁפָל הֲלֹא הִרְבֵּיתָ
קַבֵּל מִנְחָה, וְשָׂם לָבָשָׁה
מַלְכוּתְךָ עוֹז בְּיוֹם נִגְלֵיתָ
עַל שַׂרְפֵי הוֹד, פְּאֵר חָבָשָׁה
לִסְגוּלָּה לָךְ כְּבָר הוֹרֵיתָ
חֶמְדַּת זֹהַ[ר] וְלָךְ אוֹרָשָׂה
מַעְגַּל אוֹר רַב נְתִיבָתֶךָ
כְּבֵן גַּם אֲנִי לָךְ, בָּרְכֵנִי
הָאֵל וכו׳.

human understanding; in the Zohar it is referred to by such titles as *ḥokhmeta ila'ah setima'ah* ['hidden supernal wisdom']. An outstanding illustration of the original use of these terms to describe the first two sefirot and their existence in concealment is provided by Zohar III, 288*a–b* (*Idra zuta*). And see I. Tishby, *The Wisdom of the Zohar*, trans. D. Goldstein (Oxford, 1989), i. 243–6, 280–2, 293–5. Apparently the description of the hidden sefirot was placed first as an introduction to the revelation of God and of divine wisdom at the giving of the Torah.

From the lowly man From Moses, who was distinguished for his humility.

and there At Mount Sinai. The description of the giving of the Torah follows aggadic midrashim. The expression 'Your sovereignty' refers to the Shekhinah in her identity as the sefirah Malkhut.

The pleasantness of Splendour The text reads *ḥemdat zh*; it is clear that the copyist has acidentally omitted the *r* of *zohar*. The Torah is called *ḥemdah* ['delight, pleasantness'] or *ḥemdah genuzah* ['hidden delight'] in the sources, but the phrase *ḥemdat zohar* appears to have been coined by Luzzatto.

and they were betrothed to You On the basis of Deut. 33: 4: 'Moses commanded us a law, an inheritance [*morashah*] for the congregation of Jacob', which is expounded as follows in the Talmud (*Ber.* 57*a*; *Pes.* 49*b*): 'Read this not as *morashah* but as *me'orasah* ['betrothed', fem. sing.].' In the Talmudic gloss the reference is to the Torah, but Luzzatto applied it to Israel, who are here called *segulah* ['treasured possession'] in the feminine, in consequence of Hos. 2: 21–2. But this application of the text may exist in some older source.

Bless, O bless Your treasured possession
Again show favour and rejoice in us
Let their heart hold fast Your acts of kindness
Reveal the treasures which are hidden
Let come the man who showed his zeal for You
The man to whom the covenant gives strength, but peace for us
One son You have, the nation of Your witnesses
By every righteous act, long since, they showed their faithfulness to You
Let me see Your greatness and rejoice in it
The time has come, it is already time, be gracious to me
God who etc.

[Underwritten with the initials of the Hebrew words 'Ended and completed, thanks be to God the Creator of the universe'.]

[*Structure and metre of the poem.* The opening stanza has four lines of alternately nine and ten syllables, and serves as a refrain. The body of the poem consists of nine stanzas, six with ten lines and three with eight. Each line consists of four *tenuot* [long vowels] followed by a *yated* [a foot consisting of one short vowel and one long vowel] and three *tenuot*, except for the last line in each stanza, which consists of *yated* and *tenuah*, *yated* and two *tenuot*, *yated* and *tenuah*.]

Your treasured possession Your people Israel; see above.

the treasures The secrets of the Torah, which are hidden until the coming of the Redeemer.

[O bride, all my delight]

[101v] GROOM O bride, all my delight is in you
When will your beauty sate me?
BRIDE My beloved, all my soul is yours
When will you console me?
G. Fair one, let me see your face
B. My beloved, make me happy
See, I am yours alone
See, I am yours alone

O bride The bride and bridegroom in this dialogue are the divine couple, the Holy One, blessed be He, and the Shekhinah, when they are cut off from each other.

let me see your face Cf. S. of S. 2: 14.

בָּרֵךְ בָּרוּךְ סְגוּלָּתֶךָ
תָּשׁוּב תִּרְצֶה וְתִשְׂמַח בָּנוּ
יִתְמָךְ לִבָּם נְדִיבוֹתֶיךָ
וּצְפוּנִים גַּל אֲשֶׁר נִצְפָּנוּ
יָבֹא נָא אִישׁ קְנָאוֹתֶיךָ
עוֹז לִבְרִית לוֹ, שְׁלוֹמוֹת לָנוּ
אֶחָד בֵּן לָךְ וְעַם עֵדֶיךָ
צֶדֶק כָּל לָךְ כְּבָר נֶאְמָנוּ
אֶרְאֶה אֶשְׂמַח גְּדוּלָּתֶךָ
זְמָן בָּא, כְּבָר עֵת, חָנֵּנִי
הָאֵל וכו׳

תר״שלב״ע

the man who showed his zeal for You Elijah, the herald of the Messiah. See 1 Kgs. 19: 10, 14.

to whom the covenant . . . peace for us The reference is to the dual character of Elijah in the time to come, as portrayed in the literature of aggadah and its offshoots: the man of zeal in relation to the nations and a messenger of peace for Israel. The poetic description here is based on what Scripture says of the zealous Phinehas, with whom Elijah is identified in the midrashim. Num. 25: 11–12: 'in the zeal he showed for Me . . . behold, I grant him My covenant of peace'. This line of the poem describes the covenant as a source of strength for Elijah in his war against enemies, but 'for us', Israel, it is a covenant of peace.

One son You have Israel.

the nation of Your witnesses As in Isa. 43: 10.

The time has come 'The end of days' [the time for the appearance of the Messiah—Trans.].

[כלה כל חפצי]

ח׳ כַּלָּה כָּל חֶפְצִי בָךְ
מָתַי יוֹפְיֵךְ תַּרְוִינִי
כ׳ דּוֹדִי כָּל נַפְשִׁי לָךְ
מָתַי תְּנַחֲמֵנִי
ח׳ יָפָה מַרְאֵךְ הַרְאִינִי
כ׳ דּוֹדִי נָא תְשַׂמְּחֵנִי
רְאֵה נָא אַךְ לְךָ הִנֵּנִי
ח׳ רְאִי נָא אַךְ לָךְ הִנֵּנִי

G. Fair one, how could my heart forget you
Has there departed from it
That perfect seal which you impressed on it
Has it found rest [in absence] from you
Or found relief in joy
Since the day that you were hidden [from me]

B. [My] beloved, do you not know
How I have burned for you as on a sacrificial fire
What other joy, then, have I chosen
[102r] My love, when far from you
When will the day come that I satisfy you [with my love]
Raise up this [lowly person], comfort my troubled soul

G. Fair one, I can no longer
Wait patiently; hasten
Quickly to me, arise, approach, draw near

B. My love, draw rather to yourself
[Your bride, who is] sick with love for you
Lead me, I pray you, to the light,
The light of your salvation

G. Fair one, come, I am here
Long ago we rejoiced together
Let us renew our joy for all time to come, but even more so now.

[*Structure and metre of the poem.* Thirty-one lines, most of them short lines of seven syllables (with some exceptions), a few of them longer, with eleven syllables.]

That perfect seal . . . on it As in Ezek. 28: 12 and S. of S. 8: 6. And see Zohar I, 244*a* (Tishby, *Wisdom of the Zohar*, i. 366).

Since the day that you were hidden Since you went into exile.

How I have burned . . . sacrificial fire The representation of the ardour and anguish of love as if the person in love were being consumed by fire on the altar of sacrifice is a figure which appealed to Luzzatto. See his use

ח׳ יָפָה הַאִם לִשְׁכּוֹחַ
מִלֵּב אוֹתָךְ אוּכָלָה
הַאִם מֶנּוּ אָזָלָה
תָּכְנִית חוֹתָם חָתַמְתְּ
אוֹ מָצָא לָךְ מָנוֹחַ
אוֹ אִם רָחַב לִשְׁמוֹחַ
מִיּוֹם הַעְלֵם נֶעְלַמְתְּ

כ׳ דּוֹדִי אִם לֹא יָדַעְתָּ
אִם לֹא עַל מוֹקֵד לָךְ תָּמִיד בָּעַרְתִּי
אוֹ מַה שִּׂמְחָה בָּחַרְתִּי
דּוֹד וּרְחוֹקָה מִמֶּךְ
מָתַי יוֹם אֶשְׂבָּעֶךְ
דַּלֵּה זֹאת, תְּנַחֵם נֶפֶשׁ נִבְהָלָה.

ח׳ יָפָה עוֹד לֹא אוּכָלָה
אוֹחִיל אֶתְאַפָּק, חִישִׁי
אֵלַי מַהֵר, קוּמִי קִרְבִי הַגִּישִׁי

כ׳ דּוֹדִי קָרֵב לָךְ אָתָּה
חוֹלַת יְדִידוֹתֶיךָ
לְאוֹר יְשׁוּעָתֶךָ
לְאוֹר נָא הוֹלִיכֵנִי

ח׳ יָפָה בּוֹאִי הִנֵּנִי
מֵאָז הֵן שַׂשְׂנוּ יָחַד
נָשׁוּב נָשִׂישׂ עוֹלָם, וּמַה גַּם עַתָּה.

of it in the next poem ('Open to me, my sister'). And see, in the notes on that poem, a comparable passage from *Layesharim tehilah*.

[My] love After this word the letters of the word *hu* ['he'] have been deleted.

[**approach** Hebrew *hagishi*, 'present [me]', perhaps used in place of *geshi*, 'approach', for the sake of the metre and rhyme.—Trans.]

your salvation An allusion to the Shekhinah awaiting her own redemption from captivity.

but even more so now Because the time of the Redemption has arrived.

[Open to me, my sister]

[103v] Open to me, my sister, my love
My dove, my perfect one
For my head is wet with dew
My locks with the drops of the night

Awake, my fair one, pray awake
Awake, my fair one, when will you rouse yourself from sleep?
Look on the burning heart of one who is afire for you
Spread over it the water of your consolation
Awake, see [my] soul
It is the offering burning on its altar fire
All the day and all the night
Open to me etc.

I pray you open, open, pray, the gate which shuts me out
From darkness let your light shine out to me
Amidst all tumult and disaster
Your recollection so sweet, so good, gives rest to my soul
Look upon my heart, most faithful to you
Losing itself in love for you
[104r] Musing on the praise which is your due
Day and night
Open to me etc.

Arise, my perfect one, arise, and of your kindness [grant]
My heart, which longs for you as [does the slave] for shade, the
pleasantness of your love
Distil the honey of your mouth

Open to me . . . drops of the night The first part of this verse from S. of S. (5: 2: 'I was asleep, but my heart was awake. Hark! My beloved is knocking') is omitted here, but the whole verse is given as a quotation at the end of the poem. The 'beloved' in this poem is Luzzatto. He appeals to his loved one, the Shekhinah, in her lowly condition, exiled and far from him, to take courage and strengthen him by the renewal of their love. In the second prayer for the night of 17 Shevat, the blame for the separation of the Shekhinah, 'the bride of Moses', from Luzzatto is pinned on the 'mixed multitude'—the persecutors of Luzzatto and his group, as will be explained in its proper place.

It is the offering . . . fire Here it is clear that stylistically the metaphor which represents the fire of love as the flames of an altar fire has its source in the description of the burnt offering

[פתחי לי אחותי]

פִּתְחִי לִי אֲחוֹתִי רַעְיָתִי
יוֹנָתִי תַמָּתִי שֶׁרֹאשִׁי נִמְלָא טָל
קְוֻצּוֹתַי רְסִיסֵי לָיְלָה

עוּרִי יָפָה נָא עוּרִי
עוּרִי יָפָה, מָתַי תָּקִיצִי
לֵב בּוֹעֵר לָךְ לוֹהֵט תָּשׁוּרִי
מֵי נִיחוּמַיִךְ נָא עָלָיו תָּפִיצִי
עוּרִי נֶפֶשׁ תִּרְאִי
הִיא הָעוֹלָה
עַל מוֹקֵד לָהּ
כָּל הַיּוֹם וְכָל הַלַּיְלָה
פִּתְחִי וכו׳

אָנָּא פִתְחִי, פִּתְחִי נָא סְגוֹר שָׁעַר
מִנִּי חֹשֶׁךְ אֵלַי אוֹרֵךְ יוֹפִיעַ
בֵּין כָּל שׁוֹאָה וָסָעַר
זִכְרֵךְ מָתוֹק כִּי טוֹב נַפְשִׁי יַרְגִּיעַ
שׁוּרִי לֵב נָכוֹן לָךְ
בִּידִידוּתֵךְ יִשְׁגֶּה
בִּתְהִלָּתֵךְ יֶהְגֶּה
יוֹמָם וָלַיְלָה
פִּתְחִי לִי וכו׳

קוּמִי תַמָּה קוּמִי, אָנָּא הוֹאִילִי
אֶל לֵב כַּצֵּל שׁוֹאֵף נוֹעַם דּוֹדַיִךְ
נוֹפֶת חִכֵּךְ הַזִּילִי

in Scripture. See Lev. 6: 2 [6: 9 in English versions]. The same image appears briefly in the previous poem ('O bride, all my delight'). Similar language is used by Yosher in recounting the torments of his hopeless love in Luzzatto's play *Layesharim tehilah*, pt. 1, act 1, scene 3 (*Sefer hamaḥazot*, ed. S. Ginzburg (Tel Aviv, 1927), 218): 'My blood within me is fire, my spirit a flame / and all the things I see around me, / all are wood [to feed] my embers, / to set myself alight, and burn / my soul upon the altar fire day and night.'

[the gate [*sha'ar*] which shuts me out Hebrew *segor sha'ar*. In Hos. 13: 8 *segor* is understood to mean 'enclosure'.—Trans.]

as [does the slave] for shade Job 7: 2.

Distil By emendation from *azilu* (in both G and H) to *hazili*.

Let me see your face
How long will you delay
Pray arise
For the appointed time has come
Morning has come, and also night
Open to me etc.

How long will you forbear, how long can you
Leave me dying in affliction
How can your soul not be disquieted, how can you not be wholly moved
To pity me, or how not heed
The outpouring of all my heart
[104ᵛ] Straying from its nest
A bird alone upon a roof
[Exposed] to heat by day and frost by night
Open to me etc.

Were it not that I hoped in One
I should have perished in my affliction
Truly I have waited for Him
Again to grant me [or 'He will again grant me'] the sweet fruit of my labour
[When] I shall again be satisfied by your goodness
Distress will putrefy and stink
Sorrow will flee away
Departing like a vision of the night
Open to me etc.

Hannah, when will you don your holy grace
That went into exile with you?

Let me see H: 'And let me see'.

[**Pray arise** The line reads *kumi* ('arise') *va'ed*, but the latter word makes no obvious sense here.—Trans.]

the appointed time has come The time of the Redemption. Ps. 102: 14: 'You will arise and have pity on Zion, for it is time to be gracious to her, for the appointed time has come.'

Morning . . . night Isa. 21: 12.

dying *gove'a*, misspelt with *veit* instead of *vav* (so, too, in H). And see Ps. 88: 16.

in affliction Hebrew *ben oni*, literally 'a son of affliction'; see Prov. 31: 5.

moved / To pity The phrase echoes an expression in a *piyut* in the Yom Kippur Ne'ilah [concluding] prayer.

pity [*raḥem*] G has *yaḥem*(?) [which would mean 'to warm'—Trans.]. Apparently the true reading there, too, is *raḥem*, the letter *resh* being blurred.

Straying from its nest See Prov. 27: 8.

A bird . . . roof As in Ps. 102: 8.

הַרְאִינִי אֶת מַרְאַיִךְ
עַד מָה תַעַמְדִי, נָא
קוּמִי וָעֶד
כִּי בָא מוֹעֵד
אָתָא בֹקֶר גַם לַיְלָה
פִּתְחִי לִי וכו׳

עַד מָה תִתְאַפָּקִין, עַד מָה תוּכָלִי
אוֹתִי תַעַזְבִי בֶּן עוֹנִי גּוֹוֵעַ
אֵיךְ לֹא תֵהוֹם נַפְשֵׁךְ, לֹא תִתְגַּלְגָּלִי
עָלַי רַחֵם כֻּלֵּךְ, אֵיךְ אֵין שׁוֹמֵעַ
כָּל-לֵבָב נִשְׁפָּךְ
מִנִּי קִנּוֹ נוֹדֵד
צִיפּוֹר עַל גַּג בּוֹדֵד
לַחוֹרֶב בַּיּוֹם וְקֶרַח בַּלַּיְלָה
פִּתְחִי לִי וכו׳

לוּלֵי אֶחָד קִוִּיתִי
אָז אָבַדְתִּי בְעָנְיִי
אָכֵן אֵלָיו חִכִּיתִי
יִתֵּן מִיגִיעִי עוֹד מְתוֹק פִּרְיִי
אָשׁוּב אֶשְׂבַּע טוּבֵךְ
תִּבְאַשׁ צָרָה תִּסְרַח
יָנוּס יָגוֹן יִבְרַח
יִידּוֹד כְּחֶזְיוֹן לַיְלָה
פִּתְחִי לִי וכו׳

חַנָּה, מָתַי חִנֵּךְ קֹדֶשׁ תִּלְבָּשִׁי
אִתָּךְ גָּלָה, כַּדֶּשֶׁא תִּפְרַחְנָה

to heat by day Jer. 36: 30.

I should have perished in my affliction Ps. 119: 92.

He will . . . grant [*yiten*] H has *sheyiten* ['that He will grant']. In G a letter is erased at the beginning of the word, and the copyist read it incorrectly as *sheyiten*.

will flee [*yivraḥ*] H has *yifraḥ* ['fly', or 'blossom'!].

Departing [*yidod*] H has *yudad* ['will be chased away'], as in Job 20: 8.

Hannah All the positive maternal characters in Scripture can serve as a symbol for the Shekhinah. The poet has chosen the name Hannah [*ḥanah*] here to fit with *ḥinekh* ['your grace'] which follows it.

your holy grace [*ḥinekh kodesh*] [literally, 'your grace, holiness'] The *shin* in *kodesh* is blurred and it may be that the word written was *kadosh* ['holy']. H has *bekodesh* ['in holiness']. The sense is the same in each case: when will the Shekhinah renew her holy grace, which she lost in exile?

went into exile [*galah*] H has *gilah* ['it revealed'], an obvious error.

All my bones will flourish like grass
When you acquire eternal strength
[105r] My eyes will quite forget their bitter tears
The brilliance of your rising light will breach
Every high defensive wall
O strengthen majesty
To give light with your moon by night
Open to me etc.

Return, we shall again rejoice in you, and you in us
On the hill, set firm for ever, [which is?] our whole desire
Over all the glory [will be] a canopy, happiness for us
The throng all celebrating there the splendour of our joy
In the shade of cloud and smoke
We will take our fill of love
On henna and nard
By day, and [in] the bright light of a flaming fire by night
Open to me etc.

As it is said: 'I slept, but my heart was awake. Hark! My beloved is knocking. "Open to me, my sister, my love, my dove, my perfect one, for my head [105v] is wet with dew, my locks with the drops of the night." '

Completed, praise be to God the Creator of the universe.

[*Structure and metre of the poem.* The poem opens with a verse from Scripture (S. of S. 5: 2) which is divided into three lines and serves as a refrain. The body of the poem consists of seven stanzas of eight lines. Each stanza contains some long lines and some short, but the number of syllables varies without a set pattern. In the whole poem there are nineteen lines of eleven syllables, two of ten syllables, two of nine, nine of seven, fifteen of six, two of five, and five of four.]

All my bones . . . grass As in Isa. 66: 14.

The brilliance of your rising light Isa. 60: 3.

Every high defensive wall The light of the Shekhinah will break through and bring down the walls of the Sitra Ahra and the nations of the world. Cf. Isa. 25: 12 on the destruction of the fortifications of Moab.

כָּל עֲצְמוֹתַי עֵת עוֹז עוֹלָם תְּ[י]רָשִׁי
תַּמְרוּר דִּמְעָתָם כָּל עֵינַי תִּשְׁכַּחְנָה
מִשְׂגַּב כָּל רוּם חוֹמָה
יִבְקַע נוֹגַהּ זַרְחֵךְ
חַזְקִי הוֹד בְּיַרְחֵךְ
לְהָאִיר לַיְלָה
פִּתְחִי לִי וכו׳

שׁוּבִי עוֹד נִשְׂמַח בָּךְ, תָּגִילִי בָנוּ
עַל הַר נָכוֹן עוֹלָם כָּל חֶמְדָּתֵנוּ
עַל כָּל כָּבוֹד חוּפָּה שִׂמְחָתָה לָנוּ
הָמוֹן כָּל חוֹגֵג שָׁם הוֹד רִנָּתֵנוּ
בְּצֵל עָנָן עָשָׁן
נִרְוֶה דוֹדִים
עַל כֹּפֶר וּנְרָדִים
יוֹמָם, וְנוֹגַהּ אֵשׁ לֶהָבָה לַיְלָה
פִּתְחִי לִי וכו׳

כדבר שנא׳ אני ישנה ולבי ער קול דודי
דופק פתחי לי אחותי רעיתי יונתי תמתי
שראשי נמלא טל קווצותי רסיסי לילה

תושלב״ע

the hill, set firm The Temple Mount, as in Mic. 4: 1.

Over all the glory . . . From here to the end is mostly based on Isa. 4: 5. ['The throng all celebrating' is a reference to Ps. 42: 5.—Trans.]

As it is said S. of S. 5: 2.

[Hope, hope, my heart]

[105v] Hope, hope, my heart, I will wait in hope
Hope, hope indeed, hope yet again, my light will shine
Hope until wholeheartedly I gain in hope
Strengthen yourself
Justify your Rock
My soul, in Him alone have faith, seek Him
Have faith, for He is One, you shall not be ashamed.

If you [my soul] see breakers, or a flood
If your star grows dark while in the heavens it is yet day
If every adversary, every enemy sets sharp eyes upon you
See, do not be afraid
Strengthen yourself
Justify your Rock
My soul etc.

[106r] If that for which you hoped is far away, and all your hope
Long ago dashed, [if] you see
The baldness [of your mourning] grown great as on a vulture's head, and sorrow drawing near
Be strong, do not be afraid,
Strengthen yourself
Justify your Rock
My soul etc.

If grief defiles or mars your joy
If your sighing is too much for your strength

I will wait in hope *oḥilah*; *ohilah* in the next line (see below) is a play on this word.

hope . . . my light will shine *kaveh ohilah*; between these two words a word has been erased.

my light will shine Literally 'I will shine', Heb. *ohilah* in G and H. The correct form is *ahelah*, from the root *h-l-l*. Luzzatto treated the verb as if it were from [an unused] root *y-h-l*, perhaps to improve the rhyme, or perhaps in error.

until [*ad*] H has *od* ['again', 'still'].

He is One Written over an erased word. No erasure in H.

you shall not [*al*] H has *lo*. G is correct, agreeing with *al* in Ps. 25: 2: 'My God, in You I trust, let me not be ashamed.'

If your star grows dark [*im ḥashakh kesilekh*] 'Star': literally 'constellation', 'Orion'. This follows Isa. 13: 10: 'For the stars of the heavens and their constellations will not give their light, the sun will be dark when it goes forth, and the moon will not cause its light to shine.' H has 'If darkness has covered you' [*im ḥoshekh kisah*

[קוה קוה לבי]

קַוֵּה קַוֵּה לִבִּי קַוֵּה אוֹחִילָה
קַוֵּה אַף קַוֵּה, עוֹד קַוֵּה, אוֹהִילָה
קַוֵּה עַד מִכָּל-לֵב תִּקְוָה אַגְדִּילָה
כֹּחֵךְ חַזְּקִי
צוּרֵךְ צַדְּקִי
נַפְשִׁי אַךְ בּוֹ בִטְחִי אוֹתוֹ תִדְרוֹשִׁי
בִּטְחִי כִּי אֶחָד הוּא כִּי אַל תֵּבוֹשִׁי

אִם מִשְׁבָּרִים תִּרְאִי, אִם שֶׁטֶף מָיִם
אִם חָשַׁךְ כְּסִילֵךְ עוֹד יוֹם שָׁמָיִם
אִם כָּל צָר כָּל אוֹיֵב לוֹטֵשׁ עֵינָיִם
תִּרְאִי, אַל נָא תִירָאִי
כֹּחֵךְ חַזְּקִי
צוּרֵךְ צַדְּקִי
נַפְשִׁי וכו׳

אִם תּוֹחַלְתֵּךְ תִּרְחַק וּכְבָר נִכְזָבָה
כָּל תִּקְוָתֵךְ, תִּרְאִי רַבָּה נִרְחָבָה
כַּנֶּשֶׁר קָרְחָתֵךְ, צָרָה קָרָבָה
עוּזִּי, אַל נָא תִירָאִי
כֹּחֵךְ חַזְּקִי
צוּרֵךְ צַדְּקִי
נַפְשִׁי וכו׳

אִם שִׂמְחָתֵךְ יָגוֹן יַבְאִישׁ יַפְרִיעַ
אִם אַנְחָתֵךְ רַבַּת כֹּחֵךְ תַּכְרִיעַ

lakh], apparently a misreading because of a small gap in the word *kesilekh* between *kesi* and *lekh*; or perhaps the copyist failed to understand what was meant and made what he thought was a correction.

yet [*od*] H has *ad*(?) ['until'].

If that for which you hoped . . . In the stanzas on fo. 106[r] and also at the end of the poem on fo. 107[r], the photograph, which does not cover the margin, has cut off the beginning of every line. I have made good the deficiencies by reference to H.

The baldness . . . vulture's head As in Mic. 1: 16.

Be strong [[*u*]*zi*] H has *nafshi* ['my soul']. In G, too, the last two letters could be *shi* and not *zi*, but the reading *uzi* seems to accord better with the context and with the corresponding lines in the other stanzas.

be afraid [*tiri*] Misspelt in H, here and in the subsequent stanzas, as if from the root *ra'ah* ['to see'], omitting the *yod* of the root *yare* ['to be afraid'].

mars Hebrew *yafria* ['disturbs']. In H,

Night brings you no relief, nor does the day bring calm
Rejoice, do not be afraid
Strengthen yourself
Justify your Rock
My soul etc.

Amid impenetrable darkness, be strong and hope
In all the gloom of devastation, rejoice again
Bring a purification offering of eternal hope
To God, and do not be afraid
[106ᵛ] Strengthen yourself
Justify your Rock
My soul etc.

Endure the pangs of childbirth, for you will yet give birth
Remembering your [past] salvation, do not lose hope
Lift up your eyes and look around you, look upon rejoicing
It is yours, pray do not be afraid
Strengthen yourself
Justify your Rock
My soul etc.

Those who hope will see your salvation, will see and rejoice
A great wonder they will see [performed] for them
The nation that is blind will open its eyes and accept instruction
Rejoice, for you will not be afraid
Strengthen yourself
Justify your Rock

inappropriately, *yafriaḥ* ['causes to flower', or, at best, 'causes to fly away, blows away'—Trans.].

Night brings you no relief Adapted from Lam. 2: 18. In H the negative *lo* has been deleted in error.

[**the gloom of devastation** Hebrew *emesh sho'ah*, from Job 30: 3, as understood by some.—Trans.]

Lift up your eyes Above the line, between 'lift up' and 'your eyes', there is a short word, indistinct and possibly erased.

Lift up your eyes and look around you As in Isa. 49: 18.

Lift up . . . rejoicing / It is yours [In the Hebrew the words 'lift up' and 'rejoicing' are consecutive, thus: *tis'*[*i*], *si*[*mḥ*]*ah*, and are followed in the next line by *lakh hi*, 'it is yours'.—Trans.] H has a corrupt reading: *tsh* (or *ts*) *lakh hi*, omitting the last two letters of

לַיְלָה לֹא פוּגַת לָךְ, יוֹם לֹא יַרְגִּיעַ
שִׂמְחִי, נָא אַל תִּירָאִי
כֹּחֵךְ חַזְּקִי
צוּרֵךְ צַדְּקִי
נַפְשִׁי וכו׳

בֵּין כָּל מַחְשָׁךְ סָתוּם חִזְקִי הוֹחִילִי
בֵּין כָּל אֶמֶשׁ שׁוֹאָה שׁוּבִי וָגִילִי
מִנְחַת טוֹהַר, תִּקְוַת עוֹלָם הוֹבִילִי
אֶל אֵל, כִּי לֹא תִּירָאִי
כֹּחֵךְ חַזְּקִי
צוּרֵךְ צַדְּקִי
נַפְשִׁי וכו׳

חֶבְלֵי מַשְׁבֵּר סִבְלִי כִּי עוֹד תַּמְלִיטִי
זֵכֶר יִשְׁעֵךְ תִּקְוָה כִּי לֹא תַמְעִיטִי
סָבִיב עֵינֵךְ תִּשְׂאִ[י], שִׂ[מְחָ]ה הַבִּיטִי
לָךְ הִיא, נָא אַל תִּירָאִי
כֹּחֵךְ חַזְּקִי
צוּרֵךְ צַדְּקִי
נַפְשִׁי וכו׳

יִרְאוּ קוֹיִם יִשְׁעֵךְ, יִרְאוּ יִשְׂמָחוּ
מוֹפֵת רַבָּה לָהֶם יִרְאוּ יִפְקָחוּ
הָעָם עִוֵּר עֵינָיו מוּסָר יִקָּחוּ
שִׂמְחִי, כִּי לֹא תִּירָאִי
כֹּחֵךְ חַזְּקִי
צוּרֵךְ צַדְּקִי

tis'i and the words 'look upon rejoicing' [*simḥah habiti*], evidently because in the original, in G, there is an ink stain between *tis* and *simḥah*, the letters *mḥ* in the word *simḥah* are indistinct, and the copyist could not decipher the writing.

Those who hope will see . . . This appears to be a reference to the members of Luzzatto's group, called *kovim* ['those who hope']; their salvation and deliverance from their troubles will occur at the same time as the personal salvation of their leader, and that will take place together with the messianic redemption. See above, my note on the first poem ['God who works wonders', third stanza] explaining the expression 'those who trust'.

A great wonder . . . for them Salvation will prove the rightness of the way they have pursued under the guidance of Luzzatto. Or perhaps these words refer to the 'blind people' who are mentioned immediately afterwards.

The nation . . . instruction Those who blindly oppose and persecute Luzzatto and his

My soul, in Him alone have faith, seek Him
[107r] Have faith [in Him], for He is One, you shall not be ashamed

As it is written in Your Torah 'Hear, O Israel' etc., 'Trust in the Lord for ever' etc., 'And the Lord shall be King' etc.

[*Structure and metre of the poem.* There are seven stanzas. The first one contains three lines of eleven syllables followed by a four-line refrain in which the first two lines are of four syllables and the last two of eleven syllables. The other six stanzas are on the same pattern but with the addition, before the refrain, of a line of seven syllables which recurs with variations in each stanza.]

group will open their eyes and recognize their error and their guilt.

He is One In G, written over an erased word.

you shall not [*al*] **be ashamed** H has *lo*.

As it is written Deut. 6: 4; Isa. 26: 4; Zech. 14: 9.

[110v] Poem to be Recited after the Shavuot Study Session

Alef
From [the world's] first days, from its earliest years
Since first it was inhabited by a nation
Falsehood was its inheritance, emptiness in the midst of darkness
It dwelt among shadows of deceit
While salvation was far off because of wrongdoing
And truth lay in the depths of oblivion
There was no law, no justice or righteous words
No one to mend a breach or make good disrepair.

Beit
God who seeks righteousness and loves salvation
Chose Abraham when He looked
[And saw that] his heart was prepared to destroy transgression
Justice came up at his feet and shone
For he arose [in his] time to loose the bonds of wickedness
In face of Sheol, when he descended [there], he made truth spring forth

Falsehood . . . deceit *shav* ['falsehood, emptiness'], *rik* ['emptiness'], and *kazav* ['lying, deceit'] denote idol-worship and moral corruption.

Justice [or 'righteousness'] **. . . his feet** Based on Isa. 41: 2 [where moderns translate *tsedek* as 'victory'—Trans.], which is expounded as referring to Abraham. See *Bereshit rabah*, 43: 3.

In face of [*bifnei*] The text reads *penei* ['the face of'], but the metre requires the preposition.

נַפְשִׁי אַךְ בּוֹ בִטְחִי אוֹתוֹ תִדְרוֹשִׁי
בִּטְחִי כִּי אֶחָד הוּא כִּי אַל תֵּבוֹשִׁי

ככתוב בתורתך שמע ישראל וכו׳
בטחי בה׳ עדי עד וכו׳ והיה ה׳ למלך וכו׳.

שיר לומר אחר הלימוד של שבועות

א׳

מֵרֹאשׁ יְמוֹת עוֹלָם, שְׁנוֹת קַדְמָתָה
מֵאָז הֱיוֹת תֵּבֵל לְגוֹי נוֹשֶׁבֶת
שָׁוְא יָרְשָׁה לָהּ, רִיק בְּתוֹךְ עֵיפָתָה
בֵּין צִלְלֵי כָזָב אֲשֶׁר יוֹשֶׁבֶת
כִּרְחוֹק יְשׁוּעָה מִפְּנֵי עַוְלָתָה
וּלְיַרְכְּתֵי שִׁכְחָה אֱמֶת שׁוֹכֶבֶת
אֵין חֹק וְאֵין מִשְׁפָּט וְאִמְרֵי צֶדֶק
גּוֹדֵר פְּרָצוֹת אוֹ מְחַזֵּק בֶּדֶק

ב׳

דּוֹרֵשׁ צְדָקָה אֵל וְאוֹהֵב יֶשַׁע
בָּחַר בְּאַבְרָהָם בְּעֵת הִשְׁגִּיחַ
הוּכַן לְבָבוֹ לוֹ לְכַלֵּה פֶּשַׁע
צֶדֶק לְרַגְלוֹ יַעֲלֶה יַזְרִיחַ
כִּי עֵת לְהַתִּיר קָם אֲגוּדוֹת רֶשַׁע
פְּנֵי שְׁאוֹל כִּי שַׁח אֱמֶת יַצְמִיחַ

In face of Sheol, when he descended . . . In accordance with the view of the Zohar that Abraham's descent into Egypt is to be understood as his descent to the abyss of the husks (the underworld, Sheol). The Zohar states that in contrast to Adam and Noah, whose descent was a failure and who were caught by the Sitra Ahra—the forces of evil—Abraham was saved from the seductions of the husks and, on his reascent from their domain, he continued to work with even greater vigour

His seed after him continued his righteous tradition
Establishing the foundations of the earth on truth

[111r] *Gimel*

The Lord wrought wondrously and planted among them
A people to be distinguished from the multitude of nations for ever
And, yielding their fruit like a wholly good fruit tree
[This people] had already begun to grow in greatness
When a son of villainous men sorely afflicted them
There they lost patience and their soul indeed grew weary
In the furnace into which they were delivered
To try their strength of soul, that they might be purified

Dalet

And so, when the term appointed was complete and the time came
Many were His mighty deeds and by Him they were saved
His holy right hand powerfully showed its strength
When Pharaoh and his army were plunged into the sea
Then, to satisfy her love, she [*sic*] [transported]
Her people on a wing, so that they would not tire
Then they journeyed from Rephidim and came
To Sinai as one man, and there He tested them.

for the *tikun* [setting to rights] of the world. The descent of Jacob and his sons to Egypt is explained in the Zohar as a continuation of Abraham's descent and of his work to bring about this *tikun*. From here to the end of stanza *gimel* is a poetic reworking of the Zohar I, 83*a*. For the better understanding of Luzzatto's version I will quote his source in translation from the Aramaic: 'It is all a mystery of wisdom . . . Abraham descended into the very depths [of the husks] and knew them but did not cleave to them . . . and returned to his place, to the upper level to which he had attached himself at the beginning . . . Come and see. The mystery of the matter is, if Abraham had not gone down into Egypt and had not been purified there first, he would not have had a portion in the Holy One, blessed be He. Similarly with his descendants: the Holy One, blessed be He, wished to make of them a single people, a perfect people, and to draw them near to Him. But if they had not gone down into Egypt first and been purified there, they would not have become His unique people' (Tishby, *Wisdom of the Zohar*, ii. 457). And see my explanation and additional notes, ibid.

The Lord The abbreviation *he'* in both G and H, but the metre requires three more syllables, e.g. *eloheinu* ['our God'] or a similar word.

and planted . . . nations In the days of Jacob and his sons God planted Israel among the nations as [His] own people. Or perhaps 'among them' should be read as referring to 'the foundations of the earth', i.e. in the world.

[**for ever** Here and in the last line of the poem, Hebrew *selah*, translated as traditionally understood.—Trans.]

like a . . . fruit tree When the people of Israel had begun, as it were, to produce fruit in their work of perfecting the world.

זַרְעוֹ כְּצִדְקוֹ אַחֲרָיו הִשְׁלִימוּ
אָשְׁיוֹת אֲדָמָה עַל אֱמֶת הֵקִימוּ.

ג׳

הִפְלָא ה׳ וְנָטַע בָּמוֹ
עַם מֵהֲמוֹן גּוֹיִם לְהַבְדִּיל סֶלָה
וּכְעֵץ פְּרִי אַף טוֹב בְּתֵת פִּרְיָמוֹ
לָרוֹב גְּדוּלָּתוֹ כְּבָר הֵחֵלָּה
עֵת בֶּן בְּנֵי נָבָל בְּרָע עִנָּמוֹ
שָׁם קָצְרָה רוּחָם וְנַפְשָׁם תֵּלַהּ
אָכֵן בַּכּוּר לָהֶם אֲשֶׁר נִמְכָּרוּ
לִבְחוֹן בְּעֹז נַפְשָׁם וְהִטֶּהָרוּ

ד׳

כֵּן אָז בְּהַשְׁלִים קֵץ וְעֵת הִגִּיעָה
רַבּוּ גְבוּרוֹתָיו וּבוֹ נוֹשָׁעוּ
כֹּחָהּ יְמִין קָדְשׁוֹ בְּעוֹז הוֹדִיעָה
פַּרְעֹה וְחֵילוֹ עֵת בְּיָם טוּבָּעוּ
לִרְווֹת יְדִידוּתָהּ אֲזַי ההיעה(!)
עַמָּהּ עֲלֵי אֶבְרָה וְלֹא יִיגָעוּ
אָז מֵרְפִידִים נָסְעוּ וּבָאוּ
סִינַי כְּאִישׁ אֶחָד וְשָׁם נִסָּהוּ.

a son of villainous men Pharaoh, king of Egypt; the children of Ham.

In the furnace . . . purified The exile in Egypt, where the children of Israel were held in servitude as if sold as slaves, was a furnace in which they were purified. Egypt, in Scripture (1 Kgs. 8: 51), is called 'the iron-furnace'. Cf. Luzzatto's prayer for the eve of Rosh Hashanah: 'And in the iron-furnace in Egypt in which the men of wickedness, blood, and deceit afflicted their lives . . . You wrought signs and wonders with them so as to redeem them, a nation from the midst of another nation' (fo. 66r).

her love H: 'their love'.

[**her** [feminine] **love, she** The apparent antecedent of the feminine subject 'she' is 'His right hand'.—Trans.]

[transported] Both manuscripts have the nonsense reading *hehiah*, but in G there is a stroke above the second letter *h*, undoubtedly to draw attention to the error and indicate that the word should be read as *hisiah* ['[she] made them journey']. The Harvard copyist copied G's mistake. In saying that God's right hand 'transported her people on a wing', Luzzatto was combining two different versions of the exodus from Egypt: Deut. 32: 11, 'carries them on its wing' (and see the parallel expression in Exod. 19: 4), and Ps. 78: 52, 'He transported [*vayasa*, the same verb as *hisiah*] His people like sheep' (and see the parallel expression in Ps. 80: 9). The choice of *hisiah* to go with 'on a wing' was made to provide a rhyme with the first and third lines of the stanza.

Then . . . from Rephidim From here on is based on Exod. 19, with the addition of many motifs from aggadic literature describing the giving of the Torah.

He
[All] was prepared as He commanded, and they sanctified themselves
The seed of His chosen ones declared they would obey
[111v] On the third day they drew near, they approached
When the ram's horn sounded a blast most loud
There His heavens were opened while they quaked
In them He tore many [openings to] His upper chambers
He appeared as a merciful father to His children there
And they beheld His way which had been hidden.

Vav
They saw His mighty deeds and rejoiced
And beheld His greatness, and then they knew
Their Rock was One alone, and in Him they trusted
They heard some of His holy words in fire
Their enemies and opponents retreated, fled
Then mountains fell, then were they cleft asunder
Then lofty ones were cut down, they withered like a flower
The cedars of the nations fell, brought down to Sheol.

Zayin
Their eyes beheld the King in His beauty
The chariot of God upon its bases
The [four] living creatures, each with its four faces, went to and fro
High above them rose the awe-inspiring throne
[112r] One, God spoke aloud to them
His law, and lofty are its ways
For it raised truth up to His holy heights
A time is appointed for it and [then] it will throw light reaching even to the footstool.

declared they would obey They said 'We will do and obey' [Exod. 24: 7]. I have pointed the consonants *dbrv* as *diberu* ['they spoke'], to fit the metre, rather than *devaro* ['His word'].

He tore . . . upper chambers God tore open, broke open, many entrances and stairways in the heavens by which to ascend to Him.

the King in His beauty Based on Isa. 33: 17. Here the description of God revealing Himself at Sinai as a king sitting on the throne of glory surrounded by *ḥayot* ['living creatures'] and *ofanim* ['wheels'] is based on the vision of the chariot in Ezek. 1.

its bases The feminine pronominal suffix [represented in the translation by 'its'] must be understood as referring to the *merkavah*, which is the normal word for the celestial chariot, though here the masculine *rekhev* is used. In this stanza Luzzatto has not troubled himself

ה׳

הוּכַן כְּמִצְוָתוֹ וְהִתְקַדָּשׁוּ
זֶרַע בְּחִירָיו דִּבְרוֹ לִשְׁמוֹעַ
יוֹם הַשְּׁלִישִׁי נִקְרְבוּ נִגָּשׁוּ
שׁוֹפָר בְּקוֹל חָזָק מְאֹד בִּתְקוֹעַ
שָׁם נִפְתְּחוּ שָׁמָיו בְּעֵת רָעָשׁוּ
הִרְבָּה עֲלִיּוֹתָיו בְּמוֹ לִקְרוֹעַ
נִרְאָה כְּאָב רַחְמָן לְבָנָיו שָׁמָּה
וַיֶּחֱזוּ דַרְכּוֹ אֲשֶׁר נֶעְלָמָה.

ו׳

רָאוּ גְבוּרוֹתָיו וְכֵן שָׂמָחוּ
וַיֶּחֱזוּ גָדְלוֹ וְאָז יָדָעוּ
אֶחָד לְבָד צוּרָם וּבוֹ יִבְטָחוּ
מִדַּבְּרוֹת קָדְשׁוֹ בְּאֵשׁ שָׁמָעוּ
מַשְׂטִין וְצוֹרֵר נָדְדוּ בָרָחוּ
אָז נוֹפְלִים הָרִים אֲזַי נִבְקָעוּ
שָׁם נִגְדְּעוּ רָמִים כְּצִיץ יִמָּלוּ
אַרְזֵי לְאֻמִּים עַד שְׁאוֹל נָפָלוּ.

ז׳

מֶלֶךְ בְּיוֹפְיוֹ יֶחֱזוּ עֵינֵימוֹ
רֶכֶב אֱלֹקִים עַל מְכוֹנוֹתֶיהָ
חַיּוֹת בְּאַרְבַּע סָחֲרוּ פָנֵימוֹ
רָמָה עֲלֵיהֶם כֵּס בְּאֵימוֹתֶיהָ
אֶחָד מְדַבֵּר הָאֵל בְּקוֹל אֵלֵימוֹ
דָּתוֹ, וְרָאמִים הֵם הֲלִיכוֹתֶיהָ
כִּי עַד מְרוֹם קָדְשׁוֹ אֱמֶת הִגְבִּיהָה
קֵץ לָהּ וְהִיא אוֹר עַד הֲדוֹם תַּגִּיהַּ.

unduly to observe the distinction between masculine and feminine; there are two other examples of mixed genders in the rest of the stanza.

For it raised . . . footstool The sense of these two lines is not clear. They can be understood literally: the Torah raises truth to a supreme height and spreads its light even to the lowest levels. But it may be that their meaning is mystical and messianic: the power of 'the Torah of truth' operates and exerts influence in the uppermost regions, the sefirot ('His holy heights'), and in the time to come its light will penetrate even into the realm of the husks ('the footstool'). Neither of these interpretations is free from difficulty, because Luzzatto habitually uses the word *hadom* ['footstool'] in a positive sense, especially as an epithet for the Temple, and perhaps here too the 'footstool' is a parallel to 'His holy heights'.

Het
Lo, He sought as far as [E]dom and they did not want
God to give it, still less to give it to them
Moab and Ishmael had already spurned it
Till He rejected them and let them go
Then [His] children were strong and determined
From the hand of fools they took their fortune
For themselves, and it is theirs
They alone were ready
To inherit God's courts and dwell in them.

Tet
Understanding and discernment, and a crown of wisdom,
Declaring 'We will do and hearken' they acquired honour
There their soul cleaved [to God] and was saved
[The] One [God] was the source of their strength and they have not been parted
[112v] The cup, the bowl of dregs has been prepared for the nations
They will be destroyed through their foolishness, they will be [or 'are'] brutish, stupid
[At] the time [to come] He will requite all our adversaries
Washing our footsteps in the blood of the wicked.

[*Yod*]
Jealous and avenging, God of truth, how long
Will my foe uplift himself against You and shout in triumph
From Your bosom [put forth] Your right hand which has been hidden

He sought as far as [E]dom The Hebrew *hadom* ['footstool'] has a stroke over the initial letter to indicate that the correct reading is *Edom*, substituting *alef* for *he*. The rabbis, declaring that the nations of the world refused to accept the Torah, mentioned in particular the children of Esau, the children of Lot, and the children of Ishmael; Luzzatto follows them in his enumeration of Edom, Moab, and Ishmael. 'Ishmael' is written here without an *alef*, apparently to remove the holy name of God (*El*).

still less [The Hebrew is simply *ad*.—Trans.] They did not desire the giving of the Torah in general and, in particular, did not desire it to be given to them.

let them go Dismissed them, broke off His connection with them.

Understanding . . . honour With understanding, discernment, and wisdom the people of Israel said 'We will do and obey' [homiletically interpreted as 'We will do and hear', i.e. 'We promise to perform the commandments even before we hear what they are'—Trans.] and so they earned honour. Or perhaps the meaning is that by saying 'We will do and hear' Israel earned honour, which

ח׳

הֵן עַד הֲדוֹם דָּרַשׁ וְלֹא חָפָצוּ
תִּתָּהּ אֱלֹקִים עַד תְּנֶהָ לָמוֹ
מ[ו]אָב וְיִשְׁמָעֵל כְּבָר נָאָצוּ
בָּהּ, עַד מְאוֹס בָּהֶם וְהִתִּירָמוֹ
אָז חָזְקוּ בָנִים וְהִתְאַמָּצוּ
מִיַּד כְּסִילִים לָקְחוּ טוּבָמוֹ
[לָ]הֶם, וְלָהֶם הִיא, לְבָד נָכוֹנוּ
חַצְרוֹת אֱלֹקִים יִנְחֲלוּ יִשְׁכּוֹנוּ.

ט׳

בִּינָה וְהַשְׂכֵּל אַף עֲטֶרֶת דַּעַת
עַד נַעֲשֶׂה נִשְׁמַע יְקָר יִנְחָלוּ
שָׁם דָּבְקָה נַפְשָׁם וְהִיא נוֹשַׁעַת
אֶחָד מְקוֹר עוּזָּם וְלֹא נִבְדָּלוּ
הוּכַן לְעַמִּים כּוֹס וְסַף קוּבַּעַת
יִכְלוּ בְהֶבְלָם יִבְעֲרוּ יִכְסָלוּ
הָעֵת גְּמוּל יָשִׁיב לְכָל צָרֵינוּ
לִרְחוֹץ בְּדַם רָשָׁע הֲלִיכוֹתֵינוּ.

[י׳]

קַנָּא וְנוֹקֵם, אֵל אֱמֶת, עַד אָנָה
יָרוּם לְנֶגְדְּךָ אוֹיְבִי יָרִיעַ,
מֵחֵיקְךָ יָמִין אֲשֶׁר נִטְמָנָה

embraces 'understanding and discernment' and 'a crown of wisdom'.

and they have not been parted Israel are attached to God by an inseverable bond.

The cup, the bowl of dregs The cup of staggering, of drunkenness. Here we have an amalgamation of 'the dregs of the cup of staggering' (Isa. 51: 17) with 'the bowl of staggering' (Zech. 12: 2).

. . . has been prepared for the nations As long ago as the giving of the Torah it was decreed that the nations which had rejected the Torah and deserted God would be destroyed in the time to come.

they will be brutish, stupid They will be sunk in the brutishness and stupidity of idol-worship.

[At] the time . . . He will requite The destruction of the nations will take place in the days of the Messiah, when God will punish them for their persecution of the Jews.

Washing . . . wicked Based on Ps. 58: 11: 'He will wash his feet in the blood of the wicked.'

[put forth] Your right hand Put forth Your right hand, which has been hidden in Your bosom during the period of exile, and quickly destroy [*kaleh*] the enemies of Israel. The

Make an end quickly, make known Your strength
God of vengeance, hasten the time which has been prepared
Make haste and satisfy the afflicted soul
Therefore we will wait for You, that we may be redeemed
O God who is wholly good to Israel for ever.

God is wholly good to Israel, to those who are pure of heart: Let God arise, let His enemies be scattered, and let those that hate Him flee before Him:
But the king shall rejoice in God, everyone who swears by Him shall exult, for the mouth of those who speak falsehood shall be stopped.

Completed, praise be to God the Creator of the universe

[*Structure and metre of the poem.* Ten stanzas, each of eight lines, each line consisting of two long syllables and one *yated*, two long syllables and one *yated*, and three long syllables.]

functions of waging war against these enemies and subduing them are ascribed to the right hand of the Lord in many scriptural passages. Perhaps, however, the verb *kaleh* is used here not in the sense of destruction but in that of completion, bringing something to a conclusion, and the meaning would then be 'Quickly complete the task of Your hidden right hand'.

make known Your strength The right hand of the Lord is associated with His strength in several scriptural verses. See Isa. 62: 8; Ps. 89: 14.

the time which has been prepared The time of 'the end of days', which has long been fixed and in readiness. Or perhaps the word 'prepared' in this poetic and eschatological

[115r] Poem for the Night of 17 Shevat, to be Recited during the Festive Meal

You Who keep truth for ever, O God, our hope
Bestowing in truth upon Your people Your righteous law
To You alone, to You, Lord, our eyes are turned
Truly in You alone we hope; to the people who are Your portion
Show favour, reveal Yourself to those who wait for You
You Who love good and seek it, Who speak peace

[**You Who keep truth for ever** Ps. 146: 6.—Trans.]

O God, our hope . . . As I pointed out in the section of my introduction headed '*Piyut* and two prayers for the night of 17 Shevat', this is clearly a *piyut* of Luzzatto's group, and even

כַּלֵּה מְהֵרָה, עוּזְּךָ הוֹדִיעַ
חִישׁ אֵל נְקָמוֹת עֵת אֲשֶׁר הוּכָנָה
מַהֵר וְנֶפֶשׁ נַעֲנָה תַּשְׂבִּיעַ
עַל כֵּן נְיַיחֵל לָךְ וְנִגָּאֵלָה
אַךְ טוֹב לְיִשְׂרָאֵל אֱלֹקִים סֶלָה.

אך טוב לישראל אלקים לברי לבב:
יקומו אלקים יפוצו אויביו וינוסו
משנאיו מפניו: והמלך ישמ[ח] באלקים
יתהלל כל הנשבע בו כי יסכר פי דוברי שקר:

תו״שלב״ע

sentence has a topical meaning: Hasten the Redemption now, because the way has been prepared for the coming of the Redeemer by the messianic *tikunim* carried out in Luzzatto's group.

satisfy the afflicted soul Isa. 58: 10.

[**Therefore** Hebrew *al ken*. Possibly *ki al ken*, 'because', is intended.—Trans.]

God is wholly good . . . the pure of heart Ps. 73: 1.

Let God arise Ps. 68: 2. The poem has the verb in the plural.

But the king . . . stopped Ps. 63: 12.

שיר לליל י״ז שבט תוך הסעודה

שׁוֹמֵר אֱמֶת עוֹלָם, אֵל תִּקְוָתֵנוּ
מַנְחִיל אֱמֶת עַמָּךְ מִשְׁפַּט צִדְקֶךָ
הֵן לָךְ לְבַד, הֵן לָךְ אָדוֹן עֵינֵינוּ
אַךְ בָּךְ לְבַד מִקְוֶה אֶל עַם חֶלְקֶךָ
אָנָּא רְצֵה, הוֹפַע נָא לִמְחַכֶּיךָ
אוֹהֵב וְדוֹרֵשׁ טוֹב, שָׁלוֹם מַשְׁמִיעַ

where expressions in the first person plural appear to be used in the name of the whole community of Israel, the speakers are the members of the group, while the first person singular is to be understood as the personal utterance of Luzzatto.

When will You bring Your justice, as a light to nations,
Again to rest upon Your prized possession, whom You chose long ago
Again tend your sheep, and as You used to do,
Again guard Your beloved of long ago, for whom You created the world
We pray You, the one true God, O Rock who has not changed
Remember the eternal statute which You ordained for Jacob
Your thoughts were for [our] welfare, you planned [our] good
When, O God, will You look upon us
We beg You, see how our heart is wholly Yours
Let not those who hope in You have their hopes dashed through us
[115ᵛ] To those who unify You pray give Your strength
Give a sure sign, let my enemies be shamed
Pray seek the poor who seek Your lovingkindness
Their heart, a blameless heart [and] upright, they have set [on You]
Pray be gracious to us, God, in You alone we hope
Look how we, all of us together, have desired naught but Your glory
In all our distress, have we indeed been faithless
To Your covenant? You, O Most High, are our witness
Look, You made enemies ride over our head, You set them over us
We went in terror all through fire and water
Then it was You gave the Law of truth to us
A refuge and tower eternal and a fortress of salvation
How should its proud strength still not lay low and break for ever
The pride of strangers, the staff of wickedness
O Israel's refuge, Glory of Your people [or 'towards Your eternal people']

When will You . . . nations Isa. 51: 4: 'And I will cause my justice to rest as a light to nations.' [The translation 'cause to rest' is as understood by Rashi, among others.—Trans.]

Your prized possession Israel [see e.g. Deut. 7: 6]. 'Your' is not in the manuscript though required by the metre.

[**for whom You created the world** See *Rosh hashanah* 31*a* on Ps. 24.—Trans.]

Remember . . . for Jacob An allusion to Ps. 105: 10–11: '. . . which He established as a statute for Jacob, as an everlasting covenant for Israel, saying "To you I will give the land of Canaan as your allotted portion" '.

[**Your thoughts . . . [our] good** Jer. 29: 11; Zech. 8: 15.—Trans.]

Let not . . . dashed through us Cf. Ps. 69: 7.

my enemies Luzzatto's persecutors.

upright Hebrew *yshr*, printed here as *yashar* ['upright' or, less usually, 'uprightness'], should perhaps be read as *yosher* ['uprightness'] [in which case the line might mean 'Their heart is a blameless heart, they have set uprightness firm'. For setting the heart on God—using the same Hebrew verb as here—see e.g. 2 Chr. 20: 33—Trans.].

You made enemies ride over our head See Lam. 1: 5; Ps. 66: 12.

You gave the Law of truth [*torat emet*] **to us** It appears that even this apparently transparent statement, using an expression traditionally

מָתַי לְאוֹר עַמִּים מִשְׁפָּט תַּרְגִּיעַ
שׁוּב עַל סְגוּלָּה מֵאָז בָּחַרְתָּ
שׁוּב נָא, רְעֵה וּשְׁמוֹר כִּימוֹת שָׁמַרְתָּ
שׁוּב עַל יְדִיד עַד, לוֹ עוֹלָם קָנִיתָ
נָא אֵל אֱמֶת אֶחָד, צוּר לֹא שָׁנִיתָ
אֶל יַעֲקֹב תִּזְכּוֹר חֹק לָעַד שַׂמְתָּ
הֵן מַחְשְׁבוֹת שָׁלוֹם טוֹבָה זָמַמְתָּ
מָתַי אֱלֹקִים נָא רָאֹה תִּרְאֵנוּ
אָנָּא רְאֵה כָל לָךְ נָתוּן לִבֵּנוּ
לֹא עוֹד יְבוֹשׁוּן נָא בָנוּ קֹוֶיךָ
לִמְיַחֲדִים שִׁמְךָ תֵּן נָא עוּזֶּךָ
אוֹת לָאֱמֶת הַרְאֵה, צָרַי יֵבוֹשׁוּ
אָנָּא דְרוֹשׁ דַּלִּים, חַסְדְּךָ יִדְרוֹשׁוּ
לִבָּם לֵב תָּמִים, יָשָׁר הֵכִינוּ
נָא חָנֵּנוּ אֵל, אַךְ לָךְ קִוִּינוּ
שׁוּר כִּי כְבוֹדָךְ רַק יַחְדָּיו חָמַדְנוּ
הַאִם בְּכָל מָצוֹק בָּגוֹד בָּגַדְנוּ
בִּבְרִיתְךָ עֶלְיוֹן עֵידֵינוּ[!] אַתָּה
צָרִים לְרֹאשׁ הַבֵּט הִרְכַּבְתָּ שַׁתָּה
בָּאֵשׁ וּמַיִם כָּל נִבְהָלִים בָּאנוּ
תּוֹרַת אֱמֶת הֵן אָז נָתַתָּ לָנוּ
מָעוֹז וּמִגְדּוֹל עַד וּמְצוּדַת יֶשַׁע
אֵיךְ לֹא גְאוֹן זָרִים עוֹד, מַטֵּה רֶשַׁע
יַשְׁפִּיל גְּאוֹן עוּזָּהּ, יִשְׁבּוֹר לָנֶצַח
מָעוֹז לְיִשְׂרָאֵל, אֶל עַמְּךָ נֶצַח

applied to the Torah, is intended to refer to Luzzatto's doctrine as received in the revelations of the *magid* and conveyed to the members of the group. At least the reference is to the teachings of kabbalah [*torat hakabalah*] which they studied and disseminated.

A refuge . . . salvation See Ps. 31: 3. Here the group's 'law of truth' is called 'a refuge and tower' and 'a fortress of salvation'. The phrase 'refuge and tower', which is not found in the Bible, is akin to the scriptural expression 'a tower of strength' [*migdal oz*] which Luzzatto used as the title of his well-known play. In a parable which has its origin in the Zohar and is quoted in the opening of the play—where it is introduced by the words 'In the holy Midrash there is a reference'—the 'tower of strength' is linked to the secrets of the Torah. See F. Lachower, *Al gevul hayashan vehehadash* (Jerusalem, 1951), 40–3, 80–1.

How . . . not An odd turn of speech. In context, the word 'How' should be interpreted as a wish, i.e. 'Would that the pride of strangers might no longer rule and the staff of wickedness no longer humble the proud strength of the law of truth.' [Or a rhetorical question, as in the translation?—Trans.]

Glory of Your people [*amekha netsaḥ*] Your eternal people [*amekha hanitsḥi*], [or] Eternal One [or Glory: see 1 Sam. 15: 29—Trans.] of Israel [*netsaḥ yisra'el*].

There is no falsehood in You, draw near and save us
We shall rejoice in You, we shall be glad, and in reward
[116r] Shall see Your holiness, for [our efforts] will not have been in vain
Turn evil back to good, and grief to joy
O Only One, God of Israel for ever
Let Your right hand be raised, O God, let it be strong and not grow weary
Then the hills will burst forth into joyous song
All earth and heavens, all that You made for Your renown, will rejoice
Your children will bring sacrifices of praise as their gift [to You]
Arise, [in] Your lovingkindness lead the nation You have redeemed
Reveal Yourself, pasture on high Your holy flock
Guide them with Your strength to Your holy dwelling-place.

Completed, praise be to God, the Creator of the world.

in reward . . . holiness [The Hebrew *pe'ulah* means 'action', 'activity', but also a payment or reward for action.—Trans.] By virtue of our activity we shall be privileged to see Your holiness. 'Looking upon holiness' indicates a mystical grasp of the Godhead. See above, in the notes on the poem 'God who works wonders', as to the expression 'look upon holiness'.

[Son of Joseph, the fruitful one]

[202r] Son of Joseph, the fruitful one, dear Ephraim,
Child of [God's] delight, planted for [His] glory
You shall be glad, rejoice, be happy, for sevenfold
The righteous man will be avenged, and will rise up against the barren woman's house

Son . . . Ephraim Messiah ben Joseph, who is also called 'the son of Ephraim' and 'Ephraim'. See *Pesikta rabati*, chs. 36–7. [In Gen. 49: 22 Joseph is described as a fruitful son (or tree). Here the reference to a son is transferred to Ephraim. For references to Messiah ben Ephraim, see Essay 3, n. 73, and Essay 4, n. 112.—Trans.]

The righteous man will be avenged Messiah ben Joseph is called 'righteous' after the sefirah Yesod, the supernal Righteous Being, with whom Messiah ben Joseph is associated. When the time comes for the Redemption he will be avenged upon the Sitra Ahra, at whose hands he suffered torments when he descended to the husks.

כָּזָב בְּךָ אֵין יֵשׁ, קָרְבָה וּפְדֵנוּ
נִשְׂמַח בְּךָ, נָגִיל, וּפְעוּלָּתֵנוּ
אֶת קָדְשְׁךָ נִרְאֶה, כִּי לֹא לַהֶבֶל
רָעָה לְטוֹב הָשֵׁב וּלְשָׂשׂוֹן אֵבֶל
יָחִיד מְיוּחָד, אֵל יִשְׂרָאֵל סֶלָה
תָּרוּם יְמִינְךָ אֵל, תָּעוֹז לֹא תֵלַהּ
אָז יִפְצְחוּ הָרִים רִנָּה, יָגִילוּ
אֶרֶץ שְׁחָקִים כָּל לְשִׁמְךָ פָּעַלְתָּ
זִבְחֵי תְהִלּוֹת שַׁי בָּנִים יוֹבִילוּ
קוּם, חַסְדְּךָ תַנְחֶה עַם זוּ גָּאַלְתָּ
הוֹפַע, רְעֵה מָרוֹם צֹאן קָדָשֶׁיךָ
נַהֵל בְּעוּזְּךָ אֶל נָוֶה קָדְשֶׁךָ

תר״שלב״ע

Let Your right hand . . . strong Based on Ps. 89: 14.

Then the hills . . . rejoice Isa. 49: 13.

[in] Your lovingkindness This line from here on, and the last line, are based on Exod. 15: 13.

[הבן פורת יוסף]

הַבֵּן פּוֹרָת יוֹסֵף, יַקִּיר אֶפְרַיִם
יֶלֶד שַׁעֲשׁוּעִים, מַטַּע תִּפְאֶרֶת
תָּשִׂישׂ תִּשְׂמַח תָּגִיל, כִּי שִׁבְעָתַיִם
יוּקַם צַדִּיק, וְקָם עַל בֵּית עֲקֶרֶת

will rise up against the barren woman's house [*beit akeret*] See Isa. 31: 2. Perhaps 'the barren woman' is the Sitra Ahra, so called because of its infertility: see Tishby, *Wisdom of the Zohar*, ii. 509. Or perhaps the reference is to Gog, against whom Messiah ben Joseph will fight, in accordance with Luzzatto's homily in *Tikunim ḥadashim*, 127: 'A scorpion, that is the wicked Gog, for of the snake it is said (Mishnah *Ber*. 5: 1) "Even if a snake is coiled round his heel, he must not pause in his prayer", but for a scorpion he may pause [*Ber*. 33*a*], for a scorpion [*akrav*] is [spelt with the first four consonants of] *akar bayit* [an uprooter of the house, or the barren one (masculine) of the house], of whom it is said "Against the Lord and His anointed"

When it is time to come and set a crown on the head of the
righteous man
The blessing of the mountains that brought you forth, the blessings of
the breasts
The blessings of the ancient hills, the crowning glory
Stored up for you are all things precious, Heaven's blessings

His majestic ox will be exalted together with the lion
He will scorn the tumult [or 'horde'] of foreigners, he will be tranquil
and at rest
He will condemn the snake to die, he will laugh at fear

You will scatter the army of the ruthless, the wind will carry them off
The fattest of those who are ever at ease you will deliver to destruction
You will dwell in a peaceful place, secure for ever.

[*Structure and metre of the poem.* A sonnet, each line consisting of eleven syllables.]

(Ps. 2: 2).' Cf. *Tikunei hazohar*, ed. R. Margaliot (Tel Aviv, 1948), beginning of *tikun* 21.

The blessing of the mountains . . . Heaven's blessings The description of the blessings accords with Gen. 49: 25–6 and Deut. 33: 13–16, but is an esoteric reference to the divine flow which descends from the sefirot. See Zohar I, 247*a–b*.

[From Bashan, Dan, awake]

[202v] From Bashan, Dan, awake, go up, prevail,
A roaring, rending lion, deck yourself in your grandeur
Spread your burning anger over the nation I have doomed to
destruction
On the proud neck of [that] people set your foot

From Bashan, Dan . . . Cf. Deut. 33: 22. The person addressed is Seraiah of the tribe of Dan. See the preface to 'Two messianic sonnets', p. 120 above. Yonah David, in *Tarbiz*, 31 (1962), 102–4, disputed the view that this sonnet should be understood as a messianic poem. On the basis of parallels with the opening of Luzzatto's play about Samson, *Ma'aseh shimshon*, in turns of phrase, images, and rhyme (*telah—selah*), he sought to interpret this poem as 'a sonnet to courage' written against the background of the subject matter of the play: 'The camp of Dan under the oppression of the Philistine enemy'. J. Dan has already written a soundly reasoned rejection of this opinion (ibid. 412–13). It would be possible to add much more evidence in refutation of David's arguments, but I will content myself

עֵת בֹּא עַל רֹאשׁ צַדִּיק לָשִׁית עֲטֶרֶת
בִּרְכַּת הָרִים הוֹרִים, בִּרְכוֹת שָׁדַיִם
בִּרְכוֹת גִּבְעוֹת עוֹלָם, הַדְרַת כּוֹתֶרֶת
כָּל מֶגֶד לָךְ צָפוּן, בִּרְכוֹת שָׁמַיִם

יָרוּם הֲדַר שׁוֹרוֹ עִם לָבִיא יָחַד
יָבוּז הֲמוֹן זָרִים, יִשְׁקוֹט יָנוּחַ
יִשְׁפּוֹט נָחָשׁ לִסְפּוֹת, יִשְׂחַק לַפָּחַד

תָּפִיץ חֵיל עָרִיצִים, תִּשָּׂאֵם רוּחַ
מִשְׁמַן שַׁלְוֵי עוֹלָם תִּמְסוֹר לַכָּחַד
תֵּשֵׁב בִּנְוֵה שָׁלוֹם לָעַד בָּטוּחַ.

His majestic ox Messiah ben Joseph, to whom Deut. 33: 17 is applied.

the lion Messiah ben David (Gen. 49: 9: 'Judah is a lion's whelp') or the commander of the messianic army, Seraiah of the tribe of Dan (Deut. 33: 22: 'Dan is a lion's whelp').

the snake The Sitra Ahra.

those who are ever at ease Ps. 73: 12.

[מבשן דן עורה]

מִבָּשָׁן דָּן עוּרָה, עֲלֵה הַצְלִיחָה
אַרְיֵה שׁוֹאֵג טוֹרֵף, עֲדֵה גָבְהֶךָ
הָפֵץ עַל עַם חֶרְמִי חֲרוֹן אַפֶּךָ
עַל רוּם צַוַּאר גּוֹי רַגְלְךָ הָנִיחָה

with quoting another clear parallel which occurs at the end of the play *Layesharim tehilah*, a late work by Luzzatto dating from the time of his stay in Amsterdam. This consists of the four verses beginning *ḥelek tehilah* ['renown is a part...'] and ending *al-telah* ['let it not weary'], with the rhyme-scheme *hineha*, *selah*, *hagbe'ah*, *telah*. The formal pattern of these lines, including the rhyme *selah—telah*, bears an obvious resemblance to that of the end of the sonnet we are considering, but in content and situation they have nothing in common with either the messianic sonnet or *Ma'aseh shimshon*.

deck yourself in your grandeur See Job 40: 10.

On the proud neck . . . foot Cf. Josh. 10: 24.

See the noisy foreign foes, and hiss,
A snake upon [their] path, where [you will execute] your deeds of deliverance
Against horse and rider, all your mighty acts
Where your strong hand has made all your hope spring to life.

For the enemy's protection has departed from him, surely there has begun
Help from above for you, salvation for us
You will rise up, overcome, be raised on high, and we shall be redeemed.

You will find every enemy, your hand will not grow weary;
From the battle-lines of the living God in the day they are drawn up,
A mighty warrior, leap out upon the army's head. *Selah*.

[*Structure and metre of the poem*. A sonnet, each line consisting of six long syllables, one *yated*, and three long syllables.]

A snake upon [their] path As in Gen. 49: 17.
where . . . your deeds of deliverance Where the snake, the Sitra Ahra, has been exercising dominion, you will bring salvation by your victory.
Against horse Against the captains and kings of the nations.
and rider Against the Sitra Ahra which leads them.

[The only God]

[223v] The only God, Whose throne was set firm long ago
Splendid, wondrous, You who are from everlasting
Whose glorious majesty will rule for ever
Restore the footstool which once You put at Your feet
The hill You sought out then
To be Your dwelling, pray seek it now also
We pray You, return to a people whom Your hands established
Whom You formed for Yourself, who have been faithful only to You.

Your holy children, the stock You planted,
Pray look upon them and remember them, O Saviour

The only God . . . long ago Cf. Ps. 93: 2.
the footstool The Temple, as in e.g. Ps. 132: 7.
The hill The Temple Mount or Mount Zion.
To be Your dwelling Cf. Ps. 132: 13.

הֶמְיַת צָרִים זָרִים רְאֵה, הָפִיחָה
נָחָשׁ עַל דֶּרֶךְ, שָׁם תְּשׁוּעוֹתֶיךָ
עַל סוּס עַל רוֹכֵב כָּל גְּבוּרוֹתֶיךָ
כָּל לָךְ תִּקְוָה שָׁם יָדְךָ הִצְמִיחָה

כִּי סָר מֵאוֹיֵב צֵל, הֲלֹא הֵחֵלָּה
עֶזְרָת מִמַּעַל לָךְ, תְּשׁוּעָה לָנוּ
תָּרוּם תִּגְבַּר תִּגְבַּהּ וְנִגְאָלָה

תִּמְצָא כָּל שׂוֹנֵא, יָדְךָ לֹא תֵּלַהּ
מִמַּעַרְכוֹת אֵל חַי בְּיוֹם כּוֹנָנוּ
גִּבּוֹר עַל רֹאשׁ צָבָא תְּזַנֵּק סֶלָה

Where your strong hand . . . life Through your strength you have aroused hopes of their defeat.

For the enemy's protection [literally 'shadow': Num. 14: 9] **. . . for us** The strength of the Sitra Ahra has already been undermined and signs have been seen of divine help in Seraiah's battle.

[יחיד מאז]

יָחִיד מֵאָז נָכוֹן כִּסְאֶךָ
הָדוּר נִפְלָא מֵעוֹלָם אַתָּה
וָעֶד יִמְלוֹךְ הוֹד מַלְכוּתֶךָ
הֲדוֹם הָקֵם אֶל רַגְלָךְ שַׁתָּה
אָנָּא הַר זֶה, זֶה אֶל שִׁבְתֶּךָ
דָּרַשְׁתָּ אָז תִּדְרוֹשׁ גַּם עַתָּה
נָא שׁוּב עַם יָדֶיךָ כּוֹנָנוּ
יָצַרְתָּ לָךְ, אַךְ לָךְ נֶאְמָנוּ.

יַלְדֵי קָדְשָׁךְ כַּנָּה נָטַעְתָּ
אָנָּא הַבֵּט וּפְקוֹד מוֹשִׁיעַ

Whom You formed for Yourself Isa. 43: 21.

the stock You planted Ps. 80: 16.

remember them, O Saviour O God, Saviour of Israel, remember the nation You chose from among all the nations.

The nation whom, [alone] of all the nations, You have known,
Who seek Your mercy, when will they have rest
[224r] And the one afflicted as a lamb, whom You brought low long since,
Bearing his sickness, hoping, entreating
Let us see him clad in splendour and beauty
Let him be exalted, let him be high, and let him guide us [towards] peace.

That bright light which, from the beginning, You hid away,
O only God, reveal to those who wait for You
Fill with knowledge the earth which You founded
Despoil [or 'bring into contempt'] the foreigners who took the fruit of Your vineyard
Comfort the hill of Zion, where You dwelt
Renew the wonders that have ceased
Let the afflicted nation, all its people together, again delight in You
And let them laugh at fear.

Completed, praise be to God, the Creator of the world.

[*Structure and metre of the poem.* Three stanzas, each of eight lines, each line consisting of nine syllables. In each stanza the initial letters of the lines are the consonants of the names YHVH Adonai, in their correct order in the first stanza and rearranged in the others.]

the one afflicted as a lamb The tormented Messiah, whom You have crushed and afflicted with illness since times long past, and who is waiting and praying for his recovery and his exaltation to power so that he may fulfil his mission to redeem Israel. The description of the Messiah follows that of the servant of the Lord in Isa. 53: 3–12.

Let him be exalted, let him be high As in the beginning of the description of the servant of the Lord (Isa. 52: 13): 'Behold, My servant shall

הָעָם בֵּין כָּל עַמִּים יָדַעְתָּ
דּוֹרֵשׁ חַסְדָּךְ, מָתַי יַרְגִּיעַ
וּמְעוּנֶּה שֶׂה מֵאָז הִכְרַעְתָּ
נוֹשֵׂא חָלְיוֹ, קֹוֶה, מַפְגִּיעַ
הָדָר, יוֹפִי עָלָיו תַּרְאֵנוּ
יָרוּם, יִגְבַּה, שָׁלוֹם יַנְחֵנוּ.

אוֹר בָּהִיר הוּא מֵרֹאשׁ צָפַנְתָּ
יָחִיד גַּלֵּה אֶל לָךְ יִיחֲלוּ
דֵּעָה מַלֵּא אֶרֶץ כּוֹנַנְתָּ
הָבֵז זָרִים כַּרְמָךְ חִלֵּלוּ
נַחֵם הַר זֶה צִיּוֹן שָׁכַנְתָּ
וּפְלָאוֹת עוֹד תָּשִׁיב חָדֵלוּ
יִתְעַנֵּג עוֹד עָלֶיךָ יָחַד
הָעָם עָנִי יִשְׂחַק לַפָּחַד.

תו״שלב״ע

prosper, he shall be exalted and lifted up, and shall be very high.'

That bright light The light that was created on the first day of the Creation and was hidden away to be bestowed on the righteous in time to come. See *Ḥag.* 12*a*. The hidden light occupies an important place in aggadic and kabbalistic literature.

Fill with knowledge the earth Cf. Isa. 11: 9.

[**Despoil [or 'bring into contempt']** The verbal form used by Luzzatto, *havez*, could be derived from two different roots, and is unusual for both.—Trans.]

[A Riddle in Verse]

[227r] The form of the riddle
Who are you [or 'Whoever you may be'] who seek holy things
Shut your mouths, do not hold your peace

If you seek me—[though you go] as far as all the words
You will not find me—but the head [or 'beginning'] of books
From Av ['the father'] to the eighth, [which is?] the end—most of the good sayings
Strength is his, and great is his might—a mighty man among men
Lo, a helmet of salvation is on my head—the most splendid of headgear
And in front of me I will surely set—God, who formed the lights
My hand will prevail against—every warrior [and all] enemies
My strength will again be renewed—a renewal like that of eagles

Who are you . . . who seek What merit have you, how do you dare to seek . . .? Or perhaps: When you come to seek . . . [which would favour the bracketed translation 'Whoever you may be'—Trans.].

seek holy things Seek an understanding and knowledge of the divine sefirot.

Shut your mouths, do not hold your peace For *bal* ['not'] read *lev* ['heart'], reversing the two consonants. These words are a poetic paraphrase of a sentence in *Sefer yetsirah*, 1: 8: 'Ten sefirot of [or 'founded on'] nothingness [*belimah*] [see n. 1, p. 122 above], restrain [*belom*] your mouth from speaking and your heart from thinking.' The answer to the riddle is *reshit* ['beginning'], as explained in my preface to this poem. 'The form of the riddle' indicates that the reference is to the sefirah Hokhmah ['Wisdom'], which cannot be grasped by human understanding, but which, in the lines of this riddle, is given various meanings: the word *reshit* ['beginning'], or *bereshit*, 'in the beginning' or the book of Genesis; wisdom, in the literal sense; Torah; the sefirah Hokhmah itself; the sefirah Malkhut—the Shekhinah, which is called *Ḥokhmah taḥtonah* ['the lower Hokhmah'].

but the head [or 'beginning'] of books *Bereshit*, at the head of the books of the Bible. ['Words' in the preceding line of the poem is *devarim*, which is the Hebrew title of Deuteronomy.—Trans.]

From Av ['the father'] to the eighth, [which is?] the end It appears to me that the allusions in this line are kabbalistic. With some doubt I offer the following interpretation: the sefirot from Hokhmah—which has, as it were, the status of a father [*aba*]—to Malkhut, 'the lower Hokhmah'—which is the eighth sefirah below Hokhmah (from Binah to Malkhut) and is the last of the series ('the eighth, [which is?] the end')—together constitute nine of the ten sayings ('most of the good sayings') with which the world was created [Gen. 1: 3–2: 18]. In kabbalistic lore the ten sayings are commonly identified with the ten sefirot, and Malkhut is counted as the eighth sefirah below Binah. With regard to this see Tishby, *Wisdom of the Zohar*, iii. 1253, on the mystical significance of Shemini Atseret. [On that page, first line of the penultimate paragraph, 'without the Shekhinah' is a misprint for 'within the Shekhinah'.—Trans.] This riddle in verse was certainly intended to be read in a circle of

[שִׁיר-חִידָה]

צורת החידה

מִי אַתֶּם לִקְדוֹשִׁים תְּבַקְּשׁוּן
קִפְצוּ פִּיכֶם בַּל תַּחֲרִישׁוּן

אוֹתִי אִם תִּדְרְשׁוּן – עַד כָּל הַדְּבָרִים
לֹא אֶמָּצֵא לָכֶם – כִּי אִם רֹאשׁ סְפָרִים
מֵאָב לִשְׁמִינִי סוֹף – רוּבֵּי טוּב אֲמָרִים
עוֹז לוֹ וָרָב חֵילוֹ – גִּבּוֹר בֵּין גְּבָרִים
הֵן כּוֹבַע יֶשַׁע עַל רֹאשִׁי – הוֹד פְּאֵרִים
וּלְפָנַי שֹׁם אָשִׁים – אֵל יוֹצֵר מְאוֹרִים
תָּעוֹז יָדִי אֶל מוּל – כָּל לוֹחֵם צָרִים
עוֹד יִתְחַלֵּף כֹּחִי – חַדֵּשׁ כַּנְּשָׁרִים

kabbalists belonging to the group, so that from the point of view of its content I see no difficulty in the interpretation I have suggested. But I am not happy about the reading of the word [I have vowelled] *rubei* ['most', 'the majority of'], because on the basis of the structure of the other lines it should be read *rubi* ['most of me'], a reading which does not fit my suggested interpretation.

Strength is his . . . I do not know why there is a change from first to third person in this line. It may be a slip of the pen: *lo . . . ḥeilo* instead of first person *li . . . ḥeili*. On the substance of the line: in a number of scriptural passages wisdom is bracketed with strength and might, and a wise man is called *gever* [a word which conveys the ideas of masculinity and strength—Trans.]. Here are a few such references: Prov. 8: 14, 24: 5; Job 12: 13, 34: 34.

a helmet of salvation Cf. Isa. 59: 17. Here the 'helmet of salvation' denotes the sefirah Keter which is above the sefirah Hokhmah, in accordance with one of the meanings of that expression in kabbalistic symbolism.

on my head—the most The caesura has been placed as in the manuscript, but to fit the pattern of the metre it would have had to fall between 'on' and 'my head' [*al—roshi*].

And in front . . . lights This perhaps refers to the words 'God created' (God 'who formed the lights') immediately after 'In the beginning' in the Torah. Or perhaps the subject is the sefirah Hokhmah, the source of the seven 'sefirot of the structure', from Hesed to Malkhut, which are the forces operative in the work of creation.

My hand will prevail [*ta'oz yadi*] I add here to the references I gave above on 'Strength [*oz*] is his': Prov. 21: 22, 24: 5–6; Eccles. 7: 19.

enemies [*tsarim*] The metre requires a semivowel before *tsarim* to give a *yated*, so that it appears that we should read *loḥem vetsarim* ['warrior and enemies'].

My strength . . . eagles The words are based on Isa. 40: 31, and on Ps. 103: 5: 'Your youth will be renewed like the eagle's.' In substance this line is appropriate to the Shekhinah, the lower Hokhmah, which is involved in processes of descent and ascent, weakness and recovery of strength. More precisely, it fits the angel of the Shekhinah, Metatron, who, according to the Zohar, 'is renewed in youth like the eagle and becomes young again'. See Tishby, *Wisdom of*

A place where silence is—[there?] my works are precious
I know not how to do harm—I will not turn [my] footsteps aside
My gaze is lifted high—strong every morning
I will prevail, I will take possession, I will dwell [in]—the best of the lands of the fortified
To her who is fair of form I will be sweet—she shall not weep bitterly
[227v] From my morning to my evening—raising my voice [in] joy
Reproach will be [or 'is'] far from me—I shall not be shamed for generations
In the chronicles—my praises are recorded
To the poor I [will] give my love—I [will] despise the rich
And I [will] dwell in the heart of Amon—burning between rivers
On the day when you say 'This is it'—I will rule among the pure
I will rest upon the head of the bridegroom—the first of the chief of sayings
So in the sanctuary [*bakodesh*] you will see—diadems added to his crown
In a foreign tongue *shefi* is not a cloak—but Haran companions [i.e. Haran and it are companions]

the Zohar, ii. 619. But perhaps what is meant is the daily renewal of the work of creation, which is mentioned every day in the morning prayers.

A place where silence is Silence as the realm of wisdom is appropriate both for the divine sefirah and for human wisdom ('A fence for wisdom is silence': Mishnah, ed. Danby, *Avot* 3: 14).

I know not how to do harm . . . The qualities enumerated without further definition in this and the succeeding two lines can bear both a literal and an esoteric interpretation.

I will not turn [my] footsteps aside The source is Job 31: 7: 'If my step [*ashuri*] has turned aside from the way'. On that basis the text here [*lo ateh ashurim*] would mean 'I will not turn my steps away (from the path of uprightness)'. But the first half of the line requires a parallel in the second half, and therefore it seems to me that the second half is correctly understood as meaning 'I will not turn aside, i.e. pervert, the justice due to the upright [*yesharim*]'.

the best of the lands of the fortified Possibly 'fortified lands' [*aratsot betsurot*] was in mind but had to be manipulated for the sake of metre and rhyme. 'Fortified' here is *betsurim*, masculine plural, whereas the Bible has the plural only in the feminine. Elsewhere in the poem also, masculine plural endings have been preferred for the sake of the rhyme. Every line ends in -*rim*.—Trans.]

To her who is fair . . . bitterly For this line the following doubtful explanation is the only one I can find: 'she who is fair of form' is the Shekhinah, who is consoled and encouraged by the upper Hokhmah [*ḥokhmah elyonah*] during her time of distress in exile.

From my morning . . . joy This seems to be a reference to *ḥokhmah*, wisdom in the sense of Torah, whose voice is heard all day as it is studied.

Reproach will be [or 'is'] far from me . . . This and the succeeding two lines can easily be given both a literal and an esoteric interpretation.

מָקוֹם דּוּמִיָּה שָׁם – מַעְבָדַי יְקָרִים
לִגְמוֹל רָע לֹא אֵדַע – לֹא אַטֶּה אֲשׁוּרִים
נִשְׂגָּב מַבָּטִי הוּא – חָזָק לַבְּקָרִים
אֶחְזַק אִירַשׁ אֶשְׁכּוֹן – טוּב אַרְצוֹת בְּצוּרִים
לִיפַת תּוֹאַר אֶמְתַּק – בַּל תִּבְכֶּה מְרוֹרִים
מִבָּקְרִי עַד נִשְׁפִּי – קוֹלִי גִּיל לְהָרִים
תִּרְחַק מִנִּי חֶרְפָּה – לֹא אֵבוֹשׁ לְדוֹרִים
בֵּין דִּבְרֵי הַיָּמִים – הִילּוּלַי זְכוּרִים
אֶל דַּל דּוֹדַי אֶתֵּן – אֶבְזֶה לַעֲשִׁירִים
וּלְבַב אָמוֹן אֶשְׁכּוֹן – בּוֹעֵר בֵּין נְהָרִים
תֹּאמַר יוֹם כִּי הוּא זֶה – אֶמְשׁוֹל בֵּין טְהוֹרִים
אָחוּל עַל רֹאשׁ חָתָן – רִאשׁוֹן רֹאשׁ אֲמָרִים
כֵּן בַּקֹּדֶשׁ תֶּחְזֶה – אֶל כִּתְרוֹ עֲטָרִים
לוֹעֵז שֶׁפִּי לוֹט לֹא – אַף הָרָן חֲבֵירִים

And I [will] dwell in the heart of Amon The sefirah Hokhmah, 'the ancient Torah', emanates its light and strength ('dwells') in the sefirah Tiferet, 'the written Torah', which is called Amon (this is one of the kabbalistic meanings of the name 'Amon', in consequence of the homiletic interpretations of Prov. 8: 30 at the beginning of *Bereshit rabah* [the biblical text, *va'ehyeh etslo amon*, is variously translated in the versions, for example as 'I was beside Him as a nursling', or '. . . as an architect'—Trans.]; see R. Moses Cordovero's *Pardes rimonim*, Gate 20*c*, Gate *Erkhei hakinuyim* [index of kabbalistic designations of the sefirot], under the heading *Amon*).

burning between rivers Tiferet operates from a position between Binah and Yesod, the upper and lower rivers in the world of the sefirot. Since Tiferet in its capacity as 'the written Torah' is called *esh dat* ['a fiery law'] (Deut. 33: 2) and also *nehar dinur* ['a river of fire'], it is said to be 'burning between rivers' (see Cordovero, *Pardes rimonim*, headings *or* ['light'] and *nahar* ['river']).

On the day . . . the pure On the day of the Redemption, Wisdom [*ḥokhmah*], which is Torah, will rule in Israel. Between 'this' and 'it' [*hu* and *zeh*] there is an indistinct letter, undoubtedly erased, because the metre does not allow any room for it.

[**when you say 'This is it'** The expression seems to have been borrowed from Exod. 8: 22—see e.g. the translation in the Revised Standard Version—which relates to the identification and recovery of lost articles.—Trans.]

I will rest . . . chief of sayings This refers to the *ḥatan bereshit* ['the bridegroom of Bereshit'] on Simhat Torah ['The rejoicing over the Torah'], who is crowned with 'the first of the chief of sayings', i.e. with the word *bereshit*, which is the first word in the Torah.

So in the sanctuary [*bakodesh*] . . . his crown Cf. Ps. 63: 3. Kodesh is a regular name for the sefirah Hokhmah, and 'his crown' [*kitro*] refers to the sefirah Keter which is above Hokhmah.

In a foreign tongue *shefi* is not a cloak [*Shefi* is a Hebrew word, but its meaning in Hebrew is not relevant here: see next note.—Trans.] The word *shefi* is not a cloak in Italian for the answer to the riddle.

but Haran companions [*ḥaverim*] 'Haran' should read 'Paran'. The meaning is 'But if you

Open up, come out, say to him—form ties with him
Down to the depth of evil, many—are my [*rabat—li*] gateways
We shall look upon the city of our solemn festivals—Zion the release of prisoners
The bridegroom with his bride—the upright will rejoice.

join [*meḥaberim*] Paran to *shefi* you get the solution to the riddle in Italian—*principi*.' The Italian for 'beginning' is *principio*, but the Hebrew transliteration *prnshpi*—vowelled, *prinshipi*—corresponds to the pronunciation of the word in the Judaeo-Italian dialect in Luzzatto's time and milieu. (This has been confirmed for me by an expert in Judaeo-Italian philology.) The slip of the pen by which the copyist rendered the 'Paran' of the draft as 'Haran' was apparently due to his being unconsciously influenced by the word *lot* ['cloak'] in the first half of the verse, the biblical character Lot being the son of Haran.

Open up . . . Open up the poem and tell the answer to the riddle to come out of his stronghold, since his identity has been revealed. Cf. the 'foreign-language' solution to another riddle in verse in *Sefer hashirim*, ed. Ginzburg and Klar, 45.

form ties with him Bring him together with the companions who are connected with him.

Down to the depth . . . gateways As in *Sefer yetsirah*, 1: 5: 'Ten sefirot of [?] nothingness, their measure is ten which have no end [*she'ein lahem sof*], the depth of the beginning [*reshit*] and the depth of the end [*aḥarit*], the depth of good and the depth of evil' etc. In *gematriyah*,

תִּפְתַּח צֵא תֹּאמַר לוֹ – תִּקְשָׁר לוֹ קְשָׁרִים
עַד עֹמֶק רָע רַבַּת – לִי פִּתְחֵי שְׁעָרִים
קִרְיַת מוֹעֵד נֶחְזֶה – צִיּוֹן צֵאת אֲסוּרִים
חָתָן אֶת כַּלָּתוֹ – יָשִׂישׂוּ יְשָׁרִים.

the difference ['gateways'] between the numerical value of *reshit*—the solution to the riddle—and that of *ra* ['evil'] is 642, arrived at as follows: *reshit*, on the system which treats the whole word as adding 1 to the value of its letters, has a total value of 912; *ra* (not so dealt with) has a value of 270, and the difference between them is thus 642. This is the same as the numerical value of *rabat li* ['I have many'].

the city of our solemn festivals Cf. Isa. 33: 20.

The bridegroom . . . rejoice It is probable that this riddle, too, was written for a wedding and that the bridegroom was a member of Luzzatto's group. That is to say, on the exoteric level the reference to a bridegroom and bride is to be understood literally. But the content and general sense of the poem indicate that this concluding line has a mainly mystical significance: the complete and enduring unification of the Holy One, blessed be He, and the Shekhinah in rejoicing when the Redemption takes place.

B. PRAYERS

[64r] (A) PRAYER FOR THE NIGHT OF SHAVUOT, BEFORE THE STUDY SESSION

Master of all the worlds, supreme King of kings, the Holy One, blessed be He, whose like there is none, who is first and last, from whom comes all strength and power, who gives strength to the weary, alters the celestial order, and changes the watches of the heavenly hosts.

You are the one and only God, exalted, hidden, and terrible, whose place of concealment none can reach, and no intellect can look upon Your many wonders and endure, for You are holy above all who are holy, high above all who are high, exalted above all who are exalted, upraised above all who are upraised, and Your dominion extends from beginning to end; in the greatness of Your marvellous wisdom and Your profound understanding, You foretell the end from the beginning, You look out and see ahead to the end of all generations. You chose Your people for Yourself from among all peoples, to give them Your statutes [and] commandments and Your Torah with thunder [64v] and lightning and the sound of the ram's horn from within cloud and thick darkness and burning fire, and You showed[2] them Your strength and made known to them Your exceeding greatness and bestowed on them an eternal inheritance, an inheritance of truth and faithfulness. We therefore give thanks to You, O Lord our God, and praise Your mighty, great, and terrible name, and we praise, extol, glorify, and hold in awe Your kingship and Your terrible and mighty dominion, which is unending and limitless; for You have known us of all the peoples and chosen us from among all the nations and drawn us near to Your service in truth and fear, to rejoice in Your statutes and exult in the words of Your Torah.

May it be Your will, O Lord, King of all worlds, to crown us with the crown of Your holiness,[3] to adorn us with the ornaments of Your faithfulness

[2] As stated in the prefaces to the poems (Part A of this essay), this prayer also appears in MS Harvard 54. The only noteworthy variant in that manuscript is the word for 'You showed', *hereta*, obviously a correction by the copyist, dropping the erroneous final *khaf* in G [which would make the word mean 'Your showing'—Trans.].

[3] In this messianic paragraph it is very clear that the speakers in the first person are the members of the group in Padua. Hence it is evident that the whole prayer and the poem connected with it are compositions by Luzzatto on behalf of his group and that they were recited at their gatherings for Tikun Leil Shavuot, the study session on the night of Shavuot. It is true that some of the petitions are addressed to God in the name of the whole of Israel, but equally in the rest of the liturgical writings intended for his group Luzzatto used to present the group as speaking on behalf of the Jewish people.

for ever, and to glorify us with Your great glory. By Your great, exalted, and wonderful strength draw Your prisoners[4] out of the pit, and proclaim everlasting freedom for Your people, for all nations will prostrate themselves before You and all peoples will run [to pay homage] to Your name, and they will know that You are One alone in kingship and there is none other than You. Look upon the face of Your anointed one,[5] so as to raise up our horn [= grant us strength or success] in glory and prepare for him [65^{r}] a light through Your salvation. Let all his enemies be ashamed and dismayed and let all who are incensed against him[6] be put to shame for ever. Accept our worship and rejoice over us with great compassion, for You are a high and exalted King for all generations and for ever and ever, and we look for Your salvation.

May the words of my mouth and the meditation of my heart be acceptable to You, O Lord, my rock and my redeemer.[7] In You, O Lord, I hope; You will answer, O Lord, my God.[8] As for me, I trust in Your love; my heart will rejoice in Your salvation; I will sing to the Lord, for He has dealt kindly with me.[9]

[72^{v}] (B) PRAYER FOR THE NIGHT OF 17 SHEVAT[10]

May it be Your will, Lord God, God of Israel, [73^{r}] to accept our service,[11] and bestow upon us the light of Your holiness; grant us the privilege of sanctifying Your name in Your world; save us from all sin and iniquity and from all evil; grant us the privilege of walking in Your ways in truth; reveal Your truth in Your world; remove idols from the earth; stop the mouths of those who speak falsehood; remove every lie from the world; enact anew for all Your people, the house of Israel, favourable decrees, salvation, and consolation,

[4] The 'prisoners' are the members of the group, who conducted their activities in secret for fear of their persecutors and saw themselves as imprisoned in a dungeon.

[5] As stated above in my notes on 'God who works wonders' (p. 125), Luzzatto regarded himself, and was regarded in his group, as the incarnation of Moses and superior to the two Messiahs, but in the prayers the term 'Messiah' ['anointed'] mainly refers to him.

[6] The reference is to those who persecuted and ostracized Luzzatto.

[7] Ps. 19: 15. [8] Ps. 38: 16. [9] Ps. 13: 6.

[10] On the celebration of the night of 17 Shevat by Luzzatto's group, see my preface to the '*Piyut* and two prayers for the night of 17 Shevat' (pp. 118–19 above).

[11] Even in this prayer, composed for his group as it clearly was, Luzzatto coupled with the requests specific to members of the group (their illumination by the light of divine holiness, success in their efforts to sanctify the name of Heaven in the world, the stopping of the mouths of their accusers, and the annulment of false charges) petitions on behalf of all Israel. The text of the second prayer for the night of 17 Shevat, taken from another manuscript, which is reproduced immediately below, shows that in MS Guenzburg 745 the representation of the group together with the whole of Jewry as if they were one and the same had the ulterior purpose of camouflaging the objects of the group and the mystical and messianic rituals they followed in their communal life.

and rescind every adverse decree laid upon them. Look kindly upon us and on all Your people the house of Israel; guide us and all Your people the house of Israel with great compassion, and save Your Shekhinah and Your children soon with everlasting salvation, as was said: 'Israel is saved by the Lord with everlasting salvation',[12] and 'the Lord is the true God' etc.[13]

Completed, praise be to God, the Creator of the world.

[152^r] (C) [A SECOND PRAYER FOR THE FORMAL MEAL ON THE NIGHT OF 17 SHEVAT][14]

Master of all the worlds,[15] Cause of all causes, may it be Your will to accept with favour our service and our [study of the] Torah which we offer up before You in Your great, mighty, and terrible Name *ykvk* [a substitution of *kof* for *he* in the Tetragrammaton—Trans.], blessed may it be for ever and ever, and show Your favour and joy in this meal at which we are seated before You, by shedding the light of Your unity upon us. And just as we are seated at this table to rejoice in Your Torah, so may our souls be seated at the pure table which is the Shekhinah, to be fed with the pure bread which is the threefold enunciation of God's name [the Tetragrammaton] in the scriptural blessing: 'The Lord bless you and keep you; the Lord cause His face to shine upon you and be gracious to you; the Lord lift up His face towards you and grant you peace',[16] and in 'the Lord is King; the Lord was King; the Lord will be King for ever and ever'.[17] Endow us with the Holy Spirit, so that we may be illumined by Your light and our souls be bound together with Your holiness; let our bodies be nourished with the celestial food[18] which descends from Your holy Heaven,[19] and by which our 248 organs and 365 sinews will be purified, [the food] which is *leḥem abirim* ['the food of angels'], food which is wholly assimilated by the organs of the body [*evarim*][20] and in which the Sitra Ahra

[12] Isa. 45: 17.

[13] Jer. 10: 10.

[14] This is the prayer referred to above (preface to '*Piyut* and two prayers for the night of 17 Shevat', p. 118) which appears in two manuscripts as the conclusion of a homily for the night of 17 Shevat. The text published here follows MS Oxford 2237; I mention in the notes only the more important of the variants in MS Oxford 2593. Where there is no doubt as to the correct reading of a word but MS 2237 has a letter which is indistinct or missing at the margin, I have made good the deficiency without comment by reference to MS 2593. Those variants which are quoted from the latter manuscript are distinguished by the letter B.

[15] Abbreviated to initial letters in the Hebrew text.

[16] Num. 6: 24–6.

[17] A standard expression in the liturgy.

[18] B adds *shamen* ['fat', 'rich'], a word indicating divine bounty [*shefa*].

[19] From the sefirot.

[20] BT *Yoma* 75*b*, where this exposition of the scriptural expression 'the bread of the mighty' (Ps. 78: 25) is applied to the manna, which is described as the food of the angels, i.e. spiritual sustenance. [Most of the standard English versions translate the Psalmist's expression as 'the food of the angels'.—Trans.]

['Other Side'] has no part at all, and thus the Sitra Ahra will not be able to adhere to our flesh which will have been perfected through *tikun* by Your holy light, and Your holy lights will encompass us [or crown us][21] and surround us on every side, as it is said: 'For You bless the righteous, O Lord, You encompass him with favour as with a shield.'[22] And [in response to?] this voice[23] which we lift up towards You in ceaseless [study of] Your Torah[24]—strengthen us to serve You in truth and to raise up Your holy Shekhinah [in] an ascent after which there will be no descent whatsoever, and all Your lights[25] will be united in Your unity—the Cause above all Causes, blessed be He and blessed be His name for ever and ever, hear, O Israel, the Lord is our God, the Lord is One,[26] and no adversaries shall be able to hinder us, [for they will be thwarted] by the power of Your holy name Shadai, overturner of established orders,[27] by which You will overturn the power of the wicked Sama'el and all his brood, so that they will be unable to bring any charge against us or do us any harm at all. And the light of Your Torah which is kept in store, of which it was said: 'How great is Your goodness which You have stored up for those that fear You' etc.[28]—reveal it to us by Your holy Name *yod ke vav ke* [*ke* substituted for *he*—Trans.], by which 'Behold, my servant shall prosper, he shall be exalted and lifted up, and shall be very high'.[29] Lift up our heads [152ᵛ] above every enemy through Your three Names Vaho Ani Vaho,[30] with the initial letters of which,[31] together forming *vav*, You crown the souls of Israel in order that they may cleave to Your Shekhinah. And since the descent of Moses' bride[32] from him was due to the mixed multitude who split Israel,[33] remove them from the world, as it was said of them: 'For then I

21 B: crown them.

22 Ps. 5: 13.

23 B: and because of this voice [*uvakol* instead of *vehakol*].

24 Cf. the *Takanot rishonot* ['First Rules'] of Luzzatto's group, sect. 2 (*Igerot*, i. 8).

25 B: the lights of Your holiness.

26 Deut. 6: 4.

27 The sentence may be paraphrased as follows: by the power of the name Shadai, which puts the evil spirits to flight, You will thwart the plan of the husks to frustrate our action.

28 Ps. 31: 20.

29 Isa. 52: 13.

30 Based on the expression in the Hoshanot prayers 'ani vaho hoshiah na' ['we beseech You, Lord, save']. Vaho is a name of God minus the letter *yod*; Ani consists of the consonants of Adonai without the *dalet*. According to Cordovero, *Pardes rimonim*, Gate 20c, ch. 6, under the heading *vav he" vav*, the words *ani vaho* stand for the Shekhinah and Tiferet. And see E. E. Urbach, *Ḥaza"l: pirkei emunot vede'ot* (Jerusalem, 1969), 107–8.

31 'Which' here in the singular; in B, plural.

32 The Shekhinah, Luzzatto's bride; he saw himself as the reincarnation of Moses functioning as Tiferet. See Tishby, *Netivei emunah uminut*, 186–8, 192–4, 197–201.

33 The Shekhinah departed from her bridegroom, Luzzatto, and descended to the husks. Those who were to blame for this were his opponents and the persecutors of his group, who caused a split in Israel by their action to exclude Luzzatto and his followers from the community. Luzzatto's adversaries are called a 'mixed multitude' after the 'mixed multitude' in Numbers, who levelled accusations against Moses and incited the people against him. However, it should

will remove from your midst your proudly exultant ones',[34] and Israel will be left as one nation in the land, and Moses will be united with his bride, and all Israel will be crowned anew with Your celestial crowns, and the lights of Your holy Torah will rule in the world and be constantly renewed by You, the Cause of all Causes, for of You [it is said]: 'who in His goodness renews every day the work of Creation'.[35] May Your Name be blessed for ever and ever.

(D) CONFESSIONAL PRAYERS OF LUZZATTO AND HIS GROUP

Introduction

This prayer, or series of prayers (fos. 74^r–82^v), which carries no title, differs in kind from all those that precede it, and was actually separated from them by a blank page. The series follows the pattern of the traditional *viduy* ['confession']: 'We have been guilty of sin, we have been treacherous' etc.—an alphabetical list—with one prayer for each sin. The central subject is the exile of Israel and the exile of the Shekhinah. In nearly all the prayers the following motifs recur: apology for sins, complaints about tribulations, petitions for pardon and annulment of adverse decrees, expressions of hope for early salvation. Every prayer finishes with the cry: 'For Your salvation I hope, O Lord' [Gen. 49: 18]. On the face of it this section seems to belong to a common type of extension of the traditional *viduyim*. In fact, however, it is a unique set of confessional prayers by Luzzatto on behalf of his group, reflecting their feelings at the time when they were obliged to shut themselves in and operate in secret for fear of their persecutors. In several prayers the 'confession' is clearly a dialogue between the members of the group and God. They recount the distress and suffering caused them by their persecution and complain at the success of the wicked—their opponents—who have brought disgrace upon them, forced them to hide their actions from the public and operate in dark secrecy, and thus prevented them from working to bring about the *tikun* of Israel and the Shekhinah and the hastening of the Redemption. Other prayers, on the other hand, seem to be concerned with the troubles and hopes of the Jewish people without any particular connection with the fortunes of the group. But in all the confessional prayers the concerns of the Jewish community are associated with those of the group; in other words the group, in its prayers, identified itself with the whole Jewish people, because this little group of messianic mystics in Padua regarded itself

be pointed out that the Shabateans regularly used the expression 'mixed multitude' as a term of opprobrium for those who rejected their messianic faith.

[34] Zeph. 3: 11.

[35] A quotation from the daily Shaharit prayer.

as the representative and emissary of the Jews, in charge of their defence in exile and of the actions required to bring about their redemption.

The Confessional Prayers

[74r] *Master of all worlds*, if we have been guilty of sinning towards You, and our guilt is so great, rising up to Heaven [Ezra 9: 6], that we have, by our guilt, caused You to cast down from Heaven to earth the holy Shekhinah, of whom it is said: 'He has cast down from Heaven to earth the glory of Israel'[36] and of whom it is also said: 'I went down to the feet of the mountains; the earth with its bars was about me for ever',[37] we [stand] before You in our guilt; verily You have been angry with us according to our guilt, as it is said of them: 'And there was wrath against Judah and Jerusalem according to their guilt'.[38] Will You be angry with us for ever, will You prolong Your anger to all generations [Ps. 85: 6], for if You have utterly rejected us, You have been exceedingly angry with us; why do You forget us for ever, and unendingly forsake us? Turn us back towards You, O Lord, and we will return; renew our days as of old [Lam. 5: 21–2]; in You, O Lord, do we seek refuge, and let it be said of us: 'None of those who seek refuge in Him shall be found guilty.'[39] For Your salvation I hope, O Lord.

Master of all worlds, if we have dealt treacherously against You, as it is said: 'They have dealt treacherously against the Lord, for they have borne alien children',[40] and further: 'For the house of Israel has dealt very treacherously against Me',[41] verily You have delivered us into the hands of wicked traitors and into the hands of despisers who are themselves to be despised, and it is said of us: 'For the treacherous deal treacherously, the treacherous deal very treacherously';[42] Lord God, [do not] spare all these wicked traitors [Ps. 59: 6]. Behold, we are despised and held in contempt by all who see us, [74v] not [only] by the great men of our nation but even by the common people, we are regarded as thorn[s] in their eyes, as wicked men, fools, madmen, simpletons, heretics, and, Heaven forbid, deniers of the Torah, as idolaters [?Heaven forbid], and we have no one to comfort and console us, so great is the darkness which envelops us, and there are many who wonder at us, with none to understand. We have [no one] on whom to rely, for we know that there is no understanding among us. We will, indeed, O Lord our God, hold fast to Your

[36] Lam. 2: 1. For this series of prayers I have not, in general, given biblical references except where Scripture is expressly quoted. [Some additional references have been inserted in square brackets in the text, which makes free use of scriptural language.—Trans.]

[37] Jonah 2: 7.

[38] 2 Chr. 24: 18, where the text reads 'for this their guilt'.

[39] Ps. 34: 23.

[40] Hos. 5: 7.

[41] Jer. 5: 11, but [no doubt accidentally] with a singular (feminine!) verb for the scriptural plural.

[42] Isa. 24: 16, where the word 'for' does not appear.

unity, for You are One and rule alone, and our eyes are always fixed upon You; we hope for light and there is none; not that we desire to enjoy Your light for our own benefit,[43] but only so that we may know that You have chosen us and take pleasure in our worship, for outside, the sword bereaves, words wounding as sword-thrusts are spoken by all who rise up against us [Deut. 32: 25; Prov. 12: 18]; within, one may feel the darkness which plunges us into gloom; You have made us dwell in darkness like those long dead [Lam. 3: 6], because of our sins and the sins of Your people Israel, for You are righteous, O Lord, and Your judgements are just. Look upon our affliction and see our hearts' distress, for You examine men's hearts and will not for ever lay waste, for You are merciful. Do not any longer deceive the virgin Israel, do not deal with her harshly, because You have humbled her [Deut. 21: 14]. Release, release, O Creator, the prisoners from darkness, and say to the prisoners 'Go out' [Ps. 146: 7; Isa. 49: 9] [75^r] for our eyes are turned towards You. For Your salvation I hope, O Lord.

Master of all worlds, if we have stolen aught of Your holiness,[44] giving it out to those who should not have [it],[45] as it is said: 'The spoil of the poor is in your houses' [Isa. 3: 14]—the spoil which they stole from the righteous poor man—and we have robbed [others of] justice, as it is said: 'To rob his people's poor of their right',[46] we have ourselves been oppressed and robbed day by day ever since You became angry with us, as it is said of us: 'And you shall be only oppressed and robbed always';[47] surely it is enough now, O Lord God; rescue, we pray You, the robbed from the hand of the oppressor,[48] for we have been left poor and needy, and it is said of You: 'who rescues the poor man from those that are stronger than he, the poor and needy man from those that rob him';[49] rescue us, O Lord, for we hope in You. For Your salvation I hope, O Lord.

Master of all worlds, if we have spoken slander, as it is said of us: 'And they spoke with their mouth, and with their tongue they lied to Him',[50] behold, You have made us an object of scorn and derision and the taunt of our enemies, they open wide their mouths against us, and as for Your holy

[43] Cf. the group's rules: *Takanot rishonot*, sects. 4, 9 (*Igerot*, i. 8, 9); *Takanot nosafot*, sect. 1 (ibid. 10).

[44] The manuscript has 'Your holy one', an evident error.

[45] It appears to me that this refers to the revelation of the secrets of the Torah to unworthy recipients. A person who commits this fault causes a split in the sefirot and, as it were, steals the Shekhinah from Yesod ('the righteous poor') and Tiferet ('justice'). See the comment by R. M. Zacuto on the Zohar III, 244*a* (*Raya meheimna*), quoted in *Nitsotsei orot* [a commentary by H. J. D. Azulai printed in the margin of editions of the Zohar—Trans.]; Tishby, *Wisdom of the Zohar*, iii. 1087–8. And see Zohar II, 118*a* (*Raya meheimna*), commentary on the verse 'The spoil of the poor is in your houses' (Isa. 3: 14).

[46] Isa. 10: 2 [but the biblical text reads '*my* people'—Trans.].

[47] Deut. 28: 29.

[48] Correcting the manuscript's *he'ashuk* ['the oppressed'] to *ha'oshek* ['the oppressor'].

[49] Ps. 35: 10.

[50] Ps. 78: 36. The psalm reads 'They beguiled Him with their mouth'.

Shekhinah, because of our sins, it is said of her: 'I was dumb, I did not open my mouth'.[51] Lord God, act for Your sake and not for ours, open Your mouth, judge righteously and find for the poor and needy,[52] do it for the sake of Your holy Shekhinah. How long will the adversary scoff? Will the enemy revile[53] Your name for ever? Bring her soul out of prison;[54] she constantly entreats You: 'My God, my God, why have You forsaken me? Deliver my soul from the sword, [75ᵛ] my only one from the power of the dog. Save me from the mouth of the lion; answer me [literally 'You have answered me'] from the horns of the wild oxen' [Ps. 22: 21–2]. Bring her out from between the teeth of these lions, so that it may be said of You: 'I have taken out of his mouth what he had swallowed'.[55] Why, O Lord, should You keep silence when the wicked swallows the righteous, open the mouth of this silent dove, speak kindly to her and comfort her, as it is said: 'And I spoke kindly to her'.[56] She is like a silent dove and all she has is hope. For Your salvation I hope, O Lord.

Master of all worlds, if we have perverted our path, pursuing so many paths which we did not desire, and have angered You with our evil ways, have we not seen with our own eyes many perversions of justice against Your holy Shekhinah, 'a servant-girl when she supplants her mistress',[57] many perversions of justice against our glorious Temple which was burnt down, perversion of justice against our king(s), our priest(s), our elders, our princes, our pious men, who were killed, burnt, strangled, hanged, drowned, or suffered death in many other cruel ways to sanctify Your name, the name of the one God. And it is said of us: 'He has made my paths crooked'.[58] O Lord our God, turn us back, O Lord, to You and we will return to Your g[ood] ways, and make Your face shine upon us so that we may know Your ways, open our eyes this day, open our ears for the sake of the glory of Your name, for we have placed our hope in You, O Lord, we have sought You; we beg You, do not delay, for we wait for Your salvation. For Your salvation I hope, O Lord.

[76ʳ] *Master of all worlds*, if we have acted wickedly and sinned and caused the public to commit sins such as all the sins of Jeroboam and all those who have been drawn after him up to the present day,[59] have You not given us into

51 Ps. 39: 10.

52 Prov. 31: 9.

53 Correcting the manuscript's *yena'ef* ['commit adultery'] to *yena'ets*: Ps. 74: 10.

54 Based on Ps. 142: 8, but applied to the Shekhinah by substituting 'her soul' for 'my soul'.

55 Jer. 51: 44.

56 Hos. 2: 16.

57 As in Prov. 30: 23, but giving the words a kabbalistic meaning: while the Shekhinah is in exile Lilith takes her place.

58 Lam. 3: 9.

59 Undoubtedly to be understood not as a literal reference to the sins of Jeroboam recorded in Scripture but rather as an allusion to the kabbalistic idea, developed in Shabateanism and pursued in Luzzatto's writings, that Jeroboam had been intended to be the Messiah ben Joseph and was disqualified by his sins from fulfilling his messianic role, but was destined to be revealed as the Messiah ben Joseph when his soul was restored to perfection [*tikun*] in time to come. Luzzatto's views on the messianic status of Jeroboam are considered in Essay 4 below, where I

the hands of our enemies, so that we should not be able to bring anyone back to Your good path? And in any event[60] You have requited us. O Lord God, it is enough now, O Lord, open their eyes and let them see and be ashamed and let them return to Your presence, let sinners cease from the earth and evil-doers be no more, and let Your honour be exalted through us, so that they may know that we have served You in truth, and those who truly trust in You will not be shamed. For Your salvation I hope, O Lord.

Master of all worlds, if we have been arrogant towards You, and it is said of us: 'because You knew that they acted arrogantly against them',[61] has not arrogance come, and disgrace too, through so many decrees and persecutions decreed against us, those who were for the sword, to the sword, those who were for famine, to famine, and those who were for captivity, to captivity [Jer. 15: 2], and the proud waters have passed over us [Ps. 124: 5]. O Lord God, surely we have gone through fire and water, but You will bring us out to abundance[62] and will rebuke all the arrogant who are cursed, as it is said: 'You rebuked the arrogant who are cursed, who err from Your commandments',[63] and it is further said: 'I will put an end to the pride of arrogant men' etc.[64] Even though we know the arrogance of our hearts [in presuming] to come before You and pray to You, [since we are] the smallest of those upon earth, broken vessels, [76^{v}] truly You will see that we have no one, consider that there is none to intercede, and that it is for the honour of Your holy Shekhinah that we lay our supplications before You, and we rely on Your abundant mercies. In this we trust, let us not be disappointed; do not put us to shame. For Your salvation I hope, O Lord.

Master of all worlds, if we have committed violent wrongs, and it is said of us: 'The whole earth was filled with violence',[65] have not many people afflicted us when we had wronged no one? The nations of every land have hated us with a violent hatred because we would not forsake Your unity, and we have cried out 'Violence!' day by day and hour by hour but there was no answer. O Lord God, save me from the man [or 'men'] of violence,[66] who planned to

conclude by saying: 'Probably, too, Luzzatto's disclosure [in his book *Kinat hashem tsevaot*] as "a great, great secret that Jeroboam clothed holiness in the Sitra Ahra by his worship" was a reference to the Shabatean mystical aim of destroying the world of uncleanness by introducing an excess of holiness into it.' On this basis the confessional prayer here relates to a hypothetical sin by the group in erring similarly by clothing holiness in the Sitra Ahra along with all those who were drawn after Jeroboam 'up to the present day' (apparently there is an allusion here to Shabateans in general or extremist Shabateans in particular); their excuse is that because of their persecutors they could not point the right way to those who, as mentioned above, continued in the sins of Jeroboam, and bring them to repentance.

60 The manuscript uses a standard abbreviation for this expression.
61 Neh. 9: 10.
62 Cf. Ps. 66: 12.
63 Ps. 119: 21.
64 Isa. 13: 11.
65 Gen. 6: 11.
66 As in 2 Sam. 22: 49 [where, however, the sense is 'You saved me'—Trans.]. The expression 'man of violence' could be understood here as a collective epithet for Luzzatto's persecutors,

make my footsteps stumble[67] and to turn us away from Your ways and from serving You. And that violence became a rod of wickedness.[68] It happened when the rod was turned into a serpent;[69] now, O Lord, let it turn into a rod in the hand of Your servant Moses, but let it remain a holy serpent [when acting] on behalf of holiness for ever;[70] and let it be said of it: 'Dan is a serpent on the path, a snake on the way, that bites the horse's heels so that its rider falls backwards' [Gen. 49: 17]. For Your salvation I hope, O Lord.

[77r] *Master of all worlds*, if we have uttered malicious falsehoods [Ps. 119: 69], as it is said: 'They have taught their tongue to speak lies',[71] has not a wicked man acted falsely and led the world astray with the words of a lying spirit concerning the words of the living God [which are] truth and justice?[72] And it is not in our power to make the truth known, for we have become an object of ridicule to them, and they do not know Your wonders and Your deep thoughts; for truly You have done things to us which the mind cannot endure, and which cannot be declared publicly, since we have no authority on which we can rely in order to reveal Your truth. O Lord God, our reason does not suffice [to discover] how it may be known where the truth is, save that You, in Your wonderful wisdom, will do as You have done until now. For indeed it is marvellous in our eyes that You have chosen for Your many high [purposes] men devoid of knowledge, understanding, and intelligence; it is beyond our comprehension. Is it on us that You would found the earth? And day after day we continue to marvel so greatly that we may think improper thoughts, Heaven forbid,[73] for each and every one of us knows and

but it may refer to a specific person; if so, that person would be R. Moses Hagiz. See nn. 72 and 87 below.

67 This is the only use of the first person singular in the confessional prayers (other than the refrain 'For Your salvation I hope'). It is possible that the plural was intended.

68 Ezek. 7: 11. It may be that here we are intended to read not *ḥamas* ['violence'] but *ḥomes* ['violent man'], i.e. Hagiz.

69 This certainly refers to the time of Luzzatto's capitulation in Padua in 1730. This occurrence is described by means of the kabbalistic-messianic image, very common in Luzzatto's writings, of the transformation of the staff into a snake. See Essay 4, pp. 234–7.

70 The Messiah, 'the holy serpent', will be freed from the husks, and Luzzatto, the reincarnation of the biblical Moses, will be able to act together with the Messiah and make him operate as a staff to bring about the Redemption. Or perhaps the 'holy serpent' here is Dan–Seraiah–Jekutiel, on the basis of the verse quoted: 'Dan is a serpent on the path' (Gen. 49: 17). See *Netivei emunah uminut*, 175–8, 192, 195–6.

71 Jer. 9: 4.

72 This is undoubtedly a reference to a specific wicked man, namely R. Moses Hagiz, who levelled false charges against Luzzatto's 'words of the living God' and misled the world by his lies. See n. 66 above and n. 87 below.

73 The meaning of this sentence is not clear. It could be interpreted as alluding to a renewal of the revelations of the *magid* to Luzzatto and to wonderful events witnessed by the group after Luzzatto's recovery from his defeat, especially after his marriage on 27 Av 5491 [summer 1731], which to him and his group represented his marriage to the Shekhinah. (See *Netivei emunah uminut*, 186–8.) On this interpretation the words 'that we may think . . .' should be understood

recognizes how lowly and contemptible is his worth, and that it is these in whom You take pleasure. We turn[74] to the right and there is none to help, and to the left and there is none to support us. O Lord our God, King [77^{v}] who shows us kindnesses, uncover our eyes so that we may see wonderful things out of Your Torah [Ps. 119: 18], and let Your Torah be a consolation and a delight to us, so that we may truly know that You take pleasure in us. And if You please to put us to the test, who are we that we should be able to stand the test? Indeed, many of the leading men of our nation, whose little finger is thicker than our loins, have not been able to stand before You. Lo, the heavens are not guiltless in Your eyes; in Your angels You find fault, yet our worth is accounted as nothing compared to theirs. You are our Father, answer us this day by cleaving through all darkness, by showing Your great strength, of which our forefathers told us; reveal Your glory to us and let our eyes see and our hearts rejoice in Your salvation, in the salvation of Your holy Shekhinah which waits for our salvation and redemption. How long, O Lord, shall we hope in vain, shall we hope for light but behold, there is darkness; rescue us, O Lord, from this darkness. How long, O Lord, shall we pray to You without being heard, how long, O Lord, shall we cry to You without being answered, how long, O Lord, shall we hope for good but behold, there is darkness. You know that we hope in You truly, with a whole heart and a willing mind [1 Chr. 28: 9]; and You, O Lord, have said 'Those who hope in Me shall not be disappointed'.[75] How long shall we grope [78^{r}] in darkness like blind men, how long. How long shall we suffer contempt for the sake of Your glory, how long. How long will Your name be profaned, how long. How long shall the foe utter taunts, how long. How long shall the enemy revile Your name for ever, how long [cf. Ps. 74: 10]. How long must we hide in secret places like a thief, how long. How long shall wicked men rule over us, how long. How long shall there be no hope for the poor, how long. How long will You not have compassion on us, how long shall we be regarded by our people as transgressors against You, how long. How long shall Your land lie waste, how long. How long shall Jerusalem, the holy city, lie ruined and uninhabited, how long. How long shall Your glorious house be reduced to a desolate hill where wicked men rule, how long. How long shall Your holy Shekhinah remain as a widow, how long. How long shall Your spouse be far from You, how long. How long will You not console Your beloved, how long. How long will You

as an expression of fear by the group that these events might lead them to a view of their own importance which did not match the lowliness of their true position. But it may be that the opposite is meant: the members of the group were pointing out sadly that their wonder at their lowly condition was growing from day to day, and they were afraid that (Heaven forbid) they might come to think heretical thoughts denying their mission.

[74] The manuscript has *pinu* ['our mouths]', evidently for *paninu* ['we turned'].

[75] Isa. 49: 23.

not speak tenderly to her, how long. How long shall Your dove wander [far] from her nest, how long. How long shall Your glory sit on the ground, how long. How long shall the King's daughter be captive, how long. How long shall the silent dove not open her mouth, [78v] how long. How long shall Your noble princes be in sorrow, how long. How long shall the way of the wicked prosper, how long. What can we say before You, what words can we speak and how can we clear ourselves? We do not know what to do, but our eyes are turned towards You. For Your salvation I hope, O Lord.

Master of all worlds, if we have counselled [or 'planned'] evil, having consulted for evil [with] an evil and worthless man who is guilty of giving wicked advice, and we have distanced ourselves from Your good counsel,[76] as it is said: 'Is counsel perished from the prudent?',[77] have You not shone upon the counsel of the wicked, our enemies? but let us return to You.[78] And it is said of them: 'Take counsel together, but it will be frustrated; say a word, but it will not stand, for God is with us',[79] and let us return to Your counsels, as it is written: 'I will guide you with My counsel',[80] for in You, O Lord, is our hope. For Your salvation I hope, O Lord.

Master of all worlds, if we have lied and pursued falsehood, which is the ultimate source of all uncleanness, we pray You, Lord God, turn us back to You and we will return, as it is written: 'Remove falsehood and lying from me',[81] which is a lying word against the Word of Truth; favour us with the Word of Truth from You which is the Shekhinah,[82] which unites with the King, and we will not be false to your covenant as we have been, [79r] for You, our Father, are a God of truth, as it is written: 'And also the Glory of Israel does not lie or repent';[83] save us and answer us, for our eyes are turned towards You. For Your salvation I hope, O Lord.

Master of all worlds, if we have scoffed and made mock of Your commandments, and it is said of us: 'And scoffers delight in their scoffing',[84] have we not been a byword and a disgrace among the nations, a cause for the peoples to shake their heads and mock at us and exclaim 'Aha!' We pray You, Lord

[76] A confession of hypothetical sin in case they had succumbed to the seductions of the evil inclination, Sama'el, and distanced themselves from the counsel of the Lord. [77] Jer. 49: 7.

[78] Substituting *elekha* ['to You'] for the erroneous *alekha* ['on You'] in the manuscript. The whole sentence is unclear but it can be understood as follows: You, O God, have supported the plans of our wicked enemies (as in Job 10: 3: 'And shine upon the counsel of wicked men'), and we are trying to return to You and obey You.

[79] Isa. 8: 10. [80] Ps. 73: 24.

[81] Prov. 30: 8 (where, however, a different verb is used [rendered 'remove far' in the Authorized Version]).

[82] *Emet* ['Truth'] is Tiferet, and *devar emet* ['the Word of Truth'] is Malkhut, the Shekhinah.

[83] 1 Sam. 15: 29.

[84] Prov. 1: 22 (with a slip of the pen in the manuscript: *lashon* ['tongue'] for *latson* ['scoffing']).

God, of whom it is said: 'At the scoffers He scoffs',[85] turn back [the taunts of] our enemies sevenfold upon them, so that it may be said of You: 'He who sits in Heaven laughs, the Lord scoffs at them',[86] and in place of the scoffer [*lets*] who mocks at us[87] let an advocate [*melits*] on our behalf come and stand up to comfort us, as it is written: 'If there should be an angel, an advocate on his behalf, one among a thousand',[88] a single one out of a thousand [*elef*]—by a supreme wonder [*pele*],[89] make wonderful Your kindnesses, You who save those who trust, for we have poured out our hearts like water, and our eyes look hopefully to You. For Your salvation I hope, O Lord.

Master of all worlds, if we have rebelled against You, as it is said: 'to the children of Israel, to a nation of rebels',[90] have not many evildoers rebelled against You, for they embittered our spirits,[91] saying: 'These are not the people of the Lord', for it is said of them: 'They are among those who rebel against the light'.[92] [79v] We pray You, Lord God, make their spirit rebellious, let them die thereby and not with wisdom,[93] for You are righteous, and surely we have long enough experienced the cup of staggering [Isa. 51: 17]; let us not return to folly. O Lord, save, we pray You; O Lord, grant success, so that all the nations of the earth may know that You have not forsaken us and that if we rebelled, we have repented, and that they, a stiff-necked people, would not pay heed. Reveal Your strong arm, let them see and be ashamed, for You are our God and are called the God of Israel; in You our[94] ancestors trusted, they trusted and You rescued them, and we, after them, have trusted and will not be put to shame. For Your salvation I hope, O Lord.

Master of all worlds, if we have despised Your great name, and it is said of us: 'How long will this people despise Me',[95] surely, if we have, all of us together, despised [You], we have turned back and repented, and while we have been among the Gentiles it has been said: 'Continually every day My name is

[85] Prov. 3: 34.
[86] Ps. 2: 4.
[87] It may be that the person denounced here as the 'scoffer', who jeered at Luzzatto and his group, is again R. Moses Hagiz, previously described as the 'wicked man' who slandered them (see n. 72 above). But it is more likely that the epithet 'scoffer' refers to R. Jacob Belilios, Luzzatto's principal opponent among the rabbis of Venice.
[88] Job 33: 23.
[89] *Pele* by rearrangement of the letters of *elef*. The reference is to Keter Elyon, the first sefirah, which is called Pele.
[90] Ezek. 2: 3.
[91] [Cf. Ps. 106: 33. The verb—root *m-r-h*—in other contexts is a synonym of *m-r-d*, 'to rebel'.—Trans.]
[92] Job 24: 13 (with another lapse in the manuscript: *ot* ['a sign'] for *or* ['light']).
[93] Job 4: 21, but with an odd displacement of the caesura. [The verse in Job is variously understood, but a specimen rendering, as in the Revised Standard and American Jewish versions, is: 'their tent-peg is plucked up within them [*bam*]; they die without wisdom'. Luzzatto transfers *bam* to the second half of the verse; it is not clear how he understands it.—Trans.]
[94] Hebrew (archaic) *avotemo*, no doubt a mistake for *avoteinu* ['our ancestors'].
[95] Num. 14: 11 (but the verse uses a different word for 'how long').

despised',[96] for they said: 'He has grown weak like a female, "because of the Lord's inability"',[97] and we have become an object of contempt to the lowliest in the land. We pray You, Lord God, act for the sake of Your honour, and let not nations any longer despise Your name for ever, for we are Your children and You are our Father, and they are slaves whom You made subject to the children of Israel: 'Cursed be Canaan; a slave of slaves shall he be [80^r] to his brothers',[98] for they are despised by You and rejected. Distinguish between the light and the darkness, between Israel and the nations. In You, O Lord, we hope; You will answer [cf. Ps. 38: 16]. For Your salvation I hope, O Lord.

Master of all worlds, if we have been stubborn, as it is said: 'Like a stubborn heifer, Israel has been stubborn',[99] have You not delivered us into the hands of stubborn and rebellious men and hedged our path in so that we could find no way out? We have been desolate these many, many[100] years, so that it is said of us: 'He has turned aside my paths and torn me in pieces, He has made me desolate',[101] in the midst of so many levels of uncleanness, the shadow of death, and disorder.[102] Lord God, this bitterness of death which has turned aside [towards us?],[103] remove it from us and bring us forth from darkness to great light, for You, O Lord, open the eyes of the blind, and let it be said of us: 'The people who walked in darkness have seen light';[104] for You are our God, and let it be said of us: 'This is the Lord, we hoped in Him and He has saved us, this is the Lord, in whom we hoped, let us rejoice' etc.[105] For Your salvation I hope, O Lord.

[96] Isa. 52: 5, which, however, reads 'all day long' not 'every day'.

[97] Num. 14: 16, which is expounded as follows in the Talmud (*Ber.* 32*a*): 'Now the nations of the world will say: "His strength has grown weak like a female and He cannot save [them]."' Here again, as in the other confessional prayers, the words of Scripture and of the rabbis regarding Israel and the Gentiles are applied to the members of the group and their persecutors, as is clearly shown by the rest of the sentence: 'we have become an object of contempt to the lowliest in the land'.

[98] Gen. 9: 25.

[99] Hos. 4: 16.

[100] 'Many, many': Hebrew *kamah vekhamah*, the second word being written above the line.

[101] Lam. 3: 11. The word for 'torn in pieces' is miscopied in the manuscript. [There is a play on words here: 'stubborn' and 'turned aside' are both *sorer*, but from two different roots (*s-r-r* and *s-u-r*). And the intransitive *sar*, 'turned aside', is followed by the imperative *haser*, 'turn aside, remove'.—Trans.]

[102] From this we are to understand that as a result of their persecution they sank down among the husks. And see Job 10: 22.

[103] 1 Sam. 15: 32. The words spoken there by Agag are taken by most commentators as an expression of despair ('the bitterness of death has turned towards me', 'is at hand'), whereas Ralbag (Levi ben Gershom) took it as an expression of hope ('. . . has departed'). Luzzatto, by the words 'remove it from us', is expressing a hope [rather, a petition for removal of a threat—Trans.].

[104] Isa. 9: 1.

[105] Isa. 25: 9, slightly misquoted.

Master of all worlds, if we have been guilty of iniquities before You and You have delivered us into the hand of our iniquities,[106] and it is said: '"Your iniquities and the iniquities of your fathers", says the Lord, "who have burned incense on the mountains and on the hills"',[107] have we not been taken captive because of our iniquities and sold because of them, as it is said: [80v] 'For your iniquities you were sold'.[108] Lord God, redeem Israel from all its iniquities, for You have brought upon us even all those plagues which are not written in the Torah [cf. Deut. 28: 61]; and do not any longer remember against us our former iniquities. Let Your compassion come quickly to meet us, for we are brought very low [Ps. 79: 8]. And let it be said of us: '[The punishment of] your iniquity is ended, O daughter of Zion',[109] 'and it shall come to pass on that day that search will be made for the iniquity of Israel but there will be none, and for the sins of Judah, but they will not be found, for I will pardon those whom I leave as a remnant' [cf. Jer. 50: 20], for as a hired servant waits for his wage, so do we wait for You. For Your salvation I hope, O Lord.

Master of all worlds, if we have rebelled against You, as it is said: 'Children have I reared and brought up, and they have rebelled against me',[110] did not Moses, Your servant and Your anointed,[111] suffer many torments for our transgressions, for it is said of him: 'He was wounded for our transgressions, crushed for our iniquities'[112] etc. 'and he was numbered with the transgressors'.[113] Lord God, forgive, we pray You, the transgression of Your people and the sin which they committed against You, by virtue of all the torments of the leaders of Your people, for that is Your glory, as it is said: 'And His glory [is that He] passes over transgression'.[114] And You, O Lord, whose attribute it is to forgive iniquity and pass over transgression [Mic. 7: 18], [81r] acquit us of our transgressions, and cast them into the depths of the sea in a place where they will never be remembered or thought of or called to mind,[115] and reveal that day of which it it is said: 'I will remove the iniquity of that land in one day',[116] for it is for that day that we wait. For Your salvation I hope, O Lord.

[106] Isa. 64: 6 [64: 7 in English versions].

[107] Isa. 65: 7, which, however, has the word 'together' after 'your fathers'.

[108] Isa. 50: 1. [109] Lam. 4: 22. [110] Isa. 1: 2.

[111] A letter, or two letters, erased or smudged here. Apparently the word 'suffered' had been written in the third or first person plural; what is left is third person singular. This is an important alteration. 'Moses Your servant and Your anointed' in the confessional prayer meant two persons, Luzzatto being Moses and R. Moses David Valle 'the anointed'—Messiah ben David—in their group. But to accord with the quotation from Isaiah (see next note) the plural was altered to the singular.

[112] Isa. 53: 5, slightly misquoted but sense unaffected. [113] Isa. 53: 12.

[114] Prov. 19: 11, where, however, the verb is in the infinitive, 'to pass over'.

[115] ['And cast . . . to mind' is a quotation from the Rosh Hashanah and Yom Kippur liturgy, based on Mic. 7: 19.—Trans.] [116] Zech. 3: 9.

Master of all worlds, if we have harassed [*tsararnu*] and have caused distress [*tsarot*] to Your holy Shekhinah, did not an adversary [*tsar*] and enemy enter into Your sanctuaries to revile the army of the living God, and it is said: 'Your enemies [*tsorerekha*] roared in the midst of Your meeting-place',[117] and with many troubles did they harass us within our gates, as it is said: 'Much have they harassed me ever since my youth, let Israel say',[118] her enemies saw, they laughed at her ruin. Lord God, in our straits we have called to You, O Lord: answer me, O Lord, by granting me freedom.[119] Do not forget all Your enemies, the uproar of Your attackers which ascends continually.[120] Repay anger to Your adversaries [Isa. 59: 18], be our stronghold in the day of trouble, and let the poor have hope [Job 5: 16]. For Your salvation I hope, O Lord.

Master of all worlds, if we have been stubborn, as it is said: 'They stiffened their necks',[121] did not our spirit become impatient because of cruel slavery; You have made Your people experience hardship, You have made us drink the wine of staggering.[122] [81ᵛ] Lord God, do not regard the stubbornness of this people [Deut. 9: 27], humble this uncircumcised heart of ours and give us a heart of flesh, as it is said: 'Then will your uncircumcised heart be humbled',[123] and it is also said: 'I will give you a heart of flesh',[124] so that we may serve You in truth and sincerity according to Your will, for that is our constant desire the whole day long. For Your salvation I hope, O Lord.

Master of all worlds, if we have been wicked in Your sight, as it is said: 'For there are wicked men among the peoples' [*sic*],[125] have not the wicked carried their wickedness to excess; and all the time of our tranquillity has been less than [the time] that You have placed us among all the nations and the wicked of the earth. The wicked have drawn the sword against us and bent their bows against us, to wipe out our name from the earth, and behold, these wicked men and those that are always at ease have increased their wealth.[126] Let the hope of the wicked perish; and be compassionate towards our hope(s). For Your salvation I hope, O Lord.

Master of all worlds, if we have corrupted [*shiḥatnu*] our ways, as it is said: 'Seed of evildoers, children who deal corruptly',[127] has not an enemy destroyed [*shiḥet*] Your fortresses, and it is said of them: 'They are corrupt, they do abominable deeds, none does good',[128] not even one of them. Lord God, destroy every enemy of ours, raise us out of the pit of destruction [82ʳ] and draw us near to You, and remove from us all darkness, every enemy and adversary, and every kind of cloud. Uncover our eyes so that we may see the

[117] Ps. 74: 4. [118] Ps. 129: 1. [119] Ps. 118: 5, but the psalm reads 'I called . . .'.
[120] Ps. 74: 23, but the psalm reads 'the voice of . . .' [*qol*] not 'all' [*kol*].
[121] Jer. 7: 26, 17: 23. [122] Ps. 60: 5 [60: 3 in English versions].
[123] Lev. 26: 41 [*o az*, usually understood as 'if then'. Luzzatto has only *az*, 'then'—Trans.].
[124] Ezek. 36: 26. [125] Jer. 5: 26, which reads, however, 'among my people'.
[126] Ps. 73: 12. [127] Isa. 1: 4. [128] Ps. 14: 1.

wonders in Your Torah. O Lord who opens the eyes of the blind, open our eyes, O Lord who raises those who are bowed down, lift up our horn, for behold, as the eyes of servants look towards their master, as the eyes of a maid towards her mistress, so do our eyes look towards You in hope of Your favour [cf. Ps. 123: 2]. For Your salvation I hope, O Lord.

Master of all worlds, if we have done abominable things, have gone astray, have led others astray,[129] as it is said: 'Abominable things have been done in Israel',[130] and it is said: 'Who strayed from Me when the children of Israel went astray',[131] have we not in truth strayed like a lost sheep; guide us in Your ways, make us walk straight in the path of truth, for we have no strength by reason of the many troubles of our servitude in exile and [the anxieties of] each one of us in finding enough food for his needs; for the last farthing has gone from [our] purse,[132] and there is no one on whom we can rely but You. Our Father in Heaven, answer us; our Father, answer us today; answer us, our King, answer us, You who hear the prayers of the poor, answer us, O God whose word is faithful, answer us, for we have hoped in You up to now, and we will still hope in You. For Your salvation I hope, O Lord.

But You have been just in all that has come upon us, for You have dealt truthfully and we have done wickedly.[133] But if we have sinned and transgressed Your Torah which was given with twenty-two letters, we now repent and confess before You our iniquities and the iniquity of our forefathers. Turn us back to You, O Lord, and we will return and be joyful and rejoice in You—in the twenty-two letters, in You—in Your holy name which will be revealed to us, in You—in Your holy Shekhinah, in You—in Your rejoicing, and let there be fulfilled in us the words: 'And the glory of the Lord will be revealed and all flesh will see',[134] even before the flesh, the red flesh,[135] has undergone *tikun* [has been rendered perfect], for the mouth of the Lord has spoken it;[136] speedily in our days, Amen. And as for me, may my prayer to You, O Lord, be at a time of favour; O God, in Your great mercy, answer me

[129] 'Led astray': the Hebrew verb is misspelt.

[130] Mal. 2: 11.

[131] Ezek. 44: 10. 'The children of' is not in the verse, and Ezekiel's 'from Me' has been badly copied in the manuscript (*bo'alai* for *me'alai*).

[132] An allusion to the opinion expressed in *San.* 97*a*: 'The son of David will not come . . . until [every] *perutah* has gone from [people's] purse.'

[133] [Neh. 9: 33, which in the Yom Kippur service follows the *ashamnu* ('we have been guilty') paragraph elaborated by Luzzatto.—Trans.]

[134] Isa. 40: 5.

[135] The physical body. The meaning is: reveal Your glory by proving our righteousness and the truth of the *magid*'s revelations ('for the mouth of the Lord has spoken it'), by lifting up our horn in the sight of all Israel, even before we have completed our messianic mission through the *tikun* of corporeality in the time of perfect redemption which is to come. On the expectation of the *tikun* of corporeality which Luzzatto shared with his group, see above, preface to '*Piyut* and two prayers for the night of 17 Shevat', pp. 118–19.

[136] Isa. 40, end of verse 5.

with Your sure salvation.[137] May the words of my mouth and the meditation of my heart be acceptable to You, O Lord, my Rock and my Redeemer.[138] For Your salvation I hope, O Lord.

137 'And as for me . . . salvation': Ps. 69: 14.

138 Ps. 19: 15, represented in the manuscript by the initial letter of each word in the verse.

THREE

The Messianic Ferment in Rabbi Moses Hayim Luzzatto's Group in the Light of a Messianic Marriage Contract and Messianic Poems

A. THE MARRIAGE OF MOSES–RAMHAL TO THE SHEKHINAH

In the year 5491 [1731],[1] following his first capitulation[2] at the end of 5490, Luzzatto let himself be persuaded by R. Isaiah Bassano[3] to marry Zipporah, daughter of R. David Finzi, the rabbi of Mantua. The names of the bridegroom and bride, Moses and Zipporah, reminded their companions of the biblical Moses and his wife,[4] and R. David Finzi even boasted the sobriquet 'father-in-law of Moses'.[5] The kabbalist R. Samson Hayim Nahmani,[6] a pupil

[1] J. Almanzi (in *Kerem ḥemed*, 3 (1838), 118–19) conjectured that Luzzatto's wedding took place 'in 5492 or 5493' [1732–3], whereas S. Ginzburg (in *R' mosheh ḥayim lutsato uvenei doro: osef igerot ute'udot*, ed. S. Ginzburg [hereafter *Igerot*] (Tel Aviv, 1937), ii. 425 n. 33) and B. Klar (in *Sefer hashirim*, ed. S. Ginzburg and B. Klar (Jerusalem, 1945), 170 n. 1) concluded that on 10 Iyar 5491 [late spring of 1731] he was already married, since in a letter which he sent from Mantua to his teacher on that date he referred to R. David Finzi as 'our honoured teacher and rabbi, my father-in-law, may the Merciful One guard him and preserve him in life' (*Igerot*, ii. 230). However, in the text of the *ketubah* it is plainly stated that the wedding was in Padua on 27 Av 5491 [late summer 1731], and it necessarily follows that he was betrothed in Mantua before 10 Iyar and at that date was calling his fiancée's father 'father-in-law'. The fact that the wedding took place in Luzzatto's home in Padua is also proved by his reply to the complaint about the performance of a comedy on the war of Gog (*Igerot*, ii. 238).

[2] [See Essay 1, p. 11 and nn. 22 and 61.—Trans.]

[3] *Igerot*, ii. 217–18. In that letter, which is undated, Luzzatto demonstrated by esoteric argument that 'a man who walks in the ways of the Lord' must precede union by proximity, and it was apparently for this reason that he lived in Mantua for some time before his marriage.

[4] See S. Ginzburg, *The Life and Works of Moses Hayyim Luzzatto* (Philadelphia, 1931), 52 n. 94; Klar, in *Sefer hashirim*, 123 note 1.

[5] *Igerot*, ii. 257.

[6] See M. S. Ghirondi, *Toledot gedolei yisra'el ugeonei italyah* (Trieste, 1853), 324, 325; M. Wilensky, 'Mi hu r' netanel halevi?', *Kiryat sefer*, 23 (1946), 135.

of R. David Finzi, who composed a poem in honour of the bridegroom and bride and their parents,[7] went further, and in kabbalistic allusions at the beginning of his poem he compared Luzzatto's marriage to the union of Moses with the Shekhinah:[8]

And this man Moses, his right hand has done valiantly, and through the mysteries of the chariot the ways of the world have been made his.[9] How good and how pleasant it is *for Zipporah to be the wife of Moses as of old.* The enlightened man will understand the secret of my parable, because *the bride of Moses is a garden locked*,[10] and 'the bed' in the mystery of the seal [is] 'the finest spices' in [its] inner letters.[11]

Students of the Luzzatto story did not attach any importance to the connection between Moses and Zipporah, and even Almanzi, with the words of Nahmani's poem before him, gave no particular weight to the reference. Scholars adopted a rationalistic approach and saw in the association of the names and in the allusions to their significance no more than literary playfulness or idle prattle.

A remarkable document, which I publish and elucidate here, casts fresh light—the light of a profound mystical experience—on the play on names and the significance of Luzzatto's marriage. This document is the text of Luzzatto's marriage contract [*ketubah*] with an extensive mystical interpretation in which the bridegroom himself describes his marriage as the union of Moses with his divine bride. The document appears at the end of a collection

[7] The poem was printed on a single sheet; an exemplar is in the National Library in Jerusalem. See Almanzi, *Kerem ḥemed*, 3: 118–19 and 154 n. 83. Benjacob (*Otsar hasefarim* (Vilna, 1880; New York, 1965), under letter *shin*, no. 639) has an entry for a book described as 'Poems for the wedding of R. M. H. Luzzatto by R. Solomon David Treves, R. Isaac ben R. Shabetai Marini, R. Gershon Treves, R. Abraham [*sic*] Shalom and others: Mantua, 1733, 8°'. I have not found any mention of such a book anywhere else, and it seems that it never existed but was invented on the basis of Almanzi's n. 82, which named the disciples of Luzzatto enumerated by Benjacob as having 'lifted up their voices for his wedding day', along with 'many who loved him who hid their names in their songs'. The reference 'Mantua, 1733' certainly originated in Almanzi's mistaken identification of the place and time of Luzzatto's wedding. The four poems alluded to are included in a manuscript in the Schwadron Collection in the National Library, Jerusalem. See A. Ya'ari, 'Shenei shirei ḥatunah leramḥa"l', *Kiryat sefer*, 8 (1931), 202. Jekutiel of Vilna's poem in honour of Luzzatto's wedding, which I quote below at p. 208, was not known to Almanzi.

[8] See I. Tishby, *The Wisdom of the Zohar*, trans. D. Goldstein (Oxford, 1989), i. 288–9; iii. 874–5.

[9] [Probably a play on Hab. 3: 6.—Trans.]

[10] The Shekhinah is, as it were, a virgin. See pp. 211–12 and n. 107 below. [For 'the bride . . . a garden locked, a fountain sealed', and for 'the finest spices', see S. of S. 4: 12 and 14.—Trans.]

[11] These allusions are not clear to me. Further on, another allusion by Nahmani accepts the truth of the *magid*'s revelations to Luzzatto: 'The Torah of truth was in the mouth of Moses, a legacy to him from the supernal patriarchs, "and by knowledge the rooms are filled" [Prov. 24: 4].'

of kabbalistic writings by Luzzatto,[12] and is headed: 'Writings of our teacher and master, Rabbi Moses Hayim Luzzatto'.[13]

In the Zohar and later kabbalistic literature much is said on the subject of erotic love between the righteous and the Shekhinah.[14] But because the kabbalists in general avoided any personal note in describing their mystical aims, it is hard to discover from their writings how far they actually experienced erotic communion with the Shekhinah. For this reason great importance attaches to the underlying meaning of Luzzatto's marriage contract, which although expressed in the third person and in speculative kabbalistic style, is undoubtedly an autobiographical document; it opens a window through which we may see into the depths of a Jewish mystic's soul.

It must be conceded that we cannot generalize from the level and details of Luzzatto's experience, for his attachment to his celestial bride was not simply as a kabbalist and righteous man but as Moses himself, husband of the Shekhinah. Apparently kabbalists of inferior rank to his did not earn the privilege of an actual covenant of marriage with the Shekhinah: their union was a temporary one, merely a phenomenon incidental to their earthly marriage. In a well-known section of Luzzatto's *Tikunim ḥadashim* (the profound significance of which is clear from *Sod haketubah* ['The Mystical Interpretation of the Marriage Contract'], where Luzzatto is wholly identified with the Moses of the Bible) Adam reveals the superiority of Ramhal–Moses to all other righteous men as shown by his intimate relations with the Shekhinah:

The ancestor of our ancestors, Adam, the first man, stood up and said: 'Worthy is your portion' etc. Of you it is written: 'He that is left in Zion and he that remains in Jerusalem shall be called holy' (Isa. 4: 3). For the other inhabitants of the world, when they come down to the world, part from their place on high as one leaves for

12 MS Guenzburg 376 (photograph in the Ben Tsevi Institute), fos. 174ʳ–176ʳ. The rest of the collection comprises: *Perush ha'idra raba* (fos. 8ʳ–155ʳ), finishing before the end of *Adir bamarom* as printed; *Reshit haberiah* (fos. 156ʳ–163ʳ), as in the 'pamphlet' at the end of *Pitḥei ḥokhmah vada'at* (Warsaw, 1884); *Kinat hashem tsevaot* (fos. 163ᵛ ff.), this, too, finishing before the end of the printed version. This is undoubtedly MS Coronel 28, which is described in the catalogue (London, 1871).

13 The whole collection is in the same Ashkenazic hand, and it is therefore surprising that the last composition in particular should be headed with the name of the author. The use of the word 'writings' in the plural shows that it relates to more than one composition, and it may be that in the original order *Sod haketubah* came at the beginning of the collection.

14 See Tishby, *Wisdom of the Zohar*, i. 300–2; iii. 990–3, 1357. The motifs in the Zohar were extensively developed by the scholars of Safed in their kabbalistic and ethical works. I quote as an example one paragraph from R. Elijah de Vidas's *Reshit ḥokhmah* (Amsterdam, 1708), heading 'Holiness', sect. 7 (177*a*): 'It stands to reason that anyone who does not get up [at midnight] does not desire the love of the Shekhinah at all, for the beloved who follows his loved one neither slumbers nor sleeps, so great is his love, and because this scholar does not rise, the Shekhinah complains that he has no love for her, seeing that he has deprived her of her conjugal right and is not concerned about her.'

a distant place, but you, *although you are in the world, do not part from the Shekhinah at all, like Moses the faithful shepherd*, of whom [*sic*: more accurately 'to whom'—Trans.] it was said: 'But as for you, stand here by Me' (Deut. 5: 28).[15]

This revelation occurred in the year 5489 [1729],[16] when Luzzatto was still single. His opponents charged him with being 'half a person',[17] to which he replied, in a letter to his teacher:[18] 'And if I am unmarried—so was Ben Zoma, and he was beloved of the Lord: not that I intend to remain unmarried—but [my present state] is not a disqualification.' On the basis of the foregoing revelation it appears to me that the secret of his unmarried state, too, was connected with his adhesion to the Shekhinah in the role of Moses, as in the exposition by the Zohar of the verse 'But as for you, stand here by Me'.[19] When the time came for the *tikun* of the Shekhinah at a higher stage by her redemption from captivity among the husks, he adhered to her in a different way, by the covenant of marriage through the medium of his union with his wife Zipporah.[20]

Sod haketubah stresses in several places that the *tikun* brought about by Luzzatto's marriage is the culmination of the *tikunim* to complete the redemption of the Shekhinah and subdue the Sitra Ahra ['Other Side'],

in order that all the *tikunim* which will in future be carried out may be strengthened by this *tikun* . . . [including] the *tikunim* that have not been strengthened by oath

[15] This fragment is one of those from *Tikunim ḥadashim* quoted by Almanzi (*Kerem ḥemed*, 3, 138). The book was thought to have been lost, and none of the scholars who studied Luzzatto troubled to check whether or not *Tikunim ḥadashim* in MS Oxford 1901 (Reggio Collection 31)—recorded in Neubauer's catalogue under the name of Luzzatto—is the same as the 'lost' book. When I was in Oxford I examined the manuscript and established beyond doubt that it was indeed the same. I lectured on a number of matters in connection with that book at the Congress on Jewish Studies held in Jerusalem in 5717 [1957].

Following my publication of the fact that the 'lost' book was extant, the manuscript was copied and printed (Jerusalem, 1958). In my quotations from here on, the page references are to those of the printed text. This passage appears there at p. 125. My comparison of the texts established that Almanzi had a different copy.

[16] See *Igerot*, i. 16. [17] Ibid. 78, 86, 101, 129. [18] Ibid. 114.

[19] Zohar III, 261*b*: 'From then on he separated himself entirely from his wife and attached himself and went up to another place [which was that] of a male, and not to a female. Worthy was the portion of Moses the faithful prophet, who was privileged to rise to the most exalted levels which no other son of the prophets ever achieved.' The Zohar goes on to say that Moses was raised to the rank of *ish ha'elohim* [Trans.: literally 'the man of God' (see superscription to Ps. 90), but here interpreted as] the husband of the Shekhinah.

[20] It is a characteristic line in kabbalistic doctrine that erotic communion with the Godhead does not demand sexual abstinence but, on the contrary, is generally attained through the holiness of physical married life. But it should be pointed out that Moses himself, whose attachment to the Shekhinah is expressly described as a covenant of marriage, was commanded to stay away from his wife. See Zohar III, 148*a*; *Zohar ḥadash*, ed. R. Margaliot (Jerusalem, 1953), 'Ki tetse' (*Midrash hanelam*).

and covenant . . . because when they have been included in this *tikun* there is no longer any fear that the husks will suck anything from them . . . [for] all [the *tikunim*] are to be held liable as surety for the fulfilment of this contract of marriage . . . the time is ripe for the acceptance of all these *tikunim* which come from above, since the hour is certainly propitious for him [for Moses–Luzzatto]. (fo. 175^{v})

The propitious hour is expounded expressly as falling in the year *tav tsadi alef*, i.e. (5)491 [1731],

at the time of which it is said: 'When you go forth [*tetse*, spelt *tav tsadi alef*] to war against your enemies', precisely *tetse*, to war against your enemies in a number of wars against the husks to bring back the holy Shekhinah who had gone down into exile there, 'and the Lord your God delivers them into your hand and you take them captive' by some sparks of holiness that are emitted on high; and then 'you see among the captives a beautiful woman' etc., the bride of Moses, certainly, 'and she shall be your wife'. (fo. 174^{r})

In what he says about the *tikunim* included in and performed as part of the *tikun* of the marriage, Luzzatto was referring first and foremost to the *tikunim* he had performed earlier in his group and which his persecutors had tried to block, among them the organized *tikunim* of the Shekhinah arranged in accordance with the rules of the group dating from the beginning of 5491.[21] At the end of *Sod haketubah* he explicitly mentioned his colleagues and associated them with his activity: 'for all these comrades are certainly fit and they are vessels proper to be filled with the Holy Spirit and to acquire all these *tikunim*, certainly' (fo. 176^{r}).

It can be seen from the foregoing that Luzzatto had soon recovered from the reverse he suffered in 1730, and that a year later his mystical activities in the performance of *tikunim* were crowned by a great achievement. Further signs of his fresh exaltation are evident in his letter to his teacher at the beginning of 5492 [towards the autumn of 1731]:[22]

For this I know: God is for me, the Lord is for me, I have no fear, what can man do to me? [Ps. 118: 6]. Thank God, *this Rosh Hashanah is not like last year's*, and things change from time to time, thank God. *God has already given evidence from Heaven for*

[21] See *Igerot*, i. 8–11. It should be noted that in a letter regarding the study undertaken by the group (ibid. ii. 234), Luzzatto informed his teacher that 'this study was only for the *tikun* of all Israel', concealing from him the primary purpose expressed in the group's regulations: 'for the *tikun* of the holy Shekhinah'. It was only after Bassano had again raised objections to their rules of conduct that Luzzatto sent him an accurate and detailed description (ibid. 239). Ginzburg correctly concluded (ibid. i. 179 n. 6) that the rules now in our hands were composed in Shevat 5491 [early in 1731], that is, after the severe blow inflicted on Luzzatto and his colleagues in the late summer of 1730. But there is no doubt that an organized group of mystics had formed round him much earlier. See ibid. i. 19–21, 25, 53; ii. 407–8.

[22] Ibid. ii. 235–6.

me and has justified [me] *before those who were deemed acceptable for this*, and has made known the truth exactly as it is to the pure in heart and men of truth, but I cannot say any more about that. Those who know, and those who ought to have known—let them know whether I am a wicked man or whether an evil spirit has tormented me or whether the Lord has sent me and his spirit . . . for I, thank God, am strictly observing the terms of my oath and am not giving myself the benefit of any doubt as to the law; but let them not break bounds, lest He break out against them [Exod. 19: 21–2]. For I am already full of words [Job 32: 18], and as for many who are impressed with their own wisdom, I would scorn to set them as a heel to the sole of the most junior of my pupils, who, thank God, have attained what neither they nor their leaders' leaders have attained.

This confident and aggressive trumpet-call is very different from the dejected cry of a man anxiously waiting for the compassion of Heaven in his letters dating from the autumn of 1730.[23] *Sod haketubah* hides the key to the understanding of the allusion to 'things changing': towards Rosh Hashanah 5492, i.e. in the late summer of 1731, there took place that great event, the marriage of Moses–Ramhal to the Shekhinah. The members of the group knew its mystical significance, they saw the signs, and the faith of the master and his disciples in their power and status increased.

Every line of *Sod haketubah* is steeped in messianic fervour and the sense of the end of days. The wedding was fixed to take place in the month of Av, the month of consolation, and on the 27th of that month, to correspond with 'the twenty-seven letters of the Torah, the Torah by which the Shekhinah is raised to the level of the day when "the night is as bright as day" [Ps. 139: 12]' (fo. 174^{r}). The Shekhinah had already been rescued and was freed from the power of the husks, 'because now this bride is a daughter of Israel in his *gadlut* ['spiritual maturity'], and therefore she no longer fears the husks' (fo. 175^{v}), and moreover 'all five supernal *partsufim*' [countenances of God or configurations of the sefirot], through whose *tikun* perfect and eternal redemption would come about, 'have been restored to perfection' (fo. 174^{r}), 'and this *tikun* will endure to all eternity' (fo. 176^{r}). We have here, then, an explicit attestation by Luzzatto himself to his messianic mission. I will try to clarify the obscurities in this matter in the light of *Sod haketubah* and the two messianic poems I publish here.

[23] 'For I shall wait for God [written *elok*] to do His will, because if it were not that I do not wish to speak I could, God be praised, say many times as much as I have said, but I wish to be silent until there speaks the mouth that says great things' (ibid. 216–17) [Dan. 7: 8 for the words but not the context—Trans.]; 'For I am like a dumb man who does not open his mouth; hidden among the baggage [1 Sam. 10: 22], I will not go out of the door, for that is what best befits me until God bares His arm, and it is made known that the hand of the Lord is with His servants, and He shows His indignation against His enemies [Isa. 66: 14]' (ibid. 220).

B. LUZZATTO'S MESSIANIC MISSION

The main accusation levelled against Luzzatto by his opponents related to the messianic trend of his activities, in which they saw a continuation of Shabatean messianism.[24] They claimed, moreover, that he regarded himself as the Messiah ben David, and was so regarded in his group. In 1735 the rabbis of Venice wrote that Luzzatto 'pretended to be a Messiah in Israel, a prophet, a mighty man and a warrior', and they alleged that he had declared: 'I am the anointed one [the Messiah] of the God of Jacob, [appointed] to gather together all those who are scattered.'[25] R. Jacob Emden based this accusation on indications in a letter from R. Jekutiel of Vilna, and on an explicit statement which he said was contained in a letter of 1730 from R. Elijah Ulianov (who, while living in Padua, was in personal contact with Luzzatto) to R. Mordecai Jaffe in Vienna.[26]

Scholars who made a special study of Luzzatto were divided on this issue: some accepted the allegations by his opponents,[27] while others regarded them as doubtful or rejected them outright.[28] B. Dinur went so far as to declare categorically that 'in his unceasing efforts to penetrate to the mystery of redemption Luzzatto was very far removed from those whose concern is to calculate the date [when the Redemption will occur]'.[29]

Supporters of the view that Luzzatto held himself to be the Messiah relied principally on the extracts from his *Tikunim ḥadashim* quoted in Almanzi's biography [*Kerem ḥemed*, 3 (1838)]. These extracts did, at any rate, afford sufficient grounds to confirm the claim that Luzzatto saw his own time as 'the end of days' and assigned to himself the duty of hastening 'the end' [the com-

24 See Essay 1, pp. 4–7.

25 *Igerot*, ii. 271–2.

26 See R. Jacob Emden, *Torat hakenaot* (Lvov, 1870), 111–17. A letter from R. Mordecai Jaffe to R. Jonathan Eybeschuetz, reproduced in *Luḥot edut* (Altona, 1755), 14*b*–15*a*, rejects this allegation as a total lie. But it should be pointed out that R. Moses Hagiz had referred indirectly to the letter containing the accusation as early as 1730, when he wrote that R. Elijah Ulianov had 'gone out of his mind and written things about this young man (Luzzatto) that were not right' (*Igerot*, i. 162).

27 Almanzi, *Kerem ḥemed*, 3: 115; H. Graetz, *Geschichte der Juden von den ältesten Zeiten bis auf die Gegenwart* (Leipzig, 1897–1911), x. 345; D. Kahana, *Toledot hamekubalim hashabeta'im vehaḥasidim*, ii (Tel Aviv, 1927), 4; Ginzburg, *Life and Works of Moses Hayyim Luzzatto*, 34; F. Lachower, *Al gevul hayashan veheḥadash* (Jerusalem, 1951), 67–78.

28 See E. Ph. Rothstein, *Nezir elohim* (Frankfurt, 1875), 53–4; A. Kahana, *Rabi mosheh ḥayim lutsato* (Warsaw, 1899), 73–4.

29 B. Dinur, *Bemifneh hadorot* (Jerusalem, 1955), 179. G. Vajda also expressed the opinion (in the introduction to the French translation of *Mesilat yesharim* (Paris, 1956), 6) that Luzzatto did not in the least intend to give rise to a messianic movement.

ing of the Messiah—Trans.] by disseminating the secrets of his doctrine in the community at large. Now that the whole of that book [*Tikunim ḥadashim*] has been found we have an extensive description of Luzzatto's messianic tasks. I will mention briefly the processes of the Redemption for which Luzzatto held himself responsible and which he wrote down in accordance with revelations by messengers from on high and by the souls of 'the fathers of the world', from Adam to the Messiah:

(*a*) *War against the Sitra Ahra.* Reducing the Sitra Ahra to submission,[30] breaking the power of the rulers of the nations,[31] the removal of darkness and the destruction of evil.[32]

(*b*) *Redemption of the Shekhinah.* Raising her up from among the husks and restoring her to her place,[33] mitigation of judgement and perfecting the light of the moon.[34]

(*c*) *Aid to the Messiahs.* Bringing light to the Messiah ben David and his companions living in the darkness of the husks,[35] relief of the torments of the Messiah in exile,[36] helping the Messiah ben Joseph to act against the husks and subdue the four kingdoms,[37] revelation and unification of the Messiahs.[38]

(*d*) *Redemption of Israel.* Awakening to repentance,[39] cleansing Israel of their impurity and drawing them near to God,[40] assuaging the pains of Israel, vengeance on the nations,[41] subjugating seventy nations to Israel,[42] relieving the pangs [which precede the coming] of the Messiah,[43] restoring the body to perfection [*tikun haguf*],[44] disclosure of esoteric lore from the tree of knowledge,[45] gathering in the exiles and rebuilding Jerusalem.[46]

This is an ordered messianic statement of all the steps involved in redemption of the Divinity, the cosmos, and the nation, expressly linked with personal action by Luzzatto.

[30] *Tikunim ḥadashim*, 43. The killing of the snake is described ibid. 37, and at p. 133 we read: 'Your tongue is the staff of God which split the sea of the Torah, and through which were revealed many secrets which had been hidden above, certainly the staff by which the serpent was turned into a staff, so that in this way all the other sides were subjected to the holy side.' Here too there is a clear allusion to his identification with Moses.

[31] Ibid. 92, 134.

[32] Ibid. 10, 80, 141–2.

[33] Ibid. 10, 13, 37, 78–9, 141, 143–4.

[34] Ibid. 140–1.

[35] 'And now with this brightness of yours you shine on *m'b'd* [the Messiah ben David] who is in darkness, he and some others, of whom it was said: "The people who walked in darkness" etc. (Isa. 9: 1); now it grows light for them little by little, later on it will be fully light for him [*sic*]' (ibid. 127). See pp. 9–17 above.

[36] *Tikunim ḥadashim*, 140, 142.

[37] Ibid. 141, 143.

[38] Ibid. 5, 10, 127. And see *Igerot*, i. 97.

[39] *Tikunim ḥadashim*, 128–9, 141.

[40] Ibid. 80, 142–3.

[41] Ibid. 142.

[42] Ibid. 92.

[43] Ibid. 128–9.

[44] Ibid. 110.

[45] Ibid. 6, 78.

[46] Ibid. 75–6, 142.

But in *Tikunim ḥadashim* there are no clear signs of the cultivation of a messianic movement. There are no calculations of the end of days[47] and no explicit personal messiahship. Scholars focused their attention mainly on two passages in which they found support for the idea that Luzzatto was to appear as Messiah ben David. According to one of these,[48] Luzzatto would bring the Shekhinah out of exile: 'Elijah the faithful prophet stood up and began to speak thus: "Worthy is your portion, for you have been a support to the Shekhinah in exile and now you are a throne of honour for her, and when she comes out of exile you will lead her."' The second passage, already considered in Section A of the present essay,[49] is the allusion to Luzzatto's identification with Moses, which was interpreted by reference to the well-known idea that Moses, the original redeemer, would be the Messiah in the final redemption.[50] F. Lachower was the only scholar who saw the importance of the kabbalistic writings of Luzzatto and his group for the understanding of his character and his literary activity. Lachower came to the conclusion that 'In the period of his great awakening, Luzzatto regarded himself as a sort of reappearance in new clothing, or a new *ibur*—a reimpregnation of the soul, as understood by kabbalah—of "the faithful shepherd": Moses, the hero of the Torah', and that the many homilies on 'the subject of the messiahship of Moses in Luzzatto's kabbalistic works' were written 'apparently in reference to his own name'.[51]

Lachower was undoubtedly correct in his principal conclusion that Luzzatto identified himself with Moses, who would act as redeemer in the final redemption as he had done before. This is now confirmed by *Sod haketubah*. But the evidence on which he based his conclusion is defective in several respects. *Razin genizin*,[52] the book from which he derived most of his indications, is attributed by him to R. Israel Hezekiah Treves, a disciple of Luzzatto, as recorded on the printed title-page, and on the basis of this attribution it may be argued that the contents of the book do not prove Luzzatto's own beliefs and outlook. Lachower's explanations of the passages he quotes are in general reasonable, but he did not entirely extract their hidden meanings, and he is silent on the pieces which contribute most to the support of his thesis. And lastly: Lachower pointed out[53] that 'Luzzatto's mystical works waver between Joseph, David, and Moses on the question of the identity of

[47] In one of his letters in which he ostensibly dissociated himself from calculations of the end of days, Luzzatto hinted that he engaged in such calculations but that he concealed them in his writings: 'And I have never disclosed the end. On the contrary: anything which makes even the slightest approach to this question is hidden behind "etc." or the symbol "*s*" [= *sod*, 'mystery'], or the expression "and it is hidden and sealed so that it cannot be understood"' (*Igerot*, i. 95). And see ibid. 48, 56, 86.

[48] *Tikunim ḥadashim*, 13.

[49] See pp. 190–3 above.

[50] See pp. 192–3 above.

[51] Lachower, *Al gevul hayashan veheḥadash*, 68.

[52] Printed with Luzzatto's *Likutei torah* and *Megilat setarim* under the title *Megilat setarim verazin genizin* (Warsaw, 1889).

[53] *Al gevul hayashan veheḥadash*, 77.

the future Messiah, and he found a basis . . . on which to unite the messiahship of Joseph and David and to place Moses at the head of both.' But he did not properly address the difficulty this involved, and although he found two Messiahs side by side with Moses in Luzzatto's writings, he adopted the simple view of Luzzatto as Messiah. The whole issue therefore requires fresh consideration.

Razin genizin, which is a remnant of a work on the weekly portions of the Torah in the language of the Zohar, was attributed to Treves on the title-page of the printed edition because 'written on them [the *Razin*, 'the secrets'—Trans.] in manuscript was the word "Israel" '. However, a comparison of the language, style, and content with the writings of Luzzatto, and especially with *Tikunim ḥadashim*, shows conclusively that we have before us parts of a large book composed by Luzzatto himself at the dictation of the *magid*, which is perhaps connected with the treatise on the Torah [*Ḥibur al hatorah*] mentioned several times in his letters.[54] [But see Essay 6, n. 76.—Trans.] The name 'Israel' certainly refers not to the author but to a disciple who copied the work or kept it in his possession. In the same way the last pieces in the series are headed with the name of R. Jekutiel in manuscript,[55] and these are undoubtedly by the author of the whole book.

This book contains many passages which throw light on the reappearance and activity of Moses 'at the end of days' and hint at his identity with Luzzatto. I will quote and offer brief explanations of five such passages which were not mentioned at all by Lachower, and will also deal with the obscurities and contradictions in them.

[54] See *Igerot*, i. 19, 31, 52–3, 70, 75. Luzzatto's *Likutei kabalah* (MS Adler 886, Library of the Jewish Theological Seminary, New York) is a collection of short discourses in Hebrew on scriptural verses, resembling in content and form the discourses in *Razin genizin*, and one of them (fo. 45^{r}) really does belong with the series of discourses on 'Moses' veil', some of which are considered below.

[55] *Razin genizin*, 105. In MS Oxford Heb. f. 120 I found a *Sefer hakavanot shel kol hashanah* ['*Kavanot* for the Whole Year'] of Luzzatto's circle. Apparently this is the *Kitsur sefer hakavanot* prepared by Luzzatto himself (see *Igerot*, ii. 353). The title-page is inscribed 'By the noble and exalted writer [of this], Solomon Treves', whereas the colophon says: 'Completed on the fifth day [Thursday], 13 Shevat, in the year [Ps. 145: 18] "*karov h' kol* [*sic*] *kore'av lekhol asher yikra'uhu* ***be'emet***" [(5)493 (1733)] [in *gematriyah*, *kol* plus the letters with dots over them, here indicated by bold type, equals 493—Trans.]. I, the young [in knowledge—an expression of humility—Trans.] Israel Hezekiah, son of my lord and father Michael Treves, may his Rock preserve him in life, wrote all this here in Padua at the desire of the learned physician, our honoured teacher R. Jekutiel Gordon of Vilna, and presented them [*sic*] to him. May it be His will that they may avail to confer merit on the many and that [Isa. 53: 10] the Lord's cause may prosper by his hand; amen, may that be His will' (fo. 117^{r-v}). This shows that Luzzatto's pupils used to write their name on their teacher's works, and perhaps deliberately suppressed Luzzatto's name. Apparently the book was given to R. Jekutiel as a parting gift when he was about to leave Padua. With regard to his return to Poland, see *Igerot*, ii. 241, 270.

According to one of these passages,[56] the light of Moses during the period of exile is covered over by the darkness of the serpent's skin, but when that period ends he clothes himself in his *ibur*; this at first is like a veil and a glass which does not shine, but at the time of the Redemption, after undergoing *tikun* and attaining perfection, 'it will be a mirror of light, from which the light of Moses will be revealed to others'. Then Moses himself will be revealed and will radiate his own light, but his *ibur* will shine together with him. When he first dons his *ibur*, and he himself is weak, the light of the *ibur* is similarly faint, but

> when the time of the deliverance came, that hand had to be strengthened, for it is written (Isa. 35: 3): 'strengthen the weak hands', and they are two hands, *one on his side and one on the side of his ibur*, for when he was impregnated with it, he was in the mystical condition of the beginning, and that hand was weak, but 'at the time of the end' that hand was strengthened . . . and from his side the hand of his *ibur* was also strengthened . . . at that time two lights appeared in the world, from Moses and his *ibur*.

The reference here to Moses' *ibur* tells us that it would appear and act in two stages, at different levels of strength: immediately before the Redemption when Moses was hidden, and at the time of the Redemption when he would be revealed. The first stage was in the hidden state of 'the beginning' and the second stage would follow 'at the time of the end'. There is no doubt that here Luzzatto is also speaking about himself, but his position is not clear. It is uncertain whether the two stages represent transformations of the *ibur* at different times or whether they are different levels of its development during a single period; and it is hard to decide whether Luzzatto saw himself as Moses' *ibur* or as Moses himself who was to be revealed. The former interpretation is more probable, since the reference to the state of the *ibur* in the first stage uses the present tense. The *Ḥibur al hatorah* is one of the first books written at the dictation of the *magid*, and it seems that in the first years after the *magid* revealed himself, until Luzzatto's elevation to the rank of Moses himself in *Sod haketubah*, Luzzatto was destined, or destined himself, for the position of Moses' *ibur*, functioning as his emissary and executive before the Redemption and his partner and second in command in the Redemption itself.

In the second passage[57] Moses' *tsinor* ['conduit'] stands in place of his *ibur*. Of the two 'lights' in the verse 'Let there be light, and there was light', the first is interpreted as referring to the two Messiahs who are one Messiah, and the second as relating to Moses,

> and at the end of day[s] those two lights [will] join together as one and deliverance will be completed by them, *for through the strength of Moses* [exercised] *by his tsinor the two Messiahs will be* [literally 'are'] *strengthened* and by him [they will be] made one . . .

[56] *Razin genizin*, 50. [57] Ibid. 51.

for Moses will come and by his *tsinor* will be joined to the two Messiahs and will lead them according to his will, and deliverance will be completed, [that is] certain.

The motif of the strengthening, unification, and guidance of the two Messiahs by Moses 'at the end of days' recurs repeatedly in Luzzatto's messianic writings, but in a few places this function is expressly assigned to Luzzatto himself.[58] According to this passage, these actions will be carried out by Moses' *tsinor* in his presence and through his strength, and again it is doubtful whether, in this description, Luzzatto is Moses or his *tsinor*.

The third passage[59] deals with Moses 'at the end of days' being clothed in the character of possessor of 'the secret of hope', whose function is to strengthen the hope of redemption in the hearts of Israel. Even during the period of exile Israel were sustained by the sparks of hope which were given off by the light of Moses, but Moses himself was covered by the darkness of the husks; it was only by force of his hope that light was drawn down to him from above, and therefore his light was alternately revealed and hidden. It would not be so 'at the end of days':

And as for this expression of Scripture (Exod. 34: 35): 'Until his going in to speak with him', this applies to the end of days, *for one will arise who is the mystical embodiment of hope and Moses has clothed himself in him and spoken with him in secret*, for the verse says 'with him' without mentioning a name. Thus Israel are strengthened by him with his hope, and it is said of him 'For Your salvation I hope, O Lord' (Gen. 49: 19), and the secret is for the wise. And so it will no longer be necessary for Moses to converse in the mystery of the hidden and the revealed as he did on account of hope, for there is already (some)one in the world who is working for it, and it can be revealed that hope is already present.

The figure of the possessor of hope fits very well with Luzzatto's appearance on the scene and his activity, and similarly the remark that Moses 'spoke with him in secret' matches the revelations experienced by Luzzatto, for one of the principal characters who appeared in his visions and spoke with him was 'the faithful shepherd'.

In the fourth passage[60] a new image is used to describe Moses' deputy: the throne of Moses. Just as Moses endured the anguish of exile for the *tikun* of the Shekhinah, who had been blemished by the sin of the golden calf, and he subdued the husks and the members of the 'mixed multitude',

just so did someone do who is a throne for him, for he forsook everything for the love of the Shekhinah, and he made seven [stages], corresponding to the seven who entered into covenant(s),[61] to restore the stages of the Shekhinah, and that is the secret of

[58] See above, text referring to n. 38. [59] *Razin genizin*, 51–2. [60] Ibid. 59–60.

[61] A midrashic source shows that this is a reference to the three patriarchs and Moses, Aaron, Phinehas, and David (Judah David Eisenstein, *Otsar midrashim* (New York, 1915), 163). And see Menahem Azariah da Fano's *Ma'amar hanefesh* (Piotrków, 1903), iii, ch. 1. Two homilies in

'seven years' (Gen. 29: 18). And him, too, the Sitra Ahra cannot overcome, for it is written: 'Many waters cannot [quench love]' (S. of S. 8: 7); for he gives up his home for the sake of the Shekhinah, and the secret is for the wise.

Here there is an express reference in the present tense to a living person, written while Luzzatto was still a bachelor; the text therefore suits his condition and is consistent with the secret of his having remained unmarried because of his love for the Shekhinah, a matter which I have considered above.[62] True, in view of Luzzatto's age at the time there was no need for seven years of celibacy; however, it seems that the number of years is not to be taken literally, but refers to the seven stages of the Shekhinah, as explained at the beginning of this passage with regard to Moses himself.

In the fifth passage, too,[63] the last on this subject, 'the throne of Moses' first makes its appearance to help the two Messiahs in their destruction of Amalek. Just as at the time of the giving of the Torah Moses brought the two Messiahs into action, 'now just as in the past Moses gave strength to the two Messiahs to destroy Amalek, who was the first to make war with him, and the secret of this is *his throne which awakened the tikun in time past*, and the secret is for the reapers of the field,[64] and afterwards Moses himself needed the two Messiahs to be united with the Shekhinah'. The action of the 'throne', which, acting as Moses, performs its mission of destroying Amalek, is described in the present tense ('now')[65] and even in the past ('which awakened the *tikun* in time past'), and probably refers to Luzzatto himself. The piece which follows on the same page enumerates four eschatological stages which will precede the destruction of the world: '*now* by the destruction of Amalek, *afterwards* by the time of the King-Messiah, after that by the time of Gog, and after that by the time of the great judgement day'. It may therefore be said that the revelation of 'Moses himself' is here assigned to the second stage, 'the time of the King-Messiah', when he will unite the two Messiahs with the Shekhinah.

This brings us back to the marriage contract in *Sod haketubah*. Several references to the bridegroom Moses are coupled with mention of 'his aspects', and in one place the hidden meaning of Moses' 'aspects' is explained:

In this there is a perfect union *verily with Moses* in all his aspects . . . 'Your [the bride's] food': the mystery of this is manna, through the merit of Moses, 'your clothing', this is in allusion to the poor man 'lowly and riding on an ass' [*Messiah ben David*; the quotation is from Zech. 9: 9] . . . 'the supply of your needs': alluding to Seraiah, a fru-

Luzzatto's *Likutei kabalah*, MS Adler 886, fo. 49^{r-v}, mention '*tikunim* performed by the seven who entered into the covenant'. And see n. 103 below.

[62] See p. 193 above.

[63] *Razin genizin*, 96.

[64] 'The field': *ḥakla* [Aramaic], misspelt as *ḥalka* [almost the Hebrew equivalent—Trans.].

[65] This passage is the tenth in a series of eleven, in all of which the destruction of Amalek and the performance of other acts of *tikun* are described as occurring in the present.

gal supply. 'And coming in to you': this is *M*[essiah] *b*[en] *J*[oseph] Yesod, by whom the intercourse is performed. (fo. 174^{v})

What all this tells us is that 5491 [1731] was the year in which 'the time of the King-Messiah' arrived, and that thereupon Luzzatto himself was revealed as 'verily Moses'—the mystical embodiment of Moses—and carried out the function he had previously assigned to 'Moses himself': he raised up all the other redeemers with him and joined them with himself in his union with the Shekhinah.

But one alteration in *Sod haketubah* needs explanation: what is the significance of the messianic group of four as against the trio of whom we have read until now, and what kind of being is Seraiah, who has been added to the three redeemers? This quartet and their joint union with the Shekhinah are not an innovation of *Sod haketubah*: their significance is explained in Luzzatto's kabbalistic writings. The passage most relevant for our present purpose[66] reads as follows:

And indeed they are the four heads branching out from the river which flows out of Eden to water the garden; they have perfected the beauty of the eyes of the woman of worth, the crown of her husband, *Moses and the two Messiahs and Seraiah, for their union with her is in the mystery of moshe"h eḥa"d*;[67] eye to eye they will see to the beautification of the eyes of Moses' bride, while he says to her through them (S. of S. 4: 1): 'Lo, you are fair, my love'—his love in very deed.

The four redeemers are also mentioned in the two passages which follow this one,[68] with a description of their connection with the Shekhinah, the bride of Moses, and the expression 'your eyes are doves [*yonim*]' is expounded as applying to Seraiah:

'Your eyes are doves' relates to Seraiah, for *yonim* is connected in meaning with *hona'ah* ['deception'] [the verbal root of which is *y-n-h*—Trans.]: these eyes smile at the evil spirits, the *ḥitsonim* ['the external ones'], while the latter are in control, in order actually to deceive them so that they are not on their guard against them, until their measure is full and they are defeated by Seraiah with the flaming sword which turns every way, which is verily the sword of the *yonah*.[69] And the hidden meaning of this is 'the staff [or 'tribe'] of Dan, the glorious rod',[70] for that is the secret of the rod,

[66] *Razin genizin*, 106.

[67] Apparently this is an allusion to the interpretation of the word *eḥad* ['one'], as in *Razin genizin*, 58–9: 'Love is one, [i.e.] *eḥ"d*'' [*eḥad* is separated into the letters *alef-ḥet* (*aḥ*, 'brother'?) and *dalet* (= 4)—Trans.], here applied to the quadruple love of Moses–Ramhal for the Shekhinah.

[68] Ibid. 106–7.

[69] [*ḥerev hayonah*, Jer. 46: 16: 'the oppressing sword'. The Targum renders it 'the enemy's sword'.—Trans.]

[70] An intentional alteration of the scriptural text (Jer. 48: 17): 'The staff of strength [= 'the strong staff'], the glorious rod'.

that he will actually be the instrument with which to subdue the idolaters and beat them about the head.

And it is he 'who gathers his strength and shows his might all day long to perfect the Shekhinah in her *tikunim* and beautify her with her adornments until she is *yafah veyafah* ['twice beautiful': the word is used twice in S. of S. 1: 15—Trans.] . . . and since you are *yafah veyafah* and the numerical value of *yafah* [95], repeated, is *kets* [*kof tsadi* = 190], an end [*kets*] has been put to your darkness'. The substitution of 'the staff of Dan' for 'the staff of strength' in the verse from Jeremiah indicates that Seraiah is of the tribe of Dan and that he fulfils the role of the staff of Moses.[71] Another of Luzzatto's writings[72] which is mostly concerned with the character and role of Seraiah begins his description thus: '"Now Naomi had a kinsman of her husband", Moses [her husband] who with his staff divided the sea; this is of course Seraiah of the family of Dan, who will rescue Israel from the hand of those who despoil them when he is the commander of the army of the Lord.'[73]

To sum up: from the time that he began to act in accordance with the revelations of the *magid*, Luzzatto appeared among his group as the representative of the biblical Moses through the mystery of his embodiment of the *ibur*, and in 1731 he was raised to the rank of Moses himself. But in identifying himself with Moses he did not regard himself as Messiah ben David—which would have accorded with the conventional opinion prevalent even in Shabatean doctrine—but held the view expressed in *Raya meheimna*[74] that Moses was above the Messiahs, his destiny at the end of days being to lead and unite the redeemers and help them to fulfil their mission in matters both revealed and occult.

This conclusion raises a new question: were the two Messiahs and Seraiah—the connection of all of whom with Moses is described in the great-

71 The homilies on the mystery of Dan as the staff of Moses which turned into a snake appear to be connected with Seraiah. See *Tikunim ḥadashim*, 103–4; *Razin genizin*, 76–9.

72 *Megilat setarim* on Ruth, 47–50. This composition, and the pieces on Seraiah in *Razin genizin*, are in Hebrew. They may have been written in 1731 after Luzzatto had been forbidden to write compositions in the language of the Zohar, whence the strong connection between them and *Sod haketubah*.

73 Seraiah of the tribe of Dan makes his first appearance as a partner to the Messiah ben Joseph, 'to wreak vengeance and wage war on the other nations', in the Zohar III, 194*b*, and the verse 'his rider falls backwards' (Gen. 49: 17) is expounded in relation to him. On the basis of the Zohar, *Galei razaya* (Mogilev, 1812), 43*b–c*, says that Samson 'in the time of the Messiah ben Ephraim will transmigrate (with God's help, blessed be He) and come with him and be the commander of his army, and he will be called Seraiah; this is he whom Jacob blessed, who "bites the horse's heels so that its rider falls backward", that is the snake that he was riding over. For Your salvation I wait, O Lord.' This passage is quoted in *Yalkut re'uveni* (Prague, 1660), heading 'Messiah', sect. C. And see R. Nathan Spira, *Megaleh amukot* (Lublin, 1884), on 'Vayera', 21, and on 'Vayeshev', 87.

74 See Zohar II, 119*b*–120*a*; III, 153*b*; etc.

est detail—living persons in Moses' group in Padua, or is it possible that they did not exist except in the prophetic vision of Luzzatto, who announced their imminent arrival and was waiting for them to reveal themselves? In my opinion, once the identity of Moses with Luzzatto has been established, the descriptions themselves, especially in *Sod haketubah*, prove that his messianic partners were actual persons living and working alongside him. But with regard to the two Messiahs I have no need to rely on reasoning alone. In my research I have found conclusive proofs that the Messiah ben David was R. Moses David Valle, one of the leaders of Luzzatto's group. As for the identity of Seraiah of the tribe of Dan, in that case, too, I have found evidence amounting almost to a certainty: the commander of the messianic army in Luzzatto's group was R. Jekutiel of Vilna. The most problematic figure is that of the Messiah ben Joseph, on whose identity I refrain for the time being from expressing any opinion.[75]

The messianic role of R. Moses David Valle needs more extensive consideration than would be appropriate here,[76] and with regard to him I shall therefore note only two matters to supplement my explanation of *Sod haketubah*. On the identification of Jekutiel as Seraiah, however, I shall have more to say in the next section, in connection with the messianic poems.

In 1730 [*tav tsadi*, 5490] Valle affirmed in two places that the Messiah ben David would reveal himself publicly in the following year. The text of the first passage[77] reads as follows:

> And in the year *tav tsadi alef*, he [Messiah ben David, called the *mevarer* [here rendered as 'the winnower'—Trans.]] will illuminate the world with his lamp which has been prepared for him, for the holy spirit is already resting upon him in the year *tav tsadi* . . . and nations will walk by his light, and kings by the brightness of his sunrise, as it is written (Isa. 51: 4): '*For Torah shall go forth* [*tetse*, i.e. *tav tsadi alef*] *from me, and my justice as a light to the nations* [by which] *I will give them rest.*'

The second passage is a fragment placed between a consideration of the stages of the *tikun* and an interpretation of the suffering of the Messiah. It reads thus:[78] 'And the winnower [in the year *tav tsadi*] is not yet revealed, because the fourth husk has not yet sufficiently undergone *tikun* . . . but next year [*tav tsadi alef*] . . . in that year the winnower reveals himself with an

[75] On the Shabatean character of the Messiah ben Joseph in Luzzatto's writings, see p. 273 ff. below.

[76] In my lecture to the 1957 Congress on Jewish Studies in Jerusalem I presented some of the evidence I had obtained from the works of R. Moses David Valle which are held in manuscript in the British Museum, and I hope in the near future to clarify this complex matter in writing. [See Essay 6 below.—Trans.]

[77] MS BL Add. 27160, fo. 314^{r}. I found conclusive evidence that in his remarks on 'the winnower' in these passages and elsewhere, Valle was referring to himself.

[78] Ibid., fo. 503^{v}.

additional soul, which is the mystery of *ḥayah yeḥidah* [the two highest parts of the soul, 'the living one' and 'the only one', are joined together here—Trans.], soul [added] to soul.'[79] What this means is that before Luzzatto's capitulation at the end of 5490 [late summer 1730] it had already been determined in Luzzatto's group that the end of days would be reached in 5491, and the great *tikun* of the union of Moses and of the three redeemers with the Shekhinah in Luzzatto's marriage was the realization of what had been expected and promised in the inward realm of their mystical experience.

The traces of that experience are preserved in Valle's writings. In his intimate personal notes[80] he alludes to the processes of his erotic communion with the Shekhinah around the day of Luzzatto's marriage: 'On the 25th(?)[81] of that month [Av 5491] the matter of the kisses[82] and the blessing Sheheheyanu ['Who has kept us alive']'; 'This day, 28 Menahem [Av],[83] communion [*devekut*] in love, destruction of the unclean spirit and delight in [divine] favour'; 'This day, 5 Elul, the news of the *kinyan* ['acquisition': the formal transfer of money or an article such as a ring—Trans.] with a full purse, *erusin* ['betrothal'], and the time for the *nisu'in* [the stage which completes the marriage]'; 'This day, the 11th of the month [Elul], the union in love and the promise concerning the revelation soon to come, amen, may it be His will'. These hints of what he experienced do not lend themselves to full interpretation but it is clear that they describe the stages of Valle's ascent, from his coming together with the Shekhinah in kisses to the experience of complete union. The closeness of the time to the date of Luzzatto's *ketubah* is certainly not coincidental, and therefore these notes must be seen as the reflection of the event of *Sod haketubah* in the soul of the Messiah ben David, who was put by Luzzatto at the head of those invited to take part with him in the *tikun* of the Shekhinah. Valle gave emphasis to the messianic character of the shared communion [*devekut*] by placing 'the promise concerning the revelation soon' immediately next to 'the union in love'.

[79] The *yeḥidah* is the soul of the Messiah.

[80] Valle's notes, which together constitute a sort of mystical diary, are dealt with in Essay 7 below. The four quoted here are in MS BL 387, fos. 52^v, 58^v, 65^r, 69^r.

[81] [The query is Tishby's: the date is twice given as '20th' in Essay 7, text following references there to nn. 125 and 343.—Trans.]

[82] So, too, Luzzatto, in *Sod haketubah*, fo. 175^r, writes that his union with the Shekhinah is 'precisely in the mystery of speech, the union of the kisses'.

[83] The day after Luzzatto's wedding.

C. MESSIANIC FIGURES IN LUZZATTO'S POEMS

[The following three paragraphs are all quoted verbatim in Essay 2 above, pp. 120, 121.—Trans.]

Luzzatto's poetry as hitherto known to us does not give expression to his love of the Shekhinah and the messianic visions by which he was possessed and which inspired him with such fervent devotion. Did Luzzatto the poet really stifle or silence his mystical and messianic aspirations and experiences, which without doubt were what he valued most highly and held most sacred for many years? This would be surprising, but a 'hidden treasure' which I chanced upon and have been able to identify has shown that any such assumption is unwarranted. The discovery is a collection of religious poems and prayers by Luzzatto[84] which may entirely alter our assessment of the character of his poetic œuvre. In these compositions the poet-artist and the kabbalist-seer, between whom many scholars had sought to draw a distinction, are united. Here I publish only two messianic sonnets[85] which contribute to the clarification of the problems involved in *Sod haketubah*.

The first sonnet is a blessing and message of encouragement for the Messiah ben Joseph. The term 'Messiah' is not used, but unmistakable expressions such as 'Son of Joseph, the fruitful one, dear Ephraim' and 'his majestic ox will be exalted', as well as the content of the poem as a whole, show clearly that the warring and avenging Messiah is meant. The poet expresses joy at the coming of the time of vengeance and redemption and declares his confidence that the Messiah ben Joseph will successfully complete his mission by subduing his opponents and will dwell 'in a peaceful place, secure for ever'. The poem is replete with kabbalistic and messianic symbols, such as the epithet 'tsadik' for the Messiah ben Joseph on the basis of his mystical status in relation to the sefirah Yesod, the names *beit akeret* [the barren woman's house] and 'serpent' for the forces of evil, and the description of the divine flow which descends upon the head of the Messiah. The poem is founded on an apocalyptic sense that the end is at hand and that the wars leading to it will terminate in the victory of the Messiah.

The second sonnet concerns Dan, that is, Seraiah, the commander of the army of the Messiah [ben Joseph]. The identity of Dan with Seraiah is proved

[84] MS Guenzburg 745 (photograph, Ben Tsevi Institute).

[85] I hope to be able soon to publish all the important compositions in this collection, making clear their authorship by Luzzatto, their meaning, and their importance. [See Essay 2 above, and in particular the foreword by the editor of *Molad*.—Trans.]

by a description of his deeds, by the allusions to the scriptural words [Gen. 49: 17] 'its rider falls backward', and especially by the last verse 'a mighty warrior, leap out upon the army's head'. Here some of the events are described in the present tense and even in the past, and the verses of the third stanza put it beyond doubt that Seraiah is very much alive and has already begun to operate successfully.

The messianic sonnets are followed in the collection by two poems (fos. 203^r–204^v) bearing the name 'Jekutiel of Vilna'. The second poem was doubtless written for Luzzatto's wedding. The subject of the first poem is not clear, but from the names mentioned in it, it appears to me that it was composed as a song of praise for R. Moses David Valle. Both poems have a messianic ring to them and bring in the name 'Dan'. In the first poem:

> The mighty warrior and marksman will yet rest
> When the days of service come fully to an end . . .
> Now to confound the foe, subdue the enemy
> He will settle [in their home] those who are lowly,
> they will be raised high for ever . . .
> Judah with Joseph will rejoice over Dan . . .
> O Almighty, bring back the bird's young to the nest.

The last stanza of the second poem:

> Much will we sing in the city where David dwelt
> Who begot me all these in joy?
> Lo, this Dan who leaps out, we will rejoice in honour
> Moses and Tsipor, he has the strength of the miraculous staff
> Great and honoured King of all kings
> May He soon rebuild the beautiful city.

In both poems the content is obscure, perhaps intentionally, or else because of the writer's inability to express his ideas clearly within the constraints of the metre, but there is no doubt that Dan, Judah, and Joseph are Seraiah and the two Messiahs, and that 'Dan who leaps' is Seraiah. In both places the mention of Dan comes as a surprise, and the context, especially in the second poem, shows that Dan is another name for the author, that is to say that Seraiah is Jekutiel.[86]

This hypothesis is strongly supported in the writings of R. Moses David Valle by a splendid hint as to the identity of the mystical embodiment of Dan. He writes:[87]

> It is well known that Gog is from the far north, and that perhaps he is the king of Poland, [Poland being] mystically understood as the land of Magog; and Dan is a

[86] It may be that the words 'the miraculous staff', too, are an allusion to Dan–Seraiah, who is the staff of Moses.

[87] MS BL Add. 27160, fo. 928^v.

snake opposed to a snake whose head he is to smash, for his forehead is stronger than the forehead of the unclean snake. Therefore *the mystical embodiment of Dan came out of the kingdom of the king of Poland and was born in his land.* That is [what is meant by] 'From the forest itself [comes] the axe [that] will go into it',[88] and he will get strength from all the twelve tribes[89] to overcome the unclean snake which is Gog, the letters 'Gog' [*gimel vav gimel*] amounting to 12 in the mystery aforesaid. And perhaps that is why he rouses himself to quarrel with Israel more than do all the other kings; first, the Poles are by nature more insane than all others, and secondly, the mystical embodiment of Dan was born in his kingdom and because of [God's] majesty he can do nothing.[90]

Seraiah, 'the mystical embodiment of Dan', who is the holy snake opposed to the unclean snake,[91] was born in Poland and left that country, and in order to complete his task of 'overcoming the unclean snake who is Gog',[92] he is to acquire strength from the other tribes. From the messianic atmosphere in Luzzatto's group and from Valle's writings it appears that 'the mystical embodiment of Dan' was in Padua in the person of Jekutiel of Vilna.

Further, it is a necessary conclusion from the special status of Jekutiel in Luzzatto's group that he was assigned a principal part in the messianic battle. In his well-known letter to R. Mordecai Jaffe—which was certainly not written on impulse by an enthusiastic admirer but was planned in the group to spread the first news that the Redemption was being prepared in Padua[93]—Jekutiel indicated that Luzzatto had allotted an important secret mission to him: 'And he told me also that there was a great secret [reason for] my having found my way here to study with him, for there is nothing without a cause. He also told me about my soul and my *tikun* that I was to perform.'[94] He was chief assistant to Luzzatto in the running of the group at Padua and was appointed to oversee the procedures of the *tikun* together with Luzzatto and R. David Moses Valle,[95] i.e. with Moses and the Messiah ben David. This status is well suited to Dan–Seraiah, who functions as 'the staff of Moses'.[96]

The identification of Jekutiel with Seraiah also clarifies an obscure point in the instructions given to him by Luzzatto at the behest of the *magid*. In his

88 See *San.* 39*b*.

89 There may have been representatives of the tribes in Luzzatto's group alongside the redeemers.

90 See Job 31: 23.

91 See above, text referring to nn. 30 and 71.

92 Luzzatto, too, connects the war against Gog with Seraiah. See *Megilat setarim* on Ruth, 49.

93 In spite of Luzzatto's disavowals, it seems to me that the letter was written at the command of the *magid*. See *Igerot*, i. 24, 26, 30, 68, 70, 72, 90.

94 Ibid. i. 19. And see ibid. i. 31; ii. 408. On the special *tikunim* that were given to him, see ibid. i. 30–1, 53.

95 Ibid. i. 9–12.

96 It appears that even on his return to Poland he was given a special task, that of acting as Luzzatto's envoy, as is shown by R. Israel Treves's allusion (p. 199 and n. 55 above): 'May it be His will that they [Luzzatto's *kavanot* which were handed over to Jekutiel] may avail to confer merit on the many and that the Lord's cause may prosper by his hand.'

letter to Vienna Jekutiel wrote:[97] 'I also, out of my great love of the Torah, intended to give up secular studies, until he told me and it was told me according to the word of the *magid*: "Take hold of the one but do not withdraw your hand from the other [cf. Eccles. 7: 18], for a reason which remains in my keeping."' The rabbis of Venice, who of course were not impressed by the *magid*'s 'reason which remains in my keeping', were outraged by this strange instruction.[98] But if Jekutiel was regarded as Seraiah we can understand the *magid*'s hidden meaning. In another revelation he taught that although secular subjects 'result from the union of Sam[a'el] and Nuk[ba]' and the keen pursuit of such subjects had been responsible for Israel's exile,

> there is someone [or 'there are those'] who grappled with them with regard to whom it was said 'You shall not learn to do' (Deut. 18: 9), 'but as for you, learn [in order to understand and teach]',[99] for this was someone who grappled with them in order to seize Sam[a'el] and Nuk[ba] by means of them as one seizes dogs by the chain round their necks, and this was someone who did not turn his feet away from the Torah but undoubtedly was firmly attached to it and seized these dogs again.[100]

In the hands of a select few,[101] who, along with their study of the Torah, occupy themselves with secular studies with holy intent for the purpose of making war on the Sitra Ahra, the secular studies become a chain with which to capture those dogs, Sama'el and Lilith.[102] One passage makes explicit use of the metaphor of the chain in a description of the actions of Dan–Seraiah at the end of days. For the duration of the period of exile the chain lost its strength and the Shekhinah, Moses' bride, was deprived of her authority, but at the time of the Redemption 'thus this bride gives the chain to one who is fitted to bind the seventy nations with it, and thus [in the verse] (Mic. 7: 14) "Shepherd Your people with Your rod", *the rod* [is] *undoubtedly from Dan's side*, for in him is leadership from Moses' side. And that is for Israel, but as for the idolatrous nations, "you shall break them with a rod of iron" (Ps. 2: 9).'[103]

[97] *Igerot*, i. 19.

[98] Ibid. ii. 273. In mid 5490 [spring 1730] Jekutiel told R. Isaiah Bassano that he had largely given up the study of secular literature because he was too busy copying the works of Luzzatto, 'and I turn my attention [to such literature] only twice a week for lack of leisure' (ibid. i. 98).

[99] *Shab.* 75*a*.

[100] *Tikunim ḥadashim*, 130–1.

[101] The words *da man* [translated 'this was someone'] may relate to a single person, Seraiah–Jekutiel. [The verbs in the quotation are in the singular.—Trans.]

[102] This idea shows the influence of the spirit of Shabateanism.

[103] *Razin genizin*, 102. Luzzatto's *Likutei kabalah*, after mentioning the *tikunim* performed by 'the seven who entered into the covenant', refers in the past tense to the action taken by Seraiah to subdue the seventy princes and nations, by the power of Moses, in support of the Messiahs: '"And in all the great terror" [Deut. 34: 12], that is, the great fear to which Seraiah subjected the princes and the seventy nations. "Wrought by Moses", that is, Seraiah, who is the mystical embodiment of Moses, from whom all the *tikunim* come, undoubtedly Moses. "In the sight of all Israel", that is, the two Messiahs, because all the *tikunim* which he performed were for the

Jekutiel therefore needed to continue with secular studies and carry out the instruction 'take hold of the one but do not withdraw your hand from the other', so as to be able to fulfil the mission of Seraiah, which was also outlined for him in the sonnet for Dan:

> You will rise up, overcome, be raised on high, and we shall be redeemed.
> You will find every enemy, your hand will not grow weary;
> From the battle-lines of the living God in the day they are drawn up,
> A mighty warrior, leap out upon [the enemy] army's head.
> *Selah*.

LUZZATTO'S MARRIAGE CONTRACT AND ITS MYSTICAL INTERPRETATION [*SOD HAKETUBAH*] (MS GUENZBURG 376)

[174^{r}] *For the Unification of the Holy One, blessed be He, for His sake and for the sake of all Israel*

The writings of our teacher and master,
RABBI MOSES HAYIM LUZZATTO

The mystical meaning [*sod*] of the *ketubah* [is] *katuv* ['written'] with a letter *he*,[104] for the Shekhinah until now has been like the words of a sealed book, but now, by force of the *tikunim*,[105] [it is] *katuv*, written with the deliberate addition of a *he*. '**On the fourth day** of the week', the mystery of this is:

purpose that the two Messiahs, who were hidden in exile, might be revealed' (MS Adler 886, fo. 49^{r}). In another homily the *tikunim* performed by Seraiah together with his partners are described in the present tense: '"And those who turn the many to righteousness" [Dan. 12: 3], these are Seraiah and the other six shepherds, who turn Israel to righteousness in order to bring them out of exile by the power of their *tikunim*. Of them it is said [as in *Avot* 5: 18, where the reference is to Moses] "righteous and making the many righteous", for the righteousness [or 'merit'] of the many depends on them' (ibid., fo. 53^{r}). It is said by our rabbis that the seven shepherds are Adam, Seth, Methuselah, Abraham, Jacob, Moses, and David, who will help the Messiah at the time of the Redemption. See e.g. *Suk*. 52*b*. The description of Seraiah as chief of the shepherds who work by their *tikunim* for the ending of the Exile creates the impression that Luzzatto saw members of his group as the seven shepherds, and perhaps also labelled them as 'the seven who entered into the covenant'. See p. 201 and n. 61 above.

104 'Written with a letter *he*': the Shekhinah, which is represented by a letter *he* in the Tetragrammaton YHVH, was concealed in exile but has left her concealment and been revealed by virtue of the *tikun* executed by this *ketubah*.

105 The reference is to the *tikunim* of the Shekhinah performed in Luzzatto's group. See *Igerot*, i. 8–13; ii. 234.

a virgin should be married on the fourth day;[106] [this applies] because the Shekhinah is a virgin and no man has known her.[107] Although government is the responsibility of the seven lower [sefirot], there are indeed times when the Shekhinah is among three, when they are behind *n"h"y"* [Netsah, Hod, Yesod].[108] There she is below Yesod, and that is according to custom.[109] The mystery of '**on the sixth day** of the week' is thus explained: the seven lower ones [sefirot] are the mystical seven days of the week and Yesod is the sixth; this is while she is a widow,[110] as it is said of her[111] 'she has become like a widow'; but when she becomes of equal worth to the King, then she joins with *ḥg"t* [Hesed, Gevurah, Tiferet][112] and there she is on the fourth day [which corresponds to Tiferet—Trans.], because *ḥg"t* become the chariot of the four living creatures[113] precisely on the fourth day of the week. '**The seven** and twentieth day of the month of Menahem [Av]', the mystery of this is 'Let them bring me pure [*zakh*, letters *zayin kaf*] olive oil',[114] by all the twenty-seven [*kaf zayin*] letters of the Torah, the Torah by which the Shekhinah is raised to the level of the day[115] when 'the night is as bright as day' [Ps. 139: 12]. '**Of the month** [*ḥodesh*]', in which there occurs the renewal [*ḥidush*] of the moon,[116] that is certain. '**Menahem**', [the month of Av] to which [the command to] 'Comfort, comfort my people'[117] [applies] 'and in Jerusalem you shall be comforted'.[118] The mystery of this is 'Everyone who mourns for Jerusalem will be worthy [or privileged] to see her joy'.[119] 'Everyone who mourns for Jerusalem' refers to this month in which 9 Av

[106] Mishnah *Ket.* 1: 1. The date of the *ketubah*, 27 Av 5491, fell on a Wednesday ('the fourth day').

[107] While the Shekhinah is separated from her husband she is as if a virgin because she does not allow the Sitra Ahra to have sexual contact with her. See Zohar III, 89*b*–90*a*, 180*b*, 276*a*; Tishby, *Wisdom of the Zohar*, i. 378; R. Shalom Buzaglo, *Mikdash melekh*, iv (Żółkiew, 1794), 49*b*–50*a*.

[108] The lower sefirot from Hesed to Yesod—the six 'end ones' [*ketsavot*]—govern the world together with the Shekhinah. During the time that their stature is diminished the six shrink into three, the sefirot Netsah, Hod, and Yesod, and then the Shekhinah's position below Yesod is *beshishi beshabat*: literally 'on the sixth day of the week', i.e. the sixth of seven. This condition of the six 'end ones' is called 'three entirely contained in three' [*gimel kalil begimel*]. See R. Hayim Vital, *Ets ḥayim* (Korets, 1782), 'gate' headed *Sha'ar hakelalim*, ch. 9.

[109] *Shulḥan arukh*, 'Even ha'ezer', 64: 3: 'And so the custom spread of weddings taking place on the eve of the Sabbath.'

[110] Parted from her husband Tiferet.

[111] Lam. 1: 1.

[112] [Tishby's note expanding the abbreviation *ḥg"t* has been incorporated in the translation of the text.]

[113] See Tishby, *Wisdom of the Zohar*, ii. 588–9.

[114] Exod. 27: 20; Lev. 24: 2. Both verses read 'bring you'.

[115] The Shekhinah, which is the principle of night, is raised to the level of Tiferet, the principle of the day, by the power of the letters of the Torah, which [including the five final forms—Trans.] number 27—*kaf zayin*. In *gematriyah* this is *zayin khaf* = *zakh* ['pure']. And see Luzzatto's *Razin genizin*, 52, where this verse and its context are expounded in relation to the soul of Moses.

[116] The renewal of the strength of the Shekhinah.

[117] Isa. 40: 1. [*menaḥem* = 'the comforter'.—Trans.]

[118] Isa. 66: 13.

[119] *Ta'an.* 30*b*.

falls, a day on which a number of calamities occurred, both new and old; but he will be worthy, certainly, because he purifies himself, as it is said of him: 'For he is like a refiner's fire',[120] in these twenty-seven days in which pure olive oil [is] beaten for the light [Exod. 27: 20], beaten and subjected to various poundings and calamities suffered by the mourner. 'For the light', certainly, for then the eyes of the blind will be opened and he will be privileged to see her joy; to see, literally, by means of a number of lights which are revealed here today to give light to our eyes.

'**The year** five thousand four hundred and ninety-one since the creation of the world', five thousand certainly, for all five supernal 'countenances' [*partsufim*] have been restored to perfection by *tikun* in the mystery of Arikh Anpin, five thousand in the mystery of Malkhut,[121] the letter *he* of *behibaram* ['when they were created', Gen. 2: 4], meaning *behe bera'am* ['with *he* He created them'].[122] Similarly, Scripture says[123] 'Here is [spelt *he alef*, pronounced *he*] seed for you; sow the land.' What is meant by 'sow the land'? That by this union of Moses with his bride you shall sow the land,[124] the bride of Moses certainly, at the time of which it is said: 'When you go forth [*ki tetse*] to war against your enemies',[125] precisely *tetse*, to war against your enemies in a number of wars against the husks to bring back the holy Shekhinah who had gone down into exile there, 'and the Lord your God delivers them into your hand and you take them captive' by some sparks of holiness that are emitted on high; and then 'you see among the captives a beautiful woman' etc., the bride of Moses, certainly, 'and she shall be your wife'.

'**The year**' in which she becomes a full year of twelve months.[126] [That is to say,] certainly *he-t-ts-a* [numerical value 5491], *he* [5] as in the '*he lakhem*' of 'here is [seed] for you; sow the land', *t-ts-a* [491] in which we shall go out [*netse*] to war, and she will be your wife. '**According to the reckoning** which

120 Mal. 3: 2. The verse refers to the messenger of the covenant who [verse 1] will clear the way before God. Luzzatto applied it [and the saying quoted from *Ta'anit*: see preceding note] to himself: he had mourned and suffered over the destruction of the Temple and the exile of the Shekhinah, the Jerusalem of the upper world, and now, through her *tikun* by his marriage to her, he would 'be privileged to see her joy'.

121 The *tikun* of all the five 'countenances' [*partsufim*] of God was completed by the *tikun* of the Shekhinah, who is called (the letter) *he*. [And *he* as a numeral = 5.—Trans.]

122 See *Bereshit rabah* 12: 10.

123 Gen. 47: 23.

124 The Shekhinah is the bride of Moses, and is, metaphorically, land sown by Luzzatto's marriage to her. See Tishby, *Wisdom of the Zohar*, i. 282, 288–9.

125 Deut. 21: 11. The word *tetse* ['you (will) go out': the numerical value of its letters is 491—Trans.] is expounded as a reference to the year 5491, the year of the *ketubah*, when the final war against the husks, to redeem the Shekhinah and the sparks, was being waged with greater vigour than ever.

126 According to the Zohar III, 277*b*–278*a* (*Raya meheimna*), the Shekhinah in her *tikun* [restoration to perfection] as a bride is metaphorically a year of twelve months.

we reckon here in Padua', which adds up to the same total as *tsiyah* ['dry ground'],[127] as it is said:[128] 'He grew up before Him like a young plant and like a root from dry ground.' 'The reckoning which we reckon', we[129] and not others, certainly; here [*poh*] in Padua, where the mouth [*peh*, same spelling] was opened,[130] precisely here. **'Whereas** Moses' in all his aspects[131] **'said** to the virgin' whom no man had known, the bride of Moses, **'be** my wife' in perfect union, to bring about the marriage on high, everlasting and without end. '**According to the law** of Moses and Israel', [according to the la]w[132] on her part, [174[v]] a fiery law to them,[133] and Moses for himself and all his aspects, and Israel in the comprehensive sense of the strength of all Israel, in the name of all Israel, that is certain. 'And I will work for you and honour and feed and provide for you': I will work by means of many commandments in the Torah and by good deeds to satisfy the needs of this bride, as it is said with regard to her: 'And with all kinds of work in the field'.[134] 'I will work' relates to Moses specifically, as it is said: 'The king makes himself a servant to the field.'[135] And I will honour, through honouring the Shekhinah in every detail. And I will feed: this is the mystery of the beast which ate a thousand hills every day, 'behemoth on a thousand hills',[136] *ese"v* [an acronym for] *ikar shekhinah bataḥtonim*[137] ['from the very beginning the Shekhinah was among "those below", the inhabitants of this world']. And I will provide: by drawing the flow of divine bounty from above and also from below to sustain the One

[127] The numerical value of 'Padova'—*pe alef dalet vav vav he*, plus one for each of its six letters—is 108, which is the same as that of *tsiyah—tsadi yod he*, plus one for each of its three letters. The religious awakening in Padua in the wake of Luzzatto's *tikunim* is compared to making the desert bloom. See *Igerot*, i. 53–4, 70, 73, 88. This application of the term *tsiyah* to Padua makes it clear that *Razin genizin*, 105, similarly refers to the *tikunim* of Luzzatto and his group: 'From what place did she [the Shekhinah] rise up? From the wilderness; this is the secret meaning of "wilderness and dry ground [*tsiyah*]", for there these *tikunim* were performed and from there she rose up, and the secret is for the wise.'

[128] Isa. 53: 2.

[129] Apparently this refers to Luzzatto's group, who calculated that 'the end of days' would occur in 5491. See p. 205 above.

[130] An allusion to the *magid*'s revelations to Luzzatto.

[131] Messiah ben David, Messiah ben Joseph, and Seraiah, as explained further on. And see pp. 202–3 above.

[132] Only the last letter (*tav*) of the word *kedat* is legible.

[133] Deut. 33: 2. The Shekhinah is, as it were, the fire of the attribute of judgement, and it was through her that the Torah was given.

[134] Exod. 1: 14.

[135] Eccles. 5: 8. Moses is king as mystically representing Tiferet, and his marriage with the Shekhinah is like the cultivation of a field.

[136] Ps. 50: 10. In the aggadah (*Vayikra rabah*, end of ch. 22) the verse is expounded as referring to a beast which 'lies on a thousand hills and a thousand hills grow all kinds of herbage for her and she eats [it]'. In the Zohar the aggadah is explained as meaning that the Shekhinah is fed on angels. See Tishby, *Wisdom of the Zohar*, ii. 624.

[137] *Bereshit rabah* 19: 7. The acronym *ayin s(h)in beit* [*esev*, 'herbage'] shows that the herbs which feed the Shekhinah are made to grow by the deeds of the *taḥtonim* [the inhabitants of this world].

on high. 'You', because all the works and deeds [of] the *taḥtonim* are her due, certainly. 'According to the [prescribed] practices [*halakhot*] of Jewish men who work for and honour and feed and provide for their wives in truth'. The mystical significance of this is 'You shall not turn aside from what they tell you',[138] for we learn from the mouth of our sages, of blessed memory, how to serve the Shekhinah, that is certain, through various rulings [*halakhot*] and decrees which they issued[139] for us: they were Jewish men coming from the exile of Judah who had been in Babylonia and returned in [the time of] the Second Temple, for we have nothing from the ten tribes. Now all the work of the inhabitants of this world causes the king to do different work in the world above, the king is made a servant to the field, for everything derives from the arousal brought about here below, and the mystery of this is 'in truth', and this seal of the king in the mystery of T[ifere]t[140] is the seal of the Holy One, blessed be He, [which] is truth.[141] **'And I have given** you in silver [*kesef*] two hundred *zuzim*, which is your due as ordained by the Torah.' The mystery of this is 'I have waited patiently for the Lord',[142] and also 'Because you are filled with longing [*nikhsof nikhsafta*, same root letters as *kesef*] for your father's house',[143] for two desires[144] are needed, certainly, to draw forth and arouse desire on high. And Hesed, so far as concerns *kesef*,[145] is forty-eight[?][146] worlds of longing [*kisufin*], which are two hundred by reason of the joining together of m[ale] and f[emale],[147] each of them a hundred cubits high,[148] for the Shekhinah alone is a hundred cubits, but when she is joined with Yesod, he being a hundred and she a hundred, together they make two hundred. The reason for all this is simply that it 'is proper for you in accordance with the Torah', because she comes together with the King from time to time and is entitled to consideration in compliance with the Torah, her root in T[ifere]t being backed by the authority of the Torah. They are *zuzim* for the reason that the numerical value of *zayin vav zayin* is the same as *ḥet yod* (*ḥay*)[149] in allusion to Yesod[150] when he is joined with his female counterpart,

138 Deut. 17: 11.

139 Manuscript singular verb corrected to plural.

140 Hebrew letters *tav"tav* [t-t], standing for Tiferet, as King, the Holy One, blessed be He, and truth.

141 *Shab.* 55*a*.

142 Ps. 40: 2.

143 Gen. 31: 30.

144 On the part of the male and of the female.

145 The drawing forth of Hesed, represented by *kesef* (as if *kosef*) in the sense of *kisufim* ['longing'].

146 *mem-ḥet*. Apparently *yod-ḥet* (18) is intended: see Zohar I, 24*a*; *Zohar ḥadash*, ed. Margaliot, *tikunim*, 117*d*; etc. Or perhaps the Aramaic *matan* (200) is meant: see Zohar I, 97*b* (*Midrash hanelam*).

147 *dalet vav"nun* = initials for Aramaic *dukhra venukba*, male and female.

148 Apparently on the basis of the idea that each sefirah contains the whole system of sefirot, as do also all these secondary sefirot, so that every sefirah consists of 10×10.

149 [The numerical value of *zuz* is 20 (7+6+7); that of *ḥay* is 18 (8+10). Parity could be obtained by a device of *gematriyah*, giving an additional value of one to each letter of *ḥay*.—Trans.]

150 Yesod is called *ḥay olamim* ['the eternally living'].

that is certain. '**And your food** and your clothing and the supply of your needs and coming in to you as is the way of all the earth': in this there is a perfect union verily with Moses in all his aspects. The mystery of this is 'he shall not diminish her food, her clothing, and her conjugal rights',[151] and although food, clothing, and conjugal rights are only three, nevertheless they have been divided into four to correspond with the four aspects of Moses. '**Your food**': the mystery of this is manna, through the merit of Moses,[152] 'your clothing' [*kesutaykhi*], this is in allusion to the poor man 'lowly and riding on an ass' [153] of whom it is said: 'for that is his only covering [*kesuto*], for he is poor and his heart is set upon it'.[154] 'And the supply of your needs': alluding to Seraiah,[155] a frugal supply. 'And coming in to you': this is M[essiah] b[en] J[oseph][156] Yesod, by whom the intercourse is performed. 'As is the way of all the earth' in that the Shekhinah is renewed again 'so that your youth is renewed like the eagle's',[157] for all her aspects are gathered together, all the earth,[158] and the mystery of this is: 'After I have grown old I shall have pleasure after the manner of women.'[159]

'And this virgin **desired to consent** and you became my wife', for it is written: 'I adjure you . . . not to awaken or arouse love until it please',[160] and now perfect desire has been aroused 'and you have become my wife'—specifically 'mine'—she has been given into his hand. The mystery of this is 'The righteous man [*tsadik*] rules over the Fear of God'[161] which is the Shekhinah. '**And this** is the dowry which she has brought to him from her father's house in silver, in gold, in jewellery, in clothing, and in bedding requisites', [175^r] for all the *tikunim* will touch, in the world above, one light which is contained

[151] Exod. 21: 10.

[152] Cf. *Igerot*, i. 38, where it is hinted that the *tikun* carried out by Luzzatto with his Zoharic treatise is 'like the mystery of the manna which came by reason of the merit of Moses, in whom is included the whole of the 600,000, and who draws forth the flow of the intercourse through the power of all of them collectively'. Generally speaking *mem-nun* as an abbreviation stands for *mayin nukbin* ['female waters'], the flow imparted by the righteous to arouse the Shekhinah to couple with her husband.

[153] Messiah ben David.

[154] A conflation of two verses: Exod. 22: 26 and Deut. 24: 15.

[155] Commander of the army in the days of the Messiah. See n. 73 above.

[156] Messiah ben Joseph, corresponding to Yesod.

[157] Ps. 103: 5.

[158] Aramaic *ara*. The sparks of the Shekhinah, who is called *erets* ['earth'] in Hebrew, are redeemed with her in her renewal.

[159] A conflation of Gen. 18: 12 and 11. [The rhetorical question in Genesis, 'Shall I have pleasure?', appears to be taken here as a statement: 'I shall'.—Trans.]

[160] S. of S. 2: 7.

[161] 2 Sam. 23: 3 [as probably intended to be understood here: 'rules over' instead of 'rules in'; and Tsadik is another name for Yesod—Trans.]. The Fear of God [*yirat elohim*] is the level of the Shekhinah, which is the milder attribute of Judgement.

in the mystery of Ima (Mother), its name being *aḥarit hayamim* ['the end of days'],[162] and when this bride ascends on high all these *tikunim* come out and become a dowry for her, because they have not been lost, Heaven forbid. And the mystery of 'which she brought him from her father's house' [is] the supernal Mother, in the mystical understanding of 'His house—that is, his wife'.[163] But because the powers of Aba [Father] and Ima are considered together as one, both silver and gold are referred to, Hesed and Din—Lovingkindness and Judgement, these being general aspects of both Aba and Ima.[164] But these are followed by jewellery, clothing, and bedding, which pertain to Ima alone, Ima who lent a garment to a daughter by the power of the *ḥashmal* which radiates from her,[165] and Ima 'made him a little coat'.[166] 'Bedding requisites [*shimushei de'arsa*]': these are sixty warriors who guard the bed,[167] specifically described as *shimushim*, for they are important servants [*shamashim*]. As is well known, they are those referred to in 'Look, it is Solomon's bed; around it are sixty warriors' etc.[168] See, they are the beginnings of the *tikunim* carried out in the world below, and they say 'We [or 'they'] have given you what was yours,[169] jewellery etc. [and] bedding requisites'. '**Fifty** *litrin*' [*librae*, 'pounds'], because the *he* of Malkhut is supplemented by all its sefirot through the power it receives from Ima 'from her father's house' etc., and is made *nun* [50] by Ima, a final ['straight'] letter *nun* [ן].[170] 'God settles those who are solitary in a house'[171] for the purpose of this union, for what had been *dakh* ['oppressed'] by the *mem resh* of Amalek proves not to be so and is overturned so that just as *he* becomes *nun*, so the *dakh* ['oppressed'] becomes *ram* ['high'].[172] This has the same numerical value as *litra* spelt without a *yod*, for that is how *litrin* is written [below]. '**And**

[162] Binah, mother of the lower sefirot and source of freedom and redemption, contains a light called *aḥarit hayamim* ['the end of days'], which serves as a repository for all the *tikunim* carried out with the aim of redeeming the Shekhinah. Now, with the completion of her *tikun* by her marriage to Luzzatto, these would be given to her as a dowry.

[163] Mishnah *Yoma* 1: 1. Ima is Binah, the wife of Aba, who is Hokhmah.

[164] Aba is the root of Hesed, mercy, and Ima is the root of Din, judgement.

[165] See I. Tishby, *Torat hara vehakelipah bekabalat ha'ar"i* (Jerusalem and Tel Aviv, 1942), 69–71, 75–6, 104, 112–13.

[166] 1 Sam. 2: 19. By an obvious error Luzzatto has put the verb in the masculine.

[167] See Zohar II, 51*a*; III, 60*a*; etc.

[168] S. of S. 3: 7.

[169] Mishnah *Eruv.* 10: 15. The bridegroom receives back the results he has achieved on high by his *tikunim*.

[170] Malkhut, the letter *he* (5), is multiplied by ten when it is completed by its sefirot, and reaches the level of *nun* (50), which is the letter of Binah.

[171] Ps. 68: 7. By virtue of their union 'the solitary ones' Tiferet and Malkhut are enabled, with the help of Binah (who is also called Elohim ['God']), to set up home in the domain of that sefirah.

[172] The bridegroom, Moses–Luzzatto, had been sunk in depression during the rule of the husk Amalek; 'Amalek' in *gematriyah* is 240, the same as *mem-resh*, which spells *mar* ['bitter']. Now the bridegroom is freed, overcomes the husk, and instead of being *dakh*

the bridegroom' in all his aspects '**desired**', for the desire must be on both sides, and in Moses, too, desire had not hitherto been awakened; but now 'he desired and [accordingly] assigned to her an additional fifty *litrin* of his own'; for his root in Ima[173] was also *nun* and he, too, had been *dakh* and is [or 'was'] now *ram*. And then a perfect union takes [or 'took'] place so as to destroy the wicked Lilith[174]—whose name amounts to 480[175]—through the strength of *ram*: 'O Lord, Your hand is lifted up but they do not see',[176] that is certain. In total, a hundred *litrin* of silver. The mystery of this is: 'Open your mouth for the dumb',[177] 'Open your mouth, O righteous judge',[178] for the mouth [*peh*] of the dumb Moses has been opened, and the bride, too, has opened her mouth. The word *sakh* ['sum'], which has the numerical value [80] of the letter *pe* [pronounced similarly to *peh*—Trans.], also means *dibur hakol* ['saying everything'], and *hakol* has the same letters as *kalah* ['bride']; so that *sakh hakol* ['the sum of everything', 'the total'] is what is said by the bride, the sum of everything certainly in perfect union. A hundred *litrin* of silver, for the perfect union of male and female [results in] a perfect form: 'Male and female He created them and He called their name Adam';[179] then the left is sweetened by the right and the female is bound up with the male and the silver of the whole [*kesef hakol*, instead of *sakh hakol*, 'the total'] is Hesed.

'**And thus spoke** Moses, the aforesaid bridegroom', in all his aspects, for the words must be uttered by the mouth for union to take place, certainly, and the mystery of this is 'Open your mouth, righteous judge', for when the words of the male are brought together by the unifying action of the female [we have] 'righteous judge', justice and righteousness together.[180] 'And thus he spoke', precisely in the mystery of speech, the union of the kisses.[181] **'The responsibility of this marriage contract and of this dowry I have accepted for myself and my heirs after me'**, and the mystery of this is 'under oath and covenant' to fortify this dowry against the husks by every means so as to

['oppressed, lowly'] (numerical value 24), he becomes *ram* ['high'], reversing the letters of *mar*. *Ram* has a numerical value ten times that of *dakh*, the same factor as in the change of the bride, the Shekhinah, from *he* to *nun*. On the destruction of the husk Amalek at the time of the Redemption, see Luzzatto's *Megilat setarim verazin genizin*, 16–17, 91–6. In 1730 Luzzatto wrote a treatise devoted to the verse 'the Lord will have war with Amalek' [Exod. 17: 15]: see *Igerot*, i. 153.

173 *Alef-yod*, not marked as an abbreviation but clearly meant to be an abbreviation for Ima.

174 Indicated by the abbreviation *lamed-yod*.

175 Twice the numerical value of *ram*.

176 Isa. 26: 11.

177 Prov. 31: 8.

178 Prov. 31: 9 reads *shefot tsedek*, an imperative verb ['judge [in] righteousness'], which should be read instead of the text here [*shofet tsadik*]. Further on the word *tsedek* is expounded in relation to the Shekhinah.

179 See Gen. 5: 2.

180 Justice is Tiferet and Righteousness is Malkhut.

181 The utterance by the mouth symbolizes a kiss. On the union of kisses, see Zohar II, 124*b*, 146*a*–147*a*, 253*a*–255*a*, 256*b*. And see Luzzatto's *Tikunim ḥadashim*, 71.

prevent them from abstracting any of it, Heaven forbid. Thus the reason for saying 'The responsibility for this contract' etc. is in order to detail every item so that they should not be able to acquire control over them, Heaven forbid. And he[182] includes all Israel, for they are his children because of the power of the Torah which he gave them, 'my heirs after me'. He says 'my heirs' and not 'my children', because they are not strictly his children but his heirs: 'Moses commanded us a law, an inheritance—*morashah*—for the congregation of Jacob',[183] precisely 'my heirs' through the mystery of this bride, who is referred to in the scriptural verse by the word *morashah*. You are to read not *morashah* but *me'orasah* ['betrothed'].[184] **'To be paid out of all** the finest things of the land, the property and possessions which I have under all the heavens, whether acquired or in future to be acquired by me, and whether real or personal property', so as to include all the beauty of [175v] the *tikunim* which have been carried out [and] which will be perfected by this *tikun*. 'Property' means the *tikunim* which have been performed in holiness, and 'possessions' means the sparks acquired from the husks. He says 'which I have[185] under all the heavens' because with regard to the *tikunim* which have not[186] yet ascended to Heaven to be stored in the treasury of 'the end of days'[187] one must be fearful lest the husks acquire control over them, Heaven forbid. 'Which I have under all the heavens', i.e. at the level of Z-A,[188] and the mystery of this is 'for everything [*kol*] in the heavens',[189] 'body', and 'covenant' are accounted as one,[190] 'all the heavens'. '[Whether acquired] or in future to be acquired by me', in order that all the *tikunim* which will in future be carried out may be strengthened by this *tikun*, and in particular [the sparks] from the husks in the mystery of acquisition as we have said. The expression also includes the *tikunim* that have not been strengthened by oath and covenant. 'Possessions whether real or personal', certainly, because when they have been included in this *tikun* there is no longer any fear that the husks will suck anything from them. **'All of them** are to be held liable as surety for the fulfilment of this contract of marriage and **this** additional undertaking', for certainly the payment of the wife's[191] dowry takes precedence over the demands of every creditor. It is to be observed that the Sitra Ahra is called

[182] The bridegroom, Moses–Luzzatto. [183] Deut. 33: 4. [184] *Ber.* 57*a*.

[185] In the manuscript there is a blank space showing that a word has been omitted; I have supplied the word which fits the context. So, too, with the words 'acquired' and 'the sparks' enclosed in square brackets below.

[186] Correcting a misspelling of *lo* in the manuscript, which reads 'to him' where 'not' was clearly intended. [187] See n. 162 above.

[188] Ze'ir Anpin, who is called *shamayim* ['Heaven']. [189] 1 Chr. 29: 11.

[190] Zohar III, 223*b* (*Raya meheimna*) etc. Yesod is called *kol* ['everything']; *guf* and *berit* ['body' and 'covenant'] are Tiferet and Yesod.

[191] Correcting a clerical error in the manuscript (*sheha'ishah* where *ha'ishah* was meant).

marei deḥov ['creditor': a literal Aramaic equivalent of the Hebrew *ba'al(ei) ḥov*; see below], and is always seeking to take a number of things which belong to Israel as repayment of debt; but now that all the *tikunim* are committed to the dowry of this bride and her marriage contract, she always takes precedence wherever she sees[192] that the creditor [*haba'al ḥov*] is stretching out his hand to take, for everything is liable to her prior claim, certainly. '**And even** the cloak on my shoulders': the mystery of this is 'You have let men ride over our heads',[193] for the Sitra Ahra is in the end a servant enslaved to this bridegroom in all his aspects. As our rabbis, of blessed memory, said,[194] if Adam had not sinned the serpent would have been a faithful servant, and a servant in relation to his master is like an instrument with which he can do his will. This servant, be it noted, is a *golem*, for it is formless, and only a *golem* has no form;[195] and it is a cloak [*gelima*], the outermost garment of a man, for the husk surrounds the exterior of the fruit. Now while the servant is under the hand of his master, matters proceed as they should, but during the exile the *golem* mounts up on [his master's] shoulders and weighs very heavily; [thus] 'You have let men ride over our heads'. Nevertheless he is always a servant and will again become enslaved; therefore even this servant is made subject to this marriage contract, [in the words] 'even the *gelima* on my shoulders', for the servant must receive a wage from his master's money[?],[196] certainly. '**In my life and in my death**', in life and in death. 'From this day and for ever', because even when dead[197] he performs a number of *tikunim* and these, too, are included in this *tikun*, for they are numerous and great *tikunim* and you can have no control over them, Heaven forbid, for the words 'free among the dead'[198] which our rabbis explained as meaning: 'When a man dies he is freed from the obligation to perform the commandments'[199] do not apply to Moses, who lives always: righteous people in their death are called living. And [the contract] says 'from this day and for ever' because Scripture says: 'Like the days of a tree shall the days of my people be',[200] so that Moses will never again die, that is certain.[201] '**And the responsibility** for

192 Correcting another error: *shehro'ah*, which does not make sense, should read *shehi ro'ah*.

193 Ps. 66: 12.

194 See *San.* 59*b*.

195 The idea of the Sitra Ahra as a formless *golem* is one of the principles of Nathan of Gaza's kabbalah. See H. Wirszubsky, 'Hate'ologyah hashabeta'it shel natan ha'azati', *Keneset*, 8 (1944), 227–31.

196 The manuscript has *mmn*, apparently for *mamon* [or *mimamon*].

197 During the exile, while Moses was dead. In *Raya meheimna*, and—under its influence—in Luzzatto's writings, a great deal is said about the metamorphoses of Moses and his *tikunim* throughout the generations.

198 Ps. 88: 6.

199 *Shab.* 30*a*.

200 Isa. 65: 22. 'Tree' is an allusion to Moses, as explained in *Megilat setarim* on Ruth, 45: ' "One" is Moses, who is a single tree, the initials of the words *mekom shipul ha'ets* ['the place at the base of the tree'] spell *Mosheh*.'

201 This seems to be a declaration of Luzzatto's belief in his immortality, now that Moses' metamorphoses have reached finality in him at the end of days.

this contract and this supplementary undertaking has been accepted by the aforesaid bridegroom', Moses in all his aspects, for to accept this bride requires acceptance in the heart, and indeed the time is ripe for the acceptance of all these *tikunim* which come from above, since the hour is certainly propitious for him. '**As is the obligation** in all marriage contracts and supplementary undertakings which are customary with regard to the daughters of Israel', for there must certainly be an obligation so as to prevent the external forces of evil [*haḥitsonim*] from attaching themselves, Heaven forbid. And it says 'daughters of Israel' because now this bride is a daughter of Israel in his *gadlut* ['spiritual maturity'].[202] Therefore she no longer fears the husks as was the case in the time of Dinah, [176ʳ] for then she was the daughter of Jacob, for it was said of her: 'Because he had committed an outrage in Israel by lying with Jacob's daughter',[203] for she could not enter into a bond as she can now that she is a daughter of Israel. That is why it says 'like the obligation etc. customary with regard to the daughters of Israel', for that is where the whole obligation and the strict oath exist, that is certain. '**Which are made** according to the ordinance of our sages, of blessed memory, not as a nominal security or a merely formal deed', certainly according to the ordinance of our sages, of blessed memory, with all their edicts against the serpents, of which creatures it was said: 'He who breaks down a wall, a serpent shall bite him'.[204] 'Not as a nominal security', this is a reference to the Sitra Ahra, which ostensibly offers bonds to give an impression of security but these have no support—castles in the air—there is nothing in them on which one can rely—a broken reed, for they have no proper support but are only nominally securities; whence the contract says 'not as a nominal security'. And this bond and deed are completely voluntary, not imposed by force as is done by the Sitra Ahra, the boor [who] beats [his wife] and then copulates with her.[205] And the underlying meaning of 'a formal deed' is a deed drawn up and entered into by force contrary to law, and so here 'not a merely formal deed', certainly. '**And the acquisition of responsibility** [*kinyana*] by the transfer of a token from Moses as[206] the aforesaid bridegroom [has taken place].' These are the witnesses: heaven and earth, a single act of transfer, a transfer specifically from Moses etc. to bring the lights down into this world below. '**To** this **virgin**',

[202] According to Lurianic kabbalah the name 'Israel' denotes Ze'ir Anpin (Tiferet) when it is in its state of spiritual maturity [*gadlut*], whereas it is called Jacob when in the spiritually immature state. At the time which, for the *ketubah*, is the present, that being the time of the Redemption, Ze'ir Anpin is in a state of perfect spiritual maturity, and the Shekhinah is in an exalted condition as 'the daughter of Israel'. See Luzzatto's *Kelalei ḥokhmat ha'emet*, 46 (printed with *Milḥemet mosheh* (Warsaw, 1889)).

[203] Gen. 34: 7.

[204] Eccles. 10: 8.

[205] *Pes.* 49*b*.

[206] Correcting manuscript *befi'* to *beḥi'* [= *beḥinat*] ['in the capacity of'].

for the Shekhinah is present among the inhabitants of this world [*ayin shin"beit*, meaning *ikar shekhinah bataḥtonim*], and the *taḥtonim* must undertake the acquisition for the sake of this bride so that she [the Shekhinah] may rest upon them. '**All** [*kol mah*] that is written and expressly stated above', certainly, 'in all'—*bekhol mah*—this is Yesod, the line of existence of everything, *berit* ['covenant'] certainly, and *kol* has reference to Yesod, who will after this be called Kol. *Guf* and *berit* ['body' and 'covenant'] are accounted as one, and the mystery of this is '*mah* ['what'] is his name and *mah* is the name of his son',[207] [which is] the Tetragrammaton with each of its letters spelt out,[208] everything certainly just as it has already been prepared above in Heaven before the King, for everything has already been done above before it descends to this world. '**In all**[209] that is written and expressly stated [*meforash*, verbal root *parash*] above', certainly, for there the lights are spread out more [*mitparesim*, verbal root *paras*], and the mystery of this is 'They shall spread the garment before the elders of the town'[210]—['They' meaning] the father and mother [*alef vav alef* = *aba ve'ima*], certainly—'and expressly stated above', precisely 'above'.[211] '**With an article** fit to be used as the token of acquisition', for all these comrades[212] are certainly fit and they are vessels proper to be filled with the Holy Spirit and to acquire all these *tikunim*, certainly. '**And all is valid and enduring**', Yesod has now risen to be joined in marriage, for he rules[213] and has control over all the husks, and this *tikun* will endure to all eternity, and all is valid and enduring, certainly. '**Witnesses**': the heavens and the heavens of heavens and all their host, and the earth and all that is on it and the seas and all that is in them.

[The two messianic poems from MS Guenzburg 745, and the notes on them, printed at this point in the Hebrew essay were also included in Essay 2 above, pp. 158–63, and have therefore not been reproduced here.—Trans.]

207 Prov. 30: 4 [literally 'What is his name and what is the name of his son?'—Trans.]. 'He' and 'his son' are Tiferet and Yesod.

208 [Spelt out thus: the letter *yod* = *yod vav dalet* (20), letter *he* = *he alef* (6), letter *vav* = *vav alef vav* (13), letter *he* again (6)—Trans.], this has the same numerical value as *mah* (45). Since it is the name of the six sefirot from Hesed to Yesod it belongs to both Tiferet and Yesod, and in the scriptural verse the word *mah* ['what'] is an allusion to it [therefore read 'His name is *mah* . . .'—Trans.]. See Luzzatto's *Kelalei ḥokhmat ha'emet*, 52 (printed with *Kinat hashem tsevaot* (Warsaw, 1888)); *Razin genizin*, 106.

209 [**In all**: traditional *ketubot* have 'according to all'.—Trans.]

210 Deut. 22: 17.

211 'Above' meaning in the realm of the sefirot or the *partsufim*, the 'countenances' of God.

212 The members of Luzzatto's group.

213 ['He rules': *sorer*, apparently as a play on *sharir*, 'valid'.—Trans.]

FOUR

Luzzatto's Attitude to Shabateanism

THE controversy over R. Moses Hayim Luzzatto which agitated European Jewry in 1730 and 1735–6 was dominated from beginning to end by the charge of Shabatean heresy brought against him. But this central issue has never as yet been investigated; indeed the world of Luzzatto's thought is still a closed book so far as concerns scholarly study. Nearly all scholars have agreed that the allegation of a link between Luzzatto's activities and the Shabatean movement was malicious or mistaken, but this consensus has not been critically examined on the basis of the documents and writings available to us. Yet it is very important to clarify this problem for the light it can cast both on the personality of Luzzatto and on the history of the Shabatean movement and its offshoots.

A. THE CHARGE OF SHABATEAN HERESY AGAINST LUZZATTO

The first letter in which R. Moses Hagiz brought his accusations against Luzzatto was dated 9 Heshvan 5490 [autumn 1729]. In it he transmitted to Venice a copy of a letter from R. Jekutiel of Vilna on Luzzatto's revelations, and called for 'enquiry and investigation and for this evil company to be rooted out before it can spread among the common people in its evil',[1] but made no mention of Shabateanism. Shortly afterwards, however, Hagiz, or some other zealot, explicitly raised the suspicion that Shabatean heresy was involved, as can be seen from a report on the evidence given by the emissary from Safed, R. Raphael Israel Kimhi, to the rabbis of Venice at the beginning of the controversy. The report says of R. Jekutiel's letter that 'it contained no

[1] *R' mosheh ḥayim lutsato uvenei doro: osef igerot ute'udot*, ed. S. Ginzburg [hereafter *Igerot*] (Tel Aviv, 1937), i. 20. And see M. Benayahu, 'Ha"magid" shel ramḥa"l', in I. Ben-Zvi and M. Benayahu (eds.), *Sefer zikaron liyeshayahu zoneh/Isaiah Sonne Memorial Volume* (= *Sefunot*, 5) (Jerusalem, 1961), 297–336, which presents new documents and additional explanations relating to the Luzzatto affair.

mention *of anything to do with a prophet or Sh*[abetai] *Ts*[evi], but only praises of the gentleman [Luzzatto] of the highest order'.[2] Added to this, the denial of the charge of Shabateanism by Luzzatto in his letter to Hagiz[3] and by R. Isaiah Bassano in his letter to the rabbis of Venice[4] shows clearly that the suspicion of Shabateanism was raised from the start to motivate the witch-hunt.[5] From then on this allegation was never allowed to drop, although it was only in the second stage of the controversy, during the persecutions and rabbinic bans of 1735, that it was brought into prominence and formulated as a definite accusation.[6]

However, examination of the charges shows that the accusers had no substantial evidence. In most of the documents we find vague declarations and exaggerations, without even any attempt to offer proofs. Only two of the accusers had something to say worth study and discussion: R. Moses Hagiz and R. Jacob Emden. These two scholars, who were experts on kabbalah and Shabateanism and specialized in deciphering hidden Shabatean allusions, made definite accusations and tried to support them.

R. Moses Hagiz, citing a treatise based on the revelations of the *magid* which Luzzatto had sent to Hamburg, claimed to have found 'that its entire essence was nothing but an apology for the apostasy of Shabetai Tsafia ['Shabetai dung'], whom they call "our G–d"'.[7] R. Jacob Emden relied on two short passages, one in a letter from R. Jekutiel to Vilna and one in a leaf from *Zohar tinyana* which accompanied that letter:

> In saying with regard to the matter of Sh.Ts. that it was a mistake, he [Jekutiel quoting Luzzatto] did not say, as he should have done, that it was false and that his messiahship was a falsehood and his faith an absolute lie . . . and who knows what he meant in attributing the mistake to him, *whether perhaps he thought that* [Shabetai Tsevi] *was the Messiah ben Joseph and* [Luzzatto] *was reserving to himself the kingship of the Messiah ben David*, and he was hinting at this at the end of his Zoharic tract, *Dayar vesoher* ['Inmate and Jailer'], copied above, when he said 'the prison shall be enslaved by you', by which is meant the raising of the Shekhinah from the dust and the arrival of the Redemption, 'by the strength of that splendour [*zohar*] of yours and the Messiah ben David who is in righteousness [*betsedek*]', and it is well known that the heretics use the word *tsedek* to allude to Sh.Ts., may the name of the wicked rot.[8]

Taking their stand against the accusers, R. Isaiah Bassano and Luzzatto stoutly rejected the charge of Shabateanism.[9] Even outside the context of the argument with his accusers Luzzatto dissociated himself from the Shabateans

2 *Igerot*, i. 21.
3 Ibid. 24.
4 Ibid. 61.
5 See also Bassano's letter to Luzzatto, ibid. 29–30.
6 See ibid. ii. 309–19, 368, 376, 383, 392.
7 Ibid. i. 161, and see ibid. 126, 159, 164.
8 R. Jacob Emden, *Torat hakenaot* (Lvov, 1870), 111.
9 See *Igerot*, i. 24, 60–1, 134, 171.

and referred to them in derogatory terms.[10] In Sivan 5490 [mid 1730] he began writing a book entitled *Kinat hashem tsevaot* ['The Zeal of the Lord of Hosts'],[11] most of which was directed against the Shabateans. This book, part of which was printed and part of which I have found in manuscript,[12] is full of denigration of 'the pursuers of the deer' [*rodefei hatsevi*, i.e. the followers of Shabetai Tsevi].[13] In other books too, written after *Kinat hashem tsevaot* between 1731 and 1734 when the heat of the controversy had subsided, Luzzatto continued to denigrate the Shabateans.[14]

On the face of it, it would seem clear that Bassano's vigorous defence together with Luzzatto's denial and his anti-Shabatean activity countervail the charges of his accusers, shaky as those charges are for lack of evidence. We do not now have the offending document by Luzzatto or the proofs offered by Hagiz of its Shabatean meaning, and Emden, for his part, put forward his accusation as a conjecture based on obscure allusions.

But the actual letters contain information from Bassano and Luzzatto themselves which undermines any confidence that Luzzatto completely rejected Shabateanism, and which confronts us with a difficult problem. R. Isaiah Bassano's attitude to Luzzatto's activity is not faithfully reflected in his stand against the accusers: his love of his pupil and his devotion to him moved him to conceal the doubts which are repeatedly revealed in his intimate letters to Luzzatto—doubts which are also relevant to the question of Shabateanism. The same is true of Luzzatto, who, in his letters to Bassano, spoke more frankly about his ideas and aims than he did in addressing strangers, though he kept some secrets even from his teacher.[15]

In several letters, Bassano wrote that he too had misgivings lest the Sitra Ahra ['Other Side'] might play some part in the *magid*'s appearance to

[10] Ibid. 84, 112.

[11] Ibid. 153, 155, where Luzzatto indicated that the anti-Shabatean part of the book had two purposes: to cleanse texts of the Zohar of Shabatean distortions, and to rescue souls trapped by Shabatean heresy, 'for many have gone astray who are the wisest of the wise; and in western countries, like those who entered the ark, they are innocent of this mistake'.

[12] In the printed version the text breaks off in the middle of a sentence, and by way of conclusion the following words are added: 'Understand and the cause of the Lord will prosper in your hands.' In MS Oxford 2237 the whole work appears on fos. 203^r–246^r, and fos. 227^r onwards are missing in the printed version. However, the manuscript itself has lacunae after fos. 230^v and 235^v and at the end. From several indications it is evident that this copy was produced in Luzzatto's school. On fos. 230^r–235^v the handwriting is different, and the hand that penned those folios, apparently that of Luzzatto himself, also made some marginal additions on fo. 227^r. The part that was not printed contains an extremely strong anti-Christian polemic, and it appears that those comments were the main reason for the truncation of the printed version.

[13] See *Kinat hashem tsevaot* (Warsaw, 1888), 1–3, 14, 15, 17–21, and in the manuscript continuation, fos. 227^v–228^r, 237^v–238^r.

[14] *Adir bamarom* (Warsaw, 1886), 192; end of the introduction to *Kela"ḥ pitḥei ḥokhmah*.

[15] See *Igerot*, i. 32, 48, 53, 56, 91, 95, 106–7.

Luzzatto.[16] In one letter he told Luzzatto explicitly that his doubts were connected with the distinctly messianic character of the *magid*'s revelations:[17] 'But I find it disturbing that your words constantly return to the matter of the Messiah, for that is one of the things which raise doubt whether the matter does not contain some admixture of the Sitra Ahra: for that is one of the undoubted signs that the *magid* is in darkness, Heaven forbid, it being the way of the other sides [*sitrin aḥrin*] *to confuse people's minds by speaking of the Messiah so as to make Israel stumble.*' And if, here, he contented himself with a hint and refrained from any explicit mention of Shabateanism, he spoke plainly in a later letter:[18]

Know that I have heard from reliable informants that *during the time of the Tsevi* there were, in the land of the East, many great heart-searchers[19] on whom the spirit rested when they prostrated themselves,[20] and they composed great and terrible works in ancient language which were wondrous in the eyes of all who saw them; *chief of these was R. Nathan*, who wrote profound discourses. He himself used to say that, following in the footsteps of the Ari [Luria], may he be remembered for life in the world to come, he [R. Nathan] had set out to explain what Luria had not explained and reveal what he had not revealed, and had developed Luria's principles in his [Nathan's] books *Sefer haberiah* ['The Book of Creation'] and *Zemir aritsim* [a title taken from Isa. 25: 5], which are in our possession; moreover, he made many turn back from sin and gave *tikunim* to tens of thousands of people. He also used to say that the souls of the righteous revealed themselves to him—and nevertheless, in the end it all came to nothing and was lost, to say nothing of the events it led to. *Well, then: what difference is there between the two cases?* Only that all R. Nathan's words were along lines drawn towards the single point of the Tsevi, which is not so in your case. *But in any event, who is to decide?* And you should not complain so much about the unbelievers or the doubters, for *a burnt child dreads the fire.*

Thus Bassano saw a close resemblance between Luzzatto and the Shabatean visionaries, and even *a precise parallel between him and Nathan of Gaza*; and although Luzzatto's innovative interpretations were not directed 'towards the single point of the Tsevi', his teacher still asked: 'who is to decide?'—in other words, who could vouch for the intentions behind the secrets of his doctrine—and showed understanding for people's suspicions.

Indeed, it is precisely Luzzatto's standpoint in relation to Nathan of Gaza which shows that his attitude to Shabateanism was complex. The little he said on this subject was charged with meaning and is worth quoting in full.

16 See ibid. 86, 103–4, 146.
17 Ibid. 86.
18 Ibid. 104–5.
19 [A play on Judg. 5: 16, which, taken out of context, could be so read.—Trans.]
20 ['prostrated themselves': *nefilat apayim*, 'falling on one's face', a description of the posture in which some mystics sought to commune with the upper world through meditation.—Trans.]

In a letter written at the beginning of the controversy[21] he says: '*On R. Nathan's yiḥudim and the words he has spoken I will say nothing in writing*, but face to face, with God's help, I will inform your Honour of a true word which the Lord in His kindness has revealed to me, for no man knew the ways of His designs.' We do not have Bassano's questions on 'R. Nathan's *yiḥudim* and his words', but it is clear from what Luzzatto says that Nathan of Gaza's activity and innovations occupied his mind and that their inner meaning was disclosed to him by the *magid*. Because of the nature of the secret he was obliged not to communicate it in writing for fear that it might come into the hands of his opponents and strengthen the case against him. Evidently it explained the significance of the Shabatean prophet's activity by reference to God's designs. Luzzatto replied in the same guarded language to his teacher's arguments that his activity was similar to that of Nathan of Gaza:[22] '*But with regard to R. Nathan I cannot reply to your Honour in writing*; but face to face, if the Lord grants, I will reveal it to you faithfully; *for I must be cautious in this matter*—since, as your Honour knows, others have already saddled me with the baseless charge that I confirm what he says.'[23] Not only did he not indignantly reject the comparison with Nathan of Gaza but he even hinted at a secret explanation which he could not reveal in writing because it might strengthen the hands of those who accused him of asserting that Nathan spoke the truth. He did, indeed, describe the allegation as baseless, but a secret explanation is not an outright contradiction.

Part of that secret is revealed in another letter:[24]

> *With regard to the writings of that R. Nathan* I would say that even though their basis is falsehood and lying which cannot stand scrutiny—*there is no harm in putting them away*, which is equivalent to their burial; they will then be hidden from all eyes, so as to remove a stumbling-block from before the blind. But as there is no falsehood which does not contain an element of truth—*in those, too, there will be found some word of good*; and face to face I will tell your Honour how it comes about that true words may be found within falsehood. And therefore *whoever is wise can certainly eat their inner substance and throw away their husk*, like R. Meir who learned from Aher [Elisha ben Avuyah].

The letter from Bassano to which this is a reply has not come down to us, but its contents can be guessed. In face of the new storm which had blown up over Shabateanism he had asked Luzzatto's opinion whether the writings of Nathan of Gaza in his possession ought not to be destroyed. Luzzatto replied that duty could be done *by putting them away without destroying them*, in order

[21] *Igerot*, i. 42.

[22] Ibid. 114.

[23] Apparently this refers to an accusation made by two Venetian rabbis, Belilios and Merari, to whom Luzzato replied that 'the allegation on the subject of Nathan of Gaza was completely false and erroneous' (ibid. 76).

[24] Ibid. 152.

to hide the evil and falsehood in them from foolish people who were liable to stumble, but keeping them for study by the wise who could extract the kernels of truth and so profit from the good contained in the Shabatean writings. The opinion that in Nathan of Gaza's revelations there was a mixture of good and bad, truth and falsehood, had been expressed about thirty years previously by a Shabatean in the circle of R. Benjamin Hakohen.[25] For our purpose what is most important is Luzzatto's verdict that scholars could learn from Nathan of Gaza's writings and 'eat their inner substance'. This is an acknowledgement that he found a positive content in the Shabatean writings and learned from them. The writings of the Shabatean prophet are mentioned once more in connection with Luzzatto's treatises against the Shabateans:[26] 'It would be well *if your Honour were to bring the writings of Nathan with you when you come*, for I may get material from them, too, to help with my reply to him and his compositions in that book of mine.'[27] Here he was asking for the writings in order to condemn and throw away their husk, but to judge from his approach he certainly intended to eat their inner substance.

The foregoing makes it clear that Emden's instinct had not misled him when he scented danger in Luzzatto's outlook as reflected in his characterization of Shabateanism—reported in R. Jekutiel's letter—not as false and lying but as a mistake. That was not a chance remark: in all of Luzzatto's letters and treatises which were not known to Emden, and even in his sharpest criticisms of Shabateanism, the Shabatean heresy is repeatedly described as a mistake or a blunder. In some places the origin and significance of the mistake are explained. We now know that the mistake Luzzatto saw was the destruction of the good and true 'inner substance' by its introduction into a 'husk' of evil and falsehood.

Luzzatto himself has provided us with the key to his attitude to Shabateanism. The starting point of our investigation is the question: what did he accept and what did he discard, what did he admit as 'inner substance' and what did he reject as 'husk'? To elucidate this question fully would require an exhaustive comparison of Luzzatto's doctrine of the Messiah and the Redemption with Shabatean doctrine. Here I necessarily restrict myself to a few essential points. I will concentrate on two elements fundamental to Shabateanism: the descent of the Messiah to the husks, and transgressions for the sake of *tikun* ['restoration to perfection']. Luzzatto himself made these elements the target of his polemic against Shabateanism, and my investigation will be based on an examination of the arguments in his book *Kinat hashem tsevaot*, supplemented by explanations drawing on other works.

[25] See G. Scholem, *Ḥalomotav shel hashabeta'i r' mordekhai ashkenazi* (Jerusalem, 1938), 50, 52–5, 81–3, 88.

[26] *Igerot*, i. 155.

[27] It appears that Luzzatto repeated this request in an enigmatic sentence, ibid. 157.

B. THE PATHS OF THE MESSIAHS AMONG THE HUSKS

In Luzzatto's view the essence of the Shabatean heresy was a distorted perception of the descent of the Messiah to the husks. He argued that actually the Messiah does not descend to the husks while he is in this world, but the superior soul [*yeḥidah*] which is to reside in the Messiah is sunk among the husks together with the Shekhinah and the souls of the righteous, 'and there they suffer from lack of light and many kinds of distress, and they are called sufferers of illnesses who suffer the sins of Israel. Chief of them all is the King-Messiah, that is, the *yeḥidah* created long ago which is about to become a crown for the redeemer with which he will redeem Israel, and the *yeḥidah* stands in the clothing and lack of light mentioned above.'[28]

For the purpose of explaining the true meaning of the Messiah's descent to the husks Luzzatto examines various modes of existence experienced by souls in the realm of the Sitra Ahra. The first is before they come into the world, when they are among the husks because of Adam's sin. Such souls 'are not in the category of sufferers of illnesses but are in the mystical condition of victims of oppression'. They are marred by their contact with the forces of evil, and 'when they enter this world they are persecuted by the Sitra Ahra and need [to accomplish] a great *tikun* by their deeds in order to be restored from that condition to their perfection'. The second mode is the association of the souls of the wicked with the Sitra Ahra in their sins. This occurs first in this world,[29] 'for the husk interferes in the existence of the soul while it is still in the body . . . and it is delivered into the hand of the Sitra Ahra'. This bond continues even after the death of the wicked, whose souls go to Gehenna and are subjected there to the authority of the Sitra Ahra until they are purified. The third mode is that in which the souls of the righteous exist after they leave this world. The righteous man 'has already separated himself from the Sitra Ahra and he cleaves to his holy root' by virtue of his good deeds; therefore the Sitra Ahra has no authority to take hold of his soul when it leaves this world. But 'sometimes that soul descends and clothes itself in the husk, in such a way that the Sitra Ahra surrounds it . . . and, while not adhering to the soul at all, deprives it of the light which ought to be revealed to it in accordance with its merit'.[30] These souls, in partnership with the Shekhinah, fulfil a mission to preserve exiled Israel by bearing the burden of their sins.

[28] *Kinat hashem tsevaot* (1888), 16.

[29] Ibid.

[30] Ibid. The text, here as in the other quotations below, has been corrected to agree with the manuscript.

The soul of the Messiah is unique. It dwells among the husks before entering this world, not, however, as an oppressed soul but to fulfil a mission like the souls of the righteous.[31] Because of this the husks are unable to mar its perfection, for 'the Messiah's soul is of the nature of the *yeḥidah*, which is free and *has no concern with this* [with oppression on account of Adam's sin], for it has to come into the world only to crown the Messiah *and not to undergo tikun*. Therefore it is in the category of those who suffer illnesses, and indeed chief of them all.'[32] The *yeḥidah* existed in Adam before he sinned, and if he had not stumbled 'the messianic *tikun*' would have occurred at the very beginning, but 'by reason of his sin the *yeḥidah* immediately departed, and it is that *yeḥidah* that is proper to be given afterwards to the King-Messiah in order to restore matters to the necessary state of perfection [*tikun*]'. Ever after the first sin there were ups and downs of *tikunim* and misdeeds, until, with the destruction of the second Temple, the misdeeds became by far the stronger,

> and now the Shekhinah is in the midst of the husks and power has been given to all degrees of impurity to dominate Israel. But the above-mentioned *yeḥidah* and the other sufferers of illnesses together stand next to her clothed, like her, in the husks, where they suffer great torments and their mystical condition is lack of light and diminution of the divine flow. But by this means Israel is given strength to endure the exile . . . and when he [the Messiah] is revealed, his *tikun* will bring about the *tikun* of all Israel and he will prepare them all for redemption.[33]

Thus Luzzatto set important limits to the Shabatean doctrine of the Messiah. His reservations were: (*a*) the descent of the Messiah to the husks is quite unconnected with his existence in this world; (*b*) even in the world of the souls his descent leaves him unmarred; therefore he has no defect of his own to repair by *tikun*, and when he is revealed his *tikun* will be meant only for the redemption of Israel.[34]

In explaining the source of the Shabateans' mistake, Luzzatto taught that there were risks attached to any consideration of the seizure of holiness by the husks, and in particular to consideration of the exile of the Shekhinah; those who contemplated these matters without proper preparation could be caught by the Sitra Ahra in its net and brought to entertain false beliefs. It was from such flawed consideration that the Shabatean heresy sprang; in

[31] 'If the Messiah had not undergone these torments, then Israel, Heaven forbid, would have perished, whereas through his sharing their affliction, and even more through his suffering on their behalf, although they remain poor and lowly in their exile, they continue to exist and they have been granted readiness for redemption' (*Kinat hashem tsevaot*, MS, fo. 241^{r}).

[32] *Kinat hashem tsevaot* (1888), 16.

[33] *Kinat hashem tsevaot*, MS, fos. 239^{v}–240^{r}.

[34] The principal idea in these reservations—the descent of the *yeḥidah* to the husks in the world of the souls—had already been expressed before *Kinat hashem tsevaot* was written. See *Ma'amar hage'ulah* (printed with *Da'at tevunot* (Warsaw, 1889)), 22–3; *Igerot*, i. 83–4.

other words, it was an error in their understanding of the secrets of kabbalah concerning the relations between holiness and impurity.[35]

However, it is clear in spite of those reservations that Luzzatto adopted a fundamental principle of Shabatean doctrine, accepting it as 'inner substance' to be cleansed of its husk.[36] The few allusions in the Zohar[37] and in Lurianic kabbalah[38] to the soul of the Messiah among the husks do not match Luzzatto's views: many of his motifs are to be found only in Shabatean literature. I examine here a number of topics which bear the imprint of Shabatean doctrine. For the most part, of course, they appear with alterations and nuances which are original contributions by the Paduan kabbalist.

Take the idea that the Messiah's soul, before it comes into the world, undergoes torments in the realm of the Sitra Ahra, where it struggles to subdue the husks and carry out *tikunim* in preparation for the Redemption. This idea is itself not Lurianic: it has its source in the innovations of Nathan of Gaza and his disciples,[39] but Luzzatto's reservations changed its original form. In *Kinat hashem tsevaot* and *Ma'amar hage'ulah* his attitude also differs from that of the Shabatean scholars in regard to the time when the Messiah's soul descended to the husks. According to Nathan of Gaza and his disciples the descent took place during the processes of Creation, in the *tsimtsum* [God's withdrawal into Himself] or the breaking of the vessels. Luzzatto, on the other hand, declares that the soul of the Messiah had been dwelling with the Shekhinah among the husks since the destruction of the Temple on account of Israel's sins. It seems to me, however, that Luzzatto was here camouflaging his true view. What he really believed flashes out at us from the pages of *Adir bamarom* in a strange description of the processes of *tsimtsum* and the breaking of the vessels[40] into which he has slipped a piece of

[35] *Kinat hashem tsevaot* (1888), 14, 15. And see I. Tishby, *Torat hara vehakelipah bekabalat ha'ar"i* (Jerusalem and Tel Aviv, 1942), 88 n. 1.

[36] It should be pointed out that in Luzzatto's works the idea of the descent of the Messiah to the husks is not tied to criticism of the Shabateans but is a basic element of all his books dealing with messianic subjects: *Megilat setarim verazin genizin* (Warsaw, 1889), *Ma'amar hage'ulah*, and *Adir bamarom*, as well as works which were hidden away and still exist only in manuscript. *Razin genizin*, consisting of cycles of discourses on verses of the Pentateuch and the Song of Songs in the language of the Zohar, is attributed on the title-page to R. Israel Hezekiah Treves, a pupil of Luzzatto, but I have no doubt that the printed text, which is very important for the doctrine of the Messiah in particular, is among the remnants of the works composed by Luzzatto at the behest of the *magid*.

[37] Zohar III, 279*a* (*Raya meheimna*).

[38] See G. Scholem, *Shabetai tsevi vehatenuah hashabeta'it bimei ḥayav* (Tel Aviv, 1957), i. 45, 49–50, 248–9. Luzzatto's opinion that the highest aspect of the Messiah's soul, the *yeḥidah*, is sunk among the husks is absolutely contrary to Lurianic kabbalah.

[39] See Scholem, *Shabetai tsevi*, i. 244–51; ii. 705–6.

[40] *Adir bamarom*, 189–208. The description is based on verses from the biblical account of the Creation and on the stories of the patriarchs. I will summarize one of the main points, the description of the *reshimu* or the *tehiru* in the space vacated by the *tsimtsum*. The space as it was

Shabatean theology in coded language, as I shall elaborate elsewhere. In that work[41] there is an allusion to the Messiah fighting with Satan, in the space vacated by the *tsimtsum*, in order to bring about the *tikun* of the *reshimu* [a residue of the divine light left behind in the primordial space], 'to restore it from its Satanic character to the character of the Messiah' in the mystical meaning of the verse 'The spirit of God hovered over the surface of the water'. This allusion is rooted in Nathan of Gaza's doctrine—which derives its support from the same verse—on the position of the Messiah's soul in the *tehiru* [the primordial space].[42]

Luzzatto made no attempt at all to deny or tone down the reality of the hold exercised by the husks on the soul of the Messiah. On the contrary, he taught explicitly that while the control of the husks over the Shekhinah was apparent rather than real, the soul of the Messiah was literally bound to their authority and its beauty was in fact marred. He wrote:[43]

> But indeed you need to know that all this is in regard to Malkhut, who appears on the face of it to have suffered injury, but this is not actually so, *but with regard to the Messiah it is really so*. Thus the Sitra Ahra laughs even at the Shekhinah, but in truth it is not as it appears to the Sitra Ahra, for they are mistaken in this, but as for the Messiah, it is really so, because he must indeed accept affliction in order to repair the faults of Israel. Hence 'his form, disfigured, lost the likeness of a man';[44] this surprising statement is not an empty figure of speech but a statement of the truth, for he is indeed disfigured, [that is] certain.

The position of the Messiah among the husks is described as 'like an armed man in the bowels of a lion',[45] a comparison which admirably fits the description of Shabetai Tsevi's position among the husks in Shabatean literature. The Shabatean source is also evident in the description of the Messiah's sufferings. What afflicts him most is that the light of the Torah is hidden from him and his intellectual grasp is reduced: 'And now I will tell you what is meant by the torments of the Messiah and the others who suffer illnesses: because of Israel's sins, the access to the bounty of the Torah to which their

before the entry of the 'straight line' of light is described as darkness where Satan dwelt. The *reshimu* in it is a mixture of good and evil in which the element of evil predominates, and therefore it partakes of the nature of Ur of the Chaldees, and the entry of the line into it is symbolized by the casting of Abraham into the fiery furnace. The work is full of surprising images and symbols like these, presented in a vague and confused fashion, and it is quite impossible to grasp their meaning except in the light of Nathan of Gaza's doctrine. See H. Wirszubsky, 'Hate'ologyah hashabeta'it shel natan ha'azati', *Keneset*, 8 (1944), 214–18, 227–31; Scholem, *Shabetai tsevi*, i. 242–4.

41 *Adir bamarom*, 192.

42 See G. Scholem, *Be'ikevot mashiaḥ* (Jerusalem, 1944), 17–19, 28, 99, 105.

43 *Kinat hashem tsevaot*, MS, fo. 246r.

44 Isa. 52: 14.

45 *Razin genizin*, 61. Cf. *Igerot*, i. 111.

rank would entitle them is diminished';[46] 'And the King-Messiah is in the tomb, of which it is said "His grave was made with the wicked"[47] in the mystery of the great concealment, so that even this access, in the mystery of *sekhel* ['intellect'] spelt with the left-hand letter *sin*,[48] is greatly reduced for him.'[49] Luzzatto here applies to the Messiah what was said in *Raya meheimna*[50] in relation to Moses in exile; such transferences are frequent in Shabatean literature.[51]

These descriptions in *Kinat hashem tsevaot* of the condition of the Messiah among the husks are such as to raise doubts whether the opinion expressed by Luzzatto at the beginning of his attack on the Shabateans—that the husks do not harm the Messiah's soul and that it does not need purification or correction as a result of its contact with them—reflected his genuine view or whether it was not simply advanced by way of polemic. These doubts are reinforced by an important statement on the falls [*nefilot*] endured by the Messiah, mystically understood as abortions [*nefel*], in a letter to R. Isaiah Bassano. Deriving his support from Lurianic kabbalah with regard to the sifting of the sparks, Luzzatto has this to say on the subject of the Messiah:[52]

Since, as we know, the King-Messiah is perpetually shut in by a tight seal, *it sometimes happens*, because of the sins of Israel, *that when he ascends to be purified and to be born* in the mystical meaning of 'I have this day given birth to you',[53] the Sitra Ahra is not willing to desist from shutting him in, *and then he must—Heaven forbid—fall again as he did before, and the husks are further strengthened, too*. You will understand, learned Sir, that this is a great and profound secret which I have disclosed to you, and you will realize that this was the source of many of the calamities decreed upon Israel, Heaven forbid, for the most part at a time intended for the coming of the Messiah, *for the impregnation* [*ha'ibur*] *occurred and then came the fall* [the abortion: *nefilah*]. But I cannot go much further into this even though these things are old; one should not say too much about them.

It was not for nothing that Luzzatto repeated his statement that this was a deep secret and should be kept hidden, for we have here a description of the Messiah among the husks which closely resembles Shabatean descriptions. The Messiah is a captive in the realm of the Sitra Ahra, 'shut in by a tight

46 *Kinat hashem tsevaot*, MS, fo. 241r.

47 Isa. 53: 9.

48 Luzzatto is here distinguishing between *sekhel* spelt with a 'left-hand' initial letter *sin* [שׂ], this being the degree of understanding during the exile, and the same word substituting a 'right-hand' letter [*shin* (שׁ)], which is the degree of understanding, derived from the hidden light, that the Messiah will be privileged to acquire at the time of the Redemption.

49 *Kinat hashem tsevaot*, MS, fo. 243v.

50 Zohar III, 125*b*, 280*a*, etc. See *Igerot*, i. 111.

51 See R. Jacob Sasportas, *Tsitsat novel tsevi*, ed. I. Tishby (Jerusalem, 1954), 260–2; H. Wirszubsky, 'Ha'ide'ologyah hashabeta'it shel hamarat-hamashiaḥ', *Zion*, 3 (1938), 230–3.

52 *Igerot*, ii. 224. On the Lurianic view of the purification of souls in the course of gestation, see Tishby, *Torat hara vehakelipah bekabalat ha'ar"i*, 124 n. 6.

53 Ps. 2: 7: 'I have this day begotten you.'

seal', and the husks acquire strength from their hold on his soul, which they defile. At appropriate moments, 'at a time intended for his coming', he tries to free himself and 'be purified', in the process of gestation in the Shekhinah, from the dross of defilement which clings to him, so that he may be born and fulfil his mission as redeemer of Israel. But because of Israel's sins the Sitra Ahra succeeds in seizing him, and he falls repeatedly, 'and the husks are further strengthened, too'. Thus, instead of redemption, calamities befall Israel. We have here the fall of the Messiah in the world of souls following the failure of the efforts at redemption on account of Israel's sins, paralleling the failure and fall of Shabetai Tsevi in this world.

A principal motif in Luzzatto's doctrine of the Messiah which is clearly coloured by Shabateanism is the description of the Messiah as a snake [*naḥash*] on the basis of the numerical equality in *gematriyah* of the two words [*mashiaḥ* and *naḥash* both equal 358—Trans.] and the explanation of his situation and actions in relation to the husks by the mystery of the changing of the staff into a snake and the snake into a staff. After examining the aspects of staff and snake in the state of Judgement [*din*] residing in the Shekhinah, which is symbolized by the letters *dalet* and *nun* in the name Adonai,[54] Luzzatto has this to say:[55]

> Against this [the situation where the Sitra Ahra gain the upper hand and the staff is turned into a snake—Trans.] there is the Messiah, and that is the *yeḥidah* which is made ready to crown the two Messiahs. This, too, belongs to the mystery of the staff . . . for in its place stands the Messiah, and by force of his authority he subdues the nations and raises up all the necessary *berurim* [sparks which he sifts out]; but when the staff is transformed *the Messiah too has the numerical value of naḥash*, a snake, *and the tikun is conveyed to him in a different way, in that he must go and clothe himself in the husks* and be confined to prison there, deprived of light and the divine flow, and those are the diseases which he bears.[56] And I say to you that that is what is meant by the statement that he sits at the gate of Rome;[57] and that is exactly what is meant by 'his grave was made with the wicked'[58] . . . and from there he sifts out the sparks which Israel needs.

Thus the soul of the Messiah operates in two ways in order to prepare the Redemption: in the mystical form of the staff when it is standing in its place and ruling from above over the Sitra Ahra and the enemies of Israel, and in the mystical form of the snake when it is among the husks and subjected to them. True, even in the capacity of a snake the Messiah performs *tikunim* to subdue evil: 'for the snake itself can be a good *tikun* by overturning evil; and know that the King-Messiah must stand in this relationship during the Exile, precisely in order to overturn evil so that it is below the good . . . It is in this

[54] See also *Razin genizin*, 76–7, 79.

[55] *Kinat hashem tsevaot* (1888), 19.

[56] [See Isa. 53: 4: 'he bore our diseases'.—Trans.]

[57] *San.* 98*a*.

[58] Isa. 53: 9.

regard that the King-Messiah must gather strength in this mystery of the snake which has the numerical value of *mashiaḥ*',[59] for even in the midst of the husks 'the King-Messiah, who stands in the mystical form of the snake, gathers strength in holiness and the Sitra Aḥra cannot detach him'.[60] But this *tikun* is not of a high order, because the Messiah suffers torments and his strength is sapped:

Now all this applies to the Messiah in his mystical capacity as the snake; in that capacity, while he is in exile, he binds the husks together [and places them] below holiness, and then he is said[61] to be 'free among the dead'; it is to this that Scripture alludes in the verse 'He has made me dwell in darkness like those who are long since dead',[62] but he has no power to perform a *tikun* by way of fulfilment of a commandment[63] but [only] by way of the Torah, of which it is said[64] 'And nothing is left except this Torah'.[65]

The transformation of the staff into a snake creates a dangerous situation, as is said in relation to Moses: 'But when he cast the staff to the ground and was no longer holding it, it reverted to its previous appearance and became a snake. Then Moses fled from it, for he saw that this made it a place of great danger; this refers to the breaking of the tablets when Moses cast them from his hands, for that is actually when there occurred the incident of the staff that turned into a snake.' The tablets were broken because the letters of the seventy-two-lettered Divine Name had left them, 'And when they depart, the Shekhinah descends to the lower world and there is death, *and thenceforward the Messiah is given this attribute of existing in the mystical character of a snake*.'[66] We see here that the transformation into a snake inflicts a grievous blemish, even a sort of death, on the Shekhinah and the Messiah. But with regard to the Shekhinah Luzzatto tried, in this matter as in his description of her descent to the husks,[67] to remove the blemish:

This secret is the staff [*mateh*] which turned into a snake, and they brought it about; but it was not, as the Sitra Aḥra thought, God's staff (Heaven forbid) that was turned into a snake, but the blemish was inflicted on the staff of a *mazeh* [a priest, 'one who sprinkles' water of purification: a play on the identical spelling in Exod. 4: 2 of *mazeh beyadekha*, 'What is this in your hand?'—Trans.] and thereby it was turned into a snake . . . but the holy Shekhinah is pure on all sides and no harm at all can reach there.[68]

[59] *Adir bamarom*, 192. [60] Ibid. 194. [61] Ps. 88: 6. [62] Lam. 3: 6.

[63] This reference to the mystery of the *mitsvah* is undoubtedly to be understood symbolically, as no *tikun* can take place through the fulfilment of practical commandments in the world of the souls.

[64] The *piyut Zekhor berit avraham* ['Remember the covenant with Abraham'] [see the Yom Kippur Ne'ilah (concluding) service—Trans.].

[65] *Adir bamarom*, 194. [66] *Kinat hashem tsevaot* (1888), 19–20.

[67] See above, text referring to n. 43. [68] *Razin genizin*, 66–7.

The case is different with the Messiah, on whose transformation into a snake Luzzatto expresses no reservations, leaving it to be understood that the injury is deserved.[69]

The description of the Messiah as a snake, in the sense of a holy snake which fights against the impure snake, is found in early sources,[70] but only in Shabateanism does it become a major principle linked to the descent of the Messiah to the husks. On the other hand the transformation of the staff into a snake is nowhere connected with the Messiah except in Shabatean literature.[71] In the Zohar it is Metatron who is transformed,[72] and in Lurianic kabbalah it is the husk Nogah,[73] not the Messiah. The main supporting evidence offered by Luzzatto[74] was the daring description in the Zohar of the Shekhinah and the Sitra Ahra joined to each other as the head and tail of the snake,[75] but it is clear that his true source is not that passage but the developed view which he found in Nathan of Gaza's doctrine of the Messiah, the 'inner substance' of which he absorbed. It will add emphasis to the Shabatean nature of this innovation if I quote one of the few references I have found in Lurianic kabbalah alluding to the transformation of the Messiah into a snake. In a homily on Samson there is a statement that Jacob, when he saw that he had fallen into sin, said 'For Your salvation I hope, O Lord', 'for [I hope] not in him *whom I thought to be the Messiah; he was transformed into a snake* [*mashiaḥ nehpakh lenaḥash*], for the numerical value in *gematriyah* [of

[69] In *Adir bamarom*, 192, in pointing to the numerical equivalence of *naḥash* and *mashiaḥ* ['snake' and 'Messiah'], Luzzatto also remarks on the equivalence in *gematriyah* of *satan* [359] and *mashiaḥ* [358 plus 1 for the word itself]: 'for in the external realm he becomes *satan* and in the internal realm he becomes *mashiaḥ*'. I have not found any source for the latter surprising piece of *gematriyah*. It is more daring than *mashiaḥ–naḥash*, since the Messiah as a snake can be depicted as 'the holy snake', whereas no such favourable interpretation is possible if he is cast as Satan. It is true that a contemporary of Shabetai Tsevi who knew him before 1665 preached a daring sermon on 'Satan in holiness'. See Scholem, *Shabetai tsevi*, i. 139. Together with the *gematriyah mashiaḥ* = *satan*, Luzzatto also gives *ya'akov* × 2 = *hasatan* [364]; this last I have found in R. Nathan Spira's *Megaleh amukot*, 'Vayishlaḥ'.

[70] See Scholem, *Shabetai tsevi*, i. 249 n. 1.

[71] See Scholem, *Be'ikevot mashiaḥ*, 65, 115–16, 124; G. Scholem, 'Perakim apokaliptiyim umeshiḥiyim al r' mordekhai me'aisenshtat', in *Sefer dinaburg* (Jerusalem, 1948), 253–4.

[72] See I. Tishby, *The Wisdom of the Zohar*, trans. D. Goldstein (Oxford, 1989), ii. 629. In *Tikunei hazohar*, ed. R. Margaliot (Tel Aviv, 1948), *tikun* 60 and others, this inversion was applied to everyone: when a man rules over the evil inclination the snake turns into a staff, when he submits to the evil inclination the staff turns into a snake. See Tishby, *Wisdom of the Zohar*, iii. 1429.

[73] R. Hayim Vital, *Ets ḥayim* (Korets, 1782), Gate 49, ch. 2 etc. And see Tishby, *Torat hara vehakelipah bekabalat ha'ar"i*, 69–72.

[74] *Adir bamarom*, 192–3, 197.

[75] Zohar III, 119*b*. And see Tishby, *Wisdom of the Zohar*, ii. 469. This passage is also cited in connection with the Messiah and the snake in R. Israel Hazan's *Perush mizmorei tehilim* (MS Jewish Theological Seminary, New York, Kaufmann 255, fo. 8^{v}, photo Schocken [Schocken Institute, Jerusalem]).

mashiaḥ and *naḥash*] is the same, and his feet were cut off'.[76] Here the change into a snake is given as the reason for the removal of the messiahship from Samson, whereas in Shabatean doctrine and in Luzzatto's writings the transformation is a *tikun* imposed on the Messiah as a messianic duty.

In the matters so far discussed I have dealt only with the Messiah ben David, but most of them also apply to Moses and the Messiah ben Joseph, who are his associates in the Redemption according to Luzzatto's view, and who, similarly, are described in Luzzatto's writings as fighting against the husks and active among them. Shabatean literature, too, speaks of the *tikunim* of Moses and the Messiah ben Joseph among the husks, but Moses appears there as identical with the Messiah ben David in the final Redemption,[77] and the Messiah ben Joseph, in general, appears as a hazy subsidiary figure.[78] Luzzatto, on the other hand, generally speaks of a messianic triad whose three members all occupy an important place; and in the context of the war against the husks he says many things about the Messiah ben Joseph which do not apply to the Messiah ben David and which are of great interest for the help they give in clarifying Luzzatto's attitude towards Shabateanism.

Out of the wealth of ideas on the functions of Moses in the final Redemption I propose to deal with only one point here. In a description of the special activity of Moses among the husks there is an image certainly drawn from a specific Shabatean source. The strength of the Messiah ben David, whose work of sifting the sparks while he is among the husks is conducted at an external level, is called *shevet* [another word for a staff—Trans.],

> but in the case of Moses, who is swallowed up among them, his sifting is done at an internal level, because his strength is called *meḥokek* [in the Pentateuch, a lawgiver, or his staff or sceptre, but the root *ḥ-k-k* means 'to engrave or hollow out'—Trans.]; for he is situated there *like a worm inside a fruit*, which eats what is found within it and leaves nothing of it but its husk; in the same way what Moses does inside the husks is *to hollow out* [Aramaic *leḥakaka*] *their insides*, [therefore] certainly *meḥokek* ['one who hollows out'].[79]

[76] R. Hayim Vital, *Sefer halikutim* (Jerusalem, 1913), Judges, 75*a*. And see ibid., Isaiah, 81*c*, in connection with Hezekiah. R. Israel Hazan's remarks, quoted by Scholem in *Shabetai tsevi*, ii. 745, are not, as Scholem thought, a Shabatean distortion of the midrash with regard to Samson's messiahship, for *Bereshit rabah* 98: 14 (numeration as in the Theodor–Albeck edn.) states explicitly that Jacob 'regarded him as the King-Messiah', but what Hazan says does distort the passage in *Sefer halikutim* relating to the Messiah and the snake.

[77] See Scholem, *Shabetai tsevi*, i. 247; ii. 629–30; Wirszubsky, 'Ha'ide'ologyah hashabeta'it shel hamarat-hamashiaḥ', 230–3.

[78] See G. Scholem, 'Perush mizmorei tehilim meḥugo shel shabetai tsevi be'adrianopol', in *Alei ayin: minḥat devarim lishelomoh zalman shoken aḥarei mele'ot lo shivim shanah* (Jerusalem, 1948–52), 175; Scholem, *Shabetai tsevi*, ii. 771–3. The only people who had much to say about him were Cardozo, who thought he was himself the Messiah ben Joseph, and those Shabatean scholars for whom Shabetai Tsevi had become the Messiah ben Joseph. See Scholem, 'Perakim apokaliptiyim umeshiḥiyim al r' mordekhai me'aisenshtat', 241–3.

[79] *Razin genizin*, 72.

This description first appears, in a slightly different form, in a work by R. Abraham Peretz of Salonika, a pupil of R. Nathan of Gaza, written to explain Shabetai Tsevi's actions after his conversion to Islam as hidden activity among the husks;[80] Luzzatto transferred the image from Shabetai Tsevi to Moses.

On the subject of the Messiah ben Joseph, Luzzatto repeatedly emphasizes that he is the leading character in the battle against the husks, and it is in him principally that the transformation into a snake occurs: 'And from then onwards this characteristic of appearing in the mystical capacity of a snake is given to the Messiah, *especially to the M*[essiah] *b*[en] *J*[oseph], who is the mystical embodiment of the left.'[81] Because his root is in the left, in the realm of strict judgement, he is exposed to grave danger by his contact with the Sitra Ahra, and suffers blemishes on many occasions in his vicissitudes in this world and in the descent of his soul to the husks. The main respects in which Luzzatto differed from the Shabateans' view of the Messiah concerned the restriction of the Messiah's contact with the husks to the world of the souls, and the inability of the husks to inflict any blemish on him or do him harm: Luzzatto regarded these limitations as inapplicable to the Messiah ben Joseph. Sometimes, too, the latter's image as portrayed by Luzzatto was very close to that of the Shabatean Messiah. We therefore need to examine in more detail the description of this messianic character in Luzzatto's writings.

The Messiah ben Joseph has a long pedigree, a history of alternations between misdeeds and rectification [*tikun*]. The first link in the chain is Adam's sin. Adam's duty was to join together the tree of knowledge and the tree of life, which mystically represent the realms of the exterior and the interior. But his sin widened the separation between them and put evil in control of the exterior. The exterior was quite literally blemished, and the interior too suffered from the separation. It was then that there was determined the manner of achieving *tikun* through the two Messiahs, who themselves bore the character of the exterior and interior: 'Since then the *tikun* has been prepared in the mystical mission of the two Messiahs . . . for the Messiah ben Joseph mystically represents the left, and he bears the character of the exterior *which needs all these tikunim*, and the Messiah ben David mystically represents the right which needs to be joined to it [to the left—Trans.], and the Redemption [will then be] complete.'[82] Thus the Messiah ben Joseph is blemished and subjected to the authority of the Sitra Ahra from the beginning of his hidden existence, because the root of his soul bears the character

[80] In *Igeret magen avraham me'erets hama'arav*, ed. G. Scholem (*Kovets al yad*, NS 2 (12); Jerusalem, 1937), 138, Shabetai Tsevi among the husks is described as being 'like a worm developing inside wood; on the outside the wood may be, to all appearances, sound and beautiful and strong, but when it is split open it is found to be all rotten and worm-eaten, as we know'.

[81] *Kinat hashem tsevaot* (1888), 20.

[82] Ibid. 20–1.

of the exterior, in the tree of the knowledge of good and evil.[83] The characteristics of the exterior and interior entered the world in Cain and Abel, but instead of *tikun*, 'there, too, things went wrong'.[84] Cain's sin led to the Messiah ben Joseph's having to turn into a snake to fight the Sitra Ahra: 'It is necessary that you should know that there is a great deal for the Messiah ben Joseph to do in regard to this matter, and this arose because of the mystical relationship to the left, that is, to Cain, for that is where the snake discharged its filth, *and he needs to cleanse himself of it* and thereby cleanse the world.'[85] The first task of the Messiah ben Joseph is to cleanse himself of the snake's filth which clings to him on account of Cain; only after his own *tikun* will he be able to cleanse the world and act as redeemer.[86]

The next stage of the attempt at *tikun* through the two Messiahs was with Joseph and Judah, through the agency of the matriarchs Leah and Rachel, who likewise represent the interior and exterior. The *tikun* was first hindered by the separation resulting from the sale of Joseph into slavery in Egypt. Taking advantage of the separation, the Sitra Ahra tried to sabotage the *tikun*, seeking to lead Joseph astray—Joseph being the mystical essence of the Messiah ben Joseph's messiahship—by tempting him into sin with Potiphar's wife. Joseph saved himself from committing the sin but stumbled in thought, which led to the involuntary emission of ten drops of semen. It was on account of these that the blemish was inflicted on the Messiah ben Joseph and he was condemned to death, '*for it was as Messiah ben Joseph that he was blemished* and he himself should have died after all'; but the decree was executed upon the ten martyrs,[87] 'all of whom go to make up this *tikun* of the Messiah ben Joseph'. Chief among them was 'R. A[kiva] ben Joseph, who was an aspect of Messiah ben Joseph himself'.[88] But between Joseph's downfall

[83] R. Hayim Vital, in *Likutei torah* (Vilna, 1880), end of 'Ezekiel', says: 'The Messiah ben David is from the side of the tree of life . . . but the Messiah ben Joseph is from the side of the tree of knowledge.'

[84] *Kinat hashem tsevaot* (1888), 21. Nehemiah Hayon, in his *Divrei neḥemyah* (Berlin, 1713), 4*a*, quotes Luria as saying that 'Messiah ben David was descended from Abel and Messiah ben Joseph from Cain', but I have failed to find this text in the Lurianic literature.

[85] *Kinat hashem tsevaot* (1888), 20. In the printed edition the text is incomplete and corrupt.

[86] On the two Messiahs in the character of Cain and Abel, and the bringing of the Redemption through the *tikun* of Cain by the Messiah ben Joseph, see *Razin genizin*, 67–8.

[87] The ten martyrs [enumerated in the Yom Kippur *piyut*, *Eleh ezkerah*—Trans.] are often linked with the sin of Joseph in Lurianic kabbalah. See [R. Hayim Vital's] complete *Sefer hagilgulim*, chs. 41–4.

[88] A passage in *Sefer hagilgulim*, ch. 41, and in *Sefer halikutim*, 'Vayeshev', 23*c–d*, says of R. Akiva that 'he was a spark of the Messiah', but appears to mean the Messiah ben David. That is also how the passage in question was understood by R. Israel Hazan, who took 'the declaration of the rabbi, may he be remembered for the life of the world to come', that R. Akiva was a spark of the Messiah and explained it as applying to Shabetai Tsevi. See Scholem, 'Perush mizmorei tehilim', 175. On the basis of the sources I have quoted, Scholem's remark (ibid.) that 'no

through sinful thought and R. Akiva's martyrdom some grievous sins were committed which increased the Messiah ben Joseph's burden of guilt. The sin of the golden calf by which Israel stumbled, after reaching the highest level of *tikunim* in the giving of the Torah, is connected with the Messiah ben Joseph; for the calf 'is the mystical representation of "the face of the ox on the left side"[89] which is the Messiah ben Joseph', and the sin of the golden calf was responsible for the most grievous misdeed in the incarnations of the Messiah ben Joseph—Jeroboam's sin, 'for afterwards came Jeroboam, *who himself was the Messiah ben Joseph*, and sinned against his mystical mission by making the calves'.[90]

Most of the items in this account are to be found as isolated ideas scattered through earlier sources,[91] but their concentration in the person of the Messiah ben Joseph and their combination into a running biography of his incarnations are innovations by Luzzatto. His purpose was simply to explain Jeroboam's sin and its connection with the Messiah ben Joseph, the same sin to which the Shabateans linked the mystery of Shabetai Tsevi's apostasy. At the beginning of his discussion of the Messiah ben Joseph, Luzzatto quoted the saying in *Raya meheimna*[92] that Jeroboam, by his sin, 'had to be profaned by idolatry,[93] he and [his] seed'. He added:

This saying is truly one to inspire fear, for it appears from it that had it not been for the sufferings of Moses *it would have been necessary for the Messiah ben Joseph to be profaned by idolatry*, and this provides an opportunity for heretics to gain the ascendancy: they would say that because the generations changed and behaviour varied according to the actions of people in this world the sufferings of Moses were not enough, so that finally the thing had to be done by Shabetai Tsevi. Such words are certainly false and misleading because they are against the Torah of Moses, but at any rate we do need to explain the true meaning of what was said by R. Simeon bar Yohai, of blessed memory.[94]

such statement exists in the name of Luria or Vital' needs correction. In the teachings of Nathan of Gaza I have found a statement that 'his [R. Akiva's] soul is the soul of the Messiah ben Joseph'. See Scholem, *Be'ikevot mashiaḥ*, 44–5. Perhaps the source is R. Menahem Azariah da Fano's *Kanfei yonah* (Korets, 1786), i, ch. 3, where it is said that R. Akiva 'was [i.e. would have been] the Messiah ben Joseph of that generation if they had deserved it'.

89 Ezek. 1: 10.

90 *Kinat hashem tsevaot* (1888), 21–2.

91 See nn. 83, 84, 87, 88 above.

92 Zohar III, 276*b*.

93 Later editions of the Zohar have the abbreviation *be'aku"m*, literally 'by the worship of stars and planets', but in the first editions, those of Mantua and Cremona, the text reads *be'a"z* [as quoted in the Hebrew text of Tishby's essay], literally 'by foreign worship'. Apparently Nathan of Gaza had not read the latter version, which better fits the Shabatean purpose of demonstrating a mystical link between Shabetai Tsevi's apostasy and this passage; witness the addition in his quotations of the expression 'among the nations'.

94 *Kinat hashem tsevaot* (1888), 20.

Luzzatto explains the influence of Jeroboam's sin on the fate of the Messiah ben Joseph as founded on Jeroboam's messiahship:

Know that all these things that we say about Jeroboam or about any of the others who are said to be the Messiah ben Joseph are not said with regard to the *yeḥidah* itself, which is not put into the man who is worthy of it until the *tikun* is complete . . . but it is upon the roots of the souls [*neshamot*] which are fit and ready to be redeemers in their generation that the *yeḥidah* which rests upon and crowns the Messiahs comes to rest, so that *when we say of Jeroboam that he is the Messiah ben Joseph*, we mean the root which was truly the one worthy that this *yeḥidah* should rest upon it; it is called, as it were, a branch of it [of the *yeḥidah*], for it is its instrument. And it was this [root] that had to clothe itself in a Gentile body as was said above,[95] in the same way as Jeroboam clothed holiness in defilement by making the calves, because of which R. Akiva and his colleagues had to be handed over to death. It is, indeed, certain that this is a blemish which affects the root itself because its instrument is thus blemished, and correspondingly he, too [Messiah ben Joseph], had to be defiled, Heaven forbid, by the Sitra Ahra.[96]

Hence the soul of the Messiah ben Joseph is active in this world before the Redemption and is liable to suffer blemish. This does not apply to the *yeḥidah* itself—we have learnt to the contrary in relation to the Messiah ben David—but the blemish inflicted on the soul that is worthy of the messiahship affects the *yeḥidah* too, because the soul is, as it were, an instrument and branch of the *yeḥidah*. Therefore even at the time of the Redemption the Messiah ben Joseph, as the Messiah in actual possession of the *yeḥidah*, would necessarily be defiled by Jeroboam's sin.

In this passage Luzzatto does not differentiate between Jeroboam and 'all the others who are said to be the Messiah ben Joseph', those whom he goes on to call 'the men of the messiahship' who 'are always found in every generation'. But in fact Jeroboam's messianic status differs from that of the other 'men of the messiahship'. In explaining the expression in the Zohar that 'he and his seed' had to be defiled, Luzzatto declares that Joseph is *sod hameshiḥut*, the mystical embodiment of the messiahship, and that Ephraim and his descendants, the seed of Joseph, are the various incarnations of the men of the messiahship. Basing himself on this distinction, he writes:[97]

Because of Jeroboam's sin, he and his seed, being the two aspects, the messiahship and the souls of the messiahship, should have been defiled by idolatry . . . and I tell you *that Jeroboam was already prepared for, and close to receiving, the messiahship*, though he had not yet received it, but because he was close to doing so the souls of

[95] Luzzatto had previously explained that 'the holy soul of Jeroboam which departed from him when he sinned had been required to be clothed in a Gentile body and afterwards to leave that body and enter a Jewish one; the Gentile was R. Akiva's father, on leaving whom it entered R. Akiva's body, and there it was restored to its perfect state [*nitkenah*]'.

[96] *Kinat hashem tsevaot* (1888), 22.

[97] *Kinat hashem tsevaot*, MS, fo. 227^{r-v}.

Joseph and Joseph's son Ephraim joined him as is necessary for whoever earns the privilege of receiving the messiahship. However, because, meanwhile, he had brought a blemish upon himself, *they, too, became blemished, and then, Heaven forbid, all should have been defiled, the messiahship and its branches*, but the power of Moses' sufferings mended matters so that this would not happen but the messiahship would be saved and, for the seed, there would be the matter of R. Akiva ben Joseph which I have mentioned, and that would suffice.

Hence Jeroboam had already actually attained the level of Redeemer and been joined by the soul of Joseph, who was 'the mystical embodiment of the messiahship', and therefore his failure would necessarily have involved the defilement of the Messiah ben Joseph by idolatry.

A passage which, in the printed version, is in part omitted and in part corrupt, clarifies the nature of the defilement for which the Messiah ben Joseph had been destined: *he should have been defiled by Christianity*:

If he [the Messiah ben Joseph], Heaven forbid, had been defiled, as should have been the consequence of Jeroboam's sin, this would have been a great disgrace, because *that man* was condemned [to be plunged] into boiling excrement, which was the foulest filth in the husk, and if the Messiah ben Joseph had had to be defiled he would have had to clothe himself there, Heaven forbid,[98] *in such a way that the Nazarene*[99] *himself would acquire some power from his action in clothing himself*, and then he [Jesus] would have come and clothed himself in the wicked Armilus in time to come, and by the power he had acquired from this action he would have done wonderful things in the world as Jeroboam's calf had said.[100] This would have been an exceedingly great disgrace and an unparalleled sorrow, Heaven forbid, for Israel; and the Messiah ben Joseph himself after receiving the messiahship would have had to die, in order to set this matter right, through Armilus himself who would have come in his strength. And this, too, would have been a desecration for him . . . but the strength of the torments suffered by Moses prevented the Messiah ben Joseph from being thus defiled, and so the blemish remained only in the instrument of the messiahship, namely the soul of Jeroboam himself. For this reason R. Akiva and his

[98] From the context it appears that not only was the soul of the Messiah ben Joseph obliged to clothe itself in the husk of Jesus, but in this world, too, he [the Messiah ben Joseph] had to be defiled by engaging in 'foreign worship' [see n. 93 above] in Christianity. Nathan of Gaza taught that the soul of Shabetai Tsevi was clothed in the husk of Jesus of Nazareth, but 'he would bring about his *tikun*'. See Scholem, *Shabetai tsevi*, i. 231–2, 247, 252. Luzzatto describes the donning of the husk of Jesus as a dreadful defilement for which the Messiah had been marked out without any mission to bring about *tikun*.

[99] The Hebrew word *notseri* ['Nazarene'] is deleted in the manuscript, and in the margin the consonants *tet he gimel mem* are substituted; this is a transcription into the code known as *atbash* (*alef* for *tav*, *beit* for *shin*, etc.). Similar coded substitutions occur elsewhere in the manuscript, especially in the polemic against Christianity.

[100] Luzzatto, basing himself on *San.* 107*b*, had earlier declared that 'Jeroboam's calf said "I am the Lord your God" '.

colleagues died, but the messiahship itself will not be profaned and the Messiah ben Joseph will be saved from death.[101]

However, the death of R. Akiva and his colleagues did not wipe out the blemish in 'the instrument of the messiahship', and the soul of the Messiah ben Joseph must transmigrate and suffer in every generation in 'the men of the messiahship'. The nature of his transmigrations and sufferings is explained in a letter from Luzzatto to his teacher:[102]

> But the portion which falls to the Messiah ben Joseph is that he [must] clothe himself completely in all those souls which are worthy to be the Messiah ben Joseph, so, however, that it [his soul] lacks all power to act, and thereby suffers all those deaths, unlike the Messiah ben David. And the essence of his suffering is the lack of strength, for all the [exalted] levels are present in that man but they are altogether hidden and he is quite without strength . . . The Messiah ben Joseph should have received the light of the Torah in great abundance, but since he is shut off only a little light reaches him.

The sufferings of the Messiah ben Joseph are the very sufferings of the Messiah ben David's *yeḥidah* among the husks, the lack of strength and the diminished light of the Torah, and Luzzatto himself in this passage points out the parallel and the difference: 'But the Messiah ben David, too, suffers illnesses, but in a different way, not in this world but above.' Thus the sufferings of the Messiah ben Joseph in his transmigrations, too, are caused by the husks laying hold of his soul in every generation.

We do, indeed, read in other writings [by Luzzatto] of the Messiah fighting in the depths of the husks and needing to be cleansed of the filth that sticks to him. Luzzatto uses this mystical approach to explain the birth of Jacob as relating to the Messiah ben Joseph:[103]

> And afterwards Messiah ben Joseph comes forth, his hand grasping Esau's heel; the Sitra Ahra has a hold on the heels of holiness at the lower levels, and accordingly *the Messiah ben Joseph must go into all parts of the husk, even the heels*, to extract every good part of it, for which reason 'his hand grasps the heel of Esau', *and that is the underlying meaning of 'on the heels of the Messiah'*,[104] that it is necessary to subdue these heels.

The Messiah ben Joseph *exercises cunning in his fight against the Sitra Ahra and uses flattery* in order to get the sparks out of their possession: 'And the Messiah who sees that [the Sitra Ahra] has this prize which he seeks, some

[101] *Kinat hashem tsevaot* (1888), 22; in the manuscript, fo. 227^r.

[102] *Igerot*, i. 84. For the source of the idea that the Messiah ben Joseph is reincarnated in every generation and suffers martyrdom repeatedly, see Scholem, *Shabetai tsevi*, i. 44–5.

[103] *Megilat setarim*, 7.

[104] [This seems to be a literal understanding of the words *be'ikevot mashiaḥ*, 'on the advent of the Messiah', in Mishnah *Sot.* 9: 15.—Trans.]

lights of holiness, *approaches him with flattery* in accordance with the verse "with the crooked you are devious"[105] in order to recover these sparks, but the Shekhinah is there watching over him to see that nothing untoward happens to him and he does not fall into their hands, Heaven forbid.' Earlier in the same document Rebecca's pregnancy is explained as a reference to the purification of the Messiah ben Joseph in the process of conception in the Shekhinah: 'Because the Messiah had been inside the husk he had to be carried in the womb in order to repel a kind of darkness that clung to him.'[106] There is no mention here of the Messiah ben Joseph's transmigrations, and it is therefore impossible to determine from the context whether the reference to his war with the husks relates to this world or to the world of the souls, but on the basis of what we learn from *Kinat hashem tsevaot*, as well as from indications in other works which I cannot go into here, it may be assumed that what is meant is war and defilement in this world.

I have dealt at some length with the topic of the Messiah ben Joseph because it again makes it clear, and if anything even clearer, that the very passages in which Luzzatto dissociates himself from Shabateanism conceal evidence of his affinity to it and his absorption of its doctrine. The portrayal of the Messiah ben Joseph in Luzzatto's writings resembles in major outlines that of Shabetai Tsevi in Shabatean literature: a blemished soul which has transmigrated successively into many notable persons and has experienced torments, temptations, and failures;[107] he has been condemned to profanation by idolatry;[108] his war against the Sitra Ahra is waged in the depths of the abyss, where he carries out the *tikun* involving the heels;[109] he fights with cunning and flattery, i.e. to all appearances adapting himself to the husks;[110] he is turned into a snake and the filth of the husks sticks to him. It is true that *Kinat hashem tsevaot* adds an important distinction which turns the whole matter on its head from a practical point of view, namely that unlike Shabetai Tsevi the Messiah ben Joseph is saved from the defilement which was to have been his lot, but so far as ideas are concerned the features the two have in common are unaffected.

It appears that the central motif here, *the messiahship of Jeroboam*, is also derived from a Shabatean source. My efforts have failed to find in any Lurianic source the daring idea that Jeroboam was actually the Messiah ben Joseph and that only his sin prevented his messiahship from being realized. Even in the Shabatean writings so far published or studied there is no mention of this. The idea has its roots in an opinion common in Lurianic litera-

[105] Ps. 18: 27.
[106] See also *Razin genizin*, 108–9.
[107] See Scholem, *Shabetai tsevi*, i. 231–2; ii. 688–9; Scholem, 'Perush mizmorei tehilim', 175.
[108] See pp. 240–1 above.
[109] See Scholem, *Shabetai tsevi*, i. 244–5, 259.
[110] See ibid. ii. 686–7, 734–40.

ture and based on the Zohar[111] that the holy soul which departed from Jeroboam because of his sin entered his son Abijah and was destined to become the soul of the Messiah ben Joseph. The most extreme version that I have found states that in time to come 'Jeroboam will undergo *tikun* [i.e. his imperfection will be corrected] and he will be the Messiah ben Joseph',[112] but this is still a long way from ascribing the messiahship to Jeroboam in his lifetime. I have, though, found the subject dealt with in a Shabatean work composed by a member of a circle close to Luzzatto: the responsa of R. Elijah Mojajon of Ancona to R. Benjamin Hakohen on questions of Shabatean kabbalah.[113] In one of the responsa (fos. 5^r–6^r) the sins of Solomon in marrying foreign wives, and the sins of idolatry of the kings of Israel and Judah, Jeroboam, Ahab, and Manasseh, are explained as a failure in the act of *tikun* the Messiah was required to perform, in that they planned to destroy the Sitra Ahra by cramming it with sins to increase its size until it burst from superabundance. The explanation is built entirely on remarks by Nathan of Gaza in the homily *Raza demalka meshiḥa*, of which we have only extracts preserved in manuscript.[114] I reproduce below a paragraph, important for our present purpose, the substance of which is explicitly credited to R. Nathan:

You, Sir, already know our teacher and master R. Nathan's explanation *that no one who is a king can* [endure] *if there is no spark of the King-Messiah*[115] *in him*. Now the

111 *Zohar ḥadash*, ed. R. Margaliot (Jerusalem, 1953), end of 'Balak'.

112 The kabbalist R. Nathan Spira's *Megaleh amukot* on 'Va'etḥanan', *ofan* ['wheel'] 155. In *ofan* 252 of that work, the author writes that 'Jeroboam in *gematriyah* equalled *merkavah teme'ah* ['impure chariot'], [which was the same as] *kelev ra* ['wicked dog']' [all three having the numerical value 322—Trans.], and the spark of holiness in him was given to Abijah, 'who was the Messiah ben Joseph'. The complete *Sefer hagilgulim*, ch. 67, says: 'Jeroboam's soul, which fled from him before he sinned, will in time to come transmigrate into the Messiah ben Ephraim', the soul in question being the one which entered Jeroboam's son Abijah. There is indeed an allusion in the writings of R. Menahem Azariah da Fano to Jeroboam as a candidate for the messiahship in his lifetime, but the reference there is to the role for which he had been destined before the division of the kingdom: *Em kol ḥai*, iii, sect. 10: 'The Holy One, blessed be He, sought to make him [Rehoboam] the Messiah, with Jeroboam as his deputy.' And see *Ḥikur din*, iv, chs. 16–17. These two works could have served as a source for the alteration in the character of the Messiah ben Joseph as seen by the Shabateans, who turned him into a sort of viceroy to the King-Messiah. See Scholem, *Shabetai tsevi*, ii. 773. Apparently R. Mordecai Eisenstadt's promise to R. Abraham Rovigo similarly related to the position of the Messiah ben Joseph as viceroy.

113 MS Guenzburg 517 (Moscow), from a photograph in the Ben Tsevi Institute in Jerusalem. These responsa by Mojajon are very important for the development of the Shabatean kabbalah of Nathan of Gaza's school.

114 See G. Scholem, 'Te'udot shabeta'iyot ḥadashot mis' "to'ei ruaḥ"', *Zion*, 7 (1942), 183–5. From the passage reproduced here it is clear that the book is entitled *Raza demalka meshiḥa* and not *Raza dema'aseh merkavah* [which has the same initial letters—Trans.]. See Scholem, *Shabetai tsevi*, ii. 693 n. 3. The work is referred to by its correct name ibid. 246 n. 3.

115 The manuscript abbreviates to *mem-he* (*melekh hamashiaḥ*).

kings of Israel and Manasseh wanted the *tikun* to be effected by them *because there was a root of the King-Messiah in them*, and, wishing to be like him, they entered a husk to perfect it so that it should afterwards be broken open and all would be set right [*yetukan*]. Now Jeroboam entered there and, once in, he could not get out because it was not yet time, and he remained there.

Similarly with Ahab and Manasseh. 'You will find the account of this mystery, Sir, in the treatise *Raza demalka meshiḥa* which was composed by our teacher and master, R.N.'[116] At the end of this explanation there is an indirect reference to the subject which is our main concern: 'But after Solomon the mystical embodiment of Joseph took his [Solomon's] place, for, *as you already know, Jeroboam was the mystical embodiment of the Messiah ben Joseph*, and a word to the wise . . .'. The remark 'as you already know' here alludes no doubt to a previous responsum or some other Shabatean source in the hands of R. Benjamin Hakohen where the mystery was further explained. Probably, too, Luzzatto's disclosure as 'a great, great secret that *Jeroboam clothed holiness in the Sitra Ahra* by his worship'[117] was a reference to the Shabatean mystical aim of destroying the world of uncleanness by introducing an excess of holiness into it.

Finally it should be emphasized that in his interpretation of the ancient sources Luzzatto followed in the footsteps of Shabatean exegesis. If he had not accepted the interpretations of Nathan of Gaza and his colleagues, who saw allusions everywhere to the descent of the Messiah to the husks, he could have disposed of most of the difficulties without complications and forced explanations. Here are some examples of the strong influence of Shabatean interpretation on Luzzatto. The verse 'the spirit of God hovered over the surface of the water'[118] is explained as alluding to the soul of the Messiah among the husks.[119] The description of the servant of the Lord in Isaiah 52–3, which Shabatean theologians saw as mirroring the image of Shabetai Tsevi,[120] is applied by Luzzatto in many of his writings to the Messiah among

[116] Several passages in the full text of the discourse, which I cannot reproduce here, show clearly that this composition by Nathan of Gaza was the source of Nehemiah Hayon's homily in his *Divrei neḥemyah*, 81*a*–82*a*, quoted by G. Scholem in 'Mitsvah haba'ah ba'averah', *Keneset*, 2 (1937), 375–7. The idea at the end of Hayon's discourse on the penitent is present in a passage from the same composition by Nathan reproduced in a Shabatean anthology in notebook form (MS Columbia University, X893/Z8, vol. i, no. 20, fo. 2^r, photo Scholem). Similarly, the remarks of R. Elijah Hakohen of Smyrna—the Shabatean nature of which has already been dealt with by G. Scholem—on the sins of the kings of Israel are drawn from this source. See G. Scholem, 'R' eliyahu hakohen ha'itamari vehashabeta'ut', in S. Lieberman (ed.), *Alexander Marx: Jubilee Volume on the Occasion of his Seventieth Birthday*, Hebrew vol. *Sefer hayovel likhevod aleksander marks* (New York, 1950), 459–61.

[117] *Kinat hashem tsevaot* (1888), 22.

[118] Gen. 1: 2.

[119] *Adir bamarom*, 192; *Igerot*, i. 122. See p. 232 above, text between references to nn. 41 and 42.

[120] See Scholem, *Shabetai tsevi*, ii. 689–90.

the husks[121] and, using Nathan of Gaza's typological method of interpretation, he adds Jonah in the sea to the series of characters who symbolize the Messiah sunk in the abyss of the husks. 'Truly many of the most important of these matters are contained in the prophecy of Isaiah ch. 53 in the verse [actually 52: 13—Trans.] "Behold, my servant shall prosper", and also in the prayer of Jonah when he is in the sea, *which is the selfsame matter as the Messiah in the midst of the husks.*'[122] A clear illustration of Luzzatto's attitude, showing him interpreting the Zohar in the spirit of Shabatean exegesis, is provided by the following polemical introduction:[123]

The second passage is in the same chapter in *Raya meheimna* 282*a*, where it says: 'The wicked servant-girl is a grave and in it she imprisons her mistress' etc., *from which it would appear that this is how it must be for the Messiah, who is mystically equated with the Shekhinah*:[124] he must clothe himself in a husk, that is, *in Shabetai which is the husk Ishmael*, and this is an allusion to the diminished state of the moon as explained in that passage; but the edifice collapses of itself because of what I have told you, namely that everything said here relates only to the soul of the Messiah and not to the body of the man who is worthy to be the Messiah.

This passage in the Zohar contains no reference to the Messiah but deals entirely with the exile of the Shekhinah. The plain meaning of the text, according to which Shabetai [Saturn] is Lilith, has nothing to do with the husk Ishmael, but since Luzzatto accepted the Shabatean interpretation which departs from the plain meaning,[125] he had to shelter behind his expressed reservation that the words were meant to apply to the soul of the Messiah in the upper world.

[121] See *Razin genizin*, 72–8, a series of homilies on 'Behold, my servant shall prosper'.

[122] *Kinat hashem tsevaot*, MS, fo. 240^r.

[123] Ibid., fo. 228^r.

[124] It is very common to find the Messiah placed at the level of the Shekhinah in Shabatean literature. See Scholem, 'Perush mizmorei tehilim', 182–3, 185, 192–5, 200–2, 204; *Shirot vetishbaḥot shel hashabeta'im*, ed. M. Attias and G. Scholem (Tel Aviv, 1948), 32, 34, 35, 49, etc. This, again, is a teaching which issued from Nathan of Gaza. In the notebook collection referred to in n. 116 above there is a quotation attributed to *Raza demalka meshiḥa* which reads as follows: 'The King-Messiah is Malkhut, the uppermost degree of the world of emanation . . . he is the Shekhinah herself' (MS Columbia University, X893/Z8, fo. 10^v), and the same idea recurs ibid., fos. 14^r and 21^r. Nathan took as his authority the Zohar I, 238*a*; II, 127*b*. And see Wirszubsky, 'Ha'ide'ologyah hashabeta'it shel hamarat-hamashiaḥ', 232; Ya'el Nadav, 'Rabi shelomo ailyon vekunteresav bekabalah shabeta'it', in I. Ben-Zvi and M. Benayahu (eds.), *Sefer hayovel lishene'ur zalman shazar/Shneur Zalman Shazar Jubilee Volume* (= *Sefunot*, 3–4) (Jerusalem, 1959–60), 324–5.

[125] See Wirszubsky, 'Ha'ide'ologyah hashabeta'it shel hamarat-hamashiaḥ', 230–1.

C. THE MYSTERY OF SIN FOR A HOLY PURPOSE [*AVERAH LISHEMAH*]

Luzzatto's outlook on the commission of sins for the sake of *tikun* will occupy no more than a short section, but is very important and most instructive. We find ourselves here, beyond the limited and speculative area of messianic doctrine, in the realm of practical Shabateanism, which embarked on a wide-ranging attempt to undermine the foundations of the Jewish religion and Jewish ethics.

After condemning the Shabateans for turning sins for the sake of *tikun* into virtuous acts [*mitsvot*], since 'it is impossible for a sin to be a *mitsvah*', Luzzatto quotes a famous saying which, on the face of it, supports Shabatean lawlessness:

> It is true that there is one saying by our rabbis, of blessed memory, which seems to us like a very serious difficulty, namely their observation with regard to Jael[126] that 'greater is a sin for a holy purpose than a *mitsvah* which is not for a holy purpose'. If so, it is possible for a fault to be a *tikun*, but you need to understand that there are many distinctions to be drawn in this, and anyone who considers it with less than hair's-breadth precision is likely to fall into deep pits, Heaven forbid.[127]

The distinctions are illustrated by the actions of Esther and Jael. Both actions are connected with the exile of the Shekhinah, but 'Esther acted under compulsion [*ones*], and Jael's action was a sin for a holy purpose'.

Esther's action is explained as an event symbolizing the condition of the Shekhinah during its exile. Just as Esther was enslaved to Ahasuerus, but when he sought to have intercourse with her by force a she-devil came and took her place[128] so that she was not sullied, so too the Shekhinah, who is delivered into the hands of Sama'el, is protected from the filth which he seeks to cast upon her by intercourse, 'and this is called *ones* ['rape, compulsion'], which the Sitra Ahra wishes to force upon her but fails to do'. On the other hand Jael copulates with Sisera of her own free will for the sake of *tikun* in order to draw the Sitra Ahra away from the Shekhinah and prevent it from interfering with the celestial intercourse of the Shekhinah with her husband Ze'ir Anpin:

> In any event [the celestial couple] were stirred to union [*yiḥud*] and the Sitra Ahra did not lay hold on holiness in the upper world, but on the contrary she [Jael], by

126 *Naz.* 23*b*.

127 *Kinat hashem tsevaot* (1888), 17. All the passages quoted below are from that work, pp. 17–18. There are also passages in Luzzatto's other writings and in those of members of his group which are relevant to the question of sinning for the sake of *tikun*, but I have not the space to deal with them here.

128 See Zohar III, 276*a* (*Raya meheimna*).

force of her *tikunim* and her merit, took this matter upon herself so that she herself gained no pleasure, as is written in the Talmud,[129] because he cast filth upon her but the sanctuary on high remained holy and the impulse to union was aroused there.

According to this explanation Jael's action does indeed show that *a fault can be a tikun* and a sin can be a virtuous act. What, then, is Luzzatto's complaint against the Shabateans? The answer is that Jael's action was 'the mystery of *hora'at sha'ah*', a decision dictated by the exigencies of the hour, and therefore 'it cannot be repeated, but one may do it only once and then immediately return to the observance of all the commandments . . . but it should not be possible to change the prescribed order, for that would be called an alteration of the Torah, which cannot be altered under any circumstances'. Hence 'you will know and understand how false and deceitful is the edifice of these sins, a bait laid by the accuser who lies in wait with his yoke for the hearts of the simpletons who forget God,[130] [causing them] to transgress contemptuously every law and judgement, not for one day or two, nor for a month, but for "all the days of [their] empty lives" etc.' Another reservation by Luzzatto is that

> all that I have said can only apply to females, who are passive recipients [*karka olam*, 'ground in its natural state'] in whom there exists the matter I have mentioned, but it cannot apply to males, *since for them a forbidden union is no tikun at all*, but the righteous man must beware of the Gentile woman and draw back and not be contaminated; and even as regards all the other commandments which are of less weight than the prohibition of such a union the rein is not relaxed so as to permit them to be altered, Heaven forbid, except where *the dictates of the hour* require an alteration appropriate to the situation.

From the negative statement we can deduce the positive: *the sin of a forbidden union can serve as tikun for females, and other transgressions can do so for males too, where required by hora'at sha'ah, the dictates of the hour.*

This is a most surprising attitude to find in an anti-Shabatean composition, all the more so when we know that even the reservation as to 'the dictates of the hour' is contained in the writings of Nathan of Gaza, who sheltered behind that reservation to justify the transgressions of Shabetai

[129] *Naz.* 23*b*.

[130] In the manuscript there are two interesting deletions at this point. After the word 'God' the following was written and then crossed out: 'for even if a *tikun* were found to exist in a sin committed for a holy purpose [*lishemah*] the strap would not be loosened [i.e. the restraint would not be removed]'. Above the deleted line was written: 'It must be observed that the statement which praised the commission of a sin for a holy purpose as being at the dictates of the hour did not on that account make it legally permissible', and these words too were crossed out. These efforts at modifying the draft, which were ultimately dropped altogether, testify to the author's anxiety to avoid expressly admitting the possibility of *tikun* through sin committed for a holy purpose. It is probable that the words were written and deleted on the personal instructions of Luzzatto.

Tsevi:[131] '*There is no limit to the number of commandments which can be nullified by reason of hora'at sha'ah*; therefore anyone who believes in the King-Messiah should not question how he can be the Messiah when he commits a number of transgressions and a number of other people act on what he says, *because he can reply that it is hora'at sha'ah*.' Further on Nathan is so bold as to use the principle of *hora'at sha'ah* even to justify mass apostasy at the command of the Messiah.[132] It is true that extreme Shabateans no longer relied on *hora'at sha'ah* but actually reached the point of permitting transgressions 'all the days of their empty lives', but it is clear that Luzzatto's attempt to justify 'transgressions for the sake of *tikun*' by bringing them within the dispensation of *hora'at sha'ah* was a broken reed, a weak defence intended to distance its author from the Shabatean heresy.

The truth of the matter is that Luzzatto went beyond the bounds of 'the dictates of the hour' and opened the way to forbidden unions by females as an obligatory *tikun*. In explaining the principle of *averah lishemah*, transgression for a holy purpose, in relation to Jael 'so that she should not, Heaven forbid, make the mistake of these simpletons who stray from following the Lord to pursue licentiousness', he wrote:

Know that the beginning of corruptness was the snake's copulation with Eve when he cast filth on her, because of which she afterwards descended into the midst of the husks as mentioned above. Now this blemish cannot be repaired except in the manner referred to in the scriptural verse 'The women will be violated'.[133] It means that *in the end this matter must be* [dealt with] *in this world, that the sinner must bear his sin and* [thereupon] *the blemish departs from the root, for in the world above the snake is in constant pursuit because of this, and when he is given, in the world below, a share in Israel who have sinned, he will complete the accusation in the world above*, and much great suffering will be caused to the holy women, the women of Israel, who will be obliged to endure this bad business. And you will see that the beginning of the corruption was 'They raped women in Zion',[134] and *therefore the end of the sifting will be 'and the women will be violated'*. But know that even this suffering cannot occur except at the very end, when the *tikun* is about to be completed, as is said in relation to that time: 'She laughs at the last day',[135] for the strength is already great *and that deed causes no blemish above but, on the contrary, effects tikun*. And I will tell you how it effects *tikun*: by this deed those impure creatures will receive all the filth remaining from the beginning, whereas all the good they contain will go out of them and be taken into holiness. And the mystery of all this is that the Sitra Ahra must be given its due share, but *in order for tikun to take place it must be done here below and not on high*.

[131] Wirszubsky, 'Ha'ide'ologyah hashabeta'it shel hamarat-hamashiaḥ', 233.

[132] Ibid. 233–4. And see ibid. 226. Even before the apostasy, R. Jacob Sasportas had protested against the resort to 'the dictates of the hour' to justify Shabetai Tsevi's 'strange deeds'. See *Tsitsat novel tsevi*, ed. Tishby, 118, 150, 165.

[133] Zech. 14: 2.

[134] Lam. 5: 11.

[135] Prov. 31: 25, rendered literally.

This paragraph, which exhibits all the ingredients of typical Shabatean paradox, presents, in a quiet and straightforward style, a principled justification for declaring sexual transgressions holy, and even for regarding sin in general as holy. The subject it considers is Jael's giving herself to Sisera, and therefore the discussion is limited to sins of unchastity by females, but the principle that 'the Sitra Ahra must be given its due share' and that for the benefit of the *tikun the gift of transgressions* must be made 'below and not on high' can apply to any sin at all according to whatever may be required for the *tikun*, and so an opening is provided for the most far-reaching inversion of values. Such a statement could well have been written in the school of Nathan of Gaza, and even extreme Shabateans could have prided themselves on having composed it.

True, Luzzatto hedged this doctrine about with a number of limitations: 'But this is the point, that it will not be able to succeed even *by way of punishment*, as I have said, except *at the end of the tikun* when it is about to be completed, and in the sense that it should be done with all these safeguards and *tikunim*, and nevertheless only *in accordance with the dictates of the hour* and not for any regular rule of conduct based on it, Heaven forbid.' However, these limitations have not much force. Actions which are essential for the completion of the *tikun*, because that is how 'the end of the sifting' must be, are undoubtedly not in the category of the dictates of the hour in the literal sense of that term. By the words 'by way of punishment' Luzzatto apparently meant that the *tikun* would be effected through the rape of 'the women of Israel' by Gentiles, but the explanation is linked specifically to Jael, who did not act under compulsion as Esther did but voluntarily committed a transgression for a holy purpose; and where 'punishment' and compulsion apply to the circumstances there is no point in requiring 'that it should be done with all these safeguards and *tikunim*'. As for the restriction to 'the end of the *tikun*', which is emphasized in the body of the text also, this again is not a genuine limitation, because the Shabateans, and Luzzatto too, regarded their time as the end of days, i.e. the period of 'the end of the *tikun*'.

It need hardly be said that if such a document had fallen into the hands of people like Hagiz and Emden who were on the lookout for damning evidence, they would have made the most of it to disgrace Luzzatto and intensify their persecution of him. Even R. Samson Morpurgo, a moderate opponent of Luzzatto, defended him against rabbinic bans and the burning of his books as heretical only because 'he has not "cut the shoots", he has not permitted things which are forbidden and he has not declared the impure to be pure',[136] but if he had known that Luzzatto had advanced arguments to

[136] *Igerot*, ii. 363. And see ibid. i. 129–30; ii. 389–90.

justify transgressions for the sake of *tikun*, he would have allied himself wholeheartedly with the persecutors.[137]

On the other hand it is clear that it did not occur to Luzzatto to teach transgression for the sake of *tikun* as a practical matter, and that he did not see anything to take exception to in his words, or detect the obvious sting in them: witness the fact that when he had written his *Kinat hashem tsevaot* and while the storm of opposition to him was raging, he sought to get the book printed and circulated,[138] undoubtedly on the naive assumption that its publication would help to end the calumny and silence the controversy. This astounding naivety poses a difficult psychological problem. I am inclined to think that it may be traced to the inspiration of the *magid*, who also impelled him to write the anti-Shabatean book.[139] The powerful impression made on him by the divine revelation penetrated his entire being and blunted his critical faculty. At that time, before the investigation in Padua, he was doing nothing at all without the orders or approval of the *magid*, and most of his actions show signs of an inner compulsion.[140] If my conjecture is correct, it would explain a number of surprising Shabatean elements in his writings: they sprang from the depths of his soul and were not altogether under his conscious control.

It should be pointed out that a similar hypothesis is already hinted at by R. Moses Hagiz in his comments on the treatise which Luzzatto himself sent to Hamburg and in which Hagiz found a justification of Shabetai Tsevi's apostasy. He wrote:[141] 'In this manner and with these heretical gyrations and this apology [for the apostasy of Shabetai Tsevi] this boy's treatise goes round and round, *his magid having misled him into sending it to us so as to reveal the secret in his heart* through this novel idea brought into being by this boy.' From Luzzatto's letters to his teacher we know that the letter to Hamburg and the treatise which accompanied it were indeed sent at the command of the *magid*;[142] and when his teacher rebuked him for sending the treatise with-

137 Even though ignorant of such pronouncements, he doubted the genuineness of Luzzatto's opposition to Shabateanism. See ibid. ii. 281.

138 See ibid. i. 153–4, 155–6.

139 See ibid. 155.

140 I will cite a few sentences as examples: 'And truly, as to what the Lord may bring my way in regard to this—I give it no thought at all; only when it is time to reply will I hear what the Lord God says to me in His kindness towards me, *and what He commands me I will do*. I know that He turns matters to suit His designs [*mesibot mithapekh betaḥbulotav*, Job 37: 12, where the meaning is doubtful—Trans.], and all that He does I accept as good . . . *what He commands me I will do*, and nothing more' (*Igerot*, i. 107); 'He turns matters [as He wills], *even against my will He desired to reveal His mysteries*, and He put into the heart which He had given [sc. the thought] to send words flying to the ends of the earth. And when I asked Him: Shall I let letters go or not? He said: Let them. What can I do, then, except stand upon my watch *to hear what He says and do it*?' (ibid. 150).

141 Ibid. 159.

142 Ibid. 75: 'You see, all these are things *I have done upon command*.'

out a commentary, Luzzatto replied: 'Know, honoured and learned Sir, that I was so commanded.'[143] It may be that Hagiz's intuition was correct in principle and that the Shabatean content in which he saw 'the secret in the heart' of Luzzatto was not without significance.

In any event, now that analysis of Luzzatto's own words has exposed motifs which are unmistakably Shabatean, R. Isaiah Bassano's penetrating question[144] again raises itself: '*Well, then: what difference is there between the two cases?* Only that all R. Nathan's words were along lines drawn towards the single point of the Tsevi, which is not so in your case. *But in any event, who is to decide?*' The question for us is: was Luzzatto's doctrine of the Redemption, permeated as it was with Shabatean ideas, entirely divorced from historical Shabateanism, or did he slip 'the point of the Tsevi' into his philosophy and his messianic vision? I shall try to answer that question in continuing my examination of the Luzzatto affair.

143 Ibid. 114.

144 Ibid. 105. And see pp. 225–6 above, paragraph following reference to n. 15.

FIVE

Features of the Shabatean Movement and the Portrayal of Shabetai Tsevi in the Writings of Luzzatto and his Disciples

THE charges of Shabatean heresy in the campaign against Luzzatto which erupted at the beginning of 5490 [late 1729] were based on the assumption that his activity as head of a group, and as a man favoured with a *magid*, was intended to hasten the second advent of Shabetai Tsevi so as to complete the redemption which the Shabateans believed had begun in 1665–6. Luzzatto vigorously rejected the charges, and in the second half of 5490 [mid 1730], when the attacks and the threats against him were intensified, he wrote his *Kinat hashem tsevaot* ['The Zeal of the Lord of Hosts'], in which he expressed his strong opposition to Shabateanism and set out a broad range of kabbalistic and messianic arguments intended to prove its falsity and the dangers it involved. His opponents, however, gained the upper hand, and they twice succeeded in forcing his submission: on 3 Av 5490 [17 July 1730] in Padua and on 17 Tevet 5495 [1 Jan. 1735] in Frankfurt am Main.

The opinion prevalent among scholars has been that the accusations of Shabateanism, or of affinity with that movement, against Luzzatto and his group were false and malicious, and there were some scholars who denied that the activities of the group showed any tendency to active messianism, whether or not connected with Shabateanism. My researches, in the course of which I have discovered and studied hitherto unpublished documents by Luzzatto, have led me to entirely different conclusions.

I will indicate briefly those of my main conclusions that have already been published.[1] From the time that the *magid* appeared to him in 1727, Luzzatto

[1] The most important of my essays for the conclusions given here are 'Yaḥaso shel r' mosheh ḥayim lutsato el hashabeta'ut', *Tarbiz*, 27 (1958), 334–57 (included in my book *Netivei emunah uminut* (Ramat Gan, 1964), 169–85, 316–22) [Essay 4 above]; 'Hatesisah hameshiḥit beḥugo shel ramḥa"l le'oram shel ketubah veshirim meshiḥiyim', in S. W. Baron *et al.* (eds.), *Sefer-yovel leyitsḥak ber bimelot lo shivim shanah/Yitzhak F. Baer Jubilee Volume on the Occasion of his Seventieth Birthday* (Jerusalem, 1960), 374–97 (included in *Netivei emunah uminut*, 186–203, 322–31) [Essay 3 above]; 'Demuto shel rabi mosheh david vale (ramda"v) uma'amado baḥavurat

was seized with a powerful messianic urge, which developed into a restless ferment of speculative and practical activity directed towards speeding the completion of the Redemption in his own lifetime. This messianic ferment, with peaks and troughs according to the circumstances, continued without a break until Luzzatto went to Amsterdam in 1735. Actually the messianic awakening in Padua had begun a few years before 1727, at least in the written word, in the compositions of R. Moses David Valle (Ramdav). These, written both before the appearance of the *magid* to Luzzatto and contemporaneously with his revelations, were similarly composed under the inspiration of a spirit from above whom Valle, in his writings, called 'the *mashpia*', 'the transmitter of the divine flow'. Within Luzzatto's group a messianic command structure emerged consisting of four personalities: Moses, chief of the redeemers elect, and his embodiment in Luzzatto, their leader; Messiah ben David, Valle; Messiah ben Joseph, apparently R. Isaiah Romanin; Seraiah of the tribe of Dan, Messiah ben Joseph's military commander, R. Jekutiel of Vilna.

On the question of attitude to Shabateanism, I have shown that Luzzatto had made a deep study of the writings of the Shabatean scholars, above all those of Nathan of Gaza, long before he began on his book *Kinat hashem tsevaot*, and there is no doubt that the members of the group also read Shabatean writings. In his letters Luzzatto's attitude to the works of Nathan of Gaza was explicit and positive, with the reservation that Nathan's doctrine was a mixture of good and bad, and that it was desirable to sort out and absorb the good in it and reject the bad; 'to eat the inner substance', as it were, and 'throw away the husk'. The influence of the Shabatean 'inner substance' was so strong that even the treatise he wrote to refute Shabateanism contains numerous traces of Shabatean ideas, and it includes, in a formulation of his own, an endorsement of the main principle of Shabatean ideology: the Messiah is sunk among the husks and fights against them in their own domain for the sake of *tikun* and redemption. It is true that in discussing the points of contact between his outlook and Shabatean messianism Luzzatto stressed that there were profound contrasts between them: truth and faithfulness on the one side, falsehood and heresy on the other. But I have shown that in important matters his emphasis on the contrasts does not stand closer inspection; its purpose was apologetic, and even his denunciations and rejections reveal that he had 'eaten its inner substance'.

With regard to historical Shabateanism, which Luzzatto pilloried unreservedly in his explicit oral statements, I have so far done no more than allude

ramḥa"l', in S. Ettinger, H. Beinart, and M. Shtern (eds.), *Sefer zikaron leyitsḥak ber/Yitzhak F. Baer Memorial Volume* (= *Zion*, 44 (1979)) (Jerusalem, 1980), 265–302 [Essay 6 below]. References below to essays included in my *Netivei emunah uminut* give the title of the book and the page numbers. For the conclusions I summarize here I do not give individual references.

to the fact that, although his writings avoid direct mention of Shabateanism, they conceal evidence of a certain positive evaluation of the Shabatean system.[2] I examine that question here.

I rely on two sources: (*a*) *Ma'amar hage'ulah* ['On the Redemption'], a comprehensive and wide-ranging treatise mentioned in a letter from Luzzatto dated 18 Kislev 5490 [Dec. 1729] to his teacher, R. Isaiah Bassano, listing for the first time items he had composed since the advent of the *magid*;[3] (*b*) messianic homilies included in the collection *Razin genizin*, which, like Luzzatto's Zoharic compositions, are written in Aramaic. These may be remnants of the treatise on the Torah which he wrote at the dictation of the *magid*, or they may have been written by a few of his pupils or by one of them, R. Israel Hezekiah Treves.[4] However that may be, it is clear, in my opinion, that they were written at about the time when *Ma'amar hage'ulah* was composed, and at any rate before Luzzatto's first capitulation in July 1730, when he undertook to refrain from writing compositions in the language of the Zohar. Certainly the ideas and inclinations of the leader of the group are reflected in the content of the homilies. My discussion will be centred on two homilies from two sections; the content of these, again, ties them closely to the time of *Ma'amar hage'ulah*.

A. THE SHABATEAN MOVEMENT: THE STAGE OF *PEKIDAH* ['VISITATION'] IN THE REDEMPTION

At the beginning of *Ma'amar hage'ulah*[5] there is a description of the principal disorders which characterize the low ebb to which all realms of existence had sunk in exile ever since the destruction of the Temple as a result of Israel's sins: (*a*) 'Hiding the face' in the lights, i.e. the divine sefirot, which caused the

2 See Essay 6, addendum to n. 37.

3 See *R' mosheh ḥayim lutsato uvenei doro: osef igerot ute'udot*, ed. S. Ginzburg [hereafter *Igerot*] (Tel Aviv, 1937), i. 31. *Ma'amar hage'ulah* was written either before *Tikunim ḥadashim* or shortly afterwards, i.e. it was composed at the latest at the beginning of 5490 [Sept. 1729], and my impression is that the whole of it is one of the revelations of the *magid*. This is one of the few works of Luzzatto dating from before his capitulation in Av 5490 [July 1730] which have been preserved in manuscript. It was published by R. Samuel Luria at the head of the writings which he added to *Da'at tevunot* (Warsaw, 1889). The title *Ma'amar hage'ulah* alone will be used here. Its pages in the printed edition are numbered 1–24. With regard to *Tikunim ḥadashim* see my *Netivei emunah uminut*, 323 n. 13, and Essay 6, pp. 321–3. The page references given below for the passages from *Tikunim ḥadashim* relate to the printed version (Jerusalem, 1958).

4 See Essay 6, n. 76. The homilies were printed in *Megilat setarim verazin genizin* (Warsaw, 1889) [hereafter *Razin genizin*].

5 See *Ma'amar hage'ulah*, 1–3.

closure of the entrance and the blocking of the channels through which the divine flow descends to the Shekhinah and through her to her branches—the angels, humans, particularly Israel, and the other creatures. But the main channel was not completely blocked, and a flow limited to the amount essential for the existence of the world continued to pass through it. (*b*) Consolidation and strengthening of the battle formation of the forces of uncleanness, and the fall of parts of the lights, i.e. fragments of vessels and sparks, into the abyss of the husks. This disorder also resulted in the strengthening of the Gentile nations who were linked to the Sitra Ahra ['Other Side']. (*c*) The descent of the Shekhinah herself, together with her accompanying holy forces, into exile in the dominion of the Sitra Ahra. (*d*) The subjugation of the people of Israel by the nations, who enslaved them and subjected them to harsh decrees and torments. The third of these disorders, the exile of the Shekhinah, was the most serious, because it injured the divine force charged with responsibility for the governance of the world, and the descent of the Shekhinah to the realm of the forces of uncleanness led the Sitra Ahra to believe that responsibilities had been reallocated and that the functions of the Shekhinah had been transferred to it.

The correction of the disorders will take place in the Redemption in two stages at different times, the first stage being *pekidah* and the second *zekhirah* [two words for 'remembrance', the first, however, meaning also e.g. 'visitation', and so translated here—Trans.]. The 'visitation' is a temporary redemption, only transitory and partial, and the principal events comprised in it take place unremarked, on the internal level. Most of the beginnings of the Redemption on this level will continue in existence into the future, but externally no trace of them at all can be detected. In the description of the temporary nature of the 'visitation' the 'internal level' is defined as the source of the souls of Israel in the world above.[6]

At the end of the period of the 'visitation' darkness reigns in the world and the Torah is forgotten in Israel:

> Therefore [because of the deficiencies of the redemption in the 'visitation'] it is followed by darkness, and so great is the darkness that the Torah is forgotten more and more, every hand has lost its strength and every arm is weak, until eternal light shines out, and therefore the prophet ends by saying: 'Though I dwell in darkness, the Lord is a light to me'; here he is speaking of this darkness which is renewed after the visitation to which he has already referred: 'Though I have fallen, I shall arise.' (pp. 5–6)

[6] 'But there are two things you need to know: [first], that the "hiding of the face" was removed only deep within, in the place of the souls of Israel, and not externally in the place of the servants and soldiers, and you should also know what is meant by "within"; and secondly, that the opening was only of short duration and did not continue but did its work and the gate has been closed again after it until a redeemer arises [to bring redemption] for ever' (ibid. 3). And see ibid. 5.

The verse alluded to here (Mic. 7: 8) is quoted in full as a rubric at the head of the treatise: 'Do not rejoice over me, my enemy; though I have fallen, I shall arise; though I dwell in darkness, the Lord is a light to me.'

Of the four dislocations of order in the Exile none is corrected even temporarily in the 'visitation' except the first, that is, the closing of the gate and the blocking of the channels of the divine flow, and even that is not completely corrected. But limited though that correction is, it acts in certain important ways in three spheres.

The first of these spheres is the exile of the Shekhinah. Her condition among the husks is eased by a process of illumination which nullifies her isolation and her separation from the masculine sefirot and brings about a temporary union [*zivug*] between her and the sefirah Yesod:

The truth is that when the desire arose in the presence of the Only Ruler to redeem the Shekhinah and Israel, strength went forth from Him and began to descend through all the levels from level to level . . . When the strength drawn from the perfect root reached the Righteous One—the Tsadik [Yesod], who is called 'the redeeming angel' [Gen. 48: 16] in the Torah—this light descended and was revealed to the Shekhinah, his spouse, and it gave her strength which had not been granted to her from the day that Israel was exiled until that day. Then there took place a union such as had not occurred from the day aforesaid until now . . . With the arrival of this Tsadik who entered into union with the Shekhinah, the blockage which, as I have said, had been created previously was opened up, and there was no longer any hiding of the face as there had been. (p. 3)

The direct contact is with the sefirah Yesod, but the motive force for the opening of the gate in the 'visitation' is the shining of lights from the sefirah Hokhmah, and the Shekhinah senses and hears from afar the participation of the sefirah Tiferet in the union.[7]

In this sphere [the exile of the Shekhinah—Trans.] the temporary redemption is called 'the arising of the Shekhinah from the dust':

I will tell you what this arising is: there had been nothing but darkness and gloom for Israel, and they had had no one to comfort them in their great sorrow and distress, which increased from day to day. Hence their soul sank down into the dust, that is, the husks, and when the time comes for the Tsadik to be united [with the Shekhinah] as I have mentioned, a comforter is found for them and *the Shekhinah*

[7] 'When the time for the "visitation" arrived, T-t [Tiferet] awoke for the first time and sent Yesod down to the Shekhinah who was standing at the edge of the darkness. When she saw him she knew that it was T[ifere]t who had awakened although it was only Yesod who had come down, and that is why [Scripture, S. of S. 2: 8] said: "Hark! My beloved", who is Tiferet. The meaning is: "I hear the voice of my beloved." The truth is that she heard it only from afar and it was only Yesod who drew near to her, and it was of him that she said: "Here he comes, leaping over the mountains, bounding over the hills"' (ibid. 6). On the light of the sefirah Hokhmah, see ibid. 4–5.

arises from this dust, and she gathers strength even though she is among the husks, for she has not yet gone forth, but she is not as she was before, brought low and moaning and, as it were, weltering in her distress, for now she has taken on the light of sovereignty and lacks nothing except the revelation of her reign to all the nations and all the rulers, which she will show them at the time of the remembrance [*zekhirah*] speedily in our days.[8] (p. 4)

Further on it becomes clear that the temporary union with Yesod brings about the complete liberation of that aspect of the Shekhinah which is identified as her soul—her *nefesh* or her *neshamah*—and only in her corporeal aspect does she have to wait until the time of the 'remembrance' for complete redemption.[9]

The second sphere in which the 'visitation' brings light is the situation of the souls of the Messiahs. The existence of the souls of the Messiah ben Joseph and the Messiah ben David among the husks occupies a central position in Luzzatto's doctrine of the Redemption.[10] Here I propose to indicate only the little that he says on the situation of the Messiahs in connection with redemption in the 'visitation'.

The Messiahs are portrayed as the feet of the Shekhinah,[11] and in that capacity they are sunk lower and are more afflicted among the husks than she is. But the divine flow which descends on her from the light of Hokhmah reaches them, too, and benefits them in their lowly position.[12] Action is also undertaken to hasten the time of the remembrance when the Messiah ben David will come and redeem Israel:

Understand this well, that from the time of the visitation onwards the crown for the Messiah has begun to be constructed. This crown is known to be the *yeḥidah*,[13] and in the time between the visitation and the remembrance the man who has been ordained to carry out the Redemption is designated to undergo *tikun* and be ready for what he is to do. Therefore in those days he will ascend by infinitely great degrees, for then the Supreme King of kings will crown him with his glorious crown. (p. 6)

The third sphere of eschatological actions in the 'visitation' encompasses the souls of Israel. *Ma'amar hage'ulah* deals separately with two kinds of soul;

8 For a description of the arising of the Shekhinah, see also ibid. 5.

9 See ibid. 5, 8.

10 See Tishby, *Netivei emunah uminut*, 172–82.

11 'There is one other blemish, and that is the washing of the feet. It is known that the hold exerted by [the forces of] uncleanness is upon these feet. It is written: "Her feet go down to death" [Prov. 5: 5], and the two Messiahs are these two feet which are to redeem Israel, but when the blemish grows strong in their root, they will be unable to muster the strength to carry out the redemption. Hence Scripture says: "I have washed my feet, how can I soil them?" [S. of S. 5: 3], which is actually a figure of speech, and it is as if it said: "I have soiled my feet, how can I wash them?"' (*Ma'amar hage'ulah*, 4–5).

12 See ibid. 5.

13 The *yeḥidah* [literally 'the only one'—Trans.] is the highest part of the soul of the Messiah. On its position and activity among the husks until the complete Redemption, as described in *Kinat hashem tsevaot*, see Tishby, *Netivei emunah uminut*, 172–3.

each kind undergoes *tikunim* specific to it: (*a*) Souls which dwell among the husks and have not yet entered the world. Some of them are of very inferior quality, the others are highly superior. Because of their deep inferiority or their great merit the Sitra Ahra does not allow them to leave its domain, and only with the help of the light given by Yesod in the temporary marriage do they begin to gain their freedom and be born into the world.[14] (*b*) The souls of the children of Israel which live in this world at the time of the 'visitation'. Of these it is said:

[14] These two kinds of soul and the distinction between them are described in obscure terms, and their meaning needs to be clarified by reference to several sources. Explanatory comments have been added to the following extract from *Ma'amar hage'ulah*, 6.

> But in the visitation it is not so [not as it is in the 'remembrance'], for the *tikun* has not yet properly arrived, and here, therefore, Scripture says [S. of S. 2: 8]: 'leaping over the mountains, bounding over the hills'. These mountains and hills are the dark mountains and gloomy hills of the husks, and because Israel are imprisoned there he leaps over them. But now I will explain this matter to you thoroughly, and you will grasp an exceedingly great hidden truth: that some souls have been oppressed in the recesses of these mountains since ancient times, and to this day they have not left there because of the preponderant strength of the forces of uncleanness who will not allow them to leave, but they will leave before our redemption. And how will they be able to leave if they have been unable to do so up to the present? It will be by the great light which shines upon them in the visitation, for then the Righteous One [Yesod] to whom I have referred will leap over all the mountains and all the hills where those souls are, and when he arrives there, those souls will receive light from him and very great strength, and that strength will enable them to leave there. But the Righteous One will not stay long on the mountains and hills, for before the husk can become aware of his presence he must go on his way. *You must realize that most of these souls are of the same generation as the Messiah; you already know why he is called a contemporary among the souls.* But other very great souls, too, will go forth from then onwards in their proper time to undergo *tikun* so that the world will be full of a great and powerful light.

Comments: The 'oppressed souls' are the worst of the souls which fell among the husks, having been shed from the soul of Adam (which was the soul of all humanity) as a result of his sin in the Garden of Eden. Because of the inferiority of these souls the husks are able to exercise a firm hold on them, and they cannot enter the world until the time of the Redemption. In Lurianic kabbalah they are called the souls 'of the heels' because of their lowly status with respect to both their origin in the limbs of Adam and their location in *adam beliya'al* [Adam Belial], who is the demonic parallel of the divine Adam Kadmon. See I. Tishby, *Torat hara vehakelipah bekabalat ha'ar"i* (Jerusalem and Tel Aviv, 1942), 103–4, 124–5, 134–40; G. Scholem, *Shabetai tsevi vehatenuah hashabeta'it bimei ḥayav* (Tel Aviv, 1957), i. 32–5, 39–40. The representation of souls of this kind as 'of the same generation as the Messiah' evolved from Nathan of Gaza's *Derush hataninim*. See G. Scholem, *Be'ikevot mashiaḥ* (Jerusalem, 1954), 44–6, 50–2; Scholem, *Shabetai tsevi*, i. 244–5, 258–60. The allusion to the great souls held captive by the husks is founded on Lurianic kabbalah, according to which even souls of the utmost holiness fell, on account of Adam's sin, into the realm of the Sitra Ahra, which refused to release them from its control. See Tishby, *Torat hara vehakelipah*, 131–2; Scholem, *Shabetai tsevi*, i. 49–50. Detailed descriptions of the kinds of existence led by souls among the husks are given in Luzzatto's *Kinat hashem tsevaot*. See *Ginzei ramḥa"l*, ed. H. Friedlaender (Benei Berak, 1980), 94–5, 129–30.

Know that when the lights shine with this desire and longing, there will be drawn from them to all the souls of Israel a great and powerful light, and even though knowledge of it is not revealed, nevertheless their souls will have received this illumination and there will be put into their hearts [the desire] to return to the Lord their God and to seek Him . . . and therefore *there will be an awakening of redemption and repentance in Israel*, and thence [comes] the vision for the appointed time [Hab. 2: 3] and holiness will be sanctified. (p. 5)

I quote below in full Luzzatto's summary of the matters relating to the 'visitation'. For our present purpose the addition at the end of the summary is particularly important:

And now I will sum up for you in a few words all that I have said to you so far, to ensure that you understand the matter correctly and do not err or stumble: the conclusion we have reached is that the visitation is a correction [*tikun*] of one disorder [resulting] from the Exile, namely the hiding of the face and concealment of the light. Therefore the Righteous One [the Tsadik] will come down and join himself to Malkhut, and there she will receive strength and might from him and will arise from the dust. Then all the souls which are sunk in darkness will likewise gather strength and leave there, and the Messiah will perfect [*yetaken*] himself and prepare himself to become a redeemer. Something else takes place in this period and is included in the *tikunim* of the Messiah, although I did not explain it above, namely the binding of the souls of all Israel in the crown which is being prepared for the Messiah, whereby *the desire of all the people* [is turned] *towards their shepherd, and their love for him and faith in him is very great.* This will result in perpetual peace and tranquillity. All this is deep within and is not revealed outwardly. (pp. 6–7)

It is clear that the 'something else' appended to the summary and presented as new information does not relate to the souls that had been sunk among the husks until the 'visitation' but to the messianic awakening of 'all the people' in this world. The statement that 'this . . . is not revealed outwardly' refers only to the existence of 'perpetual peace and tranquillity'.

Apart from the homilies of *Razin genizin*, which I shall consider in connection with the character of Shabetai Tsevi, the only passage in the other compositions of Luzzatto known to me in which I have found the topics of the 'visitation' and the 'remembrance' is *tikun* 29 in *Tikunim ḥadashim*,[15] which was composed in 1729 and played an important part in the controversy. *Tikun* 29 begins as follows:

'And for all the strong hand',[16] for at the time when it came about that the Shekhinah went down among the husks it was said of her (Jonah 2: 7): 'I went down

[15] See n. 3 above. *Otserot ramḥa"l*, ed. H. Friedlaender (Benei Berak, 1986), 149, in the context of an allusion to the Messiah ben Joseph, has the following: 'For thus is the end of the *tikun*—in the mystery of remembrance, not in the mystery of visitation.'

[16] Deut. 34: 13, the last verse in the Pentateuch, which begins every *tikun* in *Tikunim ḥadashim* and to which each *tikun* is applied.

to the feet of the mountains; the bars of the earth closed me in for ever', that is the wicked Lilith who planned to exert her strength against the Shekhinah so that she could not rise from there. But 'You raised my life up from the pit'. When was that? [It means] the Lord my God, when there were joined together as one [His names] *Y-k-v-k* [and] *Elokim*, the complete name [with the pious substitution of *k* for *h*—Trans.], at which time it was said of Him: 'He raises the poor up from the dust' (Ps. 113: 7). And that is 'Your hand', on the part of I[ma] etc.,[17] *and that is the visitation.* 'And for all the strong hand': the hand [*yad*] is the *yd* of Shaday [the Almighty], by which [was conveyed]: 'Shake yourself from the dust' (Isa. 52: 2). Afterwards she [the Shekhinah] remained down there until she was totally perfected as was fitting. Thus 'He raises the poor up from the dunghill' (Ps. 113: 7), *this is the remembrance. 'And for all the great terror'*, at the time of which it is written: 'The nations will fear the name of the Lord' (Ps. 102: 16). (pp. 54–5)

This paragraph does not expressly state that 'visitation' and 'remembrance' are separate stages of the processes of redemption, but the principles of the view spelt out in *Ma'amar hage'ulah* are present in its clear allusions: in the 'visitation' the Shekhinah is lifted from the dust by her union with Yesod, whose name is Shaday ('the *yd* of Shaday'), but after that union she remains below among the husks; only in the 'remembrance' will she succeed in being raised up in perfect redemption.

*

Ma'amar hage'ulah speaks of the stage of the 'visitation' in the past and future tense by turns, but it is clear that it refers to processes and events that have already taken place, for Luzzatto's group expected that the complete redemption foretold in the descriptions of the 'remembrance' would begin very soon, following closely on the time when the *Ma'amar* was written; the time for it is repeatedly defined in the writings of R. Moses David Valle as the years 5490–1 [1730–1].[18]

17 [The initials *alef yod*, representing Ima, could also be understood as standing for *et yadekha*, 'Your hand'.—Trans.] The word *yadekha* ['Your hand']—interpreted here in relation to the action of Ima–Binah, in the 'visitation'—is apparently a reference to the scriptural verse (Ps. 145: 16) 'You open Your hand and satisfy every living thing', which this *tikun* goes on to apply (on p. 55) to the source of the divine flow to the Shekhinah in the 'visitation'. The printed version and the copy in MS Oxford 1901, fos. 45^{v}–46^{r}, spell *yadekha* as if it were plural ['Your hands'].

18 See Essay 6, Section D. It is true that the terms 'visitation' and 'remembrance' as used to indicate stages of the redemption are found in the Zohar I, 119*a*, but there they refer to two successive stages separated by only six and a half years, and they are assigned to the years 60 and 66 of the sixth millennium [5060 and 5066 = 1300 and 1306]. With the passage in the Zohar as his starting point, R. Abraham Halevi transferred the stages of the 'visitation' and the 'remembrance' to the years 5284 and 5291 [1524 and 1531], in his own period. See G. Scholem, 'Hamekubal r' avraham ben eli'ezer halevi', *Kiryat sefer*, 2 (1925–6), 132, 136–7. According to *Ma'amar hage'ulah*, on the other hand, there was a long interval of darkness and gloom between the two stages, and the start of the redemption in the course of the 'visitation' was brief and transitory.

So far as concerns the external aspects of the 'visitation', its main lines are *a strong reawakening among the Jewish people to the prospect of redemption and repentance which had been interrupted by the rule of darkness and gloom*; its outstanding characteristic is its reflection of the historical Shabatean movement at its height, in the years 1665–6, and of the grave crisis into which that movement was plunged by Shabetai Tsevi's conversion to Islam and the continuation of Israel's unmitigated distress and exile. Luzzatto declared that the 'visitation', in spite of the darkness of the exile that followed it, constituted the beginning of the Redemption because in it, on the internal plane, some of the disorders of the exile were actually corrected, and on the external plane it served as a preparation for complete redemption. These dicta of his undoubtedly show him evaluating historical Shabateanism as a first step in the eschatological process and one which was of great importance in Jewish history. We must therefore examine what stage in the evolution of Shabateanism formed the background to the viewpoint expressed in *Ma'amar hage'ulah*, and where we can find the sources which nurtured that viewpoint. The main point arising in both these questions is *in what ways Shabatean messianism envisaged the redemption of the Shekhinah*, the beginning of which Luzzatto saw as the principal *tikun* to have occurred in the 'visitation', and which he called 'the arising of the Shekhinah from the dust'.

The first news of the change for the better in the position of the Shekhinah on the advent of the Messiah Shabetai Tsevi—at any rate according to the chronological order given in the documents before us—is contained in a letter from Nathan of Gaza to Raphael Joseph Chelebi in Cairo, written about the end of 5425 or the beginning of 5426 [early autumn 1665],[19] which says: 'You will certainly know that *there is no spark of the Shekhinah among the external forces of evil* [the *ḥitsonim*], and the worlds are now . . . as they are on the eve of the Sabbath.' In that letter Nathan made a connection between these changes and some practical consequences in the religious life of the kabbalists: the annulment of Luria's *kavanot* in the prayers, 'since the worlds exist in a different way, and it is as if one were to perform a weekday task on the Sabbath'. But the worlds had not yet really reached the status of the Sabbath which was required for the Messiah's rise to power and for the beginning of the redemption of Israel, which according to Nathan's letter were due to take place 'a year and some months hence'. From other writings by Nathan of Gaza and from events in the progress of the movement we learn that to attain these goals it was necessary to rescue other souls and sparks of holiness which were still sunk among the husks: the responsibility for their redemption was laid upon the children of Israel. To this end Nathan composed and circulated

[19] Many copies of this letter are extant in print and in manuscripts. The most important versions are J. Sasportas, *Tsitsat novel tsevi*, ed. I. Tishby (Jerusalem, 1954), 7–12; and Scholem, *Shabetai tsevi*, i. 219–23, with an extensive explanatory supplement, 223–35.

'penitential *tikunim*', and he succeeded in inspiring a messianic religious awakening which was both powerful and widespread.[20]

In his kabbalistic-messianic work *Derush hataninim*, written in 5426 [1666], at the latest before the month of Av [summer], Nathan of Gaza declared that the *tikun* of the Shekhinah had occurred in 5417 [1657], at the time when Shabetai Tsevi was still a wanderer, driven out and persecuted for his 'unholy acts'. Nathan coupled with this announcement a practical consequence for the religious way of life: the annulment of the *tikun ḥatsot* [prayers at midnight] and other practices expressing mourning for the exile of the Shekhinah.[21] This teaching fits very well with the annulment of the fast of 17 Tamuz in 1665, just before Shabetai Tsevi left Jerusalem on his way to Smyrna, and it is probable that the mourning practices were annulled at about the same time. In Turkey Shabetai Tsevi annulled all the fasts in the calendar in 1666, and the culmination of the change from mourning to joy was reached on 9 Av, about a month before his apostasy in the middle of Elul 5426 [late summer 1666].[22]

The belief that there had been a real beginning to the Redemption on the internal, divine level, with a change in the situation of the Shekhinah, stirred the hearts of the faithful. The strength of the feelings it aroused that the end of days was at hand and that a change had occurred in the 'order of the worlds' was a principal factor in the emergence and crystallization of the Shabatean messianic sect, in spite of the apostasy of their Messiah-to-be and the falsification of the prophetic tidings, as was first explained in Gershom Scholem's famous essay 'Mitsvah haba'ah ba'averah'.[23]

Nathan of Gaza, in documents he wrote before and after the apostasy, spoke of the complete redemption of the Shekhinah without laying down any limitations or defects requiring to be made good.[24] But in practical terms he

[20] See I. Tishby, 'Tikunei teshuvah shel natan ha'azati', *Tarbiz*, 15 (1944), 161–80 (included in my *Netivei emunah uminut*, 30–51, 280–3; references below to these *tikunim* are to the page numbers in that book); Scholem, *Shabetai tsevi*, i. 235–40.

[21] See Scholem, *Be'ikevot mashiaḥ*, 14–15. Nathan said that just as on Sabbath eve, immediately before the Sabbath begins, 'the worlds ascend and then the Shekhinah is not, Heaven forbid, in exile, so, truly, from the year 5417 . . . the holiness of the Sabbath began and the Shekhinah rose from exile, and it is inappropriate to weep and lament for the exile of the Shekhinah'. According to other sources the redemption of the Shekhinah and the annulment of the prayers at midnight began in 5418 [1658]. See Scholem, *Shabetai tsevi*, i. 129–32; and see n. 24 below.

[22] See Scholem, *Shabetai tsevi*, i. 192–3, 203, 335–6; ii. 513–18, 526–9.

[23] G. Scholem, 'Mitsvah haba'ah ba'averah', *Keneset*, 2 (1937), 347–92 (included in his book *Meḥkarim umekorot letoledot hashabeta'ut vegilguleiha* (Jerusalem, 1974), 9–67). And see Scholem, *Shabetai tsevi*, ii. 580–3.

[24] Writing with regard to the year 1665 in his letter to Raphael Joseph, Nathan was categorical in his statement: 'Know, of a certainty, that there is no spark of the Shekhinah among the forces of evil.' See above, text referring to n. 19. In *Derush hataninim* he used the expression 'the

limited the immediate consequences [of the redemption] to changes in *kavanot* and in the wording of prayers and the annulment of the fasts and mourning practices; and although his teaching included the reception of a new spiritual Torah and the annulment of commandments, these were events he saw as deferred to the future time when Shabetai Tsevi's fight against the husks would end in complete victory and Shabetai would be revealed in outward reality in his active role as the redeemer. However, after the apostasy the movement split into two streams, the extreme and the moderate, within which there were ideological and practical differences and nuances which multiplied and grew stronger in the course of time under the influence of events. Both sides diverged from Nathan's teachings to a greater or lesser extent, although they recognized his eminence as a prophet and his authority as a guide.

To appreciate the Shabatean background to Luzzatto's outlook in *Ma'amar hage'ulah*, we need to concentrate on the nature of moderate Shabateanism, which may also be called hasidic, in its Italian form as practised in the circles of R. Benjamin Hakohen of Reggio [Rabakh] and R. Abraham Rovigo of

Shekhinah rose from exile': see n. 21 above. In later compositions written a few years after Shabetai Tsevi's apostasy, Nathan says that the Shekhinah left the husks in 5417 or 5418 and her redemption was completed in 5420 [1660], whereupon she returned to her place in the divine order. See G. Scholem, 'Te'udot shabeta'iyot ḥadashot mis' "to'ei ruaḥ"', *Zion*, 7 (1942), 183; and his *Be'ikevot mashiaḥ*, *derush hamenorah*, 118–19. In a most important document written after 5431 [1671], when Shabetai Tsevi had directed that 9 Av should be celebrated with seven days of rejoicing like the festival of Passover, Nathan declared that the Shekhinah had been redeemed upon the advent of the Messiah. He backed this pronouncement with a lengthy justification, and he strongly rejected the argument that the redemption of Israel must precede the redemption of the Shekhinah because she needed to be with them and protect them in exile. See G. Scholem, 'Igeret natan ha'azati al shabetai tsevi vahamarato', *Kovets al yad*, NS 6 (16) (1966), 447–50 (included in his book *Meḥkarim umekorot*, 263–6; references below are to the page numbers in the book). Scholem declared (*Meḥkarim umekorot*, 234) that this pamphlet in the form of a letter was 'a sort of circular to the faithful'. M. Benayahu, 'Hatenuah hashabeta'it beyavan', *Sefunot*, 14 (1971–8), 337, disputed this statement, and on the basis of two occurrences of the expression 'Furthermore, he argued' (*Meḥkarim umekorot*, 262, 263), he wrote: 'However, there is no doubt that this composition is a reply to a believer assailed by many doubts.' But he did not take account of the fact that the expressions 'he argued' are closely followed (on p. 264) by 'The aforesaid scholar argued'. All three expressions refer to a discussion between Nathan and a rabbinical emissary from Jerusalem about three months before the text under consideration was written, as is explicitly stated earlier in the same document: 'three months ago an emissary came here from Jerusalem (may it be rebuilt and established speedily in our days) and raised a new question which had not been settled to his satisfaction by anything we had said . . . and I replied . . .' (p. 261). Together with the replies to the emissary's arguments we find mention of oral debate with other interlocutors: 'There are some who ask . . . and I have replied . . .' (p. 266); 'Moreover, many asked . . . and I said . . .' (p. 268). These references show that Scholem was correct in his assertion that what we have here is not really a letter at all but a pamphlet for circulation, motivated by the large number of questions and doubts troubling Shabateans around Nathan.

Modena. Its main principles were *acceptance that the Shekhinah truly rose from the dust* through the merit of Shabetai Tsevi's messianic activity, and *expectation of complete redemption at his second coming*. But their belief was accompanied by question marks, perplexity, and switches of opinion from time to time as to the correct understanding of these principles and their proper influence on the religious way of life.

R. Benjamin's perplexity—which we may also take as evidence of Rovigo's perplexity, in view of the close alignment between their Shabatean beliefs—is exemplified by two letters of his written fifteen years apart. The first one, dating from 5437 [1676–7] and addressed to an admired Shabatean personality whose identity is not clear, was undoubtedly composed before it was known in Italy that Shabetai Tsevi had died in Albania on Yom Kippur of that year. In it R. Benjamin, having received glad tidings, declared his hope that Shabetai Tsevi would soon bring the Redemption, but asked at the same time whether it was still necessary to continue with the prayers at midnight and Luria's *kavanot*.[25] This shows that for an unknown period between the apostasy and the arrival of the new tidings he had been led by disappointment to revert to these practices, contrary to the teachings of Shabetai Tsevi and Nathan of Gaza. The second letter, written in Shevat 5451 [early 1691], was addressed to R. Heschel Tsoref, the Shabatean seer of Vilna. In that letter R. Benjamin sought advice particularly on the question whether 'they' were correct in the practice they had followed 'for some years past' of treating Luria's *kavanot* as annulled in accordance with Nathan of Gaza's instructions, 'since the Shekhinah has already risen from the dust'.[26] The text shows that confusion existed as to the very questions of the Shekhinah's arising and the prohibition of mourning for the destruction of the Temple.

For our present purpose particular importance attaches to the revelations of two preachers ['*magidim*'],[27] R. Baer Perlhefter and R. Mordecai Ashkenazi, who were active in the school of R. Abraham Rovigo in Modena, the first of them from 1676 to 1681 and the second from 1696 until his departure for Israel in 1702 in the group which went with Rovigo.[28] I shall deal with the well-known revelations of Perlhefter in Section B, where I consider the questions involved in the way that Shabetai Tsevi was perceived.[29] Here I confine my attention to an anonymous 'maggidic' revelation, as yet

[25] See Tishby, *Netivei emunah uminut*, 230–1 and n. 37.

[26] See Aron Freimann, *Inyenei shabetai tsevi* (Berlin, 1912/13), 107.

[27] [Human '*magidim*' are preachers, unlike Luzzatto's *magid*, who was his messenger from Heaven; but both Perlhefter and Ashkenazi were credited with knowledge of Heaven's intentions.—Trans.]

[28] See I. Tishby, 'Ha"magid" hashabeta'i harishon beveit midrasho shel r' avraham rovigo', *Zion*, 22 (1957), 21–55 (included in my *Netivei emunah uminut*, 81–107, 295–305; references below are to the page numbers in that book); G. Scholem, *Ḥalomotav shel hashabeta'i r' mordekhai ashkenazi* (Jerusalem, 1938).

[29] See below, text referring to nn. 87–9.

unpublished, in MS Jerusalem 1466 8°, fos. 214v–218r, which is of the same type as Perlhefter's revelations and in my opinion is by him. In giving information about the two '*magidim*' it says clearly that R. Benjamin Hakohen was enthusiastic about them and believed in the statements they made during the times when they were active in Modena.[30] The revelation in MS Jerusalem 1466, like the other messianic revelations by Perlhefter which have been preserved, is written in a clumsy and opaque style full of obscure allusions. I will quote and, so far as I can, annotate where necessary, three passages which have an important bearing on the stages of the Redemption and the arising of the Shekhinah.

This referred solely to the revelation of the Messiah . . . and it was simply remembrance in its ordinary sense as is alluded to in the verse 'I will remember my covenant with Ya'akov [Jacob]',[31] where the letter *vav* of Ya'akov is a hidden reference to the sixth millennium . . . Afterwards the Fear of Isaac[32] will be aroused, and after that the Constant Love [*ḥesed*] of Abraham,[33] for it is from Hesed that *the Remembrance for ever* will come to pass in Israel. (MS Jerusalem 1466, fo. 215r)

Three stages are referred to here. First, 'remembrance' in its ordinary sense, used in relation to Jacob—the sefirah Tiferet and its offshoot Yesod. This stage is the beginning of the Redemption. Third, 'the Remembrance for ever' related to Abraham—the sefirah Hesed—which is the complete Redemption. Between these is an intermediate stage related to Isaac—the sefirah Gevurah. The first and third stages are respectively the Shabatean movement before the apostasy, and the renewal and completion of the processes of redemption. The intermediate stage, symbolized by 'the Fear of Isaac' which is active within it, is the interval extending from the Redeemer's fall among the husks to their subjugation and the correction of the blemish of the apostasy through the force of the divine attribute of Judgement. We are told openly that these are stages in the development of the Shabatean movement; there is no attempt at disguise, and the manuscript even uses the name Shabetai to refer to the Messiah in his lowly state.

The passage I have quoted goes on immediately to say:

Now the remembrance [in its ordinary sense] is a hidden reference to the beginnings of conception and the months of pregnancy with the Messiah, when Yesod remembers Rachel and visits and impregnates her, and when that holy seed is absorbed, *which reveals light in the world in body and soul here below* while the spirit of the Messiah, with regard to whose body here below it was said: 'The spirit of

30 See Tishby, *Netivei emunah uminut*, 95–7; Scholem, *Ḥalomotav*, 32–3.

31 Lev. 26: 42. [The Masoretic text here spells Ya'akov plene, i.e. with penultimate letter *vav*—which has the numerical value 6.—Trans.]

32 Gen. 31: 42.

33 In Mic. 7: 20, 'the constant love *for* Abraham'.

wisdom will rest upon him' etc.,[34] is still hidden in the womb of Ima, in the hidden meaning of the closed *mem* in *lemarbeh hamisrah* ['of the increase of government . . .'],[35] until there takes place there the nine months' gestation alluded to in the *tikunim* (Z[*ohar*] *ḥ*[*adash*] 5*d*).[36] At the same time the realm of the wicked one will be extended nine months . . . and then she 'like a woman with child, when she is near her time, will cry out, writhing in her pains'.[37] At that time there will be pang after pang, with no relief between one and the next. (MS Jerusalem 1466, fo. 215r–v)

We learn from this passage that in the first stage no direct contact is made with Jacob–Tiferet, who acts, however, through the agency of Yesod in the marital union of the latter with the Shekhinah, who is symbolized as Rachel. But the purpose of the union—the birth of the Messiah, represented by the birth of Joseph, to bring about the Redemption—was not properly achieved at that stage. True, the Messiah was in existence in this world in body and soul, and in these forms he was vouchsafed some illumination, but 'the spirit of the Messiah', without which there could be no real redemption, was not present in him but remained as a foetus in the womb of the Shekhinah for the nine months of pregnancy. During those months she and the Messiah were in distress, suffering torments from the assaults of 'the realm of the wicked one', i.e. Lilith, as is clearly stated in the passage immediately following the extract just quoted, and elsewhere: the people of Israel, too, were enslaved and humiliated in exile. For this reason all the processes taking place at this stage 'are called birth pangs, by which is meant the birth pangs of the Messiah',[38] and the actual birth will only occur when Jacob–Tiferet is an active participant in the union.

Before that time, i.e. before 'the Remembrance for ever', the Shekhinah will not have been redeemed, and this '*magid*' therefore insists on the observance of mourning for her exile and condemns those who cancel it:

It is necessary to pray at that time to Ze'ir [Tiferet] that he may take part [in the union] with her, for the key to the birth is in his hand, and so long as he does not

[34] Isa. 11: 2; actually 'The spirit of the Lord will rest upon him, the spirit of wisdom and understanding'.

[35] Isa. 9: 6 [the 'closed *mem*' is the final form (ם) of the letter, anomalously written in the middle of the word in the Masoretic text.—Trans.]: 'Of the increase of government and of peace there will be no end upon the throne of David and on his kingdom.' For messianic explanations of the 'closed *mem*' in this passage, see I. Tishby, *Meshiḥiyut bedor gerushei sefarad uportugal* (Jerusalem, 1985), 124 n. 69, and 154–5.

[36] See *Zohar ḥadash*, ed. R. Margaliot (Jerusalem, 1953), 97*d*–98*a*, which refers to nine months during which the Shekhinah is pregnant with the Messiah. The reference '*Z"ḥ 5d*' relates to the printed edition of Venice, 1658.

[37] Isa. 26: 17, which, however, reads 'she writhes, cries out'.

[38] MS Jerusalem 1466, fo. 216r. In the passages quoted here references to the Messiah without further definition relate, in general, to Shabetai Tsevi in his capacity as Messiah ben Joseph. And see below, text referring to nn. 91–9.

take part she remains in the exile of the husk, which is a placenta [consisting of] an iron wall which separates them [Israel] from their Father in Heaven, and the wall [*ḥomat*] of iron is the seal [*ḥotam*] of the womb. At that time there occurs [the distress of] 'the afflicted one, storm-tossed and unconsoled',[39] and *we must share in her suffering, turn our thoughts towards her and bewail her distress* . . . for until that righteous man [*tsadik*] comes forth[40] we must not rest or cease from mourning for her suffering. Therefore, as for those who erred and thought that this now was the time of the complete Redemption and inserted their hands into the womb to receive the Messiah before his time, the serpent comes from there and bites them, as you will see . . . and therefore I have set out to warn you and help you not to be tripped up by the stumbling-block over which they came to grief by mistakenly fixing a definite time for the Messiah, who penetrates to the bottom of the abyss, where there is that snake which bites them because they did not wait for the snake to bite the supernal placenta from which the spirit of the Messiah will be born.[41] Now the Shekhinah is still in the abyss, and the Messiah has reached the gates of *hamavet* ['death'], whose letters *hmvt* spell *tehom* ['the abyss'] . . . and [they shall] serve the

[39] Isa. 54: 11.

[40] This refers to the exit, from imprisonment among the husks, of Shabetai Tsevi–Messiah ben Joseph, who is linked with the sefirah Yesod–Tsadik.

[41] The biting of the womb of the Shekhinah by the snake, which is mentioned twice in this revelation, requires explanation. An aggadic passage in the Talmud (*BB* 16*b*) relates that because the womb of the hind is narrow, she has difficulty in giving birth, and the Holy One, blessed be He, appoints a dragon to bite open her womb. On the basis of this aggadah the Zohar states in several places that the snake, the Sitra Ahra, shares in the parturition process of the Shekhinah by biting her womb. The text of the Zohar makes explicit reference to the birth of the souls; the main idea is the existence of close contact between the Sitra Ahra and the Shekhinah which arises from the desire and ability of the Sitra Ahra to take part in the flow of holy influence, as I explained in my book *The Wisdom of the Zohar*, trans. D. Goldstein (Oxford, 1989), ii. 754–5. And see further ibid. 755–7. Two passages in the Zohar which are most important in this connection, II, 219*b*–220*a* and III, 249*a*–*b*, are translated and explained in *Wisdom of the Zohar*, ii. 738–40 and i. 393–6. The Zohar itself contains few eschatological allusions to the participation of the snake in the birth of the souls, but in *Raya meheimna* (Zohar III, 67*b*–68*a*, 249*a*) the whole concept is applied to the birth of the two Messiahs, i.e. the snake's bite is the birth pangs of the Shekhinah in bringing the Redemption. In the school of Nathan of Gaza the motif of the snake-bite was used to justify the apostasy of the Messiah, Shabetai Tsevi, on the grounds that, by the apostasy, the Sitra Ahra brought down upon the Shekhinah the torments necessarily involved in the processes of redemption. See Scholem, *Shabetai Tsevi*, ii. 692, referring to a passage in MS Jewish Theological Seminary, New York, Kaufmann 255, fo. 17[r]. In the revelation we are considering, an opposite line of thought is pursued: Shabetai Tsevi's apostasy and its results were eschatological torments preceding the Messiah's birth which was to be induced by the bite of the snake; those who believed that, with the events in question, the Redemption had occurred, were mistaken and exposed themselves to injury by the bite of the Sitra Ahra because 'they inserted their hands into the womb to receive the Messiah before his time'. The author of the revelation was of the opinion that the snake's bite at the time of the birth of the Messiah would bring about the self-destruction of the Sitra Ahra, and indeed *Raya meheimna* (Zohar III, 68*a*) says: 'At that time . . . the snake will pass away from the world.'

Lord with fear,[42] when she is in exile among the nations, because *so long as her children are in exile she lies in the dust*, and then you must fulfil the verse 'Arise, cry out in the night, at the beginning of the watch'.[43] However, when her victory shines out like the brightness of day[44] and the city of Jerusalem is rebuilt and the Shekhinah returns[45] to her place and all people gather together to be with her, then indeed the words of the prophet will be fulfilled:[46] 'Who are these flying like a cloud', *yod he vav he*,[47] all of whom [together] will be perfect compassion, and it is to this that Scripture alludes in the verse 'with compassion [*raḥamim*] I will gather you',[48] and then—forget the lamentations, shed the ashes [*efer*], and take the diadem [*pe'er*, the letters of *efer* rearranged]. (MS Jerusalem 1466, fo. 217^{r-v})

Since it is reasonable to assume that Rovigo and R. Benjamin accepted the views and teachings contained in this revelation, it must be concluded that round about the year 1680 a reversal of attitudes in fact occurred in the centre of Shabateanism in Italy. True, there remained an unshaken expectation that there would be a second coming by Shabetai Tsevi in the course of the complete Redemption, but the duty to mourn for the destruction of the Temple and the Exile was reintroduced, and from this point of view Shabetai Tsevi and Nathan of Gaza, both of whom ordered the annulment of the fasts and mourning practices, were regarded as errant and misleading. After Perlhefter left Modena the local Shabateans did, indeed, cancel these observances again, apparently from 1682 onwards, but their hearts were not fully in this reform, as is shown, in my opinion, by the confusion expressed in R. Benjamin's letter of 1691.

The revelations of the second '*magid*' of Modena, R. Mordecai Ashkenazi, in 1696–9, have been considered in detail and his views and teachings with regard to Shabatean messianism clarified in Gershom Scholem's comprehensive study.[49] The episode of the new '*magid*' proves conclusively that before his appearance on the scene the fasts and mourning practices had again been cancelled by Rovigo and R. Benjamin, which confirms the assumption I made in the preceding paragraph. There were even some 'believers' in their circle who went so far as to turn 9 Av into a day of feasting and rejoicing.[50] However, Rovigo, and his colleagues too, plied R. Mordecai unceasingly with questions, because they harboured doubts. That '*magid*' evaded many of the

42 Cf. Ps. 2: 11.

43 Lam. 2: 19, which, however, has the plural 'watches' [*ashmurot*], not the singular [*ashmoret*]. The reference is of course to the recitation of the midnight prayers.

44 As in Isa. 62: 1.

45 Misspelt in the Hebrew.

46 Isa. 60: 8.

47 The letters of the Tetragrammaton, each spelt out in full (*y* = *yod vav dalet*; *h* = *hy* [twice], *v* = *vyv*) have the total numerical value of 72, the same as *av* ['cloud']. So spelt out, the Tetragrammaton represents perfect compassion [*raḥamim*].

48 Isa. 54: 7: 'with great compassion I will gather you'.

49 See Scholem, *Ḥalomotav*, esp. 37–52.

50 See ibid. 51, 97.

questions,[51] but in relation to the position of the Shekhinah and its bearing on practical conduct he was unequivocal.

His main teachings in this regard were the following.[52] It is an unshakeable truth that the Redemption began with the events of 1666 and that the Shekhinah rose from the dust, but her rise was partial and limited in two respects: (*a*) she rose only from the lower dust, but in the realm of the upper dust, at a high level which the Sitra Ahra had succeeded in penetrating, she had not been freed;[53] (*b*) even this partial rise was flawed, in that it was

[51] See ibid. 38–46. The '*magid*' did not respond to Rovigo's pressing requests to clear up the problematic aspects of Shabetai Tsevi's personality and the course of his life—problems referred to as 'the matter of the *amirah*' [an acronym for *adonenu malkenu yarum hodo*, 'our lord and king, may his glory be exalted'—Trans.] or 'the matter of the Messiah'—but it is clear that he cast no doubt on the belief that Shabetai Tsevi was the past Messiah and the Messiah to come.

[52] In addition to the explanatory material noted above, Scholem published a long discourse from this document in *Ḥalomotav* as appendix B, pp. 79–100, most of which consists of a detailed consideration of the position of the Shekhinah and of connected theological and practical questions.

[53] See ibid. 50–1, 80–1, 85–9, 91–4, 98. After the publication of the notebook containing the revelations of R. Mordecai Ashkenazi, it transpired unexpectedly, from a letter written by R. Hayim Malakh to R. Benjamin and Rovigo at the end of 5456 or the beginning of 5457 [autumn 1696], that the distinction between 'the lower dust'and 'the upper dust' in relation to the arising of the Shekhinah originated in a teaching attributed to Shabetai Tsevi himself. See G. Scholem, 'Igeret me'et r' ḥayim malakh', *Zion*, 11 (1946), 173–4 and n. 47. The attribution to him of this distinction, modifying the news of the Shekhinah's arising, is certainly not fictitious. It is clear that it was a pronouncement made towards the end of his life when he was in Albania, and it is on all fours with the moderating instruction in his letter to Nathan of Gaza from his place of exile, according to which, although five afflictions must be undergone on 9 Av, 'because now the hour requires it', it was 'even now' forbidden to weep and mourn. See Scholem, *Meḥkarim umekorot*, 272–3. In my opinion the undated letter from Nathan published in A. Amarillo's essay 'Te'udot shabeta'iyot miginzei rabi sha'ul amarilyo', in I. Ben-Zvi and M. Benayahu (eds.), *Sefer zikaron liyeshayahu zoneh/Isaiah Sonne Memorial Volume* (= *Sefunot*, 5) (Jerusalem, 1961), 253–4—which stated that five afflictions must be undergone 'without weeping and lamentation'—was written between 1674 and 1676 in response to the instruction from Shabetai Tsevi in his letter from Albania, and not in 1667 as assumed by Amarillo, ibid. 240. But it must be pointed out that even in the late letter considered here, Nathan again stressed his view 'that the Shekhinah ascended to her original source and is not dwelling in exile'. See n. 24 above. If, therefore, we are to accept as correct the report quoted by Benayahu ('Hatenuah hashabeta'it beyavan', 408) from the writings of R. Abraham Miranda, to the effect that 'the elders of Jerusalem' testified 'that our teacher R. N[athan] had retracted his opinion and said that the worlds had returned to their place in the world to come, and this is alluded to in *Ḥemdat yamim*, "*Siaḥ hasadeh*"', then we must hold that this radical shift in Nathan's views occurred after Shabetai Tsevi's death. 'The elders of Jerusalem' here of course means R. Jacob Algazi, who according to my conclusions headed the group which composed *Ḥemdat yamim*, and his friends in Jerusalem. In this connection see the evidence presented, *passim*, in my essays 'Hanhagot natan ha'azati, igerot rabi mosheh zakut vetakanot rabi ḥayim abulafiyah besefer ḥemdat yamim', *Kiryat sefer*, 54 (1979), 585–610; '"Shalshelet yuḥasin" shel "mori" va' "a[vi]-a[vi] mori" beduyim hamutsavim besefer ḥemdat yamim', *Tarbiz*, 50 (1981), 463–514.

achieved by the Shekhinah's own exertions and not by the action of the Holy One, blessed be He, i.e. her union with Tiferet did not take place. These defects manifested themselves externally in the continued exile of Israel, without whose redemption there could be no ascent of the Shekhinah and no renewal of unity and harmony in the divine order. Therefore, for the time being, the fasts and other mourning customs must not be annulled. On the contrary, it was a holy duty to observe them, and even to add other acts of repentance, in order to hasten the complete Redemption above and below. These directions did, indeed, run counter to the instructions of Nathan of Gaza; he was an exalted tsadik and a true prophet and his instructions and guidance, in general, were and remained valid, but evil spirits were mixed with his holy spirit and led him to err and lead others into error.[54]

Rovigo found it difficult to reconcile himself to the instruction that the prophet Nathan's orders must be annulled, and even after he had succumbed to the influence of the '*magid*' he tried to steer a middle course by odd compromises like fasting and mourning on 9 Av in private, without going to the synagogue.[55] But the '*magid*' prevailed; R. Benjamin apparently adopted the same course as his colleague, and Shabateanism in its Italian centre was restricted in practice to looking back with nostalgia and forward with hope.

The view of the 'visitation' in *Ma'amar hage'ulah* is very close in principle, and on some important specific points too, to the assessment of the start of the Redemption, and its interruption in 1666, in the revelations of the two Shabatean '*magidim*' who preceded Luzzatto in Italy. It is unnecessary to go over in detail the lines they pursue in common, which will have been made clear by the account given above.[56] They do also differ substantially on many

[54] See Scholem, *Ḥalomotav*, 50, 53–4, 81–2, 88. H. J. D. Azulai recorded hearing R. Jacob Hazak quote Luzzatto's *magid* as having made a similar assessment of Nathan of Gaza's mystical grasp, meaning, in that context, his reception of revelations from on high: 'And N-B's [Nathan Benjamin's] grasp [of this] was mixed with *sta* [Sitra Ahra].' See M. Benayahu, 'Ha"magid" shel ramḥa"l', in I. Ben-Zvi and M. Benayahu (eds.), *Sefer zikaron liyeshayahu zoneh/Isaiah Sonne Memorial Volume* (= *Sefunot*, 5) (Jerusalem, 1961), 335. And see below, text referring to n. 82.

[55] See Scholem, *Ḥalomotav*, 51, 87–8, 97–8.

[56] Nevertheless I will offer a few examples. The words for the stages of the Redemption used by Luzzatto and in Perlhefter's revelation are similar: 'visitation' and 'remembrance' in the one case, 'remembrance in its ordinary sense' and 'eternal remembrance' in the other. Both Luzzatto and Perlhefter emphasized the occurrence of the union between Yesod and the Shekhinah in the first stage, and presented the association of Tiferet with the Shekhinah as a principal factor in bringing about the complete Redemption in the second stage. Similarly R. Mordecai Ashkenazi in his revelations said that the main flaw in the first stage was the lack of the union between Tiferet and the Shekhinah, but in place of the action of Yesod at that stage R. Mordecai spoke of the Shekhinah's rising by her own effort, using the increased strength she received from above without being raised up by Tiferet, with whom her union would take place in time to come. For the distinction between the Shekhinah's rising by her own effort [as in R. Mordecai's version] and her being raised up, the first revelation by Luzzatto's *magid*—on

matters, but equally there are conspicuous differences between the teachings of R. Mordecai Ashkenazi and those of R. Baer Perlhefter. It may be that Luzzatto had read the revelations of the two earlier '*magidim*', which were kept among R. Abraham Rovigo's private papers in Modena,[57] and it is fair to assume that there were also copies of the revelations in the great collection of Shabatean writings in the library of R. Benjamin Hakohen. In any event it is clear to me that Luzzatto was aware of their existence, knew the trend of the ideas and teachings they contained, and developed them in accordance with his own particular outlook.

B. SHABETAI TSEVI—THE PROFANED MESSIAH BEN JOSEPH

Ma'amar hage'ulah refers only once to the identity of the redeemer at the stage of the 'visitation', and then only in the following brief and unclear terms: 'Know that the visitation [is] by Yesod, as I have told you, and the revelation of the remembrance [is] by *t"t* [Tiferet], and therefore those two actions confer strength on the Messiah ben Joseph and the Messiah ben

the New Moon of Sivan 5487 [summer 1727]—is important. Its main item of information was that the Holy One, blessed be He (Tiferet), would soon raise up the Shekhinah by union with her. It is in these terms: 'Come and see: in the former exile it was never stated that the Holy One, blessed be He, would come and raise up the *matrona*, [although] they did raise her up, but in the present exile He will certainly come and raise her from the dust.' See Benayahu, 'Ha"magid" shel ramḥa"l', 328–9. In 1727 the *magid* had not yet revealed the secret disclosed and expounded in *Ma'amar hage'ulah*—a revelation similar in content to those of R. Mordecai Ashkenazi—namely that in the latter exile, too, there was a limited redemption of the Shekhinah, without her being raised up by Tiferet, in the 'visitation' stage, i.e. in 1665–6. It should be pointed out that according to *Ma'amar hage'ulah* the situation of the Shekhinah between the two stages was better than that described in the revelation in MS Jerusalem 1466, for according to that manuscript 'she was lying in the dust', whereas Luzzatto declared that she was upright and protected in the realm of the husks. See above, text referring to nn. 8 and 43. In *Ma'amar hage'ulah* there is not the slightest mention of changes in the *kavanot* of prayer or of the annulment of the fasts and mourning practices, and it is obvious that at that time, while awaiting the complete Redemption, Luzzatto's group were careful to refrain from violating any commandments or hallowed customs for messianic reasons. This attitude was in line with the instructions of the two earlier '*magidim*' in the circles of Rovigo and R. Benjamin Hakohen.

[57] Perlhefter's revelations and the notebook [*pinkas*] containing R. Mordecai Ashkenazi's revelations were preserved with the private papers of R. Abraham Rovigo in Modena and in R. Benjamin Hakohen's library. See Scholem, *Ḥalomotav*, 6, 55–6, 61; G. Scholem, 'Perakim apokaliptiyim umeshiḥiyim al r' mordekhai me'aisenshtat', in *Sefer dinaburg* (Jerusalem, 1948), 238 and n. 6; and his 'Igeret me'et r' ḥayim malakh', 168, with reference to MS Jerusalem 1466.

David to do valiantly for the future redemption.'[58] Those who are well versed in such matters will understand that the Messiah ben Joseph is at the level of Yesod and that the Messiah ben David is at the level of Tiferet, and hence that the redeemer in the 'visitation' was the Messiah ben Joseph. But nothing is said, even by so much as a hint, about the actions of the Messiah ben Joseph in the course of the 'visitation' or his fate at that time and in the period of darkness which followed it. Wherever else the Messiah ben Joseph is mentioned in the descriptions of the 'visitation' he is coupled with the Messiah ben David and no reference is made to him separately. Only in the presentation of the 'remembrance' do we find descriptions of the characters and functions of the two Messiahs which draw clear distinctions between them, and even there the characterization of the Messiah ben Joseph displays none of the traits of Shabetai Tsevi.

The picture is different in other writings by Luzzatto. As I concluded in a previous study, 'the portrayal of the Messiah ben Joseph in Luzzatto's writings shows outstanding similarities to the image of Shabetai Tsevi in Shabatean literature'.[59] For that conclusion I relied, *inter alia*, on a few hints supplied by homilies in *Razin genizin*, the collection I mentioned at the beginning of the present essay.[60] But the passages to which I referred in my previous study are not, by themselves, enough to establish the identity of the Messiah ben Joseph with the historical Shabetai Tsevi: they need to be supported by clearer statements. And indeed there are definite statements which put the matter beyond doubt in two homilies in *Razin genizin*. I explain below the content of these homilies.

The first homily[61] is the ninth in a cycle of expositions of verses on the birth of Joseph[62] and of the verse: 'Is Ephraim my dear son; is he the child of my delight?'[63] The whole homily is centred on the 'visitation' and 'remembrance' stages of the Redemption in accordance with their description in *Ma'amar hage'ulah*. It begins by saying: 'Come and see, the beginning of the *tikun* takes place in the mystery of the visitation, its end and perfection occur in the mystery of the remembrance.' The birth of Joseph is perceived as a description of the advent of the Messiah ben Joseph in the two stages of the Redemption, but in the 'visitation' no actual birth took place, because neither the Shekhinah nor the Messiah ben Joseph had yet emerged from the realm

[58] *Ma'amar hage'ulah*, 3. The words 'as I have told you' relate to remarks which immediately precede this about the temporary union of Tsadik–Yesod with the Shekhinah in the 'visitation'.

[59] Tishby, *Netivei emunah uminut*, 180, and see ibid. 177–81. At p. 170 I quoted the opinion of R. Jacob Emden that Luzzatto might have regarded Shabetai Tsevi as the Messiah ben Joseph. The results of my investigation, as made clear here, show that Emden had hit the mark.

[60] See above, text referring to n. 4.

[61] *Razin genizin*, 69–70.

[62] Gen. 30: 22: 'God remembered Rachel and God heeded her prayer and opened her womb.'

[63] Jer. 31: 19. [On this translation of the verse, see below, text immediately following the reference to n. 71.—Trans.]

of the husks, from whose control they had only been freed for the time being and in secret. Rachel, who symbolizes the Shekhinah, was silenced and powerless during the Exile, and it was said of her: 'like a ewe that is silent before her shearers'.[64] In the 'visitation' she recovers somewhat, to the extent that she achieves a temporary union with Yesod, but because this union is broken off and her isolation continues, she still complains: 'I called him but he did not answer me.'[65] For this reason the story of the birth of Joseph opens with the words: 'And God *will remember* Rachel', meaning remembrance in time to come [reading *veyizkor*, future, instead of *vayizkor*, past—Trans.], and the words with which the story continues, similarly taken as future tense: 'And God will heed her', refer to the complete redemption which is expected. Furthermore, the biblical description of the birth—'He opened her womb and she conceived and bore a son'[66]—is itself read as in the future tense referring especially to the 'remembrance'. The Messiah ben Joseph did appear in the 'visitation' and begin to perform *tikunim*, but because the *tikunim* were interrupted and were fulfilled only in secret, the womb was not opened at that time and the birth did not take place. At that stage the Messiah ben Joseph was regarded as an embryo, and only in the 'remembrance', when his *tikunim* would be out in the open and complete, would it be said of him that he was actually born.[67]

According to another version presented in this homily, the 'visitation' was in the nature of a 'first coming in [*biah*]' from the left, the attribute of Din (Judgement), and in the 'remembrance' there would be a 'second coming in'[68] from the right, the attributes of Hesed and Rahamim (Mercy and Compassion), and then the Messiah ben David would emerge from the husks

64 Isa. 53: 7. [The misspelling here—*ne'elamah* not with an *alef* but with an *ayin*, which would make it read *na'alamah* ('was hidden')—is presumably a printer's error.—Trans.]

65 S. of S. 5: 6.

66 Gen. 30: 22–3.

67 'At that time she conceived and bore a child, that is, Messiah ben Joseph, whose *tikunim* began from the time of the visitation, and *the mystery is for the wise*, but because they were hidden and not revealed he was regarded as being like an embryo which is in its mother's womb and has not been born, but when the time of the remembrance arrived and all his *tikunim* would be revealed, then [the words of Scripture would apply]: "she bore [him]", that is certain' (*Razin genizin*, 69–70). The connection made between the birth of Joseph and the advent of Shabetai Tsevi–Messiah ben Joseph closely parallels Perlhefter's revelation in MS Jerusalem 1466, both in its general lines and in detail. See above, text referring to nn. 34–8.

68 The source of the expressions 'first coming in' and 'second coming in' is a rabbinic saying in *San.* 98*b*. There they refer to the entry of Israel into the Land of Israel: a splendid 'first incoming' in the days of Joshua and a lesser 'second incoming' in the days of Ezra. But the word *biah*, literally 'coming in', also has a sexual connotation, and here the reference is to the two divine unions with the Shekhinah, the first and inferior union to generate the Messiah ben Joseph and the second, superior one to generate the Messiah ben David. The 'second *biah*' was described as 'the perfect union', and in the light of what is said in *Ma'amar hage'ulah* the perfect union is the union of Tiferet with the Shekhinah. See n. 7 above.

and bring perfect redemption. That is why Rachel, upon the blemished birth of Joseph–Messiah ben Joseph, said: 'May the Lord add [*yosef*] another son to me',[69] that is, she prayed that the Messiah ben David would be born soon. This version supplements the previous one without any essential alteration: the proper birth of Joseph–Messiah ben Joseph will occur at his second advent, when 'another son', the Messiah ben David, is born and is revealed for the first time so that he may fulfil his mission.

The connection with historical Shabateanism, which is shown by the division of the Redemption into the stages of 'visitation' and 'remembrance' as explained at length in *Ma'amar hage'ulah*, appears all the more clearly in the interpretations of the verses 'God has taken away my shame'[70] and 'Is Ephraim my dear son?'

Rachel's reference to her shame is to be understood as relating to the disgrace brought upon the Shekhinah and the people of Israel by the ability of the Sitra Ahra to frustrate the Messiah ben Joseph's *tikunim* during the 'visitation'; this disgrace will be removed by the second appearance of the Messiah ben Joseph in the 'remembrance'.[71] The tidings brought by the prophet Jeremiah [in unpointed Hebrew his rhetorical question can be read as a statement—Trans.], 'Ephraim is my dear son', are intended to teach that the Messiah ben Joseph will be exalted in the 'remembrance' and will earn the great love of the Holy One, blessed be He, *thanks to the torments he suffered from curses and insults during the 'visitation'*. The term 'child of [my] delights'—the Hebrew uses the plural—indicates that even the *tikunim* of the Messiah ben Joseph in the 'visitation' are accounted as 'a delight of redemption'.[72] The curses and insults heaped upon Shabetai Tsevi after his apostasy

[69] Gen. 30: 24.

[70] Gen. 30: 23.

[71] 'At that time [in the 'remembrance'] [the verse] "God has removed my shame" [will apply], for during the whole of the visitation *tikunim* were performed, but because the strength of the Sitra Ahra was great there were *tikunim* which were begun and not finished, as is known. This caused great disgrace. But in the time of the remembrance when the strength of the Sitra Ahra has been weakened thus, all the *tikunim* will be completed and the disgrace will be made to pass away, [so that] "God has removed my shame", certainly' (*Razin genizin*, 70).

[72] '"Ephraim is my dear son", this is Messiah ben Joseph whose *tikunim* began from the time of the visitation; he endured many curses and insults, and nevertheless held fast to *tikunim* and with great love strengthened himself to bear the afflictions of the Exile, and because of this he is dear to the Holy One, blessed be He . . . "The child of [my] delights", two delights, one from the visitation and one from the remembrance' (ibid.). In most of the descriptions of the Messiah ben Joseph in the other homilies in this and other series, his image is not matched to the historical or legendary image of Shabetai Tsevi. This is because the Messiah ben Joseph is depicted in various guises reflecting the messianic-kabbalistic opinion, expressed repeatedly in the writings of Luzzatto and his disciples, that he transmigrates and reappears in every generation. But adequate proof of the identification of Shabetai Tsevi with the Messiah ben Joseph is afforded even by a single homily when it reflects his personality as clearly and precisely as any mirror. And see n. 81 below on the many aspects of the priestly mitre in one series of homilies in which the first

form the subject of many deeply embittered comments in Shabatean literature.[73]

The second homily I consider here[74] is the first of a series of interpretations of the verses 'You shall place the mitre on his head and put the holy diadem on the mitre'[75] and 'A virtuous wife is the crown of her husband but one who acts shamefully is like rottenness in his bones.'[76] Quantitatively, most of the homily is concerned not with those verses but with verses which describe the birth of Moses, the placing of the child in the ark at the river's edge, and his being drawn out of the water,[77] and only in the last paragraph are the key verses expounded. But the content of that paragraph, which constitutes the main point of the homily, is summed up in the opening sentence: 'This is said of the Messiah ben Joseph, for all the trials and tribulations that befell him in the time of the Exile will become a crown upon his head in the time of the Redemption.' The terms 'visitation' and 'remembrance' are not found anywhere in the homily, but from its content it is to be understood that 'the time of the Exile' refers principally to the stage of the 'visitation' and 'the time of the Redemption' is the stage of the 'remembrance'.

The homily expounding the matters connected with the birth of Moses is a very complicated one, and I will confine myself to providing a short paraphrase of its contents, inserting a few expository details where needed for the understanding of the context. The Messiah ben Joseph, represented by the child Moses, was 'in the mystical state of impregnation [*ibur*]' until his root Tsadik–Yesod revealed itself in his person, whereupon it was said of him that he was born and entered the world. With the light that he received from his divine root he performed *tikunim* of redemption, but when 'those months and those years'[78] had passed it became clear that it was not yet time, and

homily directs attention towards the Shabatean 'mystery of the mitre', whereas the others in the series make no connection between the mitre and the image of the Messiah.

[73] The Shabateans did indeed find evidence in pre-Shabatean sources for the belief that the Messiah would be tormented by curses and insults. One of the sources on which they placed great reliance is an extended version of the prophecy of Zerubabel which was reproduced as part of *Heikhalot rabati*. This stated that the Messiah would be called a robber and an apostate. Scholars declared this text to be a Shabatean forgery. See Scholem, *Shabetai tsevi*, ii. 625–7. It has recently been found included in a pre-Shabatean manuscript as part of the Heikhalot literature, apparently dating from the end of the fifteenth or the beginning of the sixteenth century. See B. Richler in *Kiryat sefer*, 58 (1983), 195. But the context of the allusions in the homily in *Razin genizin* shows clearly that there they refer to the scorn poured upon the Messiah ben Joseph–Shabetai Tsevi.

[74] *Razin genizin*, 86–7.

[75] Exod. 29: 6.

[76] Prov. 12: 4.

[77] Exod. 2: 2–6.

[78] In the episode of the infant Moses the scriptural text (Exod. 2: 2) says: 'She hid him for three months.' The words 'those years' are added to indicate the messianic activity of Shabetai Tsevi in 1665–6. And possibly the combination of 'months' and 'years' contains an echo of Nathan of Gaza's announcement in his letter to Raphael Joseph: 'A year and some months from today he will take over the government from the Turk.' See Sasportas, *Tsitsat novel tsevi*, ed. Tishby, 10.

because of the grave accusations raised by the Sitra Ahra he was deprived of the power to continue with his *tikunim*. He was therefore forced to hide his light in the Shekhinah, who was exiled to the realm of the husks, and to go down himself to the brink of the river, which is the stormy sea of the forces of impurity.[79] The Sitra Ahra, by means of its accusations, was able to triumph over the Messiah ben Joseph because he had not yet attained his full messianic rank, but when he attained it the power of the Sitra Ahra would be weakened, and at the time of the Redemption the Shekhinah, called 'the daughter of Pharaoh', would come down to him and draw him out of the river.[80] At the end of the homily on the child Moses–Messiah ben Joseph we find this: '*When he was among the husks he was called many bad names*, but when he comes out [future tense—Trans.] thus, [the words of Scripture will apply:] "She [the Shekhinah] called his name Mosheh [Moses], 'because I drew him out [*meshi-*

[79] The placing of the infant Moses in the ark at the river's edge had already been interpreted as the descent of Moses–Messiah to the husks in *Galei razaya*. See *Galei razaya* (Mogilev, 1812), 6*c*–7*a* (ed. Rachel Elior (Jerusalem, 1981), 19–21). The revelations of R. Mordecai Eisenstadt, written in Italy about 1680, say that the concealment of the Messiah 'now' is on the pattern of the concealment of the infant Moses in the ark. See Scholem, 'Perakim apokaliptiyim', 246. But it appears that in those revelations the reference is to Eisenstadt, whom they present as the Messiah ben David, and not to Shabetai Tsevi, who is there regarded as the Messiah ben Joseph. See below, text referring to nn. 88–9. However, a homily by a scholar of the Doenmeh sect shows clearly that the Shabatean system of thought applied the concealment of Moses in the ark to the descent of Moses–Messiah–Shabetai Tsevi to the husks. See Y. Molkho and R. Schatz, 'Perush "lekh lekha" lihudah levi tovah', in I. Ben-Zvi and M. Benayahu (eds.), *Sefer hayovel lishene'ur zalman shazar/Shneur Zalman Shazar Jubilee Volume* (= *Sefunot*, 3–4) (Jerusalem, 1959–60), 469–71. The homily in question slips an allusion to the name of Shabetai Tsevi into its interpretation of this topic: '"And with pitch [*zefet*]", this is the brightness [*nehiru*] which was hidden in him, *zefet* with substitution of related letters' (*Razin genizin*, 86). Replacing the dental consonant *zayin* with another dental, *shin*, and the labial *pe* with another labial, *beit*, turns *zefet* into *shabat*. Shabetai Tsevi himself connected *shabat* with his name, and this application of *shabat* is common in Shabatean literature. See Scholem, *Shabetai tsevi*, ii. 422, 490, 521, 628, 742, 747.

[80] The following examples will illustrate the complexities of the exegesis in this homily, which is remarkable for its use of *gematriyah* and letter substitution: 'This is as is written in Scripture: "She took an ark of *gome* ['papyrus reeds'] for him." What is *gome*? It is *dam* ['blood'; the consonants of *dam* have the same numerical value, 44, as those of *gome*], because until now he has been *dam* and not *Adam*, for which reason accusations could prevail against him. "And she covered it with *ḥemar* ['bitumen' or 'clay']"; this is the *raḥam* [Aramaic, 'womb': Hebrew *reḥem*; same three consonants as *ḥemar*] of *Avraham*, of whom [it was said]: *raḥem araḥamenu* etc. ['I will surely have compassion on him': Jer. 31: 19—the verse beginning 'Is Ephraim my dear son . . .'] and this *raḥam* turned into this ark to save him from the Sitra Ahra, but he is *ḥemar* and up to now has not achieved his full perfection, and when he is perfected *ḥemar* will be made into *raḥem* in perfect *tikun* . . . "To know what [*mah*] [would become of him]", for the accusation was entirely because Adam was not perfected. All this is alluded to in the word *gome* as I say, but when Adam is perfected the Sitra Ahra will be weakened. That is why [Scripture is to be understood as saying] "to know [that] he will become *mah*", precisely *mah* [which has the same numerical value as *adam*]' (*Razin genizin*, 86).

tihu] of the water'", for he was no longer among the husks who had been hiding him.' The expectation that the profaned Messiah would emerge from the husks and be revealed as an active and successful redeemer constitutes the essence of the eschatology of the Shabatean movement after Shabetai Tsevi's apostasy and death.

Two verses are expounded as referring to the deliverance and exaltation of the Messiah ben Joseph: 'You shall place the mitre . . .' (Exod. 29: 6) and 'A virtuous wife . . .' (Prov. 12: 4). The mitre, which was 'the esoteric symbol of the exile, on account of which he suffered trials and tribulations', would be 'a crown upon his head, which is his salvation'; with regard to this the verse says '. . . the holy diadem on the mitre'. The Messiah ben Joseph would be raised to the rank of husband of the Shekhinah. Lilith had wished to be 'like rottenness in his bones', to rob him of the light of the Torah which was his life by nullifying the *tikunim* he had performed to bring about the Redemption; but she would be put to shame because the Holy One, blessed be He, desired that the Messiah ben Joseph should take up where he had left off, that is, that he should complete the redemptive *tikunim* which he had begun before his descent to the husks.

The underlying Shabatean meaning breaks to the surface throughout the homily, and is daringly expressed in the declaration that the mitre, which brought down calamities on the Messiah ben Joseph in exile, would later confer holiness on him and give him strength to fulfil his messianic mission.[81] The expression most commonly used in Shabatean literature to present Shabetai Tsevi's apostasy as a messianic process is 'the mystery of the mitre'. According to the homily, the lack of perfection in the personality of the Messiah ben Joseph was an important cause of his profanation and self-degradation by his descent to the husks; but by virtue of the torments he suffered and by achieving perfection while among the husks, that is to say by continuing the struggle against them and overcoming them, he held on to his future role as Messiah.

Evidence has come down to us from Luzzatto's school to support the hypothesis that the assessment of Shabetai Tsevi's apostasy in the homily discussed here is in fundamental agreement with Luzzatto's own thinking. In 1776 H. J. D. Azulai recorded in his diary, in coded language, information given to him in Padua by R. Jacob Hazak on the *magid*'s revelations to

[81] In the other homilies in the cycle there is no connection between the mitre and the figure of a Messiah. In four homilies (nos. 3, 4, 5, 9) the mitre is treated as a reference to the Shekhinah. The other explanations are: *Malka kadisha* [the Holy King (Tiferet)], *Kise hakavod* [the Throne of Glory], *Yirat hashem* [Fear of the Lord], *Nehiru de'i'* [The Light of Ima = Binah], *Resha dela ityeda* [the Beginning which has not been made known] (apparently the sefirah Keter), a canopy over the heads of the righteous in the world to come or the root of the souls. And see n. 72 above.

Luzzatto. He wrote: '*ve-a*' [an abbreviation for *ve'amar*, 'and he said'; the *magid* is meant] that *shts* [Shabetai Tsevi], because [he] was revealed earlier, was captured by *sta* [Sitra Ahra]'.[82] The 'capture by *sta*' of course means Shabetai Tsevi's apostasy, and 'earlier' means 'too early': he was intended for messiahship and worthy of the role, but the Sitra Ahra succeeded in preventing him from fulfilling his mission and took him captive because he had revealed himself prematurely, for, as stated in the homily, it was not yet time and he had not attained his full messianic stature. Two fundamental points present in the homily are missing from Azulai's note: (*a*) Shabetai Tsevi was the Messiah ben Joseph; (*b*) his descent to the husks as an apostate did not nullify his messianic status, and he was destined to be revealed for the second time and fulfil his mission in the complete Redemption.[83] Azulai was apparently not informed of these points because they were out of date and had quite lost their significance in Padua since the decline in active messianism in Luzzatto's group.

*

The first to reduce Shabetai Tsevi to the rank of Messiah ben Joseph, shortly after his apostasy and as an incidental result of it, was another Shabetai. Shabetai Raphael was a young man who emigrated from Greece to the Land of Israel and there, according to his own account, was in close contact with Shabetai Tsevi and Nathan of Gaza in 1665, when the Shabatean movement was actively growing. He left for Italy, apparently in the summer of 1666, where he spread the tidings of the Redemption. During 1667, when news of Shabetai Tsevi's apostasy was circulated, Shabetai Raphael was in Italy, but from the information we have we cannot determine his immediate reaction to this drastic turn of events. It was only later, after his arrival in Amsterdam at the beginning of 5428 [early autumn 1667], that he is known to have expressed the novel idea that the apostate Shabetai Tsevi was the Messiah ben Joseph, the suffering Messiah, and that the Messiah ben David would soon appear and bring the Redemption, perhaps hinting that he himself was destined for the role of the superior in rank of the two redeemers. At the same time as conducting his messianic propaganda, he claimed to have prophetic and magical powers, and his activity aroused fierce controversy: many Ashkenazim were attracted to him and gave him their support, others opposed him, and the heads of the Spanish and Portuguese community drove

[82] See Benayahu, 'Ha"magid" shel ramḥa"l', 335. And see n. 54 above.

[83] These ideas are found in both of the homilies I have considered, both of which, even if not written by Luzzatto, certainly reflect his views. These homilies leave no room for Benayahu's interpretation of the veiled reference in Azulai's notes as meaning that according to Luzzatto's *magid* Shabetai Tsevi's messianic status had been entirely annulled on account of his apostasy. See Benayahu, 'Ha"magid" shel ramḥa"l', 320.

him out of Amsterdam. Shabetai Raphael turned for help to R. Jacob Sasportas, and met him while in Hamburg. Sasportas had much to say about Shabetai Raphael and gave a detailed account of his actions and escapades.[84] For our purpose it is sufficient to make it clear that Shabetai Raphael and his activity, ideas, and opinions represent an episode of no importance beyond the time and places of its occurrence.

The Shabatean background to Shabetai Tsevi's demotion from Messiah ben David to Messiah ben Joseph in Luzzatto's group, like the background to the stages of 'visitation' and 'remembrance' which I considered in Section A above, is evident in Italy in the circles of R. Abraham Rovigo and R. Benjamin Hakohen. But this downgrading is rooted entirely in the revelations of R. Baer Perlhefter, the first Shabatean '*magid*' who was active in Modena.[85] Here, in contrast to the obscure circumstances of Shabetai Raphael's declaration, it can be seen clearly how the change in the perception of Shabetai Tsevi's functions arose and developed as a result of critical events and processes in the history of Shabateanism.

In 1673, when the sect of 'believers' had already been established in Turkey and Greece, and to a certain extent in other countries too, Shabetai Tsevi was exiled to Albania. This caused fresh confusion among the members of the sect and strengthened the expectation of early redemption. Men of note who had been in close contact with Shabetai Tsevi in Adrianople [Edirne] and with Nathan of Gaza in Greece moved to Italy. Prominent among them was R. Meir Rofe of Hebron, who settled in Livorno in 1674. He and his associates whipped up the ferment in the Shabatean cells in Italy. On Yom Kippur 5437 [autumn 1676] Shabetai Tsevi died in Albania, but in Italy conflicting rumours were circulated as to his condition, and it was not until the middle of Elul 5437 [nearly a year later] that it was confirmed that the exiled Messiah had departed this life.

At that time the '*magid*' R. Baer Perlhefter had become a leading light in the school of R. Abraham Rovigo, and the 'believers' turned to him with questions, seeking revelations on the position as existing and foreseen. The content of his answers varied from time to time as changes occurred in the realities of the external situation. His first message was that Shabetai Tsevi would not die and would quickly complete the Redemption. At the end of 5437 [autumn 1677], when it was beyond doubt that Shabetai Tsevi was dead, the '*magid*' announced, in conformity with a saying in the Zohar, that the Messiah was hidden in the Garden of Eden in the palace called Kan Tsipor ['Bird's Nest'], and declared that in twelve months' time he would again be

[84] The Shabetai Raphael story is told at considerable length and extensively documented in Sasportas's *Tsitsat novel tsevi*, ed. Tishby, 271–89. Scholem (*Shabetai tsevi*, ii. 664–76) gave a detailed explanation of it by reference to Sasportas and other sources.

[85] See above, text referring to nn. 28–48.

revealed and fulfil his eschatological functions. Finally, apparently in 1679, Perlhefter made the surprising revelation that Shabetai Tsevi was the Messiah ben Joseph and the herald of the Redemption; in accordance with the fate assigned to the Messiah ben Joseph he had to die, and only when the Messiah ben David appeared would he return to life and complete the tasks of the Messiah ben Joseph. The devout Shabatean R. Meir Rofe sharply rejected the transformation of Shabetai Tsevi into the Messiah ben Joseph, and there were certainly other 'believers' who rebelled against the injury to his messianic rank. Rovigo, however, acquiesced in the reduction of Shabetai Tsevi's status, as will be apparent from what I say below, and it is probable that R. Benjamin Hakohen associated himself with Rovigo's approval of the declaration by the '*magid*'.[86]

The revelations to which I have so far referred are not extant, and are known to us only from R. Meir Rofe's reactions to them in his letters to Rovigo. But a series of revelations has been preserved which were written about the same time: this was towards the time when R. Mordecai Eisenstadt of Prague arrived in Italy with the object of performing *tikunim* in Rome, the centre of Christianity, for the downfall of the kingdom of Satan and the establishment of the kingdom of the house of David. R. Mordecai was known in the second half of the 1670s, in Ashkenazi countries and in Italy too, as a man with a messianic mission. At first, it appears, he claimed to be the Messiah ben Joseph.[87] Only after the death of Shabetai Tsevi did he seek to crown himself as Messiah ben David, whereupon, in 1680, he was invited to Italy on Perlhefter's initiative to begin his activity as redeemer. It was he who wrote the 'maggidic' revelations we are now considering.[88] These declared that when the Messiah ben David, Mordecai, succeeded in overcoming the obstacles, the Messiah ben Joseph, Shabetai Tsevi, would emerge from captivity among the husks and join with the Messiah ben David in bringing the complete Redemption.

Gershom Scholem published these complicated revelations and headed them with a study in which he explained their subject matter and the problems they involved, and cleared up some important but enigmatic details to the extent that it was possible to do so. By way of example I will quote here a short paragraph[89] which explicitly presents Shabetai Tsevi as Messiah ben Joseph and Mordecai as Messiah ben David:

[86] On the matters which I summarize briefly here, see *Netivei emunah uminut*, 81–5, and my article 'Igerot rabi me'ir rofe lerabi avraham rovigo mishenot tala"h–ta"m [5435–40]', in I. Ben-Zvi and M. Benayahu (eds.), *Sefer hayovel lishene'ur zalman shazar/Shneur Zalman Shazar Jubilee Volume* (= *Sefunot*, 3–4) (Jerusalem, 1959–60), 74–7.

[87] See Scholem, 'Perakim apokaliptiyim', 242.

[88] See Tishby, *Netivei emunah uminut*, 100–1.

[89] Scholem, 'Perakim apokaliptiyim', 250. And see, ibid., the references given in the notes.

What [is meant by] 'I will not be false to David' [Ps. 89: 36]? Simply that when people see that the Messiah ben Joseph has fallen into the pit of the wicked maid-servant, who is Hagar, they will say 'There is no hope; even if another Messiah comes, who is David, he too will fall, for they all tell lies and say that they are the Messiah, and nothing they say is true.' It is concerning this that it says 'I will not be false to David'; *if the thing appears to be false with regard to the Messiah ben Joseph, it will not appear false with regard to the Messiah ben David* . . . I will not attempt [to persuade] people to think on this account that his words are false, as they thought in the case of the herald—who was one of the sons of the sons of Rachel [***m**ibenei* ***v**aneha* ***s**hel* ***r**aḥel*], the initials of which spell *mevaser*, a herald, and are the initial letters in reverse order of ***r**ishon* ***s**habetai* ***b**a'aḥaronah* ***m**ordekhai*—'first Shabetai, finally Mordecai'.

I will add part of the anonymous revelation in MS Jerusalem 1466 which, as I said in Section A above, is of the same type as the printed revelations of Perlhefter and is shown to belong with them by content and form alike.[90] In the passage I quote (with omissions where indicated), the references to the two Messiahs display parallels with and novel departures from the other revelations:

At that time he is called the Messiah *bar niflei* [or 'the Messiah is called *bar niflei*'] [literally 'son of the fallen'—an untimely birth][91] . . . [We] must pray that he does not fall altogether, and many prayers and entreaties are needed to conciliate the Shekhinah and her children . . . At that time, when the snake desires to copulate with Eve, she says: 'Do not look upon me [thus] because I am dark',[92] for that wicked female, the wicked maidservant, the star Shabetai [Saturn],[93] is the maidservant when she displaces her mistress,[94] who is Queen Sabbath [*shabat malketa*], *after whom the Messiah who is to come is called Shabetai*. At that time this maidservant [*shifḥah*] becomes the freedom [*ḥufshah*, by rearrangement of the consonants of *shifḥah*—Trans.] of those three, the Destroyer, Wrath, and Anger, which encircle her, and that is when the crown has fallen from our head[95] . . . Because of this the chasm of the great deep, wherein is the snake, is open, and ox and ass fall into it: these two are combined in Moses [***mosheh***] in the hidden meaning of 'they fall into it [*venafelu* ***shamah***]'. And *because the fall of the Messiah ben Joseph is certain but the Messiah ben David depends on repentance which is in doubt*, Scripture says 'and an ox or

[90] See above, text referring to n. 30.

[91] A name applied to Shabetai Tsevi in his fallen state, from *San.* 96*b*, where it is used for the Messiah [but there probably does not mean 'fallen'—Trans.]. Here the reference is to Shabetai Tsevi's fall by apostasy. And see Scholem, 'Perakim apokaliptiyim', 261–2, where the name *bar niflei* is applied both to Shabetai Tsevi–Messiah ben Joseph and to R. Mordecai–Messiah ben David.

[92] S. of S. 1: 6.

[93] Lilith, who overpowers the Shekhinah, Queen Sabbath. See Zohar III, 281*b*–282*a* (*Raya meheimna*).

[94] Prov. 30: 23.

[95] Lam. 5: 16.

an ass falls into it',[96] since that mixed multitude gore the Messiah ben Joseph like an ox but they treat the Messiah ben David as an ass which breaks its bone but the body remains alive . . . and when the bone of *ḥamor* ['ass'] is broken by uprooting the [letter] *ḥet* in the mystery of *akrav* ['scorpion'],[97] *Mor remains, in the mystery of mor deror* ['flowing myrrh'][98] *of Mordecai* . . . And at what time will the *ḥet* of *ḥamor* be destroyed so that *mor deror* is left? At the time when Ze'ir [Tiferet] gives the childless Rachel the key which will open the closed *mem* [ם] and turn it into *this* kind of *mem*: מ.[99] (MS Jerusalem 1466, fos. 216r–217r)

The difference between the fall of Messiah ben Joseph—Shabetai—and that of Messiah ben David—Mordecai—is clearer in one of the revelations which appeared in print, though even there it is lamely expressed:[100] 'For the secret purpose of these Messiahs is to don the clothing of the husk in order to subdue it . . . but the Messiah ben Joseph . . . goes to the husk in dress and in action and he enters there by two falls . . . but in the case of the Messiah ben David there is only one fall, namely in regard to dress, which envelops the body like a booth [*sukah*].' Earlier in this document it says: 'The Messiah ben David, too, will change his dress and don Esau's clothes . . . and people will wonder greatly at this', that is, when the Messiah ben David, Mordecai, goes to Rome to perform redemptive *tikunim* he will disguise himself by dressing as a Christian, but the hope is that he will be saved from a second fall—apostasy. With regard to this the manuscript revelation says 'The Messiah ben David depends on repentance which is in doubt', and although, through his fall in the matter of dress, he suffers torments, 'the body remains alive'.[101] The effect of the fall of the Messiah ben Joseph, Shabetai Tsevi, is equated to his being gored by an ox, which also injured both the Shekhinah and the Jews, but did not deprive him of his role as Messiah in time to come. Rovigo endorsed Perlhefter's revelations that Shabetai Tsevi was the Messiah ben

[96] Exod. 21: 33. The exposition of this verse applying the reference to the ox and the ass to the two Messiahs is based on Zohar III, 279*a* (*Raya meheimna*). And see Scholem, 'Perakim apokaliptiyim', 252–3, 262, where the verse is expounded in various ways as applying to the Messiahs.

[97] Akrav is one of the names of the husks, who, while they are in control, cause holiness to be uprooted by adding the letter *ḥet* of *ḥamets* ['leaven'] to the Messiah Mor so that he becomes *ḥamor*, as just indicated above; but 'in the mystery of *akrav*' is an allusion to the *tikun* consisting of the uprooting of the injurious letter *ḥet* and the overcoming of the husks by the Messiah Mor–Mordecai.

[98] As in Exod. 30: 23, expounded as referring to the name Mordecai. See *Ḥul.* 139*b*.

[99] See n. 35 above.

[100] Scholem, 'Perakim apokaliptiyim', 252–3. And see ibid. 241–3.

[101] In the imaginary descriptions of the risks undertaken by the Messiah ben David, Mordecai, in going to Rome, there are obvious echoes of the action of Nathan of Gaza at the Vatican in 1668. Nathan, too, 'fell' in the matter of dress: it was said of him that 'he cut off his beard and put on fine clothes'. See Tishby, *Netivei emunah uminut*, 59–60. On the information available to us, R. Mordecai Eisenstadt never went to Rome, and he left Italy in 1682. Perlhefter left shortly before him, and this messianic awakening quickly came to an end.

Joseph in a letter to R. Mordecai Eisenstadt written in the week of the Torah portion 'Vayakhel' [Exod. 35: 1–38: 20], 5440 [early 1680], in which he said: '*It has already become clear to us here that Shabetai Tsevi is no more than the Messiah ben Joseph*, and he will not reveal himself until the Messiah ben David reveals himself, at which time the words of the verse "The flowers appear on the earth"[102] will be fulfilled.' On the face of it the context in which this statement was made is surprising, since immediately before it Rovigo says:

I also have to tell Your Excellency this: people lately arrived here testify that R. Nathan has left the congregation of Sofia and gone to Salonika, and that before leaving he delivered a sermon rebuking the community and commanding them to do penance. He told them that Shabetai Tsevi was certainly alive and he was going to meet him, and said that he was coming [or 'had come'] from across the river Sambatyon.[103]

I am of the opinion that these two pieces of information are connected with a letter from Eisenstadt to Rovigo dating from 5439 or the beginning of 5440 [late 1679] in which he announced that he was the Messiah ben David and promised that Rovigo was to be viceroy in his messianic kingdom.[104] The paragraph quoted above from Rovigo's letter, written in Adar 5440 [spring 1680], was intended to strengthen Eisenstadt's confidence in himself as candidate for the senior messiahship, on the basis that Shabetai Tsevi, although he was alive and would soon reveal himself, was 'no more than the Messiah ben Joseph'.

The Shabatean documents written after 1682 which have been preserved among the private papers of Rovigo and R. Benjamin Hakohen, and which include a notebook containing the revelations of R. Mordecai Ashkenazi from 1696 to 1699, show that the two scholars reverted to the belief that Shabetai Tsevi would be revealed as the Messiah ben David, and the '*magid*' in question [R. Mordecai Ashkenazi] did not oppose this belief.[105]

In the controversy of 1713–14 in which Nehemiah Hiya Hayon was attacked, R. Benjamin Hakohen dissociated himself personally from the Shabatean propagandist but refrained from signing the *ḥerem* [writ of excommunication] against him and his writings. From the documents relating to the controversy, including R. Benjamin Hakohen's letters, it is absolutely clear that at that time, less than fifteen years before the first appearance of Luzzatto's *magid*, R. Benjamin still belonged to the camp of the moderately

102 S. of S. 2: 12.

103 The letter is included in MS BL Or. 9165, fo. 97^{r-v}. The two portions of the paragraph discussed here are reproduced in my *Netivei emunah uminut*, 229. And see ibid. 101–2, and 303 n. 144. The whole letter has been published by Benayahu, 'Hatenuah hashabeta'it beyavan', 414–15.

104 See Tishby, *Netivei emunah uminut*, 102, 229.

105 See above, text referring to nn. 49–54, and see also n. 51.

devout Shabateans.[106] As far as I know, nothing has been discovered on R. Benjamin Hakohen's attitude to the status of Shabetai Tsevi as Messiah after the Hayon controversy, but from the standpoint he adopted in that controversy it is reasonable to assume that in spite of the perplexities and uncertainties by which he was exercised, he continued to harbour a belief in the tenets of Shabateanism, both in its historical and in its ideological aspects, until he died in Shevat 5490 [early 1730].[107] Correspondence between R. Benjamin Hakohen and Luzzatto—the one elderly and invalid, the other ebullient and communicating his enthusiasm to others—and references to the two in other letters[108] show a relationship of mutual esteem between them from which, in my opinion, important conclusions may be drawn concerning the attitude of each: R. Benjamin, for his part, hoped that ultimately the Redemption which had been cut short by Shabetai Tsevi's apostasy and death would be completed through the messianic activity of Luzzatto under the inspiration of his personal *magid*; Luzzatto, on the other hand, regarded R. Benjamin as a righteous and saintly man, one of the last of those who kept alive the embers of active messianism, and one greatly pained by the sins of Israel which had disrupted the beginning of the Redemption and prevented its completion. Luzzatto therefore hoped that the personal merit and spiritual heritage of this distinguished 'believer' would help him, Luzzatto, to restore the ruins of the task begun by the Messiah ben Joseph—Shabetai Tsevi—and bring it to completion within the messianic system set up in his school in Padua.[109]

[106] See M. Friedmann, 'Igerot befarashat pulmus neḥemyah ḥiya ḥayon', *Sefunot*, 10 (1966), 500–2, 564–5, 592.

[107] Ginzburg (*Igerot*, i. 87) gives the exact date: Friday night, the Sabbath of the Torah portion 'Beshalaḥ', 5490.

[108] All but a few of these references were recorded by Ginzburg, ibid., indexes, 482, under *R' binyamin hakohen (haraba"kh)*.

[109] R. Benjamin Hakohen's Shabateanism was an open secret in Italy, and was not unknown to his friends in other countries too, but because of his eminence as a Torah scholar and kabbalist and his high religious and moral way of life, they glossed over his allegiance to the camp of the excommunicated 'believers'. Even the persecutors who accused Luzzatto of Shabatean heresy, such as the rabbis of Venice and R. Moses Hagiz, referred to R. Benjamin by most honourable titles. See e.g. *Igerot*, i. 18, 161, 166. Luzzatto wrote to R. Benjamin at the end of Heshvan 5487 [autumn 1726], in terms of the greatest respect, to ask him for his solution of some kabbalistic problems. He received a reply at the beginning of the following month (Kislev) expressing R. Benjamin's esteem and support for the young kabbalist. See ibid. 5–8. The personal note struck in these letters shows that at that time, about half a year before the *magid* first appeared to Luzzatto, the two were already in direct touch with each other. It is probable that they met and became friends while Luzzatto was on a visit to his teacher, R. Isaiah Bassano, who had succeeded to his father-in-law's rabbinical office in Reggio. It was only on a visit to Reggio in 1729, about two years after the appearance of the *magid* and shortly before that development was publicized in the letters of R. Jekutiel of Vilna, that Luzzatto disclosed to his teacher 'in a whisper' the fact of his kabbalistic activity under the inspiration of the *magid*. Remarkably, it appears

on the face of it that even then he kept the news of the *magid* from R. Benjamin Hakohen. The reason for this concealment, as is shown by letters written at the beginning of the controversy in 1730, was Luzzatto's fear of appearing to boast of a great mystical attainment to the greatest living tsadik, a man who was a light to his generation. In Luzzatto's words: '*For you are head of the tribes of Israel*, and the Lord has granted you the distinction that your good name already extends to the uttermost parts of the earth' (ibid. 38, in the letter to R. Benjamin in which he first described how the *magid* had revealed himself to him). [He and R. Benjamin address each other in the third person—'for he is' etc.—Trans.] The most important sentence linking his concealment of his mystical elevation with his admiration of R. Benjamin is contained in an earlier letter to Bassano in which he explained the moderate tone of his reply to Hagiz's accusations. It reads as follows: 'And truly, *if it were not for my respect for the holy old man, the revered rabbi his father-in-law (may the merciful God preserve him), who I know is most dear to his Master, and for whose sake I have kept myself hidden up to the present day—for it is proper that I should accord respect to a teacher*—I would have shown Hagish [*sic*] what would become of his dreams and whose word would stand—his or the Lord's' (ibid. 27).

In spite of R. Isaiah Bassano's admiration and affection for his outstanding pupil, he was sceptical of the modus operandi Luzzatto adopted at the behest of the *magid*, regarding whom he expressed serious reservations, especially because of the fiery messianism displayed in his revelations. See my quotation and comment in *Netivei emunah uminut*, 170–1. R. Benjamin, on the other hand, on learning what had occurred in Padua, hesitated only briefly before accepting the news with enthusiasm, and appealed to 'the man with the *magid*' to lay bare the roots of his soul and reveal why he, R. Benjamin, was afflicted with his grave illness. He alluded clearly to his hope that the actions taken on the authority of the *magid* would lead to the fulfilment of the missions assigned to the Messiah. I will mention the two most important allusions of this kind. In a letter to Luzzatto expressing his excitement at the news of the appearance of the *magid* and seeking to learn more and 'to understand the root and nature of the matter', he wrote: 'For I know you to be of noble spirit, a man of understanding, possessed of wisdom and sound knowledge; is it really true that newcomers have brought with them the secrets of the Merciful One?—It had not occurred to me that *the time had come to establish it* [*et lekhonenah*]' (*Igerot*, i. 45). The phrase I have emphasized is an adaptation of the words of Ps. 102: 14: 'You will arise and have mercy on Zion, for it is time to show favour to her [*et leḥenenah*], for the time has come.' What R. Benjamin says here refers to Luzzatto's statement (*Igerot*, i. 37–9) that whereas the *tikunim* of R. Simeon bar Yohai and Luria on behalf of the Jewish people were temporary and no longer effective, 'now, it being the Lord's will to do good to his people, He has been pleased to reveal another new light like the Zohar . . . and He, in his mercy, has chosen me'. In other words, through the help of the *magid* Luzzatto was able to perform lasting and final *tikunim* of redemption. The second eschatological allusion by R. Benjamin in a letter to Luzzatto reads as follows: 'And we shall be privileged very soon to see, in our lifetime, a Zohar composed by you, the shining of your lamp which will never be extinguished, *and through your merit the sanctuary and the porch will be rebuilt*' (ibid. 48). The underlying meaning of these allusions by the veteran 'believer' was that here at last was an end to the tribulations and disappointments associated with the expectation of the Redemption, and the action which had begun in 5425–6 [1665] was likely to reach a successful conclusion very soon. With regard to R. Benjamin's complaints about his dreadful sufferings, not only on account of the physical pain but because, to his great misfortune, they deprived him of the ability to fulfil important *mitsvot*, Luzzatto wrote to him: 'Because of our iniquities, it was he who bore our sins [*sic*; in Isa. 53: 4, 'our illnesses'—Trans.] and suffered our pains' (*Igerot*, i. 38–9); 'As I live, the holy speaker [the *magid*] spoke thus to me, that they exist only because of the sin of this generation and to correct it . . . and [it is] your righteousness, learned Sir, which stands today as an atonement for all Israel, may the Lord grant you life; because this generation is unworthy, many are the afflictions imposed on

As we conclude this section, it may be remarked that even the compositions Luzzatto wrote in the years following his first capitulation in Av 5490 [late summer 1730] are full of ardent messianic aspirations; some of them show clear signs that the inspiration of the *magid* was still having a powerful effect, and traces of the influence of Shabatean ideas can also be detected in them. But I have found nothing in them which would testify to a positive relationship to historical Shabateanism like the indications, both open and concealed, in the writings considered in the present essay. It may be that in consequence of the shocks of the investigations and bans in 1730, Luzzatto and his group cut themselves off entirely from the vicissitudes of the real-life history of Shabateanism; at any rate they avoided any written hint of a positive attitude towards it.

you' (ibid. 47). Subsumed in these justifications of divine judgement is the great consolation that it was not in vain that the suffering tsadik had toiled and taken pains over decades to restore that generation to perfection and advance the redemption of Israel. As R. Benjamin himself said: 'I have placed myself in peril in the paths of the Lord, as is known' (ibid. 46), for the time had come when his devotion would bear fruit, and very soon, during the year 5490 [1730], as Luzzatto's group believed, the perfect Redemption would ensue.

SIX

Rabbi Moses David Valle (Ramdav) and his Position in Luzzatto's Group

A. THE GENESIS AND DEVELOPMENT OF LUZZATTO'S GROUP

An appendix to the rules of Luzzatto's 'holy society' in Padua prescribes the order in which seven members were to be seated at the table presided over by Luzzatto when they were engaged in their joint studies. It goes on to say:

And two have been selected together with their teacher, Rabbi Moses Hayim, to supervise and to strive with all their might to ensure that these arrangements [in the rules] are properly observed, for the glory of the Lord G–d of [*elokei*] Israel and for the glory of His Shekhinah . . . and the three of them have signed this undertaking . . . our honoured teacher and rabbi R. Moses Hayim son of our honoured teacher R. Jacob Hai Luzzatto; our honoured teacher the learned R. Y-k [Jekutiel] son of the pious teacher and rabbi, R. Judah Leib of Vilna; the honourable Mr Moses Valle son of our honoured teacher R. Samuel Valle. [Their titles are abbreviated to initial letters in the Hebrew.—Trans.][1]

Three copies of the rules[2] have been preserved, complete as to all their parts, including the document appointing the supervisors. None of the three

[1] *R' mosheh ḥayim lutsato uvenei doro: osef igerot ute'udot*, ed. S. Ginzburg [hereafter *Igerot*] (Tel Aviv, 1937), i. 9–10.

[2] Almanzi Collection, British Library, the source of the printed version; MS Cincinnati 501, fos. 330^r–334^r, appendix to commentary on *Idra raba*, copy made in Luzzatto's school; MS Oxford 2237, fos. 100^r–104^r, R. Jekutiel's copy. I am grateful to the directorate of the Hebrew Union College Library for sending me in 1958 a photograph of MS Cincinnati 501, which I had sought from them for the purpose of my researches into Luzzatto manuscripts. The documents in the printed version are: *Takanot rishonot* ['First Rules']; *Nosafot letakanot yeshivat ramḥa"l* ['Additions to the Rules of Luzzatto's Academy'], including the seating order of the members and the appointment of the supervisors; *Takanot nosafot* ['Additional Rules']; *Vezeh mishpat hab'h't* [error for *hab'h'm* (= *beit hamidrash*)] *hakadosh hazeh* ['This is the Practice of this Holy *beit midrash*']. In the other two copies the document setting out the seating arrangements and the appointment of supervisors appears at the end. I. Sonne and M. Tsevat pointed out

bears a date. S. Ginzburg correctly determined that *Takanot rishonot* ['First Rules'] were drawn up in Shevat 5491 [early in 1731].[3] It is clear, however, that the group was in existence long before the introduction of the rules as we now have them, and it is important to know the processes by which the group came into existence and took shape if we are to understand the position of Valle within it.

In the letters available to us dating from the end of 5489 to Av 5490 [early autumn 1729 to late summer 1730] which deal with the first stage of Luzzatto's activities, culminating in his being investigated and obliged to capitulate in Padua, he appears as the leader of an organized group and is so described; some of these letters also tell of earlier activity by him as leader of a group. The most detailed retrospective information, in which the members of the group are named, is contained in a letter from Luzzatto to his teacher written in Tevet 5490 [end of 1729–beginning of 1730]:

[Of] the colleagues who are with me, may the Lord preserve them, the first [in rank] are two: our honoured teacher R. Isaac Marini and our honoured teacher R. Isaac Treves, who are privy to every secret and who look within; they are [such men as are] followed by all who are upright in heart [cf. Ps. 94: 15], everyone who is wise and understanding. And there are also our honoured teacher the learned R. Moses David Valle, and our honoured teacher the learned R. Jacob Forti [known also as Hazak], and our honoured teacher the learned R. Isaiah Romanin, and our honoured teacher the learned Mordecai Ferrarese, and our honoured teacher the learned Jekutiel Ashkenazi . . . and our honoured teacher R. Solomon Dina. And after them fine young men, each according to his capacity.[4] (*Igerot*, i. 53)

In a letter dated 1 Adar 5490 [spring 1730] about the *magid* who had appeared to him, Luzzatto wrote:

At first I told none of this even to my close companions; only afterwards when I had been so commanded did I tell the wise and understanding Isaac Marini, our honoured teacher and rabbi, may the Merciful One preserve and bless him, and the wise young man, our honoured teacher R. Treves, may the Merciful One preserve and bless him, and they and I together undertook to meet for regular daily study. (Ibid. 70)

Hence the first cell was set up in secret at the end of 5487 [early autumn 1727], shortly after the first appearance of the *magid*. Gradually the circle was

some of the differences between the Cincinnati manuscript and the printed version in their article 'Some Luzzatto Manuscripts', *Studies in Bibliography and Booklore*, 2 (1955–6), 158. The seven named as seated at the table were the seven members who signed the 'first rules'.

[3] See *Igerot*, i. 179 n. 6.

[4] Not all the members mentioned here were signatories to the rules. See n. 6 below. *Igerot*, i. 122, mentions three members to whom R. Isaiah Bassano asked Luzzatto to convey his greetings: Marini, Treves, and Valle.

widened, and at the end of 5489 [early autumn 1729], following the propagandizing letters of R. Jekutiel of Vilna, an extensive movement grew up round Luzzatto in Padua, and the organization, limited and secret in its beginnings, branched out and gave rise to a network of groups at various levels.[5]

In spite of the severe restrictions imposed on Luzzatto in Av 5490 [late summer 1730] his group did not disband and he continued as their teacher and leader, but was careful not to let his mystical and messianic activity be publicly known, as he wrote in his letter of 5 Heshvan 5491 [autumn 1730]:

[5] The close-knit group, sometimes called a yeshiva [academy], continued to occupy itself mainly with kabbalah, and only selected individuals, tried and tested, took part regularly in its studies. But temporary access was also granted to favoured visitors from Padua and elsewhere. Outside the limited circle of the group, Luzzatto taught the revealed Torah, preached admonitory sermons, and gave penitential *tikunim* to all who asked. The students of the revealed Torah were divided into groups according to the level of their knowledge and understanding. Here, by way of example, are two passages which support this account: 'Many of the young men, God be praised, turn back from sin and come to learn and to receive answers, to such an extent that I am obliged, with God's help, to establish another study session; for the room is not big enough, and also the Talmud class is not suitable for all comers. For this reason I shall leave the Talmud students in one of my rooms, and in another room I shall hold an easier class suited to its audience. But *the students of* [esoteric] *wisdom are the friends, may their Rock preserve them and grant them life*, who put their study first and their livelihood second, doing their stint day by day; the physician Dr Ferrarese, too, comes every night to study wisdom, and Rabbi [Shabetai] Marini has also made arrangements to come' (*Igerot*, i. 32); 'I still hold fast to my integrity, concealing what the Ancient of Days has concealed; and the secret of the Lord [which he reveals] to those who fear Him [cf. Ps. 25: 14] I have not expounded in public, as has been maliciously imputed to me by dishonest men; for if people anxious to receive the word of the Lord come together to hear my lessons—all I shall place before them is moral rebuke and admonition . . . for they [Luzzatto's kabbalistic works] have been given only to the remnant whom the Lord calls, experts in wisdom and knowledge, *those who stand in the council of the Lord, who learn with me how to walk in His ways*' (ibid. 133). It is true that, prima facie, a few expressions seem to show that instruction in the revelation of the *magid* was open to all: this statement, for example: 'I am only a revealer of wisdom who has been commanded in the name of the Lord to make known and reveal to His children His great and glorious majesty . . . Whoever is willing to believe—let him come and rejoice in the joy of the Lord, and whoever will not believe—let him bask in his disbelief and stay at home' (ibid. 42). It seems to me, however, that statements such as this are to be classed as rhetorical and should not be seen as confirming the allegation by Luzzatto's opponents that in his haste to disclose secrets to the community he cast off all restraint. But a paragraph in the confessional prayers by Luzzatto in MS Guenzburg 745, fo. 75^{r}, which begins 'Master of all the worlds, if we have robbed You of any of Your holiness [taking *kidushekha* or *kedoshekha*, 'Your sanctification' or 'Your holy one', as an error for *kedushatekha*] by disclosing to anyone to whom it is not right to do so . . .', shows that after a time, when his group was in difficulties, he was afraid that he might have fallen into error by 'revealing secrets of the Torah to people unworthy to receive them', for 'one who stumbles in this regard causes division among the sefirot and, as it were, robs Yesod and Tiferet of the Shekhinah'. That is how I interpreted that paragraph in a note on the confessional prayers included in my essay 'Tefilot miginzei r' mosheh ḥayim lutsato' [Essay 2, n. 45—Trans.].

'For now I am absolutely resolved to conceal and keep hidden . . . until the Lord's time, for the Lord will grant wisdom *and I and my companions, all of them holy, will possess it, and the stranger with us shall have no share in it*' (*Igerot*, ii. 219). Shortly afterwards he decided, under the pressure of circumstances, to organize a clandestine mystical order on a new pattern set out in the rules of Shevat 5491 [early in 1731], with the mission to strive hard and constantly for the *tikun* of the Shekhinah and the Jewish people and so hasten the messianic Redemption. At first the order consisted only of the seven signatories to the 'first rules', who had been chosen from among his trusted associates,[6]

[6] That is to say, 'the holy society' of those working for the *tikun* of the Shekhinah was formed as a solid nucleus within the group of 'students of wisdom'. This emerges clearly from Luzzatto's first announcement of the introduction of new arrangements in his school: 'And therefore we have applied ourselves to the establishment of a course of study [in the literature of the Zohar] which will be conducted with no pause whatsoever, in the following manner: we have chosen seven [of us], who have volunteered for the purpose, to undertake among themselves that there will always be some of them studying from morning to evening, they will never be silent' (*Igerot*, ii. 234). The other 'students of wisdom' continued to study as before, without the intensive series of messianic *tikunim*, and they were even allowed when necessary to stand in for a member of the secret order, as stated in their rules, *Takanot rishonot*, sect. 7: 'That each one of the members, *even if he is not one of the holy society, shall at times be privileged* to study on a temporary basis instead of him and this shall be considered as if one of the holy members themselves were studying' (*Igerot*, i. 9). Thus the earlier group had split into two groups of mystics functioning on two different levels. In the references to the seven chosen members who signed the 'first rules' there is no mention of three prominent persons who were named as senior members of the group in 1730: Valle, Isaiah Romanin, and (see preceding note) Mordecai Ferrarese. In the printed copy the 'additional rules' [*Takanot nosafot*] are shown as signed by 'our honoured teacher the learned R. Isaiah son of the Hon. Joseph', who, to judge from his father's name, is the Isaiah Romanin who is known to us, and the next signatory is 'Isaiah son of the Hon. Abraham'. But in the other two copies (see n. 2 above) the name 'Isaiah ben Joseph' is absent. The only Isaiah in MS Cincinnati 501 is 'our honoured teacher the learned R. Isaiah son of our honoured teacher R. Abraham', while the only one in MS Oxford 2237 is 'our honoured teacher and rabbi, R. Isaiah son of our teacher the rabbi R. Abraham Romanin'. This indicates that the member in question, who is not known to me from any other source, belonged to the Romanin family, but that the name 'Isaiah ben Joseph' got into the printed copy by mistake. I discuss below (text referring to nn. 32–5 with nn. 36 and 37) why the names of R. Moses David Valle and R. Isaiah Romanin are missing. Among the other signatories to the 'additional rules' were 'the Hon. Mordecai son of the Hon. Raphael . . . the Hon. Mordecai son of the Hon. Ben Tsiyon', but neither of them is 'our honoured teacher the learned R. Mordecai Ferrarese' who is mentioned in the letter of Tevet 5490 (*Igerot*, i. 53). The last-mentioned is certainly the physician Mordecai Ferrarese who qualified as a doctor in Padua on 4 December 1714 and whose father's name was Jacob. On him, see A. Modena and E. Morpurgo, *Medici e chirurghi ebrei dottorati e licenziati nell'Università di Padova dal 1617 al 1816* (Bologna, 1967), 74–5, no. 187; M. Benayahu, 'R' avraham hakohen mizante velahakat harofe'im-hameshorerim bepadova', *Hasifrut*, 26 (1978), 117. We must therefore conclude that 'the physician Dr Ferrarese' previously mentioned (*Igerot*, i. 32) as a scholar not belonging to the group who 'came every night to study wisdom' (see preceding note) remained a visiting member and that when the group was reconstituted in 1731 he was not included in it. The existence of a

but within a few months they were joined by other members who, having passed the test, signed the 'additional rules' [*Takanot nosafot*].[7]

R. Moses David Valle's name was unknown to the general public in connection with the controversies surrounding Luzzatto. Nor did he leave his mark on the internal life of the group or in its history as reflected in the collection of letters in our possession. Apart from his service as supervisor in the school, he was not identified with any specific task.[8] The impression was

close friendship between Luzzatto and Ferrarese is confirmed by Almanzi's note (quoted in *Sefer hashirim*, ed. S. Ginzburg and B. Klar (Jerusalem, 1945), 220): 'A poem . . . on the day when the honourable Mordecai Kohen son of the honourable R. Menahem was adorned with the crown of philosophy and medicine, and Ramhal presented the poem to the distinguished scholar, the physician our honoured teacher the learned R. Mordecai Ferrarese, the mentor of his loving friend [the graduate].'

7 In the documents available to us the earliest information on the expansion of the 'holy society' is contained in a letter from Luzzatto to his teacher written during the intermediate days of Passover 5492 [1732], where he says: 'I tell you truly, at first I had only seven comrades who accepted [the conditions], and with them I shared every secret. Then came newcomers longing for that which is holy, and before they, too, accepted [these conditions] I taught them only superficialities and did not dare reveal anything [secret] to them, but once they had given their acceptance I no longer, thank God, had any fear' (*Igerot*, ii. 241). This letter was written as an apology for the arrangements in the rules which had led to complaints and with regard to which R. Isaiah Bassano had asked for clarification. On the basis of the sentences I have quoted and the content of the letter as a whole, I am of the opinion that it was written an appreciable time after the accession of the members who signed the 'additional rules', and meanwhile the framework of 'the holy society' had been further expanded in accordance with section 9 of those rules: 'That anyone who wishes to join with them later on shall be [accounted] as one of them under all the conditions already specified' (ibid. i. 11). However, the original seven members continued as a group with superior rights even after the expansion of the framework, as stated in section 8: 'They [those joining the group] undertook that if the holy members who were the first signatories needed to perform some secret action in the house of prayer [initials *beit he tav* = *beit hatefilah*, but 'the house of study', *beit he mem—beit hamidrash*—is meant] which could not be revealed to them, they would leave with no complaints whatever' (ibid.). In the letter I have quoted here, and in one which precedes it (ibid. ii. 236–7), reference is also made to the study of the revealed Torah in company with 'the holy society' and with outside groups, but in both letters Luzzatto emphasizes strongly that in his view the study of the Gemara and the laws of halakhah are subsidiary matters, a demeaning necessity, as it were, and that his mission is 'to understand and discern the depth of the secrets of His Torah [for the *tikun* of the Shekhinah] . . . and I shall leave the straw and chaff which is fit for cattle [the literal understanding of Scripture]—to the cattle, and [sc. reserve] what is fit for man [the esoteric meaning]—for man' (ibid. 240). And see Essay 1, pp. 41–2. The claim by I. Sonne in 'Avnei binyan (te'udot leḥeker ramḥa"l veḥugo)', *American Jewish Yearbook* (1935), 218–21, that the study of halakhic matters was a principal element in Luzzatto's school, is no more than an exercise in apologetics divorced from reality. And see Essay 8, n. 20.

8 The only document signed by Valle relating to the controversy is the 'Testimony of the heads of the congregation of Padua in the matter of Ramhal's bookcase' dated 19 Tevet 5495 [Jan. 1735] (*Igerot*, ii. 293–4). This document was written at the request of R. Isaiah Bassano, and it was signed by scholars of the congregation in the following order: 'Shabetai son of our honoured teacher the learned R. Isaac Marini (may the memory of that righteous man be for a

therefore created that he was a figure on the fringe of the group and its affairs, involved only as one of the rank-and-file students taught by Luzzatto and subject to his authority. And indeed he is so described in most research studies if they mention him at all. It is true that R. Hananel Neppi spoke highly of him:

I have heard wonderful reports of his Torah knowledge, his piety and holiness; he was an outstanding pupil and faithful member of the household [i.e. a faithful adherent] of the godly *tana* [scholar and authoritative teacher] our teacher and rabbi, the holy R. Moses Hayim Luzzatto (may he be remembered for blessing in the life of the world to come), and he was a man of wide scholarship, a wonderful preacher, and a godly kabbalist . . . a leader of the prayers in a Sephardi synagogue; he studied Torah standing up and did not go to bed at night until all the Jews of the holy congregation had returned home safely, and he prayed for them that no evil should befall them and that the Lord in his mercy should protect them.[9]

In that description, which is undoubtedly based on a faithful Paduan tradition, Valle is represented as having been a saintly guardian of the congregation during his lifetime. For generations after his death they kept his memory alive, and they made it their custom to recite the 'prayer over the graves of the righteous' (Luzzatto's composition intended for all righteous men) 'over the grave of the physician R. Moses David Valle'.[10] But even in Neppi's panegyric Valle is described in relation to Luzzatto as no more than 'an outstanding pupil and faithful adherent'.

This portrayal lessens his stature and detracts from his true position in the group. Only in Almanzi's biography do we find a few items of information which could place the relationship between Valle and Luzzatto on a different footing, but they are contained in scattered and obscure remarks *obiter*, and researchers have not grasped their importance. In my researches I have discovered further information which sheds new light on Valle's personality and his position in the group, and I shall consider these sources together in order to determine his true place in the group's history.

blessing), servant of the holy congregation; Jacob Israel son of our honoured teacher the learned Abraham Hazak (may the memory of that righteous and holy man be for a blessing); Isaiah son of our honoured teacher R. Joseph Romanin, may his memory be for a blessing; Moses David son of our honoured teacher Samuel Valle, may his Rock protect him and preserve his life; Isaac Shabetai son of the honourable R. Judah Rocca'. R. M. D. Valle's father died on 14 Kislev 5496 [Nov. 1735], as is noted on a copy of his tombstone inscription kept in the office of the Padua congregation which I read on my visit there in 1977.

[9] H. Neppi, *Zekher tsadikim liverakhah* (printed with M. S. Ghirondi's *Toledot gedolei yisra'el uge'onei italyah*) [hereafter Neppi–Ghirondi] (Trieste, 1853), 247, 249. The inscription on Valle's tombstone, which is quoted there, describes him as 'the distinguished and learned physician, the godly kabbalist, our honoured teacher the exalted and holy rabbi Moses David Valle, may the memory of that righteous man be for a blessing; departed to his eternal home, year [5]537 [1777]'.

[10] J. Almanzi, biography of Luzzatto [hereafter 'Almanzi'], *Kerem ḥemed*, 3 (1838), 140 n. 41.

B. A GROUP OF KABBALISTS UNDER VALLE'S LEADERSHIP IN THE SOCIETY OF SEEKERS OF THE LORD

In his description of Luzzatto's young days Almanzi writes:

Each day M.H.L. used to go and study in the Society of *Those who seek the Lord* (now known by the name of *Metivei tsa'ad* ['Those who take good steps']) [both names emphasized in the original] [for these names, see Prov. 28: 5 and 30: 29—Trans.], and there he became closely attached to those men of renown who walked in [the way of] the Torah of the Lord, teaching the children of Israel both the written and the oral Torah, I mean R. Israel Hezekiah Treves, the physician R. Moses David Valle, and R. Jacob Hazak [Forti] . . . All three were learned in the ways of kabbalah. When M.H.L. told them of his longing to go deeply into these matters they became his friends and colleagues. They chose one place in that society and one place in his house where they could meet in conclave, and they began to study the books of the Ari [Luria], the Remaz [R. Moses Zacuto], and other kabbalists.[11]

This description would make it appear that they set apart one place for the study of kabbalah in the *beit midrash* ['house of study'] of the 'Society of Seekers of the Lord' and another in Luzzatto's home at the same time. I am in no doubt, however, that here Almanzi has confused the order of events. The information that the young Luzzatto embarked on studies in a communal *beit midrash* in company with men who were his superiors in kabbalistic knowledge derives from a tradition which was current in the Paduan community. The *beit midrash* of the 'Seekers of the Lord' was still in existence under a different name at the time Almanzi wrote his biography, and in the margin of his observation that 'they chose one place in that society' he remarked with disgust:

To this day that place [the special room to which the group of kabbalists withdrew to study] remains permanently closed . . . the ignorant are afraid to go near it, and avoid the doorway for fear that some disaster may befall them if they enter it . . . Are these people friends of ours? You fools, when will you grow wise?[12]

[11] Ibid. 114. In the orders of prayer in some manuscripts it is recorded that it was customary to recite Luzzatto's prayers for the eves of Rosh Hashanah and Yom Kippur over Valle's grave. See M. Benayahu, 'Tefilot shenityaḥasu leramḥa"l ve'einan lo utefilot shelo nizkar bahen shemo vehen lo', *Sinai*, 78 (1976), 223, 234–9.

[12] Almanzi, 130 n. 15. The name *Metivei tsa'ad* tells us that R. M. S. Ghirondi, too, was referring to Luzzatto's period of study in the *beit midrash* of the Seekers of the Lord when he wrote at the beginning of the collection entitled *Likutei kabalah* (MS Jewish Theological Seminary, New York, Mic. 1599, previously MS Adler 886) that Luzzatto 'flourished like a cedar in Lebanon'

However, for proof of the existence of a *beit midrash* in Luzzatto's father's house Almanzi relied on letters written later,[13] whereas, as I shall show, the *beit midrash* was certainly not set up when Luzzatto was taking his first steps in the world of kabbalah but rather when he had attained a higher level of mystical understanding. Thus Almanzi's further statement, in the paragraph I have quoted, that 'he [Luzzatto] was head of them all' etc., does not fit the period of study in the Society of Seekers of the Lord but should be applied to subsequent stages.[14] On the basis of what we know of the three personalities whom the young Luzzatto joined in order to embark on an exploration of the hidden depths of kabbalah, it is clear that the man who headed the group in kabbalistic expertise was Valle, who had already produced some works on kabbalah when Luzzatto was still a stripling.[15] This was known to Almanzi, as

[*parah ke'erez balevanon*] (a dot over the last letter of each word, indicating that those three letters spell *ḥazan*, alludes to Luzzatto's service as cantor and prayer-leader: see Almanzi, 115) 'in the great synagogue of the Ashkenazi congregation *and in the* [house of] *study of the hasidim which is called Lekaḥ tov* ['good doctrine'] *and Metivei sa'ad* [*sa'ad* = 'assistance'; Almanzi's version has *tsa'ad*, 'step', in agreement with the text of Prov. 30: 29] here in this city, which may God protect, and there he taught the science of truth [kabbalah] to his pupils, may the memory of those righteous men be for a blessing, and he was privileged to hear the voice of an angel and holy being from Heaven coming down to reveal to him the secrets and mysteries of the Torah'. But this account altogether distorts the picture, for it is quite clear that the *magid's* revelations were communicated and learnt in the *beit midrash* in Luzzatto's own home. In his biography of Luzzatto Ghirondi made no mention at all of the '*beit midrash* of the hasidim' and spoke only of the one which Luzzatto opened in his home, but in this case also the description is confused and contrary to the facts. See *Kerem ḥemed*, 2 (1836), 55.

[13] See Almanzi, 131 n. 16; 160–1 nn. 102, 104.

[14] Following Almanzi's misleading description, A. M. Habermann added complication to confusion with regard to study in the Society of Seekers of the Lord. See *Sefer leshon limudim*, ed. A. M. Habermann (Jerusalem, 1945), pts. 2 and 3, introd., p. 8.

[15] The two manuscript volumes of *Sefer halikutim* were composed in 1717–18, when Luzzatto (born 1707) was 10 or 11 years old and Valle (born 1696) was 21 or 22. See n. 70 below and text referring to nn. 77–95. According to Modena and Morpurgo, *Medici e chirurghi*, 73–4, no. 184, Valle was awarded his medical doctorate on 22 Oct. 1713 (the beginning of Heshvan 5474). This date is questionable, because it would mean that he completed his studies at the university at the age of 18. R. Jacob Hazak was older than both Luzzatto and Valle—he was about six years Valle's senior—but his forte was principally halakhah. See Neppi–Ghirondi, 148, 150; M. Benayahu, *R' ḥayim yosef david azulai* (Jerusalem, 1959), 70 n. 73. I have no information on the age of R. Israel Hezekiah Treves, but from Almanzi's description there is no doubt that he too was some years older than Luzzatto. Mention should be made of another three personalities known to have been senior members of Luzzatto's group who were older than he was: (*a*) R. Isaiah Romanin: see M. Benayahu, 'Ketavav shel yeshayah romanin mipadova', *Bar-Ilan*, 14–15 (1977), 181, 187; (*b*) R. Jekutiel of Vilna: see Essay 8, n. 126; (*c*) R. Isaac Marini: two proofs of his seniority: he was a student at the university in 1716, when Luzzatto was in his eleventh year (see n. 54 below); and a mention of R. Isaiah Bassano's poem on the occasion of Marini's wedding, in the early version of *Leshon limudim* (pt. 2, *limud* 5, p. 47), which was compiled in 1724, shows that his marriage took place in Luzzatto's seventeenth year or earlier (as

is shown by his remark that Valle was 'Luzzatto's *teacher* [*rav*—the emphasis is mine] and subsequently his colleague in matters of kabbalah'.[16]

We cannot determine with certainty when Luzzatto entered upon his studies with the Society of Seekers of the Lord, but several items of information combine to point to the most probable time. R. Isaiah Bassano, who was rabbi of Padua from 5475 to 5482 or the beginning of 5483 [1715–22], stated explicitly that Luzzatto, while a student in his school, read some kabbalistic works which he found there and was greatly attracted to them, and then 'his thoughts extended into the valley of secrets, he delighted in love of them, he took his fill of love'.[17] R. Jekutiel of Vilna, writing at the end of 5489 [late summer 1729], said: 'Even earlier, when he was 14 years old, he knew all Luria's works by heart.'[18] Although this is late hearsay evidence and third-hand at that, contained in a letter written in hyperbolic language for propagandist purposes, it is undoubtedly based on a kernel of fact, and we are at least entitled to conclude from it that in 1721 or thereabouts Luzzatto was already at home in the study of kabbalah.[19] This conclusion is reinforced by the distinctly kabbalistic character of the author's introduction to the second part of *Leshon limudim* in its first edition, which was written in 1724.[20] On the

was realized by B. Klar: see *Sefer hashirim*, ed. Ginzburg and Klar, 43–4). The editor, A. M. Habermann, published Bassano's poem as an appendix to *Leshon limudim* (69–77).

16 Almanzi, 140 n. 41.

17 *Igerot*, i. 59. For the years of Bassano's service as rabbi in Padua, see M. Wilensky, 'Letoledotav shel r' yeshayah bassan', *Kiryat sefer*, 27 (1951), 113–14.

18 *Igerot*, i. 19.

19 It is fair to assume that in that year, when he was only 14, it was still beyond him to compose kabbalistic works, and indeed we learn as much from the information I have quoted above in the text of the present essay. It is true that one of the copies of *Masekhet rosh hashanah* (MS Oxford 2307, fos. 1^r–15^v, second foliation) is annotated at the end: 'This day, the first day [i.e. Sunday], 28 Elul, year 5481 [1721], in Padua', but in the 5480s 28 Elul fell on the first day of the week only in 5487, whereas in 5481 it fell on the Sabbath. Hence 5481 should have read 5487: a slip of the pen by the copyist. M. Benayahu, *Kitvei hakabalah sheleramḥa"l* (Jerusalem, 1979), 64, recognized the inconsistency but nevertheless held obstinately to the defective date. *Masekhet rosh hashanah* was published recently in duplicated form as an appendix to *Sefer kitsur hakavanot*, ed. H. Friedlaender and Y. Spiner (Benei Berak, 1978), 173–82. And see ibid., introd., pp. 13, 16. Benayahu, not content with endorsing the obvious error, went further and by a flight of his imagination dated to 5481 the composition of *Asarah pirkei mishnah* ['Ten Chapters of Mishnah'], a systematic summary of the principles of Lurianic kabbalah which Luzzatto included in *Ma'amar havikuaḥ*. See *Kitvei hakabalah*, 123–4. And see Essay 1, pp. 50–3 and n. 157.

Benayahu's book was published in the second half of February 1979, more than a month after the present essay was handed over for publication. Wherever, therefore, I have found it necessary to refer here to the new book I have added a note or a supplement to a note in square brackets. See also Essay 10, n. 10.

20 F. Lachower, in his essay 'Besha'ar hamigdal' ['At the Gate of the Tower'] (in his *Al gevul hayashan vehehadash* (Jerusalem, 1951), 32–6), brought these two points together to show that, contrary to the opinion which was current among scholars, Luzzatto had engaged in the study

1. Jottings and kabbalistic drawings by the young Luzzatto (MS Jewish Theological Seminary, New York, Mic. 1615)

2. Jottings and kabbalistic drawings by the young Luzzatto
(MS Jewish Theological Seminary, New York, Mic. 1615)

basis of the foregoing I assume that Luzzatto began his study of kabbalistic texts in 1720, when he reached bar mitzvah age, and that this was the time when he joined the circle of students of kabbalah in the Society of Seekers of the Lord.

I have found strong support for the information given by Almanzi in a surprising source. At the beginning of MS Jewish Theological Seminary, New York, Mic. 1615, which contains R. Hayim Vital's *Otserot ḥayim* with many marginal notes and comments in Luzzatto's hand,[21] an inscription inside the cover reads: 'This book belongs to me, Mosheh Hayim Luvzzatto[?]', and on another line: 'I, Mosheh Hayim Luvzzatto[?],[22] bought this *Sefer halekatim*[?] ['book of gleanings'].'[23] On the same page there are diagrams of the sefirot as a chain and in the form of circles and straight lines as in Lurianic kabbalah, and scribbled letters and words, lines and dots. The succeeding page too (fo. 1^r), on the folio before the beginning of the kabbalistic work, has a few drawings and doodles of the same kind, together with remarks on holy names, and words and names of persons in Italian,[24] and is annotated: 'This book belongs to the Society of Seekers of the Lord', followed by the initials *yod tsadi vav*, meaning 'may their Rock and Redeemer protect them' or 'may their Rock protect them and preserve them in life'. These jottings and diagrams are clearly by an unskilled hand, and the drawings of the sefirot should be seen as amateurish efforts by the youthful Luzzatto as he felt his way into the esoteric field of kabbalah.[25] Evidently the young novice in the study of

of kabbalah at a very early age. However, Lachower made no mention of the information on Luzzatto's study of kabbalah in the Society of Seekers of the Lord, which lends strong support to his argument.

[21] It is probable that the notes in question served as a basis for the 'commentary on the beginning of *O[tserot] ḥ[ayim]*' (*Igerot*, ii. 220; and see ibid. 263).

[22] At the foot of the page the name is clearly written with two *vavs*: Lvvtsato.

[23] The composition is headed in square Hebrew characters *S' a[lef] ḥ[et]* [= *Sefer otserot ḥayim*] followed, in Italian Hebrew cursive, by *Likutei hakdamat hakabalah* ['Selections for an Introduction to Kabbalah'].

[24] The name Salomon Racach Paduwa should be particularly noted; the wealthy philanthropist Solomon Rakah is mentioned many times as a patron of Luzzatto and his group, but in the available documents dating from 1730 onwards he is described as a resident of Venice, where he maintained a yeshiva. See *Igerot*, headings 'Rakah' and 'Shelomo Rakah' in the indexes; Essay 8, p. 428 and n. 67; p. 440 and n. 115. From Luzzatto's jottings it would appear that he was previously a resident of Padua. It is therefore probable that he was also a patron of the Society of Seekers of the Lord and first came into contact with Luzzatto and his group in the 1720s in Padua.

[25] I publish these two pages here in facsimile (Plates 1 and 2). I am most grateful to the directorate of the library of the Jewish Theological Seminary, New York, and in particular to its director Dr Menahem Schmelzer, for their kindness in photographing this manuscript and others in their collection for me during my time as visiting professor at that institution in 1967, and in granting me permission to publish them wholly or in part. Apparently a misunderstanding of these jottings was responsible for M. Benayahu's absurd pronouncement that Luzzatto's

kabbalah, after joining the study group in the Society of Seekers of the Lord, handed over to the society a book which he had bought.

The 17-year-old Luzzatto's growing strength in the field of kabbalah manifested itself not only in speculative ideas which he expressed in the first edition of *Leshon limudim* but also in mystical activities he undertook with the aim of attaining a higher understanding of esoteric wisdom. In 1730, in a letter to R. Benjamin Hakohen telling how the *magid* had revealed himself to him,[26] he wrote: '*For years* I diligently occupied myself with *yiḥudim*, performing them at the rate of one almost every quarter of an hour, as indeed is still, thank God, my constant practice', and, he said, by virtue of his 'constant practice of *yiḥudim*' he was privileged to receive revelations from on high. The reference is to 'years' before the New Moon of Sivan 5487 [early summer 1727] and is apt for the year 5484 or at latest 5485 [1724–5]. The fact that he was inspired to perform *yiḥudim*, with its results in the manifestation to him of the *magid* and of angels and souls of the righteous, is understandable in the light of teachings in the literature of kabbalah, especially R. Hayim Vital's *Sha'ar ruaḥ hakodesh*, and also against the background of occurrences which were frequent in the Shabatean movement in general and in Shabatean circles in Italy in particular.[27] But it is reasonable to assume that

group, in its new incarnation in 1731, 'was called "The Society of Seekers of the Lord"' (*Sinai*, 82 (1978), 42). [My surmise has proved correct. See Benayahu, *Kitvei hakabalah*, 116–17, which in addition to this misunderstanding contains other oddities: there is no mention of Luzzatto's personal jottings with their immature handwriting, or of his diagrams; Almanzi's remarks are quoted only in an aside (ibid. 57 n. 23), and the important information I have quoted in my present essay is entirely omitted; the name 'Society of Seekers of the Lord' becomes forthwith the regular name for Luzzatto's group, and thus there is conveyed to the reader the remarkable discovery that the prayers and poems in MS Guenzburg 745 include compositions written 'for the day when the Society of Seekers of the Lord was founded' (ibid. 99)—which are actually the prayer and *piyut* for the night of 17 Shevat! And see also ibid. 192, 258.]

26 *Igerot*, i. 39.

27 Revelations through '*magidim*' and in other ways were common and played central parts in the Shabatean movement at its inception and in the course of its development. The best-known of the personalities on whose revelations detailed information has been preserved in Shabatean literature are Nathan of Gaza and A. M. Cardozo. See G. Scholem, *Shabetai tsevi vehatenuah hashabeta'it bimei ḥayav* (Tel Aviv, 1957), under the appropriate headings in the indexes; M. Benayahu, 'Hatenuah hashabeta'it beyavan', *Sefunot*, 14 (1971–8), similarly. The *batei midrash* of R. Abraham Rovigo in Modena and R. Benjamin Hakohen in Reggio served as ports of call for itinerant preachers and places of abode for regular revelators. As we know, the aged R. Benjamin Hakohen lived to welcome Luzzatto's *magid*, and asked to be blessed with a knowledge of his revelations. See *Igerot*, i. 45–9 etc. Luzzatto met R. Benjamin Hakohen face to face when he visited Reggio in 1729, and may perhaps have been in close contact with him earlier. On the same visit, which took place before the publication of the affair of the *magid* in the letters of R. Jekutiel and its repercussions, Luzzatto disclosed the secret in confidence to R. Isaiah Bassano alone. Later on he apologized for having concealed it from R. Benjamin, whom he looked up to and admired as his teacher, as he said when writing with regard to R. Moses

the revelations from on high which were astir in Valle's soul during the existence of the group studying kabbalah in the Society of Seekers of the Lord played an immediate and direct part in raising the level of Luzzatto's mystical understanding. I report on those revelations below.

We may fairly take it that Luzzatto's performance of *yiḥudim* and the appearance to him of the *magid* took place in the privacy of his home in his father's house. Of course, outside the hours when he shut himself away to perform *yiḥudim*, he continued his study of kabbalah. But it is hard to decide whether he still did so in the Society of Seekers of the Lord or whether, from the time when he began the 'constant practice' of *yiḥudim* in his home, he carried on his studies at home too and withdrew from the communal *beit midrash*, and if so, whether he studied on his own at that time or drew away his friends to join him. Two important documents are directly relevant to this question, but their content is problematical and no firm conclusions can be drawn from them. In a letter to the rabbis of Venice dated 3 Shevat 5490 [early 1730], R. Isaiah Bassano wrote [stringing together biblical quotations in traditional rabbinic rhyming prose—Trans.] that, after he left Padua,

He [Luzzatto] pitched the tents of his palace, and all who sought the Lord would seek his dwelling-place, and he put forth his shoots, and his springs were spread abroad, and his delight day by day, together with his companions and friends, was to set up the tabernacle of the Torah, in the fear of the Lord [which] is pure, in study and in deed, a pleasing odour, a fire-offering.[28]

A letter to the rabbi of Hamburg, printed under the heading 'The rabbis of Padua to R. Ezekiel', but actually written in Luzzatto's group by R. Isaiah Romanin, who signed it as 'scribe of the yeshiva of Padua' on behalf of the yeshiva committee, reads as follows:

When the ark set forth, the ark of God, our honoured teacher and rabbi the above-mentioned R. I. B[assano], from our holy congregation to the holy congregation of Reggio, may its glory increase—in his *beit midrash* he [Luzzatto] spent much time

Hagiz's denunciation of his activity: 'And truly, if it were not for my respect for the holy old man, the revered rabbi his father-in-law (may the merciful God preserve him), who I know is most dear to his Master, *and for whose sake I have kept myself hidden up to the present day—for it is proper that I should accord respect to a teacher*—I would have shown Hagish [*sic*] what would become of his dreams and whose word would stand—his or the Lord's' (*Igerot*, i. 27). And see ibid. 26, 28–31, 36. For our purpose, therefore, great importance attaches to the two Shabatean '*magidim*' who were active in Rovigo's *beit midrash*, in whom R. Benjamin believed and to whose teachings he listened with enthusiasm. See 'Ha"magid" hashabeta'i harishon beveit midrasho shel r' avraham rovigo', in I. Tishby, *Netivei emunah uminut* (Ramat Gan, 1964), 95–8; G. Scholem, *Ḥalomotav shel hashabeta'i r' mordekhai ashkenazi* (Jerusalem, 1938), 32–3. It should be remarked that Nathan of Gaza's *yiḥudim* were discussed in correspondence between R. Isaiah Bassano and Luzzatto on the revelations of Luzzatto's *magid*. See Essay 4, pp. 225–8.

[28] *Igerot*, i. 59.

in privacy and seclusion, making his study of the Torah his occupation, not resting night or day. There God was revealed to him in the year 5487 [1727], as indeed he told us in truth and sincerity after disclosing [his secret] to us; for he had kept [it] closely concealed for about two and a half years, keeping secret this great thing that God had done for him.[29]

On the face of it these two documents would appear to show clearly that from about 1724, when Luzzatto began to occupy himself with *yiḥudim*, it was also at home that he studied. However, the two descriptions do not tally with regard to the manner of his study. According to Bassano's account it appears that at that time he began to function as head of a group, whereas according to Romanin he at first 'made his . . . Torah his occupation' 'in privacy and seclusion', and only some time later, after the *magid* had appeared to him, did he become a teacher and leader, first to individual companions and then to a wider public. Bassano's description is certainly inaccurate, for it is perfectly clear that Luzzatto's public activity did not begin before 5489 [1729]. From the content of the letter it is evident that the writer was giving a compressed account, with abbreviations and omissions, and the remarks I have quoted are appropriate to the period after the appearance of the *magid*. Nor had Romanin any intention of presenting Luzzatto's opponents with a detailed report on the stages of his development, and his account does not exclude the possibility that from 1724 to 1727 Luzzatto continued to study with the group in the *beit midrash* of the Seekers of the Lord. I am inclined to come down in favour of that possibility, and we have an important document dated 13 Tishrei 5486 [autumn 1725]—before the appearance of the *magid*—which in my opinion supports my interpretation. The document is an official one issued by the rabbis and lay leaders of the Paduan community,[30] headed by R. Shabetai Marini, who had decided

to crown with the crown of *ḥaverut* [i.e. to confer the title of *ḥaver* on] the under-named three distinguished and valued men, because ever since their youth God has planted in their hearts [the desire] to understand and be wise, to listen to and learn the word of the Lord [which is] tried and tested: our honoured teacher R. Isaiah—may his Rock protect him and preserve him in life—son of our honoured teacher R. Joseph Romanin, of blessed memory, and the *ḥakham* ['sage'] [the emphasis is mine—I.T.] our honoured teacher R. Moses David son of our exalted and honoured teacher R. Samuel Valle, may his Rock protect him and preserve him in life, and our honoured teacher R. Moses Hayim son of the exalted and honoured R. Jacob Hai Luzzatto, may his Rock protect him and preserve him in life. Having

[29] Ibid. 87. For the style in which the letter is written and signed, see ibid. 95, 107, 132.

[30] This document is in the *pinkas* [official record] of the congregation. I copied it from a photograph in the General Jewish History Archive in Jerusalem (microfilm HM 3123). It has been published in facsimile and in Italian translation. See P. Nissim, 'Sulla data della laurea rabbinica conseguita da Moshé Chajim Luzzatto', *Rassegna mensile di Israel*, 20 (1954), 499–503.

seen that they are accomplished rabbinical scholars worthy of ordination by reason of their excellent character, erudition, understanding, and activities which *are well known*, as is the fact that their deeds will draw them near [to God], since they have determined to make their [study of] Torah their occupation, the aforesaid eminent gentlemen [the authorities—Trans.] have ordered that henceforth, with God's help, the names by which they shall be called, especially for the purpose of calling them up to read the Torah, shall be the eminent *ḥaver* Rabbi Isaiah Romanin, may his Rock protect him and preserve him in life, the eminent *sage* the *ḥaver* Rabbi Moses David Valle, may his Rock protect him and preserve him in life, and the eminent *ḥaver* Rabbi Moses Hayim Luzzatto, may his Rock protect him and preserve him in life.

From the triple 'crowning' ceremony and the praise of the laureates, and particularly the observation that 'they had determined to make their study of Torah their occupation', it is evident that they engaged in Torah study in a group. In my opinion we have here the nucleus of Valle's group in the Society of Seekers of the Lord in the last stage of its existence before it was superseded by Luzzatto's newly formed group.[31] Valle's pre-eminent position

[31] See above, text referring to nn. 4 and 5. At first sight it may seem odd that the group certificate granting *ḥaverut* makes no mention of R. Israel Hezekiah Treves and R. Jacob Hazak, who are enumerated by Almanzi together with Valle as the students of kabbalah in the Society of Seekers of the Lord who were joined by Luzzatto. The explanation is that R. I. H. Treves was not yet considered qualified to receive the title, while R. J. Hazak, who is regularly referred to in the letters and in the rules as 'our honoured teacher the sage, rabbi', had certainly received it before 5486, the date of this certificate. R. Isaiah Romanin, whom Almanzi does not name as one of the 'Seekers of the Lord', probably joined that group after Luzzatto. It is to be supposed that R. Isaac Marini, who became a confidant of Luzzatto on an equal footing with R. Treves immediately after the appearance of the *magid*, was another member of the Society of Seekers of the Lord. His name, too, is missing from the certificate, because he had not yet attained the level of *ḥaver* in halakhic studies. R. J. Hazak was granted *hatarat hora'ah* [rabbinic qualification; literally, authorization to give halakhic rulings] with the title of *harav hakolel* ['the learned rabbi'] in Elul 5497 [1737], and at the same time the title of *ḥaver* was conferred on R. Isaac ben R. Shabetai Marini, R. Israel Hezekiah Treves, R. Samuel Hai Ka"ts (one of the cantors), and R. Solomon ben R. Jacob Menahem Treves. This collective certificate of ordination is likewise preserved in the communal record and there is a photograph of it in the General Jewish History Archive in Jerusalem (microfilm 3116). The four *ḥaverim* are referred to as pupils of R. J. Hazak in this certificate, which notes them as being 'two pairs of our rabbis, *ḥaverim* listening to his words of wisdom'. However, it is certainly no coincidence that all five ordinees belonged to Luzzatto's group, which, as will become clear, was headed by Valle after Luzzatto left Padua in 1735, and the ordination is to be understood as intended additionally to honour the group of pupils who were taught kabbalah and the ways of piety by Luzzatto and Valle. The information on R. Isaac Marini and R. Solomon Treves in this document should be added to their description in the essay by M. Benayahu, 'Shirim leyom ḥatunato shel ramḥa"l', in *Shai leheiman: meḥkarim basifrut ha'ivrit shel yemei habeinayim (Sefer haberman)/Papers on Medieval Hebrew Literature Presented to A. M. Habermann (A. M. Habermann Jubilee Volume)* (Jerusalem, 1977), 53–5, where the ordination certificate is not mentioned.

among the *ḥaverim* is given emphasis in the certificate by its application of the title 'the sage' [*heḥakham*] to him alone.[32]

[32] Apparently Valle was already married at the time of his ordination. This is not simply an opinion based on his age—he was 30 years old in 1726—but is founded on factual information. In one of the personal notes interspersed in his writings he says: 'This day, 20 Iyar [5487/1727], being the day *asher yuladti ben* [understood, ungrammatically, as meaning 'when a son was born to me'—Trans.] . . .' (MS BL 385, fo. 625ᵛ). This information refutes M. Benayahu's assertion in 'Shirei ḥupah ḥadashim leramḥa"l', *Hasifrut*, 24 (1977), 96, that Valle 'was married in Venice in the middle third of the month of Sivan in 5490 [1730]' on the basis of a mention of 'the honourable Moses David's wedding' in Venice in a letter of 26 Sivan 5490 (*Igerot*, i. 153). How little reliance can be placed on this is also shown by the way the bridegroom is referred to ['the honourable Moses David'—Trans.], for in the letters R. Moses David Valle is given his proper title, 'our honoured teacher, the sage, rabbi', together with his family name. In the document appointing the supervisors, too, which on p. 10 of the printed version calls him 'our honoured teacher, rabbi', the copy in MS Cincinnati 501 has 'our honoured teacher, the sage, rabbi' (fo. 334ʳ). It is therefore probable that 'the honourable Moses David' was a young Paduan or Venetian man who is unknown to us. The name Moses David seems to have been common in the region. Close to a mention of the poems written for Valle's wedding (with no indication of when it took place) which were the basis of Benayahu's assertion, there is a reference to the young man Moses David Anzolin of Venice. See M. Soave, 'Letter (no. 15) to M. Steinschneider', *Vessillo israelitico*, 28 (1880), 175. Moreover, to back his assertion Benayahu wrote that 'Valle's diary for that year (5490), which is interspersed in his writings on Scripture in the British Museum's manuscripts, is full of references to marriage'. Nothing of the sort. The references to 'the kisses', '*devekut* in love', 'betrothal and a time for wedding', and 'the marriage in love' occur in Valle's diary from 25 Av to 11 Elul 5491 [1731], spanning the date of Luzzatto's wedding on 27 Av 5491. In Essay 3, p. 206, I quoted the text of four notes in MS BL 387 (fos. 52ᵛ, 58ᵛ, 65ʳ, 69ʳ) which are relevant to this matter, indicating their date and explaining their significance. In the diary entries for 5490 there is no mention of weddings or marriages, and for Sivan, the alleged month of Valle's marriage, there is only one sentence, which heads his commentary on the Book of Esther and reads as follows: 'On 20 Sivan—and I shall rejoice in the Lord, I shall exult in the God of my salvation' (MS BL 386, fo. 548ᵛ). (Benayahu gave no references for the entries for 5490 which were allegedly 'references to marriage', but as was his wont with 'discoveries' founded on air, he cast his eyes far into the future and referred the reader to an essay that is still to come: see his 'Shirei ḥupah', n. 15.) Even if we were nevertheless to concede the possibility that the bridegroom 'the honourable Moses David' was Valle because he might have been widowed or divorced and have remarried in 5490, it must still be said that to shift to 5490 the timing of certain notes in order to tilt the balance, when it is absolutely clear that they were written in 5491, constitutes a deliberate 'scientific' deception. On the essential point in Benayahu's essay: it will be clear to every intelligent reader that to take a poem which in the manuscript is underwritten with the name of its author, 'Jekutiel of Vilna' (as is also the epithalamion for Luzzatto which immediately follows it), and to present it as a poem written by Luzzatto for Valle's wedding, is nothing more than an idle fiction. See Essay 3, p. 208, where I described Jekutiel's composition as a poem in praise of his colleague Valle, and quoted some sample verses copied from the photograph of MS Guenzburg 745 obtained by the Ben Tsevi Institute.

C. THE SPECIAL STATUS OF VALLE IN LUZZATTO'S GROUP

In information about Luzzatto and the members of his group dating from and after the first appearance of the *magid*, we are repeatedly told that their place of study and the scene of their activity was his father's house, where a regular *beit midrash* was maintained throughout the vicissitudes of the group even after Luzzatto left Padua.[33] In other words, the students of kabbalah removed to that house from the Society of Seekers of the Lord and became disciples of their young colleague, 'the man with the *magid*'. However, R. M. D. Valle, who in my opinion was head of the study circle in the Society of Seekers of the Lord, did not lose his special status when the circle ceased to exist, but continued to operate in close association with Luzzatto as an unacknowledged partner in the leadership of the group, and after a while, when Luzzatto settled in Amsterdam, succeeded him as head of the group. I will indicate the main evidence for these conclusions.

1. Valle, who was appointed together with Luzzatto and R. Jekutiel of Vilna to supervise the arrangements of the group, was not a signatory to the rules and was not named as one of the members allotted a seat at the table at which their studies were led by Luzzatto.[34] The absence of the name of the supervisor seems surprising and calls for explanation, since he was of course one of those who 'pledged faithfulness[35] to the covenant' and regularly took part in the studies and activities of the group.[36] In my opinion the explanation of the mystery is that Valle was not regarded as an ordinary member but was almost equal in rank to the leader of the group, Luzzatto, who was similarly not a signatory to the rules. As regards the allocation of places at the table, we must

[33] See *Igerot*, ii. 322. R. Isaac Marini, who in 1736 leased or rented the house from Luzzatto's father when the latter moved to Amsterdam, and who promised 'to watch over the doors of the *beit midrash*', was described as the *gevir* ['magnate'] without any further title. This description does not fit R. Isaac ben Shabetai Marini, who was one of the heads of the group and one of Luzzatto's closest confidants, and it therefore seems to me that the person who rented the property was R. Isaac ben Aaron Marini.

[34] See n. 2 above. Similarly, in the letter of Passover 5492 to his teacher [n. 7 above] Luzzatto did not include Valle in the number forming his group, for he wrote: 'at first I had only seven comrades . . . and with them I shared every secret', meaning the seven comrades who signed the rules and were seated in order at the table.

[35] '*koretei emunah*' as in the printed copy of the rules. The other two copies have *koretei amanah* ['those who entered into an agreement'], which is the correct reading.

[36] We still have a homily of his which he preached to 'attentive colleagues' at a gathering of the group for the festive meal on the night of 17 Shevat 5492 [1732]. See Essay 2, p. 119.

take it that while studies were in progress Valle would have been sitting in a separate area assigned to him for the performance of special messianic *tikunim*, since he was destined shortly to be revealed and become active as the Messiah ben David.[37]

[37] It seems to me that we can dispose in the same way of the similar problem with regard to R. Isaiah ben Joseph Romanin, who is not mentioned in the documents which date from 5491, as I explained in n. 6 above. This scholar was a friend and companion of Luzzatto even before 1727 and appeared as scribe [*sofer*] of Luzzatto's yeshiva in 1730, when he defended Luzzatto in public (see above, n. 29 and text referring to nn. 30–1). He was certainly one of the secret order from the start, and his very omission from the list tells us that he was regarded as being of superior rank to the seven colleagues who were named. In Essay 2, p. 125, I quoted a paragraph from the writings of Valle and pointed out: 'We have here an explicit statement that the two Messiahs [ben Joseph and ben David] . . . were present in Luzzatto's group in Padua.' The paragraph in question was written in Elul 5491 [early autumn 1731]. I have been unable to find any clear information showing which one of the group was the Messiah ben Joseph but several clues (see n. 100 below) provide grounds for supposing that R. Isaiah Romanin was their candidate for the role of the warrior Messiah. If my supposition is correct, we must take it that Romanin–Messiah ben Joseph, too, would have sat in an area separate from the rest of the members of the group, alongside Valle–Messiah ben David. In Essay 4 above I summed up my consideration of the Messiah ben Joseph in these words: 'The portrayal of the Messiah ben Joseph in Luzzatto's writings resembles in major outlines that of Shabetai Tsevi in Shabatean literature' (p. 244). And in Essay 3, where I wrote 'his [Luzzatto's] messianic partners were actual persons living and working alongside him' and 'the most problematic figure is that of the Messiah ben Joseph, on whose identity I refrain for the time being from expressing any opinion' (p. 205), I referred the reader to my discussion of 'the Shabatean character of the Messiah ben Joseph in Luzzatto's writings' (p. 205 n. 75). I thereby offered a hint to the perceptive that in my opinion Luzzatto believed that with the appearance of Shabetai Tsevi the Messiah ben Joseph had been revealed, but that through force of circumstances he had sunk down among the husks and had been unable to complete his mission. Thus the Messiah ben Joseph in Luzzatto's group was regarded as a reincarnation of Shabetai Tsevi, and when he was freed from the fetters of the Sitra Ahra he would succeed in fulfilling his messianic mission. I have since gathered a great deal of material which confirms my opinion and I am about to clarify the matter in full in an essay entitled 'Demuto shel shabetai tsevi vehatenuah hashabeta'it betorat hage'ulah shel ramḥa"l' [apparently a superseded title for what is now Essay 5 above—Trans.]. Following my hints, Y. Liebes has drawn attention to, and explained, several passages in Luzzatto's writings which point in that direction. See his essay 'Sefer "Tsadik yesod olam": mitos shabeta'i', *Da'at*, 1 (1978), 94, 96, 111, nn. 112, 119, 187. And see below, addendum to this note.

Addendum to n. 37

I present here in general outline two texts from cycles of homilies written in Aramaic. In both of them the personality and fate of the Messiah ben Joseph reflect the image and actions of the historic Shabetai Tsevi as these are depicted in the doctrine and literature of Shabateanism. The first text (*Megilat setarim verazin genizin* (Warsaw, 1889), 69–70) is 'the 9th interpretation' in the commentary on the verses 'God remembered Rachel' (Gen. 30: 21) and 'Ephraim is my dear son' (Jer. 31: 19 [understood as a statement—Trans.]). It begins by declaring that the messianic redemption is coming to fulfilment in two stages, 'visitation' and 'remembrance', and goes on to describe them as being, as it were, a 'first coming' and a 'second coming'. The 'visitation' is the beginning of the eschatological *tikun* and is only a temporary and hidden

2. Explicit testimony to his exalted position in the group is given by two unique mystical and messianic documents which were in the possession of Almanzi but have been lost. This is how Almanzi described their contents:

> *A discussion* . . . for the *tikun* ['making good the wrong done'] of the sale of Joseph in which Ramhal takes the lead, *and second to him R. Moses David Valle* [the emphasis is mine—I.T.] and after them all their colleagues speak in reply, and by joining together with the Shekhinah they annul this iniquity and all the sin of the house of Israel from Adam, the first man, up to that time . . . *A deed* . . . *done by Ramhal and R. M. D. Valle* which is similar [in purpose—Trans.] to the discussion, to hurl ballista stones to strike the enemies, the fifth 'army' [*ma'arakhah*] and the wicked Armilus, *and these stones will afterwards be great stones for the foundation of the House.*[38]

redemption which is discontinued for fear of the Sitra Ahra. 'But in the time of the remembrance it will not be so, for at that time everything will be brought into the open, and what was done in secret at the time of the visitation will be revealed.' At the time of the 'visitation' it is the Messiah ben Joseph who is active. When his *tikunim* are halted by the power of the Sitra Ahra the failure of the humiliated redeemer is a source of great shame, and he is subjected to taunts and curses, 'for the *tikunim* of this Messiah ben Joseph began from the time of the visitation and *he suffers many taunts and curses* . . . for this began at a time of affliction and secrecy, afflicted he certainly was'. In the perfect redemption which would occur in the time of the 'remembrance' with the appearance of the Messiah ben David, the shame would be removed and it would be revealed that the Messiah ben David was and remained 'Ephraim my dear son'. The second text (*Megilat setarim verazin genizin*, 86–7) appears at the beginning of the homilies on 'You shall put the mitre' (Exod. 29: 6) and 'A woman of worth is the crown of her husband' (Prov. 12: 4). It says that at the first coming of the Messiah ben Joseph 'the time was not yet complete and *many strong accusations were heaped upon him*' which forced the humiliated Messiah to hide his light in the realm of the Sitra Ahra. '*While he was among the husks he was called by many bad names.*' The act of concealing the infant Moses in the ark and laying him 'on the bank of the river' (Exod. 2: 3) is applied to the descent of the Messiah ben Joseph to the husks, and therefore 'when he emerges thus, she will call him "Moses [*mosheh*], because I drew him out of the water [*meshitihu*]"' (Exod. 2: 10). The surprising ending is this: 'With regard to this mystery it is written: "You shall put the mitre" etc.; this is the secret of the exile because of which he suffered trials and torments, and it is a crown on his head, for that is his deliverance, for which reason Scripture says "the holy crown upon the mitre".' As is well known, 'putting on the mitre' [or 'turban'] was an expression of unmistakable meaning, commonly used in Shabateanism for the apostasy of the Messiah. The distinction between the period of the 'visitation' and that of the 'remembrance' is the central pivot of Luzzatto's thought in his *Ma'amar hage'ulah*, which was composed in Kislev 5490 [end of 1729] or earlier, at the height of his overt messianic activity. The descriptions of the 'visitation' in that work clearly match the course of the Shabatean movement as perceived by some of its thinkers and adherents, but the personal features of the Messiah ben Joseph–Shabetai Tsevi are more masked than in the homilies. The whole affair is noteworthy for the influence of the writings of A. M. Cardozo and the revelations of R. Baer Perlhefter, who was active as a man with a *magid* in the circles of R. Abraham Rovigo and R. Benjamin Hakohen, as I show in the essay I have mentioned [Essay 5 above—Trans.]. On the question whether the homilies are the work of Luzzatto himself or were written by members of his group, see n. 76 below.

[38] Almanzi, 131 nn. 18–19, where the titles of the documents are given emphasis. I am grateful to my friend Professor Shimon Halkin for his observation that the strange expression 'the

In these documents, both in the first one which mentions but does not name the members of the group, and in the second in which they play no part, Valle appears as Luzzatto's partner in kabbalistic *kavanot* and acts of magic for the rectification [*tikun*] of sins and for war against the Sitra Ahra ['Other Side]' in order to hasten the Redemption. The time when these documents were written is not known, but from unpublished manuscripts by Luzzatto which I discovered in the course of my researches and which shed fresh light on his activities and on the clandestine life of the group in 1731–4, it seems to me that the actions described here were among those carried out at that time to speed the arrival of the 'end of days'.

3. In all the writings by Valle that I have examined I have found four mentions of Luzzatto in contexts where novel kabbalistic ideas are quoted in his name. I reproduce here the important parts of each of these:[39]

It has been known for some time that all the affairs of the world are overseen and arranged by His names which issue forth among them, to each one according to its ways . . . according to the combination [in force] in each month . . . Some of this *I received from my dear friend and companion the learned and wise R. Moses Hayim Luzzatto*. But we need to know in addition that governance by the glorious Name constantly goes round the whole twenty-four hours of the day and night, too.

I received from my dear friend Ramhal [the knowledge] that the four parts, skin, flesh, sinews, and bones, correspond to the four *partsufim* ['faces, configurations'],

fifth *ma'arakhah*' means the fifth sphere, the place of the planet Mars according to the Ptolemaic system which was widely known among Jewish scholars. What is meant is that according to our apocalyptic sources the wicked Armilus, who came from Rome, was to kill the Messiah ben Joseph. In Luria's *kavanot* it is said that he ordered his disciples to pray for the Messiah ben Joseph that this should not happen. Mars [*ma'adim*] was of course regarded as the power in charge of war, destruction, and bloodshed. In my opinion he is taken here as the partner of Armilus in the sense of the combination Edom–Rome–Christianity, and it is possible that by 'Armilus' Luzzatto and Valle meant the Pope. The purpose of the attack on 'the enemies' with 'ballista stones' was to bring about the complete Redemption without the death of the Messiah ben Joseph. See Ben Yehudah dictionary under *ma'adim*; R. Margaliot, *Malakhei elyon* (Jerusalem, 1945), under 'Armilus', 213–14; D. Tamar, *Meḥkarim betoledot hayehudim be'erets yisra'el uve'italyah* (Jerusalem, 1970), 170–1. The annulment of the sin of selling Joseph was certainly another act of *tikun* to save the Messiah ben Joseph's life.

[39] References for the four extracts, in the order in which they are quoted, are as follows: MS BL 385, fos. 721^{v}, 865^{v}; MS BL 386, fos. 229^{v}–230^{r}, 383^{v}. In this connection I should mention a surprising point which is hard to explain. At the beginning of the first volume of the British Museum collection (MS 385) there are some entries in a hand which differs from the rest and looks like Luzzatto's writing: some lines on combinations of letters and on magical formulae (fos. 4^{r}, 5^{r}) and three pages (fos. 7^{v}–8^{v}) headed: 'I copied [this] from the book *Mevo she'arim*.' The works by Valle in which this material was inserted were written in 1722, and if indeed the additions were made by the 15-year-old Luzzatto, we may conclude that Valle, the head of the group in the Society of Seekers of the Lord, handed over his writings for study by the youngster who was learning kabbalah with him, and allowed him to make additions of his own.

Z[e'ir] and his female partner N[ukba], A[ba], and I[ma], which are the four letters of the Tetragrammaton, as we know.

Moreover: *kimeḥolat* ['like the dance of . . .'] is written in the defective form [i.e. with the omission of the *vav* representing the vowel 'o'][40] so as to allude to Mahalat the daughter of Ishmael who is the mystical representation of the city of Constantinople, sister of Nevayot, he being mystically identified with the beguiler Muhammad, *as was conveyed to me by my dear friend the learned Ramhal, may the Merciful One guard him and bless him.*

And the hidden meaning of this is: one needs to know that Tevet and Shevat, Tamuz and Av, are, in mystical terms, the N[etsah] H[od] of the months, as is known to kabbalists, and there during the exile the snake bites and the lion rends, and were it not for the Lord who is for us, they would swallow us alive. And that is the hidden meaning of 'who bites the horse's heels, so that its riders fall backwards',[41] for the snake bites N[etsah] and H[od] in order to topple Yesod, who is their rider, *as I am told has been said by the learned sage Ramhal* with regard to this verse.

The last of the above pieces is centred upon the *mevarer* [rendered here as 'the winnower'—Trans.], who is *sod hamelekh*, that is, mystically identified with 'the King', in other words Valle in his capacity as Messiah ben David,[42] who in two months of the year clashes with 'two forces of impurity who desire to overcome him; these are the snake in the month of Tevet and the lion in the month of Av'. Two of the four passages quoted were written in 5488 [1728] and two at the end of 5489 [late summer–early autumn 1729]; all of them, therefore, after the *magid* had made his appearance and before that event became known to the people of Padua, and all of them at the time when Luzzatto's group was active in secret and Valle was involved in it. The references to Luzzatto are couched in language which points to a relationship of colleagues studying together and would not be appropriate for a pupil receiving instruction from a teacher.

4. In Valle's writings, where he describes the stages of the eschatological *tikunim* and reveals his growing messianic strength, the times and processes

40 S. of S. 7: 1 [on the Shulamite. Without the *vav*, the word could be read in isolation as *kemaḥalat*.—Trans.]. For Mahalat the daughter of Ishmael, see Gen. 28: 9. Basing himself on Luzzatto's statement, Valle went on to say: 'Accordingly this indicates that Shulamit will be the mystical representation of Jerusalem when the time comes for her to govern as a ruler over kingdoms, just as she is at present Mahalat, the mystical representation of Constantinople. And the reason she is called Mahalat of the two camps is that in her there is a memorial of the two camps of Esau [Rome—Trans.] and Ishmael, for she first came into the hand of Esau, and the emperor Constantine named her Constantina [Constantinople], after his own name . . . [and] although she afterwards came into the hand of Ishmael, Esau's power of evil did not leave her, for each man helped the other, each one encouraged his brother, in raising up the edifice of defilement.'

41 Gen. 49: 17; not, however, 'riders' but 'rider'.

42 See Section D below, and text referring to nn. 77–95.

he specifies should be seen as contributions to autobiographical statements (as will be proved by the passages quoted at the end of the present essay), and they are linked to the activities of Luzzatto and the vicissitudes of Luzzatto's group. Here are some passages which show that Valle worked in step with Luzzatto in independent personal *tikunim* for the advancement and realization of their messianic missions:

The suspension of the lights by the Sitra Ahra [continued] until the year 5481 [1721] . . . for in 5482 the lights began to be revealed to the winnower for the purpose of the winnowing,[43] and until 5487 he had not begun his return to Ramah

[43] The revelation of divine lights for the purpose of the winnowing was accomplished through a celestial force—called the *mashpia* ['transmitter of the divine flow'] in the intimate personal notes interspersed in Valle's writings—which strengthened Valle's spirit and disclosed secrets to him. I quote below seven such notes dating from 1722 to 1725 which go some way towards clarifying this complex and ramified matter. (It is some time since I announced—see *Netivei emunah uminut*, 326 n. 77—that I was engaged in clearing up the entire problem of Valle's mystical and messianic diary and was preparing a complete collection of the notes in question for publication in a critical edition. For the time being see the further examples below, nn. 102–4.) [But now see also Essay 7 below.—Trans.]

(*a*) 'Year 5482 [1722], the Lord, blessed be He, has had compassion on me and has brought me forth from curse to blessing and from darkness to great light' (MS BL 385, fo. 9^{r}); (*b*) 'From here onward in the year 5483, *when the light was dimmed* by the curtain of the separating clouds, but *the mashpia remained* and went running back and forth' (ibid., fo. 62^{v}); (*c*) 'At this time in the month of Shevat [5483/late winter–early spring 1723], I was visited in the pit of my sorrows and anointed with the oil of joy which was poured on my head from on high' (ibid., fo. 127^{r}); (*d*) 'Now began the days of adversity in the days of Tevet, *when the mashpia departed altogether* and I fell from a high roof into a deep pit, year [5]484. May the Lord, blessed be He, have mercy on me' (ibid., fo. 305^{r}); (*e*) 'At this time, in the days of Tishrei, the Lord in his compassion for me brought healing to my wound *and the mashpia returned*, year [5]485 [autumn 1724]' (ibid., fo. 391^{r}); (*f*) 'This day, the tenth day of Marheshvan [5485], I have been relieved a little of my sorrow and distress and of the hard labour that I was made to do [by the Sitra Ahra]. May the name of the Lord be blessed from now and for ever, blessed be He who bestows good on the undeserving and has bestowed all good on me, for the *mashpia grows ever stronger* as the hand of the Lord is good to me' (ibid., fo. 404^{r}); (*g*) 'Blessed be God who has not turned away my prayer, nor His lovingkindness from me. This day, 15 Tevet [5485/Dec. 1724], I have found some rest for my soul, for the accusation(s are) growing ever weaker and *the mashpia is growing ever stronger* against my enemies. My foot stands on level ground, in the assemblies I will bless the Lord' (ibid., fo. 446^{v}). Here, by way of example, is one sentence in which the shining of lights and the revelation of secrets of the Torah are combined and are taken by Valle, 'the winnower', as a justification for attributing prophetic rank to himself: 'For he has reached [so far as] face to face *to receive his lights and his teachings from his supernal teacher*, as in the verse "The spirit of the Lord speaks through me and His word is upon my tongue [2 Sam. 23: 2]"' (MS BL 387, fo. 43^{v}). I shall explain elsewhere the prophetic and messianic connections in Valle's writings and in his personality.

On the question of the anointing in the third of the above notes it should be observed that in Shabatean literature there are repeated descriptions of the anointing of Shabetai Tsevi in various ways and at various times as a mystical and visionary experience which takes place in his soul or as a miracle which is witnessed by the public. In the calendar of the sect the date of the

from the winnowing towards the left . . . and in 5489 the winnowing was entirely finished, and now in 5490 the winnower returns to his root with the fourth husk [Nogah, 'brightness'], which is eaten together with the fruit, and he is brought ever closer to perfect *tikun*, when Nogah is like a bright light.[44] (MS BL 386, fo. 344[r])

The processes of *tikun* in the Godhead and in the worlds are bound up with the personal situation of the winnower. Until 1721 he was sunk among the husks,[45] where he and the divine lights were together subjected to the authority of the Sitra Ahra. From 1721 to 1727 he battled among the husks, with varying success, to winnow the sparks by means of the forces of the divine attribute of Judgement [Din]. In 1727, at the time when the *magid* appeared to Luzzatto and the 'maggidic' group was set up in secret, the winnower began to rise from the abyss of the husks and to lift the sparks up to their divine source with the aid of the attributes of Mercy and Compassion—Hesed and Rahamim. In 1729, when the news of the *magid*'s revelations and of the accompanying messianic activity had begun to spread beyond the boundaries of the clandestine group, the winnowing of the sparks was completed. In 1730 [5490], when the group was operating openly and its influence reached its peak, 'the winnower returned to his root' and the time of the Redemption and of complete *tikun* began with the transformation of the 'brightness' husk, Nogah, into a holy force.[46]

The turning-point reached in 1727 is thrown into prominence by the clear-cut distinction between the processes of the struggle which preceded it and those of the redemption which followed it: 'In this year [1730] the perfect *tikun*. First there was the world of *tohu* ['desolation'] from the year 83 to the year 87 [1723–7], and from 87 to the year [of] *pedut* ['redemption'; numerical value 490, i.e. year 5490] there was the world of *tikun*' (MS BL

anointing is given as 21 Sivan. See R. Jacob Sasportas, *Tsitsat novel tsevi*, ed. I. Tishby (Jerusalem, 1954), 16, 94–5; Scholem, *Shabetai tsevi*, 112–13, 130. Here are two descriptions comparable with the reference to the anointing in Valle's note: 'They saw [at the festive gathering for the night of Shavuot in Gaza] what looked like drops of oil dripping from his [Shabetai Tsevi's] head, and the prophet [Nathan] told them that he was being anointed from Heaven' (*Tsitsat novel tsevi*, 16); '*bezot* [literally 'with (or in) this', but the numerical value of *zot* is 408; hence *bezot* = 'in 5408' (1648)] he [Elijah] anointed the Redeemer, the King-Messiah, with the oil of joy and happiness' (*Shirot vetishbaḥot shel hashabeta'im*, ed. M. Attias and G. Scholem (Tel Aviv, 1948), no. 192, p. 177; as in the corrected version in Scholem, *Shabetai tsevi*, 113 n. 3).

44 The words are those of Hab. 3: 4, *nogah ka'or tihyeh* ['[His] brightness is like a light'].

45 His descent among the husks began in 5475 [1715]. See n. 78 below.

46 On the nature of the 'brightness' husk and its position in the realms of uncleanness and holiness, see my explanation in I. Tishby, *The Wisdom of the Zohar*, trans. D. Goldstein (Oxford, 1989), ii. 463–4; I. Tishby, *Torat hara vehakelipah bekabalat ha'ar"i* (Jerusalem and Tel Aviv, 1942), 69–72, 110–13, 141–2. On 'his return to Ramah' and the return of the winnower to his root, see n. 92 below.

386, fo. 446[r]).[47] Immediately before this passage there is a reference to the year 5486 as included in the opening stage of the *tikun*. This is the year when the title of *ḥaver* was conferred on Valle and Luzzatto, and when Luzzatto was engaged in the performance of *yiḥudim* to bring the holy spirit to rest upon him:

In the year[s] 86 and 87 . . . the winnowing from the world of Nukba [the female] was completed, and afterwards in 5488 Yesod was revealed and brought down to begin the winnowing from the world of the male, until it was completed in the present year, which is the year of redemption [*pedut*, 5490], when T[ifere]t is revealed to raise up the fallen Tsadik and Tsedek [Yesod and Malkhut]. (MS BL 386, fo. 434[r])

In describing the *tikunim* performed in 5488, Valle makes a clear reference to the activities of the group:

They [the years of exile imposed upon Israel] came to an end actually in 5488, *when the awakening and the tikunim of the redemption began with increased vigour . . . when the great tikunim in honour of God began in secret.* (MS BL 387, fo. 3[v])

These words, which disclose the fact that the clandestine group intensified its activity on *tikunim* in 1728, were written at the end of Sivan or the beginning of Tamuz 5491 [summer 1731],[48] about a year after Luzzatto's first capitulation in Padua, and they serve to show that the underground messianic activity in 1731 was regarded as a direct continuation of the secret stirrings and public ferment in the years 1727–30. Indeed, the year 5491 [1731] is said in many places to be the time of the complete Redemption, in accordance with Luzzatto's mystical marriage contract, even in documents written

[47] For the meaning and applications of the terms 'world of *tohu*' and 'world of *tikun*' in Luria's kabbalah and in discussions of the special virtue of his kabbalah, see my essay 'Ha'imut bein kabalat ha'ar"i lekabalat harema"k bikhetavav uveḥayav shel r' aharon berekhyah mimodena', *Zion*, 39 (1974), 8–11, 20–1, 78–81. Valle transferred these terms not only to his activities aimed at universal *tikun*—divine, cosmic, and human—but also, in the rest of the sentence quoted here, to his own *tikun*, represented as the *tikunim* of the three parts of the soul of the winnower: 'for the *tikun* of Malkhut in the first place and the winnowing of the sparks of the *nefesh*, together with the *tikun* of the *nefesh* of the winnower, occurred in the year[s] 87 and 88, and the *tikun* of the *ruaḥ* and the winnowing of its sparks and the *tikun* of the *ruaḥ* of the winnower occurred in the year 89, and now in the year *hatamim* ['perfect'; numerical value 5490], this is the *tikun* of the *neshamah* with the winnowing of its sparks and the *tikun* of the *neshamah* of the winnower'.

[48] In his homiletical justification for fixing 5488 as the year in which the exile ended, Valle relied on what 'we have already said in another place', by which he meant a document written between the New Moon of Heshvan and the New Moon of Adar 5488 [winter 1727–8] (MS BL 385, fo. 734[r]). That document, however, only contains a calculation of 'the end of days' unrelated to the performance of *tikunim*. Hence the mystical and eschatological activity which was intensified about half a year after the *magid* first appeared to Luzzatto was due to the belief that 5488 was the right year in which to hasten the Redemption.

in 5490.[49] These extracts—merely a few of the many which could be quoted—suffice to show that at every stage Valle, as Messiah ben David, acted as an almost equal partner to Luzzatto's Moses[50] in mystical preparations to speed the Redemption.

5. In most of the correspondence between Luzzatto and his pupils which still survives there are prominent mentions of 'our *aluf* the physician' or 'the *aluf*, the physician' [*aluf*, meaning *inter alia* 'chief', is an honorific for a distinguished scholar—Trans.] and in some of the letters it is clear that the reference is to a member who has taken Luzzatto's place as leader of the group. S. Ginzburg made the quite unfounded statement that 'apparently the physician was Ferrarese',[51] whereas B. Klar asserted[52] that 'the *aluf*, the physician' was R. Isaac ben Shabetai Marini, on the basis of the information that 'the wealthy R. Isaac Marini' leased or rented Luzzatto's father's house in 1736 in order 'to watch over the doors of the *beit midrash* . . . to meditate on his Torah together with attentive companions'.[53] This assertion can immediately be dismissed: side by side with 'our *aluf* the distinguished physician' there is a reference to 'our respected colleague, our honoured teacher, the sage R. Isaac',[54] who is certainly R. Isaac ben Shabetai Marini. From Valle's personal standing it is clear that the honorific title 'our *aluf*' fits him extremely well. An entry in his writings indicates exactly when he was appointed as head of the group: 'This day, 11 Tamuz [5497/summer 1737], I have been brought into the holy *beit midrash* to teach and supervise' (MS BL 388, fo. 113^r).

49 See the two passages I quoted in Essay 3, pp. 205–6, in connection with my consideration of Luzzatto's marriage contract.

50 See Essay 3, pp. 190–206.

51 *Igerot*, ii. 435 n. 190. M. Benayahu adopted Ginzburg's erroneous opinion, without acknowledgement, and in his essay 'R' avraham hakohen mizante', 117, he flatly declared: 'R. Mordecai Ferrarese was one of the members of Luzzatto's group, and after Luzzatto left Padua R. Mordecai Ferrarese became head of the group.' Here again (see n. 32 above), he adopted the principle of 'supporting an unproven statement by an unproven statement', and relied for his proof on an essay that has still to see the light of day (see 'R' avraham hakohen mizante', n. 38). And see n. 6 above.

52 See *Sefer hashirim*, ed. Ginzburg and Klar, 43.

53 *Igerot*, ii. 322. In my opinion (see n. 33 above) the house was let to R. Isaac ben Aaron Marini, who was a junior member of the group and was certainly not regarded by them as 'our *aluf*'.

54 *Igerot*, ii. 399. The references to R. Isaac Marini in the letters and other documents known to me give no indication that he was a physician. B. Klar's description 'the physician Isaac ben Shabetai Hayim Marini' is apparently based on Almanzi (141 n. 48) and J. H. Schorr (his words are quoted in *Sefer hashirim*, ed. Ginzburg and Klar, 27). The records in Modena and Morpurgo, *Medici e chirurghi* (no. 100, p. 411), make it clear that R. Isaac Marini was registered at the university in 1716 but did not complete his studies. R. Isaac ben Aaron Marini, another who was not a physician, is similarly mentioned alongside 'our *aluf* the physician' (see quotation below, text referring to n. 56).

Apparently the appointment of a replacement for Luzzatto was deferred until it was clear that he did not intend to return from Amsterdam to Padua.[55]

The references to 'our *aluf* the physician' in the letters are an important source of information about Valle. I will quote and elucidate them in chronological order. The first of these references occurs at the end of Luzzatto's farewell letter 'to the holy colleagues, members of our *beit midrash*, may the Merciful One protect and preserve them', written in Bolzano when he was on his way from Padua to Amsterdam, on 10 Kislev 5495 [Nov. 1734]:

> Above all, greet our *aluf* the physician, may the Merciful One protect and preserve him, and also convey my greetings to His Honour the Rabbi Marini, may the Merciful One protect and preserve him, and the physician Samuel Hai Ka"ts [*ka"ts* = *kohen tsedek*] and his father, the physician, may their Rock protect and preserve them, and the physician Samuel Cohen, and the rabbi, R. Isaac Rocca, and R. Isaac ben Aaron Marini, may the Lord protect him, and *s(h)in"shin* [?my greetings to you also].[56]

This tells us that Valle had been regarded by the group as 'our *aluf*', and had been so described, before Luzzatto left Padua, and that Luzzatto counted himself as one of the *aluf*'s admirers.[57] The other persons mentioned by name were singled out because they were only associates outside the circle of the 'holy colleagues', while 'our *aluf*' received separate mention because of his special status within the group. About a year and a half before the leadership was finally transferred to Valle, Luzzatto wrote, in a letter of 18 Heshvan 5496 [autumn 1735] (in which he urged the members of the group to continue to operate as they had been doing in spite of the insults and threats of their opponents, 'and any excommunication, any ban, any curse is permitted to you, forgiven you, allowed you [i.e. you may accept them—Trans.]'):[58] 'All of us, and in particular my lady wife, send you [plural] our greetings; my greetings to our *aluf* the physician, may the Merciful One protect and preserve him.'[59] Again, at the end of the latest letter of his to Padua which we have, dated 26 Adar I 5499 [spring 1739] and addressed to 'the pleasant companions, members of my *beit midrash* at Padua, may the Merciful One protect and preserve them', he particularly mentioned Valle: 'And to the *aluf*, the physician, may the Merciful One protect and preserve him, sheaves of good

[55] Before Valle was chosen to head the group, it had continued to function under the care of R. Jacob Hazak, as appears from Hazak's letter of the New Moon of Adar 5496 [spring 1736] to R. Isaiah Bassano. See *Igerot*, ii. 416.

[56] Ibid. 282. And see ibid. 435 n. 191.

[57] It may be that this title was conferred on him in recognition of his messianic mission, in the same way that the Shabateans, as instructed by Nathan of Gaza, used to refer to Shabetai Tsevi by the epithets 'the beloved' and 'our beloved'. See my essay 'Te'udot al natan ha'azati bekhitvei rabi yosef ḥamits', in *Netivei emunah uminut*, 287 n. 95.

[58] See Essay 8, n. 38, and Essay 1, n. 61.

[59] *Igerot*, ii. 323.

wishes.'[60] In the three letters from members of the group which mention 'our *aluf*' he is clearly described as their actual head, but from what is said in the letters it emerges that he was unsuccessful in holding them together and getting them to operate properly under his leadership:

Our *aluf*, His Excellency the physician, may the Merciful One protect and preserve him, sends his greetings. And the happy man, the respected magnate Solomon Rakah, may the Merciful One protect and preserve him, was married on the day of Purim, having been bereaved of his first wife, and he wished our *aluf* the physician to recite the marriage blessing; this was a great wonder to everyone; it can only have been the hand of God that did this, and he did him great honour. (*Igerot*, ii. 399; 27 Adar 5498 [spring 1738])

The honour which the celebrated magnate accorded to 'our *aluf*' was seen as help from Heaven to raise and strengthen the depressed status of the group. This letter already hints that there had been a downturn in the life of the group.[61] The letter which immediately follows it says explicitly that the activity of the group was in crisis, the main cause being the absence of Luzzatto's leadership and the inability of 'our *aluf*' to cope:

And how greatly we grieve over your departure, for since then, for our many sins, we have lacked everything, especially in regard to the science of truth [kabbalah], which has been left in a corner, and the study of the Zohar is conducted under a number of difficulties . . . *and our aluf, His Excellency the physician (may the Merciful One protect and preserve him), at whose word we go out or come in, does not know what to do*. We have conveyed your greetings to His Excellency the physician aforesaid, and he, in return, sends many good wishes to you, Sir. (*Igerot*, ii. 399; 28 Sivan 5498 [summer 1738])

[60] *Igerot*, 401. It should be noted that in this letter, written fully a year and a half after Valle had been made responsible—undoubtedly with Luzzatto's approval—for 'teaching and supervising', Luzzatto still addresses the members of the group as 'members of my *beit midrash*', and in the body of the letter, too, he expresses himself as their leader, sending instructions to them from a distance. The content of the letter is itself of great interest, for in spite of the bans and prohibitions on his teaching kabbalah whether in writing or orally, and on the study of kabbalistic works composed by him, he wrote to his pupils: 'Be aware that the Lord takes pleasure in His world only if His servants acknowledge His glory and exalt His greatness *and take delight in the hidden depths of His secrets*. Now the[se] little openings that have been opened for us into the ways of the Lord from the beginning so that we may walk in the paths of His mysteries in truth, *do not forsake them and let not the*[se] *things depart from your hearts*, but at least do not lose what you have been able to grasp . . .'. The 'little openings' into the mysteries of the Godhead are undoubtedly to be understood as the secrets of the Torah which they learnt from Luzzatto by word of mouth or from his writings, including the revelations of the *magid*, copies of which they kept in their possession and which they constantly studied. See my essays referred to in n. 58 above.

[61] On R. Solomon Rakah and his ties of friendship with Valle, see the references I gave in n. 24 above.

The last reference to this situation is contained in a letter from R. Jacob Hazak dated the 22nd day of the Omer [7 Iyar] 5504 [late spring of 1744], which was sent, or was intended to be sent,[62] on behalf of the members of the group to the Land of Israel—undoubtedly Acre (*Igerot*, ii. 402)—and in which, while they acknowledge and express thanks for the receipt of 'your delightful letters . . . by the hand of the distinguished magnate our honoured teacher R. Solomon Rakah, may the Merciful One protect and preserve him', they complain that 'the study of the Zohar is being carried on under difficulties, but not all day long, because the number of students has decreased and it is beyond us to form part of the sector of those who are perfect [apparently a play on the grammatical term for regular verbs, *gizrat hashelemim*—Trans.]'. Valle is again mentioned: 'Our *aluf*, His Excellency the physician, may the Merciful One protect and preserve him, has instructed us to convey his greetings to you and all the members of your household.'[63]

6. Although the group was on the verge of disintegration in 1744, it can be established on the basis of external literary evidence that it remained active for at least a few years longer under the leadership of Valle, partnered, apparently, by R. Israel Hezekiah Treves. The evidence is contained in a sonnet by Ephraim Luzzatto.[64] The years during which he was resident in Padua are not exactly known, but on the basis of dates indicated in scholarly studies,[65] it is reasonable to conclude that the poem was written in or about the period 1750–3, a few years after M. H. Luzzatto's death.[66] It is worth quoting the sonnet in its entirety together with its heading:

These are the names of the men learned in the Torah, our honoured teacher R. Moses Valle and our honoured teacher R. Israel Treves, residents of Padua, who *take sweet counsel* [*yamtiku sod*] *together* [the emphasis is mine—I.T.] each Sabbath at the time of Minhah [the afternoon service]. ['yamtiku sod'—see Ps. 55: 15—could be understood as 'sweeten esoteric wisdom'.—Trans.]

62 See *Igerot*, ii. 448 n. 405.

63 In this letter, and in this letter alone, Luzzatto is addressed as 'our teacher and *aluf* [followed by the initials representing 'our honoured teacher and rabbi, Rabbi'], Mosheh Hayim, may the Merciful One protect and preserve him'.

64 *Eleh benei hane'urim* (London, 1768), no. 50; *Shirei efrayim lutsato*, ed. and intro. J. Fichman (Tel Aviv, 1942), 78. I have also commented on this sonnet in Essay 10, n. 80.

65 See Betsalel (Cecil) Roth, 'Kavim lidemuto shel efrayim lutsato', in Sh. Abramson and A. Mirsky (eds.), *Sefer hayim shirman/Hayyim (Jefim) Schirmann Jubilee Volume* (Jerusalem, 1970), 364. I can see no grounds for Roth's opinion that the sonnet was written in honour of a new society founded by Valle and Treves 'for the study of the Torah on the Sabbaths at Minhah time'.

66 M. Benayahu, in his essay 'Aliyato shel haramḥa"l le'erets yisra'el', in Z. Warhaftig and Sh. Y. Zevin (eds.), *Mazkeret: kovets torani lezekher yitsḥak aizik halevi hertsog* (Jerusalem, 1962), 471–3, concluded that Luzzatto died in Acre in 1744, contrary to the generally accepted opinion that dated his death to his fortieth year (1746 or 1747).

1 Sabbath by Sabbath, two are they
2 who search out that which is hidden, in company with the throng,
3 fearless in spirit and unperturbed
4 though their ways lead through a great sea.
5 Lo, they have set a limit to the time they speak
6 from after the Minhah service until it has grown dark;
7 so sweet and pleasant are their words
8 that vainly one would seek another man like them.
9 The one, when he speaks, distils honey,
10 the other stands day by day in the counsel of God
11 and breaks the teeth of the wicked.
12 The one glorifies the Torah side by side with the other.
13 None understands the law of Moses as does Israel
14 None has arisen in Israel like Moses Val.

A marginal note against verse 11 reads: 'This is the husk, as understood by those who have esoteric knowledge.' From what we know about Valle it is clear that verses 10–11 refer to him. Probably the young poet was allowed to attend the gatherings of the group and listen to their leaders teaching the secrets of the Torah, and understood or was told that Valle's purpose was to subdue the Sitra Ahra by the *kavanot* he introduced into his homilies.

D. FEATURES OF VALLE'S KABBALISTIC WRITINGS AND OF HIS MYSTICAL AND MESSIANIC CHARACTER

Almanzi's allusions to Valle contain information on his extensive literary remains, most of which we still have. The power of Valle's writings, the originality of his grasp, and the mystical experiences reflected in his numerous compositions are such that we can clearly recognize the intellectual and spiritual qualities which earned him the admiration of the group and his superior position among them. To quote Almanzi:

Of the learned Valle's writings I have under my hand eight parts containing about 8,000 folios actually in his handwriting, most of them kabbalistic in nature. He also composed seventy *tikunim* in the Holy Tongue on the verse 'And in all the mighty hand' [Deut. 34: 12], a discussion in Italian on faith, written when he was 25 years old, in seven parts or days, called 'I sette giorni della Verità', consisting of about 400 folios, and other books.[67]

The writings assembled in the thousands of pages of the eight volumes are, except for a few sections or items, of a single literary genre: homiletic expositions of the books of the Bible, mainly in mystical terms, most of them structured compositions, with or without titles, but in part consisting of disconnected interpretations of the Scriptures, the sayings of the sages, and the Zohar, not cast in any literary mould and generally slipped in among structured compositions. Some of the books of the Bible are expounded more than once in works devoted specifically to them which were written at different times; the later compositions are not corrected or reworked versions of their predecessors but new commentaries.

The eight volumes were acquired by the British Museum and were lying neglected in their library (MSS BL 385–92). While staying in England in 1956 I began to examine them, and have since been engaged in studying them and elucidating their subject matter.[68] Most of the compositions in these volumes bear dates, and even those which do not can be dated by reference to the dates of personal notes written into them or adjoining them. This massive literary output was all produced over the forty-five years from 1722 to 1767, i.e. from the author's twenty-sixth year to his seventy-first, about ten

[67] Almanzi, 130 n. 14. S. D. Luzzatto, in his review of Almanzi's library, described the eight volumes in greater detail. See *Hamazkir. Hebräische Bibliographie: Blätter für neuere und ältere Literatur des Judenthums*, vi, ed. M. Steinschneider (Berlin, 1863), 49–50. On the basis of the personal notes written into the compositions in question, some examples of which he gave, S. D. Luzzatto concluded: 'It seems to me that the kabbalist desired and hoped that he would be visited by the *magid* or by one of the manifestations of the Holy Spirit at some other level . . . and sometimes, as it seems to me, he wrote down the verses that he read in a dream.' In relation to his namesake he wrote: 'He [Valle] was one of Ramhal's companions but does not mention him; only in Part I, folio 5, does he refer to the vowelling of the 42-letter Name "from the words of a kabbalist spoken to him by a *magid*", and this is undoubtedly a reference to Ramhal.' Both the statements in this sentence are erroneous: Ramhal is explicitly mentioned four times (see above, text referring to nn. 39–42), and the 'words of a kabbalist spoken to him by a *magid*' certainly do not relate to Ramhal, for they are quoted from a text written in 1722, five years before the *magid* appeared to Ramhal.

[68] I am greatly indebted to the directorate of the British Museum Library, who, on the occasion of my visits in 1956 and subsequent years as well as in response to requests I sent them from Jerusalem, kindly provided me with photographs of writings by Valle and Luzzatto and of other writings in the Library's collection, with permission to publish them in whole or in part. Of the results of my comprehensive research, all that I have so far committed to print are a few remarks in the course of my essays on Luzzatto and his group. But I have given detailed oral clarifications of some important questions in my lectures, especially at the fifth Congress of Jewish Studies in 1969 on the subject of 'R. Moses David Valle of Padua's Doctrine of the Redemption and its Relationship to Shabateanism', and under the auspices of the Israeli Academy of Sciences in 1971 on 'The Mystical and Messianic Personality of R. Moses David Valle, One of the Leaders of Ramhal's Group in Padua'.

years before his death. In the course of my researches I found the big Italian book, written in dialogue form, in the library of the Jewish Theological Seminary in New York,[69] and seven small volumes in Hebrew, all seven being additional compositions which Almanzi did not have.[70] Of these compositions, *Sefer halikutim* was produced before Valle began to write the works in the collection; so too, apparently, was the dialogue in Italian;[71] three compos-

[69] MS 2213, the gift of H. G. Friedman. The composition in Italian receives the following mention in MS BL 386: '. . . which we have previously explained in the composition "The Seven Days of Truth" which we wrote in the language of the Gentiles' (fo. 137v). This remark relates to the explanation of the division of 'the body of the earth' into continents 'just like the body of man': Asia, Africa, and Europe correspond to the head, the upper torso, and the abdomen, 'and America . . . is the mystical representation of the heels in darkness, for which reason they dwelt in darkness for a long time and their inhabitants [were] the most brutish of the people as is the natural condition of the heels, and they were discovered at the heels of the Messiah [i.e on the approach of his footsteps—Trans.]'.

[70] I will list them in chronological order: Jewish Theological Seminary, New York, MSS Kaufmann 462, *Sefer halikutim*, 2 vols., 1717–18; Kaufmann 27 (expositions of Ecclesiastes, Song of Songs, Psalm 45), 1758–9; Kaufmann 26 (exposition of Proverbs), 1769; Mic. 1053 (expositions of Psalms, Song of the Sea, Song of Deborah, Obadiah, 'And Moses entreated . . .' [Exod. 32: 11]), 1771; Mic. 1051 (expositions of Judges, Esther, Ruth, Samuel, Kings, Hosea), 1771, 1772, 1773; Mic. 1052 (expositions of the Twelve Prophets, of the complete Book of Psalms, of Psalms up to the middle of Psalm 38), 1773–4. The year 5534 [1774] occurs only in two diaristic notes at the head of fos. 38v and 78v in the first half of the complete exposition of Psalms, which is undated at beginning and end. It is therefore possible that the second exposition of Psalms, which breaks off in the middle of a psalm or is partly missing and is the last composition to have come down to us, was written after 1774 and that Valle died before he could finish it. There are also personal notes in the other two volumes in the New York manuscripts [Mic. 1053 and 1051], three dated 1771 and two dated 1772. Of the total of seven such notes, three are written in coded language using initials which I cannot interpret, the other four express personal experiences in plain language. I will quote one note which contains a reference to a mystical experience as well as initials of unknown meaning: 'On 7 Tevet [5531/Dec. 1770], ascent of my soul [brought about] by *mem"he* [45—the 45-letter Name], blessed be the Lord God of Israel *alef yod alef"shin lamed*' (MS Mic. 1053, fo. 54v). The presence of notes of this kind in these late writings is surprising, since in vol. VIII of the volumes in the British Museum Library [MS BL 392] there are only three factual notes, and in the compositions in the Kaufmann manuscripts I have found none at all. What they show is that even in the last years of his life Valle was still moved by mystical impulses. There is a copy of the MS Kaufmann 27 exposition of the Song of Songs in MS Mic. 1054. In a foreword to the copy, which, from the handwriting, appears to have been made by R. M. S. Ghirondi, Valle is described as Luzzatto's 'confidant'. The end of the copy is missing, the last pages having apparently been lost. This is the only copy so far known to me made from writings which can be ascribed with certainty to Valle. And see below, ends of nn. 76 and 99. *Sefer halikutim* is mentioned in a description of Valle's works in Neppi–Ghirondi, 249.

[71] The author headed the book with a note in Italian saying that he had written it at the beginning of 5482 [autumn 1721] after reaching the age of 25, and he added in Hebrew 'that up to now [*ad koh* (*k'h* = 25)] the Lord has helped me and so, in His great mercy, may He always help me'. Taking the year of his birth as 5456 [1696], this indication of his age would make him 25 in 5481 [1721], when he began to be freed from his sufferings under the rule of the husks,

itions contained in one volume were written in 1758–9 and for some unknown reason were not included in the large collection, and the compositions in four volumes were written in 1769–74, after the collection had been completed.

The only work hitherto published under Valle's name is one which, in the printed version, is entitled *Shivim panim al pasuk aḥaron shebatorah venikra beshem tikunim ḥadashim*.[72] The manuscript from which this was printed exists in Valle's handwriting, with no indication of his name and no title, as MS Jerusalem 5217 8° (fos. 217^{r}–260^{r}); it is not one of the group of writings I have described, but its parts are copied or mentioned in MS BL 387. The *tikunim* are inserted, *passim*, into a commentary on Psalms written in 1731–2.[73] From the manner in which they are presented we may conclude

but on the method of calculation used in his Hebrew writings he was 26 years old in that year. See n. 78 below. I am indebted to Professor G. Sermoneta for acquainting me with the exact meaning of Valle's note in Italian.

[72] Printed as a separate section (pp. 3–44) in *Megilat setarim verazin genizin*. According to the pagination the composition should have a title-page of its own, but in the copies I have examined I have not found one. In a note at the end, the editor, R. Samuel Luria, tells how he knows that the author was Valle. (See M. Benayahu's explanation for the absence of the title-page in his book *Kitvei hakabalah*, 39 n. 37.)

[73] In this commentary on Psalms, as in many other such commentaries by Valle, the scriptural passages expounded are presented out of sequence, and expositions of individual sections or psalms are separated by expositions of passages from other books of the Bible or by various other items unconnected with what precedes or follows. At the end of the commentary the author says: 'With this I have completed the commentary on this subject and also the commentary on the whole Book of Psalms . . . and I have called this work *Sefer hahoda'ah* ['The Book of Thanksgiving'] . . . This work was completed on 25 Elul in the year 5492 [early autumn 1732]' (MS BL 387, fo. 290^{v}). The greater part of the commentary is contained in MS BL 386, which ends at fo. 967^{v}. From the reference to the years 1731–2 I was able to determine that the commentary began with the Hallel psalms, nos. 113–18 (fos. 641^{v}–667^{v}). Two sections—Ps. 119: 59–176 and the *Shir hama'alot* ['Song of Ascents'], Pss. 124–34—do indeed appear further back (fos. 276^{r}–334^{r}, 335^{r}–378^{v}), and it is probable that in referring to 'the commentary on the whole Book of Psalms' Valle was including the sections written from about the end of Elul 5489 to about the middle of Tevet 5490 [autumn 1729 to end of 1729], but as they are separated from the exposition of the Hallel psalms by hundreds of folios (384^{r}–641^{r}) which include four compositions complete in themselves (commentaries on Ecclesiastes: *Sefer hahanhagah* ['The Book of Guidance']; on Ruth: *Sefer hage'ulah* ['The Book of Redemption']; on Esther: *Sefer hayeshuah* ['The Book of Salvation']; on Jonah: *Sefer hahashgaḥah* ['The Book of Providence']) I have not taken them into account. At the end of the Jonah commentary it is noted that it was completed on 14 Elul 5490 [early autumn 1730]. It follows that the compilation of the commentary on Psalms in the form that I have referred to took two years, from the beginning of Elul 5490 to the end of Elul 5492.

I list here the places in MS BL 387 where the *tikunim* are mentioned (their numerical order is indicated in parentheses): 102^{r-v} (1, 2), 114^{v}–115^{r} (3), 187^{v}–188^{r} (4, 5), 192^{r-v} (6, 7), 198^{r-v} (8, 9), 201^{r-v} (10), 203^{v} (11), 204^{v} (12), 207^{v}–208^{r} (13, 14), 213^{v} (15, 16), 217^{r} (17, 18), 218^{v} (19, 20), 220^{v} (21, 22), 223^{v} (23, 24), 226^{v} (25, 26), 231^{r} (27, 28), 235^{v} (29, 30), 238^{r} (31, 32), 242^{r} (33, 34),

that the collection of *tikunim* was written before 1732 and that Valle, having kept it for a time, decided to insert its constituent parts, most of which applied to verses of the Psalms, into his expositions of the appropriate psalms.[74] This composition differs in form and content from Luzzatto's *Tikunim ḥadashim*, but the arrangement of both in the form of seventy expositions of a single verse on the pattern of *Tikunei hazohar*, substituting the last verse in the Pentateuch for the first, shows that there is a relationship of interdependence between them. Luzzatto wrote his composition recording the words of angels and the souls of the righteous, revealed to him through the medium of the *magid*, in the second half of 5489 [spring–summer 1729], as stated in R. Jekutiel's letter: 'And now they have commanded him to compose seventy *tikunim* on the verse "All the mighty hand" which ends the Torah.'[75] Since Valle reproduced the sections of his composition only in the

245^{v} (35), 249^{r} (36, 37), 249^{v} (38, 39), 253^{v} (40, 41), 254^{v} (42, 43), 260^{v} (44–7), 264^{r} (48, 49), 266^{v} (50, 51), 269^{r} (52, 53), 272^{r} (54, 55), 275^{r} (56, 57), 277^{v} (58–60), 280^{v} (61, 62), 284^{v} (63–5), 289^{r} (66–70).

[74] *Tikunim* 1–12 are reproduced verbatim and in full in the composition as printed. *Tikunim* 13 and 14 are copied only in part, and in place of the missing portions we find: 'All the rest I have written above in the commentary on the verses', and: 'The explanation of these verses I have written above.' *Tikunim* 15–70 are mentioned and the verses expounded in them are recorded but without any word of the content of the *tikunim*. In other words Valle inserted parts of his composition, with changes in form, into his commentary on the Psalms, but reproduced the full text of the parts which were unsuited to his commentary in his *Tikunim ḥadashim*. On a quick examination I have not found any links between the subject matter of the *tikunim* which are mentioned and the expositions of the psalms which they adjoin, and there is no clear reason for them to have been scattered in the various places in the text which I indicated in the preceding note. [M. Benayahu, discussing this compilation of *tikunim* by Valle in his book *Kitvei hakabalah*, entangles himself in a web of errors. I have not the space to go into detail here and shall confine myself to indicating some important cases in which he has gone badly astray. (*a*) The *tikunim* mentioned *passim* in the commentary on the Psalms are presented as revelations from above, disclosed to Valle, we are to suppose, while he was writing the expositions which adjoin the references to the *tikunim* (see *Kitvei hakabalah*, 39–41). Through failure to understand the nature of the mystical revelations which are explained and reproduced in part in the present essay, the *tikunim* are treated as attached to them though they have nothing in common with them. (*b*) The set of *tikunim* is described as having been composed by bringing together separate revelations in adapted and edited form after the completion of the commentary on Psalms at the end of 5492 [early autumn 1732] (see ibid. 41, 257). The manner in which the *tikunim* are quoted or mentioned in their numerical order, as I have described in this and the preceding note, and their insertion among the expositions of the psalms on no systematic pattern and without any connection with the verse 'In all the mighty hand' which serves as a fixed framework for every item, show clearly that the *tikunim* were composed before the commentary. (*c*) The declaration that 'Valle composed *tikunim* in Aramaic too, and their language, style, and content are fully equal to the book called *Razin genizin*' (ibid. 32) does not begin to be sustainable. Both compositions are available in print; the discerning reader can easily satisfy himself that none of Valle's *tikunim* is the equal of the Aramaic discourses in the collection in *Razin genizin*, and with respect to language and style there is not even any real similarity between the two works.]

[75] *Igerot*, i. 19. And see ibid. 16.

part of his commentary which he wrote in 1732, we can conclude that it was composed in 1731, after Luzzatto's capitulation in Padua, when the group were operating underground. In view of the particular nature of Valle's writings, which I consider below, I am of the opinion that his *Tikunim ḥadashim* was not produced simply as an imitation of Luzzatto's Zoharic work of that name but had a practical eschatological purpose, which was to help in reviving and realizing the messianic aim that Luzzatto's *Tikunim ḥadashim* had been intended to promote but that had been frustrated by the decrees imposed on him in Av 5490 [summer 1730].[76]

[76] See Essay 3, pp. 196–8. At pp. 199–202 I quoted Aramaic compositions printed in *Razin genizin* in which, side by side with Moses, there appears a secondary figure described as being a sort of *ibur* of Moses [a reimpregnation of his soul], his *tsinor* ['conduit'], his garment, or his throne, and I found it difficult to decide 'whether Luzzatto saw himself [before his marriage in 1731] as Moses' *ibur* or as Moses himself who was to be revealed' (p. 200 above). On the basis of my study of additional sources, especially the writings of Valle, I have come to the conclusion that Luzzatto's identification with Moses as chief of the redeemers preceded the 'mystical marriage contract' of 1731, and that in Moses' companion we are apparently to recognize one of the senior members of the group. On the other hand I must qualify as open to question my assertion that in the Aramaic cycles in *Razin genizin* 'we have before us parts of a large book composed by Luzzatto himself at the dictation of the *magid*' (p. 199 above). I do not exclude the possibility that they are parts of works by Luzzatto's pupil R. Israel Hezekiah Treves, or perhaps by a few pupils, written in Luzzatto's *beit midrash* under the influence of his Zoharic compositions. [M. Benayahu, in the course of a detailed description of the collection in MS Jerusalem 5217 8°, gave reasons which led him to the categorical conclusion that the scriptural expositions and the Hebrew and Aramaic homilies collected in *Megilat setarim verazin genizin* were for the most part not the work of Luzzatto but that of his pupils. See *Kitvei hakabalah*, 28–39, 42–5. In my opinion, Benayahu's reasons still leave the identity of the author open to doubt, but even if we tip the balance against Luzzatto's authorship of these and similar writings, it is clear that their principal ideas and motifs reflect his opinions and inclinations. We may therefore turn to them for support in clarifying his views. I am about to consider these questions in more detail in my essay 'Derushei kabalah "magidiyim" miginzei ramḥa"l' ['Kabbalistic "Maggidic" Homilies from the Unpublished Manuscripts of Luzzatto'].]

Three homilies on Song of Songs 4: 1—'Behold, you are fair, my love'—which are printed in *Razin genizin*, 106–7, next to a cycle of homilies in Aramaic on the same verse, and which in the original (MS Jerusalem 5217 8°, fos. 55^{r}–56^{v}) are in Valle's handwriting, also appear in MS BL 387, fos. 54^{v}–55^{v}. Two other homilies, on Genesis 30: 22—'God remembered Rachel'—which are printed (*Razin genizin*, 107–9) under the heading 'Omissions relating to the portion "Vayetse" [Gen. 28: 10–32: 3]' and appear, separately from each other, in the Jerusalem manuscript in Valle's hand (the first at fos. 57^{r}–58^{r}, the second at fo. 88^{r-v}) are included in his writings in MS BL 386, the first with many alterations, additions, and changes of order in two homilies on the same verse (fos. 902^{v}–904^{v}), and the second almost word for word (fo. 913^{r-v}). These texts are very similar in form and content to Aramaic homilies in a cycle on the same verse (*Razin genizin*, 42–72). In view of these findings it may be supposed that other homilies and commentaries in the Jerusalem manuscript which are not in Valle's handwriting, both some which have been printed and some which have not, contain some of his innovative insights into the Torah which were copied and studied in the group. And see n. 99 below. [M. Benayahu surmised that the homilies in Valle's handwriting were incorporated in his compositions, but since

As a solid basis for identifying Valle's personal image in what he says about the winnower I will quote a passage which contains an undoubtedly autobiographical description specifying the year of the winnower's birth, and will place alongside it two quotations relating to his age in 5489 [1729]:

The winnower himself was born in the year tav nun vav [(5)456 / 1696], to which there is a reference in 'Ascribe [*tenu*, spelt *tav nun vav*] strength to God', and he is alluded to in the verse 'For a child is born to us, a son is given to us',[77] *lanu* ['to us', spelt *lamed nun vav*] twice, first in its literal sense and secondly to allude to the year *nun vav* in which he was born. *And in* [5]*475* [1715] *his troubles began, he being then 20 years old*,[78] and that is alluded to in 'I the Lord will hasten it *be'itah* ['in its time', taken as *be*-, 'in', plus the letters *ayin tav he* = 475—Trans.]'.[79] *And in 5481* [1721] *his*

he, Benayahu, did not know where they were, he delivered himself of the vague and unsupported statement, in regard to the expositions of 'Behold, you are fair, my love', that 'their author is Valle and the commentaries themselves are contained in his large compilation in the British Museum's manuscript' (*Kitvei hakabalah*, 34 n. 20). At pp. 41–2 he also mentioned the expositions of the verse 'God remembered Rachel' which I have dealt with above, and the exposition of Deuteronomy 25: 19: 'When the Lord your God gives you rest . . .' (MS Jerusalem 5217 8°, fos. 89^{r}–90^{v}), but cautiously avoided saying that they were included in the collection of Valle's compositions in the British Museum. I should therefore add that the British Museum collection does include the exposition of the command in Deuteronomy to blot out the remembrance of Amalek (MS BL 386, fos. 848^{r}–849^{r}, 850^{r-v}, dated the beginning of Adar II 5491 [spring 1731]), but in addition to normal textual variants there are important differences between the two versions, which it would be out of place to go into here. The findings above reinforce my hypothesis that Valle circulated his writings among the group and that they studied them.]

It should be pointed out that I. Sonne, in his essay 'Avnei binyan (te'udot leḥeker ramḥa"l veḥugo)', published, in Hebrew translation from the Italian, a memorial eulogy on Luzzatto which he attributed to R. M. D. Valle because it was 'in a collection of various pieces ascribed simply to *Valle* [emphasized in the original], containing various extracts from homiletic and ethical writings in Hebrew and Italian' (ibid. 219). In the light of my investigations I have come to the conclusion that the eulogy cannot reasonably be ascribed to Valle, because the declaration by the eulogist: 'I must grieve for him more than others do, because I was privileged to serve him for many years, day and night' (ibid. 223) does not fit the relationship between Valle and Luzzatto. But probably all or most of the other writings that were in the collection were by Valle and were autographs or else copies made by the group. The manuscript of the eulogy was preserved among Sonne's literary remains and found its way to the Ben Tsevi Institute, but the other parts of the collection have not been found and its exact contents are unknown. See Benayahu, 'Aliyato shel haramḥa"l le'erets yisra'el', 469; Essay 8, n. 20. [For different reasons, Benayahu has since retracted his agreement with Sonne's attribution of the eulogy to Valle, and is of the opinion that the eulogist was R. Michael Terni. See *Kitvei hakabalah*, 29–32.]

77 The two verses expounded in relation to the winnower's year of birth are Ps. 68: 35 and Isa. 9: 5.

78 In calculating his age he included both the calendar year of his birth and the calendar year he had reached. By 'the beginning of his troubles' in 5475 [1715] is meant his sinking down among the husks and his subjection to their authority, without being able to fight them and raise sparks of holiness from within them.

79 Isa. 60: 22.

light began to sparkle,[80] when he was aged 26 [*kaf vav*], corresponding to the numerical value of the Tetragrammaton, and the owner of the vineyard girded himself to destroy its thorns, for which reason *it was said to the winnower*[81] *in 5482*: 'Make haste, my love, and be like a gazelle or a young hart on the hills of Beter',[82] for he went down into the world of Nukba [the female] and was rebuilding it for seven years[83] until the year of *hatamim* ['the perfect one'; numerical value 5490], but first *it was said to him* in order to strengthen and encourage him: 'The mandrakes give forth their fragrance, and at our doors are all precious fruits, new and old, which I have stored up for you'[84] . . . and as soon as his light began to sparkle in 5481 [1721] his winnowing began, and because at that time it was among the interposing forces of evil [the *ḥitsonim*, 'the external ones'] that he was winnowing, there is an allusion to his situation in Scripture: 'Your life shall hang in doubt [*telu'im*] before you.'[85] *Telu'im* has the numerical value 481, which is the year [(5)481] in which the winnowing was begun among the *ḥitsonim* by the son of Perez, and the insolent dogs[86] interposed and blocked his light. And now in 5489[87] the news has been received that the winnowing is quite finished, and henceforward in the year *hatamim*, 5490 [1730], the Merciful One, blessed be He, will establish Jerusalem and make it the glory of the earth. (MS BL 386, fos. 284ᵛ–285ʳ)

80 This refers to the beginning of the illumination he received from the supernal force called the *mashpia*, the transmitter of the divine flow, in his personal notes. See n. 43 above.

81 This expression and numerous similar ones in Valle's writings indicate revelations which he received from on high. Some of the statements quoted as announcements to the winnower and supplemented by explanatory comment appear in the personal notes scattered through the manuscript at the tops of pages and between the lines. It may be inferred that the rest of these obscure allusions to the revelations were explained in the expository texts themselves.

82 S. of S. 8: 14, which, however, reads 'on hills of spices'. 'Beter' is taken from the similar verse 2: 17.

83 There are references in many places to seven years of *tikun* with varying fortunes in the fight against the forces of the Sitra Ahra. The years in question are sometimes given as 5482–9 [1722–9], sometimes as 5481–8. Some passages explain that until 5488 he was acting for the *tikun* solely of the Shekhinah, and that in 5489 he also winnowed the sparks belonging to the male sefirot Yesod and Tiferet, and corrected [*tiken*] the defects in them. Here the action is described as 'going down' into the world of the female because the winnower was at the levels of Yesod and Tiferet, who are higher than the Shekhinah, and he was descending to her place of exile among the husks to achieve her *tikun* and raise her up, but the period of years is put at 5482–9.

84 S. of S. 7: 14. In his notes on the revelations this verse was entered in 5483 [1723] (MS BL 385, fo. 81ʳ).

85 Deut. 28: 66.

86 Literally 'dogs fierce of soul', a name given to the husks, taken from Isa. 56: 11 [where the sense is 'greedy'—Trans.]. A note written in 5484 [1724] reads: 'This day on the fast of the fourth month [17 Tamuz], the insolent dogs smote me, they wounded me and stoned me. Blessed be the Lord who has not made me a prey for their teeth' (MS BL 385, fo. 372ʳ). In the Zohar, and in a *piyut* by Luria for the 'third meal' on the Sabbath, the name is *kalbin deḥatsifin* ['dogs who are insolent'].

87 5490 deleted and 5489 written above the line. This passage is shown by the dates of the notes which precede and follow it (MS BL 386, fos. 275ᵛ, 293ᵛ) to have been written at the end of 5489 [late summer–early autumn 1729].

And now [(5)489] in the winnower's 34th [*d"l*] year 'there was hope for the lowly [*dal*] and all wickedness stopped its mouth',[88] and when the year *hatamim* [5490] came, it was said of it: 'You shall be whole-hearted [*tamim*] with the Lord your God',[89] for the winnowing is finished [*tam*], and completed is the union of the beloved couple Z" and N"[90] the Lord your God, He has swallowed up [or 'will swallow up'] death for ever, and the Lord God will wipe away tears from every face.[91] (Ibid., fo. 286[v])

And thus *the winnower was promised that he would return to his root*[92] which is the mystery of the T[ifere]t [Glory] of divine favour in the months of *gadlut* ['spiritual

[88] A conflation of Job 5: 16 and Ps. 107: 42.

[89] Deut. 18: 13.

[90] Ze'ir and Nukba, Tiferet and Malkhut, to whom are ascribed two names of God—YHVH and Elohim ['the Lord God'].

[91] Isa. 25: 8, where the text has *Adonai YHVH* and is read as *Adonai Elohim*, but here piously rendered as *H' Elokim*. [The tense in Isaiah is 'prophetic perfect'; Valle could have taken it as past or future.—Trans.] This verse, in the last-mentioned form, is quoted in MS BL 386, fo. 318[v], as having been said to the winnower: 'The winnower himself, when his work was finished, put out his hand and took from the tree of life also and ate and will live for ever, for he had previously *been told*, in order to comfort him [on account of] his deeds and the toil of his hands, "He will swallow up death for ever, and *H' Eloki"m* will wipe away tears from every face".'

[92] To judge from the date of a note on a neighbouring page (MS BL 386, fo. 313[v]) these words were written at the end of Tishrei 5490 [autumn 1729]. The promise was fulfilled before Sivan [early summer 1730]. A note reads: 'At this time [5490/1730], in the month of Adar, I received tidings which made known to me that I had returned to my root' (ibid., fo. 440[v]). The two dates are reconciled in a passage written a few days before the one quoted here from fo. 310[r] of the manuscript: 'And so the winnower *in the months of gadlut* ['spiritual peak': Nisan, Iyar, Sivan], in which T[ifere]t holds sway, *will return to his gadlut* and he will rest in glory, for an end will be made of all the husks which have tormented him and they will be quite destroyed from off his head, for the winnowing among them was completed in this present year of *pedut* ['redemption'; numerical value 490] and they were thrown on to the refuse heaps in the month of Adar *at the end of the period of katnut* ['low spiritual state'], *so that he might return on high entirely to his root*' (ibid., fo. 304[v]). A passage quoted above (text referring to n. 44), which was written in Kislev 5490, says simply 'now in 5490 [1730] the winnower returns to his root'. The same passage states that in the year 5487 there occurred 'the beginning of his return to Ramah' [cf. 1 Sam. 7: 17; *ramah* means 'a height'—Trans.]. A note [by Valle] makes it clear that this expression refers to his ascent to the Shekhinah, which was completed at the beginning of 5488: 'This day, in the year 5488, the New Moon of Marheshvan [autumn 1727], the completion of the winnowing, *and his return to Ramah*, for his home [his spouse, the Shekhinah] is there' (MS BL 385, fo. 705[v]). To sum up, his expectations were supported by his mystical experiences: his personal ascent to be received into his divine root in Tiferet, which was directly connected with the completion of his mission to perform *tikunim* and destroy the husks, began in Adar 5490 and reached its pinnacle in Sivan.

Low levels and peaks, the alternation of *katnut* and *gadlut*, in the spiritual life of the winnower (one of whose titles, constantly used, was 'the tsadik', the righteous man) are a frequent concept in Valle's writings. His use of *katnut* and *gadlut* to indicate conditions of human existence is different beyond compare from the common use of these terms in Lurianic sources, and has an extremely close affinity, both taken as a whole and in detail, with the ideas of *katnut* and *gadlut* in hasidic literature. See my essay 'Harayon hameshiḥi vehamegamot hameshiḥiyot bitsemiḥat

peak': see n. 92—Trans.], and especially in the month of Sivan, which is T"t' at its peak, for Nisan and Iyar are the arms [Hesed and Gevurah]. And further, *it was said to him* that the days of his affliction were of the number of ***alpayim veshesh me'ot*** [2,600],[93] whose initial letters spell *asham* ['guilt-offering'], to which there is an allusion in the verse *im tasim asham*,[94] and he was *in the 34th* [letters *dalet lamed* = 34] *year of the number of his years*, corresponding to *dal* in the scriptural 'There was hope for the lowly [*dal*] and wickedness stopped its mouth',[95] and forthwith 'he will see his seed, he will prolong his days'[96] in the place of length of days, the mystery of the Ancient One. (Ibid., fo. 310^r)

These passages prove beyond any possible doubt that wherever in Valle's writings there is a reference to 'the winnower' or, as he is frequently called, 'the winnower tsadik' or just 'the tsadik'—the righteous man—or 'the tsadik who brings about *tikun*', 'the tsadik put to the test', 'the afflicted tsadik', or the like, the author is referring to himself,[97] even where there are no clear

haḥasidut', *Zion*, 32 (1967), 14–15 n. 77. I shall be clarifying this matter in an essay entitled 'Yeridat hatsadik va'aliyato bekhitvei r' mosheh david vale: degamim le'inyenei torat hatsadik haḥasidit' ['The Descent and Ascent of the Tsadik in the Writings of R. Moses David Valle: Patterns Corresponding to the Hasidic Doctrine of the Tsadik']. For the present I shall content myself with drawing attention to references in Valle's *Shivim panim*, where see *tikunim* 30, 33, 41, 46, 58, 65.

93 'The number of days of his affliction' covers the years 1722–9, when he was at war with the husks to raise up the sparks of holiness imprisoned in their domain. See n. 83 above.

94 Isa. 53: 10 [variously understood, but literally perhaps: 'The Lord desired to crush him, he made him ill, (to see) if his soul would offer (or make itself) a guilt-offering'—Trans.]. Valle of course saw in the servant of the Lord his own image as the Messiah suffering and operating among the husks. The descriptions of the events in the life of the winnower state repeatedly that he is sorely tested by the temptations of the husks and that sometimes they succeed in drawing him into the actual commission of sins. I have no doubt that that is what is meant by the allusion to the mystery of 'if [his soul] would offer a guilt-offering'.

95 Here Job 5: 16 is quoted verbatim. The application of the term *dal* ['lowly, poor'] to the winnower to indicate the age at which he completed the *tikun* in 1729 is in tune with his announcement that *dal ve'evyon* ['poor and needy'] in Psalms refers to the Messiah ben David and the Messiah ben Joseph who are sunk among the husks and will be freed from their dominion in Padua. See Essay 2, p. 124, note on 'Or what . . . bowed down'. [I have since found strong support for my explanation that Luzzatto, too, was referring to the two Messiahs in the poem 'God who works wonders' when he wrote 'the poor man crushed, the lowly poor bowed down'. In the book *Takta"v tefilot leramḥa"l*, ed. S. Ulman (Benei Berak, 1979), prayer 'Va'etḥanan' ['And I entreated'] (sect. 515), 348, we find: 'Two Messiahs of whom it was said "Who raises up the lowly [*dal*] from the dust, who lifts the poor [*evyon*] from the refuse heap" [Ps. 113: 7]'. A massive liturgical collection written by Luzzatto in 1732 and discovered recently is full of ideas and motifs of great importance for their bearing on the whole of his output. See Benayahu, *Kitvei hakabalah*, 188–94, 280–8.]

96 A continuation of the quotation from Isa. 53: 10.

97 As well as these, 'the Messiah' without qualification, 'Messiah ben David', and even Ze'ir Anpin, Tiferet, and Yesod, are sometimes used to refer to Valle the winnower, but no autobiographical significance should be ascribed to these names except where the context makes the intention absolutely clear. It is hard to determine without extensive and meticulous research

signs of actuality such as indications of years which correspond to the years of his life. That is to say, the personalities of antiquity become prototypes of Valle in expositions of Scripture which set out to show that hidden within the 'plain meaning' of the biblical text is a deeper message foretelling what will take place in Padua 'at the end of days' in the soul, way of life, and actions of the winnower-Messiah. What is more, the Scriptures also allude to what will befall the members of the group. Some of Valle's remarks on Moses, the Messiah ben Joseph, and Seraiah are certainly intended to refer to Luzzatto, to the member of the group whom they regarded as personifying the Messiah ben Joseph, and to R. Jekutiel of Vilna,[98] and the life of the group and Valle's senior status in it are reflected with great clarity by references to the comrades of the winnower as 'the seven who made a covenant',[99] 'the righteous

exactly when Valle became inwardly aware of his messianic mission and how long it continued to inspire him. From his notes it would appear that this spiritual awakening began in 1721 or 1722, but in the texts themselves the signs of intense messianism and references to the activity of the winnower first become prominent in 1726 or thereabouts, and only in retrospective accounts does Valle ascribe any eschatological significance to his actions and state of mind in earlier years. From a rapid reading of the last volumes in the British Museum collection and of the late compositions not in that collection, my impression is that even into old age his hope of realizing his messianic mission continued quite unabated, and he may have retained it to the end of his life.

[98] On the question of the identity of the Messiah ben Joseph in the group, see n. 37 above and n. 100 below. As regards Seraiah–Jekutiel, see *Netivei emunah uminut*, 192–6. I have since become convinced that the three homilies on 'Behold, you are fair, my love' in *Razin genizin*, with their account of 'Moses, the two Messiahs, and Seraiah' which I quoted ibid. 192 as paralleling the messianic group of four in Luzzatto's 'Mystery of the Marriage Contract', are the work of Valle; so that on this subject also, the two men are in accord. See n. 76 above.

[99] In *Netivei emunah uminut*, 327 n. 99, in quoting extracts from MS Jewish Theological Seminary Mic. 1599, I said that 'Luzzatto saw members of his group as "the seven shepherds", and perhaps also called them "the seven who entered into the covenant"'. I have come to the conclusion that in that sentence 'perhaps' should be altered to 'certainly'. 'The seven who entered into the covenant' are the seven members who signed the rules of the group drawn up in 1731, before whose names is written: 'The signatories *who entered into an agreement* [see n. 35 above] *on this covenant* were . . .' (*Igerot*, i. 9); and the foreword to the rules states: 'These are *the words of the covenant*, the statutes, ordinances, and laws which the holy comrades have undertaken to observe' (ibid. 8). A further proof: in an appendix to the rules it is recorded that 'the other ordinances of silence are written in *the book of the covenant* which they have signed in their own hand' (ibid. 12). (This sentence also appears in the copy of the rules in MS Cincinnati 501, but is missing in Jekutiel's copy in MS Oxford 2237.) The subject of 'ordinances of silence' would be out of place among the ground rules which have come into our hands, and it seems more likely that the reference is to a secret document which has not been preserved. The existence of esoteric rules which were kept hidden is proved by a fragment at the end of the rules in the Cincinnati copy (fo. 334^{r}) consisting of the opening two lines of a document: 'The ordinances of the writing[?] [*ha(ket)ivah*] / Every night they will come (to) the house of the hasid . . .'. (The page is moth-eaten and torn and the end of the second line is missing, but it is clear that the copying was broken off, for the space from that line to the bottom of the page is blank. In other words the copyist decided, apparently on instructions from the heads of the group, to

performers of *tikun*', etc. I will quote as examples several passages written between the middle and end of 5491 [spring–early autumn 1731], i.e. after the attempt made in Av 5490 [late summer 1730] to dissolve the group. These examples add to our information about the atmosphere which prevailed in the clandestine messianic movement in Padua, on whose manner of

suppress the document.) At the end of Jekutiel's copy only the first word has been copied (*mishpetei* ['the ordinances of . . .']). In any event the name 'book of the covenant' fits the title 'those who entered into the covenant' which was conferred on the elite members of the group. The passages on 'those who entered into the covenant' which I cite in the course of this essay reinforce this conclusion. It should be pointed out that Moses and the two Messiahs are separated from the group of seven whereas Seraiah is one of their number; this accords with the identification of the redeemers in my explanation. The seven senior members were also honoured as 'shepherds'.

Luzzatto says in his commentary on *Idra raba*: 'Know that wherever men join together in assemblies for the sake of Heaven' the alliance is [brought about] 'by Yesod . . . and a sign of this is *berit* ['covenant'], for a covenant is a bond [*masoret*, the word used with *berit* in Ezek. 20: 37—Trans.], a binding together [*kesher*] of those who enter into it . . . and when the assemblies are formed here below, the light of this *berit* of Yesod [which represents the male organ in the sefirotic system—Trans.] shines among them and joins them together into a unity [so that] they are included in the generality of the covenant' (*Adir bamarom* (Warsaw, 1886), 19). It appears that in saying this, he has in mind the organization of his group by the covenant made in 1731. Moreover, allusions of his in the same work show that he saw his group as the image of R. Simeon bar Yohai's group and that he sought to understand and explain its current trials and tribulations as a reflection of those endured by its ancient predecessor. On the basis of his distinction between two stages in the existence of R. Simeon bar Yohai's group—'For at first, although there were comrades in his presence engaged in studying the secrets of the Torah, no strong alliance was formed among them except in this matter of the assembly [*idr'*]' (ibid. 18; and see ibid. 20)—he set out to establish a general principle with regard to mystical societies: 'So long as the group is, as it were, temporary, that is, that there is no fixed arrangement between them but they meet in this way to associate with each other, then there is only the one bond [*kesher*] in their root . . . *and then there may still, Heaven forbid, be accusations in the mystery of sheker* ['falsehood'], *Heaven forbid, and the tikun is not so strong unless a perfect bond* [*kesher*] *is established between them . . . a covenant* supported on two pillars so that there is no fear of its falling' (ibid. 19). In other words: the establishment of his group on a foundation of solid regulations in Shevat 5491 [early 1731] was pictured by Luzzatto as if it were an action undertaken by R. Simeon bar Yohai at a meeting of the Idra, the great assembly, and its purpose was to strengthen the bond [*kesher*] against the disasters of the accusations by *sheker* which shook the group in Av 5490 [late summer 1730]. And see Essay 8, n. 19.

The collection in the New York manuscript is entitled *Likutei kabalah misefari[m] yekari[m]* ['Selected Kabbalistic Writings from Treasured Books]', and R. M. S. Ghirondi, who attributed it to Luzzatto, headed it with an 'important notice': 'Everything written in this holy book is entirely the teaching of . . . our master Moses Hayim Luzzatto, may the memory of that righteous and holy man be for a blessing', but from its contents it is clear to me that this is an anthology compiled by the group, in which homilies by Valle and by Luzzatto are mingled indiscriminately. Some homilies (fos. 29^r–32^v) are in Luzzatto's handwriting, the rest are copies. As for the passages on the *tikunim* of 'those who entered into the covenant' and 'shepherds', I am of the opinion that they are homilies by Valle. I shall deal elsewhere with this anthology and throw further light on its nature.

existence light has been cast for the first time by unpublished material discovered in recent years.

1. MS BL 386, fo. 935ᵛ:

Any kingdom which has not the following three things has no real substance [*ein bo mamash*]. They are: a king, a viceroy, a military commander [*melekh*, *mishneh*, *sar tsava*], whose inital letters spell *mamash* ['reality'], and when they are lacking in Israel, *mamash* becomes *shamem* ['desolate'] . . . and now that they are returning, *shamem* will be turned into *mamash* speedily in our lifetime: 'king' is Messiah ben David, 'viceroy' is Messiah ben Joseph,[100] the military commander is Seraiah, [the initial letters of] these constituting *mamash* in the mystery of which I have spoken.

This passage states clearly that there are three persons in the group who are competent to fulfil the functions of authority required for the establishment of the messianic kingdom. It was written at the end of Iyar 5491 [early summer 1731], about three months before Luzzatto's marriage, by which the *tikun* to hasten the Redemption was carried out as described in 'the mystery of the marriage contract' [see Essay 3 above—Trans.]. Moses in the person of Luzzatto, who is above the three signified by *mamash*, is not mentioned here, but his existence and his position at the head of the ladder of messianic rank are self-evident. As early as the beginning of 5490 [autumn 1729] Valle was declaring with complete confidence that in 5491 he would be revealed as the redeemer of Israel and would establish the messianic kingdom.[101] In his personal notes there is no explicit mention of the critical events culminating in Av 5490 [late summer 1730] when the rabbis' investigation led to Luzzatto's capitulation, but whereas the notes Valle made in 5490 are full of joy over the realization of his messianic mission,[102] from the end of 5490 onwards he

[100] Sometimes the Messiah ben Joseph, too, is called 'king'. The following strange note is therefore of great interest: 'This day, 4 Nisan [5491], the year of *Yeshayah"u ha"melekh* [King Isaiah], the numerical value of whose letters is 5491 [taking the letter *he* of *hamelekh* as 5,000—Trans.]' (MS BL 386, fo. 882ᵛ). In my opinion this is a reference to R. Isaiah Romanin, whom I suppose to have been regarded as the Messiah ben Joseph, and the *gematriyah* in the note is a declaration of his 'coronation' in 5491 [1731]. See n. 37 above. I would draw attention to two other indications which may be seen as supporting my hypothesis: (*a*) Romanin's father's name was Joseph; (*b*) 'Ephraim', a name applied to the Messiah ben Joseph in the writings of Luzzatto and Valle on the basis of midrashim, has a numerical value, on the 'small numbers' system of *gematriyah* [counting tens and hundreds as ones—Trans.] and counting the name 'Ephraim' itself as a unit, equal to the numerical value of 'Isaiah', spelt *yeshayah*. These indications may seem flimsy and forced, but in view of the atmosphere which prevailed among the group it is reasonable to suppose that they may have interpreted congruences of this sort as signs of Romanin's messiahship. At any rate it is appropriate to point them out in addition to the other evidence I have presented.

[101] See *Netivei emunah uminut*, 193. The two passages which I quoted there were written at the end of Tishrei 5490 and in Iyar of that year [autumn 1729 and early summer 1730].

[102] Here are some examples from the notes: 'At this time, the day of blowing the horn in "the perfect year" [*hatamim*, the perfect one, numerical value 5490] . . . When my enemies have

hinted at the existence of obstacles which it would need strenuous efforts and the compassion of Heaven to overcome.[103] But his belief in his messiahship and in the imminence of the Redemption was unshaken, and we even come across outbursts of joy and triumph, especially just before and after Luzzatto's wedding.[104]

turned back, they have stumbled and perished before You, but I shall rejoice in the Lord, I shall exult in the God of my salvation' (MS BL 386, fo. 293ᵛ); 'At this time, the tenth day, Yom Kippur [10 Tishrei], I received tidings of riches and favour, and nations shall come to your light, and kings to the radiance of your sunrise' (fo. 299ᵛ); 'At this time, on the feast of ingathering [Tabernacles] of the year of redemption [*pedut*, numerical value 490], blessed are You, O Lord, who restores His Shekhinah to Zion. And righteous men will rejoice and exult before God and be filled with joy and happiness' (fo. 303ᵛ); 'Blessed be the Omnipresent, blessed be He, blessed be He who keeps His promise to those that fear Him. At this time on the days of solemn assembly and rejoicing: the mother of the children is joyful, *haleluyah*, and let them say among the nations: "The Lord reigns"' (fo. 309ᵛ [309ʳ in the 'Complete List of Diary Entries' in Essay 7—Trans.]); 'This day, the 14th day [of Heshvan], Arise, go through the length and breadth of the land, you [are] Messiah' (fo. 324ᵛ); 'Ask of me and I will give you nations as your inheritance and the ends of the earth as your possession' (fo. 331ᵛ); 'At this time, 20 Kislev, in this year the king will obtain favour from the Lord' (fo. 355ᵛ); 'This day on the fast of the 10th [day of Tevet], I have prepared a lamp for my anointed' (fo. 376ᵛ); 'This day, 27 Iyar, the Lord has said to me "You are My son", You have established the earth and it stands firm' (fo. 524ᵛ).

103 For example 'At this time, at the end of the month of Elul: the word of the man who has been raised on high, I have laid help on a mighty man' (MS BL 386, fo. 657ᵛ); 'This day, at the close of the tenth day, in the year 5491: put your hope in the Lord, be strong and let your heart take courage, and put your hope in the Lord, God will send His mercy and His truth' (fo. 670ᵛ); 'On 24 Kislev at the close of the holy Sabbath: He will bring them to His holy border [Ps. 78: 54 interpreted as future—Trans.], the Stone of the Strayers has been washed away' [see Mishnah *Ta'an.* 3: 8—Trans.] (fo. 749ᵛ); 'This day, 2 Tevet: may strict Judgement altogether cease this year, for the New Year and Yom Kippur atone' (fo. 759ᵛ); 'At this time, in the month of Adar: the Lord will protect you from all evil, He will protect your soul' (fo. 827ᵛ); 'The Lord your God [has been] with you, you have lacked nothing. And in seven [troubles] no evil shall touch you' (fo. 831ᵛ); 'For He has rescued me from every trouble, and my eye has seen [the downfall of] my enemies' (fo. 834ᵛ); 'I sought the Lord and He answered me and rescued me from all my fears' (fo. 835ᵛ); 'This day, the 7th of the month [Nisan]: You have saved me and revived me' (fo. 886ᵛ); 'At this time, the end of the month [Nisan]: the spider [or 'lizard'] has been killed and will no longer be taken in [the] king's palaces' [see Essay 7, n. 98—Trans.] (fo. 909ʳ).

104 For example 'On 24 Marheshvan [5491/late autumn 1730]: The Lord will fulfil all your petitions; now I know that the Lord has saved His anointed [*meshiḥo*]' (MS BL 386, fo. 717ᵛ); 'This day, 15 Kislev, the new mitre, kings shall see and rise, princes [shall see] and bow down' (fo. 740ᵛ); 'This day, 21 Tevet [misspelt, *tav* and *tet* reversed] at the close of the holy Sabbath: I have prepared a lamp for my anointed, his enemies I will clothe in shame, but on him his crown will shine' (fo. 781ᵛ); 'This day, the 28th of the aforesaid month: With joy and gladness of heart by reason of the abundance of everything' (fo. 786ᵛ); 'This day, the day of Purim: Who begot me these? Happy are all who wait for Him, The living, the living, he shall thank You, as I do This day' (fo. 861ᵛ); 'This day, the 10th of the month [Nisan]: the great *kesher* ['bond'], a star has stridden forth out of Jacob and a sceptre has arisen from Israel' (fo. 892ʳ); '. . . and on the last night of Passover, unification [*yiḥud*] of the lights, with mirth and songs, tambourine and harp'

2. MS BL 386, fo. 877^{r}:

Here, too, the text is speaking of the Messiah ben Joseph and the seven who made a covenant, who are called *rabim*, [not in the sense 'numerous' but] in the sense of greatness, as in *rabei hamelekh* ['the king's chief officers'] [Jer. 39: 13]. When they see Messiah ben David, *who is the King*, emerging from the husks after undergoing many great and grievous troubles, they too will be afraid because they have to go down into unclean depths in the world of Nukba to perform their *tikun*, but they will trust in the Lord . . . and He will not forsake them, and the forces of evil ['the external ones'] will not prevail over them, Heaven forbid.

This homily dating from the end of Adar II 5491 [spring 1731] turns upon Psalm 40: 4: 'Many [*rabim*] will see and fear, and will put their trust in the Lord.' The preceding and following verses of the Psalm, which are expressed in the singular, are interpreted as applying to '*the winnower, Messiah ben David* . . . who overcame the forces of evil and rose from death to life'.

3. MS BL 386, fo. 935^{r}:

For they have conspired against you with one accord, they have made a covenant against you[105] . . . that is to say, they ['the external ones', the forces of evil] all conspired to band together at the lowest depth of uncleanness . . . and together they have made a covenant to prevail, as if that were possible, against the Shekhinah and the holy Yesod, but it will not succeed, because *seven who have made a covenant on the side of holiness have already taken up their stand aganst them*, to make an end of the enemy and the vengeful.

This paragraph (which is adjoined by the passage on the Messiah ben David, the Messiah ben Joseph, and Seraiah, whose initial letters constitute the 'reality' [*mamash*] of the messianic kingdom) explains the purpose of the covenant made by the signing of the rules of the group in Shevat 5491 [early 1731]. The senior members of the clandestine group stand in relation to 'the winnower, Messiah ben David' as do ministers to the king; their cooperation with him, when they descend to the husks to achieve the *tikun* of the

(fo. 901^{v}); 'At this time, 3 and 4 Tamuz: the double assurance, stand firm and see the salvation which the Lord will work for you this day' (MS BL 387, fo. 8^{v}); 'This day, on the tenth day, year 5492, the crown has been completed, and the Holy Spirit announces: I have laid your foundations with sapphires' (fo. 92^{v}); 'This day on the day of Hoshana Raba [seventh day of Tabernacles]: the [sc. decree of] rest has been sealed, and they shall no longer behave presumptuously' (fo. 100^{r}); 'This day, 22 Tevet, For the Messiah has come [or 'is coming'] and proclaims freedom' (fo. 171^{v}); 'At this time in the days of Nisan: the divine flow drawn down and existence for ever, the gateway to love, I have set you over my household' (fo. 218^{v}); 'This day, 26 Menahem ['the comforter', Av]: Hallel [psalms of praise] and jubilee and release from everything' (fo. 271^{r}). On Valle's notes relating to Luzzatto's marriage, see *Netivei emunah uminut*, 193–4.

105 Ps. 83: 6. This exposition was written at the end of Iyar 5491 [early summer 1731].

Shekhinah and for their own benefit, becomes clearer in the light of important additional information in the passages quoted below.

4. *Megilat setarim*: *Shivim panim*, *tikun* 60 (p. 39):

The holy Yesod [the winnower], who is afflicted[106] under his [Sama'el's] hand and is subjected to his authority, is sad and grieves most greatly over the success of the wicked one . . . and why does the Holy One, blessed be He, desire it to be so? . . . because the supreme Overseer wishes to trap these villains in their own craftiness[107] and wicked devices, and in the very cauldron in which they intend to boil *the righteous who are engaged in tikun*, they themselves in fact are boiled, for the fall of the righteous man[108] was itself his remedy [*takanato*] . . . and it is the downfall of 'the external ones' [the forces of evil] . . . and humility comes before honour[109] to *the righteous* who abase themselves to the ground to bring about *tikun* for the Shekhinah, and the Holy One, blessed be He, raises them up to the heights by the power of the strong hand and the great and terrible deeds of *the Lawgiver, the faithful member of His household, whose hand was certainly in all the tikunim to bring them to their due completion.*

Here the supremacy of Luzzatto as Moses is given prominence; all the *tikunim* performed in the group, even those of Valle the Messiah ben David, are operated and achieve their purpose by his power.

5. *Megilat setarim*: *Shivim panim*, *tikun* 65 (p. 41):

Come and see: this matter is the mystical expression of the call by the righteous winnower to all the other *righteous men engaged in tikun* to bow their shoulders to bear the troubles of the[ir] trial, for it is all for their benefit so that they may distinguish between good and evil and in the end be sated with enjoyment of the good . . . for it is good for man that he should know good and know evil and turn himself back to the good, and that is the secret of faith[110] . . . That is the point [*ta'am*] of what the psalmist says here: 'O taste [*ta'amu*] and see that the Lord is good',[111] that is to say, taste the evil of the husk and you will see clearly that the taste of holiness is the only good and there is nothing better in all existence.

The author goes on to explain that 'the troubles of the trial' means the descent 'to the state of *katnut* ['minority', i.e. spiritual immaturity], for then man must contend with the external ones who intervene against him', and if the man who descends does not stumble into sin through the enticements of the husks he 'is raised to the state of *gadlut* ['majority', spiritual

106 Further on he is called 'the afflicted tsadik'.

107 The expression is based on Job 5: 13.

108 The theme of 'the fall of the tsadik [the righteous man]' or 'the descent of the tsadik' in order to rise again and raise up the Shekhinah, to achieve her *tikun* and subdue the Sitra Ahra, runs like a continuous thread through Valle's writings, and at any rate from the phenomenological point of view, the significance of the idea in his philosophy must be seen as a link between Shabateanism and hasidism.

109 Prov. 15: 33; 18: 12.

110 From Zohar II, 34*a*. Valle was fond of this quotation and used it repeatedly in his writings. And see Tishby, *Wisdom of the Zohar*, ii. 457.

111 Ps. 34: 9.

maturity]'.[112] Here the author is saying that 'the righteous winnower' urges 'the righteous men engaged in *tikun*' to follow him down to the husks. The experience of evil is not only for their personal benefit—it is not simply a descent to the lowest level of 'minority' for the purpose of rising to the heights of 'majority': its main purpose is to rescue and restore to perfection the Shekhinah who is held captive among the husks.[113] On the other hand, 'the troubles of their trial' alludes to the sufferings caused to the group by bans and persecution. This allusion is more manifest in the last two of the present set of examples.

6. MS BL 386, fo. 927^r:

And then he said: 'Remember, O Lord, the taunts [endured by] Your servants',[114] on behalf of all Israel who are insulted and do not insult, who hear the taunts of the nations and do not reply, but all the more so *the servants, who are those engaged in the tikun and the winnowing, who suffer so many taunts and curses* and do not abandon their work for the honour of the Holy One, blessed be He and His Shekhinah; even more so the winnower himself who has actually borne in his bosom every kind of husk that exists in order to put an end to them and correct their imperfection [*letakenam*].

The faithful servants of the Lord, and above all their leader the winnower, who continue to engage in *tikunim* in their Paduan *beit midrash* despite being

[112] The whole of *tikun* 65, with a few alterations, is introduced into the commentary on Psalm 34 (MS BL 387, fos. 271^v–272^r). See above, text referring to nn. 73–4. The actions of the 'righteous men engaged in *tikun*' are also described in *tikunim* 8, 9, 35, 42.

[113] In a parallel text this topic is specifically linked, on the basis of the passage from the Zohar quoted here [see n. 110], with action by the righteous to join the Shekhinah among the husks and share in her affliction in order to raise her up and be raised up themselves: 'The mystical significance of this matter is that faith is the secret quality of Nukba . . . and anyone who wishes to be put to the test and be raised up by her must know good and evil just like her . . . and it is impossible to pass to life except by way of death or to good except by way of evil, and this is the secret of faith, that she, too, tastes good and evil just as they do' (MS BL 386, fos. 121^v–122^r). In the same connection, another text describes the situations of 'the righteous man' when he is sunk among the husks and when he is elevated to the realm of holiness: 'Come and see the mystery of this matter: when *the righteous man* was in the midst of the husk [singular—Trans.] all his organs were sunk in it from head to foot, whereas when he returns into holiness he is brought totally inside so that all his organs are contained within the supernal holiness, and then he understands and knows the difference between the husk and holiness and gives praise and thanks to his Supreme Helper, with whom there is none to compare. That is the mystical significance of the verse [Ps. 35: 10]: "All my bones shall say, O Lord, 'Who is like You?'" And the reason for making *the righteous man* traverse two paths is in order to perfect him, in the mystery of the saying by our rabbis: "It is good for a man to know good and know evil and turn himself back to good", and that is the secret of faith; it is to that that Scripture alludes in the verse [2 Chr. 12: 8]: ". . . that they may know My service and the service of the nations [Chronicles has 'kingdoms'] of the countries", which is exactly for the above-mentioned purpose in the mystery of which I have spoken' (*Shivim panim, tikun* 48).

[114] Ps. 89: 51. This exposition was written in Iyar 5491 [late spring–early summer 1731].

humiliated, vilified, and assailed by taunts and curses, epitomize in their lives the suffering and faithfulness of the people of Israel in exile.[115] The text goes on to say that it was the forces of evil called 'the external ones' who taunted them, but in the minds of the members of the group their [human] opponents were pictured as emissaries of the Sitra Ahra, and they saw the attacks aimed at subduing and silencing them as a war waged against them in two demonic realms: in revealed existence, by the rabbis of Venice and R. Moses Hagiz and their supporters, and in concealed existence, by Sama'el and his forces.

7. MS BL 387, fos. 87^r–88^r:

Now as to what is written after that: 'Trust in Him at all times, O people',[116] etc., this is [said by] the winnower, who has proved by his own experience how great is the merit of trust . . . he therefore gives *all his companions* also the confidence to trust at all times in his trust and gather strength, [trust] in the Shekhinah who rests upon them that she will not forsake them at any time, even in time of trouble, that is certain . . . Moreover: to devote their soul to sanctifying the divine Name just as he has devoted his, and to offer up . . . their *nefesh*, their *ruaḥ*, and their *neshamah* [the three aspects of the soul] [as] female waters for the *tikun* of the Shekhinah. And this is the mystical significance of 'your heart', which means all their inwardness whether good or bad . . . the good inclination and the evil inclination . . . for in reward for this, even evil is ultimately turned into good just as he himself [the winnower] was turned . . . and *they will not be afraid of the accusation made when they are humiliated and brought low*, for the Shekhinah herself, who rests upon them, will shelter them as she did him, and the accusation against them will fail . . . As for what it goes on to say: 'Men of low degree are but wind, men of high degree are falsehood', etc., this is the winnower himself speaking to *the righteous performers of tikun*, assuring them that they should not be afraid of the accusation by the external ones and by all the forces of the worthless villain ['the man of Belial'], the evildoer, for they are all wind and falsehood . . . and then the winnower himself speaks again to the rest of *the righteous performers of tikun* . . . If you see great prosperity in the edifice of the husk . . . do not let your heart pay heed to this and do not cease from or forsake your *tikunim* and your good deeds on that account.

This comprehensive and detailed text, written in Elul 5491 or early 5492 [late summer–early autumn 1731], and here reproduced with omissions for the sake of brevity, states explicitly that 'the righteous performers of *tikunim*' are the 'companions' of the winnower, and speaks of their being 'humiliated and brought low' because of 'the accusation'. The language of Scripture, 'men of low degree are wind, men of high degree are falsehood', is applied to

[115] See Essay 2, pp. 154–5, at the beginning of the notes on the 'Poem for the night of 17 Shevat'. I have dealt more extensively with this in my essay 'Tefilot miginzei r' mosheh ḥayim lutsato', now with the printers for publication in *Molad* [and now Essay 2, Part B, above; and see the foreword by E. Broido at p. 114].

[116] Ps. 62: 9. The other scriptural allusions in this text relate to the same psalm.

'the accusation by the external ones' and to 'the forces of the worthless villain', but it is clear that Valle was referring mainly to the literal meaning of the verse and was seeking to designate as 'wind and falsehood' the accusations and calumnies of actual 'men of low and high degree' who were striking at the life of 'the holy society' and decreeing that they should cease their *tikunim* and good deeds. Here Valle's special status in the group is clearly delineated in various of its aspects, some of which also appear in the other texts I have quoted: by his addresses to the members he gave them encouragement and strengthened their confidence, in spite of their lowly condition; by the ways in which he fought against the husks he set them an example and taught them what they should do to achieve the *tikun* of the Shekhinah and hasten the Redemption; and even his instructions to serve the Lord with their evil inclination in order to change evil into good are derived from what occurred in the life of the winnower, 'who was himself changed'. In other words, Valle's functions were not limited to supervising the maintenance of the arrangements laid down in the rules of the group: he also oversaw, alone or in partnership with Luzzatto,[117] the conduct of esoteric activities not mentioned in the rules.

These passages and the information I have extracted from them are the merest fraction of what may be learnt from R. Moses David Valle's writings about the redeemers and their associates who were active in Padua. To sum up, the spiritual autobiography of the Messiah ben David of Luzzatto's group, which is enfolded in the thousands of pages of Valle's esoteric teachings, also serves to acquaint us with the aims, experiences, and mystical and messianic activities which went to make up the secret life of the group and which in small part have been considered in the present essay. They are likely to be far more extensively revealed by a full study of the writings in that collection.

[117] See above, text referring to n. 38.

SEVEN

Rabbi Moses David Valle's Mystical-Messianic Diary: A Record of Spiritual Experiences and Visions

INTRODUCTION

A. A DESCRIPTION AND CHARACTERIZATION OF THE ENTRIES

VALLE's extensive kabbalistic-messianic œuvre, which I described at p. 318 ff. above in Essay 6,[1] makes a unique contribution to the literature of Jewish mysticism by its dated personal notes, the great majority of them concerning spiritual experiences and visions, interpolated in his works of scriptural exegesis, between the lines and at the top of pages. Together these notes, which are spread over several decades, constitute a sort of mystical and messianic journal. In the same essay and in earlier ones I alluded to the nature and general significance of the 'diary entries', quoting some passages as examples. I pointed out that many of these entries recurred in the body of the compositions, introduced by expressions such as 'It was said to the winnower' and

[1] The main theme of that essay is Valle's assignment of the kingship of the house of David to himself, as proved by the descriptions of the figure of 'the righteous winnower' in his compositions, and the group's recognition of his messianic status. M. Zlotkin, in his bibliography *Otsar hasefarim: ḥelek sheni* (Jerusalem, 1965), 250–1, says at the end of the item *Pe'*[*rush*] *al hatanakh ler"m david vale* ['Bible Commentary by R. M. D. Valle']: 'The commentary on Isaiah is printed in the book *Asarah me'orot hagedolim*, by R. H. Y. I. Gad, 5713 [Johannesburg, 1952].' There is no commentary on Isaiah in that book.

accompanied by explanatory comments, and that side by side with these, many revelations which were not noted between the lines or in the margins were quoted and explained.[2] In this essay I will classify and explain the separate entries, making extensive use of quotations to support my interpretations.[3]

The entries number more than 270. All of them, except for seven late entries made in 1771–4, are contained in the eight large volumes which were in Almanzi's library in Padua and passed into the possession of the British Library in London.[4] The dates of those in the eight volumes range from 1722 to 1766, but in several years during this long period there are no entries at all, while in some there are only isolated examples. The main concentration in terms of both number and content occurs in the years 1723–42, with particular frequency and importance between 1729 and 1735, i.e. from the time when Luzzatto and his group began their public messianic activity until his departure from Padua to live in Amsterdam.[5]

In general the scattered entries may be divided into three groups, two large and one small:

1. Notes of spiritual occurrences written in the writer's personal style, expressing emotions and moods, such as sorrow and joy, depression and enthusiasm, uncertainties and mental struggle, hopes and disappointments, pleas for help and salvation, and the receipt of promises and consolation. Expressions of emotions are sometimes explicitly associated with dreams and visions, the allusions to which are generally brief and obscure. Some of the entries of this kind also contain biblical quotations.
2. Biblical verses or parts of verses, singly or joined with others, verbatim and with nothing added.
3. Notes of actual events or details of a factual kind, mostly personal or family matters, or information relating to members of the group in Padua. The few entries in this category are mostly in the last volumes of the set in the British Library.

[2] See Essay 6, nn. 43, 70, 81–7, 92, 97, 100–4. And see also Essay 3, pp. 204–6.

[3] In quoting from the diary entries I shall confine myself, in general, to their essentials, omitting subsidiary matter. I shall publish elsewhere further studies in clarification of the diary, reproducing the entries in full and in chronological order. [See the 'Complete List of Diary Entries' below.—Trans.] I am most grateful to the directorate of the British Library, who on the occasion of my visit acceded to my request for photographs of Valle's writings and gave me permission to publish them in whole or in part.

[4] See Essay 6, pp. 318–20 and n. 70.

[5] The only information on these diary entries, before I took up my study of Valle's writings, was that contained in S. D. Luzzatto's review of Almanzi's library. See *Hamazkir. Hebräische Bibliographie: Blätter für neuere und ältere Literatur des Judenthums*, vi, ed. M. Steinschneider (Berlin, 1863), 49–50; and Essay 6, p. 318 and n. 67.

In the light of the unmistakable character of the entries in the first group, all recording mystical experiences which bear the stamp of revelations from on high, there can be no doubt that the verses in the second group are not mere quotations but are expressions in scriptural language of mystical experiences and visions. The content of the verses testifies to the correctness of this assumption, and it is completely confirmed in the text of the compositions, where verses in the entries are interpreted as revelations of hidden truths.

Before I consider entries of these two sorts relating to experiences and visions, I will quote and comment on passages from the third group, namely remarks relating to external events.[6] I have chosen as examples allusions whose meaning is not obvious and which have a bearing on the life of the group.[7]

Two entries written in the middle of 5491 and early in 5492 [spring 1731 and autumn/winter 1731–2], express praise of a Moses in the group, and it is worth giving some thought to what they mean.

II 828^{r}: [5491] From Moses to Moses, none has arisen like Moses.[8]

III 159^{v}: This day, the New Moon of Tevet [5492/Dec. 1731], manifestation of the light of Moses, and truth springs out of the ground.[9]

From adjacent entries bearing dates, the aphorism 'From Moses to Moses . . .' can be dated to Adar 5491 [spring 1731]. The personal and self-related character of the entries as a whole might be thought to indicate that the second Moses was Valle. But Luzzatto's status as the embodiment of the biblical Moses, superior to the two Messiahs in the group, was undoubtedly known to Valle and accepted by him,[10] and tips the balance in favour of the assumption that the second Moses was Luzzatto.

[6] Where I give references for diary entries and compositions in the eight volumes in the British Library, MSS 385–92, I refer to the volumes by consecutive roman numerals, thus: I = MS 385, II = 386, and so on. [Folio numbers are indicated by arabic numerals.—Trans.]

[7] In Essay 6, n. 32, I quoted a personal, familial note by Valle in which he mentioned incidentally that on 20 Iyar 5487 [1727] a son had been born to him. His remark is reproduced in full below, text referring to nn. 67–70. In entries relating to 1731, 1733, and 1734 (III 128^{v}, 427^{v}, 430^{v}, 689^{v}) he says that in each year a son was born to him. As is shown by the entries and their dates, the second son died before he could be circumcised.

[8] See T. Preschel, 'Mimosheh ve'ad mosheh lo kam kemosheh (gilgulah shel imrah)', *Hado'ar*, 48 (1969), 627–8.

[9] Ps. 85: 12.

[10] See Essay 3, pp. 190–206. *Sod haketubah* ['The Mystical Interpretation of the Marriage Contract'] (Essay 3, pp. 211–22), written at the time of Luzzatto's marriage, seven or eight months after the diary entry we are considering, was certainly an open secret to the members of the group, and in particular to Valle and R. Jekutiel of Vilna, who, for the group, were the Messiah ben David and Seraiah, commander-in-chief to the Messiah ben Joseph, and they knew, earlier than this, that Luzzatto represented the biblical Moses. And see Essay 8, pp. 413–15.

The second of the two entries supports this assumption, for in the matter of the manifestation of Moses' light the reasonable choice is between the Moses of Exodus and Luzzatto. According to the first of these possible choices, it would have to be said that this is an allusion to a collective mystical experience in which the light of the biblical Moses was revealed to the inward eyes of the members of the group. On the second of these possibilities, the reference would be to the brilliant light of Luzzatto in the group. In either event, 'truth' [*emet*] in the scriptural quotation which is attached to the 'manifestation of the light of Moses' means the sefirah Tiferet, the domain of Moses in the celestial system. 'Springs out of the ground', however, is another ambiguous expression: 'the ground' [*erets*] may be Malkhut, the Shekhinah who dwells with the Moses of Exodus and with Moses Luzzatto, or it may indicate the lowly state of the biblical Moses, afflicted in his various incarnations, or of the persecuted and reviled Moses Luzzatto.[11]

Four entries date from the first quarter of 5492 [last quarter of 1731], and these contain important evidence on the crystallization and activity of the group after Luzzatto's first capitulation at the end of 5490 [late summer 1730]:[12]

[11] In spite of these considerations, which appear to me to be soundly based, one cannot entirely dismiss the possibility that in both of these diary entries the problematic Moses is Valle, because the winnower, too, is described by him as a spark of Moses in the sense of a Moses–Messiah. Here is a paragraph which also contains additional pointers to Valle's self-image and to the revelations he received from on high: 'And with the breath [*ruaḥ*] of his lips he will slay the wicked [Isa. 11: 4, on the 'shoot from the stock of Jesse'], this is said with regard to the Messiah ben David. Since his root is from the breath [*hevel*] of his mouth, he will slay the wicked, that is, the husk, with his lips, for *he* [the husk] *is a spark of evil* whose power is in his mouth. Because of him kings will shut their mouths [Isa. 52: 15, on 'the servant of the Lord'], kings indeed. Moreover: what does "kings" mean? Rabbis [on the basis of *Git.* 62*a*], for they will see things which have not been told them [Isa. 52: 15], miracles and wonders performed by him. For thus was it said to the winnower: Your right hand will teach you fearsome deeds [Ps. 45: 5], and they will behold things they have not heard of [Isa. 52: 15], in the sense of the inwardness of wisdom, for he is crowned with *ḥayah yeḥidah* [the 'living' and the 'only', the two highest parts of the soul—Trans.] and no secret is withheld from him; the key of the house of David is on his shoulder, and he shall open, and none shall shut, and he shall shut, and none shall open [Isa. 22: 22]' (II 434^{r}). This paragraph is taken from the commentary on Ecclesiastes, which was written in the first half of 5490 [late 1729–early 1730]. The 'kings–rabbis', who saw the winnower's miracles and wonders and heard him expound the secrets of kabbalah, were certainly the members of the group. There is an allusion to Valle's occupation in the teaching of kabbalah in an entry made a short time before he began to write the commentary on Ecclesiastes: 'This day, the New Moon of Kislev [5490] [end of 1729], new propositions from the inwardness of wisdom' (II 337^{v}). On *ḥayah yeḥidah* as parts of the soul, see below, text referring to n. 105, and the note itself.

[12] It is worth quoting here a remarkable and important, if thinly veiled, description of the group in an exposition of Psalm 8 which, to judge from the date on an adjoining entry, was written in Iyar 5491 [late spring–early summer 1731], shortly after the group began its clandestine

III 104^{v}: The blessings of Heaven greeted me, and now, on Shabat Bereshit [5492] [the Sabbath following Simhat Torah, 'the Rejoicing over the Law', i.e. autumn 1731—Trans.], Elijah blessed me through Jacob Hayim.

We can decipher this obscure entry with the aid of a note in R. H. J. D. Azulai's diary recording something said to him by R. Jacob Hazak in 1776: 'The *magid* [Luzzatto's *magid*] said that Elijah reveals himself to si[gnor] Castel-Franco, who has achieved great insights, and in dreams on Sabbath

activities under the rules drawn up in Shevat 5491. See Essay 6, pp. 289–94. The description reads as follows: 'Indeed it was God's wish to complete this great *tikun* [the completion of the winnowing of the good from the bad and the union of the Shekhinah with Tiferet and Yesod] by the hand of actual babes and sucklings, who are *the righteous performers of tikun*, who are truly babes in years but nevertheless suck the milk of the supernal wisdom which is the wisdom of kabbalah. And that is the underlying meaning of the verse [Ps. 8: 3]: "Out of the mouths of babes and sucklings You have founded strength." And the reason these babes and sucklings were chosen rather than veteran scholars as would have been appropriate was in order to "silence the enemy and the vengeful" [Ps. 8: 3], who is the wicked *sm'* [Sama'el], an adversary and an enemy and vengeful, that is certain . . . for if veteran scholars were occupied in this science, the *tikun* would not suffice to stop the mouth of the accusing enemy and stir [God's] mercies and bring forth the Redemption, because they [the veterans] would be following their normal practice, and their awakening here below does not strengthen the beings on high as much as does the awakening here below of babes and sucklings, whose normal practice this is not but who nevertheless choose the wisdom of kabbalah and the ways of holiness in preference to [their] nature and the evil inclination which is strong in their young days . . . for it is a most wonderful thing that babes and sucklings should be awakened to complete the *tikun* of the world, which is why some of them have been chosen to be *messiahs and prophets and fighters against "the external ones"* [the forces of evil] . . . It was concerning this great thing that the prophet said: Jacob will not now be ashamed, nor will now his face grow pale, for when he sees his children, his actual children, the work of his hands, in my midst, they will be sanctifying my name, *performing the sanctification of the Lord by their right choice and sacrificing themselves for the sanctification of the Name*, and so giving holiness strength to prevail and spread in the world [Isa. 29: 22–3, with alterations and expository additions]. And that is the underlying meaning of "They will sanctify the Holy One of Jacob and stand in awe of the God of Israel" [Isa. 29: 23]' (II 932^{v}).

The expression 'the righteous performers of *tikun*' is very common in Valle's writings. I have previously shown that it serves to signify the members of the group. See Essay 6, pp. 327–35. I have no doubt that 'the wicked *sm'*, an adversary and an enemy and vengeful', alludes additionally to the persecutors of Luzzatto and his group, chief among them R. Moses Hagiz and the rabbis of Venice. Valle regarded them as representatives of the Sitra Ahra ['Other Side'], whose fault it was that the 'righteous performers of *tikun*' were humiliated and condemned to suffer for the sanctification of the Name. See Essay 6, pp. 332–5. The remark that there were 'messiahs' in the group tells us that alongside the Moses of Luzzatto and the Messiah ben David of Valle there was also a Messiah ben Joseph, a reborn Shabetai Tsevi who in his previous existence had been destined to be the Messiah ben Joseph but had not succeeded in fulfilling his destiny. In my opinion this second Messiah in the group was R. Isaiah Romanin. See Essay 6, n. 37 and addendum; n. 100. The reference to 'prophets' among 'babes and sucklings' in the group shows

and New Moon sees Ezekiel.'[13] Valle's diary entry makes it clear that the connection of R. Jacob Hayim Castel-Franco, one of the important personalities in the group, with the prophet Elijah was not confined to the receipt of personal revelations, but that he also served as an intermediary between the prophet and members of the group, or at any rate bestowed a blessing on Valle in the name of Elijah.

III 108^{r}: This day, the New Moon of Heshvan [5492/autumn 1731], we arrived at the holy lodging-place whose banner and emblem are *berakha"h tova"h* ['a good blessing'].

III 149^{v}: At this time, the night of the close of the holy Sabbath, 16 Kislev [5492/end of 1731], the day was declared holy by the acclamation of the members.

III 155^{v}: This day, 28 Kislev [5492], love and brotherhood, peace and friendship.

I do not know whether 'the holy lodging-place' actually means an inn where the members of the group met together or is only a symbol for a divine home. In the latter case the reference would certainly be to the ascent of the soul and [its] adherence [*devekut*] to the Shekhinah, which would also fit the emblem 'a good blessing'. In any event it is clear that this entry denotes a collective mystical experience shared by the group when they arrived 'at the holy lodging-place'. That is also the general meaning of the sanctification of the day at the close of the Sabbath 'by the acclamation of the members', and it is probable that the reference in the third entry to harmonious relations within the group is similarly an allusion to cooperation in mystical matters.

The following three entries are from the years 5496–7 [1735–7], the years of the bans and persecutions which followed the investigation of Luzzatto in Frankfurt am Main in 5495, when he was on his way from Padua to Amsterdam:

III 854^{v}: This day, 20 Heshvan [5496/autumn 1735], the night of the holy Sabbath, the Kedushah ['Sanctification'] aloud and in public, God is with you in all that you do.[14]

that it was not only Luzzatto and Valle who were regarded as possessing the spirit of holiness and prophecy. [On Valle as prophet—Trans.], see below, pp. 352–6. The whole paragraph reproduced above gives powerful expression to the consciousness of their messianic mission which inspired the group of Paduans looking out for the Redemption.

[13] Quoted in an addendum to M. Benayahu's essay 'Ha"magid" shel ramḥa"l', in I. Ben-Zvi and M. Benayahu (eds.), *Sefer zikaron liyeshayahu zoneh/Isaiah Sonne Memorial Volume* (= *Sefunot*, 5) (Jerusalem, 1961), 335. And see ibid. 315, 317–18.

[14] Gen. 21: 22.

III 864v: This day, 27 Shevat [5496], I rejoiced over the *ry"k* [see below] and said: My brethren, my brethren, say to God 'How fearsome are Your works.'[15]

IV 113r: This day, 11 Tamuz [5497], I have been brought into the holy *beit midrash* to teach and supervise.

Apparently the words 'the Kedushah aloud and in public', with the verse which follows them, mean that for Valle, his recitation aloud of the 'holiness' blessing in the [silent] Sabbath-eve Shemoneh Esreh prayer ['The eighteen benedictions'] in the group's *beit midrash* was a mystical act which brought him an assurance from above that he was about to achieve his aspiration and inherit Luzzatto's position as leader of the group. But the third entry shows that this assurance was not fulfilled until Tamuz 5497 [summer 1737], and in fact, even after he was appointed 'to teach and supervise', he was not a success as head of the group.[16] The *ry"k* mentioned in the second entry is R. Jekutiel [Yekutiel] of Vilna, who left Padua for Poland in 1733; this entry tells us that while the storm-winds raged round Luzzatto and his writings and disciples both at home and in eastern Europe,[17] the joyous news reached Padua that

[15] Ps. 66: 3. The rest of the verse reads: 'Through the greatness of Your strength Your enemies come cringing to You'.

[16] See Essay 6, pp. 314–18.

[17] See *R' mosheh ḥayim lutsato uvenei doro: osef igerot ute'udot*, ed. S. Ginzburg [hereafter *Igerot*] (Tel Aviv, 1937). The fiercest document issued in eastern Europe against Luzzatto and his group is the excommunication by R. Aryeh Leib, rabbi of the communities of Glogau and Lvov and brother-in-law of R. Jacob Emden, dated 3 Tamuz 5495 [summer 1735], addressed to 'the rabbis, the great scholars of Israel for Greater Poland and Lesser Poland', and requesting *inter alia* 'that the edict be proclaimed in all the provinces of Polonia on the eve of every New Moon that this heretic [Luzzatto] and his disciples and his retinue of evildoers and his faction be excommunicated and outlawed, set apart and separated from all the holiness of Israel, and that all his books and writings be condemned as books of infidels and sorcerers to be burnt' (*Igerot*, ii. 309–10). The first document we have on the participation of the Polish rabbis in the campaign against Luzzatto is the proclamation by R. Eleazar of Kraków, when he was still rabbi of the congregation of Brody, in his own name and that of 'the distinguished rabbis who sit in judgement' (ibid. 317–18). In the proclamation they associate themselves with the bans contained in 'the pronouncement by Rabbi Ezekiel Katzenellenbogen and R. M. Hagiz', which was addressed to 'all the great rabbis and leaders of the holy congregations in the diaspora of Poland and Ashkenaz [the German-speaking countries], may their Rock and Redeemer preserve them, and particularly the great rabbis of the Land of Israel, may it be rebuilt and established speedily in our days, and the great rabbis and leaders of the holy congregation in Turkey, may the Lord preserve them, and the great rabbis of all Italy, may the Lord preserve them' (ibid. 289–91). The pronouncement in question was written in the week of the *parashah* [Torah reading] 'Vayigash' [Gen. 44–7] 5495, about a fortnight before Luzzatto's confession in the Frankfurt investigation which was concluded 'in the *parashah* "Shemot" [beginning of Exodus] on the third day of the week, 17 Tevet of this year 495 [1 Jan. 1735] in the abbreviated numeration', and the text of the proclamation by the rabbis of Brody in the week of the *parashah* 'Mishpatim' 5495 [five weeks after 'Shemot'] shows clearly that they were still unaware of the investigation and confession in Frankfurt. R. Eleazar wrote in his proclamation: 'If there should be a meeting

the confidant of Luzzatto and his group was acting on their behalf in Poland and succeeding in curbing the fierce attacks on them.[18]

The last two factual entries I quote here are from the years 5512 and 5515:

V 258^{v}: This day, 8 Marheshvan [5512/autumn 1751]: it will certainly be my good fortune to go to the Land of Israel, but I do not know whether now or later.

VII 451^{r-v}: On the last day of Tishrei, 5515 [autumn 1754], Shelomoh Rakah, my dear friend, died [above the line the initials *nun ayin*, 'may his soul rest in Eden'], and may God, blessed be He, help me, for He is Lord of everything and everything is from Him.

On the face of it there is nothing to link these entries, especially as they were written three years apart. But from the information brought to light in the course of my researches it appears that they are of one piece, and are connected with the relations between Valle and R. Jekutiel of Vilna. The wealthy philanthropist R. Solomon Rakah, originally of Padua and later resident in

of a council of scholars in our province, I must travel to the meeting-place, perhaps we might be able to stand in the breach'; but his desire to submit the Luzzatto affair to the Council of Four Lands for judgement was not fulfilled. And see two further documents by R. Eleazar written in Elul 5495 [late summer 1735] (ibid. 318–20), and the testimony in the 'endorsement by the emissaries of Safed' of Tamuz [summer] 5495 (ibid. 315–17) 'that the great and pious *gaon*, renowned in his generation, the *av beit din* [president of a rabbinical court] in Israel, our honoured teacher and rabbi R. Eleazar of Kraków, may the Merciful One preserve and bless him, in the holy congregation of Brody, he and his court of justice in an assembly of elders on this matter in [5]490 and now again, decreed the excommunication of HM"L [*sic*] and his books and all his writings, [ordering] that they be not remembered or brought to mind among the congregation of Israel, and that they be treated in the manner appropriate for the books of sectarians [*minin*]; and they placed a strict ban on anyone who studies or has in his possession any book or writing written by this heretic [*apikoros*] HM"L'. In his bans on Luzzatto and on Luzzatto's writings, R. Eleazar expressed in the clearest terms his strong opposition to Shabateanism and its aftergrowths. I therefore see no basis for the assertion by Y. Barnai, in his book *Yehudei erets-yisra'el bame'ah hayod"ḥet* (Jerusalem, 1982), 86–9, that R. Eleazar's attitude to Shabateans and Shabateanism was ambivalent, and that 'side by side with his opposition' he also felt 'a certain sympathy' with them. A remarkable turn of events should be noted: during the years of Luzzatto's residence in Amsterdam (1735–43) there arrived to take up office in that city, one after the other, the two men who had been his principal accusers in the campaign against him in Poland: R. Eleazar of Kraków was rabbi of the Ashkenazi community from 1736 to 1740 and R. Aryeh Leib of Glogau and Lvov succeeded him in 1741. And see Y. Bartal, 'Aliyat r' elazar me'amsterdam le'erets-yisra'el bishenat tak"a', in Y. Michman (ed.), *Meḥkarim al toledot yahadut holand*, iv (Jerusalem, 1985), 7–19.

[18] See Essay 8, pp. 414–18, 426–41, and esp. 435–7; Essay 10, pp. 487–92. In 1736 action to counter the attacks on Luzzatto in eastern Europe was also taken by people visiting Italy from Poland who became sympathizers of Luzzatto and his group. See *Igerot*, ii. 340–2, letter of 12 Kislev 5496 [end of 1735] from R. Hayim Falk of Lublin to R. Isaiah Bassano. And see also Essay 10, n. 10.

Venice, was a patron of Luzzatto's group from its inception until he died.[19] The first time that R. Jekutiel returned to Italy it was on a journey undertaken on behalf of the community of Brisk (Brest-Litovsk) in 1751–2, when he was given a letter of recommendation by the community and rabbis of Venice (New Moon of Shevat, 5512 [1752]). On the second occasion he arrived in Venice in 5515, intending to travel from there to the Land of Israel and establish a yeshiva in Hebron funded by R. Solomon Rakah, but he learned on arrival that the philanthropist had died, and he settled instead in Venice.[20] The plan to set up the yeshiva in Hebron was probably conceived in 5512 [1751–2], or possibly earlier, and from Valle's diary entry in 5512 we may infer that he too intended to go up to the Land of Israel and take part in the pious initiative. However, the entry in 5515 on the death of R. Solomon Rakah is enough to indicate that the project was cancelled.

To begin my consideration of entries recording mystical experiences whose visionary character is beyond doubt, I will quote some passages which show what kind of spiritual events these were.

1. Conveying tidings

Five entries from 5486 to 5495 [1725–autumn 1734]:

I 504^{r}: This day, the night of 22 Kislev [5486/Nov. 1725], I received tidings that my labours had been rewarded. May Your lovingkindness comfort me in accordance with Your promise to Your servant.[21]

II 299^{v}: This day, the 10th of the month, Yom Kippur [5490/1729], I received tidings of riches and favour. And nations shall walk by your light, and kings by the brightness of your sunrise.[22]

II 440^{v}: At this time, in the month of Adar [5490/1730], I received tidings which made known to me that I had returned to my root.[23]

III 716^{r}: This day, the night of 10 Menahem [the end of the fast of 9 Av], I received tidings by these and similar expressions, the windows of Heaven were opened,[24] *un mondo di* revelations from the *mashpia*,

[19] On R. Solomon Rakah and his links with Valle and R. Jekutiel, see Essay 8, p. 428 and n. 67, p. 440 and n. 115; and Essay 6, n. 24 and p. 316.

[20] See Essay 8, pp. 428–9, 440; and see S. Eidelberg, 'Igeret shenishleḥah mivenetsiyah lemets bemaḥatsit hame'ah hayod"ḥet (letoledot ḥayav shel harofe r' yekutiel gordon)', in Saul Lieberman (ed.), *Salo Wittmayer Baron: Jubilee Volume on the Occasion of his Eightieth Birthday*, iii [Hebrew section] (New York, 1975), 1–6.

[21] Ps. 119: 76. This is Valle's expression of his wish that the news be confirmed. I shall not add comments of this kind except where they are needed to clarify the revelation.

[22] Isa. 60: 3.

[23] See Essay 6, p. 312 and n. 46; p. 326 and n. 92.

[24] This is the exact expression used with regard to the Flood, Gen. 7: 11. Similar in form is Isa. 24: 18: 'For windows on high are opened and the foundations of the earth quake'. But the

blessed are You, O Lord, who comfort all mourners, blessed is He who revives the dead,[25] according to the suffering is the reward,[26] amen, may this be His will.

III 746v: This day, the New Moon of Heshvan in the perfect year [*temima"h*, 'perfect', numerical value 495], I received tidings that I had entered the hall of the sapphire pavement.[27]

2. Assurances

Three entries, one each from the years 5485, 5487, 5491 [1725, 1727, 1731]:

I 456r: It is a night of watching unto the Lord[28] [eve of Passover 5485], when the Lord my God lightened my yoke and assured me in His great lovingkindness that the time is near for His salvation to come and His righteousness to be revealed.[29]

I 607r: At this time, in the month of Adar [5487], he is assured that he has earned a place in the world to come.

III 8v: At this time, on 3 and 4 Tamuz [5491]: the double assurance, stand firm and see the salvation which the Lord will work for you this day.[30]

3. Visitations

Two entries, one in 5483 and one in 5485 [1723 and 1725]:

I 127r: At this time, in the month of Shevat [5483], *I was visited* in the pit of my sorrows and anointed with the oil of joy which was poured on my head from on high.[31]

scriptural source which comes nearest in sense to what is meant here is Ezek. 1: 1: 'The heavens were opened and I saw visions of God'. Valle, spontaneously breaking into Italian, goes on to describe the visions as, in effect, a torrent of revelations from his *mashpia*, whence the association with the Flood. Apparently the words he heard from on high are not reproduced in his note, in which the quotations simply express the enthusiasm stirred by his experiences. Possibly, however, the words 'by these and similar expressions' refer to scriptural quotations in the composition itself at this point, where verses from Isaiah 49 are expounded.

25 The blessing 'Who revives the dead' is quoted in another entry in a different context. See below, text referring to n. 147, and the note itself.

26 [*Avot* 5: 23.—Trans.]

27 The hall of the sapphire pavement is the lowest in the ascending order of seven halls described in the Zohar, and is the first stage in the divine order through which the soul ascends. See I. Tishby, *The Wisdom of the Zohar*, trans. D. Goldstein (Oxford, 1989), ii. 591–2.

28 Exod. 12: 42.

29 Isa. 56: 1, altering 'My' to 'His'.

30 Exod. 14: 13. The plural form of address here and in other similar entries is probably directed to the members of the group.

31 See Essay 6, n. 43; below, text referring to n. 52, and the note itself; and n. 72.

I 461^{v}: Do not rejoice over me, O my enemy; though I have fallen, I shall rise again.[32] On the evening of 4 Iyar [5485] *I was visited* and sanctified.

4. Instructions

One entry, in 5492 [1732]:

III 250^{r}: On 22 Sivan, because they strengthened holiness upon me and *instructed me* to announce that the Sitra Ahra ['Other Side'] would no longer prevail over me.[33]

5. Visual revelation

One entry, in 5485 [end of 1724]:

I 441^{r}: At this time, in the days of Tevet, to strengthen weak hands and tottering knees,[34] *the Lord showed me* the good of the land for a while, and [it] departed to await its time.

All the entries in the above set of examples bear the unmistakable hallmark of aural or visual revelations. Some are attributed to 'the Lord' or 'the Lord my God', others are reported in the impersonal plural hinting at unspecified supernal forces, but most are not related to any source.

In seventeen entries spread over the years 5491–5501 [1731–41] there are references to dreams, some in clear and plain language, others vague and obscure. None of the dreams is ascribed to any particular source. I will quote the 'dream' texts verbatim, in general restricting my comments to short explanations in the notes, so far as such explanations are necessary and possible.

II 901^{v}: On the seventh night of Passover [5491/1731], the dream of *mt*' [Metatron], But You, O Lord, be gracious to me and raise me up.[35] And on the day of the homily on the eighth night, Awake, north wind, and come, south wind, etc.[36] And on the last night of

[32] Mic. 7: 8. This verse has no bearing on the revelation itself but is quoted to explain the significance of the visitation and sanctification.

[33] He appears to mean that even at his lowest ebb among the husks he will stand firm and will not sin.

[34] Cf. Isa. 35: 3.

[35] Ps. 41: 11. Possibly the verse itself was spoken in the dream, but the connection between it and the revelation of Metatron is not clear.

[36] S. of S. 4: 16, which continues: 'Blow upon my garden, so that its spices may flow out. Let my beloved come to his garden and eat its precious fruit.' It is to be supposed that, in the dream, the whole verse was recited, and in the symbolism of kabbalah it would mean the marital union of Tiferet and Yesod (the beloved) with the Shekhinah (the garden), with the assistance of Gevurah and Hesed (North and South). But the diary entry probably relates mainly to Valle's erotic communion [*devekut*] with the Shekhinah; he saw himself as the representative and

Passover, unification [*yiḥud*] of the lights with mirth and songs, tambourine and harp.[37]

III 76ʳ: On 18 Elul [5491], the dream about R. Simeon bar Yohai.[38]

III 101ʳ: On the night of Shemini Atseret [eighth day of Tabernacles], the day of solemn assembly [5492], the dream of the Lady [*gevirah*], the treasury of all precious things.[39]

III 206ʳ: At this time, in these days of Purim [5492], the dream of Elijah, and wings like the wings of a stork,[40] [the wings] of a bird of the air [*le'of hashamayim*; but possibly *la'uf hashamayim*, 'to fly heavenward'—Trans.].

III 360ᵛ: On the night of 7 Kislev [5493], the dream of the circumcision in joy to strengthen the *tikun*.[41]

III 730ᵛ: At this time, at the close of the holy Sabbath on the night of 28 Elul [5494], the dream of the killing of ten enemies[42] and joyful thanksgiving.

III 736ʳ: At this time, on the night of the Day of Atonement [5495/1734], the dream of perfect healing.[43]

III 833ʳ: This day, 28 Menahem [Av 5495/1735], the dream of the star with regard to the request[44] for long life and to receive the divine flow of good.

embodiment of Tiferet and Yesod, especially in relation to the Shekhinah, as will become clear in the course of our detailed consideration. Apparently he attributed the dream in which he experienced the divine union to the merit of the sermon he preached in the group's *beit midrash* on the eighth day of Passover, which he called 'the day of the homily'. In another entry the latter part of the verse ('Let my beloved come to his garden and eat its precious fruit') is quoted without any relationship to a dream, and there Valle is undoubtedly alluding to an erotic mystical experience of his own. See below, text referring to n. 161.

[37] '*Yiḥud* of the lights' means unification of the divine forces in the whole sefirotic system. The phrase 'with mirth . . . and harp' is taken from Laban's words to Jacob (Gen. 31: 27), but I cannot see any connection of substance with the context here.

[38] Immediately after this there is a quotation from Scripture which may also have been heard in the dream: 'But My servant Caleb, because he had a different spirit' (Num. 14: 24). The rest of the verse reads: 'and has followed Me wholeheartedly, him will I bring to the land which he entered and his children shall inherit it'; hence the dream about R. Simeon bar Yohai was interpreted as a promise that the messianic expectations of Luzzatto and his colleagues would soon be fulfilled.

[39] Hos. 13: 15. 'The Lady' is undoubtedly the Shekhinah, and the words of Scripture are quoted to convey the delight of union with her.

[40] As in Zech. 5: 9. An indication that he saw Elijah flying.

[41] See n. 121 below, explanation of the entry regarding 'the *tikun* of the circumcision'.

[42] Presumably a reference to the forces of the ten sefirot of uncleanness.

[43] For the end of this entry, see below, text referring to nn. 80–1.

[44] A request apparently through the intermediary of the star.

IV 73^{v}: The night of the close of the holy Sabbath, 21 Adar II [5497], a dream[45] that the Messiah is coming [or 'has come'],[46] let us hope for good fortune, let us act and succeed.[47]

IV 140^{r}: On the third day of the festival [of Tabernacles], the night of the holy Sabbath [5498/1737], I prayed this prayer in a dream, upon my knees before the tree of life, calling aloud: May it be Your will, O Lord my God, to pardon me for all the sins I have committed before You from the day I came into existence on this earth until this day, and not to let me sin any more for the rest of my days, and[48] let me not be in need of the gifts of mortals or of their loans, for their gift is small and their disgrace is great, but only of Your hand, which is full and generous, rich and open, so that I may not be ashamed in this world or be put to shame in the world to come, and hearken to my prayer. Thus far my prayer.

IV 153^{v}: This day, 26 Shevat [5498/1738], a dream about reward for the work,[49] the lifting of the ewer, and the preparation of the throne.

IV 158^{v}: This day, 11 Nisan [5498], the dream of the circuit [of the synagogue] in the matter of *kash kasheh*[?],[50] and the acknowledgement from 'There is none like our God' to 'We will give thanks to our Saviour'.

IV 161^{r}: On the night of 21 Nisan [5498], a dream of the subduing of the angels[51] in the matter of its repetition[?] [the reading *hishanoto* is doubtful], and every month fresh joy.

45 [Adar II: a leap year has two months of Adar.—Trans.] He writes *halom* ['hither'], with initial letter *he*: no doubt a slip of the pen. Substitution of *ḥet* gives 'dream'.

46 The reference to the Messiah in the third person might be thought to show that in 5497 he had already given up his belief in his own destiny as Messiah, but later entries and descriptions of the winnower's functions and activities in the years following 5497 are against such a conclusion. See below, text referring to n. 110.

47 The expression of hope is undoubtedly external to the dream.

48 From here on the sentence is based on the words of the grace after meals.

49 This undoubtedly refers to the completion of the works of *tikun*, whose substance is hinted at in the obscure expression 'the lifting of the ewer and the preparation of the throne'.

50 I do not know what this means, or what the connection is between the circuit and the *piyut* 'There is none like our God' which is recited at the end of the Sabbath morning service. ['We will give thanks to our Saviour' ends the third verse of that *piyut*.—Trans.]

51 'The angels' are probably the angels of destruction. The words which follow may mean that this dream recurred and that its repetition causes 'fresh joy' every month, in accordance with Gen. 41: 32: 'As for the doubling of Pharaoh's dream, it means that the thing has been firmly determined by God, and God will very soon do it.' For the source of the expression 'every month fresh joy', see I. Davidson, *Otsar hashirah vehapiyut* (New York, 1970), ii. 29, under *Bekhol ḥodesh*.

IV 250^{v}: This day, 9 Iyar [5499], a dream of the anointing[52] by the Father, and the promise completed.

IV 400^{v}: This day, 28 Elul [5500], the great dream with the doubled call: O Lord, save Your people, the remnant of Israel.[53]

IV 444^{v}: At this time, the end of the month [Nisan 5501], Now his head [in the 'Complete List' below, 'my head'—Trans.] will be lifted up,[54] and the dream [that] the fowl which shakes its face[?] [the reading *tarnegola demena'ara anpa* is doubtful—Trans.][55] has gone [or 'will go'] forth to freedom.

IV 463^{v}: This day, the New Moon of Tamuz [5501], a good dream came to me a second time, and also it was said: Lo, I have made him a witness to the nations, a prince and commander to the nations.[56]

I found from Valle's writings that he thought of dreams as a low rung of dubious worth on the ladder ascending to the receipt of revelations. Here is what he said in the commentary on the Song of Songs which he wrote in 5489 [1729] when at the height of his mystical and messianic activity in Luzzatto's group and in the full vigour of his own literary creativity, about two years before the first dream mentioned in the diary:

The mystical significance of the dream has long been known, [namely] that it is *gadlut* ['spiritual maturity'] enclosed in *katnut* ['spiritual immaturity'], and in *katnut* the 'external ones', the forces of evil, have a strong position, they being the mystery of chaff and straw, concerning which it was said by our rabbis: 'Just as there can be no corn without straw, so there can be no dream without idle details',[57] which are the 'external ones' who take hold during the time of *katnut* in the mystery mentioned above. (II 142^{r})

However, even if he still kept to this evaluation, it stands to reason that the dreams he committed to writing in his diary were regarded by him as 'corn free of straw' and that he did not doubt their truth.

I incline to the view that, apart from this handful of revelations which are expressly ascribed to dreams, all the mystical experiences and occurrences

[52] This undoubtedly means 'the anointing with oil from on high' (see above, text referring to n. 31; and n. 72 below). Apparently 'the father' [*ha'av*] is the sefirah Hokhmah, which is called Aba, and 'the promise completed' is the fulfilment of Valle's messianic destiny.

[53] Jer. 31: 6.

[54] Ps. 27: 6 ['. . . my head . . .'].

[55] This phrase, heard or seen in the dream, occurs repeatedly, with the addition of the words 'from the ashes', in midrashim on the resurgence of Jerusalem from its ruins at the time of the Redemption. See *Bereshit rabah*, ed. Theodor–Albeck, 75: 1, and the remarks ibid., p. 878. Valle appears to have applied it to himself as the Messiah-to-be.

[56] Isa. 55: 4.

[57] *Ber.* 55*a*.

mentioned in the diary took place while he was awake. This assumption hardens into certainty in the case of eight entries made in 5483–7 [1722–3 to 1727] in which there appeared the spiritual force called the *mashpia*, which by the measure of its presence and the degree to which it was active determined the peaks and troughs in Valle's life. I will quote and elucidate the main points in these entries, which, in addition to their mention of the *mashpia*, contain matter of great importance for our present purpose.[58]

I 82^{r} [or I 62^{v}: see below in the 'Complete List of Diary Entries'—Trans.]: From here onward in the year 5483, when the light was dimmed [above the line: 'by the curtain of the separating clouds'], but the *mashpia* remained and went running back and forth.

I 305^{r}: [In different ink: initials *beit ayin" he*, 'for my many sins'] Now began the days of adversity in the days of Tevet, when the *mashpia* departed altogether [above the line in different ink: 'and I fell from a high roof into a deep pit'], the year 484 in the abbreviated numeration [5484] [in different ink: 'May the Lord, blessed be He, have mercy on me'].

I 391^{r}: At this time, in the days of Tishrei, the Lord in his compassion for me brought healing to my wound and the *mashpia* returned, the year 485 in the abbreviated numeration.

I 404^{r}: This day, the [letter erased and 'tenth' written below the line] day of Marheshvan [5485], I have been relieved a little of my sorrow and distress and of [two letters erased, and above the line is written: 'the hard labour that I was made to do' [Isa. 14: 3]]. May the name of the Lord be blessed from now and for ever,[59] blessed be He who bestows good on the undeserving and has bestowed all good on me,[60] for the *mashpia* grows ever stronger as the hand of the Lord is good to me.

I 446^{v}: Blessed be God who has not turned away my prayer, nor His lovingkindness from me.[61] This day, 15 Tevet [5485/Dec. 1724], I have found some rest for my soul, for [above the line: 'the accusation(s are) growing ever weaker'] and the *mashpia* is growing ever stronger against my enemies.[62] My foot stands on level ground, in the assemblies I will bless the Lord.[63]

[58] Five entries mentioning the *mashpia* are among the examples I quoted in Essay 6, n. 43.

[59] Ps. 113: 2.

[60] The blessing Hagomel (on delivery from danger), omitting the divine name and declaration of God's kingship.

[61] Ps. 66: 20.

[62] Apparently plural [*oyevay*]. See Isa. 42: 13. [Singular (*-iy*) and plural (*-ay*) suffixes are indistinguishable in unvowelled text.—Trans.]

[63] Ps. 26: 12.

I 524r: This day in Adar II [5486], at the close of the holy Sabbath, the evening of the reading of the scroll of Esther, the *mashpia* grew exceedingly strong,[64] in accordance with the word of the Lord which is sure, on 13 Adar, and they were to be despoiled of their possessions.[65]

I 568v: At this time, in the month of Tishrei, year 5487, the strength of the *mashpia* will increase to prevail against my enemies, and as for the oppressor, his strong strides will be cut short, and disaster is made ready to lame him.[66]

I 625v: This day, 20 Iyar [5487], the day on which a son was born to me,[67] the oppressor ceased[68] and the *mashpia* was at rest and I went forth from under an iron yoke[69] to life, healing is near and the gates of light are opened, the light growing ever brighter until it is bright day.[70]

The years 5483–7 when Valle made these explicit references to his relationship with the *mashpia* saw the main stages of his progress towards liberation from the husks into whose depths he had sunk in 5475 [1715]. (He had begun to shake off their yoke and ally himself with the holiness of the Godhead in 5481.[71]) Nothing is said about the nature and rank of the *mashpia*, but from the entries I have quoted and from adjoining entries with subject matter resembling that contained in references to the *mashpia*, it can be concluded that it was perceived as a personal representative of a hidden non-divine source such as an angel or the soul of a tsadik[72] through which divine lights and revelations from on high were conveyed to Valle. Its special function was to protect Valle from the forces of the Sitra Ahra and strengthen him in his war against them, and it occasionally fulfilled this function even at times of great stress when it could not maintain the link between its protégé and celestial sources.

64 [*gavar ve'avar*, 'was strong (or prevailed) and passed (or overflowed)'. Words probably paired for assonance.—Trans.]

65 Esther 8: 11.

66 Based on Job 18: 7 and 12 [on the rendering of which the versions vary—Trans.].

67 See Essay 6, n. 32, and n. 7 above.

68 Cf. Isa. 14: 4.

69 For the expression 'an iron yoke' see Deut. 28: 48; Jer. 28: 14.

70 Cf. Prov. 4: 18.

71 See Essay 6, pp. 307–14, 324–5.

72 The *mashpia*, then, is to be characterized as akin to a *magid*. But throughout his diary Valle avoids using the word *magid*. The sole exception is an opaque allusion in the poetic language of Scripture, in an entry made in 5492 [1732]. This was about five years after his last mention of the *mashpia*, which, as I shall show, marked the end of the *mashpia*'s activity. The exceptional entry (III 271v) reads as follows: 'On the 17th of the month [Av 5492] *magid mishneh ashiv lakh* [Zech. 9: 12] ['(I) declare I will restore double to you', but could be construed as 'I will give you back a second *magid*'—Trans.], and the remedy by the pouring of oil.' 'The pouring of oil' may mean anointing from on high. See Essay 6, n. 43, and nn. 31 and 52 above.

In the first and last of these eight entries the light is associated with the *mashpia* in two contrasting situations. In the first, we are told: 'the light was dimmed . . . but the *mashpia* remained . . .'. In other words, even when the light lost its brilliance, the *mashpia*, though weakened, continued to be active. The last entry, on the other hand, describes the light as shining strongly, with no need for any special activity by the *mashpia* because the forces of oppression and darkness had been silenced, as Valle says: 'the oppressor ceased and the *mashpia* was at rest . . . and the gates of light are opened, the light growing ever brighter until it is bright day'. It is probable that the last-mentioned announcement, which was written in Iyar 5487 [early summer 1727], was not intended to indicate an event of temporary duration but reported the beginning of a fundamental and permanent change, in that and the following year, in which Valle felt himself to have been completely freed from the rule of the husks[73] and so no longer needed the protection of the *mashpia*. The joyful announcement of the flood of uninterrupted light is, indeed, also found, with minor changes in the description, in Heshvan 5487 [autumn 1726] shortly before the time of the entry I have quoted, and again after it in Nisan 5488 and Tishrei 5489 [spring and autumn 1728]:

I 572^{v}: At this time in the month of Marheshvan [5487/1726], the adversary and enemy is growing ever weaker, and *the gates of salvation are opened*, the light growing ever brighter until it is bright day.

I 821^{r}: At this time, in the month of Aviv [Nisan 5488] [*aviv* also means 'spring'—Trans.], the raging waters have ended and been cut off, and *the gates of light and joy are opened*, growing ever brighter until it is bright day.

I 957^{v}: At this time, in the month of Tishrei, 5489, *the gates of holiness are opened*, the light growing ever brighter until it is bright day.

The opening of 'the gates of holiness', which are at a higher level than 'the gates of salvation' and 'the gates of light', also marked the opening of a new era in the stages of Valle's inspiration and spiritual attainment. At the

[73] See Essay 6, pp. 310–14, where I consider the relationship between the events in Valle's life in these years and the appearance of the *magid* to Luzzatto, the crystallization of the group in 1727–8, and the beginning of their open messianic activity in 1729. The diary entry shows that the cessation of activity by the *mashpia*, which was connected with Valle's elevation to a higher level of spiritual attainment, occurred just before the *magid*'s first appearance to Luzzatto on the New Moon of Sivan 5487 [1727]. In parallel with these developments, taking place internally and externally, Valle's contact with the sefirot Yesod and Tiferet was being established and he was acquiring strength at their level, as was clearly indicated for the first time in the following entry: 'This day, in the year 5488, the New Moon of Marheshvan, the completion of the winnowing, and his return to Ramah [or 'to the height'], for his home is there' (I 705^{v}). And see Essay 6, n. 92; and text referring to n. 119 below.

beginning of 5489 [autumn 1728] the holy spirit entered into him, and in 5492 he rose to the rank of prophet. Here is a series of entries explicitly testifying to the activity of the holy spirit and the prophetic power in his soul:

II 2r: At this time, in the month of Heshvan [5489/1728], there rested upon him the spirit of the Lord, the spirit of wisdom, etc.[74]

II 364v: This day, 30 Kislev [5490/Dec. 1729], the spirit of the Lord spoke through me and His word was upon my tongue.[75]

III 92v: This day, the tenth day [of Tishrei; the Day of Atonement], year [5]492 [autumn 1731], the crown has been completed, and the holy spirit [*resh"he*, the initial letters of *ruaḥ hakodesh*] announces: 'I have laid your foundations with sapphires.'[76]

III 173r: [Tevet 5492/Dec. 1731–Jan. 1732] Complete redemption by prophet and messenger; 'prophet' is the righteous winnower, with whom the [divine] word communes, and he is called a *navi* ['prophet'] because those are the letters of *niv alef* ['the saying of the One'], for he earns the privilege of communicating [literally 'the saying of the lips from'; see Isa. 57: 19] what he receives from the One and Only One, for glory clothes itself in him, and glory—the wise shall inherit it;[77] and 'messenger' is Elijah, who reveals himself with him to bring perfect joy into the world.[78]

III 486r: This day, the New Moon of Tamuz [5493/summer 1733], the holy spirit is roused to revive the spirit of the humble and revive the heart of the broken.[79]

III 736r: At this time, on the night of the Day of Atonement [5495/autumn 1734], the dream of perfect healing, and *the h*[oly] *s*[pirit][80] And the Lord's cause will prosper in our hands.[81]

III 760r: At this time, the night of the holy Sabbath, 24 Kislev [5495/Dec. 1734], Can we find such a man, in whom there is *the spirit of God*?[82]

74 Isa. 11: 2. We also have here an unmistakable hint of messianism, since the whole chapter is a vision of the redemption of Israel and the world when the 'shoot from the stock of Jesse' makes his appearance. [In Isaiah the tense is understood as future, but the verb there could be read as future, present, or past.—Trans.]

75 2 Sam. 23: 2. Another clear hint of messianism, for this is the beginning of 'the last words of David', which the scriptural verse introduces as 'the saying of the man raised on high, the anointed of the God of Jacob'.

76 Isa. 54: 11 [where the tense is 'prophetic perfect', i.e. 'I will . . .'—Trans.].

77 Cf. Prov. 3: 35.

78 Followed by initials standing for 'speedily in our days, amen, may this be His will'.

79 Isa. 57: 15. The task of restoring Valle's courage at times when he was troubled and broken in spirit, which until 5487 [1727] was represented as the particular responsibility of the *mashpia*, is here ascribed to the holy spirit.

80 Sc. 'announces'.

81 Isa. 53: 10, substituting 'our hands' for 'his hand'.

82 Gen. 41: 38.

IV 138ʳ: At the close of the Day of Atonement [5498/1737], thrice *kadish* [or 'holy'], and from the pit He raised him to great deeds, from time to time *he prophesied.*

VII 601ʳ: On the festival of Tabernacles in the year 5516 [1755], [letters] *he nun dalet"beit*[83] *alef tav ayin" beit vav pe yod kaf ayin.*

The first entry in which Valle classes himself as a prophet (III 173ʳ) requires comment. It is not actually a diary entry: it is undated and in style it differs from the other entries. References to himself in the third person are indeed very common in other entries, but only in this one does he describe himself as 'the righteous winnower', a name he regularly uses in his compositions to camouflage his own identity. On the other hand this paragraph is conspicuous by its deliberate separation from the body of the text to which it has been added (the commentary on the Psalms): it is written at the top of the page and, like many of the diary entries, has no connection with what precedes or follows it; the last letter of each word is preceded by *gershayim* [a double apostrophe].

The paragraph is also of considerable interest in relation to the doctrine of the Redemption. Its attribution of prophetic rank to the Messiah is found in the sources,[84] and expositions of the eschatological events promised in Malachi 3 commonly identify the prophet Elijah, who is mentioned at the end of the chapter [which appears as chapter 4 in English versions—Trans.],

[83] Initials of *hineh natati devaray befikha* ['behold, I have put my words into your mouth'], said when Jeremiah was consecrated as a prophet (Jer. 1: 9). The letters which follow are undoubtedly also initials. The first three may stand for *al tira avdi* ['do not be afraid, My servant'] (Isa. 44: 2; Jer. 30: 10, 46: 27–8). It is worth noting that in 5516 Valle still regarded himself as a prophet, but was careful to use coded language in referring to his prophetic rank.

[84] Maimonides deals directly and incisively with this. See *Igeret teiman* ['Letter to Yemen'], iv, in *Igerot haramba"m*, ed. M. D. Rabinowitz (Jerusalem, 1960), 177–9; *Mishneh torah*, 'Hilkhot teshuvah' ['Laws of Repentance'], 9: 2. And see A. J. Heschel, 'Al ruaḥ hakodesh bimei habeinayim (ad zemano shel haramba"m)', in S. Lieberman (ed.), *Alexander Marx: Jubilee Volume on the Occasion of his Seventieth Birthday*, Hebrew vol. *Sefer hayovel likhevod aleksander marks* (New York, 1950), 175–208. This is a comprehensive survey of the appearance in public of men favoured with the holy spirit and the gift of prophecy, and also deals with links between the attainment of the holy spirit and prophetic powers, on the one hand, and the arousal of messianic fervour, on the other. To a limited extent in the body of his essay, and to a much greater extent in the notes, the author extended his consideration beyond the time of Maimonides, but these digressions are marred by imprecision and by surprising omissions. At pp. 186–7 he writes: 'Mysterious men who rose to fame as prophets are apparently no longer to be found after the twelfth century. A few who appeared subsequently did not achieve recognition by this title.' At n. 74 he remarks: 'Such as the prophet of Avila', and there is no mention at all of R. Abraham Abulafia, the famous prophesying kabbalist and creator of prophetic kabbalah. In that selective study no place is found, of course, for Nathan of Gaza and the other prophets of Shabateanism and its offshoots, and their existence is slurred over in the strange and evasive remark: 'See also *Me'ore'ot tsevi*, Warsaw 5598 [1838], *nun"alef, beit*, ff.'

with the messenger in the first verse.[85] But the prevailing opinion is that the renewal of prophecy will begin with the appearance of Elijah to announce the Redemption and pave the way for the kingdom of the Messiah,[86] whereas here the renewal of prophecy is reinforced by the personality of the Messiah = the righteous winnower = Valle, and Elijah's task, as a messenger who brings salvation, is to help the Messiah = the prophet.

The same paragraph throws important light on Valle's view of his prophetic rank and how he attained it. Prophetic inspiration reaches him through the Shekhinah, who dwells within him and regarding whom it is said here, using the names she bears in the literature of kabbalah, that '*the word* communes with him', 'for *glory* clothes itself in him'. The source of his prophetic gift is represented by the name 'the One and only One', which fits the sefirah Keter.[87] From these descriptions it appears that after his elevation to full prophetic and messianic rank in 1729–30, the Shekhinah took the place of the *mashpia* in his moods and mystical experiences.

B. THE MAIN CONCERNS OF THE DIARY ENTRIES

The motif most common in the entries is *conflict*, described as war against a single enemy or many. The fight is carried on for years without remission, with successes and failures alike indecisive: sometimes the hero of the struggle prevails, sometimes it is the enemy who gains the advantage. The enemy appears under various names and descriptions, for example oppressor, the vile one, Amalek, the accuser, spider [or 'lizard': *semamit*]; his partners or assistants are evildoers, greedy dogs, raging waters, and a variety of terrifying creatures. The descriptions of the conflict often convey impressions of strenuous efforts by an enslaved and tormented prisoner struggling in a dark pit, in an asphyxiating dungeon, in fetters and bearing a heavy yoke, striving to free himself and emerge from darkness into light.

In the entries I quoted in Section A above we have already encountered some of the descriptions of the struggle, especially in the passages relating to the *mashpia*. In those entries, and even more so in those I quote below, it can

[85] See *Seder eliyahu raba veseder eliyahu zuta: hamuva'im beshem tana devei eliyahu*, ed. M. Ish-Shalom (Vienna, 1902), introd., 19–20.

[86] See e.g. *Midrash tehilim*, ed. S. Buber (Vilna, 1891), Ps. 3: 7; Maimonides, *Mishneh torah*, 'Hilkhot melakhim' ['*Halakhot* Relating to Kings'], 12: 2.

[87] According to the opinions commonly expressed in kabbalistic doctrine, the direct source of prophecy is in the sefirot Netsah and Hod, and its supreme source is in the sefirah Binah.

be clearly seen that the enemy is not a being of flesh and blood and that his assistants do not have a real existence in the world of nature, but are demonic forces, monsters of Sheol lodged in the author's soul and seeking to subject it to their control. In a few entries the enemy is mentioned by his proper name, 'the husk' or the Sitra Ahra, and sometimes we hear anguished cries by the diarist to the angels to deliver him from his distress:[88]

I 9ʳ: Year 5482 [1722], the Lord, blessed be He, has had compassion on me and has brought me forth from curse to blessing and from darkness to great light.[89]

I 372ʳ: This day on the fast of the fourth month [17 Tamuz 5484/1724], the insolent dogs[90] smote me, they wounded me[91] and stoned me.[92] Blessed be the Lord who has not made me a prey for their teeth.[93]

I 478ᵛ: At this time, in the month of Menahem [Av 5485/1725], the fetters on my neck were slackened[94] and the burning in my loins was relieved.[95]

I 516ᵛ: This day, 7 Adar [5486/1726], the Lord [added above the line: 'my God'] presented me with the key to my redemption.[96]

I 530ᵛ: At this time, in the month of Ziv [Iyar 5486], Amalek and all his forces set out to do battle with me.

I 542ᵛ: This day, the New Moon of Menahem [Av 5486], after I had endured so many troubles and evils without number, the Lord my

88 Some of the entries quoted here speak of states of distress without mentioning an enemy, but even in those it is clear that the distress is caused by the demonic enemy within.

89 This is the very first of the entries, and it marks the beginning of Valle's emergence from the abyss of the husks, in which he had been sunk since 5475 [1715]. Thenceforward he fought with varying success to achieve his complete freedom. See Essay 6, pp. 310–14, 324–6.

90 Isa. 56: 11: 'the greedy dogs [who] do not know what it is to be satisfied'. In the literature of kabbalah the husks are frequently described as dogs. See the interpretations of this verse in the Zohar, II 121*b*; III 63*a*, 80*a*, 259*b*; Luria's phrase 'those insolent dogs' in the *piyut Benei heikhla*.

91 S. of S. 5: 7: 'The watchmen going round the city found me, they beat me, they wounded me.'

92 Lam. 3: 53: '[My enemies] have cut off my life in the pit and cast a stone [or stones] upon me.'

93 Ps. 124: 6, with substitution of 'me' for 'us'. The previous verse reads: 'Then the raging waters would have gone over us.' This entry is an excellent example of the combination of parts of verses from different books of the Bible, with slight changes, to form a single sentence expressing the spiritual experiences of the writer.

94 Based on Isa. 52: 2 [as written (*ketiv*) but not as read—Trans.]: 'The fetters on your neck have been loosened, O captive daughter of Zion.'

95 Based on Ps. 38: 8: 'My loins are full of burning and there is no soundness in my flesh.'

96 This is followed by a passage of prayer bringing in the words of Ps. 142: 8: 'Free my soul from prison.'

God roused [above the line: 'my spirit'] as a man is roused from his sleep,[97] and gave my hand strength to overcome my enemies.

II 909^{r}: At this time, the end of the month [Nisan 5491/1731], the spider [or 'lizard'] has been killed and will no longer be taken in [the] king's palaces.[98]

III 304^{v}: This day, in the year 5493 [1732], being the morrow of the fast of the tenth day [the Day of Atonement], adjuration of the Prince of the Countenance [Metatron] to spread his wings over one who has suffered many troubles and desires to rest and ascend.

III 434^{v}: At this time, on the night of watching [Passover 5493/1733], the power of the husk has been broken, and sweet is the light, and it is pleasant for the eyes to see the sun.[99]

III 750^{v}: At this time, the end of the month of Heshvan [5495/1734], Behold, my covenant was with him,[100] the prosecutor has become counsel for the defence.[101]

III 781^{v}: This day, 8 Adar [5495], the time has come for [my] release from prison.

III 849^{r}: This day, on the festival of Shemini Atseret [the eighth day of Tabernacles: 5496/1735], going up and calling aloud[102] to Michael and Metatron.

[97] As in Zech. 4: 1: 'And the angel who spoke with me returned and roused me as a man is roused from his sleep.'

[98] Reversing the sense of Prov. 30: 28, which reads: '. . . the *semamit* ['spider' or 'lizard'] which you may take in the hand, yet she is in kings' [the Hebrew has singular 'king's'] palaces'. In the midrashim this is interpreted as the destruction of the Temple by the kingdom of Edom = the *semamit* = Esau. See *Bereshit rabah*, ed. Theodor–Albeck, 66: 7, and the remarks ibid. In this note by Valle of the vision he experienced the *semamit* is apparently Lilith, by whose death the hold of the forces of uncleanness on the world of the sefirot was brought to an end. It may be that by 'king', which in the symbolism of kabbalah is the sefirah Tiferet, the divine male principle, the diarist also meant the King-Messiah; in other words 'the king's palaces' are the recesses of the soul of Valle, 'the righteous winnower', who was saved from Lilith's claws.

[99] Eccles. 11: 7.

[100] The nearest to a word-for-word equivalent in Scripture is Mal. 2: 5. From the context here it appears that the reference is to a renewal of the ancient covenant made with Noah (Gen. 9) and Abraham (Gen. 17), by virtue of which the charges against Valle, and perhaps against the whole of Israel, were silenced.

[101] This expression owes its origin to the rabbinic saying (*Ber.* 59*a* and elsewhere): 'A prosecutor cannot become counsel for the defence', which it converts from a negative to a positive. On the role of the Sitra Ahra as prosecutor and how to appease it, see Tishby, *Wisdom of the Zohar*, ii. 452–4, 509–11.

[102] Undoubtedly a call for help.

IV 119^{v}: This day, on the fast of the fifth month [9 Av 5497/1737], Mercy has been aroused and is extended more and more, to free the captive from prison.[103]

IV 494^{v}: At this time, between New Year and the tenth day [the Ten Days of Penitence ending in the Day of Atonement] in the year 5502 [1741], the vow of *s"y* [or *sy'*][104] which subdues the Sitra Ahra and gladdens the soul.

The entries relating to the conflict were written during the years from 5482 to 5502 [1722–41]. However, a distinction must be drawn between the years before 5488 and those which followed. Until 5488 nearly all the entries were concerned with the conflict, which is described as a personal battle for the salvation of the combatant's soul. From 5488 onward, however, references to conflict grow progressively fewer, and even those entries can be seen to relate principally to a messianic war for the Redemption of Israel and the *tikun* of the world, of the Shekhinah, and of the divine order.

This brings us to the question of messianism, which is the main motif in the entries from 5488 onward. Some of these clearly present the writer as the redeemer of Israel, either by explicit mention of the Messiah or by pointing to messianic qualities and actions. Here are some examples of personal entries of this kind:

I 794^{v}: At this time, on the days of Purim [5488], on my head is the living [and] only one [*ḥayah yeḥidah*].[105]

II 324^{v}: This day, the 14th day [Heshvan 5490/autumn 1729], Arise, go through the length and breadth of the land,[106] you [are] Messiah.

[103] Isa. 42: 7. Cf. n. 96 above.

[104] If this reading is correct it is to be supposed that the reference is to R. Jacob Hayim Castel-Franco, who was referred to as *sy'* (*si'*: Signor) in H. J. D. Azulai's record of a statement by R. Jacob Hazak. See Benayahu, 'Ha"magid" shel ramḥa"l', 315; and above, text referring to n. 13.

[105] See n. 11 above. In Luria's kabbalistic writings it is stated that 'the soul's soul', which is higher than the *nara"n* of Emanation [*nara"n*: the three parts of the soul, *nefesh*, *ruaḥ*, *neshamah*—Trans.], was not given even to Moses, and that only the Messiah will be privileged to receive it. See [Vital's] *Sefer hagilgulim* (Przemyśl, 1875), ch. xix, 20*b*–21*b*, and *Sha'ar hagilgulim*, ii (Przemyśl, 1875), ch. xii, 30*b*–*c*, ch. xiii, 31*b*–*c*. It appears to me that according to these sources the Messiah's great superiority over Moses in the matter of 'the soul's soul' will extend also to [exclusive] possession of the powers of the *ḥayah* and the *yeḥidah*, but according to one interpretation by R. Hayim Vital in *Sefer hagilgulim* the *ḥayah* was also given to Enoch. Luzzatto developed *in extenso* a view of his own on the *yeḥidah* as the soul of the Messiah or the Messiahs. See Essay 4, pp. 229–42 and the notes to that essay; see also Essay 3, pp. 205–6. At any rate, according to the statement here that *ḥayah yeḥidah* rested on Valle's head, these two powers were acquired uniquely by the Messiah ben David. And see G. Scholem, *Shabetai tsevi vehatenuah hashabeta'it bimei ḥayav* (Tel Aviv, 1957), i. 33, 42, 45.

[106] Gen. 13: 17.

[Last letter of each word from 'Arise' onward separated by double apostrophe.]

II 355^{v}: At this time, 20 Kislev [5490/Nov. 1729], in this year the king will obtain favour from the Lord.[107]

II 740^{v}: This day, 15 Kislev [5491/Nov. 1730)], the new mitre,[108] kings shall see and rise, princes [shall see] and bow down.[109]

III 645^{r}: At this time, in these days of Purim [5494/spring 1734], Return, my son, return, the gates of Jerusalem have been opened for you.

A few entries mention the Messiah in the third person, but even these clearly refer to Valle himself.[110] Here are three examples:

III 171^{v}: This day, 22 Tevet [5492/Jan. 1732], For the Messiah has come [or 'is coming'] and proclaims freedom.

[107] Based on Prov. 12: 2: 'A good man will obtain favour from the Lord.' It is perfectly clear that 'the king' substituted for 'the good man' is Valle himself.

[108] In Scripture the only adjective found with 'mitre' is 'pure': 'They placed the pure mitre on his head' (Zech. 3: 5). In Nathan of Gaza's letter of 1668 to R. Joseph Hamits—the first document to offer a justification of Shabetai Tsevi's apostasy, arguing that he was 'good within but his clothes were bad'—the Shabatean prophet paraphrased this verse: 'Although he placed the pure mitre on his head, it was not on that account that his holiness was profaned' (R. Jacob Sasportas, *Tsitsat novel tsevi* ['The Fading Flower of Tsevi (= his beauty; a play on Isa. 28: 4)'], ed. I. Tishby (Jerusalem, 1954), 206). And see ibid. 259–62; I. Tishby, 'Te'udot al natan ha'azati bekhitvei r' yosef ḥamits', *Sefunot*, 1 (1957), 80–117 (included in my *Netivei emunah uminut* (Ramat Gan, 1964), 52–80); Scholem, *Shabetai tsevi*, ii. 628–31, 728–36, 744–5, etc. Apparently we are to understand from 'the new mitre' that in Valle's messiahship the blemish of Shabetai Tsevi's bad clothing, the Ishmaelean mitre, was rectified. It is true that in the writings of Valle which I have examined I have not found any reference to the person of Shabetai Tsevi or to the Shabatean movement on the historical or factual plane, whereas Luzzatto referred to them frequently, directly and indirectly, either to approve or to criticize. But Valle's ideas and visions are full of the spirit of Shabatean messianism in manifold forms, and his own self-image displays distinguishing features clearly modelled on the Shabatean Messiah. It is therefore not surprising that hints of the rectification [*tikun*] of Shabetai Tsevi's apostasy found their way into Valle's messianic spiritual experiences and thence into his writing. On traces of historical Shabateanism in Luzzatto's writings, see Essay 4 above; Essay 6, n. 37 and the addendum to that note. I dealt there, *inter alia*, with a homily by Luzzatto or members of his school, alluding to the *tikun* of the mitre of Shabetai Tsevi, whom Luzzatto regarded as the Messiah ben Joseph, and I undertook to consider the matter exhaustively in my essay 'Shabetai Tsevi and the Shabatean Movement in Luzzatto's Doctrine of the Redemption' [apparently now Essay 5 above—Trans.]. I have alluded, *passim*, to parallels with Shabatean messianism in Valle's writings, and this is another matter which I wish to expand upon in a separate essay. And see nn. 116, 134, 150, 165 below.

[109] Isa. 49: 7. By quoting this verse Valle gives himself the status of king of kings, as befits the Messiah ben David.

[110] See above, text referring to n. 46, and the note itself.

III 747^{r}: This day, the third of the month [Heshvan 5495/autumn 1734], . . . May You [or 'You will'] soon make the offshoot of David spring up,[111] Yinon[112] and Elijah do I send.

IV 191^{v}: This day, the eve of the New Moon of Menahem [Av 5498/summer 1738], the [appointed] time of Redemption, and the redeemer has come [or 'is coming'].

Several entries describe the fulfilment of messianic missions, such as the incoming of the ten tribes, perfect liberty, abolition of Christianity:

IV 200^{v}: At this time, the night of 15 Elul [5498/late summer 1738], the ten tribes have come.[113]

III 271^{r}: This day, 26 Menahem [Av 5492/summer 1732], Hallel [psalms of praise] and jubilee and release from everything.[114]

II 749^{r}: On 24 Kislev, at the close of the holy Sabbath [5491/Nov. 1730], He will bring them to His holy border,[115] the Stone of Strayers has been washed away.[116]

[111] The beginning of one of the blessings in the Shemoneh Esreh prayer ['The eighteen benedictions'].

[112] A name of the Messiah in the Talmud and midrashim, based on Ps. 72: 17: *yinon shemo* ['May his name endure', but can be read as 'His name is *yinon*'—Trans.].

[113] In H. J. D. Azulai's diary R. Jacob Hazak is recorded as saying that Elijah told Luzzatto of his visit to the ten tribes and gave him information about them. See Benayahu, 'Ha"magid" shel ramḥa"l', 317, 335. In 5498 [1738], when Luzzatto was living in Amsterdam and Valle was acting as leader of the group in Padua, he [Valle—Trans.] had a vision of the arrival of the tribes in his area of activity, doubtless to assist in the fulfilment of his messianic mission.

[114] 'Release from everything', linked here with the jubilee year, refers to liberation from enslavement to foreign kingdoms and the rule of the husks.

[115] Ps. 78: 54, where the verb is properly understood as past tense and refers to the conquest of the land after the exodus from Egypt.

[116] This is certainly a reference to Christianity. Valle's writings contain many harsh strictures on Christianity, and on Jesus in particular. But on the plane of personal messianism, where it might have been least expected, we find positive assessments of Jesus, or at any rate an ambivalent attitude which has parallels in the Shabatean ideology of Nathan of Gaza. This is a matter with extensive ramifications, and I will confine myself here to two paragraphs assessing Jesus' beginnings and his ultimate destiny in the days of the Messiah.

'We have said in another place [not found by me—I.T.] that *the mamzer* [child of a forbidden marriage] *was fit to be the Messiah ben Joseph*, for a learned *mamzer* takes precedence over an ignorant high priest [as stated in Mishnah *Hor.* 3: 8], but he did himself injury by his impudence . . . and he therefore became a *mum zar* [a strange or foreign blemish] *and fell from the* [sefirah] *Yesod of holiness to the Yesod of the husk*, who is the veritable villain' (II 881^{r}). This pronouncement contains an extremely favourable assessment of Jesus at his original level as compared with Nathan of Gaza's teaching in *Derush hataninim* that Jesus was Shabetai Tsevi's husk and that the Messiah's task was to bring about his *tikun*. See G. Scholem, *Be'ikevot mashiaḥ* (Jerusalem, 1944), 43. On the *tikun* of Jesus, see below, in the second quotation from Valle. Luzzatto, too, noted a connection between the Messiah ben Joseph and Jesus, but only in a negative sense. In

VII 93[v]: On 25 Heshvan, year 5513 [autumn 1752], the Messiah said to the Pope: Abase yourself so that the feet of holiness may tread upon your head.[117]

his opinion the Messiah ben Joseph was to have been profaned by clothing his soul in Jesus, but was saved by the sufferings of Moses from this dreadful profanation. See Essay 4, pp. 242–3. '"Until Shiloh comes, and unto him there shall be an assembly of nations" [Gen. 49: 10 (one of several suggested translations of this verse, taking Shiloh as the Messiah—Trans.)], meaning that the evil of the nations will come to him, which is to say, the husk of each nation, the purpose being to restore it to perfection . . . and by the hand of the redeemer all the nations have been perfected, and His mercy and goodness, blessed be He, will be seen and revealed for all, jointly and severally, and all the ends of the earth will acknowledge to Him [that] everything was for their good, *even Haman who was hanged and Jesus who was crucified*, for [the Lord] is good to all, and His mercy is over all his creatures [Ps. 145: 9], and He ruined in order to make good . . . even those who were sentenced by a court of law [Haman and Jesus] met their end so that their bodies might be handed over to the Sitra Ahra and their souls be saved, and *in the world of recompense they will drink the* [cup] *of consolation instead of the cup of staggering which they drank at the time of their death* . . . [at] the end of all flesh [the Sitra Ahra] has taken what belongs to it in the smitten body, and the [mouth] of the accuser is stopped, and the holiness of the oppressed is hidden in a place where the hand has no control over it, and they have eaten their due portion and their share in the final perfection of the world with eternal joy, when they will awaken from their sleep' (II 44[v]–45[r]). [Variation of tenses as in the Hebrew.—Trans.] At the start of the Shabatean movement, in a letter to Raphael Joseph written at the end of 5425 or the beginning of 5426 [late summer–early autumn 1665], Nathan had already ascribed to Shabetai Tsevi the mission of bringing about Jesus' *tikun*, and he held to this ascription in *Derush hataninim*, as I have pointed out in the present note. But I doubt if there is a statement anywhere in Nathan's writings that the purpose of putting Jesus to death was to save his soul and keep him holy until the resurrection of the dead. However, so far as concerns the ultimate destiny of Jesus, an opinion even more favourable than that of Valle was expressed in *Sefer hameshiv*, a pre-Shabatean source dating from the generation of the Spanish expulsion, which implied that the Christian Messiah would be transformed into the Messiah ben Joseph. See M. Idel, 'Hayaḥas lanatsrut besefer hameshiv', *Zion*, 46 (1981), 84–8. That early work may perhaps be the source of Luzzatto's opinion, mentioned above, on the profanation for which the Messiah ben Joseph had been destined but was saved. On the other hand, Valle's own writings contain remarks the very reverse of what is said in the paragraph I have quoted here. For example, as against the idea that the Messiah's mission is to bring about the *tikun* of the nations, Valle speaks elsewhere of the destruction of the nations in time to come. Here again his indecision has important parallels in Shabateanism. See Scholem, *Shabetai tsevi*, ii. 714–19, 736–7. And see n. 108 above, and nn. 134, 150, 165 below.

[117] I am indebted to Professor Reuben Bonfil for drawing my attention to the information in A. Milano, *Storia degli Ebrei in Italia* (Turin, 1963), 601, which shows what prompted the vision of the Pope's humiliation by the Messiah. Milano relates that in 1668 Pope Clement IX required the Jews of Rome to pay a tax towards the carnival festivities in place of their previous liability to take part in the carnival games, and the payment was accompanied by a humiliating ceremony: the rabbi of the congregation and the heads of the Roman ghetto were obliged on that occasion to make humble speeches to the dean of the Conservatori or the senator, who, according to a widespread but unconfirmed tradition, placed his foot on the rabbi's neck to mark the servile status of the Jews. On the basis of this tradition it is to be assumed that the trampling underfoot of the Pope by the Messiah was intended to represent his humiliation in equal measure.

I have no doubt that even in this late entry, written about seven years after the death of Luzzatto, by which time the group under Valle was much enfeebled, Valle saw himself as the Messiah in the vision in which he required the Pope to submit to him, the purpose being to impose his authority on the head of the Christian Church in preparation for the forthcoming Redemption. In other words, as late as that year he was still inspired by faith in his messianic destiny. That faith may have taken fire anew as a result of his meeting with R. Jekutiel of Vilna in 1752, which moved him to plan to emigrate to the Land of Israel with his colleague in order to hasten the Redemption.[118]

In another group of entries the Redemption is alluded to in mystical messianic images such as the completion of the raising of the sparks, *tikunim*, the strengthening and unification of the forces of the Godhead:

I 705^{v}: This day, in the year 5488 [1727], the New Moon of Marheshvan, the completion of the winnowing, and his return to Ramah, for his home is there.[119]

III 82^{v}: The Lord your God will circumcise your heart and the heart of your offspring [the Hebrew is marked with dots over letters which spell Elul, indicated here by bold type, thus: *umal . . . et levavekha ve'et levav zarekha*],[120] the initial letters of Elul. This day, 25 Elul [5491/1731], the *tikun* of the circumcision. [In the 'Complete List' below, '*tikun* and the circumcision'.—Trans.][121]

III 232^{r}: In the month of Ziv [Iyar 5492/late spring 1732] on the 10th of the month the power of the *yiḥud* began to prevail. [On *yiḥudim*, see Essay 1, pp. 50–60.—Trans.]

[118] See above, text referring to nn. 19–20.

[119] 1 Sam. 7: 17. And see Essay 6, p. 326 and n. 92; and n. 73 above.

[120] Deut. 30: 6.

[121] This *tikun* signifies the ending of Lilith's hold on the sefirot and the soul of the winnower, as stated in the passage I reproduce here from the commentary on the Psalms. The extract I quote was written at the beginning of 5491 [early autumn 1730], to judge from the dates of entries which adjoin it: 'Moreover: "The earth saw and trembled" [Ps. 97: 4], the underlying meaning of this is the unclean earth, which is the wicked maidservant [Lilith], who flees from her mistress [the Shekhinah] when she sees the *tikun* of holy ranks . . . and therefore to [*sic*] the winnower also . . . the maidservant was bound to him at first in order [for him] to winnow out her inner substance, and he was told: Behold, I have given my maidservant into your bosom [cf. Gen. 16: 5], and the maidservant herself is to be understood as the foreskin which covers the covenant and which will be removed from him at the completion of the *tikun*, whereupon he will again couple with the *gevirah* [the Lady, the Shekhinah] to bring laughter and joy into the world. And *that is an esoteric reference to Abraham's circumcision*, after which Isaac was born to him by his wife Sarah who was in literal fact the *gevirah*; and *our father Abraham was occupied at that time with his* [*own*] *tikun and that of the winnower who would issue from his loins*' (II 700^{r}). 'The *tikun* of the circumcision' is the subject of the 'dream of the circumcision in joy' quoted above, text referring to n. 41.

IV 212ʳ: This day, 26 Marheshvan [5499/1738], Behold, a day is coming for the Lord,[122] to restore to Yesod what he had given out for the sake of Malkhut.[123]

In many of Valle's diary entries his messianic activity is described in terms of processes linked to *devekut* and *tikun*, and *devekut* is presented as a relationship of distinctly erotic love between the winnower and the Shekhinah. These elements are also central to Luzzatto's doctrine of the Redemption, as is made clear in my extensive treatment of the matter in Essay 3 above.[124] In that essay I quoted four of Valle's diary entries written in Av and Elul 5491 [late summer 1731], which I explained as allusions to 'the processes of his erotic communion with the Shekhinah around the day of Luzzatto's marriage'.[125] Because of their great importance in the present context I reproduce them again here at the head of the following examples, in chronological order:

III 52ᵛ: On the 20th [previously given as '25th(?)'—Trans.] of that month [Av 5491] the matter of the kisses and the blessing Sheheheyanu ['Who has kept us alive'].

III 58ᵛ: This day, 28 Menahem [Av 5491/1731], communion [*devekut*] in love, destruction of the unclean spirit and delight in [divine] favour.

III 65ʳ: This day, 5 Elul [5491], the news of the *kinyan* ['acquisition'; the formal transfer of money or an article such as a ring] with a full purse, *erusin* ['betrothal'], and the time for the *nisu'in* [the stage which completes the marriage].

III 69ʳ: This day, the 11th of the month [Elul 5491], the union in love and the promise concerning the revelation soon to come, amen, may it be His will.

III 73ᵛ: This day, the 15th of the month [Elul 5491], the sending of the light of rest to dwell [on me], On the day he earns it you shall pay him his wage etc.[126]

122 Zech. 14: 1.

123 The restoration of the flow which the divine male had sent down to the husks when the Shekhinah was living in exile among them. See Tishby, *Wisdom of the Zohar*, i. 384; I. Tishby, *Torat hara vehakelipah bekabalat ha'ar"i* (Jerusalem and Tel Aviv, 1942), 75, 85–9, 119–20.

124 And see also Essay 1, pp. 4–7 and n. 128; and Essay 10.

125 See Essay 3, p. 206.

126 Deut. 24: 15. The proximity of this entry to the preceding ones, which speak plainly of *devekut* in union with the Shekhinah, leaves no doubt that 'the light of rest' is another reference to delight in the love of the Shekhinah. The biblical verse is quoted as a way of saying that on the very day that he has performed acts of *tikun*, Valle is rewarded with a mystical erotic experience. And see below, text referring to n. 138.

III 218v: At this time, in the days of Nisan [5492], the divine flow drawn down and existence for ever, the gateway to love, I have set you over my household.[127]

III 535v: This day, the 20th of the month [Elul 5493], under the propitious sign of twelve choice fruits,[128] I gave my daughter to this man.[129]

III 866v: On 6 Adar [5496] at the close of the holy Sabbath, love from now and for evermore.

Most of the messianic entries were written in the years 5488–92 [1728–32] in which messianic fervour reached its peak in Luzzatto's circle in general and Valle's writings in particular. In the treatises themselves erotic communion [*devekut*] joins with eschatological *tikun* to form a major element in Valle's mystical thought which could be, and deserves to be, the subject of an exhaustive study, both on its own account and to assist in determining the relationship between hasidism and his writings. This in my opinion could also help to resolve the controversial issue of the position of messianism in

[127] Based on 1 Chr. 17: 14, using the same Hebrew verb: 'I will establish him [Solomon] in my house and my kingdom for ever.' In Valle's note 'my house' means the Shekhinah.

[128] As I understand it, the 'twelve choice fruits' have their origin in the kabbalists' custom of putting twelve loaves on the table for Sabbath meals in accordance with teachings in the literature of the Zohar, the ideas of which, and their practical application, were extensively developed in Lurianic 'conduct' writings. The oldest Zoharic source is *Zohar ḥadash*, ed. R. Margaliot (Jerusalem, 1953), *parashah* 'Aḥarei', section *Sitrei torah* ['Secrets of the Torah'], 47*c–d*. *Sitrei torah* is one of the parts of the main body of the Zohar attributable to Moses de León; its teachings were then included in the offshoots of the Zohar: *Raya meheimna* (Zohar III, 245*a*) and *Tikunei hazohar*, ed. R. Margaliot (Tel Aviv, 1948), *tikun* 47, 84*a–b*. And see Margaliot's comments in *Nitsotsei zohar* [a commentary by H. J. D. Azulai printed in the margin of editions of the Zohar—Trans.]. In Lurianic literature the principal sources for the mystical explanation of this custom are [Vital's] *Sha'ar hakavanot* (Jerusalem, 1902), 72*a–b*, and *Peri ets ḥayim* (Korets, 1782 etc.), *sha'ar hashabat*, ch. 17. Both in the literature of the Zohar and in Lurianic literature there are descriptions of twelve loaves as ornaments or gifts for the Shekhinah in preparation for her union with her divine husband. In this connection particular attention should be drawn to a stanza in a *piyut* by Luria for the Sabbath evening meal, which is the Shekhinah's meal (*ḥakal tapuḥin kadishin* ['a field of holy apples']): 'The Shekhinah will be adorned / with six loaves to a side / With *vavs* she will be bound / and with *zayins* of assemblies' [*vav* and *zayin*: the sixth and seventh letters of the alphabet—Trans.]. And see M. Benayahu, *Sefer toledot ha'ar"i* (Jerusalem, 1967), 330, 340–1, 342–3, 350; Y. Liebes, 'Zemirot lise'udot-shabat sheyised ha'ar"i hakadosh', *Molad*, NS 4 (27) (1972), 547, 550. Valle used the expression 'choice fruits' to emphasize the erotic element, borrowing the phrase from S. of S. 4: 13, 16; 7: 14, and applying it to the pleasure of the Shekhinah in her loving relationship with him. The entry was written on a weekday, to mark his spiritual experience of union with the Shekhinah on that day.

[129] Deut. 22: 16. This is an example of the use of a scriptural verse in a context which is poles apart from that of the original. The verse is taken from the passage relating to a false accusation against a hated wife but is here applied to the beloved Shekhinah.

hasidism.[130] Here I quote two paragraphs to illustrate this important question, one on the erotic nature of *devekut* and one on the links between *devekut* and messianism:

Come and see *how great is the power of love*, which ruins the ranks [possibly 'wall'—*shurah* for *shur*—Trans.] and destroys the walls of the *ḥitsonim* [the 'external' forces of evil] and *constantly presses forward until it reaches perfect devekut*, which is the veritable cleaving of spirit to spirit; the proof is 'He will kiss me with the kisses of his mouth',[131] and the secret of that is 'Mouth to mouth I speak with him'.[132] And although the righteous man is never forsaken in the midst of trouble, for there are channelled down to him the supernal flows from the left side, which is the esoteric meaning of 'wine that gladdens',[133] to revive his soul and restore his spirit, nevertheless he is disquieted and has no rest, that is certain, and all this is worth nothing to him, for many are his sighs and his heart is faint whenever he sees his dove, his beloved, far from him, for it is union with her that gladdens his soul with perfect happiness more than does wine . . . and therefore he constantly knocks and presses until he reaches his spouse and overcomes all that would prevent him, and *comes into the chamber to his wife to lie with her, beside her, and be with her on the bed of love*, for your love is better than wine.[134] (Valle, *Shivim panim*,[135] *tikun* 11, p. 8)

At the end of *tikun* 11 there is an explicit statement that the above refers to 'the righteous winnower', i.e. to Valle himself. It reads as follows: 'Everything is in the power of Moses; that is the hidden meaning of "in all the strong hand and in all the great and terrible deeds which Moses did",[136] for it

[130] See I. Tishby, 'Harayon hameshiḥi vehamegamot hameshiḥiyot bitsemiḥat haḥasidut', *Zion*, 32 (1967), 1–45; G. Scholem, 'The Neutralization of the Messianic Element in Early Hasidism', *Journal of Jewish Studies*, 20 (1969), 25–55; G. Scholem, *The Messianic Idea in Judaism, and Other Essays on Jewish Spirituality* (New York, 1971), 176–202.

[131] S. of S. 1: 2 [with the verb taken as future tense—Trans.].

[132] Num. 12: 8, translated literally.

[133] Based on Ps. 104: 15: 'And wine that gladdens the heart of man'. Wine is a symbol for the sefirah Gevurah, which is 'the left side'. Valle delivered a homily for the *tikun* called 'the mystery of the wine that gladdens' to the Paduan group at their formal meal on the night of 17 Shevat, but this referred to the sanctification of corporeality by the actual drinking of wine. See Essay 2, p. 119; and Essay 10, pp. 519, 525.

[134] S. of S. 1: 2. Cf. text referring to n. 165 below. The description of 'the winnower–the Messiah–Valle' as husband of the Shekhinah, with sexual symbols so frank as to present their mutual relations as relations of sensual physical love, must be seen as revealing traces of Shabatean messianism. It is true that in the literature of kabbalah in general, and especially its mythical currents, notably in the Zohar and Lurianic literature, one of the outstanding features new to Judaism is the breaking of the bounds of modesty by kabbalistic erotic symbolism in relation to the various aspects of the Godhead, which extends even to marital intercourse between the righteous and the Shekhinah; but Shabatean literature went much further than had been common in previous kabbalistic writing. At any rate, here again I know of no precedent for Valle's self-image other than the messianic figure of Shabetai Tsevi. And see nn. 108, 116 above; nn. 150, 165 below.

[135] Printed in *Megilat setarim verazin genizin* (Warsaw, 1889).

[136] Deut. 34: 12.

is Moses alone who has the great power *to raise up the righteous winnower in*[*to*] *his house of rest* and destroy the enemies who face him.'[137]

All this good that is finally mine[138] was brought about for me by the great *devekut* with which I cleaved to Your name, the mystery of the Shekhinah and the house of the Lord, and now I dwell there on a throne of glory . . . *in reward for the great devekut* . . . and as for what Scripture goes on to say, 'Happy is the man whose strength is in You' etc.,[139] *this relates to the winnower himself*, who winnowed out the strength which was in the hands of Esau and which was given to him, and *happy is that man who clung to Him, blessed be He, as a girdle clings to a man's waist*[140] . . . Great and important is the eminence of this man, for *all the winnowed sparks* in whose heart are the highways of holiness . . . to return to their place and their root in Ramah ['on high'] in the inwardness of holiness, *all of them shall be equal and in agreement, their hearts united as one heart, which they shall make a fountain for this man who for their sake has taken on the burdensome business of winnowing* . . . *for this man will be be their head and become like a fountain which is the supernal source* shedding its flow upon them, and all of them will receive the flow from him and be under his oversight . . . and just as he was clothed in all the curses when he was in the husk, so he will wrap himself in a garment of all the blessings in great abundance when he has cleared a way for the redeemed to pass through[141] . . . (III $65^{r\text{–}v}$)

We have here a close connection between personal *devekut*, the raising of sparks, and the elevation of the winnower-Messiah to the level of divinity in the process of redemption.

I conclude this survey of the subjects of the diary entries with some examples to illustrate the use of scriptural verses verbatim without alterations or additions. This is a large category, about equal in bulk to the entries recording spiritual experiences and visions in Valle's characteristic style. It spans a considerable period, from 5483 to 5531 [1723–71], almost fifty years. The entries I quote are arranged here by subject in the order in which I have dealt with those subjects in this section.

1. Conflict, and deliverance from enemies

I 784^{v}: For You have been my help (New Moon of Adar) [5488/1728] and in the shadow of Your wings I rejoice.[142]

II 322^{v}: This day, the 10th of the month [Heshvan 5490/autumn 1729], O Lord, You have raised my soul up from Sheol.[143]

137 These remarks about Moses probably also refer to Luzzatto, the eschatological incarnation of Moses who headed the messianic group. See above, text referring to n. 10, and the note itself.

138 This is a reference to *tikunim* in the world of the sefirot and the elevation of the man by whom they were performed, earlier described in the commentary on Psalm 84, the psalm from which an extract is quoted here. The speaker in the first person is David, but it is expressly stated that King David and the winnower, Valle, are one and the same.

139 Ps. 84: 6.

140 Jer. 13: 11.

141 As in Isa. 51: 10.

142 Ps. 63: 8.

143 Ps. 30: 4.

II 834^{v}: [Adar 5491/early 1731], For He has rescued me from every trouble, and my eye has seen [the downfall of] my enemies.[144]

2. Personal messianism and the Redemption of Israel

I 101^{r}: [5483/1723] You shall be over my household, and according to your word shall all my people be ruled.[145]

II 57^{v}: At this time in the month of Shevat [5489/early 1729], You are a priest for ever, after the manner of Melchizedek.[146]

II 158^{r}: On the night of keeping the festival [Passover 5489/1729], blessed be the reviver of the dead,[147] for Your dew is as the dew of light, and the earth shall bring the dead to birth,[148] and the children of Zion shall rejoice in their king.[149]

II 321^{v}: This day, the 9th of the month [Heshvan 5490/autumn 1729], His clothes were white as snow with the clouds of Heaven.[150]

[144] Ps. 54: 9. [145] Gen. 41: 40. [146] Ps. 110: 4.

[147] The conclusion of the second blessing in the Shemoneh Esreh prayer, omitting the direct address to God. Its intention here is to convey the news that the resurrection is about to take place. See above, text referring to n. 25.

[148] Isa. 26: 19. The verse begins: 'Your dead shall live, my corpses shall arise; awake and sing, you dwellers in the dust'. [149] Ps. 149: 2, adding 'and' at the beginning.

[150] A combination of two fragments from verses in Daniel. I will quote the two verses in full and explain why the diary entry combines them: 'I looked, until thrones were placed, and *the Ancient of Days sat; his clothes were white as snow* and the hair of his head was like clean wool; his throne was flames of fire, its wheels were burning fire' (Dan. 7: 10); 'I saw in visions of the night, and *behold, with the clouds of Heaven there came one like a son of man, and he reached the Ancient of Days* and was presented to him' (Dan. 7: 13). The two fragments have different subjects in Daniel, and their fusion into a single sentence is intended to indicate that there is an essential link between the Messiah and the Ancient of Days. The existence and significance of this link are made clear in the treatises themselves; it can be seen to present a remarkably close parallel to the Shabatean belief in the deification of the Messiah. In Essay 6 (see pp. 324–33), I drew attention in several places to Valle's identification with the sefirot Yesod and Tiferet in regard to his root in them, his operation as their representative, his calling himself by their names, and his ascent to take his place with them. In that essay I avoided saying explicitly that in many of Valle's expositions he equates himself so closely with divine forces as to deify himself, my reason being that I plan to include a clarification of this important issue in a comprehensive study of the relationship between the ideas of the winnower's messianism and those of Shabatean messianism. But the diary entry just quoted, which alludes to the high point of Valle-the-Messiah's deification, obliges me to deal with its subject matter before completing the study in question. In the present context I will confine myself to quoting one outstanding paragraph.

'Now this verse [Isa. 52: 13, on the servant of the Lord] alludes to all the ascents of the winnower . . . he shall be exalted and lifted up, and shall be high [the levels of the Shekhinah and Yesod and Tiferet, the supernal sefirot] *and finally he rises from this level to the supreme rank of the Ancient of Days*, in accordance with what is said [in Dan. 7: 13]: "He reached the Ancient of Days", which is the secret meaning of "he shall be exalted and lifted up, and shall be very high". And in the same way it is written of him [Ps. 8: 6]: "You have made him a little lower than [a] god [*elokim*]", for *he is like elokim among the dwellers in this world by his high eminence*, as it is said

II 717^{v}: On 24 Marheshvan [5491/1730], The Lord will fulfil all your petitions, now I know that the Lord has saved his anointed.[151]

II 781^{v}: This day, 21 Tevet [misspelt] [5491/Dec. 1730] at the close of the holy Sabbath, I have prepared a lamp for my anointed, his enemies I will clothe in shame, but upon him his crown will shine.[152]

III 523^{v}: On 22 Menahem [Av 5493], I will turn the speech of the nations to a pure speech, that they may all call on the name of the Lord.[153]

V 864^{v}: This day, 21 Sivan 5510 [1750], You will arise and have mercy on Zion, for it is time to show favour to her, for the time has come.[154]

3. Cleaving [*devekut*] to the Shekhinah—spiritual experiences, erotic and mystical

I 81^{r}: [5483/1723] The mandrakes give forth their perfume etc., both new and old, [which] I have laid up for you, my beloved.[155]

II 744^{r}: This day, the 19th of the month aforesaid [Kislev 5491/Nov. 1730], This is my beloved and this is my companion, O daughters of Jerusalem.[156]

III 36^{v}: On 2 Menahem [Av 5491/1731], the night of the holy Sabbath, Because you are precious in my eyes, [and] are honoured, and I love you.[157]

[Zech. 12: 8]: "And the house of David [shall be] like *elokim*." And as to *his being slightly lower than elokim, this is because he exists in physical form*, which is not the case with the *elokim* themselves, who are the highest servants whose dwelling is not with flesh [Dan. 2: 11] . . . You have put everything under his feet [Ps. 8: 7], Israel and the nations of the world, and, as we have said, he ascends to the level of the Ancient of Days, *so that the whole structure of the ten sefirot is actually put under his feet*' (II 933^{v}).

Valle tried to moderate and soften the winnower's astounding boast by saying that the *elokim* were 'the highest servants', but the paragraph makes it clear that in this context the 'servants' are the divine sefirot. On the deification of the Messiah in Shabateanism, see Scholem, *Shabetai tsevi*, i. 223–6, 252–6; ii. 698–9, 745–7, 786–7, etc.; and his 'Berekhyah rosh hashabeta'im besaloniki', *Zion*, 6 (1941), 181–91. The deification of the Messiah in Valle's writings is an extreme example of this viewpoint, in his own independent and original formulation. And see nn. 108, 116, 134 above; n. 165 below.

151 Ps. 20: 6–7 [understood as 'The Lord will . . .' rather than 'May the Lord . . .'—Trans.].

152 Ps. 132: 17–18.

153 Zeph. 3: 9. In these diary entries this is the only allusion to the *tikun* of the Gentiles as a messianic mission, but in the treatises themselves it plays an important part in Valle's doctrine of the Redemption. And see n. 116 above.

154 Ps. 102: 14.

155 S. of S. 7: 14. The words omitted are 'and at our doors are all choice fruits'. This is the third entry of all. The second entry (I 62^{v}) is annotated 'In the year 5483 [1723]', and the sixth one (I 127^{r}) is annotated 'in the month of Shevat' of the same year. And see below, text referring to nn. 162–4.

156 S. of S. 5: 16.

157 Isa. 43: 4. The second part of the verse reads: 'I will give men in exchange for you, and peoples in exchange for your life'.

III 161v: This day, the 4th of the month [Tevet 5492/Dec. 1731], And thus the maiden came to the king; all that she asked for was given her.[158]

III 538v: This day, the 16th of the month [Elul 5493/1733], 'I have come to my garden, my sister, my bride', up to 'Eat, friends, drink your fill, beloved ones [or 'drink your fill of love']'.[159]

III 700v: This day, 4 Tamuz [5494/1734], This now is bone of my bones and flesh of my flesh.[160]

IV 442v: On Passover, year 5501 [1741], Let my beloved come to his garden and eat its precious fruits.[161]

*

The entries quoting Scripture which I have reproduced are no more than a handful drawn from a great number of such entries. In the case of many of the verses and accompanying parts of verses used in the entries, their intended meaning is obscure, and it is even hard to know what the allusions in them relate to. Even with those quotations whose primary meaning is plain, like the examples I have given here, their application in detail is often felt to be unclear. However, the obscurities in many of the verses are clarified in the text of the treatises. In some cases the explanations are related to the diary entries by remarks such as 'It was said to the winnower', but in others the interpretations of the verses stand alone with no mention of their having been spoken to Valle.

I will end my consideration of this subject by reproducing an interpretation of 'The mandrakes give forth their perfume', the verse which appears in the first of the entries to quote Scripture and with which I began the preceding examples on *devekut* and erotic experiences in such entries.[162]

The mandrakes give forth their perfume and at our door are all choice fruits, both new and old, which I have laid up for you, my beloved.[163] The word 'mandrakes' [*duda'im*] is derived from *dodim* ['love']; these are the love [*ahavim*] of Yesod, who was seeking love from his spouse the holy Malkhut, as was said above, and took very great pains for her sake and *exposed himself to enormous danger in the depths of the husk in order to winnow*. And it is this love, which had already been tried and tested and found strong as a mirror of cast metal [Job 37: 18], that gave forth a sweet perfume

[158] Esther 2: 13. 'The king' here probably means the King-Messiah, Valle.

[159] S. of S. 5: 1. The words omitted read: 'I have gathered my myrrh with my spice; I have eaten my honeycomb with my honey, I have drunk my wine with my milk.' In Scripture the verse concludes: 'Drink abundantly (drink and grow drunk), beloved ones.' Apparently Valle in adopting the plural form ('friends', 'beloved ones') at the end of the verse is addressing the members of the group, who will share in the mystical experience. See n. 30 above.

[160] Gen. 2: 23. An allusion to the origin of the Shekhinah in the sefirah Yesod, the winnower —Valle—being her incarnation.

[161] S. of S. 4: 16. See n. 36 above. [162] See above, text referring to n. 155. [163] S. of S. 7: 14.

in the midst of holiness to reward him for what he had done, so that he might come into the chamber to his wife and delight with her in all kinds of choice fruits, in return for his service and the suffering and distress of all kinds which he endured. For no longer will sin be found crouching at the door as in former times, because the winnower has overcome it by his toil and the work of his hands, and he will master it[164] and trample on it, and will find instead of it, at that door, that all kinds of choice fruits have flourished; these are the mystical manifestation of the blessings with which *the King-Messiah* will be blessed by all the holy ranks which draw all good down to him, in place of all the evil that was drawn to him by the polluting ranks at the time of his troubles. (II 258^{v})

The winnower-Messiah is presented here in distinctly sexual images as the husband of the Shekhinah, bound to her by a powerful love, in the role of the sefirah Yesod. He is rewarded for his exertions to free her from the domination of the husks by being allowed the delight of sexual union with her; and in subduing the Sitra Ahra he advances the processes of Redemption and universal *tikun*.[165]

This exposition is taken from a commentary on the Song of Songs entitled *Et dodim* ['A Time for Love'], which, to judge from the dates of adjoining entries, was composed in the second half of 5489 and completed before the end of that year [summer or early autumn 1729], i.e. about six years after the first entry relating to the mandrakes was written. It would not make sense to suppose that in 5483, in the first stages of his struggle to overcome his demonic enemies, Valle was already crediting himself with the messianic and divine qualities described in the exposition we are considering, but it is clear that at that time, while he was ascending from the husks, he underwent an

164 As was said by God to Cain, Gen. 4: 7. The words of Scripture are applied to the situation of the winnower-Messiah among the husks, who, before they are subdued, do him injury and threaten to gain complete control over him. And see the next note.

165 Cf. text referring to n. 134 above. The description of the winnower-Messiah's mission in descending to the husks, with its emphasis on his exposure to danger and his suffering—one of many such descriptions in Valle's works—displays clear traces of the Shabatean ideological treatment of Shabetai Tsevi's actions among the husks, especially in its explanation and justification of the Messiah's apostasy. One of the principal sources of our information on such views is an exegetical work by R. Israel Hazan of Kastoria, who was a pupil and confidant of Nathan of Gaza. See G. Scholem, 'Perush mizmorei tehilim meḥugo shel shabetai tsevi be'adrianopol', in *Alei ayin: minḥat devarim lishelomoh zalman shoken aḥarei mele'ot lo shivim shanah* (Jerusalem, 1948–52), 178–94. Hazan visited R. Benjamin Hakohen and R. Abraham Rovigo in Italy and disclosed his Shabatean views to them, and apparently also left some of his own writings with them or sent them on after his return to Turkey. See Scholem, ibid. 181; and his 'Te'udot shabeta'iyot al r' natan ha'azati miginzei r' mahalalel halelyah be'ankona', in *Harry Austryn Wolfson: Jubilee Volume on the Occasion of his Seventy-Fifth Birthday*, iii (Jerusalem, 1965), 240 and n. 29; M. Benayahu, 'Hatenuah hashabeta'it beyavan', *Sefunot*, 14 (1971–8), 241–3. I would suppose that Valle read R. Israel Hazan's writings and drew some important ideas from them. And see above, nn. 108, 116, 134, 150.

erotic and mystical spiritual experience involving the Shekhinah, and gave expression to it in the verse from the Song of Songs.[166]

THE COMPLETE LIST OF DIARY ENTRIES

A wide selection from these entries is quoted in my Introduction, where they are grouped according to the themes identified in my research and are supplemented by comments and explanations. In those cases I shall generally do no more here than give references to the Introduction (indicated by the one word 'above'). As before (n. 6 above) the references are to the eight volumes of Valle's manuscripts in the British Library: thus I = MS 385, II = MS 386, etc.

I 9^{r}:[167] Year 5482 [1722], the Lord, blessed be He, has had compassion on me and has brought me forth from curse to blessing and from darkness to great light.

I 62^{v}:[168] [In the Introduction the reference is given as I 82^{r}—Trans.] From here onward in the year 5483, when the light was dimmed [above the line: 'by the curtain of the separating clouds'], but the *mashpia* remained and went running back and forth.

I 81^{r}:[169] The mandrakes give forth their perfume etc., both new and old, [which] I have laid up for you, my beloved.

I 93^{r}: I will make all my goodness pass before you.[170]

166 I shall be clarifying the nature of the links connecting Valle's written works with his spiritual experiences and the revelations with which he was inspired (both those recorded between the lines and those only referred to in his commentaries) in the continuation of my study of this Paduan Messiah's mystical diary.

167 This is one of fourteen entries (I 9^{r}, 372^{r}, 478^{v}, 516^{v}, 530^{v}, 542^{v}; II 909^{r}; III 304^{v}, 434^{v}, 750^{v}, 781^{v}, 849^{r}; IV 119^{v}, 494^{v}) quoted above, text referring to nn. 88–104; and see those notes. The first entry of the set is also quoted in Essay 6, n. 43.

168 Inserted between the end of one topic and the beginning of the next. This is one of eight entries (I 62^{v}, 305^{r}, 391^{r}, 404^{r}, 446^{v}, 524^{r}, 568^{v}, 625^{v}) quoted above, text referring to nn. 58–70. And see the text referring to nn. 71–3, and the notes themselves. Four of the entries in this set are also quoted in Essay 6, n. 43.

169 This is one of seven entries (I 81^{r}; II 744^{r}; III 36^{v}, 161^{v}, 538^{v}, 700^{v}; IV 442^{v}) quoted above, text referring to nn. 155–61.

170 Exod. 33: 19.

I 101r:[171] You shall be over my household, and according to your word shall all my people be ruled.

I 127r:[172] At this time in the month of Shevat, I was visited in the pit of my sorrows and anointed with the oil of joy which was poured on my head from on high.

I 196v (in the middle of the page): At a time of good omen, In the beginning God created [or 'When God began to create'],[173] year 5483, New Moon of Iyar [late spring 1723].

I 305r:[174] [In different ink: initials *beit ayin" he* (*ba'avonotai harabim*, 'for my many sins').] Now began the days of adversity in the days of Tevet, when the *mashpia* departed altogether [above the line in different ink: 'and I fell from a high roof into a deep pit'], the year 484 in the abbreviated numeration [5484] [in different ink: 'May the Lord, blessed be He, have mercy on me'].

I 360r (foot of the page): At a time of good omen, year 484 [spelt *pd"t* instead of *tp"d*; *pedut* means 'redemption'—Trans.], 4 Tamuz [summer 1724].

I 372r:[175] This day on the fast of the fourth month [17 Tamuz], the insolent dogs smote me, they wounded me and stoned me. Blessed be the Lord who has not made me a prey for their teeth.

I 391r [176] (in the middle of the page and the middle of the line): At this time, in the days of Tishrei, the Lord in his compassion for me brought healing to my wound and the *mashpia* returned, the year 485 in the abbreviated numeration [autumn 1724].

I 404r [177] (below the top two lines of the page): This day, the [letter erased and 'tenth' written below the line] day of Marheshvan [5485], I have been relieved a little of my sorrow and distress and of [two letters erased, and above the line is written: 'the hard labour that I was made to do']. May the name of the Lord be blessed from now and for ever, blessed be He who bestows good on the undeserving and has bestowed all good on me, for the *mashpia* grows ever stronger as the hand of the Lord is good to me.

I 441r:[178] At this time, in the days of Tevet, to strengthen weak hands and tottering knees, the Lord showed me the good of the land for a while, and [it] departed to await its time.

[171] This is one of eight entries (I 101r; II 57v, 158r, 321v, 717v, 781v; III 523v; V 864v) quoted above, text referring to nn. 145–54.

[172] This is one of two entries (I 127r, 461v) quoted above, text referring to nn. 31–2. The first one is also quoted in Essay 6, n. 43.

[173] Gen. 1: 1.

[174] See n. 168 above.

[175] See n. 167 above. This entry is also quoted in Essay 6, n. 86.

[176] See n. 168 above.

[177] See ibid.

[178] This entry is quoted above, text referring to n. 34.

I 446^{v}:[179] Blessed be God who has not turned away my prayer, nor His lovingkindness from me. This day, 15 Tevet [5485/Dec. 1724], I have found some rest for my soul, for [above the line: 'the accusation(s are) growing ever weaker'] and the *mashpia* is growing ever stronger against my enemies. My foot stands on level ground, in the assemblies I will bless the Lord.

I 456^{r}:[180] Blessed be the Lord, my rock, who trains my hands for battle, my fingers for war.[181] My mouth shall be filled with Your praise, and with Your glory all day long,[182] who saves the poor from one too strong for him, the poor and needy from his despoiler.[183] It is a night of watching unto the Lord [eve of Passover 5485/1725], when the Lord my God lightened my yoke and assured me in His great lovingkindness that the time is near for His salvation to come and His righteousness to be revealed. My Father, my God and the rock of my salvation,[184] remember my affliction and my misery, the wormwood and the gall,[185] [when] I said 'Let us appoint a chief'.[186] May the glory of the Lord endure for ever, may the Lord rejoice in His works.[187]

I 461^{v}:[188] I will bless the Lord at all times; His praise shall always be in my mouth.[189] Do not rejoice over me, O my enemy; though I have fallen, I shall rise again. On the evening of 4 Iyar I was visited and sanctified. My soul shall glory in the Lord; the humble shall hear and be glad.[190]

I 471^{r}: I will extol You, O Lord, for You have lifted me up, and have not let my enemies rejoice over me. O Lord my God, I cried to You and You have healed me.[191] At this time in the days of Sivan, the Lord my God has awakened my spirit, for I have tasted a little honey and my eyes have grown bright.[192] How sweet to my palate are Your

[179] See n. 168 above.

[180] This is one of three entries (I 456^{r} [in part], 607^{r}; III 8^{v}) quoted above, text referring to nn. 28–30. [181] Ps. 144: 1. [182] Ps. 71: 8. [183] Ps. 35: 10.

[184] Ps. 89: 27: 'He will call to Me: You are my Father, my God and the rock of my salvation'; referring to King David, who is called *mashiaḥ* ['anointed'] several times in this psalm. Here are two of these 'messianic' expressions: 'I have found David My servant, with My holy oil I have anointed him' (verse 21); '. . . with which they revile the footsteps of Your anointed' (verse 52).

[185] Lam. 3: 19.

[186] Based on Num. 14: 4: 'They said to each other: "Let us appoint a chief and return to Egypt".' Apparently Valle means that when he felt afflicted and depressed, there were times when he lost hope in the Redemption. [187] Ps. 104: 31.

[188] See n. 172 above. [189] Ps. 34: 2. [190] Ps. 34: 3. [191] Ps. 30: 2, 3.

[192] Based on 1 Sam. 14: 29: 'And Jonathan said: My father has troubled the land, see how my eyes have brightened because I took this little taste of honey.'

words, sweeter than honey to my mouth.[193] I will thank You, O Lord my God, with all my heart, and I will glorify Your name for ever,[194] for He stands at the right hand of the poor man, to save him from those who would condemn his soul.[195]

I 478^{v}:[196] At this time, in the month of Menahem [Av], the fetters on my neck were slackened and the burning in my loins was relieved. I will thank the Lord for His righteousness, and will sing praise to the name of the Lord, Most High.[197]

I 490^{v}: At this time in the month of Tishrei, year 5486 [autumn 1725], with the renewal of the year my affairs have been renewed for the better, for the distress and suffering are growing continually less and the accusation continues to diminish, until a spirit is poured upon me from on high,[198] and [He] brings me out into the light [in which?] I shall see His salvation.

I 504^{r}:[199] This day, the night of 22 Kislev, I received tidings that my labours had been rewarded. May Your lovingkindness comfort me in accordance with Your promise to Your servant.

I 516^{v}:[200] This day, 7 Adar, the Lord [added above the line: 'my God'] presented me with the key to my redemption. Let Your hand be ready to help me, for I have chosen Your precepts,[201] support me, so that I may be saved, and I will always occupy myself with Your statutes.[202] Bring my soul out of prison, to give thanks to Your name; righteous men will crown [me?], when You deal bountifully with me.[203]

I 524^{r}:[204] I will give thanks to the Lord; though You were angry with me, Your anger turned back, and You comforted me.[205] This day in Adar II [5486], at the close of the holy Sabbath, the evening of the reading of the scroll of Esther, the *mashpia* grew exceedingly strong, in accordance with the word of the Lord which is sure, on 13 Adar, [when] they were to be despoiled of their possessions. The Lord will complete [His purpose] for me; O Lord, Your

193 Ps. 119: 103, which has singular 'Your word' with plural verb.

194 Ps. 86: 12.

195 Ps. 109: 31.

196 See n. 167 above.

197 Ps. 7: 18.

198 Based on Isa. 32: 15: 'Until a spirit is poured upon us from on high and the wilderness becomes a fruitful field'.

199 This is one of five entries (I 504^{r}; II 299^{v}, 440^{v}; III 716^{r}, 746^{v}) quoted above, text referring to nn. 21–7.

200 See n. 167 above.

201 Ps. 119: 173.

202 Ps. 119: 117.

203 Ps. 142: 8. [The meaning is doubtful: 'will crown' has no clear object in the psalm.—Trans.]

204 See n. 168 above.

205 Isa. 12: 1 (which begins: 'I will give thanks to You').

mercy endures for ever; do not abandon the work of Your hands.[206]

I 526^{r}: Who would not fear You, O King of the nations? For that is Your due; for among all the wise ones of the nations and all their royalty there is not Your like.[207] You are great, and great is Your name in might.[208] This day, the 29th of the month aforesaid, the night of the close of the holy Sabbath,[209] the Lord my God strengthened my right hand to overcome my enemies and subdue those who rose against me. All nations surrounded me, but in the name of the Lord I cut them off.[210] I will thank You for ever because You have done it, and I will place my hope in Your name, because it is good, in the presence of Your pious servants.[211]

I 528^{r}: I will thank the Lord with all my heart; I will recount all Your wonderful deeds | I will rejoice and exult in You, I will sing praise to Your name, O most High | [above the line: 'when my enemies have turned back, they have stumbled and perished before You'].[212] It is the Passover of the Lord, who passed over and saved,[213] [You are] my Father, my God and the rock of my salvation,[214] and He [has] commanded that the beloved of my soul be rescued from the hand of her enemies.[215] I have brought His deliverance near, it is not far off, and His salvation will not delay.[216] Rejoice in the Lord and be glad, you righteous, and sing for joy, all men of upright heart.[217] The Lord redeems the soul of His servants, and none of those who trust in Him shall be found guilty.[218]

I 530^{v}:[219] At this time, in the month of Ziv [Iyar], Amalek and all his forces set out to do battle with me. Praised is the Lord, on whom I call, and I shall be saved from my enemies.[220]

I 542^{v} [221] (from the fifth line on, with an asterisk above the line): At a time of good omen, amen, may it be His will. This day, the New Moon of Menahem [Av 5486], after I had endured so many troubles and evils without number, the Lord my God roused [above the line:

206 Ps. 138: 8 (which has Hebrew plural, 'works'). 207 Jer. 10: 7. 208 Jer. 10: 6.

209 'the night . . . Sabbath', here as elsewhere, represented by the initials of the Hebrew words.

210 Ps. 118: 10. 211 Ps. 52: 11. 212 Ps. 9: 2–4.

213 Valle here combines and adapts two extracts from Scripture (Exod. 12: 27, Isa. 31: 5), taking a reference to the Passover deliverance of the children of Israel in Egypt and transferring it to the future deliverance of Jerusalem. 214 Ps. 89: 27. See n. 184 above.

215 Adapted from Jer. 12: 7: 'I have forsaken My house, I have abandoned My heritage, I have given the beloved of My soul into the hand of her enemies.'

216 Isa. 46: 13 (which has, however, 'My deliverance . . . My salvation').

217 Ps. 32: 11. 218 Ps. 34: 23. 219 See n. 167 above.

220 Ps. 18: 4. 221 See n. 167 above.

'my spirit'] as a man is roused from his sleep, and gave my hand strength to overcome my enemies. See my affliction and my misery and forgive all my sins | See how many are my enemies, and the violent hatred with which they hate me,[222] See how I love Your precepts; O Lord, in Your lovingkindness grant me life.[223] But as for me, who am poor and needy, the Lord will think of me, You are my help and my deliverer; O my God, do not delay.[224] Accept, O Lord, the willing offerings of my mouth, and teach me Your laws.[225]

I 568ᵛ:[226] At this time, in the month of Tishrei, year 5487 [autumn 1726], the strength of the *mashpia* will increase to prevail against my enemies, and as for the oppressor, his strong strides will be cut short, and disaster is made ready to lame him. Happy is he whose help is the God of Jacob, whose hope is in the Lord his God.[227] Let Your lovingkindness, O Lord, be upon us, as we have hoped in You.[228]

I 572ᵛ:[229] Sing to the Lord, praise the Lord, for he has rescued the soul of the poor from the hand of evildoers.[230] At this time in the month of Marheshvan [5487/autumn 1726], the adversary and enemy is growing ever weaker, and the gates of salvation are opened, the light growing ever brighter until it is bright day. My soul will glory in the Lord; the humble will hear and be glad.[231] Be strong and let your heart take courage, all you who hope in the Lord.[232]

I 607ʳ:[233] --* At this time, in the month of Adar [5487/spring 1727], he is assured that he has earned a place in the world to come *--

I 612ᵛ (asterisk over the middle of the first line): I will extol You, O Lord, for You have lifted me up, and have not let my enemies rejoice over me. | O Lord my God, I cried to You and You have healed me | O Lord, You have raised my soul up from Sheol, You have saved my life so that I should not go down into the pit.[234] It is a night of watching [eve of Passover] unto the Lord,[235] who has kept His promise, my Father, my God and the rock of my salvation.[236] O Lord, Your lovingkindness endures for ever, do not abandon the

222 Ps. 25: 18–19.
223 Ps. 119: 159.
224 Ps. 40: 18.
225 Ps. 119: 108.
226 See n. 168 above.
227 Ps. 146: 5. Valle has *ad* ['until', 'up to'] for scriptural *al* ['on', whence 'in'].
228 Ps. 33: 22.
229 This is one of three entries (I 572ᵛ, 821ʳ, 957ᵛ) quoted above, text following the reference to n. 73.
230 Jer. 20: 13.
231 Ps. 34: 3.
232 Ps. 31: 25.
233 See n. 180 above.
234 Ps. 30: 2–4.
235 Exod. 12: 42.
236 From Ps. 89: 27. See n. 184 above.

work of Your hands,[237] for His lovingkindness is great towards us, and the truth of the Lord endures for ever. Praise the Lord.[238] Give thanks to the Lord, for He is good, for His lovingkindness endures for ever.[239] I am poor and needy; O God, hasten to me; You are my help and my deliverer; O God, do not delay.[240]

I 625v [241] (asterisk above the line): I will bless the Lord at all times; His praise shall always be in my mouth.[242] This day, 20 Iyar [5487], the day on which a son was born to me, the oppressor ceased and the *mashpia* was at rest and I went forth from under an iron yoke to life, healing is near and the gates of light are opened, the light growing ever brighter until it is bright day. The Lord is a doer of righteous deeds, and executes justice for all who are oppressed.[243] He saves them from the sword of their mouth, and the needy from the hand of the strong, | so there is hope for the poor, and wrongdoing stops its mouth.[244]

I 705v:[245] This day, in the year 5488, the New Moon of Marheshvan [autumn 1727], the completion of the winnowing [*gemar haberur*, with the letters *mr* run together with *hb*], * [erasure, followed by] and his return to Ramah, for his home is there.

I 784v:[246] For You have been my help (New Moon – – –*– – – Adar) [5488: see text referring to n. 142 above—Trans.] and in the shadow of Your wings I rejoice.

I 794v:[247] At this time, on the days of Purim [5488], on my head is the living [and] only one [*ḥayah yeḥidah*: see n. 11 above—Trans.].

I 821r:[248] Bless the Lord, O my soul; and all that is within me, bless His holy name.[249] I will rejoice and exult in You, I will sing praise to Your name, O Most High | When my enemies have turned back, they have stumbled and perished before You | For You have upheld my right and my cause, You have sat on the seat of judgement as a righteous judge | You have rebuked nations, You have destroyed the wicked, You have blotted out their name for ever and ever.[250] At this time, in the month of Aviv [Nisan 5488/1728], the raging

[237] Ps. 138: 8, altering plural 'works' to singular [as do the English versions—Trans.].

[238] Ps. 117: 2. [239] Ps. 118: 1. [240] Ps. 70: 6.

[241] See n. 168 above. This entry is also quoted in Essay 6, n. 32. [242] Ps. 34: 2.

[243] Ps. 103: 6. [244] Job 5: 15–16.

[245] This is one of four entries (I 705v; III 82v, 232r; IV 212r) quoted above, text referring to nn. 119–23. The first of those entries is also quoted in Essay 6, n. 92.

[246] This is one of three entries (I 784v; II 322v, 834v) quoted above, text referring to nn. 142–4.

[247] This is one of five entries (I 794v; II 324v, 355v, 740v; III 645r) quoted above, text referring to nn. 105–9. [248] See n. 229 above. [249] Ps. 103: 1. [250] Ps. 9: 3–6.

waters have ended and been cut off, and the gates of light and joy are opened, growing ever brighter until it is bright day. Who can tell the mighty deeds of the Lord, or utter all his praise?[251] I will give thanks to You, for I am fearfully and wonderfully made; wonderful are Your works, and that my soul knows right well.[252] I will come with [praise of] the Lord God's mighty deeds, I will tell of Your righteousness, Yours alone.[253] O God, [you are] terrible out of your holy place; the God of Israel, it is He who gives strength and power to the people. Blessed be God.[254]

I 928^{v}: 21 Elul, He looses the bonds of kings and binds a girdle on their loins[255] *– –

I 957^{v}:[256] Bless the Lord, O my soul; and all that is within me, bless His holy name.[257] At this time, in the month of Tishrei, 5489 [autumn 1728], the gates of holiness are opened, the light growing ever brighter until it is bright day. My mouth shall be filled with Your praise, and with Your glory all day long.[258]

II 2^{r}:[259] – –* At this time, in the month of Heshvan [5489], there rested upon him the spirit of the Lord, the spirit of wisdom, etc. *– –

II 57^{v}:[260] – –* At this time in the month of Shevat [5489/spring 1729], You are a priest for ever, after the manner of Melchizedek *– –

II 81^{v}: – –* This day, 7 Adar, The living, the living, he shall thank You, as I do this day[261] *– –

II 158^{r}:[262] – –* On the night of keeping the festival [Passover], blessed be the reviver of the dead, for Your dew is as the dew of light, and the earth shall bring the dead to birth, and the children of Zion shall rejoice in their king *– –

II 218^{r} (dashes and an asterisk above the entry): This day, 22 Sivan, the cloud covered the tent,[263] for the higher ones [above the line: 'will'] cover the lower ones, [but] the Lord is a God of justice, happy are all who wait for Him.[264]

[251] Ps. 106: 2. [252] Ps. 139: 14. [253] Ps. 71: 16. [254] Ps. 68: 36.
[255] Job 12: 18. [256] See n. 229 above. [257] Ps. 103: 1. [258] Ps. 71: 8.
[259] This is one of nine entries (II 2^{r}, 364^{v}; III 92^{v}, 173^{r}, 486^{r}, 736^{r}, 760^{r}; IV 138^{r}; VII 601^{r}) quoted above, text referring to nn. 74–83. [See in particular n. 74.—Trans.]
[260] See n. 171 above. [261] Isa. 38: 19. [262] See n. 171 above.
[263] Exod. 40: 34: 'The cloud covered the tent of meeting, and the glory of the Lord filled the tabernacle.' Exod. 40: 35 continues: 'And Moses could not enter the tent of meeting, because the cloud dwelt on it and the glory of the Lord filled the tabernacle.'
[264] The last two clauses are from Isa. 30: 18: 'Therefore the Lord will wait to show you favour, and therefore He will be exalted and show you mercy, for the Lord is a God of justice, happy are all who wait for Him.' As I understand it, what this entry tells us in terms of Valle's spiritual

II 239ʳ: – –* Do not rejoice over me, O my enemy; though I have fallen, I shall rise again,[265] * This day, the eve of the fast of the fourth month [17 Tamuz], for the Lord has helped me.[266]

II 255ᵛ: – –* On 7 Menahem [Av], He has delivered my soul in safety from the war against me[267] *– –

II 275ᵛ: – –* At this time, at the end of the month of Elul, I am my beloved's and my beloved is mine[268] – –

II 293ᵛ: At this time, the day of blowing the horn [Rosh Hashanah], year *hatami"m* ['the perfect year'; numerical value of *h-t-m-y-m* is 5490], you shall be wholehearted [*tami"m*, 'perfect'] with the Lord your God[269] and the Lord shall be one and His name one.[270] When my enemies have turned back, they have stumbled and perished before You,[271] but I shall rejoice in the Lord, I shall exult in the God of my salvation.[272]

II 299ᵛ:[273] – –* This day, the 10th of the month, Yom Kippur, I received tidings of riches and favour. And nations shall walk by your light, and kings by the brightness of your sunrise *– –

II 303ᵛ (dashes and asterisk above the entry): At this time, on the feast of ingathering [Tabernacles] of the year *pedu"t* [5490/1729; 'redemption', numerical value 490], blessed are You, O Lord, who restores His Shekhinah to Zion.[274] And righteous men will rejoice and exult before God and be filled with joy and happiness.[275]

II 309ʳ (asterisk precedes the entry): Blessed be the Omnipresent, blessed be He, blessed be He who keeps His promise to those that fear Him.[276] At this time on the days of solemn assembly and rejoicing [Shemini Atseret and Simhat Torah]: the mother of the children is

experiences is that the higher sefirot are concealing ('covering with a cloud') the lower sefirot (Yesod and Malkhut, the glory of the Lord) from Moses (Valle), and he is waiting for the renewal of his link with the divine powers.

265 Mic. 7: 8. [Also quoted at I 461ᵛ, text referring to n. 32 above.—Trans.]

266 As in Ps. 118: 13: 'You have thrust hard at me, to make me fall, but the Lord has helped me.'

267 Ps. 55: 19.

268 S. of S. 6: 3; in Hebrew, four words, whose initials spell 'Elul' and are marked off by Valle with apostrophes.

269 Deut. 18: 13.

270 As in Zech. 14: 9.

271 Ps. 9: 4.

272 Hab. 3: 18. There is a quotation from this entry in Essay 6, n. 102. [And cf. I 528ʳ and I 821ʳ above.—Trans.]

273 See n. 199 above. This entry is also quoted in Essay 6, n. 102.

274 The blessing Retseh ['Accept, O Lord'] in the Shemoneh Esreh prayer.

275 Ps. 68: 4. This entry is quoted in Essay 6, n. 102.

276 Taken from the blessings in the Passover Haggadah.

joyful, *haleluyah*,[277] and let them say among the nations: 'The Lord reigns'.[278]

II 313^{v}: * At this time, the last day of the month of Tishrei, on the night of the holy Sabbath, This is the man in whom I delight[279] *

II 321^{v}:[280] – – This day, the 9th of the month [Heshvan], His clothes were white as snow with the clouds of Heaven – –

II 322^{v}:[281] – – This day, the 10th of the month, O Lord, You have raised my soul up from Sheol – –

II 324^{r}: – – This day, the 13th, the stone which the builders rejected has become the chief cornerstone[282] – –

II 324^{v}:[283] This day, the 14th day, Arise, go through the length and breadth of the land, you [are] Messiah – –

II 329^{r}: * This day, the 21st day, at the close of the holy Sabbath, Before I formed you in the womb I knew you, I appointed you a prophet to the nations[284] *

II 331^{v}: * Ask of Me and I will give you nations as your inheritance and the ends of the earth as your possession[285] *

II 337^{v}: * This day, the New Moon of Kislev, new propositions from the inwardness of wisdom[286] *

II 355^{v}:[287] – –* At this time, 20 Kislev, in this year the king will obtain favour from the Lord.

II 364^{v}:[288] – –* This day, 30 Kislev, the spirit of the Lord spoke through me and His word was upon my tongue – –*

II 376^{v}: – –* This day on the fast of the 10th [day of Tevet], I have prepared a lamp for my anointed[289] – –*

II 379^{v}: At this time, the 13th day [of Tevet], I will call to the corn and will increase it,[290] and I will remove the northern one far from you ['you' plural, as in Joel—Trans.][291] – –*

[277] An application of Ps. 113: 9.

[278] 1 Chr. 16: 31. The whole of this entry is quoted in Essay 6, n. 102.

[279] Divine proclamation with regard to Valle.

[280] See nn. 171 and 150 above.

[281] See n. 246 above.

[282] Ps. 118: 22.

[283] See n. 247 above. This entry is also quoted in Essay 6, n. 102.

[284] Jer. 1: 5, omitting the middle of the verse: 'and before you left the womb I consecrated you'. This entry on 21 Heshvan 5490 [autumn 1729], more than two years before the entry in Tevet 5492 (III 173^{r}), may be an earlier allusion to Valle's consciousness of his prophetic rank.

[285] Ps. 2: 8. This entry is quoted in Essay 6, n. 102.

[286] See n. 11 above.

[287] See n. 247 above, and text referring to n. 107. This entry is also quoted in Essay 6, n. 102.

[288] See n. 259 above, and text referring to n. 75.

[289] Ps. 132: 17. This entry is quoted in Essay 6, n. 102.

[290] Ezek. 36: 29.

[291] Joel 2: 20.

II 440^{v}:[292] – –* Bless the Lord, O my soul, and forget not all His benefits; He forgives all your iniquity, He heals all your diseases, He redeems your life from the pit, He crowns you with lovingkindness and mercy.[293] At this time, in the month of Adar, I received tidings which made known to me that I had returned to my root [this sentence is written over an erasure]. Purge me with hyssop, that I may be clean; wash me, that I may be whiter than snow | let me hear joy and gladness, let the bones which I have broken rejoice.[294] The Lord will complete [His purpose] for me; O Lord, Your mercy endures for ever; do not abandon the work of Your hands.[295]

II 471^{v}: – –* On the night of keeping the festival [Passover], Behold, you are fair, my beloved, and pleasant,[296] his belly is polished ivory etc.[297] *– –

II 506^{v} (at the head of the commentary on Ruth): – –* This day, on the Second Passover [14 Iyar], Then I said: Behold, I have come, in a scroll of a book it is written concerning me[298] *– –

II 524^{v}: – – This day, 27 Iyar, the Lord has said to me: 'You are my son',[299] You have established the earth and it stands firm[300] – –

II 548^{v} (at the head of the commentary on Esther): And I in the Lord – – on 20 Sivan – – shall rejoice, I shall exult in the God of my salvation.[301]

II 573^{v}: This day, 14 Tamuz, See, the smell of my son is like the smell of the field which the Lord has blessed.[302]

II 657^{r} (one line, above which there appears: – – –*– – –): – – At this time, at the end of the month of Elul, The word of the man who has been raised on high,[303] I have laid help on a mighty man[304] – –

II 670^{v} (two lines, above which there appears: – –*– –): This day, at the close of the tenth day [the Day of Atonement, 10 Tishrei] in the year

[292] See n. 199 above. This entry is also quoted in Essay 6, n. 92.

[293] Ps. 103: 2–5. Verse 4 is quoted twice.

[294] Ps. 51: 9–10, which reads '. . . which You have broken'. [The final letter *yod* which makes the verb appear a first person may be simply a slip of the pen.—Trans.]

[295] Ps. 138: 8. [Quoted above, text referring to n. 206.—Trans.]

[296] S. of S. 1: 16.

[297] S. of S. 5: 14. The verse ends: 'overlaid with sapphires'.

[298] Ps. 40: 8. ['The Second Passover': as ordained in Num. 9: 9 ff.—Trans.]

[299] Ps. 2: 7.

[300] Ps. 119: 90. This entry is quoted in Essay 6, n. 102.

[301] Hab. 3: 18. This entry is quoted in Essay 6, n. 32.

[302] Gen. 27: 27 (which reads: '. . . a field . . .').

[303] 2 Sam. 23: 1 (which reads: '. . . and the saying . . .' and continues: 'the anointed of the God of Jacob').

[304] Ps. 89: 20. The verse concludes: 'I have exalted one chosen from the people'. Verse 21: 'I have found David, My servant, with My holy oil I have anointed him.' Part of this entry is quoted in Essay 6, n. 103 [but there given as fo. 657^{v}—Trans.].

[5]491 [1730], put your hope in the Lord, be strong: and let your heart take courage, and put your hope in the Lord.[305] (Second line): – – G–d [*elokim*] will send His mercy and His truth[306] – –

II 717^{v} [307] (one line, above which: – –*– –): On 24 Marheshvan, The Lord will fulfil all your petitions | Now I know that the Lord has saved his anointed.

II 740^{v}:[308] – – This day, 15 Kislev, the new mitre, kings shall see and rise, princes [shall see] and bow down – –

II 742^{v}: – – This day, 17 Kislev, He brought them to His holy border[309] – –

II 744^{r}:[310] This day, the 19th of the month aforesaid [Kislev], This is my beloved and this is my companion, O daughters of Jerusalem – –

II 749^{r}:[311] – – On 24 Kislev, at the close of the holy Sabbath, He will bring them to His holy border, the Stone of Strayers has been washed away – –

II 759^{r}:[312] – – This day, 2 Tevet, may [strict] Judgement altogether cease this year, for the New Year and Yom Kippur atone – –

II 781^{v}:[313] – – This day, 21 Tevet [misspelt, *tav* and *tet* reversed] at the close of the holy Sabbath, I have prepared a lamp for my anointed | his enemies I will clothe in shame, but on him his crown will shine – –

II 786^{r}: – – This day, the 28th of the aforesaid month, With joy and gladness of heart by reason of the abundance of everything[314] – –

II 821^{v}: – –* This day, 5 Adar, I have called you by your name, you are mine[315] *– –

II 827^{v}: – –* At this time, in the month of Adar, the Lord will protect you from all evil, He will protect your soul[316] *– –

II 828^{r}:[317] – –* From Moses to Moses, none has arisen like Moses – –*

II 831^{v}: – –* The Lord your God [has been] with you, you have lacked nothing.[318] And in seven [troubles] no evil shall touch you[319] *– –

305 Ps. 27: 14.
306 Ps. 57: 4. This entry is quoted in Essay 6, n. 103.
307 See n. 171 above. This entry and the next one are quoted in Essay 6, n. 104.
308 See n. 247 above.
309 Ps. 78: 54.
310 See n. 169 above.
311 This entry is quoted above, text referring to nn. 115–16 (and see n. 116), and [as fo. 749^{v}—Trans.] in Essay 6, n. 103.
312 This entry is quoted in Essay 6, n. 103.
313 See n. 171 above. This entry is also quoted in Essay 6, n. 104.
314 Deut. 28: 47, where it is part of the rebuke 'Because you did not serve the Lord your God with joy . . .'. Here undoubtedly used in a favourable sense.
315 Isa. 43: 1.
316 Ps. 121: 7. This entry is quoted in Essay 6, n. 103.
317 This is one of two entries (II 828^{r}, III 159^{v}) quoted above, text referring to nn. 8–9.
318 Deut. 2: 7.
319 Job 5: 19. This and the next two entries are quoted in Essay 6, n. 103.

II 834^{v}:[320] – –* For He has rescued me from every trouble, and my eye has seen [the downfall of] my enemies *– –

II 835^{r}: – –* I sought the Lord and He answered me and rescued me from all my fears[321] *– –

II 843^{v}: – –* Its height is as half its length and as half its breadth, there is substance in his words, acquit him[322] *– –

II 848^{r}: – – This day, 1 Adar II, Instead of copper I will bring gold[323] – –

II 851^{r}: – –* Instead of your fathers there shall be your sons, you will make them princes in all the earth[324] – –*

II 857^{v}: – –* The Lord has established His throne in the heavens, and His kingdom rules over all[325] *– –

II 861^{v}: – –* This day, the day of Purim [14 Adar II], Who begot me these?[326] Happy are all who wait for Him,[327] The living, the living, he shall thank You, as I do This day[328] – –*

II 877^{v}: – –* This day, the last day of the month of *ve*Adar [Adar II], Your kingdom is an everlasting kingdom,[329] the Lord [is] one and His name one[330] – –*

II 882^{v}: – –* This day, 4 Nisan [5491], the year of *Yeshayah"u ha"melekh* [King Isaiah], the numerical value of whose letters is 5491 [taking the letter *he* of *hamelekh* as 5,000—Trans.].[331] – –*

[320] Ps. 54: 9. See n. 246 above. [321] Ps. 34: 5.

[322] I do not know what this obscure entry means. I would conjecture that it relates to an ascent of the soul experienced by Valle, and that it may perhaps allude to things said with regard to him by an angel in one of the *heikhalot* ['heavenly palaces']. [323] Isa. 60: 17.

[324] Ps. 45: 17. [325] Ps. 103: 19. [326] Isa. 49: 21. [327] Isa. 30: 18.

[328] Isa. 38: 19. This entry contains two allusions to the numerical value 36: 'these' [*eleh*], written here *ele"h* to mark its significance, and 'the living, the living', similarly written *ḥa"y, ḥa"y* (18+18). [329] Ps. 145: 13.

[330] Zech. 14: 9: 'On that day the Lord will be one and His name one.'

[331] In Essay 6, n. 100, I quoted this entry and remarked on it: 'In my opinion this is a reference to R. Isaiah Romanin, whom I suppose to have been regarded as the Messiah ben Joseph, and the *gematriyah* in the note [the diary entry] is a declaration of his "coronation" in 5491 [1731].' In n. 37 to that essay I explained Romanin's important position in Luzzatto's group and stated that 'in my opinion Luzzatto believed that with the appearance of Shabetai Tsevi the Messiah ben Joseph had been revealed, but that through force of circumstances he had sunk down among the husks and had been unable to complete his mission', and my conclusion was that 'the Messiah ben Joseph in Luzzatto's group [i.e. Romanin] was regarded as a reincarnation of Shabetai Tsevi'. It should be added that there are strong links between R. Isaiah Romanin and a collection of Shabatean writings which I discovered in MS Oxford 2239. In Neubauer's catalogue the collection itself was attributed to Romanin. In my publication 'Te'udot al natan ha'azati' (*Netivei emunah uminut*, 52–80, and the notes ibid. 283–95) I proved that Neubauer's attribution was incorrect and that the author of the collection was R. Joseph Hamits, but I made it clear that Romanin knew and understood the Shabatean content of the writings and that his

II 886v: – –* This day, the 7th of the month [Nisan]: You have saved me and revived me[332] – –*

II 892r: – –* This day, the 10th of the month: the great *kesher* ['bond'], a star has stridden forth out of Jacob and a sceptre has arisen from Israel[333] – –*

II 897v: – –* At this time, the night of watching [Passover night], That night the king could not sleep.[334] Who will remove the dust from your eyes[335] *– –

attitude towards them remained positive long after the messianic ferment in Padua had subsided (see *Netivei emunah uminut*, 52, 55, 58). Such an attitude accords well with my hypothesis as to his Shabatean messianic status in Luzzatto's group. (And see the addendum to this note at the end of the 'Complete List of Diary Entries').

Addendum to n. 331

In this connection I must remark here on the curious fate, in the writings of Mosheh Idel on R. Abraham Abulafia's kabbalistic doctrine, of the conclusion I reached in my research that the collection in MS Oxford 2239 was the work of R. Joseph Hamits. In my essay in *Netivei emunah uminut* (55–6) I pointed out that Hamits's ideas betray the conspicuous influence of 'R. Abraham Abulafia's prophetic kabbalah and his "science of combination"'; and 'passages by Abulafia or members of his school are copied with additions and supplementary matter, and the author follows Abulafia in his fondness for "combinations of Names" and *yiḥudim* and the use of *gematriyah* and notarikon'. My remarks of course attracted the attention of Idel while he was researching Abulafia, and in the light of those remarks he produced a detailed account of the influence of Abulafia's kabbalah on the collection in question. But—*mirabile dictu*—while he quoted the Abulafian passages in the collection as 'Selections by Hamits' or 'An anthology of writings by Abulafia compiled by R. Joseph Hamits', giving references to MS Oxford 2239, he failed to mention my essay on the character of the collection and the identity of its author. See the following by Mosheh Idel: (*a*) *The Mystical Experience in Abraham Abulafia* (New York, 1988), 44 n. 31 (text: p. 20); 64 n. 1 (text: 53–4); 65 n. 15 (text: 56); 168 n. 231 (text: 122); (*b*) *Haḥavayah hamistit etsel avraham abulafiyah* (the Hebrew edition of the work just mentioned) (Jerusalem, 1988), 22 n. 31 ('Selections by Hamits'); 43 n. 1 ('Selections by R. Joseph Hamits from the writings of Abulafia'); 46 n. 14 ('Selections by R. Joseph Hamits'); 106 n. 231 ('Selections by Hamits'); (*c*) *Language, Torah and Hermeneutics in Abraham Abulafia* (New York, 1989), 135 n. 84 (text: p. 2); 146 n. 71 (text: 14); 154 n. 104 (text: 20); 188 n. 7 (text: 83); 197 n. 128 (text: 118). In these tortuous references the attribution of the MS Oxford 2239 collection to R. Joseph Hamits is portrayed as if it were a marvellous discovery generated in Idel's mind by a flash of intuition. It is true that the description 'Selections by R. Joseph Hamits' for the Abulafian passages in the collection first appeared in Idel's doctoral thesis 'Kitvei r' avraham abulafiyah umishnato' (mimeographed; Jerusalem, 1976), 31, and thereafter *passim*, and he did, as in duty bound, give a reference to my essay at the beginning of the thesis. But in preparing an adapted and extended version of his study of Abulafia's writings he suppressed the scholarly basis for identifying the 'selections by Hamits', which I had formulated and explained in detail in my essay, and he appropriated my discovery to himself. And see my essays 'Hafikhah beḥeker hakabalah', *Zion*, 54 (1989), 209–22 (on Idel's book *Kabbalah: New Perspectives*); 'Ḥadeshanut medumah beḥeker hakabalah', *Zion*, 54 (1989), 469–91.

332 This entry is quoted in Essay 6, n. 103.

333 Num. 24: 17. This entry is quoted in Essay 6, n. 104.

334 Esther 6: 1.

335 Mishnah *Sot.* 5: 2.

II 901v[336] (four lines, headed by: – –*– –): I will bless the Lord, Who has given me counsel; in the nights also my inward parts instruct me. My mouth shall be filled with Your praise, and with Your glory all day long.[337] On the seventh night of Passover [5491/1731], the dream of *mt'* [Metatron], But You, O Lord, be gracious to me and raise me up. And on the day of the homily on the eighth night, Awake, north wind, and come, south wind, etc. And on the last night of Passover, unification of the lights with mirth and songs, tambourine and harp.

II 909r:[338] – –* At this time, the end of the month [Nisan], the spider [or 'lizard'] has been killed and will no longer be taken in [the] king's palaces *– –

II 932r: – –* This day, 20 Ziv [Iyar], And [upon] all the fish of the sea; they are given into your hand[339] *– –

III 8v:[340] At this time, 3 and 4 Tamuz: the double assurance, stand firm and see the salvation which the Lord will work for you this day.

III 36v:[341] On 2 Menahem [Av 5491/1731], the night of the holy Sabbath, Because you are precious in my eyes, [and] are honoured, and I love you.

III 51r: This day, 18 Menahem [Av], True instruction was in his mouth, and no wrong was found on his lips.[342]

III 52v:[343] On the 20th of that month [Av 5491] the matter of the kisses and the blessing Sheheheyanu ['Who has kept us alive'].

III 58v: This day, 28 Menahem [Av 5491], communion [*devekut*] in love, destruction of the unclean spirit and delight in [divine] favour.

III 65r: This day, 5 Elul [5491], the news of the *kinyan* ['acquisition'] with a full purse, *erusin* ['betrothal'], and the time for the *nisu'in* [the stage which completes the marriage].

III 69r: This day, the 11th of the month [Elul 5491], the union in love and the promise concerning the revelation soon to come, amen, may it be His will.

[336] This is one of seventeen entries (II 901v; III 76r, 101r, 206r, 360v, 730v, 736r, 833r; IV 73v, 140r, 153v, 158v, 161r, 250v, 400v, 444v, 463v) quoted above, wholly or in part, in the text referring to nn. 35–56. Part of this one is also quoted in Essay 6, n. 104.

[337] Pss. 16: 7, 71: 8. [On the rest of this entry, see nn. 35–7 above.—Trans.]

[338] See n. 167 above. This entry is also quoted in Essay 6, n. 103.

[339] Gen. 9: 2.

[340] See n. 180 above. This entry is also quoted in Essay 6, n. 104.

[341] See n. 169 above.

[342] Mal. 2: 6. Here apparently relates to Luzzatto.

[343] This is one of eight entries (III 52v, 58v, 65r, 69r, 73v, 218v, 535v, 866v) quoted above, text following the reference to n. 125. The first four are also quoted in Essay 3, text beginning with the reference to n. 80.

III 73^{v}: This day, the 15th of the month, the sending of the light of rest to dwell [on me], On the day he earns it you shall pay him his wage etc.

III 76^{r}:[344] On 18 Elul, the dream about R. Simeon bar Yohai, But my servant Caleb, because he had a different spirit.[345]

III 82^{v}:[346] The Lord your God will circumcise your heart and the heart of your offspring [the Hebrew is marked with dots or strokes over letters which spell Elul], the initial letters of Elul. This day, 25 Elul, *tikun* and the circumcision.

III 92^{v}:[347] This day, the tenth day [of Tishrei; the Day of Atonement], year [5]492 [autumn 1731], the crown has been completed, and the Holy Spirit [*resh"he*, the initial letters of *ruaḥ hakodesh*] announces: 'I have laid your foundations with sapphires.'

III 100^{r}: This day on the day of Hoshana Rabah [seventh day of Tabernacles]: the [sc. decree of] rest has been sealed, and they shall no longer behave presumptuously.[348]

III 101^{r}:[349] On the night of Shemini Atseret [eighth day of Tabernacles], the day of solemn assembly, the dream of the Lady [*gevirah*], the treasury of all precious things.

III 104^{v}:[350] The blessings of Heaven greeted me, and now, on Shabat Bereshit [first Sabbath after Simhat Torah], Elijah blessed me through Jacob Hayim.

III 108^{r}:[351] This day, the New Moon of Heshvan [5492/autumn 1731], we arrived at the holy lodging-place whose banner and emblem are *berakha"h tova"h* ['a good blessing'].

III 128^{v}: This day, 22 Marheshvan, good fortune has come to me on the day of the circumcision.

III 149^{v}: At this time, the night of the close of the holy Sabbath, 16 Kislev [5492/Dec. 1731], the day was declared holy by the acclamation of the members.

III 155^{v}: This day, 28 Kislev, love and brotherhood, peace and friendship.[352]

[344] See n. 336 above. [345] See n. 38 above. [346] See n. 245 above.

[347] See n. 259 above. This entry and the next one are also quoted in Essay 6, n. 104.

[348] Deut. 17: 13. [349] See nn. 336 and 39 above.

[350] This entry is quoted above, text referring to n. 12. And see text referring to n. 13, and the note itself.

[351] This and two of the three succeeding entries (III 149^{v}, 155^{v}) are quoted above, text following the reference to n. 13.

[352] [A quotation from the 'Seven Blessings' of the marriage ceremony.—Trans.]

III 159^{v}:[353] This day, the New Moon of Tevet [5492/Dec. 1731], manifestation of the light of Moses, and truth springs out of the ground.

III 161^{v}:[354] This day, the 4th of the month [Tevet 5492], And thus the maiden came to the king; all that she asked for was given her.

III 171^{v}:[355] This day, 22 Tevet [5492/Jan. 1732], For the Messiah has come [or 'is coming'] and proclaims freedom.

III 173^{r} [356] (at the top of the page, without any apparent connection with what precedes and follows): Complete redemption by prophet and messenger; 'prophet' is the righteous winnower, with whom the [divine] word communes, and he is called a *navi* ['prophet'] because those are the letters of *niv alef* ['the saying of the One'], for he earns the privilege of communicating [literally 'the saying of the lips from'; see Isa. 57: 19] what he receives from the One and Only One, for glory clothes itself in him, and glory—the wise shall inherit it; and 'messenger' is Elijah, who reveals himself with him to bring perfect joy into the world, speedily in our days, amen, may it be His will. [Every word in this passage is written with a double apostrophe before the last letter, to emphasize its significance.—Trans.]

III 174^{v}: This day, the 26th of the month, I opened to my beloved.[357]

III 184^{v} (in the middle of the page): On the night of the 17th -- and wine that gladdens the heart of man[358] -- of the month of Shevat.

III 187^{v}: On the 20th of the month, the night of the holy Sabbath, Behold, I am coming to you in a thick cloud, so that the people may hear etc.[359]

III 206^{r}:[360] At this time, in these days of Purim, the dream of Elijah, and wings like the wings of a stork, [the wings] of a bird of the air [*le'of hashamayim*; but possibly *la'uf hashamayim*, 'to fly heavenward'—Trans.].

III 218^{v}:[361] At this time in the days of Nisan [5492]: the divine flow drawn down and existence for ever, the gateway to love, I have set you over my household.

353 See n. 317 above.

354 See nn. 169 and 158 above.

355 This is one of three entries (the others are III 747^{r}, IV 191^{v}) quoted above, text referring to nn. 110–12. This one is also quoted in Essay 6, n. 104.

356 See n. 259 above, and text referring to nn. 77 and 78.

357 S. of S. 5: 6.

358 Ps. 104: 15.

359 Exod. 19: 9. The verse continues: 'when I speak with you, and also that they may believe in you for ever'.

360 See n. 336 above.

361 See n. 343 above. This entry is also quoted in Essay 6, n. 104.

III 220^{v}: On the night of keeping the festival [Passover], come out, you daughters of Zion, and see King Solomon with the crown with which his mother has crowned him etc.[362]

III 228^{r}: This day, 4 Ziv [Iyar], the supernal bride has come [or 'is coming'] to her husband's house, I am the Lord your God, who brought you out etc.[363]

III 232^{r}:[364] In the month of Ziv [Iyar], on the 10th of the month, the power of the *yiḥud* began to prevail.

III 250^{r}: The living, the living, he shall thank you, as I do this day,[365] on 22 Sivan, because they strengthened holiness upon me and instructed me to announce that the Sitra Ahra would no longer prevail over me, I will rejoice in the Lord, I will exult in the God of my salvation | God, the Lord, is my strength, He has made my feet as fleet as hinds, and sets me on [my high places?—reading not clear]. For the director of music, on stringed instruments.[366]

III 263^{v}: This day, 25 Tamuz, And God said: 'Let there be light', and there was light.[367]

III 265^{r}: I have done what is just and right; do not abandon me to my oppressors,[368] eve of the New Moon of Menahem [Av].

III 271^{r}:[369] This day, 26 Menahem [Av], Hallel [psalms of praise] and jubilee and release from everything.

III 271^{v}: On the 16th of the month [Av] *magid mishneh ashiv lakh* [construed as 'I will give you back a second *magid*'—Trans.],[370] and the remedy by the pouring of oil.

III 280^{r}: On 10 Elul, And let me not see this great fire any more, lest I die.[371]

III 281^{r}: (And the Lord will remove all illness from you),[372] (I have instructed you in the way of wisdom).[373]

III 286^{r}: This is my resting-place.[374]

III 289^{v}: This day, 24 Elul, And eats it and lives for ever.[375]

[362] S. of S. 3: 11. The verse ends: 'on his wedding day, the day of his gladness of heart'.

[363] Exod. 20: 2, which continues: '. . . of the land of Egypt, out of the house of bondage'.

[364] See n. 245 above.

[365] Isa. 38: 19. See n. 328 above.

[366] Hab. 3: 18–19: '. . . makes me tread on my high places. For the director . . . on my stringed instruments'.

[367] Gen. 1: 3.

[368] Ps. 119: 121.

[369] This entry is quoted above, text referring to n. 114; and in Essay 6, n. 104.

[370] Zech. 9: 12. This entry is quoted in n. 72 above [where the date is given as the 17th—Trans.]; see that note and the text referring to it.

[371] Deut. 18: 16.

[372] Deut. 7: 15.

[373] Prov. 4: 11.

[374] Ps. 132: 14.

[375] Gen. 3: 22.

III 304v:[376] This day, in the year 5493 [1732], being the morrow of the fast of the tenth day [the Day of Atonement], adjuration of the Prince of the Countenance [Metatron] to spread his wings over one who has suffered many troubles and desires to rest and ascend.

III 360v:[377] On the night of 7 Kislev [5493], the dream of the circumcision in joy to strengthen the *tikun*.

III 427v: This day, the second day [Monday], 7 Nisan, *bishe'at to"v* [?'may the hour be propitious': but see III 430v—Trans.], a male child was born to me,[378] Give thanks to the Lord, for He is good, for His mercy endures for ever.[379]

III 430v: On the day of the holy Sabbath, being Shabat Hagadol ['the Great Sabbath', the last before Passover], *bishe'at to"v* [?here expressed in resignation—Trans.], the child died. The Lord gave and the Lord has taken away, blessed be the name of the Lord.[380]

III 434v:[381] At this time, on the night of watching [Passover], the power of the husk has been broken, and sweet is the light, and it is pleasant for the eyes to see the sun.

III 486r:[382] This day, the New Moon of Tamuz, the holy spirit is roused to revive the spirit of the humble and revive the heart of the broken.

III 523v:[383] On 22 Menahem [Av], I will turn the speech of the nations to a pure speech, that they may all call on the name of the Lord.

III 534r: This day, 6 Elul, the sons of the Palace [*heikhal*] who long to see the radiance of *z"a* [Ze'ir Anpin] will be [or 'let them be'] here at this table etc.[384]

III 535v:[385] This day, the 20th of the month [Elul], under the propitious sign of twelve choice fruits, I gave my daughter to this man.

III 538v:[386] This day, the 16th of the month [Elul], 'I have come to my garden, my sister, my bride', up to 'Eat, friends, drink your fill, beloved ones [or 'drink your fill of love']'. [This entry is out of date order, but bears the same reference and date where quoted at p. 369 above.—Trans.]

III 549v: On the night of the holy Sabbath, 3 Tishrei, year 5494 [autumn 1733], I have separated you from the peoples, to be Mine.[387]

[376] See n. 167 above.
[377] See n. 336 above, and n. 121.
[378] See n. 7 above.
[379] Ps. 106: 1 and others.
[380] Job 1: 21.
[381] See n. 167 above, and text referring to n. 99.
[382] See nn. 259 and 79 above.
[383] See nn. 171 and 153 above.
[384] Luria's *piyut* for 'the third [Sabbath] meal'. The verse ends: 'on which the King's name is engraved'.
[385] See n. 343 above.
[386] See n. 169 above.
[387] Lev. 20: 26.

III 591ʳ: The Lord bless you.[388]

III 605ᵛ: – –* At this time, on the night of the holy Sabbath, 6 Tevet, I will not again smite every living thing as I have done[389] – –*

III 645ʳ:[390] – –* At this time, in these days of Purim [5494/spring 1734], Return, my son, return, the gates of Jerusalem have been opened for you *– –

III 663ʳ: * At this time, the sixth night of Passover, All the works of Creation were created in the form they desired [*tsivyonam*], were created with their consent [*datam*], were created in their full stature [*komatam*],[391] the initial letters of these making up *tsedek* ['justice'], I have cleared the house[392] *– –

III 689ᵛ: Give thanks to the Lord, for He is good, for His mercy endures for ever.[393] This day, 4 Sivan, year 5494 [1734], on the night of the holy Sabbath, in the darkness of the morning [i.e. before dawn], a male child was born to me.[394] May the Holy One, blessed be He, grant him life and preserve him for His service and the study of His Torah; let him be called in Israel by the name Samuel Hayim, and may the Lord, blessed be He, command that there be bestowed on him His blessing of life for ever.

III 700ᵛ:[395] – –* This day, 4 Tamuz, This now is bone of my bones and flesh of my flesh *– –

III 706ʳ: – –* This day, 15 Tamuz, I will give peace in the land[396] *– –

III 711ᵛ: – –* This day, the New Moon of Menahem [Av], on the night of the holy Sabbath, You will reign over all that your soul desires[397] *– –

III 716ʳ:[398] – –* This day, the night of 10 Menahem [the end of the fast of 9 Av], I received tidings by these and similar expressions, the windows of Heaven were opened, *un mondo di* revelations from the *mashpia*, blessed are You, O Lord, who comfort all mourners, blessed is He who revives the dead, according to the suffering is the reward, amen, may this be His will. *– –

III 717ᵛ: – –* This now is bone of my bones and flesh of my flesh[399] *– –

388 Num. 6: 24 (the priestly blessing) and others.

389 Gen. 8: 21, with slight textual variations which do not affect the meaning.

390 See n. 247 above.

391 *RH* 11*a*, *Ḥul.* 60*a*, with alteration of the order to yield the word *tsedek*; apparently a reference to the Shekhinah, one of whose names is Tsedek.

392 Gen. 24: 31.

393 Ps. 106: 1 and others.

394 See n. 7 above.

395 See n. 169 above.

396 Lev. 26: 6.

397 2 Sam. 3: 21.

398 See n. 199 above.

399 Gen. 2: 23.

III 728ᵛ: – –* At this time, the end of the month of Elul, Great peace have those who love Your Torah,[400] Behold, I give him my covenant of peace[401] *– –

III 730ᵛ [402] (four lines; the dashes and asterisks are at the beginning and end of lines 1 and 4): – –* At this time, at the close of the holy Sabbath on the night of 28 Elul, the dream of the killing of ten enemies and joyful thanksgiving * O Lord my God, You are very great, You are clothed in glory and splendour | Wrapping Yourself in light as in a garment, stretching out the heavens like a curtain,[403] His work is glory and splendour and His righteousness endures for ever.[404] And at first I said; and my sword – –* drawn in my hand.[405] And all the enemies of the Lord will be destroyed. Amen, may it be His will *– –

III 731ᵛ: – –* At this time, on the Day of Memorial [Rosh Hashanah], I have called you by your name, you are Mine,[406] year [5]495 [1734/5] under a propitious sign, amen, may it be His will *– –

III 736ʳ:[407] – –* At this time, on the night of the Day of Atonement, the dream of perfect healing, and the h[oly] s[pirit] and the Lord's cause will prosper in our hands *– –

III 746ᵛ:[408] – –* This day, the New Moon of Heshvan in the perfect year [*temima"h*, 'perfect', numerical value 495], I received tidings that I had entered the hall of the sapphire pavement. [Followed by the initial letters of] Give thanks to the Lord, for He is good, for His mercy endures for ever[409] *– –

III 747ʳ:[410] – –* This day, the third of the month, the night of the holy Sabbath, May You [or 'You will'] soon make the offshoot of David spring up, Yinon and Elijah do I send *– –

III 750ᵛ:[411] – –* At this time, the end of the month of Heshvan, Behold, my covenant was with him, the prosecutor has become counsel for the defence *

III 756ᵛ: – –* At this time, in the month of Kislev, a well of living waters, and flowing streams from Lebanon[412] *– –

III 760ʳ:[413] – –* At this time, the night of the holy Sabbath, 24 Kislev, Can we find such a man, in whom there is the spirit of God *– –

[400] Ps. 119: 165. [401] Num. 25: 12. [402] See n. 336 above.
[403] Ps. 104: 1–2. [404] Ps. 111: 3.
[405] In Num. 22: 23 and 31, Josh. 5: 13, and 1 Chr. 21: 16, 'And his sword drawn in his hand', said of the angel of the Lord. [406] Isa. 43: 1.
[407] See nn. 259 and 336 above, and text referring to nn. 80–1. [408] See n. 199 above.
[409] Ps. 106: 1. [410] See n. 355 above; for Yinon, n. 112.
[411] See nn. 167, 100, 101 above. [412] S. of S. 4: 15. [413] See n. 259 above.

III 769^{r}: – –* [May it be] under a propitious sign, on the day of the fast of the tenth [of Tevet] of the year of *hapedu"t* ['the redemption', numerical value 5490] *– –

III 781^{r} [previously given as 781^{v}—Trans.]:[414] – –* This day, 8 Adar, the time has come for [my] release from prison *– –

III 790^{r}: – –* On 18 Nisan in the year of the redemption [*ha'pe'd'u't'*, 5490] *– –

III 790^{r}: – –* At this time, in the days of Passover, For He has rescued me from every trouble,[415] and has delivered us from our enemies[416] *– –

III 833^{r}:[417] – –* This day, 28 Menahem [Av], the dream of the star with regard to the request for long life and to receive the divine flow of good *– –

III 843^{v}: – –* Under a propitious sign, on the Day of Memorial [Rosh Hashanah] of the year 496 according to the abbreviated reckoning, which is the numerical equal of *ba" zema"n hayeshua"h* ['the time of salvation has come', or 'is coming'][418] *– –

III 849^{r}:[419] – –* This day, on the festival of Shemini Atseret, going up and calling aloud to Mi"khael and Metat"ron *– –

III 854^{v}:[420] – –* This day, 20 Heshvan, the night of the holy Sabbath, the Kedushah ['Sanctification'] aloud and in public, God is with you in all that you do *– –

III 864^{v}:[421] – –* This day, 27 Shevat, I rejoiced over the *ry"k* and said: My brethren, my brethren, Say to God 'How fearsome are Your works' *– –

III 866^{v}:[422] – –* On 6 Adar at the close of the holy Sabbath, love from now and for evermore *– –

[414] See n. 167 above. [415] Ps. 54: 9. [416] Ps. 136: 24. [417] See n. 336 above.

[418] The edicts of excommunication against Luzzatto following his enforced confession at the Frankfurt inquiry on 17 Tevet 5495 culminated in stringent bans applying to his whole group from 3 Tamuz 5495 onward. See n. 17 above. It therefore seems to me that the information that 'the time of salvation is coming', given in this entry at Rosh Hashanah 5496 as the equivalent in *gematriyah* of that year, alludes first and foremost to the deliverance of Luzzatto and his group from the troubles of their persecution. The group's response to the comprehensive ban was forcefully expressed in a letter of protest dated 21 Tishrei 5496 [autumn 1735] written and signed by R. Jacob Hazak 'in the name of all the members' and addressed to 'our rabbis the luminaries of the Diaspora'. The letter was published by Ginzburg in *Igerot*, ii. 320–1, under the heading 'Hitnatselut talmidei ramḥa"l' ['Apologia by Luzzatto's Pupils'].

[419] See n. 167 above.

[420] This is one of three entries (III 854^{v}, 864^{v}; IV 113^{r}) quoted above, text referring to n. 14.

[421] See the preceding note. [422] See n. 343 above.

III 868r: – –* On 20 Adar, the night of the holy Sabbath, the King has brought me into his chambers,[423] and the blessing 'At whose word all things come into being' *– –

IV 73v:[424] – –* The night of the close of the holy Sabbath, 21 Adar II [5497], a dream that the Messiah is coming [or 'has come'], let us hope for good fortune, and let us act and succeed.

IV 113r:[425] This day, 11 Tamuz, I have been brought into the holy *beit midrash* to teach and supervise.

IV 119v:[426] – –* This day, on the fast of the fifth month [9 Av], Mercy [Hesed] has been aroused and is extended more and more, to free the captive from prison, blessed be the Lord for ever, amen and amen[427] *– –

IV 119v (in the margin): – –* Which they and their forefathers have not known,[428] initial letters *Eliyah"u* [Elijah], final letters *ra"u he"m* ['they have seen'] *– –

IV 127v: – –* At this time, in the month of Elul, my son the messenger of the Lord *– –

IV 131r: – –* This day, 18 Elul, Beloved above and a delight below[429] *– –

IV 131v: – –* This day, 24 Elul, Wisdom and knowledge are given you[430] *– –

IV 135v: – –* On the Day of Memorial [Rosh Hashanah] of the year 5498 [autumn 1737], I will give him an everlasting name which shall not be cut off[431] *– –

IV 138r:[432] – –* At the close of the Day of Atonement, thrice *kadish*, and from the pit He raised him to great deeds, from time to time he prophesied – –*

IV 140r:[433] – –* On the third day of the festival [of Tabernacles], the night of the holy Sabbath, I prayed this prayer in a dream, upon my knees before the tree of life, calling aloud: May it be Your will, O Lord my God, to pardon me for all the sins I have committed before You

423 S. of S. 1: 4.

424 See n. 336 above.

425 See n. 420 above. This entry is also quoted in Essay 6, text referring to n. 55.

426 See n. 167 above.

427 'Blessed . . . amen' (Ps. 89: 53) indicated by the initials of the Hebrew words.

428 Jer. 9: 15: 'asher lo yade'u hemah va'avotam', with a stroke over the initial and final letters of each word. The verse in full reads: 'I will scatter them among the nations whom they and their forefathers have not known, and I will send the sword after them until I have made an end of them.' It is not clear what connection was seen by Valle between the scriptural quotation and the allusions he identified in the initial and final letters.

429 *Ber.* 17*a*. [A stroke after the first letter of each word in the Hebrew quotation draws attention to the fact that the initials spell 'Elul'.—Trans.]

430 2 Chr. 1: 12.

431 Isa. 56: 5.

432 See n. 259 above.

433 See n. 336 above.

from the day I came into existence on this earth until this day, and not let me sin any more for the rest of my days, and let me not be in need of the gifts of mortals or of their loans, for their gift is small and their disgrace is great, but only of Your hand, which is full and generous, rich and open, so that I may not be ashamed in this world or be put to shame in the world to come, and hearken to my prayer. Thus far my prayer. And every word of God is pure, He is a shield to all who take refuge in Him[434] *– –

IV 145^r: – –* On 8 Marheshvan, the night of the holy Sabbath, a star has stridden forth,[435] and I asked for [or 'sought'] a king *– –

IV 146^v: – –* This day, 18 Marheshvan, In all My house he is the most trusted[436] *– –

IV 147^r (at the head of a passage in the middle of the page): At this time in Venice.

IV 147^r (at the head of a passage in the middle of the page) [the same as the previous reference—Trans.]: At this time in Conegliano, end of Marheshvan.

IV 152^r (at the beginning of a passage, in different ink): At this time in Venice, 9 Shevat.

IV 152^r (at the end of the passage, in different ink): On the 10th of the month I returned to my home, with God's help.

IV 153^v:[437] – –* This day, 26 Shevat, a dream about reward for the work, the lifting of the ewer and the preparation of the throne *– –

IV 158^v:[438] – –* This day, 11 Nisan, the dream of the circuit [of the synagogue] in the matter of *kash kasheh*[?], and the acknowledgement from 'There is none like our God' to 'We will give thanks to our Saviour' *– –

IV 161^r:[439] – –* On the night of 21 Nisan, a dream of the subduing of the angels in the matter of its repetition(?—I.T.), and every month fresh joy[440] *– –

IV 167^v: – –* On 6 Iyar, the night of the holy Sabbath, Go, eat your bread with joy etc., for God has already accepted your deeds[441] *– –

IV 191^v:[442] – –* This day, the eve of the New Moon of Menahem [Av], the [appointed] time of redemption, and the redeemer has come [or 'is coming'] *– –

434 2 Sam. 22: 31 and Ps. 18: 31 [and see above, text referring to n. 48, and the note itself—Trans.].

435 Num. 24: 17.

436 Num. 12: 7.

437 See nn. 336, 49, 50 above.

438 See ibid.

439 See ibid.

440 See n. 51 above.

441 Eccles. 9: 7. The words omitted are: 'and drink your wine with a merry heart'.

442 See n. 355 above.

IV 192^{v}: – –* This day, 5 Menahem [Av], there are no more stumbling-blocks, they have been sweetened one and all, behold, thus shall be blessed the man who fears the Lord[443] *– –

IV 200^{v}:[444] – –* At this time, the night of 15 Elul, the ten tribes have come *– –

IV 204^{v}: – –* Year 5499 during the Ten Days of Penitence, You raised my life up from the pit,[445] and I will make of you a great nation[446] *– –

IV 205^{r}: – –* Between the tenth of the month [the Day of Atonement] and the Festival [Tabernacles], *yisom* [or *yishom* or *yisum*], he will rest, he enters, and they enter[447] *– –

IV 209^{r}: – –* This day in Venice, the fifth day [Thursday], 9 Marheshvan, [may it be] of good omen and a good sign, amen, may it be His will *– –

IV 212^{r}:[448] – –* This day, 26 Marheshvan [5499/1738], Behold, a day is coming for the Lord to restore to Yesod what he had given out for the sake of Malkhut *– –

IV 217^{v}: – –* Today, 22 Kislev, I returned to my home, may the name of the Lord be blessed from now and for ever *– –

IV 233^{v}: – –* In Adar I, I have called you by your name, you are Mine[449] *– –

IV 238^{v}: – –* At this time, in the days of Purim, with regard to you Isaiah said: 'Israel in whom I will be glorified'[450] *– –

IV 250^{v}:[451] – –* This day, 9 Iyar, a dream of the anointing by the Father, and the promise completed *– –

IV 266^{r}: – –* At this time in the month of Tamuz, Long live the king, long live the king[452] *– –

IV 267^{v}: – –* This day, 8 Tamuz, You will arise and have mercy on Zion etc.,[453] For you shall go out with joy etc.[454] *– –

IV 276^{v} (at the head of the commentary on Samuel): Who saves those that take refuge[455] – –*– – On 29 Tamuz 5499 [late summer 1739] (second line, below the asterisk): Sing a new song to the Lord,[456] blessed be the Lord.

443 Ps. 128: 4.

444 This entry is quoted above, text referring to n. 113.

445 Jonah 2: 7.

446 Exod. 32: 10.

447 Obscure allusions. [The context gives no guidance on how to read or what is meant.—Trans.]

448 See n. 245 above.

449 Isa. 43: 1.

450 Isa. 49: 3.

451 See n. 336 above.

452 2 Sam. 16: 16.

453 Ps. 102: 14. The verse ends: 'for it is time to be gracious to her, for the time has come'.

454 Isa. 55: 12, which continues: 'and be led forth in peace'.

455 Ps. 17: 7.

456 Isa. 42: 10, Ps. 96: 1, and others.

IV 276[v] [the same as the previous reference—Trans.]: – –* This day, the New Moon of Menahem [Av], blessed be the Lord, Behold your God[457] *– –

IV 280[r]: – –* This day, 12 Menahem [Av], Behold, I am sending you Elijah the prophet etc.[458] *– –

IV 295[v]: – –* Year 5500, Tishrei [autumn 1739], on the day of the fast [of Gedaliah], Your righteousness is like the mighty mountains, Your judgements [are like] the great deep; man and beast[459] You save, O Lord[460] *– –

IV 316[v]: – –* On 23 Kislev, greater shall be the glory of this house etc. and in this house I will grant peace[461] *– –

IV 319[r]: – –* This day, 2 Tevet, Then my soul will rejoice in the Lord, it will exult in His salvation,[462] the seventh year is approaching[463] *– –

IV 345[v]: – –* This day, the eve of Passover in the year 5500 [1740], Nothing will be lacking there[464] *– –

IV 346[v]: – –* At this time, during the days of Passover, the sign of the *lulav* ['palm branch'],[465] I will do you no more harm,[466] And you shall be like a well-watered garden and like a spring of water etc.[467] *– –

IV 398[v]: – –* This day, 17 Elul, On the day of your watchmen your salvation has come[468] *– –

IV 400[v]:[469] – –* This day, 28 Elul, the great dream with the doubled call: O Lord, save Your people, the remnant of Israel *– –

IV 401[v]: – –* On the night of the Day of Memorial [Rosh Hashanah], year 5501 [1740], Let my beloved come to his garden and eat its precious fruits[470] *– –

IV 411[v]: – –* On 26 Marheshvan, Hark! My beloved! Behold, he comes, leaping over the mountains, bounding over the hills[471] *– –

457 Isa. 35: 4, which continues: 'will come with vengeance'.

458 Mal. 3: 23 [4: 5 in non-Jewish versions], which ends: 'before the coming of the great and terrible day of the Lord'.

459 In the Hebrew, initial letters only.

460 Ps. 36: 7.

461 Hag. 2: 9: 'Greater shall be the latter glory of this house than its former [glory], says the Lord of Hosts, and in this place I will grant peace, says the Lord of Hosts.'

462 Ps. 35: 9.

463 Deut. 15: 9, which continues: 'the year of remission'.

464 Deut. 8: 9, substituting third person verb for second person: 'You will lack nothing there'.

465 It is not clear what this 'sign' signifies.

466 1 Sam. 26: 21.

467 Isa. 58: 11, which ends: 'whose waters do not fail'.

468 Based on Mic. 7: 4, which reads: 'The day of your watchmen, of your visitation, has come.'

469 See n. 336 above.

470 S. of S. 4: 16.

471 S. of S. 2: 8.

IV 415v: – –* At this time, in the month of Kislev, Long live the king, long live the king,[472] Wisdom and knowledge are given you[473] *– –

IV 442v:[474] – –* On Passover, year 5501 [1741], Let my beloved come to his garden and eat its precious fruits *– –

IV 444v:[475] At this time, the end of the month [Nisan 5501], Now my head will be lifted up, and the dream [that] the fowl which shakes its face[?] [the reading *tarnegola demena'ara anpa* is doubtful—Trans.] has gone [or 'will go'] forth to freedom *– –

IV 463v:[476] – –* This day, the New Moon of Tamuz [5501], a good dream came to me a second time, and also it was said: Lo, I have made him a witness to the nations, a prince and commander to the nations *– –

IV 478v: – –* This day, 17 Menahem [Av], Open to me the gates of righteousness, I will enter into them and give thanks to the Lord[477] *– –

IV 494v:[478] – –* At this time, between New Year and the tenth day [Yom Kippur: the Ten Days of Penitence] in the year 5502 [1741], the vow of *s"y* [or *sy'*] which subdues the Sitra Ahra and gladdens the soul *– –

IV 510v: – –* At this time, in the month of Kislev, Now my head shall be lifted up,[479] Ask of God good understanding to serve You and fear Your name *– –

IV 530r: – –* This day, 5 Adar I, But there is a friend who sticks closer than a brother[480] [written ***v****eyesh* ***o****'hev* ***d****'avek* ***me****'aḥ*; total value of the first letters is 45 (*mem he*)], giving the Name *mem"he* which is the distinctive quality of my soul[481] *– –

IV 550r: – –* At this time, the night of 7 Nisan, return home and thanksgiving: Blessed be the Lord who has delivered my soul from all trouble[482] *– –

472 2 Sam. 16: 16.

473 2 Chr. 1: 12.

474 See n. 169 above.

475 See nn. 336 and 55 above.

476 See ibid.

477 Ps. 118: 19. [The numeral '17' is here written *to"v* ('good': *tet vav+beit* = 15+2).—Trans.]

478 See nn. 167 and 104 above.

479 Ps. 27: 6, which continues: 'above my enemies round about me'.

480 Prov. 18: 24.

481 'The Name *mem"he*' (numerical value 45) is the Tetragrammaton with each letter spelt out in full (*yod he vav he*, where each vowel in *he vav he* is represented by *alef*). One of the latest entries says: 'On 7 Tevet [5531/Dec. 1770], ascent of my soul [brought about] by [the Name] *mem"he*' (MS Jewish Theological Seminary, New York, Mic. 1053, fo. 54v). Thus some thirty years later he still felt a strong personal bond between his soul and the Name *mem"he*. And see n. 528 below.

482 2 Sam. 4: 9; 1 Kgs. 1: 29, substituting 'Blessed be the Lord' for 'As the Lord lives'.

IV 593^v: – –* At this time, within the straits [the three weeks from 17 Tamuz to 9 Av], Arise, shine, for your light has come,[483] come in, ye beloved of the King *– –

IV 597^v: – –* This day, 19 Menahem [Av], But the stone that struck the image became a great mountain and filled the whole earth[484] *– –

IV 615^v: – –* This day, the last in the month of Elul, See, I have removed your iniquity from you and will clothe you in fine robes[485] *– –

IV 616^v: – –* At this time, the night of the close of the Day of Memorial [Rosh Hashanah] of the year 5503 [autumn 1742], O afflicted one, storm-tossed and unconsoled, I will set in fair colours etc.[486]

IV 749^v: – –* At this time, in the month of Tishrei of the year 5504, You crown the year with Your goodness,[487] a mantle of salvation instead of a gloomy spirit[488] *– –

IV 795^v: – –* At this time, in the month of Shevat, Sinners shall cease from the earth, and the wicked be no more; bless the Lord, O my soul. *Haleluyah*[489] *– –

IV 809^r: – –* This day, the New Moon of Adar, Now the king's compassion has been aroused,[490] Those who fear You shall see me and rejoice because I have hoped in Your word[491] *– –

IV 904^v: – –* At this time, in the Ten Days of Penitence of the year 5505 [autumn 1744], The Lord has sworn by His right hand and His strong arm: Never again will I give etc.[492] *– –

IV 996^v: – –* At this time, in the month of Iyar, year 5505 [early summer 1745], He will deliver him, for He takes delight in him[493] *– –

IV 1056^r: – –* At this time, in the year 5506 [1745], between New Year and the tenth day [the Ten Days of Penitence], the prayer with the

[483] Isa. 60: 1. In the Zohar (see III *6b*, 89*a*, 118*a*) the verse refers to the rescue of the Shekhinah by those who are loved by the King, her husband, Tiferet. They are invited to go in to her in language which is unmistakably Zoharic. Here it is meant to apply principally to Valle himself. [484] Dan. 2: 35. [485] Zech. 3: 4.

[486] Isa. 54: 11. The second half of the verse reads: '. . . will set your stones in fair colours and lay your foundations with sapphires'.

[487] Ps. 65: 12. [488] Isa. 61: 3, substituting 'salvation' for 'praise'.

[489] Ps. 104: 35. [In context, the verse means 'may sinners cease', but the verb can be read (and Valle may have meant it) as an indicative.—Trans.]

[490] Undoubtedly Zoharic language. Apparently this is meant to refer to the increase in joy said in the Talmud [*Ta'an.* 29] to begin with Adar. [491] Ps. 119: 74.

[492] Isa. 62: 8: 'Never again will I give your corn to be food for your enemies.'

[493] Ps. 22: 9. [In context, the verse means 'let Him deliver him'. Cf. n. 489 above.—Trans.]

Tetragrammaton vowelled as in the word *yehavekha* ['your burden'],[494] that the Name might guard me from all evil and guard my soul,[495] and I was answered with light and delight, bringing consolation and joy.

V 241^v:[496] – –* At this time, in the month of Tishrei in the year 5512 [autumn 1751], My soul will rejoice in the Lord, it will exult in His salvation *– –

V 258^v:[497] – –* This day, 8 Marheshvan [5512]: it will certainly be my good fortune to go to the Land of Israel, but I do not know whether now or later.

V 864^v:[498] – –* This day, 21 Sivan 5510 [1750], You will arise and have mercy on Zion, for it is time to show favour to her, for the time has come.

VI 61^v: – –* At this time, between New Year and the tenth day [the Ten Days of Penitence] in the year 5509 [1748], I will comfort them and give them joy in place of their sorrow,[499] The glory of Lebanon shall come to you[500] *– –

VI 211^v: – –* At this time, in the month of Tamuz [5507/1747], Come in, ye beloved of the King, come in,[501] For the sake of my brothers and friends, let me speak peace concerning you[502] *– –

VI 247^r: – –* At this time, in the year 5508 between New Year and the tenth day [the Ten Days of Penitence, 1747], God is not man, that He

494 As in Ps. 55: 23: 'Cast your burden upon the Lord and He will sustain you; He will never let the righteous be shaken.'

495 See Ps. 121: 7.

496 In vols. V–VI the entries, in groups or singly, are in reverse chronological order. In consecutive date order they would be arranged thus: VI 420^v, 540^v—Shevat 5506, Tishrei 5507; VI 211^v, 247^r, 254^r—Tamuz 5507, Tishrei 5508; VI 61^v—Tishrei 5509; V 864^v—Sivan 5510; V 241^v, 258^v—Tishrei, Heshvan 5512. The reason for the altered order is as follows: the two volumes, which contain commentaries on the Pentateuch, are arranged in the order of the Five Books (vol. V, Genesis and Exodus; vol. VI, Leviticus, Numbers, Deuteronomy) but they were composed in reverse order, as is shown by the notes at the ends of the commentaries. Here are the references: 'This commentary [on Genesis] was completed on 23 Sivan, year 5512' (V 419^r); 'This commentary [on Exodus] was brought to completion on 4 Tishrei, year 5511' (V 754^v); 'It [the commentary on Leviticus] was completed on 13 Sivan, year 5509' (VI 180^v); 'It [the commentary on Numbers] was completed on 8 Sivan 5508' (VI 377^r); 'It [the commentary on Deuteronomy] was completed on 3 Sivan, year 5507' (VI 645^v). Thus, in the British Library manuscripts, Valle copied these commentaries in the opposite order from that in which he had originally written them, and into each commentary he copied his personal notes in positions intentionally corresponding to their positions in the original.

497 This entry and VII 451^{r–v} are quoted together above, text following reference to n. 18. And see text referring to nn. 19 and 20.

498 See n. 171 above.

499 Jer. 31: 12.

500 Isa. 60: 13.

501 See n. 483 above.

502 Ps. 122: 8.

should lie, etc.,[503] Behold, I received a command to bless; He has blessed etc.[504]

VI 254^{r}: – –* On 26 Tishrei, year 5508, Delight in the Lord and He will grant you your heart's desires[505] *– –

VI 420^{v}: – –* This day, 13 Shevat, year 5506, I have said to you: 'You are my servant',[506] Israel, in whom I will be glorified, you are my servant[507] *– –

VI 540^{v}: – –* In the month of Tishrei in the year 5507 [1746], Sing to the Lord, for He has done gloriously; this is made known in all the earth[508] *– –

VII 93^{v}:[509] – –* On 25 Heshvan, year 5513 [autumn 1752], the Messiah said to the Pope: Abase yourself so that the feet of holiness may tread upon your head.

VII 451$^{r–v}$:[510] [451^{r}] On the last day of Tishrei, year 5515 [1754], Shelomoh Rakah, my dear friend, died [above the line the initials *nun ayin*, 'may his soul rest in Eden'], and may God, blessed be He, help me, [451^{v}] for He is Lord of everything and everything is from Him. Heal me, O Lord, and I shall be healed; save me, and I shall be saved; for You are my praise.[511]

VII 599^{r}: – –* At this time, the close of the Day of Atonement, year 5516 [1755], The Lord bless you and keep you[512] *– –

VII 601^{r}:[513] – –* On the festival of Tabernacles in the year 5516, [letters] *he nun dalet"beit alef tav ayin" beit vav pe yod kaf ayin* *– –

VII 734^{v}: This day, 20 Menahem [Av], Behold, I give him my covenant of peace[514] *– –

VII 735^{v}: – –* This day, the 21st of the aforesaid month, there came a stormwind and damaged a number of the houses of the Gentiles but there was no damage to Israel, praise be to the Creator of the world[515] *– –

503 Num. 23: 19, which continues: 'or a son of man, that He should repent'.

504 Num. 23: 20. The verse ends: 'He has blessed and I cannot revoke it'.

505 Ps. 37: 4.

506 Isa. 41: 9. The verse ends: 'I have chosen you and have not cast you off'.

507 Isa. 49: 3: 'And He said to me: "You are my servant Israel, in whom I will be glorified".'

508 Isa. 12: 5.

509 This entry is quoted above, text referring to n. 117. And see text referring to n. 118 above, and the note itself.

510 See n. 497 above.

511 Jer. 17: 14. [This sentence, turned into the plural 'heal us' etc., forms part of the daily Shemoneh Esreh prayer.—Trans.]

512 Num. 6: 24.

513 See nn. 259 and 83 above.

514 Num. 25: 12. [Cf. text referring to n. 401.—Trans.]

515 'Praise be . . .' etc. represented by the initials of the Hebrew words.

VII 751^{v}: – –* Between New Year and the tenth day [the Ten Days of Penitence], year 5517 [1756], Go, eat your bread with joy, etc.[516] *– –

VII 753^{v}: – –* At this time, between the tenth day and the Festival [Tabernacles], there shall rise for you who fear My name etc.,[517] Who restores His Shekhinah to Zion[518] *– –

VII 770^{v}: – –* At this time in Venice, at the end of Heshvan [above the line: '5517'], It is the blessing of the Lord which makes rich, and toil adds nothing to it [or 'He sends no sorrow with it'][519] *– –

VII 771^{v}: – –* This day, the New Moon of Kislev, I returned to my home in peace, Give thanks to the Lord, for His mercy endures for ever[520] *– –

VII 805^{r}: This day, 17 Tevet, I was in Venice.

VII 807^{v}: This day, 25 Shevat, I returned to my home. [Initial letters of] Blessed be He who gives strength to the weary and strengthens those who are weak[521] *– –

VII 906^{r}: * From this time in the month of Tishrei, year 5518 [autumn 1757], The Lord our God be with us as He was with our forefathers.[522]

VII 910^{v}: – –* This day in the year 5518, 2 Heshvan, the Lord said to him, Peace[523] *– –

VII 911^{v}: – –* This day, 5 Heshvan, Open to me the gates of righteousness, I will enter them and give thanks to the Lord[524] *– –

VII 1027^{r}: – –* On the day of the New Moon of Elul 5518 [late summer 1758], I will heal their backsliding, I will love them freely, for My anger is turned away from them[525] *– –

VIII 115^{r} (at the top of a page and the beginning of a topic, in different ink): At this time, in Verona in the house of my relative Samuel Valle, in the month of Iyar, year 5520 [1760].

[516] Eccles. 9: 7. The verse ends: 'and drink your wine with a merry heart, for God has already accepted your deeds'. [Cf. text referring to n. 441 above.—Trans.]

[517] Mal. 3: 20 [4: 2 in non-Jewish versions], which continues: 'a sun of righteousness with healing in its wings'.

[518] Conclusion of the blessing Retseh ['Accept with favour Your people Israel and their prayer'] in the Shemoneh Esreh.

[519] Prov. 10: 22.

[520] Ps. 106: 1 and others.

[521] Isa. 40: 29, preceded by the word *barukh* as in the early morning blessing which reproduces the first half of the verse.

[522] 1 Kgs. 8: 57.

[523] Judg. 6: 24 [where it means: 'and he [Gideon] called it "The Lord–peace".'—Trans.].

[524] Ps. 118: 19.

[525] Hos. 14: 5.

VIII 115^{v} (middle of the page, beginning of a topic): This day, 29 Iyar, the Lord, blessed be He, returned me to my home, to life and peace.

VIII 728^{v}: At this time in the month of Kislev, year 5526 [end of 1765], change of place and change of fortune for the better. God is not man, that He should lie.[526]

SEVEN DIARY ENTRIES IN THE MANUSCRIPTS OF THE JEWISH THEOLOGICAL SEMINARY, NEW YORK

I am grateful to the directorate of the Library of the Jewish Theological Seminary, New York, for their permission to publish these manuscripts.

MS Mic. 1053, fo. 49^{r}: On 7 Heshvan [5531/1770], My eyes are ever towards the Lord, for He will free my feet from the net.[527]

Ibid., fo. 54^{v}:[528] On 7 Tevet [5531/Dec. 1770], ascent of my soul [brought about] by [the Name] *mem"he*, blessed be the Lord, God of Israel,[529] [letters] *alef yod alef"shin lamed*.[530]

MS Mic. 1051, fo. 6^{v}: At the end of the month of Nisan 5531 [1771], Your salvation, O Lord, will lift me high.[531]

Ibid., fo. 78^{v}: 11 Sivan 5532, [initials] *lamed yod alef alef kaf yod alef ḥet vav" alef mem yod he*.[532]

Ibid., fo. 83^{v}: At this time, the night of the aforesaid day [21 Tamuz 5532], [initials] *tav ayin"beit tsadi leil* [or *layil*] *vav alef"yod lamed*.[533]

MS Mic. 1052, fo. 38^{v}: At this time, in the month of Heshvan 5534 [autumn 1773], See now that I, I am He,[534] I will show you marvellous things.[535]

Ibid., fo. 78^{v}: 5534, [initials] *beit resh ḥet"tet* (?—the reading is doubtful) [initials] *ayin"yod kaf yod"ḥet yod"mem alef"nun yod alef"alef vav"ayin tsadi"vav ḥet yod"alef*.[536]

[526] Num. 23: 19.
[527] Ps. 25: 15.
[528] This entry is quoted in Essay 6, n. 70. And see n. 481 above.
[529] 1 Sam. 25: 32 and others.
[530] The meaning is unknown.
[531] Ps. 69: 30, which reads, however: 'Your salvation, O God . . .'.
[532] The meaning is unknown.
[533] The meaning is unknown.
[534] Deut. 32: 39.
[535] Mic. 7: 15, substituting 'show you' for 'show him'.
[536] Meaning of initials unknown.

EIGHT

How Luzzatto's Kabbalistic Writings were Disseminated in Poland and Lithuania

A. COMBINED EDITIONS OF *MESILAT YESHARIM* AND *DEREKH ETS ḤAYIM* AND THEIR EVOLUTION

Derekh ets ḥayim[1] ['The Way of the Tree of Life'] is a booklet on ethical topics, chief of which are sin and repentance, the battle against the evil inclination, Torah and commandments, and methods of studying kabbalah. It belongs in content and style to the body of literature openly concerned with kabbalistic ethics, unlike Luzzatto's other ethical works, particularly *Mesilat yesharim* ['The Highway of the Upright'] and *Derekh hashem* ['The Way of the Lord'], part IV, in which the author's approach to kabbalistic ideas and concepts is camouflaged. This booklet was originally intended to serve as an introduction to *Kela"ḥ pitḥei ḥokhmah* ['138 Gateways to Wisdom'], Luzzatto's main systematic work on speculative kabbalah, as he says explicitly at the end of *Derekh ets ḥayim*: 'And I have compiled, along with the present work, the 138 gateways to wisdom which I found in an ancient document, and these are great keys to the Science of Truth.'[2]

In 1785, when *Kela"ḥ pitḥei ḥokhmah* was published in full, *Derekh ets ḥayim* was printed at its head under the title 'Introduction by the author', but the 'introduction' had been printed and published some twenty years before as an addendum to the second edition of *Mesilat yesharim* (Zholkva [Żółkiew], 5526 [1766]), and it continued to be printed thus in a considerable propor-

[1] In some editions the work is called *Derekh ets haḥayim*, and sometimes both forms of the name are used indiscriminately.

[2] Luzzatto's *Kela"ḥ pitḥei ḥokhmah* (Korets, 1785), 8*b*.

tion of the editions of *Mesilat yesharim* even after it had been printed in its proper place at the head of the '138 Gateways'.[3] In my researches I found that the editions of *Derekh ets ḥayim* appended to *Mesilat yesharim*, especially those of Zholkva and Shklov, contained complications and obscurities which have not hitherto been understood. My study of the difficulties led me to realize that their solution would be of great importance, extending even beyond the field of bibliography, as will become clear from what follows.

The editions of *Mesilat yesharim* jointly with *Derekh ets ḥayim* which are of particular interest for the purpose of my investigation are those which appeared up to 1835. In chronological order they are: Zholkva 5526, 5528, 5530, 5542 [1766, 1768, 1770, 1782];[4] Shklov 5544, 5555 [1784, 1795]; Grodno 5555; [Zholkva] 5569 [1809]; Shklov 5595/1834, four printings all showing that year of publication in both styles.[5] To these may be added,

[3] A detailed bibliography of Luzzatto's works is given in N. Ben-Menahem's *Kitvei rabi mosheh ḥayim lutsato* (Jerusalem, 1951). In addition to the 'addenda and corrigenda' at the end (pp. 149–75), many descriptions and remarks in that book need to be further corrected or supplemented. In this essay I shall deal with only some of the bibliographical questions, to the extent necessary for the present purpose.

[4] These editions are described in N. Ben-Menahem's article 'Arba mahadurot shel "mesilat yesharim", zolkva', *Areshet*, 1 (1959), 479–80. The first three are also listed in Ben-Menahem, *Kitvei rabi mosheh ḥayim lutsato*, where his description of the 5526 edition is incomplete and lacks the year of publication (pp. 143–4), the 5528 edition is mentioned without any details (p. 70), and the 5530 edition is described (p. 143) in more detail than in *Areshet*. Ben-Menahem does not record the source of his description of the 5526 edition, but he was kind enough to inform me orally that it is based on the copy which he saw in the library of the Lubavitcher Rebbe in New York. At present this is the only copy known to us, and I have therefore been unable to examine that edition. [But now see pp. 451–2 below, '*Mesilat yesharim*, Edition of Zholkva 5526'.—Trans.] R. Uri Tsevi Rubinstein, in his *Siftei yeshenim*, ii (Zholkva, 1806), 27, no. 67, refers to '*Mesilat yesharim* [by] our teacher Rabbi Moses Hayim Luzzatto . . . [initials for] Zholkva print 5526', and the book was certainly in the hands of the writer. J. Fuerst, too, notes after the first edition: 'Żółkiew 1766' [= Zholkva 5526], but he may have copied that from *Siftei yeshenim*. The catalogue of the books left by R. Meir Lehren, R. Akiva Lehren, and R. Moses de Lima in Amsterdam, which were put up for auction by J. L. Joachimsthal between 13 Feb. 1899 and 2 Mar. 1899, lists the following on p. 85 at no. 1553, after '*Mesilat yesharim*, Amsterdam 1740': 'The same, and at its end "*Derekh ets ḥayim*" on the study of kabbalah, Zholkva 5526.' It is to be hoped that this copy has been preserved in some west European library. The description of the edition of 5530 was taken by Ben-Menahem from Hayim Lieberman's note of a copy of the book in the library of the Lubavitcher Rebbe. That description does not record *Derekh ets ḥayim* and does not indicate the number of pages. But the New York Public Library has this edition, and the Library's *Dictionary Catalog of the Jewish Collection*, xii (1960), 10827, notes that the book has 72 pages, exactly the same number as Zholkva 5528, which has *Derekh ets ḥayim* at its end.

[5] See Ben-Menahem, *Kitvei rabi mosheh ḥayim lutsato*, 76–8, 162, where three printings are listed. Two are arranged identically, page for page and line for line, except only for a difference in the appearance of the title-page, and they give the year as 5595 and 1834; the third printing is set in different type and in a completely different format, and the year is given only as

doubtfully, Vilna (undated), which 'was printed by the great rabbinic sage Menahem Man, son of our teacher and master R. Barukh, may the memory of that righteous man be for a blessing', it being impossible at present to determine its date of printing even approximately. It may have been a few or many years before 1835 or a few years after 1835.[6]

The title-page of the Zholkva edition of 5526 tells us that it 'was sent for printing by the humble hasid, the great rabbi, our teacher and rabbi R. Elijah, son of our teacher and rabbi R. Israel (may he be remembered for life in the world to come), of the holy congregation of Brisk of Lithuania [Brest-Litovsk], son-in-law of the great and famous *gaon*, our teacher and rabbi R. Nahman (may he be remembered for life in the world to come), *av beit din* [president of the rabbinical court] and head of the yeshiva of the said holy congregation'.[7] The editor-publisher added an introduction (from which

1834. The National and University Library in Jerusalem has a copy of a third printing of the same sort as the first two (5595 and 1834). In all the printings the date of censorship is 30 *santiabr* 1834. It seems that the book was printed several times in succession over a period of some years and that for reasons connected with the censor's licence the publishers continued to print the same year on the title-page.

[6] I. Rivkind, in *Kiryat sefer*, 15 (1938–9), 498, no. 2, notes this edition as 'Vilna, no date (about 5559) [1799]'. The index of the National Library in Jerusalem gives it as 'between 5563 and 5577 [1803–17]'. Ben-Menahem at first registered the date erroneously, in his book (*Kitvei rabi mosheh ḥayim lutsato*, 109), as 'between 5663 and 5677', but in the light of an observation by H. Lieberman he amended this to 'the time of printing must be put earlier' (p. 170). It is clear that the earliest possible time is 5563, because the printer's father, who is referred to as deceased on the title-page ('may the memory of that righteous man be for a blessing'), died in that year. But there is no reason to fix 5577 as the latest date. That date was taken by the National Library from a misstatement in H. D. [Bernard] Friedberg's *Toledot hadefus ha'ivri bepolonya* (Antwerp, 1932), 88, on the period during which the Vilna printing house bearing Menahem Man ben Barukh's name was in operation. Friedberg removed the incorrect information in the second edition of his book (Tel Aviv, 1950). On the information available to me the latest date of printing must be taken as the year when R. Menahem Man died, which is shown on the printer's gravestone as 5602, and therefore the period should be defined as 'between 5563 and 5602 [1803–42]'. See H. N. Maggid-Steinschneider, *Ir vilna* (Vilna, 1900), 200–3. Some books printed after his death do indeed show his name on the title-page, in the following form: 'Vilna, at the printing works of R. Menahem Man ben R. Barukh, may his memory be for a blessing, and R. Simhah Zimel ben R. Menahem Nahum, may his memory be for a blessing.' (The examples I have seen are: *Midrash rabah* with *Eshed haneḥalim*, 5603–5; *Mesilat yesharim*, 5604; *Devir*, 5604.) It seems probable, however, that a book which shows R. Menahem Man's name without that of his partner was printed during his lifetime. His name certainly continued to be printed until the death of his partner R. Simhah Zimel in 5605 [1845]. See Friedberg, *Toledot hadefus ha'ivri bepolonya* (Tel Aviv, 1950), 125–8.

[7] [A. L. Feinstein's] *Ir tehilah* (Warsaw, 1885), 32, numbers among the sages of Brest-Litovsk in the fifth century [evidently the century beginning 5501 (1740)—Trans.] 'the saintly rabbi, our teacher R. Elijah ben Israel, publisher of the book [called] *The Old Mesilat yesharim*'. Apparently this information came from a letter from R. Joseph Levinstein of Serotsk which said: 'Further, the title-page of *The Old Mesilat yesharim* carries the statement: "Published by

Ben-Menahem quoted a few lines, with some omissions), in which he said: 'I have found . . . some writings by the author [Luzzatto] . . . among them . . . the book *Pitḥei ḥokhmah* ['Gateways to Wisdom']', but because he could not afford to publish *Pitḥei ḥokhmah*, he decided to publish 'for the second time' *Mesilat yesharim* with the addition of *Derekh ets ḥayim*, in the hope that the profits would enable him 'to open up wisdom', i.e. to publish Luzzatto's '138 Gateways'.[8]

the humble hasid, the great rabbi, our teacher R. Elijah ben Israel, may his memory be for a blessing, of the holy congregation of Brisk of Lithuania"' (ibid. 163). It is hard to tell whether '*The Old Mesilat yesharim*' means the edition of 5526 or that of 5595, which I consider below. It appears to me that R. Levinstein had not himself seen the book, for he does not quote what the title-page goes on to say, namely that R. Elijah was the son-in-law of R. Nahman, rabbi of Brest-Litovsk (who is frequently mentioned in *Ir tehilah*). R. Noah Weintraub's book *Me'orei eliyahu* (Jerusalem, 1932), 3 n. 3, gives a genealogy which mentions 'the *gaon* our teacher Rabbi Eli[jah], may his memory be for a blessing, *av beit din* of the holy congregation of Kobrin, who was descended from the Shakh [Shabetai ben Meir Hakohen]', and it goes on to say: 'And the said *gaon* R. Eli[jah] was son-in-law of the holy rabbi, the *gaon* R. Nahman, *av beit din* of the holy congregation of Brisk.' This is a case of mistaken identity, for the father of R. Elijah of Kobrin (the R. Elijah who wrote *Mikhtav eliyahu* (Hamburg, 1715)) was named Aryeh Leib, and it is also clear from other considerations that these were two different persons.

[8] One of the traditions handed down in relation to the Vilna Gaon tells of his admiration for *Mesilat yesharim*: 'I heard from the great *gaon*, R. Eliezer Gordon (may his memory be for a blessing), who was *av beit din* and head of the yeshiva of Telz [Telšiai] in Lithuania, an oral tradition that when the book *Mesilat yesharim* was published, *its author being then no longer living*, and the Gra [the Gaon R. Elijah] read the words of that book, he said that a great light had shone out into the world, and he taught it orally a hundred and one times, and paid a substantial sum for that book' (R. Moses Rosenstein, *Yesodei hada'at*, i (Warsaw, 1935), 2; Rosenstein was an old pupil of R. Simhah Zisl of Kelme). This tradition, which comes from a reliable source, gives us reason to suppose that the edition of *Mesilat yesharim* read by the Gra was that of Zholkva 5526, the first to appear after Luzzatto's death. It may be that the 'substantial sum' he paid 'for the book' was given to help R. Elijah of Brisk to publish the '138 Gateways'. (The tradition is also quoted, with minor differences, and with the remark 'I heard this from great men', at the beginning of R. Isaac Malzan's foreword to Luzzatto's *Derekh hashem* (Jerusalem, 1914).) And see n. 132 below. The Gra had manuscripts of kabbalistic works by Luzzatto in his library, as is recorded on the title-page of Luzzatto's *Pitḥei ḥokhmah vada'at* (Warsaw, 1884): 'This has been published for the first time from a manuscript that was laid up in the manuscript collection of the saintly Gaon R. E[lijah] (may his memory be for a blessing) in Vilna.' And see B. Landau, *Hagaon heḥasid mivilna* (Jerusalem, 1967), 121–2 n. 30 and 179 n. 10. Another tradition relates: 'I heard that when the Gra, may his memory be for a blessing, obtained Luzzatto's writings on the *Id[ra] r[aba]*, he put on festival clothing in his honour and to mark the joyous occasion' (R. Isaac Malzan, foreword to *Derekh hashem*: see above). I see no reason to doubt the principal item of information in this report, namely that Luzzatto's commentary on *Idra raba* (see n. 19 below) was acquired by the Gra in manuscript. The position of the Gra and his pupils in regard to the teachings of kabbalah, and their attitude to messianic ideas and aims in general and to Luzzatto's messianic kabbalah in particular, are still *tabula rasa* so far as concerns scholarly research. Without clarification of these matters our picture of the Gra's personality and historical influence must remain defective.

The Zholkva edition of 5528 is quite different. There is no mention of the editor, R. Elijah of Brisk, on the title-page, which (referring to *Mesilat yesharim*) reads instead: 'And because its great usefulness and importance are not available [to the public], we have printed it [by a grammatical slip, the text reads 'we have been printed'] a second time in a small volume so that everyone can carry it in his pocket and study it at all times, and the earth will be full of knowledge and they will go up to Zion with joyful song.' The editor's introduction is omitted too, and after the words at the end of the first treatise 'And herewith the book *Mesilat yesharim* is concluded', which were undoubtedly in the Zholkva edition of 5526 also, the second treatise is added under the title *Sefer derekh ets haḥayim* ['The Book of the Way of the Tree of Life'], without any indication that it is an introduction to the '138 Gateways to Wisdom'. On the contrary, in the concluding remarks in Luzzatto's epilogue, which were printed at the end of the first edition of *Mesilat yesharim* (Amsterdam, 5500 [1740]) and here are placed after *Derekh ets ḥayim*,[9] a significant change is introduced. Whereas, in the original, Luzzatto of course speaks only of *Mesilat yesharim*, here we read: 'The author says: Now I will thank the Lord, I will sing praises [to Him] because His mercies have helped me until the present time to publish this my book *Mesilat yesharim and the book Derekh ets ḥayim* [Tishby emphasizes the phrase 'and . . . *ḥayim*'—Trans.], which I have composed for personal study' etc. The purpose of this spurious addition is clear: *Derekh ets ḥayim* is put forward as having been published together with *Mesilat yesharim* in 5500, during Luzzatto's lifetime.[10]

All the editions I have enumerated above which include *Derekh ets ḥayim*,[11] except for Shklov 5595 and the undated Vilna edition (on both of which I shall have more to say below), are in the same form as the Zholkva edition of

[9] The titles of both treatises were printed in large type.

[10] Eliezer [Leser] Rosenthal, who had the Zholkva edition of 5528 but knew nothing of Zholkva 5526, noted with surprise the addition of *Derekh ets ḥayim* with an epilogue by Luzzatto, and was equally surprised that 'the printer did not mention who composed this work and how it came into his hands'. The suspicions thus aroused, together with other suspicions he propounded with regard to the printing of the complete version of *Kela"ḥ pitḥei ḥokhmah* (Korets, 5545), led him by a strange train of thought, 'enlightened' as it were, to affirm that 'any eye that looks critically into the inwardness of this volume will see that these two books [*Derekh ets ḥayim* and *Kela"ḥ pitḥei ḥokhmah*] are not the work of R. Mosheh Hayim but that some Polish hasid borrowed a great man's name [to enhance the reputation of his own book]'. See M. Roest, *Catalog der Hebraica und Judaica aus der L. Rosenthalischen Bibliothek* (Amsterdam, 1875), ii, Hebrew appendix, 221, no. 1155. And see ibid. 349, no. 1790, on *Kela"ḥ pitḥei ḥokhmah*; and n. 46 below.

[11] As will be evident from n. 4 above, I have been unable to examine Zholkva 5530. In a copy of Zholkva 5542 which is in the possession of Mr Ben-Menahem and which I have inspected, the last pages are missing, and therefore I have not seen the text of the concluding words in Luzzatto's epilogue. On present information there is no reason to think that these editions

5528 in every respect I have mentioned, without any alteration. Similarly in the editions printed between 5528 and 5595 [1768–1835] without *Derekh ets ḥayim*—Lvov 5553; Poretsk 5576; Józefów 5587, 5595[12]—it is clear from the text of the title-pages that their archetype is Zholkva 5528. Only two reprints were published outside eastern Europe: Mantua 5541, Lunéville 5566. These were based on the Amsterdam first edition and were completely independent of Zholkva.

The Shklov editions of 5595 have an unexpected feature: the title-page records that the book was sent for printing by R. Elijah of Brisk, word for word as on the title-page of Zholkva 5526, even to the printer's mark. Between the title-page and Luzzatto's introduction there is another page headed 'Publisher's Foreword' which contains the extracts quoted by Ben-Menahem from the publisher's foreword in Zholkva 5526. On the page before the beginning of *Derekh ets ḥayim* there is another foreword by 'the publisher', with no separate heading, but above it, as at the top of all the other pages of the treatise, is the title 'Sefer derekh ets ḥayim' (or sometimes 'haḥayim').[13] It is clear to me that R. Elijah of Brisk's two forewords were printed here in the same form as in Zholkva 5526, and that if any material changes were made in them, which I think unlikely, they would have been by way of omission and not addition.[14] The Zholkva edition [of 5526—Trans.]

differ in any way from Zholkva 5528. In the copy of [Zholkva] 5569 in the National Library, Jerusalem, the last two pages, 61–2, have been torn out, and the same pages are missing from the copy in the library of Dr I. Mehlman in Jerusalem. In the copy in the Ben Tsevi Institute, Jerusalem, the two pages are torn and tattered and the greater part of them is missing, but from what is left I was able to establish that Luzzatto's epilogue was printed in the same version as in Zholkva 5528. The whole of the Shklov edition of 5555 is the same as Zholkva 5528 except that *Derekh ets ḥayim* is followed by the words: 'Ended and completed, praise be to God the Creator of the universe' and the colophon 'by the workman' etc. as noted in Ben-Menahem, *Kitvei rabi mosheh ḥayim lutsato*, 74; and the final words in Luzzatto's epilogue are absent. Prima facie one might conclude that the omission here represents the beginning of an intentional 'correction' of the Zholkva 5528 forgery, but such a conclusion would not be safe. The last page is full to the very last line, and there may have been a technical reason for omitting the words, namely in order not to have to add a page especially for them. [When [the Hebrew original of] this essay had already been set in type the National Library in Jerusalem received a photograph of a complete copy of Zholkva 5569 from the library of the Hebrew Union College, Cincinnati, and it has been confirmed that the text of the epilogue is the same as in Zholkva 5528.]

[12] Since *Derekh ets ḥayim* is not printed in these editions they end with the words 'And herewith the book *Mesilat yesharim* is completed', and the conclusion, with Luzzatto's epilogue, is dropped.

[13] The final words of Luzzatto's epilogue as printed here are of course the true version and do not have the added phrase 'and the book *Derekh ets ḥayim*'.

[14] Ben-Menahem, in his description of Zholkva 5526 in *Areshet*, did not point out that there was also a publisher's foreword at the beginning of *Derekh ets ḥayim*, nor did he mention the

may have contained letters of approval which were omitted in 5595.[15] Thus after seventy years a text was reprinted which, in its time, had been rejected and virtually lost without trace.

The undated Vilna edition has a character of its own. It differs both from Zholkva 5526/Shklov 5595 and from Zholkva 5528 and its offshoots, and has elements of each. The title-page is similar to that of Zholkva 5528 but is not identical: 'And because of its great usefulness and importance in the service of the Lord, previous [editions] have long been exhausted, and because many people are anxious to have access to it, we have reprinted it so that everyone who has the fear of the Lord in his heart may study it at all times and there may be fulfilled through us the verse "and the earth will be full of knowledge" [cf. Isa. 11: 9] and we may be privileged to go up to Zion with singing, amen *selah*.' There is no mention of the editor, R. Elijah of Brisk, and his first foreword is not there. But *Derekh ets ḥayim* is preceded in full by the same foreword as in Shklov 5595, minus his name, and the final words of Luzzatto's epilogue have been stripped of the spurious addition. It is clear that the editor of the undated Vilna edition deliberately took the odd decision to suppress R. Elijah of Brisk's name and remove his first foreword but put in his second foreword. If the Vilna edition was earlier than 5595, we have here a first step towards the reintroduction of the Zholkva version of 5526; if it was later, the Vilna edition represents a retreat from the revival of the complete Zholkva 5526 version.

In any event the Shklov 5595 version had no successor, whereas the 'mixed' version in the undated Vilna edition became the archetype of most of the editions which combined *Mesilat yesharim* with *Derekh ets ḥayim*. To mention only a few details: in the first three editions printed after that of Vilna,[16] the editor's foreword to *Derekh ets ḥayim* appeared in full just as in the Vilna edition, whereas the fourth one printed only [part of] the first sentence of

close correspondence between that edition and those of Shklov 5595. In *Kitvei rabi mosheh ḥayim lutsato*, however, he wrote (p. 77) that in Shklov 5595 there were 'a few words by the publisher' at the beginning of *Derekh ets ḥayim*, and also said that 'the publisher's foreword in these three Shklov editions had previously been printed in the Zholkva editions [*sic*: the singular was intended] I have noted above, p. 143 no. 252, and it may have been taken from an earlier edition' (ibid. 162). He meant Zholkva 5526, whose publication date he did not know at the time.

[15] In the years following the Frankist apostasy, people in Poland were careful not to print kabbalistic books, or ones which bordered on kabbalism, without rabbinic letters of approval. It is reasonable to assume that they would not have ignored this precaution when they sent to the printers a kabbalistic work by Luzzatto, who, in his time, was accused of Shabateanism and whose writings were placed under stringent bans. See pp. 414–20 below.

[16] The three editions are Zhitomir 5607 [1847] and two which lack publisher's name and year of publication (Königsberg, apparently between 5611 and 5618).

R. Elijah of Brisk's foreword: '. . . This is an introduction to *Sefer pitḥei ḥokhmah*, which is founded on the *Sefer ets haḥayim* of our teacher R. H[ayim] V[ital], may he be remembered for life in the world to come',[17] as if this were an introduction written by Luzzatto. Again and again since then, right up to the present, the printers have copied the undated Vilna edition, complete with the introduction to *Derekh ets ḥayim* written by the editor of Zholkva 5526. Thus the name of R. Elijah of Brisk, the man who took pains to reissue *Mesilat yesharim*, publish *Derekh ets ḥayim*, and add forewords to each, was expunged and forgotten; but his foreword to *Derekh ets ḥayim*, robbed of its author's name, was preserved and has been reprinted dozens of times. This unattributed foreword, proclaiming the extraordinary merits and holiness of Luzzatto and his doctrine, has been transmitted from generation to generation, as will be shown, but to this day no scholar has asked who and what sort of a man its author was, and what he meant by the words near the beginning: 'And I have already declared my purpose in the introductions [*sic*: the singular was intended]—that it is my wish to have the book printed in order to lead the public to virtue, to open the eyes of the blind.'

B. THE GENERAL ATTITUDE TO THE BANS ON LUZZATTO'S WRITINGS IN POLAND AND LITHUANIA

Before I turn to the identity of the editor-publisher of Zholkva 5526, his personality, and his motives, I must deal with some other questions which arise from my bibliographical researches in the previous section. What were the reasons for altering the Zholkva 5526 text to that of 5528? Why the return to the rejected text in 5595, after two generations? And why was that version

[17] See *Mesilat yesharim* (Lyck, 5618 [1858]), 41*b*. Clearly the publisher of this edition intentionally omitted all the rest of the foreword. Attention should be drawn here to an exceptional version of *Derekh ets ḥayim* now in the National Library in Jerusalem, to which it passed from the collection of M. Gaster. The copy in question consists of ten folios in a small format, and comprises only *Derekh ets ḥayim*, with no title-page, no publisher's foreword, and no pagination. It is possible, however, that R. Elijah of Brisk's foreword was printed at the beginning of the work and is missing from the copy we have. The pages are each headed 'Ets ḥayim'. From the style of the lettering it is clear that it was printed in eastern Europe. At the end of the work, which finishes on fo. 10^{r}, a misquotation has crept in which I have not found in any other edition: 'And

again displaced, retaining no more than a scrap of the foreword to *Derekh ets ḥayim*? In answering these questions we shall pass from the complexities of editions and editors to another complicated problem of great importance in the history of eighteenth-century Jewish religion and thought, namely the controversy over Luzzatto and its consequences, and we shall examine the attitude of Polish and Lithuanian Jewry to the proscribed works of that messianic kabbalist during the early years of hasidism.

All the evidence points clearly to the fact that the transition from the 5526 version to that of 5528 was not the result of a voluntary decision by the publishers but was forced by a ban imposed by a Jewish censorship body. We do not know who the Jewish censors were but clearly their reasons for disqualifying the 5526 version arise from the content of R. Elijah of Brisk's forewords. I set out and explain below the main points in these forewords.

1. Praise of Luzzatto's writings and his doctrine

There is no proper worship of God without knowledge of the wisdom of kabbalah, 'and my tongue will utter truth, for I have turned my heart to those who have understanding, and wisdom is not found [among them] and they do not understand its secret as it really is, for the Ari [Luria], may he be remembered for life in the world to come, clothed these matters in several garments, and the student must remove the covering from the words spoken in the language of allegory'. There is a risk, therefore, that anyone studying Lurianic kabbalah will fall into the error of materialization. But now he has found guidance to the true understanding of Luria's kabbalah in the writings of Luzzatto which have come into his possession:

> I have found that which my soul loves, writings by the rabbi-author, may he be remembered for life in the world to come, and among them I have found the book

when you have become fluent in the aforesaid 138 gateways of *enlightenment*' (instead of 'wisdom'). On fo. 10v there is a paragraph printed in characters squarer and larger than those in the main body of the treatise. I will quote the words of the conclusion, omitting most of the scriptural verses: 'Let trust in the Lord, blessed be He, and hope in Him not depart from the heart of man . . . and according to the greatness of his fear, he will add strength to his trust . . . *and our opening remarks have already enlightened us as to the mitsvah of fear and service* . . . for remembrance leads to performance . . . and because of this Elijah the prophet will come . . . therefore each of us should remind his brother and his neighbour of the words of the Torah of our God, and all Israel are responsible for each other, as it was said: "Each man helps his neighbour, and says to his brother: Be strong" [Isa. 41: 6]. Ended and completed, praise be to God, the Creator of the world.' Clearly this paragraph is presented as if it were written by Luzzatto to form his conclusion to *Derekh ets ḥayim*. It may be that, in this version also, *Derekh ets ḥayim* was printed as an appendix to *Mesilat yesharim*, and that 'our opening remarks' means Luzzatto's introduction to *Mesilat yesharim*.

Pitḥei ḥokhmah ['Gateways to Wisdom'], which is a commentary on R. H[ayim] V[ital]'s *Ets ḥaḥayim* and in which he explains each matter separately . . . All of the aforesaid [the mystery of the *yiḥud* and the mystery of evil] you will understand from his book clearly and not in riddles, you will understand the allegory of the ancients, the words of the Ari and his disciples.[18]

In other words, the only key to the thorough understanding of the 'science of truth' is contained in the kabbalistic works of Luzzatto. The writer only mentions *Pitḥei ḥokhmah* explicitly, but his allusion to 'writings' in the plural shows that he had a number of Luzzatto's treatises, and he makes a passing reference to one other, the commentary on *Idra raba* which was later published under the title *Adir bamarom* (Warsaw, 1886): 'And see *Id*[*ra*] *r*[*aba*], the commentary of the rabbi-author.'[19]

2. Information on the exalted personal merit of Luzzatto and how his doctrine was founded on revelations from on high

For as for this man MOSES, **we know what became of him** [a play on Exod. 32: 1—Trans.], **for Elijah (may he be remembered for life in the world to come) revealed himself to him at all times, and each and every matter was expounded**

[18] *Mesilat yesharim* (Shklov, 1834), first foreword, 2*a*–*b*. Where the text of a parallel edition is superior, I use it without comment. (Wherever italic is used for emphasis in a quotation, throughout this essay, the emphasis is mine; all quoted words in larger letters [here represented by small capitals—Trans.] or in bold type are as in the original.)

[19] Ibid. 2*a*. The commentary on *Idra raba* was composed in Italy in 5491 [1731], and not in 1740 or thereabouts as G. Scholem supposed in *Bibliographia Cabbalistica* (Berlin, 1933), 200, no. 62, before the letters in *R' mosheh ḥayim lutsato uvenei doro: osef igerot ute'udot*, ed. S. Ginzburg [hereafter *Igerot*] (Tel Aviv, 1937) were published. See *Igerot*, ii. 230, 231, 399. *Adir bamarom* as printed has the following parenthesis at the top of p. 21: '(The beginning of the book, up to this point, was printed in Pressburg in 5633 [1873], and is in everybody's hands.)' I have found no mention of the existence of this first publication in bibliographies, nor do they address themselves to the remark I have quoted. Before the end of the fragment printed in Pressburg (*Adir bamarom*, 19–20) there is a passage which affords an ideological basis in kabbalah for the exalted mission of mystical groups—in Luzzatto's words, 'assemblies for the sake of Heaven'—which are founded on a covenant among their members, in the mystery of the sefirah Yesod, 'for a covenant is a binding together of those who make it and Yesod is the covenant'. They operate within a fixed organizational framework, 'establishing a perfect bond with each other'. I therefore imagine that the source of this fragment was a copy, made in one of the groups led by R. Jekutiel of Vilna which I consider in Section C below (see pp. 426–33), which found its way to Pressburg (or to an editor in Vienna who had it printed in Pressburg) and was published there long after it was written. It is probable that the few pages in question were not printed as a separate booklet but were appended to another book which was 'in everybody's hands'. To date, my efforts to trace this have been unsuccessful. And see nn. 47 and 132 below.

by Moses according to [the four methods known by the acronym] ***parde"s*****,**[20] **as is known to students of** THE TORAH OF MOSES;[21]

All his words are the words of the Holy Spirit, and I have reliable testimony from *geonim* [senior rabbinic authorities] of the holy congregation of Amsterdam that from the days of Moses until Moses none has arisen like Moses.[22]

Clearly, in mentioning the appearances of Elijah and referring to the Holy Spirit the writer discreetly avoided direct reference to the revelations of the *magid* whose words Luzzatto wrote down in his treatises. The larger letters used to emphasize 'Moses' and 'the Torah of Moses', and the terms of the extravagant praise said to have been bestowed by the sages of Amsterdam, were meant to be understood as allusions to the embodiment of the biblical Moses in Luzzatto.[23]

3. Denunciation of Luzzatto's accusers and argument in his defence

When I saw members of our people who spoke insolently against the righteous, with pride and arrogance, saying: 'Was it only with Moses that the Lord spoke? Surely the Torah was given to us too, to expound in forty-nine ways [*Bamidbar rabah*

[20] I. Sonne discovered, in manuscript, part of R. Moses David Valle's memorial eulogy on Luzzatto, and in his essay 'Avnei binyan (te'udot leḥeker ramḥa"l veḥugo)', *American Jewish Yearbook* (New York, 1935), 218–25, he published that fragment in Hebrew translation from the Italian, with some omissions. [As to its authorship, however, see Essay 6, n. 76.—Trans.] (Sonne remarked that 'the document is in a collection of various pieces attributed to Valle, without chapter and verse, including various extracts from homiletic and ethical writings in Hebrew and Italian' ('Avnei binyan', 219); but among the manuscripts he left, which are now in the Ben Tsevi Institute, Jerusalem, there are only the folios of the fragmentary eulogy. The complete collection may possibly still be found somewhere.) The eulogy states: 'There are four methods of interpretation altogether, and commentators on Scripture made a mnemonic of the initials of these: *parde"s* [*peshat*, *remez*, *derush*, *sod*—plain sense, allusion, homily, esoteric meaning]. The excellent rabbi [Luzzatto] was prepared to interpret any saying about which he was asked by [all] the four methods mentioned' (ibid. 221). Hence R. Elijah of Brisk was referring to the oral teaching methods used by Luzzatto in his school in Padua, and the words which follow ('. . . as is [or 'was'] known to students of the Torah of Moses') actually relate to Luzzatto's pupils, regarding whose studies R. Elijah had information from a reliable source, as explained at pp. 426–8, 439 below. In my opinion the wording and content of the eulogy show that it was delivered before a large audience in Padua, contrary to Sonne's view ('Avnei binyan', 223 n. 29) that it 'took place in Luzzatto's school in the circle of his friends and pupils'. The eulogy does indeed have some important things to tell us about the arrangements for study and the practices followed in Luzzatto's school. But the conclusions which may properly be founded on the eulogy are the reverse of those of Sonne, who sought, by tendentious interpretation of Valle's description, to show that Luzzatto's school was fundamentally the same as other *batei midrash* ['houses of study'] in Italy, that 'his [Luzzatto's] general "teaching" on all weekdays was entirely based on the revealed [Torah]—halakhah and ethics—and *only on the Sabbath did he establish a place for esoteric study* for his friends' (ibid. 220). These and similar remarks are far removed from the true spiritual character of Luzzatto and the members of his group.

[21] *Mesilat yesharim* (Shklov, 1834), first foreword, 2*b*.

[22] Ibid., second foreword, 52*b*.

[23] See I. Tishby, *Netivei emunah uminut* (Ramat Gan, 1964), 186–94.

2: 3] and to explain it like him', I determined to offer something from the Torah of Moses, namely the above-mentioned *Derekh ets ḥayim*, from which the children of Israel would acquire instruction in the knowledge of the truth, for not so is [the] servant [sc. 'of the Lord'] Moses, for in all he is trusted;[24] he conceals two handbreadths and reveals one handbreadth, all his words are the words of the Holy Spirit . . . And now, you children of Israel, do not say, concerning everything the people say, that it is right because a surpassing spirit is in them;[25] in it [in controversy] our fathers and forefathers stumbled, and because of it our city was destroyed, yet still Satan dances among us, dividing our hearts; and each man asserts his authority over his neighbour, saying: 'I will rule', and every day they cry 'Give, give'.[26]

The author of the forewords himself adopted the practice of 'revealing one handbreadth and concealing two'. On the face of it the accusers' allegations are reduced to the fact that they are not prepared to acknowledge the supreme greatness of Luzzatto. But it is evident that the lips which [as in Ps. 31: 19—Trans.] 'spoke insolently against the righteous' slandered Luzzatto and rejected his writings and his doctrine as heretical. There is no doubt that the remarks in the forewords were also directed against accusations in R. Elijah of Brisk's own time and place.

4. The distribution of Luzzatto's writings to end the controversy and hasten the Redemption

And I said in my heart: When will I create a lasting reputation for him in Israel by spreading his thoughts among the public so that the earth will be full of knowledge. And even though I cannot afford it [literally 'the bundle of money is not in my sack': see Gen. 42: 35], I have therefore thought it right to print this book [*Mesilat yesharim*] a second time . . . And now, our brethren, O children of Israel, know of a certainty that I have taken a vow that all the profit which falls to my lot—its fruit will be holy, so that no extraneous matters shall be mixed with the rejoicing it occasions but [it will be used] only to open up wisdom and instruction for His holy people. And thus we shall be privileged to see His holy house and the earth will be full of knowledge, [as] it is said: 'For then He will turn all the peoples' etc.; and it is said: 'On that day the Lord will be One and His name One', amen, may it be His will.[27]

No man has taken to heart why it is that the harvest is past, the summer is ended, and we have not been saved, and there is never a day whose curse is not greater than

[24] Varied from Num. 12: 7: 'Not so [i.e. not like other prophets] is my servant Moses; in all my house he is trusted.'

[25] Adapted from Isa. 8: 12 ('Do not call conspiracy all that this people call conspiracy') and Dan. 6: 4. He means that the charge of conspiracy (or treason) against Luzzatto by 'the people', i.e. by his opponents, is rooted in their pride and arrogance.

[26] *Mesilat yesharim*, second foreword, 52*b*.

[27] Ibid., first foreword, 2*b*. ['For then He will turn all the peoples . . .' is a misquotation of Zeph. 3: 9, which reads literally: 'For then I will turn to the peoples a pure lip', i.e. God will make their speech pure.—Trans.]

the curse of the day before, and there has arisen upon us all the groaning[28] of which the prophets spoke, and there has been no cure for our wound . . . My intention has been to make known to everyone the words of this little book [*Derekh ets ḥayim*] and create a reputation for it[29] like that of the greatest ones in the land; perhaps in this way we may succeed in straightening the crookedness hidden among us, such as baseless hatred and all that derives from it. May it be His will to fulfil in us the verse spoken by the prophet: Ephraim will not envy Judah etc. And it is said: The children of Judah and the children of Israel will be gathered together and will appoint one head for themselves. And it is said: On that day the Lord will be One and His name One; amen, may it be His will, speedily in our days, amen.[30]

In my opinion the messianic note on which the two forewords conclude is not a mere matter of form but has real significance. It reflects the stirring of messianism in the minds and actions of Luzzatto and his circle: the propagation of Luzzatto's holy writings to explain and spread the light of kabbalah would help to hasten the Redemption.

*

For a proper appreciation of R. Elijah of Brisk's daring in expressing himself as he did, we must examine the general attitude to Luzzatto and his writings at the time of the edicts of excommunication against him, in 5495–6 [1735–6] and the years which followed.

The bans, which were aimed mainly at preventing the distribution and printing of the 'sectarian' writings, were imposed not only on the 'heretic' and 'criminal transgressor' 'the wicked M.H.L., may his spirit and soul perish', but on anyone who helped him to print his writings or studied them or kept them in his possession. The general edict of excommunication by the sages of Ashkenaz and Poland which was published to the Jewish community said:

The decree has been issued by the [rabbinical] court of justice to all the congregation of Israel wherever they live, that there shall not be seen or found among them a Jew or Jewess who has the presumption to assist the said criminal transgressor to print any one of his books or writings of any kind whatsoever . . . nor [shall any] give support to miscreants who study his books or writings of any kind whatsoever . . . And furthermore, that all his books, his writings, his poems and songs [or 'psalms'], in sum, all his compositions of any kind whatsoever, shall be treated as the books of infidels and heretics which, as well as any mention of them, are destroyed by burning, so shall all these words of his be condemned to be consumed by fire, so that no Jew shall stumble because of them today or ever . . . And any man who is so presumptuous as to disobey, let him fall into pits, never to rise, and into

[28] Another version reads 'the signs' [*ha'otot*] instead of 'all the groaning' [*kol ha'anaḥot*].

[29] Perhaps this is intended to apply not only to the book but also to Luzzatto. [The Hebrew could be read, without alteration, as 'for him'.—Trans.]

[30] *Mesilat yesharim*, second foreword, 52*b*.

the nets of the great and terrible excommunications decreed by the shields of the earth and the outstanding men of our generation.[31]

Of those who were personally responsible for the excommunications, one who was outstanding for his inquisitorial zeal was R. Aryeh Leib [Loewenstamm], 'who resides at present in the holy congregation of Glogau, and whose influence extends as far as the holy congregation of Lvov and district',[32] who decreed 'that assemblies be assembled [i.e. that public meetings be held] . . . and that the decree be announced in all the provinces of Poland on every eve of New Moon, to excommunicate, banish, set apart, and separate this heretic and his disciples and his retinue of evildoers and his faction from all the holiness of Israel, and all his books and writings shall be condemned to be burnt as the books of sectarians [*minim*] and sorcerers'.[33] Apparently he did not succeed in putting his design into execution even for a short time, because many important rabbis in Poland and Lithuania were not happy with the persecution of Luzzatto and the banning of his writings, and it is noteworthy that the Luzzatto controversy was never considered in the Council of the Four Lands.[34] On the other hand it should be pointed out that, in contrast to the Hayun controversy of earlier times and the Eybeschuetz controversy which came later, in Luzzatto's case not a single rabbi stood up to defend him in public, still less did anyone issue decrees to counter the excommunications.[35] Even in Italy the dispute was limited to one

[31] *Igerot*, ii. 326–7. ['Nets' (*rishtot-*): a play on the two meanings of *ḥerem*, 'excommunication' and 'net'. 'Shields of the earth': Ps. 47: 10.—Trans.]

[32] Brother-in-law of R. Jacob Emden. In 1740 he was appointed rabbi of Amsterdam.

[33] *Igerot*, ii. 310. I will quote another example from the excommunication signed by two rabbinical emissaries from Safed who, relying on the authority of R. Eleazar of Brody, wrote that that celebrated rabbi and his court 'made a decree excommunicating HM"L [*sic*], his books, and all his writings, to the end that they be not brought to mind or remembered among the congregation of Israel, and that they be condemned as is appropriate for the books of sectarians; and imposed a strict decree of excommunication on anyone who studies or possesses any book or writing written by this heretic [*apikoros*] HM"L . . . and they added force to their words by determining with all severity that the writings and books of the said HM"L be not remembered or brought to mind among the congregation of Israel, now or ever, and they imposed a duty on anyone who has any of them to execute the sentence of burning them and remove them from the world, leaving no way open by which he might be allowed to retain them' (ibid. 316). This document is full of the most virulent curses and imprecations.

[34] See *Pinkas va'ad arba aratsot*, ed. I. Halpern (Jerusalem, 1945), 509, no. 980.

[35] One of the reasons for this surprising state of affairs was that whereas Hayun and Eybeschuetz defended themselves vigorously, Luzzatto, from the time of his arrival in Amsterdam in the autumn of 1734, imposed on himself an outward attitude of complete submission, and bore the curses and imprecations hurled at him with silent contempt. See *Igerot*, ii. 299–300, 303–5, 323–5, 358. The 'kindest' remark by Luzzatto's persecutors during their campaign against him appears in a letter from R. Jacob Hakohen Poppers of Frankfurt am Main to R. Samson Morpurgo in Ancona. He writes that if the box of banned writings is sent to his

'procedural' point: those who took the stricter view demanded that the writings be burnt, the more lenient would be satisfied with putting them beyond reach in a genizah or burying them.[36]

And yet during his time in Amsterdam (1734–43) Luzzatto earned respect, repute, and great admiration among the Sephardi community, and no one in any Jewish congregation anywhere uttered a word against the new books he wrote and published in Amsterdam before he left for the Land of Israel: *Mesilat yesharim* (5500 [1740]), *Derekh tevunot* (5502), *Layesharim tehilah* (5503). Even R. Jacob Emden, who was unsparing in his castigation of Luzzatto, said of the last years of his life: 'From then on [from the time of his arrival in Amsterdam] we heard nothing from him that was bad, and he published two small treatises which he had written, *Mesilat yesharim* and *Derekh tevunot*, with which I could find no fault.'[37] It would be a mistake, however, to think that this tolerant attitude applied retrospectively to the works written before 1734, or indeed that there was any change in the prohibitions on writings which Luzzatto ascribed to the revelations of the *magid*. There is no mention of either withdrawal or relaxation of the bans.[38] Emden, having

court 'to peruse them and debate to what [fate] they should be sentenced, whether burning or burial in waste ground, so that they shall never be remembered or brought to mind, then certainly the land, God willing, will be at peace, with no cry of distress and no breach, in such a way that if HM"L conducts himself from now on in the way of uprightness and there are no longer heard from him any of the things he said previously, and he fulfils the oath he swore before me and a properly constituted court of this place, then he will be at rest and the world will be at rest, and [he] will not again go out [= stray] through obstacles and stumbling-blocks, and the crooked heart will depart from us, and [He] will give truth to Jacob' (ibid. 393). Even bittersweet words such as these, which were intended to pacify the uneasy feelings of 'moderate' Italian rabbis like R. Samson Morpurgo, evoked complaints on the part of R. Moses Hagiz and the rabbis of Venice. See ibid. 394–8.

[36] See ibid. 329, 332–3, 335, 342–3, 344, 348–9, 365, 385, 388–90, 421.

[37] R. Jacob Emden, *Zot torat hakenaot* [hereafter *Torat hakenaot*] (Altona, 1752), 57*b*.

[38] It is only in Luzzatto's letter of Marheshvan 5496 [autumn 1735] to his pupils in Padua that we learn in so many words of his own dismissal of the bans: 'Let not your hearts fall because of all those who taunt and revile, and do not draw up battle lines against them, for all their curses are less than nothing, and are accounted as worthless. They may curse—and God the Most High will bless, *and every ḥerem and every niduy and every curse is permitted you, forgiven you, allowed you*' (*Igerot*, ii. 323). Apparently, in Luzzatto's *beit midrash* ['house of study'] and in the circles of Luzzatto's pupils and admirers elsewhere in Italy, the excommunications were regarded from the first as wicked libels—as witness the originals and the numerous copies of Luzzatto's writings which were preserved in spite of the bans and hyperboles of the Venetian rabbis (see ibid. 276, 327–30). It is true that at the height of the controversy, on 8 Av 5495 [summer 1735], R. Jacob Hazak told R. Isaiah Bassano: 'My Witness is in Heaven—in the heights is my Witness—that from the day our honoured teacher and rabbi, R. Moses Hayim, went away, neither I nor my friends of my own age (being his pupils who learnt "the science of truth" from him) any longer study his writings . . . for our honoured teacher and rabbi aforesaid collected and gathered to himself all the writings, and the *beit midrash* was emptied of all the books . . .

made the favourable comment on Luzzatto quoted above, goes on to say: 'It is quite evident that there was great heresy [*minut*] in Luzzatto's heart, and it struck evil roots in this world',[39] and he expresses severe criticism of Luzzatto in several other places, both on the strength of his own opinion and as conveyed in letters and information received.[40] Luzzatto's pupils and admirers in Amsterdam had in their possession several compositions by him on various topics, but not until 1783 did they publish four small works: *Derekh ḥokhmah*, *Ma'amar al hahagadot*, *Ma'amar ha'ikarim*, and *Ma'amar haḥokhmah: or haganuz*, of which only the last-named ['Wisdom: The Hidden Light'] was truly kabbalistic.[41] The rabbis who wrote the letters of approval, and the publisher too, were lavish in their praise of the author, and slipped into their comments some dark allusions to the controversy and the suppression of Luzzatto's writings,[42] but they did not dare come out into the open to defend him and denounce his persecutors.

[but] of this we have kept hold, and with the Lord's help we have not let it go: to study the plain text of the book of the Zohar, the holy of holies, in a voice which never ceases [an expression borrowed from *Mo'ed katan* 18*b*—Trans.]' (ibid. 301–2; and see ibid. 321, 416). One must question how far this declaration corresponds to reality; at any rate it is not to be supposed that the members of the group in Padua refrained from studying Luzzatto's kabbalistic writings for very long.

39 *Torat hakenaot*, 58*a*.

40 See ibid. 63*a*; *Sefat emet uleshon zehorit* (1752), [19]*b*; *Akitsat akrav* (1753?), 17*a*; *Aspaklaryah hame'irah* (appendix to *Sefat emet uleshon zehorit* (Lvov, 1877)), 96*a* (first printed 1752); *Edut beya'akov* (1756), 42*b*, 68*b*; *Shevirat luḥot ha'aven* (1756), 40*b*; *Sefer shimush* (1758–62?), 68*a*; *Beit yehonatan hasofer* (1763?), 6*a*; *Hitabekut* (1762–9), 84*b*. I have given the dates of printing as in Y. Raphael, 'Kitvei rabi ya'akov emden', *Areshet*, 3 (1961), 231–76.

41 *Ma'amar haḥokhmah* is one of the works based on the revelations of the *magid*. See *Igerot*, i. 31, 102, 114.

42 See the letters of approval [*haskamot*] by R. David Hakohen d'Azevedo and R. Abraham Toviana, the publisher's foreword, and *Zimrat ha'ara"sh* by David Franco Mendes. R. Saul, rabbi of the Ashkenazi community in Amsterdam, also gave his approval to the printing of the treatises, and wrote at the beginning of his *haskamah*: 'I remember that when I was in the land of my birth [Poland] in my young days, there rose the sun of the scholar, the celebrated rabbi, our teacher, Rabbi Moses Hayim Luzzatto, may his memory be for a blessing; he shone forth in his country, the land of Italy, and *we heard in our country, too, that the man Moses was very great and excelled in everything*. And later, when I came here, I heard of his might from great sages and scholars who knew him, how great was his strength for Torah, his heart like the heart of a lion [a pun on 'Ari'] in *gemara* and reasoning, sharp in debate and widely read, and, moreover, excelling in every branch of learning and knowledge, and was above all of us with [regard to] the paths of the Merciful One among the reapers of the field. He entered the *pardes* [engaged in esoteric philosophy] and came out unscathed [*Ḥag.* 14*b*].' R. Saul was born in 1717, and his father was R. Aryeh Leib of Glogau (one of the leading scholars of Poland), who issued a *ḥerem* [decree of excommunication] against Luzzatto in the sharpest terms, and heaped scorn upon him (see pp. 416–17 above). When R. Aryeh Leib died in 1755, R. Saul was invited to Amsterdam to succeed him. The testimony of R. Saul that in his young days Luzzatto gained a great reputation in Poland was an attempt to extinguish the memory of past events by denying the truth. There were even efforts to reconcile his declaration with the facts by saying that his

In 5526 [1766] R. Elijah of Brisk naively thought—and so, certainly, did the printers in Zholkva[43]—that, with the lapse of thirty years since Luzzatto's writings were banned, the time had come to right what he and they saw as a wrong by glorifying the personality and activities of Luzzatto and publishing his brilliant writings on kabbalah. But his great admiration for Luzzatto blinded him to the true situation. Contemporaries of his, men unknown to us but influential in their time, were unhappy about the printing of Luzzatto's kabbalistic works, and learnt with displeasure of R. Elijah of Brisk's intention to publish the '138 Gateways to Wisdom'; still less were they ready to entertain his description of the excommunicated kabbalist as a man of God. As a result of this opposition the printers were forced to put away R. Elijah of Brisk's edition, with the forewords in which he sought to inspire others with his own enthusiasm; and, as they were unwilling to drop the publication of *Derekh ets ḥayim*, they had to hide its true nature and falsely present it to the public as having been printed as an appendix to *Mesilat yesharim* in 5500 [1740] and distributed ever since without complaint. Thus the first attempt to rehabilitate Luzzatto and his kabbalistic writings, and lend sanctity to his name and his doctrine, foundered and was forgotten.

These conclusions from the disappearance of the 5526 Zholkva edition of *Mesilat yesharim* receive strong support from another quarter. In 5545 [1785] a second attempt was made, in line with R. Elijah of Brisk's intention and supported by a direct quotation from his remarks. In that year the '138 Gateways to Wisdom' was published, with letters of approval from R. Moses Yom Tov, '*dayan* [judge in the rabbinical court] of the holy congregation of Korets', and R. Jacob Joseph, '*magid* of the holy congregation of Ostrog', author of *Rav Yeivi* and one of the disciples of the Maggid of Mezhirech. The publisher, R. Gedaliah ben Elyakum of Korets,[44] at the beginning of his foreword, reproduced a passage in praise of Luzzatto from R. Elijah of Brisk's first foreword, without mentioning R. Elijah's name: 'Behold, I desired truth with my innermost being [cf. Ps. 51: 8], and by painstaking search I have found the words of a holy mouth, a godly man, this man Moses, we know what became of him, because Elijah revealed himself to him at all times, and each and every matter was expounded by Moses by *parde"s* [see n. 20 above],

memory of his early days related to the years before the turmoil and excommunications of 1735. This concealment of the truth, or blurring of the facts, should anyway be understood as prompted by concern for communal harmony.

[43] In 5494 [1734] they had been preparing to print the Zohar, with Luzzatto's *magid*-inspired commentary, in Zholkva (or Kraków). See *Igerot*, ii. 264, 270. I propose to deal with this in another essay continuing my account of the dissemination of Luzzatto's writings.

[44] In 5541 [1781], jointly with R. Abraham ben Yitshak Eisik, he published R. Eisik Tyrnau's *Sefer minhagim* ['Book of Customs'] in Korets. See A. Tauber, *Meḥkarim bibliografiyim* (Jerusalem, 1932), 22–3, no. 8. I have been unable to find the book.

as is written in the introduction to his book Mesilat yesharim.' He then quoted the following testimony:

When I heard from his [R. Joseph Jacob of Ostrog's] own mouth, and not from anything he had written, that he heard from a holy mouth, a holy light [a hasidic rabbi], whose soul is in the treasuries on high, I mean our honoured guide and rabbi Dov the *magid* of the holy congregation of Mezhirech, who said of this author that his generation was not worthy to understand his righteousness and asceticism, and therefore many of our people, out of their great lack of knowledge, spoke insolently against the righteous, which is against the law—see how great a man testifies [in his favour], namely the said rabbi whose reputation reaches [here] from afar, and greater are the righteous in their death etc. [*Ḥul.* 54*a*: 'Greater . . . than in their lifetime']. And he is an authority worthy of our trust, *and let the voices cease.*

R. Gedaliah now turns back to R. Elijah of Brisk, and this time he quotes a passage from R. Elijah's second foreword: 'For not so is Moses my servant, in all My house he is trusted,[45] *as is written in his book in the printer's foreword to Derekh ets ḥayim*, where it says: "I have reliable testimony from *geonim* of the holy congregation of Amsterdam that from the days of Moses until Moses none has arisen like Moses. And now, you children of Israel, do not say, concerning everything this people say," etc.' He goes on to quote the words of R. Elijah with alterations and additions. The main addition is of great interest: 'The man Moses was very humble, more than any man etc., and therefore he himself did not send any of his writings to be printed; this work was done for him by others who were eager for his words, the words of the living God; all his words are the Holy Spirit, and *it is not by human intellect that they must be understood but only by faith, faith in the wise*, whose words are all coals of fire, and beware lest you be burnt etc. [*Avot* 2: 10].'

This foreword by a man who, as well as being a hasid of the Maggid of Mezhirech and of one of the Maggid's disciples, was also an enthusiastic admirer of Luzzatto, shows that even in 5545 [1785] voices were still being raised against Luzzatto. R. Gedaliah sought to silence them—'Let the voices cease'—and add lustre to Luzzatto's name by the use of favourable remarks taken from R. Elijah of Brisk's forewords and by quoting the Maggid of Mezhirech's praise of Luzzatto's great eminence and the Maggid's denunciation of Luzzatto's vilifiers. On the other hand he tried to mask the severity of the opposition to Luzzatto by falsifying the facts, saying that it was because of his great humility that 'he himself did not send any of his writings to be printed', and not because the sages of his generation condemned them

[45] Here 'my servant' as in Num. 12: 7. In *Mesilat yesharim* (Shklov, 5595) the text varies from Scripture: 'For not so is [the] servant Moses, for in all he is trusted.' See above, text referring to n. 24, and the note itself.

to be destroyed. Finally he called for Luzzatto's writings and doctrine to be accepted 'by faith, faith in the wise', a requirement which is common in hasidic literature in relation to the doctrine and practices of the tsadikim. R. Gedaliah said nothing about the source of the manuscript which he had sent to be printed.[46] But on the basis of the strong link between his foreword and the forewords to *Mesilat yesharim* and *Derekh ets ḥayim* in the Zholkva edition of 5526, it is to be supposed that the manuscript possessed by R. Elijah of Brisk and prepared for publication by him, or a copy of that manuscript, is the one published in Korets in 5545.[47]

Similarly R. Jacob Joseph of Ostrog, in his letter of approval, expresses the greatest admiration for Luzzatto and his writings, especially *Kela"ḥ pitḥei ḥokhmah*, and he, too, uses the words of R. Elijah of Brisk to support his views:

And it was also with Moses that the Lord spoke 138 gateways to wisdom, which are the openings to the holy book *Ets ḥayim* by the Ari, may he be remembered for a bless-

[46] E. Rosenthal, in a Hebrew appendix to M. Roest's catalogue of his collection (*Catalog der Hebraica und Judaica*, ii. 349, no. 1790), remarked that 'neither the printer [the publisher, R. Gedaliah] nor the writers of the *haskamot* ['letters of approval'] said anything to us about how the manuscripts came into their hands', and came to the conclusion that the whole book was a hasidic forgery purporting to be by Luzzatto. See n. 10 above.

[47] It should be pointed out that the writers of the letters of approval, and the editor too, entirely ignored Luzzatto's statement at the end of *Derekh ets ḥayim* that this book was based on a text which he found 'in an ancient document *Kela"ḥ pitḥei ḥokhmah*', and from the tone of their remarks it is apparent that they regarded the whole book as Luzzatto's own work. This is true also of the allusions by R. Elijah of Brisk mentioned at p. 412 above. Their assumption was undoubtedly correct, and the question is: what prompted Luzzatto to take the uncharacteristic step of inventing a story about 'an ancient manuscript' and disguising his own original thoughts as a commentary on an ancient text? The answer is to be found in an argument used by Luzzatto in letters to his teacher, R. Isaiah Bassano, early in 5491 [autumn 1730], shortly after his capitulation at the end of 5490 (see *Igerot*, i. 176–7; ii. 410–11): 'The truth is that with regard to commentaries I am not bound by my oath at all, but only with regard to new compositions . . . for truly whatever is not a new composition but a commentary on the words of the ancients is not subject to any prohibition whatever' (ibid. ii. 222; and see ibid. 219, 221–2, 222–3), so that in asking his teacher to approve the distribution of copies of commentaries, he was not in breach of his obligation. In other words, he had to invent 'an ancient document' in order to legitimize the book and permit its circulation. The same point arose in connection with the commentary on *Idra raba* (see nn. 19 above and 132 below) and led to some tension between Luzzatto and his teacher when Luzzatto sought permission to deliver a copy of it to his father-in-law, R. David Finzi, and Bassano was reluctant to give his consent (see *Igerot*, ii. 230, 231–2). In my opinion that book too is, for the most part, really a treatise dressed up as a commentary: around phrases or short sentences from the Zohar are arrayed many pages of exposition, and sometimes there is no connection between the 'exposition' and the alleged 'source'. The documents prove, in my opinion, that Luzzatto regarded the undertaking he gave in Padua as of questionable validity because he had signed it under duress, so that it was permissible to find ways round it, or even contravene it if there was no alternative. The same attitude to his undertaking was adopted by the members of his group.

ing, *and there has already been printed, at the end of the book Mesilat yesharim* [in the editor's foreword to *Derekh ets ḥayim* in the edition of 5526], [a tribute to] the nature, quality, and great virtues of the book, [*words*] *which in part issued from the mouth of a holy one, Moses spoke them from his own mouth*[48] with kindly intent to [open the ways] into the profundities of the book *Ets ḥayim* by the Ari, may his memory be for a blessing, and he brought them out by 138 [gateways] by this path to explain deep secrets . . . and all these were done by his hand, *and all these were the word of the Lord.*

On the face of it the expressions 'it was also with Moses that the Lord spoke' and 'all these were the word of the Lord' are simply rhetorical. But it seems to me that the obscure words 'which in part issued from the mouth of a holy one, Moses spoke them from his own mouth' should be taken as an allusion to the *magid*'s revelations to Luzzatto; if so, this would mean that R. Jacob Joseph of Ostrog regarded the '138 Gateways to Wisdom' as a work dictated or inspired by the *magid*; and the expressions 'it was also with Moses that the Lord spoke' and 'the word of the Lord' should be understood in that context. It is probable, too, that the Maggid of Mezhirech's declaration relayed by R. Jacob Joseph of Ostrog is connected with R. Elijah of Brisk's forewords: the expression 'and therefore many of our people, out of their great lack of knowledge, spoke insolently against the righteous, which is against the law' sounds like a paraphrase of the foreword to *Derekh ets ḥayim*: 'When I saw members of our people who spoke insolently against the righteous, with pride and arrogance'.

The second stage of the attempts to end the aspersions against Luzzatto and reinstate him as a 'godly kabbalist' ended in partial success. The '138 Gateways' was distributed and continued in circulation without giving rise to protests, and it was followed by the publication of another kabbalistic work by Luzzatto, *Ḥoker umekubal* ['Philosopher and Kabbalist'].[49] But it is this very edition of the '138 Gateways' that demonstrates the activity of a Jewish censorship intent on ruling out extravagant praise of Luzzatto and silencing

[48] *Mipi atsmo*, as in *Meg.* 31*b*. The corresponding Tosefta says: 'Moses spoke them of his own accord [*me'atsmo*], and by the Holy Spirit.' Here the meaning is that the words conveyed to Luzzatto 'from the mouth of a holy one' were uttered or written by Luzzatto 'from his own mouth'. The words 'from the mouth of a holy one' could indeed be interpreted as relating to Luria, but I am still of the opinion, as I go on to say below, that we have here an allusion to the revelations of the *magid*.

[49] Printed in Shklov in 5545 [1785]. The printers had previously owned a printing works in Korets. See A. Ya'ari, 'Hadefus ha'ivri bisheklov', *Kiryat sefer*, 22 (1945–6), 50. The title-page of the book states that Luzzatto is well known 'for his books, the book *Kela"ḥ pitḥei ḥokhmah* and the book *Mesil[at] yesharim*', which tells us that *Ḥoker umekubal* was published after *Kela"ḥ pitḥei ḥokhmah*, and yet the letter of approval by R. Issachar Baer ben R. Leib, 'who was previously *av beit din* in the holy congregation of Slutsk, and is at present in the holy congregation of Shklov', is written in routine terms and restrained style, even though he had before him the glowing approval by R. Jacob Joseph of Ostrog.

the voices raised against his accusers. The foreword by the publisher, R. Gedaliah ben Elyakum of Korets, which I have dealt with in some detail, is to be found in only some of the copies, whereas in others it has been omitted and the page left blank.[50] Clearly the object of deleting the foreword was to prevent the reading public from seeing 'undesirable' material which those responsible for the printing had regarded as worthy and necessary. While printing was in progress someone had commented on the danger inherent in the content of the foreword, and the people concerned had yielded to pressure and removed it.[51] This incident sheds light on the withdrawal of the 5526 edition of *Mesilat yesharim*, from the forewords to which the writer of the foreword to the '138 Gateways' drew most of his text, as indeed he acknowledged. Thus, even in 5545, the time had still not come when Luzzatto could be publicly praised in such terms as had been used by R. Elijah of Brisk; even the patronage of the teachers of hasidism was not enough to save R. Gedaliah's foreword, in spite of the fact that hasidism was in the ascendant in and around Korets at the time.[52]

In 5595, some seventy years after the withdrawal in Zholkva of R. Elijah of Brisk's edition with his forewords to *Mesilat yesharim* and *Derekh ets ḥayim*, and fifty years after the deletion of the publisher's foreword from *Kela"ḥ pitḥei ḥokhmah* in Korets, a combined edition of *Mesilat yesharim* and *Derekh ets ḥayim* was published in Shklov in the version which had been put away and forgotten. We have no means of knowing now on whose initiative this unusual step was taken, and we are ignorant of what motivated it. The Shklov edition of 5595 contains no contemporary letter of approval and no new foreword, and from the text of the title-page one could fall into the error of thinking that the editor, R. Elijah of Brisk, had seen to the printing of the book and written his forewords in 5595.

[50] See Ben-Menahem, *Kitvei rabi moshe ḥayim lutsato*, 170. The National Library in Jerusalem has examples of both kinds, i.e. with and without the foreword. I have seen these. Where the foreword appears, it is on fo. 2^r, and 2^v has the beginning of the text of Luzzatto's *Derekh ets ḥayim*. If the foreword had been printed on a separate folio it would certainly have been torn out, and we should have been left with no clear sign of Jewish censorship.

[51] It is probable that the text of R. Jacob Joseph of Ostrog's letter of approval was similarly regarded as objectionable but was left untouched out of respect for him. On the other hand there is no doubt that the 'publisher's foreword' rejected as unfit for publication was written with the knowledge and encouragement of R. Jacob Joseph, who was a man of importance in the hasidic movement.

[52] The printing houses in Korets served as a main centre for the printing of kabbalistic and hasidic books, and most of the writers of the letters of approval were hasidic scholars. See Tauber, *Meḥkarim bibliografiyim*, 15–52; A. J. Heschel, 'Letoledot r' pinḥas mikorets', in *Alei ayin: minḥat devarim lishelomoh zalman shoken aḥarei mele'ot lo shivim shanah* (Jerusalem, 1948–52), 225–6, and 239–40 nn. 124–32. There is nothing in the arguments of H. Lieberman, 'Legende un emes vegn die hasidishe drukereien', *YIVO-bleter*, 34 (1950), 192–8, to disprove the hasidic character of the Korets printing houses.

It may be that the Shklov printer-publisher R. Isaac ben R. Manin, or whoever got him to print the book in the version of Zholkva 5526, had family connections or some other reason for wanting to revive recollections of the editor and honour his memory. It stands to reason, however, that the main motive was to bring to public notice the information which had lain hidden on Luzzatto's greatness and the holiness of his doctrine, and to remove every trace of the ignominy which his opponents had heaped on him and his activities. Undoubtedly the move to restore Luzzatto to favour and strengthen his influence was still in the nature of 'a word in season'. Of the three kabbalistic works by him which had been published up to 5545, only two were reprinted before 5595—*Ma'amar hahokhmah*[53] and *Ḥoker umekubal*;[54] there was no second printing of *Kela"ḥ pitḥei ḥokhmah* until sixty-four years after its publication in Korets.[55] The decades following 5545 saw an enormous strengthening and expansion of the hasidic movement, and yet a kabbalistic book endorsed by R. Jacob Joseph of Ostrog and recommended by the Maggid of Mezhirech failed to be republished during this period. This is instructive; it shows, in my opinion, that at that time there was still some unwillingness to countenance the distribution of Luzzatto's kabbalistic writings.[56] The fact that new kabbalistic works by Luzzatto which existed in manuscript in eastern Europe were not published until some of them appeared in print in the second half of the nineteenth century[57] reinforces the conclusion that

[53] 2nd edn.: [Zholkva] 5559 [1799]. See Ben-Menahem, *Kitvei rabi mosheh ḥayim lutsato*, 19–20, no. 14. At p. 31, no. 36, Ben-Menahem also notes '[Lvov 5560]', but I doubt the existence of such an edition.

[54] Lvov 5560. See Ben-Menahem, *Kitvei rabi mosheh ḥayim lutsato*, 40, no. 57, and 155. I have not seen the editions of Zholkva 5570 and Lvov 5570 which he notes at pp. 40–1, nos. 58–9. It seems to me that Lvov 5570 'came into existence' through a mistake in a note in M. Frestadt's German-language introduction to *Ḥoker umekubal* (Leipzig and Königsberg, 1840), p. xiv, where Frestadt says he knows of, but has not seen, a Lvov edition of 1810. This is certainly an error for 1800, i.e. 5560. Apparently the imaginary Lvov edition of 5570 'gave birth' to Zholkva 5570.

[55] Czernowitz 5609. See Ben-Menahem, *Kitvei rabi mosheh ḥayim lutsato*, 112–13, no. 225. I fear that the edition of Kraków 5590 together with *Derekh ḥokhmah* and *Ma'amar al hagadot*, under the title of *Sheloshah sefarim niftaḥim* ['Three Opened Books'], which he notes at p. 122, no. 238, never saw the light of day.

[56] It is apparently no coincidence that the second edition of *Kela"ḥ pitḥei ḥokhmah* (Czernowitz, 5609) did not include the publisher's foreword from the Korets edition, but it [the foreword] was printed in an edition giving no place or year of publication (but conjectured by bibliographers to have been published at Johannisburg *c.*5620 [1860]), and in a Kraków edition of 5640. Nothing is to be learnt from the absence of that foreword in the Warsaw edition of 5648 [1888]. Its editors, R. Samuel Luria and his assistants, were not dependent on the testimony of the Korets publisher for support, since they were conducting their own vigorous campaign to clear Luzzatto's name and assert his saintliness on the basis of information and documents which had come into their possession. The letters of approval in the first edition were omitted from all the other editions.

[57] I propose to deal elsewhere with late publications of Luzzatto's kabbalistic writings.

Luzzatto's status as a 'kosher' kabbalist was not yet sufficiently established. Publication of R. Elijah of Brisk's forewords could therefore be expected to advance the aims of Luzzatto's admirers.

We have no evidence of any opposition to the edition of 5595. On the contrary, we may fairly assume from the appearance of four printings in a single year, or showing the same year on the title-page, that the book was purchased and distributed in large numbers, and it seems probable that it was precisely the praise of Luzzatto in the unknown forewords that attracted its readership. It should not be overlooked, however, that the full text of the forewords was not subsequently reprinted as in the editions of Shklov 5595; the foreword to *Derekh ets ḥayim* alone, in the form in which it appeared in the undated Vilna edition, was reprinted many times. I have already indicated in Section A[58] that I cannot determine whether the Vilna edition preceded or followed Shklov 5595. But in either event it seems that even after 5595 some people were still hesitant about Luzzatto's personality and doctrine, and the printers therefore chose to compromise: they removed the first foreword, which had placed a declaration of Luzzatto's greatness as a godly kabbalist in a prominent position at the front of the book, but they printed the second foreword, with its extravagant praise, because it was tucked away between *Mesilat yesharim* and *Derekh ets ḥayim*.[59]

C. R. ELIJAH OF BRISK: A SENIOR MEMBER OF R. JEKUTIEL OF VILNA'S GROUP

Who was the editor of Zholkva 5526 who set himself the aim of disseminating Luzzatto's writings and doctrine and glorifying his name and fame? How and where did he come by the 'find' of Luzzatto manuscripts which had been banned and hidden away? Where did he get 'reliable testimony from *geonim* of the holy congregation of Amsterdam that from the days of Moses until Moses none has arisen like Moses'? Did he act on his own initiative, or might he have had partners in his propagandist work? I found answers to these questions in items of information scattered through the writings of R. Jacob Emden which are reinforced and confirmed by the conclusions I have reached in the course of my research.

58 See pp. 405–6, 410–11 above.

59 By the time that it would have been possible to publish R. Elijah of Brisk's two forewords without fear of the consequences, they had disappeared from view and been forgotten.

A letter from R. Isaac ben Meir of Prossnitz, *av beit din* of Biała, to R. Aryeh Leib, *av beit din* of Amsterdam,[60] says:

Let this be known to all the children of Israel, what the unclean calls the one who cries 'unclean, unclean', with reference to the man Ry"kutiel [*sic*] the physician, who is mentioned in the book *Torat hakenaot* ['(This is) the Law of Jealousies'],[61] and was previously in the holy congregation of Shklov in Russia, and afterwards for some time in the holy congregation of Brisk, *and had with him the writings of the young man Hayim Luzzatto, and there were drawn to learn from him h"t*[62] Hayim, *the rabbi R. Eli*[jah], *son-in-law of the gaon the av beit din* [of Brisk], *our teacher and master R. Nahman, may the Merciful One preserve and bless him*, and several other men who were caught in the trap with him, and they had all his aforesaid writings copied by the copyist our teacher and master Hayim, who *lk"k*[63] as a tutor with the said rabbi Israel [*sic*],[64] and this was the reason for the beginning of the mischief wrought in the holy congregation of Brisk.[65]

[60] The two rabbis were sons-in-law of the Hakham Tsevi [Tsevi Hirsch Ashkenazi] and brothers-in-law of R. Jacob Emden. R. Isaac of Biała was a loyal ally of Emden in the Eybeschuetz controversy and was one of his chief informants on the events in the communities of Poland and Lithuania. See B. Wachstein, *Die Grabschriften des alten Judenfriedhofes in Eisenstadt* (Vienna, 1922), 78; *Pinkas va'ad arba aratsot*, ed. Halpern, index of personal names, under heading 'Isaac ben Meir, *av beit din* of Biały'.

[61] In connection with the controversy over Luzzatto and R. Jekutiel's activity in Shklov, which I consider below. See Emden's *Torat hakenaot*, 44*b*–48*b*, 50*b*–55*a*, 57*b*–58*a*.

[62] Possibly *hatalmid* ['the student'], who would not be the same as 'the copyist our teacher and master' mentioned further on. But *h"t* could be interpreted as *hamarbits torah* ['the teacher of Torah'], in which case the two may be identical.

[63] Possibly a mistake for the letters *lamed ayin ayin = le'et atah* ['at present']. Or possibly *lk"k = likehilat kamenets* ['to the congregation of Kamenets'] (see the following note), and a word should be added: 'who [went] to the congregation of Kamenets'.

[64] At the beginning of the letter the writer says of him: '... who was *av beit din* of the holy congregation of Kamenets and has now been appointed a trustee of the house of Israel of the four lands', adding that he promised to support Emden and not Eybeschuetz. He was rabbi of Kamenets-Podolsk. See *Pinkas va'ad arba aratsot*, ed. Halpern, 401, 407, 531. This tutor-copyist, who moved from Lithuania to Podolia, could have served as an important channel for the dissemination of Luzzatto's kabbalistic writings in the centres of the nascent hasidic movement. See pp. 444–8 below.

[65] R. Jacob Emden's *Edut beya'akov*, 68*b*. 'The beginning of the mischief' appears to mean the decree of excommunication against the detractors of R. Jonathan Eybeschuetz which was received by the rabbis and communal leaders of the regions of Lithuania 'on the third day [Tuesday], 5 Kislev 512 in the abbreviated numeration [i.e. 5512 = end of 1751] here in the holy congregation of Mir, may our Rock and Redeemer preserve it'. The signatories were from five large Lithuanian communities; two of them were from Brisk. The decree was supported by a document from 'the rabbis, counts, officers, magnates [and] leaders of the holy congregation of Lithuanian Brisk [Brest-Litovsk]' dated 17 Adar 5512 [spring 1752], very strongly worded and bearing eleven signatures. The two documents were printed in Eybeschuetz's book *Luḥot edut* (Altona, 5515 [1755]), 37*a*–39*a*. R. Isaac of Biała saw in these bans the influence of R. Jekutiel and his group. The powerful impression created by the decree of the Mir conference is shown by the efforts of Emden and his supporters to invalidate it. See *Edut beya'akov*, [70] (50)*a*–[70]

The letter was written in connection with the Eybeschuetz controversy. The extract I have quoted served as introduction to a warning against the danger foreseen from R. Jekutiel's journey from Brisk to the Land of Israel, because according to the writer's information he operated while in Brisk as one of the leaders of the 'faction' supporting R. Jonathan Eybeschuetz. The letter goes on to make this clear:

The man [Eybeschuetz] wrote him [Jekutiel] a friendly letter, with many flattering remarks, [urging that] our teacher and rabbi, the said R. E. [Elijah], should become actively involved and propagate lies in exchange for a bribe[66] . . . And when he [R. Jekutiel] went to the Land of Israel, and a certain wealthy man from Italy[67] gave him support by giving him 300 thaler every year to be sent to Hebron, [the arrangement being] that he would head the man's *beit midrash* ['house of study'], and he went on his voyage bearing Micah's graven image,[68] not to[69] lead everyone astray as did R. Isaiah the son-in-law of R. Judah Hasid, who [plural] sinned there[70] in belief in Sh[abetai] Ts[evi], may the name of the wicked rot.[71]

Without realizing it, R. Isaac of Biała was giving us important information about R. Elijah of Brisk: he was one of the heads of a restricted group round R. Jekutiel of Vilna who were engaged in the study of Luzzatto's doctrine from writings in the possession of R. Jekutiel; the members of the group made copies of Luzzatto's writings; the group sided with R. Jonathan Eybeschuetz and worked on his behalf in the controversy.

R. Elijah's father-in-law, R. Nahman Sirkin, was one of the greatest rabbis of his generation. He came to Brisk from Zamość in 1718 and was rabbi of

(53)*b*; *Shevirat luḥot ha'aven*, 45*a*. I propose to deal at greater length elsewhere with R. Jekutiel's activities in eastern Europe on his return from Padua. Here I consider them only so far as they are relevant in the present context.

66 According to R. Isaac of Biała's communication, this was an attempt to bribe the rabbi of Brisk, R. Nahman, to sign the declaration drawn up by supporters of Eybeschuetz. See n. 73 below. Here we are given to understand that, to this end, R. Jonathan sought the intervention of R. Elijah, R. Nahman's son-in-law, through the good offices of R. Jekutiel. R. Jekutiel left on his mission on 23 Iyar 5511 [late spring 1751] (see p. 437 below). R. Jonathan Eybeschuetz's letter may have reached him some months before his departure, because he sent many urgent letters to Poland after the start of the controversy early in 5511 [autumn 1750]. See *Edut beya'akov*, 29*b*.

67 R. Solomon Rakah of Venice, who was a patron of Luzzatto and the members of his group. See *Igerot*, ii. 216, 244–5, 399, 400, 402, 415, 423; M. Benayahu, 'R' yitsḥak karigal be'italyah', *Otsar yehudei sefarad*, 1 (1959), 31; M. Benayahu, 'Aliyato shel haramḥa"l le'erets yisra'el', in Z. Warhaftig and Sh. Y. Zevin (eds.), *Mazkeret: kovets torani lezekher yitsḥak aizik halevi hertsog* (Jerusalem, 1962), 470. And see below, pp. 439–40 and n. 115.

68 Apparently 'Micah's graven image' [Judg. 18] was the bundle of Luzzatto's writings.

69 To make sense in this context, words such as 'one must beware and warn others' need to be inserted before 'not to'.

70 It is not clear whether 'there' means that it was in the Land of Israel, R. Jekutiel's destination, that the members of R. Judah Hasid's group 'sinned', or whether it was in the communities of Ashkenaz in which R. Isaiah and his associates propagated Shabateanism and through which R. Jekutiel would pass on his way to the Holy Land.

71 *Edut beya'akov*, 68*b*.

the city for some forty years until his death in 1757. He left no written works but some letters of approval by him have been preserved and a great deal of information about him has been collected.[72] The most important information for our present purpose is contained in Emden's writings, particularly where he quotes letters from R. Isaac of Biała, who repeatedly emphasizes that people who were at R. Jonathan Eybeschuetz's beck and call tried to draw the great rabbi R. Nahman to their side with gifts of money and get him to sign a document in favour of Eybeschuetz, but he stood firm and was not to be tempted.[73] In other words, R. Nahman resisted the attempts of R. Jekutiel's faction, including his own son-in-law R. Elijah, to persuade him to join them in public support of R. Jonathan Eybeschuetz.

R. Elijah's brother-in-law R. Mordecai ben R. Nahman, author of *Mayim amukim* (Zholkva, 5520 [1760]), married the daughter of R. Gershon Nathan ben R. Betsalel, one of the leaders of the Zholkva community.[74] In his 'author's foreword' he describes in glowing terms the time he spent as a young man living in his father-in-law's house and studying in the Zholkva *beit midrash*.[75]

[72] See A. L. Feinstein, *Ir tehilah* (Warsaw, 1885), 29–30, 130, 142, 144–5, 149, 157, 178–9, 181, 184–5, 187, 192–3, 203; I. T. Eisenstadt and S. Wiener, *Da'at kedoshim* (St Petersburg, 1897–8), 158; *Pinkas va'ad arba aratsot*, ed. Halpern, 390, 398. The name Sirkin is apparently derived from the fact that R. Nahman was a descendant of R. Joel Sirkes, the author of *Bayit ḥadash*.

[73] The story is repeated many times in R. Isaac of Biała's letters and in references to his letters: 'This will leave you in no doubt: in [regard to] a document that was sent from the holy congregation of Brisk, the *gaon* our teacher and rabbi was not willing to append his signature, and there was a certain emissary who wanted to give the honourable rabbi thirty ducats, but he refused to put forth his hand to add his signature to theirs, and some of them would not send him *mishlo'aḥ manot* [the gifts of food exchanged at Purim] and became his enemies. In spite of this he remained firm in his righteousness' (*Torat hakenaot*, 65*a*); 'We shall prove to the honoured counts, officers, leaders, congregational heads, and the great rabbis of the land that one of his [Eybeschuetz's] disciples wanted to give a bribe of thirty ducats to a man unique in this generation, the honoured and renowned *gaon*, the exilarch, our teacher and rabbi R. Nahman, may the Merciful One preserve and bless him, *av beit din* and head of the yeshiva of the holy congregation of Brisk, to get him to add his signature to theirs and confirm their falsehoods' (*Edut beya'akov*, 66*a*). And see *Torat hakenaot*, 64*b*; *Edut beya'akov*, 67*b*, 69*a*, 69*b*; *Shevirat luḥot ha'aven*, 45*a*. See also n. 66 above. It must be conceded, however, that R. Isaac of Biała's hope that 'his in-law the old *gaon* our teacher and master R. Nahman would write and sign a *ḥerem* [edict of excommunication] against the man who was (to begin with) a writer of amulets' (*Edut beya'akov*, 68*a*) was not fulfilled, and it appears that right up to his death R. Nahman refrained from any public intervention in the dispute. R. Isaac of Biała's extreme respect and admiration for R. Nahman Sirkin rules out any suspicion of his making unfounded accusations against R. Elijah of Brisk. On the contrary, it certainly pained him to declare that R. Nahman's son-in-law was one of those caught in R. Jekutiel's net.

[74] A letter of approval by R. Samson Maisels, rabbi of Zholkva, describes R. Mordecai as 'son-in-law of the honoured, the distinguished and renowned rabbi, our teacher R. Gershon Nathan son of R. Betsalel of our congregation, an elder who sits in the yeshiva continually, who ever since his youth has [bowed] his shoulder to bear the yoke of the Torah'.

[75] In that foreword he writes: 'I remember the days of old when I was in my prime, in God's company . . . a meeting-place for scholars . . . this is the law of the house of these two

Apparently even after he left Zholkva he continued to live in the area: he died on 24 Shevat 5525 [early 1765] 'in Pomorin, in the vicinity of Lvov'.[76] Thus R. Elijah of Brisk had family connections, and perhaps also colleagues and friends,

brothers-in-law, namely my father-in-law the distinguished rabbi our teacher and master R. Gershon Nathan, may he be remembered for life in the world to come, and his brother-in-law our distinguished and outstanding teacher and master Enoch Henokh, may his memory be for a blessing, in these brothers-in-law a most felicitous match occurred . . . there were seats there for our rabbis and their studies, and a *beit midrash* for *perushim* ['separated ones', people who had left home to study—Trans.], that is, [who have become *perushim*] out of love, the Lord loves the gates of Zion—those who are distinguished for their occupation with the law [*halakhah*] [*Ber.* 8*a*, referring to Ps. 87: 2.—Trans.] . . . While I was there I was in my father-in-law's home as mentioned . . . our teacher and master R. Benjamin Ze'ev, may his memory be for a blessing, son-in-law of the magnate our teacher and master E[noch] Henokh aforesaid, may his memory be for a blessing, bound the sources of the streams and brought hidden things to precious light [*o"r yekaro"t*][Job 28: 11, with *or yekarot*, literally 'the light of precious things', very freely adapted from Zech. 14: 6; and see below in this note—Trans.].' On R. Gershon Nathan and his brother-in-law R. Enoch Henokh see S. Buber, *Kiryah nisgavah* (Kraków, 1903), 21, sect. 3, paras. 58, 59; 29, sect. 8, para. 89; 67–8, sect. 50, paras. 251, 253, 255; Ts. H. Horowitz, *Kitvei hageonim* (Piotrków, 1928), 32–4. Apparently it was this Mordecai ben R. Nahman who, according to Buber (*Kiryah nisgavah*, 56, sect. 40, para. 213), 'was a signatory in a *pinkas* ['register'] . . . to a promissory note dated [Sunday], New Moon of Kislev 5484 [end of 1723], together with other leaders of the congregation'. His relative and friend R. Benjamin Ze'ev was the R. Joseph Benjamin Ze'ev who wrote *Or yekarot* (first printed Zholkva, 1732, together with a work by his father, under the title *Livyat ḥen ve'or yekarot*). The extract I have quoted goes on to recount that the two friends were preparing to write a book jointly on 'the Gemara with Rashi's commentary and Tosafot' entitled *Mayim amukim*, but 'the partnership broke up'. This foreword contains an interesting description of the methods of study in the Zholkva *beit midrash*: 'They were sitting in separate groups, each man seeking his own subject, each of them according to his strength in the path of their [*sic*] learning, one being concerned with the occult, another attracted to aggadah; I said to them "No, for halakhah [study of the law and its application] is my purpose."' R. Mordecai devoted himself entirely to the study of halakhah, and saw no need to look beyond it, unlike his brother-in-law R. Elijah of Brisk, who was seized by 'concern with the occult' and worked for that interest with great enthusiasm. In *Torat hakenaot*, 72*b*, Emden praises 'our honoured teacher, the rabbi R. Henokh of Zholkvi [*sic*]' for his opposition to the Shabateans. But the Zholkva *beit midrash* was one of the important centres of Shabatean activity in Poland. The extreme Shabatean propagandist R. Hayim Malakh lived there during 5455–6 [1695–6] in close contact with R. Gershon Nathan, an important communal leader and future father-in-law of R. Mordecai Sirkin, and R. Gershon at that time loyally shared Malakh's heretical messianic beliefs. See G. Scholem, 'Igeret me'et r' ḥayim malakh', *Zion*, 11 (1946), 169, 174; G. Scholem, *Ḥalomotav shel hashabeta'i r' mordekhai ashkenazi* (Jerusalem, 1938), 10–11; G. Scholem, 'Hatenuah hashabeta'it bepolin', in I. Halpern (ed.), *Beit yisra'el bepolin*, ii (Jerusalem, 1954), 55, 57–8, 60–2. Among the students in the 'separate groups' studying 'the occult' and aggadah in the *beit midrash*, from whose interests the elderly R. Mordecai emphasized that he had distanced himself in his youth, there were probably some Shabateans. R. David, R. Jacob Emden's brother, was another son-in-law of R. Gershon Nathan. See Buber, *Kiryah nisgavah*, 68, para. 253; Horowitz, *Kitvei hageonim*, 33–4.

[76] See Horowitz, *Kitvei hageonim*, 140, where he gives the text of the inscription on R. Mordecai's gravestone. But Horowitz did not know that R. Mordecai ben R. Nahman of Brisk was the selfsame R. Mordecai, son-in-law of R. Gershon Nathan of Zholkva, that he mentions at

in Zholkva and its environs, and it may be that his relatives and friends helped to further his plans for the printing and distribution of Luzzatto's works.

R. Jekutiel's activity in Shklov, where he lived before coming to Brisk, is dealt with in intricate detail in two books by R. Jacob Emden.[77] In both places he relies on oral information obtained in Altona from 'the exalted and eminent scholar [*aluf*] our honoured teacher and rabbi, R. Gedaliah son of our teacher and rabbi R. Isaac Halevi',[78] who was in personal contact with R. Jekutiel in Shklov. The first version is an account of testimony given unofficially and not dated,[79] whereas the second version is a protocol of evidence delivered formally 'before a session of three [judges]' on 18 Iyar 5513 [late spring 1753]. However, the testimony in the first case, too, was given 'under solemn oath'. In both cases the evidence was taken in the *beit midrash* in Altona, and in both cases the investigators were headed by R. Jacob Emden. In wording and content there are fairly important differences between the two, but in essentials they do not contradict each other. The main purpose of the depositions was to charge R. Jekutiel with having taught heretical messianic beliefs and opinions and conducting obscene sexual practices in his group. These matters are not within the scope of my consideration here, and I shall confine myself to the clarification of a few points which afford parallels to information about R. Jekutiel's group in Brisk: the existence of a group led by him, their study of Luzzatto's works, and links between R. Jekutiel and R. Jonathan Eybeschuetz.

I quote verbatim and in order the main passages relating to these matters in both versions:

(*Torat hakenaot*) Long and wordy were the efforts by which he [Jekutiel] thought to tempt him to become one of his company . . . and *he said that he had associates, and the chief of them was R"J*[80] . . . He also testified that this fool who earns disgrace [Prov. 3: 35], when he was in Solkov,[81] had an evil company of students, young men who studied kabbalah with him . . . they had a distinctive little cap on their heads, made of

p. 33 of his book (see nn. 74 and 75 above). Two other sons of R. Nahman of Brisk, R. Jacob and R. Joshua Heschel, were residents of Shklov and died there, the first in 1789 and the second in 1805, and a record also exists of another son-in-law, R. Nathan Neta of Brisk, a *kohen*, son of R. Isaiah of Shebreshin [Szczebrzeszyn]. See Eisenstadt and Wiener, *Da'at kedoshim*, 162; S. Berman and M. Rabinowitz, 'Mishpeḥot k"k sheklov', *Kovets al yad*, NS 1 (11) (1936), 152, 170; Feinstein, *Ir tehilah*, 157, 181, 203. No one, however, remembered to number R. Elijah of Brisk among the members of R. Nahman Sirkin's family. It may be of interest that two of R. Nahman's sons lived in Shklov, the area where R. Jekutiel was active before he came to Brisk.

[77] *Torat hakenaot*, 57*b*–58*a*; *Beit yehonatan hasofer*, 6*a*–*b*.

[78] In *Torat hakenaot* he is referred to by the initials *mem he resh* [= 'our teacher the rabbi'] *gimel* (Maharag), with no explicit mention of his name.

[79] From the fact that the testimony is juxtaposed to a report of R. Jekutiel's arrival in The Hague at the time the book was being printed, it appears that it was taken at the end of 5511 or the beginning of 5512 [i.e. in the last few months of 1751].

[80] R. Jonathan Eybeschuetz, as is spelt out in the second version.

[81] Shklov is meant.

black samite in a special likeness,[82] the same for all of them, so that they should be able to recognize each other by their signs when they met . . . *Indeed he* [Jekutiel] *carried about with him a very thick manuscript book, and said that it was the work of his teacher, Luzzatto, from which he prayed and offered praise and which determined everything he did, and he studied this manuscript book with pupils and associates listening to him.*

(*Beit yehonatan hasofer*) He [the witness] declared, on his faith and his Judaism, how when he was in Sklov [*sic*], R. Jekutiel the physician of Vilna[83] was there, a man who had been in Italy, in Padua and Mantua,[84] and had served that man Hayim Luzzatto . . . and had learnt from him all the matters which engaged him, and *brought with him a book written by the said heretic Hayim, an enormous volume*, and began to lead the said R"G astray . . . and tempted the said R"G to meet him privately in a remote spot where people would not notice, and the man R"G got a boat in which, while floating on the water, *Jekutiel the physician aforesaid revealed to him all the mysteries he had received from his teacher the heretic Luzzatto, whom he praised highly, saying that he had several times heard a voice issuing from Heaven which said: Peace to you, Rabbi . . . and he* [Jekutiel] *wanted to hand over to him* [the witness] *yiḥudim on which he should concentrate with his eyes closed*, whereupon immediately a roomful of mice and cats[85] would come, in order to nullify thought,[86] and by this means he would see wonders of wonders. *He also told him that R. Jonathan Eybeschuetz was one of their company and a member of their sect*; although he had never seen him they knew each other very well *and letters sped back and forth between them* . . . R"G also reported that this fool of a quack doctor set up an association based on his creed, and they called themselves a *ḥevrah kedeshah*[87] . . . The *ḥevrah* of the prostitute were identified by their samite *kapplakh* [little caps, 'kappels'; this and the word 'samite' are in Yiddish as locally pronounced—Trans.], the same for all of them, and by other signs by which they could recognize each other, including their footwear.

R. Jekutiel's group is portrayed here as an organized clandestine mystical order. It is hard to understand why they should need special clothes as private

[82] *Temunah*; standard Hebrew would use *tsurah* ['shape' or 'form'].

[83] In *Torat hakenaot* Jekutiel is called Kusel [Ashkenazi Yiddish pronunciation] the physician. Hence he practised medicine in Shklov too.

[84] Luzzatto lived in Mantua for a while before his marriage to the daughter of R. David Finzi, rabbi of that city. See Essay 3, nn. 1 and 3. It appears that he again lived there for a time after his wedding on 27 Av 5491 [late summer 1731], and was perhaps put up in his father-in-law's house on several occasions. See *Igerot*, ii. 230–3, 353. Evidently R. Jekutiel was in contact with him there.

[85] The testimony would certainly have spoken of angels and holy souls and the like, and was garbled by Emden in his characteristic way.

[86] Perhaps this means getting rid of the disturbing thoughts which are called 'extraneous thoughts' in *musar* books, and especially in hasidic literature; or it may refer to a state of ecstasy in which intellectual thought ceases to be possible.

[87] They called themselves *ḥevrah kedoshah* ['a holy company'], but here the 'defective' spelling (omission of the letter *vav*) is deliberately used so as to read *kedeshah* ['temple prostitute']. This is not merely a term of derision, for the text goes on to say that 'they hired a prostitute to be shared by them all', or, as *Torat hakenaot* puts it, 'They had a Gentile prostitute in their fellowship, shared by all of them.' The significance of such charges against R. Jekutiel's group and the problem of their veracity will be considered by me elsewhere.

recognition signs. Their distinctive garb, which I see no reason to question, may be interpreted in two ways: (*a*) it is incorrect to explain it as a recognition sign; the purpose of uniformity in caps and shoes was precisely to provide the group with a uniform; (*b*) if these articles were indeed recognition signs, we must conclude that they were needed because R. Jekutiel's 'sect' consisted of several groups, some of them outside Shklov. It is to be supposed that the group in Brisk, too, was organized and clandestine. R. Jekutiel had served as a sort of master of ceremonies in Luzzatto's secret group in Padua,[88] and from the testimony relating to Shklov it is clear that in the areas where he was active he tried to establish new groups under his personal leadership on the pattern of his teacher's 'holy company'.[89] The study of Luzzatto's kabbalistic writings had to be kept secret in Brisk too. As to the manner of its study, which was apparently similar in the two cities, the testimony relating to Shklov provides us with most important information: R. Jekutiel had 'an enormous volume' containing manuscripts, and perhaps not only one volume;[90] it was from his teacher's writings that R. Jekutiel 'prayed and offered praise, and they determined everything he did'; which is to say that the writings by Luzzatto in his possession included prayers and *piyutim*[91] and instructions on conduct and mystical activities; in teaching the members of his group R. Jekutiel did not confine himself to theoretical study but imparted *yiḥudim* and mystical *kavanot* for the elevation of the soul and the reception of revelations and visions; the kabbalistic doctrine they learnt in the group contained unmistakably messianic elements;[92] R. Jekutiel revealed secrets

[88] The rules of Luzzatto's group were written down and preserved in various versions. See *Igerot*, i. 8–13; A. L. Frumkin, *Toledot ḥakhmei yerushalayim*, ii (Jerusalem, 1928), 135–8. The text of the rules copied by Frumkin from MS Oxford 2237 contains important variants from that in *Igerot*, but the copy is marred by omissions and errors, and I have it in mind to republish the document in a complete and accurate version.

[89] The 'holy' character of Luzzatto's group is given great prominence in the 'rules': 'the holy members', 'the holy *beit midrash*', 'the holy study', 'the holy table', and other expressions of holiness. See also *Igerot*, i. 53–4; ii. 234–5, 239, 240–1. And see n. 19 above.

[90] It may be that the bundle of documents from Padua in R. Jekutiel's possession also contained writings by members of Luzzatto's group. I have in mind particularly R. Moses David Valle, who had written many extensive works—which have been preserved in manuscript—before R. Jekutiel left Padua. Valle and Jekutiel operated jointly as heads of Luzzatto's group. See *Igerot*, i. 10; Frumkin, *Toledot ḥakhmei yerushalayim*, ii. 138; Tishby, *Netivei emunah uminut*, 192–6; Essay 6, p. 306 ff.

[91] In a collection of manuscripts by Luzzatto and members of his group, I discovered a rich store of Luzzatto's liturgical compositions, in verse and poetic prose. I lectured on these some years ago [in 1961: see the foreword to Essay 2—Trans.] at the Institute of Jewish Studies in Jerusalem. I hope I shall be able to publish the texts and my researches on them in the near future.

[92] From the descriptions in the testimony from Shklov it is clear that R. Jekutiel had copies of works dictated by the *magid*, most of which had a strongly messianic bent, and these, too, were studied in his group. We know from other sources that when he was in Padua R. Jekutiel was keen to collect numerous copies of Luzzatto's writings in preparation for his return to Poland,

drawn from his recollections of Luzzatto's personality and of his *beit midrash*, in the course of which he 'praised Luzzatto highly' and told of the revelations of the *magid*, who was called 'a voice from Heaven' [*bat kol*] in the testimony relating to Shklov. In my opinion it may be assumed without hesitation that all this applies equally to the activity of the group in Brisk, in which R. Elijah participated. In the reverse direction, it appears to me that the information about the copying of Luzzatto's writings by members of the group, of which Emden speaks only in a letter about Brisk, is just as valid for the group in Shklov. Finally, the testimony in relation to Shklov also casts fresh light on the connections with R. Jonathan Eybeschuetz. R. Jekutiel's activity in Shklov certainly pre-dated by a few years the quarrel over the amulets [see *Encyclopaedia Judaica*, vi. 1076—Trans.] which began in 1751. It follows that the correspondence between R. Jekutiel and R. Jonathan at first had no connection with the dispute,[93] and it was therefore natural for R. Jonathan, when

and his friends gave him additional copies as parting gifts. Undoubtedly most of these were copies of works transmitted in the name of the *magid*. See *Igerot*, i. 98; ii. 408; Tishby, *Netivei emunah uminut*, 325 n. 53, and 327 nn. 92, 94. The strong messianic urge which animated the thoughts and actions of Luzzatto and the members of his group was also trenchantly expressed in *Derekh ets ḥayim*—published in 5526 [1766] from a manuscript originating in R. Jekutiel's school—and especially at the end of the work, in the explanation of the need and duty to study kabbalah: 'We take this as a principle, that for every generation in whose days the Temple is not rebuilt, it is as if the Temple was destroyed in their days, because they had a choice and could have brought about the rebuilding of the Temple by their good deeds . . . and by performing great *tikunim* through concern with our Torah . . . particularly the study of the science of truth, which is the study of kabbalah, which is chief of all *tikunim*, as the holy rabbi, R. Simeon bar Yohai, may his memory be for a blessing, said explicitly: [quoting in Aramaic] that by it Israel will come out of exile, [then in Hebrew] through the merit of studying kabbalah Israel will come out of exile . . . and look, this science [*ḥokhmah*] is left aside and no one seeks it out . . . that we need to seek for *tikunim* by which all that has been done wrongly will be set right, for by this means our Messiah will come.' And see n. 129 below.

[93] Emden records two interesting pieces of information about personal contact between Luzzatto and R. Jonathan Eybeschuetz: 'Mark this too: once there passed this way a man in whose very name is impurity, Mosheh Hayim Luzzatri [*sic*], who trod the paths of heresy [but while *minut*, 'heresy', may be meant, *minit*, 'sexual', is written] according to the edict of excommunication printed concerning him by all the great rabbis of the land. When he arrived at the house of that abominable man [Eybeschuetz] he stood before him in public and spoke these words: "When a holy and pure man passes our way", and we here were amazed by this, but now the matter has been settled quite simply' (*Sefat emet uleshon zehorit*, [19]*b*, in a letter from R. Nehemiah Reischer of Metz); '(Truly, as to his [R. Jonathan's] so insistently demanding rectification of the wrong done to M.H.L., we know from a report from the Land of Israel that M.H.L. died there and that among his writings they found recorded in manuscript that he had spent eight days with the heretic [R. Jonathan] on sorcerers' affairs)' (*Shevirat luḥot ha'aven*, 40*b*). These two reports certainly relate to the time when Luzzatto was living in Amsterdam, but it cannot be determined whether they refer to one meeting or two. The meaning of 'sorcerers' affairs' is not clear. It may refer to practical kabbalah, e.g. amulets, or it may be another name for Shabateanism in Emden's lexicon. H. J. D. Azulai, in his notes in cipher (quoted in

the dispute broke out, to seek help from the friend and ally who was living and working in Brisk. The statement that R. Jonathan, in his letter to R. Jekutiel, appealed 'with many flattering remarks' for the support of R. Elijah of Brisk[94] shows that he had previously received details of the activity of R. Jekutiel and his group.

The information I have extracted in this review is based on a few short fragments which happened to find their way into R. Jacob Emden's denunciatory books. The evidence with regard to Shklov was taken and recorded some years after the event, and the information on the students of Luzzatto's kabbalah in Brisk reached Emden in a letter written in 1755,[95] when R. Jekutiel had already left Brisk for good. Had it not been for R. Jacob Emden's fanatical zeal in hunting down every man infected with sympathy for R. Jonathan Eybeschuetz, we should have heard nothing about R. Jekutiel's groups in Shklov and Brisk. Even now our knowledge is of the slightest, and the information we do have is more often than not obscure.

The meagreness of our information is particularly striking when it is considered that more than twenty years elapsed between the autumn of 1732, when R. Jekutiel left Padua,[96] and his departure from Brisk in 1755. Where

M. Benayahu's essay 'Ha"magid" shel ramḥa"l', in I. Ben-Zvi and M. Benayahu (eds.), *Sefer zikaron liyeshayahu zoneh/Isaiah Sonne Memorial Volume* (= *Sefunot*, 5) (Jerusalem, 1961), 335), recording what R. Jacob Hazak told him in Padua in 1776 about divine revelations to Luzzatto, has this to say: 'The *magid* said that Rabbi Jonathan's attainment [with regard to the holy spirit, revelations from on high] was but small, he knew the Talmud but was not a wonder.' (The punctuation is of course mine, as in the other quotations in my essay, but it seems clear to me that the word 'small' goes with 'attainment' and not with the knowledge of the Talmud.) Azulai's note shows that even before Luzzatto left Padua in 1735—that is to say, during the years when R. Jonathan Eybeschuetz was still living in Prague, not long after the first stories of his connection with Shabateanism which were silenced among the public at large by his excommunication of the Shabateans in 1725—Luzzatto and the members of his group were already giving thought to R. Jonathan's personality and the standard of his mystical attainments, and they may have corresponded with each other. It is probable that R. Jekutiel, on his travels as an emissary in 1751–2, met R. Jonathan. See pp. 437–9 below.

94 See above, text referring to n. 66.

95 See *Pinkas va'ad arba aratsot*, ed. Halpern, 401–2, no. 735, and 531.

96 See *Igerot*, ii. 241, 270. R. Jekutiel was awarded his doctorate of philosophy and medicine in the University of Padua on 16 October 1732. See D. Kaufmann, 'Contributions à la biographie de Mosé Hayyim Luzzatto, Yekutiel Gordon et Mosé Hages', *Revue des Etudes Juives*, 23 (1891), 256. Apparently he returned home soon afterwards. See Tishby, *Netivei emunah uminut*, 325 n. 53. In Av 5490 [late summer 1730], just after Luzzatto's first capitulation on the 3rd of that month (see *Igerot*, i. 176–7; ii. 410–11), R. Samson Morpurgo, writing to R. Moses Hagiz with regard to R. Jekutiel, recommended that 'if perchance, on his safe return to his people and his land, he should pass within your holy camp [Morpurgo addresses Hagiz courteously in the third person—Trans.], or in the neighbourhood of those cities, that you may be active [or 'that there should be someone to be active'] on his behalf, to help and be his spokesman and advocate' (*Igerot*, ii. 214). But his return to Poland was put off until the beginning of 5493 [autumn 1732].

did he live and what did he do during that long spell? When he returned to Poland, did he immediately settle in Shklov or did he move from place to place? We have not the least idea. After the storm over Luzzatto had subsided, it would have seemed to his opponents that his 'heretical' writings and false doctrine had been finally laid to rest in the soil of Frankfurt am Main and on the book-burning pyres of that community and others, in obedience to the demands of the excommunicators.[97] They would therefore have seen no need to keep track of the movements and activities of R. Jekutiel of Vilna. Hence great importance attaches to two pieces of information from Luzzatto's circle in Padua, brief and obscure though they are. The first of these derives from a private jotting by R. Moses David Valle,[98] one of the leaders of Luzzatto's group: 'This day, 27 Shevat [5496], I rejoiced over the *ry"k* [R. Jekutiel] and said: My brethren, my brethren, say to God "How fearsome are Your works".' The style shows that it does not relate to a visionary experience, as do most of Valle's private jottings, but is one of the entries which deal with an actual occurrence in the physical world. In Shevat 5496 [early spring 1736] the dispute over Luzzatto was raging, and the rejoicing in Padua over R. Jekutiel may have been due to something important he did in Poland for the benefit of Luzzatto or the members of Luzzatto's group, who, like their leader, were vilified and excommunicated.[99] At any rate this tells us that R. Jekutiel was not sitting idly by, and that Luzzatto's group were following his activities with interest. The second item of information is in a postscript to a letter of 28 Sivan 5498 [summer 1738] from Luzzatto's pupils in Padua to their teacher in Amsterdam: 'Since the magnate R. Solomon Rakah,[100] may the Merciful One preserve and bless him, has been informed that the learned R. Jekutiel has arrived in those parts, we beg you *to let us know what sort of person he is and what is his occupation* [in other words, 'tell us all about him'—Trans.], and why he has disappeared until now, *and whether he is still faithful to our covenant*.'[101] Apparently there had been no communication between the group in Padua and R. Jekutiel since the glad tidings of Shevat 5496, and there may possibly have been no strong connection between them even earlier than that. The group's concern that R. Jekutiel might have abandoned his faithfulness to their covenant shows clearly that they valued his loyalty greatly and hoped it would contribute to the advancement of their aims and aspirations. Was the news of R. Jekutiel's visit to

[97] See *Igerot*, ii. 395–8.

[98] Jottings such as this are scattered through Valle's manuscript works; taken together they form a sort of mystical diary of great importance. I propose to publish them as a unit [now Essay 7—Trans.]. See Tishby, *Netivei emunah uminut*, 193–4.

[99] See *Igerot*, ii. 320–1, 323–4. And see pp. 416–18 above.

[100] See p. 428 and n. 67 above, and pp. 439–40 below.

[101] *Igerot*, ii. 400. Luzzatto's pupils took it for granted that R. Jekutiel and Luzzatto would meet.

'those parts', i.e. the environs of Amsterdam, genuine or a fabrication? And if the visit really took place—where did R. Jekutiel come from, where did he arrive, and what was the purpose of his journey? We must leave these questions unanswered, but we have found a clear answer to the question asked by the worried Paduan group: R. Jekutiel was not false to their covenant, and twenty years after leaving Padua he was still working energetically to disseminate Luzzatto's writings and win adherents to his teachings.

The clearest factual information we have, thanks to well-authenticated documents from various sources, tells of R. Jekutiel's mission on behalf of the community of Brisk in 5511–12 [1751–2]. *Torat hakenaot*[102] relates that while that book was being printed 'there arrived here the emissary who occasions our concern, the quack doctor Kusel who was sent from Brisk and had been in The Hague, where he was shown honour on the strength of *recom[en]datsiehn*'.[103] The certificate confirming his mission,[104] which was written and signed in Brisk on 23 Iyar 5511 [late spring 1751], with the addition of endorsements from the communities of Breslau, Glogau, Lissa (Leszno), Berlin,[105] Vienna,[106] and Venice,[107] was printed as a leaflet in

[102] p. 58*a*, in small type in the 'printer's foreword', after the testimony on R. Jekutiel's activity in Shklov.

[103] Emden goes on to say that 'he was put up in the home of a distinguished communal leader, whose wife he tried to rape . . . as that highly respected man told us himself'. This kind of information in Emden's writings must be treated with scepticism when not confirmed by another source. In the present case it is clear that even if Jekutiel did come under suspicion, there were no consequences, for he continued his travels on behalf of Brisk without interference and received help wherever he went.

[104] The printed document is in the collection of Mr Abraham Schischa in Letchworth. See Benayahu, 'R' yitsḥak karigal be'italyah', 31 n. 21.

[105] R. Mordecai of Lissa and R. David of Berlin were shown as signatories. Both were among Luzzatto's excommunicators but adopted a moderate attitude compared with the others, and it is possible that R. Mordecai's name was inserted in error in the ban and that he gave no support to it. See *Igerot*, ii. 308–9, 327, 439 n. 258, 441–2 n. 304. R. Jekutiel also visited Metz. See n. 119 below.

[106] Recommendation dated 24 Tishrei 5512 [autumn 1751]. The signatories were the magnates Abraham Sinzheim and Zalman Sinzheim. It was certainly on this visit that R. Jekutiel wrote a short composition in the form of a *piyut*, at the head of which he says: 'I have been moved [literally 'It is my portion, said my soul'—cf. Lam. 3: 24] to compose all the deeds of *Megilat ester* [the Scroll (Book) of Esther] on the letters of the word *megilah* forward and backward from beginning to end, and it was possible to write it in honour of the eminent prince and leader in Israel, the celebrated magnate, the honourable rabbi R. Solomon Zalman *Sega"l* Sinzheim. [This is] my memorial for all generations, and this is my name, Jekutiel son of the saintly teacher and rabbi Judah Leib of Vilna, doctor, of the holy congregation of Brisk of Lithuania, may God preserve it.' The composition was written in pointed Hebrew on parchment in the form of a scroll (MS Oxford 2430), and has been printed under the title *Mishloaḥ manot* ['The Sending of Portions'—Esther 9: 22] (Vienna, 1879). On the magnate R. Solomon Zalman Sinzheim, see B. Wachstein, *Die Inschriften des alten Judenfriedhofes in Wien*, ii (Vienna, 1917), 398 n. 5.

[107] Recommendation dated New Moon, Shevat 5512 [early 1752]. Among the signatories were R. Jacob Belilios, the chief of Luzzatto's enemies and persecutors from 1730 onwards, and

Mantua.[108] Travelling together with R. Jekutiel on this journey in aid of the distressed Brisk community was 'the rabbi, the great luminary, outstanding in his Torah scholarship and fear of Heaven, the erudite, the uprooter of mountains [i.e. a great dialectician], learned in all things, our honourable teacher and master R. Gershon, *av beit din* of the holy congregation of Wysokie (may their Rock and Redeemer preserve them), who was formerly *av beit din* of the holy congregation of Plotsk and district (may their Rock and Redeemer preserve them)', as he is described in the certificate.[109] Heading the signatories from Brisk was 'the humble Nahman son of the celebrated *gaon*, our teacher, the rabbi Samuel Tsevi (may the memory of that righteous man be for a blessing), residing at present here in the aforesaid holy congregation', the rabbi of the community. His name was followed by sixteen others, rabbis and communal leaders.[110]

The very fact that R. Jekutiel was chosen 'to go to and fro over a wide area, the countries of Ashkenaz and Italy and Spain', as the certificate puts it, to act as an emissary of the community of Brisk, shows that he had already been living in Brisk for some years, and that they knew him well and trusted him. But his description and titles tell us much more:

Who is this who comes from the tens of thousands of holiness, whose mouth speaks wisdom and tells [*magid*] his thoughts,[111] who strides in the greatness of his strength, pleasant(?)[112] are the sweet things expressed in his speech [a paraphrase of S. of S. 5: 16—Trans.], his sword on his side; we refer to the wonderful rabbi, the perfect sage of wide learning, on his head a glorious diadem, the crown of the Torah and the crown of a good name, perfect in beauty, sharp in intellect, pure, entirely holy to the Lord, *doktor*, the expert physician, approved as a man and approved as a hundred [*sic*: *keme'ah* instead of *kame'a*, 'an amulet', as in *Shab.* 61: 'the man is approved and the amulet is approved' for healing purposes—Trans.],

R. Solomon Halevi Minzi (Minz) and R. Moses Menahem Merari, both of whom also took part in the campaign against Luzzatto. See *Igerot*, index of names. Apparently they were prepared, in the interests of the Brisk community, to overlook the hostility they had shown to Luzzatto and Jekutiel a few years earlier; they may also have felt regret for what they had done.

[108] See I. Sonne, 'Avnei binyan letoledot hayehudim be'italyah', *Horeb*, 6 (1942), 112–14. The emissaries also visited Ferrara, where they received a recommendation from R. Isaac Lampronti. This was published in Sonne's article.

[109] I have reproduced his personal titles in full for the purpose of comparison with those of R. Jekutiel, which I give below. In addition to his titles there are words of praise for him as *moreh hora'ah* [an arbiter of practical questions in accordance with Jewish law] in his congregation.

[110] Eight of these were among the eleven additional signatories to the Brisk *ḥerem* of 1751 in support of R. Jonathan Eybeschuetz, which was printed in *Luḥot edut*, 37*b*–39*a*. See n. 65 above.

[111] This may allude to his activity as a preacher [*magid*] and 'rebuker of the congregation' [*mokhiaḥ*] in Brisk. See p. 440 below.

[112] The text reads *arekhu* or *erko* [neither of which makes sense here]; apparently *arevu* ['are pleasant'] was intended; a reference to the pleasant words of Torah which issued from his mouth.

our honoured teacher and rabbi Jekutiel, son of our saintly teacher and rabbi Judah Leib of the honourable citizens of the holy congregation of Vilna, *doktor* of our congregation, may his Rock and Redeemer preserve him.

These titles for a 'layman' who held no religious office in the community go beyond the generous expressions of praise by which an emissary would be dignified in order to help him to succeed in his mission. Their particular importance will be apparent if they are compared with the titles attached to his partner in the mission, R. Gershon, which are of a routine nature although he was the rabbi of the community. Especially notable are the expressions 'comes from the tens of thousands of *holiness*', 'sharp in intellect, pure, *entirely holy to the Lord*', which show, in my opinion, that 'the expert physician' was regarded as a healer of souls and was considered holy even outside the limited confines of his own group. It is clear at any rate that if R. Isaac of Biała not only knew of the existence of a group whose members studied and copied Luzzatto's kabbalistic writings but even knew their names, the same information would have been known to the rabbi, R. Nahman Sirkin, father-in-law of R. Elijah, that active member of the group, and to the other leaders of the community. It follows that the rabbis and communal leaders of Brisk were not in the least troubled by the bans and curses laid on Luzzatto's works and on people who studied and distributed them. On the contrary, they looked upon those activities with a kindly eye and admired the head of the group, R. Jekutiel of Vilna.

It is to be supposed that R. Jekutiel completed his mission before the end of 5512 [late summer 1752] and returned to Brisk. In 1755 he left Brisk, intending to 'go up' to the Land of Israel, as related in the letter from R. Isaac of Biała,[113] but failed to reach his destination and was obliged to settle in Venice. His attempt to emigrate to the Land of Israel and his enforced settlement in Venice are described in an interesting autobiographical document written some ten years after his return to Italy, i.e. about 1765.[114] According to R. Jekutiel himself he did not proceed beyond Venice because when he

[113] See pp. 426–9, 435 above.

[114] MS Oxford 2237, fos. 15ʳ–16ᵛ. The document is the 'foreword by the author-compiler', actually an autograph by R. Jekutiel written as an introduction to a compilation of laws and methods of study for his pupils, but only part of the compilation has been preserved. The first part of the foreword, which is the important part as to personal information, was printed in Frumkin's *Toledot ḥakhmei yerushalayim*, ii. 139, but the text is truncated and corrupt, there is no comment on the nature of the document, and no indication that its substance was understood. Frumkin presented the autobiographical material as 'his [Jekutiel's] fortunes and misfortunes up to his arrival in the city of Padua', i.e. before 1728, and so led others into making the same mistake. A complete and corrected text of this document ought to be published. At the end of the foreword the letters *pe"kof* appear; it is hard to decipher their meaning, but the time of writing is determined by the statement 'I have spent these past ten years [in the Torah Or *beit midrash* in Venice] and have not succeeded in raising up pupils with a mastery of the Torah' (fo. 15ᵛ).

arrived there he learned that the magnate Solomon Rakah, whose promise of support in the Land of Israel he had relied on in starting his journey, had departed this life.[115] With the help of 'the princes and leaders of the people' he began teaching in the '*beit midrash* called Torah Or ['the Torah is light']', which was founded by R. Solomon Rakah, 'there to sit constantly engaged in Torah and the service of Heaven, and anyone seeking the Lord in order to study could come and study free of charge'. Particularly important for our present purpose is the beginning of the document,[116] which tells of R. Jekutiel's situation and his activities while in eastern Europe:

I make mention of the Lord's kindnesses and his praise is constantly in my mouth, for his mercies have not ceased from me throughout my life, and he has marvellously performed miracles and wonders for me, my own eyes, not those of another, have seen how whenever my soul was bowed down to the ground and I said: Now I have fallen and shall not rise again, He raised me up from the dust and set me among princes, while I was still in my own country, the land of my birth, when nearly all the great men of the land came often to my door. And also I called at the head of every busy street [Prov. 1: 21] in the midst of assembly and congregation with moral rebuke in the language of the learned which the Lord has given me, [and] in the language of that land,[117] and I showed favour to neither old nor young, neither the venerable and wise nor the ignoramus. My skill in medicine, too, stood me in good stead, even though I did not regard it as a profession or a craft, but only as the skill of a healer and a device for collecting money and receiving 'the reward for going' [*Avot* 5: 14] and the reward for pleasant speech.

We see from this that he experienced ups and downs but sometimes achieved an honoured position in society; and as we have also seen, he was held in similar high regard in Brisk. It is important to note that he also acted as a preacher and 'rebuker' in the congregation. His activity in the groups with which he was associated is not even hinted at here.

It is clear, however, that he saw that activity as his principal mission, and that, of course, is our main concern at present. By getting to know R. Jekutiel's work as head of a group in Brisk we have been given answers to the questions I put at the beginning of this section. R. Elijah 'found' Luzzatto's kabbalistic works in the collection of writings which R. Jekutiel brought with him from Padua; it was from Jekutiel that he received authori-

[115] The day of his death is noted by R. Moses David Valle in one of his manuscript entries: 'On the last day of Tishrei, year 5515 [autumn 1754], Shelomoh Rakah, my dear friend, died (may his soul rest in Eden), and may God, blessed be He, help me, for he is Lord of everything and everything is from Him. Heal me, O Lord, and I shall be healed; save me, and I shall be saved; for You are my praise.' And see p. 428 and n. 67 above.

[116] MS Oxford 2237, fo. 15^r. Some words in the manuscript are deleted and there are additions above the line, but I have not indicated such details here and have incorporated the additions in the text.

[117] Undoubtedly Yiddish.

tative news of what the exiled kabbalist was doing, of his exalted status, and of the admiration in which he was held by the sages of Amsterdam; and R. Elijah, in his efforts to publish the 'hidden' writings and disseminate knowledge of Luzzatto's kabbalah, was continuing the work of R. Jekutiel of Vilna.

But one question remains open, and at present can only be given a conjectural answer based on impressions and personal judgement: did R. Elijah act as an individual on his own initiative or were there others who shared in his propagandist work? Since it has been made clear that there was a group interested in disseminating Luzzatto's kabbalistic writings in Brisk, and it has been shown that R. Elijah belonged to that group, the question should be formulated differently: what happened to R. Jekutiel of Vilna's group after its leader left Brisk? Did it break up, was it wound up, did its activities cease, or did it continue to operate and foster the cult of Luzzatto's personality and doctrine under another leader, or as a group of friends with common views and aims but no particular leader? If we were to try to decide this question by drawing analogies from the fate of other groups of the same kind, we could find a wide variety of examples which give different answers. It seems to me, however, that we can find reasonable grounds for a decision in the following points: (*a*) One of the principal bases for the existence of the group in Brisk was the study of Luzzatto's 'hidden' writings, and since there were still copies in the possession of members of the group, there remained a strong justification for its continuance. (*b*) R. Elijah of Brisk's cry in his foreword to *Mesilat yesharim*: 'And I said in my heart: When will I create a lasting reputation for him in Israel by spreading his thoughts among the public so that the earth will be full of knowledge?'[118] shows that his ambition to publish Luzzatto's kabbalistic writings and extend the influence of his doctrine to the wider community was exercising him long before 5526 [1766], and his aspiration was probably shared by the other members of the group in Brisk. I incline to the opinion that his partners in this aspiration remained faithful to it even after [his departure in] 1755, and that when he left for Zholkva to begin putting it into execution his companions stood by him and did all they could to help him. (*c*) The wish to right the wrong done to Luzzatto by his excommunication and the banning of his writings was another fundamental reason for the existence of the group. This was certainly a strong emotional factor in people who had learnt of Luzzatto's greatness and of what had befallen him from R. Jekutiel of Vilna; and since, in the years following R. Jekutiel's departure from Lithuania, nothing had been done to ease the bans, it is to be supposed that the members of the group would not have discontinued their efforts to achieve the desired rehabilitation.

[118] See p. 415 above.

To reinforce these considerations I will add one matter which has not been discussed and indeed has remained unknown until now. From the latest evidence which had been available on the life of R. Jekutiel in Venice after 1755, which dated from 1760, it appeared that at that time he was supplementing his income by copying manuscripts.[119] I have dealt above with the document he wrote in 1765 or thereabouts,[120] but prayers preserved in manuscript[121] make it clear that he lived for years after that. At one point he says:

You are the Healer of all flesh and Worker of wonders; behold, it is time that You healed all the afflicted and the stricken and sufferers of torments with the King-Messiah. Heal us, O Lord, and we shall be healed, save us and we shall be saved, for You are our praise. And if You wait for the perfect repentance of Your people Israel, all the years in the world will not suffice for them, for behold, *a thousand and seven hundred and four years are the days of our exile*, and it is impossible to unite them [the people] all in perfect repentance, for You have dispersed us to the four corners of the earth, and we have nothing except our hope in You that You, Lord God, will act and sprinkle clean water upon us to cause us to return to You.[122]

The date is 5532 [1772]. Another prayer refers to the year 5533 three times, here too in terms of the number of years of the Exile:

Even one who does not believe in their [Israel's] redemption—judge him leniently, for who can believe [after] so long an exile . . . for a thousand and 705 years have gone by, we have not seen our signs, there is no longer any prophet, nor is there with us anyone who knows how long [Ps. 74: 9] . . . and how many troubles we have endured and persecutions of thousands and tens of thousands who have been killed or burnt to death for the sanctification of Your name . . . and You have not avenged them or Your Torah. *In view of those many years, a thousand and 705 years*, it is beyond me to understand how they remain Jews with all the wickedness they suffer from the nations[123] . . . And who is like Your people Israel, a nation unique on earth, who are not swallowed up among the Gentiles and remain one nation wherever they are

[119] See Benayahu, 'R' yitsḥak karigal be'italyah', 30–1, 34. E. Carmoly's *Itinéraires de la Terre Sainte* (Brussels, 1847), 229, gives the content of a letter in manuscript which was written by R. Mordecai di Padova, a resident of Venice, to B. Shapira in Metz on the subject of support for the yeshivas of Tiberias and Jerusalem. R. Mordecai said in that letter that he had consulted the physician Jekutiel Gordon of Vilna, who had been living in Venice for the past three years as a member of the Torah Or *beit midrash*, and Jekutiel had praised B. Shapira, whom he had got to know when he passed through Metz on his mission on behalf of the community of Brisk. (I am obliged to Dr M. Benayahu for drawing my attention to Carmoly's book.) Carmoly thought that the letter was written in 1756, but it is clear from the number of years that R. Jekutiel had lived in Venice that the correct date is 1758. See pp. 439–40 above.

[120] See p. 439 above.

[121] R. Jekutiel's prayers are interesting and important from several points of view, and I hope to publish them together with other writings by him.

[122] MS Oxford 2237, fo. 109^{v}.

[123] Ibid., fo. 125^{v}.

and are killed for the sanctification of Your name, *a thousand and 705 years* [are] *the days of this evil which has faced us.*[124]

In prayers of confession and thanksgiving for recovery from sickness as an old man, R. Jekutiel relates that he survived serious illnesses at the age of 80 and over.[125] Apparently R. Jekutiel was a few years older than Luzzatto.[126] At any rate it is clear that he died after 5540 [1780], and it may have been after 5545 [1785]. We must therefore ask: was his contact with his comrades and pupils in Brisk and elsewhere in Lithuania completely broken off for as long as twenty-five to thirty years? The question cannot be firmly decided without documentary support, but one may reasonably speculate that they were sometimes in touch with each other by correspondence, and perhaps that he sometimes found a way of sending his allies copies of additional kabbalistic writings by Luzzatto which R. Jekutiel was keen to distribute and the members of his groups were anxious to obtain.[127]

[124] Ibid., fo. 129^{r}. The complete prayer is at fos. 125^{r-v}, 129^{r-v}. When the manuscript was bound the two folios were separated. Two fragments of this prayer were printed in *Toledot ḥakhmei yerushalayim*, ii. 139–41, in transposed order and in ignorance that they belonged to a single prayer. The text of the copies is badly mutilated, and the date is wrong. Frumkin erroneously read *tav shin" he* ('705') as *tav samekh" he* ('465'), and because he had determined, on the basis of an imagined chronology, that the prayer was written in 5496 (*tav tsadi vav*: 1736), he proposed to 'correct' the year to read 'a thousand and *tav resh samekh" he*' ('665')! And see Sonne, 'Avnei binyan letoledot hayehudim be'italyah', 113 n. 1. Sonne accepted Frumkin's erroneous conclusion that the prayer was composed while R. Jekutiel was in Padua with Luzzatto's group, and he added 'explanations' which compounded the error; for example, he understood 'one who does not believe in their [Israel's] redemption' as meaning Jews who had been attracted to the Christian faith under the influence of missionaries in Italy, and he understood R. Jekutiel's intention as being to offer a defence of such Jews! (ibid.).

[125] 'You have shown wonderful kindness towards me in granting me a complete cure, for no one would believe that a man of 80, old and full of years, would recover from an illness [so] grave and great' (MS Oxford 2237, fo. 117^{r}). And see ibid., fos. 131^{r}, 137^{r}. At fos. 137^{v}–138^{v} there is a second prayer of thanksgiving for having survived a later illness.

[126] He was married before he came to Padua, as is shown by his request in 1730 to pass a letter on to his wife (see *Igerot*, ii. 263). The statement in his letter to R. Joshua Heschel, *av beit din* of Vilna, at the end of 5489 [late summer 1729] that the Lord had brought it about 'that He prevented my footsteps from making their way [to Padua] . . . in years past' (ibid. 407) also goes to show that he was born a few years before 5467 [1707], the year of Luzzatto's birth. He appears to have arrived in Padua at the end of 5488 or the beginning of 5489 [late summer–early autumn 1728]. See *Igerot*, i. 30–1, 70.

[127] It is true that documents written by R. Jekutiel which have been preserved in manuscript show that he was in a difficult financial situation in Venice, and apparently the members of his group in Brisk were not well-to-do either. Nevertheless they were able to find the means to pay the expenses of correspondence and the dispatch of copies, just as they managed to pay for the making of the copies in Brisk. On the basis of the documents mentioned I surmise that R. Jekutiel would also have liked to establish a mystical group in the Torah Or yeshiva in Venice but was unable to do so. His pupils did not make the progress in their studies he would have wished, and they left the *beit midrash* at an early age and went into business.

I will conclude with a very difficult and important question: is there not reason to think that there was contact, perhaps on a personal level too, between the members of R. Jekutiel's group—or between R. Elijah of Brisk and his colleagues after they parted from R. Jekutiel—and members of active hasidic groups which were taking shape in the regions of Podolia and Galicia at that time? In trying to answer this question we are groping in the dark wherever we turn. The truth is that whereas we have legends which have been handed down, documented information on the inner lives, aims, and activities of the hasidic groups during the early years of hasidism is scarce and is no more reliable than the information we have on R. Jekutiel and his groups. It need hardly be added that there are no factual data on relations between the two types of group. The only area where we have a documentary basis for our consideration is the *beit midrash* of the Maggid of Mezhirech, who, with his disciple R. Jacob Joseph of Ostrog and his disciple's hasid R. Gedaliah ben Elyakum of Korets, showed admiration for Luzzatto and sought to improve his public image and distribute his 'hidden' writings, drawing support, avowed or not, from the words of R. Elijah of Brisk.[128] It could be argued that their only connection consisted in reading R. Elijah's forewords to *Mesilat yesharim* and *Derekh ets ḥayim* and acquiring information and opinions from that source. But in my opinion there are signs which point to the existence of some links, extending beyond the printed forewords, with admirers of Luzzatto who had first-hand knowledge of details unknown in Poland of his life and hardships, his successes and setbacks, his writings and his doctrine. I find it hard to imagine that it was solely on the 'publisher's foreword' that the Maggid of Mezhirech based his declaration that 'his [Luzzatto's] generation was not worthy to understand his righteousness and asceticism' and that his persecutors, the rabbis of Poland and Ashkenaz, calumniated him 'out of their great lack of knowledge'. I would think it even harder to say that the praise lavished on Luzzatto and his kabbalah in R. Jacob Joseph of Ostrog's letter of approval—which appears also to contain allusions to the revelations of Luzzatto's *magid*—is related to R. Elijah of Brisk's forewords alone, owing nothing to any close contact with people familiar with authoritative sources.[129] And lastly: the enthusiastic references

[128] See pp. 420–3 above.

[129] In R. Jacob Joseph of Ostrog's letter of approval in the first editions of R. Hayim Vital's *Ets ḥayim* and *Peri ets ḥayim* (both Korets, 5542 [1782]), he praises the distribution of printed versions of books of kabbalah, taking as his authorities the ruling by R. Isaac de Lattes in the foreword to the Zohar (Mantua, 1558) and R. Hayim Vital's foreword to *Ets ḥayim*. He writes: 'Especially as we see with our own eyes that this observation is from Heaven, as He revealed His secret to the Tana, the holy light, the rabbi Simeon bar Yohai (may he be remembered for life in the world to come), that this knowledge might be revealed in the footsteps of the Messiah [i.e. when the Messiah is on his way].' This messianic note well befits a scholar who was closely in tune with the activity and kabbalistic teachings of Luzzatto. As this sentence was written by a

in the foreword by the publisher of *Kela"ḥ pitḥei ḥokhmah*, R. Gedaliah ben Elyakum, cannot, in my opinion, be explained as a puff to promote the sales

disciple of the Maggid of Mezhirech it is also of interest in connection with the debate among scholars on the attitude of hasidism to messianism. See I. Tishby, 'Harayon hameshiḥi vehamegamot hameshiḥiyot bitsemiḥat haḥasidut', *Zion*, 32 (1967), 1–3, 29–45. There is nothing novel in the content of the declaration by 'Rav Yeivi' [R. Jacob Joseph] which I have quoted; it merely paraphrases *Tikunei hazohar*, R. Isaac de Lattes, and R. Hayim Vital. But that precisely is what makes it important for the study of hasidism. A hasidic declaration in the spirit of those sources does not square with the opinion that there was a shift in hasidism towards a deliberate neutralization of messianic aims and that aspirations to hasten 'the end of days' were thrust out of sight. The clash with that opinion is particularly striking if the words of R. Jacob Joseph are considered against the latest formulation of the theory of neutralization in Rivkah Schatz-Uffenheimer's *Haḥasidut kemistikah* (Jerusalem, 1968), 170: 'The echoes of the watchword of the author of the *Tikunim*, that "by this work [the Zohar] they will emerge from the Exile", which R. Isaac de Lattes used to support his polemic permitting the printing of the Zohar, or the echoes of R. Hayim Vital's campaign to clear the way for Luria's kabbalah in the name of the messianic idea, are no longer current coin in hasidic thought.' For 'Rav Yeivi', on the contrary, those echoes really were 'current coin', since he used them to justify the printing of books of Lurianic kabbalah: 'And therefore I said, concerning the good workman, may He add to your strength in Torah; and I agree with the rabbis, the lights of the Exile, who preceded me, both in their authorization of the printing and in their decree with regard to the protection of copyright.' On the messianic aims which underlay the printing of the Zohar by R. Isaac de Lattes and his faction, see I. Tishby, 'Hapulmus al sefer hazohar bame'ah hashesh-esreh be'italyah', *Perakim*, 1 (1967–8), 141, 153–8.

If I may turn here to a related matter: while studying R. Jacob Joseph of Ostrog's letter of approval [see the beginning of this note—Trans.] I came across several pieces of bibliographical information which also have some importance by reason of their content and which may suitably be examined here although they are not relevant to the main body of the present essay. The National Library in Jerusalem has three Korets editions of both *Ets ḥayim* and *Peri ets ḥayim*: *Ets ḥayim*—5542, 5544, 5545–6; *Peri ets ḥayim*—5542, 5545, 5546. (*Peri ets ḥayim* 5546 is not in Tauber's study *Defusei korets* ['Books Published in Korets'], which I have mentioned several times [but not in these essays, though Tauber is mentioned in nn. 44 and 52 above—Trans.].) The first three letters of approval, written in 5541 (by *Mar* Hayim of Zanz and *Mar* Moses Ostrer, the two sages of the Brody *klaus*, and *Mar* Abraham Mordecai, *av beit din* of Zholkva) and printed in *Ets ḥayim* and *Peri ets ḥayim*, edition of 5542, praise the editor, R. Isaac Halevi of Satanov, the well-known *maskil*, who numbered among his 'hobbies' an interest in printing kabbalistic books. However, in the letters of approval by R. Jacob Joseph of Ostrog and his hasidic friends, R. Asher Tsevi and R. Samson of Ostrog, and in the letter of approval from the sages of the Ostrog *klaus*, all dated 5542 and printed together with the first three, there is no mention of the editor's name. The omission is certainly not accidental. Indeed in 5545 these hasidic scholars, headed by R. Jacob Joseph, gave their blessing to a different editor in their new letters of approval for the third editions of *Ets ḥayim* (5545–6) and *Peri ets ḥayim* (5546), and this time they added emphasis to the mention of his name: 'The distinguished, the celebrated, the hasid, the venerable, our teacher and rabbi, R. Simeon of the holy congregation of Korets'. But in the second edition of *Peri ets ḥayim* (5545) I found a strange complication. In that edition the letters of approval from the first edition (5542) were printed unaltered save for the omission of the one from the sages of the Ostrog *klaus*, just as in the second edition of *Ets ḥayim* (5544), but in this case, below the commendations, there was a statement which I will reproduce in full: '[I] add to the first ones these, having by our labours found a [copy of the] book, *P*[*eri*] *e*[*ts*] *ḥ*[*ayim*],

of a new book. They seem to me rather the heartfelt words of a man who was genuinely concerned for the fate of both the book and its author and was anx-

most carefully revised, which has been copied from a manuscript of the late rabbi, hasid, and kabbalist, our teacher R. Shabetai Rashkover, may his memory be for a blessing, all of whose writings can be considered to be sound, since, as is known, his reputation is firmly based, and what is well known requires no proof. There are also added in this book some observations by disciples of the Ari [Luria], may his memory be for a blessing, which no eye had seen at the time of the first edition. If anything had been added anywhere from the fresh insights of our teacher R. Shabetai himself, we would not have wished to commit them to print, but only the observations of the disciples of the Ari, may his memory be for a blessing. However, if there should be found some difficult question and answer signed "Shabetai", let it be known that it is an accidental error, for we did not order any additions to be inserted in the writings of the Ari other than the observations of his distinguished disciples who are known to everybody, and let no man other than them lift his hand to compose a complete item or an addition except in a separate book with the approval of the sages of the generation.' (In connection with the dissemination of Luzzatto's kabbalistic works it is important to note that the year in which this statement was published also saw the publication in Korets of the '138 Gateways to Wisdom', which was described as a commentary to *Ets ḥayim*, and was indeed printed as 'a separate book with the approval of the sages of the generation'. See p. 420 above.) Even a superficial examination is enough to show that the text of this edition differs substantially from that of the first edition. The content of the letters of approval printed here would oblige us, on the face of it, to reach the surprising conclusion that R. Isaac of Satanov, the *maskil*, replaced the previous version by the one in the copy made by R. Shabetai of Rashkov, who was a friend of the Ba'al Shem Tov and the hasidic movement, and that the statement I have reproduced was written by the maskilic editor. However, from the third edition of *Peri ets ḥayim* (5546), which also contains R. Shabetai of Rashkov's version but with new letters of approval and (like the third edition of *Ets ḥayim*, 5545–6, described above) bears the name of the hasidic editor R. Simeon, it is perfectly clear to me that the hasidic editor was also responsible for the preparation of the second edition of *Peri ets ḥayim* (5545). In other words, the coupling of R. Isaac of Satanov with the manuscript from the literary remains of R. Shabetai of Rashkov is just a bibliographical curiosity which has no foundation in fact, and at present it is hard for me to suggest any reasonable explanation for the confusion. On R. Isaac of Satanov and his writings, see I. Zinberg, *Toledot sifrut yisra'el*, v (Tel Aviv, 1959), 118–22; S. Werses, 'Al yitsḥak satanov veḥiburo "mishlei asaf"', *Tarbiz*, 32 (1963), 370–92. See also Lieberman, 'Legende un emes vegn die ḥasidishe drukereien', 193, 197, 207. It appears to me that Satanov used Luzzatto as a stylistic model in some of his books. He may have had before him some works by Luzzatto in manuscript; at any rate he had knowledge of Luzzatto's activity and his writings in the field of kabbalah from books by Emden, and he certainly knew the '138 Gateways' and *Ḥoker umekubal*, which were printed in 5545 [1785]. Apparently, when he wrote *Kunteres misefer hazohar ḥibura tinyana* (Berlin, 1783) and in his imitations of the Psalms in *Zemirot asaf* (Berlin, 1793) Satanov's mental picture was of Luzzatto's *Zohar tinyana* and book of psalms, a few fragments of which have been preserved, but there is no essential resemblance between the books of the two authors. The '138 Gateways' provided Satanov with a specimen of an allegedly ancient source accompanied by a commentary credited to the writer (see n. 47 above). In Satanov's *Imrei binah* (1784), which is arranged in the form of a dialogue between 'Jedaiah, [the man] of great understanding, and Noam, the man of faith', on the relations between scholarly research and kabbalah, I see a resemblance to Luzzatto's *Ḥoker umekubal*. (If *Imrei binah* really was printed in 5544 [1784], as stated—in the abbreviated form '544'—on the title-page, it was published before *Ḥoker umekubal*. It should be observed that a manuscript of *Ḥoker umekubal* was in the possession of R. Solomon Dubno, a member of the

ious to imbue its readers with a sense of the extraordinary greatness of both. In the light of these indications I am of the opinion that the most satisfactory answer to the question is obtained if we are prepared to accept the hypothesis that the hasidic personalities referred to, and perhaps some of their close associates, were on friendly terms with the propagandists of Luzzatto's *beit midrash* and his pupils, R. Jekutiel of Vilna and R. Elijah of Brisk and their colleagues, and lent a sympathetic ear to the praises they heard from those quarters. If that is the case, R. Gedaliah ben Elyakum's addition to the words of R. Elijah of Brisk: 'this work [of printing Luzzatto's writings] was done for him by others who were eager for his words, the words of the living God',[130] and the use of the plural in this addition, are not mere rhetorical flourishes

circle of *maskilim* in Berlin in Satanov's time; and a copy of that manuscript, noted at its end that it was made in 1786 in Frankfurt am Main for R. Wolf Heidenheim, is in MS Oxford 2285, fos. 1^r–19^r.) Luzzatto's book was also printed in a reworked version under the title *Milḥemet mosheh* (Warsaw, 1889) with the addition of a foreword by the anonymous editor, who presented himself as a pupil of Luzzatto. That version, which I regard as of doubtful authenticity [but see Essay 1, n. 167—Trans.], also appears in MS Oxford 1306 (fos. 113^r–140^r), where it is headed by the title *Imrei binah*—the same title as Satanov's book—in a different handwriting from that of the text of the manuscript. It is not impossible that R. Isaac of Satanov had a hand in the editing of the reworked text. And see N. Ben-Menahem, 'Kol shaḥal: shirei efrayim lutsato', *Kiryat sefer*, 44 (1969), 560–2.

It should be pointed out that R. Isaac Eisik Haver [Wildmann], who wrote important commentaries on kabbalistic writings by the Vilna Gaon (his teacher was R. Menahem Mendel of Shklov, one of the Gaon's leading pupils, who saw to the editing and publication of the Gaon's works), regarded the printing of books of Lurianic kabbalah as creating a stumbling-block. In his book *Magen vetsinah* ([Königsberg?], n.d.), 4*b*, he wrote: 'Head of all sin in putting into print the words of the Ari (may his memory be for a blessing) was that wicked man and heretic of Satanov, as is well known.' But he found retrospective justification for the printing, quoting in support the fact that 'there have already been published the words of the rabbi, the godly hasid, R. M. H. Luzzatto, may his memory be for a blessing, in his treatises which are more precious than all the delightful things of the world, [the man] who, in relation to certain matters, revealed the depth of their meaning' (ibid.; and see ibid. 59*a*–61*b*). At about the same time we hear from within the hasidic movement that R. Abraham Joshua Heschel of Apta refused to sign a letter of approval for the publication of a new edition of *Ets ḥayim* and *Peri ets ḥayim* which had been prepared for printing by R. Tsevi Hirsch of Zhidachov with the object of hastening the Redemption, and it was also said that the Tsadik of Apta 'cursed even the original printers who printed those holy books' (letter from R. Tsevi Hirsch of Zhidachov to R. Abraham Joshua Heschel of Apta, in [Heschel's] book *Eser kedushot ler' yisra'el berger* (Piotrków, 1906), 35). It is hard to establish the year in which the letter was written, because the words at its head which ostensibly give the year in *gematriyah* (*asher yidvenu libo*), if taken with no omissions, yield [5]611 [1851]! And see A. Marcus, *Haḥasidut* (Tel Aviv, 1954), 164, 166–7. (This book was originally written in German and published as a complete work in 1901. The text of the Hebrew translation is defective and corrupt, as was pointed out by G. Scholem in his essay 'Aharon markus vehaḥasidut', *Beḥinot*, 7 (1954), 3–8, but for the present purpose I see no reason to refer the reader to the German original.)

130 See p. 421 above.

but are meant to refer to the existence of a group of people 'eager for his words', of whom R. Gedaliah was one, and who knew and consented to what he was doing.[131]

[131] Aaron Marcus, whose extreme admiration for Luzzatto was expressed in wild exaggerations—a characteristic of his whether apportioning praise or blame—and who attributed marvellous new ideas to him without the least foundation in fact, repeatedly emphasized his view that, greatly to the credit of the hasidim, the Maggid of Mezhirech's statement in his favour and the publicity the Maggid gave to *Kela"ḥ pitḥei ḥokhmah* led to the lifting of the bans on Luzzatto's kabbalistic writings and rescued them from total destruction. See Marcus's book *Haḥasidut*, 68–9, 224, 280, 287, 324. (On new ideas in science and philosophy attributed to Luzzatto, see ibid. 78–9, 166, 207, 251, 280, 299, 311, 324–6, 355, 373, 405; A. Marcus, *Hartmann's inductive Philosophie im Chassidismus*, i (Lemberg, 1889), 19–29, 83.) Marcus's admiration for Luzzatto reached its peak in his Hebrew book *Keset hasofer* (Kraków, 1912). Here his praise of Luzzatto (whom he generally calls 'the Rav, may he be remembered for life in the world to come' without naming him) is quite unbounded, and is accompanied by numerous extracts from his works, most of them lengthy. I will content myself with reproducing one passage which is of great interest in the present context. After pointing out the superiority of 'the words of the Rav, may he be remembered for life in the world to come' over the words of other kabbalists, Marcus writes that their high value had not been recognized except 'in the eyes of the nobles of the children of Israel, the honourable rabbis of all the exiles, the rabbis R. Baer [the Maggid of Mezhirech] and the Gra ['the Gaon R. Elijah', the Vilna Gaon], may their memory be for a blessing, who, even though a mountain had been raised between them by slanderers, men of baseless hatred . . . both of them saw the great nobility of the wisdom of the Rav, may he be remembered for life in the world to come', and it was brought about by Heaven 'that the Rabbi, the great Maggid, rescued the book *Kela"ḥ pitḥei ḥokhmah* like a brand plucked from the fire, and ordered his pupil and servant, author of the book *Divrat shelomoh* [R. Solomon of Lutsk], to print it, and so it was printed in 5548 [*sic*: actually 5545 [1785], the last digit being not *ḥet* but *he*]; and had it not been for this we would have had no means of answering their [the Gentile scholars'] new learning [in the natural sciences]' (p. 12*a*). In point of fact there is no basis for claiming that the rescue of Luzzatto's writings and their preservation for future generations should be credited to the teachers of hasidism, but nevertheless the following grain of truth can be found in what Marcus says: in 1785 hasidim tried to get the excommunications annulled, and apparently they planned to publish other kabbalistic writings by Luzzatto in addition to *Kela"ḥ pitḥei ḥokhmah*, but the same opposition that led to the deletion of the 'publisher's foreword' frustrated their plan. At any rate it seems to me that in what he says, Marcus is transmitting a feeling of admiration by hasidim for Luzzatto which he got to hear of while on his visits to tsadikim in Poland.

However, among the teachers of hasidism in Poland at about the time in the nineteenth century that Marcus was living there, there were some who took exception to Luzzatto's kabbalistic writings. In *Netiv mitsvoteikha* (Part 'Hatorah', Path A, sect. 32), R. Isaac Eisik of Komarno named *Kela"ḥ pitḥei ḥokhmah* and *Ḥoker umekubal* as examples of 'books of the moderns' which it was 'dreadfully dangerous to peruse even in a cursory manner', as I pointed out in my essay 'Harayon hameshiḥi vehamegamot hameshiḥiyot bitsemiḥat haḥasidut', 41 n. 180. The same hasid-kabbalist also made similar remarks, express or implied, elsewhere in his books. I will quote one sentence of express condemnation: 'In this matter, do not be so foolish as to be a kabbalist and peruse the books [plural] *Ḥoker umekubal*, on worthless matters' (*Heikhal haberakhah* (Lemberg, 1866), 'Va'etḥanan', 27*d*). It is fair to presume that R. Tsevi Hirsch of Zhidachov, R. Isaac Eisik of Komarno's teacher, also rejected Luzzatto's kabbalah. In his sharp attack on the Habad school of thought, without mentioning Habad by name, he wrote of explanations of

It is common knowledge that both the Vilna Gaon and his pupils were great admirers of Luzzatto, and their admiration was not limited to the Luzzatto of the ethical teachings in *Mesilat yesharim* but extended to him as a teacher of kabbalah. According to a reliable tradition, the Gaon 'said of him [Luzzatto] that he knew the underlying meaning of the Ari's writings (for the Gra, may his memory be for a blessing, said that the writings of the Ari were entirely allegorical)'.[132] It is therefore appropriate to contrast the viewpoint

'the words of the Zohar and the *Idrot* and the words of the Ari, may his memory be for a blessing, who speaks of the *partsufim alef beit yod" ayin* [the 'countenances' of God *atsilut, beriah, yetsirah, asiyah*: Emanation, Creation, Formation, Making] and they [those who offer these explanations] say that this is all by way of allegory and subtle distinction and cleverness in the service of God, and they explain matters as allegories by means of intellectual examination'. Of such explanations he said that this was a way 'close, Heaven forbid, to heresy, may the Merciful One deliver us' (*Hakdamah vederekh le'ets hahayim* (Lemberg, 1870), sheet 4, 3*b*; and see ibid. 6, 4*d*–7, 1*a*). From the substance of his remarks and in view of his pupil's outlook it appears to me that this denunciation was directed against Luzzatto's writings too. A. Marcus strongly disapproved of R. Tsevi Hirsch of Zhidachov's attitude (see *Haḥasidut*, 123, 157–9, 163, 269). Attention should also be drawn to another contrast between Marcus, quoting his chief teacher in hasidism R. Solomon of Radomsk, and R. Tsevi Hirsch of Zhidachov. R. Tsevi Hirsch, in his letter to R. Abraham Joshua Heschel of Apta, was severely critical of *Mikdash melekh*, the famous commentary on the Zohar by R. Shalom Buzaglo, and had this to say on the author and his book: 'We do not know whether he was properly ordained as a rabbi and is fit to be trusted . . . I have looked at the marginal comments in *mk"m* [*Mikdash melekh*] and find that he made no corrections at all in them . . . I will show the *admor* [the addressee] numerous cases in which opinions in the marginal comments in *mk"m* are mistaken . . . really inverting the facts . . . turning and confusing' (Heschel, *Eser kedushot ler' yisra'el berger*, 36–7). Similarly *Ateret tsevi*, R. Tsevi Hirsch's commentary on the Zohar, is full of criticisms of *Mikdash melekh*. Marcus, on the other hand, in his commentary to R. Jacob Halevi of Marvege's *She'elot uteshuvot min hashamayim* (Tel Aviv, 1957), 34–5, wrote: 'As was said by the holy man of God, our teacher and rabbi, the rabbi R. Solomon Hakohen of Radomsk, the work and the author are of completely unequal greatness, for the [author of] *Mikdash melekh* [was] a very simple man, but expert in matters of detail, and composed a commentary which is indispensable for the study of the Zohar.'

132 In Luzzatto's *Derekh tevunot* (Jerusalem, 1880), 38*b*, in a letter of 17 Iyar 5619 [early summer 1859] from R. Abraham Simhah of Mestislav, nephew of R. Hayim of Volozhin. The writer quoted these words of the Gra as having been reported by his uncle. Cf. the remarks of R. Elijah of Brisk in his foreword to *Mesilat yesharim*: 'For the Ari, may he be remembered for life in the world to come, clothed these matters in several garments, and the student must remove the covering from the words spoken in the language of allegory', and 'you will understand from his [Luzzatto's] book clearly and not in riddles, you will understand the allegory of the ancients, the words of the Ari and his disciples'. See pp. 412–13 above. It should be observed that the discussion of Luzzatto's commentary on *Idra raba* applies to a manuscript. The commentary was printed under the title *Adir bamarom* in 1886, twenty-seven years after the letter was written, and the reported conversation had taken place long before that. There were many copies of this work in circulation among the Gaon's pupils before it was printed; it was much admired by them and they quoted freely from it. It should be noted here that R. Abraham Simhah, in reporting his conversation with his uncle, added: '(for I have seen several copies of this manuscript and all of them alike break off with the subject unfinished, and although it occupies more than 68 quarto leaves, it is a commentary to the extent of only about two [and] a half leaves from

of R. Hayim of Volozhin, a pupil of the Gaon, with that of the Maggid of Mezhirech and his disciples, in the matter of the dispute over Luzzatto and the banning of his works. R. Hayim's nephew (his brother's son) relates that after his uncle had agreed with him that Luzzatto's expositions of *Idra raba* 'are all awe-inspiring revelations from the world above',

> I went on to say to him that I was very upset by the charges brought against so godly a man, and he replied: 'It is not for us to consider the matter or think about it at all, for have we not seen that with regard to those of his works against which there have been no accusations, it has been decreed from Heaven that they should be revealed in the world, and those against which there have been accusations (the Psalms and his *tikunim* on the verse "and in all the mighty hand" [Deut. 34: 12]) have not been revealed in the world.'[133]

In spite of their recognition of Luzzatto's holiness and superlative merit, going so far as to acknowledge that his writings on kabbalah were 'awe-inspiring revelations from the world above', it will be observed that in regard to the accusations and accusers R. Hayim adopts an attitude of caution and reserve which leaves room for him to justify the action of Luzzatto's opponents on the basis [of the Hillel–Shammai ruling—Trans.] that 'these and those are the words of the living God'. Clearly this attitude is intended to avoid any offence to the rabbis who placed a ban on Luzzatto's writings. It seems to me that a comparison of the remarks just quoted with the sharp condemnation of Luzzatto's opponents by the Maggid of Mezhirech, both orally and in print, many years before R. Hayim's conversation with his nephew, can help us to appreciate the significance of that early hasidic counter-attack and see it in its proper light.

As I have said, at this stage I offer it as no more than a hypothesis that there were contacts between the founders of hasidism and the members of R. Jekutiel of Vilna's group. But one thing I am prepared to say without reservation: if it becomes clear that there are points of contact and close parallels between the ideas in Luzzatto's kabbalistic writings and those in the literature of hasidism which could point to a relationship of source and derivation, the existence of such a relationship should not be dismissed by arguing that the relevant works by Luzzatto were hidden away during the early growth period of hasidism and could not have served as sources for its doctrine. The matters

the beginning of the *Idra*, and it is not known whether he, may his memory be for a blessing, did not write any more on this topic, or whether it is our misfortune that his holy words on the whole of the *Idra* have not been discovered)'. The scope of the book in print corresponds approximately to this description. At least one manuscript which has been preserved contains much more than the printed version. I plan to publish the additional material. And see above, p. 413 and n. 19, and n. 47.

[133] *Derekh tevunot*, 38*a–b*. And see the foreword to Luzzatto's *Derekh hashem* (Jerusalem, 1914).

I have raised in the foregoing consideration certainly suffice to support the modest conclusion that the first hasidim read 'hidden' works of kabbalah by Luzzatto and were influenced by them.

This brings us, then, to the large question: is there a strong kinship of ideas between the two areas under discussion? The answer to this must depend on a critical comparison of the main elements of early hasidic literature with the principal ideas in the ramified literary output of Luzzatto and the members of his group, in print and in manuscript.[134]

MESILAT YESHARIM, EDITION OF ZHOLKVA 5526

After I had sent this essay to be printed, I learned that the library of [the yeshiva] Ets Hayim in Amsterdam had a copy of *Mesilat yesharim* and *Derekh ets ḥayim* in the combined edition of Zholkva 5526 which had been withdrawn as a result of Jewish censorship and lost to sight as I explained above. Meanwhile a photograph of it has been received in the National and University Library in Jerusalem, and I append a few details.

This may be the copy put up for auction in Amsterdam in 1899 (see n. 4 above). At the top of the title-page is a signature: 'Shelomoh midubno' [Solomon of Dubno], and the book was undoubtedly bought by that well-known *maskil* shortly after it was published in 1766. This supplements the testimony quoted in n. 129 above that Solomon Dubno handed over a manuscript of Luzzatto's *Ḥoker umekubal* to be copied in Germany. We know of his admiration for Luzzatto and Luzzatto's literary works from his introduction to his edition of *Layesharim tehilah* (Berlin, 1780). The two items of information I have given show that he was also interested in Luzzatto's ethical and kabbalistic works.

Of course this edition does not contain the spurious addition 'and the book *Derekh ets ḥayim*' which appears at the conclusion of Luzzatto's epilogue in the edition of Zholkva 5528 (see pp. 408 and 420 above). The book is not headed with any letters of approval, and there are no differences of substance in R. Elijah of Brisk's forewords as compared with the Shklov editions of 5595 (see pp. 408–10 above).

I note here three readings in the foreword to *Derekh ets ḥayim* which are relevant to the quotations included in my essay: 'I have already declared my purpose in the introduction [singular] to the book . . .' (see p. 411 above); 'For not so is [the] servant Moses . . .' (see p. 415 above [which has the same

[134] I am at present engaged in the preparation of a comparative study along these lines. [See now Essay 10.—Trans.]

reading—Trans.] and n. 24; pp. 420–1 and n. 45); 'there has arisen upon us all the groaning . . .' (see p. 416 and n. 28).

NOTES IN CLARIFICATION OF THE COMMENTS ON P. 452 [OF *KIRYAT SEFER*, 45 (1970)] RELATING TO LUZZATTO AND R. JEKUTIEL GORDON OF VILNA

[On the page referred to, H. Lieberman quotes from a comment on *Ḥoker umekubal* in an unpublished manuscript by 'Habad's great teacher, the author of *Tsemaḥ tsedek*' (Menahem Mendel Schneersohn) as follows: 'Although his remarks are not entirely directed towards hasidism, they are only partly true.' And from the same manuscript: 'But [as for] what the *Ḥoker umekubal* says . . . there is a flaw in what he says.'

On the same page of *Kiryat sefer*, E. Kupfer notes that in MS Oxford Heb. f. 120 (photocopy in the National and University Library, Jerusalem), I. H. Treves refers to 'the learned physician our honoured teacher, R. Jekutiel Gordon of Vilna', 'which shows that Jekutiel's family name was Gordon'.—Trans.]

(*a*) The remarks by the author of *Tsemaḥ tsedek* on Luzzatto's *Ḥoker umekubal* which are quoted by H. Lieberman in his comment add an interesting nuance from an important source to the evaluation of the book among hasidim. But I doubt whether that expression of reserve should be seen simply as 'the opinion of Habad' in the sense of an absolute and unambiguous opinion of the teachers of Habad hasidism, even in regard to that book, still less in regard to Luzzatto's kabbalah in general. *Ḥoker umekubal* was written as a popular and apologetic treatise, and it may be that Luzzatto himself would have been prepared to acknowledge that 'there was a flaw in what he said'. The main kabbalistic work by Luzzatto which was widely available in Poland and Lithuania—and one which was greatly admired both in the Maggid of Mezhirech's *batei midrash* and in those of the Vilna Gaon—was the '138 Gates of Wisdom'. I pointed out in n. 131 above that in my opinion R. Tsevi Hirsch of Zhidachov coupled the teachings of Habad with Luzzatto's kabbalah in his attack on the explanation of the Zohar and Luria's writings 'by means of intellectual examination'. On the basis of my comparative study of the sources I am of the opinion that the first teachers of Habad hasidism, particularly R. Shneur Zalman of Lyady and R. Aaron Halevi of Starosielce, followed Luzzatto in several important matters. I propose to examine and clarify the relationship between their ideas in a study devoted to that subject.

(*b*) E. Kupfer's 'discovery' that a reference in MS Oxford Heb. f. 120 shows 'that R. Jekutiel of Vilna's family name was Gordon' is no discovery at all. About eighty years ago, in 1891, David Kaufmann published the contents of an official document on the award to Jekutiel Gordon of a doctorate of medicine in the University of Padua; ever since then every schoolboy learning about Luzzatto has known for a certainty that R. Jekutiel's family name was Gordon, and the surname appears again and again in studies and discussions on R. Jekutiel (see e.g. under 'Gordon' in the indexes to *Igerot*, and in my *Netivei emunah uminut*). In the present essay, the very one on which Kupfer comments, I quoted Kaufmann's essay, and the name Jekutiel Gordon occurs in my quotation (see n. 96). I also mentioned 'the physician Jekutiel Gordon of Vilna' in n. 119. And lastly: the passage in the Oxford manuscript from which Kupfer copied an extract to prove his 'discovery' was published some years ago in full and with explanatory comments in my essay 'The Messianic Ferment in Rabbi Moses Hayim Luzzatto's Group' [now Essay 3 above]; see n. 55 to that essay.

One must protest at this unseemly haste to publish observations of the kind described which are based on no more than a glance at a manuscript, unsupported by study and verification or any knowledge of the subject.

NINE

'Kudsha berikh hu orayta veyisra'el kola ḥad': The Origin of the Expression in Luzzatto's Commentary on *Idra raba*

A

The well-known saying that the Holy One, blessed be He, the Torah, and Israel are a unity is much quoted—either as in the title of this essay or in some variant of it—in late homiletic and ethical literature, where it is attributed to the Zohar or left unattributed; but it is not to be found in the Zohar. The passage in the Zohar which comes nearest to it in sense speaks of strong links between the three constituents of the union,[1] but of course a link is not the same as unity.

B. Dinur remarked that 'the genesis of this dictum needs particular examination. It appears to be late and may perhaps be simply a product of that generation [the period of the Ba'al Shem Tov].'[2] G. Scholem went further and asserted categorically that the problematic dictum was first voiced by the Ba'al Shem Tov. After declaring that 'the well-known saying that the Holy One, blessed be He, the Torah, and Israel are one was quoted by all the disciples of the Besht in the [Aramaic] language of the Zohar, and sometimes as being a saying of the Zohar', Scholem remarked that the statement of the Zohar on the links between the three constituents—the statement which was the source of the dictum as to their unity—'was still a long way from the bold version *which the Besht was the first to formulate*' (the emphasis is mine—I.T.).

[1] Zohar III, 73*a*: 'There are three levels, linked with one another: the Holy One, blessed be He, the Torah, and Israel.' The Zohar goes on to say that the link consists in the dual aspect of all three—the hidden and the revealed. See I. Tishby, *The Wisdom of the Zohar*, trans. D. Goldstein (Oxford, 1989), iii. 1086.

[2] B. Dinur, *Bemifneh hadorot* (Jerusalem, 1955), 212 n. 27, where Dinur quoted two versions of the formula in hasidic literature, one in *Degel maḥaneh efrayim* and one in *Keter shem tov*. See nn. 17 and 22 below.

Scholem quoted this as a foremost example of what he had found to be one of the Besht's outstanding characteristics, namely 'his special power . . . to phrase his utterances in the spirit of the classical aphorists . . . to impart a fresh aspect to the words of the ancients by slightly altering them', and he criticized the caution shown by Dinur, 'who sensed this, but refrained from drawing the conclusion required by an examination of the sources, that it was the Besht himself who introduced and disseminated this "saying"'.[3]

I have examined the sources and have been surprised to find that they do not accord with Scholem's assertion that the saying was frequently used in the writings of 'all the disciples of the Besht'.[4] It is also quite wrong to present the expression as having been formulated by the Besht. My investigation has shown that most of the Besht's disciples did not use it at all, and it is rare even in the writings of his disciples' disciples. Moreover, even the idea of the unity of the three is not to be found in most of the early books of hasidism, and the concept of the threefold bond which is expounded in the Zohar is not mentioned in those books or else is given no place of importance in them. To assess the significance attaching to the absence of the formula of unity I will concentrate on the writings of two leaders of hasidism after the Besht, R. Jacob Joseph of Polonnoye and R. Dov Baer, the Maggid of Mezhirech, while to demonstrate the ways in which the formula was used in the literature of hasidism I will consider *Degel maḥaneh efrayim*, the book by the Besht's grandson R. [Moses Hayim] Ephraim of Sudylkov, which is in fact the only source relevant to our present purpose in the writings of the teachers of hasidism who were pupils of the Besht.[5]

[3] G. Scholem, 'Demuto hahistorit shel r' yisra'el ba'al shem tov', *Molad*, 18 (1960), 354 and n. 62.

[4] Scholem is correct so far as concerns the partial formulation 'The Holy One, blessed be He, and the Torah are one', which appears repeatedly in the books of the earlier and later hasidic writers and which does not appear in the Zohar in that form. But this formulation is also common outside hasidism, and in sense it is indeed based on the Zohar. See Tishby, *Wisdom of the Zohar*, iii. 1086; and pp. 462–6 below. The most important identifications of the Torah with the Holy One, blessed be He, in the Zohar are II, 60*a*, 90*b*. In a few hasidic books I have found a different partial formulation: the unity of Israel and the Torah. R. Gedaliah of Lunietz, in his *Teshuot ḥen* (Berdichev, 1816), 'Tazria', 21*c*: 'It appears that this has to do with "This is the Torah of man" [2 Sam. 7: 19, literally understood—Trans.], that Israel and the Torah are one [literally 'it is one'].' R. Ze'ev Wolf of Zhitomir, in his *Or hame'ir* (Korets, 1798), 'Bereshit', 2*b*: 'And the Torah and Israel are one [literally 'they are one']'. R. Joseph Bloch, in his *Ginzei yosef* (Lvov, 1792), 'Nitsavim', 80*b*, has this formula in Hebrew instead of Aramaic: 'The main thing is that the Torah and the soul of Israel are a unity.'

[5] From a quick examination of the works of the disciples of the Besht's disciples it appears to me that even in them the formula we are looking for occurs in scattered references which can only be found by meticulous search. I will quote two books from the school of the Maggid of Mezhirech by way of example. An isolated mention in R. Menahem Mendel of Vitebsk's *Peri ha'arets* (Kopust, 1814): 'It is well known, six hundred thousand are the souls of Israel, so, too,

The Torah is one of the central topics of the four books by R. Jacob Joseph of Polonnoye which are the main source of the earliest doctrine of hasidism in general and the ideas of the Besht in particular, but their discussions turn on the position occupied by the commandment to study the Torah, the ways of fulfilling it in everyday life, the merits of the Torah, and its functions in the relations between man's soul and God, especially in the attainment of *devekut*, either as compared with other religious values such as prayer and fear of Heaven or in partnership with them. The tripartite connection is faintly seen in the descriptions of *devekut*, where the possibility of *devekut* and its realization by means of the Torah is explained by reference to the divine root of the Torah and of the souls of Israel or to the presence of the light of Ein Sof in the letters.[6] But even the Zohar's declaration of the links between the three sides is absent from R. Jacob Joseph's writings, and it need hardly be added that they contain no mention of the formula of threefold unity ascribed to the Besht. In a few passages they do speak of the bonds between the Holy One, blessed be He, the Torah, and Israel, and there are allusions to the words of the Zohar, but in his proof of the existence of the bonds R. Jacob Joseph skirts round the express statement in the Zohar and makes use of another source by means of forced homiletic explanations.[7] Even the partial formula-

are the letters of the Torah, *as it is well known* that the Torah, the Holy One, blessed be He, and Israel are [literally 'it is'] all one, and it is Israel who are the essence of the Torah' ('Beha'alotekha', 17*a*). In R. Ze'ev Wolf of Zhitomir's *Or hame'ir*, a work of some size, I found the saying in two sections: '*It has long been known* that the Holy One, blessed be He, and the Torah and Israel are one [literally 'they are one', *inun ḥad*] . . . *as in the saying of the Zohar*, the Holy One, blessed be He, and the Torah and Israel are one [*ḥad inun*; otherwise identical with the first quotation]' (a homily for Passover, 93*c*–94*a*); '. . .You [plural] must of necessity be a unity with the Holy One, blessed be He, so as to be part of God above, *and the Holy One, blessed be He, and the Torah and Israel are one* [*ḥad inun*], and since this is so, its purpose is to rebuke them—"Why are you lazy and [why do you] neglect to submit your necks to the service of your Lord?"—and it is this negligence that delays the footsteps of the harbinger, as already mentioned' ('Ekev', 207*c*). Here the saying is slipped into a hasidic-messianic homily aimed at arousing people to serve the Lord with fervour and *devekut* in order to hasten the Redemption.

6 See R. Jacob Joseph of Polonnoye's *Toledot ya'akov yosef* (Korets, 1780), foreword, 1*a*–6*d* (on the basis of the author's commentary on Ps. 107, which has no connection with the well-known commentary ascribed to the Besht); 'Vayetse', 24*b*, 25*a*; 'Yitro', 49*b*; 'Va'etḥanan', 168*d*–169*a*; and others.

7 In 'Va'etḥanan' (ibid. 168*c*–169*a*) he quotes from Tosafot *Ḥag.* 3*b* (text 'Who is like You?'): 'Three testify concerning each other, the Holy One, blessed be He, and Israel and the Sabbath', to prove the threefold bond by casuistic exposition: '*edut* ['testimony'] means joining together' [apparently relying on another meaning of the verbal root *ud*—Trans.] and 'The joining together of the Holy One, blessed be He, and the Sabbath is the seventy faces of the Torah'. The explicit saying in the Zohar is not even hinted at here. The foreword (ibid. 4*c*) quotes the words of the Zohar (III, 73*b*) on the attachment of Israel to the Torah and to the Holy One, blessed be He, by the sign of the covenant [circumcision], and the author arrives at a trinity of the Holy

tion 'the Holy One, blessed be He, and the Torah are one' does not appear in his books, although in some places he does identify the Holy One, blessed be He, with the Torah.[8] These findings show that R. Jacob Joseph did not know the formula of threefold unity.

In the homilies of the Maggid of Mezhirech, oneness plays a greater part, but he comes nearer to the formulae considered above only to the extent that he specifies the relationship between the Torah and the Godhead. The formula 'The Holy One, blessed be He, and the Torah are one' is repeated several times,[9] and his explanation of the meaning of the formula[10] places greater emphasis on the divine virtues of the Torah and the idea of unity. But nowhere does the Maggid expand this unity to include Israel.[11] The dictum

One, blessed be He, the Torah, and the Sabbath by introducing the words 'That is to say, the Sabbath is the name of the Holy One, blessed be He', which are not in the original. The words quoted from the Zohar are a continuation of the passage containing the formula 'There are three levels, linked with one another: the Holy One, blessed be He, the Torah, and Israel' (III, 73*a*), but there is no mention of that formula anywhere in the homily. In *Toledot ya'akov yosef*, 'Yitro', 51*c*, an indirect reference to the section of the Zohar in question occurs where 'hidden and revealed' are noted as a shared characteristic of the Holy One, blessed be He, man, and the Torah, but this blurs the formula of the threefold link. For the inclusion of the Sabbath in the trinity see also ibid., 'Shofetim', 183*c*; *Ben porat yosef* (Korets, 1781), foreword, 5*c*.

[8] *Toledot ya'akov yosef*, 'Shofetim', 183*c*: 'For the Holy One, blessed be He, and His name are one and the Torah consists entirely of His names, blessed be He; this being so, the Torah is the Holy One, blessed be He.' And see ibid., 'Vayikra', 71*d*.

[9] All the references are to *Magid devarav leya'akov*—the first and most authoritative of the printed collections of the Maggid's homilies—second edition (Korets, 1784), which is an enlarged edition. The formula occurs at 2*b*, 4*a*, 10*a*, 19*a*, 21*a*, 22*b*, 27*b* (twice), 32*b*, 41*a*–*b*. The Zohar is not recorded as a source, but in two places there is an explicit indication that what we have is a quotation: 22*b* (the abbreviation *arza"l*, 'our rabbis, may their memory be for a blessing, said'), and 32*b* (*vav alef yod*' [= *ve'ita*, 'there is a saying']).

[10] Here is the explanation given at 22*b*: 'As to this, our rabbis, may their memory be for a blessing, said that the Torah and the Holy One, blessed be He, are [literally 'it is'] all one; He, blessed be He, the Ein Sof, has no parts; so, too, the Torah has no parts, [since] every part of a commandment is included in the 613. The reason is that the whole force of the performer of the act forms a simple unity with that which is acted upon, only the concrete manifestations of the act are separated . . . and when man performs the commandments with fervour and desire and with his will to fulfil the will of the Holy One, blessed be He, they are uplifted to the primordial will, where all the 613 commandments and all the letters of the Torah are a simple unity.' A similar explanation is given at 10*a*, 27*b*. Thus the name 'the Holy One, blessed be He' in the formula is applied to Ein Sof, who is understood as the source of the Torah, and the Torah is united with Ein Sof. And see n. 28 below.

[11] In the writings of the Maggid's disciples we find the unity of the two altered to a unity of three by bringing in the soul, or Israel, without changing the formula. I will give two examples: 'This is well known, that the Torah and the Holy One, blessed be He, are [literally 'it is'] all one; consequently—and this is due to the holy soul—when he attaches himself to the holy letters by that share of divinity which is within him, he raises the words up on high and they cleave to His unity, blessed be His name, and it is the union of the Holy One, blessed be He, and His

of the Zohar on the threefold links is not mentioned, and in the only two places which make clear the relationship of Israel, the Torah, and the Holy One, blessed be He, there is no reference to the Zoharic formula.[12] It is self-evident that here, too, it would be futile to search for the dictum on the unity of the three.

Since the saying we are looking for is not to be found in the writings of R. Jacob Joseph of Polonnoye and the Maggid of Mezhirech and the other disciples of the Besht,[13] it comes as a surprise to find the extensive and varied use made of it in R. Ephraim of Sudylkov's *Degel maḥaneh efrayim*. In that book there are nine expressions of the 'unity of three';[14] the formula of the unity of the Holy One, blessed be He, and the Torah appears in six passages, in three of which the unity of the two turns into a trinity in mid-discourse,[15]

Shekhinah in which he unites the holy Torah and his holy soul with the Holy One, blessed be He, by the study of the Torah and by prayer' (R. Elimelekh of Lyzhansk, *No'am elimelekh* (Tarnów, 1904), 'Metsora', 59*b*); 'The point is that each individual member of Israel has the root of his soul in the Torah which is the root of all the roots of all the souls of Israel, and thereby the souls of Israel will be united with the Lord, blessed be He, when they engage in [the study of] the Torah, for the Torah and the Holy One, blessed be He, are one [*ḥad hu*], for it would be impossible for the world to exist if the Holy One, blessed be He, were not united with the Torah' (R. Nahum of Chernobyl, *Me'or einayim* (Slavuta, 1798), 'Tetsaveh', 64*d*–65*a*).

[12] See *Magid devarav leya'akov*, 47*b*–48*a*, 50*a*–*b*.

[13] I have, however, found the complete formulation in the notebooks containing the sayings of R. Phinehas of Korets, who was a disciple and colleague of the Besht: 'It is necessary to know the secret of the names which issue from the holy Torah; and the Holy One, blessed be He, and Israel and the Torah, all of it is one' (*Nofet tsufim* (Piotrków, 1911), 39); 'It is on the tsadik that the conduct of the world depends, for the Holy One and the Torah and Israel, all is one' (ibid. 54, sect. 75). The sayings of R. Phinehas of Korets have come down to us as oral traditions in the name of his disciples and their disciples, in various versions and sometimes with serious errors, and therefore they need critical study to determine how far they are authentic and accurate. But there is no doubt that in its substance the formula of 'the unity of the three' comes close to the spirit of R. Phinehas, and it accords with the lavish praise of the Torah and Israel in his sayings. I will quote by way of example one trenchant passage which contains the partial formula of unity: 'When the Holy One, blessed be He, gave the Torah, all the world was filled with Torah, for the whole earth is full of His glory [Isa. 6: 3] *and the Torah and the Holy One, blessed be He, are one*, and now there is nothing in which there is not the Torah of the Lord, and that is [what is meant by] "In all your ways know Him" [Prov. 3: 6], and anyone who says that the Torah is one thing and worldly affairs are another is an infidel' (M. E. Gutman, *Rabi pinḥas mikorets: ḥayav pe'ulotav vetorato* (Tel Aviv, 1950), 29). If R. Phinehas did indeed give voice to the slogan of 'the unity of the three', he may have served as the first as well as the main channel for its dissemination among hasidim, and R. Ephraim of Sudylkov may perhaps have received it from him or from members of his circle.

[14] *Degel maḥaneh efrayim* (Korets, 1810), 'Bereshit', 1*a*; 'Ḥayei sarah', 11*c*; 'Va'era', 34*c*; 'Beshalaḥ', 40*d*; 'Ki tisa', 51*c*; 'Aḥarei mot', 65*d*; 'Balak', 79*d*; *haftarah* to 'Ki tavo', 97*b*; *Likutim*, 108*a*.

[15] Unity of two which does not merge into a trinity: 'Terumah', 46*c*; 'Ki tisa', 50*a*; *Likutim*, 'Ḥayei sarah', 101*b*. Unity of two merging into a trinity: '[Our sages succeeded] in explaining

and in two adjacent paragraphs we find a partial formulation in the Aramaic of the Zohar: 'Kb"h [Kudsha berikh hu] veyisra'el kola ḥad' ['the Holy One, blessed be He, and Israel, all is one'].[16] The 'unity of three' version is given in two forms: 'The Holy one, blessed be He, and the Torah and Israel, are all of them [*kulho*] one', and the same, substituting 'the souls of Israel' for 'Israel'. Most of the passages are not attributed to any source; sometimes they are introduced by the comment 'It is well known . . .', but the Zohar is mentioned four times as the source—twice for the threefold version,[17] once for the Holy One, blessed be He, and the Torah,[18] and once for the Holy One, blessed be He, and Israel.[19]

The importance of the formula of unity in *Degel maḥaneh efrayim* lies not only in the frequency of its use but also in the ways in which it is used and the ideas with which the author associates it. R. Ephraim repeatedly explains its significance and emphasizes its importance. Most of his explanations are not

every obscure saying in the law of the holy Torah, because there rested upon them the power of God, *He and the Torah being all one* and the light of their soul also, this is *the threefold cord* which will not be broken to all eternity' ('Ekev', 91*b*); 'The Torah and the Holy One, blessed be He, it is [*kulo*] all one, and the root of his [the Jewish man's] soul is also from the Torah; if so, how can the Jewish man be separated from the Torah and the Holy One, blessed be He?' (*Likutim*, 107*c*, and similarly 107*c*–*d*).

16 'Balak', 78*d*, 79*a*.

17 'It is well known *that in the holy Zohar it is written*: "The Holy One, blessed be He, and the Torah and the souls of Israel, are all one." And this should be understood to mean that the life of Israel derives, as it were, from the essence of the Holy One, blessed be He . . . And this Torah is man . . . for the Torah is verily the essence of man, for see, the Holy One, blessed be He, and the Torah and Israel are all one' ('Bereshit', 1*a*); '"And the fellowship of the King is with him" [Num. 23: 21, as understood by Rashi and here—Trans.] is to be explained by what is said in the holy Zohar: "The Torah and the Holy One, blessed be He, and Israel are all one" . . . for it is impossible to separate [them], because they [the Torah and the Holy One, blessed be He, according to R. Ephraim's interpretation of Num. 23: 21] are verily within him' ('Balak', 79*d*). Dinur (*Bemifneh hadorot*, 212 n. 27) remarked on the departure from the usual form (substituting 'the souls of Israel' for 'Israel') in the first quotation of the 'threefold' formula attributed to the Zohar, and deduced that 'from this it can also be seen that the saying is new'. But he overlooked the second quotation described as being from the Zohar, which is exactly in the traditional form. The authors of homiletic works had no compunction in altering the text of quotations to suit their purpose. And see pp. 462–3 below.

18 'And in the holy Zohar, too, there is [the statement that] the Holy One, blessed be He, and the Torah are all one, and when he [or one] studies Torah for the sake of the Holy One, blessed be He . . . he thereby acquires [it: the object of the verb is not expressed—Trans.] for the Holy One, blessed be He, just as described above' ('Terumah', 46*c*).

19 'The Lord, blessed be He, separated and set apart the nation of the children of Israel . . . so that they and He should adhere each to the other as all one, as is said in the holy Zohar, the Holy One, blessed be He, and Israel, all is one' ('Balak', 78*d*). It is possible that the words of the Zohar 'The Holy One, blessed be He, and *Keneset yisra'el* are called one' (III, 93*b*) served as the source of this formula, although there *Keneset yisra'el* [literally 'the assembly of Israel'] means the Shekhinah.

original,[20] but some unusual ideas and some trenchant turns of phrase are brought to bear on the pattern of unity.[21]

R. Ephraim, who as a boy and young man lived close to the Ba'al Shem Tov and received instruction and words of Torah from him, made a point of including in his book sayings of the Besht of which he had personal knowledge, or which were recorded in the writings of R. Jacob Joseph of Polonnoye, or which he had heard from members of his grandfather's circle, and he was punctilious in stressing that these were sayings of the Besht. But in quoting the sayings on unity in the typical Aramaic of the Zohar he never mentioned the Besht. Hence the silence of the Besht's disciples and the statements by his grandson lead to the same conclusion: the formula of threefold unity was not enunciated by the Besht[22] and did not germinate in the soil of

[20] For example, the root of the souls of Israel in the Torah; the parallel between man and the Torah in the 248 [organs in the body, corresponding to the number of positive commandments—Trans.] and 365 [sinews, corresponding to the negative commandments—Trans.]; the 600,000 letters in the Torah and the 600,000 roots of the souls in Israel; every Jew has hold of one letter of the Torah; cleaving [*devekut*] to the Torah and to the Holy One, blessed be He. These ideas are common in the literature of kabbalah and hasidism, and the principal sources on which the hasidim drew were R. Isaiah Halevi Horowitz's *Shenei luḥot haberit* (known as *Shela"h*) (1st edn. Amsterdam, 1648) and R. Abraham Azulai's *Ḥesed le'avraham* (Amsterdam, 1685). See nn. 23, 29, 58 below.

[21] One idea which is out of the ordinary is that 'the unity of the three' provides a guarantee to the sinners of Israel that they will repent: 'Accordingly it is a great principle that even a man who is a great sinner is then called a spark of Israel and has in him a divine part from above and will certainly turn back in penitence in spite of himself' ('Balak', 79*d*). And see *Likutim* [in *Degel maḥaneh efrayim*—Trans.], 107*c*–*d*. Noteworthy turns of phrase and descriptions: 'The secret of his divinity is hidden in the Torah itself and in the mystery of the soul of man' ('Beshalaḥ', 40*d*); '*Man is the Holy One, blessed be He*, as the Tetragrammaton, blessed be He, with each letter spelt out in full to give the Name *mem he* [numerical value 45] which is the numerical value of *adam* ['man'] . . . and when man occupies himself with the Torah for its own sake, to observe it and to do it, then he draws all his organs near to their root . . . to the Torah . . . and he and the Torah become one in perfect union and unity, like the union of man and wife' ('Aḥarei mot', 65*d*).

[22] At first sight it would seem possible to invoke R. Aaron Hakohen of Apta in support of the attribution of the formula of threefold unity to the Besht. In R. Aaron's *Keter shem tov*, ii (Zholkva, 1795), in a section which opens with remarks described as 'by the Besht, may he be remembered for life in the world to come', we find the following: 'The letters of the Torah are the chambers of the Holy One, blessed be He, into which He transmits the emanation of His light, *as is written in the Zohar* "the Holy One, blessed be He, and the Torah, all is one", and into them a man must put all the devotion [*kavanah*] which is the soul . . . and that is the *devekut* ['cleaving together'] [expressed by] "*the Holy One, blessed be He, and the Torah and Israel, all is one*".' In *Or haganuz* (Zholkva, 1800), which was printed anonymously but is by the same author, the same quotation appears with an explicit attribution to the Besht: '[That is] *what is said in the name of the Besht, may his memory be for a blessing*: the letters in the Torah are vessels and chambers of the Lord, blessed be He . . . and that is the cleaving together [expressed by] "the Holy One, blessed be He, and the Torah and Israel, all is one"' (end of 'Mikets'). But R. Aaron turns out to be an unreliable source, and his quotation of the aphorism and its context

hasidism but reached R. Ephraim of Sudylkov and some of his contemporaries from some external source. The other teachers of hasidism of his time who knew the saying did not attach any special importance to it and mentioned it without emphasis or left it out of their homilies altogether, unlike R. Ephraim, who was enthused by it and saw it as a firm peg on which to hang hasidic ideas and slogans.[23]

'in the name of the Besht' is based on a distortion. The beginning of the section 'by the Besht' in *Keter shem tov* is from *Tsava'at hariba"sh*, but its continuation from 'when he thinks evil thoughts' to 'he will see many of the upper worlds' is taken from the words of the Maggid of Mezhirech in *Magid devarav leya'akov*, 5*a*; and in the Maggid's text there is no mention of the formulae of unity: the fragment from 'as is written in the Zohar' down to 'and Israel, all is one' is an interpolation. In *Or haganuz* the formulae of unity attributed to the Besht are tacked on to a short sentence from the Maggid's discourse. The interpolated fragment also appears, with no indication of its source, in R. Aaron's *Ner mitsvah*, which was printed from a manuscript (Piotrków, 1911). There are three further references to the formula of threefold unity in *Or haganuz*: 'As is said in the holy Zohar, the Holy One, blessed be He, and the Torah, all is one, whence the Holy One, blessed be He, the Torah, and Israel, who is His soul, all is one' ('Bereshit'; allegedly quoting the Besht); 'And they, by combinations of letters . . . for they have in them the power and vitality to create that man, Adam, [creating] existence out of nothingness [*yesh me'ayin*], and give him life, for the Torah and the Holy One, blessed be He, and Israel, all is one' ('Vayeḥi'; allegedly from the *Tanya*); 'The light of the Godhead is bound upon his soul, and the Holy One, blessed be He, the Torah, and Israel becomes all of it one' ('Matot'; no mention of source). R. Aaron of Apta was an irresponsible collector, and he excelled all others in 'enriching' the Besht with sayings not attributed to him in any source. It follows that Dinur (*Bemifneh hadorot*, 198 n. 19) is in error in his opinion of the importance of *Or haganuz* 'as a source for the history of hasidism', but the book deserves meticulous study from a bibliographical point of view. And Dinur, in citing a remark in the rabbi of Zholkva's letter of approval that 'the book was written a long time ago and has long since gained renown', is relying on a misquotation of the source, for what the letter of approval says is '[he] gained renown with a book which was written long ago', which is certainly a reference to *Keter shem tov*. And see S. M. M. Wodnik, *Sefer ba'al shem tov*, i (Łódź, 1938), 249, heading (*d*). The author noted that R. Aaron of Apta made unfounded attributions to the Besht.

[23] I have not here touched upon books written in a hasidic environment during the early development of hasidism. The question of the absence or presence of the formulae of unity on the fringes of hasidism is an important one which needs thorough study as a separate matter, but I would be remiss not to mention R. Barukh of Kosov (whom I considered, together with his writings, in my essay 'Harayon hameshiḥi vehamegamot hameshiḥiyot bitsemiḥat haḥasidut', *Zion*, 32 (1967), 24–9), because his standpoint is very important for our present purpose. R. Barukh devoted a great deal of attention to the relation between the Holy One, blessed be He, the Torah, and Israel. His writings deal with it in a number of places, comprehensively and in depth, in discussions aimed at clarifying it, and he points to the principal sources in the literature of kabbalah: *Shenei luḥot haberit*, especially the treatise *Toledot ha'adam* at the beginning of that work, and R. Abraham Azulai's *Ḥesed le'avraham*, in the part entitled *Ein hakore*, particularly *nahar* ['stream'] 18 and 21. I give here references to the main passages in R. Barukh's writings which deal with this issue: *Yesod ha'emunah* (Czernowitz, 1854), 82*c*, 89*a–c*, 90*b–c*, 101*b–c*; *Amud ha'avodah* (Czernowitz, 1854), 34*b*–36*a*, 111*b*–112*c*, 120*a–d*. R. Barukh repeatedly stresses that the three constituent parts are interlinked in perfect unity and essential identity as one. Invoking the Zohar, he cites the saying on the the threefold links in Part III,

B

The other side of the coin of 'threefold unity' is its existence in treatises and settings inconsistent with its attribution to the Besht and his disciples, namely in writings by mitnagedim belonging to the school of the Gaon of Vilna.

In the writings of R. Hayim of Volozhin [Hayim Volozhiner], the greatest of the Gaon's disciples, the formula is used four times, once in *Nefesh haḥayim*, in its traditional form but with no indication of its source, and three times in *Ruaḥ ḥayim*[24] in an altered form, two of them in the name of the

73*a*. His quotation, however, is not exact, but is altered so as to convey the meaning of unity. Whereas the Zohar says: 'There are three levels, linked with one another: the Holy One, blessed be He, the Torah, and Israel', R. Barukh writes: 'As is well known, the Zohar says: *There are three bonds of faith* [*kesharin dimeheimanuta*], the Torah, the Holy One, blessed be He, and *keneset yisra'el* [the Jewish people]' (*Yesod ha'emunah*, 101*c*). That version appears also in four passages in *Amud ha'avodah* (34*c*, with references to *Shenei luḥot haberit*: 111*b–c* twice, 112*c*, 193*a*), but in the second passage the words 'all of them are one' are added at the end, while the fourth one adds 'all is one'. At first sight it seems as if the departures from the text of the Zohar were not deliberate but were due to quotation from memory, for R. Barukh had difficulty in explaining the reading *keneset yisra'el*. However, the expression 'three bonds of faith' does not occur anywhere in the Zohar but is a well-known Shabatean theological catchword on threefold unity in the Godhead (Atika Kadisha, Malka Kadisha, and the Shekhinah). On the other hand, contrary to the general opinion of students of Shabateanism that the expression and the nature of the divine 'trinity' are entirely a Shabatean fabrication, it must be said that these do have a footing in the Zohar: 'For on this depends celestial faith: on Atika Kadisha, on Ze'ir Anpin, and on the field of [sacred] apples' (II, 88*a*) [see Tishby, *Wisdom of the Zohar*, iii. 1287—Trans.]; and 'three levels of faith' (204*b*). The Shabateans, however, substituted 'bonds' for 'levels' and turned bonds into unity, and so coined the formula (in Aramaic) 'three bonds of faith which are one'. R. Barukh of Kosov, who was strongly opposed to Shabateanism, came under the influence of this formulation by his opponents and adopted the same attitude as they did towards the 'trinity' of the Holy One, blessed be He, the Torah, and Israel. Basing himself on the phrase 'three bonds of faith', once in the full Shabatean version 'Three bonds of faith *which are one*' (*Amud ha'avodah*, 120*b*), he wrote: 'Hence the Torah and the Holy One, blessed be He, and *keneset yisra'el*, that is, the souls of Israel, *all is essentially one* but the Torah is the generality and so, too, the Holy One, blessed be He, is the generality, and the souls are individuals and are included in the generality in simple unity' (ibid. 34*c*). It is probable, too, that the altered version of the description of the threefold connection in the Zohar is itself taken from a Shabatean source. Cf. A. M. Cardozo's version of the aphorism, quoted in n. 58 below. But the exact standing of the formula of threefold unity in the writings of R. Barukh of Kosov is difficult to determine. Why are the concluding words 'all of them are [or 'all is'] one', which turn 'three bonds' into a unity of the three, absent in three passages but appended to the formula in two others? I would surmise that R. Barukh knew two formulae which altered the substance of the original expression in the Zohar: (*a*) beginning with 'Three bonds of faith' and without 'all of them are one' at the end; (*b*) 'all of them are one' without 'three bonds'. R. Barukh adopted the 'three bonds' but sometimes added 'all of them are one'.

[24] On the genesis and the component parts of this book, which had its origin mainly in R. Hayim's oral lessons on the tractate *Avot* edited by his son, R. Isaac, from notes, see N. Lamm, *Torah lishemah bemishnat r' ḥayim mivolozin uvemaḥashevet hador* (Jerusalem, 1972),

Zohar and one with no attribution: (*a*) 'As to this, the proper life, light, and existence of all the worlds depend entirely on our occupying ourselves properly with it [the Torah], for *the Holy One, blessed be He, and the Torah and Israel, all is one*, because the supernal root of the soul of each member of Israel is firmly attached and held fast to one letter of the Torah so that in very deed they become one';[25] (*b*) 'All the worlds were created only for the sake of the Torah and those who believed in it . . . and therefore the Holy One, blessed be He, and the Torah and those who believe in it, all is one, *as is written in the Zohar*';[26] (*c*) 'But the matter is *as written in the holy Zohar*: the Holy One, blessed be He, and the Torah and those who occupy themselves with it, it is one, for it is well known that He and His will are one and the Torah is His will and the souls are firmly attached [*devukim*] to Him, blessed be His name.'[27]

R. Hayim of Volozhin's hyperbolic appraisal of the Torah, which equates the root of its existence with the Godhead, is one of the best-known of its kind. In all his writings he repeatedly emphasizes the unity of the Holy One, blessed be He, and the Torah, quoting the Aramaic formula 'Kudsha berikh hu veorayta ḥad hu' ['. . . it is one'] or parallels such as 'the Holy One, blessed be He, and His word are one', and 'the Holy One, blessed be He, and His will are one', and also gives explanations of the idea without any fixed formula. The highest level of his superlatives, which is unusual in discussions of the merits of the Torah before R. Hayim, confers on the root of the Torah a status above the world of emanation [*atsilut*] and fixes it in the realm of Ein Sof.[28] He also devotes considerable attention to the strong links between

75–6. Lamm was right to declare as he did that this work was not to be relied upon for accuracy in detail, but it seems to me nevertheless that we may take it as a fact that R. Hayim was heard to ascribe the 'threefold' aphorism to the Zohar.

[25] *Nefesh haḥayim* (Vilna, 1837), Gate [*sha'ar*] 4, xi, 100. I give references to the second edition because the first edition did not print the introductory chapters to Gate 4. See Lamm, *Torah lishemah*, 39.

[26] *Ruaḥ ḥayim* (Vilna, 1859), 35*d*.

[27] Ibid. 38*b*. This version of the formula is quoted on a previous page (37*a*) with no indication of its source. In *Pe*[*rush*] *me'aḥi hager"a z"l* ['Commentary by the Brother of the Late Vilna Gaon'] on tractate *Avot*, printed in R. Joseph Hayim Segal's book *Tosefot ḥayim* (Lublin, 1906; 1st edn. 1904), 19*c*, I found the following: 'As is written in the Zohar, the Holy One, blessed be He, and the Torah and Israel, it is one', which made me think that R. Abraham, the Gra's brother, must be added to the list of those who quoted the declaration of threefold unity. But on further study I realized that the *Perush me'aḥi hager"a z"l* is entirely an abbreviated and variant version of *Ruaḥ ḥayim* that had been attributed, in error or with intent to deceive, to the brother of the Gra. Lamm, *Torah lishemah*, 75, remarked on the existence of *Ruaḥ ḥayim* in various manuscript versions but did not identify the commentary in *Tosefot ḥayim*, which existed in print, as another version.

[28] Lamm, however, was in error when he wrote (*Torah lishemah*, 80–1) that in this matter R. Hayim made a daring innovation unparalleled in the literature of kabbalah and hasidism. There are statements in hasidic books which link the spiritual root of the Torah to Ein Sof or

Israel and the Holy One, blessed be He, on the one hand, and between Israel and the Torah on the other, and on the relationship between the three exalted entities, explicitly quoting, in one case, the words of the Zohar on the threefold links.[29] Several scholars have discussed these matters at some length,[30]

the light of Ein Sof. See nn. 6 and 10 above. But there is no need to look for hidden sources or parallels: R. Hayim specifically indicated his source in kabbalistic literature, but Lamm did not grasp the significance of the allusion. The sentence quoted by Lamm—'The supernal root of the holy Torah is in the highest of the worlds which are called the worlds of the Ein Sof'—continues as follows: 'the mystery of the secret garment mentioned in the secrets of the wonders of wisdom which is part of the doctrine of our teacher, the Ari, may he be remembered for blessing, and which is the beginning of the mystery of the letters of the holy Torah' (*Nefesh haḥayim*, Gate 4, x, 99; and see ibid., Gate 4, xxvi, 115–16). By 'the mystery of the secret garment' is meant the central idea of Lurianic kabbalah in the version of R. Israel Saruk, according to which, in the events which preceded the *tsimtsum*, there was created a garment described as woven of the divine letters of the original Torah, and Saruk's disciples speak explicitly of 'the worlds of the Ein Sof'. See G. Scholem, 'Yisra'el sarug: talmid ha'ar"i?', *Zion*, 5 (1940), 230–4; G. Scholem, *Kabbalah* (Jerusalem, 1974), 131–3. Among members of the school of the Vilna Gaon the doctrine of the garment was regarded as belonging to the esoteric part of Lurianic kabbalah. R. Isaac Eisik Haver [Wildmann], in *Pitḥei she'arim* (Warsaw, 1888), 15*b*, wrote: 'This is known from the mystery of the world of the garment which was revealed by the Ari's disciples, about which we do not wish to speak.' But in *Beit olamim* (Warsaw, 1889) he showed no hesitation in dealing with matters connected with the mystery of the garment, and even devoted a special section to them (pp. 189 ff.). In my essay 'Ha'imut bein kabalat ha'ar"i lekabalat harema"k bikhetavav uveḥayav shel r' aharon berekhyah mimodena', *Zion*, 39 (1974), I consider anew several questions relating to the dissemination in Italy of Saruk's version of Lurianic kabbalah.

[29] *Nefesh haḥayim*, Gate 1, xvi, margin. Lamm, in his explanation of this matter (*Torah lishemah*, 53, 90–1), failed to distinguish between the connection defined in the Zohar and existence as an essential unity, and he ascribed to the Zohar the view that the three sides constituted a single identity. On the other hand, he sought to detect in R. Hayim an unwillingness to accept the 'mystical perception' of identity, which he attributed to an inclination to regard the position of Israel in the triple order as merely an attachment by way of the study of the Torah. R. Hayim did, indeed, emphasize the practical aspect in several places, and made use of a formula in that sense in the Aramaic of the Zohar: 'For Israel are attached to the Torah and the Torah to the Holy One, blessed be He' (*Nefesh haḥayim*, Gate 1, vi, 23). That formula is also found in the homilies of R. Shneur Zalman of Lyady (e.g. *Torah or* (Kopust, 1837), 'Mikets', 72*b*; *Likutei torah* (Vilna, 1904), 'Tazria', 23*a*), but I have not found it in the Zohar; and see *Shenei luḥot haberit* (1698), i, 'Toledot adam', 3*a*. Lamm, however, here blurred the meaning of the passages in which R. Hayim was clearly referring to identity—passages which Lamm himself considered elsewhere—and he also diverted from its plain sense the expression in the Zohar 'The Holy One, blessed be He, and *keneset yisra'el* are called one' (III, 93*b*), which is a clear reference to the Holy One, blessed be He, and the Shekhinah. In the same way he misinterpreted R. Hayim's remarks, based on the Zohar, on the unity of the Holy One, blessed be He, and His will, where the will represents, by its nature, the light of Ein Sof or Keter. The fact is that R. Hayim went beyond the Zohar and turned the connection into unity. His knowledge of the formula of the triple link certainly helped him on his way.

[30] In addition to Lamm, *Torah lishemah*, mention should be made of Y. Ben-Sasson, 'Olamam haruḥani umishnatam haḥinukhit shel meyasedei hayeshivah halita'it', in *Ḥinukh ha'adam veyi-*

but they have left untouched the formula of triple unity in R. Hayim of Volozhin's two books.

There is no doubt that R. Hayim did not get the formula from hasidic literature. Even if it were present in the works of the early hasidim, which R. Hayim undoubtedly read in order to acquaint himself with their viewpoint,[31] there was no need to assume that someone so strongly opposed to hasidism[32] was indebted to its spokesmen for a daring aphorism on a matter

udo (Jerusalem, 1967), 172–7; I. Etkes, 'Shitato ufa'olo shel r' ḥayim mivolozin kiteguvat haḥevrah ha"mitnagedit" laḥasidut', *Proceedings of the American Academy for Jewish Research*, 38–9 (1972), 23–31.

[31] In *Nefesh haḥayim*, Gate 4, xxviii, 117–18, a sentence in parentheses quotes a hasidic book in the following terms: 'And not as I saw in a book written by one who had investigated the question why the science of kabbalah is called *nistar* ['hidden, esoteric'] . . . and he explained it as he did'. Lamm (*Torah lishemah*, 86 n. 53) gave the correct source, but because he relied on information at second hand, he mistakenly took this to be a reference to the Besht. The direct source is *Likutim yekarim* (Lvov, 1792), 22*d*; the passage begins 'I will explain to you, my dear friend, and the words are those of R. Meshulam Feivush of Zbarazh, quoting R. Menahem Mendel of Peremyshlyany'.

[32] In recent times researchers have greatly played down R. Hayim of Volozhin's opposition to hasidism. According to the descriptions by Lamm (*Torah lishemah*, 9–16, 18–25, 42–4, 59–62, 221–3) and Etkes ('Shitato ufa'olo', 21–3), the moderate and restrained tone of R. Hayim's polemic shows that in spite of his strong objection to the principles of hasidic doctrine his attitude to the hasidim was one of forgiveness and understanding because he regarded them as people who had fallen into error but whose religious deviations were made with holy intent—'for the sake of Heaven'. Lamm went further and, arguing step by step, gradually turned R. Hayim from a strong mitnaged into a man who saw both points of view, and then into a sympathizer of the hasidim and hasidism. In Lamm's opinion R. Hayim set himself the task of '*drawing the hasidim nearer* [the emphasis is mine—I.T.] while strenuously opposing hasidism', and it was an aspiration of his that 'the two separate streams should be able to exist together' (*Torah lishemah*, 61). Not content with this, Lamm went on to declare that R. Hayim, in his complaints against the neglect of the study of halakhah [the law in practice] in the written and oral Torah and against excessive occupation with 'books on fear [of Heaven] and ethics', had in mind '*particularly* the hasidic ethical books which were acquiring a growing reputation', and that 'by expressly associating these books of hasidism with the other books on ethics written long ago . . . *he invested them with legitimacy and authority*' (ibid. 222–3). This is not the place to enter into a lengthy refutation of Lamm's view on this issue, which I regard as an apologetic array of weak and mostly self-defeating arguments. I will deal only with the main argument, which at first sight looks convincing, and will give my opinion. Lamm alleges that R. Hayim 'consistently' refers to the hasidim by 'an expression which describes them in laudatory terms: "those who desire to draw near to God" ', and he quotes as examples two extracts to prove that in this description 'the allusion to the hasidim is clear and unambiguous' (ibid. 43–4). In fact the two examples constitute the total use of this 'consistent' description, for I have not found it anywhere in the book except in those two extracts: one (introduction to Gate 4, viii, 91) on missing the time for prayer, the second (Gate 4, i, 93) on excessive study of 'books of fear and ethics'. However, it is quality, not quantity, that is decisive, and from the practical point of view there is certainly some positive element of esteem in the description. The second extract says clearly: 'The Lord will forgive them, for *their intention is for His sake, blessed be He*.' But the question is

which was central to his outlook. Still less is there any call for such an assumption in view of the fact that the formula of threefold unity is only found in *Degel maḥaneh efrayim* and among the disciples of the Besht's disciples, as I explained in the previous section of this essay, and R. Hayim would certainly not have thought those teachers of hasidism worthy of serving him as a source. The only disciple of the Maggid of Mezhirech whose influence could conceivably be traced in R. Hayim's writings is R. Shneur Zalman of Lyady. But the 'threefold' formula is not to be found either in the *Tanya*, which R. Hayim certainly read, or in R. Shneur Zalman's homilies,[33] some of which he may have got to know from manuscripts or reports. On the other hand, the fact that the formula exists in hasidic literature rules out the possibility that it was coined by R. Hayim himself.

whether these words really refer to the hasidim. In my opinion *most of the anti-hasidic rebukes in Nefesh haḥayim were directed towards those who were attracted to hasidism*, especially people round the author who were inclined to follow the ways of the new movement; he addressed himself to them gently in order to rescue them from its dangers and return them to the right path. It seems to me that even where he was clearly referring to hasidim, as in his allusions to tsadikism (Gate 1, xxii, 45–6; Gate 3, ix, 76–7) and to the belittlement of Torah scholars (introduction to Gate 4, iii, 86–7), the purpose of the rebuke was to deliver a warning to people who felt drawn towards hasidism. It is precisely in the two passages which mention the quest to draw near to God that I find support for my new approach to the understanding of the polemics in *Nefesh haḥayim*. In both places R. Hayim's personal experience is referred to by the words 'I have seen with my own eyes'. The first passage alludes to his having spoken to those who had been drawn to hasidism by the evil inclination, from whose enticements he would certainly have tried to rescue them: 'My eyes have seen many who desire to draw near to God and who stumble with the above-mentioned words which *they spoke to me from their heart*' (Gate 4, viii, 91). His true attitude to the hasidim and to the teachers of hasidism as such found expression in his impassioned defence of his teacher in his foreword to the Gaon's *perush* ['commentary'] on *Sifra detseni'uta* (Vilna and Grodno, 1820): '[That] which has come to my ears, the calumny of many, ignoramuses, worthless people, in the remotest provinces, who have never seen the light of his teaching and his holiness, men without a yoke [*beli ol*; he meant Belial], whose mouth and tongue, by their pomposities, besmirch the saints of Heaven, dead flies [paraphrasing Eccles. 10: 1] causing to stink and bubble the holy ointment of our great teacher, may he rest in Eden.' There is no substance in Lamm's attempt to blunt the sharpness of this attack. As I understand it, not only did R. Hayim of Volozhin regard the hasidim as ignorant and insolent, but he also looked upon them as agents of the evil inclination lying in wait for the souls of those 'who desired to draw near to God'; and it was only out of politeness and because he aimed to educate those who had strayed into error that he restrained his language in *Nefesh haḥayim*.

[33] I have examined R. Shneur Zalman's writings but did not have the space to consider them in the previous section. Here I will confine myself to two remarks: (*a*) The partial formula 'The Torah and the Holy One, blessed be He, all is one' occurs several times in the *Tanya*, but there is no trace of the Zohar's pronouncement on the threefold links. (*b*) In the homilies an important part is played by the threefold links defined in the Zohar, which is quoted verbatim or paraphrased. The main references are: *Torah or*, 'Mikets', 52*c*, 72*b*; *Likutei torah*: 'Vayikra', 5*c*; 'Tazria', 23*a*; 'Beḥukotai', 45*a*; 'Nitsavim', 46*a*; 'Vezot haberakhah', 94*a*; S. of S. 16*d*. But I did not find any attempt to pass from the concept of connections to that of unity and identity. And

Further valuable evidence for the dissemination of the 'threefold' formula in the writings of the mitnagedim is given in the works of the kabbalist R. Isaac Eisik Haver, a disciple of a disciple of the Vilna Gaon.[34] R. Isaac, most of whose extensive works are devoted to explaining the Gaon's kabbalistic allusions and disseminating his doctrine,[35] was much concerned with a proper appreciation of the Torah and applied himself to explaining ways of studying it.[36] On examining his writings I found the formula of triple unity at least six times, three of them with an express attribution to the Zohar:

1. 'For the soul of the Jew [together] with the Torah is all one, *as is said in the holy Zohar* "the Torah and the Holy One, blessed be He, and Israel, all is one" [*orayta vekb"h veyisra'el kola ḥad*].'[37]
2. 'And so, too, is adherence to the Torah, which is as if one adhered, as it were, to the Shekhinah, for the Torah and the Holy One, blessed be He, and Israel, it is one.'[38]
3. 'It is as I have said above: the souls of Israel are from *z"a* [Ze'ir Anpin], and on this *they said in the Zohar* "The Torah and the Holy One, blessed be He, and Israel, it is one", for the whole Torah and its commandments are dependent on *z"a*, and Israel are there, too, and therefore *z"a* is also called Israel.'[39]
4. 'The point is that *it is known* that the Torah and the Holy One, blessed be He, and Israel, it is one, and the 600,000 letters in the Torah are the 600,000 souls of Israel that fell among the husks when the vessels were broken . . . and therefore for so long as they were sunk among the husks it was not time to give the Torah to Israel.'[40]

see n. 29 above. It is also worth noting that the author of *Tsemaḥ tsedek* [Menahem Mendel Schneersohn], who edited the homilies and added a great deal of material of his own, did not quote the statement on triple unity anywhere in his supplementary remarks.

[34] His teacher was R. Menahem Mendel of Shklov. See R. Isaac Eisik's remarks in his foreword to his *Magen vetsinah* (place and year of publication not given, no author's name; certainly printed during the lifetime of the author, hence no later than 1852); and the remarks of his disciple R. Isaac Kahana in his foreword to *Sefer yetsirah* with the Vilna Gaon's commentary (Jerusalem, 1874/5).

[35] See the lists of his compositions in his son R. Joseph's foreword to *Masekhta atsilut* together with his commentary *Ginzei meromim* ([Johannisburg], 1864), in his son R. Moses' foreword to *Pitḥei she'arim*, and in his son-in-law R. Isaac Tsevi Halevi's foreword to his commentary *Or torah* on *Ma'alot hatorah*, by the Gaon's brother Abraham, which were printed together under the title *Amudei hatorah* (Jerusalem, 1880).

[36] He followed in the footsteps of R. Hayim of Volozhin, either mentioning him or his book or without acknowledgement. He was not a pupil of R. Hayim but certainly kept in contact with him and admired him. In *Magen vetsinah*, 54*b*, he heaped extravagant praise on him, stressing his merits in the teaching of Torah, his conduct, and his leadership.

[37] *Amudei hatorah*, 5*a*.

[38] Ibid. 19*a*.

[39] *Beit olamim*, 140.

[40] Ibid. 151–2.

5. 'The root of the ancient Torah is in the *tsimtsum* ['contraction'] of Ein Sof *b"h* [*be'olam hamalbush*, 'into the world of the garment'][41] . . . The Torah is the mystical Name *m"h* [45, the numerical value of the Tetragrammaton when each letter is spelt out in full—Trans.] which was revealed after the *tikun* of the world, and at that time Israel was called *adam*, which has the same numerical value . . . and is also called children of the Omnipresent in the mystery of the Divine Name of fifty-two letters [*b"n* = 52; *ben* = 'son'], and when Israel join with the Torah it is the marriage of the Divine Name *m"h* with *b"n* . . . and *that is why they said in the Zohar* "The Torah and the Holy One, blessed be He, and Israel, it is one".'[42]

6. 'This is because the whole is made up of three aspects, *as they said*, "The Torah and the Holy One, blessed be He, and Israel, it is one".'[43]

In the case of R. Isaac Eisik Haver, too, it is quite evident that he did not get the saying from the literature of hasidism, nor was he influenced by that literature in his ideas. His teacher, R. Menahem Mendel of Shklov, was an unbridled opponent of hasidism;[44] R. Isaac Eisik pursued the same course and remained an out-and-out mitnaged to the end of his life. This became clear to me when I examined his writings, which are strewn with examples, open or veiled, of anti-hasidic argument. I will quote two such examples from his *Or torah*: (*a*) Study of the Torah for its own sake and not for its own sake:

Let not a man say 'Because I cannot study [it] properly for its own sake, it is better for me that I should not study at all', Heaven forbid, as was thought by many, and they strayed from the path, for that is the way of the evil inclination, to blind a man's eyes and, in speaking of what is good, tell him that it is evil etc.[45]

(*b*) Condemnation of the neglect of Torah study in the pursuit of fervour and *devekut*:

And thus whoever follows his intellect in the worship of the Lord,[46] which is not in accordance with the ways of the Torah which our holy sages handed down to us by

[41] As the text goes on to explain. And see n. 28 above.

[42] *Beit olamim*, 191.

[43] *Pitḥei she'arim*, 11*a*. The wording of the quotation is the same in every case except one, where 'it is one' is replaced by 'it is all one'. And see below, p. 470 and n. 52, and p. 474.

[44] See his sharply polemical letter of 1805 to a relative who was inclining towards hasidism. The letter is reproduced in M. Wilensky's *Ḥasidim umitnagedim* (Jerusalem, 1970), i. 315–18.

[45] *Amudei hatorah*, 10*b*. This passage displays the clear influence of R. Hayim of Volozhin. At p. 61*c* there is another sharp polemic on the same subject (Torah for its own sake and otherwise) with an explicit reference to *Nefesh haḥayim*.

[46] This remark, astonishing at first sight, that the hasidim follow their intellect, is intended to mean that they distance themselves from the values of the Torah and ancient tradition and accept beliefs and ways of life thought up by their leaders, the tsadikim. Similar remarks can be found in anti-hasidic polemical writings, and even more in works never published that I have

word of mouth and which they received, one from the mouth of another, from its origin in the primordial quarry, the mouth of the Lord, nor does it accord with the words of the later sages who delved into the holy Torah and embellished it in accordance with the laws transmitted to us in the *Sh*[*ulḥan*] *a*[*rukh*] which has been placed before us, and he thinks other thoughts, even though he thinks that the essence of worship is to be in [a state of] *devekut* and religious fervour all day long and that one should desist from such study of the Torah, this stems from the counsel of *s"m* [Sama'el] and his company, [Sama'el] who sweetens his ways for him, and he wallows in mud and mire, which are verily murky waters. And therefore the man who walks uprightly and is concerned for his soul and the honour of his Maker will distance himself from new sects which are constantly coming into existence,[47] and which say 'This is the way in which you should walk, it is the essential principle of worship'. My son, do not walk in the way with them, withhold your foot from their path, and do not turn aside (Heaven forbid) from the way beaten out for the many since ancient times, to walk in other ways which are most dangerous, and then it will be well with him [*sic*].[48]

This venomous attack on hasidism follows a sharp denunciation of the *maskilim* who 'occupy themselves with the accursed science of *flisofya* [for *filosofiyah*]' and end 'in denying the living God', and whose way and whose scholarship are labelled 'murky waters' and 'mud and mire'. Again, in his will (written on the eve of Rosh Hashanah 5613 [autumn 1852], just before his death),[49] R. Isaac Eisik, in a warning to his sons to keep away from evil and dangerous company, bracketed together *maskilim* who were drawn after 'books written by the unfit, by authors who are the wicked men of our people' and hasidim, members of 'the new sects which have come into existence because of our many sins'. This militant mitnaged would certainly not have been willing to accept an idea or a theological teaching from the writings of the hasidic 'heresy'.

found in manuscript. The most important of such works, which is still unpublished and was previously unknown, is *Milḥamot hashem*, by R. Meir ben Elijah, which exists in two copies in the manuscript collection of the National Library in Jerusalem. It is a complete book of some size and of great importance. I lectured on it at the Schocken Institute in Jerusalem in 1971, when I described the book, which had been catalogued as a work completed in Jerusalem in 1892, and I demonstrated that the author was the grandson of the Gaon of Vilna's brother Abraham and that it had been written in Lithuania in approximately 1835, before the author emigrated to the Land of Israel. I am engaged at present in the preparation of the book for publication in a critical edition.

[47] This refers to the proliferation of tsadikim and their courts. In R. Isaac Eisik Haver's time new dynasties, most of them offshoots of Karlin–Stolin hasidism, were beginning to flourish in Lithuania and the territories under its control. See W. Z. Rabinowitsch, *Haḥasidut halita'it* (Jerusalem, 1961), 111–54; I. Tishby, 'Tsevi herman shapira—kesofer haskalah', *Molad*, NS 4 (27) (1972), 574–7.

[48] *Amudei hatorah*, 31*a–b*, and see ibid. 6*a–b* (Torah and *devekut*), 58*d* (Torah and prayer).

[49] The will was printed at the end of *Beit olamim*, in which see sect. 7.

The facts stated lead inevitably to the conclusion that the expression of the 'threefold unity' entered the literature of hasidim and mitnagedim from a common source, outside their domain, which preceded the emergence of hasidism and mitnagedism. The source was without doubt acceptable to both of the opposing movements.

C

There is indeed such a source going back to before the time of the Besht and the Vilna Gaon, and it is extant in print, but up to now it has escaped the notice of researchers. It is in M. H. Luzzatto's commentary to *Idra raba*,[50] which was printed as *Adir bamarom* (Warsaw, 1886) and has also been preserved in manuscripts.[51] The saying is given in Hebrew, together with an explanatory comment. I reproduce the main part here:

They *said in the Zohar that the Holy One, blessed be He, and the Torah and Israel, it is one*[52] . . . But you must know that the souls come out of the lights, and in truth, out of all the lights, from the beginning of *atsilut* [the world of emanation] to the end of *asiyah* [the world of making], souls have come forth . . . And indeed you must always keep in mind this principle, that the lights of the sefirot change[53] to match the [soul] which is to be born from them. And the emission of light from the sefirot for [the purpose of] bringing forth the souls is the most fundamental emission beside which all others are like branches, and this outspreading of the lights in order to bring forth the souls [occurs] with new strength, [no punctuation in the Hebrew—Trans.] certainly in them alone[54] [is] the strength they need for themselves, and this outspreading is the Torah which has as many parts as there are souls which issue from them.[55] That is why it was said that the Torah is the root of the souls of Israel. It follows that there are three things, the lights, the souls that issue from them, and the outspread of the lights to make the souls, and these three things are the Holy One, blessed be He, the Torah, and *Keneset yisra'el*.[56] And understand this well.[57]

[50] The book was written in Italy in 1731. See Essay 8, pp. 412–13 and n. 19.

[51] The extract quoted here is in MS Guenzburg 376, fo. 47^{r-v}, and MS Warsaw 149, fo. 49^{r-v}. The text is the same in both manuscripts. I have indicated in the notes where the manuscripts differ substantially from the printed version.

[52] Hebrew *eḥad hu*. In the manuscripts: . . . *hakol davar eḥad* ['it is all one thing']. The printed version corresponds to the Aramaic *ḥad hu*, the manuscripts to the Aramaic *kola ḥad*.

[53] Manuscripts: ' . . . that the emission of light from the sefirot . . . changes'.

[54] The manuscripts, instead of *levad* ['alone'], have *milevad* ['apart from'] [and the text would then read: '. . . certainly with new strength in them, apart from the strength they need for themselves'—Trans.].

[55] The reference is to the 600,000 letters of the Torah, corresponding to the 600,000 roots of the souls of Israel.

[56] The printed version gives the Aramaic version of the formula; the manuscripts have it in Hebrew.

[57] *Adir bamarom*, 61.

This passage proves conclusively that the formula in question was committed to writing in Padua in 1731, about ten years before the Besht appeared on the scene, and it seems to have been an original idea of Luzzatto's.[58] But in order to understand how the formula was disseminated in Poland and Lithuania, I need to examine an important question: how did it get into hasidic and mitnagedic circles from a manuscript which had been put away unpublished?

I have shown elsewhere[59] that the Vilna Gaon and R. Hayim of Volozhin had Luzzatto's commentary to *Idra raba* and that both of them admired it

[58] There is a formula which comes close to the statement of threefold unity, without attributing it to the Zohar, in R. Hayim Vital's *Sha'ar ruaḥ hakodesh* (Jerusalem, 1912), 42*b*. Vital's remarks preceding and following the formula are also of interest in connection with Luzzatto's explanation. He says: 'Know that the Torah is the quarry of all the souls of Israel, for from it they were hewn, and therefore *the Torah is one Torah and Israel is one nation and the Holy One, blessed be He, is One* [as in the Sabbath afternoon prayer: 'You are One and Your Name is One, and who is like Your people Israel, a nation one (i.e. unique) on the earth'], and this is mystically equated with the [group of] six sefirot *ḥaga"t neh"i* [Hesed, Gevurah, Tiferet; Netsah, Hod, Yesod] in which the written Torah is rooted . . . and they represent [the] 600,000 roots of souls . . . and similarly there are 600,000 interpretations of the written Torah for each and every verse . . . It follows that each and every soul of the 600,000 souls of Israel has one [i.e. its own—Trans.] path in the whole Torah according to the distinctive quality of the root of his soul.' It must be supposed that Luzzatto had *Sha'ar ruaḥ hakodesh* in manuscript, and he may have set out to achieve a synthesis between Vital's remarks and the extensive discussion in *Shenei luḥot haberit* (i. 3*a*–19*a*) on the statement relating to the threefold bonds. In these two works, then, we may see a pair of sources which spurred Luzzatto to attribute the doctrine of threefold unity to the Zohar. As a matter of fact the 'bonds' had already been converted into 'unity' in a Hebrew paraphrase of the words of the Zohar before Luzzatto, in a work by the Shabatean Abraham Miguel Cardozo. If we assume that Luzzatto read Cardozo's writings—which seems very probable in view of what we know of his position with regard to Shabateanism in general and the writings of Nathan of Gaza in particular (see Essay 4, esp. pp. 224–8)—we have here a direct source for the phrase he coined in the name of the Zohar. In the homily *Kodesh yisra'el lashem reshit tevuato* [Jer. 2: 3], printed in G. Scholem's essay 'Shenei mekorot ḥadashim lidiat torato shel avraham mikha'el kardozo', Cardozo says: 'Now you will understand their saying (may they be remembered for blessing) [Zohar III, 73*a*] "*There are three bonds which are one, the Holy One, blessed be He, and the Torah and Israel*" [the emphasis is mine—I.T.]. One of these is Israel, which is one nation, the Torah is one, for the Holy One is called Torah and is also called Israel, and if there were no Israel there would be no Torah and if there were no Torah there would be no Israel and if there were no Torah there would be no creatures and if there were no creatures the Holy One, blessed be He, would not be called God . . . *See, just as the Holy One, blessed be He, and the Torah and Israel are bound together and they are a unity in bereshit* ['in the beginning'], the Holy One, blessed be He, is the beginning [or 'first'] of everything, Israel is the beginning, the Torah is the beginning' (I. Ben-Zvi and M. Benayahu (eds.), *Sefer hayovel lishene'ur zalman shazar/Shneur Zalman Shazar Jubilee Volume* (= *Sefunot*, 3–4) (Jerusalem, 1959–60), 256). Establishing a relationship of source and derivation between Cardozo and Luzzatto in this matter enables us to understand very well why Luzzatto used Hebrew for the statement he attributed to the Zohar. And compare Cardozo's version of the Zoharic statement with that of R. Barukh of Kosov quoted in n. 23 above.

[59] See Essay 8, n. 8 and pp. 449–50.

greatly. I add here some information on the use made of the book by former pupils of the Gaon. MS Jerusalem 3177 8° contains *Sefer habahir* with two commentaries: *Or layesharim*, by a pupil of the Rashba [R. Solomon ben Abraham Adret, thirteenth century],[60] which was edited by R. Moses Solomon of Tulchin, a pupil of the Gaon, with the addition of his own marginal comments; and *Or layehudim*, by R. Zadok ben Noah Bloch, a pupil of R. Hayim of Volozhin. The manuscript is print-ready, and the title-page shows it as having been written in Ivanits in 5564 [1804]. On the reverse of the title-page is a letter of approval from R. Hayim of Volozhin, written in his own hand in 1811.[61] And remarkably, R. Zadok Bloch's commentary quotes passages from Luzzatto's manuscript commentary to *Idra raba*, three times giving the name of that book and twice mentioning Luzzatto's book without naming it.[62] I reproduce here the way in which he prefaced each of these quotations in the book which had been got ready for publication: 'The saintly rabbi, our teacher and rabbi R. M. Luzzatti, may his memory be for a blessing, wrote in a commentary to the holy *Idra raba* which is still in manuscript . . . and see what is said at length in that treatise by the aforesaid saintly man, and you will find that which will quench your thirst . . . as the aforesaid saintly rabbi explained there at length' (fo. 5^r); 'The saintly rabbi, the kabbalist, our teacher and rabbi, R. M. Luzzatti, may his memory be for a blessing, wrote at length in his introduction to the holy *Idra raba*' (fo. 12^v); 'In a book written by the kabbalist [spelt defectively] rabbi, our teacher and rabbi, R. M. Luzzatti, may his memory be for a blessing, which is still in manuscript, he

[60] This is the same commentary as *Or haganuz*, which was printed long afterwards (Vilna, 1883), with the addition of 'some marginal comments and explanations by the Gra'; but the editor did not use the version in this manuscript.

[61] B. Landau specified the works included in this manuscript and published R. Hayim of Volozhin's letter of approval in his book *Hagaon heḥasid mivilna* (Jerusalem, 1967), where see pp. 363–4, 384. But his description of the contents of the manuscript is confused and inaccurate, and the copy of the letter of approval is marred by errors at the end.

[62] R. Zadok Bloch also quotes passages from a kabbalistic book by Luzzatto entitled *Mesilah ha'olah b*[*eit*]*"a*[*lef*] (apparently Beth-El: 'A Highway which Goes Up to Beth-El'), which is not known to me from any other source: 'On this, the saintly rabbi, our teacher and rabbi, R. M. Luzzatti [*sic*], may his memory be for a blessing, enlarged in his book, still in manuscript, which is to be entitled *Mesilah ha'olah b"a*, and there he showed, with proofs that are plain to those who have found knowledge [Prov. 8: 9] . . .' (fo. 12^r); 'The kabbalist rabbi, our teacher and rabbi, R. M. Luzzatti, may his memory be for a blessing, enlarged on this matter in his book [in] manuscript entitled *Mesilah ha'olah b"a*' (fo. 23^v); 'As was explained to us at length by the godly kabbalist, our teacher and rabbi, R. M. Luzzatti, may his memory be for a blessing, in his book [in] manuscript *Mesilah ha'olah b"a* . . . as he explained there at length' (fo. 29^v). This pupil of R. Hayim of Volozhin was zealous in his concern for the copying and distribution of any of Luzzatto's kabbalistic writings which came his way in manuscript. *Ḥoker umekubal*, ed. M. Frestadt (Leipzig and Königsberg, 1840), was printed from a copy of a manuscript made by R. Zadok Bloch which reached the editor from the Volozhin yeshiva via R. Jacob Kaplan of Minsk. See the introduction to that work, p. xiv, and the note on pp. 45–6 of the text itself.

explains at length these things in *Ra*[*ya*] *m*[*eheimna*] . . . by a marvellous mystery' (fo. 17ᵛ); 'As explained at length in the commentary to the holy *Idra raba*, a manuscript by the saintly kabbalist our teacher and rabbi, R. M. Luzzatti, may his memory be for a blessing' (fo. 24ᵛ); 'The rabbi, the kabbalist, our teacher and rabbi R. M. Luzzatti, may his memory be for a blessing, wrote at great length on the subject of study for the sake of Heaven' (fo. 30ʳ). R. Hayim of Volozhin, who endorsed the publication of the extracts from Luzzatto's *Idra raba* commentary with the highest praise, had certainly studied that book and was well versed in its subject matter. In the *Likutim* [a collection of extracts] at the end of R. Menahem Mendel of Shklov's *Mayim adirim* (Warsaw, 1885), 83*d*, we find: 'And now I will reveal to you the secret of the war of the Lord, although it has already been explained in part by the great kabbalist R. Moses Hayim Luzzatto, may the memory of that righteous and holy man be for a blessing, in his commentary on the *Idra*, though for sound understanding it needs to be further considered, and between him and me the correct conclusion will be reached.' R. Isaac Eisik Haver, in his commentary to *Likutei hager"a* (Warsaw, 1889), remarked: 'This is a profound mystery explained in the writings of the kabbalist rabbi the [*sic*] Luzzatti in his commentary on the *Idra raba* on the mystery of the battle which is mentioned in several places in the *Tikunim* and the *Raya meheimna* and the Zohar.' And lastly: R. Isaac Eisik Haver's son, son-in-law, and pupil testify that he wrote a great commentary on Luzzatto's commentary on *Idra raba*. The first two, in listing his works, include 'also an extensive commentary on the commentaries of the watcher and holy one [Dan. 4: 10] the R. M. H. Luzzatto, may his memory be for a blessing, on the *Idrot*';[63] '. . . and a commentary on the words of the watcher and holy one, the R. M. H. Luzzatto, may his memory be for a blessing, on the *Idrot*'.[64] Haver's pupil, R. Isaac Kahana, who 'went up' to Jerusalem and settled there, numbers among the books which his teacher sent him for study, apparently while he was still in the Diaspora, 'another book by the rabbi Ramhal, may his memory be for a blessing, namely his commentary on *Idra raba*, part of it with the commentary of our master and teacher [*admo"r*], may his memory be for a blessing'.[65] In the light of these facts it is clear that Luzzatto's commentary on *Idra raba* was widely available to scholars of the Vilna Gaon's school—an open book from which any who wished could copy and publish as they pleased.

The circulation of the book among hasidim is a more difficult question. I have no factual information additional to that given in my previous essay[66] to

63 Introduction by the author's son Joseph to the commentary *Ginzei meromim* on *Masekhta atsilut*.

64 Introduction by R. Isaac Tsevi Halevi, R. Isaac Eisik Haver's son-in-law, to *Amudei hatorah*.

65 Introduction to *Sefer yetsirah* with the Vilna Gaon's commentary.

66 See Essay 8, pp. 420–3, 444–8.

show that members of the school of the Maggid of Mezhirech knew of the existence of Luzzatto's commentary to *Idra raba* and were aware that R. Elijah of Brisk had it in manuscript. The fact that the dictum 'the Holy One, blessed be He, the Torah, and Israel, all is one' is quoted in Aramaic in the works of hasidim shows, in my opinion, that some of the teachers of hasidism took it directly from Luzzatto's book and others received it at second hand. The book is full of difficult and complex Lurianic terms and concepts; many hasidic scholars would not have been capable of understanding it properly, and it is certain that only a few individuals read it carefully from beginning to end. This, I think, provides a reasonable explanation for the limited use of the dictum of threefold unity in the literature of hasidism.

A final question: why the change of language from the Hebrew original in Luzzatto's book to the Aramaic version of the dictum in customary use? The answer is that readers translated the dictum into Aramaic in order to 'give it back' its 'original' character. Convincing proof of this is furnished by R. Isaac Eisik Haver's explanatory comments when quoting the formula in his *Pitḥei she'arim*:[67]

> And therefore it [the Torah] was given by the hand of Moses our teacher, peace be upon him, for it contains all the 600,000 souls of Israel . . . the meaning is that the whole is divided into three aspects, *as they said* [in Aramaic]: 'orayta vekb"h veyisra'el ḥad hu' ['the Torah and the Holy One, blessed be He, and Israel, it is one'], that is to say, the lights, which are all the matters we are speaking about in the sefirot and the countenances of *atsilut* ['Emanation'], and that which is drawn down from them is the souls, and the Torah is the drawing down of the lights to the souls, *as was said by the pious and godly man our teacher and rabbi, R. M. H. Luzzatto, may his memory be for a blessing, in his writings*, and thence it is the root of all the souls of Israel.[68]

This explanation is a summary of the words of Luzzatto in the commentary to *Idra raba*,[69] and the vague expression 'his writings' is meant to refer to that work: that is to say, the formula in Aramaic is a direct translation of Luzzatto's Hebrew.[70]

It appears to me that in tracing the problematic dictum to its source in Luzzatto's writings, I have not only settled an individual literary and intellectual problem but have also found one link in a long chain. At the end of my essay on the dissemination of Luzzatto's kabbalistic writings I wrote: 'if it becomes clear that there are points of contact and close parallels between the

[67] See nn. 28 and 43 above. [68] *Pitḥei she'arim*, 11*a*. [69] See p. 470 above.

[70] The translation of the formula makes two alterations which need explanation. The change in word order, substituting 'the Torah and the Holy One, blessed be He' for 'the Holy One, blessed be He, and the Torah' is understandable: R. Isaac Eisik Haver preferred to make the Torah the first of the 'trinity' in order to emphasize its divine level. But it is hard to understand why, here in particular, he should have dropped the words 'in the Zohar'. The omission may possibly have been a printer's error.

ideas in Luzzatto's kabbalistic writings and those in the literature of hasidism which could point to a relationship of source and derivation, the existence of such a relationship should not be dismissed by arguing that the relevant works by Luzzatto were hidden away during the early growth period of hasidism and could not have served as sources for its doctrine'.[71] In laying bare the varied fortunes of the dictum 'kub"h orayta veyisra'el kola ḥad' I have proved that at any rate the Besht's grandson and members of the third generation in the history of hasidism took up an important idea from a work by Luzzatto which had been put away unpublished. My researches have led me to the opinion that the influence of Luzzatto's writings, and together with them those of his colleague R. Moses David Valle, was not limited to isolated sayings, and that it has left its mark on substantial elements of hasidic doctrine.[72] I offer the present essay as an introduction to an extensive examination of my hypothesis.

ADDENDA

I. THE THREEFOLD UNITY IN THE HOMILIES OF THE MAGGID OF MEZHIRECH, IN *OR TORAH*, AND IN *OR HA'EMET*

In my discussion of the Maggid of Mezhirech in this essay[73] I asserted that in spite of the part played by oneness in his homilies, they did not contain the dictum on threefold unity but only the formula of the unity of two, 'the Holy One, blessed be He, and the Torah are one' [*kub"h veorayta ḥad*]. In making this assertion I pointed out that I was basing myself on *Magid devarav*

[71] Essay 8, p. 450.

[72] The following are some basic topics on which I perceive a strong link between the literature of hasidism and the writings of Luzzatto and the members of his circle: the nature of *devekut*, its processes, and what it is intended to achieve; the purification of corporeality and turning evil into good; the descent of the tsadik and the stages of spiritual 'immaturity' and 'maturity' in his descent and ascent. As regards the last-mentioned topic, one of the principal sources for which in hasidism is, in my opinion, found in the writings of R. Moses David Valle, I have already published part of my evidence orally in my lectures at two conferences, one at the World Congress on the Science of Judaism and the other at the Israeli National Academy of Science in Jerusalem. There are also clear signs of Luzzatto's influence in some characteristic ideas of the Habad movement: among others, one of the central ideas in the writings of R. Aaron Halevi of Starosielce—that when bringing evil into existence God created its opposite so that it could be annulled in time to come—is rooted in the view of evil and the purpose of its existence in Luzzatto's doctrine.

[73] [Which had already been published.—Trans.] In *Kiryat sefer*, 50 (1975), 482.

leya'akov (Korets, 1784), because it was 'the first and most authoritative of the printed collections of the Maggid's homilies'.[74] On a quick examination of the other two collections, *Or torah* (Korets, 1804) and *Or ha'emet* (Husiatyn, 1899), I did not find any differences of substance so far as concerns the formulae of unity, and I therefore saw no need to deal with them. But after the present essay had been printed I found that there are two homilies in *Or ha'emet* (one of them is also in *Or torah*) which contain the formula of threefold unity. In view of this finding I must moderate the categorical assertion I made with regard to the Maggid of Mezhirech.

I reproduce the two passages here:

> If he performs it [if he fulfils a commandment (*mitsvah*)] with his own advantage in mind, he has thereby created a separation, *for the Torah and the Holy One, blessed be He, and Israel, all is one* [*kola ḥad*]; it follows that if he performs it properly, the *mitsvah* and the Holy One, blessed be He, become all one. (*Or ha'emet*, 57)

> For the Holy One, blessed be He, wished to sift out of Egypt all the sparks which occurred in the breaking of the vessels . . . that is to say, this would be the sifting by which He introduced these words and letters into the Torah . . . and that is the hidden meaning of one of the narratives of the Torah, apart from other mysteries which are alluded to in narratives, [mysteries] quite without number in every single letter, for *the Holy One, blessed be He, and the Torah and Israel, it is one* [*ḥad hu*]. (Ibid. 150, and *Or torah*, at head of the *parashah* 'Bo')

Both works quote the dictum on threefold unity without indicating its source or connecting it in any way with the Besht.

Since both collections were late publications, edited and printed after the death of the pupils of the Maggid to whom the collectors of the homilies were related—R. Isaiah of Dunayevtsy for *Or torah* and R. Levi Isaac of Berdichev for *Or ha'emet*—it may be that the formula of threefold unity in the Maggid's homilies resulted from the addition of 'Israel' to the dual version by copyists or editors. But in the absence of any evidence to support this we are not entitled to contradict the traditions that have come down to us. This would indicate that the dictum on threefold unity was known to the Maggid of Mezhirech, and that at times he used it in his homilies. If so it must be assumed that the Maggid himself saw it in Luzzatto's commentary to *Idra raba*. On the basis of these considerations the Maggid could be regarded as a principal channel for the dissemination of the dictum in hasidic circles, perhaps in parallel with R. Phinehas of Korets.[75]

[74] n. 9 above. [75] See n. 13 above.

II. ON THE WAYS IN WHICH USE WAS MADE OF THE CONCEPT OF 'THREE BONDS OF FAITH', AND OF THE EXPRESSION ITSELF

In my note on R. Barukh of Kosov,[76] who described the relationship of the Holy One, blessed be He, the Torah, and Israel as 'three bonds of faith', I observed that this expression is a well-known Shabatean theological catchword, and although I found a foothold for it in the 'three levels of faith' of the Zohar II, 204*b*, the fact that R. Barukh of Kosov used the exact words used by the Shabateans showed that this anti-Shabatean scholar 'came under the influence of this formulation by his opponents'. That observation needs to be corrected and supplemented both as regards the use of the expression in R. Barukh of Kosov's writings and as regards its substance in the Zohar and Shabatean literature.

I must first correct my mistaken assertion that 'the expression "three bonds of faith" does not occur anywhere in the Zohar'. The expression occurs in at least two passages in the main body of the Zohar with minor variations: (*a*) II, 38*a*, says that the Egyptians enslaved Israel with the help of three forces of uncleanness from the sefirotic system of the Sitra Ahra ['Other Side'] which were called *telat kesharin* ['three bonds' or 'three knots'],[77] and it was only through the merit of '*the three bonds* [*kitrei*; *ketar*, *kitra* is an Aramaic synonym of *kesher*—Trans.] *of faith*', Abraham, Isaac, and Jacob, that they were freed; (*b*) III, 36*a*, in considering the fact that the Torah begins with the letter *beit* [***B****ereshit*], comments: 'And because it [the Torah] is the Holy Name, it began with *beit*, which is the whole of the Holy Name *in the three bonds of faith*.' Nevertheless the formula 'three levels of faith', to which I drew attention, is interesting. In the Zohar the expression *telat kitrei*, and apparently *telat kishrei* also, means the sefirot Hesed, Gevurah, and Tiferet,[78] a combination which does not represent the Shabatean trinity. 'Three levels', on the other hand, refers to the *partsufim* [divine 'countenances'] Atika Kadisha, Ze'ir Anpin, and the Shekhinah, as explained in the extract I quote from the Zohar II, 88*a* [in n. 23 above], which relates the three Sabbath meals to these three *partsufim*—the *partsufim* which constitute the Shabatean trinity.

[76] n. 23 above.

[77] Zohar II, 38*a* and 40*b*.

[78] The comments of the Zohar on the three bonds [*telat kishrei*] are made in the name of R. Eleazar, and they are applied to the 'trinitarian' explanation of the letter *beit*, based on its shape [ב], as previously reported in the name of R. Judah: '*Beit*, two "roofs" [horizontal strokes] and one which joins them together . . . one for Heaven and one for earth and the Holy One, blessed be He, joins them together.' Apparently the 'trinity' here means Binah, Tiferet, and Malkhut. And see p. 483 below.

However, in order to clarify the nature of the Zoharic sources from which the Shabateans derived their catchword 'three bonds of faith', and to understand the ways in which it is connected with the statements in the Zohar, we must turn to the literature of Shabateanism. I will consider here the writings of Nehemiah Hayon, who disseminated in print the Shabatean 'mystery of the Godhead' [*sod ha'elohut*], central to which was the 'three bonds of faith'; *Shem olam* (Vienna, 1891), by R. Jonathan Eybeschuetz, who followed in Hayon's footsteps in the development of Shabatean theology;[79] and the subject of the trinity in the Frankists' 'principles of the faith'.

Hayon issued a stern ruling on the supreme importance of belief in the 'three bonds of faith': 'Therefore anyone who denies this belief is not one of the children of Israel, and all the *mitsvot* he has performed during his lifetime are not counted in his favour, and he is shut out of all the doors of that world even if he has accumulated all the *mitsvot* in the world.'[80] He therefore found it necessary to prove in detail that this belief, which could be seen as leaning towards Christianity, sprang from a trustworthy source, and he undertook a sort of research study, exhaustive in its scope, to uncover in the Zohar the roots of the belief he professed.[81] Some of the passages he gathered to justify this belief had already been quoted and explained in his little book *Raza deyiḥuda* (Venice, 1711), but here he presented his extensive array of sources in systematic order with the object of providing an answer to three questions: (*a*) 'First of all we will cite passages to establish whether there are three bonds of faith';[82] (*b*) 'Now I must tell you to whom the three bonds of faith relate, and how this is reconcilable because they are three which constitute one';[83] (*c*) 'Now we must tell you that it is the three bonds that are the essence of the faith of Israel.'[84]

To show that the 'three bonds of faith' do exist in the Godhead, Hayon cited numerous proof-texts from all parts of the Zohar, but the passages which include the forms *telat kishrei* and *telat kitrei* for the bonds and *telat dargei* for the levels are not among them.[85] It is hard to imagine that these expressions in particular, which come closest to the Shabatean catchword, escaped Hayon's notice. It seems more likely to me that they were knowingly omitted because Hayon's object was not to find an identical terminology in the Zohar but to authenticate the belief in the unity of a divine trinity; and the element of unity is, indeed, present in the passages which he brought

[79] See M. A. Perlmutter, *R' yehonatan aibeshits veyaḥaso el hashabeta'ut* (Jerusalem and Tel Aviv, 1947), 182–265.
[80] *Oz lelohim uveit kodesh kodashim* (Berlin, 1713), 87*b*–88*a*.
[81] 'Therefore, in order to break the teeth of infidels I have been obliged *to gather all the passages which relate to the matter of the three bonds of faith*' (ibid. 83*a*).
[82] Ibid.
[83] Ibid. 84*b*.
[84] Ibid. 87*b*.
[85] Some of the passages cited contain the expressions *telat kesharin* [for 'three bonds'] or *kishra demeheimanuta* ['the bond of faith'] which occur in many places in the Zohar, but they do not have the phrase 'three bonds of faith' or the like.

together,[86] whereas that element is absent from the references to 'three bonds'(whether *kishrei* or *kitrei*) and 'three levels'.

In answering the question what made up the divine trinity Hayon found himself in difficulties, because in the sections of the Zohar where the unity of three is spelt out, the three constituent parts are not the same as in the Shabatean version, and in some sections on unity which do correspond to *partsufim* in the Shabatean trinity, we find only a duality: Atika Kadisha and Ze'ir Anpin.[87] It was only by subjecting vague or obscure statements to forced interpretations that Hayon could 'discover' what he was looking for. In this matter he therefore relied chiefly on the section relating to the Sabbath meals in the Zohar II, 88*a–b*,[88] with which the formula 'three levels of faith' is associated, and the parallel section in III, 288*b* (*Idra zuta*), because, although they contain no mention of the threefold unity, they present the combination of the *partsufim* Atika Kadisha, Malka Kadisha, and Matronita[89] as the very basis of the Jewish faith. And so in the third stage of his argument, in which he set out to prove the centrality of the belief in the 'three bonds of faith', Hayon again cited the section on the Sabbath meals as his principal evidence.[90]

[86] The majority of those that relate to unification [*yiḥud*] as the purpose of reciting the Shema are quoted or referred to in Tishby, *Wisdom of the Zohar*, iii. 971–3.

[87] Hayon saw the difficulty and tried to resolve it: 'It must be said that when, in the Zohar, Atika Kadisha appears next to Z[e'ir] A[npin], it is speaking of Malka Kadisha and His Shekhinah . . . that is, Atika Kadisha is called Malka Kadisha and His Shekhinah is called Ze'ir Anpin' (*Oz lelohim*, 85*a*).

[88] Hayon calls it 'first of the first' [i.e. the most important—Trans.] (ibid.).

[89] These are the names in *Idra zuta* which most closely fit the customary Shabatean terminology. Elsewhere Hayon dealt with the difference in the names of the male and female *partsufim* in the two passages in the Zohar, and drew a distinction between the nature of the two pairs: 'And [as to] what was said in "Beit kodesh hakodashim" ['The house of the holy of holies'] [*Oz lelohim*, 75*d*] that the upper Shekhinah is the Shekhinah of Malka Kadisha, and the lower Shekhinah is the Shekhinah of Ze'ir Anpin, and that therefore Jacob took Leah and Rachel to wife, the reason is that just as Malka Kadisha clothes himself in Ze'ir Anpin, so his Shekhinah clothes herself in the Rachel of Atsilut . . . and therefore you will find in both places in the Zohar concerning the three meals that sometimes it calls them Ze'ir Anpin and the field of sacred apples, and sometimes it calls them Malka Kadisha and Matronita . . . but the answer is as we have said, that their external aspect is called Ze'ir Anpin and the field of sacred apples, and their inward aspect is called Malka Kadisha and Matronita' (*Oz lelohim*, 78*a–b*). It appears to me that we have here the source from which both R. Jonathan Eybeschuetz and R. Jacob Koppel Lipschuetz of Mezhirech developed the idea of the upper and lower Shekhinah in their Shabatean writings. See my essay 'Bein shabeta'ut laḥasidut' in my *Netivei emunah uminut* (Ramat Gan, 1964), 221, and 339–40 in the notes.

[90] See *Oz lelohim*, 87*b*–88*a*. Nor did Hayon produce any new evidence from the Zohar in his *Hatsad tsevi* (Amsterdam, 1714), 27*b*–31*a*, where he replied to the attack on his belief in the trinity in R. Tsevi Ashkenazi's pamphlet *Le'einei kol yisra'el* (see Aron Freimann, *Inyenei shabetai tsevi* (Berlin, 1912/13), 120–1; and see n. 96 below). But in that reply there was no mention of the formulae of the three bonds and the three levels (*telat kishrei*, *telat kitrei*, and *telat dargei*) which I have

R. Jonathan Eybeschuetz, who had before him the extracts from the Zohar collected in *Oz lelohim*, indicated in general terms that the 'three bonds [*kishrei*] of faith' were referred to in the Zohar, in *Tikunei hazohar*, and in other kabbalistic books, but he stressed a few sources in particular.[91] The sources he named are: (*a*) Zohar, *parashah* 'Bo'. By this Eybeschuetz undoubtedly meant an outstandingly trinitarian statement, dealing with the *kavanah* of unification in reciting the Shema, at the end of the *parashah* in the Zohar (II, 43*b*) [see Tishby, *Wisdom of the Zohar*, iii. 972—Trans.]; and he may also have been alluding to the statement on the three bonds [*kitrei*] of faith (II, 38*a*) ignored by Hayon.[92] (*b*) The two *Idrot*, especially *Idra zuta*. In fact *Idra raba* contains only one clearly trinitarian passage,[93] whereas in *Idra zuta* there are trinitarian references in plenty.[94] (*c*) The passages in the Zohar on the Sabbath meals which I considered above. As R. Jonathan puts it: 'As is well known, the Zohar explains [that there are] three bonds of faith, and *Tikun shabat* will prove that the three meals allude to A[tika] K[adisha], Z[e'ir] A[npin], and Nukba.'[95]

All the polemics attacking Hayon which I have examined pillory the belief in the trinity expressed in his books as a disgraceful and dangerous heresy, but the ways in which they condemn it are not uniform, and it is interesting to note what use is made of the formula 'three bonds of faith' in their different reactions. The greatest of his opponents—R. Tsevi Ashkenazi,[96] known as

considered here; and for the elements which constitute the belief in the trinity he again relied mainly on the sections relating to the Sabbath meals, but added as further evidence the instruction in *Sefer tikunei shabat*, on the basis of Luria's hymns, that each of the three meals should be devoted to one of the *partsufim* which make up the Shabatean trinity (*Hatsad tsevi*, 27*b*). In this connection the originality of his *Hatsad tsevi* consists chiefly in linking the trinity to the kabbalistic ideas in the works of Radbaz [R. David ben Solomon ibn Abi Zimra] and Cordovero (ibid. 29*a*–30*b*) and accordingly setting up a new trinitarian pattern: 'light, substance, and root'.

[91] See *Shem olam* (Vienna, 1891), 31, 32, 121,197, 236, 252, 253–4.

[92] See pp. 478–9 above. The statement on unification in the Zohar (II, 43*b*) is also not to be found in Hayon's writings, and it is hard to understand why he omitted it. That statement was prominent among the arguments in support of the belief in the trinity submitted by the Frankists at the disputation in Kamenets. See R. Jacob Emden's *Sefer shimush* (Amsterdam [actually Altona], 1758–[1762]), 41*b*; M. Balaban, *Letoledot hatenuah haferankit* (Tel Aviv, 1934–5), i. 146, 154.

[93] See Zohar III, 142*b*.

[94] See ibid. 288*a*–*b*, 289*b*, 292*b*, 296*b*.

[95] *Shem olam*, 254. And see ibid. 31. By *Tikun shabat* he means the teachings in *Sefer tikunei shabat* based on Luria's Sabbath hymns. Cf. the remarks by Hayon in *Hatsad tsevi*, cited in n. 90 above. Traces of the additions made by Hayon in *Hatsad tsevi*, and of his characteristic turns of phrase, can be identified in several places in *Shem olam*.

[96] In an addendum to his ruling he gave exact references to statements on the last pages of Hayon's *Oz lelohim*, saying that they were 'great heresies which it is forbidden for Israel to commit to writing' (Freimann, *Inyenei shabetai tsevi*, 120). However, not only did he not mention the 'three bonds' formula but he nowhere specified that his remarks applied to the belief in the trinity, and he was silent on the proof-texts adduced by Hayon from the Zohar. In a passage beginning 'These three transgressors of Israel' in the pamphlet *Piska min shemaya* (printed as an

Hakham Tsevi, R. Moses Hagiz in some of his works opposing Hayon,[97] R. Joseph Ergas,[98] and R. David Nieto[99]—condemned Hayon's remarks on

appendix to *Shalhevet yah* (Amsterdam, 1714)), Hayon wrote that R. Tsevi Ashkenazi, having moved to London from Amsterdam as a result of the dispute [described in *Encyclopaedia Judaica*, iii. 734—Trans.], 'sowed heresy there . . . for the said author [the author of *Oz lelohim*: Hayon] supports his case with the words of the Holy Zohar, old and new and *Tikunim* new and old [but by a misspelling *yeshanim* ['old'] is turned into *yeshenim* ['sleeping']] and *Raya meheimna*, but he [Ashkenazi] stood the matter on its head and "took her to be a harlot" [Gen. 38: 15]. What did he do? He said to them: "Know that these books were written 300 years ago and they are not by R. Simeon ben Yohai and his companions and disciples", and he quarrelled over it and called its name *sitnah* ['enmity']. [See Gen. 26: 21.] Further, he opened wide his mouth and said: "Why do they bring me proofs from the Zohar? Let them bring me proofs from *Moreh nevukhim* ['The Guide of the Perplexed']."' Of course the reliability of Hayon's reports is questionable, but there is certainly a grain of truth in his testimony here. And see R. Tsevi Ashkenazi's responsa *She'elot uteshuvot* (Amsterdam, 1712), later printed under the title *Shu"t ḥakham tsevi*, no. 36, where he asserts that 'even if the words of the Zohar were the opposite of those of the *posekim*, we should not abandon the words of the *posekim* for esoteric interpretations of the Torah'. He concludes with a forceful anti-Shabatean declaration: 'And that is the foundation of our holy Torah, for otherwise you would be allowing every individual to take the law into his own hands and follow his understanding of the Zohar, whether good or bad. And for our many sins, that is the cause of great breaches, for I myself have seen how many people have transgressed the laws, altered the statutes [Isa. 24: 5], in reliance on the words of the Zohar or *Raya meheimna* according to their opinion of its meaning, an opinion infected by a commentary on the words of the Zohar or *Raya meheimna*. And Heaven forbid that any such thoughts should have occurred to the authors of the Zohar and *Raya meheimna*.' This responsum was written in Altona in 1706, before the beginning of the Hayon dispute. Apparently R. Jacob Emden [son of R. Tsevi Ashkenazi—Trans.] followed in his father's footsteps not only in attacking Shabateans but also in questioning the antiquity of the Zohar in order to undermine the Shabateans' case. Cf. Emden's remarks on the Zohar in *Sefer shimush*, 37*a*–*b*, 40*b*, 48*b*.

[97] In *Milḥamah lashem veḥerev lashem* (Amsterdam [actually London], 1714), 5*b*, he wrote: 'As if this trouble were not enough for him, he compounded the mischief and sinned in believing in a trinity like the uncircumcised. You of this generation, see who and which one of the kabbalists it is who has written this lying foreword expressing belief in a trinity like idol-worshippers.'

[98] In *Tokhaḥat megulah* (London, 1715), 12*b*, he wrote: 'Moreover, at the end of this accursed book he enlarged on this, stating that the God of Israel was one composed of three . . . and as if the storm and trouble aroused by this heresy were not enough, he collected all the statements in the holy Zohar that might prove to people who are weak-sighted and ignorant like him that the truth is as he says, but anyone versed in the secrets of the Torah will know in truth that he has preached rebellion against the Lord, for which no atonement is possible.' Ergas goes on to prove (ibid. 12*b*–14*a*) from the writings of kabbalists that it is forbidden to take the trinitarian statements of the Zohar literally.

[99] In *Esh dat* (London, 1715), 13*a*–23*b*, Nieto discusses at length the criticism of the writings in which Hayon expressed his belief in the trinity. His main conclusion is the same as that of R. Joseph Ergas, that to understand the expressions in the Zohar as trinitarian amounted to rank heresy. But Ergas relied on kabbalistic ideas to support the interpretation of the descriptions in the Zohar as allegorical, whereas Nieto contrasted the literalists' views with those of the kabbalists; and although he declared that 'there is no difference between the literalists and the kabbalists

the trinity indirectly, or at any rate without mentioning the formula in question. Some people rejected the belief in the trinity outright, and categorized the formula 'three bonds' also as a Shabatean forgery.[100] Others, such as

with regard to the Godhead' (ibid. 27*b*, no. 57), in fact he favoured bringing the words of the Zohar into line with the views of the literalists. The rule he adopted was 'that it is impossible that so great and holy a *tana* as R. Simeon ben Yohai should have written anything in his book contradicting a principle on which everything depends' (ibid. 15*a*, no. 94; and see ibid. 21*b*, no. 150).

[100] R. Gabriel Pontremoli gave trenchant expression to this opinion: 'And, having believed in a duality, what he added to his sin [was] the transgression of believing in a third one, *calling them three bonds of Meheimanuta dekhula* ['The Faith of All'—the title of a book for which Hayon claimed authorship—Trans.] . . . One who believes this throws down and lays low the wall of the Torah and its true faith . . . and is very close to the faith of those who believe in a trinity [the Christians] . . . It seems to me that anyone who believes in this triad [believes in] *a falsehood and a lie . . . things which come from we know not where, or whither they are going, or from whose womb they sprang*, and anyone who gives heed to *these fictions* and places his belief in them I call the simpleton who believes everything [Prov. 14: 15]' (*Milḥamah lashem veḥerev lashem*, 19*b*–20*a*). And see the remarks by R. Samson Morpurgo, ibid. 12*b*. A pamphlet in MS Oxford 2409, fos. 2r–16v, says bluntly that the belief in the trinity, and the formula 'three bonds of faith', are a fabrication by Hayon. Here are three extracts from the pamphlet:

(*a*) 'These three things are too wonderful for me . . . they are the three bonds of faith, and heresy and idol-worship; we have never seen or heard anything as bad as these, they have not been mentioned in any book which is called by the name of Israel, and it has never entered the mind of any authority on religious law to allow the one and only God to be brought out of the domain of the one into the domain of the many' [a play on the legal expressions for the private and the public domain—Trans.] (fo. 10r).

(*b*) To Hayon's allegation that 'just as there are three bonds of faith, there are three bonds of falsehood [the Christian trinity], as is [stated] in the Zohar, *Shemot*, 243*b*' (*Oz lelohim*, 82*b*), this is the reply: 'What is the point of the deceiver's saying these things with his deceit and the forger with his forgery, when we have the holy Zohar before us, and there, in *Shemot*, there is nothing of all these, and the three bonds of faith are not mentioned, and there is nothing about falsehood at all . . . and *possibly it does not occur anywhere else in the Zohar, either*' (ibid.).

(*c*) As to Hayon's reliance on 'all the statements relating to the matter of the three bonds of faith', the pamphlet answers: 'He tried to invoke a great authority, namely the holy Zohar, by the slenderest of niceties—thin, and shrivelled by the east wind [Gen. 41: 6] . . . for after all, the contemptible likeness of *these three bonds*, the invention of his lascivious heart, is *not mentioned in any book*, whether by the ancients or by later writers, but only in the words of this idolater who has imputed things which are not right to the Lord our God' (fo. 13r).

Following the pamphlet in the manuscript (fos. 25v–26r) is a letter signed by David Lopez Jesurun, written in Amsterdam in 1725. The pamphlet was composed at the time of the Hayon dispute, apparently at the end of 5474 [early autumn 1714], because it mentions Hayon's *Hatsad tsevi* (fos. 27, 28), which was printed in that year. Its author may have been one of the scholars of the Portuguese community in Amsterdam, but was certainly not Jesurun, who wrote the letter. Jesurun was a pupil of R. Solomon Ayllon, who was the Shabatean rabbi of the Portuguese Jews in Amsterdam and who campaigned in defence of Hayon. See I. S. Emmanuel, 'Ḥakham david lopes yeshurun unesiato la'arets', in *Minḥah le'avraham: sefer yovel likhevod avraham elmalyah* (Jerusalem, 1959), 90–2. The letter was chiefly taken up with extravagant praise of R. Solomon Ayllon's character and his greatness as a Torah scholar, and with censure of the addressee, R. Aaron Bueno de Mesquita, for daring to deride Ayllon on a halakhic point. The pamphlet,

R. Moses Hagiz in one treatise[101] and R. Joseph Fiametta-Lehavah, rabbi of Ancona, in a letter to R. Solomon Ayllon,[102] cited the formula without dissenting from it, but declared that the meaning Hayon ascribed to it was based on a false interpretation. However, these scholars, too, gave no references for the occurrence of the formula in the Zohar.

One mention of 'three bonds of faith' [*telat kishrei meheimanuta*] in the Zohar which was passed over in silence by Hayon and Eybeschuetz was placed foremost in the public disputation which took place in Kamenets in 1757 between the anti-talmudic Frankists and the talmudist rabbis. The Frankists, setting out the principles of their faith, gave as their fifth principle the unity of the Lord 'with three countenances [*partsufim*] equal to each other and with no separation between them', and as their first evidence of the unity of the trinity they cited the statement in the Zohar (III, 36*a*) on the fact that the Torah begins with the letter *beit*, with slight inaccuracies at the end of their quotation so that it read 'which is the holy name of the three bonds of faith'.[103] The rabbis, fearful of the institutions of the Catholic Church under whose aegis the disputation took place, avoided a response to this statement of principle and the Christianizing principles which followed it.[104] R. Jacob Emden, who published the principles together with their Frankist expositions and his detailed criticisms, replied to the Frankists' use of the quotation from the Zohar:

on the other hand, describes Ayllon's rabbinical court as 'a court of idolaters, lawless lawmakers who call the arrogant happy in the pits of heresy' (fo. 2ʳ).

[101] In *Shever poshe'im* (Amsterdam [actually London], 1714), 38 (photocopy, Jerusalem 1970), he wrote: 'For the reason the ancients called that crown [Keter] Elyon is that it is the first cause in relation to all the other sefirot that were divided into three [*nishtaleshu*; but he may have intended *nishtalshelu*, 'evolved'] from it and by means of it until they came to stand as three from three, three of the first three, *which are the three bonds of faith*, as is known to those who are familiar with occult wisdom [kabbalah] and the like.' What he seems to mean is that the true 'three bonds of faith' are the three groups of three in the sefirotic system (Keter Elyon, Hokhmah, Binah; Hesed, Gevurah, Tiferet; Netsah, Hod, Yesod). And see ibid. 62.

[102] Fiametta wrote: 'Also, as to his dilating in words from which transgression is not lacking [Prov. 10: 19] *on the three bonds of faith*, we have read, and read a second and third time, these words in the Zohar, just as he has, but in a way which is upright in the eyes of God and man' (M. Friedmann, 'Igerot befarashat pulmus neḥemyah ḥiya ḥayon', *Sefunot*, 10 (1966), 582). There are also various references to the subject of the three bonds of faith ibid. 527, 542, 559, 580, 597.

[103] R. Jacob Emden, *Sefer shimush*, 39*b*. And see p. 477 above. It should be noted that the Frankists did not include in their evidence the passages in the Zohar on the three Sabbath meals.

[104] See A. J. Brawer, 'Makor ivri ḥadash letoledot ferank vesiato', *Hashiloaḥ* (Odessa), 33 (1917), 340; A. Kraushar, *Ferank va'adato*, trans. N. Sokolov (Warsaw, 1896), 89; Balaban, *Letoledot hatenuah haferankit*, i. 147. The rabbis behaved similarly at the disputation in Lvov. See Brawer, 'Makor ivri ḥadash', 444; Balaban, *Letoledot hatenuah haferankit*, ii. 241.

What they [the three bonds] refer to is the three supernal attributes, namely Hesed, Din, Rahamim, which are known as three lines in the holy tree and are also known as right, left, and middle . . . and that is [what is meant by] the expression which ends with: 'the Holy Name in the three bonds of faith', for certainly He, may He be exalted, dwells in them and binds them together . . . and if a stumbling-block is placed before those who err in their heart by its words 'the Holy Name in the three bonds of faith', you have a ready answer, for it also says that the whole Torah is the Holy Name.[105]

Another answer has been preserved, which is important on account of its author—R. Hayim Hakohen Rapoport, rabbi of Lvov, who was a persecutor of the Frankists before the disputation at Kamenets[106] and was the chief speaker against them at the Lvov disputation in 1759. In the *Likutim* appended to his homilies[107] he says:

As for their [the Frankists'] saying that 'three bonds of faith' are mentioned in several places in the Zohar, they do not know and do not understand, for this is nothing but a reference to the sefirot, as it says 'that is the holy name in the three bonds' etc.; and it is well known that 'the name' means the sefirot, but the Holy One, blessed be He, is one alone . . . and how can these misguided people say that there is a trinity, Heaven forbid.

Before and after this paragraph there are answers to some unquestionably Frankist arguments, and in some of them the 'misguided people' are addressed in the second person.[108]

In the light of the foregoing review it would seem at first sight that R. Barukh of Kosov's use of the formula 'three bonds of faith' should not be

[105] *Sefer shimush*, 39*b*.

[106] See ibid. 2*b*–3*a*. R. Hayim was the first signatory to the edict of excommunication [*ḥerem*] against the Frankists which was promulgated in Brody in 1756 and was issued in print. (The text of the *ḥerem* was republished by Joseph Kohen-Tsedek in *Otsar ḥokhmah*, 1 (1859), 22–9, and in Kraushar's *Ferank va'adato*, 77–81, reprinted by the translator N. Sokolov.)

[107] *Zekher haḥayim: derushei r' ḥayim kohen rapoport* (Lemberg, 1866), 68*a*–*b*.

[108] N. Sokolov, in his 'Translator's Note' to Kraushar's *Ferank va'adato*, 145–6, drew attention to the anti-Frankist passages in *Zekher haḥayim*, and asserted that 'in the *Likutim*, 67–9 [but read 68] we find traces of the disputation' in Lvov. It appears to me that this assertion is inaccurate. In the first paragraphs of the *Likutim* (67*a*–*c*) R. Hayim deals with an issue which no one mentioned in the public disputations with the Frankists: support for the standpoint of the 'Hakham Tsevi' in the Hayon dispute that 'the secrets of the Torah may only be learnt from one who is recognized for his *kashrut* [i.e. as being above reproach in beliefs and practices—Trans.]' (67*c*). Other matters, the question of the three bonds of faith, and the opposition to the oral law in general and the Talmud in particular, relate to the Frankist arguments at Kamenets. On the other hand, in one paragraph, the one beginning with 'six millennia the world has existed' (67*c*), the year 5519 [1759] is named. I am therefore of the opinion that there have come down to us in the *Likutim* some remnants of notes made by R. Hayim Rapoport, between the times of the two public disputations, for the purpose of internal argument against the Frankists and in preparation for the public battle of words in Lvov in which he was to take part.

seen as a sign that he had been influenced by his Shabatean opponents; the connection of the formula to the triad of the Holy One, blessed be He, the Torah, and Israel could be explained as a development of the idea that the Torah, with its divine status, is 'the whole of the Holy Name in the three bonds of faith'.[109] But R. Barukh's active concern with Shabateanism and Frankism, his opposition to Shabatean and Frankist doctrine, and the close similarity of his formulation of the triad 'the Holy One, blessed be He, the Torah, and Israel' to A. M. Cardozo's version,[110] leave it open for us to imagine that we can detect an echo of the style of the Shabateans in his choice of words. It should be noted that a similar phenomenon appears in R. Barukh's writings on a different topic. M. Piekarz has shown that the idea in Hayon's homiletic book[111] that a man must commit one deliberate sin in order to be able to fulfil the *mitsvah* of repentance was taken up by R. Barukh of Kosov in his writings.[112] This idea also appears in books by non-Shabateans and even by anti-Shabateans, but a whiff of Shabatean antinomianism can be detected in it, and I have in fact found a condemnation of the idea as a Shabatean heresy in the following criticism of *Divrei neḥemyah* by an anonymous scholar from Amsterdam: 'Moreover, he [Hayon] says that the sages said that in the place where penitents stand it is impossible for the perfectly righteous to stand, and that it is good to commit a sin in order to be able to repent and enjoy perfect bliss; and many other heresies which originated in the time of Sh[abetai] Ts[evi], and which I read at that time when he threw the world into turmoil.'[113] The fact that R. Barukh of Kosov did not shrink from including this teaching in his writings lends support to the opinion that scraps of terminology and ideas infiltrated them from Shabatean works.

[109] Zohar III, 36*a*. See p. 477 above.

[110] See nn. 23 and 58 above.

[111] See *Divrei neḥemyah* (Berlin, 1713), 85*d*–86*a*.

[112] See M. Piekarz, 'Radikalizem dati bimei hitpashetut haḥasidut: torat "kaf remiyah" bekhitvei eli'ezer lipman mibrodi', *Molad*, NS 6 (30) (1975), 423–4. The whole issue is considered ibid. 420–7.

[113] Friedmann, 'Igerot befarashat pulmus neḥemyah ḥiya ḥayon', 522. This letter was translated from the Italian: 'I have not found [this] in *Divrei neḥemyah*' (ibid., n. 68). R. David Nieto, in *Esh dat*, 15*b*, basing himself on a homily by Hayon in *Divrei neḥemyah*, 'Nitsavim', 81*c*, wrote as follows: 'He wote explicitly that it is permitted to commit transgressions unashamedly with the object of turning back in repentance.' Hayon replied to this in a note in his own hand in a copy of the book now in the National Library, Jerusalem: 'No such thing, it [*Divrei neḥemyah*] only said what was said by sages: Great is a transgression for the sake of Heaven etc. And what was said in *parashat* 'Ha'azinu' [*Divrei neḥemyah*, 85*d*–86*a*, the point dealt with in the present essay, text referring to n. 111], that it is necessary to commit one sin in order to fulfil the commandment "you shall return" [Deut. 4: 30, 30: 2], "none is so righteous on earth" etc. ['. . . that he does (only) good and does not sin'—Eccles. 7: 20].' This note is quoted in I. E. Herling's 'He'arot neḥemyah ḥiya ḥayon bikhetav yado lesefer esh dat ler' david nieto', *Kiryat sefer*, 15 (1938–9), 134, but Herling did not realize that the allusion 'what was said in *parashat* "Ha'azinu"' refers to the homily in *Divrei neḥemyah*.

TEN

Traces of Luzzatto's Influence in Hasidic Doctrine

Dedicated to
PROFESSOR G. VAJDA
on his attaining the age of 70

A. CHANNELS OF INFLUENCE

Studies of the origins of hasidism have assigned no more than a peripheral position to Rabbi Moses Hayim Luzzatto (Ramhal). Eliezer Tsevi Zweifel[1] and some researchers after him drew attention to a few parallels between the words of the teachers of hasidism and the words of Luzzatto, and postulated that certain of his ideas had been absorbed into hasidic doctrine. Gershom Scholem, on the other hand, completely rejected any suggestion that Luzzatto's influence had helped to shape the features of hasidism.[2] The arguments for and against turned solely on Luzzatto's *Mesilat yesharim*, and in particular on the merit of the 'holy man' [*kadosh*] in ch. 26 at the end of the book. Even those of his kabbalistic writings and speculative and ethical works which have long been known and are available in print were not considered in this connection. The reason for the restriction of the discussion to *Mesilat yesharim* was the prima facie reasonable assumption that writings which had been banned when they were written and had been put away in manuscript could not have been known to the founders of hasidism.

The only assertion that hasidism is rooted to a large extent in Luzzatto's philosophy is contained in the enthusiastic declaration by Bialik, in his essay '"Habaḥur mipadova"' ['"The Young Man[3] from Padua"'], that Luzzatto should be seen as the father of the three main streams of Judaism in modern times:

[1] In *Shalom al yisra'el*, iii (Vilna, 1873), 18, 25–7.

[2] G. Scholem, '"Devekut" o "hitkasherut intimit im elohim" bereshit haḥasidut: halakhah uma'aseh', in his *Devarim bego* (Tel Aviv, 1976), 328–9.

[3] [*Baḥur* also denotes 'bachelordom'. Opponents of Luzzatto using this term would have had both senses in mind.—Trans.]

All three of these channels [the school of thought of the Vilna Gaon and his disciples, the Enlightenment (Haskalah), and hasidism] have their source in the soul of Luzzatto . . . and it was he who set the pattern for the three great schools of the Gra, the Besht, and Ben-Menahem [Mendelssohn], he was their father and first begetter.[4]

We do not know the source of this declaration: was it brilliant intuition or an echo of traditions that Bialik had received from mitnagedic and hasidic circles? In any event its general terms and lack of detail afforded no basis for scholarly study.

I could see as soon as I began my researches into Luzzatto's kabbalistic writings, more than twenty years ago, that in many respects there was an essential relationship between them and the literature of hasidism. This recognition was strengthened when I discovered some unknown compositions in manuscript and realized that they were rich in parallels and points of contact with hasidism. However, before I could clear up the problem of Luzzatto's influence on hasidism I needed to determine whether there was proof that his kabbalistic writings were accessible to the fathers of hasidism.

I examined this question in my essay 'How Luzzatto's Kabbalistic Writings were Disseminated in Poland and Lithuania'.[5] The following were my main conclusions:

1. R. Jekutiel of Vilna, who from 1729 to 1733 was one of the most important members of Luzzatto's group in Padua, was active from 1733 to 1755—the period of the beginnings of hasidism—in the leadership of groups in Shklov and Brisk [Brest-Litovsk] and possibly elsewhere in eastern Europe; in these groups he taught Luzzatto's kabbalistic writings, which he had brought with him, and he distributed copies of them which found their way to areas where hasidism was developing.

2. R. Elijah of Brisk, one of the chief members of R. Jekutiel's group, was anxious to achieve the rehabilitation of Luzzatto and to print some of the latter's kabbalistic writings which had been withheld from publication and which he had in manuscript. With this aim he published a second edition of *Mesilat yesharim* in Zholkva, eastern Galicia, in 5526 [1766], at the time when the Maggid of Mezhirech was active as leader of the new hasidic movement, in order to prepare the way for the printing of Luzzatto's *Kela"ḥ pitḥei ḥokhmah* ['138 Gateways to Wisdom'], which was in R. Elijah's possession. His attempt failed because there were influential circles who were still not ready to accept Luzzatto as 'kosher' and recognize his greatness.

[4] H. N. Bialik, '"Habaḥur mipadova"', in *Kol kitvei ḥ"n bialik* (Tel Aviv, 1938), 229.

[5] Originally published as 'Darkhei hafatsatam shel kitvei kabalah leramḥa"l bepolin uvelita', *Kiryat sefer*, 45 (1970), 127–54. [Now Essay 8 above.]

3. Some twenty years later *Kela"ḥ pitḥei ḥokhmah* was printed by a hasidic publisher (Korets, 5545 [1785]) with the enthusiastic endorsement of R. Jacob Joseph of Ostrog, a disciple of the Maggid of Mezhirech. The hasidim on whose initiative the book was published shared R. Elijah of Brisk's ambition to dispose of slanders against Luzzatto's character and give wide publicity to his kabbalistic ideas. Apparently there were contacts between R. Elijah and the Maggid of Mezhirech and his disciples, and the book was printed from a copy which the hasidim received from R. Jekutiel's school.

4. These facts and hypotheses clarified the background to the defence of Luzzatto by the Maggid of Mezhirech, who was quoted in the publisher's foreword to *Kela"ḥ pitḥei ḥokhmah* as having 'said of this author that his generation was not worthy to understand his righteousness and asceticism, and therefore many of our people, out of their great lack of knowledge, spoke insolently against the righteous, which is against the law'. I showed that this sentence is a paraphrase of remarks by R. Elijah of Brisk in his introduction to *Mesilat yesharim* which was dropped from subsequent editions, and I concluded that the Maggid of Mezhirech set out to defend Luzzatto on the basis of information from Luzzatto's admirers and unpublished kabbalistic writings which had been handed over to him and had excited his admiration.

On continuing my investigations I found further evidence that kabbalistic writings by Luzzatto which had been put away in manuscript were in circulation during the beginnings of hasidism. The following are the main new items of evidence.

1. In MS Mosad Harav Kook 252, Jerusalem, there is a collection of Luzzatto's writings which was copied in Lvov in 1781, four years before *Kela"ḥ pitḥei ḥokhmah* was printed in Korets.[6] I will deal with that collection in greater detail elsewhere. Most of the writings in it were printed after the time when it [*Kela"ḥ pitḥei ḥokhmah*] was written. They include the '138 Gateways' [*petaḥim*] without the extensive commentary, thus only a small fraction of the book with the commentary; and one part of the commentary on *Idra raba*, a truncated version of the commentary printed as *Adir bamarom* (Warsaw, 1886). I mention these two in particular because R. Elijah of Brisk had them both, so that they probably reached the Lvov copyist via R. Jekutiel's school. Not only do the works by Luzzatto in this collection not bear his name but their authorship is deliberately disguised, especially so in the two compositions just mentioned. The '138 Gateways' are ascribed to R. Meir Poppers, and the part of the commentary on *Idra raba* is headed 'Copy from the commentary on the *Idra* by the great and godly philosopher and kabbalist who learned from the mouth of the servants of the Most High

[6] See Essay 1, pp. 53–4 and n. 162.

[the ministering angels]'. Thus, on the one hand, we have proof in this collection that copies of Luzzatto's works were being circulated in hasidic areas in the early days of hasidism; on the other hand my conclusion is reinforced that shortly before *Kela"ḥ pitḥei ḥokhmah* was printed, the banning of Luzzatto's works had not been forgotten in Poland, and the people who were circulating them were fearful of possible intrigues by his enemies. Hence the hasidim, in printing one of his main kabbalistic works, took measures to free it from the presumption of being a forbidden book and remove any doubt as to its fitness for publication.

2. Important and authoritative information is contained in a letter of 24 September 1781 from Moses Mendelssohn to the German philosopher Herder.[7] In the course of comments on Luzzatto's personality and what had befallen him, Mendelssohn said: 'Seine cabbalistischen Manuscripte werden nunmehr in Polen fleissig studirt.' The word *nunmehr*, 'now', was intended to convey that in spite of the persecution of Luzzatto and the campaign against him in which his writings were banned, those writings were in the hands of students of kabbalah in Poland for whom they were an attractive subject of study. The letter is dated 1781, but the information it gives clearly reflects a situation which had existed in Poland for a considerable time, and it need scarcely be pointed out that the Besht and his associates and disciples were numbered among the students of kabbalah.

3. In Adar 5494 [spring 1734], when the Besht was at most a leader of one of the pre-hasidic groups, letters were sent on behalf of 'the sages of Poland, and principally the *av beit din* of the holy congregation of Zholkva who was previously *av beit din* of the holy congregation of Apta', expressing the wish that Luzzatto be asked to interpret a passage from the Zohar which was forwarded as a sample, 'their purpose being chiefly that as the Zohar has been reprinted in the holy congregation of Zholkva in a most beautiful edition, they have therefore made the foregoing request, since it is their wish to print an interpretation of it'.[8] The rabbis of Venice expressed the fear that the plan

[7] I am grateful to Professor Alexander Altmann for drawing my attention to this important information. The letter was reproduced in Moses Mendelssohn, *Gesammelte Schriften*, xiii. *Briefwechsel*, III, ed. A. Altmann (Stuttgart, 1977), 25–6. The sentence I quote is on p. 26. And see Altmann's note, ibid. 353. In Essay 8, end of n. 129, I noted that two Polish *maskilim*, R. Isaac of Satanov and R. Solomon of Dubno (both of them friends of Mendelssohn), had read unpublished writings by Luzzatto; R. Solomon of Dubno also distributed manuscript copies of *Ḥoker umekubal* in Germany.

[8] *R' mosheh ḥayim lutsato uvenei doro: osef igerot ute'udot*, ed. S. Ginzburg [hereafter *Igerot*] (Tel Aviv, 1937), ii. 264. The request came in two successive letters from R. Hayim Alshukh (Alsheikh) of Breslau to R. Solomon Zalman of Lvov, who was living in Venice. This shows that R. Solomon Zalman, who in 1735 energetically supported the rabbis of Venice in their destruction of Luzzatto's status, was still regarded as a trusted friend of his in the spring of 1734. A reference to the letters (ibid. 270) says that 'they wish *in the holy congregation of Kraków* to print the

to publish the Zohar with Luzzatto's commentary had been inspired by the propaganda of R. Jekutiel, who had returned to Poland from Padua in 1732.[9] This is quite possible, and if so it would mean that when R. Jekutiel came back to Poland he started his activity in eastern Galicia, near places where hasidism was developing. But it is hard to imagine that R. Jekutiel's praise of Luzzatto would alone have been enough to persuade 'the sages of Poland' to formulate and propose so ambitious a plan. It is reasonable to conclude that earlier, apparently in 1730, before the edict which banned Luzzatto's writings and prohibited his kabbalistic activities, information about the Paduan 'man with the *magid*' and copies of his works must already have reached Poland and convinced the 'sages' that he was one of the great kabbalistic scholars of the age.[10] This opinion is reinforced by the fourth item of information which I quote here.

book of the Zohar and to print the interpretation by MH"L', but there is no doubt that the first version is the correct one. The rabbi of Zholkva—described as 'the brother of the distinguished magnate, our teacher and rabbi, R. Yuda, son of our teacher and rabbi R. Hirsch Witsches (may he be remembered for life in the world to come) of Apta'—was R. Isaac Segal Landau, uncle of R. Ezekiel Landau, the author of *Noda bihudah* and one of the chief supporters of R. Jonathan Eybeschuetz when Eybeschuetz was under attack twenty years later. See D. Kahana, *Toledot hamekubalim, hashabeta'im vehaḥasidim*, ii (Tel Aviv, 1927), 52, 145–6; *Pinkas va'ad arba aratsot*, ed. I. Halpern (Jerusalem, 1945), index.

[9] 'Who knows whether Jekutiel, who has departed for Poland, has not sown some thorns and nettles of his own' (*Igerot*, ii. 270). And see Essay 8, pp. 435–6 and n. 96.

[10] The information I have dealt with here is quoted and discussed in M. Benayahu's new book *Kitvei hakabalah sheleramḥa"l* (Jerusalem, 1979), 218, for the purpose of solving the mystery of the 'report transmitted in the name of R. Moses Hagiz' that Luzzatto 'wanted to print forthwith the Zohar that he had composed in Padua'. In Benayahu's opinion this false report stemmed from something that actually happened, namely that 'on 3 and 8 Adar II 5494 [spring 1734] *R. Jekutiel let it be known* [the emphasis in every case is mine—I.T.] that the *av beit din* of Zholkva *had sent him* a passage from the book of the Zohar . . . *and asked him to send it* to Ramhal', but 'this was only a reference to an obscure passage in the original Zohar which they had been unable to interpret'; the content of the letters which had been sent through the agency of R. Hayim Alsheikh was known to Luzzatto's opponents, and '*R. Jekutiel's* infelicitous *language* was misinterpreted' to mean that they [those who sent the letters—Trans.] intended to print a comprehensive commentary by Luzzatto on the Zohar. Benayahu found support for his explanation in the description of the incident by the rabbis of Venice in the letter from which I quoted an extract in n. 8 above, and he repeated: 'That passage from the Zohar *was sent to R. Jekutiel* so that he might send it on to Ramhal.'

In fact there is no need for surprise at R. M. Hagiz's communication of the report, by way of warning, to a Jew from Padua to whom he spoke in 1735 (see *Igerot*, ii. 414; M. Benayahu, 'Shevuat ramḥa"l laḥdol mileḥaber sefarim al-pi ha"magid", mahutah vetotse'oteiha', *Zion*, 42 (1977), 36 n. 47), because before the episode of the Beit Din in Frankfurt accusations were being circulated that Luzzatto was going to have his 'unfit' works printed and published in Amsterdam, and even his enforced submission did not put an end to the unease. See *Igerot*, ii. 259, 268, 274–5, 285–6, 308, 309, 315, 326, 331, 356. However, the method adopted to clear up the imagined mystery in a book which purports to be a scholarly and critical study is itself astonishing. The attribution of the letters to R. Jekutiel is a complete fiction which runs quite counter to what is said in the texts, and could only have been written on the naive and odd assumption that its authenticity would not be checked. The writer of the letters who says explicitly 'The sages of Poland *asked me* . . . and he [the rabbi of Zholkva] *asked me* to send to the holy congregation of Padua, to Si[gnor] Moses Hayim Luzzatto' (ibid. 264), was certainly no mean person, and from his description as 'a man from Poland who is called the rabbi, R. Hayim son of Mar Benjamin Alsheikh' (ibid. 270), it is probable that he is the R. Hayim, of the line of the Alsheikhs of Lublin, who in 1742–5, in Fürth, published *Teshuat yisra'el*, a translation from Italian and Latin into Yiddish of three works on the blood libel. See J. Shatzky, *Pinkes* (New York, 1927), 12–19; J. Rosenthal, in *Areshet*, 2 (1960), 161. I am also inclined to think, in spite of several difficulties, that it was he who wrote the letter of 12 Kislev 5496 [Nov. 1735] to R. Isaiah Bassano, written while the writer was in Italy, which was signed by 'Hayim son of our teacher and rabbi, R. Benjamin (may the memory of that righteous man be for a blessing), of the stock of Falk (may he be remembered for life in the world to come), of Lublin' (*Igerot*, ii. 340–2). In that letter he informed Bassano that he had written in defence of Luzzatto 'to the sages of Ashkenaz . . . and especially before the sages of Poland in the Council of Four Lands', and that his representations had been accepted 'and there is no longer such an outcry against him there in Poland', while on the other hand he strongly condemned R. Solomon Zalman of Lvov to whom R. Hayim Alsheikh's letters were sent in 1734. (R. Hayim Alsheikh's forewords in Hebrew and Yiddish to the rare book, which I have read in the National and University Library's copy in Jerusalem, help to confirm my two identifications, which shed light on an otherwise unknown personality, but this is not the proper place to go into further detail.) As to the significance of the request from Zholkva—anyone who reads the texts just as they are, stripped of fanciful distortions, can see clearly that they wanted to publish a full commentary on the Zohar by Luzzatto and that the piece in question was sent to him so that they could get a specimen of his method of interpretation. Luzzatto did indeed do a great deal of work on explaining the literature of the Zohar in writing. Apart from explanations of individual passages scattered through his letters, and the commentary on *Idra raba* which has been preserved, we know from a letter dated 12 Elul 5490 [late summer 1730] from R. Jekutiel that his teacher had 'begun to explain the book of the *Tikunim* of Rabbi Simeon bar Yohai' (*Igerot*, ii. 263); and in the introduction to *Derekh tevunot* (Minsk, 1836) the publisher enumerates four kabbalistic works by Luzzatto which were in his possession, among them 'a manuscript of an interpretation of *Sifra detseni'uta*' which is not known to us from any other source and which apparently reached Minsk from R. Jekutiel's group via the Vilna Gaon's school. (The other works mentioned there, which were printed some time later, were: 'a manuscript of the book *Kinat hashem tsevaot*, a manuscript interpretation of the *Idrot*, a manuscript of *Kelalei hakabalah*'.) Finally, mention should be made of a section of commentary on the Zohar entitled *Ma'amar p[arashat] mishpatim*, as yet unpublished, in MS Oxford 2593 (fos. 135^r–147^v), to which I alluded in Essay 1, p. 19, n. 59, and which I proposed to elucidate in my further consideration of the manuscripts in that collection. [Now see the material added as Section XI of Essay 1.—Trans.] To return to Benayahu: in order to create an impression that there could be a causal connection between the request of 1734 and the report of 1735, he passed over in silence the fact that Hagiz announced in the same breath that Luzzatto was also intending to print 'a new *Tehilim* ['Book of Psalms'] containing 150 psalms' (*Igerot*, ii. 414). And last of all, this instructive sentence: 'Could it occur to anyone that in communities which had banned Luzzatto's writings they would permit the publication of *the commentary against which their anger had been chiefly directed*?' Here a Zoharic work by Luzzatto, *Zohar tinyana* or *Tikunim ḥadashim*, which had been the object of protests both written and oral, has been artfully substituted for a commentary on the original Zohar which was not even hinted at in the undertaking signed at Padua in Av 5490 [late summer 1730] or in polemical writings up to 1735, while Luzzatto claimed, with the approval of his teacher,

4. In a letter of 7 Shevat 5496 [early 1736] R. Moses Hagiz reported that there were many copies of Luzzatto's writings in his neighbourhood, mentioning in particular *Tikunim ḥadashim* and '*Seder hak"n mizmorim* ['Order of the 150 Psalms'], which is also in our hands'. He said:

> He has composed treatises and spread them among the masses, as we see every day from the *kilkulin* [literally 'misdeeds'][11] which people bring or send me from all of these countries, crying out to us . . . and every report of having seen a copy which reaches us writes that it is signed with his name in his own handwriting.[12]

These works, which were pronounced unfit for publication and banned in the investigation carried out at Padua in Av 5490, would certainly not have been distributed by R. Jekutiel in the years immediately following the investigation, even though Luzzatto did not regard himself as bound by the undertaking he had been forced to sign.[13] It must therefore be said that before the issue of the decree requiring them to be hidden away, copies had been forwarded to the German-speaking countries, and undoubtedly also to Poland, through other channels.

that he had not been placed under any prohibition on composing and distributing kabbalistic commentaries. See Essay 8, n. 47. In 1734, therefore, when the echoes of the controversy of 1730 had long since died away, Luzzatto's sympathizers among the scholars of Poland believed and expected that he would respond to their request and agree to compose a commentary on the Zohar for publication.

Benayahu's book was published in the second half of Shevat 5739 [Feb. 1979], more than six months after the present essay was delivered to the editorial board of *Zion*. A considerable proportion of my discoveries published in my essay 'Kovets shel kitvei kabalah miginzei ramḥa"l' [Essay 1 above], which was in the hands of the reading public by Sivan 5738 [June–first days of July 1978], are incorporated in his book, just as I wrote them or in altered form, but my essay is mentioned only once (p. 8 n. 2), with the remark that the author had read it 'at the time of printing' [presumably, when his book had gone or was going to press—Trans.]; thereafter there is no reference to it whatever. The result is that anyone who reads the book without my essay will be quite unaware that it makes wholesale use of the results of my research. Similarly with my essay 'Shirim ufiyutim miginzei r' mosheh ḥayim lutsato' [Essay 2, Part A above], to the contents of which Benayahu helped himself with both hands, and in which I had published a critical edition of ten poetic works which are dealt with in his book: my essay receives no mention. And see below, additional matter in nn. 12 and 53, and n. 72.

11 A term of dishonour for the *Tikunim ḥadashim* [*tikun*, 'repairing, setting right'; *kilkul*, 'ruining, commission of a misdeed'—Trans.].

12 *Igerot*, ii. 368–9. [Benayahu ignored the important information in this letter. In dealing with Luzzatto's book of psalms he quoted one sentence from the letter, cutting out Hagiz's statement that *Seder hak"n mizmorim* ['Order of the 150 Psalms'; Tishby emphasizes the words *hak"n mizmorim*—Trans.] was in his hands, and on the basis of the mutilated quotation he delivered himself of this verdict: 'There is no doubt that he was only sent those psalms which were printed' (*Kitvei hakabalah sheleramḥa"l*, 246–7).]

13 See Essay 8, p. 418, n. 38 (with regard to the Frankfurt condemnation of Luzzatto's works to be burnt); pp. 421–2, n. 47 (with regard to the Paduan edict that his works were to be hidden away); and Essay 1, pp. 19–20 and n. 61.

Even after the removal of the obstacle which prevented researchers from investigating the relationship between hasidism and Luzzatto's kabbalistic writings, we are faced with great difficulties in undertaking a comparative study. In addition to the writings which have long been available in print, there is a wealth of material, stored away in manuscripts to which no author's name was attached, which I have discovered in my researches over the last twenty years or more, among them esoteric works yielding important new insights into Luzzatto's thought processes and his output in the field of kabbalah. Altogether this is a fairly substantial body of writings, some of them no doubt written under the inspiration of the *magid* before and after the Paduan decree, and although they were produced by a single author, they are many-sided and complex, because they are written in various forms and styles, and the ideas they present are not uniform or consistent.[14] The works in print and manuscript have, so far, not been the objects of systematic research even as individual productions, apart from some studies relating to the doctrine of Redemption. That being so, it is impossible to undertake even part of an exhaustive comparative study within the scope of this essay, and all I can achieve here must necessarily be no more than a beginning.

In my essay on the source of the dictum 'The Holy One, blessed be He, the Torah, and Israel are all one',[15] which is quoted in some hasidic literature as a formula coined by the Zohar and was attributed to the Ba'al Shem Tov by Scholem, I showed that the dictum appeared, with an attribution to the Zohar, in Luzzatto's commentary on *Idra raba*, and found its way from there both into hasidism and into the school of the Vilna Gaon. Similarly there are parallels and points of contact in many details, some of which I have dealt with elsewhere.[16] However, in my opinion Luzzatto's influence is not limited to certain details: traces of his personal philosophy can be observed in speculative systems which are central to the doctrine of hasidism. Towards the end of my essay on the Zoharic dictum [and in n. 72 to that essay—Trans.] I remarked on some major topics in the treatment of which I see a strong connection between the literature of hasidism and the writings of Luzzatto and his colleague Moses David Valle: 'the nature of *devekut*, its processes, and what it is intended to achieve; the purification of corporeality and turning evil into good; the descent of the tsadik and the stages of spiritual "immaturity" and "maturity" in his descent and ascent'. I shall concentrate here on two topics: worship through corporeality, and *devekut*. These two are interconnected, and in certain respects to which I draw special attention they merge into one.

[14] A large and important proportion of the 'hidden' works is contained in MS Oxford 2593, most of the writings in which have already been examined in Essay 1 above.

[15] *Kiryat sefer*, 50 (1975), 480–92; now Essay 9 above.

[16] See Essay 1, pp. 5–7, 37–8, 41–2, 46–8, and especially the notes.

I set out below the ideas of hasidism in a brief survey based on points made and explained in scholarly studies.[17] I classify these points and add explanatory comments on their substance but not on textual questions. However, in my detailed consideration of Luzzatto's views I also add extracts from the literature of hasidism for the purpose of comparison.[18]

B. PRINCIPLES OF WORSHIP THROUGH CORPOREALITY AND *DEVEKUT* IN HASIDISM

In essence, the idea of worship through corporeality means doing away with the separation between sacred and profane by endowing actions intended to satisfy ordinary human needs and reap material benefits, and organs and objects which man uses in such actions, with the special virtues and values attaching to divine worship. Underlying this doctrine is a spiritualistic view that existence here on earth is wretched and defective and in need of rectification [*tikun*] and raising up. This existence has its origin and root in supernal spiritual and holy powers; its defects and degeneracy were created with deliberate intent by the Godhead or came about in the processes of development, and man's function is to correct and perfect them. The execution of this task is the aim of worship through corporeality, which is generally expressed in the catchword 'In all your ways know Him' (Prov. 3: 6).

The relationship between man and God in worship through corporeality is given varied and even contradictory descriptions. With regard to the doctrine of hasidism itself as well as in the clarification of the relations between it and the views of Luzzatto, two approaches must particularly be noted: (*a*) The use of ordinary material objects is capable of bringing them into the service of God; in this respect they are like objects which are used in the ful-

[17] The following is a selection of studies in which the topics of *devekut* and worship through corporeality are variously approached and considered in detail from various points of view: M. Buber, *Befardes haḥasidut* (Jerusalem, 1945); Scholem, '"Devekut" o "hitkasherut intimit im elohim" bereshit haḥasidut', 325–50; G. Scholem, 'Hatsadik', in his *Pirkei-yesod behavanat hakabalah usemaleiha* (Jerusalem, 1976), 213–58; J. Weiss, 'Reshit tsemiḥatah shel haderekh haḥasidit', *Zion*, 16 (1951), 46–105; Rivkah Schatz-Uffenheimer, *Haḥasidut kemistikah: yesodot kevi'etistiyim bamaḥashavah haḥasidit bame'ah hayod"ḥet* (Jerusalem, 1968); M. Piekarz, *Bimei tsemiḥat haḥasidut: megamot rayoniyot besifrei derush umusar* (Jerusalem, 1978); I. Tishby and J. Dan, 'Ḥasidut', in *Ha'entsiklopedyah ha'ivrit*, xvii (1965), 760–822.

[18] Lack of space precludes my dealing here with the perception of the Creation and the governance of the world, including divine immanence, with which the ideas of *devekut* and worship through corporeality are connected both in the literature of hasidism and in Luzzatto's writings.

filment of *mitsvot*; that is to say, man can and must draw near to God in everyday physical actions just as he draws near to his Master in performing *mitsvot*, studying the Torah, and praying. (*b*) Man can and must elevate physical matter so that it approaches the level of spirituality. This action, which the teachers of hasidism used to characterize as the transformation of matter into form, is directed in the first place towards the physical state of the person performing it, but it also elevates and refines material things outside personal existence, and promotes the *tikun* of the universal corporeality which lies beyond human existence. In the realm of human existence this action is also presented as having a social mission: drawing ordinary people, who are called 'men of matter', towards the level of possessors of special virtues, 'men of form'.[19] The second approach by its very nature encompasses a change in material things, in which their coarseness and murkiness pass away or are purified. The sources sometimes speak of *the sanctification of corporeality*. This change accords well with the first approach, which places worship through corporeality in the same category as *avodat hakodesh* [prayer and observance of the commandments].

In order to purify or sanctify corporeality man must infuse external material action with internal spiritual activity. Internal activity is mostly described in three ways: (*a*) an intention to put care of the body and the satisfaction of physical needs to work in preparing and assisting the soul in its service of the Lord; (*b*) an intention to raise up sparks of holiness submerged in material things; (*c*) combination of corporeal activity with the attachment [*devekut*] of the soul to the Godhead. The inclusion of physical occupations in *devekut*

[19] I have not dealt above with two modes of action which figure prominently in scholarly studies as principal ways of worship through corporeality. These are: (*a*) service of the Lord in *devekut* while the organs of the body are engaged in physical acts, the mind being diverted from these acts and the soul entirely cut off from what is taking place on the material plane; (*b*) the conferment of happiness and pleasure on the body by satisfying its desires with lesser physical enjoyments, so as not to disturb the soul in its aim of achieving exalted spiritual happiness and pleasure in communion with the Godhead. These two modes of action bring no change for the better in the inferior and blemished status of corporeality; all they do is prevent harm to spirituality by keeping corporeality at a distance. Moreover, the second mode even strengthens corporeality in performing and fostering its defective activity. I regard this mode, the common example of which in practice consists in giving pleasure to the body on the Sabbath by additional eating and drinking, as a variation of the instruction in the Zohar that Sama'el should be given some share in the *mitsvot* so that he might be kept busy with his pleasures and not have time to interfere with Israel's contact with the Holy One, blessed be He. See my explanation in I. Tishby, *The Wisdom of the Zohar*, trans. D. Goldstein (Oxford, 1989), ii. 452–4. In this line of thought, therefore, corporeality is perceived as akin to the Sitra Ahra ['Other Side'], and its negative quality remains unchanged even when its ability to lead the soul astray is inactivated. It is true that in hasidic sources the slogan 'In all your ways know Him' is applied to these modes of action too, and they are brought within the category of worship through corporeality. But by their nature they belong mainly to the domain of methods of *devekut*; at any rate they do nothing to elevate corporeality and make it part of the actual worship of God.

accords with their being placed on the level of Torah study, *mitsvot*, and prayer, which hasidism requires to be performed with *devekut*. The intention of helping in the service of the Lord fits well with the purification of matter. Correspondingly, the transformation of matter into form is described as the submission of the body to the soul. On the other hand the raising of sparks, by its nature, can act in two different ways: it can serve as a higher stage in the purification of matter or a lower stage in the sanctification of corporeality.[20]

The teachers of hasidism are divided in their evaluation of worship through corporeality as compared with *avodat hakodesh* [see above], and one author goes so far as to give contradictory assessments. On the one hand worship through corporeality is described as equal in merit, or even superior, because it requires greater effort and makes it possible to achieve the highest degree of *tikun* of man and the world; on the other hand we find instructions to limit worship through corporeality to stated situations in which it is impossible to perform *avodat hakodesh*, and it is presented as inferior worship at the level of *katnut* ['spiritual immaturity'].

The obligation of *devekut* in the service of the Lord, in all its shades of meaning in the literature of hasidism, is itself connected with malfunctions in material existence on earth. In essence the soul is a pure and holy spiritual entity, a part of God above, and in its own existence in the heights it is inseparably attached to its divine source. Therefore, in its worldly existence in the body, it is in a state of exile and servitude. In this condition a threefold mission is laid upon it: its own redemption by freeing itself from the fetters of earthliness; secondly, by raising itself up, the *tikun* of the body and the materiality of this world; thirdly, the pinnacle of its actions, the *tikun* and redemption of the Shekhinah and of the divine sparks, which, like it, are in exile in material existence and in the abyss of the husks, and whose complete *tikun* carries with it the Redemption of Israel. The *devekut* of the soul is the force behind the execution of this mission.

Devekut can exist and be active in three situations: in *avodat hakodesh*; in leisure hours when one is alone; in the course of physical activities, either by oneself or in company with others. With regard to *avodat hakodesh* the teachers of hasidism had to wrestle with the problem of the relationship between the study of the Torah and *devekut*; they found it difficult to square the intellectual discipline of study with the emotional enthusiasm of *devekut*, but, in

[20] An opinion commonly expressed in published studies is that the raising of sparks is a constant and necessary factor in worship through corporeality. This is a generalization. J. Weiss, in several places in his essay 'Reshit tsemiḥatah shel haderekh haḥasidit', remarked that the introduction of corporeality into the service of God and the raising of sparks are not inseparably linked, and at one point he declared: 'It is possible to describe the essence of hasidism without recourse to the doctrine of the sparks' (p. 101). That sentence went too far, but he could correctly have made such an assertion if it had been limited to a number of principles of hasidic doctrine, among them worship through corporeality and *devekut*.

spite of the difficulties, they sought and found solutions which kept the two values together. In descriptions of *devekut* in physical activities, they went in two completely opposite directions: on the one hand, the separation of corporeality from spirituality in order to remove obstacles from the path of *devekut*; on the other, the combination of body and soul so closely that corporeality is sanctified by *devekut*.[21]

The ideal aimed at, as declared in hasidic literature, is constant *devekut*; that is, strong and uninterrupted contact between the soul and the Godhead in the three situations I have mentioned. It sometimes seems that the teachers of hasidism presented constant *devekut* as an aim which could be fully realized in man's life in this world. But the words which create this impression are no more than an expression of a wish by people who knew and acknowledged that it was only possible to fulfil it in part. The literature of hasidism offers many different explanations as to why, so long as the soul is in a living body, it is out of the question to maintain constant *devekut*, and it is even said that its achievement in the life of this world is undesirable. The unbroken communion [*hityaḥadut*] of the soul with its divine source is an eschatological goal which will be realized in the days of the Messiah and the life of the world to come.

C. CORPOREALITY AND *DEVEKUT* IN *MESILAT YESHARIM*

I begin my consideration of Luzzatto with his *Mesilat yesharim* ['The Highway of the Upright'] because it was published in 1740 and was reprinted in Poland in 1766 and the years immediately following, and it is very probable that contemporaries of the Ba'al Shem Tov in and outside the hasidic movement, and perhaps the Besht himself, read it and could have been influenced by it. Another reason for beginning with *Mesilat yesharim* is that Scholem, in concluding that Luzzatto had no influence on hasidism, relied on that work and on that work alone, as I shall make clear at the end of the present section; and therefore, as my purpose is to determine if there was such influence, I must first explain the ideas in *Mesilat yesharim* which relate to corporeality and *devekut*.

The book was certainly composed in Amsterdam shortly before it was printed there, i.e. a few years after the storm of controversy, persecution, and bans of 1735–6. It is clear that in these circumstances Luzzatto was forced not only to avoid expressing speculative kabbalistic ideas but also to keep

[21] See n. 19 above.

kabbalistic elements out of ethical writings. He did, indeed, show great caution, testing and refining his words in a process of self-censorship, but he nevertheless slipped into them some allusions to important points in the spirit of kabbalistic ethics.[22] One of the outstanding examples of this is provided in his references to *devekut*, on which he places emphasis as a holy duty and a vital element in the service of the Lord. There is no doubt that wherever he mentions it he is referring to mystical *devekut*, though its intensity may vary in degree.

In his introduction Luzzatto laid it down that for the proper service of the Lord it was essential that 'fixed arrangements should be made for study and learning with regard to issues of perfection of service, love, fear, *devekut*, and all the other attributes of a hasid'; and he declared that the most important aspect of the service of the Lord was 'the *devekut* and the ardour in our souls [joining us] with Him, blessed be He, and with His Torah'. As regards reverence for God's majesty, one of the two pillars of *devekut*, his introduction declares that it must be present in the soul '*over every movement one sets out to make*, all the more so when one speaks before Him in prayer or one is occupied with His Torah'. We have here an allusion to constant readiness for *devekut* even at times of physical activity.

Chapter 1, which is concerned with 'an explanation of the whole duty of man during his life on earth', says that in man's preparations in this world for the delight in the radiance of the Shekhinah for which the soul is destined in the world to come, 'true perfection is nothing else than cleaving [*devekut*] to Him, blessed be He'. The way to *devekut* is the conquest of one's impulses by

[22] Luzzatto had already adopted this course, though not as meticulously as in *Mesilat yesharim*, in works he wrote in Padua in 1731–4, notably *Da'at tevunot*, and also in *Derekh hashem*, which in my opinion was also written in Padua. On *Da'at tevunot*, see Essay 1, p. 31 and n. 97, and pp. 36–8. R. David Meldola, one of the two editors of the first edition of *Mesilat yesharim*, who was one of Luzzatto's close friends in Amsterdam, remarked in his foreword that whereas *Reshit ḥokhmah* and similar ethical works could only be understood by people well versed in 'esoteric lore'—the secrets of the Zohar and Lurianic kabbalah—'this admirable book', on the other hand, 'may be read with ease even by anyone who is not qualified to grasp more than the plain meaning of a text'. But Meldola knew very well that Luzzatto was first and foremost a kabbalist, and, alluding to his great distinction, wrote of him 'that from Moses to Moses none has arisen so wise as Moses'. The principal editor, R. Jacob Bashan, emphasized Luzzatto's greatness as a kabbalistic scholar, to which he specifically related *Mesilat yesharim*, in the rhymed encomium at the end of his foreword [each verse is divided into four pairs of words, of which the first three pairs rhyme and the fourth ends in *-rim* in keeping with the title of the book—Trans.]: '*And he cleaved to his Maker / with full-throated praise / and set free his tongue / to explain secrets // and he delved and he dug / in revealed and occult / and explained and interpreted / precious words //* and composed [*tiken*] psalms / prayers set in order / to the Creator of lights / and Searcher of innermost thoughts // and he cleansed by his faith / and increased his merit / by giving to his congregation / *Mesilat yesharim*.' By 'psalms' and 'prayers' the writer appears to have meant kabbalistic poems and prayers by Luzzatto of the kind which I discovered in MS Guenzburg 745 and which I published in part in Essay 2 above.

removing 'physical desires', and its results are the elevation of the person, of material things, and of the whole world:

If he exercises self-control and cleaves to his Creator, and uses worldly things only as an aid to serve his Creator, he is uplifted and the world itself is uplifted with him, for all creatures are greatly exalted when they serve the perfect man who is sanctified in sanctifying Him, blessed be He.

The attainment of *devekut* is a function of the soul and is bound up with the performance of *mitsvot*, but the preparations for it must enter into every physical occupation, the intention being to help the soul to reach that condition, as is re-emphasized at the end of the chapter. In this way man applies the power of *devekut* to sublimate personal and universal corporeality.[23]

On the virtues of the hasid (the pious man), we are told that in whatever he does he will always conquer his impulses; 'even in bodily and material actions' his intentions will be 'on the side of wisdom and fear' or 'on the side of wisdom and worship'; that is, to aid in the service of the Lord, in which sense the scriptural verse 'In all your ways know Him' is applied (ch. 16). In his study of the Torah, in his performance of *mitsvot*, and in prayer he must act with a lively awareness of the fear due to God's majesty. The hasid's love of the Lord, and the *devekut* and joy which are presented as its offshoots, are described as activities charged with emotion so great as to amount to ecstatic fervour, even coloured with eroticism. Here are two extracts by way of example:

Devekut consists in this, that a man's heart cleaves so closely to His name, blessed be He, that he turns aside from heeding anything else, and that is what the allegory in the words of Solomon (Prov. 5: 19) is meant to convey: 'A lovely hind, a graceful doe, let her breasts satisfy you at all times, and be intoxicated with love for her always' . . . and in the Jerusalem Talmud[24] they said: 'R. Hanina ben Dosa was standing and praying and a [poisonous] lizard came and bit him and he did not

[23] The actions and attributes required here in 'the whole duty of man during his life on earth' correspond, though with certain differences, to the qualities and the ways of serving the Lord attributed to the man ranked as 'pure' and 'pious' [*ḥasid*], which are set out in detail where he is described (chs. 13 ff.). However, with regard to the élite who attain the standard of a hasid there is no statement that material things and the whole world are uplifted by their merit. On the contrary, ch. 26, where the 'pure man' is compared with the 'holy man', says that at a level lower than holiness there can be no essential improvement in materiality itself. Yet in the description of what occurs in beings who 'serve the perfect man who is sanctified in sanctifying Him, blessed be He', there is a similarity to the words used in referring to the activity of the 'holy man'. See below, text referring to n. 29. We learn from this inconsistency that Luzzatto covered up in the body of the book what he briefly revealed in his introduction: that every Jew can and must work to elevate corporeality by directing ordinary bodily activities upwards as an aid to *devekut* in the service of God [*avodat hakodesh*]. This approximates to one of the ways of worship through corporeality in hasidism, as I made clear in the previous section.

[24] *Ber.* 5: 1.

interrupt his prayer' etc. . . . and concerning *devekut* we have been warned many times in the Torah . . . and the meaning of all these verses is the same, which is the *devekut* with which man cleaves to Him, blessed be He, so that he cannot be separated or move away from Him. (Ch. 19)

For the more deeply a man succeeds in entering into the inward knowledge of His greatness, blessed be He, the more will joy increase within him . . . Scripture says (Ps. 71: 23): 'My lips shall sing with joy when I sing psalms to You; so shall my soul, which You have redeemed.' In other words, joy grew so strong within him that his lips moved of their own accord and sang joyously while he was engaged in praising Him, blessed be He; and all this out of the great fervour with which his soul burned in its joy before Him. (Ibid.)[25]

The intention [*kavanah*] which is to be desired in the hasid when he is worshipping in love and *devekut* is of great importance. Anyone whose aspiration is 'to purify his soul before his Creator so that it may be worthy . . . to behold the beauty of the Lord, to visit his Temple' [Ps. 27] misses the real target, for 'after all, his worship is for his own benefit'. The end to be desired is that 'he should long for the Redemption because it will bring exaltation for the honour of His name, blessed be He . . . and he should always pray for the Redemption of Israel and the restoration of the honour of Heaven to [its] exalted level' (ch. 19). 'The honour of His name' and 'the honour of Heaven' are *veiled references to the Shekhinah*, and these instructions mean that there ought not to be any intention to gain personal benefit by elevating and perfecting the soul which enters into *devekut*; one should rather make *devekut* and love of the Lord work to hasten the messianic redemption for the sake of the *tikun* of the Shekhinah and her return to her place in enduring marital union.[26] Thus we have here a camouflaged paraphrase of the fundamental

[25] With regard to the circumstances and times of the hasid's *devekut*, *Mesilat yesharim* says: 'The ultimate goal of this personal quality is that a man should cleave in this way to his Creator *at all times and at every hour*; though indeed, *at least during worship*, if he loves his Creator—he will certainly have this *devekut*' (ch. 19). It is not clear whether constant *devekut* ('at all times and at every hour')—which is represented as the pinnacle which a possessor of the qualities of *ḥasidut* could and should attain—means *devekut* in worldly pursuits, which according to ch. 26, as I will show, can be achieved only by the 'holy man'. If that is its meaning, this sentence hints at the possibility of worship through corporeality with *devekut* at a lower level than that of the 'holy man', a possibility which Luzzatto intentionally leaves vague. Alternatively, it may refer to *devekut* of the individual in his leisure hours. Cf. Maimonides' instruction to people of intellectual attainment: *Guide of the Perplexed*, iii, ch. 51. And see n. 23 above.

[26] In the Maggid of Mezhirech's *hanhagot* ['rules of conduct'], which have been printed and are preserved in various manuscript versions, there are passages which in my opinion are directly derived from *Mesilat yesharim*. One of the most interesting and important passages is virtually a paraphrase of the words of Luzzatto which I have quoted in the text of this essay. I will quote here the main sentence in the version entitled *Kelalim nora'im* which was printed at the end of R. Hayim Haykel of Amdur's *Ḥayim vaḥesed* (Warsaw, 1891): 'Even if he does many things and makes many preparations *in order to be able to worship with devekut and have pleasure in*

principle in the rules of Luzzatto's messianic group which were drawn up in Padua in 1731 soon after the group went underground. The rule reads as follows: 'To perform their service before the Lord in truth and sincerity and with perfect love *without any expectation whatsoever of reward for themselves*, but only for the *tikun* of the holy Shekhinah and the *tikun* of all Israel.'[27]

This brings me to the last chapter (26), which contains a detailed description of constant *devekut* and the sanctification of corporeality as virtues of the 'holy man'. This is how they are described:

this worship, he is worshipping for his own benefit, whereas the essential point is that all his worship should be for the benefit of the Shekhinah, and not even to a small extent for his own benefit' (p. 79*a*). Two differences from *Mesilat yesharim* should be noted: the explicit mention of the Shekhinah instead of 'the honour of His name' and 'the honour of Heaven', and the omission of the desire for the messianic redemption which is expressed and emphasized in Luzzatto's teaching.

[27] *Igerot*, i. 10, *Takanot nosafot* ['Additional Rules'], sect. 1; and see ibid. 8–9, *Takanot rishonot* ['First Rules'], sects. 4, 9; and Essay 1, p. 5, n. 16. In the printed version of the rules the messianic aim is obscured, and there is no explicit reference to *devekut* either as the noun or in the form of the verb *davak* ['to stick, adhere'] from which it is derived. But its substance, together with the expectation of early redemption, is given prominence in an important paragraph which has been preserved in two other copies, with some differences between them: R. Jekutiel's copy in MS Oxford 2237, fos. 103^{v}–102^{r} (the folios are bound out of order), and a copy made in Luzzatto's school which is appended to the commentary on *Idra raba* in MS Cincinnati 501. My thanks are due to the directorate of the Hebrew Union College Library for making their photograph of this manuscript available to me in 1958 for the purposes of my research into Luzzatto's writings.

I reproduce this paragraph (which in the printed version is at 12*b*) in Jekutiel's version:

And then let them bow their heads and prepare themselves to learn and to listen to the new insights which their rabbi, our teacher and rabbi, R. Moses Hayim, will teach them, in fear and awe. And then our honoured teacher, the learned R. Jekutiel, will say these four things to the members: 1. *Take heed to be awaiting and expecting the salvation of the Lord in perfect expectation and strong hope*. 2. Submit yourselves to the Lord of all things and let your soul be silent as the dust and pour out the prayer of the poor man before the Lord your God in your heart. 3. Love the Lord your God with perfect love, with a sincere heart and a willing soul. 4. *Cleave* [*hidabeku*] *to your God and live*. And then our teacher and rabbi, R. M.H., their teacher [one word indistinct], *will expound*. And while he is *speaking* [and expounding] *the new insights* let one man [stand?] at the regular chair of study where the book of the Zohar is studied without interruption.

A. L. Frumkin, in *Toledot ḥakhmei yerushalayim*, ii (Jerusalem, 1928), 137–8, reproduced a corrupt version of this paragraph, with an addition ('vayehi mikets' to 'nikhnesah uva'ah') which does not belong to the rules. This is a ceremonial announcement to the members of the group, in which the listeners are instructed to put themselves into a spiritual state of readiness for redemption and of collective *devekut* in preparation for hearing new insights into the Torah from the lips of their teacher and rabbi. The description of Luzzatto's mystical discourses to his group as a central feature of their activities is found only in Jekutiel's version. And see n. 80 below. I am about to publish the rules of the group in a critical edition taking account of all three copies which have survived. [This does not appear to have been published, but the rules are referred to at the beginning of Essay 6.—Trans.]

That a man should be entirely separated and removed from materiality and constantly cleave at all times and in every hour to godliness . . . and even when he is engaged in physical acts which are necessary for the sake of his body, let his soul not move from its supreme *devekut* . . . and see, when a man is sanctified with the holiness of his Creator, *even his physical acts change back into veritable things of holiness.*

This does not apply to the man who has the virtues of piety, whose highest level, in what concerns his physical acts, is purity:

As for the pure man, his material acts are only those which are necessary, and he himself only intends them to fulfil his essential needs, so that thereby they are removed from the category of the evil in materiality and they remain pure, but they have not attained the status of holiness, *because it would be better if it were possible to do without them.*[28]

The attribute of holiness is represented as the ascent of a creature of flesh and blood to a level above anything earthly or human:

The holy man who cleaves constantly to his God and whose soul walks among those ideas which are true in the love and fear of his Creator is regarded as if he walks before the Lord in the lands of life [applying Ps. 116: 9—Trans.] while he is still here in this world . . . until, in the result, it is as if he is actually joined with the angels on high while he is still in this world.

The physical activities of a man of this quality are equivalent to the service of the priests in the Temple. The food and drink which he consumes are uplifted and sanctified like sacrifices and libations:

Because of this, to every thing in the world which they use, once they have adhered to His holiness, blessed be He—to every such thing which has been privileged to serve as an instrument for the tsadik's use, exaltation and advantage accrue . . . so much so that the material things which serve as instruments for his use are exalted to a greater degree than the degree by which he descends from his *devekut* and his elevated status in using material things.[29]

[28] R. Hayim Haykel of Amdur, in some teachings which he included in a polemical letter, said it was obligatory to behave in the manner of the 'pure man': 'One must be careful to take for the body only what is needed for it to live so that it may do the will of the Creator; certainly if it were possible to keep the body alive without this it would be more desirable, and whatever he can do to reduce [such actions] he will do' (*Ḥayim vaḥesed*, 75*d*–76*a*). But this instruction to practise abstinence, and other teachings in the same letter, should be seen as having an apologetic purpose. Many remarks in the book itself show clearly that the author was not content to see the tsadik solely as a purifier but credited him with great ability to refine and sanctify corporeality. Those remarks more accurately fit the picture of R. Hayim Haykel that we have from the available information.

[29] See n. 23 above. It should be noted that the 'holy man' who is superior to the hasid is here called a 'tsadik', although ch. 13 emphasizes that a tsadik has an inferior status to a hasid. Thus even in *Mesilat yesharim* Luzzatto uses the term 'tsadik' in different senses. And see n. 45 below.

The preparations necessary to attain this rank are 'solitude and great asceticism' and study of the secrets of the Godhead, Creation, and divine providence. But purification and sanctification in practice cannot occur without divine help, and therefore the matter 'begins with endeavour and ends as a gift'.

*

Gershom Scholem, arguing in his essay '"Devekut"' from the foregoing two points in this chapter [26] of *Mesilat yesharim*—the exalted personal level attributed to a person who succeeds in combining physical things with the worship of the Lord and sanctifying them, and the statement that these qualities are conferred by divine grace—asserted: 'It is impossible to see Luzzatto's book as a literary source for the change of direction by hasidism: the reverse is true.' His reasons were that for Luzzatto *devekut* was still the last stage, 'the special grace which is shown to the hasid', and that Luzzatto did not draw social conclusions from *devekut* in physical activities.[30] His assertion is based on the assumptions that in hasidism '*Devekut* is the starting point and not the end; anyone can put it into practice at once',[31] and that the teachers of hasidism applied the term as a practical concept on the social plane. In discussing the relationship between hasidism and Luzzatto Scholem speaks of *devekut* pure and simple, and *devekut* in physical actions, in the same breath, as if the general and the particular were identical.

These assumptions are, at best, of limited validity, and Scholem himself did not stick to them consistently. In the same essay we read that 'the link between *devekut* and asceticism and solitude which is constantly stressed in the ethical writings of the kabbalists still dominates the eighteenth-century literature of hasidism',[32] and—expressed more emphatically—in relation to the doctrine of the Maggid of Mezhirech, 'He does not alter the basic meaning of *devekut* as a description of inward contemplation whose main aspect is dialogue in seclusion with the Lord. *This is not a social concept*' (the emphasis is mine—I.T.).[33] In saying this he negates his assumption that 'anyone can put it into practice at once'. And indeed the sources repeatedly tell us that only individuals of superior merit are capable of fulfilling the *mitsvah* of *devekut* properly. Here, for example, is one sentence from the writings of R. Jacob Joseph of Polonnoye: 'If so, it is not in every man to fulfil the commandment "to Him you shall cleave"; not even in a learned scholar but only in a chosen few, [a man] who has cast the things of this world behind him.'[34] It is true that R. Jacob Joseph does not everywhere declare himself in favour of such strictly exclusive limits to *devekut*, but he undoubtedly avoids throwing it open to all without suitable preparation. Even in expressions such as this:

30 '"Devekut" o "hitkasherut intimit im elohim" bereshit haḥasidut', 328–9.
31 Ibid. 331.
32 Ibid. 332.
33 Ibid. 340.
34 *Tsafenat paneaḥ* (Korets, 1782), 75*d*.

'The purpose of all the 613 commandments is to enable us to cleave to Him, blessed be He, and to love Him',[35] he clearly means that only a person who has prepared himself properly can realize the purpose. With regard to *devekut* in the course of physical activity, which is only one particular path on the route of *devekut*, R. Jacob Joseph writes that it is the special virtue of 'hasidim and prophets'.[36]

Thus, even on the sole basis of the virtues of the 'holy man' in *Mesilat yesharim* in relation to the sanctification of corporeality by *devekut*, there are grounds for assuming that hasidism was influenced by Luzzatto. So far as concerns the refinement and elevation of corporeality through *devekut* in the service of God, there are clear and close points of contact in other chapters of that work which I have discussed and which are not mentioned in Scholem's essay. The actions in question are there attributed to people who are certainly no different in essentials from people described as acting similarly in the literature of hasidism.

D. REFINEMENT AND ELEVATION OF CORPOREALITY IN KNOWN WORKS BY LUZZATTO

In a considerable proportion of Luzzatto's printed works, and particularly in *Derekh hashem*, *Da'at tevunot*, and his set of kabbalistic 'principles',[37] he sets out a systematic, comprehensive, and well-defined view on the purification of matter, comparable to the transformation of matter into form in hasidism, and on the functions of *devekut* in bringing it about. I summarize his view below, with verbatim extracts and explanatory comments.[38]

35 *Toledot ya'akov yosef* (Korets, 1780), introd., 2*d*.

36 *Ketonet pasim* (Lvov, 1866), 8*b*. It should be added that according to the literature of hasidism constant *devekut*, which is ascribed [in *Mesilat yesharim*] to the 'holy man' in his performance of physical acts, is quite impossible to achieve even in *avodat hakodesh* [prayer and observance of the commandments]. See above, end of the previous section. This means that in his requirement of *devekut* in *Mesilat yesharim*, ch. 26, Luzzatto is not more moderate than the teachers of hasidism but more extreme.

37 By this I mean the work reprinted as *Kelalim rishonim* ['First Principles'] in *Sefer hakelalim*, which was published as an appendix to *Da'at tevunot*, ed. H. Friedlaender (Benei Berak, 1973). The editor declared in his introduction (p. 14) that these 'principles' summarized in unquestionably kabbalistic terms the set of ideas which Luzzatto explained in speculative style in the dialogue *Da'at tevunot*. And see Essay 1, p. 31 and n. 97, and pp. 36–9.

38 The matter presented here in outline, and also the perception of evil and matters associated with evil which I do not consider in this essay, include many great principles of Luzzatto's kabbalistic doctrine. These speculative ideas require detailed, rigorous, and extensive examination both in themselves and in relation to hasidism.

In the Creation the Holy One, blessed be He, acted with shining face and with hidden face. When His face gave light, it produced spiritual existence with perfect qualities, including the soul, and when His face was hidden there was created a material being with defects; of this kind is the body.[39] The purpose of the creation and existence of corporeality with its defects and impurities is to enable the world to acquire perfection and perfect purity by doing away with those defects. With this object man was created with the dual qualities of spirituality and corporeality, and he was given the power of choice so that in exercising it for the good he would purify and elevate corporeality, first in his own physical being and then in the whole world:

And He made the pure soul, which was hewn from under the Throne of Glory, and brought it down and breathed it into this body *to purify and sanctify* the body . . . for the ultimate purpose of the soul's entry into the body is not to enable the body to live this empty life: the essential purpose of its entry is literally to purify the body . . . [so as] to become like the ministering angels.[40]

He therefore decreed and ordained that there should be created things of perfection and things of imperfection, and a creature [man] was created to have within it the potential for both things equally, and the creature was given means by which it could acquire perfection for itself and remove its defects, whereupon it would, in so far as that were possible, become like its Creator and be worthy to cleave to Him and enjoy His benefits.[41]

By exercising the opportunity for *devekut* embedded in his soul, man would become like the Godhead, acquire part of the divine perfection, and reach the supreme level of virtue by perfecting himself and all of imperfect Creation.

If Adam had stood the test and fulfilled his mission, individual and general corporeality would have been purified and elevated at the very time that the cosmos came into existence. Because he fell into sin, it was decreed that the processes of purification and elevation should take place slowly and gradually in this world and should only be completed at the time of the resurrection of the dead and the renewal of the world. Therefore, when the soul descends into the body, it reduces its strength and light, for if it were to dwell in the body in its full radiance and power, the purification would be completed at once by its action:

This is the principle: the body—is created dark and defective, and can be purified by the soul. The soul—is great in origin, but diminishes itself when it enters the body, so as not to purify it too greatly all at once and alter it from its original condition; but little by little will do what is necessary within it by good deeds.[42]

39 See *Da'at tevunot*, 62–3.
40 Ibid. 55. And see ibid. 3–9.
41 *Sefer derekh hashem* (Amsterdam, 1896), pt. i, ch. 2, sect. 2.
42 *Da'at tevunot*, 61.

The soul, weakened at the beginning of its time in this world, exists in the body 'expelled and thrust out of its natural condition into a condition which is its opposite', but if it exerts itself and musters its strength so as to fulfil its mission to purify and elevate, 'it will weaken the power of the darkness of materiality more and more until the body is left no longer darkened, and then the body will be able to ascend with it and be illumined with the supernal light, instead of its [the soul's] being, as it was at first, darkened and brought low together with the body'.[43]

The graduated stages of *tikun* are as follows: domination of the body by the soul through good traits and good deeds; adherence [*devekut*] of the soul to its divine source through study of the Torah, observance of the commandments, and prayer; the strengthening and perfection of the soul by *devekut*; drawing lights and divine flow down to the body and to corporeality in order to promote purification, and so on through these stages again and again. Here are two descriptions of the cyclic movements in the actions of *tikun* and *devekut*:

He, blessed be His name, bestows His influence on those below only according to their readiness; it therefore concerns the tsadikim that they themselves should go on improving [*metakenim*] this dark nature little by little, for to the extent of the improvement they make in it—to that extent will the Lord, blessed be He, send down new and splendid flows, equal in value to the preparation and improvement made in the nature of those below . . . it behoves the tsadikim to go on making preparation after preparation, *tikun* after *tikun*, in the existence of those below, and correspondingly the Lord, blessed be He, will send down one flow after another, adding exaltation to exaltation . . . and this will continue until the time of the Redemption, for that is the ultimate purpose of the Exile, to remedy what had been done wrong . . . and when this has been completed—then we shall be redeemed with a perfect redemption.[44]

When the tsadikim perform this service [the removal of the defects in Creation] the supernal Unity will be aroused . . . until *tikun* is added to the whole of Creation equal in value to that service, for there is no service which does not add *tikun* to the world by some revelation of His unity, blessed be He, because it is that which removes the separation between mankind and the Creator and causes mankind to cleave to the supernal glory [the Shekhinah] . . . At first the adherence of the souls to His holiness, blessed be He, will grow in strength like a part which is joined to its whole . . . and through the strength of that adherence the Holy One, blessed be He, will bestow on the Assembly of Israel and on all that He has brought into existence a flow of holiness, that is to say, a divine and spiritual flow, and a flow of blessing which will even influence success in this world. And when those below cleave to Him, blessed be He, with loving *devekut*, the Holy One, blessed be He, will awaken

[43] *Sefer derekh hashem*, pt. i, ch. 4, sect. 2.
[44] *Da'at tevunot*, 172–3.

love between Him and them and will look favourably on their service . . . for it is by virtue of this favour that their service benefits the *tikun* of Creation.[45]

The second of these descriptions brings to the fore the factors which immediately affect the *tikun* of Creation—*devekut* by the souls and the drawing down of a flow of holiness and blessing in the present—whereas the first description lays more emphasis on the eschatological aspect, a series of preparations for the completion of the *tikun* by the messianic Redemption. Both views, however, are described as the two sides of the same coin.

The lower stage, the purification of corporeality by the domination of the soul over the body, consists essentially in two aspects of corporeal action for the sake of Heaven: man's use of material things in order to fulfil the commandments, and his intention, in satisfying his needs and his physical pleasures, to contribute to the service of the Lord. The intention of acting for the sake of Heaven confers on physical activities a status equal to fulfilment of the commandments:

When man uses [the things of] the world in this way the result will be that that use itself works [towards] perfection as I have explained, and it will confer true merit on him such as is conferred for the performance of all the commandments . . . and we, as a result, shall be exalted by this deed and the world itself will be exalted by it because it will help man when he serves his Creator, blessed be His name.[46]

In every kind of corporeal action the degree of *tikun* varies according to the nature of the doer and the deed:

Not all men are equal, and not all deeds are equal . . . two persons may speak, eat, and drink at the same table, and the consequences generated by the deeds of the one may rise to the highest heavens while the consequences of the other's deeds do not rise to any height even approaching them . . . for it is the circumstances of the doer and of the thing done, and the accompanying conditions, which affect and alter the consequences of the deeds . . . for a deed done by an ordinary man will not be like one done by a Torah scholar; nor will a deed by the Torah scholar who is less holy be like the deed of one who is holier than he is, or the deed of such a holy man like that of one who is holier, one of the remnant whom the Lord calls [Joel 3: 5 (2: 32 in non-Jewish versions)], and so on up to Moses our Master, peace be upon him.[47]

[45] Ibid. 179–80. In this book men of distinction who are capable of performing *tikunim* and fit to enter into *devekut* are regularly called 'tsadikim'. In *Sefer derekh hashem* men at various levels of spiritual merit are as a rule simply called 'the man' [*ha'adam*]. These two descriptions are also used regularly or intermittently in Luzzatto's other kabbalistic writings. As I have explained in *Wisdom of the Zohar*, iii. 1410–16, early kabbalistic literature, including the Zohar, similarly uses the term 'tsadik' more often than 'hasid' to denote a person of superior spiritual merit, and there is nothing essentially new in the way these terms are used in the literature of hasidism. And see n. 29 above.

[46] *Sefer derekh hashem*, pt. i, ch. 4, sect. 7. Cf. above, text referring to n. 23.

[47] *Da'at tevunot*, 108–10. The reference to the pre-eminence of Moses in this context is in line

The higher stage, *devekut* in prayer and in observance of the commandments, is portrayed as an equal partnership between the souls and the Holy One, blessed be He, in perfecting Creation and governing the world. The speculative dialogue expresses this idea obliquely: 'The *tikun* of Creation is, as it were, shared between the Holy One, blessed be He, and the righteous, for it can only be completed by both. And, as it were, the community of Israel feel themselves on terms of familiarity with the Holy One, blessed be He, *like a wife with her husband*, because they [Israel] have a share in the *tikun* of the world itself', and the righteous, by virtue of their partnership with the Holy One, blessed be He, 'enjoy the radiance of the Shekhinah with joy and head held high'.[48] Obviously this refers to mystical communion by the souls, but the nature of the bond is not made altogether clear; the erotic character of the communion is forgotten almost as soon as mentioned, and instead of the relationship between wife and husband there is talk of the relationship between servant and master, and bonds of friendship. On the other hand, in the corresponding passage in the kabbalistic 'Principles' [see n. 37—Trans.], where the ideas of Lurianic kabbalah are explained ('The meaning of back to back, face to face, and the sawing [apart]'), the ways of communion are set out in descriptions of the marital union of Nukba ['the female'] with Ze'ir Anpin. Dynamic and active *devekut* of the soul, bound up with its perfection of itself and of all creatures through acts of *tikun*, is, so to speak, union face to face:

When those below are in their perfect state they approach Him, blessed be He, with the familiarity of a wife to her husband, and He turns to them in love, and this is a condition in which Nukba is face to face with Ze'ir Anpin.

There is also a constant natural *devekut* between the souls of Israel and the Holy One, blessed be He, but it is static and passive, with no acts of *tikun* and no mystical marriages, and this is characterized as a union back to back:

They cleave to Him, blessed be He, because the soul is a part of God on high, and in this respect they will never be separated, and therefore, even when Nukba is back to back—the two have one wall [i.e. they have the same dwelling—Trans.], for

with Maimonides' remark in *Guide of the Perplexed*, iii, ch. 51, that it was the special merit of Moses and the patriarchs that their ordinary physical activities 'were wholly a great service [of the Lord]'. See my explanation in *Wisdom of the Zohar*, iii. 977–81. We have here an indirect reference to the possibility of sanctifying corporeality in everyday activities. There are similar hints scattered through the books we have been considering.

48 *Da'at tevunot*, 168. Further on, the partnership relation is spelt out more clearly: 'The Holy One, blessed be He, assigns part of His actual management powers to the community of Israel [*keneset yisra'el*], making them partners with Him in perfecting the world, so that He, blessed be He, will undertake *tikun* on the one side and they on the other, and by Him and by them complete *tikun* will be achieved' (p. 173).

there is a kind of bond imprinted between the supernal holiness, all of His lights, blessed be He, and the souls of Israel—there is no separation between them.[49]

The mystery of the 'sawing' in Lurianic kabbalah, which originally meant the separation of Nukba from back-to-back union in order to unite her with her husband face to face,[50] is explained as the transition of the soul from natural passive *devekut* to voluntary active *devekut* in which the soul works for the *tikun* of the world in partnership with the Holy One, blessed be He, like a wife with her husband:

This [the process of sawing] is what gives the root of those below a strength which does not need light from on high but is imprinted in themselves, so that they act not with strength enforced on them but with freely chosen strength . . . to come into the presence of the King and be regarded by Him as a wife is by her husband . . . and it is that [the voluntary act] which is more beneficial to all Creation and imparts perfection to it as I have said, so that they become partners with Him, blessed be He, in maintaining and perfecting His world.[51]

[49] In analysing the text of the Zohar I came to the conclusion that 'it is possible to distinguish between natural association [*dibuk tivi*], that is, the continuous link that exists between the Holy One, blessed be He, and the faithful souls of Israel . . . and the creation and development of a special *devekut* through a concentrated religious effort' (*Wisdom of the Zohar*, iii. 995). Luzzatto emphasized this distinction in the clearest terms.

[50] See I. Tishby, *Torat hara vehakelipah bekabalat ha'ar"i* (Jerusalem and Tel Aviv, 1942), 77–8.

[51] *Da'at tevunot, Sefer hakelalim* ['The Principles'], 276–7. In describing *devekut* as a union of the soul with the Holy One, blessed be He, Luzzatto is not simply drawing an analogy: he means that when the soul is elevated it elevates the Shekhinah and shares in her union with her husband. The reality of the union in *devekut* is given further emphasis in the explanation of 'the union of kisses and *yesodot* ['elements'—the forces of fertilization and increase]':

> The kisses are for perfect adherence [*hitdabekut*], and the *yesodot* are to form fruit, and that is the *devekut* with which the Holy One, blessed be He, attached [*hidbik*] Israel to Himself, and that is truly the meaning of 'Let him [here possibly interpreted as 'he will'—Trans.] kiss me with the kisses of his mouth' [S. of S. 1: 2]. *It is out of that great devekut that they perform their tikunim*, for they must first be bound together with the supernal lights in a perfect bond, a double bond, and then they will be able to perform their *tikunim*, whose purpose is to increase holiness and the supernal light out of the great love which the Holy One, blessed be He, will awaken in them, and then He will look with favour on their service. (Ibid. 280)

The concept of erotic *devekut* usually serves to describe the bonds between the soul and the Shekhinah as the love of a male for a female, as I explained in *Wisdom of the Zohar*, iii. 990–3 [a parenthesis: 'devekut be'ahavah'—'*devekut* in love'—in the Hebrew original is missing from p. 990 of the English version—Trans.], and in Essay 3, pp. 190–5, 200–6, 211–22. Here the soul in the state of *devekut* is portrayed as the wife, on the basis of the exposition of the Song of Songs as an allegory of the love of the Assembly of Israel and the Holy One, blessed be He. This interpretation as the union of the two divine personages can be understood in two ways: on the one hand it can be seen as a sensual realization of the mystical experience in *devekut*; but on the other, it constitutes a sublimation of the mythical erotic descriptions in Lurianic kabbalah. Luzzatto's application of Lurianic ideas on the Godhead to the relations between man and God, which we frequently encounter in these 'Principles' and in other works by him, is also very

It follows that although the complete *tikun* of human and cosmic existence by constant and perfect *devekut* is an eschatological aim, man is still capable, even during the periods of exile, of acting in close partnership with the Godhead and bringing himself and the world nearer to the perfection of the messianic era by partial *tikunim* effected when the soul is exalted in temporary *devekut*.

This comprehensive system is similar in its general pattern, and even in certain details, to the descriptions of the rises and falls of human and cosmic existence in Lurianic kabbalah. But there the central axis is the fall of the sparks and their raising up, whereas Luzzatto emphasizes the defects of corporeality and its purification, and the raising of the sparks is replaced by *devekut* as a principal instrument in acts of *tikun*. In his speculative treatises too, Luzzatto's explanations of Lurianic terms and concepts relegate the topic of the sparks to the sidelines. In the present context we need not pursue the question why Luzzatto drew a veil over the act of raising the sparks, which ever since the spread of Lurianic kabbalah had been a major element in the literature of kabbalah, in kabbalistic ethics in general and the stirrings of messianism in particular. For our purpose the main point is the relationship between hasidism and Luzzatto in this regard: on the one hand, what they have in common—the central position of *devekut* in the service of the Lord; on the other, the differences between them—the frequency of references to the raising of the sparks and the comparative lack of explicitly messianic tendencies in hasidic doctrine. In view of the clear traces of Luzzatto's influence I am of the opinion that these differences should not be seen as fundamental contradictions but as changes of form and as a concealment or softening of the intense messianism which is evident in Luzzatto's writings.[52]

important for our understanding of the links between his writings and the literature of hasidism, because—as several studies have shown—it is a prominent feature of hasidic thought that kabbalistic theosophical ideas and expressions are transferred to the plane of mystical anthropology. I propose to examine this issue in a separate study. For the time being, see Essay 1, p. 48, and, in the present essay, text referring to n. 65.

[52] The messianic significance of the idea of *devekut* in Luzzatto's kabbalah is of great importance in connection with the difference between Professor Gershom Scholem's views and mine over the status of messianism in hasidism. See my essay 'Harayon hameshiḥi vehamegamot hameshiḥiyot bitsemiḥat haḥasidut', *Zion*, 32 (1967), 1–54; G. Scholem, 'The Neutralization of the Messianic Element in Early Hasidism', *Journal of Jewish Studies*, 20 (1969), 25–55. This is not the place to debate this issue to a conclusion: I plan to discuss the matter further in an essay entitled 'Ge'ulah peratit uge'ulah kelalit besifrut haḥasidut uvimekorot kedam-ḥasidiyim' ['Individual Redemption and General Redemption in the Literature of Hasidism and in Pre-Hasidic Sources']. In the present essay, therefore, I have mentioned and shall continue to mention my findings with regard to the links between *devekut* and messianic-eschatological *tikun* as findings in the speculative and literary field without expressly relating them to the disagreement.

E. *DEVEKUT* IN PHYSICAL ACTIVITIES AND THE SANCTIFICATION OF CORPOREALITY IN UNPUBLISHED WRITINGS BY LUZZATTO

There are no explicit references to *devekut* in physical activities and the sanctification of corporeality in any of Luzzatto's printed works except *Mesilat yesharim*, ch. 26. But these matters figure prominently in several of his writings which were put away unpublished, and his descriptions of their nature and their merits contain data of great importance which show how the teachings of hasidism have their roots in Luzzatto's thinking.

At the beginning of a treatise on Jeremiah 9: 22–3 ('Let not the wise man glory in his wisdom . . . but let him that glories glory in this, that he understands and knows Me'),[53] Luzzatto declares that the prophet's instruction means 'that mankind should occupy themselves in [acquiring] the knowledge of His glorious greatness', and that it is impossible to achieve this end through learning to understand the nature of the commandments and getting to know 'the order of their performance in all their details', that is, by studying halakhah. It is necessary, therefore, to discover in the Torah itself the knowledge of 'His greatness, blessed be His name, and the mystery of His wonderful deeds', which lies beyond the commandments contained in the Torah.

'The mystery of true faith', which is hidden in the secrets of the Torah, resides in understanding the holiness of the Deity and the holiness of Israel. God chose Israel in order 'to make them holy exactly as He is holy', and He 'desires them [to be] below like the ministering angels above'. For this purpose He created the world and imbued it with His love and holiness. The holiness of God and the angels, with which Israel must sanctify themselves and which they must imitate, is explained in accordance with the dictum of the sages:[54] 'He is holy, His way is in holiness, His speech is in holiness', etc. This is how it is put:

[53] This treatise is in MS Oxford 2593, fos. 75^r–76^v. See Essay 1, pp. 46–8. [I pointed out there that it was a treatise that stood alone. M. Benayahu, on the contrary, asserts in *Kitvei hakabalah sheleramḥa"l*, 153–4, that this text on Jeremiah's 'Let not the wise man glory . . .' was a first introduction to *Ma'amar havikuaḥ* ['The Discussion'], which follows it in the Oxford collection and is in a different hand. His 'discovery' is quite baseless. The treatise contains no mention of 'The Discussion', it has none of the characteristics of an introduction either in form or in content, and nowhere is any hint to be found that Luzzatto wrote two introductions to the dialogue. See above, n. 10 and the addition to n. 12; and n. 72 below.]

[54] JT *Ber.* 9, *halakhah alef*, with alterations.

All their concerns and actions must be veritably things of holiness, that is to say, it is not enough for the things they do to be physical acts like those of all other men; even though these fulfil commandments which must be observed, that is not enough for their performance by a people who are holy exactly like the ministering angels. (fo. 75^{v})

Just as among angels there is no distinction between sacred and profane, so Israel, too, must make equal in holiness their fulfilment of the commandments, material things, and actions taken to satisfy their physical needs. This extreme demand is based on an interpretation of the verse 'In all your ways know Him':

And although the verse can also be interpreted to mean that it is enough to intend one's action to be for the sake of Heaven, that is, one will eat in order to live and serve the Lord, this is not its essential meaning, but all actions [must] be really things of holiness. (Ibid.)[55]

[55] R. Jacob Joseph of Polonnoye's book *Toledot ya'akov yosef* (Korets, 1780) contains parallel passages which in substance are paraphrases of Luzzatto with some modifications:

A great principle: In all your ways know Him, and as was said by Maimonides [*Mishneh torah*, 'Hilkhot de'ot', 3: 2–3] one should have the intention in all your [*sic*] ways [to act] for the sake of Heaven etc. *But to me* [the meaning] *seems deeper*: just as there is an intention in spiritual things in the Torah and prayer and the fulfilment of the commandments . . . to winnow the sparks . . . so, too, is the intention in material things, in eating, drinking, and all kinds of work . . . and when Scripture says 'In all your ways know Him' it means unification [*yiḥud*] of the Holy One, blessed be He, and his Shekhinah by the raising up of female waters [*mayin nukbin*, represented by the initial letters *m"n*] through the winnowing of the sparks, and understand this well. ('Bo', 40*d*)

For this is a great principle: in everything you do for the sake of Heaven, see to it that at the moment of your doing it, it is done for the service of the Lord; even in eating, so that one should not say that one is eating for the sake of Heaven because it will give strength afterwards to serve the Lord; although that is also a worthy intention, the essence of perfection is nevertheless that it involves a deed directly [intended] for the sake of Heaven, namely the raising up of sparks. ('Mishpatim', 59*b*, a report 'in the name of the rabbi and preacher Menahem Mendel' of Bar)

And see Weiss, 'Reshit tsemiḥatah shel haderekh haḥasidit', 72–3. The main idea, presented in one passage as the original thought of the author and in the other as 'a great principle' enunciated by the Maggid of Bar, is fundamentally the same in both cases, and is in line with Luzzatto's teaching. The only difference between them and Luzzatto is that according to the two hasidic teachers the transformation of corporeality from profane to sacred comes about through the intention to raise up sparks, whereas according to Luzzatto the sanctification of corporeality is achieved by *devekut* (see above, end of Section D). The exposition in R. Jacob Joseph's own version comes closer to Luzzatto by linking the distinction between the two ways of elevating corporeality to different interpretations of the verse 'In all your ways know Him'. Is it by chance that two hasidic scholars expressed an idea and drew a distinction so like those in an unpublished work by Luzzatto? On the face of it, it might be thought that all three could have drawn on an older source, but only if such a source were surprisingly to come to light could this be treated as a real possibility.

Because that is the level of merit intended for Israel,

Therefore the most important thing that a man must understand is the meaning of His holiness, blessed be He, which spreads through His world and by which Israel have been sanctified, what the meaning of this holiness is and what its ways are and how it spreads and how one prepares to encounter it so as to be properly sanctified by it. (Ibid.)

Anyone who does not know these things is described as walking in darkness like a blind man, for he does not know anything, why he is alive, why he exists in the world, and still less what it is on which the whole world is based (fo. 76[r]).

All-embracing holiness is attained by perfect *devekut*, but those who are smitten with blindness

do not see and do not know the way of holiness at all, nor [do they know anything of] cleaving to Him, blessed be He, whereas Scripture commands us: 'to Him you shall cleave' [*uvo tidbak*—Deut. 10: 20]. Although the verse is interpreted[56] as fulfilled by a person who cleaves to 'the disciples of the wise' [Torah scholars], in the end Scripture does not depart from its plain meaning [*Shab.* 63*a*], *and the truth is that Israel must really cleave to Him in perfect devekut*, so as to know and walk in the ways which are particularly His and which accord with His holiness. And that is why [the rabbis] said[57] that the Song of Songs is holy of holies, for it is founded precisely on this point and expresses this love and all the endeavour with which the Lord, blessed be He, seeks [to bring Israel] to cleave[58] to His holiness. Israel[59] must therefore respond in parallel with this by turning their desire towards Him *and cleaving to His holiness in real devekut*. (fo. 76[v])

The darkness of exile made Israel 'forgetful of this way' and 'sunk in sleep', but Heaven forbid that we should remain and cause others to remain in darkness: 'on the contrary, we should open blind eyes to see the Lord's love and to know holiness and its ways and truly be sanctified by it. *That is indeed the essence of the holy science of truth* [kabbalah], for it is nothing but an explanation of the meaning of this holiness' (ibid.). There are, it is true, 'differences in the ordering of affairs' between the time when Israel were living on their own soil and the period of exile, 'but nevertheless, even while God hides His face from them, [it is possible] for them to acquire holiness, and afterwards, when they receive their reward in the time to come, [to have it] for all eternity' (ibid.).

This is how Luzzatto sums up at the end of this short work, which consists wholly of rebuke and guidance on matters of holiness in corporeality and *devekut*:

[56] See *Sifrei* on Deut., *Ekev*, 49.

[57] Mishnah *Yad.* 3: 5.

[58] The text says 'seeks to cleave', but the intention is clear.

[59] [Note 59 is missing from the published text, but no doubt pointed out an inadvertent repetition of the word 'Israel'.—Trans.]

It follows that the whole science of truth is based upon this one issue, the issue of the holiness of Israel, how the Holy One, blessed be He, cleaves to them out of His holiness, and how Israel must cleave to His holiness, blessed be He, with their desire and their service, and how on this depend all the affairs of the world and every creature from the beginning of their existence and for ever and ever. (Ibid.)

These words speak for themselves, and their great importance for our purpose needs no explanation. But it is worth adding a few comments in clarification of certain points. Other points will be explained after my consideration of a parallel text immediately below.

1. Israel. The whole treatise deals with the holiness of Israel and their *devekut*, and there is no mention of the soul. Why does the author base himself on the relations between God and the people of Israel and not the children of Israel as individuals? Israel is often identified with individual Jewish souls in Luzzatto's other writings, and so here, too, not because of any lack of precision in his terminology, but in order to stress that every soul of Israel is only one of the particles that make up the whole of the Assembly of Israel. In the present context the point also has another significance: the assumption that collective *devekut* is possible in Jewish groups.[60]

2. The eschatological aspect. In several places the holiness and *devekut* which it is Israel's task to realize in this world are said to be in the nature of beginnings and preparations for their perfect and eternal fulfilment in the time to come. Here, to add to the quotations already given, is a sentence which places the greatest emphasis on this line of thought: 'Because, in future, they [Israel] would sin, He provided [for them to experience] some great vicissitudes until ultimately Israel would undergo perfect *tikun*, and this holiness would spread among them for ever and ever' (fo. 76^{r}). One often finds particular attention directed to the eschatological future in discussion of the issue (considered in Section D above) of the *tikun* of the body and the world through the refinement of corporeality by *devekut* in the service of God [*avodat hakodesh*]. It need hardly be added that in Luzzatto's writings this point of view is clearly messianic. Similarly, hasidic literature repeatedly asserts that the values and virtues which are important—among them *devekut* and the *tikun* of the Shekhinah and of all Creation by raising up the sparks and by worship through corporeality—will be maintained and perfected in the era of universal Redemption. In my opinion such statements are not to be regarded as empty words but are a genuine expression of eschatological messianism.

*

60 See Section F below, descriptions of *devekut* in Luzzatto's group.

The second work which centres on the sanctification of corporeality and on *devekut* is the introduction to *Ma'amar havikuah* ['The Discussion'], the dialogue which was printed and circulated under the title *Ḥoker umekubal* ['Philosopher and Kabbalist']. The introduction, which was originally intended to show the greatness and beauty of kabbalah [*ḥokhmat hasod*, 'esoteric wisdom'], was written in 1732 but did not appear in the dialogue as printed and its existence was for many years unknown.[61] It begins with a description of the manifestation of the Shekhinah at the giving of the law on Mount Sinai. At the time of the Creation the Holy One, blessed be He, hid His governance of the world from the earth and its inhabitants, and they could not see or understand 'where the things of this world were rooted and [on what] they hung' (fo. 109^r). When the Torah was given to Israel 'He revealed His mystery to them' (fo. 108^r), and the secret of the close relationship between the world and Israel and the Shekhinah was handed down from generation to generation in the secrets of the Torah. But from the time that they went into Exile 'wisdom began to depart from Israel' and they 'sink down and walk in this great darkness in every generation and are far from the holy Shekhinah', even though their own holiness is unimpaired. Through the mercy of Heaven 'the plain meaning of the Torah' has been preserved in Israel without interruption and a close affinity has been established between them and God 'at least [on the level of] His hiding His face', but in the absence of esoteric wisdom they are prevented from 'shining with the [divine] light of life' and 'delighting in the pleasure of the knowledge of His glory, blessed be He, in which knowledge the thirst of the soul is quenched and its hunger satisfied by the light of the holy Shekhinah' (fos. 109^v–110^r).

The soul and the body correspond to the esoteric and literal meanings of the Torah, and their condition depends on the way in which the Torah is studied. If a man 'engages in the study and consideration of the secrets of the Torah', not only does his soul receive 'light and divine flow on the level appropriate to the soul', but his body, too, benefits from that level, and scholars versed in kabbalah 'are all sanctified with supreme holiness', but as for anyone who concerns himself only with the literal meaning, 'even his soul is reached only by the flow appropriate to the body'. Since kabbalah is being studied less and less in Exile, faults are increasing in Israel and the world, for 'there is no *tikun* for the holy Shekhinah except through the secrets of the Torah' (fo. 110^{r-v}).

This opening in praise of kabbalah is followed by an account of its superiority over literal interpretation by its sanctification of corporeality. I quote here, in order, some extracts from this part, which constitutes the kernel of the introduction:

[61] The introduction is in MS Oxford 2593, fos. 108^r–115^r. See Essay 1, pp. 49–50 and 57 and n. 174.

According to the plain meaning all the things of this world are physical things and defects in man . . . and anyone who desires to be a *hasid* cannot but separate himself from pleasures as far as possible and enjoy only whatever is essential to keep himself alive . . . then he will be a hasid who has turned away from evil, and [his] action will remain good . . . and it will also be found to be a service to the Lord because he is taking this action in order to live to serve his Creator, but the action itself will none the less remain a human defect, and if it had been possible to do otherwise it would have been better . . . *kabbalah is greater*, for *by its nature the actions themselves revert to goodness and* [become] *the highest tikunim*; this is so because the Supernal Will provided *for the things of this world to be sanctified by the use man makes of them for his needs and enjoyment* . . . and that is because man was given the power to draw down the strength and light of the Shekhinah by means of his soul, and He gave him all the things of the world for his use because thereby they too would undergo *tikun*, and the holy strength that he drew down would extend to them too . . . When the [corporeal] deed is done in the proper way it will, itself, become a *tikun* . . . and then man, in his deeds, will become like a veritable angel of the Lord of Hosts. Thus the science of truth explains the meaning of holiness and the influence of God, blessed be He, over His creatures and His cleaving to them . . . for what the Holy One, blessed be He, desires most in His world is that all the things of the world should be veritable *tikunim* and things of holiness . . . for the Supernal Will desired to draw man near to Him, so as to rest upon him and cleave to him . . . and therefore He provided this man with great ways and marvellous statutes by which to perfect himself and his place, which is this world, and the Shekhinah conducts herself towards this man . . . so as *to sanctify him and everything associated with him* . . . and the totality of these ways and statutes is this science of truth . . . meaning the spread of His holiness, blessed be His name, in His world, and His cleaving to those He has created. (fos. 110^{v}–112^{r})

I comment below on some important points in this part of the introduction.

1. *Devekut.* *Devekut* is explained here as a meeting of man with the Godhead in which the power and light of the Shekhinah are drawn down to the soul and spread to the body and the whole world. By virtue of man's use of corporeal things in accordance with the teachings of 'the science of truth', the Shekhinah rests upon corporeality, which is sanctified and shares in the holiness of the souls.[62] *Devekut* occurs in the very act of engaging in the study of

[62] According to the descriptions here and in Luzzatto's other writings, the sanctification of corporeality means endowing corporeal things and actions with divine holiness and bringing them close to the level of spirituality in their worldly existence, in preparation for a complete change in their nature from corporeality to spirituality in the final Redemption. So too in the literature of hasidism one can find evidence of a similar point of view in those writings in which worship through corporeality is not associated with the raising of sparks. See n. 20 above.

occult wisdom.[63] By contrast, the benefit of studying the plain meaning of the Torah is limited to rescuing man from sin and establishing indirect contact between him and God by the fulfilment of the commandments. In Luzzatto's other writings, too, *devekut* is generally described as the contact of the soul with the Shekhinah, not, however, only with her presence on earth, but also above by the ascent of the soul, and there are even some references to its ascent as high as Ein Sof.[64] There is a similar range of ways of *devekut* in the literature of hasidism.

2. *Tikunim*. In this work Luzzatto clearly relates all stages and processes to *tikun*: the Shekhinah, man, and the world need *tikun*; the soul has the mission of performing *tikun*, and corporeal things can and must serve as *tikunim*; the

[63] Similarly R. Menahem Mendel of Peremyshlyany said that 'the esoteric content of the whole of the Zohar and the writings of the Ari, may he be remembered for a blessing, is built entirely on the attachment [*devekut*] of the Creator to whoever is worthy of being attached [to Him] and beholding the celestial chariot' (in R. Meshulam Feivush [Phoebus] Heller of Zbarazh's *Yosher divrei emet* (Munkács, 1905), 18*d*; and see Scholem, '"Devekut" o "hitkasherut intimit im elohim" bereshit haḥasidut', 340–1). However, unlike Luzzatto, Menahem Mendel and his pupil Meshulam Feivush Heller taught that 'both through the revealed Torah and through the hidden Torah he attaches himself, but through the hidden Torah a more wonderful *devekut* will be achieved' (*Yosher divrei emet*, 12*d*). In their opinion *torah lishemah* [Torah study for its own sake] is study of both the revealed and the hidden for the sake of *devekut*, and R. Meshulam Feivush testifies that he also heard the Maggid of Mezhirech say that in *torah lishemah* in this sense, *devekut* is the inwardness of the Torah which is learnt (ibid. 13*c*; and, more briefly, ibid. 8*a–b*). And see ibid. 11*b*–15*a*, 25*d*–26*a*. Moreover, R. Menahem Mendel reported the Besht as saying that *torah lishemah* with *devekut* earned the student 'the ability to purify many secular things' (ibid. 17*c*). The authentic traditions in *Yosher divrei emet* refute the opinion common among present-day researchers of hasidism that R. Menahem Mendel preached the pursuit of Torah study and *devekut* as two separate matters. In support of the teaching repeated here that study must be conducted with *devekut*, the writers cite 'what was said by the Ari, may his memory be for a blessing, which was quoted in the little book *Sha'arei tsiyon*' (ibid. 12*c*). This is a reference to R. Hayim Vital's report in *Sha'ar ruaḥ hakodesh* (Jerusalem, 1912), 11*a*, of a statement by the Ari, which was reproduced with certain changes in R. Nathan Nata Hannover's *Sha'arei tsiyon* (Amsterdam, 1671 and other editions), end of Gate 2: 'He [the Ari] used to say that essentially the *kavanah* of reading the Torah to attain understanding depends on this, that he concentrates wholly on binding his soul *so as to make it cleave to its root* by [his] occupation with the Torah in order to perfect the supernal tree *and to restore supernal man to perfection*.' A statement in these terms is also to be found in Luria's *Shulḥan arukh*, which was likewise printed and disseminated long before the emergence of hasidism (Kraków, undated; Frankfurt an der Oder, 1691; and others), *Kavanat talmud torah*, sect. 2. Piekarz, *Bimei tsemiḥat haḥasidut*, 359–60, drew attention to three non-hasidic ethical books which quoted this teaching. The discovery that it is mentioned in a hasidic book and is there connected with the ways of study prescribed by the teachers of hasidism helps to confirm its identification as a direct source used by them to back the obligation to study the Torah with *devekut*. It is noteworthy, too, that in the early Lurianic source quoted above, which the teachers of hasidism explicitly relied on as authoritative, *devekut* and *tikun* are presented as interlinked activities, carried out together.

[64] See Essay 1, p. 38; Luzzatto's *Adir bamarom* (Warsaw, 1886), 35–8; n. 51 above; etc.

sanctification of corporeality and *devekut* are both acts of *tikun*. We have here another example of the close interaction of *devekut* and *tikun*.

3. The essence of kabbalah; holiness; *devekut*. Both this work and the treatise on Jeremiah 9 described above lay emphasis on signposting the proper way to serve the Lord, by the sanctification of corporeality and by *devekut*, as being the essence of 'the science of truth'. Elements of kabbalistic doctrine are transferred from the theosophical to the human plane, to the life of man himself and the relations between him and God[65]—a shift formulated here as a great principle. The parallel with hasidism is evident. True, there is a great difference between the teachers of hasidism and Luzzatto, who was unquestionably a kabbalist and wrote kabbalistic books, on the model of the Zohar and the writings of Cordovero and Luria, which are full of specific kabbalistic terms and concepts; his 'Discussion' too, the introduction to which we have been considering, sets out to explain the principles of speculative kabbalah to the *ḥoker* ['philosopher'] in all its details. But the introduction, after describing the greatness of kabbalah, concludes by saying that the main purpose achieved by studying it is that when a person understands it properly 'his heart will be fired with love for the holy Shekhinah, desiring only to conduct himself in all his ways as a hasid ['saintly person'] with[66] his Maker and to give satisfaction to his Creator'. In other words, the value of the knowledge gained in the science of kabbalah resides in the fact that it renders the soul fit to cleave to the Shekhinah and restore her towards perfection [*letakenah*] by raising her up and preparing for her marriage in the upper world.

4. Degrees of *ḥasidut*. The two levels of service of the Lord described in the unpublished works considered above are paralleled by the two levels in *Mesilat yesharim*. The description of 'the hasid according to the plain meaning' [i.e. one who interprets the Torah literally—Trans.] even contains some verbal correspondences to the portrayal of the hasid in the printed book, and the man who serves the Lord with *devekut* and sanctification of corporeality in the way prescribed by kabbalah fits the picture of 'the holy man' in the book.[67] But alongside the similarities there are some conspicuous differences: 'the hasid according to the plain meaning' is compared to 'a blind man in darkness', and his soul is brought down to the lowly level of the body, whereas the hasid in *Mesilat yesharim* is a man of high spiritual rank whose soul, ascending in *devekut*, works for the *tikun* of the Shekhinah and Israel, even though he does not achieve the sanctification of corporeality. A fundamental difference which concerns us is that here the ability to sanctify corporeality is

[65] See n. 51 above.

[66] [Here, no doubt, 'in the eyes of his Maker'. The verb *mitḥased* and the preposition 'with' are borrowed from 2 Sam. 22: 26; a borrowing of form rather than of meaning.—Trans.]

[67] See above, text referring to nn. 28–9.

not peculiar to holy men whose high merit is comparable to that of Enoch and Elijah in aggadic midrashim and kabbalistic literature; nor is it bestowed as an act of grace. Anyone who is prepared to devote himself to the study of kabbalah and serve the Lord in accordance with its teachings can reach this level, and every Jew must prepare himself to attain it. True, both of the unpublished works say that those who sanctify corporeality are elevated to the rank of angels, which is similar to what is said of 'the holy man' in *Mesilat yesharim*, but here the angelic rank remains within the bounds of nature and ordinary human existence, whereas the printed book speaks of 'angelhood' at a superhuman level.[68]

F. RITUALS IN LUZZATTO'S GROUP DESIGNED TO SANCTIFY CORPOREALITY BY *DEVEKUT*

We learn from other unpublished writings that this viewpoint did not remain purely theoretical but was put into practice by Luzzatto and the members of his circle in rituals which they instituted for their group. Three homilies, a prayer, and a *piyut* for the night of 17 Shevat which have come down to us attest the existence of such a ritual in a festival peculiar to the group, and they reveal its meaning. One homily, minus the author's name, is in the collection in MS Oxford 2593 (fos. 129^{r}–143^{r}). At its head has been written: 'Se'udat leil to"v bishevat ['formal meal for the night of 17 Shevat'; *to"v*, spelt *tet vav beit*, equals 17 but also 'good'—Trans.] 5493'. This untitled homily, which has also been preserved in a copy made by R. Jekutiel of Vilna,[69] was undoubtedly composed by Luzzatto. Another of the homilies, by R. Moses David Valle, one of the leaders of Luzzatto's group, was written and delivered at a festive gathering of the group in 5492 [1732], and is inscribed: 'On the night of the 17th [*yod"zayin*] of the month of Shevat, and wine gladdens the heart of man.'[70] Thc third homily does not give the author's name or any indication that it relates to 17 Shevat,[71] but from its content it is clearly of the same kind

[68] As regards *Mesilat yesharim* it seems probable that the sanctification of corporeality was hedged about with severe limitations in order to hide or camouflage the author's real views. But I do not know why, in works written at about the same time as the introduction to 'The Discussion' or earlier, Luzzatto said nothing explicit about the sanctification of corporeality or about *devekut* in physical activity.

[69] MS Oxford 2237, fos. 149^{r}–152^{v}.

[70] MS BL 387, fos. 184^{v}–185^{r}. And see Essay 2, pp. 118–20.

[71] MS Jerusalem 5217 8°, fos. 16^{r-v}, 23^{r}. Between fos. 16 and 23 the binders erroneously included remnants of the revelations by the *magid* which were noted down by Luzzatto. These

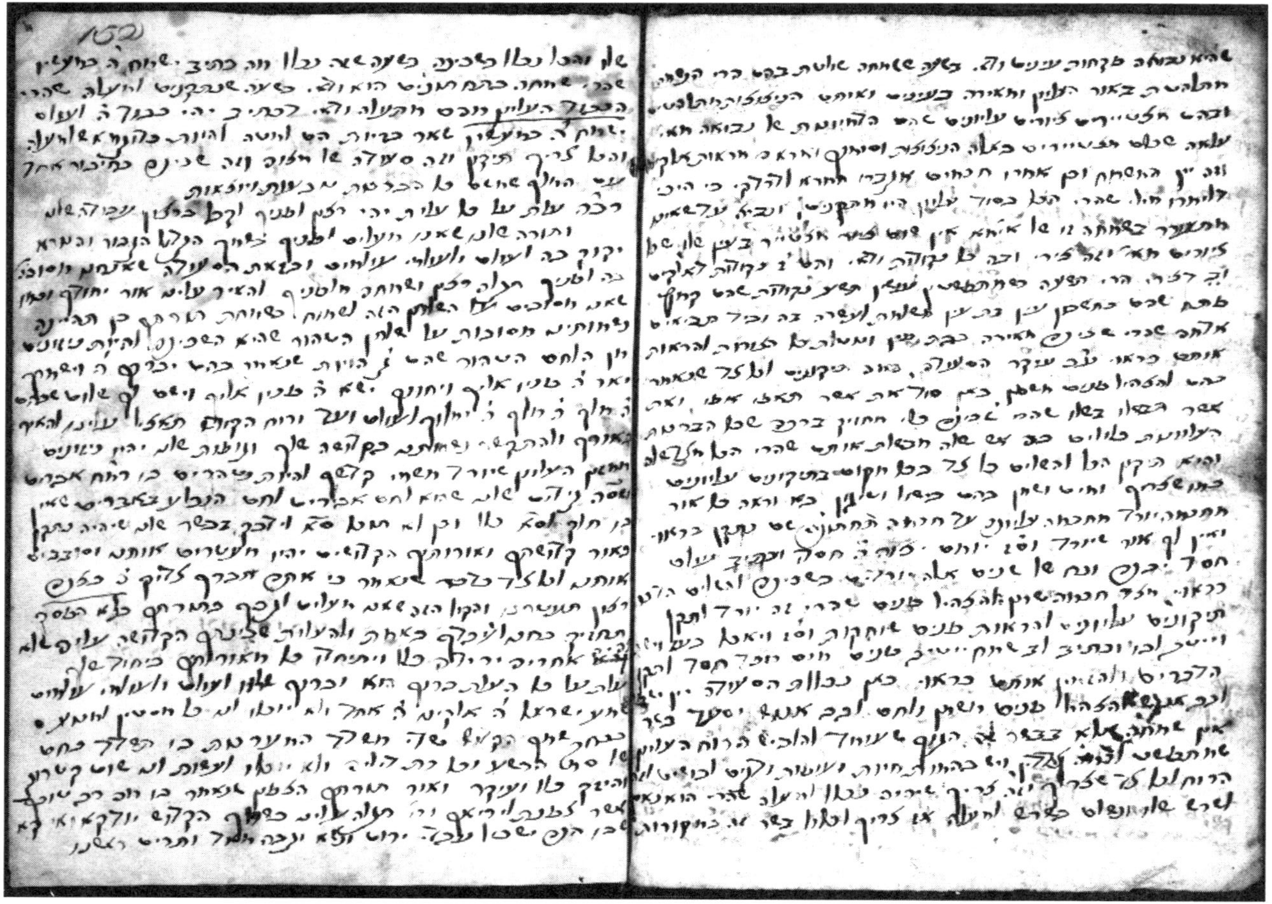

3. Folio from the homily for the ceremonial meal of the night of 17 Shevat: handwriting of R. Jekutiel of Vilna (MS. Reggio 32, folios 151v–152r, Bodleian Library, University of Oxford (MS Oxford 2237))

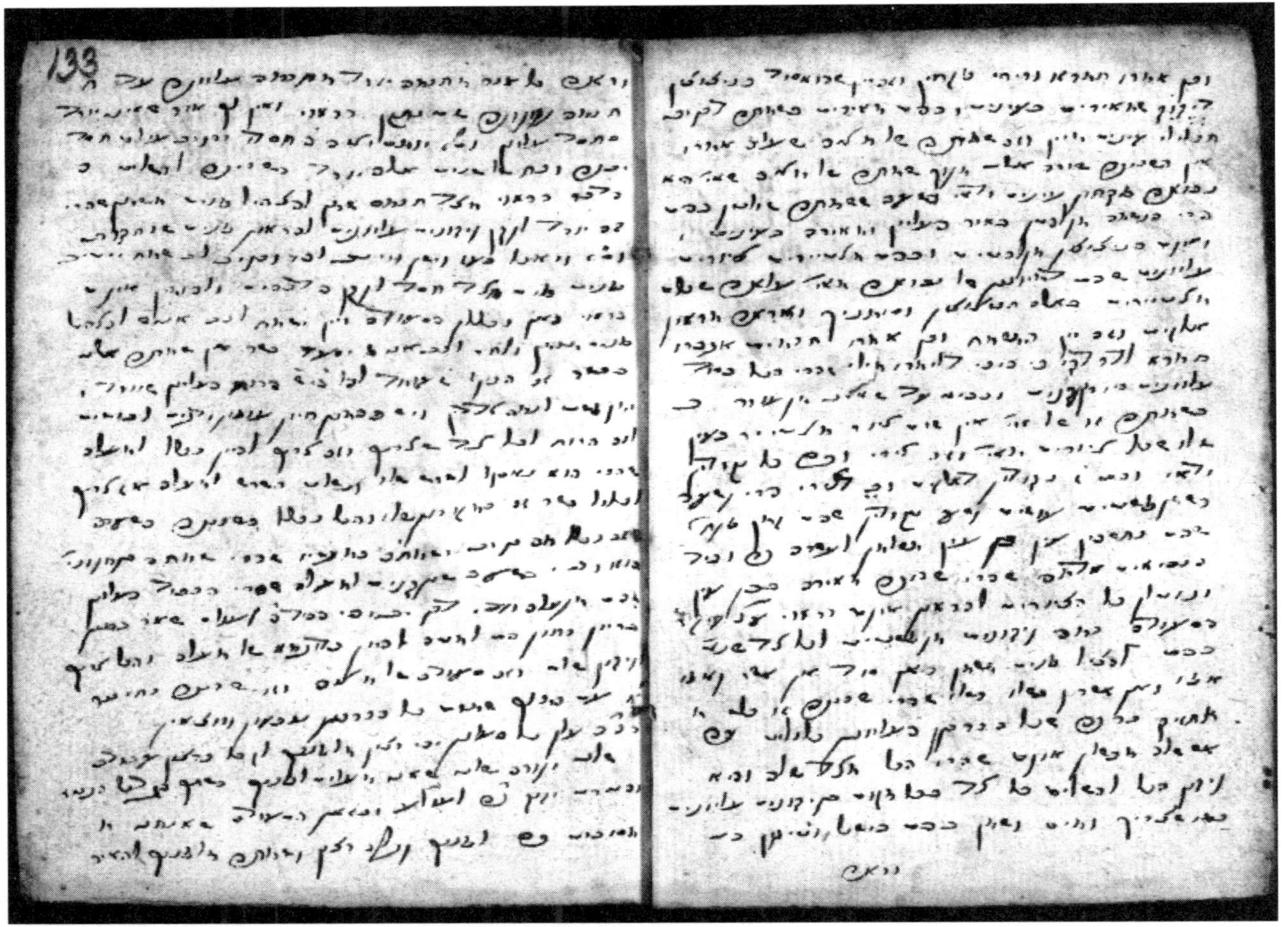

4. Folio from the homily for the ceremonial meal of the night of 17 Shevat: the disputed handwriting (MS. Opp. Add. 80, folios 132v–133r, Bodleian Library, University of Oxford (MS Oxford 2593))

as the two specifically composed for this occasion, and it was certainly written and delivered orally by one of the senior members of the group.[72]

have been published by M. Benayahu in 'Ha"magid" shel ramḥa"l', in I. Ben-Zvi and M. Benayahu (eds.), *Sefer zikaron liyeshayahu zoneh/Isaiah Sonne Memorial Volume* (= *Sefunot*, 5) (Jerusalem, 1961), 328–35. The homily is based on Eccles. 9: 7: 'Go, eat your bread in joy and drink your wine with a cheerful heart, for God has already approved your deeds.' There is another copy of the homily, with minor differences, in the same handwriting, in the collection in the Jerusalem manuscript, fos. 303ᵛ–304ʳ, in a series of homilies on scriptural verses, headed 'Ecclesiastes 9'. Probably the first copy is the version which was heard by the group on the night of 17 Shevat, and it was afterwards added to a number of expositions of other verses.

72 Following my discovery of the homilies by Luzzatto and R. M. D. Valle for the ceremonial meal held on the night of 17 Shevat, and my account of their main lines in Essay 2 above, M. Benayahu dealt with the three homilies examined here in his essay 'Piyut, tefilah uviduy mikivshono shel ramḥa"l shene'emru baḥavurah berosh hashanah leyisudah', *Sinai*, 82 (1978), 42–5, but he forgot to mention my essay. And see n. 10 above. As regards the third homily he stated that the man who wrote and preached it was R. Michael Terni, and in the light of what is said in Benayahu's new book *Kitvei hakabalah sheleramḥa"l*, 29, this seems to me a reasonable statement. But, most surprisingly, his essay attributes the homily of 5493 [1733] which has been preserved in two manuscripts to R. Jekutiel, on the basis of an assumption that the copy in MS Oxford 2593 is also in his handwriting. In his book, Benayahu enlarged on this assumption and tried to apply it to most of the compositions in that collection: see *Kitvei hakabalah sheleramḥa"l*, 80–90. I see no grounds for identifying the handwriting—which he described (ibid. 80) as 'Italian-Ashkenazi, and more Italian than Ashkenazi'—as R. Jekutiel's. In the facsimiles of R. Jekutiel's authentic handwriting and of the doubtful hand which are there reproduced together (ibid. 82–4) the differences are incomparably greater than the similarities. The difference is most marked in the two copies of the homily for the night of 17 Shevat, which can be compared word by word. I publish here, side by side, two folios (Plates 3 and 4), a comparison of which, in my opinion, completely negates the assumption that their handwriting is identical. I am obliged to the curators of the Bodleian Library in Oxford for making photographs of the two manuscripts to help me in my research and for granting me permission to publish them. Variations in the text also show that they were not written by the same man. However, even if we could concede, for the sake of argument, that Jekutiel altered his handwriting from time to time and made verbal additions and deletions in the homily, there would still be no justification for taking the writer to be the author in the absence of any convincing evidence drawn from the content or the form. If that line were to be pursued to its 'logical' conclusion we should be obliged to accept R. Jekutiel as the author of all the compositions in MS Oxford 2593 in the same 'Italian-Ashkenazi' hand which are not known from other sources to be the work of Luzzatto—for instance the collections of homilies and the 'Discussion between the Soul and the Intellect' [see Essay 1, p. 30 ff.—Trans.]. Not only did Benayahu himself not go as far as this, but even with regard to compositions in MS Oxford 2237 which are undoubtedly in R. Jekutiel's handwriting, he was careful not to credit R. Jekutiel with authorship of Luzzatto's work. See *Kitvei hakabalah sheleramḥa"l*, 91, 94. He even arbitrarily deprived Jekutiel of the credit for a halakhic work which Jekutiel wrote for the purpose of instructing his pupils in Venice and prefaced with a 'foreword by the author-compiler'; and by an elaborate and convoluted structure of subtleties Benayahu sought to attribute it to Luzzatto. See ibid. 92–4, 237; and Essay 8, pp. 439–40 and n. 114. In fact the attribution of the homily of 5493 to R. Jekutiel will not stand examination. Both its style and its content as described above are overwhelming testimony to the fact that we have here a work unquestionably by Luzzatto and not by his disciple from Vilna, who in both language and ideas was completely dwarfed by his giant of a master and certainly could not compare with him in the writing of a kabbalistic work.

Luzzatto's homily is the longest and most profound, and explains in detail the purposes of the *tikunim* at the meal, the ways in which they were performed, and the results of carrying them out. The main purpose was *the tikun of the Shekhinah*, and in order to explain how this was done at the meal, the homily begins with an account of the position of the Shekhinah and her rises and falls in the divine system and in her relation to the worlds and living creatures. The principles of kabbalistic theory underlying worship through corporeality at this meal may be summarized as follows: it was through the Shekhinah that the worlds were brought into existence and all living creatures are rooted in her, and the purpose of their existence is 'to show His unity as including those who have been created out of Him' by attaching those below to the Shekhinah, so fulfilling the verse 'May the whole earth be full of His glory' (Ps. 72: 19). By this attachment the Shekhinah undergoes *tikun* to such an extent that she is elevated 'above everything . . . and all the worlds and all levels are none other than the perfection of Malkhut' (fo. 129^{r-v}). The task of bringing about these conditions had been placed on Adam, but because he fell into sin, the Sitra Ahra ['Other Side']—the forces of evil—grew in power and caused a separation above and below: above, the Shekhinah was separated from her husband and from Binah, the upper Shekhinah; and below, living creatures, including man, were cut off from the Shekhinah, their divine source. The *tikun* of the Shekhinah and of Creation by renewing the bond between them, which will be completed in the messianic Redemption, has been made the responsibility of Israel; and one of the means of achieving it is by the consumption of food accompanied by holy *kavanot* at the meal, by which the diners and the foods they eat will be illuminated by divine lights and will become part of those lights.

The description of the *tikunim* clarifies the significance of the sanctification of corporeality according to kabbalah, which was expounded in the works I considered in Section D above. Every thing in the world reflects a certain sefirah or process in the sefirotic system according to the symbolism of kabbalah, and in line with the relationship of source and derivation between beings in the upper world and those below, every thing in the world has a root above. Therefore, when material things are used, one must have the intention in one's heart to direct them towards the divine powers which they represent. In this way they undergo *tikun* and sanctification by being elevated to their source and by drawing light and divine flow down to themselves, while at the same time *tikun* is undergone by the beings in the upper world, especially the Shekhinah, in whom all creatures are rooted and who includes them all. Worship through corporeality at the meal has even greater merit because it is accompanied by blessings and words of Torah said at the table which symbolizes the Shekhinah.

Luzzatto gives details of the food and drink served to the group at the holy meal, describing the kabbalistic symbolism involved and the steps taken in the preparation, cooking, baking, and frying, and every item and every action acquires *a sacramental character* in its description. As illustrations of these remarkable statements on the sanctification of the meal I quote here the descriptions of the *tikun* with bread and wine and the *tikun* with meat:

The mystery of the meal depends on two things, bread and wine, one being the Shekhinah and the other I[ma].[73] When they are joined together as one, all the *tikunim* in the world are accomplished by them. And the table is the Shekhinah, at which man takes the creatures of this world below and makes use of them in order to accomplish *tikun* above. The entire *tikun* is a cup of blessing,[74] and that is this table at which words of Torah are spoken, for the whole Torah is the names of the Holy One, blessed be He, all of which shine upon this table with the letters of the Torah, for the table receives them by way of the mystery of the creatures each one of whom is rooted above in the name proper to it . . . and bread is the entirety of the creatures who are included in the mystery of the Shekhinah. (fos. 131^{v}–132^{r})

Meat: there can be no festivity without meat;[75] this is the body which is to clothe the spirit from above which comes down and spreads out on various sides, and there are animals, domestic and wild, birds, and fish which are garments for this spirit on whatever side is necessary . . . It is necessary, then, for this meat to be integrated with its sources, and all is included in the Shekhinah. (fo. 133^{r})

The homily ends with a prayer[76] in which the participants in the meal ask for *tikun* and sanctification for their souls and bodies and strength to accomplish the *tikun* of the Shekhinah with an everlasting (i.e. a messianic) *tikun* by virtue of their unceasing study of the Torah at the table during the meal:

Show Your favour and joy in this meal at which we are seated before You, by shedding the light of Your unity upon us. And just as we are seated at this table to rejoice in Your Torah, so may our souls be seated at the pure table which is the Shekhinah . . . Endow us with the holy spirit, so that we may be illumined by Your light and our souls be bound together with Your holiness; let our bodies be nourished with the celestial manna [here *man*, 'manna'; on p. 174 above, *mazon*, 'food'—Trans.] which descends from Your holy Heaven . . . and thus the Sitra Ahra will not be able to adhere to our flesh which will have been fed [*nizon*; on p. 175 *nitkan*, 'perfected through *tikun*'—Trans.] by Your holy light, and Your holy lights will encompass them [our organs] and surround us on every side[77] . . . And [in response to] this voice which we lift up towards You in ceaseless [study of] Your Torah[78]—

[73] The sefirah Ima–Binah. [74] A symbol for the Shekhinah. [75] See BT *Pes.* 109*a*.

[76] Subsequently published in *Molad*, NS 8 (31) (1980), and now in Part B of Essay 2 (pp. 174–6 above).

[77] For a description of the state of *devekut* in kabbalistic sources and in hasidic literature as enwrapment in the light of the Shekhinah, see Scholem, '"Devekut" o "hitkasherut intimit im elohim" bereshit haḥasidut', 329–30. [78] In accordance with the group's rules. See *Igerot*, i. 8.

strengthen us to serve You in truth and to raise up Your holy Shekhinah [in] an ascent after which there will be no descent. (fo. 133^{r-v})

The prayer makes explicit what, in other parts of the homily, can be gleaned from between the lines and from the descriptions: the *tikunim* in every area of existence which were to lead to the harmony and unity of the worlds and man with the Shekhinah, and of the Shekhinah with the sefirotic system right up to Ein Sof, were performed by the group at their meal in collective mystical *devekut*, in a spirit characterized by fervour and the shedding of corporeality.

R. Moses David Valle, at the beginning of his short homily, describes the ceremonial meal of the night of 17 Shevat as a *se'udah shel mitsvah* [a meal to mark a religious occasion] which 'these holy companions hold on this night . . . to perform *tikunim* for the sake of Heaven'. His homily is based on the verse 'There is joy for a man in the utterance of his tongue, and a word in season, how good it is' (Prov. 15: 23), concentrating on the *tikun* which is 'the mystery of the wine that gladdens'. From the point of view of worship through corporeality its main point is that joy in drinking 'the wine that gladdens' arouses the soul to produce new insights into the Torah 'by way of the mystery of the parting of the lips', and the power of these insights is such as to perfect in Heaven the holy intercourse between Tiferet and Malkhut, who correspond to voice and speech.

The third homily is also short and simple, but it is very important for our purpose because it deals with a matter closely parallel to the treatment of the 'holy man' in *Mesilat yesharim*. Its subject is the *tikun* of the celestial marriage by bread and wine. To the question: 'Surely eating and drinking are material and physical things which the Sitra Ahra enjoy, and a man ought to distance himself from them and not draw near to them?', the answer is that while the Temple stood, sins were atoned for and the *tikun* of the celestial union achieved

by sacrifices offered on the altar . . . and now the table accomplishes that, because by the act of eating, when a man eats in holiness and purity, and especially if the meal is a *se'udat mitsvah*, the celestial union takes place, and then the lights multiply and mercy increases, and by the power of that mercy the sins are expiated and the *tikun* is properly completed by way of the mystery of the supernal unification which is revealed.[79]

Thus, in order for a man to be able to sanctify the material things which he uses and raise them to the level of sacrifices and libations, he need not be a holy person 'who cleaves constantly to his God and whose soul walks among "those ideas that are true"' in fulfilment of Luzzatto's teaching in chapter 26

79 The homilist relied here on the authority of the saying by our sages: 'So long as the Temple stood, the altar atoned for Israel, and now a man's table atones for him' (BT *Ber.* 55*a*).

of *Mesilat yesharim*. All that is required of him, at any rate with regard to eating and drinking, is that he should observe holiness and purity in his actions and, in doing them, know how to direct his intentions 'for the sake of the unification of the Holy One, blessed be He, and His Shekhinah', as in the standard formula used in kabbalah and in hasidism.

I am of the opinion that the meal of the night of 17 Shevat was only one of the holy meals celebrated in Luzzatto's group. From one of the rules of the group we learn that it was Luzzatto's regular practice to speak 'words of Torah' at the third (Sabbath) meal in his *beit midrash*, and that the 'holy companions' were in duty bound to come and listen to their teacher's homilies on those occasions. The rule reads as follows: 'It shall be obligatory for all to be present, unless prevented by causes outside their control, on every holy Sabbath day after the Minhah prayer in this holy house of prayer [represented by the initials *b-h-t* for *beit hatefilah*, but *beit hamidrash* ['house of study'] is meant] during the study period of our honoured teacher and master, their rabbi, may his light shine.'[80] As I have said, Luzzatto's homily for the night of 17 Shevat was in the hands of R. Jekutiel of Vilna, and it is probable that he instituted, in his groups, the customs and ceremonies he had learnt from his master while in Padua. It may therefore be conjectured that a relationship of source to derivation is to be detected in the similarities between the practices in Luzzatto's group—the holy meal, the delivery of 'words of Torah' at the

[80] *Igerot*, i. 10, 'Supplementary Rules', para. 6. In R. Jekutiel's copy the text of this paragraph is different, and makes it quite clear that it refers to new Torah insights presented orally at the third (Sabbath) meal. His version reads: 'It shall be obligatory on all the undersigned to come at least on every holy Sabbath day to hear [?: apparently the word 'to learn' had been written and then altered] the new insights [*hidushim*, with first letter *he* instead of *ḥet*] which our teacher and rabbi, their master R. Moses Hayim, learns[?] *and speaks about on the Sabbath afternoon between Minhah and the evening prayer*' (MS Oxford 2237, fo. 103ʳ). In the copy of the group's rules at the end of MS Cincinnati 501, the text is as in the printed version. It is possible that R. Jekutiel introduced alterations to make clear to his groups what it was that was studied between the Sabbath Minhah and Ma'ariv services in Luzzatto's group. And see n. 27 above. A sonnet by Ephraim Luzzatto proves, in my opinion, that long after R. M. H. Luzzatto had left Padua his friends and disciples continued to come together in the *beit midrash* on the Sabbath for 'the third meal', during which the heads of the group presented new kabbalistic insights into the Torah. At the head of the poem we are told: 'These are the names of the men, learned in the Torah, our honoured teacher R. Moses Valle and our honoured teacher R. Israel Treves, residents of Padua, who *take sweet counsel together Sabbath by Sabbath at the time of Minhah*.' The following are the verses which concern us here: 'Sabbath by Sabbath, two are they / who search out what is hidden, in company with the throng / . . . / Lo, they have set a limit to the time they speak / from after the Minhah service until it has grown dark' (*Shirei efrayim lutsato*, ed. J. Fichman (Tel Aviv, 1942), 78). (In my essay on R. Moses David Valle, which is about to be published in the Festschrift in honour of Professor Isaac Baer's ninetieth birthday [but the Festschrift had finally to appear as a memorial volume (Jerusalem, 1980); the essay is translated as Essay 6 above; see text there referring to n. 66—Trans.], I said 'it is reasonable to conclude that the poem was written in or about the period 1750–3'.)

table, and the sanctification of the food and drink and of the participants—and the holy meals in the presence of the leaders of the congregation in hasidism, which we know were conducted from the very beginning of the movement.[81]

CONCLUSIONS

1. On two central issues, the elevation and sanctification of corporeality and the perception and evaluation of *devekut*, we have established that there is a close affinity in principles and in details between the literature of hasidism and the writings of Luzzatto.

2. Compositions by Luzzatto which had been condemned to be left in manuscript were circulating in hasidic neighbourhoods in the early days of hasidism, and one of the most important of his works on kabbalistic doctrine, the '138 Gateways to Wisdom', was printed by hasidim of the school of the Maggid of Mezhirech, relying on their master's approval of the writings and ideas of the outlawed kabbalist to justify its publication. The parallels and points of contact should not, therefore, be ascribed to derivation from a common source, but should be seen as evidence of Luzzatto's influence in hasidic doctrine.

3. We do not know, and shall never be able to determine for certain, what exactly were the writings and information which reached the nascent hasidic movement and were absorbed into it, and what was the measure of their influence. But in my opinion it is clear that important ideas and practices passed to the first hasidim from Luzzatto's writings, from members of his circle, and from his practical example, and became basic principles in the doctrine of hasidism and in its ways of life.

[81] See J. G. Weiss, 'A Circle of Pneumatics in Pre-Hasidism', *Journal of Jewish Studies*, 8 (1957), 206–8; A. Wertheim, *Halakhot vahalikhot baḥasidut* (Jerusalem, 1960) [English version, *Law and Custom in Hasidism*, trans. Shmuel Himelstein (Hoboken, NJ, 1992), iii. 226–8, 248–54].

Appendix

ORIGINAL HEBREW TITLES OF THE ESSAYS IN THIS VOLUME, AND THE PUBLICATIONS IN WHICH THEY FIRST APPEARED

1. 'Kovets shel kitvei kabalah miginzei ramḥa"l bikhetav-yad oksford 2593', *Kiryat sefer*, 53 (1978), 167–98. (Four sections added, approximately another thirty pages in the Hebrew.)
2. 'Shirim ufiyutim miginzei rabi mosheh ḥayim lutsato (bikhetav-yad gintsburg 745)', *Molad*, NS 7 (30) (1976), 346–72 [Part A]; 'Tefilot miginzei r' mosheh ḥayim lutsato', *Molad*, NS 8 (31) (1980), 122–32 [Part B].
3. 'Hatesisah hameshiḥit beḥugo shel ramḥa"l le'oram shel ketubah veshirim meshiḥiyim', in S. W. Baron *et al.* (eds.), *Sefer-yovel leyitsḥak ber bimelot lo shivim shanah/Yitzhak F. Baer Jubilee Volume on the Occasion of his Seventieth Birthday* (Jerusalem, 1960), 374–94; reprinted in *Netivei emunah uminut*, 186–203, 322–31.
4. 'Yaḥaso shel r' mosheh ḥayim lutsato el hashabeta'ut', *Tarbiz*, 27 (1958), 334–57; reprinted in *Netivei emunah uminut*, 169–85, 316–23.
5. 'Kavei hatenuah hashabeta'it udemuto shel shabetai tsevi bekhitvei ramḥa"l vetalmidav', in Menahem Ben-Sasson, Robert Bonfil, and Joseph R. Hacker (eds.), *Tarbut veḥevrah betoledot yisra'el bimei habeinayim: kovets ma'amarim lezikhro shel ḥayim hilel ben-sason/Culture and Society in Medieval Jewry: Studies Dedicated to the Memory of Haim Hillel Ben-Sasson* (Jerusalem, 1989), 687–715.
6. 'Demuto shel rabi mosheh david vale (ramda"v) uma'amado baḥavurat ramḥa"l', in S. Ettinger, H. Beinart, and M. Shtern (eds.), *Sefer zikaron leyitsḥak ber/Yitzhak F. Baer Memorial Volume* (= *Zion*, 44 (1979)) (Jerusalem, 1980), 265–302.
7. 'Yoman misti-meshiḥi ḥavayati veḥezyoni / lerabi mosheh david vale (ramda"v)'. The Introduction was first published as 'Reshimot ḥavayatiyot veḥezyoniyot shel r' mosheh david vale (ramda"v): hamashiaḥ hameyu'ad baḥavurat ramḥa"l', in M. Idel, W. Z. Harvey, and E. Schweid (eds.), *Sefer hayovel lishelomoh pines: bimelot lo shemonim shanah/Shlomo Pines Jubilee Volume: On the Occasion of his Eightieth Birthday*, ii (Jerusalem, 1990), 441–72. [The 'Complete List' was apparently not previously published.—Trans.]

8. 'Darkhei hafatsatam shel kitvei kabalah leramḥa"l bepolin uvelita', *Kiryat sefer*, 45 (1970), 127–54. Addenda: 'Sefer mesilat yesharim, mahadurat zolkva tak-kha"v', ibid. 300; 'Havharot lehe'arot be'inyenei ramḥa"l ver' yekutiel gordon mivilna (re'eh le'eil a' 452)', ibid. 628.

9. ' "Kudsha berikh hu orayta veyisra'el kola ḥad": mekor ha'imrah beferush "idra raba" leramḥa"l', *Kiryat sefer*, 50 (1975), 480–92. Addenda: ibid. 668–74.

10. 'Ikevot rabi mosheh ḥayim lutsato bemishnat haḥasidut', *Zion*, 43 (1978), 201–34.

Glossary

Aba 'Father': the 'countenance' (*partsuf*) of God corresponding to Hokhmah, the second sefirah.

aggadah Anecdote, narrative, legend, and also other material in the Talmud not directly concerned with the application of the law.

Amidah 'Standing': the 'eighteen benedictions' prayer (actually nineteen on weekdays, seven on Sabbaths) recited standing.

Ari (the Ari) Isaac Luria (*ha'elohi rabi yitsḥak*, 'the godly rabbi Isaac').

Arikh Anpin The 'Slow to Anger', the Forbearant: in the upper sefirot, representing mercy and compassion. Also called Atika Kadisha, 'the Holy Ancient One'.

Ashkenaz The German-speaking countries of Europe. **Ashkenazim**: Jews who live in or come from those countries or from eastern Europe.

atsilut 'Emanation': the first of the four worlds of 'emanation, creation, formation, and making'.

Av The fifth month reckoning from Nisan; the eleventh reckoning from Tishrei. 9 Av (Tishah Be'av), the date on which the first and second Temples were destroyed, is a day of fasting and mourning in the Jewish calendar.

av beit din President of a rabbinical court (*beit din*, literally 'house of judgement').

beit midrash (plural *batei midrash*) 'House of study': a house or room used for the study of Torah and rabbinical literature.

Besht (the Besht) R. Israel ben Eliezer, 'the Ba'al Shem Tov' ('Master of the Divine Name').

Binah 'Understanding': the third of the ten sefirot.

breaking of the vessels Vessels in all the sefirot were intended to receive the light which flowed from Ein Sof in the process of Creation. The light proved too strong for the vessels in the lower sefirot and shattered them.

Council of Four Lands Jewish self-governing body, responsible for relations with the Polish government and for internal matters, from the mid sixteenth century until 1764. The 'four lands' were the provinces of Great Poland, Little Poland, 'the Lvov area' (Galicia), and Volhynia.

devekut (from the verb *davak*, 'stick' or 'adhere') Cleaving to God in intense devotion. See the discussion in Essay 10.

Din 'Stern Judgement': the fifth of the ten sefirot.

Doenmeh A sect, founded by followers of Shabetai Tsevi after his apostasy, nominally converted to Islam but privately continuing an attachment to Judaism.

Ein Sof The Infinite; God Transcendent.

Four Lands See 'Council of Four Lands'.

gaon 'Excellence', 'excellency'. As a title, first applied to heads of academies in Babylonia; later, to outstanding Talmudic scholars.

gemara 'Completion', 'learning': the Talmud (q.v.), more particularly the discussions and decisions etc. of the rabbis.

gematriyah Interpretation of words and phrases in Scripture, and of names, dates, etc., by equating them with other Hebrew words whose letters have the same total numerical value as in the expression interpreted. See 'numerical values'.

Gevurah 'Might': another name for the sefirah Din.

golem An automaton, made by kabbalistic or miraculous means, which served its human maker.

Gra (the Gra) The Vilna Gaon, R. Elijah ben Solomon (*hagaon rabenu eliyahu*).

Habad (*ḥokhmah*, *binah*, *da'at*: wisdom, understanding, knowledge) The hasidic movement founded by R. Shneur Zalman of Lyady.

ḥakham Wise or learned man, sage. A title of respect accorded to rabbis in Sephardi communities.

halakhah Jewish law in its practical application.

ḥashmal In Ezekiel 1, a radiant substance, understood as electrum, in the celestial chariot. In the Zohar, sparkling lights in the chariot. Plural ***ḥashmalim***: in the medieval work *Berit menuḥah*, angelic creatures, 'possessors of the power and the dominion' (Essay 1, n. 262).

hasid A pious man. An adherent of the hasidic movement. A disciple of a tsadik.

hasidism 'A movement of Jewish spiritual revival which began in southeastern Poland during the second half of the eighteenth century and came to be characterized by its charismatic leadership, mystical orientation and distinctive pattern of communal life' (A. Rapoport-Albert (ed.), *Hasidism Reappraised* (London, 1997), introd.).

Haskalah 'Enlightenment': a movement which sought to open up Jewry to the influence of Western culture.

ḥaver 'Colleague': a title bestowed on scholars of distinction.

ḥayah 'The living one': one of the two highest parts of the soul, the other being *yeḥidah*, 'the only one'.

heikhalot 'Palaces'. **Heikhalot literature**: writings relating to the seven successive heavenly palaces beyond the last of which is the Throne of Glory.

ḥerem Excommunication, ban.

Hesed 'Mercy', 'lovingkindness': the fourth of the ten sefirot.

ḥitsonim 'External ones': the forces of evil.

Hod 'Majesty': the eighth of the ten sefirot.

Hokhmah 'Wisdom': the second of the ten sefirot.

Hoshana Rabah 'The Great Hoshana [*hosha na*, 'save, we pray You']': seventh day of Tabernacles, with special ceremonies and prayers for salvation.

ibur 'Impregnation': the reimpregnation of a soul into the body of another person.

Idra raba*, *Idra zuta 'The Great Assembly', 'The Lesser Assembly': two of the divisions of the Zohar.

Ima 'Mother': the 'countenance' (*partsuf*) of God corresponding to the sefirah Binah.

kavanah (plural *kavanot*) 'Intention', 'devotion'. Mystical meditation.

kelipot (singular *kelipah*) 'Shells', 'husks': the forces of evil.

Keter 'Crown': the first of the ten sefirot.

ketubah Marriage contract.

klaus*, *kloyz Small house of prayer used by hasidim.

Lilith The consort of the wicked angel Sama'el.

ma'aseh merkavah The structure, or the making, of the chariot. See Essay 1, pp. 80–4.

magid 'One who declares or announces'. In everyday use, a preacher. In kabbalah, a messenger from Heaven.

Malkhut 'Sovereignty': the tenth sefirah. Identified with the Shekhinah, the Divine Presence.

mashpia The transmitter of the divine flow: M. D. Valle's word for the spiritual force which brought him inspiration and revelations from Heaven.

maskil 'Enlightened': a person identifying himself with the Haskalah movement (see above).

mevarer 'One who sorts or sifts out': a term applied by Valle to his own function of recovering sparks of holiness to return them to their root. Translated in these essays as 'winnower'.

Mishnah A compilation of the Jewish oral law supplementing the biblical commandments and codified about the end of the second century CE. It is divided into six orders (*sedarim*), each of which is subdivided into tractates (*masekhtot*), which in turn are divided into numbered paragraphs. Each such paragraph is called a *mishnah* (plural *mishnayot*).

mitnaged An opponent of hasidism.

mitsvah (plural *mitsvot*) A commandment. Applied to all the 613 commandments identified in the Pentateuch, and to their fulfilment; also extended to meritorious deeds.

musar 'Reproof': ethical teachings.

nefilat apayim 'Falling on one's face': in a kabbalistic context, the bowed posture adopted by some mystics seeking to commune with the upper world through meditation.

Ne'ilah 'Closing': the concluding prayer ('at the time of the closing of the gate') on the Day of Atonement.

Netsah 'Endurance for ever': the seventh of the ten sefirot.

Nogah 'Brightness': the name of one of the husks of evil. (In other contexts, the planet Venus.)

notarikon A device which takes every letter of a word as an initial or abbreviation of some other word.

Nukba 'The female'. **Nukba deze'ir**: the 'countenance' (*partsuf*) of God corresponding to the tenth sefirah, Malkhut (the Shekhinah), which is the female counterpart of Ze'ir Anpin. But Nukba elsewhere means Lilith (q.v.).

numerical values The twenty-two letters of the Hebrew alphabet are used as numerals. The first ten, *alef* to *yod*, represent the numerals 1 to 10. Teens are made up of *yod* and the letter representing the appropriate digit, except that 15 and 16 are usually *tet vav* and *tet zayin* (9+6 and 9+7) to avoid spelling a name of God. The letters *kaf* to *kof* stand for 20 to 100; *resh*, *shin*, *tav* for 200, 300, 400; intermediate and higher numbers are made up by combining letters.

Omer, days of The period of seven weeks to be counted day by day from the second night of Passover (taken as 'the Sabbath' referred to in Lev. 23: 15 when a sheaf (*omer*) from the barley harvest was offered) until the festival of Shavuot.

partsufim 'Faces': 'countenances' of God corresponding to the sefirot.

pilpul (from *pilpel*, 'pepper') Argument based on subtle distinctions.

piyut A religious poem intended for use in the liturgy.

posek (plural *posekim*) A rabbi whose ruling (*pesak*) on the practical application of Jewish law is regarded as authoritative, within his community or more widely.

Rahamim 'Compassion': the sixth sefirah, also called Tiferet (q.v.).

reshimu A residue of divine light remaining in primordial space after the withdrawal of Ein Sof into Himself (*tsimtsum*) in the process of Creation.

Sama'el Leader of 'the other side', the forces of evil.

sefirot (singular sefirah) The ten attributes or powers through which Ein Sof (God the Infinite) manifests Himself. In descending order, they are: 1 Keter Elyon, the supreme crown; 2 Hokhmah, wisdom; 3 Binah, understanding; 4 Hesed, lovingkindness; 5 Din, stern judgement; 6 Rahamim, compassion; 7 Netsah, endurance for ever; 8 Hod, majesty; 9 Yesod, foundation (of the world); 10 Malkhut, sovereignty, identified with the Shekhinah, God's presence.

sevara Conclusions reached by reasoning.

Shabat Bereshit The first Sabbath after Tabernacles, when the annual cycle of Pentateuch readings begins in the synagogue with *bereshit*, 'in the beginning', Gen. 1: 1 to 6: 8.

Shabat Hagadol 'The great Sabbath': the Sabbath immediately before Passover.

Shaharit The morning prayers (*shaḥar* means 'dawn').

Shavuot 'Weeks': Pentecost. See 'Omer, days of'.

Shekhinah (from the verb *shakhan*, 'dwell') The Divine Presence. See 'Malkhut'.

Shema, the The three paragraphs Deut. 6: 4–9 (beginning 'Hear [*shema*], O Israel'), Deut. 11: 13–21, and Num. 15: 37–41, which are recited together in morning and evening prayers.

Shemini Atseret The eighth day (*shemini*) of Tabernacles, a day of 'solemn assembly' (*atseret*).

Shemoneh Esreh 'Eighteen': the 'eighteen benedictions'. See 'Amidah'.

Sitra Ahra 'The Other Side': the forces of evil.

Talmud The Mishnah (q.v.) together with the discussions and decisions of the rabbis on its practical application, but branching out into ethics, theology, sayings of the rabbis, anecdote, and legend (aggadah). There are two versions: the Babylonian and the Jerusalem Talmud, the Babylonian Talmud being the more comprehensive and accepted as generally more authoritative.

tana (plural *tana'im*) Strictly, one of the teachers in the first two centuries CE whose rulings on the practical application of Jewish law were incorporated in the Talmud. It could, however, be applied hyperbolically to a much admired teacher such as Luzzatto.

tehiru The primordial space.

Tiferet 'Beauty', 'Splendour': a male sefirah, the sixth in order (known also as Rahamim) and the spouse of the Shekhinah.

tikun Repair, restoration, perfection; actions designed by the mystics to raise up the Shekhinah from her exile among the husks and restore her to her perfect state.

Tikunei hazohar One of the books of the Zohar. A series of commentaries, each called a *tikun*, on Gen. 1–6: 8.

Tikun Leil Shavuot A night-long study session on the night of the festival of Shavuot.

Torah 'Instruction'. Applied not only to the written and oral law but also to a person's knowledge or study of the Torah or to an authority's teachings or doctrine.

tsadik Righteous; a righteous man. In hasidism, a spiritual leader revered by his followers.

Tsadik Another name for the sefirah Yesod. **Tsadik yesod olam**: 'Tsadik the foundation of the world'.

tselem An 'image' unique to every individual which facilitates the joining of soul to body. Souls descending from paradise to join the body clothe themselves in the *tselem*; on leaving the body at its death, they clothe themselves in the perfected *tselem*.

tsimtsum The contraction of Ein Sof into Himself to make room for Creation.

yated A metrical foot consisting of one short vowel and one long vowel.

yeḥidah 'The only one': one of the two highest parts of the soul, the other being *ḥayah*, 'the living one'.

yeshiva An academy for Jewish religious studies.

Yesod The ninth of the ten sefirot. See 'Tsadik'.

yiḥudim (singular *yiḥud*) 'Unifications'. See Essay 1, pp. 59–60.

Ze'ir, Ze'eir Anpin 'The impatient': a designation for the six lower sefirot, not counting the Shekhinah.

Zohar 'Splendour', 'brilliance': title of the most celebrated of all kabbalistic works, first brought to notice in the thirteenth century but authorship traditionally ascribed to R. Simeon ben Yohai, second century CE.

Bibliography

MANUSCRIPTS

Ben Tsevi Institute, Jerusalem, I. Sonne papers. Hebrew translation from Italian of a eulogy on Luzzatto (published in *American Jewish Yearbook* (1935): see under Sonne in 'Works Cited' section below).

BL: British Museum manuscripts now in the British Library

385–92. Eight volumes by Moses David Valle on the books of the Bible with additional material on rabbinic literature and the Zohar. MS 387 contains a homily by Valle for the night of 17 Shevat 5492 (1732).

860. Luzzatto's *Da'at tevunot*, under the title *Vikuaḥ shebein hasekhel vehaneshamah* [Discussion between the Intellect and the Soul].

1075. Copy of Luzzatto's *Milḥemet mosheh* made by J. Almanzi in 1830.

Add. 27160. Writings by Moses David Valle.

Or. 9165. Contains letter from R. Abraham Rovigo to R. Mordecai Eisenstadt (early 1680) describing Shabetai Tsevi as Messiah ben Joseph.

Or. 10860 (Gaster Collection). See below under Oxford Heb. f. 120.

Cincinnati 501 (Hebrew Union College Library, Cincinnati). Contains Luzzatto's commentary on *Idra raba*, and the rules of the Paduan 'holy society'.

Columbia University, New York

17 *alef* 893. Contains Luzzatto's *Yiḥud hayirah* with his commentary.

X893/Z8, vol. i, no. 20. A collection of Shabatean writings. Contains Nathan of Gaza's *Raza demalka meshiḥa* [Mystery of the King-Messiah], fragments.

Guenzburg 376 = Coronel 28, London (photo in Ben Tsevi Institute, Jerusalem). Kabbalistic and other writings by Luzzatto, including his mystical marriage contract and commentary on *Idra raba*. (The commentary on *Idra raba* is also in MS Warsaw 149.)

Guenzburg 517, Moscow (photo in Ben Tsevi Institute, Jerusalem). Elijah Mojajon of Ancona, responsa to R. Benjamin Hakohen on Shabatean kabbalah.

Guenzburg 745 (photo in Ben Tsevi Institute, Jerusalem). Poems and *piyutim* by Luzzatto and others.

Harvard 54 (Houghton Library, Harvard University). A collection of Luzzatto's writings. Includes *mishnayot* appended to the lost work *Mishkenei elyon* [The Dwelling of the Most High]; and the *Vikuaḥ* [Discussion] between 'Mar Yanuka' and 'Mar Kashisha' ['Mr Child' and 'Mr Old'].

Jerusalem: Jewish National and University Library

1466. A 'revelation', believed to be by R. Baer Perlhefter, giving information about Perlhefter and R. Mordecai Ashkenazi as '*magidim*'.

2365. Contains Luzzatto's *Vikuaḥ* [Discussion] between 'Mar Yanuka' and 'Mar Kashisha' ['Mr Child' and 'Mr Old'].

2517 8° (previously MS Warsaw). Contains work incorrectly named *Kelalim rishonim* [First Principles]. See Essay 1, n. 97.

3177 8°. *Sefer habahir*, with commentaries *Or layesharim* [Light for the Upright], edited by Moses Solomon of Tulchin, and *Or layehudim* [Light for the Jews], by Zadok ben Noah Bloch.

5217 8° (previously MS Warsaw). Contains Moses David Valle's *Shivim panim* (see below under Valle) and an anonymous homily on Eccles. 9: 7, probably composed for the night of 17 Shevat (see Essay 10, nn. 71, 72).

Manuscript collection. Meir ben Elijah's *Milḥamot hashem* [Wars of the Lord]. Two copies; catalogued as completed in Jerusalem in 1892.

Schwadron Collection. Contains four poems for Luzzatto's wedding, by R. Solomon David Treves and others.

Jewish Theological Seminary, New York

2213. Gift of H. G. Friedman. Moses David Valle's *I sette giorni della Verità*.

Adler 886: see Mic. 1599 below.

Kaufmann 26. Moses David Valle's exposition of Proverbs (1769).

Kaufmann 27. Moses David Valle's expositions of Ecclesiastes, Song of Songs, and Psalm 45 (1758–9).

Kaufmann 255 (photo in Schocken Institute, Jerusalem). Contains R. Israel Hazan's *Perush mizmorei tehilim* [Commentary on Psalms].

Kaufmann 462. [Moses David Valle's] *Sefer halikutim* [The Book of Gleanings], 2 vols.

Mic. 1051. Moses David Valle's expositions of Judges, Esther, Ruth, Samuel, Kings, Hosea (1771–3).

Mic. 1052. Moses David Valle's expositions of the Twelve Prophets, Psalms (complete), Psalms (to Psalm 38) (1773–4).

Mic. 1053. Moses David Valle's expositions of Psalms, Song of the Sea, Song of Deborah, Obadiah, Exod. 32: 11 (1771).

Mic. 1054. Copy of the MS Kaufmann 27 exposition of Song of Songs.

Mic. 1585. Five prayers, from *Ḥibur al hatorah* [Treatise on the Torah]? (Luzzatto autograph?)

Mic. 1599 (previously MS Adler 886): *Likutei kabalah* [Gleanings from Kabbalah]. Writings by M. H. Luzzatto and M. D. Valle.

Mic. 1615. Contains Vital's *Otserot ḥayim*.

Mic. 4022. Contains letters from Luzzatto.

Mantua (Comunità Israelitica?) 112. Contains Luzzatto's *Yiḥud hayirah* with his commentary.

Montefiore 111 (microfiches at the Jewish National and University Library, Jerusalem, and the Oxford Centre for Hebrew and Jewish Studies). Collection of eighteenth-century letters and responsa, including letter (second half of 1730) from R. Isaac Pacifico to R. M. Hagiz about Luzzatto.

Mosad Harav Kook, Jerusalem, 252. Collection of Luzzatto's writings (authorship disguised) copied in Lvov in 1781. Includes *Kela"ḥ pitḥei ḥokhmah* [138 Gateways to Wisdom] without commentary, and part of his commentary on *Idra raba*.

Oxford: Bodleian Library (four-digit numbers refer to the entries in Neubauer, *Catalogue of the Hebrew Manuscripts in the Bodleian Library*)

1306. Contains a copy of Luzzatto's *Milḥemet mosheh* [The War of Moses] headed *Imrei binah* (title of a book by Isaac Satanov).

1901 (Reggio Collection 31). Luzzatto's *Tikunim ḥadashim* [New *tikunim*].

2237. A collection of writings by R. Jekutiel and Luzzatto. Includes *Kinat hashem tsevaot* [The Zeal of the Lord of Hosts] and, in R. Jekutiel's hand, Luzzatto's *Vikuaḥ* [Discussion] between 'Mar Yanuka' and 'Mar Kashisha' ['Mr Child' and 'Mr Old'].

2239. A collection of Shabatean writings, attributed by Neubauer to R. Isaiah Romanin but identified by Tishby as being by R. Joseph Hamits.

2285. Contains Luzzatto's *Ḥoker umekubal* [Philosopher and Kabbalist].

2307. Contains Luzzatto's *Da'at tevunot* [Knowledge with Understanding], *Kaf-dalet kishutei kalah* [Twenty-Four Ornaments of the Bride], and *Masekhet rosh hashanah* [Tractate 'New Year'].

2409. Contains anti-Hayon pamphlet of 1714, author perhaps Amsterdam Portuguese; and letter of 1725 from David Lopez Jesurun.

2430. Contains Jekutiel of Vilna's *piyut* based on the letters of 'Megilah'. See also under Jekutiel in 'Works Cited' section below.

2593 (= Opp. Add. 8° 79). The collection of Luzzatto's writings which is the subject of Essay 1.

Heb. f. 120 (photocopy in the Jewish National and University Library, Jerusalem). *Sefer hakavanot shel kol hashanah* [The Book of *kavanot* for the Whole Year] (= *Kitsur sefer hakavanot*: see under Luzzatto in 'Works Cited' section below). (Also in MS BL Or. 10860, without title-page or title.)

Oxford-Hirsch 1 (the location of this manuscript has not been traced). Luzzatto's *Da'at tevunot*, under the title *S[efer] havikuaḥ leramḥa"l* ['The Discussion' by Ramhal].

Warsaw (Jewish Historical Institute?)

99. A copy of Luzzatto's *Milḥemet mosheh*, with introduction by a disciple.

149. Contains Luzzatto's commentary on *Idra raba*.

174. Contains Luzzatto's *Da'at tevunot*.

WORKS CITED

AARON HAKOHEN OF APTA, *Keter shem tov* [The Crown of a Good Name] (Zholkva, 1795).

—— *Ner mitsvah* [The Commandment is a Lamp] (Piotrków, 1911).

—— *Or haganuz* [The Hidden Light] (Zholkva, 1800 (author's name not printed); also Vilna, 1883, 'with comments by the Gra [Vilna Gaon]').

Alfa beita deven sira [Ben Sira's Alphabet], ed. M. Steinschneider (Berlin, 1858).

ALMANZI, J., Biography of R. Moses Hayim Luzzatto of Padua: Hebrew 'letter', untitled, in *Kerem ḥemed*, 3 (1838).

—— *Toledot r' mosheh ḥayim lutsato* [Life of R. Moses Hayim Luzzatto] (Lemberg, 1879).

ALSHEIKH, H[AYIM], *Teshuat yisra'el* [The Salvation of Israel] (Fürth, 1742–5). Described as a rare book: a copy is in the Jewish National and University Library in Jerusalem.

AMARILLO, A., 'Te'udot shabeta'iyot miginzei rabi sha'ul amarilyo' [Shabatean Documents from the Collection of R. Saul Amarillo], in I. Ben-Zvi and M. Benayahu (eds.), *Sefer zikaron liyeshayahu zoneh/Isaiah Sonne Memorial Volume* (= *Sefunot*, 5) (Jerusalem, 1961).

APTOWITZER, A., 'Beit hamikdash shel malah al pi ha'agadah' [The Temple on High according to the Aggadah], *Tarbiz*, 2 (1931).

ASHKENAZI, MORDECAI, *Eshel avraham* [Abraham's Tamarisk] (Fürth, 1701).

ASHKENAZI, TSEVI, *Le'einei kol yisra'el* [In the Sight of All Israel], pamphlet published in A. Freimann, *Inyenei shabetai tsevi* [Matters concerning Shabetai Tsevi] (Berlin, 1912/13).

—— *She'elot uteshuvot* [Responsa] (Amsterdam, 1712).

—— *She'elot uteshuvot ḥakham tsevi hashalem* [The Complete Responsa of Tsevi Ashkenazi] (Debrecen, 1942).

AVIVI, YOSEF, 'Kavanat haberiah beḥiburei ramḥa"l' [The Purpose of the Creation in Luzzatto's Works], *Hamayan* (Tamuz 5745 (1985)).

—— 'Ma'amar havikuaḥ leramḥa"l' [Luzzatto's 'The Discussion'], *Hamayan* (Tishrei 5735 (1974)).

AZULAI, ABRAHAM, *Ḥesed le'avraham* [Lovingkindness to Abraham] (Amsterdam, 1685).

AZULAI, HAYIM JOSEPH DAVID, *Shem hagedolim* [Bibliography], ed. I. Benjacob (Vilna, 1856).

Babylonian Talmud (English trans.: London, 1935–52).

BAHYA IBN PAKUDA, *Ḥovot halevavot* [Duties of the Heart], Hebrew translation from Arabic by Judah ibn Tibbon, with English translation by D. Habermann (Jerusalem and New York, 1996).

BALABAN, M., *Letoledot hatenuah haferankit* [A Contribution to the History of the Frankist Movement] (Tel Aviv, 1934–5).

BARNAY, I., *Yehudei erets-yisra'el bame'ah hayod"ḥet* [Jews in the Land of Israel in the Eighteenth Century] (Jerusalem, 1982).

BARTAL, Y., 'Aliyat r' elazar me'amsterdam le'erets-yisra'el bishenat tak"a[lef]' [R. Eleazar of Amsterdam's Emigration to the Land of Israel in 5501 (1741)], in Michman (ed.), *Meḥkarim al toledot yahadut holand.*

BARUKH OF KOSOV, *Amud ha'avodah* [The Pillar of Worship] (Czernowitz, 1854).

—— *Yesod ha'emunah* [The Foundation of Faith] (Czernowitz, 1854).

Beit hamidrash [The House of Study], ed. I. H. Weiss (Vienna, 1865). A periodical.

BENAYAHU, M., 'Aliyato shel haramḥa"l le'erets yisra'el' [R. Moses Hayim Luzzatto's Emigration to the Land of Israel], in Z. Warhaftig and Sh. Y. Zevin (eds.), *Mazkeret: kovets torani lezekher yitsḥak aizik halevi hertsog* [In Memoriam: A Torah Anthology in Memory of Isaac Halevi Herzog] (Jerusalem, 1962).

—— 'Ha"magid" shel ramḥa"l' [R. Moses Hayim Luzzatto's '*magid*'], in I. Ben-Zvi and M. Benayahu (eds.), *Sefer zikaron liyeshayahu zoneh/Isaiah Sonne Memorial Volume* (= *Sefunot*, 5) (Jerusalem, 1961).

—— *Haskamah ureshut bidefusei venetsiyah* [Copyright, Authorization, and Imprimatur for Hebrew Books Printed in Venice] (Jerusalem, 1971).

—— 'Hatenuah hashabeta'it beyavan' [The Shabatean Movement in Greece], *Sefunot*, 14 (1971–8).

—— 'Ketavav shel yeshayah romanin mipadova' [The Writings of Isaiah Romanin of Padua], *Bar-Ilan*, 14–15 (1977).

—— *Kitvei hakabalah sheleramḥa"l* [Luzzatto's Kabbalistic Writings] (Jerusalem, 1979).

—— 'Piyut, tefilah uviduy mikivshono shel ramḥa"l shene'emru baḥavurah berosh hashanah leyisudah' [*Piyut*, Prayer, and Confession from the 'Hidden' Writings of Luzzatto, Recited in the Group on the Anniversary of its Foundation], *Sinai*, 82 (1978).

—— 'R' avraham hakohen mizante velahakat harofe'im-hameshorerim bepadova' [R. Abraham Hakohen of Zante and the Group of Doctor-Poets in Padua], *Hasifrut*, 26 (1978).

—— *R' ḥayim yosef david azulai* (Jerusalem, 1959).

—— *R' ya'akov vilna uveno veyaḥaseihem lashabeta'ut* [R. Jacob Wilna and his Son and their Connections with Shabateanism] (Jerusalem, 1954).

—— 'R' yitsḥak karigal be'italyah' [R. Isaac Carigal in Italy], *Otsar yehudei sefarad*, 1 (1959).

—— *Sefer toledot ha'ar"i* [The Book *Toledot ha'ar"i* ('Life of Luria')] (Jerusalem, 1967).

BENAYAHU, M., 'Shevuat ramḥa"l laḥdol mileḥaber sefarim al-pi ha"magid", mahutah vetotse'oteiha' [Luzzatto's Sworn Undertaking to Cease Writing Books at the Dictation of the '*magid*': Its Nature and its Results], *Zion*, 42 (1977).

—— 'Shirei ḥupah ḥadashim leramḥa"l' [New Wedding Poems by Rabbi M. H. Luzzatto], *Hasifrut*, 24 (1977).

—— 'Shirim leyom ḥatunato shel ramḥa"l' [Poems for Luzzatto's Wedding Day], in *Shai leheiman: meḥkarim basifrut ha'ivrit shel yemei habeinayim (Sefer haberman)/Papers on Medieval Hebrew Literature Presented to A. M. Habermann (A. M. Habermann Jubilee Volume)* (Jerusalem, 1977).

—— 'Tefilot shenityaḥasu leramḥa"l ve'einan lo utefilot shelo nizkar bahen shemo vehen lo' [Prayers Attributed to Luzzatto which are not by him and Prayers in which his Name is not Mentioned but which are by him], *Sinai*, 78 (1976).

—— 'Tefilot veyiḥudim lahasagah shel ramḥa"l' [Prayers and *yiḥudim* as Aids to Luzzatto's Grasp of the Divine Mysteries], in *Temirin: Texts and Studies in Kabbala and Hasidism*, ii (Jerusalem, 1981).

BEN-ISH, A., 'Te'udot letoledot ramḥa"l' [Luzzatto: Biographical Documents], *Metsudah*, 3–4 (1945).

BENJACOB, I., *Otsar hasefarim* [A Bibliography] (Vilna, 1880; New York, 1965).

BEN-MENAHEM, N., 'Arba mahadurot shel "mesilat yesharim", zolkva' [Four Zholkva Editions of *Mesilat yesharim*], *Areshet*, 1 (1959).

—— *Kitvei rabi mosheh ḥayim lutsato* [The Writings of R. Moses Hayim Luzzatto] (Jerusalem, 1951).

—— 'Kol shaḥal: shirei efrayim lutsato' [The Voice of a Lion: Poems of Ephraim Luzzatto], *Kiryat sefer*, 44 (1969). Article on the 1796 edition of Ephraim Luzzatto's poems.

BEN-SASSON, Y., 'Olamam haruḥani umishnatam haḥinukhit shel meyasedei hayeshivah halita'it' [The Spiritual World and Educational Doctrine of the Founders of the Lithuanian Yeshiva], in *Ḥinukh ha'adam veyi'udo* [The Education and Mission of Man] (Jerusalem, 1967).

BEN YEHUDAH, ELIEZER, *Milon halashon ha'ivrit hayeshanah vehaḥadashah* [Dictionary of the Hebrew Language, Ancient and Modern], 17 vols. (Jerusalem, 1910–59).

Bereshit rabah [Genesis Rabbah], ed. J. Theodor and Ch. Albeck (Berlin, 1928–9; Jerusalem, 1936).

Berit menuḥah [Covenant of Rest] (Amsterdam, 1648; Jerusalem, 1973).

BERMAN, S., and M. RABINOWITZ, 'Mishpeḥot k"k sheklov' [Families of the Holy Congregation of Shklov], *Kovets al yad*, NS 1 (11) (Jerusalem, 1936).

BERNSTEIN, S., *König Nebucadnezar von Babel* (Berlin, 1908).

BIALIK, H. N., '"Habaḥur mipadova"' ['The Young Man from Padua'], in *Kol kitvei ḥ"n bialik* [Collected Writings] (Tel Aviv, 1938).

BLOCH, R. JOSEPH, *Ginzei yosef* (Lvov, 1792). Commentary on the Torah.

BRAWER, A. J., 'Makor ivri ḥadash letoledot ferank vesiato' [A New Hebrew Source Contributing to our Knowledge of Frank and his Sect], *Hashiloaḥ* (Odessa), 33 (1917).

BUBER, M., *Befardes haḥasidut* [In the 'Orchard' of Hasidism] (Jerusalem, 1945).

BUBER, S., *Kiryah nisgavah* [Lofty City] (Kraków, 1903).

BUZAGLO, R. SHALOM, *Mikdash melekh* [Royal Sanctuary] (Żółkiew, 1794).

CARO, JOSEPH, *Magid meisharim* [[I] Tell what is Right] (Amsterdam, 1708).

—— *Shulḥan arukh* (Amsterdam, 1757–85). 'A Table Laid': an authoritative codification of Jewish law.

CORDOVERO, R. MOSES, *Derishot be'inyenei hamalakhim* [Expositions Relating to the Angels], published in Margaliot, *Malakhei elyon*.

—— *Pardes rimonim* [An Orchard of Pomegranates] (Kraków, 1592; Munkács, 1906).

DAN, J., 'Bein shir meshiḥi lesoneta ligevurah' [Messianic Poem versus Sonnet to Valour], *Tarbiz*, 31 (1962). An answer to the following item.

DAVID, Y., 'Shir meshiḥi o soneta ligevurah?' [Messianic Poem or Sonnet to Valour?], *Tarbiz*, 31 (1962).

DAVIDSON, I., *Otsar hashirah vehapiyut* [Thesaurus of Poetry and *piyut*] (New York, 1970).

DE VIDAS, ELIJAH, *Reshit ḥokhmah* [The Beginning of Wisdom] (Amsterdam, 1708).

DINUR, B., *Bemifneh hadorot* [At the Turning-Point of the Generations] (Jerusalem, 1955).

DOV BAER OF MEZHIRECH [the Maggid of Mezhirech], *Magid devarav leya'akov* [He Declares His Words to Jacob], 2nd (enlarged) edn. (Korets, 1784); ed. Rivkah Schatz (Jerusalem, 1976).

—— *Or ha'emet* [The Light of Truth] (Husiatyn, 1799).

——*Or torah* [The Light of the Torah] (Korets, 1804).

EIDELBERG, S., 'Igeret shenishleḥah mivenetsiyah lemets bemaḥatsit hame'ah hayod"ḥet (letoledot ḥayav shel harofe r' yekutiel gordon)' [A Letter Sent from Venice to Metz in the Middle of the Eighteenth Century: Biographical Information on the Physician R. Jekutiel Gordon], in Saul Lieberman (ed.), *Salo Wittmayer Baron: Jubilee Volume on the Occasion of his Eightieth Birthday*, iii [Hebrew section] (New York, 1975).

EISENSTADT, I. T., and S. WIENER, *Da'at kedoshim* [The Wisdom of Holy Men] (St Petersburg, 1897–8).

EISENSTEIN, JUDAH DAVID, *Otsar midrashim* [Thesaurus] (New York, 1915).

ELIJAH BEN SOLOMON ZALMAN: see under Vilna Gaon.

ELIMELEKH OF LYZHANSK, *No'am elimelekh* (Tarnów, 1904).

ELIOR, RACHEL, *Torat ha'elohut bador hasheni shel ḥasidut haba"d* [The Theory of Divinity in the Second Generation of Habad Hasidism] (Jerusalem, 1982).

EMDEN, R. JACOB [asterisked dates are as in Raphael, 'Kitvei rabi ya'akov emden'].

—— *Akitsat akrav* [The Sting of a Scorpion] (Amsterdam, 1753?*).

—— *Aspaklaryah hame'irah* [The Shining Mirror] (Altona, 1753*); as appendix to *Sefat emet uleshon zehorit* [The Language of Truth and the Silken Tongue] (Lvov, 1877).

—— *Beit yehonatan hasofer* [The House of Jonathan the Scribe] (1763?*).

—— *Edut beya'akov* [A Testimony in Jacob] (Altona, 1756*).

—— *Hitabekut* [The Wrestling [of 'the man' (Gen. 32) with Jacob] (Altona, 1762*).

—— *Sefat emet uleshon zehorit* [The Language of Truth and the Silken Tongue] (Altona(?), 1752; Lvov, 1877*).

—— *Sefer shimush* [A Handbook] (Amsterdam [actually Altona], 1758–62?*).

—— *Shevirat luḥot ha'aven* [The Breaking of the Tablets of Evil [the title is a play on *luḥot ha'even*, 'the tablets of stone']] (Zholkva [actually Altona], 1756*).

—— *Zot torat hakenaot* [This is the Law of Jealousies [Num. 5: 29]] (Altona, 1752). Also published as *Torat hakenaot* (Lvov, 1870).

EMMANUEL, I. S., 'Ḥakham david lopes yesurun unesiato la'arets' [*Ḥakham* David Lopez Jesurun and his Journey to the Land of Israel], in *Minḥah le'avraham: sefer yovel likhevod avraham elmalyah* [An Offering to Abraham: Festschrift in Honour of Abraham Elmaleh] (Jerusalem, 1959).

Encyclopaedia Judaica, 16 vols. (Jerusalem, 1971–2).

EPHRAIM [MOSES HAYIM EPHRAIM] OF SUDYLKOV, *Degel maḥaneh efrayim* [The Banner of the Camp of Ephraim] (Korets, 1810).

ERGAS, J., *Tokhaḥat megulah* [Open Rebuke] (London, 1715).

ETKES, I., 'Shitato ufa'olo shel r' ḥayim mivoloz'in kiteguvat haḥevrah ha"mitnagedit" laḥasidut' [The Doctrine and Work of R. Hayim of Volozhin as a Response of Mitnagedic Society to Hasidism], *Proceedings of the American Academy for Jewish Research*, 38–9 (1972).

EYBESCHUETZ, R. JONATHAN, *Luḥot edut* [Tables of Testimony] (Altona, 1755).

—— *Shem olam* [Everlasting Renown] (Vienna, 1891).

FEINSTEIN, A. L., *Ir tehilah* [City of Renown] (Warsaw, 1885).

FINE, L., 'The Practice of Yihudim in Lurianic Kabbalah', *Jewish Spirituality*, 2 (1987).

FREIMANN, ARON, *Inyenei shabetai tsevi* [Matters Concerning Shabetai Tsevi] (Berlin, 1912/13).

FRIEDBERG, H. D., *Toledot hadefus ha'ivri bepolonyah* [History of Hebrew Printing Houses in Poland] (Antwerp, 1932; Tel Aviv, 1950).

FRIEDMANN, M., 'Igerot befarashat pulmus neḥemyah ḥiya ḥayon' [Letters Relating to the Hayon Controversy], *Sefunot*, 10 (1966).

FRUMKIN, A. L., *Toledot ḥakhmei yerushalayim* [Lives of the Sages of Jerusalem], ii (Jerusalem, 1928).

FUERST, J., *Bibliotheca Judaica*, 3 vols. (Leipzig, 1849–63; repr. Hildesheim, 1960).

GABBAI, R. MEIR IBN, *Avodat hakodesh* [Sacred Service] (Venice, 1567–8).

GAD, HAYIM YOSEF ISAR BEN YITSHAK HALEVI, *Asarah me'orot hagedolim* [The Ten Great Luminaries] (Johannesburg, 1952). Bible commentary.

Galei razaya [Revealer of Secrets]: see next item.

Galya raza [Revelation of a Secret] (Mogilev, 1812); ed. Rachel Elior (Jerusalem, 1981) as *Galei razaya*.

GEDALIAH OF LUNIETZ, R., *Teshuot ḥen* [Cries of 'Grace'] (Berdichev, 1816).

GHIRONDI, JOSEPH, 'Al devar toledot hagaon r' mosheh ḥayim lutsato . . .', *Kerem ḥemed*, 2 (1836). Two biographical letters on Luzzato.

GHIRONDI, MORDECAI SAMUEL, *Toledot gedolei yisra'el ugeonei italyah* [Lives of the Great Rabbis of Israel and the Great Sages of Italy] (Trieste, 1853). Printed together with H. Neppi's *Zekher tsadikim liverakhah* (see below).

GINZBURG, S., *The Life and Works of Moses Hayyim Luzzatto* (Philadelphia, 1931).

GOTTLIEB, E., 'Ma'amrei ha"pikudin" shebazohar' [The 'Commandments' Sections in the Zohar], *Kiryat sefer*, 48 (1973). Also in *Meḥkarim besifrut hakabalah*.

—— *Meḥkarim besifrut hakabalah* [Studies in the Literature of Kabbalah], ed. Y. Hacker (Tel Aviv, 1976).

GRAETZ, H., *Geschichte der Juden von den ältesten Zeiten bis auf die Gegenwart*, 11 vols. (Leipzig, 1897–1911).

GUTMAN, M. E., *Rabi pinḥas mikorets: ḥayav pe'ulotav vetorato* [Rabbi Phinehas of Korets: His Life and Work and his Doctrine] (Tel Aviv, 1950).

HAGIZ, M., *Milḥamah lashem veḥerev lashem* [War for the Lord and a Sword for the Lord] (Amsterdam [actually London], 1714).

—— *Shever poshe'im* [Destruction of Transgressors] (Amsterdam [actually London], 1714).

Hamazkir. Hebräische Bibliographie: Blätter für neuere und ältere Literatur des Judenthums, ed. M. Steinschneider and J. Benzian (Berlin, 1858–82).

HANNOVER, NATHAN NATA, *Sha'arei tsiyon* [The Gates of Zion] (Amsterdam, 1671).

HAVER, ISAAC EISIK [WILDMANN] OF KOMARNO, *Amudei hatorah* [Pillars of the Torah] (Jerusalem, 1880).

—— *Be'er yitsḥak* (Warsaw, 1889). Commentary on Vilna Gaon, *Likutei hager"a*.

—— *Beit olamim* [An Everlasting House] (Warsaw, 1889). Commentary on *Idra raba*.

—— *Ginzei meromim* [The Treasury on High] ([Johannisburg], 1864). Commentary on the kabbalistic work *Masekhta atsilut*.

—— *Heikhal haberakhah* [The Palace of Blessing] (Lemberg, 1866). Commentary on the Torah.

—— *Magen vetsinah* [Buckler and Shield] ([Königsberg?], n.d. [before 1853], without author's name; repr. Benei Berak, 1985).

HAVER, ISAAC EISIK, *Netiv mitsvoteikha* [The Path of Your Commandments] (n.p., n.d.).

—— *Pitḥei she'arim* [Gateways] (Warsaw, 1888).

HAYIM HAYKEL OF AMDUR, *Ḥayim vaḥesed* (Warsaw, 1891).

HAYIM OF VOLOZHIN [VOLOZHINER], *Nefesh haḥayim* (Vilna, 1837).

—— *Ruaḥ ḥayim* (Vilna, 1859).

HAYON, NEHEMIAH, *Divrei neḥemyah* (Berlin, 1713).

—— *Hatsad tsevi* [Hunter of 'the Deer'] (Amsterdam, 1714).

—— *Oz lelohim uveit kodesh kodashim* [Strength for God and The House of the Holy of Holies] (Berlin, 1713).

—— *Raza deyiḥuda* [The Mystery of the *yiḥud*] (Venice, 1711).

—— *Shalhevet yah* [A Flame of the Lord] (Amsterdam, 1714).

HAZAN, R. ISRAEL, *Perush mizmorei tehilim* [Commentary on Psalms]. See 'Manuscripts' section above, Jewish Theological Seminary, New York, MS Kaufmann 255.

HELLER, MESHULAM FEIVUSH (PHOEBUS), OF ZBARAZH, *Yosher divrei emet* ['Uprightly, Words of Truth'] (Munkács, 1905).

Ḥemdat yamim [The Most Desirable of Days] (Smyrna, 1731/2, printed by I. J. ben Yom Tov Algazi; Venice, 1758).

HERLING, I. E., 'He'arot neḥemyah ḥiyah ḥayon bikhetav yado lesefer esh dat ler' david ni'eto' [Comments by R. Nehemiah Hiyah Hayon in his Own Hand on R. David Nieto's Book *Esh dat*], *Kiryat sefer*, 15 (1938–9).

HESCHEL, A. J., 'Al ruaḥ hakodesh bimei habeinayim (ad zemano shel haramba"m)' [On the Holy Spirit in the Middle Ages (up to the Time of Maimonides)], in S. Lieberman (ed.), *Alexander Marx: Jubilee Volume on the Occasion of his Seventieth Birthday*, Hebrew vol. *Sefer hayovel likhevod aleksander marks* (New York, 1950).

—— 'Letoledot r' pinḥas mikorets' [A Historical Study on R. Phinehas of Korets], in *Alei ayin: minḥat devarim lishelomoh zalman shoken aḥarei mele'ot lo shivim shanah* ['By a Spring' [Gen. 49: 22; letter *ayin* also = 70]: Papers Offered to Solomon Zalman Schocken on his Seventieth Birthday] (Jerusalem, 1948–52).

HESCHEL, ABRAHAM JOSHUA, OF APTA, *Eser kedushot ler' yisra'el berger* [R. Israel Berger's 'Ten Sanctifications'] (Piotrków, 1906).

HOESHKE, REUBEN: see *Yalkut re'uveni* below.

HORODEZKY, S. A., 'R' mosheh ḥayim lutsato kimekubal' [R. Moses Hayim Luzzatto as a Kabbalist], *Keneset*, 5 (1940).

HOROWITZ, ISAIAH HALEVI, *Shenei luḥot haberit* [= *Shela"h*] [The Two Tablets of the Covenant] (Amsterdam, 1648).

HOROWITZ, TS. H., *Kitvei hageonim* [Writings of the Great Rabbis] (Piotrków, 1928).

HOROWITZ, TSEVI JOSHUA BEN SAMUEL SHMELKE, *Tsava'at hariba"sh* [Testament of the Ba'al Shem Tov; Horowitz's own initials yield the same acronym, *riba"sh*] (Brooklyn, 1975).

IDEL, M., 'Hasefirot sheme'al hasefirot' [The Sefirot above the Sefirot], *Tarbiz*, 51 (1982).

—— 'Hayaḥas lanatsrut besefer hameshiv' [The Book *Hameshiv* and Christianity], *Zion*, 46 (1981).

—— *Kabbalah: New Perspectives* (New Haven, 1988).

—— 'Kitvei r' avraham abulafiyah umishnato' [The Writings and Doctrine of R. Abraham Abulafia] (doctoral thesis, mimeographed; Jerusalem, 1976).

—— *Language, Torah and Hermeneutics in Abraham Abulafia*, trans. Menahem Kallus (Albany, NY, 1989).

—— *The Mystical Experience in Abraham Abulafia* (New York, 1988); published in Hebrew as *Haḥavayah hamistit etsel avraham abulafiyah* (Jerusalem, 1988).

Igeret magen avraham me'erets hama'arav [A Letter of the Magen Avraham from the Land of the West [Abraham Miguel Cardozo]], ed. G. Scholem, in *Kovets al yad*, NS 2 (12) (Jerusalem, 1937).

ISAAC EISIK OF KOMARNO: see under Haver.

JACOB HALEVI OF MARVEGE, *She'elot uteshuvot min hashamayim* [Responsa from Heaven], ed. A. Marcus (Tel Aviv, 1957).

JACOB JOSEPH OF POLONNOYE, *Ben porat yosef* (Korets, 1781).

—— *Ketonet pasim* ['A Coat of Many Colours'] (Lvov, 1866).

—— *Toledot ya'akov yosef* (Korets, 1780).

—— *Tsafenat paneaḥ* [The name given to Joseph in Gen. 41: 45] (Korets, 1782).

JEKUTIEL (GORDON) OF VILNA, *Mishloaḥ manot* ['The Sending of Portions' (Esther 9: 22)] (Vienna, 1879). *Piyut* based on the letters of 'Megilah' (Book of Esther).

Jerusalem Talmud (Vilna, 1922–8).

JOACHIMSTHAL, J. L., *Reshimat sefarim* (Amsterdam, 1899). Auction catalogue of books *ex libris* R. Me'ir Lehren, R. Akiva Lehren, and R. Moses de Lima.

KAHANA, A., *Rabi mosheh ḥayim lutsato* (Warsaw, 1899).

KAHANA, D., *Toledot hamekubalim, hashabeta'im vehaḥasidim* [Lives of the Kabbalists, Shabateans, and Hasidim], ii (Tel Aviv, 1927).

KAUFMANN, D., 'Contributions à la biographie de Mosé Hayyim Luzzatto, Yekutiel Gordon et Mosé Hages', *Revue des Etudes Juives*, 23 (1891).

Keter shem tov: see under Aaron Hakohen of Apta.

KRAUSHAR, A., *Ferank va'adato* [Frank and his Community], trans. N. Sokolov (Warsaw, 1896). Translation of *Frank i frankiści polscy* (Kraków, 1895).

KURIYAT, R. JUDAH, *Sefer maor vashemesh* [Light and Sun] (Livorno, 1839).

LACHOWER, F., *Al gevul hayashan veheḥadash* [On the Border between Old and New] (Jerusalem, 1951).

LAMM, N., *Torah lishemah bemishnat r' ḥayim mivoloz'in uvemaḥashevet hador* [Torah Study for its Own Sake in the Doctrine of R. Hayim of Volozhin and in the Thinking of his Generation] (Jerusalem, 1972).

LANDAU, B., *Hagaon heḥasid mivilna* [The Saintly Gaon of Vilna] (Jerusalem, 1967).

LIEBERMAN, H., 'Legende un emes vegn die hasidishe drukereien' [Legend and Truth in Relation to the Hasidic Printing Houses], *YIVO-bleter*, 34 (1950).

LIEBES, Y., 'Sefer "Tsadik yesod olam": mitos shabeta'i' [The Book *Tsadik yesod olam*: A Shabatean Myth], *Da'at*, 1 (1978).

—— 'Zemirot lise'udot-shabat sheyised ha'ar"i hakadosh' [Songs Introduced by the Holy Ari for the Sabbath Meals], *Molad*, NS 4 (27) (1972).

Likutim yekarim [an anthology] (Lvov, 1792).

LUZZATTO, EPHRAIM, *Eleh benei hane'urim* [These are the Children of (our) Young Days] (London, 1768).

—— *Shirei efrayim lutsato* [Poems of Ephraim Luzzatto], ed. and intro. J. Fichman (Tel Aviv, 1942).

LUZZATTO, R. MOSES HAYIM, *Adir bamarom* [Mighty [is the Lord] on High] (Warsaw, 1886). Commentary on *Idra raba*.

—— *Da'at tevunot* [Knowledge with Understanding] (Warsaw, 1889); ed. H. Friedlaender (Benei Berak, 1973). In translation: *The Knowing Heart*, trans. Shraga Silverstein (Jerusalem and New York, 1982). See also 'Manuscripts' section above, MSS Oxford 2307; Warsaw 174; BL 860; Oxford-Hirsch 1.

—— *Derekh ets ḥayim* [The Way of the Tree of Life]; included in various edns. of *Mesilat yesharim*, beginning with the 2nd (Zholkva [Żółkiew], 1766), q.v.

—— *Derekh hashem* [The Way of the Lord] (Amsterdam, 1896); (Jerusalem, 1914), with foreword by R. Isaac Malzan.

—— *Derekh ḥokhmah* [The Way of Wisdom] (Amsterdam, 1783).

—— *Derekh tevunot* [The Way of Understanding] (Minsk, 1836; Jerusalem, 1880).

—— *Ginzei ramḥa"l*: see *Sefer ginzei ramḥa"l* below.

—— *Hakelalim harishonim* [The First Principles], repr. in *Sefer hakelalim* (see below) as *Kelalei pitḥei ḥokhmah vada'at* [Principles of the 'Gateways to Wisdom and Understanding'].

—— *Ḥoker umekubal* [Philosopher and Kabbalist] (Shklov, 5545 (1785)); ed. M. Frestadt (Leipzig and Königsberg, 1840).

—— *Kaf-dalet kishutei kalah* [Twenty-Four Ornaments of the Bride]. See 'Manuscripts' section above, MS Oxford 2307.

—— *Kela"ḥ pitḥei ḥokhmah*: see *Kof lamed ḥet pitḥei ḥokhmah* below.

—— *Kelalim leḥokhmat ha'emet/Kelalei ḥokhmat ha'emet* [Principles of Kabbalah]; included in *Kinat hashem tsevaot* and in *Milḥemet mosheh* (see below). In translation: *General Principles of the Kabbalah* (New York, 1970).

—— *Kinat hashem tsevaot* [The Zeal of the Lord of Hosts] (Warsaw, 1888). A more complete version, including a part withdrawn from circulation, is in MS Oxford 2237.

—— *Kitsur sefer hakavanot*: see *Sefer kitsur hakavanot* below. See also 'Manuscripts' section above, MSS Oxford Heb. f. 120; BL Or. 10860.

—— *Kof lamed ḥet pitḥei ḥokhmah* [138 Gateways to Wisdom] (Korets, 1785).

—— *Layesharim tehilah* [Praise (is Fitting) for the Upright], ed. Solomon Dubno (Amsterdam, 1743; Berlin, 1780). Also contained in *Sefer hamaḥazot*, ed. Ginzburg.

—— *Leshon limudim* [The Learned Tongue], ed. A. M. Habermann (Jerusalem, 1945; Jerusalem and Tel Aviv, 1951).

—— *Ma'amar hage'ulah* [On the Redemption]; printed together with Luzzatto's *Da'at tevunot* (see above).

—— *Ma'amar haḥokhmah* [On Wisdom] (Amsterdam, 1783).

—— *Ma'amar havikuaḥ* [The Discussion]. See Essay 1, nn. 94 and 95.

—— *Megilat setarim verazin genizin* ['The Scroll of Secrets' and 'Hidden Mysteries'] (Warsaw, 1889). Luzzatto or school of Luzzatto? See Essay 6, n. 76.

—— *Mesilat yesharim* [The Highway of the Upright] (1st edn., Amsterdam, 1740; 2nd edn., Zholkva [Żółkiew], 1766; and many later editions (see Essay 8)). In translation: *Le Sentier de rectitude*, trans. Aron Wolf and Jean Poliatschek, preface by Georges Vajda (Paris, 1956); *The Path of the Upright*, trans. Mordecai M. Kaplan (Northvale, NJ, and London, 1995).

—— *Migdal oz* [A Tower of Strength] (Jerusalem, 1972). Also contained in *Sefer hamaḥazot*, ed. Ginzburg.

—— *Milḥemet mosheh* [The War of Moses] (Warsaw, 1889).

—— *Mishkenei elyon* [Dwelling of the Most High]. See 'Manuscripts' section above, MS Harvard 54.

—— *Otserot ramḥa"l*: see *Sefer otserot ramḥa"l* below.

—— *Perush idra raba* [Commentary on *Idra raba*]. See 'Manuscripts' section above, MS Cincinnati 501.

—— *Pitḥei ḥokhmah vada'at* [Gateways to Wisdom and Understanding], ed. R. David Luria (Warsaw, 1884); see also *Hakelalim harishonim* above and *Sefer hakelalim* below.

—— *R' mosheh ḥayim lutsato uvenei doro: osef igerot ute'udot* [R. Moses Hayim Luzzatto and his Contemporaries: A Collection of Letters and Documents], ed. S. Ginzburg, 2 vols. (Tel Aviv, 1937).

—— *Razin genizin* [Hidden Mysteries]. Discourses on verses of the Pentateuch and Song of Songs. Ascribed on title-page to R. Israel Hezekiah Treves. Appended to *Megilat setarim* (see above).

—— *Sefer adir bamarom, ḥelek sheni* ['*Adir bamarom*, part ii': editor's title for the part of Luzzatto's commentary on *Idra raba* not included in *Adir bamarom*], ed. Y. Spiner (Jerusalem, 1988).

LUZZATTO, R. MOSES HAYIM, *Sefer ginzei ramḥa"l* [A Selection of Luzzatto's Writings], ed. H. Friedlaender (Benei Berak, 1980; 2nd edn., Benei Berak, 1984).

—— *Sefer hakelalim* [The Book of Principles] (Warsaw, 1889); appended to *Da'at tevunot*, ed. Friedlaender (see above), where it includes the piece incorrectly titled *Kelalim rishonim* [First Principles], as in MS Jerusalem 2517 8°.

—— *Sefer hamaḥazot* [The Plays], ed. S. Ginzburg (Tel Aviv, 1927). Three plays: *Layesharim tehilah*, *Ma'aseh shimshon*, and *Migdal oz*.

—— *Sefer hashirim* [The Poems], ed. S. Ginzburg and B. Klar (Jerusalem, 1945).

—— *Sefer kitsur hakavanot* [The *kavanot* in Brief], ed. H. Friedlaender and Y. Spiner (Benei Berak, 1978).

—— *Sefer otserot ramḥa"l* [A Ramhal Treasury], ed. H. Friedlaender (Benei Berak, 1986).

—— *Sha'arei ramḥa"l*, ed. H. Friedlaender (Benei Berak, 1986).

—— *Takta"v tefilot leramḥa"l* [515 Prayers by Ramhal], ed. S. Ulman (Benei Berak, 1979).

—— *Tikunim ḥadashim* [New *tikunim*] (Jerusalem, 1958). See also 'Manuscripts' section above, MS Oxford 1901.

—— *Vikuaḥ bein 'mar yanuka' u'mar kashisha'* [A Discussion between 'Mr Child' and 'Mr Old']. See 'Manuscripts' section above, MSS Oxford 2237, Harvard 54, Jerusalem 2365. Second part published, ed. Y. Spiner (Jerusalem, 1978).

—— *Zohar tinyana* [Second Zohar]. Fragments. Reproduced in Emden, *Zot torat hakenaot*.

LUZZATTO, S. D. (ed.), *Yad yosef* (Padua, 1864). Catalogue of J. Almanzi's library.

MAGGID OF MEZHIRECH: see under Dov Baer.

MAGGID-STEINSCHNEIDER, H. N., *Ir vilna* [The City of Vilna] (Vilna, 1900).

MAIMONIDES, MOSES, *Igerot haramba"m* [Letters of Maimonides], ed. M. D. Rabinowitz (Jerusalem, 1960).

—— *Mishneh torah* (Jerusalem, 1982); with English translation and notes by M. Hyamson (New York, 1937–49).

—— *Moreh nevukhim* [Guide of the Perplexed]. In translation: *The Guide of the Perplexed of Maimonides*, trans. M. Friedlaender, 3 vols. (London, 1881–5).

MARCUS, A., *Haḥasidut* [Hasidism] (Tel Aviv, 1954). Translation of *Der Chassidismus* (Pleschen [Pleszew], 1901).

—— *Hartmann's inductive Philosophie im Chassidismus*, i (Lemberg, 1889).

—— *Keset hasofer* [The Scribe's Materials] (Kraków, 1912).

MARGALIOT, R., *Malakhei elyon* [Messengers (Angels) of the Most High] (Jerusalem, 1945).

Mayan haḥokhmah [The Fountain of Wisdom] (Amsterdam, 1651).

MEIR BEN ELIJAH, *Milḥamot hashem* [Wars of the Lord]. Two copies in the manuscript collection of the Jewish National and University Library, Jerusalem. Catalogued as completed in Jerusalem in 1892.

MENAHEM AZARIAH DA FANO, R., *Em kol ḥai* [Mother of all Living]: one of the 'ten treatises' (see *Sefer asarah ma'amarot* below).

—— *Ḥikur din* [Discernment in Judgement]: one of the 'ten treatises' (see *Sefer asarah ma'amarot* below).

—— *Kanfei yonah* [Wings of a Dove] (Korets, 1786).

—— *Ma'amar hanefesh* [On the Soul] (Piotrków, 1903).

—— *Sefer asarah ma'amarot* ['Ten Sayings': ten treatises] (Lvov, 1858; Jerusalem, 1974).

MENAHEM MENDEL OF SHKLOV, *Mayim adirim* [Mighty Waters] (Warsaw, 1885).

MENAHEM MENDEL OF VITEBSK, *Peri ha'arets* [The Fruit of the Land] (Kopust, 1814).

MENDELSSOHN, MOSES, *Gesammelte Schriften*, xiii. *Briefwechsel*, III, ed. A. Altmann (Stuttgart, 1977).

MICHMAN, Y. (ed.), *Meḥkarim al toledot yahadut holand* [Studies on the History of Dutch Jewry], iv (Jerusalem, 1985).

Midrash tehilim [Midrash on Psalms], ed. S. Buber (Vilna, 1891).

MILANO, A., *Storia degli Ebrei in Italia* (Turin, 1963).

The Mishnah, trans. H. Danby (1933; Oxford, 1980).

MODENA, A., and E. MORPURGO, *Medici e chirurghi ebrei dottorati e licenziati nell'Università di Padova dal 1617 al 1816* (Bologna, 1967).

MOLKHO, Y., and A. AMARILLO, 'Igerot otobiografiyot shel kardozo' [Autobiographical Letters of Cardozo], in I. Ben-Zvi and M. Benayahu (eds.), *Sefer hayovel lishene'ur zalman shazar/Shneur Zalman Shazar Jubilee Volume* (= *Sefunot*, 3–4) (Jerusalem, 1959–60).

—— and R. SCHATZ, 'Perush "lekh lekha" lihudah levi tovah' [Judah Levi Tovah's Commentary on 'Go from your Country' (Gen. 12)], in I. Ben-Zvi and M. Benayahu (eds.), *Sefer hayovel lishene'ur zalman shazar/Shneur Zalman Shazar Jubilee Volume* (= *Sefunot*, 3–4) (Jerusalem, 1959–60).

MOSES DE LEÓN, *Mishkan ha'edut* [The Tabernacle of the Testimony]. Cited by Ibn Gabbai in *Avodat hakodesh* (see under Gabbai above). In the Jewish Theological Seminary, New York, there is a copy thought to have been published in the sixteenth or seventeenth century, and a microfilm of a manuscript.

NADAV, YA'EL, 'Rabi shelomoh ailyon vekunteresav bekabalah shabeta'it' [R. Solomon Ayllon and his 'Notebooks' in Shabatean Kabbalah], in I. Ben-Zvi and M. Benayahu (eds.), *Sefer hayovel lishene'ur zalman shazar/Shneur Zalman Shazar Jubilee Volume* (= *Sefunot*, 3–4) (Jerusalem, 1959–60).

NAHMANI, R. SAMSON HAYIM, Poem for Luzzatto's wedding, printed on a single sheet. Exemplar in the Jewish National and University Library, Jerusalem.

NAHUM OF CHERNOBYL, *Meor einayim* [The Light of the Eyes] (Slavuta, 1798).

NATHAN OF GAZA, *Derush hataninim* [Homily on the Sea Monsters], in Scholem, *Be'ikevot mashiaḥ*. See also Wirszubsky, *Al ha'ahavah haruḥanit*, and 'Manuscripts' section above, MS Columbia University X893/Z8.

NEPPI, HANANEL, *Zekher tsadikim liverakhah* [(May) the Memory of the Departed Righteous (be) for a Blessing] (Trieste, 1853). Printed together with M. S. Ghirondi's *Toledot gedolei yisra'el ugeonei italyah* (see above).

NEUBAUER, ADOLF, *Catalogue of the Hebrew Manuscripts in the Bodleian Library* (Oxford, 1886).

NEW YORK PUBLIC LIBRARY, *Dictionary Catalog of the Jewish Collection*, xii (1960).

NIETO, D., *Esh dat* [A Fiery Law] (London, 1715).

NISSIM, P., 'Sulla data della laurea rabbinica conseguita da Mosheh Chajim Luzzatto', *Rassegna mensile di Israel*, 20 (1954).

Otsar ḥokhmah [Treasury of Wisdom] (Lvov, 1859–65). A periodical.

PERLMUTTER, M. A., *R' yehonatan aibeshits veyaḥaso el hashabeta'ut* [R. Jonathan Eybeschuetz and his Attitude to Shabateanism] (Jerusalem and Tel Aviv, 1947).

PHINEHAS (PINHAS) OF KORETS, *Nofet tsufim* [Honey of the Comb] (Piotrków, 1911).

PIEKARZ, M., *Bimei tsemiḥat haḥasidut: megamot rayoniyot besifrei derush umusar* [In the Early Days of Hasidism: Trends in Speculative Thought in Homiletic and Ethical Books] (Jerusalem, 1978).

—— 'Radikalizem dati bimei hitpashetut haḥasidut: torat "kaf remiyah" bekhitvei eli'ezer lipman mibrodi' [Radicalism during the Spread of Hasidism: The Doctrine of 'the Deceitful Hand' in the Writings of Eliezer Lipmann of Brody], *Molad*, NS 6 (30) (1975).

Pinkas va'ad arba aratsot [Records of the Council of Four Lands], ed. I. Halpern (Jerusalem, 1945).

Pirkei heikhalot rabati, ed. S. A. Wertheimer (Jerusalem, 1889). See also under B. Richler below.

PRESCHEL, T., 'Mimosheh ve'ad mosheh lo kam kemosheh (gilgulah shel imrah)' [From Moses to Moses, None has Arisen like Moses (the Evolution of an Aphorism)], *Hado'ar*, 48 (1969).

RABINOWITSCH, W. Z., *Haḥasidut halita'it* [Lithuanian Hasidism] (Jerusalem, 1961).

RAPHAEL, Y., 'Kitvei rabi ya'akov emden' [The Works of R. Jacob Emden], *Areshet*, 3 (1961). A bibliography.

RAPOPORT, HAYIM HAKOHEN, *Zekher ḥayim: derushei r' ḥayim kohen rapoport* [*Zekher ḥayim*: Homilies of R. Hayim Kohen Rapoport] (Lemberg, 1866).

Raya meheimna: see under *Zohar*.

RICHLER, B., 'Al ha"hosafot hashabeta'iyot" bes' heikhalot rabati' [On the 'Shabatean Additions' in the Book *Heikhalot rabati*], *Kiryat sefer*, 58 (1983).

RIVKIND, I., 'Shiyurei sefer (be'ayot, he'arot ureshimot bibliografiyot). dalet. od totsaot mimesilat yesharim' [Literary Remnants (Problems, Comments, and Bibliographical Notes), 4. Further Results from *Mesilat yesharim*], *Kiryat sefer*, 15 (1938–9).

ROEST, M., *Catalog der Hebraica und Judaica aus der L. Rosenthalischen Bibliothek* (Amsterdam, 1875).

ROSENSTEIN, R. MOSES, *Yesodei hada'at* [Foundations of Knowledge], i (Warsaw, 1935).

ROSENTHAL, J., 'Sifrut havikuaḥ ha'antinotsrit ad sof hame'ah hashemoneh-esreh' [Anti-Christian Polemical Literature up to the End of the Eighteenth Century], *Areshet*, 2 (1960).

ROTH, BETSALEL (CECIL ROTH), 'Kavim lidemuto shel efrayim lutsato' [Some Features of Ephraim Luzzatto's Personality], in Sh. Abramson and A. Mirsky (eds.), *Sefer ḥayim shirman/Hayyim (Jefim) Schirmann Jubilee Volume* (Jerusalem, 1970).

ROTHSTEIN, E. PH., *Nezir elohim* [A Nazirite unto God] (Frankfurt, 1875).

RUBINSTEIN, URI TSEVI, *Siftei yeshenim* [The Lips of Those who Sleep], ii (Zholkva, 1806). A bibliography.

SASPORTAS, R. JACOB, *Tsitsat novel tsevi* [The Fading Flower of his Beauty [*tsevi*]], ed. I. Tishby (Jerusalem, 1954).

SATANOV, ISAAC, *Imrei vinah* [Words of Understanding] (Berlin, 1772).

SCHATZ (SCHATZ-UFFENHEIMER), RIVKAH, *Haḥasidut kemistikah: yesodot kevi'etistiyim bamaḥashavah haḥasidit bame'ah hayod"ḥet* [Hasidism as Mysticism: Quietistic Elements in Hasidic Thought in the Eighteenth Century] (Jerusalem, 1968).

SCHECHTER, S., *Studies in Judaism*, 2nd ser. (Philadelphia, 1908).

SCHOLEM, G., 'Aharon markus vehaḥasidut' [Aaron Marcus and Hasidism], *Beḥinot*, 7 (1954).

—— *Be'ikevot mashiaḥ* [In the Footsteps of the Messiah] (Jerusalem, 1944).

—— 'Berekhyah rosh hashabeta'im besaloniki' [Berekhyah, Head of the Shabateans in Salonika], *Zion*, 6 (1941).

—— *Bibliographia Cabbalistica* (Berlin, 1933).

—— 'Demuto hahistorit shel r' yisra'el ba'al shem tov' [The Historical Figure of R. Israel Ba'al Shem Tov], *Molad*, 18 (1960).

—— *Devarim bego* [Explications and Implications] (Tel Aviv, 1976).

—— '"Devekut" o "hitkasherut intimit im elohim" bereshit haḥasidut: halakhah uma'aseh' [*Devekut* or 'Intimate Communion with God' in Early Hasidism: Principle and Practice], in his *Devarim bego*.

—— *Ḥalomotav shel hashabeta'i r' mordekhai ashkenazi* [The Dreams of the Shabatean R. Mordecai Ashkenazi] (Jerusalem, 1938).

SCHOLEM, G., 'Hamekubal r' avraham ben eli'ezer halevi' [The Kabbalist R. Abraham ben Eliezer Halevi], *Kiryat sefer*, 2 (1925–6).

—— 'Hatenuah hashabeta'it bepolin' [The Shabatean Movement in Poland], in I. Halpern (ed.), *Beit yisra'el bepolin*, ii (Jerusalem, 1954).

—— 'Hatsadik' [The Tsadik], in his *Pirkei-yesod behavanat hakabalah usemaleiha* [Basic Readings for the Understanding of Kabbalah and its Symbols] (Jerusalem, 1976).

—— 'Igeret me'et r' ḥayim malakh' [A Letter from R. Hayim Malakh], *Zion*, 11 (1946).

—— *Jewish Gnosticism, Merkabah Mysticism and Talmudic Tradition* (New York, 1960).

—— *Kabbalah* (Jerusalem, 1974). In English.

—— *Major Trends in Jewish Mysticism*, 3rd edn. (New York, 1961).

—— *Meḥkarim umekorot letoledot hashabeta'ut vegilguleiha* [Studies and Sources for the History of Shabateanism and its Various Manifestations] (Jerusalem, 1974).

—— *The Messianic Idea in Judaism, and Other Essays on Jewish Spirituality* (New York, 1971).

—— 'Mitsvah haba'ah ba'averah' [A Virtuous Deed [Fulfilment of a Commandment] Brought About by a Transgression], *Keneset*, 2 (1937).

—— 'The Neutralization of the Messianic Element in Early Hasidism', *Journal of Jewish Studies*, 20 (1969).

—— 'Perakim apokaliptiyim umeshiḥiyim al r' mordekhai me'aisenshtat' [Apocalyptic and Messianic Passages on R. Mordecai of Eisenstadt], in *Sefer dinaburg* (Jerusalem, 1948).

—— 'Perush mizmorei tehilim meḥugo shel shabetai tsevi be'adrianopol' [A Commentary on Psalms from the Circle of Shabetai Tsevi in Adrianople], in *Alei ayin: minḥat devarim lishelomoh zalman shoken aḥarei mele'ot lo shivim shanah* ['By a Spring' [Gen. 49: 22; letter *ayin* also = 70]: Papers Offered to Solomon Zalman Schocken on his Seventieth Birthday] (Jerusalem, 1948–52).

—— 'R' eliyahu hakohen ha'itamari vehashabeta'ut' [R. Elijah ben Solomon Abraham Hakohen of Smyrna and Shabateanism], in S. Lieberman (ed.), *Alexander Marx: Jubilee Volume on the Occasion of his Seventieth Birthday*, Hebrew vol. *Sefer hayovel likhevod aleksander marks* (New York, 1950).

—— *Shabetai tsevi vehatenuah hashabeta'it bimei ḥayav* [Shabetai Tsevi and the Shabatean Movement during his Lifetime] (Tel Aviv, 1957).

—— 'Shenei mekorot ḥadashim lidiat torato shel avraham mikha'el kardozo' [Two New Sources for the Study of Cardozo's Doctrine], in I. Ben-Zvi and M. Benayahu (eds.), *Sefer hayovel lishene'ur zalman shazar/Shneur Zalman Shazar Jubilee Volume* (= *Sefunot*, 3–4) (Jerusalem, 1959–60).

—— 'Te'udot shabeta'iyot al r' natan ha'azati miginzei r' mahalalel halelyah be'ankona' [Shabatean Documents on R. Nathan of Gaza from the Collection of R. Mahalalel Hallelyah in Ancona], in *Harry Austryn Wolfson: Jubilee Volume on the Occasion of his Seventy-Fifth Birthday*, iii (Jerusalem, 1965).

—— 'Te'udot shabeta'iyot ḥadashot mis' "to'ei ruaḥ" ' [New Shabatean Documents from the Book *To'ei ruaḥ* ['Those who Err in Spirit']], *Zion*, 7 (1942).

—— 'Yisra'el sarug: talmid ha'ar"i?' [Israel Sarug: Disciple of Luria?], *Zion*, 5 (1940).

Seder eliyahu raba veseder eliyahu zuta: hamuva'im beshem tana devei eliyahu [*Seder eliyahu raba* and *Seder eliyahu zuta*: together known as *Tana devei eliyahu*], ed. M. Ish-Shalom [Meir Friedmann] (Vienna, 1902).

Sefer tikunei shabat (Livorno, 1836). Teachings based on Luria's Sabbath hymns.

Sefer yetsirah [The Book of Creation], with commentary by the Vilna Gaon and foreword by R. Isaac Kahana (Jerusalem, 1874/5).

SEGAL, JOSEPH HAYIM, *Tosefot ḥayim* (Lublin, 1906; 1st edn. 1904).

SHILOAH, A., *Nose'ei musikah bazohar* [Musical Subjects in the Zohar] (Jerusalem, 1977).

Shirot vetishbaḥot shel hashabeta'im [Poems and Songs of Praise by the Shabateans], ed. M. Attias and G. Scholem (Tel Aviv, 1948).

Shishah sidrei mishnah [The Mishnah], ed. H. Albeck (Jerusalem and Tel Aviv, 1956).

SHNEUR ZALMAN OF LYADY, *Likutei torah* [Selected Writings on the Torah] (Zhitomir, 1848; Vilna, 1904).

—— *Tanya* ['It is Taught': the opening word of his 'Collected Sayings'] (Slavuta, 1796; Kiryat Malakhi, 1998).

—— *Torah or* [The Torah is Light] (Kopust, 1837).

Shulḥan arukh: see above under Caro.

Shulḥan arukh ha'ar"i [Isaac Luria's *Shulḥan arukh*] (Kraków, n.d.; Frankfurt an der Oder, 1691).

Sitrei torah: see under *Zohar*.

SOAVE, M., 'Letter (no. 15) to M. Steinschneider', *Il Vessillo israelitico*, 28 (1880).

SONNE, I., 'Avnei binyan letoledot hayehudim be'italyah' [Building-Blocks for the History of the Jews in Italy], *Horeb*, 6 (1942).

—— 'Avnei binyan (te'udot leḥeker ramḥa"l veḥugo)' [Building-Blocks (Documents for the Study of Ramhal and his Circle)], *American Jewish Yearbook* (New York, 5695 (1935)). Contains translation from Italian into Hebrew of memorial eulogy (ascribed to Moses David Valle) on Luzzatto.

—— and M. TSEVAT, 'Some Luzzatto Manuscripts', *Studies in Bibliography and Booklore*, 2 (1955–6).

SPIRA, NATHAN NATA BEN SOLOMON, *Megaleh amukot* [Uncoverer of Deep Mysteries] (Kraków, 1637; Lublin, 1884).

TAMAR, D., *Meḥkarim betoledot hayehudim be'erets yisra'el uve'italyah* [Studies in the History of the Jews in the Land of Israel and Italy] (Jerusalem, 1970).

TAUBER, A., *Meḥkarim bibliografiyim* [Bibliographical Studies] (Jerusalem, 1932).

Tikunei hazohar: see under *Zohar*.

TISHBY, I. 'Darkhei hafatsatam shel kitvei kabalah leramḥa"l bepolin uvelita', *Kiryat sefer*, 45 (1970). Now Essay 8 above.

—— 'Demuto shel rabi mosheh david vale (ramda"v) uma'amado baḥavurat ramḥa"l', in S. Ettinger, H. Beinart, and M. Shtern (eds.), *Sefer zikaron leyitsḥak ber/Yitzhak F. Baer Memorial Volume* (= *Zion*, 44 (1979)) (Jerusalem, 1980). Now Essay 6 above.

—— 'Ḥadeshanut medumah beḥeker hakabalah' [Imaginary Ground-Breaking in Kabbalistic Research], *Zion*, 54 (1989).

—— 'Hafikhah beḥeker hakabalah' [An Upset in Kabbalistic Research], *Zion*, 54 (1989).

—— 'Ha'imut bein kabalat ha'ar"i lekabalat harema"k bikhetavav uveḥayav shel r' aharon berekhyah mimodena' [The Confrontation between Luria's Kabbalah and that of Cordovero in the Writings and Life of Aaron Berekhyah of Modena], *Zion*, 39 (1974).

—— 'Hanhagot natan ha'azati, igerot rabi mosheh zakuto vetakanot rabi ḥayim abulafiyah besefer ḥemdat yamim' [Nathan of Gaza's 'Rules of Conduct', the Letters of R. Moses Zacuto, and the Ordinances of R. Hayim Abulafia in the Book *Ḥemdat yamim* ['The Most Desirable of Days']], *Kiryat sefer*, 54 (1979).

—— 'Hapulmus al sefer hazohar bame'ah hashesh-esreh be'italyah' [The Controversy over the Zohar in Sixteenth-Century Italy], *Perakim*, 1 (Jerusalem, 1967–8).

—— 'Harayon hameshiḥi vehamegamot hameshiḥiyot bitsemiḥat haḥasidut' [The Messianic Idea and Messianic Tendencies in the Early Days of Hasidism], *Zion*, 32 (1967).

—— 'Igerot rabi me'ir rofe lerabi avraham rovigo mishenot tala"h–ta"m' [The Letters of R. Meir Rofe to R. Abraham Rovigo in the Years 5435–40 (1675–80)], in I. Ben-Zvi and M. Benayahu (eds.), *Sefer hayovel lishene'ur zalman shazar/Shneur Zalman Shazar Jubilee Volume* (= *Sefunot*, 3–4) (Jerusalem, 1959–60).

—— 'Ikevot rabi mosheh ḥayim lutsato bemishnat haḥasidut', *Zion*, 43 (1978). Now Essay 10 above.

—— 'Kavei hatenuah hashabeta'it udemuto shel shabetai tsevi bekhitvei ramḥa"l vetalmidav', in Menahem Ben-Sasson, Robert Bonfil, and Joseph R. Hacker (eds.), *Tarbut veḥevrah betoledot yisra'el bimei habeinayim: kovets ma'amarim lezikhro shel ḥayim hilel ben-sason/Culture and Society in Medieval Jewry: Studies Dedicated to the Memory of Haim Hillel Ben-Sasson* (Jerusalem, 1989). Now Essay 5 above.

—— 'Kovets shel kitvei kabalah miginzei ramḥa"l bikhetav-yad oksford 2593'. Now Essay 1 above. Part published in *Kiryat sefer*, 53 (1978).

—— *Meshiḥiyut bedor gerushei sefarad uportugal* [Messianism in the Generation of the Expulsions from Spain and Portugal] (Jerusalem, 1985).

—— *Mishnat hazohar*, 3rd edn. (Jerusalem, 1971; 1st edn., with F. Lachower, 1949). In translation: *The Wisdom of the Zohar* (see below).

—— *Netivei emunah uminut* [Paths of Faith and Heresy] (Ramat Gan, 1964).

—— '"Shalshelet yuḥasin" shel "mori" va' "a[vi]-a[vi] mori" beduyim hamutsavim besefer ḥemdat yamim' ['Spurious Genealogy' of 'My Teacher' and 'My Paternal Grandfather and Teacher' Inserted in the Book *Ḥemdat yamim*], *Tarbiz*, 50 (1981).

—— 'Shirim ufiyutim miginzei r' mosheh ḥayim lutsato (bikhetav-yad gintsburg 745)', *Molad*, NS 7 (30) (1976). Now Essay 2 above, Part A.

—— 'Tefilot miginzei r' mosheh ḥayim lutsato', *Molad*, NS 8 (31) (1980). Now Essay 2 above, Part B.

—— 'Te'udot al natan ha'azati bekhitvei rabi yosef ḥamits' [Documents Relating to Nathan of Gaza in the Writings of R. Joseph Hamits], *Sefunot*, 1 (1957).

—— *Torat hara vehakelipah bekabalat ha'ar"i* [The Doctrine of Evil and the Husk in Lurianic Kabbalah] (Jerusalem and Tel Aviv, 1942).

—— 'Tsevi herman shapira—kesofer haskalah' [Tsevi Herman Shapira as a Writer of 'the Enlightenment'], *Molad*, NS 4 (27) (1972).

—— *The Wisdom of the Zohar*, trans. D. Goldstein, 3 vols. (Oxford, 1989). See *Mishnat hazohar* above.

—— and JOSEPH DAN, 'Ḥasidut', in *Ha'entsiklopedyah ha'ivrit*, xvii (1965).

TSEVI HIRSCH (EICHENSTEIN) OF ZHIDACHOV, *Ateret tsevi* (1836). Commentary on the Zohar.

—— *Hakdamah vederekh le'ets haḥayim* [Introduction and Path to the Tree of Life] (Lemberg, 1870).

URBACH, E. E., *Ḥaza"l: pirkei emunot vedeot* [The Sages: An Anthology of Beliefs and Opinions] (Jerusalem, 1969).

VALLE, R. MOSES DAVID, *Shivim panim al pasuk aḥaron shebatorah venikra beshem tikunim ḥadashim* [Seventy Aspects of the Last Verse in the Torah, Entitled 'New *tikunim*']. Printed in *Megilat setarim verazin genizin* (see above under Luzzatto). See also 'Manuscripts' section above, MS Jerusalem 5217.

VILNA GAON [ELIJAH BEN SOLOMON ZALMAN], Commentary on *Sifra detseni'uta* ['The Book of Concealment': part of the Zohar] (Vilna and Grodno, 1820).

—— *Likutei hager"a* [Selected Writings] (New York, 1999). See also Haver, *Be'er yitsḥak*; and *Sefer yetsirah*.

VITAL, HAYIM, *Ets ḥayim* [Tree of Life (probably a pun on the name Hayim)] (Korets, 1782).

—— *Likutei torah* [Collected Writings on the Torah] (Vilna, 1880).

—— *Otserot ḥayim* [Treasures of Life (or more probably 'of Hayim')] (Korets, 1783). See also 'Manuscripts' section above, Jewish Theological Seminary, New York, MS Mic. 1615.

VITAL, HAYIM, *Peri ets ḥayim* [Fruit of the Tree of Life] (Korets, 1782; 1785, 1786).

—— *Sefer hagilgulim* [The Book of Incarnations] (Frankfurt am Main, 1684; Przemyśl, 1875).

—— *Sefer halikutim* [Selections] (Jerusalem, 1913).

—— *Sha'ar hagilgulim* (Przemyśl, 1875).

—— *Sha'ar hakavanot* [The 'Gate' of Mystical Meditations] (Jerusalem, 1902). The fifth of the eight 'gates' into which *Ets ḥayim* was divided.

—— *Sha'ar hayiḥudim* [The 'Gate' of Unifications] (Korets, 1783). A section of *Peri ets ḥayim*.

—— *Sha'ar ruaḥ hakodesh* [On the Holy Spirit] (Jerusalem, 1863 and 1912).

WACHSTEIN, B., *Die Grabschriften des alten Judenfriedhofes in Eisenstadt* (Vienna, 1922).

—— *Die Inschriften des alten Judenfriedhofes in Wien*, ii (Vienna, 1917).

WEINSTOCK, I., 'Perush [meḥug?] haramḥa"l lamishnah harishonah besefer yetsirah' [Commentary (from the Circle?) of M. H. Luzzatto on the First *mishnah* in *Sefer yetsirah* ['The Book of Creation']], in *Temirin: Texts and Studies in Kabbala and Hasidism*, ii (Jerusalem, 1981).

WEINTRAUB, R. NOAH, *Meorei eliyahu* [The Lights of Elijah] (Jerusalem, 1932).

WEISS, J., 'Reshit tsemiḥatah shel haderekh haḥasidit' [The Burgeoning of the Hasidic Way], *Zion*, 16 (1951).

WEISS, J. G., 'A Circle of Pneumatics in Pre-Hasidism', *Journal of Jewish Studies*, 8 (1957).

WERBLOWSKY, R. J. Z., *Joseph Karo: Lawyer and Mystic* (Oxford, 1962).

WERSES, S., 'Al yitsḥak satanov veḥiburo "mishlei asaf"' [On Isaac Satanov and his Work *Mishlei asaf* ['The Proverbs of Asaph']], *Tarbiz*, 32 (1963).

WERTHEIM, A., *Halakhot vahalikhot baḥasidut* (Jerusalem, 1960). In translation: *Law and Custom in Hasidism*, trans. Shmuel Himelstein (Hoboken, NJ, 1992).

WILENSKY, M., *Ḥasidim umitnagedim* (Jerusalem, 1970).

—— 'Letoledotav shel r' yeshayah bassan' [Biographical Notes on R. Isaiah Bassano], *Kiryat sefer*, 27 (1951).

—— 'Mi hu r' netanel halevi?' [Who was R. Nethanel Halevi?], *Kiryat sefer*, 23 (1946).

WIRSZUBSKY, H., *Al ha'ahavah haruḥanit: midivrei natan ha'azati* [On Spiritual Love: From the Words of Nathan of Gaza] (Tel Aviv, 1941).

—— 'Ha'ide'ologyah hashabeta'it shel hamarat-hamashiaḥ' [The Shabatean Ideology of the Messiah's Apostasy], *Zion*, 3 (1938).

—— 'Hate'ologyah hashabeta'it shel natan ha'azati' [Nathan of Gaza's Shabatean Theology], *Keneset*, 8 (1944).

WODNIK, S. M. M., *Sefer ba'al shem tov* (Łódź, 1938).

WOLF, R. ZE'EV, OF ZHITOMIR, *Or hame'ir* [The Shining Light] (Korets, 1798).

YA'ARI, A., 'Hadefus ha'ivri bisheklov' [Hebrew Printing Houses in Shklov], *Kiryat sefer*, 22 (1945–6).

——'Shenei shirei ḥatunah leramḥa"l' [Two Epithalamia for M. H. Luzzatto], *Kiryat sefer*, 8 (1931).

Yalkut re'uveni [A Reubenite Anthology] (Prague, 1660). A collection by Reuben Hoeshke of aggadic (anecdotal etc.) material from kabbalistic literature.

ZINBERG, I., *Toledot sifrut yisra'el* [History of Jewish Literature], v (Tel Aviv, 1959).

ZLOTKIN [ZLATKIN], M., *Otsar hasefarim: ḥelek sheni* (Jerusalem, 1965). A bibliography.

Zohar, ed. R. Margaliot, 3 vols. (Jerusalem, 1940–6). Individual parts have been published as the following:

Raya meheimna [The Faithful Shepherd], ed. R. Margaliot (Jerusalem, 1948).

Sitrei torah [Secrets of the Torah], ed. R. Margaliot (Jerusalem, 1953).

Tikunei hazohar, ed. R. Margaliot (Tel Aviv, 1948). A series of commentaries, each called a *tikun*, on Gen. 1–6: 8.

Zohar ḥadash [New Zohar], ed. R. Margaliot (Jerusalem, 1953).

For a fuller bibliography of editions of the Zohar and traditional texts, see Tishby, *Wisdom of the Zohar*, iii. 1529–31.

ZWEIFEL, E., *Shalom al yisra'el* [Peace upon Israel], iii (Vilna, 1873).

Index

Page references in italics indicate illustrations; those in bold type indicate glossary entries

T